MODERN QUALITY CONTROL

MODERN QUALITY CONTROL

Revised Edition

GLENN E. HAYES, Ed.D., P.E.
California State University at Long Beach

HARRY G. ROMIG, Ph.D., P.E.
California State University at Long Beach
Professor Emeritus

GLENCOE PUBLISHING COMPANY
Encino, California

To the Pioneers of Quality Control

Glencoe Publishing Company
17337 Ventura Boulevard
Encino, California 91316

Printed in the United States of America

Library of Congress Catalog Card Number: 81-84579

4 5 6 7 8 9 10 86 85

ISBN 0-02-828800-9

The authors thank and wish to acknowledge the following companies for contributing photographs within this text: page 420, 421, Edwards Laboratories; 428, Long Beach Naval Shipyard; 484, Electronic Memories & Magnetics Corporation; 489, Glenn E. Hayes; 558, 559, McDonnell Douglas; 564, 565 (top), Mattel Toys, a division of Mattel, Inc.; 565 (bottom), 566, Power Track Golf Company; 574, Jet Plastics; 581, McDonnell Douglas; 582, Rockwell International Corporation's Space Division; 585, McDonnell Douglas; 586, Rockwell International Corporation's Space Division; 589, Jet Plastics; 591, McDonnell Douglas; 604, Rockwell International Corporation's Space Division; 606, 607, Mattel Toys, a division of Mattel, Inc.; 608, 609, Hughes Aircraft Company; 610, Thomas Organ Company.

CONTENTS

PREFACE XIII

Part One Statistical Concepts 1

INTRODUCTION 1

1 INTRODUCTION TO QUALITY CONTROL 3

Objective 3 ■ Early History 3 ■ Origins of Statistical Methods in Quality Control 6 ■ Definition of Quality 9 ■ Definition of Quality Control 10 ■ Scope of Quality Control 10 ■ Definition of Life-Cycle Quality 10 ■ Definition of Statistical Quality Control 14 ■ Purposes of Statistical Quality Control 14 ■ Controls to Implement Quality Assurance 15 ■ Product Effectiveness 16 ■ Reliability, Maintainability, and Availability 17 ■ Organizing to Achieve Effective Quality Control 18 ■ Need for Adequately Trained Quality Control Personnel 18 ■ Mathematical Requirements in Quality Control 20 ■ Applications of Statistical Quality Control 20 ■ How To Use Statistical Tools and Tables 21

2 MATHEMATICS OF QUALITY CONTROL 25

Objective 25 ■ Fundamental Tools for Quality Control 25 ■ Improving Reading Ability 26 ■ Basis of Arithmetic Processes 28 ■ Addition and Multiplication 28 ■ Powers or Exponents 29 ■ Number Systems: Base 10 and Base 2 30 ■ Division 30 ■ Significant Figures: Rules for Rounding Off the Last Digit 31 ■ Arrays: Used in the Formation of

Frequency Distributions 32 ■ Finding Powers and Roots of Numbers 33 ■ Using Tables of Roots 38 ■ Checks on Mathematical Processes: Casting out 9's 40 ■ Logarithms 43 ■ Use of Logarithms 45 ■ Exponential (e^x and e^{-x}) and Napierian (natural) Logarithms (Base e) 48 ■ Factorials 53 ■ Combinations and Permutations 54 ■ Summary 56

3 BASIC STATISTICS FOR QUALITY ASSURANCE 61

Objective 61 ■ Why Statistical Quality Control? 62 ■ Frequency Distributions 66 ■ Graphical Presentations 72 ■ Measures of Central Tendency 89 ■ Measures of Variability or Dispersion 91 ■ Probability 95 ■ Method of Variables 99 ■ Method of Attributes 100 ■ Basic Distributions for Method of Attributes and Methods of Variables 106

4 INTRODUCTION TO CONTROL CHARTS 115

Objective 115 ■ Purposes of Quality Control and Quality Control Charts 115 ■ Nature of Control Charts 119 ■ Other Techniques for Obtaining Statistical Control 120 ■ Fundamental Basis of Control Charts 130 ■ Probabilities Associated with 3σ (Three-Sigma) Control Limits for Attributes 134 ■ Selection of Sampling Plans for Control Chart Usage as well as Inspection 152

5 CONTROL CHART FOR ATTRIBUTES 157

Objective 157 ■ Terminology 159 ■ Data for Control Charts 161 ■ Control Charts for Percent or Fraction Defective, p 162 ■ Control Chart for Number of Defectives, pn, or d 172 ■ Analysis and Interpretation of Control Charts 182 ■ Control Charts for Defects Per Unit, u, and Defects per Sample, c 193 ■ Summary, Relations for Control Charts for p, pn, u and c 201 ■ Control Charts for Demerits Per Unit, D_u 201 ■ Control Charts for Indexes, I 210 ■ Efficient Use of Control Charts for Attributes 215

6 CONTROL CHARTS FOR VARIABLES 219

Objective 219 ■ Nature of Variables Control Charts 219 ■ Control Chart for Averages Only—Variability Controlled 222 ■ Control Charts for Averages and Standard Deviations 224 ■ Control Charts for Averages and Ranges 261 ■ Case Study: Example of $\overline{X}$ and R Charts 280 ■ Use of Range for Controlling Variability When Samples Are Large 288 ■ Control Charts for Individuals for 100% Inspection for Several Characteristics 307 ■ Control Charts for Individuals and Moving Ranges ($n = 2$) 308

7 LINEAR CORRELATION 327

Objective 327 ■ Statistics Required in Correlation Studies 328 ■ Lines of Regression 331 ■ A Simple Technique to Obtain Best Linear Relation for Correlated Data 339 ■ Extension of Correlation Techniques Based on Theory of Errors 343 ■ Results of Correlation Studies 349

8 DESIGN OF EXPERIMENTS 353

Objective 353 ■ Random Numbers 355 ■ Why Experimental Tests Are Necessary 364 ■ Fundamentals of Experimentation 365 ■ Samples 366 ■ Tables of Random Numbers—Usage 367 ■ Random, Representative, Unbiased, Biased, and Other Samples 373 ■ Degrees of Freedom 375 ■ General Tests for Significant Difference 377 ■ Significant Difference Between Two Means and Two Variances 382 ■ Experimental Arrangements 385 ■ Latin Square 386 ■ Experimental Models—Classical versus Factorial Designs 387 ■ L_0 and L_1 Tests for Homogeneity 387 ■ Analysis of Variance 393

■ F-Test 394 ■ Additional Checks for Homogeneity 397 ■ Bartlett's Test 398 ■ Cochran's Test 399 ■ Compilations and Applications for Designs of Experiments with Applicable Analysis Tests 401

9 RELIABILITY AND MAINTAINABILITY ASSURANCE **411**

Objective 411 ■ System Design 415 ■ Achieving High Reliability in Certain Products 420 ■ The Failure Rate 421 ■ The Role of Statistics in Reliability 429 ■ Frequency and Probability Distributions 432

Part Two Managerial Concepts 437

INTRODUCTION 437

10 ORGANIZATION AND MANAGEMENT FOR PRODUCT ASSURANCE **439**

Objective 439 ■ Organization for Product Assurance 439 ■ Responsibilities of Quality Control Personnel 447 ■ The Working Climate 449 ■ Organizing and Planning Activities 451 ■ Organizing the Job 453 ■ Planning Work 454 ■ Achieving Efficiency 455 ■ Management-Worker Relationships 458 ■ Job Evaluation 466 ■ Job Descriptions 467 ■ Motivating Personnel 470 ■ The Quality Manager 474 ■ Research on Motivation 479 ■ Training Deterrents 486 ■ Training to Reduce Workmanship Defects 488 ■ Some Major Training Guidelines 490

11 SYSTEMS AND PROCEDURES **493**

Objective 493 ■ Industrial Systems 493 ■ The Information System 494 ■ Influences on System Performance 499 ■ Criteria for System Success 501 ■ Information for Management Decisions 502 ■ How Control Is Achieved 502 ■ Some Reasons for Loss of Control 505 ■ Overcoming Loss of Control 509

■ Forms Design and Control 510 ■ Prevention vs. Correction 512 ■ Management Support 514 ■ Role of Computers 515 ■ Dynamic Quality Control 521 ■ Requirements for the System 523

12 PROCUREMENT QUALITY CONTROL 525

Objective 525 ■ The Procurement Function 525 ■ Buying the Proper Quality 526 ■ Negotiating a Contract 538 ■ Evaluating Contractual Progress 546

13 STANDARDS FOR QUALITY 561

Objective 561 ■ The Importance of Standards 561 ■ Workmanship and Rework Standards 567 ■ Expressing Quality Standards 573 ■ Observance of Standards 576 ■ Standard Units of Measurement 578 ■ The Industrial Application 579 ■ Defining Accuracy and Precision 581 ■ Calibration 583 ■ Making Accurate Measurements 586

14 INSPECTION PRINCIPLES AND PRACTICES 595

Industrial Inspection 595 ■ Classifying Defects 598 ■ Inspection Planning 598 ■ Characteristics of a Lot 603 ■ Quantity of Inspection 604 ■ Quality Standards 605 ■ Criteria for Inspection 610 ■ Handling Rejections 614 ■ Responsibility for Quality 622 ■ Pitfalls for Inspectors 627 ■ Quality Control of Tooling 628 ■ Quality Control After Assembly Inspection 630

15 INSPECTION BY SAMPLING 635

Objectives 635 ■ Sampling Concepts 635 ■ 100% Inspection vs. Acceptance Sampling 636 ■ Criteria for Successful Inspection Sampling 638 ■ Acceptance Sampling Plans 642 ■ Probability Frequency Distributions for Attributes Inspection 654 ■ Features of MIL-STD-105 Sampling Plans 656 ■ The Dodge-Romig Tables 661 ■ Determination of Probabilities Involved in

Sampling 662 ■ Average Outgoing Quality 663 ■ Sampling Risks and Operating Characteristic Curves 675 ■ Operating Characteristic (OC) Curves 677 ■ Variables Inspection vs. Attributes Inspection 686

16 INTERNAL QUALITY AUDITS **695**

Need for Quality Audits 695 ■ Purposes for Auditing 695 ■ Typical Deficiencies Encountered—Quality Assurance Function 708 ■ Typical Deficiencies Encountered—Change Control Functions 710 ■ Typical Deficiencies Encountered—Procurement Function 711 ■ Typical Deficiencies Encountered—Measurement and Standards Functions 713 ■ Typical Deficiencies Encountered—Manufacturing In-Process Operations 719 ■ Typical Deficiencies Encountered—Training Function 721 ■ Typical Deficiencies Encountered—Quality Corrective Action System 721

17 ECONOMICS OF QUALITY CONTROL **725**

Quality Control for Profit 725 ■ Cost Records as a Control Device 725 ■ General Classification of Costs 727 ■ Cost Methods 730 ■ Quality Benefits of Standards 732 ■ Classifying and Reporting Quality Costs 733 ■ Implications of Quality Costs 738 ■ Pareto's Principle of Maldistribution 739 ■ Budgeting for Quality 741 ■ Measuring the Results of Quality Control 742 ■ Benefits of a Quality Control Program 748

BIBLIOGRAPHY **753**

Appendix A: Curve Fitting and Tables 759 ■ Appendix B: Derivations of Coefficients for Best Linear Lines of Regression 813 ■ Appendix C: Mathematical Relations and Tables of Factors for Computing Control Chart Lines 823

INDEX **837**

INDEX OF STATISTICAL TABLES

Table		Page
2.1	The Common Logarithms of e^{x} and e^{-x}	49
2.2	Common Logarithms and Natural Logarithms for the Integers 1–20 to Five Places	52
2.3	Common Logarithms of N × N! for Integers 1–20 to Ten Places	54
5.8	Three-Sigma Control Limits for Control Charts for Percent Defective	185–186
6.1	Factors for Computing Control Chart Lines	226
6.2	Factors for Computing Control Chart Lines—Chart for Individuals	227
6.6	Factors for Determining from σ' the Three-sigma Control Limits for $\bar{X}$, R, and σ Charts	230–231
6.7	Factors for Determining from $\bar{\sigma}$ the Three-sigma Control Limits for $\bar{X}$ and σ Charts	238
6.18	Factors for Estimating σ' from $\bar{R}$ or $\bar{\sigma}$	263
6.19	Factors for Determining the Three-sigma Control Limits for $\bar{X}$ and R Charts from $\bar{R}$	264
6.21	Factors for Computing Control Chart Lines—Standard Given	265–266
6.26	Factors for Computing Control Chart Lines—No Standard Given	273
6.42	Factors for Control Chart Limits Based on Medians (Using Median Range); Sample Sizes Given as Odds and Evens: 2–20	316
8.1	Random Sampling Numbers Part 1 Lines 1–25	354
	Random Sampling Numbers Part 2 Lines 26–50	355
8.18	L_0 Values[4] L_0 Five percent Values and One percent Values (n = 2 – 50)	389
8.19	L_1 Values[4] L_1 Five percent Values and One percent Values (n = 2 – 50)	389
8.27	F Distribution Table, page 1, 5% Points for Degrees of Freedom	395
	F Distribution Table, page 2, 1% Points for Degrees of Freedom	396
15.1	Table I of MIL–STD–105D: Code Letters for Sample Sizes	645
15.2	Table II–A of MIL–STD–105D: Normal Single Sampling	646
15.3	Table III–A of MIL–STD–105D: Normal Double Sampling	649
15.4	Table IV–A of MIL–STD–105D: Normal Multiple Sampling	651
15.10	Dodge-Romig Sampling Inspection Tables—	
	Single Sampling Plans AOQL = 2.0% and LTPD = 2.0%	666
	Single Sampling Table for Lot Tolerance Per Cent Defective (LTPD) = 2.0%	667

15.11 Dodge-Romig Sampling Inspection Tables—
Double Sampling Plans AOQL = 2.0% and LTPD = 2.0% 668
Double Sampling Table for Lot Tolerance Percent Defective (LTPD) = 2.0% 669
A.1 The Cumulative Normal Distribution, Parts 1 and 2 762–763
A.2 Normal Probability Function 764
A.3 Inverse of the Normal Probability Distribution
Part 1: Table of z Deviates of the Normal Curve for each Permille (3 significant figures, per thousand) of Frequency 765
Part 2: z Deviates of the Normal Distribution for P values 0.50 to 0.999999999 for most Practical Applications 766
A.4 Second Approximation Distribution, $F(z) = F_1(z) - kF_2(z)$ Tables A and B 767–768
A.5 Binomial Probability Distributions
Part 1: Individual Probabilities (n = 5, 10, 15, 20, 30, 50) 769–771
Part 2: Cumulative Probabilities (n = 5, 10, 15, 20, 30, 50) 772–774
A.6 Poisson's Exponential Binomial Limit
Part 1: Individual Terms of the Poisson Formula, $\frac{e^{-m}m^x}{x!}$ 775–780
Part 2: Tables of $\frac{e^{-m}m^x}{x!}$: Individual Terms of Poisson's Exponential Expansion ("Law of Small Numbers") 780–786
Part 3: Cumulative Terms of the Poisson Formula 787
A.7 t-Distribution—Two Forms and Different P Values
Part 1: Percentage Points of the t-Distribution $\alpha = 0.25$ to 0.0005, Probability Values 789
Part 2: Percentage Points of the t-Distribution—Values of t in Terms of A and v, A = 0.2 to 0.0999999, Probability Values 790
A.8 χ^2 Probability Function
Part 1: $Q = 0.995$ to 0.25 791
Part 2: $Q = 0.1$ to 0.0001 792
A.9 Logarithms of Factorials, $n! = \log \lfloor n$ 793–796
A.10 Logarithms of Numbers 797–798
A.11 Natural Logarithms 799
Factors for Computing Control Limits 827–829
Special Terms and Symbols Used in Appendix C 829–831

PREFACE TO THE REVISED EDITION

Quality—as it applies to products—and its control have become an integral part of the lives of both the consumer and the producer. More than ever before, quality is a key factor in the competitive marketplace. Consumers expect quality in the products they buy and exert great pressure on producers to maintain high standards of quality. Likewise, producers realize that if they are not competitive in all aspects of quality, they find it very difficult to survive.

There is a great need for people who have the necessary skills in both the technical and managerial aspects of quality control to effectively run modern businesses. The consequences of not having skilled quality people are always measured in terms of short-term and long-term profit drain for the company.

The authors of this text have taught many quality control and allied courses to students interested in industrial technology, quality control, and reliability engineering, and have found that available texts fail to meet practical training requirements. In the past, emphasis has been placed on pure theory, rather than on the application of these theories; hence, the majority of students have found most of the available texts difficult to understand and incomplete in the areas where quality control personnel most frequently need aid. Moreover, important fundamentals of mathematics as well as other prerequisites to courses offered by various colleges and industrial training programs have frequently been improperly mastered by the students. This text is designed to fill that gap by providing the foundation necessary to understand and apply statistical quality control techniques and product reliability procedures.

This textbook covers all the essential elements required to set up a system of quality control in a company. Students and managers of quality control alike will find the necessary tools and principles in this book that will be very beneficial in their understanding of the many aspects of quality control.

The book has been organized into two major parts:

Part I, which emphasizes statistical quality control for those students who need a better understanding of this subject and its applications.

Part II, which examines the management aspects of quality control. This section of the book can be used as a text for various management classes in quality control concepts.

Since the book covers all the major components of a quality control system in a company, it will also serve as an excellent reference for quality managers and other executives.

We wish to thank the authors and publishers who granted us permission to use their tables, and the publishers of this text for their interest in the project. We especially wish to thank Arvan Kent and Frank Squires for reading the manuscript and providing valuable suggestions for polishing the finished text.

PART ONE
STATISTICAL CONCEPTS

Introduction

In recent years, the concept of quality control has broadened in scope and importance in business and industry. Quality control functions that at one time were thought of as expensive burdens by industrial leaders are now not only commonplace, but are considered essential for successful operation in today's competitive market.

One trend that has focused attention on modern quality control methods is a growing awareness of the needs and demands of the customer—a trend that might be called *consumerism,* and one that is receiving much attention in and out of industry. It acknowledges the importance of customer satisfaction and recognizes that the consumer should expect to purchase safe, reliable products at fair prices. Because quality control divisions in manufacturing companies have the primary responsibility for ensuring and safeguarding quality of product, they are on the front line in winning consumer confidence.

Concurrent with the new social trends and advancing technology, an expansion has taken place in the scope of quality control functions. This has increased the need for highly qualified people to work in direct quality control areas. It has also emphasized the importance for those in related operations to have a better understanding of how the quality of product is created and safeguarded.

Among departments that typically operate in direct quality control areas are quality engineering, procurement quality control, inspection, metrology, configuration management, and reliability. In related areas, it is essential that the two departments most concerned with *creating* quality—design engineering and production—understand the functions and aims of quality control. Other departments that vitally influence the efficiency with which the company can deliver the expected product quality include purchasing, industrial engineering, marketing, contracts, and safety.

Among the most important tools used by quality control and related areas in the prevention and detection of defective units of production are various applications of statistics. Part One of this book is essentially devoted to this field, which is commonly referred to as *statistical quality control.* The most fundamental concepts are discussed first, progressing into the more complex statistical applications. The text is designed so that important definitions, symbolism, and tables are readily available to the student.

Numerous illustrations and examples of problems are presented to provide the reader with a broad and real understanding of quality control methodology. Statistical theory has little meaning in quality control without the knowledge of how to apply this theory to modern technology.

There are many places in industry where statistical quality control should be applied but is not. Conversely, there are probably places where it is applied but should not be. This may be accounted for by two major reasons:

1. Many managers both in and out of quality control work do not understand statistical control methods and therefore do not have an appreciation of their value.
2. Many people have a fine understanding of the *theoretical* aspects of statistics, but are so enamored of the pure mathematical concepts that the real value of statistics when properly *applied* to quality control is not realized.

Part One of this book has been written first to give the reader enough theory to understand the basic principles of statistical methods and then to present specific concepts and procedures that have proved effective in practical applications of statistical quality control.

CHAPTER ONE

INTRODUCTION TO QUALITY CONTROL

1.1 Objective

A company's reputation depends primarily on its ability to deliver a product of satisfactory quality to its customers. Quality control techniques are used to ensure that quality objectives are met as economically as possible, but obtaining the desired results is often a complex task. This chapter briefly traces some of the earliest uses of quality disciplines and the origins of modern statistical quality control methods. The reader is introduced to quality terminology and the different levels and facets of *quality, quality control,* and *reliability.* The use of statistical tools and operations research techniques to control and improve product quality is discussed, as well as the organizational approach for establishing quality control. The crucial role of adequately trained quality control personnel in the company organization makes clear the need for anyone seeking or making a career in these areas to learn the techniques and applications of statistical quality control.

1.2 Early History

Since the beginning of history, human ingenuity has been constantly tested to devise methods of obtaining food, shelter, and protection against enemies. Early cave people made creative use of natural resources to fulfill their basic needs and began to display an awareness of quality in the articles they produced. Improvements were made in protective armor and weapons. Metals were developed for swords and daggers that would not break in battle and that would hold a sharp edge. In fact, some of those metals (especially certain bronzes) are found to be better than similar metals produced today. Parchments and other writing materials that have not disintegrated with age were produced. Inks, made under controlled conditions, have not faded with time. Mummies, some dating back as far as 1000 B.C., were wrapped in cloths that are still in excellent condition.

During the Middle Ages, particularly the twelfth century, the guilds established standards of quality and required workers to be adequately trained. Rules were established for apprentices to become masters of their trades. Standards were also established for the finished products. This was especially true in the making of tapestries and ceramics. Early evidences of quality requirements are found in the products of China and other parts of Asia and even in some parts of Africa, as well as in Europe. In America, the ancient Mayas also made rapid developments in the arts and sciences. Based on the fact that there are 360 degrees in a circle, they developed a calendar similar to those currently in use containing approximately the same number of days in a year (360 to 366 days).

Even when one nation or area made great discoveries, it often took many years before others were able to reap the rewards of such developments, because of a great lag in methods of transportation and communication. When firearms were first developed, each gun was made individually so that parts from one gun differed greatly from similar parts on another. With the use of mercenary troops, the need for similar weapons by large bodies of troops was found especially necessary. An important offshoot of the Industrial Revolution was the interchangeability of similar parts. This marked the beginning of one of the more important phases of modern quality control. Where previously most parts were made individually by hand or possibly with the aid of auxiliary tools, machines were developed to produce similar parts. Some of the earliest of these were molds used to make containers, bowls, candles, vases and many ceramics. The churches and cathedrals contained many objects that had to be similar in nature, such as pews and chairs, stained glass windows, kneeling pads and archways. The columns in the early Greek and Roman temples were alike in most structures, and the arenas used a common type of architecture.

With the introduction of standardization and mass production came the realization that controls must be exercised in many different areas. Clothing sizes had to be standardized to assure a reasonable fit in ready-made clothing. It is now universally assumed that one can buy clothing by specified sizes and be assured that the garments will fit. In the past, most garments had to be tailor-made, and each individual spent many weary hours being fitted. Other examples of the growth of standardization are building construction from masses of lumber sawed to size and roads built with materials such as cement that are essentially homogeneous so that the strength and wearing characteristics are similar in nature.

Improvements based on successes and failures were continually being made. But, throughout these developments, no definite methodology was in effect. Railroads were built with the distances between the two rails on which the two-wheeled cars traveled differing from one railroad company to another. It became necessary to standardize on the width between rails so that cars could be transferred from one system to another. This was particularly true for freight cars, which transported goods across the various boundary lines of the various adjacent states. The development of railroads to replace the horse-drawn wagons and carriages was a great step forward. The use of steam instead of wind to propel ocean vessels led to the development of the modern ocean liners and brought nations closer together. The improvements in communications, particularly as developed in America, became a significant factor in providing more rapid improvements in technology and the production of quality products.

Technological advances occurred rather slowly over the centuries, growing out of a multitude of small improvements. Before the nineteenth and twentieth centuries, there was comparatively little technical change. But late in the nineteenth and early twentieth centuries, such innovations as telephones, diesel locomotives, reliable air travel, and automobiles were introduced. In a chain-reactionlike pattern, new materials and processes led to new ideas and inventions. Such historical milestones as the development of the atomic bomb and the manufacture of space vehicles were little more than conversational topics only a few years ago. Now, the precision and reliability with which components must perform is unsurpassed in the history of mankind. Technology has become an integral part of the everyday lives of millions of people. It furnishes a livelihood not only to those who are directly engaged in various phases of industry, but also to millions of others who are less directly related to industry itself.

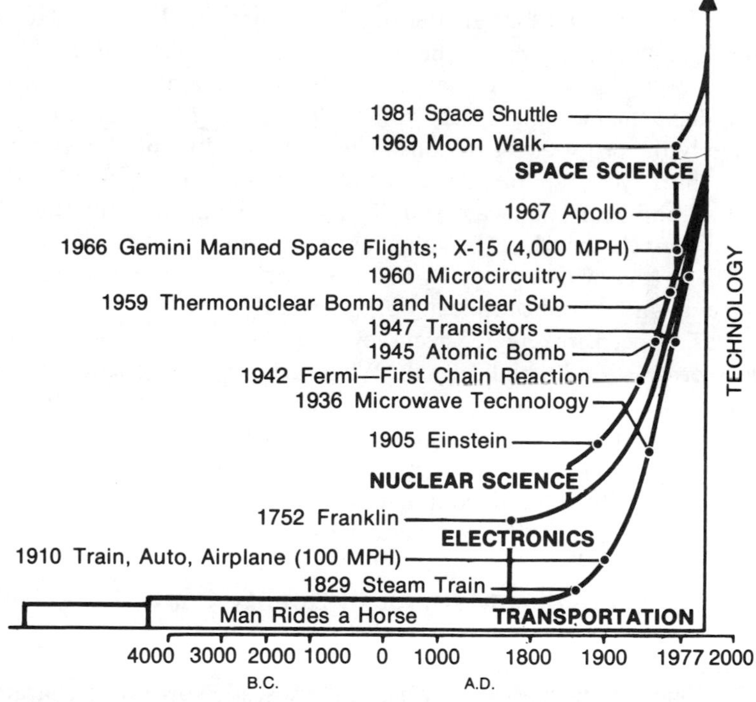

Figure 1–1 Acceleration of technology.

Figure 1-1 graphically shows how technology has accelerated throughout history. It also marks some important innovations and milestones experienced during these years. Industrial growth has accompanied technological advances. Before the twentieth century, fewer people were employed in a company and the owner was frequently both the producer and distributor of his products. The area occupied by the plant was generally small and one man could control, for all practical purposes, the activities within the enterprise. Workers not only had the opportunity to learn the skills used in the manufacture of a product, but also had some knowledge of its end use. Normally, in addition to the function of machining, a machinist performed other manufacturing operations required to produce a product. Hence, the machinist was a lathe operator, a maintenance worker, and an inspector as well. The individual work center was unspecialized; the total job called for greater operator versatility and encompassed a greater variety of equipment and tools. The machinist had flexibility to make judgments regarding both the design and manufacture of the products.

As technology advanced, it became necessary to introduce middlemen into the total economic structure. Dealers, wholesalers, and retailers all became integral parts of the producer-consumer cycle. With this broadening sphere of business activity, there was attendant expansion of industrial organization. Executives became aware that the tasks of administration and control could no longer be accomplished without greater organizational detail. In order to control activities and manage effectively, it became necessary to classify the labor force into smaller functional units. The scope of activities became less for each work center and department, and specialization for each group became greater. Where formerly the proprietor and consumer could conduct business activities in a simple and short cycle, separate departments such as finance, design, production, quality control and inspection, sales, purchasing, receiving, and shipping all were needed to effectively conduct business as companies became larger. Bigger companies, combined with a generally broader scope of business activity, greatly increased the dynamics and complexity of the overall industrial system.

An increasing need for greater accuracy and precision also was experienced during this period of industrial growth. When articles were created by artisans in early cultures, a close tolerance was considered to be not more than could be detected without the help of magnification tools. Technology had not developed to the extent that closer tolerances were needed. But as new methods, processes, and machinery were introduced, commensurate need for more accurate measurement and dimensional control was experienced.

1.3 Origin of Statistical Methods in Quality Control

Statistical methods were first applied to inspection problems in 1916 by C. N. Frazee of Telephone Laboratories. The use of the so-called operating characteristic OC curve was introduced by Frazee, who originated curves of this nature covering half the domain of the probability of acceptance range from 0 to 100%. It was necessary to obtain measures of the probability of acceptance for various sampling plans then in use. To accomplish this, F. Thorndike[1] prepared and published cumulative probability curves of the Poisson exponential distribution in the October 1926 issue of *The Bell System Technical Journal*. Tabulated values of both *Table I: Individual Terms* and *Table II: Cumulated Terms* were prepared by E. C. Molina and published in 1949.[2] These curves and tables are used today, not only in sampling inspection but in reliability engineering. These pioneers in the field of statistical quality control made it possible to develop much more rapidly the efficient sampling tables now available.

An important breakthrough in the history of quality control came in 1924 when Dr. Walter A. Shewhart, then in the engineering department of Western Electric, was given a large amount of manufacturing data to evaluate. Although a physicist rather than a statistician, Dr. Shewhart realized the best techniques that could be applied to these data were of a statistical nature. The Bell Telephone Laboratories was organized and incorporated at this time, and Dr. Shewhart became a member of its technical staff. In this capacity, he developed the concept of applying statistical methods by the use of control charts to determine whether a particular manufacturing process was controlled within chance variation limits or was out of control due to some definite, assignable causes.

The inspection department of the Bell Telephone Laboratories was organized under Dr. Reginald Jones, and Dr. Shewhart continued his studies in that group with the aid of many of the staff members of the inspection department of BTL. At that time, Harold F. Dodge and George DeForest Edwards joined Dr. Shewhart in the development of quality control within the inspection department, and were joined in 1926 by Dr. Harry G. Romig. The December 1949 issue of *Fortune* listed these men as the original developers of the quality control movement. Many others also contributed to statistical applications of quality control in the Western Electric Company. Dr. Walter Bartky of the University of Chicago, for example, acted as consultant and first developed continuous sampling methods for Western Electric's use. Two working committees were organized, one on *inspection* and one on *rating*. Standards of quality were established and millions of dollars were saved in the communications area.

While this work continued, there was very little acceptance by industry in general of quality control until the nineteen forties. The first real breakthrough was in the field of testing. A committee on methods of testing was formed; it was sponsored by the American Society for Testing and Materials and consisted of H. F. Dodge as chairman, and three other members, W. C. Chancellor, J. T. MacKenzie, and R. T. Webster. R. F. Passano and H. G. Romig were contributors in the preparation of the 1933 American Society for Testing and Materials (ASTM) manual on Presentation of Data. This included *Supplement A: Presenting Limits of Uncertainty of An Observed Average* and *Supplement B: Control Chart Method of Analysis and Presentation of Data.* This brochure was continuously upgraded and eventually became the *ASTM Manual on Quality Control of Materials* with a complete presentation of the theory of control charts and applications, an excellent reference for use in industry today.

Although the first application of acceptance sampling by the method of variables was instituted by the Bell Telephone Laboratories in 1934, the first published work was that of the doctoral dissertation of H. G. Romig dated March 1939 titled *Allowable Average in Sampling Inspection.* Following this, in the forties,

Figure 1–2 Growth in the responsibilities of the quality control organization.

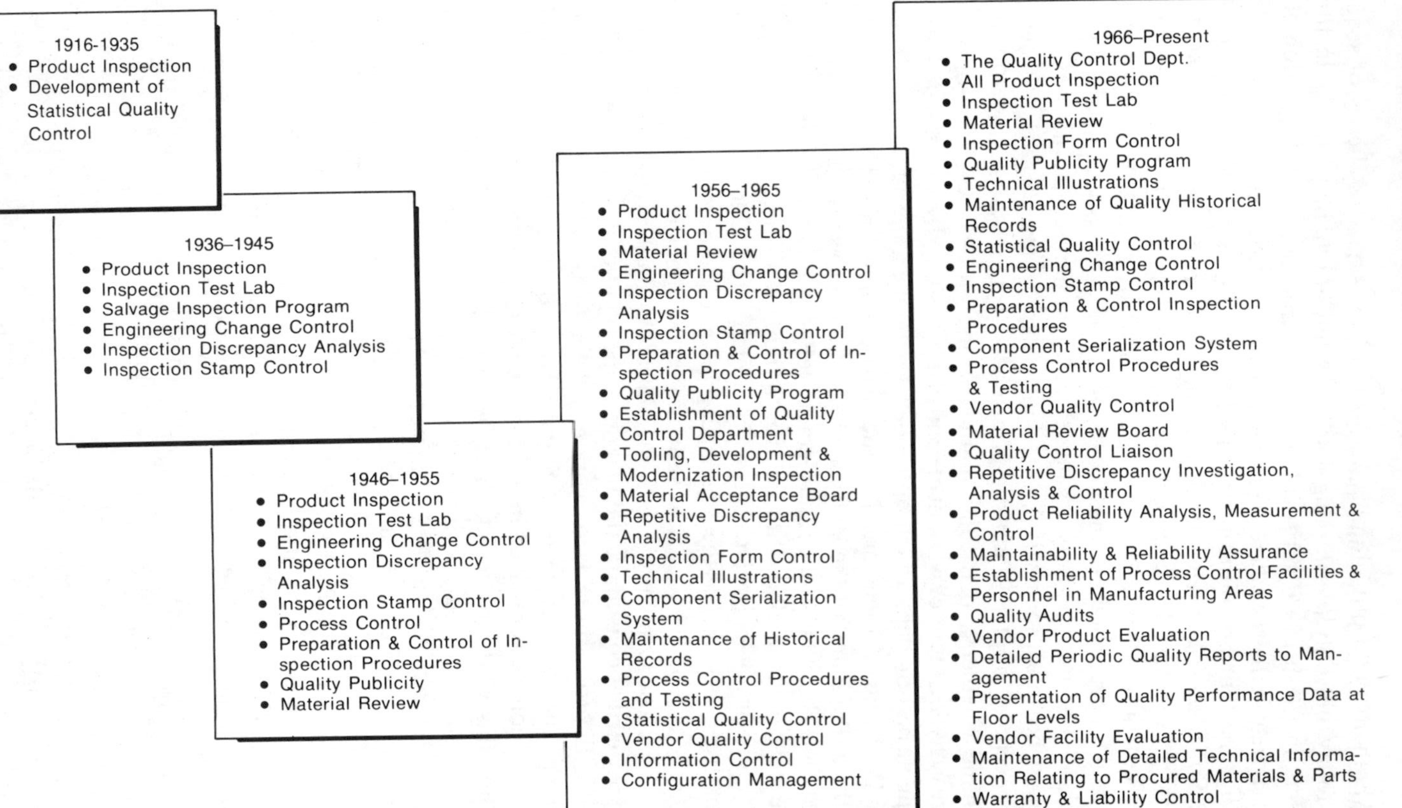

1916-1935
• Product Inspection
• Development of Statistical Quality Control
1936–1945
• Product Inspection
• Inspection Test Lab
• Salvage Inspection Program
• Engineering Change Control
• Inspection Discrepancy Analysis
• Inspection Stamp Control
1946–1955
• Product Inspection
• Inspection Test Lab
• Engineering Change Control
• Inspection Discrepancy Analysis
• Inspection Stamp Control
• Process Control
• Preparation & Control of Inspection Procedures
• Quality Publicity
• Material Review
1956–1965
• Product Inspection
• Inspection Test Lab
• Material Review
• Engineering Change Control
• Inspection Discrepancy Analysis
• Inspection Stamp Control
• Preparation & Control of Inspection Procedures
• Quality Publicity Program
• Establishment of Quality Control Department
• Tooling, Development & Modernization Inspection
• Material Acceptance Board
• Repetitive Discrepancy Analysis
• Inspection Form Control
• Technical Illustrations
• Component Serialization System
• Maintenance of Historical Records
• Process Control Procedures and Testing
• Statistical Quality Control
• Vendor Quality Control
• Information Control
• Configuration Management
1966–Present
• The Quality Control Dept.
• All Product Inspection
• Inspection Test Lab
• Material Review
• Inspection Form Control
• Quality Publicity Program
• Technical Illustrations
• Maintenance of Quality Historical Records
• Statistical Quality Control
• Engineering Change Control
• Inspection Stamp Control
• Preparation & Control Inspection Procedures
• Component Serialization System
• Process Control Procedures & Testing
• Vendor Quality Control
• Material Review Board
• Quality Control Liaison
• Repetitive Discrepancy Investigation, Analysis & Control
• Product Reliability Analysis, Measurement & Control
• Maintainability & Reliability Assurance
• Establishment of Process Control Facilities & Personnel in Manufacturing Areas
• Quality Audits
• Vendor Product Evaluation
• Detailed Periodic Quality Reports to Management
• Presentation of Quality Performance Data at Floor Levels
• Vendor Facility Evaluation
• Maintenance of Detailed Technical Information Relating to Procured Materials & Parts
• Warranty & Liability Control
• Integrated Information Systems

Dr. Abraham Wald of Columbia University developed the theory of sequential analysis. Using this theory, Dr. H. A. Freeman of Massachusetts Institute of Technology developed criteria for acceptance sampling. The combination of these results in usable tables was achieved by Albert H. Bowker and Henry P. Goode of Stanford University in 1952 in their work, *Sampling Inspection by Variables.*[3] Many other military specifications not mentioned in the footnote that are used in quality control and reliability engineering could be cited, but the aforementioned are sufficient to indicate that the military as well as industry have developed procedures and techniques that must be considered by practically all quality control personnel.

In 1946, Dr. Grant I. Butterbaugh of the University of Washington published a bibliography of statistical quality control and in 1951 published a supplement to the earlier volume. Materials covering these fields are noted in the various texts that have since been published and should be consulted. The journal of the American Society for Quality Control (ASQC), *Industrial Quality Control,* was changed to *Quality Progress* in 1967 and a quarterly technical journal, *Journal of Quality Technology,* was coincidently originated in this area. Some of the printing concerns issued journals covering quality control and mailed them to interested quality control personnel free since they contained advertisements of items that would be useful in quality control.

The Institute of Electrical and Electronic Engineers (IEEE) originally had a division covering quality control and reliability. After several years the term *quality control* was deleted. The IEEE reliability division currently publishes a journal covering quality control and reliability engineering which contains much valuable material for quality control engineers. The IEEE also sponsors an annual reliability conference, averaging more than 2,000 people in attendance, at which the latest developments in reliability as well as certain phases of quality control and operations research are presented.

1.4 Definition of Quality

Quality has been variously defined as "fitness for use," "meeting an expectation," "degree of excellence," and "conformance to a standard," along with other phrases. These all have merit, depending upon one's point of view. Two principal aspects of quality are *functional* and *appearance* criteria. Functional characteristics encompass performance factors such as reliability, durability, and maintainability, while appearance criteria pertain to cosmetic features such as color, smoothness, lines, and texture. When setting standards for quality, one must therefore prescribe either or both functional and cosmetic criteria. For example, an engineering drawing is largely a functional standard that sets forth specific tolerances within which a part must be fabricated. Auxiliary specifications further describe functional or appearance features. Only after operating and appearance standards have been established and clearly defined can conformance of items built to these standards be properly assessed.

1.5 Definition of Quality Control

The quality control organization has been identified many ways and its personnel have been called many things, but perhaps the best definition of quality control, per se, is set forth in MIL–STD–109. This definition is: "Quality control is a management function whereby control of quality of raw materials and produced goods is exercised for the purpose of preventing production of defective units." To fulfill these responsibilities, quality control organizations must use every means and device practicable to prevent, detect, and correct errors or any tendency toward errors that occur in the steps of producing hardware. This implies that to accomplish the goal of quality control, certain variables that affect quality resulting from workmanship, material, and machinery must be controlled. Workers vary in skill, materials vary in composition because of processing variations, and machines vary in performance because of variations of design, fabrication, and wear. In order to achieve quality control, variables that occur in product design, materials, processing, and fabrication must be brought under control.

Inspection is that part of quality control that pertains to detection. The total inspection operation often encompasses the appraisal of purchased parts, manufactured parts, and even parts in service. The purpose of inspection is to determine by examination of parts or witnessing of tests whether or not the product conforms to established standards of quality.

There is an integral relationship between quality control and inspection organizations, since, in order to attain control of quality, the examination of parts for the purpose of verifying their conformance is necessary. In actual practice, however, the quality control organization usually develops specifications and procedures that are carried out by the inspection personnel.

1.6 Scope of Quality Control

High product quality is achieved by maintaining a system of quality control that circumscribes the operation of effective control devices in all major functions in a company. These functions include contracts, product development, design, procurement, manufacturing, packaging, and maintainability. Throughout the period from receipt of a contract or a sales order until a customer uses the product, plans for various controls must be put into effect to achieve expected quality levels. Figure 1–3 illustrates the cycle of activities and the controls found in a typical manufacturing company. This diagram represents, in general, the phases of product development and manufacture and the applications of various degrees of quality controls.

1.7 Definition of Life-Cycle Quality

Product quality can be viewed from several perspectives. One attempts to establish quality requirements, develop and design the requirements, build the

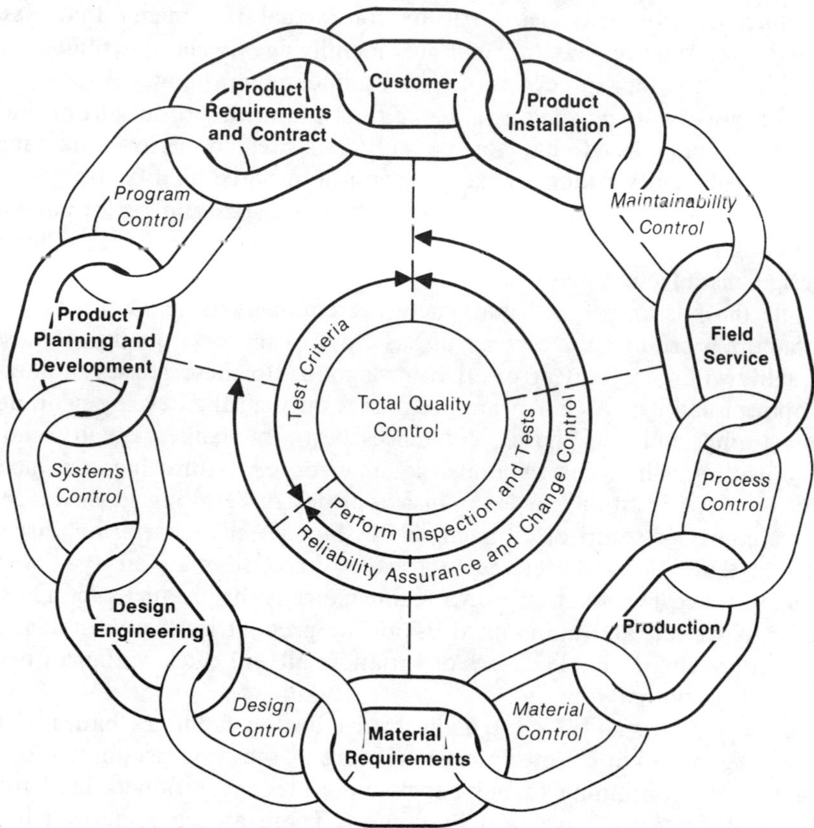

Figure 1–3 The scope of quality control.

desired features into the product, and finally market the product, even though the expectations, intentions, and realities may not coincide. In fact, it would be only by chance if they did. Fundamentally, the quality of a product can be classified in four major categories:

1. Stated quality
2. Real quality
3. Advertised quality
4. Experienced quality

Stated quality is the quality set forth in a purchase order or contract. It is the level of quality expected by the vendee or contractor from a vendor or subcontractor. It is described in drawings and specifications by terms and characteristics that can be identified and measured. It includes both the functional and esthetic attributes that can be objectively quantified and described.

Stated quality may also be thought of as the *planned* or *target* level of quality. A predetermined level of quality is defined by drawings and specifications. This level either is arbitrarily set forth in contractual statements that describe expected performance criteria without identifying specific attributes, or is developed directly through cycles of testing and drawing changes.

Real quality is the *ongoing actual quality* of a unit or product from the time it is created and placed into service until it ceases to perform its intended function. Real quality seldom, if ever, is identical to stated quality.

Predictions or expectations of product characteristics and performance may not be congruent with real quality because of the myriad variables inherent in the design, manufacture and use of a product.

While the mission of any manufacturing company is to plan, design, and manufacture a product for a given use as close to planned quality as possible, real quality will reflect any errors that have gone into these phases of hardware development and use. As hardware progresses through the development, design, manufacturing, and use phases, differences between planned quality and real quality usually will occur. A dimensional error on a drawing, an incorrect callout on a specification, an error in a tool design resulting in an inaccurate tool, an improper setup of a machine causing defective parts, an inspection procedure that allows defectives to pass, a defective material that was not thoroughly tested, lack of or improper maintenance of the product after it has been placed into service, and unintended use of the product by the consumer, along with countless unassignable causes of variation, all will cause variances between stated quality and real quality.

Predicted real quality is often illustrated by the familiar "bathtub" curve shown in figure 9-4 in chapter nine. Beginning at the time products are finally assembled and continuing through their life cycles, all products tend to have similar probabilities of successes or failures. These are characterized in three traditional stages. All products tend to experience a high probability of early failure (infant mortality), low probability of failure during the normal operating period (prime of life), and high probability of failure during the final period when degradation and fatigue occur (old age).

If the model for the bathtub curve had characteristics identical to the actual operating characteristics of a product or unit, then the actual quality line would coincide with the bathtub curve. However, the degree to which such a prediction can be accurate for any given product is predicated on (1) the degree to which *reliability* has been designed into the product (which takes into account its operating environment and use factors), and (2) the degree to which the manufacturing and quality control systems are effective in building and safeguarding the quality that has been designed into the product.

Real quality should be the same as planned quality, but because of the many variables inherent in the design and manufacturing phases of hardware development, real quality is usually to some degree either higher or lower than stated quality. A higher real quality level than that which has been planned is costly, but can help to build the reputation that the company is a producer of high quality merchandise. If real quality is lower than that which has been planned, the consequences can be even more costly. Considerable losses may be experienced through customer complaints and corrective actions as well as ultimate loss of customer goodwill.

Advertised quality is that composite of quality characteristics that an article is proclaimed to possess by a manufacturer and/or seller. These attributes are often expressed in warranties; if not, certain performance characteristics of the item are usually implied.

Advertised quality, of course, should be as close to real quality as possible. False claims about product quality, deliberate or otherwise, can result in serious problems for a manufacturer or seller. False or misleading absolute statements such as *completely safe* or *fully guaranteed* should be avoided. Numerous costly consequences may result from marketing a product that does not meet advertised quality standards.

Honest wrong beliefs about the quality of a product can also lead to costly circumstances. Results of laboratory tests may indicate that a product *should* perform as predicted, but regardless of precautions that can be taken, there is always a chance that a unit will fail. The certainty of predictions of product success is directly proportional to the amount of testing and consequent cost that one is willing to incur. Liability resulting from unsafe product operation can be financially devastating to a company if false or misleading statements have been made about quality levels. Even if a company can win a court decision, the costs for the defense actions are usually very high.

Experienced quality is that quality actually experienced by a user of a product. There are also many variables that affect this category of quality. For example, experienced quality may be defined in terms of how the product really performs, whether the product lasts a longer or shorter time than predicted or advertised, whether or not it is durable and safe for use, and the degree to which it is subjected to unintended use or abuse. Thus experienced quality may be found to be considerably different from any one or all of the aforementioned categories. If the planned quality does not account for unintended uses of a product, for example, it may have a short useful life; if safety factors have not been designed into a product, these features cannot be manufactured, and hence safety hazards will be experienced by the user; if maintainability has not been planned and designed into the product, its useful life will invariably be shortened; and if, when developing the product, it was not tested under the environmental conditions to which it will ultimately be subjected, its useful life will probably be shortened.

Abuse or misuse of the product will also shorten the normal operating period of a product, reflecting variances between real quality, stated quality, and experienced quality. It is primarily for this reason that human and maintainability factors are important considerations in early stages of product development. The primary mission of any manufacturing company is to bring these four categories of quality—stated, real, advertised, and experienced—in as close agreement as possible. This can be accomplished by:

1. Taking early preventive measures to plan quality levels on the basis of history of past products and uses of materials, etc. Customer surveys of

product uses, applications and operating characteristics, for example, often provide much relevant information about experienced quality. This feedback from users about product weaknesses, strengths, operating characteristics, and uses is vitally needed for decisions pertaining to new or revised products. In addition, such data are needed to warn the user against certain unintended uses and practices.

2. Implementing a testing program, the results of which can be used accurately to calculate reliability characteristics of components and assemblies, and producing a design with sufficient safety margins or fail safe devices.
3. Inaugurating a system of quality control that is integrated philosophically as well as functionally with procurement, development and design, and with all phases of manufacturing, and maintenance of the products. If such a system can be made efficient, the disparity between planned quality, designed quality, manufactured quality, stated quality, real quality, advertised quality, and experienced quality will be minimized.

1.8 Definition of Statistical Quality Control

The definition and principles of statistical quality control are discussed in many journals and references. One of the best is that given in the 13th volume of the latest *Encyclopedia of the Social Sciences,* page 225.[4] The following brief definition and description of statistical quality control precedes the three articles listed below, while three paragraphs in the first article covering acceptance sampling show the relationship between statistical quality control and acceptance sampling.

> STATISTICAL QUALITY CONTROL
>
> "Quality control," in its broadest sense, refers to a spectrum of managerial methods for attempting to maintain the quality of manufactured articles at a desired level. "Statistical quality control" can refer to all those methods that use statistical principles and techniques for the control of quality. In this broad sense, statistical quality control might be regarded as embracing in principle all of statistical methodology. Some areas of statistics, however, have, both historically and as currently used, a special relationship to quality control; it is these areas that are discussed in the articles under this heading. The methods of quality control described in these articles have applications in fields other than industrial manufacturing. For example, process control has been used successfully as an administrative technique in large-scale data-handling organizations, such as census bureaus. Reliability concepts are important in engineering design and seem potentially useful in small-group research.

1.9 Purposes of Statistical Quality Control

The present modern approach to quality control makes use of statistics as one of its most important tools. This is particularly true where there is ready access to computer services. One need not know the theory of computers or all the details needed to prepare the best possible computer programs, but one should appreciate the aid that computers will provide in utilizing all the data that may be accumulated in inspection, tests, and measurements. In the past, very poor records were kept of inspection results. These records usually included only such information as the number of failures and whether the lot or products submitted for acceptance were accepted or rejected. The number of units submitted and accepted were normally recorded so that payment might be made for such items. Now all possible results are recorded in detail so that such information may be given to the computing staff for their evaluation. Such data, when summarized properly, indicate whether or not a product is acceptable and what steps for better control should be taken.

It is realized that inspections must be made to determine whether to accept or reject lots of a product offered for acceptance or rejection. A sampling plan is based on the assumption that the products offered for inspection are essentially homogeneous in nature. Further, it is hoped that they are made under statistically controlled conditions. If these conditions are found to be true, then valid predictions may be made concerning the quality of the product under consideration.

A principal purpose of statistical quality control is to regulate the various processes of manufacture and assembly at desired economic levels of quality. The data obtained by inspection and test are used on the control charts to determine whether control exists at desired levels of quality and whether the industrial processes may be continued or should be stopped. Properly used, control charts indicate whether or not the resultant products will be unacceptable for use. In many companies, control charts are only applied to the processes that seem to be producing an excessive number of failures. Once statistical control is achieved, only simple inspection is applied until trouble is again encountered.

1.10 Controls to Implement Quality Assurance

It is necessary for the well-trained quality control engineer and supervisor to have sufficient command of the principles of statistical quality control to be able to apply these principles where needed. Appropriate training must be provided so that the personnel can readily apply quality control techniques in any part of the production process.

There are usually not sufficient personnel in a quality control department to monitor all phases of a company's operations. This is particularly true in production. For very critical items, some companies have used an inspector for each production worker. This is extremely costly even though very effective. A division of General Motors Corporation incorporated this one-to-one ratio when making Hyatt Bearings. The production division for Monroe calculators had almost 50 per cent of their personnel evaluating and inspecting their units in some areas to make certain they were meeting all requirements. But such procedures are usually too costly. It is more efficient to train production workers in quality control techniques so that quality control technicians merely have to spot-check the work of the production workers. This makes the production workers a part of the quality assurance team and is an effective performance incentive. This method of operation has been described in many papers, particularly in some presented in the United States by Japanese quality control supervisors. They term it the *circle* approach, in which supervisors and workers together with quality control personnel jointly discuss and check the quality of their products during all phases of production.

In some industries, statistical quality control charts for the most critical items are used by the production workers themselves. Quality control personnel lay out these charts in such a way that the worker takes little time from his production operation to maintain a quality control chart. The simplest forms of statistics are used. For example, on one vacuum tube line, the operators had to check a very critical item. After the check was made, the numerical reading found was plotted on a chart. When five readings were plotted, the middle value was circled as the median. If this median value was within the control limits prescribed by the quality control organization, the product was considered to be satisfactory for this item. If the median value was outside its control limits, the operator would call the supervisor in charge and the process would be readjusted at the desired level since it was evident that it had wandered from the desired central value.

Many simple devices of this kind are valuable aids for providing the quality assurance required for the product under consideration. In some cases, inspection and quality control may find a loose part or a part stained or painted the wrong shade. In some union shops, only production workers are permitted to correct such plainly visible defects. However, agreements can be reached in which the person finding such a minor nonconformance will correct it immediately so that it does not progress to the next operation without being corrected. Hence, procedures for simple corrective measures are often the best tools for preventing the inclusion of nonconforming units in shipments to customers.

1.11 Product Effectiveness

The term *product effectiveness* is often used in companies to indicate that the design for that particular kind of product is adequate and that the resultant product will operate effectively. In reliability texts, the term is broadened to cover more complex units and is expressed as *system effectiveness*. These terms mean that measures have been taken to have an adequate and complete program for securing products or systems that will operate and function effectively and that these results have been achieved at minimum costs. System engineers often study or test the various parts, products, or components to determine their life characteristics. When such checks are made, the units may be graded with respect to their effective usability by the consumer.

Certain phases of systems engineering and configuration management may be applied to make certain that complete procedures and methods are available and to assure that all parts and engineering changes have been properly identified and made. These evaluations, in conjunction with many kinds of reliability studies, are useful in determining what guarantees or warranties may be made for these products. In many instances, the customer may desire tabulations or reports covering the potential reliability of his product. Quality assurance techniques, which will be discussed later in this text, provide these measures.

Special techniques are required to show that the interactions between the various components of a complex piece of equipment or system are favorable rather than unfavorable. The designs may have to be reviewed in case there appear to be possible instances of incompatibility between the parts of the system. Where all components seem to meet the requirements but the system will not function, techniques for studying the various possible interactions must be applied. A reevaluation of the design may lead to improvement in the operation of the unit and increased product effectiveness. The methods used to achieve these results should be recorded.

1.12 Reliability, Maintainability, and Availability

For the effective development of quality control, many other disciplines become a part of the overall plan and program. In the early phases of production control, use was made of efficiency engineering and the techniques developed in this discipline. An efficient piece of apparatus or equipment must be reliable. To achieve reliability, care must be taken to make certain that the most important characteristics of a design are held within close tolerances to assure effective and efficient operation. The efficiency engineer has developed many effective methods to achieve these results and has attempted to obtain the best method as economically as possible. But in some cases, certain parts in a system may be made *too* reliable for their particular application. If system failure is caused by weak parts in the system, needless costs may be incurred in developing strong parts elsewhere if their potential life is only partially used. In this instance, costs to develop these high-reliability parts would not be warranted.

The goal for any group of components is to have their operating time the same so that all fail essentially at the same time. Techniques for obtaining reliable parts are discussed in this text, together with the various maintainability practices required to attain the reliabilities desired. What is most desired is that all parts are ready to go when wanted. Instant availability[5] is desired but cannot always be achieved. However, preventive maintenance measures and proper care of all parts may result in almost 100 percent availability for the system. For example, most car owners are fairly certain that their cars will operate when needed. With proper maintenance, very few cars fail to function when needed. The owner does make certain that the car has adequate gasoline, oil, and ignition at all times. If the owner is careless about looking after the battery—the source of energy for a good ignition system—the system may break down and the engine will not start.

Thus, poor maintenance practices result in lack of good availability for a car. Those in quality control work need to be conversant with actions required to provide good reliability, maintainability, and availability, and also those other factors that might cause the failure of these necessary features.

1.13 Organizing to Achieve Effective Quality Control

Although an entire chapter in Part Two of this text will be devoted to organization and management, it is desirable at this point to consider the effects of various types of organizations on the proper development of quality control. In the past, when inspection was supplemented by groups engaged in other phases of quality control, the inspector was often given the quality control responsibilities and thus was monitoring his own activities. Such self-evaluations did not result in an effective quality control program. The possible savings achieved by controlling processes at the desired levels, and thus reducing the production of nonconforming units, usually is not possible under such a pseudo-organization. When the responsibilities of quality control are given to a supervisor and his group, the supervisor must also be given the authority to effectively carry out those responsibilities. Such a quality control supervisor should be given the authority to hire employees and to terminate the employment of personnel in his department.

There are many forms of organizations that are effective. When quality control and inspection are placed under production management, the quality control program is usually ineffective. When inspectors reject articles, their decisions can be easily overruled by production if inspection is subjugated to production. In the development of the most effective use of quality control as a tool for management, the struggle for equality within production in many industries continues to be a problem.

The same holds true for reliability, as it must also be independent of the project leader. Although the project leader needs the reliability information obtained by the reliability engineering group, evaluations of design and resultant products reliability must be an independent effort to provide unbiased results for top management.

When properly organized with a suitable balance between all departments, quality control will be able to effectively control the quality of all parts as well as any resultant systems that are being developed and produced. Thus proper organization is one of the most important phases in the development of an effective quality control organization.

1.14 Need for Adequately Trained Quality Control Personnel

The majority of the tasks in quality control are relatively simple and may be easily learned. With supervision, most personnel can be trained to carry out these tasks. Quality control personnel performing work besides inspection should also become knowledgeable about inspection and testing functions in the company. Particularly in a company that produces a large variety of products, knowledge of the characteristics of these products as well as inspection techniques required to inspect and test them should not be limited to a few individuals in the quality control department. Personnel should not only be able to read blueprints and interpret specifications, but they should also be informed about measuring devices and nondestructive testing methods. Some may need to be able to evaluate soldering and welding results and to separate poor work from acceptable work. Others may need to know how to interpret X rays and other specialized inspection methods, such as those used to detect flaws and cracks in metals.

A good quality control department will provide periodical training courses in the techniques required. Where no one is qualified to train the workers in these areas, use can be made of the courses given at colleges and universities in the area, or a qualified instructor may be hired as a consultant both to train personnel and to aid in the evaluation of quality problems. Such consultants help to provide answers to problems such as complex quality control deviations that may have been introduced through purchases, production, and final assembly, as well as through carelessness of inspection personnel in making certain inspections. Many government purchase orders require that personnel be certificated and include specifications for regular training in the contract.

Manuals and procedures covering all the activities of a quality control and/or reliability organization must be well written and followed. Special methods and techniques should be clearly written and in line with all available specifications. Specific training in carrying out such operations should be provided. Courses may be scheduled during the day and after work hours and placed in effect as needed. Such courses should be tailored to the needs of the industry involved. The local sections of the American Society for Quality Control often sponsor such courses and aid the industries to secure well-trained instructors to provide the type of training required by their personnel. Many of the community colleges provide a series of courses that lead to a certificate or a two-year degree in quality control. Some four-year colleges and universities offer bachelor's and master's degrees in this field.

The American Society for Quality Control also sponsors courses given throughout the country. This society provides national certificates in both quality control and reliability. The courses offered help one to pass national examinations pertaining to these professions. Professional state licensing in quality control has gained much impetus during the last several years. California was among the first to achieve this goal.

The status of quality control is continually being improved. If those working in this area take advantage of the educational opportunities offered, they will provide better leadership and thus make quality control a truly professional vocation. The basic objectives of quality control are to improve quality standards, improve the quality of goods and services provided the consumer, and to increase the national wealth.

1.15 Mathematical Requirements in Quality Control

For most operations conducted in a quality control department, ordinary common sense is a chief ingredient in making effective decisions and judgments. However, statistical aspects often require a certain amount of mathematical proficiency. To cover possible deficiency in this area, chapter two presents the fundamentals of mathematics needed to utilize effectively the recent developments in all phases of quality control work. This includes learning to perform the four operations of addition, subtraction, multiplication, and division without error. Use must also be made of squares and square roots. Generally, tables are available that provide squares, square roots, and reciprocals. Knowledge also must be acquired concerning the nature and use of logarithms and tables in which these values are presented. Moreover, values for exponential tables based on the Poisson exponential and negative exponents for the Napierian base e, such as e^{-x}, are used extensively in reliability evaluations; a student of quality control must have a working knowledge of these tables as well as many others such as the areas under the normal law and probability values associated with the binomial relation.

Most statistical relations are simple. Control charts are based primarily on the use of measures of central tendency and measures of variability. Some knowledge of descriptive statistics is helpful but not always necessary. Distributions are based on statistical concepts developed in many fields. The normal law or "bell-shaped" distribution and the Chi-square (χ^2) distribution are used extensively. Fortunately, tables have been published that provide numerical values covering most fields of application. For finite universes, as contrasted with infinite universes, the hypergeometric distribution relation is used. To properly evaluate probability values associated with this function, some knowledge of combinations, permutations, and factorials is also needed. It must be emphasized that evaluations of all the statistical problems arising in quality control may be most readily made by using available tables. Most mathematical operations may be done with pencil and paper or carried out with little effort by using a pocket-size calculator. They are superior to the slide rule and can be operated accurately by even elementary school students. These electronic units are not easily damaged by operators under normal operation. Most industries will provide such aids to those working in processing data for control charts and sampling plans.

1.16 Applications of Statistical Quality Control

Many texts and references present results obtained by the use of the best statistical quality control techniques. The average reader often finds these cases developed in a manner too technical to understand. The case method of learning statistical quality control principles has its place, but is generally best applied to those who have already obtained engineering degrees. This text will present those cases that are needed and will show how the most efficient statistical methods may be applied to quality control. Quick and simple yet effective statistical methods known to pay large dividends to the users are stressed.

The majority of inspections are made on an acceptance–rejection basis. Units are classed as defective or nondefective, or preferably stated as nonconforming or conforming. Parts are also either accepted or rejected on the basis of lot quantities. Results of inspection may be listed in such a way that when given to a computer, immediate information concerning the process level can be obtained. Steps may then be taken to secure better control over the manufacturing processes to reduce losses. Assignable causes of nonconforming units due to random causes may also occur. Their elimination may be found to be either impossible or too costly. The detailed controls presented herein will prove very profitable in most industries.

About 5 percent of items produced require recorded, measured values to be obtained and utilized. Statistical methods used for controlling these variables at desired levels are relatively simple. In most instances computed statistical measures may be effectively applied to determine when lack of control exists. Besides the control chart method of gaining control of vital characteristics, other techniques will accomplish the same results; however, without a professional knowledge of statistics, their results are not directly seen. Among these is the *analysis of variance* technique. This method was developed in England by R. A. Fisher and makes use of the so-called F-test, an abbreviation for *Fisher test*. This technique requires numerous mathematical computations. It is best to obtain a computer program that will enter the data and provide a summary for the results of such computations. There is one form, however, that is very simple and effective. It will be presented in detail later.

Another method is the *correlation method*. Most analyses may be made by applying linear correlation methods, but the more complex problems may require the use of nonlinear correlation methods. The latter will not be discussed here; advanced texts in statistics should be consulted if more complex methods are required. Linear correlation methods do need to be understood in many quality control applications, such as interpreting the results of many nondestructive methods of testing used in place of the usual destructive tests.

1.17 How to Use Statistical Tools and Tables

Very few of the secondary schools provide an adequate foundation for the use of statistical methods. A review of many mathematical texts in intermediate algebra reveals that many books cover permutations and combinations and some cover factorials. The use of logarithms is also covered and a few cover probability and related distribution functions. So much material is required to be covered by the secondary students that chapters covering the above subjects may be treated lightly or not at all. Basic mathematics is sometimes not adequately taught.

The mathematics of statistics is readily applied. It primarily involves the proper use of addition, subtraction, multiplication, and division with some knowledge of the use of logarithms. One of the most important elements that must be learned is how to solve simple linear equations and how to set them up where required. Chapter two covers these necessary mathematical tools. When mastered, statistics becomes an enjoyable science where practical answers are obtained with ease. The prime purpose of the first part of this text is to make the application of statistical methods a pleasure and readily understood. When thus simplified, top management will more readily back the use and development of the best quality control methods. Costs will be reduced and necessary budgets for quality control can be secured more readily.

The mathematical and statistical sciences have inherited a vast library of tables covering most mathematical computations that in the past required hours of time to complete. Knowledge concerning their proper use is absolutely necessary for quality control personnel. Barlow's tables of squares, square roots, etc., were first published in 1814. Many tables of logarithms are now available. Some even give logarithms for factorials. Tables provide probability values for the normal law distribution and also give values for the combination of n things taken m at a time, used to determine the multiplying factors in the evaluation of the binomial. Tables of values for Chi-square are also available.

Besides the printed tables, use may be made of tables available in computer program libraries. Computers have had their computational time changed from milliseconds to nanoseconds and now are able to evaluate many tables that were not previously available. In quality control, where lot sizes are small, the hypergeometric distribution may be applied. Their probability values are computed either laboriously by hand, with the use of pocket computers, or by using tables giving the combination of n things taken m at a time. However, some computers have many of these values available for use by making a proper entry into their accumulated libraries. All such aids reduce the costs for obtaining the best possible controls over processes with resultant savings and increased profits.

EXERCISES

1. Based on the discussion pertaining to early history, when do you think the concept of "inspection" first was applied? Explain your answer.
2. When was the idea of statistical quality control first conceived? Who is considered to be the principal developer of statistical quality control?
3. What are the names of the two journals published by the American Society for Quality Control?
4. Define quality. What is meant by the concept of conformance? What is quality control? What is statistical quality control?
5. What is the difference between "total" quality control and "life-cycle quality"?

6. How can the effective use of statistical quality control techniques improve profit margins? Give three examples.

7. Obtain a copy of MIL–STD–109B and describe the terminology pertaining to quality control, inspection, quality assurance, and reliability.

8. Discuss the advantages and disadvantages of having a machine operator inspect his own work.

9. Discuss the pros and cons of having inspection personnel report directly to production management.

10. Write a one-page report on what you believe industrial quality control is all about.

FOOTNOTES

[1] F. Thorndike, *The Bell System Technical Journal,* October, 1926.

[2] E. C. Molina, *Poisson's Exponential Binomial Limit,* Table I–Individual Terms; Table II–Cumulated Terms, D. Van Nostrand Company, Inc., New York, 1949.

[3] Many variations of the sampling tables have been published since, such as MIL–STD–414: *Sampling Procedures and Tables for Inspection by Variables for Percent Defective* (1957); MIL–STD–690–B: *Failure Rate Sampling Plans and Procedures* (1969); MIL–STD–781–B: *Reliability Tests: Exponential Distribution* (1967); and MIL–STD–1235 (ORD): *Single and Multi-Level Continuous Sampling Procedures and Tables for Inspection by Attributes* (1962).

[4] Articles of interest are "Acceptance Sampling" by Hugo C. Hamaker, "Process Control" by E. S. Page, and "Reliability and Life Testing" by Marvin Zelen.

[5]*Availability*. "The capability of a system to perform its intended function when called upon to do so is often referred to by either of two terms: operational readiness and availability. . . . Availability is defined in terms of operating time and down time, where down time includes active repair time, administrative time and logistic time. . . . The availability of a system or equipment is the probability that it is operating satisfactorily at any point in time." per p. 7, ARINC, *Reliability Engineering,* Prentice-Hall, Inc., 1964. Its probability value is determined by equation (11.3) or equation (11.4), pp. 398–9.
"If parts are readily interchangeable and replaceable, failures may be repaired rapidly by replacing defective parts and components with operating spares. When these replacements can be performed expeditiously, we say we have high maintenance–action rate and correspondingly high availability of equipment, or simply a high availability." per p. 5 of S. R. Calabro, *Reliability Principles and Practices,* McGraw–Hill Book Company, Inc., 1962.

CHAPTER TWO

MATHEMATICS FOR QUALITY CONTROL

2.1 Objective

The field of quality assurance, encompassing inspection, quality control, reliability engineering, operations research, configuration management and kindred fields, requires the use of mathematics. It is the purpose of this chapter to review mathematical operations in such a way that even those that are not mathematically inclined will be able to perform those operations required to make quality control principles, techniques, and methods truly effective.

This chapter reviews basic mathematical processes. Also described are factorials, permutations, and combinations and their applications, along with the use of both common and natural logarithms to simplify multiplication and division.

Quality control was developed to aid production and many other disciplines to perform their functions most effectively. Practically all statistical principles and methods may be applied economically by the use of the simplest forms of arithmetical and algebraic processes. In some instances, computations may be greatly simplified by the use of higher mathematical techniques, such as analytical geometry, differential and integral calculus, and improved geometric functions. It is not necessary to be a mathematics major in order to become an excellent quality control engineer and supervisor. Applying mathematical techniques, not the theory underlying them, is the theme of this chapter.

This chapter will present a basic review covering the areas of mathematics required to carry out a good quality control program. These mathematical fundamentals should provide means to institute the necessary social, industrial, and economic controls needed to minimize costs and maximize profits.

2.2 Fundamental Tools for Quality Control

Those working in the field of quality control as well as students preparing for this work, will find it useful to review certain fundamentals in order to simplify the applications of quality control techniques. It must be emphasized that the most important technique to be applied is common sense. The methods and procedures used must be simple and be readily understood by those applying them. Final values that will aid all levels of administration should result.

One of the fundamental mathematical tools that should be used is the modern computer. It is necessary to know how a computer functions in order to utilize its help most efficiently. The information given a computer must be complete and correct in order to obtain correct answers. To obtain positive assurance that this accuracy is secured, a good operator or technician must have the ability to add, subtract, multiply, and divide accurately. Most of the errors that occur in poorly constructed quality control programs are due to simple errors in arithmetic. These should be reduced to a minimum.

Besides the ability to perform the operations of addition, subtraction, multiplication, and division correctly with a minimum of errors, a working knowledge of factorials, logarithms, ratios, ascending and descending arrays, frequency distributions, powers of numbers, squaring numbers, extracting square roots, using subscripts, exponentials and powers, the difference between straight lines and curves, what is meant by a frequency distribution, the difference between positive and negative values, how to use the constants e and pi (π), graphical representations and the use of coordinate graph paper, the meaning of the terms abscissa and ordinate, slopes, maximum and minimum values and many other mathematical terms is necessary to properly apply statistical techniques. Logarithms are a powerful mathematical tool and simplify many involved computations. All these concepts are very simple, but must be understood in order that they may be applied effectively.

Besides the ability to read intelligently, one must be able to interpret correctly what has been read. The degree to which a quality control analyst can retain facts, processes, and data largely determines how successful he will be in this work. Decisions are based on facts properly analyzed and digested, then accurately assembled into clear, concise reports. Quality control departments are often required to help in the preparation of specifications for proposals and bids. Functions relating to such specifications are discussed in more detail in chapter three, but one of the most important points in proposal preparation is the proper use of mathematical tables.

Before applying the mathematical methods described herein, the nature of the problem should be clearly understood. Those working in these areas must be able to reconstruct the problem from the written material available. One must be able to read all the material relating to the problem and thoroughly analyze the information in order to recommend the best possible solution. The final step is to write a concise report covering the nature of the problem and the recommended action that the company should take.

2.3 Improving Reading Ability

The next fundamental for constructing and operating an efficient quality control program is the ability to read instructions accurately and follow the procedures given. It may not be necessary to completely understand all the statistical theory involved in quality control work, but it is necessary to be able to read and interpret reports correctly so that accurate statistical analyses can be performed.

Recent modern methods of teaching reading have not obtained the results expected. Sight reading, not phonics, has been emphasized and courses have been offered to increase reading speed. Students attaining rapid reading skills are supposed also to have a better understanding of what they have read, but this does not always happen. The words read may be repeated but their meaning may not be clearly understood, with the result that the reader does not accurately follow the instructions and may record incorrect answers later. Some rapid readers can do the arithmetical operations demanded, but many have not learned the multiplication tables, which are basic processes required to multiply or to extract square roots. A significant weakness seems to be the inability to correctly read and interpret tables such as tables of squares, square roots, reciprocals, and even logarithms. If proper use of these tables is not made, the final results will not be accurate.

The first step that should be taken to increase the ability to read material correctly is to outline the material being read. A check may then be made of such an outline to determine if the outline is consistent with the material in the chapter. Some colleges give courses in how to study, which teach the student better concentration and the ability to understand what has been read; such a course may be related to the methods used to teach rapid reading, thus increasing the efficiency of the student. Some reading matter may be scanned, but when mathematical operations are involved, each word must be read carefully. The best technique for a reader that tends to misunderstand written material is to read the material twice through and then read and analyze each item. Such care will result in a better understanding of the material, as well as teaching the discipline in observation necessary if one is conducting inspection operations. The reading test in figure 2-1 is designed to test your ability to read accurately.

A good quality control inspector should be quality conscious. Careless personal habits carry over into work situations and can result in failure to observe defects or nonconforming items. Many wonder how it is possible to obtain products of good quality when those making and inspecting them are inefficient.

1. First read the sentence in the box below. Read once through carefully!

FINISHED FILES ARE THE RESULT OF YEARS OF SCIENTIFIC STUDY COMBINED WITH THE EXPERIENCE OF MANY YEARS.

2. Now count the F's in the sentence in the box. Count only once and do not go back and count them again.
3. Record the number of F's you have counted.[a]

Figure 2–1 Test of reacting ability and awareness.

To counteract these weaknesses, a study of the arithmetical processes in this text should prove very helpful.

At one time, those in engineering and allied sciences learned to use a slide rule to help obtain solutions to many mathematical problems. Recent developments in electronics have resulted in small pocket-sized computers that may be purchased for reasonable amounts; these are largely replacing the slide rule. Some even print the answers on a small tape. The best of these cover trigonometric functions and give squares and square root values as well as values of e^x and many other functions directly. To make the most efficient use of these machines, one must know the mathematical basis for the various functions. Results found by the use of these computers can be used to set up programs for the large computers available in industry today.

2.4 Basis of Arithmetic Processes

Our number system uses ten as a base. 1, 3, 5, 7, 9,... are called odd numbers and 2, 4, 6, 8, 10,... are called even numbers. We all have ten fingers and ten toes so we can use these as devices for counting from 0 to 20, where one considers the sum of two tens (10 plus 10) as twenty (20). The symbol + is used for the term *plus* and the symbol = is used to represent the term *equals*. The above may then be written in equation form as $10 + 10 = 20$. This illustrates simple addition.

Subtraction is the opposite of addition and may be considered the reverse of this operation since you take away units rather than adding units. For example, using the symbol − to denote subtraction, we can write $20 - 10 = 10$. This may be expressed in words as twenty minus ten equals ten. Note that the symbol + represents addition, while the symbol − represents subtraction.

2.5 Addition and Multiplication

Multiplication can be thought of as repeated additions. When two 10s are to be added, instead of using addition the notation may be changed to multiplication by using the symbol × or a dot · to denote multiplication; thus $2 \times 10 = 20$ or $2 \cdot 10 = 20$, where 20 is called the *product*. The same answer is obtained by adding 2s ten times, which may be represented by $10 \times 2 = 20$ or $10 \cdot 2 = 20$. The three terms involved are called, respectively, the *multiplier, multiplicand* and *product*. When more than two digits are involved, the arithmetical processes may be arranged differently with one term under the other so that the operations of addition, subtraction, or multiplication may be performed successively. This is helpful since provision can be made to carry over values of ten, one hundred, etc.

The process of subtraction can be treated as an additive process by determining what quantity must be added to the number being subtracted to give the original number. Or, one can use the direct subtractive process "borrowing" ten units when a particular digit is larger than the one above it. Both the additive process and the subtractive process are illustrated by the following examples:

Addition   *1. Subtraction by "Take-Away"*   *2. Subtraction by Addition*

	11				11
321 ans.	857	976	721	1551	694
+453	+694	−721	+255 ans.	−694	+857 ans.
774	1551	255	976	857	1551

1.
$$\begin{array}{rcl} 774 &=& 700 + 70 + 4 \\ 453 &=& 400 + 50 + 3 \\ \hline 321 &=& 300 + 20 + 1 \end{array} \qquad \begin{array}{rcl} 1551 &=& 1400 + 140 + 11 \\ 694 &=& 600 + 90 + 4 \\ \hline 857 &=& 800 + 50 + 7 \end{array} \qquad \begin{array}{rcl} 976 &=& 900 + 70 + 6 \\ 721 &=& 700 + 20 + 1 \\ \hline 255 &=& 200 + 50 + 5 \end{array}$$

1. 4 − 3 = **1**, 7 − 5 = **2**, 7 − 4 = **3**;
   a. Answer is 321;

   11 − 4 = **7**, 14 − 9 = **5**, 14 − 6 = **8**;
   b. Answer is 857;

   6 − 1 = **5**, 7 − 2 = **5**, 9 − 7 = **2**
   c. Answer is 255

2. 3 + **1** = 4, 5 + **2** = 7, 4 + **3** = 7;
   a. Answer is 321;

   4 + **7** = 11, 9 + **5** = 14, 6 + **8** = 14;
   b. Answer is 857;

   1 + **5** = 6, 2 + **5** = 7, 7 + **2** = 9
   c. Answer is 255

Care must be taken in multiplication of quantities involving many digits, as shown in the examples below.

Multiplication

22	22	22	748	12 345 679	12 345 679
× 13	× 45	× 48	× 659	× 9	× 36
66	110	176	6 732	111,111,111	74 074 074
22	88	88	37 40		370 370 37
286	990	1056	448 8		444,444,444
			492,932		74 074 074
					370 370 37
					1 1 1
					444,444,444

2.6 Powers or Exponents

When a number is multiplied by itself, we say the number is *raised to the second power.* If a denotes the number, then $a \times a = a^2$. The number 2 is called an *exponent.* The a term is called the base. Further examples of exponents are shown below:

$3^2 = 3 \times 3 = 9$ (read: *three squared* or *three to the second power*)

$8^3 = 8 \times 8 \times 8 = 512$ (read: *eight cubed* or *eight to the third power*)

$5^6 = 5 \times 5 \times 5 \times 5 \times 5 \times 5 = 15{,}625$ (read: *five to the sixth power*)

Since computing the cube of a number requires two multiplications, $n \times n$—giving n^2—followed by $n^2 \times n$, giving n^3. Tables like Barlow's give the answers directly, saving much valuable time. For example, suppose the cube of 1.631 is desired. If the number n is 1.631, then a decimal point would be placed after the first digit (4) after computing the cube of 1631. It is easy to determine the location of the decimal point if we note that there are three digits after the decimal point in the number; hence there must be nine digits (3 plus 3 plus 3) when we multiply $n \times n \times n$. The following multiplication will illustrate how to compute cubes of numbers and point off the decimal point correctly.

1.631	2.660 161
× 1.631	× 1.631
1 631	2 660 161
48 93	79 804 83
978 6	1 596 096 6
1 631	2 660 161
2.660 161	4.338 722 591

2.7 Number Systems: Base 10 and Base 2

Modern computers use the base 2 in making computations to solve problems; answers are written in terms of the decimal system on a binary-quinary scale rather than a decimal scale. They function on a go–no-go basis, using only the digits 0 and 1 to represent all numbers. Texts covering the operation of computers describe the binary system which follows the pattern of the abacus, the 2 to 5 bead system used for centuries by the Chinese, in detail. (See figure 2–2.) Two sets of five numbers each result in the ten basic integers used in our decimal system. Hence $2 \times 5 = 10$, the base for most mathematical calculations.

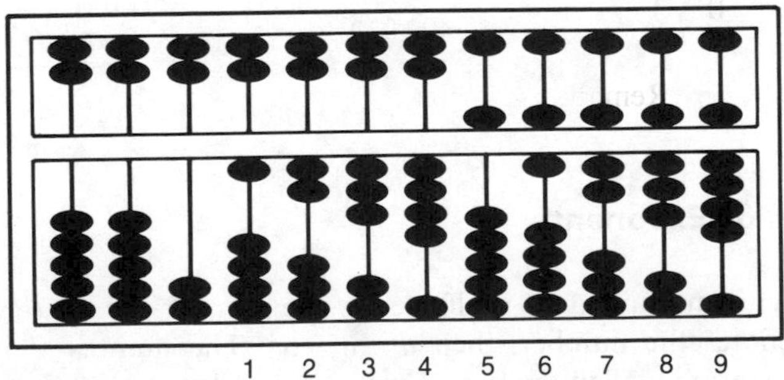

Figure 2–2 The Chinese abacus.

2.8 Division

The operation of division is the reverse of multiplication. For example, twenty divided by ten equals two and may be written as $20 \div 10 = 2$, or $20/10 = 2$, since the sum of two tens results in the number twenty $(10 + 10 = 20)$, twice as large as ten ($2 \times 10 = 20$). In learning arithmetic, division is represented by the use of two forms, one being used for small numbers and the second for large numbers. Thus 100 divided by 4 ($100 \div 4$ or $100/4$) may also be written

$$\begin{array}{r|l} 4 & 100 \\ \hline & 25 \end{array}.$$

This form does not show the division process step by step and hence is not as easy to check as the form used for more digits. Several examples given below illustrate the longer form. In some cases, the product of the *divisor* (the number used to divide) and the *quotient* (the result of the division) will exactly equal the *dividend* (the number which is being divided). In this case, the remainder is zero. The quotient is a whole number in this case. Where the divisor does not divide the dividend exactly, there is a remainder and the answer or quotient may be expressed as a whole number plus a fraction or it may be expressed as a decimal number if the division is continued. For example, if 25 is divided by 10, the quotient is 2 plus $\frac{5}{10}$ or 2.5 in the decimal notation. In this example, the dividend is 25, the divisor is 10, and the quotient is 2.5. Some quotients may be nonterminating when expressed as a decimal; for example, 4 divided by 3 gives a quotient of 1.33333..., often written $1.\dot{3}\dot{3}$, $1.\overline{3}$, or 1.3... The number of digits retained will depend on the number of significant figures that are required. The method of determining the number of significant figures to retain will be discussed in the next section.

Examples of division are shown below.

$$\begin{array}{rr}
 & 25 \\ \cline{2-2}
4 & \big)\,100 \\
 & 8 \\ \cline{2-2}
 & 20 \\
 & 20 \\ \cline{2-2}
\text{Remainder:} & 0
\end{array}
\qquad
\begin{array}{rr}
 & 4.16 \\ \cline{2-2}
15 & \big)\,62.40 \\
 & 60 \\ \cline{2-2}
 & 2\,4 \\
 & 1\,5 \\ \cline{2-2}
 & 90 \\
 & 90 \\ \cline{2-2}
\text{Remainder:} & 0
\end{array}$$

$$\begin{array}{rr}
 & 0.0416666 \\ \cline{2-2}
15 & \big)\,0.6250000 \\
 & 60 \\ \cline{2-2}
 & 25 \\
 & 15 \\ \cline{2-2}
 & 100 \\
 & 90 \\ \cline{2-2}
 & 100 \\
 & 90 \\ \cline{2-2}
 & 100 \\
 & 90 \\ \cline{2-2}
 & 100 \\
 & 90 \\ \cline{2-2}
\text{Remainder:} & 10
\end{array}$$

or 0.041667, to five significant figures.

$$\begin{array}{rr}
 & 20.88 \\ \cline{2-2}
327 & \big)\,6829.00 \\
 & 654 \\ \cline{2-2}
 & 289\,0 \\
 & 261\,6 \\ \cline{2-2}
 & 27\,40 \\
 & 26\,16 \\ \cline{2-2}
\text{Remainder:} & 1\,24
\end{array}$$

2.9 Significant Figures: Rules for Rounding Off the Last Digit

Many mathematical operations give final results that must be expressed with rounded or whole numbers rather than with fractions. In quality control, expressing numbers in decimal notation aids in the choice of final values to report. Many testing devices cannot give results accurate to more than a specified number of significant values. When only three digits are significant, recording more places indicates an accuracy that does not exist. If a dividend is correct to five significant figures but its divisor is accurate to only three significant figures, then the resultant quotient is accurate only to three significant figures, not to five. An example may clarify this. Divide 789.25 by 2.43. Its quotient carried to five significant figures is 324.79; however, since 2.43 has only three significant figures, this quotient should be rounded off to 325, which has three significant figures. Ordinarily the long form of division is used for manual computations. To conserve space, the short form is given here to illustrate the preceding example.

Divisor:	243.⟌78925.00	: Dividend	Remainder is 0.0103;
Quotient:	324.79		0.0103/2.43 = 0.0042387; hence the quotient could be written: 324.7942387

Answer to record: 325. (3 significant figures)

In all mathematical processes—and particularly in quality control work—it is necessary to check all answers for accuracy because it is easy to make mistakes that result in erroneous answers. To check division, multiplication—the reverse of division—is used. For the example above, the check is made as follows: $2.43 \times 324.79 = 789.2397$. Subtracting this value from the dividend gives: $789.2500 - 789.2397 = 0.0103$, the remainder. This agrees with the remainder shown above.

There are definite rules for rounding off the digits that exceed the reasonable number of significant figures. Physicists often round off to the nearest odd number, but the American Standards Association rounds off to the nearest even digit. Numbers ending in 5 are the ones affected by this choice of a rule. For example, the dividend 789.25, if rounded off to four significant figures, would be written 789.3 when rounding to odd values, but would be written as 789.2 per the ASA standard, which is preferred by most statisticians. The quotient would be written as 324.8, to four significant digits.

2.10 Arrays: Used in the Formation of Frequency Distributions

Numbers are often arranged in numerical order according to their magnitudes. Such an arrangement is termed either an ascending or descending array. For example, the numbers from 0 through 10 can be arranged in ascending order (0, 1, 2, 3, 4, 5, 6, 7, 8, 9, 10) or in descending order (10, 9, 8, 7, 6, 5, 4, 3, 2, 1, 0). A special case would be a way of expressing in sets the data secured from the measurement of some feature, such as the heights in inches of the boys in a class and the heights of the girls in the same class. A set is formed by the terms, numbers, letters, or any other distinct representation, recorded within brackets. Each term, even if it occurs many times, is listed only once in the set notation.

When using numbers such as the measurements of heights, an ordered set may be obtained by arranging the numbers within the brackets in either ascending or descending order. For example, if the heights of ten boys were noted as 69 inches, 65 inches, 70 inches, 71 inches, 67 inches, 70 inches, 69 inches, 69 inches, 68 inches and 72 inches, an unordered set for these data is {69, 65, 70, 71 67, 68, 72}. Note that although two 70s and three 69s were recorded as data, these two numbers are listed only once in the set. These numbers may be arranged into two different ordered sets, ascending or descending as follows: ascending order {65, 67, 68, 69, 70, 71, 72}, descending order: {72, 71, 70, 69, 68, 67, 65}.

Such basic ordered arrangements in sets are utilized in arranging data in frequency distributions. By tabulating the frequency of occurrence of similar terms, valid comparisons may be made between the observations recorded for a series of successive measurements made on one particular set and other different sets. An analysis may be made of these data by the use of the arithmetical processes of addition, subtraction, multiplication, and division.

2.11 Finding Powers and Roots of Numbers

Two other arithmetical processes must be reviewed. These are (1) obtaining the squares of a given number, and (2) obtaining the square root of any number. In many statistical operations, an average value or *mean* is found for the squares of a set of numbers. It may then be desired to find the *root mean square* (RMS) for this average value. The square root of this average value is either determined manually, read from tables of squares and square roots, or determined by a computer. The arithmetical operations are simple, but the methods used must be carefully applied to obtain valid and accurate results. To obtain the square of a number, the number is multiplied by itself or added successively as many times as the value of the number being squared. If y is the number, then its square may be represented as $y \times y$ or as y^2. For example, the square of 5 is $5 \times 5 = 25$, a product that can be found in a standard multiplication table. Expressed in terms of a sum, this number may be given as $5 + 5 + 5 + 5 + 5 = 25$.

The squares of larger numbers are found in the same manner. Thus the square of 25 is $25 \times 25 = 625$; the square of 13 is $13 \times 13 = 169$. Although one must know how to find such squares, the usual way for obtaining their values is not by performing the indicated multiplication but by looking up the correct value in a table of squares. Many texts in quality control engineering and statistics give such tables, but the most complete and extensive is Barlow's table, originally dated 1814.[1] These tables give a sufficient number of significant figures for most quality control problems.

If a number to be squared has a 5 as its last digit and only one or two digits precede the 5, as in 45 and 115, the square is found by the following rule: Multiply the digits before 5, treated as a single number *n*, by the number increased by one, multiply this product by 100, and then add the square of 5, which is always 25. Thus the square of 15 is found by finding the product $1 \times 2 \times 100$, which is 200, and adding 25, which gives 225 as the square of 15. The square of 115 is equal to

$(11 \times 12 \times 100) + 25$, which is $13{,}200 + 25$ or 13,225. Expressed as an equation, this rule is $(n5)^2 = [n \times (n + 1) \times 100] + 25$, where n is any number from 1 through 99, or even 999.

The square root of any number can be read from a table containing square roots of a number or of ten times the number. When computing the square number manually, the number is marked off in sets of two starting at the decimal point. Where no decimal point is given and the number is assumed to be a whole number, a decimal point is assumed to exist after the last digit to the right in the number. Thus 169 is considered to be 169.; 69 is taken as the first set of two digits and 1 or 01 is the second set. In practice, an apostrophe sets off the sets of two digits; thus the number 169 is marked 1′69. In some cases, a number is an *exact number* and may be considered to have almost an infinite number of significant figures. In this example, the number would be pointed off as 1′69.′00′00′00′00′00 . . . The square root of this number is 13.000000 . . .

The manual method of determining the square root of 169 as pointed off above is based on the fact that $(a + b)^2 = a^2 + 2ab + b^2$. Let a represent the ten's place and b represent the unit's place. Subtract a^2 from this relation, giving $2ab + b^2$. If this is divided by b, the quotient is $2a + b$. This is the form of the divisor of the term left after subtracting a^2. This format is the basis for obtaining the square root of a number manually. Two examples that show the application of this rule follow.

Example 1 Obtain the square root of 169 manually.

Solution As indicated earlier, set this number off as 1′69. Let a be 1. Then $1^2 = 1$. That leaves 69. The first tentative divisor is $2a$, where a is in the ten's place, so that $2a = 20$. Dividing 69 by 20 gives 3 as the possible value for b. Then $2a + b = 20 + 3 = 23$. If this is multiplied by $b = 3$, the product is 69. This is exactly equal to the value found after subtracting a^2 from the marked off number. The remainder is zero, and 13 is the square root of 169. Writing these operations down numerically yields the following:

		$a\,b$
		1 3
		$\sqrt{1'69}$
		1
$2a \times 10 =$	20	69
$b = 3$	+ 3	
$b(2a \times 10) = 3 \times$	23 =	69
Remainder =		0

In the following example, the square root of a six-digit number is to be determined by manual computation. Since we want to obtain another digit in the square root after the decimal point has been reached, a pair of zeros is added after the given number. The method given in example 1 is just extended pair by pair.

Example 2 Obtain the square root of 105,425 correct to two decimal places.

Solution To obtain a solution correct to at least two places after the decimal, the number is written as 10′54′25′.00′00. If three decimal places are desired, add another pair of zeros. Following the numerical form in example 1, but extending the successive terms from tenths to hundredths, etc., provides successive divisors.

	3 2 4 .6 9
	$\sqrt{10'54'25'.00'00}$
Trial divisors	9
	1 54
$2\cdot 3\cdot 10 + 2 = 62$	1 24
	30 25
$2\cdot 32\cdot 10 + 4 = 644$	25 76
	4 49 00
$2\cdot 324\cdot 10 + 6 = 6486$	3 89 16
	59 84 00
$2\cdot 3246\cdot 10 + 9 = 64929$	58 43 61
	1 40 39

Check solution by multiplication:

3 24.69	32 4.7
× 3 24.69	× 32 4.7
29 22 21	227 2 9
194 81 4	1 298 8
1 298 76	6 494
6 493 8	97 41
97 407	105,430.0 9
105,423.59 61	

Note that the solution is correct as the number for which the square root was desired is between the square of 324.69 and the square of 324.70.

Generally, square roots are determined from tables or by use of logarithms. However, it is necessary for those working with such numbers to be able to check tables and antilogarithms used as solutions for accuracy, as errors sometimes occur in printed tabulated values. For obtaining cube roots of numbers, the guide to the manual solution is: $(a + b)^3 = a^3 + 3a^2b + 3ab^2 + b^3$. a^3 is again subtracted, since it is the first estimated solution with a representing some multiple of ten. Dividing the remainder by b gives the proper divisor, $3a^2 + 3ab + b^2$.

The algebraic expressions that are useful guides for establishing the rules for obtaining the nth root of a number stem from raising the binomial $(a + b)$ to the nth power, i.e.,

$$(a + b)^n = a^n + \frac{n}{1!}a^{n-1}b + \frac{n(n-1)}{2!}a^{n-2}b^2 + \frac{n(n-1)(n-2)}{3!}a^{n-3}b^3 + \cdots + b^n.$$

The remainder, after subtracting a^n, divided by b is the first trial divisor of the next term in the mathematical operation. The next example illustrates the case where n is 3 and will show how to extract the cube root of a five-digit number, giving a two-digit number as an answer.

In extracting the cube root, the method detailed above for a two-digit number is followed by setting off successive parts of the number in groups of three digits.

For the general case of a two-digit number obtained as an answer, a denotes the ten's digit while b is the unit's digit. The general method of extracting the cube root of a number is outlined. With a as 30 and b as 4, we have the number 34, whose cube is 39,304.

The second example shows how to find the cube root of 39,304.

$$
\begin{array}{lll}
 & a \quad + \quad b & \\
 & \sqrt[3]{a^3 + 3a^2b + 3ab^2 + b^3} & \\
 & a^3 & \\
\hline
 & 3a^2b + 3ab^2 + b^3 & \\
3a^2 & 3a^2b & \\
\quad + 3ab & \qquad 3ab^2 & \\
\quad + b^2 & \qquad\qquad b^3 & \\
\hline
\text{Sum} \times b & & \\
 & \text{Remainder} = 0 &
\end{array}
$$

$$
\begin{array}{lllr}
 & & & a + b \\
 & & & 3\ 0 + 4 = 34 \\
 & & & \sqrt[3]{39'304} \\
a^3 = 30^3 = & & & 27\,000 \\
\hline
 & & & 12\,304 \\
3a^2 = 3(900) & = 2700 & & \\
3ab = 3(30)(4) & = \ \ 360 & & \\
b^2 = 4^2 & = \ \ \ \ 16 & & \\
\hline
 & 3076 \times (4) & & 12\,304 \\
\hline
 & & & \text{Remainder} = 0
\end{array}
$$

For any nth root, where $n = 2, 3, 4, 5, \ldots$, the method given above for square roots and cube roots of any number may be applied. As n increases in value, it becomes more difficult to accurately make the first estimate of a and later to estimate the value of b as trial divisors and part of the final answer. Tables of values of roots and powers for n greater than 4 are not generally available. Tables are available for powers up to 10 covering numbers ranging by units from 1 to 100. For most problems in quality control, squares and square roots are about the most complex values used, with the exception of an occasional application of cubes and cube root values. Three other ways may be used to find roots of numbers. Logarithms may be used, since tables with from 2 to 20 numbers in the mantissa (that part of a logarithm that is read from the tables and which is written after the decimal point following the characteristic) are available alone or in many textbooks. A second method, is to read the square root value directly from a calculator. Roots greater than two may also be determined on such modern computers. A third method is to use a slide rule. Many slide rules give both square root and cube root values as well as squares of numbers on one of the available scales. The higher powers are used very infrequently. Where it is desired to fit data with a curve generated by higher powers, use should be made of relations with powers greater than two that best fit the situation under discussion.

Square roots may also be obtained readily by utilizing one of the important characteristics of the decimal numerical system. This is termed sometimes the *odd number system of extracting square roots.* This method is based on the fact that by using the sums of successive ascending arrays of odd numbers, the number of summands used is the square root of the sum obtained. The following examples illustrate this point.

$$
\begin{array}{ll}
1 = 1 = 1^2 & \text{(1 term)} \\
1 + 3 = 4 = 2^2 & \text{(2 terms)} \\
1 + 3 + 5 = 9 = 3^2 & \text{(3 terms)} \\
1 + 3 + 5 + 7 = 16 = 4^2 & \text{(4 terms)} \\
1 + 3 + 5 + 7 + 9 = 25 = 5^2 & \text{(5 terms)} \\
1 + 3 + 5 + 7 + 9 + 11 = 36 = 6^2 & \text{(6 terms)} \\
1 + 3 + 5 + 7 + 9 + 11 + 13 = 49 = 7^2 & \text{(7 terms)} \\
1 + 3 + 5 + 7 + 9 + 11 + 13 + 15 = 64 = 8^2 & \text{(8 terms)}
\end{array}
$$

In this method, a multiplying constant (i.e., $20 = 2a$, where $a = 10$) must be utilized when carrying out the subtractive and counting operations. The number of subtractions made when counted provides the successive digits to give the square root of the original number. Successive subtractions are stopped when the number selected to be subtracted exceeds the value of the number from which the subtraction is to be made. Two examples follow. It must be noted that, except for perfect squares, the subtractive and counting process may continue until the square root obtained has the number of significant digits required. The square root of 625, a perfect square, is found as follows:

No. of subtractions per operation gives the digit for the square root:	2 5	25 is the answer; $25^2 = 625$
	$\sqrt{6'25}$	
1st subtraction:	− 1	
	5	
2nd subtraction:	− 3	
Observe that subtracting 5 gives a negative number; hence subtraction is not permitted. Subtract 20 × (No. of operations) + 1 or 20 × 2 + 1:	2 25	
	− 41	1st subtraction for 2nd operation
	1 84	
	− 43	2nd subtraction
	1 41	
	− 45	3rd subtraction
	96	
	− 47	4th subtraction
	49	
	− 49	5th subtraction
	0	Remainder

This operation is discontinued in this example when the number subtracted (49) is equal to the previous remainder obtained by subtracting 47 from 96.

If the remainder had not been zero, we would continue to subtract successively, using 20 times the number resulting from the two operations (25) plus 1, or $20 \times 25 + 1 = 501$ as the first number in the next series of subtractions.

If 625, a perfect square, were changed to 640.00 00, then the remainder would be 15 rather than 0. Then use must be made of the next set of two numbers, here

00, giving the number 1500 from which 501 is to be subtracted. 1500 − 501 gives 999. Then the next operation requires that 503 is to be subtracted from 999, giving 496. From this number 505 is to be subtracted, but such a subtraction results in a negative number. However, only one decimal value after the whole number 25 is desired. Hence this, if used, gives a third operation so the square root to three significant figures is 25.3. If this number is squared, then 25.3 × 25.3 = 640.09, which compares favorably to 640.00 00.

The above examples show in detail how to use the successive subtractions of the odd numbers, 1, 3, 5, 7, 9, 11, etc., to provide the number of successful subtractions that result in the square root of the given number. The checks by multiplication show that 25 × 25 gives 625 for the first case and 25.3 × 25.3 gives approximately 640, the second number for which a square root was obtained. The method works very rapidly on a manually operated electrical computer.

A third example is obtaining the square root of 1156. Set off groups of two: 11′56. 1, 3, and 5, are successively subtracted from 11, leaving 2 5 6 for the second operation. The first number to be subtracted is 61 (20 times 3 plus 1), since three subtractions were made, as shown by the numbers 1, 3, and 5. Now successively subtract 61, 63, 65, and 67, which totals 256, and leaves a remainder of 0. Four subtractions were made. Hence with three subtractions made in the first operation and four subtractions made in the second, the square root is exactly 34. As a check it is found that 34 × 34 gives 1156.

This quick and accurate method of extracting the square root of a number should be tried by the reader. Try the method on a much larger number such as 10′46′00′49.′64 which is also a perfect square. In this example, the first number from which 1, 3, and 5 should be successively subtracted is 10. Then from 146, successively subtract 61 and 63. The third number is 2200, from which we successively subtract 641, 643, and 645. The fourth number is 27,149, from which 6461, 6463, 6465, and 6467 are successively subtracted. The fifth number that results from these successive operations is 129,364, from which 64,681 and 64,683 are successively subtracted. Counting the operations gives 3234.2 as the square root. When this is verified by multiplication, it is found that 3234.2 × 3234.2 gives the number 10,460,049.64. When this method is used on a Monroe, Friden, Marchant, or similar computer, the machine automatically displays the number of operations used and the answer desired.

2.12 Using Tables of Roots

It is necessary to know the various methods described here which were used to determine squares, square roots, cubes, cube roots, reciprocals, and higher roots or powers. Practically, however, square root tables similar to Barlow's tables may be used to facilitate the computations if there is no access to a computer of any kind. Many texts provide tables of squares and square roots but most of these do not give a sufficient number of significant figures to make them worthwhile for many applications.

Barlow's tables are recommended for general use because they give sufficient values in various columns to cover many different cases. The column headings and values given in these tables are illustrated below, using the numbers 1600, 1631, and 1632.

No. n	*Square* n^2	*Cube* n^3	*Sq. Root* $\sqrt{n}$	*Sq. Rt. of 10n*, $\sqrt{10n}$	*Cube Root* $\sqrt[3]{n}$	*Reciprocal*
			40.	120. +	11.	0.000
1600	2,560,000	4,096,000,000	000000	6.491106	696071	6250000
...	...		...	...	...	...
1631	2,660,161	4,338,722,591	385641	7.710610 diff.	771125 diff.	6131208 diff.
1632	2,663,424	4,346,707,968	398020 12379	7.749755 3914.5	773531 2406	6127451 3757

Observe that the square root of 1631 is 40.385641.

Some editions of Barlow's tables also contain a column giving the fourth power of the number. The table from which the above was taken also includes the differences between successive values to aid in interpolation. Besides reading square roots and/or cube roots directly from such a table, it is possible to cover many numbers larger than those listed under the column "No. n" by using the number listed under n^2 for the value of n. For example, for n equal to 26,634.00, one would have to look under the value 2663, as the table does not contain 26634. The square root desired could be approximated with $\sqrt{10n}$ or 160 + 3.187009, which would be written 163.2 when rounded off to four significant figures. However, column two as shown above gives the number 26634.24 under n^2, so that n is exactly 163.2. Interpolation using this method will usually give an answer to one more significant figure. Many mathematicians and statisticians, as well as engineers, would interpolate between $\sqrt{n}$ values for 26,634 which lie between 26,630 and 26,640. Using the table from n^2 to n rather than from n to $\sqrt{n}$ provides more confidence in the fourth significant figure for this case.

Although cubes and cube roots are not used as frequently as squares and square roots, the same method for using the column covering cubes n^3 and n values rather than n and $\sqrt[3]{n}$ values will result in answers with much less error. For example, determine the cube root of 4,346.7080. The correct value will be a two-digit number, followed by a decimal point and as many significant decimal places as deemed reasonable. Reading the table under n—given to only four significant figures—the number 4347 gives for its cube root the number 16.3204 (actually 16.320365). For the number 4346, the table gives as its cube root 16.319114, so to four significant figures the answer is 16.32. Using the n^3 and corresponding n value gives an n^3 value of 4346.707968, which may be treated as 4346.7080 (the number under consideration), and an n value of exactly 16.32. The two methods verify that 16.32 is the best value to use. In practice, users of these tables apply whichever method will give the best answer without interpolation.

2.13 Checks on Mathematical Processes: Casting Out 9's

Our numerical system uses the base 10, in which each number is equal to $9X + R$, with R representing the residual. Values of R may be found directly by merely adding the digits of which the number is composed. This sum, when all the numbers which have a sum of 9 are discarded, gives the residual R. For example, $43 = 9 \times 4 + 7 = 36 + 7$ and this residual $R = 7$ equals the sum of the digits $4 + 3$. This verifies the rule given above. An example showing no residual is 72; since 7 plus 2 gives 9, which leaves a residual of 0. As a further check, note that $9 \times 8 = 72$, the number itself. All results from the operations of addition, subtraction, multiplication, and division may be readily checked by the method called *casting out 9's*,[2] which is illustrated by the following examples.

Addition

436	$4 + 3 + 6 = 13$;	$1 + 3 = 4$,	so	$R_1 = 4$
721	$7 + 2 + 1 = 10$;	$1 + 0 = 1$,	so	$R_2 = 1$
1157	$1 + 1 + 5 + 7 = 14$;	$1 + 4 = 5$,	so	$R = 5$
				$R_1 + R_2 = R$

In practice, one learns to cast out any combination of two, three, or more digits that total 9, such as 4 + 5, 3 + 6, 2 + 3 + 4, 2 + 1 + 6, etc. A number such as 436 has a residual of 4 when the 3 and 6 are eliminated. Examples for checks in subtraction follow:

Subtraction

836	$8 + 3 + 6 = 17$;	$1 + 7 = 8$,	so	$R_1 = 8$	(*Minuend*)
− 542	$5 + 4 + 2 = 11$;	$1 + 1 = 2$,	so	$R_2 = 2$	(*Subtrahend*)
294	$2 + 9 + 4 = 15$;	$1 + 5 = 6$,	so	$R = 6$	(*Remainder* or *difference*)

The usefulness of casting out 9's is shown by subtracting the residuals 8 − 2, giving 6 or R.

Sometimes the residual value for the subtrahend (R_2) is larger than that of the minuend (R_1), as in the problem 1127 − 728, where the residual for the minuend is 2, which is smaller than the residual for the subtrahend, which is 8. In this case, we add 9 to the residual R_1. This gives 11; 11 − 8 = 3. The difference is 399, which has a residual of 3 when the two 9's are eliminated. Hence we see the answer obtained by direct subtraction has the same residual value as that found by subtracting the other two residuals.

Checks by this method may also be made for multiplication, as shown in the following examples.

Multiplication

Example 3 Multiply 101 by 76. The product is 7676, the sum of whose digits is 26. Adding these digits gives 8. The multiplicand is 101, so the sum of its digits is 2. The multiplier is 76, whose digits total 13. The two digits 1 and 3 total 4. The product of these two residuals is $2 \times 4 = 8$. This checks with the first residual $R = 8$ found for the product only.

$$\begin{array}{rlllr l}
101 & 1 + 1 = 2, & & \text{so} \quad R_1 = & 2 & (\textit{Multiplicand}) \\
\times\ 76 & 7 + 6 = 13 \text{ and } 1 + 3 = 4, & & \text{so} \quad R_2 = & \times\ 4 & (\textit{Multiplier}) \\
\overline{606} & & & & \overline{8} & (\textit{Product}) \\
7\,07 & & & & & \\
7{,}676 & 7 + 6 + 7 + 6 = 26; & & & & \\
 & \quad 2 + 6 = 8, & & \text{so} \quad R = & 8 & \text{Product: Checks.}
\end{array}$$

Algebraically the multiplication desired may be made as follows: The approach used is first presented.

$$(a + b)(c + d) = ac + ad + bc + bd. \quad [9(11) + 2][9(8) + 4] = \text{Product.}$$

$$\begin{array}{ll}
a + b & \quad 9(11) + 2 \\
c + d & \times\ 9(8) + 4 \\
\hline
ac + bc & \quad 81(88) + 9(16) \\
\quad + ad + bd & \qquad\qquad + 9(44) + 8 \\
\hline
ac + ad + bc + bd & \quad 9(792) + 9(60) + 8 \\
a(c + d) + b(c + d) \quad \textit{Product} & \quad 9(852) \qquad\quad + 8 \qquad \textit{Product} \\
 & \qquad 7668 + 8 = 7676.
\end{array}$$

Example 4 Check the cube of 1631 [i.e., $(1631)^3$] by casting out 9's. The answer previously given was 4,338,722,591. Using the rules as given, we obtain the following: 4 and 3 are 7; 7 and 3 are 10, so 1 and 0 is 1; 1 and 8 is 9 and cast out; 7 and 2 give 9, which is cast out; 2 and 5 give a sum of 7; the following 9 is cast out; 7 is added to the 1, giving a final residual value of 8. Is the product obtained with this residual correct? The 6 and 3 in the number 1631 total 9, which should be cast away, leaving a sum of 1 plus 1 or 2. This value is to be cubed, giving $2 \times 2 \times 2 = 8$, which checks with the residual value for the product.

This same method for checking an answer may be applied to the process of division. Care must be used to include in the check any value that remains when a division is stopped, as that value must also be included in the count for determining residual values.

Examples are given below to show how to check answers determined by division, using the method of casting out 9's. The first example does not have a remainder and the second example does.

Division

Divide 75,200 by 25. The dividend is 75,200; the first sum of the digits is 14. 1 and 4 are then added together to give 5. However, it is wise to keep the 14 as this residual is to be divided by the residual obtained for the divisor (25), whose residual is the sum of 2 and 5 or 7. The quotient of residuals is $\frac{14}{7} = 2$ the quotient for this problem.

$$\begin{array}{lrl} & 3008 & \textit{Quotient} \\ \textit{Divisor} \quad 25 & \overline{)75200} & \textit{Dividend} \\ & \underline{75} & \\ & 200 & \\ & \underline{200} & \\ & 0 & \textit{Remainder} \end{array}$$

The residual of the quotien (3 + 8 = 11; 1 + 1 = 2), wh with the quotient $\frac{14}{7}$.

As the second example, change the dividend to 75,228; the 3009 and there is a remainder of 3. The residual for the quotient 9's is 3, but we can use the sum of 3 and 9 which is 12 as the 24, which is the residual value for the new dividend, 75,228, by 7, for the divisor, giving a quotient of 3 with a remainder of 3. T the remainder when the ordinary division is performed, carrying the quotient to four significant figures.

We can check division in the same manner as used for multiplication. *For example 1*: 75,200/25 = 3008. Multiply the residuals for the divisor and the quotient and add the remainder, if any. Following this rule gives 7 × 2 = 14, which is the sum of 7, 5, and 2—the digits for the dividend 75,200. *For example 2*: 75,228/25 = 3009 with a remainder of 3. Since the digits of the divisor are 2 and 5, following the rule gives 7 × 3 + 3 (the remainder) = 21 + 3 = 24. The residual for the dividend, whose digits are 7, 5, 2, 2, and 8, is also 24.

The procedure used in division for casting out 9's is simplified by establishing a step-by-step set of operations. Use letters to designate the sum of the digits in the three terms of each division problem and any remainder that exists after the operation of successive divisions is terminated.

Designations:	*Sum of Digits*	*Remainder*
	Dividend, D	R
	Divisor, d	
	Quotient, Q	

Relation for check: $D - R = d \times Q$, or dQ

Example 5 75,200/25 = 3,008 ($R = 0$)

Step 1. Determine sums of digits and remainder for the problem.

$$\begin{aligned} D &= 7 + 5 + 2 + 0 + 0 = 14, \quad 1 + 4 = 5; \\ d &= 2 + 5 = 7; \\ Q &= 3 + 0 + 0 + 8 = 11, \quad 1 + 1 = 2; \\ R &= 0. \end{aligned}$$

Step 2. Subtract R from D.

$$D - R = 5 - 0 = 5.$$

Step 3. Multiply d by Q.

$$dQ = 7 \times 2 = 14, \quad 1 + 4 = 5.$$

Step 4. Compare difference in Step 2 with product in Step 3. If they agree, the answer is correct.

Example 6 $75{,}228/25 = 3009$, with $R = 3$

Step 1. $D = 7 + 5 + 2 + 2 + 8 = 24, \quad 2 + 4 = 6;$
$d = 2 + 5 = 7;$
$Q = 3 + 0 + 0 + 9 = 12, \quad 1 + 2 = 3;$
$R = 3.$

Step 2. $D - R = 6 - 3 = 3.$

Step 3. $dQ = 7 \times 3 = 21, \quad 2 + 1 = 3.$

Step 4. Check. The result of Step 2 is the same as that of Step 3. The answer is correct.

2.14 Logarithms

Logarithms are one of the most useful and simple mathematical tools available to aid in completing many mathematical operations, especially multiplication and division. Logarithms are based on the fact that exponents of any constant base are additive when the exponential expressions are multiplied. Thus multiplication processes are replaced by additive processes through the use of logarithms. Usually any base may be used. Since the numerical system most universally used is the decimal system, in which the base is 10, logarithms based on powers of 10 are termed *common logarithms.* According to the *Encyclopaedia Britannica,* in 1614 John Napier published his "Canonis Descriptio" embodying his invention of logarithms. They were originally hyperbolic in nature and were modified to their present form by Henry Briggs, an English mathematician, after several conferences with Napier, and hence are sometimes called *Briggian logarithms.* Napier's logarithms were to the base e. These logarithms, discussed later in this chapter, are termed *natural logarithms* as well as *hyperbolic* or *Napierian logarithms.* The constant e used as the original base can readily be determined from the infinite series:

$$e^x = 1 + \frac{x}{1!} + \frac{x^2}{2!} + \frac{x^3}{3!} + \frac{x^4}{4!} + \cdots + \frac{x^i}{i!} + \cdots \tag{1}$$

When x is 1, the value of e is 2.718281828459045... Tables of logarithms are available for both base 10 and base e.

Since many different bases may be used for logarithms, it is necessary to give a relation that enables us to obtain logarithms to any base. If b denotes one base and b_1 denotes a second base, then a set of logarithms for a second base may be obtained from the logarithms of the first base by the following relation.

$$\log_b n = \log_{b_1} n \cdot \log_b b_1 \quad \text{(2)}$$

If the base b is 10 and the other base b_1 is e, the Napierian base, then

$$\log_{10} n = \log_e n \cdot \log_{10} e, \quad \text{where } \log_{10} e = 0.43429448190325\ldots \quad \text{(3)}$$

Most tables of logarithms give the necessary relations and factors to make such a change, but there are also a large number that do not. Many textbooks do not give these relations, which are very useful in quality control work.

In quality control and reliability engineering, e^{-x} is used more than e^x. The use of e^{-x} is covered in texts and discussions of reliability engineering and in the evaluation of mean time between failures (MTBF) values. For those having some knowledge of differential and integral calculus, it is noted that e^x is unique since it has the property that it is invariant with repeated differentiations or repeated integrations. This means that no matter how many times these operations are performed, e^x is the final answer. This characteristic is one that has made this function so useful in many mathematical developments.

In quality control, logarithms to the base 10 are most commonly used. The exponent or the power to which 10 is raised is the logarithm of the resultant number. When 10 is raised to the zero power, we have $10^0 = 1$. Thus the logarithm of 1 is 0.00000, as expressed by a five-place logarithm table using the base 10. The number before the decimal is called the *characteristic* of the logarithm and the five digits after the decimal point are called the *abscissa*; the abscissas are the numbers given in tables of logarithms. Use is made of the fact that exponents of numbers appearing as numerators of a function or fraction are considered as positive values, whereas exponents appearing on numbers in the denominator of a fraction are considered negative. This fact was used in showing that the logarithm of 1. to the base 10 is 0.

When numbers are multiplied together, their logarithms are added. What takes place is merely the adding together of the exponents or powers of 10 where $10^x = n$. A common slide rule can be used for the multiplication or division of two or more numbers because in multiplication one scale is moved so that its length on a logarithmic basis is added to the length on another scale, also marked on a logarithmic basis. To use logarithms in the multiplication of numbers, we must consult a table to find the power of 10 or logarithm which represents the multiplicand and another logarithmic number to represent the multiplier. These values are added and the resultant sum gives the logarithm that represents the product of the two numbers. As an example, $10^2 \times 10^3 = 10^{2+3} = 10^5$. This expression is another way of writing $100 \times 1000 = 100{,}000$. Thus 5 is the logarithm of the answer, 100,000. The opposite operation is applicable to division where $10^5/10^2 = 10^3$; this may also be expressed as $100{,}000/100 = 1000$. Thus $100{,}000/100 = 1000$ or 10^3. These examples show how characteristics for the logarithms of various numbers are whole numbers or integers.

So far the logarithms to the base 10 which we have examined have all been integers or whole numbers, and the corresponding values, called *antilogarithms,* have all been multiples of 10. Numbers between 1 and 10 are represented by fractional values, and are usually expressed as decimal equivalents. The number 2 may also be expressed in the form 10^x. The value of x must be determined. It may be expressed as a decimal fraction, $x = 0.30103$. Its characteristic is 0 and its mantissa, as taken from a five-place table of logarithms, is 0.30103. This means that $10^{0.30103} = 2.00000$. If the number is changed to 20, then the number 20 can be expressed as 2×10, or $10^{1.30103}$. Likewise $10^{0.47712} = 3.00000$. The numbers 2, 3, and 20 are given to six significant figures. Since only a five-place table of logarithms has been used for the values of the logarithms, these numbers should be written as 2.000, 3.000 and 20.00, to only four significant figures. The common rule to follow is that any antilogarithm is only accurate to one less number of significant figures (i.e., $m - 1$) than the number of digits listed as the mantissas in an m-digit logarithm table. Many different tables of these common logarithms are available. They are given to 4, 5, 6, 7, 10, or 20 places. Select the proper table for the nature of the data being analyzed.

Logarithms to the base 10 are usually just written as log, whereas logarithms to the base e are designated as ln or $\log_e$. Values of the logarithms to the base e are readily computed by using some series relation such as:

$$\log_e x = \ln x = \frac{(x-1)}{x} + \frac{1}{2}\frac{(x-1)^2}{(x)^2} + \frac{1}{3}\frac{(x-1)^3}{(x)^3} + \cdots \quad \text{for } x \geq \frac{1}{2} \tag{4}$$

Equation (3) presents the correct relation to change from a logarithm with base e to a logarithm with base 10. Many other forms for changing bases and deriving logarithms are given in advanced mathematical textbooks or in very large tables. One of the most important needs of a quality control technician is to be able to correctly look up logarithms of numbers as well as antilogarithms in any form of logarithmic table available or provided. The logarithm of 2 may be obtained to 20 places; as $\log_{10} 2 = 0.30102999566398119521$. If only three significant figures are desired, use 0.3010 as the log of 2.00; if four significant figures are desired, use a five-place table giving 0.30103 as the logarithm of 2.000. If nineteen significant figures are required, use the twenty-place number given above as the logarithm of 2.000000000000000000.

2.15 Use of Logarithms

Five-place common logarithm tables are most commonly used. These actually give only the mantissas of the numbers. Placement of the decimal point depends on the nature of the data and must be determined by the quality control technician. For such tables, the values found are only accurate to four significant figures. For example, determine the product of 43 by 57. Use will be made of the logarithms of these two numbers, both of which have only two digits before their decimals; thus each has 1 as its characteristic. Log 43 = 1.63347 since the characteristic of a number is one less than the number of digits in the number before the decimal point. The mantissa of 43 is listed in the appropriate logarithmic table as 0.63347. Adding this to the characteristic 1 gives log 43 as 1.63347. To obtain the logarithm of 43×57, we must add $\log 57 = 1.75587$ to log 43. Thus $43 \times 57 = 10^{1.63347} \times 10^{1.75587} = 10^{3.38934}$, since the two exponents for the base 10 must be added to obtain the desired logarithm. Thus $\log(43 \times 57) = 3.38934$. Consulting a five-place logarithmic table, or any table of logarithms that has five or more numbers tabulated as the mantissas, the antilogarithm for the product desired is found to be 2451 to four significant figures. For these simple numbers, this may be checked by direct multiplication.

$$\begin{array}{r} 43 \\ \times 57 \\ \hline 301 \\ 215 \\ \hline 2451 \end{array}$$

This agrees exactly with the product found by logarithms.

In using logarithms to solve division problems, the logarithm of the divisor must be subtracted from the logarithm of the dividend. Their difference gives the logarithm of the quotient, the answer desired. An example is given that illustrates not only the principles of division, but also shows how interpolation is used in a five-place table of logarithms to obtain the best value for the logarithm of a number with more than four significant figures.

Example 7 Divide 7824.35 by 421.22, using logarithms to the base 10 and a five-place table of logarithms, interpolating where necessary to obtain the best possible logarithms and thus the best possible value for the quotient.

Solution Although the dividend 7824.35 contains six digits, only four appear to the left of the decimal point, so the characteristic of this number is 3, one less than the number of digits. The mantissa must next be determined from the table of logarithms. The table gives the logarithm of 7.824 as 0.89343. The table also gives 0.89348 for the logarithm of 7.825. The difference between these two values is 0.00005. The number whose logarithm we desire is 7824.35; the difference between the number 7824.35 and 7824.00 is 0.35. The difference between 7825.00 and 7824.00 is 1.00, so we must add the value $0.35(0.00005) = 0.0000175$ (or approximately 0.0002) to the logarithm of 7824.00. Hence the logarithm of 7824.35 is 3.89345. The divisor 421.22 has a characteristic of 2, one less than the number of digits before the decimal point. The next step is to find the mantissa from the five-place table of logarithms. The table gives 0.62449 as the logarithm of 4.212. The logarithm of the next higher number, 4.213 is 0.62459. The difference between these two logarithms is $0.62459 - 0.62449 = 0.00010$. The divisor differs from 421.20 by 0.02 since $421.22 - 421.20 = 0.02$. Similarly, the difference between the two numbers whose logarithms were recorded is 421.30 − 421.20 = 0.10. Since 0.02/0.10 = 0.2, 0.2 of the difference between the two logarithms recorded above (or 0.2(0.00010) = 0.000020) must be added to the logarithm of 421.20. Using the characteristic determined for this number and the mantissa that results from adding the prorated difference to the smaller logarithm read from the table (i.e., 0.62449 + 0.00002 = 0.62451), we find that the logarithm of 421.22 is 2.62451. The desired quotient must now be determined.

The problem may now be expressed as $\frac{7824.35}{421.22} = \frac{10^{3.89345}}{10^{2.62451}}$. In division $\frac{x^a}{x^b} = x^{a-b}$; hence the answer to this division problem is now expressed as $10^{3.89345-2.62451} = 10^{1.26894}$.

In practice, all the detailed steps given above to show the basis for subtracting the two logarithms obtained from the table of logarithms are omitted. The shortened format shown below is used to determine the logarithm of the quotient and its antilogarithm, which is the desired quotient.

First determine the logarithm of the dividend and write that down. Next determine the logarithm of the divisor and write it under the logarithm of the dividend. Then subtract the logarithm of the divisor from the logarithm of the dividend. The difference is the logarithm of the quotient. Look up the corresponding antilogarithm, which is the desired quotient. These steps are given below.

Five-Place Log Table		*Seven-Place Log Table*	
Log 7824.35 =	3.89345	Log 7824.35 =	3.8934483
− Log 421.22 =	2.62451	Log 421.22 =	2.6245090
Log quotient =	1.26894	Log quotient =	1.2689393
Quotient =	18.57542	Quotient =	18.57545

By actual division, the quotient is 18.57544751.

Actually, for this case the quotient is good to five significant figures for the five-place log table, and to five or six significant figures for the seven-place log table. Usually an answer found by an n-place log table is good to $n - 1$ significant figures. There are some tables, however, where this may not be true if there are not a sufficient number of digits for entering the table. When linear interpolation is carried out to more than one place, the succeeding digits are questionable.

When computers are not readily available, then logarithms may be found to be the best method for obtaining the desired answers. Select a large enough table so that interpolation is reduced to a minimum. Use of logarithms when factorials are involved is covered later. Factorials are usually such large numbers that it is almost a necessity to use their logarithms in evaluating expressions used to determine the probabilities used in quality control in connection with sampling evaluations.

2.16 Exponential (e^x and e^{-x}) and Napierian (natural) Logarithms (Base e)

Where values have essentially a constant rate of increase, the curve that represents this is $y = ae^{bt}$, where a and b are constants and t denotes time. This, or some simple transformation, is called the exponential curve. This is often expressed as e^x, with $e = 2.718281828459045$. e^x may be expressed in a series form by equation (1) given earlier.

$$e^x = 1 + \frac{x}{1!} + \frac{x^2}{2!} + \frac{x^3}{3!} + \frac{x^4}{4!} + \cdots + \frac{x^i}{i!} + \cdots \tag{1}$$

In quality control and reliability engineering work, $e^{-x} = 1/e^x$ is used more frequently than e^x. e^{-x} can be expressed in series form like relation (1) above.

$$e^{-x} = 1 - \frac{x}{1!} + \frac{x^2}{2!} - \frac{x^3}{3!} + \frac{x^4}{4!} - \cdots \pm \frac{x^i}{i!} \mp \cdots \tag{5}$$

We would find e^{-1} is equal to 0.367879441171442.

An important distribution used as the limiting distribution of the binomial is the Poisson distribution, which is a discontinuous distribution with relative frequencies at integral values 0, 1, 2, 3, ..., i and is given by the relation in equation (6).

$$e^{-m}, \frac{e^{-m} \cdot m}{1!}, \frac{e^{-m} \cdot m^2}{2!}, \frac{e^{-m} \cdot m^3}{3!}, \ldots, \frac{e^{-m} \cdot m^i}{i!} \tag{6}$$

These frequencies are used as approximations to similar discontinuous probability values that should be computed when the lot size N is small and really should be used for all values of N, but may be approximated by the Poisson exponential limit or the binomial.

One of the more important functions of a complete quality control program is the evaluation of the reliability of a system comprised of numerous components, where e^{-x_i} measures the reliability of component i, where $x_i = \lambda_i t_i$ where λ_i stands for the failure rate and t_i denotes the operating time for component i. When a number of components of a system operate essentially in series, the product law applies. This product law states that the reliability of a system is the product of the reliability values of the components of the system. Since $R_i = e^{-x_i}$, then the system's reliability R is obtained from the following relation.

$$R = R_1 \cdot R_2 \cdot R_3 \cdot R_4 \cdot \ldots = \Pi R_i, \tag{7}$$

The symbol Π signifies a product and $\sum$ signifies a sum. (See equation 8.) In terms of the exponential, this product is written and evaluated as shown in equation 8.

$$R = e^{-x} = e^{-x_1} \cdot e^{-x_2} \cdot e^{-x_3} \cdot e^{-x_4} \cdot e^{-x_5} \cdots = e^{-\Sigma x_i} = e^{-(x_1 + x_2 + x_3 + x_4 + x_5 + \cdots)} \tag{8}$$

Tables for e^x and e^{-x} are available for values of x ranging from extremely small values of x to extremely large values of x, required when the product consists of only one component or is a system consisting of a large number of components or black boxes. Such tables give the probability values directly, but in many cases may not cover exactly the values covering a given product.

When the tables fail to provide the value desired or are not available, these probability values may be determined by using the logarithms of e^x and e^{-x}. The values of such logarithms may be determined from table 2.1. It gives terms which may be added together, covering all values which might occur in practice. Logarithms to ten places are also given. The range of x values is from 0.00001 to 500.00000. If smaller values of x are desired, a good approximation to use is

TABLE 2.1 The Common Logarithms of e^x and e^{-x}

x	$\log_{10} e^x$	$\log_{10} e^{-x}$	x	$\log_{10} e^x$	$\log_{10} e^{-x}$
0.00001	0.0000043429	$\bar{1}.9999956571$	0.08000	0.0347435586	$\bar{1}.9652564414$
0.00002	0.0000086859	$\bar{1}.9999913141$	0.09000	0.0390865034	$\bar{1}.9609134966$
0.00003	0.0000130288	$\bar{1}.9999869712$	0.10000	0.0434294482	$\bar{1}.9565705518$
0.00004	0.0000173718	$\bar{1}.9999826282$	0.20000	0.0868588964	$\bar{1}.9131411036$
0.00005	0.0000217147	$\bar{1}.9999782853$	0.30000	0.1302883446	$\bar{1}.8697116554$
0.00006	0.0000260577	$\bar{1}.9999739423$	0.40000	0.1737177928	$\bar{1}.8262822072$
0.00007	0.0000304006	$\bar{1}.9999695994$	0.50000	0.2171472410	$\bar{1}.7828527590$
0.00008	0.0000347436	$\bar{1}.9999652564$	0.60000	0.2605766891	$\bar{1}.7394233109$
0.00009	0.0000390865	$\bar{1}.9999609135$	0.70000	0.3040061373	$\bar{1}.6959938627$
0.00010	0.0000434294	$\bar{1}.9999565706$	0.80000	0.3474355855	$\bar{1}.6525644145$
0.00020	0.0000868589	$\bar{1}.9999131411$	0.90000	0.3908650337	$\bar{1}.6091349663$
0.00030	0.0001302883	$\bar{1}.9998697117$	1.00000	0.4342944819	$\bar{1}.5657055181$
0.00040	0.0001737178	$\bar{1}.9998262822$	2.00000	0.8685889638	$\bar{1}.1314110362$
0.00050	0.0002171472	$\bar{1}.9997828528$	3.00000	1.3028834457	$\bar{2}.6971165543$
0.00060	0.0002605767	$\bar{1}.9997394233$	4.00000	1.7371779276	$\bar{2}.2628220724$
0.00070	0.0003040061	$\bar{1}.9996959939$	5.00000	2.1714724095	$\bar{3}.8285275905$
0.00080	0.0003474356	$\bar{1}.9996525644$	6.00000	2.6057668914	$\bar{3}.3942331086$
0.00090	0.0003908650	$\bar{1}.9996091350$	7.00000	3.0400613733	$\bar{4}.9599386267$
0.00100	0.0004342945	$\bar{1}.9995657055$	8.00000	3.4743558552	$\bar{4}.5256441448$
0.00200	0.0008685890	$\bar{1}.9991314110$	9.00000	3.9086503371	$\bar{4}.0913496629$
0.00300	0.0013028834	$\bar{1}.9986971166$	10.00000	4.3429448190	$\bar{5}.6570551810$
0.00400	0.0017371779	$\bar{1}.9982628221$	20.00000	8.6858896381	$\bar{9}.3141103619$
0.00500	0.0021714724	$\bar{1}.9978285276$	30.00000	13.0288344571	$\overline{14}.9711655429$
0.00600	0.0026057669	$\bar{1}.9973942331$	40.00000	17.3717792761	$\overline{18}.6282207239$
0.00700	0.0030400614	$\bar{1}.9969599386$	50.00000	21.7147240952	$\overline{22}.2852759048$
0.00800	0.0034743559	$\bar{1}.9965256441$	60.00000	26.0576689142	$\overline{27}.9423310858$
0.00900	0.0039086503	$\bar{1}.9960913497$	70.00000	30.4006137332	$\overline{31}.5993862668$
0.01000	0.0043429448	$\bar{1}.9956570552$	80.00000	34.7435585523	$\overline{35}.2564414477$
0.02000	0.0086858896	$\bar{1}.9913141104$	90.00000	39.0864033713	$\overline{40}.9134966287$
0.03000	0.0130288345	$\bar{1}.9869711655$	100.00000	43.4294481903	$\overline{44}.5705518097$
0.04000	0.0173717793	$\bar{1}.9826282207$	200.00000	86.8588963807	$\overline{87}.1411036193$
0.05000	0.0217147241	$\bar{1}.9782852759$	300.00000	130.2883445710	$\overline{131}.7116554290$
0.06000	0.0260576689	$\bar{1}.9739423311$	400.00000	173.7177927613	$\overline{174}.2822072387$
0.07000	0.0304006137	$\bar{1}.9695993863$	500.00000	217.1472409516	$\overline{218}.8527590484$

Note: $\log e^{x+y} = \log e^x + \log e^y$. Thus, $\log e^{113.1478} = 49.139465180$.

$P = e^x = x$ when x is less than 0.00001 and $R = e^{-x} = 1 - x$ when x is less than 0.00001. When x is 0.00000001, then P also is 0.00000001 and R is 0.99999999. Table 2.1 presents, respectively, 68 ten-place logarithms for e^x and e^{-x} and uses steps of 10. Log e^{x+y} is found by adding log e^x and log e^y. Hence table 2.1 gives all the values necessary for obtaining any value of x, even those not given directly in the table. The following examples show how this principle applies.

Example 8 When $x = 1.07$, find the values of $y = e^x$ and $z = e^{-x}$ using logarithms to the base 10 from the ten-place logarithms in table 2.1. First, use all ten places and then use the table as a five-place table to illustrate the case where only four significant figures are needed in the answer.

Solution To illustrate the method and the accuracy of the results that may be obtained by using logarithms to as many places as are required, the answer is given by using all ten places given in table 2.1. The answer is also shown by using only five of the places in table 2.1. As a final comparison, values of both $y = e^x$ and $z = e^{-x}$ are given that have been taken from an extensive table for these exponential values. Actual values are given to about fifteen places in the check table.

Logarithms to ten places			*Logarithms to five places*		
x	$\log e^x$	$\log e^{-x}$	x	$\log e^x$	$\log e^{-x}$
1.00	0.4342944819	$\bar{1}.5657055181$	1.00	0.43429	$\bar{1}.56571$
0.07	0.0304006137	$\bar{1}.9695993863$	0.07	0.03040	$\bar{1}.96960$
1.07	0.4646950956	$\bar{1}.5353049044$	1.07	0.46469	$\bar{1}.53531$
	$\log y$	$\log z$		$\log y$	$\log z$

$y = 2.91537952698$; $z = 0.343008517474$ $\qquad$ $y = 2.91533$; $\qquad z = 0.343015$

The values above were determined, respectively, from a ten-place table of logarithms and a five-place table of logarithms. The values below used as a check were read from a table of the exponential functions giving values to at least fifteen places.

Check

$$y = 2.915379499976997; \quad z = 0.343008517418707.$$

Comparison

$$y = 2.91538; \quad z = 0.343009$$

Tables of the exponential functions generally provide no values for x values less than 10. Example 9 will cover a case where these logarithms provide probably the only solution.

Example 9 When $x = 24.9632$, find the values of $y = e^x$ and $z = e^{-x}$.

Solution

	Logarithms to ten places		*Answers*
x	$\log e^x$	$\log e^{-x}$	
20.	8.6858896381	$\bar{9}.3141103619$	$y = e^x = e^{24.9632}$
4.	1.7371779276	$\bar{2}.2628220724$	$y = 69403282381$
0.9	0.3908650337	$\bar{1}.6091349663$	$= 694{,}033 \times 10^5$
0.06	0.0260576689	$\bar{1}.9739423311$	$= 6.94033 \times 10^{10}$
0.003	0.0013028834	$\bar{1}.9986971166$	$z = e^{-x} = e^{-24.9632}$
0.0002	0.0000868589	$\bar{1}.9999131411$	$z = 0.00000000001440854043 6$
			$= 0.144085 \times 10^{-10}$.
24.9632	10.8413800106	$\overline{11}.1586199894$	
	$\log y$	$\log z$	

Check: 69,403,282,381 × 0.000000000014408540436 = 1.00000000000.

In determining the answers, the most important point is to determine where to place the decimal point to make the results usable.

Sometimes relations are given in terms of natural logarithms rather than the common logarithms. Unless base 10 logarithms are specifically programmed on a computer, most computers will give results in terms of natural logarithms. There are two conversion factors that may be used in such situations.

1. A common logarithm may be converted to a natural logarithm by multiplying it by 2.3025850930.
2. A natural logarithm may be converted to a common logarithm by multiplying it by 0.4342944819. Equation 3.

Tables of natural logarithms are available but usually these tables are small. Tables of the common logarithms are given in very extensive forms, alone or in many textbooks. The difference between their values is shown in table 2.2, which gives five-place logarithms of the integers 1 to 20.

One function often performed by quality control personnel is the determination of reliability values for products being life-tested. Failure rates are found in terms of the number of failures per one million (1,000,000 or 10^6) hours or cycles. The failure rate λ multiplied by the number of operations desired in terms of cycles or time t for the mission gives $x = \lambda t$; the reliability R is determined by the exponential $e^{-x} = e^{-\lambda t}$. Since table 2.1 gives the logarithms of e^{-x}, the reliability of the system consisting of i components may be determined by merely adding all the x values x_i and then evaluating e^{-x}. However, it is very desirable to note the reliability value of each component in the system. This information may make it possible to replace a component with a small MTBF value and reliability value with a better unit. An example of this usage follows.

TABLE 2.2 Common Logarithms and Natural Logarithms for the Integers 1–20 to Five-Places

Number N	Common Log	Natural Log	Number N	Common Log	Natural Log
1	0.00000	0.00000	11	1.04139	2.39790
2	0.30103	0.69315	12	1.07918	2.48491
3	0.47712	1.09861	13	1.11394	2.56495
4	0.60206	1.38629	14	1.14613	2.63906
5	0.69897	1.60944	15	1.17609	2.70805
6	0.77815	1.79176	16	1.20412	2.77259
7	0.84510	1.94591	17	1.23045	2.83321
8	0.90309	2.07944	18	1.25527	2.89037
9	0.95424	2.19722	19	1.27875	2.94444
10	1.00000	2.30259	20	1.30103	2.99573

When obtaining the antilogarithm from a table of logarithms, we must use the table that applies, i.e., the one having the same base as that being used in solving the problem with logarithms.

Example 10 We wish to determine the reliability of a system consisting of five components if it is operated 10,000 hours. Using standard test values for these components, the failure rates λ are listed[4] and multiplied by the ratio 10,000 hours/1,000,000 since failure rates are usually per million hours of operation. The x values reflect the use of this ratio. Table 2.1 provides the necessary logarithm values to obtain the desired reliability values.

Tabulation using x values for 10,000 hours of operation

Component	Failure Rate × Time, x	$\log_{10} e^{-x}$	Reliability R
A	0.005	$\bar{1}.99783$	0.99502
B	0.060	$\bar{1}.97394$	0.94176
C	0.100	$\bar{1}.95657$	0.90484
D	0.004	$\bar{1}.99826$	0.99600
E	0.001	$\bar{1}.99957$	0.99901
System	0.170	$\bar{1}.92617$	0.84366

If only the reliability of the system or a major component consisting of many parts is desired, then only those desired need be evaluated. The example above provides much more information than is usually required. Perform only those operations that are specified.

2.17 Factorials

The term *factorial* refers to the product of a set of ascending or descending numbers. Specifically, *n factorial*, sometimes written $n!$ or $\underline{|n}$, is represented by either the product:

$$n! = n \cdot (n-1)\ (n-2) \cdots 3 \cdot 2 \cdot 1 \quad \text{or} \quad n! = 1 \cdot 2 \cdot 3 \cdot 4 \cdots (n-1) \cdot n \tag{9}$$

For example, $3! = 3 \cdot 2 \cdot 1 = 6$ and

$10! = 10 \cdot 9 \cdot 8 \cdot 7 \cdot 6 \cdot 5 \cdot 4 \cdot 3 \cdot 2 \cdot 1 = 90(56)(30)(24) = 5040(720) = 3{,}628{,}800.$

The product of $10! \times 8!$ is $3{,}628{,}800 \times 40{,}320 = 146{,}313{,}216{,}000$. This product can be obtained more readily by adding the logarithms of the two factorials. This sum will give the logarithm of their product. The above product is obtained in the following way by using the logarithms of these two factorials.[5]

$$\begin{aligned} \log 10! &= 6.5598 \\ \log 8! &= 4.6055 \\ \hline \log \text{product} &= 11.1653 \end{aligned}$$

The mantissa is 0.1653. For this value, the antilogarithm may be read directly from any common log table. The product is therefore 146,300,000,000, since the characteristic for the log of the product is 11.

With only a four-place table of logarithms used, this answer differs only slightly from the more detailed answer given as a check for any computations that might be made. The difference is only 13,216,000—a very large number in itself—but relatively small when compared with the total product. Another table gives seven-place logarithms and provides a somewhat better answer for this product.

$$\begin{aligned} \log 10! &= 6.5597630 \\ \log 8! &= 4.6055205 \\ \hline \log \text{product} &= 11.1652835 \end{aligned}$$

The mantissa is now 0.1652835. For this value, the antilogarithm should be read from a seven-place common log table. Interpolating in such a table gives 146,313,200,000 as the product.

The difference from the computed value is now only 16,000, a much better answer than when using the four-place table. It is thus possible to obtain more accurate values by using a seven-place table such as that given as Table XXX of Fisher and Yates (see Footnote 5). Table XXX covers numbers from 1 to 300 and gives both factorial values and their common logarithms.

Where work in quality control requires the use of factorials and such logarithmic tables of factorials are not available, logarithms of factorials may be secured from a table giving common logarithms to as many places as desired by adding together logarithms of successive numbers. The easiest way to accomplish this is to use a pocket calculator and add the numbers given in the table. When doing this, it is simplest to start with the logarithm of 1 and successively add the logarithms of 2, 3, 4, and so forth until the n values desired are obtained. The following tabulation for log factorials based on a ten-place table illustrates the method.

N	$\log N$	$\log N!$	N	$\log N$	$\log N!$
1	0.0000000000	0.0000000000	11	1.0413926852	7.6011557180
2	0.3010299957	0.3010299957	12	1.0791812460	8.6803369640
3	0.4771212547	0.7781512504	13	1.1139433523	9.7942803163
4	0.6020599913	1.3802112417	14	1.1461280357	10.9404083522
5	0.6989700043	2.0791812460	15	1.1760912591	12.1164996111
6	0.7781512504	2.8573324964	16	1.2041199827	13.3206195938
7	0.8450980400	3.7024305364	17	1.2304489214	14.5510685152
8	0.9030899870	4.6055205234	18	1.2552725051	15.8063410203
9	0.9542425094	5.5597630328	19	1.2787536010	17.0850946213
10	1.0000000000	6.5597630328	20	1.3010299957	18.3861246170

2.18 Combinations and Permutations

Although this topic is covered in more detail in chapter three, we will introduce it briefly here. Many items or components are combined to form a single unit or system. The letters of the alphabet are combined in many ways to form words. A board of directors or committee may consist of, for example, five men. These members may be put on different committees of three, each to act on different areas of interest. How many different combinations of three each may be obtained from the five board members? This number may be found mathematically or by listing all possible arrangements by names. The number of possible arrangements by both methods should check.

Let A, B, C, D, and E denote the five different board members. The possible committees of three each may be enumerated as follows:

ABC, ABD, ABE, ACD, ACE, ADE, BCD, BCE, BDE, CDE.

Counting the above list shows that there are ten possible ways of arranging these committees. Mathematically, the number of combinations of N items taken n at a time may be determined from the following relation.

$$\textit{Combination evaluation:}\quad C_n^N = \frac{N!}{n!(N-n)!} \tag{10}$$

C_n^N can also be written as ${}^NC_n$, ${}_nC^N$ or $\binom{N}{n}$. A less common representation of a combination is $C(N, n)$. Note that this relation requires the evaluation of factorials which were covered in detail in the previous section. For small values of such factorials, since the relations are generally in fractional form, the factorials may be reduced to a few simple numbers in both the numerator and denominator, which may then be evaluated by simple multiplications and a final division. This practice will be illustrated in the examples that follow.

Permutations take account of the fact that the elements in a combination may be arranged in many different ways. For example the word *CAT* consists of three different letters. The same letters are also in the word *ACT*. These three letters also may be arranged as CTA, ATC, TCA, and TAC. This simple combination of three items arranged three at a time may be arranged in six different ways. Such possible combinations may be discovered by simply writing down all possible arrangements. However, this is time-consuming and is not recommended. Certain quality control work requires the *number* of permutations or combinations, not their composition, to determine measures of probability in sampling. For example, the coefficient of the various terms of the p binomial is determined from the combination of n items taken m at a time, expressed as C_m^n. Mathematically, the number of permutations of N items taken n at a time may be determined from the following relation.

$$\textit{Permutation evaluation:}\quad P_n^N = \frac{N!}{(N-n)!} \tag{11}$$

P_n^N can also be written as ${}_NP_n$, $P(N, n)$, or ${}^NP_n$.

In the example above concerning the number of committees of three each that could be obtained from a board consisting of five members, the number of combinations found was 10. The different ways of seating such committees is obtained by taking $10 \cdot P(3, 3) = 10 \times 6 = 60$.

In the automobile industry, engines are made with 4, 6, 8, etc., cylinders. Each cylinder is to be fired by means of a spark plug. ${}_nP_n = \dfrac{n!}{(n-n)!} = \dfrac{n!}{0!} = n!$, since $0! = 1$. For the four-cylinder motor, the number of firing orders is $4! = 24$. For the six-cylinder car, the number of firing orders is $6! = 720$, and for the eight-cylinder car, the number of firing orders is $8! = 40{,}320$.

Two more examples will help to clarify this concept. Given the five letters A, B, C, D, and E, determine the number of words consisting of two letters each that may be formed; then find the number of combinations of five letters taken two letters at a time. Since only two letters are to be used, the number of words that may be formed is the number of permutations of five letters listed two at a time. Mathematically, the number is ${}_5P_2 = \dfrac{5!}{(5-2)!}$. This may also be written $P_2^5 = P(5, 2) = \dfrac{5!}{3!} = \dfrac{5 \cdot 4 \cdot 3 \cdot 2 \cdot 1}{3 \cdot 2 \cdot 1} = 5 \cdot 4 = 20$. These may be enumerated as

AB, BA; AC, CA; AD, DA; AE, EA;
BC, CB; BD, DB; BE, EB;
CD, DC; CE, EC; DE, ED.

By inspection, it is clear that the number of combinations is half of 20, or 10. Mathematically, this means that in the relation for combinations the denominator contains also a 2!.

People who play bridge use a deck containing 52 different cards. Each hand is to contain exactly thirteen cards. How many bridge hands may be formed? This is a problem in combinations, because the arrangement of the cards in a hand has no effect on the play since any card may be played according to the rules. The solution is shown below.

$$C_n^N = C(N, n) = C(52, 13) = \frac{52!}{13! \cdot 39!} = \frac{8.0658 \times 10^{67}}{(6.2270 \times 10^9)(2.0398 \times 10^{46})}$$

$$= \frac{8.0658 \times 10^{67}}{1.27018346 \times 10^{56}} = 6.35 \times 10^{11}$$

The best way to evaluate this relation is to use the logarithms of the factorials.

log 13!	= 9.79428	log numerator = log 52!	=	67.90665
log 39!	= 46.30959	log denominator	=	−56.10387
log denominator	= 56.10387	log $C(52, 13)$	=	11.80278
		$C(52, 13)$	=	63.501×10^{10}.

These values for factorials and their logarithms were obtained from *Mathematical Tables* published by the Chemical Rubber Publishing Company. More exact values can be obtained from the Fisher and Yates tables, already listed.

2.19 Summary

The necessity for giving the mathematical techniques required in quality control work in concise form was recognized as fundamental in a text covering the introduction to statistical quality control. The field of statistics is not covered extensively in high schools or in many later mathematical courses. This section has covered certain mathematical relationships and techniques that have been deemed most useful to those working in quality assurance and reliability engineering.

It is emphasized that a knowledge of logarithms is essential, as well as of factorials, permutations, and combinations. Tables are available in many texts on statistics that make it relatively easy to obtain an answer to any of the problems in quality control without doing all the laborious computations. The use of such tables has been emphasized and a few tables have been referenced. Those working in the field of quality control should make certain that these tables are available in the library where they work and that they are available for ready access and reference. As noted, four-place logarithms may be ample for some problems, while in other situations twenty-place logarithms should be used. Where there is access to an electronic computer such as the larger machines rented on an hourly or monthly basis, the general run of problems encountered repeatedly should be programmed so that the computer may supply the answer with minimum effort on the part of quality control personnel. The new pocket-size calculators make it easier to compute problems in the field or on the production line. Answers to many important problems used to be delayed, which resulted in the production of poor-quality products. The percentage of unsatisfactory products manufactured and sold to customers should be appreciably reduced by utilizing the mathematical tools given in this section. This will result in increased profits for most industrial concerns and an increase in the national wealth.

EXERCISES

1. Add each of the following and check the results by casting out 9's.

(a)	(b)	(c)	(d)	(e)
847	489.25	0.054	827921.	45
924	329.00	0.720	72432.54	72
815	111.11	0.999	1.234	63
642	827.99	0.450		81
				1.45

2. Subtract each of the following and check results by casting out 9's.

(a) $\begin{array}{r} 425.39 \\ -121.21 \\ \hline \end{array}$ (b) $\begin{array}{r} 428.75 \\ -853.21 \\ \hline \end{array}$ (c) $\begin{array}{r} 11111.11 \\ -\ 2222.22 \\ \hline \end{array}$ (d) $\begin{array}{r} 833.42 \\ -425.4108 \\ \hline \end{array}$ (e) $\begin{array}{r} 0.4598 \\ -12.00895 \\ \hline \end{array}$

3. Multiply each of the following and check results by casting out 9's.

(a) $\begin{array}{r} 12345679. \\ \times 36. \\ \hline \end{array}$ (b) $\begin{array}{r} 42.547 \\ \times 2.121 \\ \hline \end{array}$ (c) $\begin{array}{r} 80999 \\ \times 81001 \\ \hline \end{array}$ (d) $\begin{array}{r} 6.25456 \\ \times 0.42570 \\ \hline \end{array}$ (e) $7! = 7 \times 6 \times 5 \times 4 \times 3 \times 2 \times 1 = ????$

4. Divide the following and check results by casting out 9's.

(a) $\frac{625}{25}$ (b) $\frac{81}{0.009}$ (c) $\frac{1.728}{12}$ (d) $\frac{999999999}{81}$ (e) $\frac{0.012625}{101.5}$

5. (a) Extract the square root of each of the following. (i) 625 (ii) 847 (iii) 0.000144 (iv) 0.00144 (v) 3.00000000
(b) Square each of the following numbers and check by casting out 9's. (i) 45 (ii) 115 (iii) 2.4 (iv) 1.414 (v) 3.1623

6. Determine the logarithms to the base 10 of each of the following.
(a) 100 (b) 0.425 (c) 0.000144 (d) 5289.00 (e) 4150.09

7. A building has the following dimensions: width: 80 feet; length: 120 feet; height: 10 feet.
(a) Determine how many square feet there are in this building and determine its initial cost at $32.00 per 100 square feet.
(b) Find the number of cubic feet in the building. If it takes 8 BTU (British Thermal Units) to heat this building per month per cubic foot, how much does it cost to heat the building per month at 7¢ per 1,000 BTU?

8. (a) How many combinations can be obtained from 12 letters taken (i) 4 at a time; (ii) 6 at a time?
(b) How many permutations can be obtained from 12 letters taken (i) 4 at a time; (ii) 6 at a time?

9. Bridge players are interested in the possible number of bridge hands that are possible when there are 52 cards in a deck of cards and 13 cards in each hand. Solve the relation $52!/13!39!$ by using the logarithms of factorials.

10. Using table 2.2 determine (1) the common logarithms and (2) the natural logarithms of the following: (a) 4; (b) 9; (c) 36; (d) 19; (e) 57.

11. (a) Using the common log table for e^x and e^{-x}, determine the logarithms of each of the following. (i) 101 (ii) 10.1 (iii) 15.429 (iv) 0.0235 (v) 1679.5
(b) From a five-place logarithm table, determine the antilogarithms for the five logarithms in (a) above.

12. Determine the value of each of the following. (a) $C_2^{10}(0.95)^8(0.02)^2$ (b) $C_4^{25}(0.9)^{21}(0.1)^4$

13. Determine the value of each of the following. (a) $\dfrac{e^{-2}(2)^3}{3!}$ (b) $\dfrac{e^{-1}(1)^1}{1!}$ (c) $\dfrac{e^{-5}(5)^4}{4!}$

(d) $\dfrac{e^{-0.2}(0.2)^2}{2!}$ (e) $\dfrac{e^{-2.5}(2.5)^4}{4!}$

14. Determine the value of each of the following. (a) $\dfrac{C_4^8 C_1^2}{C_5^{10}}$ (b) $\dfrac{C_4^{15} C_2^3}{C_6^{18}}$

15. The relations evaluated in exercises 12, 13, and 14 are from well-known relations used in quality control. Identify each, giving the name of the relation and its general form. (This question may not be possible to answer until you have covered the material in chapter three.)

FOOTNOTES

[a] Number of F's in figure 2–1 = 6.

[1] *Barlow's Tables of Squares, Cubes, Square Roots, Cube Roots, and Reciprocals of All Integers up to 12,500*, L. J. Comrie, Editor, 4th Edition.

[2] Further references on this topic are:
George Wentworth and David Eugene Smith, *Higher Arithmetic* (New York: Ginn and Company, 1919), 62–63, 249.
Webster Wells, *An Academic Arithmetic for Academies, High, and Commercial Schools* (Boston: D. C. Heath and Co., 1893), 29–31.
Page 32 of this second reference covers casting out 11's, sometimes used when several errors might invalidate a check by casting out 9's.

[3] Other series are: (a) $\ln(1 + x) = x - \frac{1}{2}x^2 + \frac{1}{3}x^3 - \cdots, (|x| \leq 1 \text{ and } x \neq -1)$

(b) $\ln x = (x - 1) - \frac{1}{2}(x - 1)^2 + \frac{1}{3}(x - 1)^3 - \cdots, (|x - 1| \leq 1, x \neq 0)$.

(c) $\ln x = 2\left[\dfrac{x-1}{x+1} + \dfrac{1}{3}\left(\dfrac{x-1}{x+1}\right)^3 + \dfrac{1}{5}\left(\dfrac{x-1}{x+1}\right)^5 + \cdots\right], (x > 0)$

Equation (c) is often better than equation (4). For $x = 1.5$ using 6 terms of each series equation (c) is good to 10 significant figures, where equation (4) is only good to 4 significant figures since $\ln(1.5) = 0.4054651081081644$ per 16-place $\log_e$ table.

[4] Some texts use the symbol r for hazard or failure ratio.

[5]Four-place table giving logarithms of factorials: E. L. Grant and R. S. Leavenworth, *Statistical Quality Control,* 4th Edition, Table H, 655-699.
Seven-place table giving factorials and their logarithms: R. A. Fisher and F. Yates, *Statistical Tables for Biological, Agricultural, and Medical Research,* 4th Edition (London: Oliver and Boyd, 1953), Table XXX.

$n! = \Gamma(n+1)$; many tables of $\Gamma(n)$ and $\log \Gamma(n)$ are available.

CHAPTER THREE

BASIC STATISTICS FOR QUALITY ASSURANCE

3.1 Objective

The purpose of this chapter is to supplement the mathematical methods and techniques described in chapter two and to provide the necessary statistical tools needed in quality assurance work. To be effective, quality control must have valid data, such as reports and recommendations, summarized in a useful form. Data of all kinds, especially inspection and test results, must be arranged in ordered arrays from which it will be possible to obtain the best possible representation by means of a frequency distribution. The nature of such distributions for both attributes data and variables data is covered. Relations by which data from such sources may be used in the preparation of the best possible economical sampling inspection plans as well as for control charts are given.

In quality assurance and similar areas, it is necessary to present summarized reports and recommendations of results which have been summarized by the use of the best possible statistical methods. In obtaining such summaries, use is made of computations of all kinds. Computer programs can be prepared so that computers take over the burdensome part of such tasks. Statistics are used in practically all areas. Business statistics, social statistics, engineering statistics, and many other types of statistics are based on the use of common sense and the application of a few simple statistical principles. These are explained in this chapter, so that the best possible recommendations may be available for making valid decisions. In particular, the uses of cumulative results and cumulative frequency presentations are given. These concepts are useful in deriving probability of acceptance curves, termed OC curves, used in evaluating sampling plans. Measures of central tendency are presented as well as measures of variability. From these statistics, it is possible to cover most of the problems that arise in quality control. Data can be presented graphically in accordance with standard practices. Where different methods can be used to obtain some desired result, tests must be made to determine whether one method is really significantly different from the other. Where two variables appear to be correlated, statistical methods are used to determine the extent to which correlation may exist, along with its numerical value.

The statistics necessary to solve basic problems in quality engineering are given. Later chapters cover how to prepare operating characteristic OC curves, control charts, lines of regression, and tests for significant differences. Methods of fitting curves to the data are also developed, as well as the best way to design experiments and analyze these results by the analysis of variance techniques. These statistics are presented in a manner that allows the probabilities associated with certain premises or hypotheses to be evaluated. Special situations of more difficulty are not covered, as more advanced techniques or methods may be required for many of these problems. Hence this chapter is a presentation of the fundamental statistics used in many areas of interest, but especially needed in the field of quality assurance, including reliability and audits.

3.2 Why Statistical Quality Control?

Quality and the control of desired levels of quality at specific levels are a must in industry and many other fields of endeavor. It is necessary to define and describe the proper use of these terms. *Quality* is defined by the military in DOD–D–4155.11 as "The composite of all the attributes or characteristics, including performance, of an item or product." In MIL–STD–109, quality control is defined as "A management function whereby control of quality of raw or produced material is exercised for the purpose of preventing production of defective material." The definition in figure 3–1 was obtained from the quality control department of Westinghouse. It was printed on a folded calling card so that it could be given to anyone interested

DEFINITION	EXPLANATION AND INTERPRETATION	
Quality Control is a system of INSPECTION, ANALYSIS, and ACTION applied to a manufacturing process; so that by *inspecting* the product produced, an *analysis* of its quality can be made; to determine what *action* is required on the operation, in order to maintain the desired level of quality.	**1. INSPECTION**	Either 100 percent or a small portion of the product is inspected in the regular way, using the gages and tools usually employed for this purpose.
	2. ANALYSIS	Determine the average quality and the extent of variability of quality. Inspection by the method of variables is better than the method of attributes for this purpose.
	3. ACTION	If the average quality is not satisfactory, adjust the process or tools. If the variability is not satisfactory, the machine, or process, in its present condition, is not capable of producing the desired quality level.

Figure 3–1 Westinghouse definition of quality control with explanation and interpretation.

in quality products and how quality is achieved. On the left is a definition; on the right, an explanation and interpretation of the definition. One additional area covered by Westinghouse in its quality control program was *safety*. In many other industries, the same relationship is made, since if care is exercised to prevent accidents, the same care will be carried over into the making of quality products.

Chapter two covered the nature of the mathematics that is really required in quality control work; it is now necessary to thoroughly understand the additional statistical concepts and methods that must be applied to obtain the best possible controls over processes, in order that maximum quality be obtained. What is really meant by quality? A general definition is that quality consists of those attributes that the consumer desires in the products under consideration. It is true that engineering must establish the values within which production will manufacture any given item. But these numerical measures must reflect the desires of the customer. When several characteristics considered as a composite, reflect the ultimate quality, then some suppliers will make the product to requirements; however, it may still not satisfy the customer. Another manufacturer may make the same product and it proves to be exactly what the customer desires. What causes such differences? It is these intangible interactions between various characteristics and parts that make this difference. To aid the manufacturer in making exactly what the customer desires, it is necessary to know how to handle various statistical techniques so that the supplier is certain that customer demands are really met.

The use of statistics is mainly the application of *common sense*. Mathematical techniques learned from the last chapter will help make this common-sense approach easier to follow. Processes must be controlled within specified limits to assure management that the product is really conforming to the desired standards. It is generally recognized or believed that some natural law is inherent in a process. That is, some rule, law, procedure, or technique is dominant, which when known and controlled within desired limits, makes it possible to predict future results within a band of desirable values. For example, a manufacturer needs a certain number of satisfactory components to merge with his parts; a bank needs a certain number of tellers on Fridays to handle the extra weekend load; a factory needs a certain amount of steel during the next week; and a municipality needs a certain amount of money next year to meet the actual bills as well as to meet the budget.

Quality control engineers have found that one of the easiest, quickest, and most reliable methods to separate the chaotic variations from the natural variations is the proper use of control charts. Control charts are widely used in all types of industrial work to locate sources of trouble, and to specify when and where to look for troubles and their causes. They provide a warning of imminent trouble and thus aid in averting it before it occurs. They indicate when it is desirable and profitable to change a process.

The following appeared in the July, 1946 issue of *Industrial Quality Control,* the official magazine of the American Society for Quality Control.

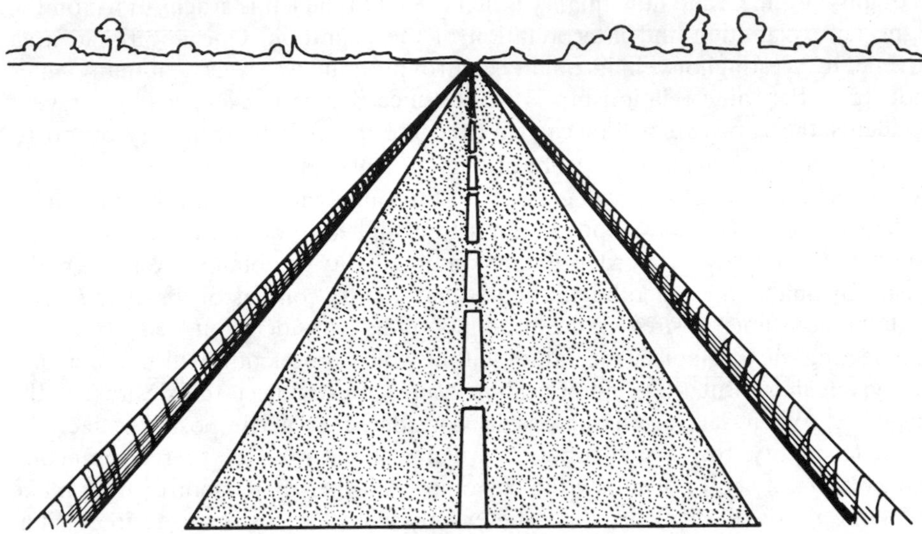

Figure 3–2 Picture of a highway.

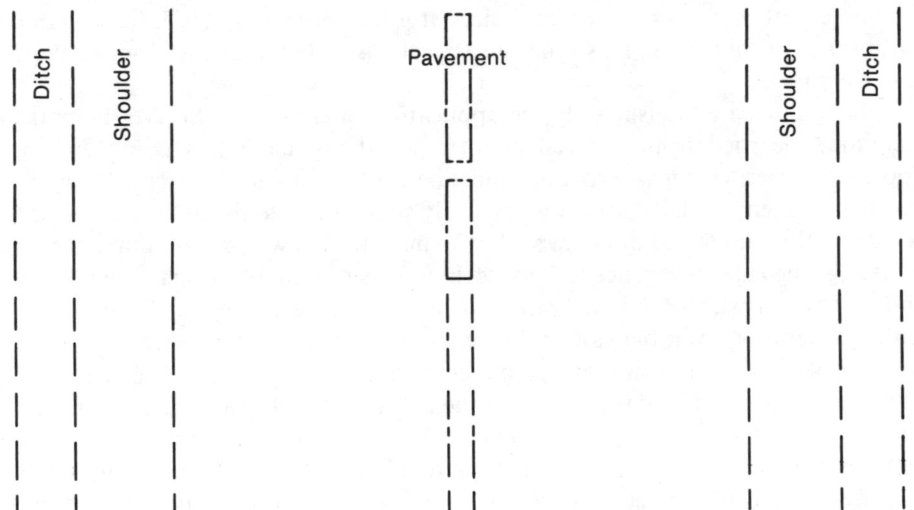

Figure 3–3 Highway diagram.

A control chart has been likened to a highway in that a highway of a certain width must be maintained to accommodate the necessities of driving vehicles. The width of the pavement necessary for a car is different from that needed for a span of mules hitched to a hay rack, although each width can probably be determined in a fairly accurate manner.

Figures 3-2, 3-3, and 3-4 show and explain a highway such as that described above. The first figure was originally drawn in three colors. The pavement is

Red	Ditch	Danger	Upper Specification Limit
Yellow	Shoulder	Caution	Upper Control Limit
Green	Pavement	Safety	Central Line
Yellow	Shoulder	Caution	Lower Control Limit
Red	Ditch	Danger	Lower Specification Limit

Figure 3-4 Highway likened to a control chart.

Figure 3-5 Possible danger from using only averages.

presented as a *green* highway, which indicates *go.* The shoulders of the highway are painted in *yellow* and indicate *caution.* The ditches on the two sides of the highway are in *red,* which indicates *danger.*

The above analogy is very helpful in understanding the use of control charts and why three-sigma control limits are used in most cases, even though two-sigma control limits may be wisely used in some situations. (These two levels for control charts are discussed later.)

Statistics are extremely useful, but must be applied properly. As shown in figure 3-5, an average may not truly indicate conditions as they exist in the entire area being considered. An illustrative story is told about a regiment of soldiers who were marching by foot from one location to another. They found a stream separating the locations, without any nearby bridge. The maps they carried indicated an average depth of three feet. Since all of the soldiers could readily wade across a stream three feet deep, the command was given to cross the stream. However, the center of the stream was over ten feet deep. Soldiers who could not swim had to be rescued by their comrades or drown. As this illustrates, more information than an average is needed in many cases. The nature of the distributions, the number of units in sample, the range of values, and the various measures of variability will be found very useful in arriving at many important decisions. The statistical methods and techniques presented as simply as possible in this book provide the necessary statistical tools required for quality assurance work and for reliability evaluations.

It is also necessary to indicate how data may best be presented graphically. Data must be ordered so that maximum use may be made of its characteristics. Data must be tallied and represented as frequency distributions. Bar charts are also very useful, especially when presented in different colors for comparison purposes. This chapter presents the basic elements of statistics and the various mathematical relations and equations required to properly evaluate most kinds of data obtained in quality control work. The most effective distributions are probability frequency density distributions where the area under the curve is exactly one. Thus frequencies must be relative frequencies in order to provide measures of probability that may be determined directly.

3.3 Frequency Distributions

Observed values or measured values, usually designated by X, are recorded as *observations.* When two supposedly correlated characteristics are treated simultaneously, one set of values is denoted by X values, while the other set of paired values is designated as Y values. When taking these values as deviations from their respective means or averages, lowercase x and/or y are used to denote such deviations. Thus $x_i = X_i - \overline{X}$, while $y_i = Y_i - \overline{Y}$, where the symbols *X-bar* ($\overline{X}$) and *Y-bar* ($\overline{Y}$) designate the respective means or arithmetic averages. The subscript i designates the ith observation or value. Data consisting of n values of X are first recorded just as they are observed. These observations are called the *raw data.*

The first step in making a frequency distribution is to rearrange the n observations in either ascending order or descending order. Such an arrangement is called an *array.* Grades or scores are usually arranged in descending order with 100 percent entered as the first value, followed in order by the smaller scores. Physical characteristics such as length, resistance, miles per hour, ages, weight, and similar items are usually arranged in ascending order. In many cases, more than one observation will have the same value. A tally of values, similar to a vote count, should be made. This tally may be a part of the process of arranging the data in ascending or descending order. The number of occurrences of the same value is called its *frequency*. The number of observations may be very large, perhaps over one hundred. For such cases, a series of consecutive values may be combined in one group or cell. The width of the group or cell might be designated as w, although some texts call the distance between the cell boundaries of consecutive groups an *interval* and denote the interval by i.

To obtain a frequency distribution that may be best interpreted statistically, it is necessary to select the best possible width of the interval. In general, the number of cells used for such distributions should be between eight and twenty. There should be very few empty cells; there should also be a sufficient number of cells to indicate some form for the distribution. A frequency distribution of only one to five cells provides a very poor measure of the variability. When the interval or cell width is too large, all the observations in a small sample might fall in only one cell. This makes it difficult to set up limits for controlling the process average.

Frequency distributions may have many different shapes. The one that is easiest to handle statistically is the normal curve, often called the *normal law curve* or *bell-shaped distribution.* This curve is symmetric, with no skewness, and theoretically has X values from minus infinity to plus infinity, although actually these limits are usually finite. It is generally given as a probability distribution, where for any sample of size n the frequencies observed for each different X value are divided by the sample size n to provide relative frequencies so that the total area under the curve is one. The sum of the frequencies observed for a range of X values is n, the size of the sample being measured or tested. If such discrete frequencies are divided by n, the relative frequencies thus found for each cell are percentages or probabilities whose sum is one rather than n. There are many other shapes that may be assumed. Some frequency distributions are rectangular, some triangular, or right triangular, some J-shaped, some exceedingly irregular with no definite shape, some exponential, and so on. The early statisticians—for example, Karl Pearson in England—represented a whole family of such distributions by a differential equation with several constants that might be varied to provide different shapes. Others used an equation as a generating function. When this function is the normal law—developed in a form like the Taylor series, using only two terms with the second multiplied by the skewness k—the distribution is called the *second approximation* or *Gram-Charlier series.* The functions with total areas under their curves equal to one are called *probability density functions.* Where the number of observations taken, n, are tallied and the respective frequencies per cell are divided by n, the total number of observations in the sample, such frequencies are called *relative frequencies*; if the sum of such relative frequencies is one, such a frequency distribution is changed into a probability density function or distribution. Other functions are the p positive binomial distribution, the Poisson exponential binomial limit, and the hypergeometric function, which are discussed in chapter four. The exponential is used in reliability probability determinations and also in the Weibull distribution. The number of these distributions may be doubled by using a logarithmic scale in place of a linear scale to represent the X values. Such a

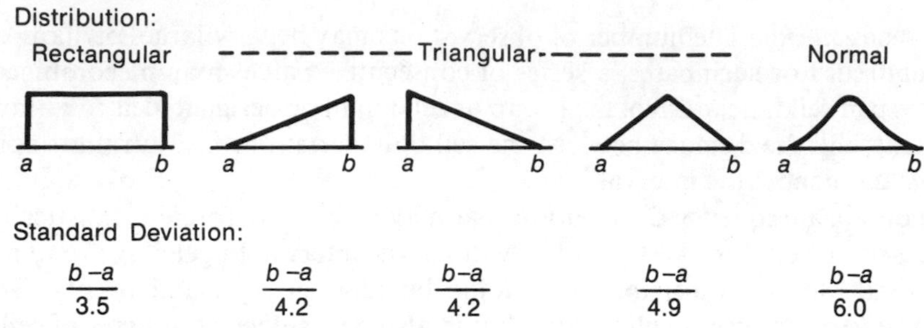

Figure 3–6 Some types of distribution and their standard deviations.

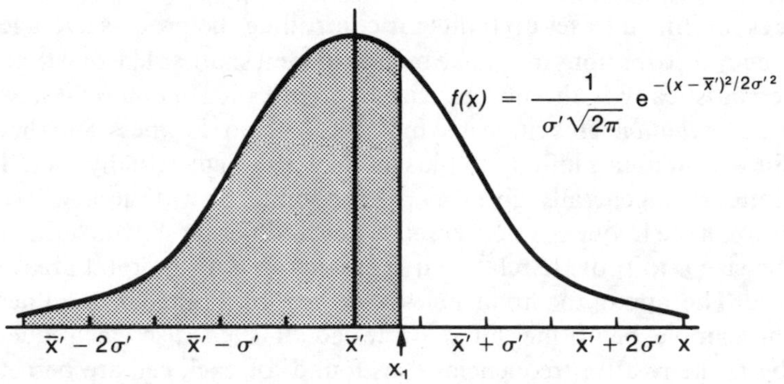

Figure 3–7 Normal distribution.

log-normal distribution fits many types of resistance measurements. Figures 3-6 and 3-7 show the shapes of many of these distributions.

The best measures of the variability of these distributions are their respective *standard deviations,* discussed more fully later in this chapter. In figure 3-6, the standard deviations of the five distributions shown are given in terms of their respective ranges, $b - a$, divided by the appropriate theoretical constant. For the normal distribution this is a practical value, because the theoretical range is from plus infinity to minus infinity and 99.73 percent of the area is between plus and minus three-sigma (three standard deviation) units. The rectangular distribution often results from successive observations obtained from a process in which tool wear may occur, with chance causes during, say, each hour of use generating a normal distribution. The peaks of such a series of successive normal distributions result in a rectangular distribution. A constant failure rate might also result in such a distribution.

In figure 3-6, two types of right triangular distributions are shown: the first form is a *left triangular distribution*; the second is a *right triangular distribution.*

The latter was used by Dr. Walter A. Shewhart and his staff of the Bell Telephone Laboratories to determine whether the averages of successive samples from such a distribution tend to be normal. This experimental approach helped to prove the feasibility of applying normal law theory to all the various average values, regardless of the shapes of the *parent populations.* The third triangular distribution in figure 3-6 is symmetric and is known as an *isosceles triangular distribution.* The last is a *normal distribution,* which is shown enlarged in figure 3-7, together with its theoretical equation. There are many other forms, such as the Chi-square (χ^2), the binomial, and the exponential distribution. These are discussed in chapter four, along with examples of their applications.

The first step in making an analysis of a mass of data is to tally the values systematically in an array as a frequency distribution. Generally the smallest value is listed first, followed by the next largest value. If the second value is the same, the value is either repeated or tallied as two observations of the same magnitude. This tabulation is continued until all the n observations are arranged in numerical order with their X values, denoting the value of the characteristic or item under consideration, listed in order with respect to their magnitudes.

Where audits are made and scores are given to vendors or products in terms of relative values where, for example, the top score is 100 percent, the array may be set up in descending order with the top score of 100 percent—or the largest percentage value—listed as the first value. This practice is also followed in the educational grading of students. In most cases in industry, the ascending-order array is used. This is illustrated in the following example.

> **Example 1** It was desired to control the diameter of a reamed oil pump shaft hole at the specified values of 0.5465 to 0.5475 inch. This is expressed as 0.5470 $\pm$ 0.0005 inch, with diameters measured to the nearest 0.0001 inch. To establish a basis for analysis, quality control engineers obtained a set of 100 measured values of the shaft hole diameters of oil pump bodies in production. Measured values are recorded only to the nearest 0.0001 inch and the range for the tolerance allowed by engineering for this diameter is only 0.0010 inch.

Table 3.1 presents these 100 observations in the order in which they were taken and recorded by quality control covering an oil pump body which has been reamed. The diameter of the reamed oil pump shaft hole is given in inches, together with the engineering specifications; hence the observed values are obtained and recorded in inches to four significant figures.

In order to make the above data in table 3.1 more meaningful, it should be arranged in a frequency distribution. This is the simplest kind of data as the process is so well controlled that no measured value is at the minimum or maximum specified limit. These data thus may be tabulated directly, with $i = 0.0001$

TABLE 3.1 Diameters of 100 Reamed Oil Pump Shaft Holes

Part Name: Oil Pump Body; Part No. 573–622 Measured to 0.0001 inch
Engineering Specifications: Limits: 0.5465–0.5475 inch; Mean Dimension: 0.5470 inch

No.	*X Value*	*No.*	*X Value*	*No.*	*X Value*	*No.*	*X Value*	*No.*	*X Value*
1	0.5469	21	0.5471	41	0.5471	61	0.5466	81	0.5470
2	0.5472	22	0.5473	42	0.5469	62	0.5469	82	0.5467
3	0.5468	23	0.5469	43	0.5470	63	0.5470	83	0.5468
4	0.5467	24	0.5471	44	0.5470	64	0.5472	84	0.5473
5	0.5470	25	0.5473	45	0.5472	65	0.5467	85	0.5468
6	0.5474	26	0.5469	46	0.5471	66	0.5469	86	0.5469
7	0.5468	27	0.5473	47	0.5467	67	0.5473	87	0.5472
8	0.5470	28	0.5467	48	0.5471	68	0.5469	88	0.5469
9	0.5471	29	0.5472	49	0.5469	69	0.5471	89	0.5468
10	0.5470	30	0.5470	50	0.5473	70	0.5468	90	0.5470
11	0.5469	31	0.5472	51	0.5467	71	0.5470	91	0.5473
12	0.5469	32	0.5469	52	0.5471	72	0.5473	92	0.5469
13	0.5470	33	0.5471	53	0.5467	73	0.5468	93	0.5469
14	0.5469	34	0.5470	54	0.5472	74	0.5471	94	0.5471
15	0.5467	35	0.5472	55	0.5468	75	0.5469	95	0.5469
16	0.5470	36	0.5468	56	0.5469	76	0.5469	96	0.5468
17	0.5469	37	0.5472	57	0.5468	77	0.5470	97	0.5472
18	0.5471	38	0.5469	58	0.5473	78	0.5469	98	0.5468
19	0.5473	39	0.5473	59	0.5470	79	0.5473	99	0.5470
20	0.5471	40	0.5470	60	0.5471	80	0.5470	100	0.5469
Sum = 10.9397		Sum = 10.9414		Sum = 10.9399		Sum = 10.9396		Sum = 10.9392	

$n = 100$; Total sum $= 54.6998$; $\bar{X} = 0.546998$.

giving nine cells when distributed. Figure 3-8 presents a tally chart showing how to tally data and arrange the data into a frequency distribution. The tally is summed, so the last column gives the frequency for each cell; the interval between each cell is 0.0001 inch.

Cumulative frequencies: Another useful form of presentation is to arrange the data as a *cumulative frequency distribution.* Two possible arrangements are (1) a *less-than* chart or distribution and (2) a *more-than* distribution. Such distributions are often termed *ogives.* Sum the tallied frequencies in ascending order or in descending order. These cumulated frequencies should actually be listed opposite the cell boundary values rather than at the mid-cell value. When plotted, they should be presented in graphical form at the cell boundary values, starting with whichever boundary provides the correct evaluation, *less-than* or *more-than.*

These cumulative frequency curves are used in many different areas. In quality control sampling inspection, these curves are plotted in terms of relative

TALLY CHART

MEASUREMENT	TALLY	FREQUENCY
	Specification Limit: Minimum 0.5465″	
0.5465		
0.5466	I	1
0.5467	卌 III	8
0.5468	卌 卌 II	12
0.5469	卌 卌 卌 卌 IIII	24
0.5470	卌 卌 卌 III	18
0.5471	卌 卌 IIII	14
0.5472	卌 卌	10
0.5473	卌 卌 II	12
0.5474	I	1
0.5475		
	Specification Limit: Maximum 0.5475″	
	Total	100

Figure 3–8 Tally with summed frequencies for data in Table 3–1; Diameter of 100 reamed oil pump shaft holes.

frequencies, rather than actual observed frequencies, so that the sum of the frequencies is 1.00 or 100%. The same concept is applied to the frequency distribution, where frequencies are also expressed as relative frequencies by dividing the number of observed frequencies in each cell by the sample size n used, or the number n of observations recorded. In figure 3-8, since the number of observations is 100, merely adding a percentage symbol changes the frequencies noted to relative frequencies, which are actually probability values. Their numerical values are obtained by dividing the observed numerical frequencies by $n = 100$.

The cumulative distribution expressed in terms of probability values gives the *probability of acceptance*, P_a value for sampling plans; such a curve is called the *operating characteristic* (OC) for the plan under consideration. Most sampling plans have their OC curves plotted so that they may be used to determine what sampling plan is best adapted to any situation.

These cumulative distributions are also used in presenting scores made in various educational tests and for the final grades of students for a given course. Such evaluations are given in terms of *percentiles*. A general division is by fourths, dividing the cumulative frequency distribution into the following percentiles: 25%, 50%, 75%, and 100%. Another favorite division is by tenths: 10%, 20%, 30%, 40%, 50%, 60%, 70%, 80%, 90%, and 100%. Is a student in the upper 10% of his class? This information is commonly desired by those interviewing candidates for various positions. It is therefore useful to present scores

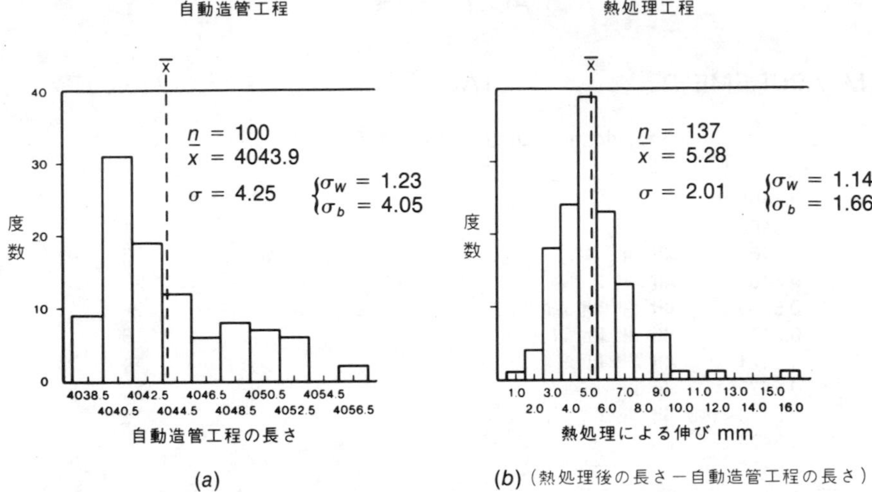

Figure 3–9 Two bar charts covering two different n values, 100 and 137.

as probability density functions or distributions rather than just as frequency distributions where the sum of the frequencies is n.

3.4 Graphical Presentations

Statistics are more readily interpreted when presented visually as graphs. One of the favorite forms is termed the *bar chart*. A bar chart or graph is presented by forming a rectangle about a base consisting of the distance between the boundary values of successive cells and making the height of the rectangle equal to the observed frequency for each cell, respectively. Where no observation exists in a cell, no rectangle will appear. For comparisons between two somewhat similar distributions, bar charts are made using half the cell width for the base of, say, the A distribution, and the other half for the B distribution against which a comparison is desired, using relative frequencies in both cases. Each rectangle is drawn and may be presented in two different colors, as clear and shaded areas, or in any other artistic manner that shows contrast.

Another form of graphical presentation is the *frequency polygon*. The frequencies of all the cells covering the distribution are plotted at the mid-cell values, respectively. The frequency is marked on the vertical at the appropriate height according to the y scale chosen. Such marks may be an x or an o. These point markers are then connected by a series of lines from point to point. Since successive frequencies are connected, these graphs are often called *line charts*. When comparing an observed frequency distribution with a selected theoretical distribution, the theoretical distribution may be drawn as a solid or dashed

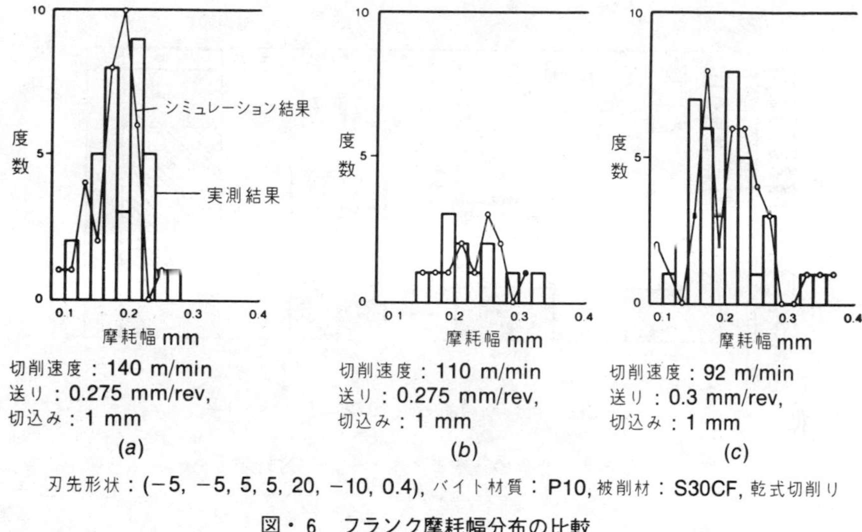

Figure 3–10 Three frequency polygons superimposed on their corresponding bar charts.

continuous smooth curve in contrast with the observed frequency polygon plotted as a probability frequency distribution. Cumulative frequency distributions and/or cumulative probability distributions may also be presented as broken-line or continuous-line graphs. Examples of the different kinds of distributions are given in figures 3-9 and 3-10 to illustrate the manner in which many types of data are graphed.

The first set of figures show the universality of the use of bar charts. They are taken from the November 1974 and January 1975 issues of the Japanese magazine, *Statistical Quality Control.* Frequency polygons are given, drawn over the corresponding bar charts. One set of bar charts shows the percentages for given parts making up a total. Another gives cumulative curves used in testing statistical hypotheses. This is another valuable use of cumulative frequency distributions.

In the bar chart in figure 3-11, each bar is similar to a circular pie, showing the percentage contribution of each part to the whole. Here four parts contribute to the total values listed for three periods, 1960, 1965, and 1970, together with an estimated value for 1980. The contribution of each part is expressed as a percentage of the whole, their sum totaling 100%.

Four figures are now given to illustrate the use of bar charts to depict various characteristics of the many distributions met in practice, as a supplement to those previously presented.

The section covering measures of central tendencies will describe all the various measures commonly used. The value of X that occurs most frequently is termed its

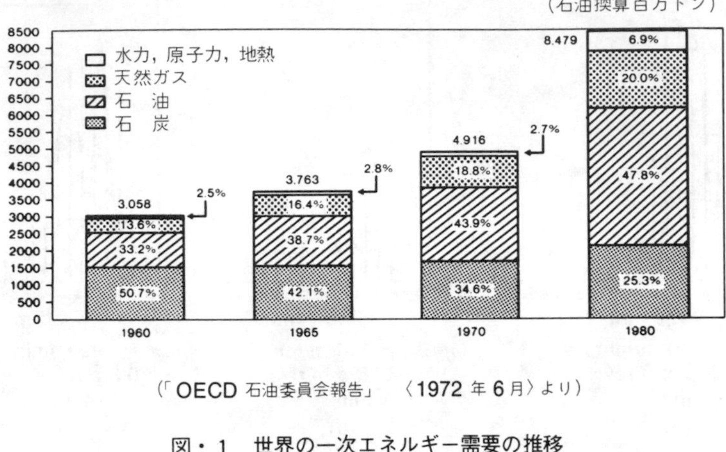

Figure 3–11 Bar chart showing actual number and percentages contributed to the whole by four periods: 1960, 1965, 1970 and 1980 (projected).

mode. Some distributions, however, may have two cells with X values that occur much more frequently than the other X values. Such a distribution is termed a *bimodal distribution* and is shown in figure 3-13. Distributions that have most of their values closely clustered about the central value are considered to have *small variability* as contrasted with distributions that have a very wide spread, with values dispersed over a very large range of X values. The latter distributions are said to have *large variability*. The bar charts in figure 3-14 illustrate such distributions.

In most cases, statisticians are primarily interested in the central value and the spread of a distribution. In mathematical terminology, these are measured by the first and second moments of the function representing the distribution. Higher moments exist, the third measuring the lack of symmetry of the distribution, termed its *skewness*. Figure 3-15 illustrates such a case by giving two bar charts, one skewed to the right called *positively skewed* and the second skewed to the left, called *negatively skewed*. Figure 3-16 illustrates these two types of distributions. Recognizing these forms helps in properly analyzing the data used in formulating such nonsymmetrical distributions. Although not used very much, the fourth moment indicates how peaked a curve may be. The degree of peakedness is called its *kurtosis*. Figure 3-16 shows both what is usually considered normal kurtosis and what might be considered more than normal. It is also possible to have some situations where there is less than normal kurtosis.

Figures 3-17 and 3-18 present the bar chart and frequency polygon that cover the data and frequency distribution for the data in table 3.1.

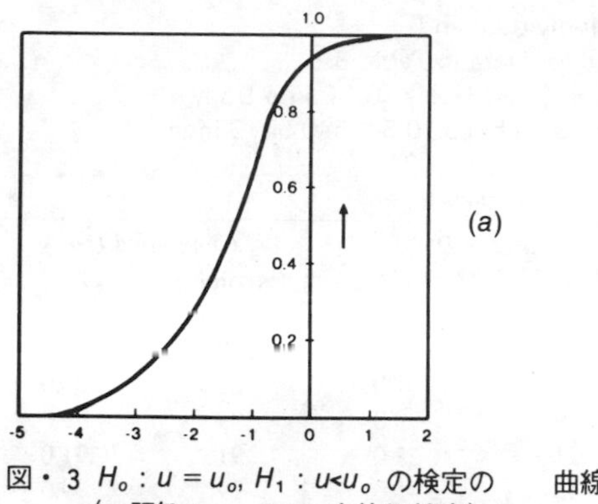

(*a*)

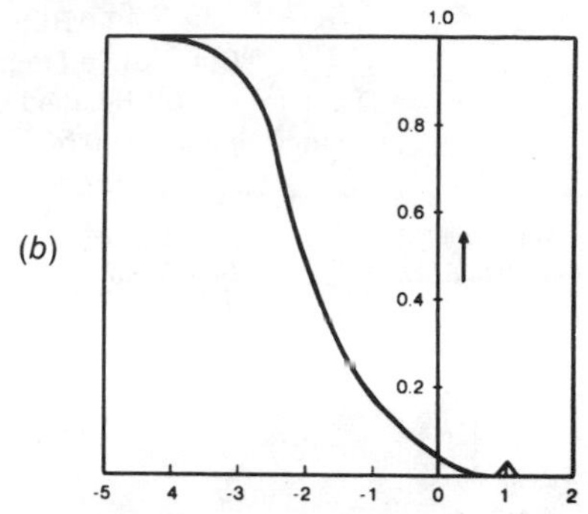

(*b*)

図・3 $H_o : u = u_o, H_1 : u < u_o$ の検定の　曲線 (既知σa = 0.05 左片側検定)

表・3 $H_o : u = u_o, H_1 : u < u_o$ の検定の検出力計算表 (2) (σ = 3.0, a = 0.05, 左片側検定 n = 9)

図・4 $H_o : u = u_o, H_1 : u < u_o$ の検定の検出力曲線 (2) (σ = 3.0, 既知, a = 0.05, 左片側検定, n = 9)

$1-\beta$	β	$u(2\beta)$	$\mu-\mu_o$
0.99	0.01	2.326	−3.97
0.95	0.05	1.645	−3.29
0.90	0.10	1.282	−2.93
0.80	0.20	0.842	−2.49
0.70	0.30	0.524	−2.17
0.60	0.40	0.253	−1.90
0.50	0.50	0.000	−1.65
0.40	0.60	−0.253	−1.39
0.30	0.70	−0.524	−1.12
0.20	0.80	−0.842	−0.80
0.10	0.90	−1.282	−0.36
0.05	0.95	−1.645	0.00

Values used for plotting each cumulative curve

Figure 3–12 Cumulative percentages for evaluating two alternative hypotheses, H_0 *vs.* H_1.

The bar chart for the data in table 3.1 is also called a *histogram.* It is defined as "a univariate frequency diagram in which rectangles proportional in area to the class frequencies are erected on sections of the horizontal axis, the width of each section representing the corresponding class interval of the variate." In some texts, such a graph is called a *block diagram.* Since cumulative distributions are so important, table 3.2 presents the cumulative frequencies in tabular form for the data in table 3.1. They are presented so that they may be used for "less-than" or "more-than" charts. Figure 3-19 shows the graphs of these two cumulative curves.

A *distribution curve* is a graph of cumulated frequencies designated as ordinates against the variate value x as abscissa, that is, the graph of the distribution function.

TABLE 3.2 Individual and
Cumulative Frequencies for Data in Table 3.1
Diameter of 100 Reamed Oil Pump Shaft Holes: Oil Pump Body
Tolerance Specified: 0.5470 ± 0.0005 inch, i.e., 0.5465–0.5475 inch

Measurement to 0.0001" Ascending Order	*Frequencies*					
	Individual		*Cumulated Down*		*Cumulated Up*	
	Actual	%	*Actual*	%	*Actual*	%
0.5465	0	0	0	0	100	100.0
0.5466	1	1.0	1	1.0	100	100.0
0.5467	8	8.0	9	9.0	99	99.0
0.5468	12	12.0	21	21.0	91	91.0
0.5469	24	24.0	45	45.0	79	79.0
0.5470	18	18.0	63	63.0	55	55.0
0.5471	14	14.0	77	77.0	37	37.0
0.5472	10	10.0	87	87.0	23	23.0
0.5473	12	12.0	99	99.0	13	13.0
0.5474	1	1.0	100	100.0	1	1.0
0.5475	100	100.0%				

Illustrations of Central Tendency

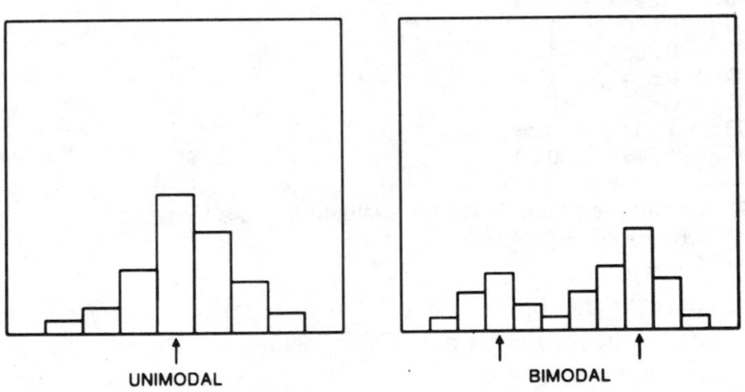

Figure 3–13 Bar charts illustrating two types of central tendency.

The distribution function $F(x)$ of a variate x is the total frequency of members with variate values less than or equal to x. As a general rule, the total frequency is taken to be one, in which case the distribution function is the *proportion* of members bearing values exactly equal to x. Similarly, to determine a cumulative distribution

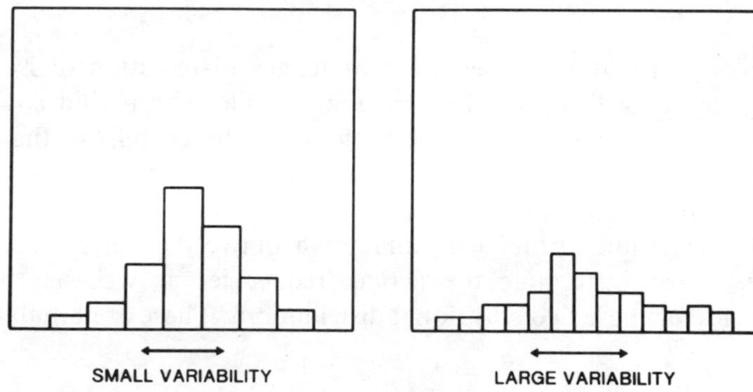

Figure 3–14 Bar charts illustrating small *vs.* large variability.

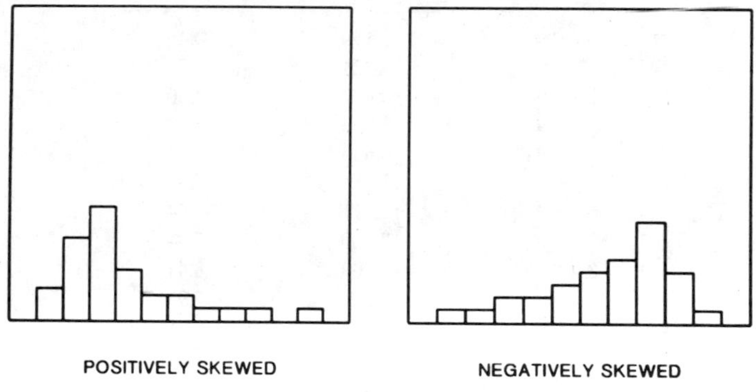

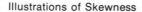

Figure 3–15 Bar charts illustrating positively and negatively skewed distributions.

for j variates $x_1, x_2, \ldots, x_j$, the distribution function $F(x_1, x_2, \ldots, x_j)$ is the frequency of values less than or equal to x_1 for the first variate, x_2 for the second variate, and so on. The curve, as noted previously, is sometimes known as an *ogive,* a name introduced by Galton because the distribution curve of a normal function is of the ogive shape. Since many distributions are not normal, the term *ogive* is better avoided or confined to the normal or near-normal case. In this discussion, the lowercase x rather than capital or uppercase X is used in the mathematical sense as the designation of a variate or variable value and designates directly observed values of characteristics tested or measured in quality control inspections or evaluations.

Example 2 Table 3.3 presents the frequency distribution of 248,707 telephone poles, classified according to length of life. The period covered is 24 years. Since the interval is one year, there will be 24 cells in the frequency distribution for these data. Using the raw data, determine the relative frequency for each of the 24 cells by dividing the recorded frequencies by n. Rearrange the interval or cell width by first using an interval of two years and then an interval of three years. Determine the actual frequencies as well as the relative frequencies for these two additional distributions. These are tabulated below.

TABLE 3.3 Frequency Distribution of 248,707 Telephone Poles, Classified According to Length of Life

Length of life (years)	*Number of poles (frequency)*	*Relative frequency, %*
0– 0.9	1,150	0.46
1– 1.9	4,221	1.70
2– 2.9	10,692	4.30
3– 3.9	13,966	5.62
4– 4.9	16,633	6.69
5– 5.9	18,211	7.32
6– 6.9	19,011	7.64
7– 7.9	19,260	7.74
8– 8.9	20,909	8.41
9– 9.9	19,879	7.99
10–10.9	20,764	8.35
11–11.9	15,454	6.21
12–12.9	14,237	5.72
13–13.9	13,779	5.54
14–14.9	9,764	3.93
15–15.9	8,534	3.43
16–16.9	7,659	3.08
17–17.9	6,918	2.78
18–18.9	4,591	1.85
19–19.9	1,798	0.72
20–20.9	815	0.33
21–21.9	313	0.13
22–22.9	102	0.04
23–23.9	47	0.02
Sum:	248,707	100.00

For comparison, graphs of the distributions based on the three different intervals covering the same data are given.

For this example covering almost 250,000 telephone poles, cumulative frequency distributions have also been determined and their values for the twenty-four cells covered in table 3.3 are given respectively in tables 3.4 and 3.5. Both actual and relative frequencies are given. Actual cumulated distributions are given in subsequent figures.

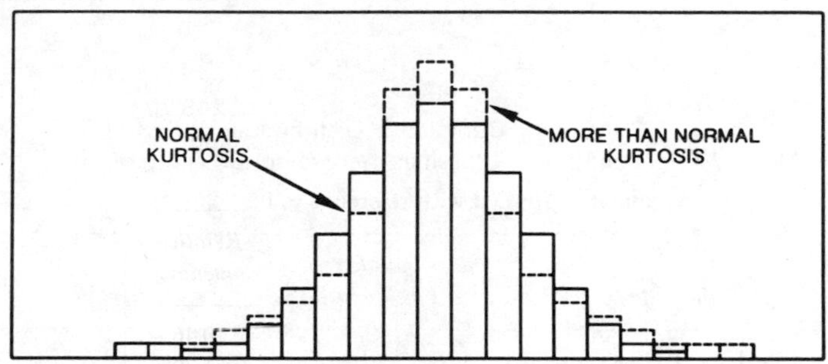

Figure 3–16 Bar chart illustrating measure of peakedness, termed *kurtosis*.

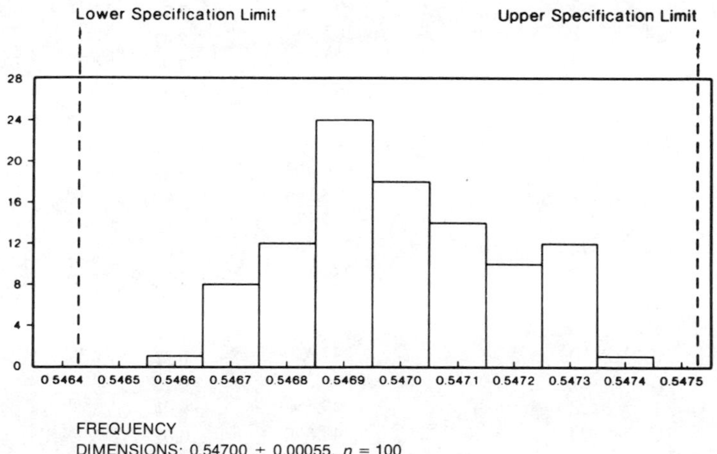

Figure 3–17 Frequency histogram.

Figure 3–20 gives a cumulative frequency distribution curve for the 248,707 telephone poles whose length of life (cumulated upward) has been tabulated. This corresponds to the second column of n values in table 3.4. Corresponding cumulative percentage values are also given in this table. Figure 3-21 gives the corresponding cumulative frequency distribution cumulated downward. Both curves are useful in forecasting future life expectancies of telephone poles in service.

In interpreting the results shown for this example in the tables and figures, note that table 3.3 shows that 1,150 poles were scrapped during the first year of use, that 4,221 were scrapped after reaching the age of one year and before reaching the age of two years, and so on. It is important to note that it is possible to cumulate a frequency series in two different ways, as illustrated. From one such table, the actual

TABLE 3.4 Cumulative Distribution of 248,707 Telephone Poles, Classified According to Length of Life

(Cumulated upward with reference to life scale)

Length of life	*Number of poles surviving (frequency)*	*Percent*
Less than 1 year	1,150	0.46
" " 2 years	5,371	2.16
" " 3 "	16,063	6.46
" " 4 "	30,029	12.07
" " 5 "	46,662	18.76
" " 6 "	64,873	26.08
" " 7 "	83,884	33.73
" " 8 "	103,144	41.47
" " 9 "	124,053	49.88
" " 10 "	143,932	57.87
" " 11 "	164,696	66.22
" " 12 "	180,150	72.43
" " 13 "	194,387	78.16
" " 14 "	208,166	83.70
" " 15 "	217,930	87.63
" " 16 "	226,464	91.06
" " 17 "	234,123	94.14
" " 18 "	241,041	96.92
" " 19 "	245,632	98.76
" " 20 "	247,430	99.49
" " 21 "	248,245	99.81
" " 22 "	248,558	99.94
" " 23 "	248,660	99.98
" " 24 "	248,707	100.00

number which fail to attain any given age may be readily determined. It is often more important to reverse the process, so that the table will enable us to immediately determine the total number above any given value. These curves are the basis of life expectancy tables used in industry, by insurance companies, or in many other applications.

The data for the length of life of 248,707 telephone poles given in table 3.3 have been arranged into three different distributions using intervals of one year, two years, and three years, respectively. Relative frequencies are used so that the area under each distribution curve is 100%. The distribution which seems to have the best eye appeal is (*b*), with a two-year interval. Distribution (*c*), with an interval of three years, has too many poles bunched in each cell for a sample of 248,707 poles.

TABLE 3.5 Cumulative Distribution of 248,707 Telephone Poles, Classified According to Length of Life
(Cumulated downward with reference to life scale)

(1) *Length of life*	(2) *Number of poles surviving (frequency)*	(3) *Percent*
0 and more	248,707	100.00
1 year " "	247,557	99.54
2 years " "	243,336	97.84
3 " " "	232,644	93.54
4 " " "	218,678	87.93
5 " " "	202,045	81.24
6 " " "	183,834	73.92
7 " " "	164,823	66.27
8 " " "	145,563	58.53
9 " " "	124,654	50.12
10 " " "	104,775	42.13
11 " " "	84,011	33.78
12 " " "	68,557	27.57
13 " " "	54,320	21.84
14 " " "	40,541	16.30
15 " " "	30,777	12.37
16 " " "	22,243	8.94
17 " " "	14,584	5.86
18 " " "	7,666	3.08
19 " " "	3,075	1.24
20 " " "	1,277	0.51
21 " " "	462	0.19
22 " " "	149	0.06
23 " " "	47	0.02
24 " " "	0	0.00

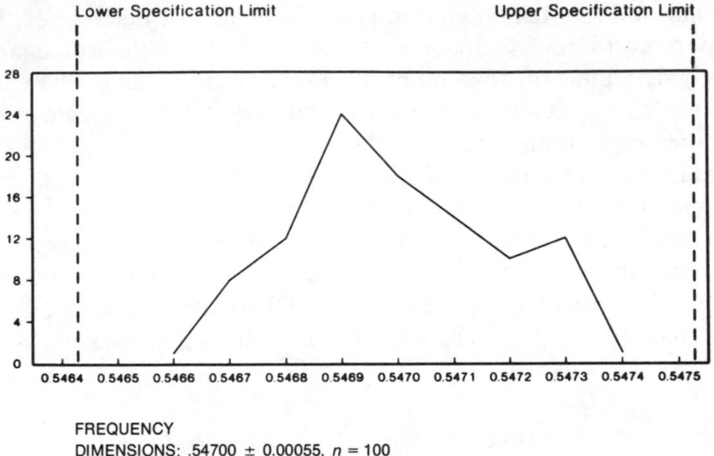

Figure 3–18 Frequency polygon.

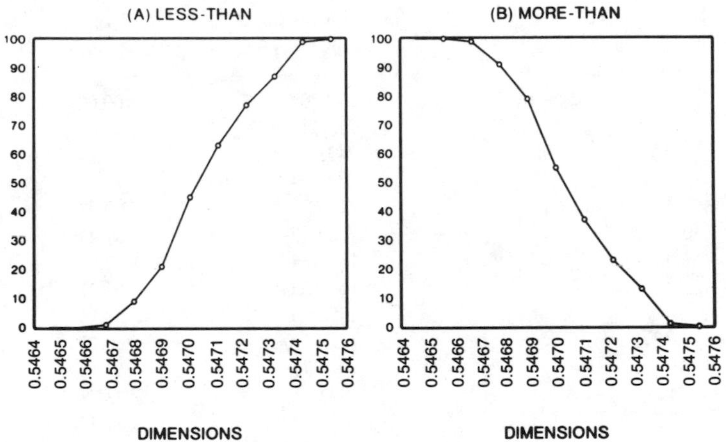

Figure 3–19 (a) Less-than, and (b) more-than cumulative distributions for Table 3–1; diameter of 100 reamed oil pump shaft holes: oil pump body.

It might be the best if the sample size were quite small. Distribution (*a*) gives more detail and may be more useful in some later studies. All distributions are close to normal, but tend to be skewed to the right.

Two examples have been presented, one with a small sample of 100 units, and the second with a sample of 248,707 units. The third example covers an intermediate value and shows additional features used in the graphical representation of various kinds of data. Table 3.6 presents the data for example 3.

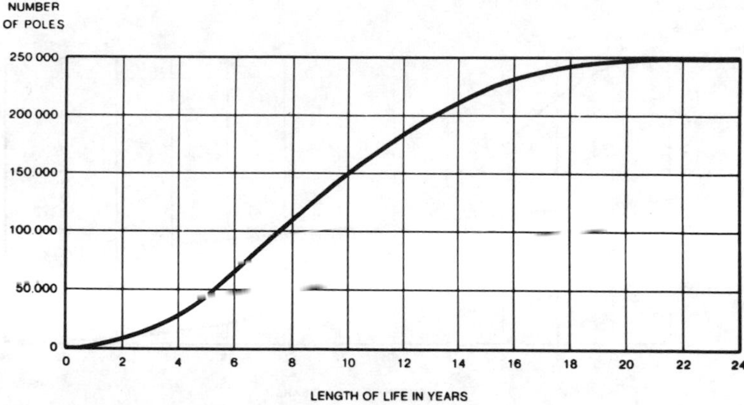

Figure 3–20 Cumulative frequency curve: distribution of telephone poles classified according to length of life (cumulated upward).

TABLE 3.6 Frequency Distribution of 269 Sawmills in the United States Classified According to Labor Cost

Labor cost (all employees) per 1,000 feet, board measure	*Number of establishments (frequency)*	*Percent*
$1.00–$1.49	3	1.1
1.50– 1.99	10	3.7
2.00– 2.49	14	5.2
2.50– 2.99	22	8.2
3.00– 3.49	38	14.1
3.50– 3.99	40	14.9
4.00– 4.49	38	14.1
4.50– 4.99	33	12.3
5.00– 5.49	20	7.4
5.50– 5.99	11	4.1
6.00– 6.49	10	3.7
6.50– 6.99	11	4.1
7.00– 7.49	8	3.0
7.50– 7.99	4	1.5
8.00– 8.49	4	1.5
8.50– 8.99	3	1.1
Sum	269	100.0

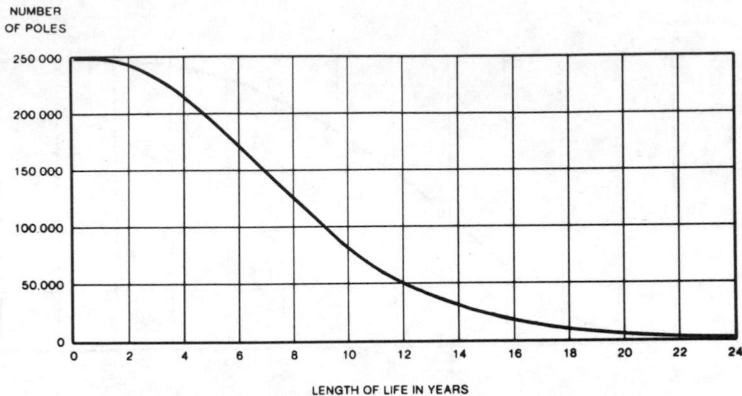

Figure 3–21 Cumulative frequency curve: distribution of telephone poles classified according to length of life (cumulated downward).

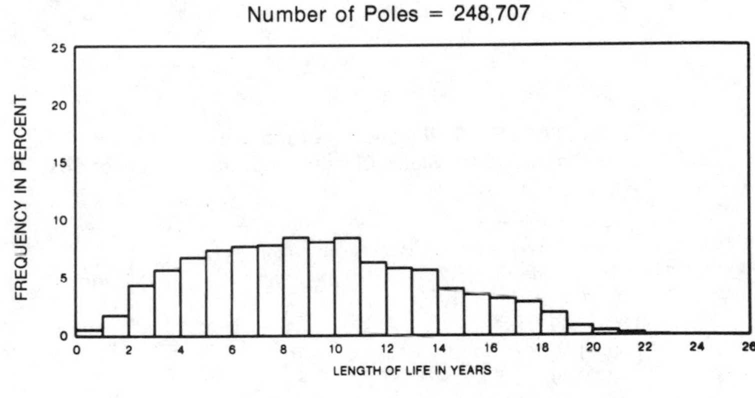

(*a*) Interval of One Year

Figure 3–22a Three frequency diagrams: comparison for probability distributions.

Example 3 Labor costs per 1,000 feet (board measure) of lumber produced by all employees at 269 saw mills in the United States were tabulated and are presented in table 3.7.[6] This article notes that there were also seven scattered cases above $9.00 in value omitted in this summary. The data are given below as a bar chart or histogram, as well as in a modified presentation where the structural relation between the ogive and the frequency curve is shown. In addition to actual observed values, these data are given in table 3.7 as relative frequencies cumulated both upward and downward.

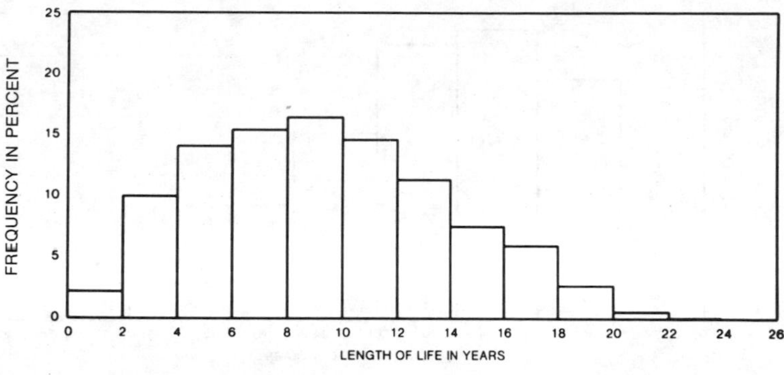

(*b*) Interval of Two Years

Figure 3–22b Three frequency diagrams: comparison for probability distributions.

TABLE 3.7 Cumulated Distributions of 269 Sawmills in the United States According to Labor Cost (all employees) per 1,000 feet, board measure: Frequencies given as Relative Frequencies.

Labor Cost (all employees) per 1,000 feet, board measure	*Actual Frequency*	*Number of establishments Cumulative Frequencies* — *Cumulated Upward*		*Cumulated Downward*	
		Actual	*Percent, %*	*Actual*	*Percent, %*
$1.00 $1.49	3	3	1.1	269	100.0
1.50– 1.99	10	13	4.8	266	98.9
2.00– 2.49	14	27	10.0	256	95.2
2.50– 2.99	22	49	18.2	242	90.0
3.00– 3.49	38	87	32.3	220	81.8
3.50– 3.99	40	127	47.2	182	67.7
4.00– 4.49	38	165	61.3	142	52.8
4.50– 4.99	33	198	73.6	104	38.7
5.00– 5.49	20	218	81.0	71	26.4
5.50– 5.99	11	229	85.1	51	19.0
6.00– 6.49	10	239	88.8	40	15.6
6.50– 6.99	11	250	92.9	30	11.2
7.00– 7.49	8	258	95.9	19	7.1
7.50– 7.99	4	262	97.4	11	4.1
8.00– 8.49	4	266	98.9	7	2.6
8.50– 8.99	3	269	100.0	3	1.1
Sum	269				

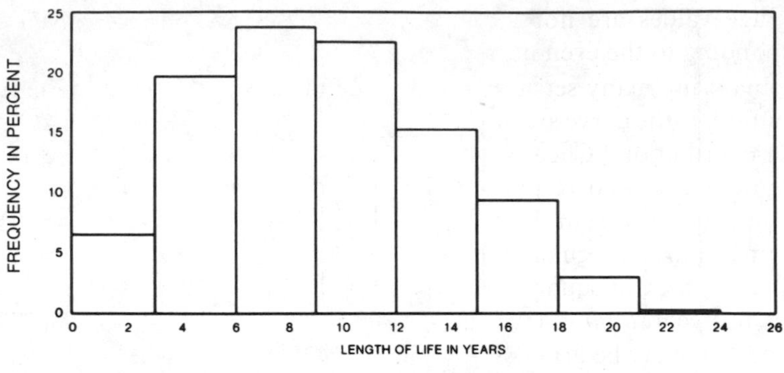

(*c*) Interval of Three Years

Figure 3–22c Three frequency diagrams: comparison for probability distributions.

Since it is desired to completely depict these data and show both individual and cumulative frequencies, a double scale is given in figure 3-23. The double scale is often used for a single line graph, but may also be used when two different line graphs are given on the same graph with the left scale applying to one curve and the right scale applying to the second curve or graph. Since table 3.7 gives cumulated frequencies in percentages, as well as in terms of observed numbers, the right-hand scale on the cumulative graph gives frequencies in percent. Thus these

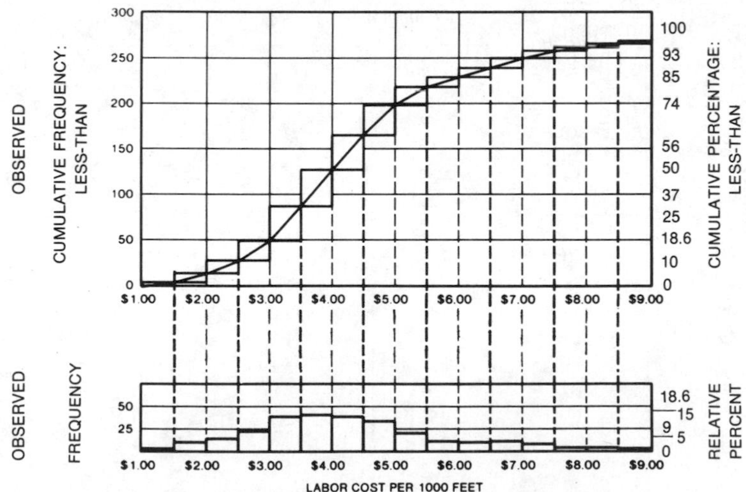

Figure 3–23 Distributions of sawmills in the United States classified according to labor cost, illustrating the structural relation between the Ogive and the frequency curve (cumulated upward).

percentage values are not given in regular intervals but are given in values corresponding to the even numerical scale (50, 100, etc.) on the left.

In analyzing many sets of data, it is desirable to determine the nature of the distribution. Is the curve symmetric? Is it shaped so that it may be assumed to be a normal distribution? Checks for determining the goodness of fit of an observed distribution with a corresponding theoretical curve, based on statistics used as parameters derived from the observations such as the normal, binomial, second approximation, rectangular, or many other types, are presented in Appendix A. The examples use the Chi-square (χ^2) distribution together with the proper value for the degrees of freedom ($m - 1$) to evaluate the probability of fit. As one check, the observed data may be graphed; the selected theoretical curve may then be drawn and superimposed upon such an observed distribution. If the probability found by the Chi-square test is small, the fit is considered poor and discrepancies between the observed frequencies and the corresponding theoretical frequencies will be readily seen by eye. For example, the distribution in figure 3-23 is apparently slightly skewed to the right and differs slightly from a symmetric normal distribution. The following additional illustration shows the application of this procedure.

Measures to the nearest 0.01 were made for an item. The range of values was from 13.13 to 13.69. These covered quality characteristic Y. For this case, 200 values were obtained; a bar chart or histogram showing these observed values is presented Figure 3-24(*b*) presents a better form for this distribution using an interval of 0.05 is equal to the sum of the values divided by n, the number of values. This has the frequency given is in terms of number observed and this scale is from 0 to 12. The second scale shown gives the relative frequencies in terms of percent, from 0 to 6 percent. Nine cells of width 0.01 are empty cells with their respective frequencies at zero. The graph has a possibility of 57 cells, for an interval of 0.01.

(*a*) Frequency Histogram
(0.01 Cell Intervals; $n = 200$; $\bar{X} = 13.41635$; $\sigma = 0.11372$)

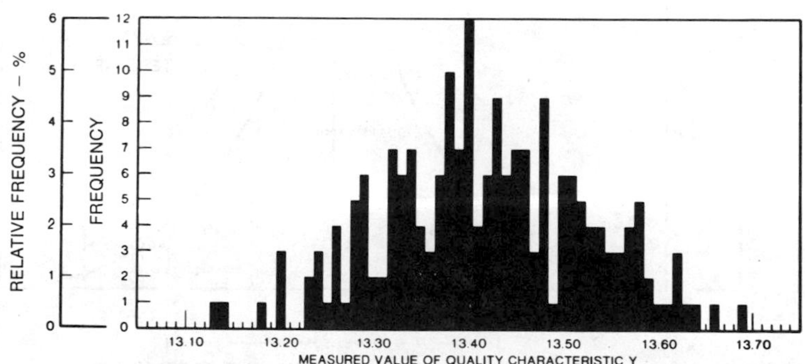

Figure 3–24 Two frequency histograms, one fitted by normal curve; theoretical normal frequencies for Sigma, σ unit scale.

Figure 3–24(*b*) presents a better form for this distribution using an interval of 0.05 for each cell. Superimposed upon this frequency histogram is a fitted normal curve. To the eye it looks very good, with only a few minor discrepancies. The sample size $n = 200$, the average $\overline{X}$, and the standard deviation of each of these two distributions are noted.

Figure 3-24(*c*) adds a theoretical normal curve and gives the theoretical frequencies to five places for the six intervals measured in 1–sigma (1σ) units. These are probability values shown as the areas between various multiples of the standard deviation, designated as sigma (σ).

(*b*) Frequency Histogram with Fitted Normal Curve
(0.05 Cell Intervals; $n = 200$; $\overline{X} = 13.4185$; $\sigma = 0.10704$)

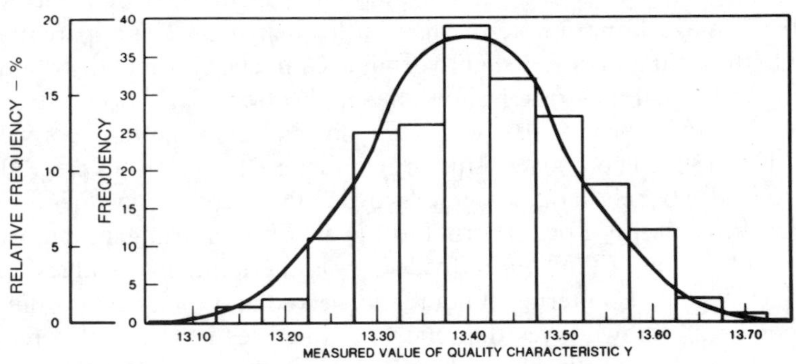

(*c*) Proportion of Total Area Under the Normal Curve

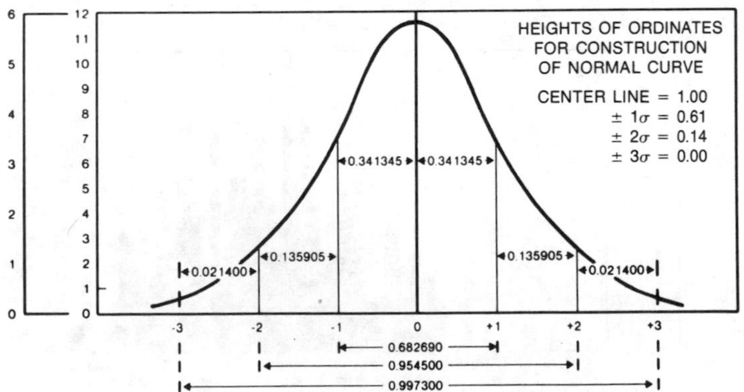

Figure 3-24 b & c Two frequency histograms, one fitted by normal curve; theoretical normal frequencies for Sigma, σ unit scale.

3.5 Measures of Central Tendency

When a sample is inspected, how many nonconforming units can you expect to find? When people are weighed in physical examinations, what are their expected weights, on the average? Such values are found by analyzing all the available data. The expected value is the *average,* a term with which nearly everyone is familiar. It is, however, one whose popular meanings are very loose and ambiguous. This term is used indiscriminately in speaking of, for example, the "average score of an examination," the "average outgoing quality level," the "mean time to failure," the "average length of life," the "average number of defectives in a set of 100 lots," and so on. Synonyms for the term in its popular usage are such expressions as *usual, representative, normal,* and *expected.* If asked to define the term more accurately, the "average" man might respond that it is the single measure or individual that best represents a group of measurements of individuals, but if asked how to select the most "representative" measure in a group of measures, he would likely become less specific.

To some statisticians and quality control personnel, *average* is a general term applying to all kinds of *measures of central tendency* derived from group data. There are several measures in common use which describe a central tendency—the arithmetic mean, the median, the mode, and the mid-range. There are other measures of central tendency, but those mentioned are most commonly used and are the measures which we will discuss in this chapter. (For such measures as the *harmonic mean,* and the *geometric mean,* consult other texts.)

The Arithmetic Mean, $\overline{X}$

As applied to quality control, the *arithmetic mean* of a series of measurements is equal to the sum of the values divided by *n,* the number of values.[7] This has been given previously as:

$$\overline{X} = \frac{\Sigma X_i}{n} \quad \text{or} \quad \overline{X} = \frac{\Sigma f_i X_i}{\Sigma f_i} \tag{1}$$

To simplify this computation, it is helpful to order the numerical data and even tabulate it in a frequency distribution before making any computations. Where computers are available, the data may be placed on IBM cards and programmed to give the desired average.

In quality control work, the arithmetic mean is usually referred to simply as the average $\overline{X}$. While the average may be computed directly from the original measures, its computation is made more convenient by not only ordering the data as an array, but also by designating the cells respectively as 0, 1, 2, 3, etc. This gives positive values and keeps the number of data small. Many texts designate a zero value near an estimate of the midpoint of the distribution and use both positive and negative numbers to obtain the average. However, fewer errors result from using as the new scale all positive numbers, designating the lowest regular cell as zero and then using this point as the origin of the new distribution on a simplified small numerical scale. The width of each cell is used together with this origin to obtain the final average value in terms of the original scale.

The Median, M_e

The *median* M_e is the value that divides the frequency distribution into two equal parts, with the number of entries below the median value equal to the number of entries above the median. When the number of data is odd, the median will be an integer. For example, for seven values the fourth value is the median. When the sample size is even, the median will not be a member of the data, but instead will be a theoretical value halfway between the entry terminating the first half of the ordered data and the first entry in the second half of these data. For example, if we have the ordered data 1, 2, 5, and 7, the median is between 2 and 5 and is half of their sum, i.e., $\frac{7}{2}$ or 3.5. If we have the data 1, 2, 5, 7, 8, and 9, the median is halfway between 5 and 7, i.e., $\frac{12}{2}$ or 6. The rule for finding the median of a set of data with n entries is as follows. Order the data. When n is odd, the median is the entry $X_{(n+1)/2}$. When n is even, the median is half the sum of the entries $X_{n/2}$ and $X_{(n/2+1)}$.

The Mode, M_o

The *mode* M_o of a frequency distribution is the value that occurs most frequently. To find the mode, tabulate the number of times each X value has been recorded. The X value having the largest frequency is the mode. In some types of distributions, when the data are arranged as an array in ascending or descending order with respect to the X values, several values of X may have the same frequency. Such distributions are called *multimodal*. When two values with the same frequency occur, the distribution is called *bimodal*; when three occur, it is called *trimodal*, etc. In some cases, when two X values have extremely high frequencies in comparison with the other X values, the distribution is considered bimodal even though the two frequencies are not identical. For example, in the data set 1, 3, 4, 4, 4, 4, 4, 4, 4, 5, 6, 7, 7, 7, 7, 7, 7, 8, 9, 10, the number 4 occurs seven times and the number 7 occurs six times. Thus this set might be termed bimodal. If only one mode is recognized, the mode is 4. For a normal law distribution which is symmetric and has only one mode, the central value is exactly the same for all these measures of central tendency; that is, the average, median, and mode are identical.

The Mid-range, X_R

The *mid-range* is the average of the maximum and minimum values in a distribution, i.e. $X_R = (X_M + X_m)/2$. For example, the mid-range for the set of numbers 1, 3, 4, 4, 4, 5, 6, 7, 7, and 8 is $(8 + 1)/2$, which is 4.5. The mode is 4, since this number occurs most frequently in the set. The average or mean is $\frac{49}{10} = 4.9$.

Since n is even ($n = 10$), the median is half the sum of the fifth and sixth numbers in the set of ordered data. The median is $\frac{(4+5)}{2} = \frac{9}{2} = 4.5$.

3.6 Measures of Variability or Dispersion

Measured values of the number of defects or defective units observed in n units will differ from sample to sample, where more than one sample of the same kind is inspected. Variations in the results may be presented graphically on a frequency distribution. The differences between the maximum and minimum values may be very large or quite small. The extent of such variations is depicted in many of the illustrations in this chapter. Those most commonly used are the *variance*, the *standard deviation* (the square root of the variance), the *mean deviation*, and the *range*.

The Variance, v

The *variance* is determined from the following relation, where X denotes a measured value for some characteristic or may be used to represent p, the fraction defective values found for a series of samples.

$$v_X = \frac{\Sigma(X_i - \bar{X})^2}{n} = \frac{\Sigma X_i^2}{n} - \bar{X}^2 \qquad (2)$$

Variances are very important because many useful features in quality control work are based on the fact that variances are additive, while other measures of variability are not. For example, when two distributions are added together, as in $Z = X + Y$, where X and Y are independent, then $v_Z = v_X + v_Y$. This use is described in more detail later. Control charts for variances in samples selected from a given universe must be used with caution, as the distribution of the variances is not normal but depends on the nature of the distribution of the parent population, the universe. The variance is used in determining the most important measure of variability, the *standard deviation*, which is the square root of the variance. This is evident since for such a measure as length, the variance is derived from squares of values and hence is given as $(\text{length})^2$, while the standard deviation is expressed in the same unit as length, and is a more practical measure.

The Standard Deviation, σ or s

The *standard deviation* is considered the best measure of variability or dispersion, because it is practically invariant with respect to sample sizes. This means that if you determine the standard deviation for a series of samples consisting of only five units and then, from the same parent population, you determine the standard deviation for a series of samples consisting of 100 units, the two sets of standard deviation values will be essentially the same. Both sets give almost the same distribution for standard deviations and provide a basis for determining the exact value for the standard deviation of the universe from which both sets of samples were selected at random. A second advantage is that the variation in further evaluations of the variability is generally smaller for the standard deviation than for any other measure now being used to measure variability. It is thus considered the most efficient measure. The relation below is generally used to determine the standard deviation.

$$\sigma_X = \sqrt{v_X} = \sqrt{\frac{\Sigma(X_i - \bar{X})^2}{n}} = \sqrt{\frac{\Sigma X_i^2}{n} - \bar{X}^2} \qquad (3)$$

When the distribution of X values is arranged in ascending or descending order as an array, then the frequency for the X_i values may be designated as f_i. This reduces the number of terms in the calculations. Equation (3) may be rewritten utilizing the f_i term.

$$\sigma_X = \sqrt{v_X} = \sqrt{\frac{\Sigma(f_i X_i - \bar{X})^2}{\Sigma f_i}} = \sqrt{\frac{\Sigma f_i X_i^2}{\Sigma f_i} - \bar{X}^2} \qquad (3')$$

where $\Sigma f_i = n$.

The theoretical tables of normal law probabilities are based on the number of standard deviation values that differ in a positive or negative direction from the mean. The standard deviation is used as the reference standard for all other measures of variability. These normal law tables are based on the assumption that the parameters of the table for the primary features are: $\bar{X}' = 0$; $\sigma' = 1$; skewness $k = 0$ (distribution is symmetric); kurtosis (degree of peakedness) $\beta_2 = 3$. Control charts in the United States are usually based on either three-sigma or two-sigma control limits about the mean, that is, $\bar{X}' \pm 3\sigma'$ or $\bar{X}' \pm 2\sigma'$. The confidence levels of these limits read from the normal law tables are, respectively, 0.9973 or 99.73% and 0.9545 or 95.45%. Many statisticians prefer to set confidence levels at levels of 0.95, 0.96, 0.98, 0.99, or some other value. To obtain these exact values, each distribution must be analyzed thoroughly to obtain an exact evaluation for obtaining the desired confidence level. Systems of causes vary so much that continual evaluations and reevaluations would be required to maintain an exact value for the confidence level or degree of belief.

Some quality control techniques require one to obtain a best estimate of the true parameters of the parent population or universe. The best estimate of the central tendency is the arithmetic mean. This value is denoted by $\bar{X}'$, using the prime notation to represent the true parameters of the universe. Similarly, the most valid estimate of the best measure of variability is σ', often denoted by s, which is determined from the following relation.

$$s = \sqrt{\frac{\Sigma(X_i - \bar{X})^2}{(n-1)}} = \sqrt{\frac{n}{(n-1)}}\sigma. \tag{4}$$

In texts in which an attempt has been made to standardize the nomenclature, s rather than σ is used. It is better practice to use the symbol σ for the statistics, although many texts use the Greek alphabet for parameters or true values and the English alphabet for the corresponding statistics. Engineering texts usually denote the computed standard deviation as σ whereas other fields may use s. In line with this practice, texts in physics and calculus designate these various parameters in terms of the lowercase Greek letter mu (μ). Then μ_0 is the sum of the frequencies and, in many cases, is equal to n, the sample size. With this notation, μ_1 denotes the arithmetic mean $\bar{X}'$ and is used in many tables. This is called a *measure of the first moment*. The second moment is designated by μ_2 and represents the variance v, so that $\sqrt{\mu_2} = \sigma$, the standard deviation. Moments higher than these, such as the third and fourth moments, provide (with suitable modifications and computations) measures of the other parameters. Only a slight knowledge of these is needed in order to use most of the tables used in quality control work.

A practical rule to follow is that the $(n-1)$ divisor should be used in the theory of estimation, when one needs to obtain the best estimates of the parameters. Besides the determination of s, the best unbiased estimate of σ' by the method of maximum likelihood, other estimates of the true value of σ' are made by dividing the value of $\bar{\sigma}$, the average of m values of σ computed from a set of samples, by a c_2 factor which is given in many tables. For samples of size n, c_2 is the average σ value for a theoretical normal law distribution, and varies with the sample sizes. Another estimate is obtained by dividing the average range $\bar{R}$ by the d_2 value corresponding to the sample size. These d_2 values are listed in tables and are theoretical values based on R values obtained from a theoretical normal law distribution. Many other methods have been proposed to obtain the best estimate of σ'. The ones listed here are those most commonly used.

The Range, *R*

The *range* R is an excellent measure of variability when the sample size is small. Since the range is based on only two values, however, it is very inefficient when the sample size from which it is determined is large. It is best used when n is ten or less, but it is often applied even with samples as large as twenty-five. The efficiency of the range is highest when the sample size is two, since all observations are used, but its efficiency drops rapidly as the sample size increases. The range is readily determined from the following relation, where X_M denotes the maximum value in a sample and X_m denotes the minimum or smallest value in the same sample.

$$R = X_M - X_m \tag{5}$$

In practice, an average value of R, termed *R-bar* ($\bar{R}$) is determined and used as an estimate of the standard deviation. The total spread about the average is termed d_2. This factor is discussed in chapter six. It is actually the theoretical average of R values for samples from theoretical normal law distribution. Some values of d_2 are noted in figure 6-5. When $\bar{R}$ is determined from a series of R values secured from a series of samples of equal size, then dividing it by the corresponding d_2 value provides an excellent estimate of the true standard deviation of the universe, designated as σ'. For example, when n is 5, then d_2 is 2.326. However, the d_2 value is approximately 6 when the sample size is 450, as shown in figure 70, page 203 of the Shewhart text, *Economic Control of Quality of Manufactured Product.* For $n = 100$, $d_2 = 5.015$ (see the Grant and Leavenworth text, *Statistical Quality Control,* Table *B*, page 644). Probability values for the distribution of the range is given for n values from 2 to 20 in Table VIII, page 60 of *Statistical Tables and Formulas* by A. Hald. In this table, w is used to designate the range. Other information about the range is given in chapter six of the present text.

When the sample size for a series of inspections is twenty-five or fifty—or better yet, some multiple of twelve—the efficiency of the range may be increased by subdividing the sample into rational subgroups and using several ranges per sample. For a sample size of twenty-five, randomly divide the sample into five subgroups of five units each and obtain five ranges; then use the average of these five ranges to estimate σ' and prepare control charts based on this better measure of variability. For samples of fifty units, five subgroups of ten each, ten subgroups of five each, or twenty-five subgroups of two each may be used. For multiples of twelve, more possible arrangements of subgroups are possible. Although the efficiency of the range is greatly improved by this procedure, the best means of using this improved procedure has not been presented generally; indeed only a limited number of papers covering these techniques has been presented. Where more efficiency is desired than would be provided by the usual range method, controls based on such subgroups will greatly improve the efficiency of the range.

The Mean Deviation, *M.D.*

The *Mean Deviation* (M.D.) is easier to compute than the variance or standard deviation, and is therefore used on occasion as a good measure of variability. $\sqrt{\frac{\pi}{2}}$ (M.D.) is a very good estimate of the standard deviation. The constant $\sqrt{\frac{\pi}{2}}$, the multiplier of the mean deviation is more easily remembered as a multiplier of 1.25 or as a divisor using 1/1.25 or 0.80. The square root of $\pi/2$ is equal to 1.253314137315500, while its reciprocal is 0.797884560802865. Actually this constant multiplier does change sometimes for a range of sample sizes. The mean deviation is easily determined because it is the arithmetic average of the deviations of all unit X values from the mean value of the n values of X (where the negative or positive sign must be disregarded as all are treated as positive values), called their *absolute values.* This relation may be expressed as follows.

$$M.D. = \frac{\Sigma|X_i - \bar{X}|}{n} \tag{6}$$

Where the X values are ordered and arranged as a frequency distribution this relation becomes

$$M.D. = \frac{\Sigma|f_i(X_i - X')|}{\Sigma f_i} \tag{6'}$$

3.7 Probability

The effectiveness of quality control has been greatly increased by adding techniques based on statistics. It is generally accepted that statistics is the collection, tabulation, analysis, and interpretation of data. Determinations of the possible chance of the occurrence of an event have been made throughout the ages. Games of chance involve the evaluation of the probability of the occurrence of a winning hand in cards, the possibility of drawing the card of highest or lowest value from a deck of cards, or the chance of tossing a particular sum on two dice thrown at random. Although these events involve probability values, definitions of probability have been omitted for years from books or texts covering statistics and related areas. Intuition is one aspect of probability. One has a strong belief that a given event will take place. This means that the probability of its occurrence is probably greater than 50%. Control limits are used to control processes. Using the control limits thus established, it is possible to make firm decisions indicating when a change should be made in the process, thereby reducing losses due to the production of an excessive number of nonconforming units. A knowledge of what probability really means and how to apply the laws of probability is necessary to effectively use these statistical tools.

The *Dictionary of Statistical Terms* by Kendall and Buckland defines probability as: "A basic concept which may be taken either as undefinable, expressing in some way a 'degree of belief,' or as the limiting frequency in an infinite random series. Both approaches have their difficulties and the most convenient axiomatization of probability theory is a matter of personal taste. Fortunately both lead to much the same calculus of probabilities."

Many authors have quite different concepts of the actual meaning of probability. One introduces the subject by asking pertinent questions. "What is statistics? How does it function? How does it help to solve certain practical problems?" In attempting to answer these questions one could say that probability and statistics are related. In general probability is the vehicle which enables the statistician to use information in a sample to make inferences or describe the population from which the sample was obtained. However, to show that in many cases the population is assumed to be known, one is only interested in calculating the probability associated with a given sample. Thus, in probability theory, one deals with both the known and the unknown. This notion of probability is covered in the preparation of control charts. In one case a standard is assumed to be known. In another case the standard used is derived from the sample, and control limits for such chance variables are derived from observed data.

Let us consider objective probability as contrasted with subjective probability. Suppose we are given an unbiased coin with two sides, which is so thin it cannot stand on edge. The probability of tossing either a head or a tail is assumed to be $\frac{1}{2}$; that is, one side up out of two possible sides. For a die with six faces (marked 1, 2, 3, 4, 5, and 6), the probability of rolling any one of these values is considered to be $\frac{1}{6}$. These probabilities are examples of objective probability. On the other hand, what is the probability that a jury will in a particular case render a decision of "guilty" or "not guilty"? What is the probability that a given group of workers will go out on strike? These probabilities are examples of subjective probability. Both subjective and objective probability may arise in quality control work. Other kinds of probability may also be met; some of these are purely mathematical probabilities. For example, odds for betting are based on mathematical values. Bets at horse races are made and evaluated on the basis of mathematical methods of computation. The laws of probability, given as axioms covering the possibility of events being independent or dependent, aid in their evaluations. The probability of a final event may depend on the possible occurrence of a series of prior events. For example, unless an automobile has gasoline in its tank, has been tuned to start, has a battery that functions, and has spark plugs with proper gaps, it will not run when the starter is activated.

Laws of Probability

1. Addition Law: The probability of realizing at least one (i.e., one *or* both) of the two events E_1 and E_2 is:

$$P(E_1 + E_2) = P(E_1) + P(E_2) - P(E_1E_2) \tag{7}$$

Example 4 If there are two cars and the probability of each car starting on a cold morning is 0.6, what is the probability of at least one of the cars starting on a cold morning?

$$P = 0.6 + 0.6 - (0.6 \times 0.6) = 1.20 - 0.36 = 0.84$$

2. Addition Law, mutually exclusive events (both cannot happen): The mathematical relation is like equation (7), except the negative term is now zero since both events cannot happen. This is the same as stating that the correlation between the two events due to independence is zero. The relation to be used is:

$$P(E_1 + E_2) = P(E_1) + P(E_2). \tag{8}$$

Example 5 A single die is thrown. What is the probability of throwing 3 or 5? The probability of throwing either a 1, 2, 3, 4, 5, or 6 is $\frac{1}{6}$. Hence

$$P = \frac{1}{6} + \frac{1}{6} = \frac{2}{6} = \frac{1}{3} = 0.33\overline{3}$$

Another example is one that results in a certain event. In tossing a coin having only two sides, with probabilities of $\frac{1}{2}$ for a head or a tail, what is the probability of throwing either a head or a tail? In this case, with only two possible events, the probability is $\frac{1}{2} + \frac{1}{2} = 1.00$, a certainty.

3. Multiplication Law: The probability that both of two events E_1 and E_2 occur is given by the mathematical relation:

$$P(E_1E_2) = P(E_2 \mid E_1)\ P(E_1) = P(E_1 \mid E_2)\ P(E_2) \tag{9}$$

Example 6 Consider a lot of ten relays, of which two are nonconforming and are classed as defective. The probability that a sample of two relays drawn at random without replacement will not contain a defective relay is equal to the probability that the second relay is good, given that the first relay was good. Let G_1 and G_2 denote the first and second good relays. Event E_1 is the occurrence of the first good relay G_1 while event E_2 is the occurrence of the second good relay G_2. Since two of the ten relays are defective, then the probability of a good relay is $(10 - 2)/10 = 8/10$. If a good relay is found in the first selection, there will remain only $8 - 1 = 7$ good relays and only $10 - 1 = 9$ relays from which to draw the second relay. This gives:

$$P(G_1G_2) = P(G_1) \cdot P(G_2 \mid G_1) = \left(\frac{8}{10}\right)\left(\frac{7}{9}\right) = \frac{56}{90} = \frac{28}{45} = 0.62\overline{2}$$

4. Multiplication Law, independent events: This is sometimes termed the *Product Rule*, as it is merely the product of the two probabilities:

$$P(E_1E_2) = P(E_1) \cdot P(E_2) \tag{10}$$

When more than two components are involved, then the product of each component's probability values gives the probability for the system as a whole.

Example 7 What is the probability of tossing five coins and obtaining five consecutive heads? The probability of a head for one coin is $\frac{1}{2}$. The solution is the product of the five probability values. Since all E_i values are equal and are $\frac{1}{2}$, then their product is:

$$P(E_1E_2E_3E_4E_5) = P(E_1) \cdot P(E_2) \cdot P(E_3) \cdot P(E_4) \cdot P(E_5) = \left(\frac{1}{2}\right)^5$$
$$= \left(\frac{1}{2}\right)\left(\frac{1}{2}\right)\left(\frac{1}{2}\right)\left(\frac{1}{2}\right)\left(\frac{1}{2}\right) = \frac{1}{32} = 0.03125$$

There are many other probability axioms or laws that might be given, but these are the most important and the ones that, in practice, will be used most of the time. For more complex axioms, consult other advanced texts in probability.

Permutations and Combinations

Many of the relations used in computing probability values involve combinations. This is true for the p binomial and also for the hypergeometric relation. The symbols and relations that are commonly used are defined below.

1. Permutation, any collection of a number of items in a definite order. *A permutation of n things taken r at a time* is an ordered selection of r of them. Various symbols such as ${}_nP_r$, P_r^n, and $P(n, r)$ are used to designate a permutation.

$$P(n,r) = n(n-1)(n-2)(n-3)\ldots(n-r+1) = \frac{n!}{(n-r)!} \tag{11}$$

NOTE: The symbol $P(n, r)$ is read as *the permutation of n things taken r at a time.* $n!$ is read as *n factorial* and means the product of the integers from 1 to n, i.e., $n! = 1 \cdot 2 \cdot 3 \cdot 4 \ldots (n-1) \cdot n = n \cdot (n-1) \cdot (n-2) \cdot (n-3) \ldots 3 \cdot 2 \cdot 1$. Note that $0! = 1$ and $1! = 1$. Factorial values are often read from tables of the Gamma function since $\Gamma(n+1) = n!$ and $\Gamma(n) = \int_0^\infty t^{n-1} e^{-t} dt$. Using equation (11), $P(n, n) = n!$ and $P(n, 0) = 1$.

Example 8 How many numbers of four different digits can be formed from the integers 1, 2, 5, 6, 7, and 8?

$$P(6,4) = 6 \cdot 5 \cdot 4 \cdot 3 = 360$$

Example 9 What 3-letter and 2-letter words (some meaningless) may be formed from the letters C, A, and T?

$$P(3,3) = 3! = 6; \quad P(3,2) = \frac{3!}{1!} = 6$$

The tabulation of these words is: CAT, CTA; ACT, ATC; TAC, TCA; CA, CT; AC, AT; TA, TC.

2. Combinations, any collection of a number of items without regard to order. *A combination of n things taken r at a time* is a selection of r of them without regard to order. Again there are many symbols, such as C_r^n, ${}^nC_r$, $C(n, r)$ and $\binom{n}{r}$, for this term.

$$C(n,r) = \frac{P(n,r)}{P(r,r)} = \frac{n!}{r!(n-r)!} \tag{12}$$

NOTE: $C(n, r)$ is read as *the combination of n things taken r at a time.* We see that $C(n, n) = 1$ and $C(n, 0) = 1$.

Example 10 How many combinations of four digits can be formed from the six integers 1, 2, 5, 6, 7, and 8?

$$C(6,4) = \frac{6!}{4!2!} = \frac{6 \cdot 5}{2} = \frac{30}{2} = 15$$

Two other axioms covering probability laws will be helpful. They are:

1. If an event E_1 can occur in n_1 ways and the event E_2 can occur in n_2 ways, which are independent of n_1, then both E_1 and E_2 can occur in $n_1 \cdot n_2$ ways.
2. If an event E_1 can occur in n_1 ways and the event E_2 can occur in n_2 ways, which are mutually exclusive of n_1, then either E_1 or E_2 can occur in $n_1 + n_2$ ways. "Mutually exclusive" means that both events cannot happen. For example, a student is thinking of going to Pasadena or to San Francisco. If he goes to Pasadena he cannot be at San Francisco at the same time and if in San Francisco he cannot be in Pasadena as they are too far apart and in different counties.

The use of these various laws of probability is covered in subsequent sections. This brief summary of the statistical techniques required in quality control and quality assurance work, as well as in reliability studies and other related areas, cannot be as detailed as those given in texts that deal entirely with statistical methods. Decisions may be made based on these various probability concepts. For example, when computations are made for an arithmetical average (or mean) and a standard deviation, what is the probability that two groups of data taken in successive months will have identically the same values for both measures? The chance of this repetition might be as small as once in a million; hence two groups of data for which this occurs will be questionable, since the second set may only be a copy of the first set.

3.8 Method of Variables

In carrying out all the different phases involved in the operation of an effective quality control program, data of different kinds must be secured. Such data are generally classed as *variables data* or *attributes data.* It is necessary to obtain such data by sampling and inspection. The results thus secured may often be classed as either a *variable* or an *attribute* since these two terms are not mutually exclusive. The two terms are often confused as their definitions overlap. A variable is a quantity which may take any one of a specified set of values. However, it is often convenient to apply the same word to denote nonmeasurable characteristics. For example, sex is a variable in this sense, since any human individual may take one of two "values," male or female. An attribute is a qualitative characteristic of an individual, usually employed in distinction to a variable or quantitative characteristic. Thus, for human beings sex is an attribute but age is a variable. Very often in statistics, attributes are dichotomous, each member of a population being allotted to one of two groups, according to whether he or she does or does not possess some specified attribute. Manifold classification can also be carried out on the basis of attributes, as when individuals are classified as belonging to various blood groups.

In quality control work, the *Method of Variables* provides a means for treating variables as well as a special case for the Method of Attributes, in which results are classified into only two classes (a *two-fold classification*). A multifold classification is used for variables. The section covering the Method of Attributes covers these features in more detail. For clarity, the term *variate* is a better designation of the data obtained by the Method of Variables, as it is known as a *random variable*. It is defined by a set of permissible values similar to an ordinary mathematical variable, and also by an associated frequency (probability) function expressing the frequency for which these values appear in the situation under discussion. However, the term *variable* is generally used in quality control. Thus the Method of Variables includes sampling by variables and variables inspection. Data thus secured are used to prepare control charts for variables. Variables inspection may only be performed to obtain data for analysis and for control charts, but it is also used in acceptance inspection where the criteria for classifying or judging a sample submitted for inspection are quantitative rather than qualitative. In this sense variable relates to a measurable quantity as distinct from an attribute.

Statistical concepts cover both variables and attributes data. The sections that follow cover techniques that apply to both types of measured values. For example, an engineering specification may provide a tolerance of 5 ohms for a 100-ohm resistor. This is used to classify resistors as either conforming or not conforming to a minimum of 95 ohms and a maximum of 105 ohms. All resistors within these limits are conforming. All others are nonconforming. This is a two-fold classification, and the handling of such a case is covered by the Method of Attributes. Where all measured values are reported and the results are handled as random variables or variates, the Method of Variables applies. Frequency distributions may be used for both cases. Thus the Method of Attributes may be considered as a special case of the Method of Variables.

3.9 Method of Attributes

In the *Method of Attributes* for statistical measurements and analysis, the data obtained are not continuous but consist of discrete values. Events that occur are classified into a two-fold classification: the event takes place or the event does not take place. If a unit is inspected for specified engineering requirements and is found to be conforming or nonconforming, it may be classed as defective or not defective; the event may be classed as a success or a failure. Mathematically, the percentage of times that the event is a success is designated as p whereas the percentage of times that it is a failure is designated as q. This results in a total of one for the sum of these two percentages, called the *probabilities of occurrence*, with $p + q = 1$.

Recall our example of tossing an unbiased coin. The probability of a head is considered to be $\frac{1}{2}$ or 0.5 and the probability of obtaining a tail is also considered as $\frac{1}{2}$ or 0.5. Their sum is obviously $\frac{1}{2} + \frac{1}{2} = 1$. A better example is to consider the probabilities involved in the game of "craps," one of the favorite games in many casinos. Most people are familiar with this game in which two dice are thrown at the same time and the sum of the numbers appearing are observed to be from two to twelve. Since each die has six faces and, for an unbiased die, the numbers are weighted equally, the probability of a 1, 2, 3, 4, 5, or 6 appearing on any face is $\frac{1}{6}$. When two dice are thrown, the odds are different; the sums can occur in thirty-six different ways, as shown in figure 3-25. The following equation represents the probabilities related to each possible sum; the sum of seven has the greatest chance of occurring.

$$P(2)+P(3)+P(4)+P(5)+P(6)+P(7)+P(8)+P(9)+P(10)+P(11)+P(12)$$

$$= \frac{1}{36}+\frac{2}{36}+\frac{3}{36}+\frac{4}{36}+\frac{5}{36}+\frac{6}{36}+\frac{5}{36}+\frac{4}{36}+\frac{3}{36}+\frac{2}{36}+\frac{1}{36}=\frac{36}{36}=1 \quad \textbf{(13)}$$

The frequency distribution in figure 3-25 is symmetric and may be assumed to be partially normal. The frequencies for the individual X values, 2 through 12

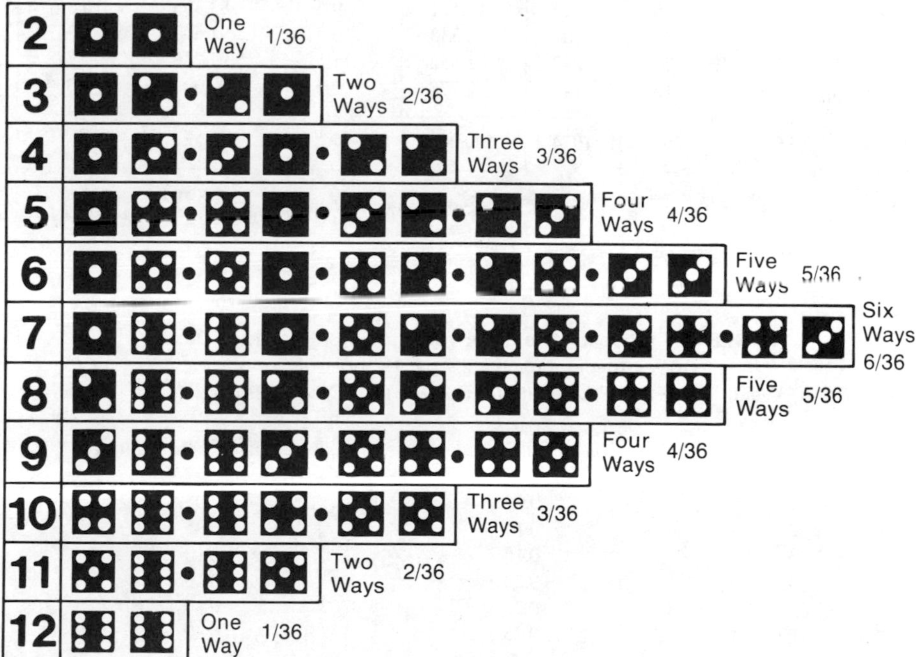

Figure 3–25 Game of craps: probabilities and possible sums for two dice.

inclusive, may be accumulated in ascending or descending arrays. This tabulation is shown in table 3.8. The cumulated results are presented on linear-probability graph paper in figure 3-26.

When unbiased dice are used, the graph of resulting cumulated distribution is a straight line over the central part of normal-linear probability graph paper. This

TABLE 3.8 Expected Individual and Cumulated Frequencies for Two Unbiased Dice in Fractions and Percentages Determination of Average, Variance and Standard Deviation

Sum of Two Dice X	*Individual Frequency i/36, f*	*Computations* $f(X)$	$f(X^2)$	*Percentage Individual*	*Cell Boundary*	*Cumulative Frequencies Percentages* *Less-than*	*More-than*
1	0	0	0	—	1.5	0.000	100.000
2	1	2	4	2.778	2.5	2.778	97.222
3	2	6	18	5.556	3.5	8.333	91.667
4	3	12	48	8.333	4.5	16.667	83.333
5	4	20	100	11.111	5.5	27.778	72.222
6	5	30	180	13.889	6.5	41.667	58.333
7	6	42	294	16.666	7.5	58.333	41.667
8	5	40	320	13.889	8.5	72.222	27.778
9	4	36	324	11.111	9.5	83.333	16.667
10	3	30	300	8.333	10.5	91.667	8.333
11	2	22	242	5.556	11.5	97.222	2.778
12	1	12	144	2.778	12.5	100.000	0.000
Sum	36	252	1974	100.000			

Average: $\overline{X} = \frac{252}{36} = 7.0$; $v = \sigma^2 = \frac{1974}{36} - (7)^2 = 54.8333 - 49.0000 = 5.8333.$

Standard Deviation: $\sigma = \sqrt{v} = \sqrt{4.3750} = 2.092$

TABLE 3.9 Probability of Face Turning Up on Weighted Dice
(*a*) Weighted approximately per Number of Spots
(*b*) Weighted so that Probability for Sum of Two Dice is Greatest for 11

Face Number	(*a*) *Individual Probabilities*	(*b*) *Individual Probabilities*
1	0.05	0.05
2	0.10	0.05
3	0.15	0.10
4	0.20	0.10
5	0.25	0.40
6	0.25	0.30
Sum	1.00	1.00

graph may readily be compared with similar distributions obtained from results obtained from biased dice of any kind. Even when a die is made very carefully and uniformly, indentations must be made and material inserted to show the number of spots. This operation might change the weight of these various surfaces. The material imbedded in the spots varies from side to side to equalize the weight. In other cases, it may be desired to make the probability of certain sums for two dice to be greater than for normal dice; this may be done by loading various sides so that the probability of certain faces turning up differs in a predictable manner. Such probabilities may be evaluated statistically and make use of the products of all possible combinations. Table 3.9 shows the probabilities for two other situations in which the dice are weighted so that the probability of each face is not $\frac{1}{6}$.

The following tables give the respective probabilities of each of the sums two to twelve, inclusive, when two dice are rolled. The possible combinations of faces are the same as for the unbiased dice shown in table 3.8. However, the probabilities

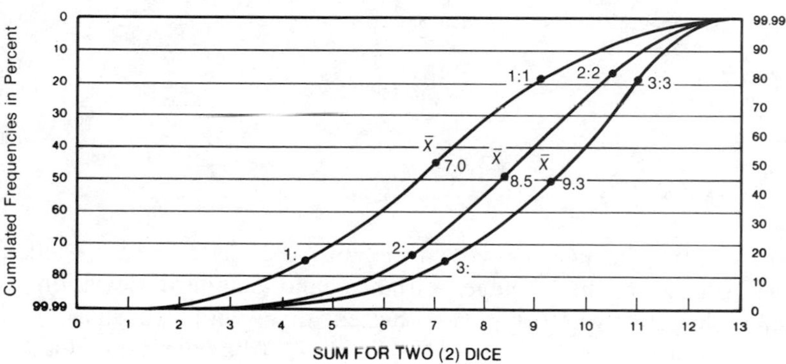

KEY:

Individual Die Face Probabilities

Die Face Value	Unbiased Curve 1	Curve 2	Curve 3
1	1/6, 0.1667	0.05	0.05
2	1/6, 0.1667	0.10	0.05
3	1/6, 0.1667	0.15	0.10
4	1/6, 0.1667	0.20	0.10
5	1/6, 0.1667	0.25	0.40
6	1/6, 0.1667	0.25	0.30

Figure 3–26 Cumulative frequency distributions (Ogives); three sets of dice, less-than and more-than curves.

will be obtained by adding the products of the occurrences of the two dice as noted. For example, for set (*b*) above an 11 can be obtained in two ways, as a 6 and 5 or as a 5 and 6; hence the probability of an 11 is 2(0.30)(0.40) = 0.24.

TABLE 3.10 Probabilities of Sums Two to Twelve, Inclusive for Two Similar Dice with Weights (*a*) shown in Table 3.9

Sum of Two Dice X	*Possible Combinations to Obtain Sum Determination of Compound Probabilities*		*Sum of Probabilities Relative Frequency*
2	1, 1	(0.05)(0.05)	0.0025
3	1, 2; 2, 1	2(0.05)(0.10)	0.0100
4	1, 3; 3, 1; 2, 2	2(0.05)(0.15) + (0.10)(0.10)	0.0250
5	1, 4; 4, 1; 2, 3; 3, 2	2(0.05)(0.20) + 2(0.10)(0.15)	0.0500
6	1, 5; 5, 1; 2, 4; 4, 2; 3, 3	2(0.05)(0.25) + 2(0.10)(0.20) + (0.15)(0.15)	0.0875
7	1, 6; 6, 1; 2, 5; 5, 2; 3, 4; 4, 3	2(0.05)(0.25) + 2(0.10)(0.25) + 2(0.15)(0.20)	0.1350
8	2, 6; 6, 2; 3, 5; 5, 3; 4, 4	2(0.10)(0.25) + 2(0.15)(0.25) + (0.20)(0.20)	0.1650
9	3, 6; 6, 3; 4, 5; 5, 4	2(0.15)(0.25) + 2(0.20)(0.25)	0.1750
10	4, 6; 6, 4; 5, 5	2(0.20)(0.25) + (0.25)(0.25)	0.1625
11	5, 6; 6, 5	2(0.25)(0.25)	0.1250
12	6, 6	(0.25)(0.25)	0.0625
		Sum	1.0000

The cumulative frequencies plotted in figure 3-26 as curve 2, together with computed values for the average, variance, and standard deviation for the distribution in table 3.10 for two biased dice with weights (*a*) thrown simultaneously, are given in table 3.11. Boundaries (showing half values) used in plotting curve 2 are given.

These results are given here to illustrate how many analyses are made. The average value for the biased dice is 8.5, whereas the average for the unbiased dice is 7, which is the usual value observed in the game of craps. The standard deviation for the biased dice is less than that of the other distribution, 2.092 compared with 2.415 for the unbiased distribution. The three-sigma control limits for individual values in both cases include most of the possible values, as the minimum sum is two and the maximum sum is twelve. These limits are:

Set 1, unbiased: $7.00 \pm 3(2.415) = 7.00 \pm 7.25$, or 0 and 14.2;
Set 2, biased: $8.50 \pm 3(2.092) = 8.50 \pm 6.276$, or 2.2 and 14.8.

It is apparent that the sum of two will occur very infrequently for the biased dice. Thus if a player throws a two, the odds of a repeat are less than $\frac{1}{300}$.

Table 3.13 gives the cumulative probabilities for the distribution given in table 3.12. Computations for the average, variance, and standard deviation also are given.

TABLE 3.11 Expected Individual and Cumulated Frequencies for Two Biased Dice; Determination of Average, Variance and Standard Deviation

Sum of Two Dice X	*Individual Frequency in %, f*	*Computations in %* $f(X)$	$f(X^2)$	*Cell Boundary* X_b	*Values for Curve 2, Fig. 3.26 Cumulative Frequencies, %* *Less-than*	*More-than*
1	0	0	0	1.5	0.00	100.00
2	0.25	0.50	1.00	2.5	0.25	99.75
3	1.00	3.00	9.00	3.5	1.25	98.75
4	2.50	10.00	40.00	4.5	3.75	96.25
5	5.00	25.00	125.00	5.5	8.75	91.25
6	8.75	52.50	315.00	6.5	17.50	82.50
7	13.50	94.50	661.50	7.5	31.00	69.00
8	16.50	132.00	1056.00	8.5	47.50	52.50
9	17.50	157.50	1417.50	9.5	65.00	35.00
10	16.25	162.50	1625.00	10.5	81.25	18.75
11	12.50	137.50	1512.50	11.5	93.75	6.25
12	6.25	75.00	900.00	12.5	100.00	0.00
Sum	100.00	850.00	7662.50			

Average: $\bar{X} = \dfrac{850.00}{100.00} = 8.5; \quad v = \sigma^2 = \dfrac{7662.50}{100} - (8.5)^2 = 76.6250 - 72.25 = 4.3750.$

Standard Deviation: $\sigma = \sqrt{v} = \sqrt{4.3750} = 2.092$

TABLE 3.12 Probabilities of Sums Two to Twelve, Inclusive for Two Similar Dice with Weights (*b*) shown in Table 3.9

Sum of Two Dice X	*Possible Combinations to Obtain Sum*	*Determination of Compound Probabilities*	*Sum of Probabilities Relative Frequency*
2	1, 1	(0.05) (0.05)	0.0025
3	1, 2; 2, 1	2(0.05) (0.05)	0.0050
4	1, 3; 3, 1; 2, 2	2(0.05) (0.10) + (0.05) (0.05)	0.0125
5	1, 4; 4, 1; 2, 3; 3, 2	2(0.05) (0.10) + 2(0.05) (0.10)	0.0200
6	1, 5; 5, 1; 2, 4; 4, 2; 3, 3	2(0.05) (0.40) + 2(0.05) (0.10) + (0.10) (0.10)	0.0600
7	1, 6; 6, 1; 2, 5; 5, 2; 3, 4; 4, 3	2(0.05) (0.30) + 2(0.05) (0.40) + 2(0.10) (0.10)	0.0900
8	2, 6; 6, 2; 3, 5; 5, 3; 4, 4	2(0.05) (0.30) + 2(0.10) (0.40) + (0.10) (0.10)	0.1200
9	3, 6; 6, 3; 4, 5; 5, 4	2(0.10) (0.30) + 2(0.10) 0.40)	0.1400
10	4, 6; 6, 4; 5, 5	2(0.10) (0.30) + (0.40) (0.40)	0.2200
11	5, 6; 6, 5	2(0.40) (0.30)	0.2400
12	6, 6	(0.30) (0.30)	0.0900
		Sum	1.0000

TABLE 3.13 Expected Individual and Cumulated Frequencies for Two Similar Biased Dice per Table 3.12; Determination of Average, Variance and Standard Deviation Values

Sum of Two Dice X	*Individual Frequency in %, f*	*Computations in %* $f(X)$	$f(X^2)$	*Cell Boundary* X_b	*Values for Curve 3, Fig. 3.26 Cumulative Frequencies, %* *Less-than*	*More-than*
1	0	0	0	1.5	0.00	100.00
2	0.25	0.50	1.00	2.5	0.25	99.75
3	0.50	1.50	4.50	3.5	0.75	99.25
4	1.25	5.00	20.00	4.5	2.00	98.00
5	2.00	10.00	50.00	5.5	4.00	96.00
6	6.00	36.00	216.00	6.5	10.00	90.00
7	9.00	63.00	441.00	7.5	19.00	81.00
8	12.00	96.00	768.00	8.5	31.00	69.00
9	14.00	126.00	1134.00	9.5	45.00	55.00
10	22.00	220.00	2200.00	10.5	67.00	33.00
11	24.00	264.00	2640.00	11.5	91.00	9.00
12	9.00	108.00	1296.00	12.5	100.00	0.00
Sum	100.00	930.00	8770.50			

Average: $\bar{X} = \dfrac{930.00}{100.00} = 9.3$; $v = \sigma^2 = \dfrac{8770.50}{100} - (9.3)^2 = 87.7050 - 86.49 = 1.2150.$

Standard Deviation: $\sigma = \sqrt{v} = \sqrt{1.2150} = 1.102$

The three-sigma control limits for the distribution (*b*) shown as curve 3 in figure 3-26 are $9.300 \pm 3(1.102)$, which gives 5.994 and 12.606. Based on normal law probabilities, the percent outside these control limits would be 0.135% for one tail and 0.27% for both tails. Thus the chance of a sum of five or less is approximately $\frac{1}{300}$.

3.10 Basic Distributions for Method of Attributes and Method of Variables

When working with attributes data, three distributions are used. The Method of Attributes is most frequently based on a two-fold classification covering any event: The event is a success or it is a failure. Products made or purchased may be satisfactory or unsatisfactory. A production line manufactures a particular product almost continuously month after month so that thousands of these same kinds of units are being produced and sold. When such large quantities are involved, the number is considered to be infinite. Hence the number produced is not considered when determining the probability of an event taking place. However, when the lot size N is 25 or 50 items, then in many cases methods which take account of the lot size should be applied.

If p is considered the probability of a failure, then the probability of a success is $1 - p$ and is called q. Thus $p + q = 1$ is the total probability of a failure and a success. (Because two terms are involved, the resultant expression, $q + p$, is called a *binomial.*) In quality control work, p is called the probability of the occurrence of a defect; hence $1 - p = q$ is the probability of the occurrence of a good unit. The sample size n denotes the number of units inspected or tested. If $n = 2$, the probability of no defects is $q \times q = q^2$, since the probability that the first unit is good is q and is also q for the second unit observed. The probability of one failure when testing two units is either qp or pq; hence the total probability is $2qp$. The probability of both units being defective is $p \times p = p^2$. These three terms are represented as $q^2 + 2qp + p^2 = (q + p)^2$, the binomial expression for a sample of two units. The general binomial relation is given in equation (14).

$$(q + p)^n = q^n + \frac{n}{1!} q^{n-1} p + \frac{n(n-1)}{2!} q^{n-2} p^2 + \cdots + p^n \tag{14}$$

This may also be written as:

$$(q + p)^n = \Sigma \, C_m^n q^{n-m} p^m = \Sigma \, C_m^n (1 - p)^{n-m} p^m. \tag{15}$$

If probability values are to have meaning and agree with actual conditions met day by day, it is necessary to have truly random samples that are representative of the product or item sampled. When large amounts are involved in lots N and samples n, treat N and n as infinite.

In applying relations for the Method of Attributes, fractional defects or partly defective units are not considered. The variant is considered to be integral or discrete. That is, only a whole number of events is used in these relations.

In the Method of Variables, distributions are continuous in nature. The classification of events is multifold. Heights of individuals could be the variable X, and could include a wide range of values. Statistical theory deals with variables as well as with attributes, although more sampling by the method of attributes occurs in practice.

The three most important distributions that must be covered in the Method of Attributes are (1) the p binomial, (2) the Poisson exponential binomial limit, and (3) the hypergeometric distribution. The first two cover infinite universes, while the third covers any finite universe. The first two, with the addition of the f binomial, may be used at times to represent the exact values given by the third distribution. These are called *probability frequency distributions,* since the sum of their frequencies is one. These frequencies may be graphed as line distributions with a y value graphed on a scale representing the relative frequency, compared with similar lines for the X or m values representing the number of successes. The X values may be ordered as $0, 1, 2, 3, \ldots, n$. Individual frequencies are tabulated and may be graphed as such in line charts. Sometimes only points are placed on such charts. Often bar charts are drawn, using cell boundaries -0.5 to 0.5 for the 0 value, 0.5 to 1.5 for the 1 value, etc. These graphs are similar to those used in the

Method of Variables. Frequencies may be cumulated and also graphed. Such points, when graphed, may be connected by dotted lines to denote lack of continuity, and may be similar to a frequency polygon. Figures 3-17 and 3-18 illustrated a bar chart and frequency polygon for variables data. Figure 3-27 presents possible line charts for attributes data.

The materials or products from which samples are selected are termed the *parent population*, the *universe of discourse*, or just the *universe*, designated as U. From such a universe, large quantities of materials (in lots of discrete sizes, submitted as lots of size N) are selected and supplied orders when requested by the purchasing department. From such lots, samples of size n are selected at random for checking and inspection. What is the nature of these universes? The basic distribution for the Method of Variables is the normal law, a symmetric bell-shaped distribution, which is also used in the Method of Attributes.

Figure 3-27 presents two charts for individual values; part a illustrates individual frequencies as lines at the integral values of X, i.e., 0, 1, 2, etc. The illustrations cover the actual frequencies for the p binomial for samples of $n = 10$ units selected at random from a process where $p = 0.20$ or 20%. The values used in these graphs are given in table 3.14. The point halfway between X integral values is used as mid-cell values for plotting *less-than* X_m and *more-than* X_m cumulated distributions, where X_m denotes these midpoints. Rounded frequency values used in plotting these graphs are included.

TABLE 3.14

p Binomial Probability Distribution for $p = 0.20$ or 20%, $n = 10$

Number of Successes X	Individual* Frequency f	Value Graphed f	Mid-Cell X_m	Cumulative Determinations Less-than X_m	Cumulative Determinations More-than** X_m	Graphed Values Less-than X_m	Graphed Values More-than X_m
0	0.1073742	0.11	−0.5	0	1.0000000	0	1.00
1	0.2684354	0.27	0.5	0.1073742	0.8926258	0.11	0.89
2	0.3019899	0.30	1.5	0.3758096	0.6241904	0.38	0.62
3	0.2013266	0.20	2.5	0.6777995	0.3222005	0.68	0.32
4	0.0880804	0.09	3.5	0.8791261	0.1208739	0.88	0.12
5	0.0264241	0.03	4.5	0.9672065	0.0327935	0.97	0.03
6	0.0055050	0.01	5.5	0.9936306	0.0063694	0.99	0.01
7	0.0007865	0.00	6.5	0.9991356	0.0008644	1.00	0.00
8	0.0000737	0	7.5	0.9999221	0.0000779	1.00	0.00
9	0.0000041	0	8.5	0.9999958	0.0000042	1.00	0.00
10	0.0000001	0	9.5	0.9999999	0.0000001	1.00	0.00
			10.5	1.0000000	0		
Sum	1.0000000						

* Table 1—Individual Terms from *Tables of the Binomial Probability Distribution*, Dept. of Commerce, National Bureau of Standards, Applied Mathematical Series 6, 1950, Government Printing Office, Washington, D.C.

** Ibid, Table 2—Partial Sums. Uses r integral values for X_m. Value for $r = 1$ agrees with that shown above for $X = 0.5$.

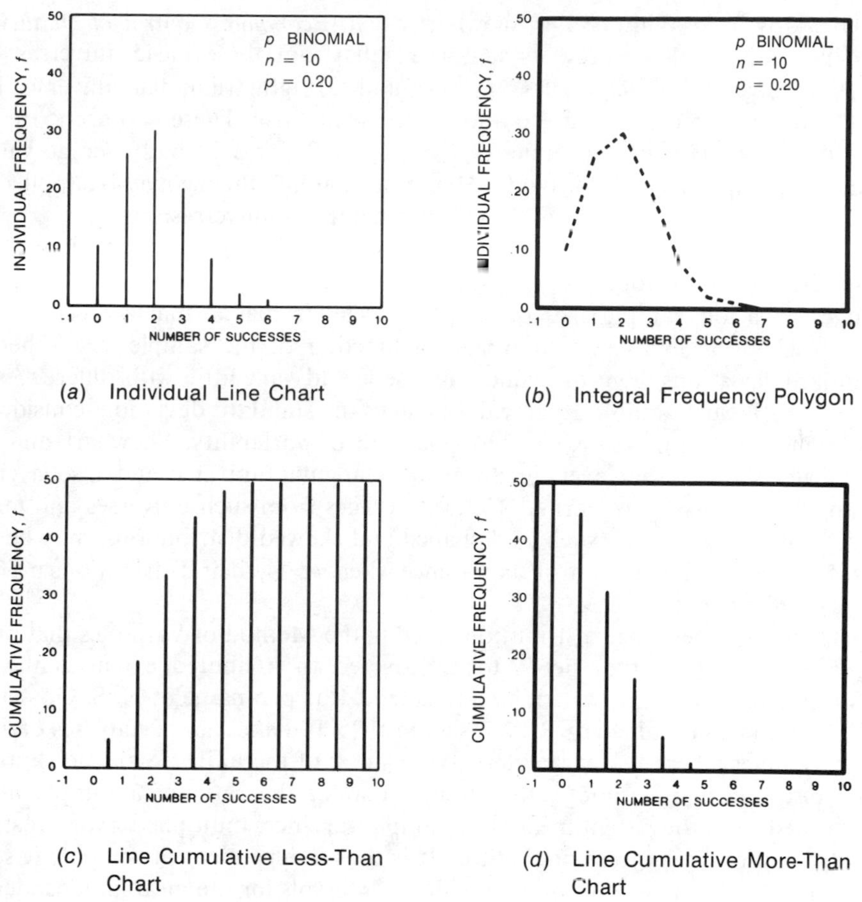

(a) Individual Line Chart

(b) Integral Frequency Polygon

(c) Line Cumulative Less-Than Chart

(d) Line Cumulative More-Than Chart

Figure 3–27 Types of charts for the method of attributes.

Most texts show cumulative values by connected points. The use of lines is the best way to show these charts when the data are attributes data. Connected cumulative curves are to be used for continuous variables distributions.

When actual characteristics have to be measured or tested in quality control work to determine whether the units inspected meet the specified requirements for such an item as weight, length, or capacitance, the Method of Variables applies. Control charts, when desired, are applied to actual data as described in succeeding sections. The nature of such distributions must be known to some degree in order to determine proper standards for control purposes. The majority of the universes or parent populations from which lots and samples are taken are essentially normal. Many quality control experts have erroneously decreed that control charts will only prove effective when the distributions covered are normal. This is not so, as was shown by Dr. Walter A. Shewhart, aided by his staff and particularly Fred Winters. Dr. Shewhart's text, *Economic Control of Quality of Manufactured Product*, presents sample results from three basic universes: (1) normal universe, (2) rectangular universe, and (3) right triangular universe. The last two are not normal and the third is not symmetric. These two are extremes (see figure 3-6). However, samples of 4, 8, 12, 16, 20, and 24 had average values that closely approached normality. Hence normal law theory may be applied to such distributions, as well as to samples from normal universes.

Figure 3-7 shows a typical normal law distribution. Figure 6-15 in chapter six also shows such a normal law distribution, which illustrates the fact that the ranges for various sample sizes for samples selected from a normal law distribution have highly variable expected ranges, a function of the sample size, whereas standard deviations from the same universe would vary little with differences in sample sizes. Such uniformity in values makes the standard deviation, considered invariant with sample size, the best measure of variability. Shewhart and his associates showed that averages from a rectangular universe and also a right triangular universe were normal. Hence, averages from such universes and many other different universes, such as J-shaped and skewed distributions, may be the basis for many different control charts since when $n > 4$, their distributions may be considered normal.

There are other basic distributions used in the Method of Variables that must be considered. One that needs to be covered to a limited extent is the "t-distribution," originally written by a "Student" (the pen-name of N. S. Gosset) in 1907, which was modified by R. A. Fisher in 1925. It makes use of statistics derived from samples where the parameters (two values) of the universe are not known. The distribution is, among other things, that of the ratio of a sample mean (measured from the parent mean) to a sample variance, multiplied by a constant, in samples from a normal population. It is thus independent of the parent scale parameter and can be used to set confidence intervals for the mean independently of the parent variance. Its t values are multiples of the sample standard deviation obtained from a sample with n degrees of freedom for various levels of significance (p). For example, where $p = 0.20$, which has a t value of 1.282 for the normal distribution, and when n is ten degrees of freedom, the multiplier t becomes 1.372; for $n = 5$ degrees of freedom, $t = 1.476$.

When testing for significant differences between means when only statistics derived from samples are available, use is often made of the t-distribution. Probability values thus found or used are more realistic.

Another distribution used in many statistical studies is the Chi-square (χ^2) distribution. It is entered on the basis of degrees of freedom involved rather than sample size and is used in testing for "goodness of fit." When f_0 denotes observed frequencies, f_t denotes corresponding theoretical frequencies, and where m cells are used, then the degree of freedom is $m = df = mt$ and the probability of fit is determined by using the χ^2 value for the $m = df$ value from the applicable table given in the relation below, the probability showing "goodness of fit" is obtained for df equal to one less than the number of cells:

$$\chi^2 = \sum \frac{(f_0 - f_t)^2}{f_t} \tag{16}$$

Most terms cover only the normal distribution. The values for the t-distribution apply to samples obtained from assumed normal distributions. However, many skewed distributions do occur. These are easily handled since probabilities may be readily computed if some information about the nature of the skewness k is known. Even if k is not computed, a graph of the distribution will show that the distribution has either positive or negative skewness. One relation that may be applied is the distribution obtained by using the normal law as the generating function; this gives the so-called *Gram-Charlier* distribution. Where k only is used as a multiplying factor, the distribution is sometimes termed the *Second Approximation.* Frequencies for this distribution are obtained from the relation:

$$P(z) = F_1(z) - kF_2(z) \tag{17}$$

where values of $F_1(z)$ and $F_2(z)$ are given in Appendix A, taken from Shewhart's text, pages 90–91. In using this relation, k may be either positive or negative. If k is negative, the two functions are added to obtain P; if k is positive, kF_2 is subtracted from $F_1(z)$, which is actually a normal distribution table. Where data are from a skew distribution, theoretical frequencies based on an assumed or computed k value may be determined. Then a test for goodness of fit may be made using the χ^2 table provided in Appendix A.

Many forms are available for simplifying the computations. Most industrial organizations will have such forms available in their mathematical, statistical, or engineering departments. The methods developed in this chapter can be used for performing computations correctly. Students may also prepare their own statistical forms or may program them for use by computers. When many computations are required, any available computer should be utilized. Many computer centers have program libraries that cover most of these longer statistical computations. By using such facilities efficiently, together with available tables, results that provide necessary quality control information will be obtained sooner and should aid in improving quality and decreasing costs.

EXERCISES

1. The following scores were made by 50 students. Ten students were selected from each of five different schools. A statistical analysis of these data is desired.
   (a) Order these data in: ascending order; descending order.
   (b) Arrange the data in two different frequency distributions using two different intervals.
   (c) Graph the two frequency distributions obtained in exercise 1(b) as: a bar chart; a frequency polygon.

TABLE A: Test Scores for Fifty Students
Ten Students from Five Different Schools

School A	*School B*	*School C*	*School D*	*School E*
80	75	90	61	76
64	55	83	69	86
74	99	85	87	81
89	76	77	83	63
78	84	73	70	84
75	79	68	76	82
69	72	71	92	70
88	65	66	67	76
71	80	79	71	79
82	85	78	94	73

2. (a) Determine the average; variance; and standard deviation for: the original fifty scores using their exact values; and for the two different frequency distributions obtained in exercise 1.
(b) Which of your two frequency distributions is the best? Why?

3. (a) Arrange the data for each of the five schools in ascending and descending order.
(b) Graph the data for exercise 3(a) in five bar charts.
(c) Graph the data for the five schools as a frequency polygon.
(d) From these graphs, does there appear to be any difference between the results from any of these five different schools?

4. (a) Make a cumulative frequency distribution for the two frequency distributions obtained in exercise 1 for both ascending and descending arrays.
(b) Make a graph of the four cumulative distributions found in exercise 4(a).

5. Assuming a normal law distribution and the averages for your best frequency distribution:
(a) What are the percentile points for $\bar{X} \pm 0.6745\,\sigma$, sometimes termed the probable error (*P.E.*) for which the normal law probability is 0.50?
(b) These limits divide the distribution into four equal areas. What percentage of the fifty scores falls in each of these four quartile areas?

6. (a) Determine the limits for the following percentiles based on the Normal Law for your $\bar{X}$ and σ values obtained from your best frequency distribution: Lower 10%; Lower 20%; Lower 30%; Upper 30%; Upper 20%; Upper 10%; and Upper 5%.
(b) Many industries and institutions of learning desire personnel that are in the upper 5% group. Considering other factors, should this rigid criterion be maintained at all costs? Are there any circumstances where other factors than just scholastic standing are more important?

7. For the distribution in example 1, determine the following.
(a) Measures of Central Tendency: average or arithmetic mean; mode; median; and mid-range.
(b) Measures of variability: variance; standard deviation; mean deviation; and range.

(c) Why are the arithmetic mean and the standard deviation the preferred measures to be used in most cases?

8. List the three primary relations used in the Method of Variables and give examples of each. The three desired for this example are: Normal Law; Chi-square (χ^2) distribution, and Student's t-distribution. How are each of these distributions used in statistics, and particularly quality control?

9. List the three primary relations used in the Method of Attributes and give examples for each. The three desired are: the p binomial; the Poisson exponential binomial limit; and the hypergeometric. Where does each of these three distributions best apply? The ones usually used are an approximation for the other two in the Poisson exponential. Explain why this is true and give an example to prove your reasons.

10. A sample of 100 resistors was selected at random from a lot of 1,000 resistors and checked for conformance to the specified resistance value. Engineering had specified for these units a resistance value of 100 ± 5 ohms, i.e., a minimum of 95 ohms and a maximum of 105 ohms. Ten resistors in the sample were found outside these specified limits, so the sample was termed 10% defective. Of these ten, there were eight resistors with resistance values greater than 105 ohms and there were also two resistors less than 95 ohms. Thus the variability of these resistors was greater than desired.

The sample of 100 resistors with ten nonconforming units was placed in a container; resistors were drawn at random and placed on a table containing 100 squares. The nonconforming resistors were marked in such a way that only the first inspector could pick them out. If twenty units are selected at random from this group of 100 resistors that consisted of ninety conforming units and ten nonconforming units, determine the following probabilities:

(a) No nonconforming units in sample, based on the binomial; based on the Poisson exponential binomial limit relation; and based on the hypergeometric relation.

(b) One nonconforming unit in sample, based on p binomial; based on Poisson exponential; and based on hypergeometric. Tabulate results for easy comparison.

11. For the histograms given in figure 3-24(a) and 3-24(b), determine the frequency distribution, listing a frequency for each cell. The sum of these frequencies for each distribution is $n = 200$.

12. Figures 3-24(a) and (b) both have average $\bar{X}$ and standard deviation σ values noted. Check these values, showing each step of your computations. Carry out one more place than given.

CHAPTER FOUR

INTRODUCTION TO CONTROL CHARTS

4.1 Objective

Consumers want to be able to purchase the best possible quality products at reasonable prices. To achieve this goal, the best and most efficient producers installed the best possible quality control systems in their plants. Quality control charts and techniques came into use, spot checks were made at frequent intervals in many industries, and corrective measures were taken when a large number of customers complained about poor quality and faulty performance.

The development and use of quality control charts has provided definite evidence to management concerning when corrective measures are necessary and should be taken. They also indicate when it would be undesirable to institute such corrective measures. When quality control charts were developed and installed at strategic points in the manufacturing process, customer complaints were greatly reduced—resulting in increased profits. The purpose of this chapter is to describe the development and nature of control charts and explain in detail where they may be applied most effectively. Also, it will cover other somewhat similar techniques and methods that are often used to replace control charts. Examples of their use will be included to provide as much detail as possible, thus making it easier to prepare all the different kinds of quality control charts which might be needed in a particular plant.

4.2 Purposes of Quality Control and Quality Control Charts

The economic development of each industry, as well as each nation, depends upon its ability to supply products and/or services that are needed by other suppliers and other nations. Where two different suppliers have essentially the same kind of product available for purchase at almost the same price, the item appearing to have the best quality and reliability is usually selected. Thus it is necessary to establish standards of quality in line with customer demands and to place this image before the potential purchasers so that the best and most economical products are manufactured and used.

Products tend to be graded automatically as to quality. When new products are placed on the market, steps are taken to bring such products to the attention of the buying public. All kinds of advertisements are presented which stress the best features of such products, especially their predominant elements of quality. For example, producers of mouthwashes stress the quality of bad breath control; some also advertise that besides the astringent quality and ability to kill bacteria and germs, their particular product is also pleasant to use. However, one older company emphasizes the fact that many hate the taste of its product but use it because it is extremely effective in controlling bad breath. For such products, quality control techniques are applied to produce a uniform product. From month to month, the end products sold must be uniform in nature to assure continuance of purchasing by the buying public. When a customer purchases a particular brand, emphasis is placed on the fact that the product purchased today is the same in most respects as the item purchased several weeks or months ago. Even with paints having the same color elements and number, control is exerted by giving each batch a separate number so that the customer may be certain that his painted surfaces are all painted with matching colors. Industries learn by experience that when they have found a product that the public likes and uses, it should not be changed from batch to batch but its uniform nature should be maintained.

The physical environment under which products are made should be controlled at the same levels at all times. The manufacturing processes should be stabilized and held as constant as possible in all phases of the production stages of manufacturing, assembly, finishing, and packing. Even when improvements are made, no adverse changes should be made in most of the components that are known to be satisfactory for customer use. One of the chief functions of quality control charts is to aid management in maintaining the quality of the products at desired levels with minimum cost.

Cost accounting is greatly aided by the use of such control charts. In the most efficient plant operations, controls are also maintained at cost centers; these cover in detail all the varying costs incurred at periodic intervals, such as every hour, with respect to all steps of the manufacturing process. Comparisons can be made of the quality history and process controls exerted by different manufacturers of the same or similar products. Inspection records are maintained for all vendors and summarized weekly, monthly, quarterly, and yearly. This makes it possible to evaluate the suppliers and rank them in accordance with both quality and costs, as well as delivery schedules. Many purchasing agents tend to place orders with the lowest bidder for a given product. Unless previous tests have shown these products as essentially equal to more expensive items with respect to all features, some additional tests and inquiries should be made to insure that the lowest bidder also provides the best value. A storage battery with an expected life of only twenty-four months may give the same performance as one with an expected life of thirty-six months and can be offered at a lower price, as its inherent costs are less, but it may not give the best value as its cost-per-month of service may be higher in the long run. Quality control, reliability, and allied departments must work with the purchasing department to obtain the best values.

Example: Selection of Components from Different Suppliers

Many examples may be cited showing the necessity of using quality control techniques prior to the issuance of the contract to evaluate the quality of products submitted by all bidders. For example, one company had an engineer who was well-trained in accounting practices, acting as its purchasing agent. In this company, manufacturing used a large number of Product X; under the previous contract, these cost 37¢ each, on the average, when purchased from Company A. A competitive bidder, which will be called Company B, offered to provide essentially the same component part for 30¢ each, a savings of 7¢ per unit. The data furnished by Company B indicated that their claim of equal quality seemed valid. Although the evidence was not conclusive, the purchasing manager gave them the contract. A few units were checked by the inspection and quality control department and were found to be very satisfactory when submitted for initial inspection. However, when the first lot was delivered, over 50% of the initial sample was found by inspection to be unsatisfactory and unusable. Company B was informed of this fact. Their reply stated that this lot was not representative of standard product and they forwarded sufficient units to replace those found defective by the purchasing company. However, this new lot—containing approximately $0.5N$ units—also contained about 50% defective units, which again were replaced. This practice was continued until N good units were obtained by the purchaser; however, the production line was shut down for some time until sufficient good parts were available for manufacture and assembly. Since inspection costs are increased due to screening and production time that has been lost, Company B's product actually is more costly than that previously furnished by Company A. The average costs per unit are shown next.

When purchasing this component from Company A, the quality of successive lots is at such a satisfactory level that lots are rejected less than 5% of the time. Using a single sampling plan of inspection, the samples used are usually less than 10% of the total units submitted; thus the cost per unit inspected is only 1¢. However, with Company B's product, practically all lots will have to be completely screened, making the inspection costs per unit 10¢. Also, a series of lots must be tested and inspected to make certain that the original N units per lot are received and also are satisfactory. The resultant costs, not considering the down-time for the period when Company B's product was being received in a series of lots, are as follows:

$$\text{Company A:} \quad C = 37¢ + 1¢ = 38¢ \text{ per unit}$$

$$\begin{aligned}\text{Company B:} \quad C &= 30¢ + 10¢ + 5¢ + 2.5¢ + 1.25¢ + \ldots \\ &= 30¢ + 20¢ = 50¢\text{, approximately per unit}\end{aligned}$$

The cost of Company B's product is 32% greater.

Many other similar examples may be obtained from industry which show that production may be operated under better controls if use is made of all the statistical techniques that are available. These are tools of production that result in decreased costs in most instances.

Example: Clerical Errors

So far the use and benefits of quality control techniques have been confined to a discussion of manufacturing practices. These same techniques are used in many other areas. One that has paid off greatly has been their application to clerical errors. The Illinois Bell System, under Howard Jones' direction, applied these techniques to many types of clerical work. It was found that many part-time workers made less errors than full-time employees, when working continuously on clerical tabulations. Thus it was found that changes in work patterns can greatly increase the efficiency of a clerical force. Plotting the percentage of errors on control charts indicates trends towards an increase or a decrease in observed defects for the work periods tested. More errors tend to creep in the last two hours of an eight-hour day in many instances. These may be reduced by changing the work assignments of those making the most errors.

Examples: Other Areas

The purity of the drugs used in medical treatments must be maintained at as high a level as possible. Companies which produce such drugs, besides using the most sterile conditions possible, also check how well these sterile conditions are maintained by means of control charts. This protects the public against poor medical materials. The same is true for surgical instruments. The food industry is also using quality control techniques in conjunction with advanced computer programs, so that food products are maintained at high standards. As part of this program, many products, such as milk products and vitamins, are dated so that they may be removed from the shelf when it is believed their quality will be degraded. For example, only about seven days under refrigeration is permitted for milk products, whereas some vitamins may not degenerate for several years. However, many consumers pay very little attention to these dates. Many states are adding special agencies to cope with these problems. Quality control departments in these critical areas can be very helpful by checking changes in quality of products stored for fairly long periods of time. Some customers have indicated in their purchase orders what deterioration is permitted after some specified period of time, such as a year or even five years. For example, some types of gyroscopes that are designed to operate at 25,000 RPM when first manufactured are required to operate at not less than 24,500 RPM after one year in storage. The same may also be true of many other products. These continued controls are part of the current programs to improve products, particularly items that affect health, purchased by all consumers. These controls result in an increased life span and better health in those areas where such controls are exercised.

4.3 Nature of Control Charts

Chapters five and six develop the two distinct types of quality control charts that are applied particularly in industry, although they may be used in any area where numerical data are obtained. These two types are:

1. Control charts for attributes, and
2. Control charts for variables.

These control charts are used under two different conditions. These are:

1. Standard given, and
2. No standard given.

Also, data are obtained in two different ways in continuous inspections. These are:

1. Samples of equal size, and
2. Samples of unequal size.

Since control charts have been developed and used, many texts have been written which discuss their applications. One of the best now available gives these techniques in great detail. It was first issued under a different title in 1934, and now has been updated and titled, *ASTM Manual on Quality Control of Materials*. It is published and distributed by the American Society for Testing and Materials. This latest edition contains most of the basic material given in the ASA (American Standards Association) Standards Z1.1, Z1.2, and Z1.3: "Guides for the Control Chart Method of Controlling Quality During Production" and "Control Chart Method of Analyzing Data." Other nations, such as Great Britain, Denmark, France, Germany, and Japan, have somewhat similar standards. Since systems are assembled from parts made in all parts of the world, and with the trend for standardizing on the metric system, there is more and more need to fully understand these basic quality control techniques. Knowledge of the *ASTM Manual* is almost a "must" in current quality control and production practices. It contains information and examples covering the use of control charts for both the Method of Attributes and the Method of Variables. Other detailed texts covering statistical quality control should also be consulted. Most give a large amount of material that is very seldom required. This text was prepared to give the rudiments of the subject for use by those who work daily in this field. It provides those working in quality control with sufficient knowledge to perform most quality control tasks required under most quality assurance programs, in line with the best configuration management methods.

In the chapter covering control charts for attributes, the following will be discussed.

1. Control charts for fraction defective, p;
2. Control charts for number of defectives, pn;
3. Control charts for number of defects per unit, c;

4. Control charts for defects per unit, u, also pn; and
5. Control charts for demerits per unit, D_u.

Such control charts will cover practically all the cases that arise in most quality control departments. How they may be made and their usage is given in detail later.

In the chapter on control charts for variables will be discussed:

1. Control charts for averages ($\bar{X}$) and standard deviations (σ);
2. Control charts for averages ($\bar{X}$) and ranges (R);
3. Control charts for medians (M_e) and ranges (R); and
4. Control charts for indexes of quality (i).

Such quality control charts for indexes and even mid-ranges are usually developed for special cases. They are covered in this text since most texts fail to cover the more fundamental economical and practical aspects of control charts. Charts for medians have been used for critical characteristics by assemblers on the production line because they can be readily understood.

4.4 Other Techniques for Obtaining Statistical Control

Many regard quality control charts as the only technique for obtaining and maintaining control of process averages. It is true that the quality control techniques are relatively simple to use and, also, to explain to top management. In control chart applications, there are two kinds of variation that need to be considered. Variations occur within units submitted together as a lot. Each unit is slightly different from its neighbor. This is measured by obtaining the standard deviation for the units in each lot. The standard deviation measures the variation within that lot for the characteristic selected as critical. All critical items are required to be tested and measured, with each such measurement recorded. Where a number of different characteristics are to be measured, the data secured are kept separate for each distinct characteristic. Industries usually purchase the same kinds of units, at intervals, in a series of lots. For each such characteristic, an average value may be found for every lot. For a set of m lots, the standard deviation value for these m average values provides a measure of the variation between lots. Then the overall variation for each such characteristic may be determined directly from the two variances (the square of the standard deviations), the measure of the variation within, and the variation between these units for the characteristic under consideration. This is the result of the additive theorem covering variances, given in equation (1).

$$v_0 = v_w + v_b, \quad \text{or} \quad \sigma_0^2 = \sigma_w^2 + \sigma_b^2, \tag{1}$$

with

$$\sigma_0 = \sqrt{\sigma_w^2 + \sigma_b^2} \tag{2}$$

From the values thus found, one can readily determine what percentage of the total variation is due to large differences in lot averages or to large differences in the quality of units in a single lot. For this purpose, we determine the numbers r_w and r_b from the relation in equation (3).

$$r_w = \frac{\sigma_w^2}{\sigma_w^2 + \sigma_b^2} = \frac{\sigma_w^2}{\sigma_0^2} \quad \text{and} \quad r_b = \frac{\sigma_b^2}{\sigma_w^2 + \sigma_b^2} = \frac{\sigma_b^2}{\sigma_0^2} \tag{3}$$

Example 1 The number of units for which measured values of resistance should be obtained is much larger than that used in this example. It would be preferable to have about $m = 25$ lots of $N = 250$ units each, from which $n = 25$ units have been measured, giving a total of 625 measurements of resistance in ohms. This example uses only $m = 10$ sets of lots with $n = 10$ units, selected at random from each lot and measured. Thus 100 measurements of resistance are available, to which the best statistical techniques may be applied. Equal sample sizes have been taken to simplify the computations. In most industries, due to differences in orders, both lot sizes and sample sizes from such lots will not be equal and the sample sizes then should be used as weighting factors.

Case 1 Data are listed below for ten different lots of equal size, from which samples of ten units each have been selected at random and measured for resistance. The resulting measurements recorded in ohms are given below. The individual

TABLE 4.1
Resistance Values in Ohms for Ten Lots, $n = 10$ Units per Lot

Sample No.	*Lot Numbers:* 1	2	3	4	5	6	7	8	9	10	*Total*
	Ohms	*Ohms*	*Ohms*	*Ohms*	*Ohms*	*Ohms*	*Ohms*	*Ohms*	*Ohms*	*Ohms*	*Ohms*
1	99	97	100	101	104	103	98	101	102	105	1010
2	98	96	97	98	102	102	101	103	99	104	1000
3	101	94	101	103	105	100	102	99	98	99	1002
4	102	98	95	97	103	100	99	100	101	101	996
5	100	95	94	104	106	99	95	96	100	98	987
6	99	99	96	95	104	100	103	97	98	103	994
7	96	96	98	97	102	96	102	103	105	102	997
8	102	94	95	98	94	95	97	104	106	103	988
9	101	93	99	99	96	102	105	99	102	99	995
10	102	98	95	98	104	103	98	98	99	96	991
Total	1000	960	970	990	1020	1000	1000	1000	1010	1010	9960
Average, $\bar{X}$:	100.0	96.0	97.0	99.0	102.0	100.0	100.0	100.0	101.0	101.0	99.60
Range, R:	6	6	7	9	12	8	10	8	8	9	83
No. of Defects, c:	0	3	1	0	2	0	0	0	1	0	7
Fraction Defective, p:	0	0.30	0.10	0	0.20	0	0	0	0.10	0	0.07

limits given in the applicable specification are 100 ± 5 ohms. The minimum value allowed is 95 ohms and the maximum value allowed is 105 ohms. The data listed have an excessive number of units outside these limits, which are considered as nonconforming units or defects.

For this example, we must first determine why there were so many resistors outside the specification limits 95.0 to 105.0 ohms. The lot numbers containing 0, 1, 2, or 3 nonconforming resistors in the respective samples from these ten lots are listed below.

Number of Nonconforming Units Resistors	*Number of Lot in Which Nonconformances Occurred, with Resistance Values*
0	1, 4, 6, 7, 8 and 10
1	3 (94); 9 (106)
2	5 (106, 94)
3	2 (94, 94, 93)

From these data the process average may be readily determined as:

$$\text{Low resistance: } \bar{p}_L = \frac{5}{100} = 0.05 \text{ or } 5.0\% \text{ Nonconforming}$$

$$\text{High resistance: } \bar{p}_H = \frac{2}{100} = 0.02 \text{ or } 2.0\% \text{ Nonconforming}$$

$$\text{Process Average: } \bar{p} = \frac{7}{100} = 0.07 \text{ or } 7.0\% \text{ Nonconforming}$$

The overall variation is measured partially by the variation between units in a sample and partially by the variation between the variance among lots. The $\bar{\sigma}_w$ within lots may be determined as the average of the ten standard deviations obtained respectively for the ten lots. The variance between lots is determined from the distribution for the ten average values. The best estimate of the true overall variance may be approximated by summing the above two variances. The actual proportion contributing to the overall variability is found by using equation (3).

Variation within lots: $v_w = 7.00$
Variation between lots: $v_b = 3.04$
Total variance: $v_0 = 10.04$

Using equation (3):

$$r_w = \frac{7.00}{10.04} = 0.697 \text{ or } 69.7\%$$

$$r_b = \frac{3.04}{10.04} = 0.303 \text{ or } 30.3\%$$

A study was made to check the above results. The overall variability was computed for the 100 observations where the overall average was 99.6 ohms. Table 4.2 presents the frequency distribution of the data for 100 resistors, covering the observed resistance values of each in ohms. The spread in individual values is from 93 to 106, with specified minimum and maximum values of 95 ohms and 105 ohms.

TABLE 4.2 Frequency Distribution of Data in Table 4.1
Computations of Statistics for Distribution Example of Short Form for Computations
Resistance Values in Ohms for 100 Units Selected from 10 Lots

Resistance X, ohms	Frequency Tabulation, f	No. of Freq. Defects		Computations			
		f	d	Var., y $y:m=1$	y^2	$f(y)$	$f(y^2)$
93	|	1	5	0	0	0	0
94	||||	4		1	1	4	4
95 Min.	𝍸 ||	7		2	4	14	28
96	𝍸 |||	8		3	9	24	72
97	𝍸 |	6		4	16	24	96
98	𝍸 𝍸 |||	13		5	25	65	325
99	𝍸 𝍸 |||	13		6	36	78	468
100	𝍸 ||	7		7	49	49	343
101	𝍸 |||	8		8	64	64	512
102	𝍸 𝍸 ||	12		9	81	108	972
103	𝍸 ||||	9		10	100	90	900
104	𝍸 |	6		11	121	66	726
105 Max.	||||	4		12	144	48	576
106	||	2	2	13	169	26	338
TOTAL:		100	7	Sum:		660	5360

Average, $\overline{X} = 93.00 + (1)\frac{660}{100} = 93.00 + 6.60 = 99.60$ ohms
Variance, $v_y = \frac{5360}{100} - (6.60)^2 = 53.60 - 43.56 = 10.04$
Standard Deviation, $\sigma_y = \sqrt{v_y} = \sqrt{10.04} = 3.17$; $\sigma_X = m(\sigma_y) = (1)(3.17) = 3.17$ ohms

In the table 4.2, the part showing the computations makes use of one method for reducing the computational work. Using 93 as the origin of a new scale with a scale width of $m = 1$ ohm, y values starting at 0 are assigned to the successive cells of this frequency distribution. Average and variance values are readily found using the frequencies assigned to the original distribution. Using the origin X_0 at 93.00, the cell width m (used as a multiplier of y values), and the average and variance values for y, average values and standard deviation values for X may then be calculated as shown in table 4.2. This method is especially adapted to the application of computers in determining the important statistics of any similar distribution.

Figure 4-1 shows the data and frequency distribution given in table 4.2 as a bar chart and also as a frequency polygon. Such illustrations show the relationship between the specified limits for individual resistors and the distribution resulting from the current manufacturing process. They indicate that this process has need of a monitoring control chart to aid the production manager to bring his process within narrower limits, in order not to have an excessive number of rejections.

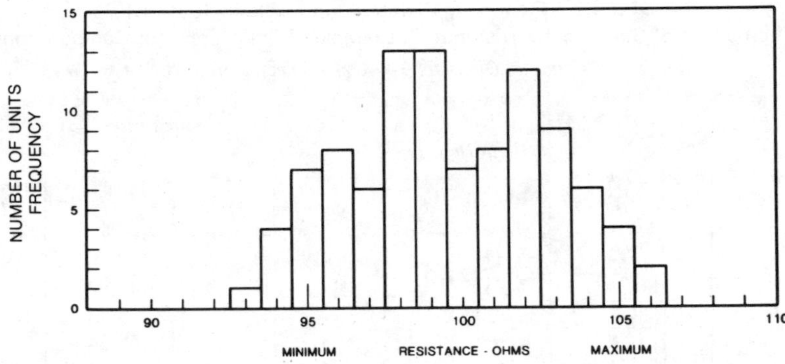

(*a*) Bar Chart or Histogram

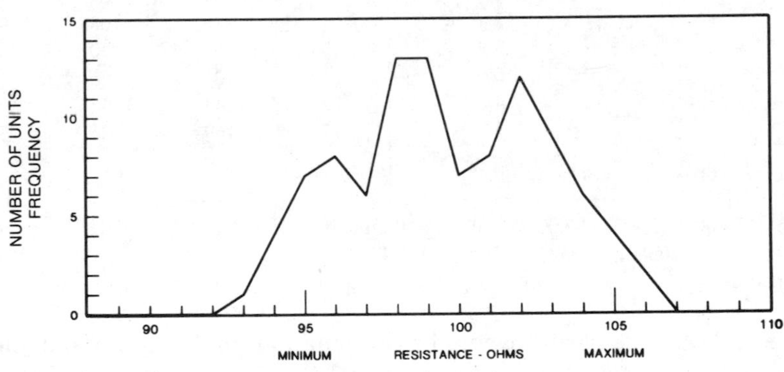

(*b*) Frequency Polygon

Figure 4–1 Bar chart and frequency polygon for 100 resistance values in Table 4–1.

Considerable time was required to compute the variances required to determine which cause contributed the most to the overall variation. Where it is desired to obtain similar results more quickly and with fewer computations, the ranges given or derived may be used. Since the sum of the ten ranges is 83, then $\bar{R}_w = \frac{83}{10} =$

8.3. These ranges may be used directly, as they are derived from ten groups having the same sample size, $n = 10$. Hence an estimate of the variability within lots is provided. These data are symmetric as there are also ten average values given, so the difference between the maximum average and the minimum average provides a range which is also based on ten values used as a measure of the variation between lots. If the sample sizes had been different, the ranges would have to be converted to standard deviations in order to be compatible, as the measures of variability should have the same common scale. The d_2 factor is the same for R_b, the range between lots, and R_w, the range within lots. For this case, the following ratios should be used.

$$r_w^* = \frac{R_w^2}{R_w^2 + R_b^2} = \frac{R_w^2}{R_0^2} \quad \text{and} \quad r_b^* = \frac{R_b^2}{R_w^2 + R_b^2} = \frac{R_b^2}{R_0^2} \tag{4}$$

Note that the range values are squared, as the ratio desired is between variances and not standard deviations. If the sample values had been different and estimates of the standard deviation were obtained, equation (3) specifies that they should be squared to obtain the ratios desired.

We can use equation (4) to evaluate the possible cause of the excessive variance experienced for these resistors. $R_b = 102.0 - 96.0 = 6.0$.

$$r_w^* = \frac{R_w^2}{(R_w^2 + R_b^2)} = \frac{(8.3)^2}{[(8.3)^2 + (6.0)^2]} = \frac{68.89}{(68.89 + 36.00)}$$

$$= \frac{68.89}{104.89} = 0.65678 \text{ or } 65.68\%$$

$$r_b^* = \frac{R_b^2}{(R_w^2 + R_b^2)} = \frac{(6.0)^2}{[(8.3)^2 + (6.0)^2]} = \frac{36.00}{(68.89 + 36.00)}$$

$$= \frac{36.00}{104.89} = 0.34322 \text{ or } 34.32\%$$

These ratios differ very little from those found from the actual variances, $r_w = 69.7\%$ and $r_b = 30.3\%$. The same conclusion is reached: The central value of this distribution is satisfactory. About two-thirds of the total variation is due to large variations that occur in a single lot or batch of resistors, which might be due to large variations in raw materials used in production. All possible causes should be studied and analyzed until the cause has been found and satisfactory corrective measures have been taken.

The conclusions reached by the above analysis are substantiated by the use of control charts. Figure 4-2 presents three control charts based on the data for resistors. In practice, only one control chart is usually made for variability. In subsequent sections, the use of these control charts is explained in detail. The first chart covers average values only. Such an average chart is supported by either a chart for ranges or one for standard deviations. The second control chart,

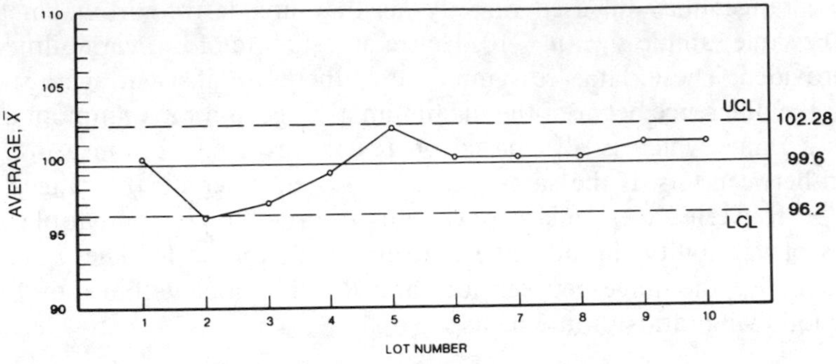

(*a*) Control Chart for Averages

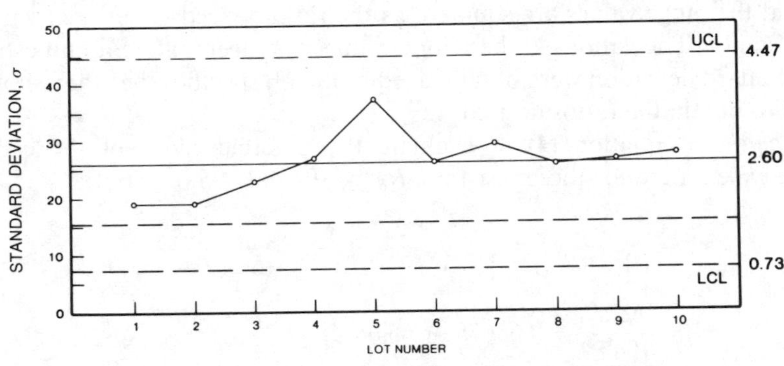

(*b*) Control Chart for Standard Deviation

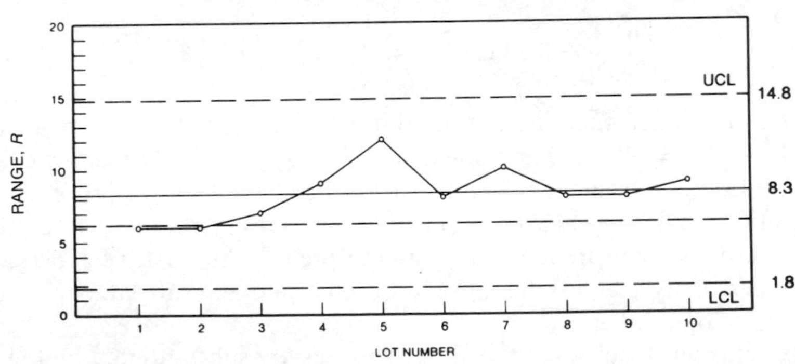

(*c*) Control Chart for Ranges

Note: Sample size is always given on control charts in industry.

Figure 4–2 Control charts based on resistance data in Table 4.1

which is slightly more efficient than the third control chart for ranges, covers computed standard deviation values. In practice either control charts for $\bar{X}$ and σ are used, or control charts for $\bar{X}$ and R are used. Figure 4-3 presents three control charts for attributes data based on these same data. Charts (*a*) and (*b*) are practically identical, since the sample sizes are equal and $n = 10$. The third chart (*c*) covers 100 individual observations.

The control charts as given in figures 4-2 and 4-3 provide the necessary information to complete the analysis of the data in the example covering resistors. A review of these charts indicates that the level given by $\bar{X} = 99.6$ is satisfactory, but that the variability is unsatisfactory. The standard deviation should be reduced to 1.70 or less for the desired $\bar{p}$ to be reduced, i.e., $\bar{p} \rightarrow 0$.

In the succeeding chapters, the detailed information presented will enable those in quality control work to set up almost all the common types of control charts used in industry. Upper control limits (UCL) and lower control limits (LCL) are derived from the standard value for the average and individual distributions as well as for either standard deviations or ranges and the measures used in the Method of Variables and the Method of Averages. Table 4.1 gives values for averages and ranges. These are shown on the control charts. Table 4.4 shows the computations of the standard deviation values plotted in figure 4-2 (*b*).

TABLE 4.3 Variances and Standard Deviation Values for Data in Table 4.1

Lot No.	*1*	*2*	*3*	*4*	*5*	*6*	*7*	*8*	*9*	*10*	*Total*
Variance: v_w	3.60	3.60	5.20	7.20	13.80	6.80	8.60	6.60	7.00	7.60	10.04
Std. Dev.: σ_w	1.90	1.90	2.28	2.68	3.71	2.61	2.93	2.57	2.65	2.76	3.17

$\bar{\sigma}_w = 2.60.$

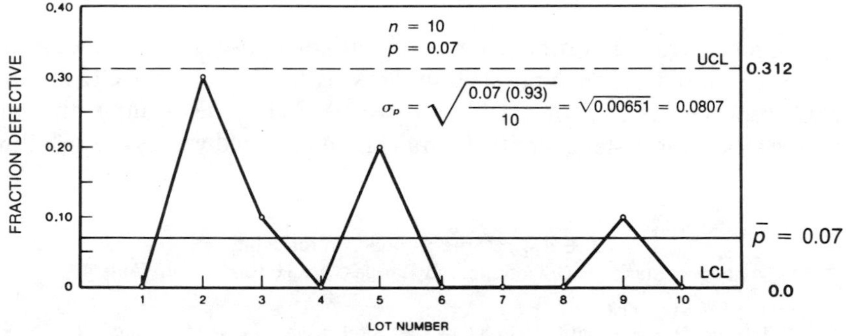

(*a*) Control Chart for Fraction Defective

Figure 4-3 Control charts for resistance data in Table 4.1.

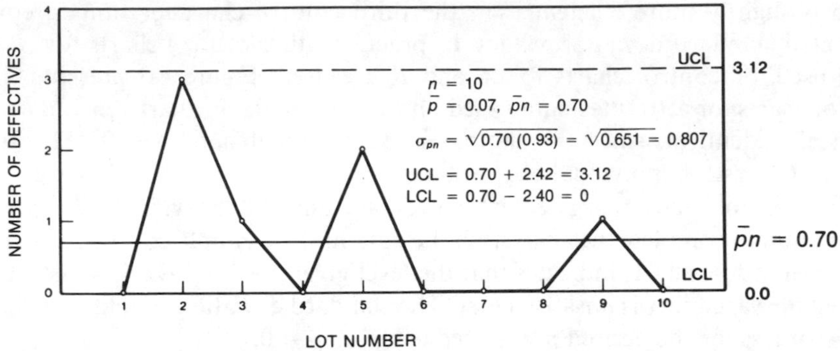

(*b*) Control Chart for Defectives

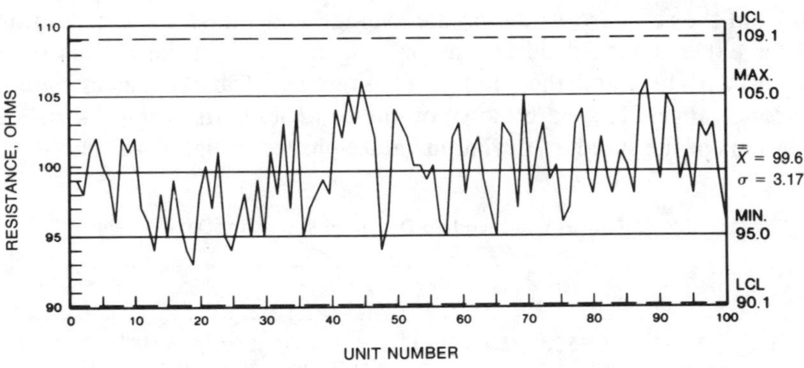

(*c*) Control Chart for Individual Units

Figure 4-3 Control charts for resistance data in Table 4.1.

The chapter covering control charts for variables discusses the factors that are to be used for different sample sizes in deriving the UCL and LCL values for all the different types of control charts. For $n = 10$ used in the example, the values of the three sets of three-sigma control limits about expected values are as follows.

TABLE 4.4 Three-Sigma Control Limits for Averages, Standard Deviations and Ranges, $n = 10$ for Data in Table 4.1

	Averages, $\bar{X}, \bar{\sigma}_w = 2.60$	*Standard Deviation*, $\sigma_w, \bar{\sigma}_w = 2.60$	*Ranges*, $R, \bar{R} = 8.3$
UCL:	$99.6 + 1.03(2.60) = 102.28$	$1.72(2.60) = 4.472$	$1.78(8.3) = 14.774$
LCL:	$99.6 - 1.03(2.60) = 96.92$	$0.28(2.60) = 0.728$	$0.22(8.3) = 1.826$

These control limits are shown in figure 4-2. Only one average, that of lot 2 (96.0), is below its lower control limit, 96.92. The cause for this low $\bar{X}$ value should be determined. However, the control charts for standard deviations and ranges are all within their control limits. Hence the results of the combined analyses for this example show that the process is 90% controlled for averages and fully controlled for variability; however, this variability is too large for the specified minimum and maximum requirements. Where customers are satisfied with a possible ten percent excessive variation in resistance values in some units, the product could be considered commercially satisfactory. Customer demands are important and in this case may be the ruling factor in forcing management to improve its process and reduce variability.

Tied in with this type of analysis for determining the cause of an excessive number of nonconforming units is the possibility of a more complete analysis by the use of the *analysis of variance* techniques. These methods are explained in detail in another chapter. Many variations of these methods are used to detect whether a significant difference between means exists from lot to lot or in manufacturing, from day to day or even from hour to hour. Some such differences may be found to exist between the different operating shifts, where more than one shift operates the manufacturing tooling. If the mean for a critical characteristic is significantly low, so that the systems or items using such a product might not operate satisfactorily, engineering must act. It must change the design and requirements to meet the demands of the customers.

Specified techniques may be applied to determine what assignable cause has been the cause of the unfavorably low values. When such an assignable cause is found by the use of these techniques, corrective measures should be taken to get the process in control at a satisfactory level. Such a cause for the example on resistors may be that the purchasing department has changed suppliers for the spools of resistance wire required in manufacturing. Or it may be that the supplier has modified his process for drawing the resistance wire or is using raw materials from different sources. Complaints from future customers are prevented by shipping no more products until the cause of the poorer quality has been found and eliminated. Modified processes will be tried and checked by either quality control charts or by some other method, such as the analysis of variance techniques. Production may again be resumed when these tests indicate that control of the process has been regained at levels desired by customers.

Another technique sponsored by some engineers, statisticians, or quality control engineers or technicians is the method of *correlation*. The details of this technique also are presented in another chapter. Checks on controls provided by correlation between some measured value and time or some other variable must be carried out in such a way as to guarantee that quality improvements are assured and may be checked by quality control charts. Trends or cycles may be a part of the manufacturing process. These should be detected by the control charts and provisions made to eliminate their recurrence.

Control charts may be used to determine whether fatigue among workers might be the cause of periodic products of poor quality. The charts may be used to evaluate the performance of various workers assigned to making such a product as the resistors. Some industries prefer to allow direct production workers to work overtime rather than hire more personnel, due to the increasing costs of fringe benefits per employee. When workers work 60 hours per week rather than the standard 40 hours, quality may suffer. Work can be rotated to reduce the fatigue factor. Work performed per hour may be plotted with control limits based on work studies. This work may be charted by persons in quality control, industrial engineering, or other personnel. In some cases, standards for such regular tasks performed in many different plants may provide standards for use with control charts. Closely allied with control charts for measuring work effectiveness is another type of sampling called *Work Sampling*.

Work sampling involves taking sample observations of performances and from this sample inferences about the percent of idle time and productive time are made. This procedure depends on obtaining truly random data over a sufficient period of time so that the evaluation is accurate and just. Industrial engineers sometimes use motion study data to evaluate work sampling inspection operations. For example, it might be found that inspectors take five minutes per unit for an effective inspection operation, whereas in another area only four minutes is used and is considered as effective as the five-minute inspection. In another study, the four-minute inspection may prove to be ineffective in reporting all the defective units that are made by the process. The results of such work studies must be carefully evaluated before valid decisions may be made as to what is the best action to take to obtain the most efficient system of testing and inspection. Control charts aid in making these decisions effective.

4.5 Fundamental Basis of Control Charts

Control chart techniques are effective because their basis is fundamentally sound. Dr. Walter A. Shewhart and his associates conducted many experiments to test their theories. Three fundamental experiments were conducted covering three different universes from which random samples were drawn. These represented a large number of units produced by a definite manufacturing process or parts that were turned out by an automatic process. The distribution of such units with respect to their most important characteristics will assume some form of a frequency distribution. Many will be essentially normal. Values selected at random from such processes when checked for goodness of fit by the Chi-square distribution against a theoretical normal law distribution, with the same mean and variance, will be found to have a high probability of fit.

Dr. Shewhart selected three distinctly different universes for his experiments. These were respectively (1) a normal distribution; (2) a rectangular distribution; and (3) a right triangular distribution. The statistics obtained are tabulated in Appendix II of Dr. Shewhart's text, *Economic Control of Quality of Manufactured*

Product. Many other texts also discuss these results. These distinctly different universes simulate those expected to be used and realized in industrial operations, as well as in clerical work. It was found in all cases that the distributions of averages closely approximated the normal law curve; hence normal law theory developed with many functional applicable tables over many years could be applied to control chart theory. Central values are established as goals. Control charts help maintain those goals.

Normal law probabilities associated with two-sigma and three-sigma control limits were used, respectively, as controls by manufacturing and by the staff. These probability values were assumed to be approximately the same as would be obtained from a theoretical normal law curve and are, respectively, 95.45% or 0.9545 for control limits using twice the standard deviation about the mean, and 99.73% or 0.9973 for control limits based upon three times the standard deviation placed about the mean. These two types of control limits proved to be very satisfactory. Processes seem to vary more with respect to level or central value than with respect to variability. Time and experience have shown that over the past fifty years such control charts have proven to be very effective in controlling the quality of many diversified events, such as manufactured products and parts or clerical errors. The only drawback is that many industries could profit by using control charts, but do not use them. Costs of many items would be much less if these statistical techniques were used in more industries and areas.

Control charts have been used very effectively with attributes data. Based on normal law probabilities, the decision to look for assignable causes when an observed average value is outside its proper control limit based on three-sigma limits means that possibly one time in three hundred no assignable cause will be found. For two-sigma limits, this possible error might be one time in twenty. When standard deviation values for distributions other than averages are used, it is necessary to know approximately how valid the assumed probability value of 0.9973 is in practice, particularly for attributes data.

The typical distribution pattern for the normal law is shown in figure 4-4. Such a distribution occurs very frequently in the various industrial practices. Variable characteristics for medicines, foods, textiles, and electrical and mechanical equipment and apparatus often assume this form. Dr. Shewhart and his associates made a distribution of chips marked with numerical values indicating their location on such a normal distribution. Figure 4-4 shows what might be termed *percentile points,* indicating what proportion of this area might occur within any selected range of values in terms of standard deviation (or σ) units. This chart was selected from a quality control procedure covering production where the pertinent statistics: (1) sample size n, (2) average $\overline{X}$, and (3) standard deviation for a particular item or characteristic may be recorded. In the Shewhart experiment, successive samples of $n = 4, 8, 12, 16, 20$, and 24, respectively, were obtained and a sufficient number of average values were obtained and checked for normality to demonstrate that the distribution of averages even for as small a sample size as four was found to be normal.

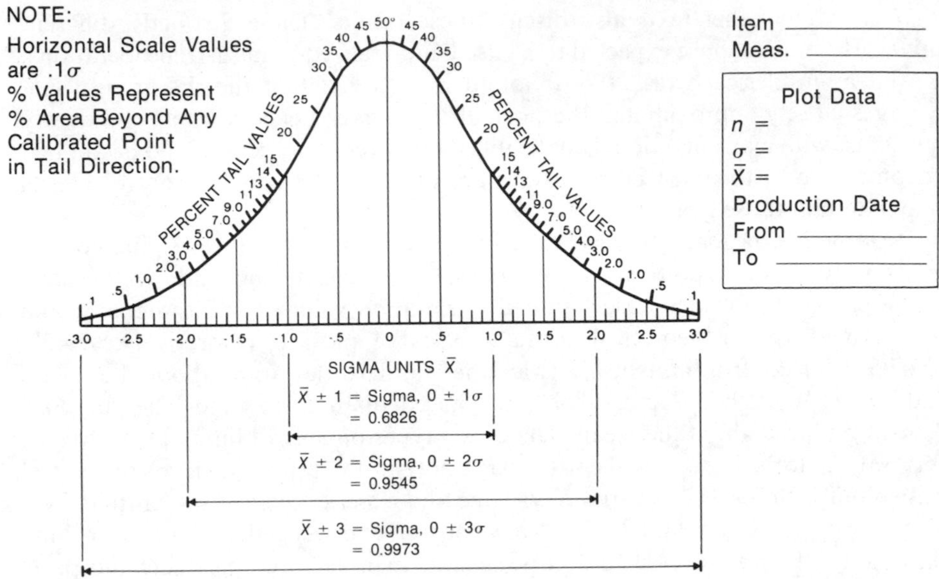

Figure 4–4 Normal distribution: probabilities for control limits based on areas under curve between designated limits.

The experiment was carried out for two non-normal distributions. Figure 4-5 shows these two possible typical universes. Figure 4-5(*a*) is a rectangular distribution while figure 4-5(*b*) is a right triangular distribution. Universes consisting of marked chips were prepared to simulate these two distributions and also samples of 4, 8, 12, 16, 20, and 24 units were drawn at random from each of these non-normal distributions. Even the distributions of averages for $n = 4$ units for each of these distributions were found to be normal. This information substantiated the control chart feature that normal law probability values may be used as a basis for statistical quality charts for averages as well as for other parameters such as the standard deviation, range, median, fraction defective, and number of defects per unit. The standard deviation for averages for samples of size n as shown previously is $\sigma/\sqrt{n}$. For most cases, the empirical choice of the control limits that should be used regularly has been established as three-sigma limits, as shown in figure 4-4, when production is well-controlled and the resultant product is essentially uniform (or *homogeneous*) and when such a system of causes has production patterns that are similar to the pattern depicted by the normal law. The shape of the distribution is symmetric and bell-shaped. Checks may be made to determine the probability that the normal law distributions best represent such distributions. How to make such checks for goodness of fit by use of Chi-square is given in detail later. It suffices here to know that such tests exist and may be used when it is necessary to know to what extent normal law theory and numerical values providing probability values for estimates of degree of conformance, fraction defective, or

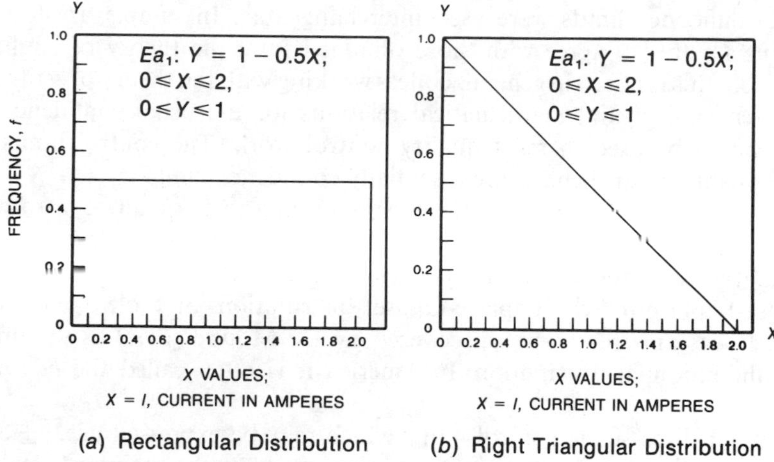

(*a*) Rectangular Distribution (*b*) Right Triangular Distribution

Figure 4–5 Method of variables—two non-normal universes.

other characteristics may be determined. These probability values are the areas under the normal law distribution for the range of $z = X/\sigma$ values found for any specific problem and are not the corresponding ordinate values. Ordinate values are used to draw the curve, whereas the area values provide the applicable probability values. In this text, only tables given area values for the normal law distribution are given. When constructing a normal law curve for a group of measurements, $\bar{X}$ and σ values are computed for these data, and for a set of equal cells the normal law area in each segment is determined from this normal law table of areas. These are the same as given in advanced texts providing a table of ordinates for the normal law. A check may be made by consulting such ordinate tables.

The system of causes operates in a random fashion resulting in a normal distribution such that the averages of samples from such a production system or universe will stay within their three-sigma control limits 99.73% of the time as shown in figure 4-4. This 99.73% or 0.9973 is termed the *degree of belief* or *confidence coefficient* and is derived from the area under a normal law distribution between the plus and minus three-sigma control limit boundaries for the range, $\bar{X} \pm 3\sigma_{\bar{X}}$. The degree of belief concept expresses the intensity of belief in the truth that the product manufactured under statistical control will stay within the confidence limits specified. These limits might be the usual three-sigma control limit values, or might be some other control limits associated with some other probability value. Thus two-sigma limits as in figure 4-4, the normal distribution, have associated with these limits a confidence value of 0.9545.

Other types of control limits may be met in practice. In 1930, R. A. Fisher introduced the concept of a *fiduciary distribution,* which is not a probability distribution in the customary sense but is derived from the distribution of estimates containing all the relevant information in the samples. In many cases, these two kinds of confidence limits were used interchangeably. In sample areas, results from fiduciary theory agree with those obtained from the theory of confidence intervals, but this is not so in general. Unless working with the theory of estimation, the simpler concept and mathematical relations for the usual confidence level derived should be used in most quality control work. The control limits used for most quality control charts are essentially confidence limits.

Since normal law theory and tables are used primarily in quality control work, those working in this field should become familiar with normal law theory. In continental writings, the distribution is often known as the Gaussian, the Laplacian, the Gause-Laplace (or the Laplace-Gause) distribution, or the Second Law of Laplace. It was apparently first discovered by De Moivre (1756) as the limiting form of the binomial distribution. In America it is often called the *bell-shaped curve*.

The usual three-sigma control limits which may be expressed as $\overline{X} \pm 3\sigma$ are also applied to statistics other than averages, such as the standard deviation, range, fraction defective, number of defects or defectives, etc., as noted previously.

Some control chart engineers would like to set definite probability values, such as 98% or 90%, on this confidence level or degree of belief. Such exact probability values will differ from case to case, as the system of causes in effect results in values which may or may not be truly random variables. Most quality control personnel should be satisfied to know that as a result of statistical studies, where three-sigma control limits are used, these limits will always contain within their upper and lower control limits at least $1 - 1/(3)^2 = 1 - 1/9 = 8/9 = 0.8889$ or 88.89% of the distribution. This is based on the Bienaymé-Tchebycheff Inequality derived by Bienaymé in the middle of the nineteenth century. It is a special case of the more general Tchebycheff Inequality. In simple language, this inequality says that "the probability that a variate will differ from the mean by more than t times its standard deviation is at most $1/t^2$ for any probability distribution." This means that the usual three-sigma control limits may be applied without any reservations. This is further verified by the consistent successes that have been achieved by their use.

4.6 Probabilities Associated with 3σ (Three-Sigma) Control Limits for Attributes

The control limits for attributes data are usually associated with three basic relations. Two of these involve no definite lot or batch size and assume that, for all practical purposes, the number of potential units in the universe or parent population is essentially infinite. ($N = \infty$.) These two are the *p binomial* and the *Poisson exponential.* The third distribution is called the *hypergeometric,* in which the lot size N is a basic part of the relation used to determine this probability distribution; hence, the universe is considered to be finite and must be described.

Advanced texts should be consulted if the complete theory behind these three relations is to be studied. The following numerical proofs should be sufficient to show the validity of control charts for such distributions.

p Binomial, $(q + p)^n$

This frequency function gives the probabilities of the occurrence of 0 through n successes when the probability of a success is p and the number of observations is n. The best measure of the central value is called p-bar ($\bar{p}$) and is exactly the p value used in the function. This $\bar{p}$ value is the expected value. It is often selected as the value at which the producer strives to maintain the product. The best measure of the variability or dispersion of this distribution is its standard deviation.

$$\sigma_p = \sqrt{\frac{p(1 - p)}{n}} \tag{5}$$

The theoretical derivation of this relation using general symbols is presented in more advanced texts. In the example below, it will be shown that this relation holds for several cases. This presentation has the advantage of making it possible to see how closely the probability of 0.9973 for the area under a normal law curve that applies to three-sigma control limits for averages is approximated by corresponding three-sigma control limits for p. If it is found that the difference is too great, then a multiplier of the standard deviation other than three might be selected to obtain the desired confidence level of 98%, 99%, or 99.73%, where possible. Since an integral number of defects or nonconforming units occur and their corresponding p values are $0/n$, $1/n$, $2/n$, ... n/n, the boundaries used to determine exact areas under the p distribution under discussion will be $-0.5/n$, $0.5/n$, $1.5/n$, $2.5/n$, etc. This makes the addition of the frequencies relatively easy. In obtaining these cumulative probabilities, it is easier to use the distribution of defects or nonconforming units d which is equal to pn. Then the boundaries for counting cumulative frequencies are -0.5, 0.5, 1.5, 2.5, ... $n - 0.5$, $n + 0.5$.

Tables for the binomial which have been computed and printed in the past fifty years are now available. The first one, covering n values from 1 to 50 in steps of one with p values from 0 to 1.00 in steps of 0.01, was derived from the Incomplete Beta function. Entering a table for terms of this function by using proper derived entries provides desired binomial probabilities. This is a government publication[1] and is readily available. An extension of this table[2] is one using n values from 50 to 100 in steps of five units with p values from 0 to 1.00 in steps of 0.01. Many texts give special tables for selected ranges of n and p values. Some tables give values for the coefficients of the binomial so that one may readily compute special cases by the use of logarithms. Computer libraries often have a large number of binomial distributions available for use that may not be in tables.

The p binomial distribution is used as a probability density function by having $q = 1 - p$, so that $q + p = 1$. Its terms are given by the following relation.

$$(q + p)^n = \sum_{m=0}^{n} C_m^n (1 - p)^{n-m} p^m = \sum_{m=0}^{n} C_m^n q^{n-m} p^m$$

$$= q^n + \frac{n}{1!} q^{n-1} p^1 + \frac{n(n-1)}{2!} q^{n-2} p^2 + \frac{n(n-1)(n-2)}{3!} q^{n-3} p^3 + \cdots + p^n, \quad (6)$$

where $C_m^n = \dfrac{n!}{m!(n-m)!}$, and $n! = n(n-1)(n-2)(n-3)\ldots 3\cdot 2\cdot 1$

The following examples show that the expected values for the average and standard deviation are given by the theoretical relations for these parameters. Note that this discussion involves true values for these measures for the binomial; hence, they are called *parameters*. If the same measures were derived from a series of sample results, they would be only approximations to the true values and would be called *statistics*. The symbol for the expected value of the central value for fraction defective for the universe or population is p'. The corresponding relation for the true standard deviation value is given by equation (5) as $\sigma'_p = \sqrt{\dfrac{p'(1 - p')}{n}}$. The prime (′) notation is used to designate the true values. When these measures are expressed in terms of defects or defectives directly, the expected value for the central value is expressed by the symbol pn. Some texts like to use the symbol c for this term, since the binomial is used to obtain the control limits for c. The corresponding theoretical relation for the standard deviation for the number of defects or defectives is given below.

$$\sigma'_{pn} = \sqrt{p'n(1 - p')}. \quad (7)$$

Example 2 Using exact frequency values derived from equation (6) for a $\bar{p}$ value of 0.10 or 10% and a sample size of $n = 5$, use direct computation to derive values of the average and standard deviation for the binomial distribution, where $\bar{q} = 1 - \bar{p} = 0.90$ or 90%. The symbol $\bar{p}$ denotes the process average as derived from data obtained in samples. For these values, the tabulation below shows exactly how these theoretical frequencies are obtained for the number of successes, X and fraction defective, $p = X/n$. Using equation (6), the frequency for each successive term of the p binomial is derived below in detail. These values could be read from a p binomial table but for large values of n, such as those values greater than 100, no tables are generally available. Any frequencies needed for determining exact control limits or for checking the efficiency of the inspection system may be determined in the same manner as shown in these computations.

TABLE 4.5 Example 2: $n = 5$, $\bar{p} = 0.10$, $\bar{q} = 1 - \bar{p} = 0.90$

P_0 = probability of 0 successes	$\bar{q}^5$	$(0.9)^5 = 0.59049$
P_1 = probability of 1 success	$5\bar{q}^4\bar{p}$	$5(0.9)^4(0.1)^1 = 0.32805$
P_2 = probability of 2 successes	$10\bar{q}^3\bar{p}^2$	$10(0.9)^3(0.1)^2 = 0.07290$
P_3 = probability of 3 successes	$10\bar{q}^2\bar{p}^3$	$10(0.9)^2(0.1)^3 = 0.00810$
P_4 = probability of 4 successes	$5\bar{q}^1\bar{p}^4$	$5(0.9)^1(0.1)^4 = 0.00045$
P_5 = probability of 5 successes	$\bar{p}^5$	$(0.1)^5 = 0.00001$
		Total 1.00000

The p binomial is a discrete frequency distribution, not a continuous frequency distribution. The latter occurs under the Method of Variables rather than the Method of Attributes. There are general theoretical values for the average value for the p binomial and also for the variance and, correspondingly, its standard deviation. We will illustrate these theoretical relations with the following computations.[3]

$$\text{Average:} \quad \bar{X} = \frac{\Sigma X_i}{n} \quad \text{or} \quad \bar{X} = \frac{\Sigma f_i(X_i)}{\Sigma f_i} \tag{8}$$

$$\text{Variance:} \quad v_X = \frac{\Sigma(X_i - \bar{X})^2}{n} \quad \text{or} \quad v_X = \frac{\Sigma f_i(X_i - \bar{X})^2}{\Sigma f_i} \tag{9}$$

$$v_X = \frac{\Sigma X_i^2}{n} - \bar{X}^2 \quad \text{or} \quad v_X = \frac{\Sigma f_i(X_c)^2}{\Sigma f_i} - \bar{X}^2 \tag{10}$$

$$\text{Standard deviation:} \quad \sigma_X = \sqrt{v_X} = \sqrt{\frac{\Sigma(X_i - \bar{X})^2}{n}} = \sqrt{\frac{\Sigma f X_i^2}{\Sigma f_i} - \bar{X}^2} \tag{11}$$

In this example, X denotes the number of successes, n denotes the number of observations, and $p = X/n$ denotes the fraction defective corresponding to X.

TABLE 4.6 p Binomial for $p = 0.10$ and $n = 5$

Number of Successes X	*Theoretical Frequency* f	*Fraction Defective* p	*Computations* $f(X)$	$f(X^2)$	$f(p)$	$f(p^2)$
0	0.59049	0	0	0	0	0
1	0.32805	0.20	0.32805	0.32805	0.065610	0.0131220
2	0.07290	0.40	0.14580	0.29160	0.029160	0.0116640
3	0.00810	0.60	0.02430	0.07290	0.004860	0.0029160
4	0.00045	0.80	0.00180	0.00720	0.000360	0.0002880
5	0.00001	1.00	0.00005	0.00025	0.000010	0.0000100
Sum	1.00000		0.50000	0.70000	0.100000	0.0280000

(a) Statistical information for number of successes, X:

Average, $\bar{X}$ or $\bar{p}n = \frac{\Sigma f_i(X_i)}{\Sigma f_i} = \frac{0.5}{1} = 0.5$, which checks with $pn = 0.1 \times 5 = 0.5$.

Variance, v_X or $\sigma_{pn}^2 = \frac{\Sigma f_i(X_i^2)}{\Sigma f_i} - \bar{X}^2 = \frac{0.7}{1} - (0.5)^2 = 0.70 - 0.25 = 0.45$.

Standard deviation, $\sigma_{pn} = \sqrt{v_X} = \sqrt{0.45} = 0.6708$, which checks with theoretical value, $\sigma_{pn} = \sqrt{pn(1-p)} = \sqrt{0.5(0.9)} = \sqrt{0.45} = 0.6708$.

(b) Statistics for fraction defective, p:

Average or expected value, $\bar{p} = \frac{\Sigma f_i(p)}{\Sigma f_i} = \frac{0.10}{1.0} = 0.10$, which checks with $\bar{p} = 0.10$.

Variance, v_p or $\sigma_p^2 = \frac{\Sigma f_i(p^2)}{\Sigma f_i} - \bar{p}^2 = \frac{0.028}{1.0} - (0.1)^2 = 0.0280 - 0.0100 = 0.0180$.

Standard deviation, $\sigma_p = \sqrt{\frac{\bar{p}(1-\bar{p})}{n}} = \sqrt{0.0180} = 0.1342$, which checks with the theoretical value above for v_p since $\sigma_p = \sqrt{v_p} = \sqrt{0.0180} = 0.1342$.

The example above checks exactly the theoretical relations and shows that they may be used at all times. Another example which follows shows how to use the available binomial tables for obtaining the probabilities required in the applications of quality control to production and inspection problems.

TABLE 4.7 p Binomial for $\bar{p} = 0.05$, $n = 20$ and $\bar{p}n = 1.00$

Number of Successes X	*Theoretical Frequency* f	*Computations* X^2	$f(X)$	$f(X^2)$
0	0.3584859	0	0	0
1	0.3773536	1	0.3773536	0.3773536
2	0.1886768	4	0.3773536	0.7547072
3	0.0595822	9	0.1787466	0.5362398
4	0.0133276	16	0.0533104	0.2132416
5	0.0022446	25	0.0112230	0.0561150
6	0.0002954	36	0.0017724	0.0106344
7	0.0000310	49	0.0002170	0.0015190
8	0.0000027	64	0.0000216	0.0001728
9	0.0000002	81	0.0000018	0.0000162
Sum	1.0000000		1.0000000	1.9499996

Average, $\bar{X} = \frac{\Sigma f_i X_i}{\Sigma f_i} = \frac{1.0000}{1.0000} = 1.0000$.

Variance, $v_X = \frac{\Sigma f_i(X_i^2)}{\Sigma f_i} - \bar{X}^2 = \frac{1.9499996}{1.0000} - (1.00)^2$

$= 1.9500 - 1.0000 = 0.9500$

Standard Deviation, $\sigma_X = \sqrt{v_X} = \sqrt{0.9500} = 0.9747$

Theoretical Values:
Average, $\bar{p}n = 0.05(20) = 1.0000$
Variance, $v_{pn} = \bar{p}n(1 - \bar{p}) = 1.00(0.95) = 0.9500$
Standard Deviation, $\sigma_{pn} = \sqrt{v_{pn}} = \sqrt{0.9500} = 0.9747$

Example 3 Example 2 used a small value of n. In this example, the sample size n is 20, a value often used in industry in many inspections of small lots. The percent defective value of 5.0% is commonly used in practice, hence it was selected as p; the fraction defective, $p = 0.05$, is one that many working students will find used where they work in industry. The theoretical frequencies of occurrences of $X = 0, 1, 2, \ldots, n$ defects or defectives, often denoted as d, are taken from the previously mentioned Bureau of Standards, *Table of the Binomial Probability Distribution.* In this example and example 4, where $n = 100$, the number of defects or defectives, $d = X$, is covered rather than the observed fraction defective, $p = X/n$.

Example 4 Using the parameters $n = 100$ and $p = 0.02$ or 2.0%, use a p binomial table to obtain the probabilities for the successive occurrences of 0 through 100 successes as determined from the p binomial relation. These probabilities provide the frequencies for obtaining defective units in inspection in a series of random samples, each containing exactly 100 units, when such samples are selected from a product containing 0.02 fraction defective units, considered as being 2.0% defective. Using these frequencies, determine the expected or average value for the number of defectives per sample and the variance and standard deviation values for this probability frequency distribution, called the p binomial. Show that these computed values agree exactly with values determined from the general theoretical relations usually used.

Solution Equation (6) in this chapter gives the relation that should be used to compute the probabilities required in example 4. However, the probabilities may also be read directly from the *50–100 Binomial Tables,* by Harry G. Romig, which was mentioned earlier. Values are given to 6 decimal places and are listed below, together with the computations requested. In this tabulation, X values are given only to $X = 12$, as the probability for 12 is only 0.000001. Values exist for X as large as 100 but its probability value is $(0.02)^{100}$, which is a very small value. Equations (8), (10), and (11) are used to determine the values for the average, variance, and standard deviation for this p binomial distribution. These results should check with the values determined by the theoretical values:

Average $= \bar{p}n$;
Variance $= \bar{p}n(1 - \bar{p})$; and
Standard deviation $= \sqrt{\bar{p}n(1 - \bar{p})}$.

TABLE 4.8 *p* Binomial for $n = 100$ and $\bar{p} = 0.02$

Success X	Theoretical Frequency f	Computations	
		$f(X)$	$f(X^2)$
0	0.132620	0	0
1	0.270652	0.270652	0.270652
2	0.273414	0.546828	1.093656
3	0.182276	0.546828	1.640484
4	0.090208	0.360832	1.443328
5	0.035347	0.176735	0.883675
6	0.011422	0.068532	0.411192
7	0.003130	0.021910	0.153370
8	0.000743	0.005944	0.047552
9	0.000155	0.001395	0.012555
10	0.000029	0.000290	0.002900
11	0.000005	0.000055	0.000605
12	0.000001	0.000012	0.000144
Sum	1.000002	2.000013	5.960113

$$\text{Average, } \bar{X} = \frac{\Sigma f_i(X_i)}{\Sigma f_i} = \frac{2.0000}{1.0000} = 2.0000.$$

$$\text{Variance, } v_{pn} \text{ or } v_X \; \frac{\Sigma f_i(X_i^2)}{\Sigma f_i} - \bar{X}^2 = \frac{5.9601}{1.0000} - (2.00)^2$$

$$= 5.9600 - 4.0000 = 1.9600.$$

Standard Deviation, σ_X or $\sigma_{pn} = \sqrt{v_X} = \sqrt{1.9600} = 1.40.$

Theoretical Values:

Average, $\bar{p}n = 0.02(100) = 2.00$, which agrees with Average above.

Variance, $v_{pn} = \bar{p}n(1 - \bar{p}) = 2.00(0.98) = 1.9600.$

Standard Deviation, $\sigma_{pn} = \sqrt{\bar{p}n(1 - \bar{p})} = \sqrt{1.9600} = 1.40.$

All computed values agree with the theoretical values as shown in this example.

Poisson's Exponential Binomial Limit, $\dfrac{e^{-pn}(pn)^m}{m!}$

Control limits can be established for many industrial cases using the Poisson exponential. To do this, it is necessary to determine what probabilities are associated with the use of three-sigma control limits. Will these confidence levels be similar to the 0.9973 associated with the normal law three-sigma control limits? An example is provided to show how to use the Poisson exponential in practice.

The Poisson exponential may often be used as an approximate relation for the p binomial or the hypergeometric distribution. Also many distributions, such as those for rubber-covered wire, are essentially the Poisson exponential. It is used as the basis for control charts for two slightly different cases:

1. Defects per unit, such as in the number of defects occurring on an electric appliance such as a toaster, refrigerator, washing machine, dryer, automatic razor, automobile, or furnace; and
2. Defects per quantities of material or product, such as in the number of insulation breakdowns along the surfaces of 100 feet of rubber-covered wire, the number of surface defects on a valuable piece of furniture, the number of large checks on units of plywood, plastic sheets, or steel plate. For these cases neither p nor n is known, but their product pn is measurable for measurable quantities such as a square yard of carpet.

Theoretically, the parameters utilized for the above distribution are:

1. *Expected value or average,* designated as $\bar{p}n$ or $\overline{pn}$ and sometimes designated as $a = pn$ or even x, as used in many tables;
2. *Variance,* sometimes designated as v_{pn}, or in the same manner as the average, $\bar{p}n$ or $\overline{pn}$; and
3. *Standard deviation,* designated as σ_{pn}, the square root of the variance v_{pn}. Usually it is written as $\sqrt{pn}$; it is actually $\sqrt{v_{pn}}$.

Tables of this distribution are available in many books of statistical tables and also in many texts covering statistics, quality control, and similar areas of knowledge. The best is E. C. Molina's tables, *Poisson's Exponential Limit: Table I—Individual Terms,* and *Table II—Cumulated Terms,* which was mentioned earlier.

The frequencies for the occurrences of $0, 1, 2, \ldots, n$ may be read from such tables. Theoretically, an infinite number of occurrences is the last term of this distribution, but actually, probabilities listed in tables soon are found to be less than 0.0000001 and hence are too small to have meaning for the larger values of X.

Example 5 Let the number of observed values for defects per unit on a product such as a tank or a complex electronic unit of equipment, a rope, or wire wound on spools be 0.05. Hence $pn = 0.05$. It is obvious that the expected value is pn, but the derivation of the variance (pn) and consequently the standard deviation $(\sqrt{pn})$ must be substantiated. If no tables are available giving the frequencies for this distribution, they may be computed term by term from the relation:

$$P_{m,pn} = \frac{e^{-pn}(pn)^m}{m!}, \tag{12}$$

where $0! = 1$, and $e^{-x} = 1 - x/1! + x^2/2! - x^3/3! + x^4/4! - \cdots$. pn may be substituted for x when computing its value in e^{-pn}. Such values may also be determined from the logarithms of e^{-x} in table 2.1. Although the x values have a range of integral values from zero to infinity, the tabulated values of computed probabilities are given in Molina's tables to only seven places for

pn values of 0.40 or less and to six places in the balance of the tables. This reduces the range of X values. For example, the greatest range is from 55 to 150, inclusive, for $pn = 100$. The X values covered by six- or seven-place probability values are nine or less for pn values that are less than 1.00. Table 4.9 starts with pn values of 0.001, then covers pn values from 0.010 to 0.40 in steps of 0.01, pn values 0.40 to 15.0 in steps of 0.1, and higher pn values to 100 in steps of 1. Throughout this text, use of proper tables is emphasized, as they save hours of laborious computations by hand.

The solution for example 5 is provided in the following tabulation, which gives the usual mathematical derivation of the expected or average value, the variance, and the standard deviation for the theoretical frequencies of the X values for which seven-place probabilities of occurrence exist for the Poisson exponential when $\overline{pn} = 0.05$.

TABLE 4.9 Poisson's Exponential Limit: $\dfrac{e^{-pn}(pn)^X}{X!}$ for $\bar{p}n$ or $\overline{pn} = 0.05$

Number of Successes X	*Theoretical Frequency* f	*Computations*	
		$f(X)$	$f(X^2)$
0	0.9512294	0	0
1	0.0475615	0.0475615	0.0475615
2	0.0011890	0.0023780	0.0047560
3	0.0000198	0.0000594	0.0001782
4	0.0000002	0.0000008	0.0000032
Sum	0.9999999	0.0499997	0.0524989
USE	1.0000	0.0500	0.0525

NOTE: In the cases below values are rounded to four decimal places. Computed statistical values provide a check against the theoretical values for the parameters of this distribution.

Expected Value:

$$\text{Average, } \bar{X} = \frac{\Sigma f_i(X_i)}{\Sigma f_i} = \frac{0.0500}{1.000} = 0.0500$$

Measures of Variability or Dispersion:

$$\text{Variance, } v_X = \frac{\Sigma f_i(X_i^2)}{\Sigma f_i} - \bar{X}^2 = \frac{0.0525}{1.0000} - (0.05)^2$$

$$= 0.0525 - 0.0025 = 0.0500$$

$$\text{Standard Deviation, } \sigma_X = \sqrt{v_X} = \sqrt{0.0500} = 0.2236$$

Theoretical Values:
Expected Value, Average, $\overline{pn} = 0.0500$
Variance, $\overline{pn} = 0.0500$
Standard Deviation, $\sigma_{pn} = \sqrt{\overline{pn}} = \sqrt{0.0500} = 0.2236$

The values obtained by mathematical computations for the parameters, average, variance, and standard deviation, agree exactly with the theoretical values. Theoretical values may be used in most cases. Computations need only be made when the distribution seems to differ markedly from the one assumed, such as the p binomial, the Poisson exponential, or normal law.

Example 5 shows a very skewed distribution, with a probability of 0.95 that no nonconforming units will be observed in the sample. Another example is given which covers a more representative value of pn that appears to exist in a large number of production processes where this probability distribution function applies. Example 6 covers a pn value of 3.9. This value of pn is used in many inspection areas where the sampling plans used are based on the concept of lot protection. When pn is 3.9, the "allowable number of defects in sample" or acceptance number c is 1, the probability of the occurrence of 0 or 1 in a sample of n units is read from the Poisson exponential table as: $P_0 + P_1 = 0.020242 + 0.078943 = 0.099185$. This is very close to the P_C value of 0.10 stipulated as the desired consumer's risk for a product of lot tolerance percent defective (LTPD) quality. This special p value is often designated as p_t. If the LTPD desired is 5.0% or 0.05, then, since pn is 3.9, the possible sample size would be $n = 3.9/0.05 = 78$, which might be rounded to 80. The single sampling plan thus determined would be $n = 80$ and $c = 1$.

If the single sampling plan noted above were applied to Vendor A in the receiving inspection area, when more than one defect was noted in the random sample of eighty units upon inspection, the lot from which the sample was selected would be rejected. If, in addition, the purchaser desired to make certain that product thus received was made under statistically controlled conditions at a level of 0.5% or 0.005 fraction defective, a control chart using three-sigma limits might be added as an additional quality-protection device. As will be shown in detail in the next chapter, these control limits would be: $\bar{p}n \pm 3\sqrt{\bar{p}n} = 0.005(80) \pm 3\sqrt{0.005(80)} = 0.40 \pm 3(0.63)$. The upper control limit (UCL) is $0.40 + 1.89 = 2.29$ defects; the lower control limit (LCL) is $0.40 - 1.89$ or 0.[4] More than two defects in sample denotes lack of control.

Example 6 Check the theoretical parameters for the Poisson exponential distribution by actual mathematical calculations for $\overline{pn} = 3.9$. For this expected value or average, the theoretical variance is $\overline{pn} = 3.9$ and the standard deviation is $\sigma_{pn} = \sqrt{\overline{pn}} = \sqrt{3.9} = 1.975$.

TABLE 4.10 Poisson's Exponential Limit: $\dfrac{e^{-pn}(pn)^X}{X!}$ for $\overline{pn}$ or $\overline{pn} = 3.9$

Number of Successes X	*Theoretical Frequency* f	*Computations* $f(X)$	$f(X^2)$
0	0.020242	0	0
1	0.078943	0.078943	0.078943
2	0.153940	0.307880	0.615760
3	0.200122	0.600366	1.801098
4	0.195119	0.780476	3.121904
5	0.152193	0.760965	3.804825
6	0.098925	0.593550	3.561300
7	0.055115	0.385805	2.700635
8	0.026869	0.214952	1.719616
9	0.011643	0.104787	0.943083
10	0.004541	0.045410	0.454100
11	0.001610	0.017710	0.194810
12	0.000523	0.006276	0.075312
13	0.000157	0.002041	0.026533
14	0.000044	0.000616	0.008624
15	0.000011	0.000165	0.002475
16	0.000003	0.000048	0.000768
17	0.000001	0.000017	0.000289
Sum	1.000001	3.900007	19.110075

Expected Value:

$$\text{Average, } \bar{X} = \frac{\Sigma f_i(X_i)}{\Sigma f_i} = \frac{3.9000}{1.000} = 3.90$$

Measure of Variability:

$$\text{Variance, } v_X = \frac{\Sigma f_i(X_i^2)}{\Sigma f_i} - \bar{X}^2 = \frac{19.1100}{1.00} - (3.9)^2$$

$$= 19.1100 - 15.2100 = 3.9000.$$

$$\text{Standard Deviation, } \sigma_X = \sqrt{v_X} = \sqrt{3.9000} = 1.975$$

These computed values for the average, variance, and standard deviation agree exactly with the theoretical values given above.

Hypergeometric, $\dfrac{C_{n-m}^{N-M} C_m^M}{C_n^N}$

When applying the Method of Attributes, samples are generally assumed to have been selected from a theoretically infinite universe or population. The relations have no N value in the factors included in their evaluation. However, many times the lot sizes submitted for acceptance or rejection or the product made on a systematic basis consist of only a small number of units, and the universe from which samples are selected is finite. Where the N value is 100 or less, the exact relation is often called the hypergeometric; all the ways in which a sample of n units may be selected from a small-sized lot containing exactly N units is considered and the number of nonconforming units is postulated to be $p_t N = M$ defects or defectives. The probability of observing exactly m nonconforming units in the sample of n units is given by the following relation, taking into account the possible ways of obtaining conforming units and the number of possible ways of obtaining nonconforming units.

$$P_{m,n;M,N} = \frac{C_{n-m}^{N-M} C_m^M}{C_n^N} \tag{13}$$

Where the manufacturing process is essentially continuous, for ease of handling, because units are very costly, or, for some other similar valid reason, the lots submitted are small, then such lots of N units each may be assumed to have come from a universe with a process average of $\bar{p}$ under controlled conditions. The distribution of nonconforming units M in lots of size N will be a p binomial distribution with possible M values from 0 to N in integral steps. Where a sample of size n is drawn at random from these lots of size N, then by the use of equation (13), the hypergeometric—the probability of getting exactly c nonconforming units in the sample of n units—may be computed for each possible M value. Such successive probabilities multiplied by the existence probabilities found from the p binomial for all M values give the same probability as that based on n alone. This is a very important fact and is usually given as a mathematical theorem. In simple terms, it means that under these conditions one must treat the distribution of the samples of n units as if they were actually selected at random from the infinite universe with process average $\bar{p}$ and then determine control chart limits based on the $\bar{p}$ binomial $(\bar{q} + \bar{p})^n$. Since the n values will be small for such cases, tables of the p binomial will usually give the probabilities needed for evaluating the sampling plan and will also aid in evaluating the confidence level for the three-sigma control charts.

Usually control chart limits will be based on the p binomial distribution even though the conditions listed above have not been satisfied. In many cases, the sampling plans given are based on the hypergeometric distribution, so it is necessary to know how to determine the expected value or average, the variance, and the standard deviation of such a distribution. No general theoretical relation has been published to date, so each case must be evaluated by the usual statistical methods with the provision that the theoretical frequencies for the probabilities of the occurrences of m or X successes, here taken as nonconforming units, are computed by equation (13). This relation may also be written in the Lagrangian form for the combination of N items taken n at a time in a manner similar to equation (13).

$$P_{m,n;M,N} = \frac{\binom{N-M}{n-m}\binom{M}{m}}{\binom{N}{n}} \tag{13'}$$

Our example uses a larger value for M than would ordinarily be expected to be maintained as a standard for a process average for most products. This level of quality will be a fraction defective value of 0.30, or 30.0% defective. The lot size is taken as $N = 20$, so that $M = pN = 0.30 \times 20 = 6.0$. The sample will be five units to simplify computations; this is also small enough so that a sample might even contain exactly five defectives.

Example 7 Given a series of lots of size N, where $N = 20$ units, each lot containing exactly $M = pN = 0.30(20) = 6$ nonconforming units. From each such lot of 20 units, a sample of five units is selected at random, hence $n = 5$. (1) Determine, using the hypergeometric relation (13), the probability of exactly $m = X$ successes, where $m = 0, 1, 2, 3, 4,$ and 5. (2) Using the probabilities found in part **(1)** as frequencies of occurrences of X successes, determine the expected average value, the variance, and the standard deviation for this distribution. (3) Determine the three-sigma control limits for this distribution for $n = 5$.

Solution Table 4.11 gives the results of the mathematical computations required for this example. Using equation (13) to determine $P_{0,5;6,20}$ as an illustration gives:

$$P_0 = \frac{5!\,15!}{20!}\,\frac{14!}{5!\,9!}\,\frac{6!}{0!\,6!} = \frac{14\cdot 13\cdot 12\cdot 11\cdot 10}{20\cdot 19\cdot 18\cdot 17\cdot 16} = \frac{1001}{7752} = 0.12912797$$

Here $\dfrac{1}{C_n^N} = \dfrac{n!\,(N-n)!}{N!} = \dfrac{5!\,15!}{20!} = \dfrac{5!}{20\cdot 19\cdot 18\cdot 17\cdot 16}$ is the first term in all the computations. The terms are reduced by division wherever possible.[5]

In table 4.11 the three-sigma control limits for this hypergeometric relation are determined from the statistics derived from N, M, n, and m for the given p value of 0.30, based on equation (13). The probability usually associated with such three-sigma control limits is 0.9973. It is considered to be the confidence level of the degree of belief P_b, assuming that the distribution is near enough to normal to use normal law probabilities in evaluating the confidence level. The upper control limit of 4.23 signifies that lack of control at the assumed level of 0.30 or 30.0% nonconforming units is indicated when all five units in the sample are found to be nonconforming. However, the proportion of the time such lack of control is indicated when it does not exist is only 0.000387 instead of the usual $1 - 0.9973 = 0.0027$, based on the normal law.

TABLE 4.11 Hypergeometric: $\dfrac{C_{n-m}^{N-M} C_m^M}{C_n^N}$, $m = X$, $N = 20$, $M = 6$, and $n = 5$; $p = 30\%$

Number of Successes X	*Theoretical Frequency* f	*Computations*	
		$f(X)$	$f(X^2)$
0	0.12912797	0	0
1	0.38738390	0.38738390	0.38738390
2	0.35216718	0.70433436	1.40866872
3	0.11738906	0.35216718	1.05650154
4	0.01354489	0.05417956	0.21671824
5	0.00038700	0.00193500	0.00967500
Sum	1.00000000	1.50000000	3.07894740

Expected Value:

Average, $\bar{X} = \dfrac{\Sigma f_i(X_i)}{\Sigma f_i} = \dfrac{1.5000}{1.0000} = 1.5000$

Measures of Variability:

Variance, $v_X = \dfrac{\Sigma f_i(X_i^2)}{\Sigma f_i} - \bar{X}^2 = \dfrac{3.07895}{1.00} - (1.5)^2$

$= 3.07895 - 2.25000 = 0.82895$

Standard Deviation, $\sigma_X = \sqrt{v_X} = \sqrt{0.82895} = 0.9105$

Three-Sigma Control Limits:

$\bar{X} \pm 3\sigma_X = 1.50 \pm 3(0.91) = 1.50 \pm 2.73 = 0$ and 4.23

In this example, a small sample of only five units is assumed to be selected at random from a finite lot of $N = 20$ units, which was supposed to contain exactly six nonconforming units. Each of the five units is inspected or tested for all specified requirements. Acceptance or rejection of the lot of twenty units will depend on the acceptance number, c, established as the criterion. In addition, the check for control should consider the process out of control when either four or five nonconforming units are found in the sample. Adding the four appears to be advisable to provide stronger controls on the process level. The percentage or fraction of the time lack of control would be checked and found to be nonexistent would be increased to $P_4 + P_5 = (0.01354489 + 0.00038700) = 0.01393189$. The confidence level is neither 0.9973 for three-sigma control limits nor 0.9545 for two-sigma control limits but $1 - 0.01393189 = 0.98606811$. Hence 0.9861 is the confidence level for this example. The upper control limit is taken as 3.5. It is not much different than the two-sigma limits of $1.50 \pm 2(0.91) = 1.50 \pm 1.82 = 0$ and 3.32. Whether the UCL is 3.5 or 3.32, nonconforming units must be treated as complete units rather than as fractional units, so action is only taken when four or five units in a lot of five units are found nonconforming.

The actual theoretical frequencies were computed in fractional form, changed to their decimal equivalents, and listed as theoretical frequencies in Table 4.11. Next, the hypergeometric relations for P_0, P_1, P_2, P_3, P_4, and P_5 were evaluated. These frequencies are given in tables 4.11 and 4.13.

TABLE 4.12 Theoretical Frequencies for Hypergeometric Relation **(13)** $n = 5$, $N = 20$, $m = X = 0$ to 5, inclusive; $M = 6$, $p = 0.30$

Probabilities as designated	*Fractional Values Multiplier* $\frac{1}{7752}{}^5$	*Decimal Equivalent*
P_0	1001	0.12912797
P_1	3003	0.38738390
P_2	2730	0.35216718
P_3	910	0.11738906
P_4	105	0.01354489
P_5	3	0.00038700
Sum	7752	1.00000000

Three other possible distributions may be used for setting control limits for the finite case. They are (1) the p binomial; (2) the Poisson exponential; and (3) the f binomial, where $f = n/N$. Consideration should be given to the possibility of using limits based upon the standard deviation values for these distributions. Each of these will be treated in sufficient detail so that this example may be used as a guide to solve similar problems in industry. Comparisons should be made between the actual, correctly computed probabilities and similar values that are derived from actual or empirical relations and used as approximations to the actual computed hypergeometric values.

(1) p Binomial for $n = 5$, $p = 0.30$; $(q + p)^n$

Expected or average value: $pn = 0.3(5) = 1.5$
Standard deviation: $\sigma_{pn} = \sqrt{pn(1 - p)} = \sqrt{1.5(0.7)} = \sqrt{1.05} = 1.025$
3-σ control limits: $1.5 \pm 3(1.025) = 1.500 \pm 3.075 = 0$ and 4.575

The frequencies of the occurrences of 0, 1, 2, 3, 4, and 5 defectives, respectively, in samples of 5 units selected at random are given in the *Tables of the Binomial Probability Distribution.* These values are tabulated in table 4.13. The confidence level for three-sigma control limits is $1 - 0.00243 = 0.99757$ where the 3-σ_X control limits are $0 - 4.6$ and $P_5 = 0.00243$.

(2) Poisson Exponential Binomial Limit for $n = 5, p = 0.30, pn = 1.5$; $\dfrac{e^{-pn}(pn)^m}{m!}$

Expected or average value: $pn = 0.3(5) = 1.5$
Standard deviation: $\sigma_{pn} = \sqrt{pn} = \sqrt{1.5} = 1.2247$
3-σ control limits: $1.5 \pm 3(1.2247) = 1.500 \pm 3.674 = 0$ and 5.174

For this case, the Poisson exponential is a poor approximation since these control limits are greater than five and thus are meaningless. For larger values of n, it is often an excellent approximation. The frequencies of the occurrences of 0, 1, 2, 3, 4, and 5 defectives, respectively, for samples of five units with a pn value of 1.5 are given in *Poisson's Exponential Binomial Limit, Table I—Individual Terms* and *Table II—Cumulated Terms,* mentioned earlier. The X values may theoretically go to infinity; hence the last probability for n possible successes usually includes the sum of all probabilities for X and greater values. These frequencies are tabulated in table 4.13 for comparison with the hypergeometric true values.

Probability values for the hypergeometric relation usually take a long time to compute by equation (13), even if log factorials are used. To reduce this labor and to make it possible to read at least some values of these hypergeometric probabilities from tables, Dean Walter W. Bartky of the University of Chicago developed empirical data for the f binomial, where $f = n/N$. In this relation, M replaces the sample size n in the binomial and f replaces p. This results in the following, f binomial from the p binomial relation $C_m^n(1 - p)^{n-m}p^m$.

$$P_{m,n;M,N} = C_m^M(1 - f)^{M-m}f^m, \quad \text{or} \quad = \binom{M}{m}(1 - f)^{M-m}f^m \tag{14}$$

In general, this relation should only be used when n is greater than M, and thus will not be very suitable for the example since n is only five, while M is six. The probabilities computed for m values of five and six are combined for $X = 5$ in the example.

Dean Bartky was a consultant for the Western Electric Company and did a large amount of development work in continuous sampling. As another method for readily obtaining hypergeometric probabilities, he developed a nomographic form of so-called *Banjo* charts using the graphed values of the Poisson exponential with a grid at right angles scaled in terms of M values. Using a straightedge, the approximation probabilities for the hypergeometric function could easily be read. With the development and availability of better computers, the use of such nomographs has decreased. They are used where computers are not available, however.

Results for this example, as determined by the f binomial, follow. A comparison will also be presented which shows the difference between the computed hypergeometric probability values and the corresponding frequencies found by these various approximations. Their use makes it possible to determine the best control limits to use when lot sizes are small and considered finite rather than infinite.

(3) f Binomial for $n = 5$, $p = 0.30$, $N = 20$, $M = 6$, and $f = 0.25$; $C_m^M(1 - f)^{M-m}f^m$

Expected or average value: $fM = pn = 0.25(6) = 1.5$

Standard deviation: $\sigma_{fM} = \sigma_{pn} = \sqrt{fM} = \sqrt{1.5(0.75)} = \sqrt{1.125} = 1.061$

NOTE: $1 - f = 1 - 0.25 = 0.75$ was used rather than $1 - p = 0.70$ in determining this standard deviation value. Since this is an empirical relation, either one might be used; however $1 - f$ is best.

$3\ \sigma$ control limits: $1.5 \pm 3(1.061) = 1.5 \pm 3.183 = 0$ and 4.683

Lack of control will be indicated for the process when five defectives are found in the sample of five units. The frequencies for this empirical f binomial are given in Table 4.13. The probability of finding five defectives in five units is 0.004639, indicating that when a judgment that lack of control exists for a level of 30.0% defective is erroneously made, this would be made only 46 times in 10,000 or 0.46% of the time. The normal law probabilities give only 0.27% as this possible probability.

Table 4.13 gives a comparison of the frequency values found by these various approximation methods and the exact hypergeometric frequencies using equation (13).

TABLE 4.13 Comparison of Computed Frequencies for Three Approximations to the Hypergeometric with Actual Hypergeometric Frequency Values Computed using Equation **(13)** with $n = 5$, $N = 20$, $p = 0.30$ and $M = 6$

		Approximations to the Hypergeometric		
Number of Successes X	*Exact Values Hypergeometric*	*p Binomial* $\binom{n}{m}(1-p)^{n-m}p^m$	$\dfrac{e^{-pn}(pn)^m}{m!}$	$\binom{M}{m}(1-f)^{M-m}f^m$
0	0.129128	0.168070	0.223130	0.177978
1	0.387384	0.360150	0.334695	0.355957
2	0.352167	0.308700	0.251021	0.296631
3	0.117389	0.132300	0.125511	0.131836
4	0.013545	0.028350	0.047067	0.032959
5	0.000387	0.002430	0.018576	0.004639
Sum	1.000000	1.000000	1.000000	1.000000

In the above example, the p binomial relation is in general the best approximation for representing the frequencies for all the six probabilities shown when compared with the corresponding hypergeometric exact frequencies. Since the M value of six exceeded the n value of five, the f binomial was not expected to be a very good approximation. It is a very good approximation for the larger frequency values for a hypergeometric relation when n is much larger than M. Two examples tabulated below illustrate this fact. The comparisons shown give actual numerical differences and the percentage of error in the various probability values found.

For very small frequencies, the percentage of error may appear to be very large; however, when the actual differences are considered, they are reasonable as they may not be much greater than the actual differences experienced in the inspection and testing operations.

TABLE 4.14 Example 1:
Differences Between Probabilities Obtained by the f Binomial Approximation and the Exact Hypergeometric Values $n = 10$, $N = 25$, $p = 0.12$ or 12.0% and $M = 3$

Number of Successes X	Computed Values		Comparison of Differences	
	True Value Hypergeometric	*Approximation f Binomial*	*Actual*	*Percentage*
0	0.1978	0.216	+0.0182	+9.2
1	0.4565	0.432	−0.0295	−6.5
2	0.2935	0.288	−0.0055	−1.9
3	0.0522	0.064	+0.0118	+22.6
Sum	1.0000	1.000		

TABLE 4.15 Example 2:
Differences Between Probabilities Obtained by the f Binomial Approximation and the Exact Hypergeometric Values $n = 15$, $N = 50$, $p = 0.10$ or 10.0% and $M = 5$

Number of Successes X	Computed Values		Comparison of Differences	
	True Value Hypergeometric	*Approximation f Binomial*	*Actual*	*Percentage*
0	0.15322	0.16807	+0.01485	+9.7
1	0.37069	0.36015	−0.01054	−2.8
2	0.32435	0.30870	−0.01565	−4.8
3	0.12777	0.13230	+0.00453	+3.5
4	0.02255	0.02835	+0.00620	+27.5
5	0.00142	0.00243	−0.00101	−41.6
Sum	1.00000	1.00000		

There are many applications of the hypergeometric probability distribution. Its use in preparing control charts is only one of these. Because of their importance, the Stanford University Press published *Tables of the Hypergeometric Distribution,* by Lieberman and Owen, in 1961. Entries in such tables will reduce the time required to apply them to the quality control programs, where lot sizes are small.

4.7 Selection of Sampling Plans for Control Chart Usage as well as Inspection

One of the most valuable probability distributions for attributes is the Poisson exponential binomial limit, $e^{-pn}(pn)^m/m!$. Tables covering this distribution are available in many texts about quality control, reliability, and statistics. One of the most valuable is the Molina Tables referred to previously. Its range of values provides pn values from 0.001 to 100, presented in various steps from 0.001 to 1.0, selected to provide a practical table that will require a minimum amount of interpolations, when necessary.

Sample sizes for control chart purposes and for individual lot protection may be quickly determined by the use of pn values selected from the Poisson exponential tables using a consumer's risk, P_C, of 0.10 associated with selected values of LTPD (lot tolerance percent defective), often designated as p_t. For the most effective use of such values, the lots submitted for inspection or test should be fairly large, equal to or greater than an N value of 100. As an aid in such a selection of LTPD, the maximum allowable number of nonconforming units in sample or the acceptance number, c, in single sampling, and corresponding n values for use in inspection and control chart usage, table 4.16 lists a series of pn values for a range of c values from 0 to 10, respectively. Where interpolation should be used to obtain a better pn value, two values of pn are listed to permit such interpolation.

If the LTPD value is stipulated as 3.0% or 0.03, and an acceptance number, c, of 1 is the most economical for the given lot size, then the sample size is 130. This value is found by using $pn = 3.9$ (from the above table), then $n = 3.90/0.03 = 130$. If, however, it is more economical to use a c value of 10, then using the pn value of about 15.45 found by interpolation for $c = 10$, $n = 15.45/0.03 = 515$. For an LTPD value of 0.03, it probably would be most economical to control the process at a level of 0.01. Control charts could then be set up by the methods covered in the next chapter for a process average $\bar{p}$ of 1.0% or 0.01 fraction defective, using the n value obtained in accordance with the method outlined above, since lot protection was already stipulated.

The fundamental procedures, methods, and techniques of inspection and testing require that we delineate the selection of the correct sampling plan for control chart use, as well as for determining the acceptance or rejection of the part or material on the line, in receiving inspection, or other inspection or test stations. Many features must be considered before making a final selection of the best sampling plan for a given situation. At present, there are many different sampling plans available; they have been updated and modified so that such standard sampling tables may be applied in many different environments. National and international standard sampling tables are being selected from available tables and standardized.

The latest techniques used to present sets of sampling plans is to describe such tables, how they are to be used, and their fundamental purpose. All the various

TABLE 4.16 *pn* Values Corresponding to *c* Values (0 to 10, inclusive) Resulting in Probability of Observing *c* or Less Nonconforming Units in Samples of Size *n*, $P_{\infty \text{ or less}} = P_C = 0.10$

Acceptance Number *c*	$a = pn$ *Values*	*Cumulative Probability Consumer's Risk*, P_C
0	2.3	0.100259
1	3.9	0.099185
2	5.3	0.101554
	5.4	0.094758
3	6.6	0.105151
	6.7	0.098808
4	8.0	0.099632
5	9.2	0.104074
	9.3	0.098650
6	10.5	0.101633
	10.6	0.096616
7	11.7	0.103453
	11.8	0.098612
8	13.0	0.099758
9	14.2	0.100264
*10	15.0	0.118464
	16.0	0.077396
*10	15.45	0.100000

NOTE: Beyond *pn* value of 15.0, values are given in units, not tenths.
* Interpolation needed for $c = 10$: Subtract 0.100000 from 0.118460. This gives 0.018460. Then subtract 0.077396 from 0.118464. This gives 0.041068. Divide 0.018460 by 0.041068. The quotient is 0.4495. Since the interval between 15.0 and 16.0 is 1.0, multiply 1.0 by 0.4495, obtaining 0.4495. Add to 15.0 giving 15.4495 by interpolation; round to 15.45, a practical value though using another table gives for $pn = 15.5$, $P_C = 0.09612$, hence $pn = 15.4132$ rather than *pn* for 15.4495 for $P_C = 0.1000$.

sampling plans have been described in this manner in this text. However, many desire to have more assurance that the choice of the best plan has been determined by the latest techniques. It has been found that the usual data and information may not be sufficient to enable one to select the most efficient and economical sampling plan for any specified set of conditions. It is necessary to make certain that sufficient data are secured for controlling the process, as well as the level of current quality. Sufficient valid and controlled data are not available usually to provide the best types of control charts as well as sampling plans. To partially compensate for this deficiency, a second document is now being standardized to provide guidelines for the standard set of sampling plans. This procedure was used with great success several years ago by the relay manufacturers in standardizing their most reliable types of relays. An international committee is working on this project.

Recently MIL–STD–105C was revised by a committee consisting of representatives from Great Britain, Canada, and the United States, who modified it slightly and issued it as MIL–STD–105D, sometimes called ABC–STD–105D, where *A* designates America, *B* refers to the British or Great Britain, and *C* refers to Canada. In 1973, *Draft International Standard* ISO/DIS *2859* was prepared which covered the material in MIL–STD–105D. It was called *Sampling Procedures and Tables for Inspection by Attributes,* and was issued as ISO/TC 69, Secretariat France, by the International Organization for Standardization. This seems to have already been tentatively approved. To aid in its use, a guideline is now being checked and modified by an international committee. It will be issued as *Guide to the Use of* ISO *2859: Sampling Procedures and Tables for Inspection by Attributes.* International recognition of such procedures and the proper use of control charts will provide better assurance of better quality products at reasonable prices. There is a stronger tendency to obtain international standards in many areas. One of the most important is in the field of quality and reliability.

EXERCISES

1. What is meant by *quality*? Give a good descriptive definition of quality.
2. Who developed the concept of control charts? In what year was this concept first presented? What is the objective of those applying quality control charts?
3. Why are control charts called *statistical quality control charts*? What probability is associated with three-sigma control limits?
4. In what areas are quality control charts applied?
5. What standards are used for control charts for attributes?
6. What standards are used for control charts for variables?
7. What distributions are associated with control charts for attributes?
8. What distributions are associated with control charts for variables?
9. When are two-sigma control charts used? Give an example.
10. When and where should control charts be used?

FOOTNOTES

[1] National Bureau of Standards, Applied Mathematics Series 6, *Tables of the Binomial Probability Distribution,* U.S. Government Printing Office, Washington, D.C. Issued January 27, 1950. Price: $2.50 (Buckram).

[2] Harry G. Romig, *50–100 Binomial Tables* (New York: John Wiley & Sons, Inc., 1953). Copies limited, available from author.

[3] Limits for summation terms such as those described in footnote 7, chapter two, are used in equation (6), but these limits are omitted for simplification from other relations presented herein. However, they are understood to be applied.

[4] In many computations of control limits, the LCL value as determined is less than zero, e.g., in the above case, 0.40 − 1.89 = −1.49. Since negative defects or fraction defectives cannot exist, zero is used as the value of the LCL in all such cases.

[5] $P_0 = \frac{1}{C_5^{20}} \cdot C_5^{14} C_0^6 = \frac{5!15!}{20!} \cdot \frac{14!}{5!9!} \cdot \frac{6!}{0!6!} = \frac{7 \cdot 13 \cdot 11}{19 \cdot 3 \cdot 17 \cdot 8} = \frac{1001}{7752}; = 0.129128$; other P_i values computed using equation (13).

CHAPTER FIVE

CONTROL CHARTS FOR ATTRIBUTES

5.1 Objective

The general principles of quality control charts were presented in the previous chapter. In this chapter, we describe how such charts may be applied when the data under consideration are *attributes* data rather than *variables* data. Relations are presented that are used to determine the statistical control limits that have been found so successful in indicating when a process deviates from its usual operating pattern and is termed to be out of control. Such controls apply not only to manufacturing data but also, when applied properly, these techniques help to reduce errors that may occur in data processing and clerical work.

Numerous examples will be included to enable the reader to set up such control charts in his own discipline and obtain the benefits that are possible when the operations are controlled within economical limits. These methods apply where the data have only a two-fold classification, such as conforming or nonconforming, good or bad, nondefective or defective, successes or failures, and the occurrence of an event or the nonoccurrence of the event. The charts as presented in this book are designed to indicate when action should be taken to correct the process. The previous chapter indicated that control limits may be based on whatever degree of belief or confidence level the user desires. In general, and in the United States in particular, these control limits are based on either two-sigma or three-sigma control limits. These limits include within their boundaries, respectively, 95.45% and 99.73% of the area under a normal law (distribution) curve. This is true because these limits are, respectively, plus or minus two standard deviation units from the mean or expected value, and plus or minus three standard units from the expected or standard value. These normal law probabilities are only approximations to the actual confidence levels, but are close enough for practical applications. Exact values are very difficult to obtain where the system of causes changes rapidly with time, within very narrow limits.

Attributes control charts cover relative values expressed as percentages, *p*, or fraction defective, *p*. Where sample sizes, *n*, are equal, some prefer to use control charts for the number of defects or defectives observed in each sample. This simplifies the computing, as it is not necessary to compute the fraction defective; the number actually determined to be nonconforming is plotted and checked against the control limits which are expressed in terms of the observed number of defects or defectives in the sample of n units. How to handle both the number of defects observed and the related number of defectives observed is considered in detail. Many references and tables which may prove helpful in applying these techniques will be cited. Examples are provided which will enable any quality control engineer or technician to set up the type of control charts that will best fit his or her operations.

In addition to control charts for p and pn, expressed in terms of percent or fraction defective and also in terms of defects per hundred units (or merely defects and defectives), there are also control charts for defects per 1,000 feet, demerits per unit, and even for various forms of quality indexes. It is expected that the examples given to illustrate the various kinds of control charts will help the reader to install such control charts in the forms applicable to attributes data.

When first introducing the concept of control charts and their applications, it was indicated that these charts are merely tools to aid the quality control engineer to perform his functions better. The controls are so established that events plotted within the three-sigma control limits are merely the result of chance variations, whereas when points are found outside these control limits, it is asserted that there should exist some assignable cause for such occurrences. Thus the charts indicate when action should be taken to seek extraneous assignable causes. Three-sigma control limits are presented in the majority of cases, but it may be desirable for those working closely with a given product or project to use two-sigma limits and seek assignable causes that occur more frequently than those needed by top management. It should be noted that when two-sigma control limits are used, one may look for assignable causes and not find them approximately 5% of the time; this is because for normal distributions, the probability associated with two-sigma limits is 0.9545. However, by utilizing three-sigma limits, where $P = 0.9973$, one may **not find** assignable causes only 27 times in 10,000 or roughly one time in three hundred. In practice, since the charts were first introduced in 1924, it has been found that in practically all cases when a point was observed outside the control limits in an unfavorable direction, one or several assignable causes were usually found when action was taken to find the assignable cause. And, when properly corrected, the process was brought within control limits, resulting in a fairly large savings for the company.

Two different types of standards are presented: (1) standard given, and (2) no standard given. In the first case, it is relatively easy to set up applicable control charts to achieve the desired results. In the second case, sufficient data must be obtained and analyzed to produce realistic standards and profitable outcomes for the company. It is noted that in many cases, standards are established that are actually too rigid and may hinder both the customer and the producer. Enforcing controls that are tighter than necessary cost too much, and if parts thus controlled are assembled with other parts that are not tightly controlled, they may wear out very early, making it necessary to replace the entire system. These tight controls are thus not truly economic levels of quality, but are instead the result of the desire of the designer to design a near-perfect product, which when used with mating parts may actually be in operation only 10% of its expected life cycle. Hence, this chapter supplements the chapter on standards and provides means of setting up attributes data for control charts that are really economic controls for the desired levels of quality demanded by consumers.

5.2 Terminology

Terms used in the preparation and application of control charts have very definite meanings. The glossary of terms given in this text should be consulted when the meaning of any term is not clear. The particular use of these terms will become apparent in studying the descriptions that follow.

In manufacturing, units may often be made that do not meet the specified requirements. Such units are not actually defective, yet they do not conform to the particular specification that has been included in the purchase order package. For example, a furniture manufacturer may be making restaurant or breakfast tables. The height of these tables is not too critical, but is set at thirty inches. The tables will not all actually be made at exactly this height. When the tables are used singly, such an actual difference in height will not matter. When such tables are put together to form a larger table, the differences in height will be important. This is particularly true in restaurants where purchases are made for tables at which both large and small groups wish to sit. For single use, the tolerance on the height of these tables might be relatively large, such as plus or minus one-fourth inch. Such a tolerance would be satisfactory for those using single tables, but a restaurant owner would find that this tolerance is too large for tables placed together, since two tables might differ by as much as half an inch in height. Hence a more reasonable tolerance would be plus or minus one-tenth inch. Two tables placed together then would differ in height by a maximum difference of only 0.20 inch. If tables were selected at random, as is usually the case, then the differences in height would be essentially negligible. Any table having a height of less than 29.9 inch or more than 30.1 inch would not be considered satisfactory. Such a table would be termed a defective.

Three terms occur in this example that should be defined. They are the terms *tolerance*, *defect*, and *defective*. *Tolerance* is any amount of deviation that is permitted from the desired or expected value for any item. Such specified limiting values result in maximum or minimum values being given. Any unit that has a value for the characteristic under consideration outside these limiting values is classed as a *defect*. Its measured or observed value does not conform to the specified limiting values and thus it is considered to be nonconforming. In our example, height is the characteristic specified. Any table not within the specified limits defined by the stated tolerances is classed as a defect. When a unit contains one or more defects, it is called *defective*. If a single table was nonconforming with respect to its length as well as its height, it contains two defects and is classed as a defective table.

The term *characteristic* is used to designate any feature, measured value, or item that is specified in describing the properties of a product or item. When many characteristics are selected to describe the quality of a product, and if two or more of these characteristics are not within specified tolerances, the unit is said to contain two or more defects and is called a *defective*. A minor defect may be overlooked. For example, when the color of a part differs very slightly from the standard color, such a defect is termed an *incidental defect* and the product is used "as is" rather than being repainted.

In production, a system of causes such as a manufacturing process may produce a series of units which all meet the specified requirements, or may produce a few that are barely outside the specified requirements. Such a production process may consistently produce a small portion of completed units that are classed as defects. A purchaser may be willing to accept such products providing that the fraction defective does not exceed some definite value, such as 2%. If the process is actually statistically controlled, then manufacturing may continue without alteration until the process actually does change in an unfavorable direction. A purchaser will buy a given number of units and request that the shipment be "as is." Thus, where N units are ordered and shipped, the quantity involved is termed a *lot* or batch. When the purchaser receives these units, he may not elect to individually inspect all of the N units for the critical characteristic specified. If he selects, for example, to inspect $f = 10\%$, this value measures the ratio of the sample size n to the lot size N, i.e., $f = n/N$. Where $N = 100$, the sample will contain 10 units. If $N = 500$, then $n = 50$. Thus a *lot* is the number of units submitted for acceptance (presumably by inspection), while a *sample* is the number of units selected at random for inspection and/or test.

Another term that is often used is *fraction defective* or *percent defective*. If one unit in a sample of ten units is inspected and found to be nonconforming, one defect or defective has been observed in the sample of ten units. The fraction defective, denoted by p, is that portion of the sample that contains defects or nonconforming units. The percent defective is determined by multiplying by 100. In this example, the fraction defective p is equal to $\frac{1}{10}$ or 0.10. Expressed in percent, this value is 10%. Fraction defective values are used when making computations.

Control charts are often made in terms of number of defects or defectives rather than the fraction or percent defective. The symbol d is often used for designating the number of defects observed, but some texts use the symbol c or pn for such charts. Thus control charts for c or pn are also described in quality control references. Since c is used also to represent the acceptance number (the maximum allowable number of defects in a sample) in sampling theory and in sampling tables, there is a great advantage in using d to represent charts for defects or defectives. Hence one must read the texts as well as the glossaries carefully, to fully understand the usage under discussion. In some texts, the symbol m is used for defects in a sample, while M is used to represent the number of defects in a lot of size N. Some texts use D in place of M when d is used in place of m. These terms are generally used when determining probabilities of acceptance and rejection, especially for finite values of M, where the hypergeometric relation is involved. For this special case

$m = pn$ and $M = pN$. Their use is described elsewhere in conjunction with a discussion of sampling inspection. Most texts have standardized on the notation used in this text.

Another term that is used is *assignable causes.* In contrast, the term *unassignable causes* is used for those causes which seem to affect each unit in a random fashion and thus are attributed to chance, because they occur only at random. An important application of control charts is to indicate when action should be taken to reduce the production of defective parts in manufacturing operations. However, they can be applied in other ways, such as in cases where an excessive number of errors are made by clerical workers. When points occur outside the control limits of acceptability, action should be taken as quickly as possible to determine the cause. Generally, after a brief study is made, at least one assignable cause is found. For example, a good trouble-shooter might find that the assignable cause of a quality problem was due to an untrained worker who started to work before completion of his training program or that it may be due to the addition of a new machine on the line which is not set up properly. Other causes might be due to poor quality components obtained from inventory or even large changes in temperature and humidity conditions. Defective parts can also be attributed to worker fatigue. Corrosion of capacitors on the line can be caused by workers with contaminant salt on their hands, a result of eating salty peanuts during their breaks. The most important fact is that where there is a definite indication of a change in the process by a control chart, action must be taken to determine the cause; a definite assignable cause should be found and corrected before production is continued.

One of the first tenets of Dr. Walter A. Shewhart's development of control charts in 1924 is that control charts offer a valuable technique based on probability theory indicating "when the results of a process are deemed to result from purely chance causes." His papers developed this theory. The first appeared in *The Bell System Technical Journal,* Vol. III, No. 1, January, 1924, and was titled, "Some Applications of Statistical Methods." This was followed by the development of the use of control charts economically in manufacturing processes. The upper and lower control limits were developed as criteria to determine when a defective was due to chance. Industry has profited greatly through the use of these techniques and the consumer has been protected against excessively defective units and products.

Shewhart showed that a cause system is in operation, resulting in a given event. This may be a report, a design, the preparation of an invoice, or the production of a simple or complex unit. Where the causes are purely random, they are called *chance causes.* By the use of modern statistical methods, criteria are provided which may be used to economically control the quality of these events and products within prescribed limits.

5.3 Data for Control Charts

In order to construct valid control charts, it is desirable to have data that are ordered in some way. In general, such data are ordered with respect to time. Rational subgroups are arranged day by day, hour by hour, or in any selected time sequence that fits the conditions. These values are plotted on the control charts and analyzed. If these data represent a well-controlled process, they will be essentially homogeneous, and the statistics derived from them, when plotted, will fall within the control limits established by the control chart method of analysis. It is easier to prepare such charts when the rational subgroups have the same number of observations per period. In process inspection, twenty-five units might be checked hourly; the number of nonconforming units observed may then be recorded together with the size of the sample in which they were found. These data will be ordered with respect to time for all operations. For such cases, the control limits from sample to sample are the same, whereas if a different number of units are inspected periodically, then the control limits will have to be modified for every point plotted to determine the proper control limits for each point and present them in graphical form.

The data should be tabulated neatly and dated so that, where possible, it may be used in conjunction with applicable computer programs for direct use in the preparation of the control charts required for controls in a particular area. In some cases, results are not only tabulated period by period but are also accumulated. The defects reported, their nature and extent, and the sample sizes used are cumulated on a weekly, monthly, quarterly, and/or yearly basis. Control limits may be modified to cover the different periods of time and the summations of the samples inspected or tested. The better type of accumulation to apply is one that may later be associated directly with definite systems of causes. It may take more time for keeping records, but it is very useful to maintain traceability of parts and processes at all stages of the operations. Later, when reports of unsatisfactory operations are received from the field, it is easier to determine why such a failure occurred and implement the best possible corrective action.

In some instances, each group of data and each characteristic under consideration are weighted equally. Each is considered to be as important as any other. However, in other cases, some characteristics are more important than others, so weighted values are used. Such weighted values may be treated the same as the simpler forms of data but are generally expressed in a different form, such as "demerits per unit." This requires the classification of defects for each component according to a definite pattern relating to their seriousness as postulated. Control charts may also be prepared for such weighted values. This case will be covered after the simpler cases have been described in detail.

Data, after being ordered, are used in the preparation of various forms of control charts for attributes. Descriptions of the more important types follow.

5.4 Control Charts for Percent or Fraction Defective, *p*

Control charts for percent defective or fraction defective, p, may be prepared for two different conditions. These are (1) standard given, and (2) no standard given. Many specifications or customers state the level of quality that must be supplied. In effect, they specify the process average value at which the producer must operate and be controlled. For example, a customer desires 500 aluminum threaded bolts two inches in length and $\frac{1}{4}$ inch in diameter, with fine threads, together with a nut that fits snugly—tight but not too tight. The buyer actually needs only 450, but is willing to allow 10% to be nonconforming to his specification. As a safety measure, he asks the supplier to control the process at a level of 5% defective for the bolts and nuts combined. The supplier then establishes controls at somewhat tighter levels.

The example above covered the first case, in which a standard was written into the contract, that is, a purchase order for 500 requiring control at 5% for each group of 100 bolts and matching nuts as made by the manufacturing process. Other buyers may be willing to buy the units as manufactured by the system of causes in effect in the operations. Other purchasers might be willing to purchase bolts and nuts of this size and variety at whatever quality level the producer deems most economical. However, they would like the product received to be uniform and thus desire the process to be controlled at some level established by the supplier. This is an example of the second case, no standard given. Past data are used to determine the quality level in effect. Lots are turned out in 100-unit lots. Sufficient data are taken and recorded by the supplier to insure that his quality control personnel can establish the most efficient quality control charts for this operation.

Standard Given

Where the percent or fraction defective desired is specified, control charts for this definite value of the process average, $\bar{p}$, may be established by using the standard deviation relation for $\bar{p}$, based on the p binomial, $(\bar{q} + \bar{p})^n$. This applies when random samples of size n are selected and measured or tested for the specified characteristics. The standard deviation σ_p, is given by the relation in equation (1), where $\bar{q} = 1 - \bar{p}$. (Since the p binomial is a probability density function, the sum of all possible occurrences must total one.)

$$\sigma_p = \sqrt{\frac{\bar{p}(1 - \bar{p})}{n}} \tag{1}$$

As noted previously, the usual control limits that have been found to be very practical limits are the three-sigma (3-σ) control limits. Many cases will be found in which the distribution for the p binomial closely approaches a normal law curve, but there are also a very large number of cases where this is not true. Irrespective of this, three-sigma control limits will be used for staff controls and two-sigma control used as limits for manufacturing controls. These control limits were initiated in 1924, so that many years of experience support the use of such limits as being very practical and economical.

True or standard values are often represented by prime values. Thus the standard value given for $\bar{p}$ may be represented as $\bar{p}'$ or merely p'. Using this notation, the control limits are:

$$\text{Upper control limit, UCL:} \quad \bar{p}' + 3\sqrt{\frac{\bar{p}'(1-\bar{p}')}{n}}$$

(2)

$$\text{Lower control limit, LCL:} \quad \bar{p}' - 3\sqrt{\frac{\bar{p}'(1-\bar{p}')}{n}}$$

Example 1 Determine the UCL and LCL values for the case discussed above, where a standard level of 5% defective is considered satisfactory. For lot sizes of $N = 500$, the sample size is a 10% sample, or 50 units.

Solution With $\bar{p}' = 0.05$, then $1 - \bar{p}' = \bar{q}' = 0.95$; $\bar{p}'(1 - \bar{p}') = 0.05(0.95) = 0.0475$.

$$\frac{\bar{p}'(1-\bar{p}')}{n} = \frac{0.0475}{50} = 0.000950 = \sigma_p^2; \quad \sigma_p = \sqrt{0.000950} = 0.030822.$$

NOTE: $\bar{p}$ is usually designated only as p', the expected value of p used as the standard value in controlling the process.
UCL: $p' + 3\sigma_p = 0.05 + 3(0.0308) = 0.05 + 0.0924 = 0.1424$, or 14.24%
LCL: $p' - 3\sigma_p = 0.05 - 3(0.0308) = 0.05 - 0.0924 = 0$, or 0%
This solution shows that when more than seven defects are observed in the sample of fifty units, the process is considered to be out of control.

Example 2 is taken from the ASTM *Manual on Control of Materials* and presents the standard p', given a control chart for p where the samples are of equal size. Since the sample sizes are equal, figure 5-1 has a single pair of values for the control limits. Also $p'n$, defects or defectives, and as noted above the corresponding three-sigma control limits for $p'n$ are the same for all samples as described in the next section. Figure 5-2 covers this.

Example 2 Table 5.1 gives the number of defectives found in inspecting a series of fifteen consecutive lots of galvanized washers for finish defects such as exposed steel, rough galvanizing, and discoloration. The nuts were of almost the same size, and a constant sample size, $n = 400$, was used for each such lot. The fraction defective p for each sample was determined by dividing the number of defectives found, pn, by the sample size n and is listed in the table. The manufacturer wishes to control his process with respect to finish for these galvanized washers at a level such that the fraction defective p' is equal to 0.0040 or 0.40% (four defective washers per thousand). The data in table 5.1 are used to set up control charts for both p and pn for the p' standard desired.

TABLE 5.1 Finish Defects, Galvanized Washers

Lot	*Sample Size,* n	*Number of Defectives,* pn	*Fraction Defective,* p	Lot	*Sample Size,* n	*Number of Defectives,* pn	*Fraction Defective,* p
No. 1........	400	1	0.0025	No. 9........	400	8	0.0200
No. 2........	400	3	0.0075	No. 10........	400	5	0.0125
No. 3........	400	0	0				
No. 4........	400	7	0.0175	No. 11........	400	2	0.0050
No. 5........	400	2	0.0050	No. 12........	400	0	0
				No. 13........	400	1	0.0025
No. 6........	400	0	0	No. 14........	400	0	0
No. 7........	400	1	0.0025	No. 15........	400	3	0.0075
No. 8........	400	0	0				
				Total....	6000	33	0.0825
				Average	400	2.2	0.0055

(1) p

Central Line

$p' = 0.0040.$

Control Limits

$n = 400$:

$$p' \pm 3\sqrt{\frac{p'(1-p')}{n}} =$$

$$0.0040 \pm 3\sqrt{\frac{0.0040\,(0.9960)}{400}} =$$

0.0040 ± 0.0095,
0.0135 and 0.

(2) pn

Central Line

$p'n = 0.0040\,(400) = 1.6.$

Control Limits

(*a*) *Exact Formula:*

$n = 400$:

$$p'n \pm 3\sqrt{p'n(1-p')} =$$

$$1.6 \pm 3\sqrt{1.6(0.996)} =$$

$$1.6 \pm 3\sqrt{1.5936} =$$

$1.6 \pm 3(1.262)$,
5.4 and 0.

(*b*) *Simplified Approximate Formula:*

$n = 400$:

Since p' is small, replace $1 - p'$ by 1.

$$p'n \pm 3\sqrt{p'n} =$$
$$1.6 \pm 3\sqrt{1.6} =$$
$$1.6 \pm 3(1.265),$$
$$5.4 \text{ and } 0.^{+}$$

Results Lack of control of quality is indicated with respect to the desired level; lots Nos. 4 and 9 are outside control limits.

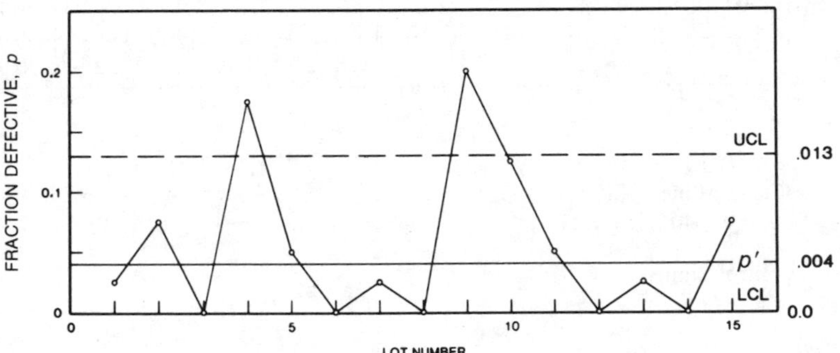

Figure 5–1 Control chart for p; samples of equal size, $n = 400$; p' given.

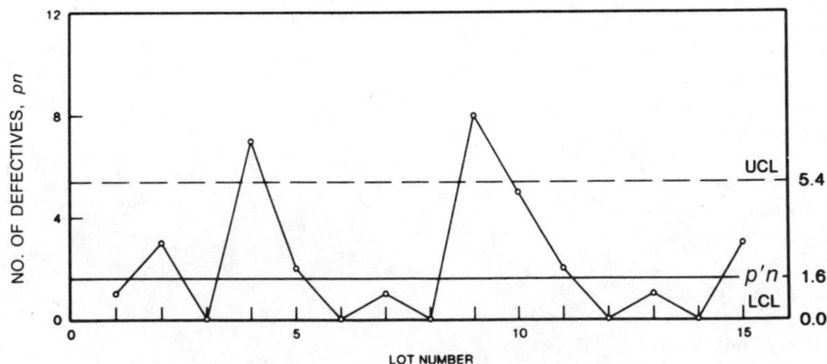

Figure 5–2 Control chart for pn; samples of equal size, $n = 400$; p' given.

The steps to be followed in setting up such control charts are very simple.

Step 1 Determine from the specification, purchase order, or customer requirements what the level of quality is in terms of percent or fraction defective desired. This is established as the p' or expected value for the control chart. It is the quality level or central value about which control limits are established.
Step 2 Determine for each sample ordered with respect to time the observed number of defects or defectives observed in each sample and tabulate.
Step 3 Determine the percent or fraction defective for each sample by dividing the number of nonconforming units, defects or defectives, by the sample size; record as p.
Step 4 Graph the p values ordered with respect to time or sample number.
Step 5 Using equation (2), determine the values of the upper control limit, UCL, and the lower control limit, LCL, and plot corresponding to the proper value of n.
Step 6 List all p values above or below their respective UCL or LCL values.

Similar steps may be written for constructing figure 5-2, the control chart for pn. For this chart, number of defectives are graphed rather than values of p, and the final control limits as well as the central standard value are given in terms of the number of defectives.

No Standard Given

Where the specifications or purchase orders do not include a desired value for the percent or fraction defective level at which control is desired, control limits should be established by the quality control department of the industry based on past data about the process involved for the product under consideration. The data used for establishing the standard should be selected from past data if it is believed that the production process has been uniform and can be considered to be operating under controlled conditions. Sometimes, during some days or weeks of the operation of a process, the data indicate a spotty condition. This results in an excessive number of defects or defectives being found by inspection and test. Omitting such data, a process average value $\bar{p}$ is computed by dividing the sum of the defects or defectives found by the sum of the sample sizes for the same periods. Thus, the desired level or standard based on past data is obtained from the relation

$$\bar{p} = \frac{\Sigma d_i}{\Sigma n_i} \tag{3}$$

This standard value is treated in the same manner as $\bar{p}'$ in computing the upper and lower control limits for the process. The values of UCL and LCL may be then computed from the same relations given in equation (2). This is shown in the next example.

Example 3 illustrates the case where the standard is derived from past data and the sample sizes are unequal in size since the lot sizes differ markedly.

Example 3 These data cover inspection results for surface defects on thirty-one lots of a certain type of galvanized hardware. Table 5.2 summarizes inspection results for these thirty-one lots. Since the total number of units in the thirty-one samples from these large lots is 19,410 and it is felt that these results came from a controlled process, the $\bar{p}$ value obtained is considered to be a good standard. Figure 5-3 presents these results on a control chart for p.

TABLE 5.2 Surface Defects, Galvanized Hardware

Lot	*Sample Size,* n	*Number of Defectives,* pn	*Fraction Defective,* p	Lot	*Sample Size,* n	*Number of Defectives,* pn	*Fraction Defective,* p
No. 1	580	9	0.0155	No. 16	330	4	0.0121
No. 2	550	7	0.0127	No. 17	330	2	0.0061
No. 3	580	3	0.0052	No. 18	640	4	0.0063
No. 4	640	9	0.0141	No. 19	580	7	0.0121
No. 5	880	13	0.0148	No. 20	550	9	0.0164
No. 6	880	14	0.0159	No. 21	510	7	0.0137
No. 7	640	14	0.0219	No. 22	640	12	0.0188
No. 8	550	10	0.0182	No. 23	200	7	0.0350
No. 9	580	12	0.0207	No. 24	330	5	0.0152
No. 10	880	14	0.0159	No. 25	880	18	0.0205
No. 11	800	6	0.0075	No. 26	880	7	0.0080
No. 12	800	12	0.0150	No. 27	800	8	0.0100
No. 13	580	7	0.0121	No. 28	580	8	0.0138
No. 14	580	11	0.0190	No. 29	880	15	0.0170
No. 15	550	5	0.0091	No. 30	880	3	0.0034
				No. 31	330	5	0.0152
				Total...	19410	267	0.01376

Central Line

$$\bar{p} = \frac{267}{19{,}410} = 0.01376.$$

Control Limits

$$\bar{p} \pm 3\sqrt{\frac{\bar{p}(1-\bar{p})}{n}}$$

For $n = 200$:

$$0.01376 \pm 3\sqrt{\frac{0.01376\,(0.98624)}{200}} =$$

$0.01376 \pm 3(0.008237) =$
$0.01376 \pm 0.02471,$
0.03847 and $0.$

For $n = 880$:

$$0.01376 \pm 3\sqrt{\frac{0.01376\,(0.98624)}{880}} =$$

$0.01376 \pm 3(0.003927) =$
$0.01376 \pm 0.01178,$
0.02554 and $0.00198.$ +

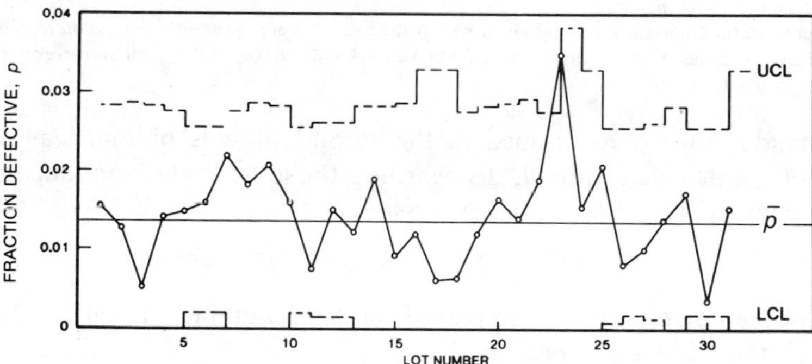

Figure 5–3 Control chart for p; samples of unequal size, $n = 200$ to 880; no standard given.

Results A state of control may be assumed to exist since 25 consecutive subgroups fall within 3-sigma control limits.

Example 4 Determine the number of defective Type A ball-point pens found by inspection during the past six months from the following listing of data; then find the process average in terms of fraction defective and also upper and lower control limits for a constant sample size of 100 pens.

TABLE 5.3 Sampling Results for Ball-Point Pens, by Weeks

Week	*Number Inspected*	*Number of Defectives*	*Fraction Defective*	*Week*	*Number Inspected*	*Number of Defectives*	*Fraction Defective*
1	300	3	0.0100	14	600	5	0.0083
2	400	5	0.0125	15	300	0	0
3	200	4	0.0200	16	300	10*	0.0333†
4	500	15*	0.0300†	17	100	2	0.0200
5	100	1	0.0100	18	300	12*	0.0400†
6	200	0	0	19	500	5	0.0100
7	400	4	0.0100	20	200	3	0.0150
8	500	6	0.0120	21	300	2	0.0067
9	400	7	0.0175	22	100	0	0
10	200	12*	0.0600†	23	400	0	0
11	100	0	0	24	200	2	0.0100
12	400	2	0.0050	25	500	5	0.0100
13	500	5	0.0100	26	300	2	0.0067
Sum	4200	64	0.0152		4100	48	0.0117

* Any period showing 3% defective or more is deemed to be out of control. Four weeks seem to have produced an excessive number of defective pens. The results for these four weeks are omitted in estimating a reasonable standard in terms of fraction defective, $\bar{p}$.

† The preliminary decision that the four weeks indicated by the asterisk were apparently out of control with respect to the desired level is verified by the control chart based on a level of $\bar{p} = 0.009$, or 0.9%. All four weeks have values above their respective UCL values.

The standard for $\bar{p}$ mentioned in the second note is obtained as follows. The sum of the defectives found, disregarding those from the four uncontrolled weeks, is obtained by the following expression:

$$(64 + 48) - (15 + 12 + 10 + 12) = 112 - 49 = 63.$$

The sum of the corresponding samples of the total number of pens inspected is provided by the following expression:

$$(4200 + 4100) - (500 + 200 + 300 + 300) = 8300 - 1300 = 7000.$$

This provides the first estimate of $\bar{p}$ as $\bar{p} = \frac{63}{7000} = 0.0090$, or 0.9%.

The upper and lower control limits for all the sample sizes listed for the twenty-six weeks are found from the relation

$$\bar{p} \pm 3\sigma_p = \bar{p} \pm 3\sqrt{\frac{\bar{p}(1-\bar{p})}{n}} \tag{4}$$

For this example, the upper and lower control limits for all the sample sizes listed for the twenty-six weeks are found from equation (4) by evaluating that part of the relation that is common to all sample sizes, giving the following:

$$\sqrt{\bar{p}(1-\bar{p})} = \sqrt{0.009\,(0.991)} = \sqrt{0.008919} = 0.094440457.$$

From this is obtained the expression $3\sigma_p = \dfrac{0.283321371}{\sqrt{n}}$. Table 5.4 gives values for the upper control limit and the lower control limit derived from equation (4) for the seven different sample sizes in the example.

TABLE 5.4 Upper and Lower Control Limits for $\bar{p} = 0.0090$

Sample Size	*Computed Values*		*3-σ Control Limits*	
n	$1/\sqrt{n}$	$3\sigma_p$	*UCL*	*LCL*
100	0.100000	0.02833	0.0373	0
200	0.070711	0.02003	0.0290	0
300	0.057735	0.01636	0.0254	0
400	0.050000	0.01417	0.0232	0
500	0.044721	0.01267	0.0217	0
600	0.040825	0.01157	0.0206	0
1000	0.031623	0.00896	0.0180	0

The distribution of the different sample sizes for the 26 weeks is:

Sample Size	*100*	*200*	*300*	*400*	*500*	*600*	*Total*
Tabulation	||||	𝍸	𝍸 |	𝍸	𝍸	|	𝍸𝍸𝍸𝍸𝍸 |
Number	4	5	6	5	5	1	26

Figure 5-4 presents a control chart for these twenty-six weeks, showing the variations in limit lines that are the result of different sample sizes. Four weeks are shown out of control. These are the four weeks that were omitted in determining the best standard for these data. The selected value for p' is the $\bar{p}$ value obtained from the twenty-two weeks assumed to have produced a uniform product, where

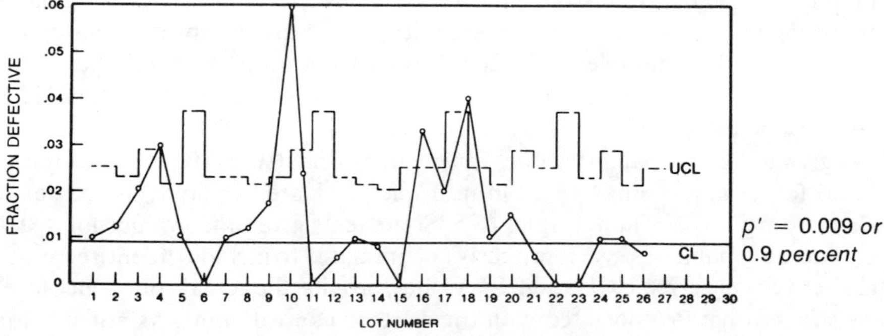

Figure 5–4 Control chart for fraction defective; unequal sample size.

statistical analysis indicates that the process is controlled. This $\bar{p}$ may be designated $\bar{p}'$ and is equivalent to a given standard p'.

5.5 Control Chart for Number of Defectives, *pn*, or *d*

It is simpler to use data obtained directly from the inspection and test areas expressed in terms of the number of defects or defectives d observed in equal samples of size n. These values may be expressed as $d = pn$, where p is the fraction defective. If p is expressed in percent, then $d = pn/100$. (The percentage symbol denotes $\frac{1}{100}$ or 0.01.) Computations are more direct when p values are expressed as decimals rather than as percentages. The correct location of the decimal point is important and is much easier to assign without error when using decimal fractions.

The central values for these control charts are established as in the previous section in two ways: (1) standard given, and (2) no standard given. The relations for determining the upper control limit and the lower control limit are based on the standard process average established from the data or prescribed, together with the sample size n. These control limits will be based on plus and minus three-sigma limits, i.e., three times the standard deviation for pn, $\sqrt{\bar{p}n(1 - \bar{p})}$, established respectively above and below the central value or standard value $\bar{p}n$. Units in each sample are assumed to have been selected at random from the process. Thus the distribution for such attributes data is the p binomial, $(q + p)^n$, where $\bar{p}'$ (or $\bar{p}$) represents the standard values for p, and $\bar{q} = 1 - \bar{p}$, resulting in a true probability frequency distribution.

The area for such a distribution between the upper and lower control limits represents the probability used to designate the confidence level or the degree of belief that in a controlled process, pn or d values will be found to occur within the boundaries of these limits. According to the multiple of the standard deviation for pn used, probability values selected from a normal law distribution are used to approximate the value of the confidence level assumed. The confidence levels as used for these control limits are thus assumed to be the same as those obtained for a normal law distribution and may be read directly from a normal law table, tabulating areas under the distribution curve for designated multiples of sigma, the standard deviation for pn. Actual probability values for the three-sigma control limits (or any other multiple of the standard deviation σ_{pn}) may be obtained by using the actual p binomial probability values for the given $\bar{p}$ and n values. These values may be calculated, but are usually available from tables of the binomial. Tables giving such probability values for p values from 0.01 to 0.99 in multiples of 0.01 and for n values from 1 to 50 in multiples of 1 are available, as well as for n values from 50 to 100 in multiples of 5. Some texts give other values for special cases. These probabilities, when properly accumulated to include the entire range of values between the given UCL and LCL values, provide the actual confidence levels, the degree of belief P_b associated with the selected control limits. As noted before, exact probability values for the range covered by the control limits are not as important as indicated in many texts because the errors actually made in taking the measurements are usually much larger than the errors when using the normal law as the distribution approximating the actual binomial. The actual determination by inspection and test, if a unit is actually nonconforming and cannot be used, is subject to many human and test-set errors. These errors are probably much larger than the errors associated with the probabilities assumed for the three-sigma or two-sigma control limits. Also, it must be noted that a probability value of 0.90, 0.95, or 0.99 has a variety of meanings when considered by different individuals.

For the p binomial, the standard deviation for pn is

$$\sigma_{pn} = \sqrt{pn(1 - p)} \tag{5}$$

When $\bar{p}$ is small (less than 0.10) in many texts the $(1 - p)$ factor is assumed to be approximately equal to one and this term is omitted in determining the control limits. The usual three-sigma control limits for $\bar{p}n$ are

$$\begin{aligned} &\text{Upper control limit, UCL:} \quad \bar{p}n + 3\sqrt{\bar{p}n(1 - \bar{p})} \\ &\text{Lower control limit, LCL:} \quad \bar{p}n - 3\sqrt{\bar{p}n(1 - \bar{p})} \end{aligned} \tag{6}$$

The $(1 - \bar{p})$ term has been retained in the above expressions. This procedure is recommended since the controls now desired are often tighter than in the past. It might be omitted when $\bar{p}$ is less than or equal to 0.04, or 4.0%. The error may actually be less than the inspection and sampling errors that might occur. The error for $\bar{p} = 4\%$, from omitting the multiplier $1 - p$ (which then equals 96%), is a different value between $\sqrt{0.04} = 0.20000$ and $\sqrt{0.04(0.96)} = \sqrt{0.0384} = 0.19596$, which is 0.00404. This divided by 0.19596 yields 0.02062 considered 2.06% error. Where the cutoff is at 0.10 or 10%, the difference is between $\sqrt{0.10} = 0.31623$ and $\sqrt{0.10(0.90)} = \sqrt{0.0900} = 0.30000$ which is 0.01623, so we have 0.01623/0.30000, which gives 0.05410 considered 5.41% error. If only a 2% error is desired, the $1 - p$ term must be included for any p value greater than 4%. If a 5% error is allowed, then $1 - p$ is added for p values greater than 10%. Care must be taken in making such a decision because there are many cases where the distribution is actually a Poisson exponential distribution in which the standard deviation does not include the $1 - p$ term. In such a distribution, the variance is pn and the corresponding standard deviation is its square root, $\sqrt{pn}$.

Under the section covering control charts for p, several illustrative examples were given. There has been no change in the relations used in determining the control limits for subsequent examples. The examples first published in the ASTM *Manual on Control of Materials* are the best illustrations of the various situations that may be actually encountered in quality control work. The American Standards Association also has used these illustrations and has amplified them in some cases. Rather than being modified, many are presented in the form originally published. Those engaged in quality control work should obtain the ASTM *Manual* and study the background for such examples. Control charts are given in this text for the majority of the examples that have been selected to illustrate the various types of situations covered by quality control. One should study especially those covering samples of unequal size. Where possible, an average sample size may be used to simplify such charts.

Example 5 The specified level for $\bar{p}'$ for defectives for Product C is 0.10 or 10%. Data for ten different lots of varying sizes, N, with different sample sizes, n, are tabulated below.

TABLE 5.5 Data for Example 5

Lot and Sample Number	*Lot Size, N*	*Sample Size, n*	*Number of Defectives*		*Variance (Std. Dev.)^2*	*Std. Dev.*	*Three Sigma Control Limits*	
			Observed	*Expected*	σ^2_{pn}	σ_{pn}	*UCL*	*LCL*
1	1,000	40	6	4.0	3.60	1.897	9.7	0
2	1,000	40	10*	4.0	3.60	1.897	9.7	0
3	4,000	100	20*	10.0	9.00	3.000	19.0	1.0
4	4,000	100	6	10.0	9.00	3.000	19.0	1.0
5	4,000	100	3	10.0	9.00	3.000	19.0	1.0
6	10,000	160	2*	16.0	14.40	3.795	27.4	4.6
7	10,000	160	5	16.0	14.40	3.795	27.4	4.6
8	2,000	75	3	7.5	6.75	2.598	15.3	0
9	2,000	75	6	7.5	6.75	2.598	15.3	0
10	2,000	75	4	7.5	6.75	2.598	15.3	0

* Outside control limits. Lots 2 and 3 above UCL; Lot 6 below LCL.

Control Limits

Sample Size, n	*Three-Sigma Control Limits:* $p'n \pm 3\sqrt{p'n(1-p')}$	*UCL*	*LCL*
40	$4.0 \pm 3\sqrt{4.0(0.9)} = 4.0 \pm 3(1.897) = 4.0 \pm 5.691$	9.69	0
75	$7.5 \pm 3\sqrt{7.5(0.9)} = 7.5 \pm 3(2.598) = 7.5 \pm 7.794$	15.29	0
100	$10.0 \pm 3\sqrt{10.0(0.9)} = 10.0 \pm 3(3.000) = 10.0 \pm 9.000$	19.00	1.00
160	$16.0 \pm 3\sqrt{16.0(0.9)} = 16.0 \pm 3(3.795) = 16.0 \pm 11.385$	27.38	4.62

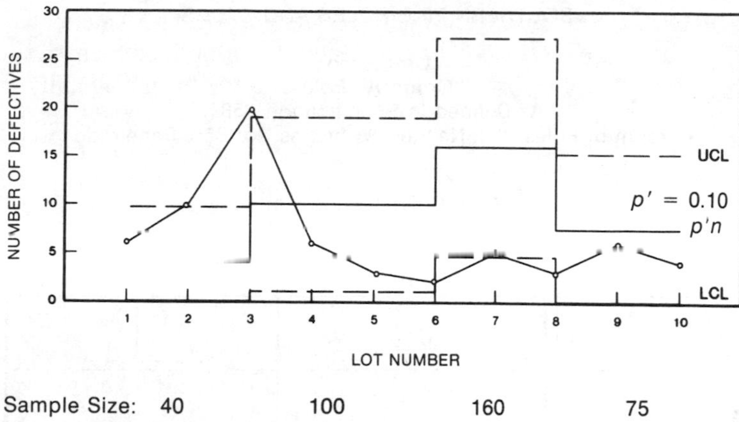

Figure 5–5 Control chart for number of defectives p'; unequal sample size, standard given.

A control chart for the above example is given in figure 5-5. Note that three of the observed number of defectives in samples are outside their respective three-sigma control limits. Samples numbered 2 and 3 are above their UCL values. Evidently some control action was taken, because succeeding samples are within their respective control limits and sample number 6 shows a value below its LCL value. This indicates that a better quality product is possible.

The next illustration covers a case where a standard derived from a large quantity of data together with the requirements of users of the product are used. Poles of different kinds are used by railroads, telegraph companies, and telephone companies. Southern pine poles are treated under pressure together with a vacuum with creosote to increase their life. Most companies use the ratio 8 : 2 or 6 : 1 for hrs. of pressure vs. hrs. of vacuum. The specification requires that the sapwood be impregnated to at least 85% of its depth or to at least 2.5 inches. The heartwood does not need to be treated. Six charts are shown using a specified p' value of 0.033 or 3.3%. The acceptance of individual lots of poles was based on a sampling plan using $n = 20$ and $c = 2$, which means that twenty poles were selected at random from a lot of poles submitted for acceptance. They were checked by an increment borer to obtain samples to be stained to show the depth of penetration of the creosote treatment. If two or less poles were found nonconforming, the lot was accepted. These measurements provided data for the charts in figure 5-6.

Figure 5-6 illustrates the case where a $\bar{p}$ is used as p'. It gives a control chart for a derived standard for percent defective selected by the purchaser as a standard for southern pine poles from three different companies supplied at five different locations. Dates and names have been modified. Points below the LCL indicate an improvement in quality submitted for acceptance.

SOUTHERN PINE POLES AND STUBS

Creosoted
"Group A" Poles
As Defined In Specification 6589
Percent of Poles With Neither 2½ Inches Nor 85% Penetration

A, B, C Creosoting Company

BRUNSWICK, GA.

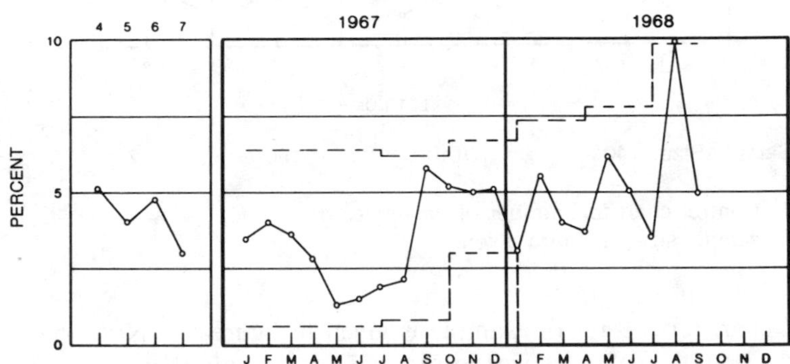

X, Y, Z Creosoting Company

BIRMINGHAM, ALA.

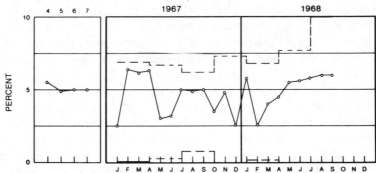

4 5 6 7
1967
1968
PERCENT
10
5
0
J F M A M J J A S O N D J F M A M J J A S O N D

Engineering Requirement for Single Pole	Minimum 2.5 Inches or 85% Sapwood Penetration
Inspection Requirement for Single Charge	Not Less Than 18 of a Sample of 20 Poles to Meet Engineering Requirement for Single Pole

Figure 5–6 Control chart for nonconforming poles classed as defectives; unequal samples per month, standard given as p'.

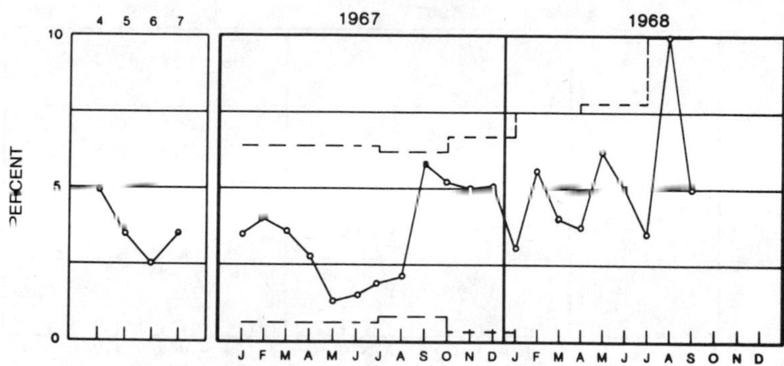

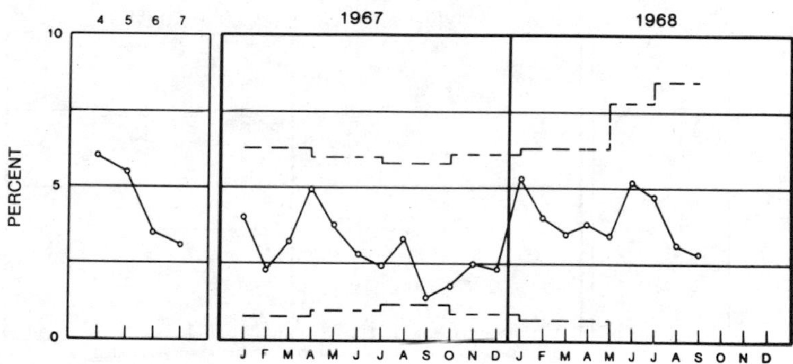

Engineering Requirement for Single Pole { Minimum 2.5 Inches or 85% Sapwood Penetration

Inspection Requirement for Single Charge { Not Less Than 18 of a Sample of 20 Poles to Meet Engineering Requirement for Single Pole

Figure 5–6 Control chart for nonconforming poles classed as defectives; unequal samples per month, standard given as p'.

Standard Given

Many purchase orders or specifications include a standard value for the fraction or percent defective that must be guaranteed by the supplier. The process must be

X, Y, Z Creosoting Company

WILMINGTON,N.C.

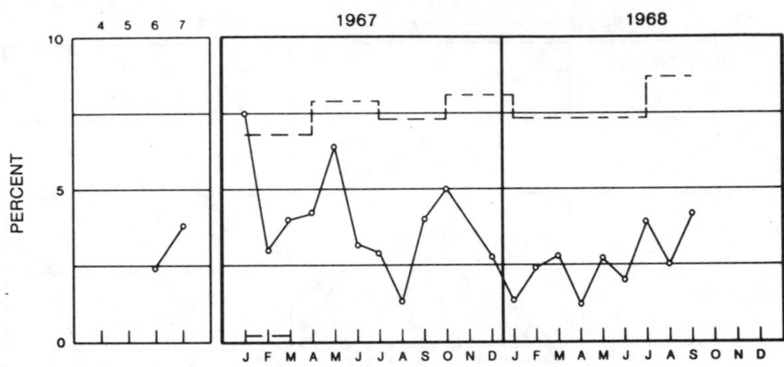

L, M, N Creosoting Company

GULFPORT,MISS.

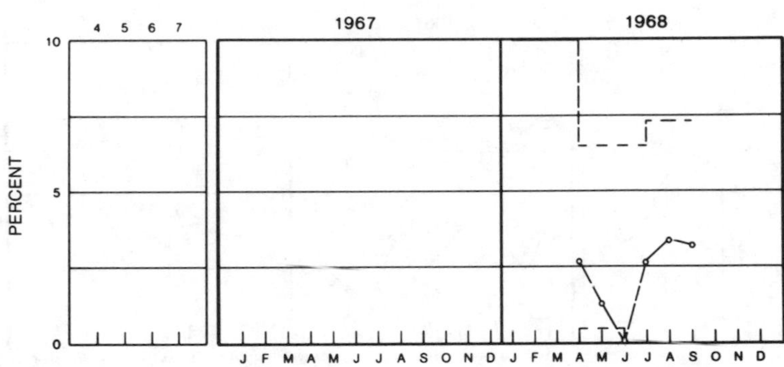

Engineering Requirement for Single Pole { Minimum 2.5 Inches or 85% Sapwood Penetration

Inspection Requirement for Single Charge { Not Less Than 18 of a Sample of 20 Poles to Meet Engineering Requirement for Single Pole

Figure 5-6 Control chart for nonconforming poles classed as defectives; unequal samples per month, standard given as p'.

controlled at a given $\bar{p}'$ value for one particular critical item or possibly for several defects. Examples of such charts are included in this chapter. Generally for such control charts, a constant $pn = d$ value is desired to avoid the necessity of stating varying central values as the expected values with three-sigma control chart limits placed about them. An example of this type of chart follows.

Example 6 For Product B, the specification requires that the process be controlled at a level of $\bar{p}' = 0.04$ (4.0%) for all defects combined and is to be given in terms of defectives. Lots of 1000 units are to be delivered; seventy-five units are to be inspected and tested for each lot. Set up a control chart for this standard, using the following data. The number of defectives, pn, is equal to d.

TABLE 5.6 Data for Example 6

Sample Number	*Observed Number of Defectives, d*	*Sample Number*	*Observed Number of Defectives, d*
1	2	11	8
2	1	12	7
3	3	13	5
4	6	14	1
5	0	15	2
6	1	16	0
7	4	17	0
8	8	18	3
9	9*	19	2
10	11*	20	1
Sum	45	Sum	29

Total Defectives $= 45 + 29 = 74$; $74 - 20^* = 54$; $\overline{pn} = \frac{54}{18} = 3.00 = \bar{d}$.

*Uncontrolled Process: These two lots were rejected.

Solution For $\bar{p}' = 0.04$, $n = 75$; p' will be used for $\bar{p}'$. $p'n = 3.00$; $\sigma_{pn} = \sqrt{p'n(1-p')} = \sqrt{3.00(0.96)} = \sqrt{2.88} = 1.697$; $3\sigma_{pn} = 5.091$.
Upper control limit, UCL, is $p'n + 3\sqrt{p'n(1-p')} = 3.00 + 5.09 = 8.09$
Lower control limit, LCL, is $p'n - 3\sqrt{p'n(1-p')} = 3.00 - 5.09 = 0$
Figure 5-7 presents a control chart for pn covering example 6.

Where the standard value of p (denoted by p') is given, it is desirable to select different sample sizes for different lot sizes. Since the observed results are given in terms of the number of nonconforming units or defectives, it is easier to just record the number of defectives found and plot them. Control charts for these unequal sample sizes must show different expected values, since $p'n$ varies with sample size.

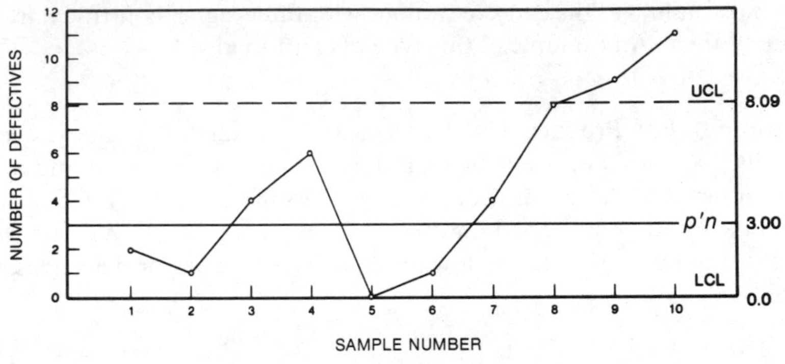

(*a*) First Ten Samples

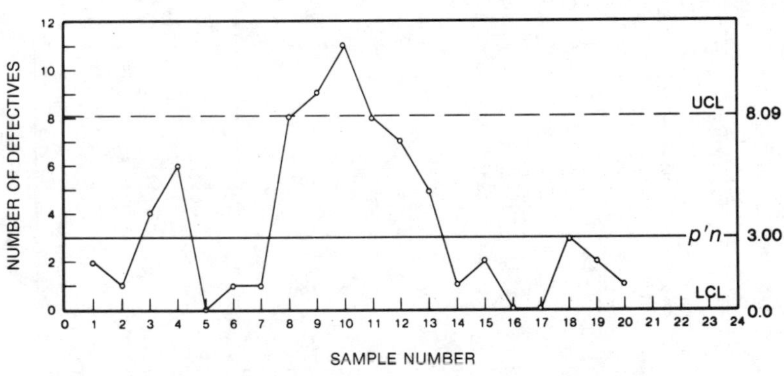

(*b*) 20 Samples Analyzed to Determine $\bar{P} + P'$

Figure 5–7 Control chart for number of defectives; sample size equal, $n = 75$. Process average from controlled data $\bar{p}n = 54/18 = 3.00 = p'n$.

No Standard Given

For most manufactured or purchased products and for most operations, the standard for the expected number of defects is not given. Standards usually are based on the desires and wants, as well as needs, of the customers. This information may be obtained from sales or customer representatives or may be derived from data secured in actual operations and/or from inspection and test. As in the previous case for fraction defective, $\bar{p}$ (designating the process average) is determined from data that was secured from products made under controlled conditions. An economical level of quality is derived from past data and experience.

In preparing control charts for such data, the control limits for the process are based on the number of defectives observed in the sample rather than the fraction defective. For this case, it is highly desirable to have the samples of equal size, although the method can be applied to samples of unequal size. Where the samples are of unequal size, it is preferable to use control charts for fraction defective. However, in establishing a standard all available data should be used. The following example illustrates this point.

Example 7 Since January 1974, Manufacturer D has been producing a product almost continuously and has been recording the number of nonconforming units that have been observed by inspection and test. He has also carefully recorded the actual number checked, together with the number of observed defectives in each sample of size *n*. He has also noted when he believes the process has been modified or is not in control. These data are given to quality control for analysis. The quality control department is to determine the most economical standard in terms of fraction defective or number of defectives for Product D based on the following data. The department is also to determine regular three-sigma control limits for a sample of 100 units.

TABLE 5.7 Number of Defectives Observed in Final Inspection for Product D; Data to Establish Process Average for Example 7

Period Month	*No. of Units Inspected*	*No. of Observed Defectives*	*Comments*
1974			
January	325	8	Process in control
February	230	6	Process in control
March	450	8	Process in control
April	150	5	Process in control
May	250	7	Process in control
June	300	32*	Process modified
July	400	28*	Corrective measures taken
August	350	20*	Process changed
September	250	26*	Poor automatic machine replaced
October	400	10	Quality improved.
November	300	7	Process controlled
December	250	4	Process controlled
1975			
January	400	5	Process controlled
February	225	4	Process controlled
March	270	3	Process controlled
April	350	6	Process controlled
May	400	7	Process controlled
Sum	5,300	186	
Uncontrolled	1,300	−106	June–Sept., 1974 Uncontrolled
Totals	4,000	80	

Best estimate of process average: $\bar{p} = \frac{80}{4000} = 0.02$ or 2.0%
Central Value or New Standard, $n = 100$: $\bar{p}_n = 0.02(100) = 2.00$
Upper Control Limit, UCL: $\bar{p}n + 3\sqrt{\bar{p}n(1-\bar{p})} = 2.00 + 3\sqrt{2.00(0.98)}$
$= 2.00 + 3\sqrt{1.96} = 2.00 + 3(1.4) = 2.00 + 4.2 = 6.2$
Lower Control Limit, LCL: $\bar{p}n - 3\sqrt{\bar{p}n(1-\bar{p})} = 2.00 - 3(1.4) = 2.00 - 4.2 = 0$

5.6 Analysis and Interpretation of Control Charts

When it is desired to establish standards based on past performance, accurate inspection and/or test data should be secured from the process currently in operation. Some of these data may come from a controlled process. In establishing a standard when some sample results are outside their respective three-sigma control limits, such results are not included in the data used to determine the desired standard. The method used is outlined below.

Step 1 Select as many consecutive samples ordered with respect to time as possible that have observed results recorded from inspections or tests on products from a seemingly controlled process or constant system of causes. From these data, determine a first estimate of the process average, $\bar{p}_1$. For units classed as defective or nonconforming as well as those classed as nondefective or conforming, determine the process average for the fraction defective by dividing the sum of the number of defectives by the sum of the sample sizes involved, i.e., $\bar{p}_1 = \Sigma d_i/\Sigma n_i$, where d denotes a defective unit and n represents the number of units in the sample in which the d defective units were observed and recorded.
Step 2 Determine, using equation (2), control limits (UCL and LCL values) for $\bar{p}_1$, using an average sample size for tentative limits and the actual sample size for exact control limits for any observed number of defectives deemed questionable. By questionable, we mean that it has a d value greater than its actual UCL value.
Step 3 Exclude samples which have p values based on d/n greater than their respective control limits. After removing the data deemed to be from an uncontrolled process, recompute the process average as $\bar{p}_2$, which will be used as a second tentative standard.
Step 4 If there still appear to be some sample points that are questionably large, redetermine their respective UCL values with $\bar{p}_2$ as the standard. Eliminate any points now shown to be greater than their respective UCL values.
Step 5 Using the remaining data—that part remaining after eliminating those data deemed to have been obtained from an uncontrolled process—determine $\bar{p}_3$. Adopt this value of p as the $\bar{p}$ to be used as a standard for control purposes.

The method outlined above was followed in obtaining the best estimate of the process average in example 7 covered in the prior section. A first estimate of the process average based on all the data was first determined for the seventeen months. Values observed and recorded for June, July, August, and September 1974 were eliminated, as these data were assumed to have been from products made under an uncontrolled process. (It had been found that one machine in the production process was old and in need of maintenance; it was termed obsolete and replaced. This change was made, resulting in an improvement in the quality of the outgoing product. Thus the system of causes was improved.) Following the method above for checking for lack of control, the first estimate of the process average for example 7 is $p_1 = \frac{186}{5300} = 0.035$. Since the sample sizes vary from month to month, the best method for a quick check for lack of control is to determine a value for the UCL based on a monthly average sample size. Such an average sample size is found by dividing the Σn_i by 17, the number of months, giving $\bar{n} = \frac{5300}{17} = 312$. Thus 300 may be used as a good approximate average value for n. For $n = 300$ the UCL value obtained by the use of equation (2) is as follows:

$$\begin{aligned}\text{UCL} &= 0.035(300) + 3\sqrt{0.035(300)(1 - 0.035)} = 10.50 + 3\sqrt{10.5(0.965)} \\ &= 10.5 + 3\sqrt{10.1325} = 10.5 + 3(3.2) = 10.5 + 9.6 = 20.1\end{aligned}$$

Correspondingly, $\text{LCL} = 10.5 - 9.6 = 0.9$.

June, July, and September have pn values greater than twenty defectives reported, while August has exactly twenty defectives recorded. These twenty defectives were observed in a sample of 350 units, greater than the 300 used to compute the UCL of 20.1. With 350 units in the sample, the UCL value will be greater, so that twenty will be within the three-sigma control limits.

Since the balance of the pn values reported and recorded for the other thirteen months are much smaller than the twenty defectives recorded for August, one should omit the evaluation of the $\bar{p}_2$ value as outlined above and determine $\bar{p}_3$ directly by ignoring the four large values of pn from the July through September 1974 data. Now check to determine whether the value of the twenty defectives reported for August is within this new UCL limit based on the new value of $\bar{p}$. This is determined by dividing 80 defectives by 4,000, the sum of the other thirteen remaining months, giving a process average of $\bar{p} = 0.02$ or 2%. The sample size for August is 350. Using these values, a new value is determined for UCL as follows:

$$\begin{aligned}\text{UCL} &= 0.02(350) + 3\sqrt{0.02(350)(1 - 0.02)} = 7.0 + 3\sqrt{7.0(0.98)} = 7.0 + 3\sqrt{6.86} \\ &= 7.0 + 3(2.6) = 7.0 + 7.8 = 14.8.\end{aligned}$$

Correspondingly, $\text{LCL} = 7.0 - 7.8 = 0$.

The August pn value of 20 is much greater than 14.8. Hence the August results are not controlled at a level of 2% and should be omitted when determining the best standard for this manufacturing process.

Control charts are used as guides to show when lack of control is indicated, based on theoretical statistical quality control principles and methods. Figure 5-8 illustrates three possible situations that might occur on various kinds of quality control charts. Seven continuous successive sample results are graphed, together with a standard $\bar{p}$ value. In addition, the upper control limits (UCL) and the lower control limits (LCL) are graphed for equal sample sizes. The first control chart (*a*) shows the percent defective in the state of statistical control. All seven points are within three-sigma control limits. The second control chart (*b*) shows: the percent defective worse than the expected value, where the last two values are greater than the upper control limit. This indicates that on an average, the process will produce more defectives than it has in the past. The third control chart (*c*) shows the percent defective value is better than the expected value. Since the last two sample results are less than the lower control limit (LCL) an improvement in the process is indicated and the process should produce less defectives than in the past, with the result that better quality, less customer complaints, and more profit will be attained by the manufacturer.

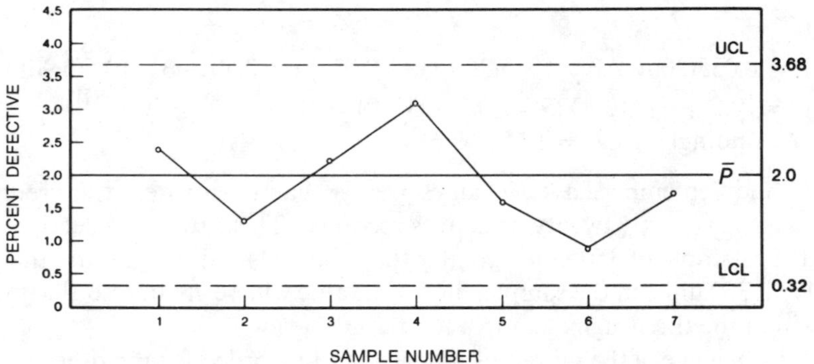

(*a*) Percent Defective in State of Statistical Control

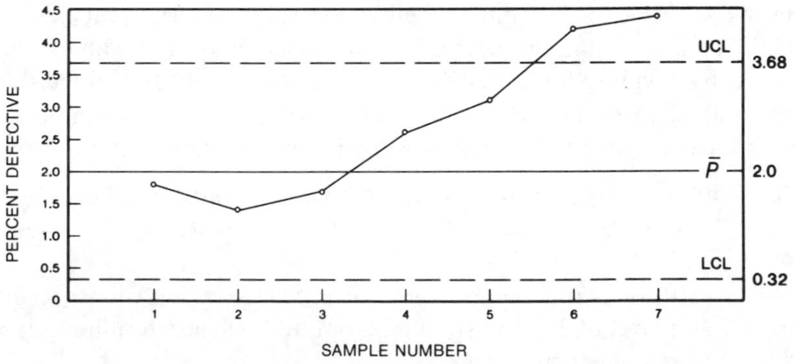

(*b*) Percent Defective Worse Than Expected

Figure 5–8 Three different cases of possible processes depicted by quality control charts for percent defective.

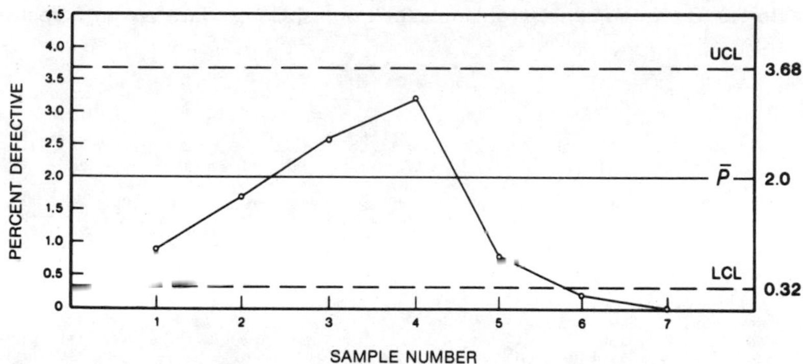

(c) Percent Defective Better Than Expected

Figure 5–8 Three different cases of possible processes depicted by quality control charts for percent defective.

TABLE 5.8 Three-Sigma Control Limits for Control Charts for Percent Defective

A. Upper Control Limit

Standard percent defective (100p')	Subgroup Size																	
	100	150	200	300	400	500	600	800	1,000	1,500	2,000	3,000	4,000	5,000	10,000	20,000	50,000	100,000
0.1	1.05	0.87	0.77	0.65	0.57	0.52	0.49	0.44	0.40	0.34	0.31	0.27	0.25	0.23	0.19	0.17	0.14	0.13
0.2	1.54	1.29	1.15	0.97	0.87	0.80	0.75	0.67	0.62	0.55	0.50	0.44	0.41	0.39	0.33	0.29	0.26	0.24
0.4	2.29	1.95	1.74	1.49	1.35	1.25	1.17	1.07	1.00	0.89	0.82	0.75	0.70	0.67	0.59	0.53	0.48	0.46
0.6	2.92	2.49	2.24	1.94	1.76	1.64	1.55	1.42	1.33	1.20	1.12	1.02	0.97	0.93	0.83	0.76	0.70	0.67
0.8	3.47	2.98	2.69	2.34	2.14	2.00	1.89	1.74	1.65	1.49	1.40	1.29	1.22	1.18	1.07	0.99	0.92	0.88
1.0	3.98	3.44	3.11	2.72	2.49	2.33	2.22	2.06	1.94	1.77	1.67	1.54	1.47	1.42	1.30	1.21	1.13	1.09
1.2	4.47	3.87	3.51	3.09	2.83	2.66	2.53	2.35	2.23	2.04	1.93	1.80	1.72	1.66	1.53	1.43	1.35	1.30
1.4	4.92	4.28	3.89	3.43	3.16	2.98	2.84	2.65	2.51	2.31	2.19	2.04	1.96	1.90	1.75	1.65	1.56	1.51
1.6	5.36	4.67	4.26	3.77	3.48	3.28	3.14	2.93	2.79	2.57	2.44	2.29	2.20	2.13	1.98	1.87	1.77	1.72
1.8	5.79	5.06	4.62	4.10	3.79	3.58	3.43	3.21	3.06	2.83	2.69	2.53	2.43	2.36	2.20	2.08	1.98	1.93
2.0	6.20	5.43	4.97	4.42	4.10	3.88	3.71	3.48	3.33	3.08	2.94	2.77	2.66	2.59	2.42	2.30	2.19	2.13
2.5	7.18	6.32	5.81	5.20	4.84	4.59	4.41	4.16	3.98	3.71	3.55	3.36	3.24	3.16	2.97	2.83	2.71	2.65
3.0	8.12	7.18	6.62	5.95	5.56	5.29	5.09	4.81	4.62	4.32	4.14	3.93	3.81	3.72	3.51	3.36	3.23	3.16
3.5	9.01	8.00	7.40	6.68	6.26	5.97	5.75	5.45	5.24	4.92	4.73	4.51	4.37	4.28	4.05	3.89	3.75	3.67
4.0	9.88	8.80	8.16	7.39	6.94	6.63	6.40	6.08	5.86	5.52	5.31	5.07	4.93	4.83	4.59	4.42	4.26	4.19
5	11.54	10.34	9.62	8.77	8.27	7.92	7.67	7.31	7.07	6.69	6.46	6.19	6.03	5.92	5.65	5.46	5.29	5.21
6	13.12	11.82	11.04	10.11	9.56	9.19	8.91	8.52	8.25	7.84	7.59	7.30	7.13	7.01	6.71	6.50	6.32	6.23
7	14.65	13.25	12.41	11.42	10.83	10.42	10.12	9.71	9.42	8.98	8.71	8.40	8.21	8.08	7.77	7.54	7.34	7.24
8	16.14	14.65	13.75	12.70	12.07	11.64	11.32	10.88	10.57	10.10	9.82	9.49	9.29	9.15	8.81	8.58	8.36	8.26
9	17.59	16.01	15.07	13.96	13.29	12.84	12.50	12.04	11.71	11.22	10.92	10.57	10.36	10.21	9.86	9.61	9.38	9.27
10	19.00	17.35	16.36	15.20	14.50	14.02	13.67	13.18	12.85	12.32	12.01	11.64	11.42	11.27	10.90	10.64	10.40	10.28
12	21.75	19.96	18.89	17.63	16.87	16.36	15.98	15.45	15.08	14.52	14.18	13.78	13.54	13.38	12.97	12.69	12.44	12.31
14	24.41	22.50	21.36	20.01	19.20	18.66	18.25	17.68	17.29	16.69	16.33	15.90	15.65	15.47	15.04	14.74	14.47	14.33
16	27.00	24.98	23.78	22.35	21.50	20.92	20.49	19.89	19.48	18.84	18.46	18.01	17.74	17.56	17.10	16.78	16.49	16.35
18	29.53	27.41	26.15	24.65	23.76	23.15	22.71	22.07	21.64	20.97	20.58	20.10	19.82	19.63	19.15	18.81	18.52	18.36
20	32.00	29.80	28.49	26.93	26.00	25.37	24.90	24.24	23.79	23.10	22.68	22.19	21.90	21.70	21.20	20.85	20.54	20.38
25	37.99	35.61	34.19	32.50	31.50	30.81	30.30	29.59	29.11	28.35	27.90	27.37	27.05	26.84	26.30	25.92	25.58	25.41
30	43.75	41.22	39.72	37.94	36.87	36.15	35.61	34.86	34.35	33.55	33.07	32.51	32.17	31.94	31.37	30.97	30.61	30.43
35	49.31	46.68	45.12	43.26	42.15	41.40	40.84	40.06	39.52	38.70	38.20	37.61	37.26	37.02	36.43	36.01	35.64	35.45
40	54.70	52.00	50.39	48.49	47.35	46.57	46.00	45.20	44.65	43.79	43.29	42.68	42.32	42.08	41.47	41.04	40.66	40.46

Continued on next page

Table 5.8 Three-Sigma Control Limits for Control Charts for Percent Defective.

	B. *Lower Control Limit*																	
Standard percent defective (100p′)	*Subgroup Size*																	
	100	*150*	*200*	*300*	*400*	*500*	*600*	*800*	*1,000*	*1,500*	*2,000*	*3,000*	*4,000*	*5,000*	*10,000*	*20,000*	*50,000*	*100,000*
0.1	0.00	0.00	0.00	0.00	0.00	0.00	0.00	0.00	0.00	0.00	0.00	0.00	0.00	0.00	0.01	0.03	0.06	0.07
0.2	0.00	0.00	0.00	0.00	0.00	0.00	0.00	0.00	0.00	0.00	0.00	0.00	0.00	0.01	0.07	0.11	0.14	0.16
0.4	0.00	0.00	0.00	0.00	0.00	0.00	0.00	0.00	0.00	0.00	0.00	0.05	0.10	0.13	0.21	0.27	0.32	0.34
0.6	0.00	0.00	0.00	0.00	0.00	0.00	0.00	0.00	0.00	0.00	0.08	0.18	0.23	0.27	0.37	0.44	0.50	0.53
0.8	0.00	0.00	0.00	0.00	0.00	0.00	0.00	0.00	0.00	0.11	0.20	0.31	0.38	0.42	0.53	0.61	0.68	0.72
1.0	0.00	0.00	0.00	0.00	0.00	0.00	0.00	0.00	0.06	0.23	0.33	0.46	0.53	0.58	0.70	0.79	0.87	0.91
1.2	0.00	0.00	0.00	0.00	0.00	0.00	0.00	0.05	0.17	0.36	0.47	0.60	0.68	0.74	0.87	0.97	1.05	1.10
1.4	0.00	0.00	0.00	0.00	0.00	0.00	0.00	0.15	0.29	0.49	0.61	0.76	0.84	0.90	1.05	1.15	1.24	1.29
1.6	0.00	0.00	0.00	0.00	0.00	0.00	0.06	0.27	0.41	0.63	0.76	0.91	1.00	1.07	1.22	1.33	1.43	1.48
1.8	0.00	0.00	0.00	0.00	0.00	0.02	0.17	0.39	0.54	0.77	0.91	1.07	1.17	1.24	1.40	1.52	1.62	1.67
2.0	0.00	0.00	0.00	0.00	0.00	0.12	0.29	0.52	0.67	0.92	1.06	1.23	1.34	1.41	1.58	1.70	1.81	1.87
2.5	0.00	0.00	0.00	0.00	0.16	0.41	0.59	0.84	1.02	1.29	1.45	1.64	1.76	1.84	2.03	2.17	2.29	2.35
3.0	0.00	0.00	0.00	0.05	0.44	0.71	0.91	1.19	1.38	1.68	1.86	2.07	2.19	2.28	2.49	2.64	2.77	2.84
3.5	0.00	0.00	0.00	0.32	0.74	1.03	1.25	1.55	1.76	2.08	2.27	2.49	2.63	2.72	2.95	3.11	3.25	3.33
4.0	0.00	0.00	0.00	0.61	1.06	1.37	1.60	1.92	2.14	2.48	2.69	2.93	3.07	3.17	3.41	3.58	3.74	3.81
5	0.00	0.00	0.38	1.23	1.73	2.08	2.33	2.69	2.93	3.31	3.54	3.81	3.97	4.08	4.35	4.54	4.71	4.79
6	0.00	0.18	0.96	1.89	2.44	2.81	3.09	3.48	3.75	4.16	4.41	4.70	4.87	4.99	5.29	5.50	5.68	5.77
7	0.00	0.75	1.59	2.58	3.17	3.58	3.88	4.29	4.58	5.02	5.29	5.60	5.79	5.92	6.23	6.46	6.66	6.76
8	0.00	1.35	2.25	3.30	3.93	4.36	4.68	5.12	5.43	5.90	6.18	6.51	6.71	6.85	7.19	7.42	7.64	7.74
9	0.41	1.99	2.93	4.04	4.71	5.16	5.50	5.96	6.29	6.78	7.08	7.43	7.64	7.79	8.14	8.39	8.62	8.73
10	1.00	2.65	3.64	4.80	5.50	5.98	6.33	6.82	7.15	7.68	7.99	8.36	8.58	8.73	9.10	9.36	9.60	9.72
12	2.25	4.04	5.11	6.37	7.13	7.64	8.02	8.55	8.92	9.48	9.82	10.22	10.46	10.62	11.03	11.31	11.56	11.69
14	3.59	5.50	6.64	7.99	8.80	9.34	9.75	10.32	10.71	11.31	11.67	12.10	12.35	12.53	12.96	13.26	13.53	13.67
16	5.00	7.02	8.22	9.65	10.50	11.08	11.51	12.11	12.52	13.16	13.54	13.99	14.26	14.44	14.90	15.22	15.51	15.65
18	6.47	8.59	9.85	11.35	12.24	12.85	13.29	13.93	14.36	15.03	15.42	15.90	16.18	16.37	16.85	17.19	17.48	17.64
20	8.00	10.20	11.51	13.07	14.00	14.63	15.10	15.76	16.21	16.90	17.32	17.81	18.10	18.30	18.80	19.15	19.46	19.62
25	12.01	14.39	15.81	17.50	18.50	19.19	19.70	20.41	20.89	21.65	22.10	22.63	22.95	23.16	23.70	24.08	24.42	24.59
30	16.25	18.78	20.28	22.06	23.13	23.85	24.39	25.14	25.65	26.45	26.93	27.49	27.83	28.06	28.63	29.03	29.39	29.57
35	20.69	23.32	24.88	26.74	27.85	28.60	29.16	29.94	30.48	31.30	31.80	32.39	32.74	32.98	33.57	33.99	34.36	34.55
40	25.30	28.00	29.61	31.51	32.65	33.43	34.00	34.80	35.35	36.21	36.71	37.32	37.68	37.92	38.53	38.96	39.34	39.54

It is often necessary to apply control charts to several characteristics at the same time, as well as to the various components making up a system. Example 8 presents such a case along with an analysis of the results, following the presentation of the data in table 5.9. Also given are standards for the three groups, designated as Group A, Group B, and Group C, and a standard for all groups combined. Note that the standard for all groups combined is less than the sum of the p' values for the three groups.

Example 8 *Control Chart for p (Fraction Rejected), Total and Components, Samples of Unequal Size.* A control device was given a 100 percent inspection in lots varying in size from about 1,800 units to 5,000 units, each unit being tested and inspected with respect to twenty-three *essentially independent* characteristics. These twenty-three characteristics were grouped into three groups designated Groups A, B, and C, corresponding to three successive inspections. A unit found defective at any time with respect to any one characteristic was immediately rejected; hence units found defective in, say, the Group A inspection were not subjected to the two subsequent group inspections. In fact, the number of units inspected for each characteristic in a group itself will differ from characteristic to characteristic; if defects with respect to the characteristics in a group occur, the last characteristic in the group having the smallest sample size is inspected 100 percent. Since 100 percent inspection is used, no additional units are available for inspection to maintain a constant sample size for all characteristics in a group or for all the component groups. The fraction defective with respect to each characteristic is sufficiently small so that the error within a group, although rather large between the first and last characteristic inspected by one inspection group, can be neglected for practical purposes. Under these circumstances, the number inspected for any group equals the lot size diminished by the number of units rejected in the preceding inspections.

Part 1 of table 5.9 gives the data for twelve successive lots of product, and shows for each lot inspected the total fraction rejected as well as the number and fraction rejected at each inspection station. Part 2 of table 5.9 gives values of p', fraction rejected, at which levels the manufacturer desires to control this device, with respect to all twenty-three characteristics combined and with respect to the characteristics tested and inspected at each of the three inspection stations. Note that the p' for all characteristics (in terms of defectives) is less than the sum of the p' values for the three component groups, since defects for more than one characteristic or group of characteristics may occur on a single unit. Control limits, lower and upper, in terms of fraction rejected are listed for each lot size using the initial lot size as the sample size for all characteristics

TABLE 5.9 Inspection Data for 100 Percent Inspection—Control Device

(1) Observed Number of Rejects and Fraction Rejected

All Groups Combined				*Group A*			*Group B*			*Group C*		
		Total Rejected			*Rejected*			*Rejected*			*Rejected*	
Lot	*Lot Size, n*	*Number*	*Fraction*	*Lot Size, n*	*Number*	*Fraction*	*Lot Size, n*	*Number*	*Fraction*	*Lot Size, n*	*Number*	*Fraction*
No. 1....	4814	914	0.190	4814	311	0.065	4503	253	0.056	4250	350	0.082
No. 2....	2159	359	0.166	2159	128	0.059	2031	105	0.052	1926	126	0.065
No. 3....	3089	565	0.183	3089	195	0.063	2894	149	0.051	2745	221	0.081
No. 4....	3156	626	0.198	3156	233	0.074	2923	142	0.049	2781	251	0.090
No. 5....	2139	434	0.203	2139	146	0.068	1993	101	0.051	1892	187	0.099
No. 6....	2588	503	0.194	2588	177	0.068	2411	151	0.063	2260	175	0.077
No. 7....	2510	487	0.194	2510	143	0.057	2367	116	0.049	2251	228	0.101
No. 8....	4103	803	0.196	4103	318	0.078	3785	242	0.064	3543	243	0.069
No. 9....	2992	547	0.183	2992	208	0.070	2784	130	0.047	2654	209	0.079
No. 10....	3545	643	0.181	3545	172	0.049	3373	180	0.053	3193	291	0.091
No. 11....	1841	353	0.192	1841	97	0.053	1744	119	0.068	1625	137	0.084
No. 12....	2748	418	0.152	2748	141	0.051	2607	114	0.044	2493	163	0.065
Total	35,684	6,652	0.186	35,684	2,269	0.064	33,415	1,802	0.054	31,613	2,581	0.082

Continued on next page

(2) *Central Lines and Control Limits, Based on Standard p′ Values*

	All Groups Combined	Group A	Group B	Group C
		Central Lines		
p' =	0.180	0.070	0.050	0.080
Lot		*Control Limits*		
No. 1	0.197 and 0.163	0.081 and 0.059	0.060 and 0.040	0.093 and 0.067
No. 2	0.205 and 0.155	0.086 and 0.054	0.064 and 0.036	0.099 and 0.061
No. 3	0.201 and 0.159	0.084 and 0.056	0.062 and 0.038	0.096 and 0.064
No. 4	0.200 and 0.160	0.084 and 0.056	0.062 and 0.038	0.095 and 0.065
No. 5	0.205 and 0.155	0.086 and 0.054	0.065 and 0.035	0.099 and 0.061
No. 6	0.203 and 0.157	0.085 and 0.055	0.063 and 0.037	0.097 and 0.063
No. 7	0.203 and 0.157	0.085 and 0.055	0.064 and 0.036	0.097 and 0.063
No. 8	0.198 and 0.162	0.082 and 0.058	0.061 and 0.039	0.094 and 0.066
No. 9	0.201 and 0.159	0.084 and 0.056	0.062 and 0.038	0.096 and 0.064
No. 10	0.200 and 0.160	0.083 and 0.057	0.061 and 0.039	0.094 and 0.066
No. 11	0.207 and 0.153	0.088 and 0.052	0.066 and 0.034	0.100 and 0.060
No. 12	0.202 and 0.158	0.085 and 0.055	0.063 and 0.037	0.096 and 0.064

combined and the lot size available at the beginning of inspection and test for each group as the sample size for that group.

Figure 5-9 shows four control charts, one covering all rejections combined for the control device and three other charts covering the rejections for each of the three inspection stations for Group A, Group B, and Group C

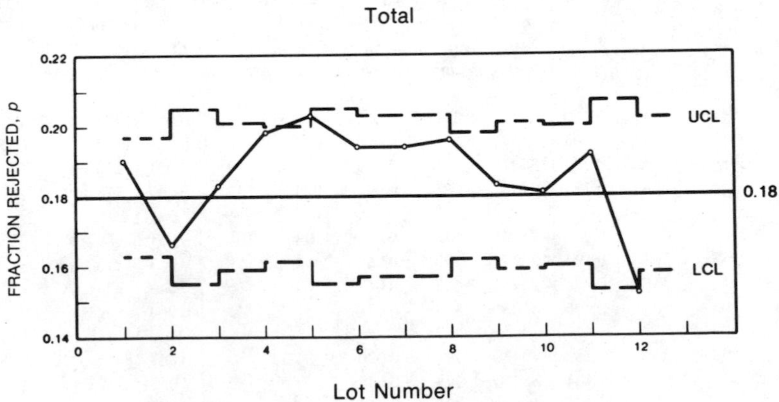

Figure 5–9 Control charts for p (fraction rejected) for total and components; sample of unequal size, n = 1625 to 4818, p' given.

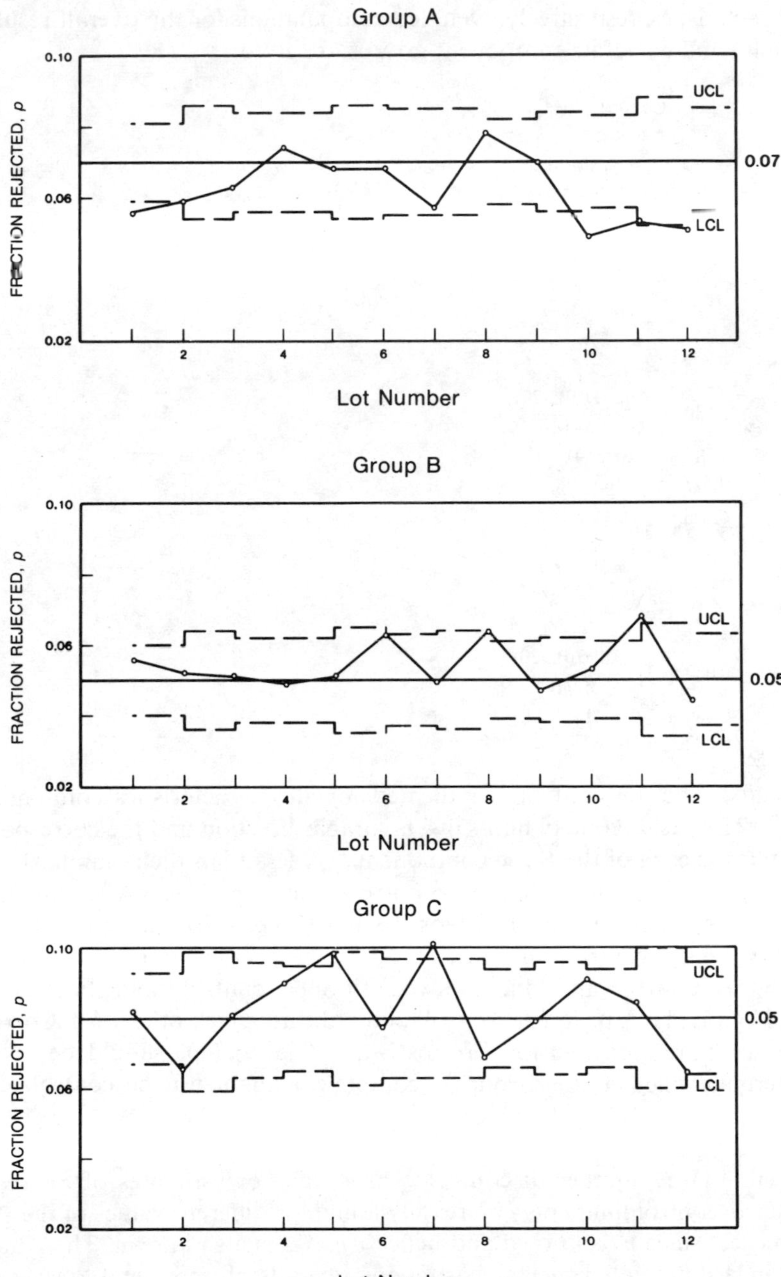

Figure 5-9 Control charts for p (fraction rejected) for total and components; sample of unequal size, n = 1625 to 4818, p' given.

characteristics, respectively. Detailed computations for the overall results for one lot and one of its component groups are given.

Central Lines
See table 5.9

Control Limits
See Table 5.9

For Lot No. 1:
Total: $n = 4814$:

$$p' \pm 3\sqrt{\frac{p'(1-p')}{n}} =$$

$$0.180 \pm 3\sqrt{\frac{0.180\,(0.820)}{4814}} =$$

$0.180 \pm 3(0.00554)$,
0.197 and 0.163.

Group C: $n = 4250$:

$$p' \pm 3\sqrt{\frac{p'(1-p')}{n}} =$$

$$0.080 \pm 3\sqrt{\frac{0.080\,(0.920)}{4250}} =$$

$0.080 \pm 3(0.00416)$,
0.0925 and 0.0675. +

Results Lack of control is indicated for all characteristics combined; lot No. 12 is outside control limits in a favorable direction and the corresponding results for each of the three components are less than their standard values, Group A being below the lower control limit. For Group A results, lack of control is indicated since lots Nos. 10 and 12 are below their lower control limits. Lack of control is indicated for the component characteristics in Group B, since lots Nos. 8 and 11 are above their upper control limits. For Group C, lot No. 7 is above its upper control limit indicating lack of control. Corrective measures are indicated for Groups B and C and steps should be taken to determine whether the Group A component might not be controlled at a smaller value of p', such as 0.06.

Where a large number of control charts for c' or estimates of c' are to be determined, control limits may be readily found for different values of the sample sizes in effect since p' is known and hence $p'n = c'$ is also known. The American War Standard presented such a chart giving two sets of upper and lower control limits. One set is the usual three-sigma control limits. The second set has a probability of 0.995 assigned to the upper control limit and 0.005 assigned to the lower control limit. Figure 5-10 presents this chart. Note that $pn = c$ is used rather than $pn = d$. The chart below may be applied to either d or c values.

Figure 5-10 shows control limits for c, which may be used to determine the control limits for the next example where both c' and u' are given as definite standards. Example 9 covers the case where standards are given and control limits are based on samples of equal size, twenty-five for each lot.

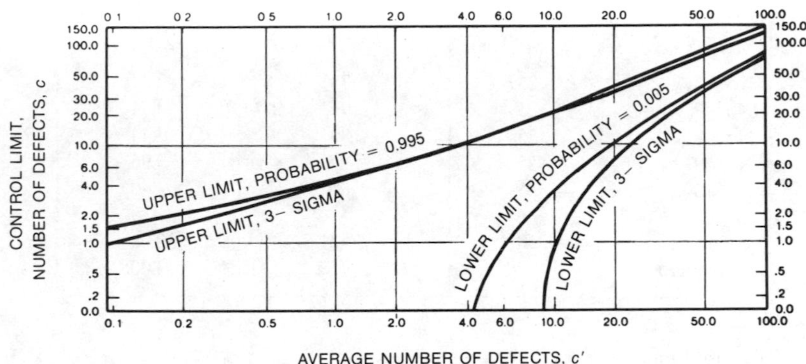

Figure 5–10 Chart for determining control limits for c, number of defects per sample.

Example 9 *Control Chart for c, Samples of Equal Size and Control Chart for u, Samples of Equal Size.* A Type D motor is being produced by a manufacturer and he desires to control the number of defects per motor at a level of $u' = 3.000$ defects per unit with respect to all visual defects. He is producing on a continuous basis and decides to take a sample of 25 motors every day, where a day's product is treated as a lot. Due to the nature of the process, he plans on controlling the product for these defects at a level such that $c' = 75.0$ defects as $u'n = c'$. Table 5.10 gives data in terms of number of defects, c, and also defects per unit, u, for 10 consecutive days. Figure 5-11 shows the control chart for c. In figure 5-12 a control chart is given for u, where the central line is $u' = 3.000$ and the control limits are:

$$u' \pm 3\sqrt{\frac{u'}{n}} = 3.000 \pm 3\sqrt{\frac{3.000}{25}} = 3.000 \pm 3(0.3464),\ 4.04 \text{ and } 1.96.$$

See figure 5-12 below for the control chart using central line $u' = 3.000$, and control limits $n = 25$. Per above computations, UCL = 4.04, and LCL = 1.96.

TABLE 5.10 Daily Inspection Results for Type D Motors in Terms of Defects per Sample and Defects per Unit

Lot	*Sample Size,* n	*Number of Defects,* c	*Defects Per Init,* u
No. 1........	25	81	3.24
No. 2........	25	64	2.56
No. 3........	25	53	2.12
No. 4........	25	95	3.80
No. 5........	25	50	2.00
No. 6........	25	73	2.92
No. 7........	25	91	3.64
No. 8........	25	86	3.44
No. 9........	25	99	3.96
No. 10........	25	60	2.40
Total	250	752	30.08
Average ...		75.2	3.008

Central Line

$$c' = u'n = 3.000 \times 25,$$
$$= 75.0$$

Control Limits

$n = 25$:

$$c' \pm 3\sqrt{c'} =$$
$$75.0 \pm 3\sqrt{75.0} =$$
$$75.0 \pm 3(8.66),$$
$$100.98 \text{ and } 49.02.$$

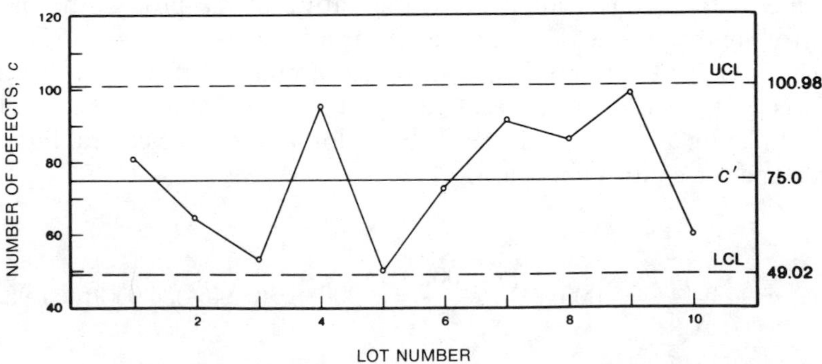

Figure 5–11 Control chart for c; samples of unequal size, $n = 25$, c' given.

Results No significant deviations from the desired level.

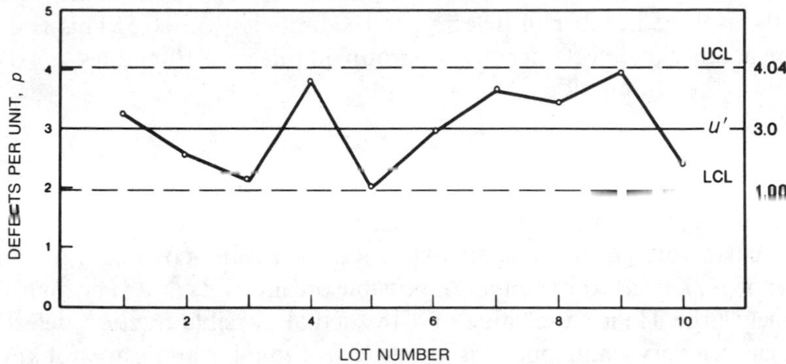

Figure 5–12 Control chart for u; samples of equal size, $n = 25$, u' given.

5.7 Control Charts for Defects per Unit, *u*, and Defects per Sample, *c*

In the prior discussion of control charts for the number of defectives, the expected value was established at $p'n$ or $\bar{p}n$, for *standard given* or *no standard given*, respectively. There often occur circumstances where more than one defect of the same kind may be observed on a unit or in a subgroup of several units. For example, a pair of matched gears consists of two gears that operate together as a unit and are treated as a single unit. In the dressmaking industry, a dress may have several defective seams. A unit that is made by riveting together several parts may have a number of defective rivets per unit on each unit inspected. An automobile, when purchased new, usually has a large number of defects on it, even though the dealer may spend considerable time in checking each car for the purchaser. Washers and nuts may be missing, some of the rheostats controlling the engine's heating and cooling system do not function, and in general, the engine is not properly adjusted and tuned to provide maximum mileage per gallon of fuel. Because of such defects, it is desirable to place control charts on each such unit in production or even on a complete system, such as a fire control system.

In many cases and for many characteristics or items, the degree of nonconformance for a unit may vary greatly. For example, a table might have on its surface a single small scratch, a large scratch, or numerous scratches of very different magnitudes. The symbol u represents the numerical magnitude for the number of defects that may occur in such instances. This measure differs from the fraction defective p, as the number of defects per unit might be very large. In other cases, this number might be quite small; many units may be perfect so that in a lot of 100 tables only five tables are scratched, each having an average of ten scratches per table. For the lot of 100 tables, however, there are only a total of fifty scratches, so that the average number of defects per 100 units is $\frac{50}{100} = 0.5$. This is denoted by $\bar{u}$. The number of defects per the subgroup, in this case 100 tables, is termed c. The following relation holds.

$$c = un \tag{7}$$

We see that $c = 0.5(100) = 50$ scratches, as noted previously.

For example, if the number of electrical breakdowns is determined by testing at a particular voltage for a particular length of rubber-covered wire, such as 5,000 feet or 10,000 feet, the number of possible breakdowns at a very high voltage is extremely large. Hence, the value of p, the actual possible fraction defective for possible cases, is very small, but pn is known even though p and n are not known. It is easier to treat this case as u and $un = c$, to differentiate it from the prior case where p and n are known and identified as actual numbers, which are finite. The first example covers the case where the standard u' is given and where the samples are of unequal size.

Example 10 *Control Chart for u, Samples of Unequal Size; Standard Given.* It is desired to control the number of defects per billet to a standard of 1.000 defect per unit in order that the wire made from such billets of copper will not contain an excessive number of defects. The lot sizes varied greatly from day to day; hence a sampling schedule was set up giving three different sample sizes to cover the range of lot sizes received. A control program was instituted using a control chart for defects per unit with reference to the desired standard. Table 5.11 gives data in terms of defects and defects per unit for fifteen consecutive lots under this program. Figure 5-13 shows the control chart for u and figure 5-14 presents a control chart for c.

TABLE 5.11 Lot by Lot Inspection Results for Copper Billets in Terms of Defects and Defects per Unit

Lot	Sample Size, n	Number of Defects, c	Defects per Unit, u	Lot	Sample Size, n	Number of Defects, c	Defects per Unit, u
No. 1........	100	75	0.750	No. 10......	100	130	1.300
No. 2........	100	138	1.380	No. 11......	100	58	0.580
No. 3........	200	212	1.060	No. 12......	400	480	1.200
No. 4........	400	444	1.110	No. 13......	400	316	0.790
No. 5........	400	508	1.270	No. 14......	200	162	0.810
No. 6........	400	312	0.780	No. 15......	200	178	0.890
No. 7........	200	168	0.840				
No. 8........	200	266	1.330	Total...	3500	3566	
No. 9........	100	119	1.190	Over-all*			1.019

$* \bar{u} = \frac{3566}{3500} = 1.019.$

Central Line

$$u' = 1.000.$$

Control Limits

$n = 100$:

$$u' \pm 3\sqrt{\frac{u'}{n}} =$$

$$1.000 \pm 3\sqrt{\frac{1.000}{100}} =$$

$$1.000 \pm 3(0.100),$$
$$1.300 \text{ and } 0.700.$$

$n = 200$:

$$u' \pm 3\sqrt{\frac{u'}{n}} =$$

$$1.000 \pm 3\sqrt{\frac{1.000}{200}} =$$

$$1.000 \pm 3(0.0707),$$
$$1.212 \text{ and } 0.788.$$

$n = 400$:

$$u' \pm 3\sqrt{\frac{u'}{n}} =$$

$$1.000 \pm 3\sqrt{\frac{1.000}{400}} =$$

$$1.000 \pm 3(0.0500),$$
$$1.150 \text{ and } 0.850.$$

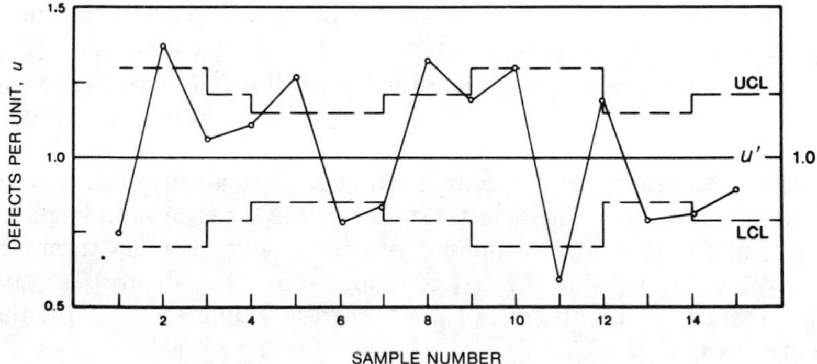

Figure 5–13 Control chart for *u*; standard given as *u'*, unequal sample size, $n = 100$, 200, and 400.

Sample Size, n	Central Line, $c' = u'n$	Control Limits $c' \pm 3\sqrt{c'}$ UCL	LCL
100	100.00	130.00	70.00
200	200.00	242.43	157.57
400	400.00	460.00	340.00

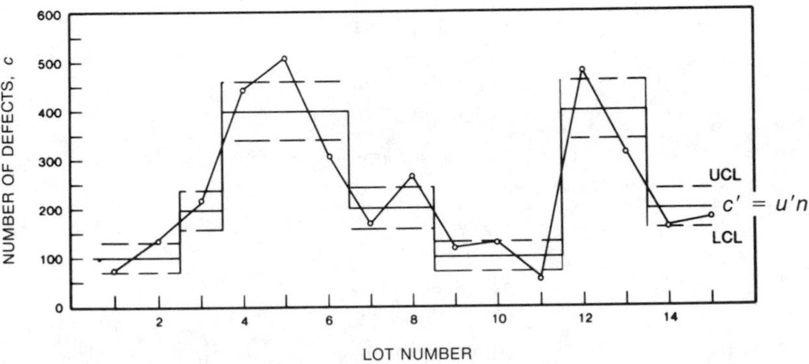

Figure 5–14 Control chart for *c;* standard given as u', samples of unequal size, n = 100, 200, and 400.

Results Lack of control of quality is indicated with respect to the desired level since lots Nos. 2, 5, 8, and 12 are above the upper control limit and lots Nos. 6, 11, and 13 are below the lower control limit. The overall level, 1.019 defects per unit, is slightly above the desired value of 1.000 defects per unit. Corrective action is necessary to reduce the spread between successive lots and reduce the average number of defects per unit.

Example 11 *Control Chart for u, Samples of Unequal Size.* Table 5.12 gives inspection results for twenty lots of different sizes for which three different sample sizes were used, 20, 25, and 40. The observed defects in this inspection cover all of the specified characteristics of a complex machine (Type A), including a large number of dimensional, operational, as well as physical and finish requirements. Because of the large number of tests and measurements required as well as possible occurrences of minor observed irregularities, the expectancy of defects per unit is high, although the majority of such defects are of minor seriousness. The defects per unit value for each sample, number of defects in sample divided by number of units in sample, was determined and these values are listed in the last column of the table. Figure 5-15 gives the control chart for u with control limits corresponding to the three different sample sizes.

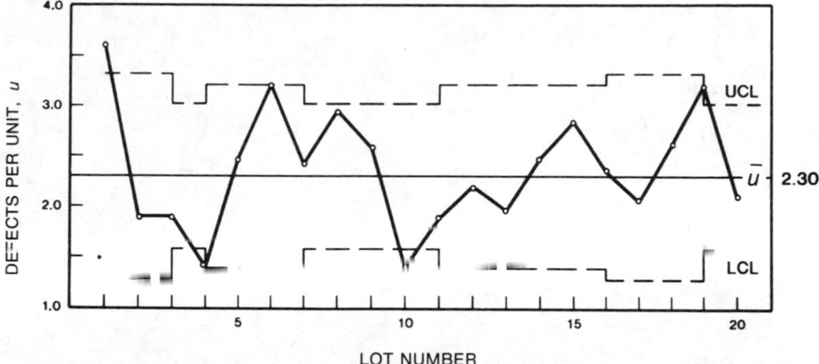

Figure 5–15 Control chart for *u;* samples of unequal size, *n* = 20, 25, 40, no standard given.

TABLE 5.12 Number of Defects in Samples from 20 Successive Lots of Type A Machines

Lot	*Sample Size, n*	*Total Defects in Sample, c*	*Defects per Unit, u*	*Lot*	*Sample Size, n*	*Total Defects in Sample, c*	*Defects per Unit, u*
No. 1........	20	72	3.60	No. 11........	25	47	1.88
No. 2........	20	38	1.90	No. 12........	25	55	2.20
No. 3........	40	76	1.90	No. 13........	25	49	1.96
No. 4........	25	35	1.40	No. 14........	25	62	2.48
No. 5........	25	62	2.48	No. 15........	25	71	2.84
No. 6........	25	81	3.24	No. 16........	20	47	2.35
No. 7........	40	97	2.42	No. 17........	20	41	2.05
No. 8........	40	78	1.95	No. 18........	20	52	2.60
No. 9........	40	103	2.58	No. 19........	40	128	3.20
No. 10.......	40	56	1.40	No. 20........	40	84	2.10
				Total...	580	1334	

Central Line

$$\bar{u} = \frac{1334}{580} = 2.30.$$

Control Limits

$n = 20$:

$$\bar{u} \pm 3\sqrt{\frac{\bar{u}}{n}} = 2.30 \pm 1.02,$$

3.32 and 1.28.

$n = 25:$

$$\bar{u} \pm 3\sqrt{\frac{\bar{u}}{n}} = 2.30 \pm 0.91,$$

3.21 and 1.39.

$n = 40:$

$$\bar{u} \pm 3\sqrt{\frac{\bar{u}}{n}} = 2.30 \pm 0.72,$$

3.02 and 1.58. +

Results Lack of control of quality is indicated; plotted points for lots Nos. 1, 6, and 19 are above the upper control limit and the point for lot No. 10 is below the lower control limit.

In the example below, breakdowns in 1,000 feet, 5,000 feet, and 10,000 feet are considered. In such cases, neither p nor n is known but only pn. Hence the actual distribution is a Poisson exponential rather than a binomial, with an expected value of pn and a variance of pn. Thus control charts for c and u are applicable.

Example 12 *Control Charts for c, Samples of Equal Size.* Table 5.13 gives the results of continuous testing of a certain type of rubber-covered wire at specified test voltage. This test causes breakdowns at weak spots in the insulation which are cut out before shipment of wire in short coil lengths. The original data obtained consisted of records of the number of breakdowns in successive lengths of 1,000 feet each. There may be 0, 1, 2, 3, . . . , etc. breakdowns per length, depending on the number of weak spots in the insulation. Such data might also have been tabulated as number of breakdowns in successive lengths of 100 feet each, 500 feet each, etc. Here there is no natural unit of product (such as 1 inch, 1 foot, 10 feet, 100 feet, etc.), in respect to the quality characteristic "breakdown" since failures may occur at any point. Since the original data were given in terms of 1,000-foot lengths, a control chart might have been maintained for "number of breakdowns in successive lengths of 1,000 feet each." So many points were obtained during a short period of production by using the 1,000-foot length as a unit and the expectancy in terms of number of breakdowns per length was so small that longer unit lengths were tried. Table 5.13 gives (*1*) the "number of breakdowns in successive lengths of 5,000 feet each," and (*2*) the "number of breakdowns in successive lengths of 10,000 feet each." Figure 5-16 shows the control chart for c where the unit selected is 5,000 feet and figure 5-17 shows the control chart for c where the unit selected is 10,000 feet. The standard unit length finally adopted for control purposes was 10,000 feet for "breakdown."

TABLE 5.13 Number of Breakdowns in Successive Lengths of 5,000 feet each and 10,000 feet each for Rubber-covered Wire

Length	*Number of Break-downs*	*Length*	*Number of Break-downs*	*Length*	*Number of Break-downs*	*Length*	*Number of Break-downs*	*Length*	*Number of Break-downs*
				(1) Lengths of 5,000 Feet Each					
No. 1.....	0	No. 13....	1	No. 25....	0	No. 37....	5	No. 49....	5
No. 2.....	1	No. 14....	1	No. 26....	0	No. 38....	7	No. 50....	4
No. 3.....	1	No. 15....	2	No. 27....	9	No. 39....	1	No. 51....	2
No. 4.....	0	No. 16....	4	No. 28....	10	No. 40....	3	No. 52....	0
No. 5.....	2	No. 17....	0	No. 29....	8	No. 41....	3	No. 53....	1
No. 6.....	1	No. 18....	1	No. 30....	8	No. 42....	2	No. 54....	2
No. 7.....	3	No. 19....	1	No. 31....	6	No. 43....	0	No. 55....	5
No. 8.....	4	No. 20....	0	No. 32....	14	No. 44....	1	No. 56....	9
No. 9.....	5	No. 21....	6	No. 33....	0	No. 45....	5	No. 57....	4
No. 10.....	3	No. 22....	4	No. 34....	1	No. 46....	3	No. 58....	2
No. 11.....	0	No. 23....	3	No. 35....	2	No. 47....	4	No. 59....	5
No. 12.....	1	No. 24....	2	No. 36....	4	No. 48....	3	No. 60....	3
Total...								60	187
				(2) Lengths of 10,000 Feet Each					
No. 1.....	1	No. 7....	2	No. 13....	0	No. 19....	12	No. 25....	9
No. 2.....	1	No. 8....	6	No. 14....	19	No. 20....	4	No. 26....	2
No. 3.....	3	No. 9....	1	No. 15....	16	No. 21....	5	No. 27....	3
No. 4.....	7	No. 10....	1	No. 16....	20	No. 22....	1	No. 28....	14
No. 5.....	8	No. 11....	10	No. 17....	1	No. 23....	8	No. 29....	6
No. 6.....	1	No. 12....	5	No. 18....	6	No. 24....	7	No. 30....	8
Total...								30	187

(1) Lengths of 5,000 Feet Each

Central Line

$$\bar{c} = \frac{187}{60} = 3.12.$$

Control Limits

$$\bar{c} \pm 3\sqrt{\bar{c}} =$$

$$3.12 \pm 3\sqrt{3.12},$$

8.42 and 0.

Results Presence of assignable causes of variation is indicated by lengths Nos. 27, 28, 32, and 56 falling above upper control limit.

(2) Lengths of 10,000 Feet Each

Central Line

$$\bar{c} = \frac{187}{30} = 6.23.$$

Control Limits

$$\bar{c} \pm 3\sqrt{\bar{c}} =$$
$$6.23 \pm 3\sqrt{6.23},$$

13.72 and 0.$^{+}$

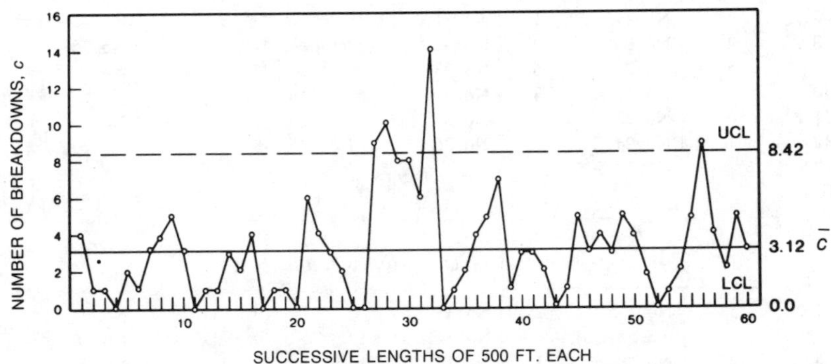

Figure 5–16 Control chart for *c*, successive lengths of 5,000 feet each.

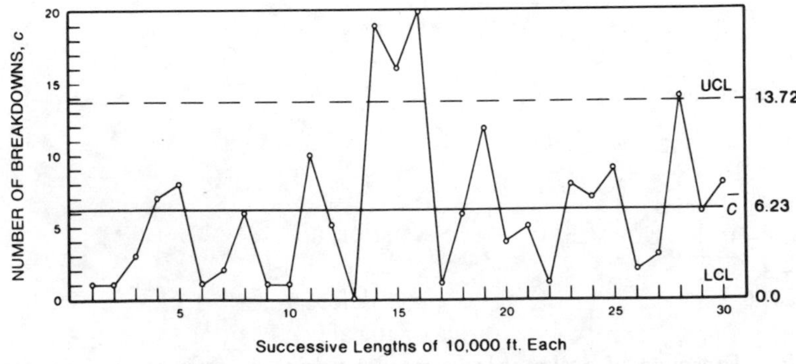

Figure 5–17 Control chart for *c*, successive lengths of 10,000 feet each.

Results Presence of assignable causes of variation is indicated by lengths Nos. 14, 15, 16, and 28 falling above upper control limit.

5.8 Summary, Relations for Control Charts for *p, pn, u,* and *c*

As an aid in the understanding and preparation of the control charts for *p, pn, u,* and *c,* a summary table is presented which provides the formulas for the central lines and for the three-sigma control limits. Two sets are given: One covers those cases where the standard is given and the second covers the case where no standard is given. They are practically identical in form. The use of *c* is especially convenient when there is no natural unit of product, as for defects over a surface or along a length, and where the problem is to determine uniformity of quality in equal lengths, areas, etc., of product. The control chart for *u* is recommended as preferable to the control chart for *c* when the sample size varies from sample to sample for conditions similar to those that also occur for control charts for *p* and *pn.* Table 5.14 gives the summary table.

5.9 Control Charts for Demerits Per Unit, D_u

When consideration is given to the fact that some defects are minor while others are very critical, it is necessary to consider the possibility of weighting many of the characteristics being tested in accordance to their importance. This allows one to make an equitable decision whether to accept or reject products on the basis of inspection and test results. If a component is finished with a paint that is slightly different than the other parts of the system, which is actually a nonconforming part for finish, the system will still function. However, if a part is broken so that it will fail to operate, that is much more critical. If there is a possibility that many units in the lot may also be so impaired that they will not function, rejection of the lot may be warranted. If parts are needed badly, then it may not be feasible to reject a lot because the finish is different and nonconforming. Several systems have been developed and placed in effect to cover these cases. A number of government documents have presented definitions covering the classification of defects according to their seriousness. MIL–STD–105D gives definitions of critical, major, and minor defects. These same definitions are repeated in MIL–STD–109B, *Military Standard Quality Assurance Terms and Definitions,* which gives MIL–STD–105 as its source.

The following definitions for critical, major, and minor defects are in effect in MIL–STD–105D.[1]

"*Critical Defect* A critical defect is a defect that judgment and experience indicate will surely result in hazardous or unsafe conditions for individuals using, maintaining, or depending upon the product; or a defect that judgment and experience indicate will surely prevent performance of the tactical function of a

TABLE 5.14 Summary of Formulas for Central Lines and Control Limits for Attributes Data

A: Control With Respect to a Given Standard (p', $p'n$, u' or c' Given)

	Central Line	*Control Limits*	*Approximation*
Fraction defective, p	p'	$p' \pm 3\sqrt{\frac{p'(1-p')}{n}}$	$p' \pm 3\sqrt{\frac{p'}{n}}$
Number of defectives pn	$p'n$	$p'n \pm 3\sqrt{p'n(1-p')}$	$p'n \pm 3\sqrt{p'n}$
Defects per unit, u	u'	$u' \pm 3\sqrt{\frac{u'}{n}}$	
Number of defects, c:			
Samples of Equal Size (c' given)	c'	$c' \pm 3\sqrt{c'}$	
Samples of Unequal Size (u' given)	$u'n$	$u'n \pm 3\sqrt{u'n}$	

B: Control—No Standard Given—Attributes Data

	Central Line	*Control Limits*	*Approximation*
Fraction defective, p	$\bar{p}$	$\bar{p} \pm 3\sqrt{\frac{\bar{p}(1-\bar{p})}{n}}$	$\bar{p} \pm 3\sqrt{\frac{\bar{p}}{n}}$
Number of defectives, $\bar{p}n$	$\bar{p}n$	$\bar{p}n \pm 3\sqrt{\bar{p}n(1-\bar{p})}$	$\bar{p}n \pm 3\sqrt{\bar{p}n}$
Defects per unit, $\bar{u}$	$\bar{u}$	$\bar{u} \pm 3\sqrt{\frac{\bar{u}}{n}}$	
Number of defects, $\bar{c}$:			
Samples of Equal Size	$\bar{c}$	$\bar{c} \pm 3\sqrt{\bar{c}}$	
Samples of Unequal Size	$\bar{u}n$	$\bar{u}n \pm 3\sqrt{\bar{u}n}$	

major end item such as a ship, aircraft, tank, missile, or space vehicle." It adds in another paragraph, "The supplier may be required at the discretion of the responsible authority to inspect every unit of the lot or batch for critical defects."

"*Major Defect* A major defect is a defect, other than critical, that is likely to result in failure, or to reduce materially the usability of the unit of product for its intended purpose."

"*Minor Defect* A minor defect is a defect that is not likely to reduce materially the usability of the unit of product for its intended purpose, or is a departure from established standards having little bearing on the effective use or operation of the unit."

Defectives are also classified and definitions are given covering them. A defective is a unit of product which contains one or more defects. Defectives will usually be classified as follows.

"*Critical Defective* A critical defective contains one or more critical defects and may also contain major and/or minor defects."

"*Major Defective* A major defective contains one or more major defects, and may also contain minor defects but contains no critical defect."

"*Minor Defective* A minor defective contains one or more minor defects but contains no critical or major defect."

For years, industry has classified defects according to their seriousness in certain areas. In most cases, critical defects are checked by all of the units involved and often by repeated inspections until there is positive assurance that all such critical defects have been eliminated. Critical defects are considered to be the most serious and differ from all the other possible defects or defectives.

Those requirements and specifications cover all the various characteristics that, if not met, may result in a nonconforming unit. Such a nonconformance is considered a defect; those defects, other than critical, sometimes are divided into four or five different classes. Demerit values are assigned to each class, as shown below.

Class of Defect	*Demerit Values* Method I, *Weight w*	Method II, *Weight w*
Major A	100	100
Major B	60	50
Minor C	25	10
Minor D	5	1
Incidental I	1	—

These demerit weights are assigned to any inspection item which is deemed to be nonconforming. Inspection defects and defectives are symbolized by *d*. Items, item by item, are considered as any characteristic or item for which inspection is made. Inspection items include all engineering requirements, finishes, standards of good workmanship, and all items which custom dictates shall be covered to provide adequate assurance of satisfactory, adequate, dependable, and economical quality. In making use of control charts for demerits per unit value, a defect is considered any failure to meet an engineering requirement or a contractual requirement, whereas a defective is any nonconforming unit containing one or more defects. A demerit is a measure of the seriousness of a failure to meet specified requirements. The demerit value for a group of defects is obtained by multiplying the number of defects in each class respectively by their demerit weights and summing such products. A demerit is often designated by the symbol D.

When it is desired to used weighted *p* values for process controls and for the application of control charts for such quality determinations, it is necessary to make a classification of defects, C/D, list for each of the components or parts involved. To aid in this classification the following definitions have been used.

Critical: Class "0" Defects, Demerit Value, 500

1. Will most certainly affect either safety of flight or proper operation of a system, e.g., timer fails to operate.
2. Affects the safety or airworthiness of the aircraft or any other factors that judgment and experience indicate would cause *immediate* harm to life or property if the aircraft or means of transportation were operated without correcting same, e.g., attitude indicator operates in reverse.

Major A: Class "1" Defects, Demerit Value, 100

1. Will surely cause an operating failure of the unit in service which cannot be readily corrected in the field, e.g., open weld, affecting operation.
2. Will surely prevent the equipment or system from performance of its tactical function and is not likely to be found at a subsequent functional test prior to delivery, e.g., excessive backlash in gears.
3. Will surely cause intermittent operating trouble, difficult to locate in the field, e.g., connection loose.
4. Will render unit totally unfit for service, e.g., lead broken.
5. Liable to cause either personal injury or property damage in service, e.g., exposed part has sharp edge; galvanized fin on case.

Major B: Class "2" Defects, Demerit Value, 50

1. Will probably cause an operating failure of the unit in service which cannot be readily corrected in the field, e.g., pointer pull-out force exceeds limit.
2. Will surely cause operating trouble which can be readily corrected in the field, e.g., resistor in accessible location—wrong resistance value.
3. Will surely cause trouble of a nature less serious than an operating failure, resulting in a failure that will initially reduce the usability of the unit of product for its intended purpose and will surely result in a loss in efficiency in operation, e.g., tight bearing.
4. Will surely involve increased maintenance or decreased life, e.g., dielectric strength less than minimum.
5. Will usually cause trouble requiring adjustment, or will result in poor service compared with normal, e.g., excessive drift, spark plug adjusted improperly.

Minor C: Class "3" Defects, Demerit Value, 10

1. May possibly cause an operating failure of the unit in service, e.g., operating voltage required exceeds maximum specified by less than 10%.
2. Likely to cause trouble of a nature less serious than an operating failure, e.g., diameter of gimbal or operating part outside specified limits.
3. Will be found during test or inspection of subassemblies, is easily repaired, and is not likely to get by system functional test, e.g., connecting plug too short.

4. Will not materially reduce the usability of the unit of product for its intended purpose, but likely to cause a loss in efficiency in operation, e.g., thickness of rotor lamination stack for motor less than specified.
5. A minor departure from established standards having no significant bearing on the effective use or operation of the unit, e.g., wrong material—commercial brass not naval brass as specified, noncorrosive steel not stainless steel as specified.
6. Variation in detail parts or subassemblies that affect only ease of assembly, or require minor adjustment during unit test, e.g., mounting holes out of alignment.
7. Likely to cause increased maintenance or decreased life, e.g., poorly soldered connection.
8. Major defects of appearance, finish, or workmanship not classified as critical or major, e.g., parts out of alignment not affecting operation (appearance only affected).

Minor D: Class "4" Defects, Demerit Value, 1 (Often called Incidental, I)

1. Will not affect operation, maintenance, or life of the unit in service, e.g., height of tube less than minimum.
2. Minor defects of appearance, finish, or workmanship, e.g., marking displaced slightly, dirt on finish of external part.

In using these definitions, it has been customary to prepare two C/D—classification of defects—lists. One covers general types of possible nonconformances; the second list covers specific requirements on particular products or components. In each of these lists, (1) general list and (2) specific lists, it is advisable to use subdivisions somewhat like the following:

Designation	*Subdivision*
1.	Electrical
2.	Mechanical requirements and dimensions
3.	Screws, nuts, and threaded holes
4.	Mounting, assembly, and miscellaneous
5.	Wiring and soldering
6.	Appearance, finish, and foreign material
7.	Marking and designation
8.	Packing and shipping

Using these designations for each subdivision possible, defects or nonconformances are classified according to the above definitions as to seriousness. When such lists are approved for use, it is then possible to set up an extremely profitable system of inspections, reports, and control charts based on demerits per unit rather than on fraction or percent defective. Such a system reduces the time and effort usually expended on minor and incidental defects and places the emphasis on the major requirements.

To obtain values of demerits per unit, D_u, it is necessary to record the inspection and test results on forms where both the class of each defect found and the size of the sample used in the inspections are noted. From these data, results of the inspection during any period may be determined from the equation

$$D_u = \frac{w_A d_A}{n_A} + \frac{w_B d_B}{n_B} + \frac{w_C d_C}{n_C} + \frac{w_D d_D}{n_D} \tag{8}$$

Where the sample sizes involved in the inspections of defects are equal, then equation (8) is simplified to the form

$$D_u = \frac{(w_A d_A + w_B d_B + w_C d_C + w_D d_D)}{n} \tag{9}$$

Standard values of p, denoted by p'_A, p'_B, p'_C, and p'_D are either established for the four classes of defects or are derived from past data as process averages. The above relations then become:

$$D'_u = w_A p'_A + w_B p'_B + w_C p'_C + w_D p'_D \tag{10}$$

For these expressions, the value of p for any class is based on the general relation involving the number of defects or defectives for any given class. The sum of the number of defects for a given class is then divided by the sum of the sample sizes in which these defects were found. Compiling such data accurately class by class provides the following general relation.

$$p_i = \frac{\Sigma d_i}{\Sigma n_i} \tag{11}$$

When establishing three-sigma control limits, it is necessary to determine how to compute the variance and standard deviation in terms of demerits per unit from these weighted p values. The variance of a linear sum of different variables is readily determined from advanced statistical theory. The relation used for its derivation makes use of partial derivatives. Although the derivation seems complex, the final value is a very simple expression. The variance of D_u is

$$v_{D_u} = \left(\frac{\partial D_u}{\partial p_A}\sigma_{p_A}\right)^2 + \left(\frac{\partial D_u}{\partial p_B}\sigma_{p_B}\right)^2 + \left(\frac{\partial D_u}{\partial p_C}\sigma_{p_C}\right)^2 + \left(\frac{\partial D_u}{\partial p_D}\sigma_{p_D}\right)^2, \tag{12}$$

where the variances of these four respective p values are given as $\dfrac{p_i(1 - p_i)}{n_i} = \sigma^2_{p_i}$.

For the D_u linear relation in equation (10), $\frac{\partial D_u}{\partial p_i} = w_i$, since $\frac{\partial p_i}{\partial p_i} = 1$ and $\frac{\partial p_i}{\partial p_i} = 0$. This results in the following relation for the variance.

$$v_{D_u} = \frac{w_A^2 p_A(1 - p_A)}{n_A} + \frac{w_B^2 p_B(1 - p_B)}{n_B} + \frac{w_C^2 p_C(1 - p_C)}{n_C} + \frac{w_D^2 p_D(1 - p_D)}{n_D} \tag{13}$$

Generally $n_A = n_B = n_C = n_D = n$, and the various p_i values are standard values. Note that the general subscript refers respectively to A, B, C, and D successively. A weighted term must be found equivalent to p in use. It is termed a standard constant and designated as C_s; it can be readily computed as follows:

$$C_s = w_A^2 p'_A(1 - p'_A) + w_B^2 p'_B(1 - p'_B) + w_C^2 p'_C(1 - p'_C) + w_D^2 p'_D(1 - p'_D) \tag{14}$$

When determining control limits for D_u, demerits per unit, the standard deviation value to be determined then uses the relation

$$\sigma_{D_u} = \sqrt{\frac{C_s}{n}} \tag{15}$$

This is a standard deviation for weighted p values similar in form to the standard deviation for p, $\sigma_p = \sqrt{\frac{p(1-p)}{n}}$, which is sometimes used as $\sqrt{\frac{p}{n}}$, when p is small and $1 - p$ may be assumed to be almost 1.

In many instances, the desired p' values for these four classes of defects are assigned definite values for general use. Satisfactory products are made when standards such as $p'_A = 0.005$, $p'_B = 0.01$, $p'_C = 0.02$, and $p'_D = 0.05$ are set as controls. Using these standards and the four classes of weights 100, 50, 10, and 1 gives standard values for D_u (using equation (10)) and C_s (using equation (14)) of $D'_u = 1.25$ and $C'_s = 76.5075$; $\sigma'_{D_u} = \frac{8.75}{\sqrt{n}}$, since $\sqrt{76.5075} = 8.74685658$. Thus a company may set standards for certain departments or manufacturing groups at $D'_u = 1.25$ and $C'_s = 8.75$. These are the values used for control limits in example 13, which follows.

The following example is set forth to illustrate the preparation of a control chart for the demerits per unit measure of quality. It is designed so that the sum of the defects for each of the four classes is such that the process average values $\bar{p}$ for the ten lots is the same as the p' values for these respective classes for the total sample size value of 2,000 units. This example illustrates both the case where standards are specified and where the process average values are used as the standards. In example 13 the sample sizes have been listed in two groups, one with five samples of 100 units each and another with five samples of 300 units each.

Example 13 A rather complex product (whose component requirements have had a classification of defects list for all items) has been produced and inspected by sampling ten lots which have been manufactured under strict controls. Table 5.15 tabulates the results of these inspections. It is desired to determine the value of demerits per unit D_u values for each lot and for two groups, where Group I covers the first five lots with samples of 100 units each, and Group II consists of five lots with samples of 300 units inspected for each lot. Control chart values should be obtained for p'_A, p'_B, p'_C, p'_D, and D'_u.

TABLE 5.15A Sample Results for Four Classes of Defects, Ten Lots with Sample Sizes of 100 and 300. Determination of Demerits per Unit Value Results for Group I, Group II, and Both Groups Combined

		Demerit Wt.	*Observed Defects*				*Fraction Defective*				*Demerits*
		w	*Major*		*Minor*		*w: 100*	*50*	*10*	*1*	*per*
Lot	*Sample*	*Class:*	*100*	*50*	*10*	*1*	*Major*	*Major*	*Minor*	*Minor*	*Unit*
No.	*Size, n*	*Demerits**	*A*	*B*	*C*	*D*	*A*	*B*	*C*	*D*	D_u
1	100	113	0	2	1	3	0	0.0200	0.0100	0.0300	1.130
2	100	92	0	1	4	2	0	0.0100	0.0400	0.0200	0.920
3	100	275	1	3	2	5	0.0100	0.0300	0.0200	0.0500	2.750
4	100	116	0	1	6	6	0	0.0100	0.0600	0.0600	1.160
5	100	137	1	0	3	7	0.0100	0	0.0300	0.0700	1.370
Gp. I	500	733	2	7	16	23	0.0040	0.0140	0.0320	0.0460	1.466
6	300	423	2	3	6	13	0.0067	0.0100	0.0200	0.0433	1.410
7	300	438	3	2	2	18	0.0100	0.0067	0.0067	0.0600	1.460
8	300	289	1	3	3	9	0.0033	0.0100	0.0100	0.0300	0.963
9	300	415	2	3	5	15	0.0067	0.0100	0.0167	0.0500	1.383
10	300	202	0	2	8	22	0	0.0067	0.0267	0.0733	0.673
Gp. II	1500	1767	8	13	24	77	0.0053	0.0087	0.0160	0.0513	1.178
All	2000	2500	10	20	40	100	0.0050	0.0100	0.0200	0.0500	1.250

* Demerits $= 100d_A + 50d_B + 10d_C + 1d_D$.

Three-sigma control limits: $1.25 \pm 3\left(\dfrac{8.75}{\sqrt{n}}\right)$ Demerits per Unit

Sample Sizes:	100	300	500	1500	2000
$\dfrac{1}{\sqrt{n}}$	0.100000	0.0577350	0.0447214	0.0258199	0.0223607
Upper Control Limit:	3.875	2.766	2.424	1.928	1.837
Lower Control Limit:	0	0	0.076	0.572	0.663

The three-sigma control limits for the four classes of defects follow.

TABLE 5.15B Sample Results for Four Classes of Defects, Ten Lots with Sample Sizes of 100 and 300. Determination of Demerits per Unit Value

Three-sigma Control Limits for p: $p' \pm 3\sqrt{\frac{p'(1-p')}{n}}$ for Four Classes of Defects, n = 100, 300, 500, 1,500, and 2,000

Standard, p'	*Class A: 0.005*	*Class B: 0.0100*	*Class C: 0.0200*	*Class D: 0.0500*
$p'(1-p') =$	0.004975	0.009900	0.019600	0.047500
$\sqrt{p'(1-p')} =$	0.07053368	0.09949874	0.140000	0.21794495
$3\sqrt{p'(1-p')} =$	0.21160104	0.29849622	0.420000	0.65383485
$n = 100$: $\frac{1}{\sqrt{100}} = 0.10$				
UCL =	0.02616	0.03985	0.06200	0.11538
LCL =	0	0	0	0
$n = 300$: $\frac{1}{\sqrt{300}} = 0.0577350$				
UCL =	0.01722	0.02723	0.04425	0.08775
LCL =	0	0	0	0
$n = 500$: $\frac{1}{\sqrt{500}} = 0.0447214$				
UCL =	0.01446	0.02335	0.03878	0.07924
LCL =	0	0	0.00122	0.02076
$n = 1500$: $\frac{1}{\sqrt{1500}} = 0.0258199$				
UCL =	0.01046	0.01771	0.03084	0.06688
LCL =	0	0.00229	0.00916	0.03312
$n = 2000$: $\frac{1}{\sqrt{2000}} = 0.0223607$				
UCL =	0.00973	0.01667	0.02939	0.06462
LCL =	0.00027	0.00333	0.01061	0.03538

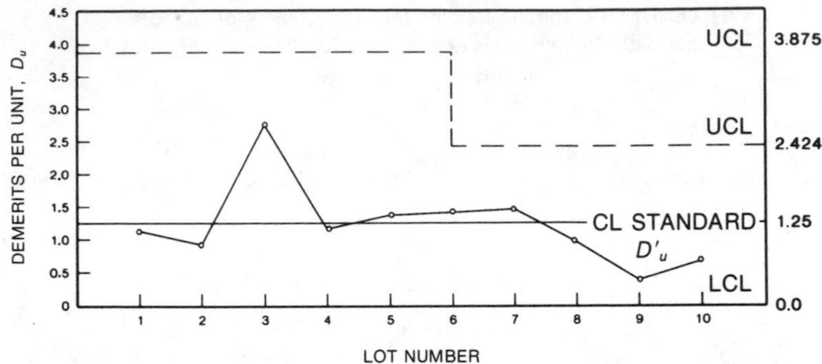

Figure 5–18 Control chart for demerits per unit; unequal sample sizes, D'_u given.

A check was made of all the various p values for each of the four classes of defects for each lot and also for the ten D_u values; all are within the control limits. This type of control should exist if the $\bar{p}$ values found for each class are to be selected as standard values for use in the future. Even in fairly well controlled manufacturing practices, now and then a point may fall outside the control limits if an assignable cause enters the manufacturing process.

These data are presented in figure 5-18 to illustrate the nature of these control charts for demerits per unit values. Control limits are given for two different sample sizes, 100 and 500. No values are outside their control limits.

Another illustration showing the use of the demerit per unit control charts is provided by example 14. It covers an actual application over a period of several years. Only a slight modification has been made so as not to indicate actual conditions under which the data were taken but excellent control is shown.

Example 14 A control chart based on tabulated data for two electrical components, fuses and protectors, is to be presented together with standards used and applicable control limits covering several years by years and also by months for two years. The two control charts for demerits per unit given in figure 5-19 show how completely a report can cover not only the quality being produced but can also present the quantities involved. In addition, expected values are given for the four classes of defects for each product, together with a summary by years for three years and by quarters for one year of the number of defects per 100 units observed. This figure is one of the best illustrations of how to utilize data most effectively.

5.10 Control Charts for Indexes, *I*

In many different operations, including quality control, index numbers are obtained in many different ways. Many, such as a food cost index and the Dow Jones Index for stock prices, take some year as a base and compare data from succeeding years with this base. Adjustments in pay are often dependent on the cost of living index. In quality control work, a standard value for D_u (demerits per unit, discussed earlier) may be established; I is then the ratio of current performance to such standard. A monthly or quarterly or even a yearly index may be secured by utilizing the appropriate data. Many desire a single index as a composite of several other indexes. Such an index might be obtained from the following relation:

$$I_0 = w_1 I_1 + w_2 I_2 + w_3 I_3 + \cdots + w_k I_k, \tag{16}$$

where the sum of the weights w_i from 1 to k equals 1, i.e., $\Sigma w_i = 1$.

In quality control work, an index of quality might be based on five major products, where a known standard has been established for each. Current performance, also measured in terms of p (fraction defective), may be compared directly with the corresponding p values already established as standards. Such an index I for these five components may be represented as:

$$I = \frac{w_1 p_1}{p'_1} + \frac{w_2 p_2}{p'_2} + \frac{w_3 p_3}{p'_3} + \frac{w_4 p_4}{p'_4} + \frac{w_5 p_5}{p'_5} \tag{17}$$

This may be expressed in an index form as:

$$I = w_1 I_1 + w_2 I_2 + w_3 I_3 + w_4 I_4 + w_5 I_5, \tag{18}$$

where

$$w_1 + w_2 + w_3 + w_4 + w_5 = \sum_{i=1}^{i=5} w_i = 1 \quad (i = 1 \text{ to } 5\text{, inclusive}) \tag{19}$$

Such I values might also be monthly indexes or index values for the four quarters in a year.

Whether a control chart is required to control the overall quality, an economic index of this same general form, or an index covering the reliability of a system,

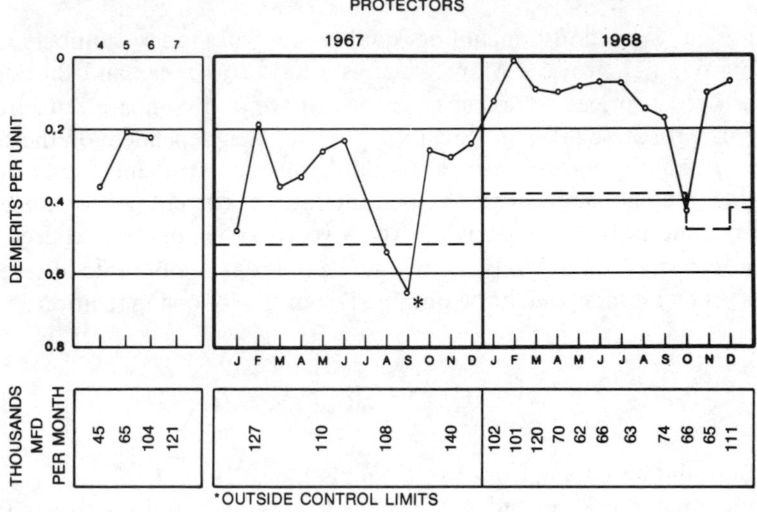

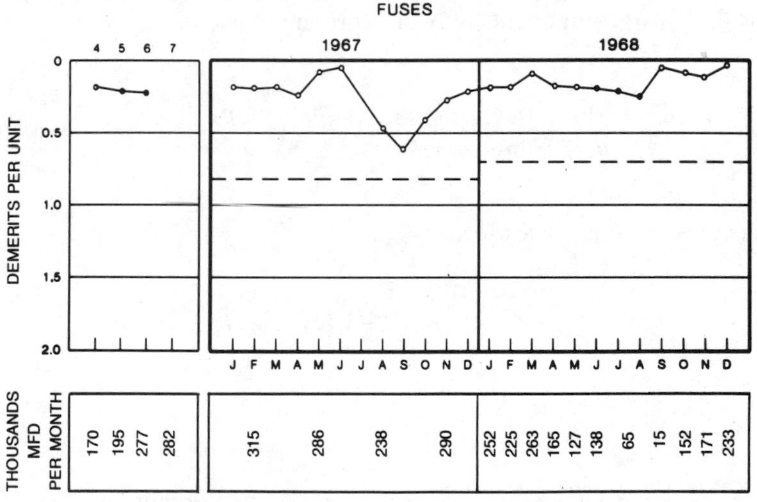

Figure 5–19 Demerits per unit control charts for fuses and protectors: standard based on past data; defects reported by classes.

FUSES ← Std. = .346

DEFECT CLASS	WEIGHT	EXPECTED	NUMBER OF DEFECTS PER 100 UNITS							
							1968 QUARTERS			
			1964	1965	1966	1967	1st	2nd	3rd	4th
A	100	.17	.11	.12	.04	.17	0	.04	0	.03
B	50	.33	.13	.17	.33	.24	.13	.10	.29	0
C	10	.09	.12	.04	.06	.08	.07	.24	.14	.19
D	1	.19	.08	.10	1.40*	.20	1.60*	.70*	1.00*	.07
Total		.78	.44	.43	1.83	.69	1.80	1.08	1.43	.29

PROTECTORS: ← Std. = .142

DEFECT CLASS	WEIGHT	EXPECTED	1964	1965	1966	1967	1st	2nd	3rd	4th
A	100	.03	.17	.15	.14	.21	0	0	0	0
B	50	.16	.32	.08	.12	.18	.03	.05	.16	.30
C	10	.27	.24	.17	.15	.40	.49	.47	.57	.25
D	1	.49	.60	.30	.50	1.00	.95*	1.35*	.32	.96
Total		.95	1.33	.70	.91	1.78	1.47	1.87	1.05	1.51

*Significantly Greater Than Expected ← STANDARD QUALITY LEVEL

CONTRIBUTION TO DEMERITS PER UNIT

Expected	1964	1965	1966	1967	Expected	1964	1965	1966	1967
.1700	.1100	.1200	.0400	.1700	.0300	.1700	.1500	.1400	.2100
.1650	.0650	.0850	.1650	.1200	.0800	.1600	.0400	.0600	.0800
.0090	.0120	.0040	.0060	.0080	.0270	.0240	.0170	.0150	.0400
.0019	.0008	.0010	.0140	.0020	.0049	.0060	.0030	.0050	.0100
.3459	.1878	.2100	.2250	.3000	.1419	.3600	.2100	.2200	.3500

Figure 5-19 (continued).

the same statistical techniques apply. It is necessary to determine the overall variance and the standard deviation of this form of index. The same theorem that was used in developing control limits for the demerits per unit charts applies here. Thus the overall variance for I is given by the relation

$$\sigma_I^2 = w_1^2\sigma_{I_1}^2 + w_2^2\sigma_{I_2}^2 + \cdots + w_k^2\sigma_{I_k}^2 = \sum_{i=1}^{k} w_i^2\sigma_{I_i}^2 \tag{20}$$

For these k indexes used as a basis for the overall index, the w_i terms may be omitted, if the weights are equal for all of the index components. This simplifies many computations. An example with five index values will illustrate the use of this method.

Example 15 For the data given in table 5.16, set up values that might be used in placing in effect a control chart for this type of index and similar indexes, that is, a control chart for an overall index based on five subindexes.

TABLE 5.16 Data for Five Indexes: Standards, Weights and Current Index Values with Sample Sizes

				Current Values and Index Value		
Index Number	*Standard* p'	*Weight* w	*Sample Size* n	p	*Index,* $I = p/p'$	*Weight* $\times I$, wI
1	0.20	0.3	100	0.18	0.90	0.27
2	0.05	0.2	64	0.07	1.40	0.28
3	0.25	0.1	144	0.30	1.20	0.12
4	0.02	0.1	225	0.022	1.10	0.11
5	0.10	0.3	49	0.17	1.70	0.51
Sum		1.0				1.29

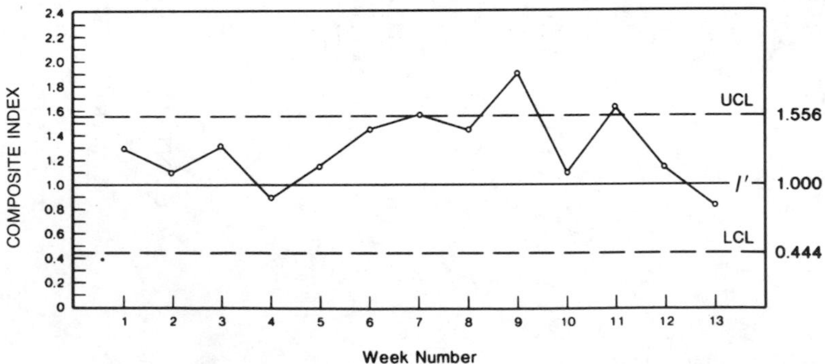

Figure 5–20 Control chart for composite index; standard given, $I' = 1.000$. Data for one quarter, 13 weeks, compiled weekly.

Expected I is $\sum w_i I_i = 1.00$; $\sigma_{I_i} = \sqrt{\frac{p_i'(1-p_i')/n}{p_i'}}$. Determine σ_I^2, then determine the standard deviation for I and the three-sigma control limits from the relation $1.00 \pm 3\sigma_I$.

NOTE: σ_I^2 must be expressed in terms of the w and p values.

From equation (20), substituting the relation for the variance for I in terms of p results in the following relation:

$$\sigma_I^2 = \left(\frac{w_1}{p_1'}\right)^2 \sigma_{p_1}^2 + \left(\frac{w_2}{p_2'}\right)^2 \sigma_{p_2}^2 + \left(\frac{w_3}{p_3'}\right)^2 \sigma_{p_3}^2 + \left(\frac{w_4}{p_4'}\right)^2 \sigma_{p_4}^2 + \left(\frac{w_5}{p_5'}\right)^2 \sigma_{p_5}^2 \quad (21)$$

Substituting the value of the variance σ_p^2 in relation (21) gives:

$$\sigma_I^2 = \frac{(w_1/p_1')^2 p_1'(1-p_1')}{n_1} + \frac{(w_2/p_2')^2 p_2'(1-p_2')}{n_2} + \frac{(w_3/p_3')^2 p_3'(1-p_3')}{n_3} + \frac{(w_4/p_4')^2 p_4'(1-p_4')}{n_4} + \frac{(w_5/p_5')^2 p_5'(1-p_5')}{n_5}. \quad (22)$$

Substituting the values in table 5.16 in equation (22) gives the following:

$$\sigma_I^2 = \frac{(0.3/0.20)^2(0.2)(0.8)}{100} + \frac{(0.2/0.05)^2(0.05)(0.95)}{64} + \frac{(0.1/0.25)^2(0.25)(0.75)}{144} + \frac{(0.1/0.02)^2(0.02)(0.98)}{225} + \frac{(0.3/0.10)^2(0.1)(0.9)}{49} = 2.25(0.001600000) +$$

$16(0.000742188) + 0.16(0.001302083) + 25(0.0000871111) + 9(0.001836735) = 0.003600000 + 0.011875008 + 0.000208333 + 0.002177775 + 0.016530615 = 0.034391731.$

Hence $\sigma_I = 0.185450$ demerits per unit. Based on this value the control limits are:

UCL: $1.000 + 3(0.1855) = 1.000 + 0.556 = 1.556.$
LCL: $1.000 - 3(0.1855) = 1.000 - 0.556 = 0.444.$

The current overall index 1.29 is well within these control limits, which are quite wide, due to the small samples that were taken to obtain some of the indexes.

This example gives all the details for obtaining these control limits. If a concern makes use of such computations on a large scale, the method should be programmed on a computer to facilitate the computations.

5.11 Efficient Use of Control Charts for Attributes

Methods and techniques for setting up all of the various kinds of control charts that might be used by small industries as well as the larger companies have been covered in considerable detail. There are sufficient examples to cover most situations that might arise in production and also in other areas where such control charts may be required. These should be considered in detail, as many have special features that apply to that particular case. This text provides many useful tables to aid in these calculations. A complete table of squares and square roots such as Barlow's tables should also be used to aid in many computations. Values should be carried out to sufficient places in the computations to provide control limits that really differentiate between controlled data and questionable data.

Where processes are well-controlled and have caused no excessive quantities of defective parts, control charts should only be applied occasionally on a check basis. Control charts prove most profitable in areas or with processes that are likely to be subject to erratic changes in quality due to many possible assignable causes. Where chance causes alone seem to be operating, it may prove very uneconomical to make use of control charts since the observed values may only fall outside the control limits due to chance.

Most presentations covering control charts do not provide methods to cover weighted values. There are sufficient examples in this text to indicate how to combine items that have very different effects on outgoing quality. The control limits for the demerits per unit charts and also for indexes cover weighted defects in sufficient detail so that a competent quality control technician should be able to establish meaningful control limits for systems and groups of components when desirable, rather than using a large number of individual charts for such operations. Thus it is possible to provide maximum profits from the proper use of the type of control chart that applies most effectively to complex plant operations.

EXERCISES

1. A company manufactured a commercial product for which sales data indicated that it could not compete with other companies effectively if more than 2% were found to be defective in the field. Thus $p' = 0.02$ or 2.0%. From each lot of 1000 units, a 10% sample of 100 units was inspected and tested. The results are as follows:

Group I			*Group II*		
Lot No.	*Sample Size, n*	*No. Defective*	*Lot No.*	*Sample Size, n*	*No. Defective*
1	100	2	6	100	5
2	100	0	7	100	6
3	100	3	8	100	7
4	100	1	9	100	9
5	100	4	10	100	3
Sum	500	10		500	30

(a) Determine the fraction defective for each lot and make a control chart for p using $p' = 0.02$ as the standard. Plot all ten values of p as computed.

(b) Is the product controlled at the desired level of $p' = 0.02$? Are any points outside their respective control limits? If not, what comments can you make about the process? Is the process better than standard?
(c) Using the same data draw on graph paper a control chart for the number of defects as listed above. Use the proper scale for the control limits and central line.

2. (a) Using the data given in exercise 1, determine if there is any significant difference between Group I data and Group II data using the relation

$$z = \frac{|p_1 - p_2|}{\sqrt{\sigma_{p_1}^2 + \sigma_{p_2}^2}} \quad \text{where} \quad \sigma_p^2 = \frac{p(1-p)}{n}. \quad \text{Use as your criterion:}$$

If z exceeds 3, then the values of p for the two groups are considered significantly different, but if z is 3 or less then the two values are considered not significantly different. Remember that the sample sizes for Group I and Group II are 500.
(b) Using the sample size $n = 500$, the total sample size for Group I and Group II, respectively determine the three-sigma control limits for p' value of 0.02. Determine the fraction defective for each group and determine if these values are within their respective control limits. As a check, determine by how many units of the standard deviation using the sample size of 500 that the p values for Group I differ from 0.02 and Group II differs from the p' value of 0.02.

3. The following data shows the number of defectives observed in a series of eight lots where the sample sizes vary a great deal as they were selected from lots of different sizes. The standard value for p is $p' = 0.10$.

Lot No.	*Lot Size, N*	*Sample Size, n*	*No. of Observed Defectives*	*Fraction Defective, p*	*Control Limits for $p' = 0.10$*	
					UCL	*LCL*
1	1,000	100	12			
2	10,000	900	99			
3	5,000	400	20			
4	1,000	100	10			
5	1,000	100	20			
6	8,000	625	100			
7	8,000	625	50			
8	5,000	400	40			
			351			

(a) Determine the fraction defective for the eight lots. Fill in the above table.
(b) Determine the UCL and LCL values for the data above and fill in the table above.
(c) Graph the data and draw in the central value, $p' = 0.10$ and the varying values of UCL and LCL for the various sample sizes.
(d) Is the process controlled? Give a brief summary of your analysis.

4. For the data in exercise 3, determine the central lines and upper and lower control limits for the number of observed defectives. Here $p'n$ is the central value. Make a control chart for number of defectives with the varying central lines and control limits.

5. List the different types of quality control charts that may be utilized when the data involved are attributes rather than variables data. These are applied when (1) a standard is specified, and (2) when no standard is given. How will you obtain a standard for each of the different types of charts you have listed? Tabulate the relations by which you establish upper and lower control limits for each of these types.

6. The following data were obtained for a process deemed to be in control. A standard value of $p'_e = \bar{p}$ was obtained from these data and used to establish control limits for this process. Analyze the following data.

   (a) Determine the values for the fraction defective and then determine the best estimate of p' from these results. Eliminate any months deemed uncontrolled in obtaining the best standard.

   (b) Using the value of p'_e obtained in part (a), determine the upper and lower control limits and tabulate.

   (c) Make a graphical presentation of your control charts plotting the twelve values of p you have tabulated together with their central line and control limits.

   (d) Make a control chart for number of defects per month. Graph and show limits.

Month	*Total Number Inspected per Month, n*	*Observed Number of Defectives per Month, c or d*	*Fraction Defective p*	*Control Limits*	
				UCL	*LCL*
January	144	12			
February	81	4			
March	100	5			
April	400	18			
May	225	9			
June	196	8			
July	64	4			
August	100	3			
September	81	7			
October	169	9			
November	400	18			
December	100	6			
Total	2060	103			

FOOTNOTES

[1] "Military Standard 105D. Sampling Procedures and Tables for Inspection by Attributes," Superintendent of Documents, Government Printing Office, Washington, D.C., 1963. (The international designation of this document is ABC-STD-105.)

+ Reproduced by permission of the American Society for Testing and Materials from copyright material STP-15C, *Manual on Quality Control of Materials.*

++ Table from *Statistical Quality Control*, by Eugene L. Grant, Second Edition, 1952, by permission of McGraw-Hill Book Company, Inc., New York.

CHAPTER SIX

CONTROL CHARTS FOR VARIABLES

6.1 Objective

This chapter describes in detail how to establish standards and control charts for variables data measurements or tests. Quality control has as one of its primary objectives the control of process averages at desired or specified levels of quality. The prior chapter explained techniques and methods to prepare control charts for attributes data only, where any unit that does not meet the specified requirement of a single characteristic is termed a *defect,* and any unit containing one or more defects is termed a *defective.* In the Method of Attributes, only one control chart is required for defectives or fraction defective, while in the Method of Variables, each important characteristic may require a separate control chart. However, variables control charts are much more sensitive and effective than attributes control charts. This chapter explains the variables control charts, how they are computed, and how to use them most efficiently. Charts similar to those in the last chapters are described and also how to compile them from all types of variables data. The method for their presentation differs markedly from prior methods, as the controls for variables must both cover process controls with respect to the proper location of central values and also provide controls for the various measures of variability or the dispersion of each characteristic under consideration.

Examples of the various types of control charts are presented in a manner which allows others to follow the steps outlined and utilize similar control charts in their occupations. Emphasis is placed on the fact that such control charts apply to any variable, whether it be obtained in manufacturing or in office work. Medical authorities may use them. Personnel offices may check the effectiveness of their rulings and determine whether there are assignable causes for an increase in absenteeism. Where attributes control charts merely indicate failures or successes, variables control charts reveal the *degree* to which something passes or fails. The merits of such control charts and their benefits are portrayed in the following sections.

6.2 Nature of Variables Control Charts

Variables data consist of all kinds of observed values. These are recorded and are analyzed by many different statistical methods. One of the best methods for determining whether products are produced under controlled conditions or under somewhat chaotic conditions is the variables control chart. As noted previously, such uontrol charts are made in a two-fold manner: (1) measures of central tendency and (2) measures of variability.

Control charts for variables may make use of extremely small samples, even as few as two observations for averages and ranges or only one value for individual observations. Attributes data obtained on such small samples provide very poor measures of the process. For samples of size two, the percent defective could only be 0%, 50%, or 100%, so that it would be very difficult to show when a production system was not controlled. On the other hand, the variables control charts will be very effective for small samples when used and compiled properly.

The different kinds of control charts for variables discussed in this chapter are:

1. Control charts for averages, $\bar{X}$;
2. Control charts for averages, $\bar{X}$, and standard deviations, σ;
3. Control charts for averages, $\bar{X}$, and ranges, R;
4. Control charts for medians, X_M, and median ranges, R_M;
5. Control charts for midranges, M, and ranges, R;
6. Control charts for individual values, X.

The ASTM *Manual on Quality Control of Materials* and other references provide control charts for many other variable items, such as moving averages. The different kinds of variables control charts listed above should provide charts sufficient for most situations. Special control charts for other situations may readily be developed, if needed.

For most of the above types of charts, four different situations may occur. Which of these are to be applied should be determined and agreed upon prior to setting up control charts for direct applications. These situations are:

(1) Standard given or specified; or (2) No standard given;
(I) Samples of equal size; or (II) Samples of unequal size.

Prime values, such as $\bar{X}'$ and σ', are usually used to designate specified standards. Where no standards are given, it is necessary to obtain standards based on the available data. The usual procedure is to obtain as much past data as possible and then check them for control. In many cases, periods will be found in which it is apparent through statistical tests that the system is out of control. These points are then eliminated from the data used to determine the desired standard. In some cases, however, there may be periods when the data indicate a better level than usual. If it is desired to tighten the standard to improve the overall quality for the characteristic under consideration, such data should be included in the final determinations. All such standards based on prior data are subject to periodic reviews to obtain the most economical possible standards. Even though lack of control is not indicated, the data should are appraised periodically.

There are many different types of data that may be analyzed by the use of control charts. When lots of resistors are successively being produced and the process by which they are produced is checked for control, the simplest method is to measure each resistor for resistance. One can thus determine how many resistors have resistance values greater than the maximum value specified and also list the number of resistors with resistance values less than the specified minimum value. The total of these divided by the number of resistors measured represents the fraction defective with respect to resistance, that is, the fraction nonconforming. However, better checks on the process will be obtained by determining successive average values of resistance for each sample selected at random from each lot. Such average values may be plotted on a control chart provided with the desired level and three-sigma control limits for the sample sizes used in these measurements. Where the dispersion or variability seems to be well-controlled at an acceptable value, it may not be necessary to also utilize a control chart for variability. If, however, variability is considered very important and a desired value has been stipulated or the current variability level for controlled product is considered to be unsatisfactory, then a control chart for standard deviation values or range values should also be used.

We will consider a slightly more complicated set of data to show the versatility in the applications of these techniques. A shoe manufacturer wants to control the sizes of his shoes. Two different characteristics are now involved. These are length, given by size number, with different scales used for children, youths, men, women, girls, and boys, and width at the toes, with widths varying from AAA to EEE using a scale of AAA, AA, A, B, C, D, E, EE, and EEE. Consider such sizes for men. Numbered sizes might be from 5 to 14, with the demand for such lengths varying greatly in different areas of the nation. Although a machine may be set to make one length and width, production may make many different sizes rather than just one. Thus, for example, a machine calibrated for 9C shoes might turn out a small number of shoes of size $8\frac{1}{2}$C, some 9C shoes, and a few $9\frac{1}{2}$C sizes. If the machines are very erratic, some shoes might be B width, some might be C width, and a very few might even be as wide as a D width. Too many variations in the size designations might result in customer dissatisfaction due to the fact that a poor fit of the correct designated size might result. In such a case, a control chart might be placed on the automatic shoe machine which seems to produce the greatest variability with respect to the two characteristics, length and width. When too much variation occurs, one or more plotted points will be found outside the designated control limits.

Consideration must be given to the amount of confidence management wishes to place on these control charts. The control limits may be set in many ways. Some like to use a constant probability value, such as 0.98, to designate what actual percentage or fraction of the distribution should fall within the designated control limits. The distribution which applies to these various kinds of quality control charts must be determined. In all cases, distributions of averages are represented by a normal law distribution, regardless of sample size, where the standard deviation for averages might be represented as:

$$\text{Standard deviation for averages:} \quad \sigma_{\bar{X}} = \frac{\sigma}{\sqrt{n}} \tag{1}$$

Tables of normal law probabilities are available in a great many texts and books containing statistical tables. Multiples of sigma may be used to obtain any level of confidence desired.

6.3 Control Chart for Averages Only—Variability Controlled

When levels must be controlled at different standard values during different periods of time, and where the variability is well controlled within satisfactory limits, then control charts need only be applied to averages. They may be more economical to maintain than those also involving variability. When at any time, it is felt that the product being inspected or tested for shipment is homogeneous, which signifies that the product is uniform in quality with respect to specified requirements, only average values need be checked for control. Their control limits are determined from the following expressions.

$$\begin{aligned} &\text{Upper Control Limit, UCL:} \quad \bar{X}^* + \frac{3\sigma}{\sqrt{n}} \\ &\text{Lower Control Limit, LCL:} \quad \bar{X}^* - \frac{3\sigma}{\sqrt{n}} \end{aligned} \tag{2}$$

where the derived standards have been designated by an asterisk (*).

When applying equations (1) and (2) to situations in which the sample sizes are equal, the control limits are constant from lot to lot or from day to day. With samples of unequal sizes, the control charts may be different from point to point. In cases where the sample sizes tend to be unequal from lot to lot or period to period, then, in practice, control charts may be established for an average n size (denoted by $\bar{n}$) and the control limits are drawn on the control chart for this value. However, when a point is found to be close to such a limit, then it is best to determine the exact values for UCL and LCL before rendering a decision with

CONTROL CHART METHOD OF CONTROLLING QUALITY
CONTROL CHART RECORD

PRODUCT – 2 ply Woolen Yarn
CHARACTERISTIC – Cleanliness after Scouring
UNIT OF MEASUREMENT – Percent Fat by Ether Extraction
SPECIFIED LIMITS – 0.1% Min. 1.0% Max.
CONTROL LIMITS – Based on Range

DEPT. – Dyehouse
NORMAL DAILY OUTPUT – 50,000 lb.
SAMPLE SIZE, GROUP OF – 5 Points by Chem. Lab.
LIMITS BY – Product Engineer

respect to control or lack of control at the current specified level. Checks for control of the process are thus performed at minimum costs without weakening the control procedures or criteria.

Figure 6-1 shows a control chart for averages only, covering fifteen months of data for two-ply woolen yarn with respect to the characteristic *cleanliness after scouring*. It illustrates what can be done effectively with such charts.

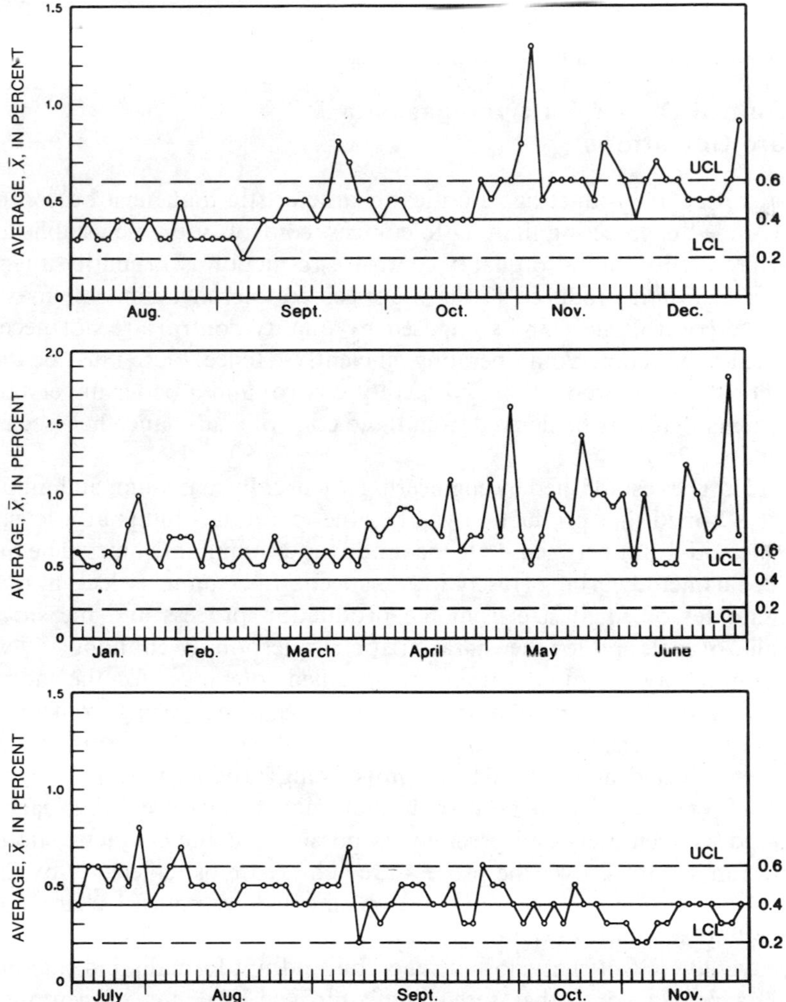

Figure 6–1 Control chart record of quality of a material: averages for 15 months only.

1. Period of normal control.
2. Change in scouring – started use of new soap.
3. Operator failed to hold specified alkali reading.
4. Faulty electrode on alkali meter – replaced.

5. Speed of yarn through bowls reduced.
6. Change in scouring – started use of another soap.
7. Causes not determined.
8. Excessive oiling of yarn due to change in method. Not accepted as cause at first by production unit. Corrected finally in August.
9. Period of experimental changes to bring about control.
10. Started change in scouring equipment – counterflow.
11. Further changes and adjustments in equipment.
12. Back in control – due to normal oiling and changes in methods.

6.4 Control Charts for Averages and Standard Deviations

Where a particular product has a critical characteristic that must be controlled within specified engineering limiting tolerances, controls must be established by not only production but also quality control. Production is primarily interested in keeping each unit produced within the specified tolerance limits. It may even feel that the control chart limits imposed by quality control are not necessary and prevent production from operating efficiently. Hence, there must be greater cooperation between production and quality control and a better understanding of the benefits that may be derived from these control charts and their seemingly tighter limits.

The tolerances established by engineering are usually maximum and minimum values; it is hoped that production will be able to produce units at a level very close to the mid-point between these maximum and minimum values. The quality control department, working closely with inspection personnel, selects at random regular samples of equal size from the production process and measures the actual value of each unit for the characteristic in question. Even though all values in the sample may be found within the specified tolerances for the individual units, quality control may find that the process is not being controlled by production at the desired level. To obtain the most effective controls, successive samples are selected at random from units being produced by the system of causes in effect. In order to be certain that such results are valid, each unit is measured as accurately and precisely as possible for the characteristic under consideration. Controls over the process are achieved most efficiently by the use of control charts for average values, supplemented by control charts for the corresponding standard deviation values for successive samples. The preceding section covered control charts for averages, but did not formally indicate how to obtain the type of averages that were being controlled. The most efficient measure of central tendencies is the arithmetic mean. It is determined from the relation

$$\bar{X} = \frac{\Sigma X_i}{n} \tag{3}$$

where X_i is the ith measurement value observed in the sample of n units. The standard deviation for averages is given in terms of the standard deviation for individual units. For setting up control charts for the averages and standard deviations of successive samples, one of the terms required is the standard deviation for individual units. This is the square root of the variance of the sample, v, and is determined from the following relation.

$$\sigma = \sqrt{v} = \sqrt{\frac{\Sigma(X_i - \bar{X})^2}{n}} \tag{4}$$

In the theory of estimation, the best unbiased estimate of the true value of the standard deviation of the entire population or universe U, denoted by σ', is obtained by using the measure *degrees of freedom,* designated as df, which is here $n - 1$, in equation (5). In engineering and quality control work, σ is used as defined above. For estimation the relation below is used.

$$s = \sqrt{\frac{\Sigma(X_i - \bar{X})^2}{(n-1)}} \tag{5}$$

Another estimate of the true value of the standard deviation is obtained from a set of data by calculating an average of the sigma values, $\bar{\sigma}$, and then using the factor c_2 (derived theoretically in advanced texts) as the average value for the sigma distribution. This applies to samples taken from a normal distribution, where the parent population has an average of zero and a value of one for σ'. This c_2 value varies with sample size, approaching one when n exceeds 100. For a sample size of 100, c_2 has a value of 0.9925. Such c_2 values are used in determining the control limits and, for each respective sample size n, are usually made a part of the multiplying factor used in determining such limits. This estimate of σ' is expressed as

$$\sigma'_e - \frac{\bar{\sigma}}{c_2} \tag{6}$$

Values of c_2 are given in table 6.1. This table summarizes most of the factors used in preparing control limits for variables. Where $\bar{\sigma} = 1$ used in preparing Normal Law tables, $c_2 = \bar{\sigma}$, the average value of the distribution of σ values for each separate value.

The cases that occur include both large and small samples of equal and unequal sizes for (1) standard given and (2) no standard given. When the standards are given, $\bar{X}'$ and σ' values are specified. If no standards are given, estimated values for such standards are derived from all available data, including the desires of potential customers. To keep control charts as simple as possible, equal sample sizes are usually specified in the procedures. When material is received from many different vendors, lot sizes may be different in size and—if control charts on vendor products are desirable—the best estimates of the possible standards are derived from weighted data. Usually the weighting factors are the differences in sample sizes. If an average of 10 ohms for a product is found for samples of 100 from one source and 9 ohms for samples of 900 from another source, control charts might be set up separately for each vendor based on their respective levels. However, a composite chart for all would be based on a level of 9.1 ohms obtained by the relation

$$\bar{X} = \frac{[100(10) + 900(9)]}{1000} = \frac{(1000 + 8100)}{(100 + 900)} = \frac{9100}{1000} = 9.1 \text{ ohms},$$

where the denominator is the sum of the numbers in the two samples from the two sources. This is the simplest and most plausible method of weighting results obtained from different sources. For standard deviation values, it is probably better to use the proper c_2 factor for each group of data involving the same sample size n. Then obtain the best estimate of σ' from the weighted averages

TABLE 6.1 Factors for Computing Control Chart Lines

	Chart for Averages			*Chart for Standard Deviations*						*Chart for Ranges*						
	Factors for Control Limits			*Factors for Central Line*		*Factors for Control Limits*				*Factors for Central Line*		*Factors for Control Limits*				
Number of Observations in Sample, n	A	A_1	A_2	c_2	$\frac{1}{c_2}$	B_1	B_2	B_3	B_4	d_2	$\frac{1}{d_2}$	d_3	D_1	D_2	D_3	D_4
2......	2.121	3.760	1.880	0.5642	1.7725	0	1.843	0	3.267	1.128	0.8865	0.853	0	3.686	0	3.267
3......	1.732	2.394	1.023	0.7236	1.3820	0	1.858	0	2.568	1.693	0.5907	0.888	0	4.358	0	2.575
4......	1.500	1.880	0.729	0.7979	1.2533	0	1.808	0	2.266	2.059	0.4857	0.880	0	4.698	0	2.282
5......	1.342	1.596	0.577	0.8407	1.1894	0	1.756	0	2.089	2.326	0.4299	0.864	0	4.918	0	2.115
6......	1.225	1.410	0.483	0.8686	1.1512	0.026	1.711	0.030	1.970	2.534	0.3946	0.848	0	5.078	0	2.004
7......	1.134	1.277	0.419	0.8882	1.1259	0.105	1.672	0.118	1.882	2.704	0.3698	0.833	0.205	5.203	0.076	1.924
8......	1.061	1.175	0.373	0.9027	1.1078	0.167	1.638	0.185	1.815	2.847	0.3512	0.820	0.387	5.307	0.136	1.864
9......	1.000	1.094	0.337	0.9139	1.0942	0.219	1.609	0.239	1.761	2.970	0.3367	0.808	0.546	5.394	0.184	1.816
10......	0.949	1.028	0.308	0.9227	1.0837	0.262	1.584	0.284	1.716	3.078	0.3249	0.797	0.687	5.469	0.223	1.777
11......	0.905	0.973	0.285	0.9300	1.0753	0.299	1.561	0.321	1.679	3.173	0.3152	0.787	0.812	5.534	0.256	1.744
12......	0.866	0.925	0.266	0.9359	1.0684	0.331	1.541	0.354	1.646	3.258	0.3069	0.778	0.924	5.592	0.284	1.716
13......	0.832	0.884	0.249	0.9410	1.0627	0.359	1.523	0.382	1.618	3.336	0.2998	0.770	1.026	5.646	0.308	1.692
14......	0.802	0.848	0.235	0.9453	1.0579	0.384	1.507	0.406	1.594	3.407	0.2935	0.762	1.121	5.693	0.329	1.671
15......	0.775	0.816	0.223	0.9490	1.0537	0.406	1.492	0.428	1.572	3.472	0.2880	0.755	1.207	5.737	0.348	1.652
16......	0.750	0.788	0.212	0.9523	1.0501	0.427	1.478	0.448	1.552	3.532	0.2831	0.749	1.285	5.779	0.364	1.636
17......	0.728	0.762	0.203	0.9551	1.0470	0.445	1.465	0.466	1.534	3.588	0.2787	0.743	1.359	5.817	0.379	1.621
18......	0.707	0.738	0.194	0.9576	1.0442	0.461	1.454	0.482	1.518	3.640	0.2747	0.738	1.426	5.854	0.392	1.608
19......	0.688	0.717	0.187	0.9599	1.0418	0.477	1.443	0.497	1.503	3.689	0.2711	0.733	1.490	5.888	0.404	1.596
20......	0.671	0.697	0.180	0.9619	1.0396	0.491	1.433	0.510	1.490	3.735	0.2677	0.729	1.548	5.922	0.414	1.586
21......	0.655	0.679	0.173	0.9638	1.0376	0.504	1.424	0.523	1.477	3.778	0.2647	0.724	1.606	5.950	0.425	1.575
22......	0.640	0.662	0.167	0.9655	1.0358	0.516	1.415	0.534	1.466	3.819	0.2618	0.720	1.659	5.979	0.434	1.566
23......	0.626	0.647	0.162	0.9670	1.0342	0.527	1.407	0.545	1.455	3.858	0.2592	0.716	1.710	6.006	0.443	1.557
24......	0.612	0.632	0.157	0.9684	1.0327	0.538	1.399	0.555	1.445	3.895	0.2567	0.712	1.759	6.031	0.452	1.548
25......	0.600	0.619	0.135	0.9696	1.0313	0.548	1.392	0.565	1.435	3.931	0.2544	0.709	1.804	6.058	0.459	1.541
Over 25......	$\frac{3}{\sqrt{n}}$	$\frac{3}{\sqrt{n}}$	......	......	......	*	**	*	**	......	......	......	......	......	......	......

$* \; 1 - \frac{3}{\sqrt{2n}}$ $** \; 1 + \frac{3}{\sqrt{2n}}$

+

of such estimates. Other texts cover this in much more detail. Since there are also errors in the measurements taken, the utmost refinement in obtaining weighted values is really not justified. A more important point is to eliminate such data as are judged to be secured from an obviously uncontrolled period of manufacture from the data used in obtaining a standard. Checks for significant differences in results will aid in the elimination of unrepresentative data.

Table 6.3 gives the formulas used to determine the control limits for samples of size n when the standards are given.

TABLE 6.2 Factors for Computing Control Chart Lines—Chart for Individuals

	Chart for Individuals	
	Factors for Control Limits	
Number of Observations in Sample, n	E_1	E_2
2......	5.318	2.660
3......	4.146	1.772
4......	3.760	1.457
5......	3.568	1.290
6......	3.454	1.184
7......	3.378	1.109
8......	3.323	1.054
9......	3.283	1.010
10......	3.251	0.975
11......	3.226	0.946
12......	3.205	0.921
13......	3.188	0.899
14......	3.174	0.881
15......	3.161	0.864
16......	3.150	0.849
17......	3.141	0.836
18......	3.133	0.824
19......	3.125	0.813
20......	3.119	0.803
21......	3.113	0.794
22......	3.107	0.785
23......	3.103	0.778
24......	3.098	0.770
25......	3.094	0.763
Over 25......	3	$\frac{3}{d_3}$

NOTES FOR TABLES 6.1 AND 6.2

NOTE 1: Values of d_3 added, covering $n = 2$ to $n = 25$.

NOTE 2: Values of d_2 and factors involving d_2 and d_3 have been extended from $n = 15$ to $n = 25$.

NOTE 3: All values in table 6.1 and table 6.2 have been computed and have been rechecked. The values in the tables were computed to enough significant figures so that, when rounded off in accordance with standard practices, the last figure in the table was not in doubt. (Except as indicated in Note 7.)[1]

NOTE 4: Following values differ from those given previously in table 6.I, Supplement B of ASTM *Manual on Presentation of Data.* Earlier values shown in parentheses ( ).

$n = 22,\ A = 0.640\ (0.639),\ n = 20,\ A_1 = 0.697\ (0.698),$
$n = 21,\ A_1 = 0.679\ (0.680),$
$n = 2,\ A_1 = 3.760\ (3.759),\ n = 18,\ c_2 = 0.9576\ (0.9577),$
$n = 15,\ A_1 = 0.816\ (0.817),\ n = 25,\ c_3 = 0.9696\ (0.9697).$

NOTE 5: Values of c_2 computed to eight places before rounding.

NOTE 6: Values of B_1, B_2, B_3, and B_4 differ from those given previously in table 6.I, Supplement B of ASTM *Manual on Presentation of Data,* being based on exact relation for σ_σ, that is,

$$\sigma_\sigma = \frac{\sigma}{\sqrt{2n}}[2(n-1) - 2nc_2^2]^{1/2}.$$

NOTE 7: Values of d_2 in column 11 and d_3 in column 13 reproduced with permission from Egon Pearson, "The Percentage Limits for the Distribution of Range in Samples from a Normal Population ($n < 100$)," *Biometrika,* Vol. 24, 1932, p. 416, Table A. This table gives d_3 to 4 significant figures for $n = 2$ to 5, inclusive and to only 3 significant figures for $n > 5$, so that the fourth significant figures for D_1, D_2, D_3, and D_4 are in doubt for $n > 5$ in table 6.1.

TABLE 6.3 Formula for Control Chart Lines—Standards Given

	Central Line	*Control Limits* — *Simplified Formula Using Factors in Table 6.1*	*Control Limits* — *Basic Formula*
For averages, $\bar{X}$	$\bar{X}'$	$\bar{X}' \pm A\sigma'$	$\bar{X}' \pm 3 \dfrac{\sigma'}{\sqrt{n}}$ .... (7)
For standard deviations, σ	$c_2\sigma'$	$B_2\sigma'$ and $B_1\sigma'$	$c_2\sigma' \pm 3 \dfrac{\sigma'}{\sqrt{2n}}$ ..... (8)[2,3]

When only observed values are available, the following relations are used. The solution of the case where the samples are unequal in size is also covered.

TABLE 6.4 Formulas for Control Limits—Standard Derived from Data

(*a*) *Samples Approximately Equal in Size:*

	Control Chart Lines — *Central Line*	*Control Chart Lines* — *Control Limits*
For averages, $\bar{X}$	$\bar{\bar{X}}$	$\bar{\bar{X}} \pm 3 \dfrac{\sigma}{\sqrt{\bar{n}}}$ .... (9)
For standard deviations, σ	σ	$\sigma \pm 3 \dfrac{\sigma}{\sqrt{2\bar{n}}}$ .... (10)

where $\bar{\bar{X}}$ = the grand average of the observed values of X for *all* samples,

$$\sigma = \sqrt{\frac{n_1\sigma_1^2 + n_2\sigma_2^2 + \cdots + n_m\sigma_m^2}{n_1 + n_2 + \cdots + n_m}} \qquad \text{(11)}$$

$$\bar{n} = \frac{n_1 + n_2 + \cdots + n_m}{m} = \text{average number of observations per sample.}$$

(*b*) *Samples Widely Different in Size:* Same as in Paragraph (*a*), except compute control limits for each sample separately, using the individual sample size, n, in the equation for control limits.

(*c*) *Samples of Equal Size:* Same as in Paragraph (*a*), except

$$\sigma = \bar{\sigma} = \frac{\sigma_1 + \sigma_2 + \cdots + \sigma_m}{m} \qquad \text{(12)}$$

$\bar{n} = n$ = number of observations in each sample.

Where the standards are not given and control charts are to be prepared for small samples of equal size, it is assumed that a set of observed values of a variable X is divisible into m rational subgroups (samples) of *equal size*, each subgroup containing $n = 25$ or less observed values.

TABLE 6.5 Factors for Control Chart Lines

	Central Line	Control Limits: Values Using Factors in Table 6.1	Control Limits: Equation
For averages, $\bar{X}$	$\bar{\bar{X}}$	$\bar{\bar{X}} \pm A_1\bar{\sigma}$	$\bar{\bar{X}} \pm 3\dfrac{\bar{\sigma}}{c_2\sqrt{n}}$ (13)
For standard deviations, σ	$\bar{\sigma}$	$B_4\bar{\sigma}$ and $B_3\bar{\sigma}$	$\bar{\sigma} \pm 3\dfrac{\bar{\sigma}}{c_2\sqrt{2n}}$ (14)[4]

where $\bar{\bar{X}}$ = the grand average of observed values of X for *all* units in the m samples,

$$\bar{\sigma} = \frac{\sigma_1 + \sigma_2 + \ldots \sigma_m}{m} \tag{15}$$

where σ_1, σ_2, etc., refer to the m computed standard deviations for the first second, etc., samples and factors c_2, A_1, B_3 and B_4 are given in table 6.1.

For *small samples of unequal size,* no general rule may be given in view of certain theoretical difficulties. The following working rule is generally satisfactory. Substitute for σ' the average value of the computed σ's for observed X values for samples of equal size n by the n value for these individual samples. Combine σ's for each subgroup. Standards and control limits may then be determined separately with little effort. Difficulties can be avoided if the samples are made of equal size for all groups where the data consist of subgroups with a different n value. The σ'_e for all subgroups combined may be obtained from the weighted average of the estimates of σ' obtained from each subgroup, using total n values for each subgroup as weighting factors.

$$\sigma'_e = \frac{\Sigma n_1\sigma'_{e_1} + \Sigma n_2\sigma'_{e_2} + \cdots + \Sigma n_m\sigma'_{e_m}}{\Sigma n_1 + \Sigma n_2 + \cdots + \Sigma n_m} \tag{15'}$$

for m subgroups is selected as an assumed standard given value with control limits of size n computed by equations (7) and (8).

In standardizing the control charts for variables data for averages and standard deviations, three documents present some of the best examples. The ASTM *Manual on Quality Control of Materials* gives condensed procedures with examples for all types of control charts. Permission has been obtained to use these examples and concepts. Dr. Romig, one of the authors of this text, served on the ASTM Committee and was instrumental in securing and preparing a large percentage of these examples and procedures, particularly those presented in the *Manual*'s appendices; hence he has selected those examples and relations that provide the best illustrative material for mastering the preparation and use of quality control charts for variables data.

The second group of standards provides examples of the use of control charts and how to prepare them and consists of three American War standards, which include many of the examples and procedures developed in the ASTM *Manual.* These are Z1.1-1941, Z1.2-1941, and Z1.3-1942, issued by the American Standards Association. Although updated from these original publications, there are very few changes in the text materials. Excerpts from these, slightly modified if necessary, are given.

Tables 6.6 and 6.7, presented in the Eugene L. Grant and Richard S. Leavenworth text, *Statistical Quality Control,* 4th edition, are reproduced by permission of the publisher and authors. **Such factors are** required for preparing control charts for $\bar{X}$ and $\bar{\sigma}$ values derived from n observed values of X. The first table is based on the fact that the standards are given so that σ' may be used with the proper multiplying factors as given in equations (7) and (8) listed in table 6.3. To avoid repetition, table 6.6 also gives the factors for use in preparing control charts for ranges covered in the next section. One advantage of tables 6.6 and 6.7 is that the n size has been extended to 100. Most tables of this nature present values of the factors for n values ending at 25 or 30 or less and do not include the larger values of n. Table 6.1 does provide for control charts for ranges for n sizes

TABLE 6.6 Factors for Determining from σ' the Three-sigma Control Limits for $\bar{X}$, R, and σ Charts

		Factors for R Chart		*Factors for σ Chart*	
Number of Observations in Subgroup	*Factor for $\bar{X}$ Chart*	*Lower Control Limit*	*Upper Control Limit*	*Lower Control Limit*	*Upper Control Limit*
n	A	D_1	D_2	B_1	B_2
2	2.12	0	3.69	0	1.84
3	1.73	0	4.36	0	1.86
4	1.50	0	4.70	0	1.81
5	1.34	0	4.92	0	1.76
6	1.22	0	5.08	0.03	1.71
7	1.13	0.20	5.20	0.10	1.67
8	1.06	0.39	5.31	0.17	1.64
9	1.00	0.55	5.39	0.22	1.61
10	0.95	0.69	5.47	0.26	1.58
11	0.90	0.81	5.53	0.30	1.56
12	0.87	0.92	5.59	0.33	1.54
13	0.83	1.03	5.65	0.36	1.52
14	0.80	1.12	5.69	0.38	1.51
15	0.77	1.21	5.74	0.41	1.49
16	0.75	1.28	5.78	0.43	1.48
17	0.73	1.36	5.82	0.44	1.47
18	0.71	1.43	5.85	0.46	1.45
19	0.69	1.49	5.89	0.48	1.44
20	0.67	1.55	5.92	0.49	1.43

n	A	D_1	D_2	B_1	B_2
21	0.65	**1.61**	**5.95**	0.50	1.42
22	0.64	**1.66**	**5.98**	0.52	1.41
23	0.63	**1.71**	**6.01**	0.53	1.41
24	0.61	**1.76**	**6.03**	0.54	1.40
25	0.60	**1.80**	**6.06**	0.55	1.39
30	0.55			0.59	1.36
35	0.51			0.62	1.33
40	0.47			0.65	1.31
45	0.45			0.67	1.30
50	0.42			0.68	1.28
55	0.40			0.70	1.27
60	0.39			0.71	1.26
65	0.37			0.72	1.25
70	0.36			0.74	1.24
75	0.35			0.75	1.23
80	0.34			0.75	1.23
85	0.33			0.76	1.22
90	0.32			0.77	1.22
95	0.31			0.77	1.21
100	0.30			0.78	1.20

$$UCL_{\bar{X}} = \bar{X}' + A\sigma'$$
$$LCL_{\bar{X}} = \bar{X}' - A\sigma'$$

(If actual average is to be used rather than standard or target average, $\bar{\bar{X}}$ should be substituted for $\bar{X}'$ in the preceding formulas.)

$$UCL_R = D_2\sigma'$$
$$\text{Central line}_R = d_2\sigma'$$
$$LCL_R = D_1\sigma'$$
$$UCL_\sigma = B_2\sigma'$$
$$\text{Central line}_\sigma = c_2\sigma'$$
$$LCL_\sigma = B_1\sigma'$$

All factors in table 6.6 are based on the normal distribution. ++

greater than twenty-five only for averages, as it is not recommended to use range values for samples larger than ten in most cases, although factors are given up to twenty-five.

Examples of control charts for averages and standard deviation values using the factors in tables 6.1, 6.6, and 6.7 are presented after table 6.7. These may be used as guides in preparing similar control charts in any industry. It must be noted that such control charts may be applied whenever a series of observations are made for any variable X.

Table 6.6 presents the factors that are used to determine control limits for averages, standard deviations, ranges when σ' is specified as well as $\bar{X}'$. This is

Average control charts were used very early without corresponding control charts for standard deviations. The Bell Telephone Laboratories Quality Assurance Department issued a quarterly quality report covering products manufactured by the Western Electric Company. The following is one page, extracted by permission, from one of their quarterly reports. It illustrates the use of different control limits for samples of unequal size, where the standard deviation is assumed to be controlled.

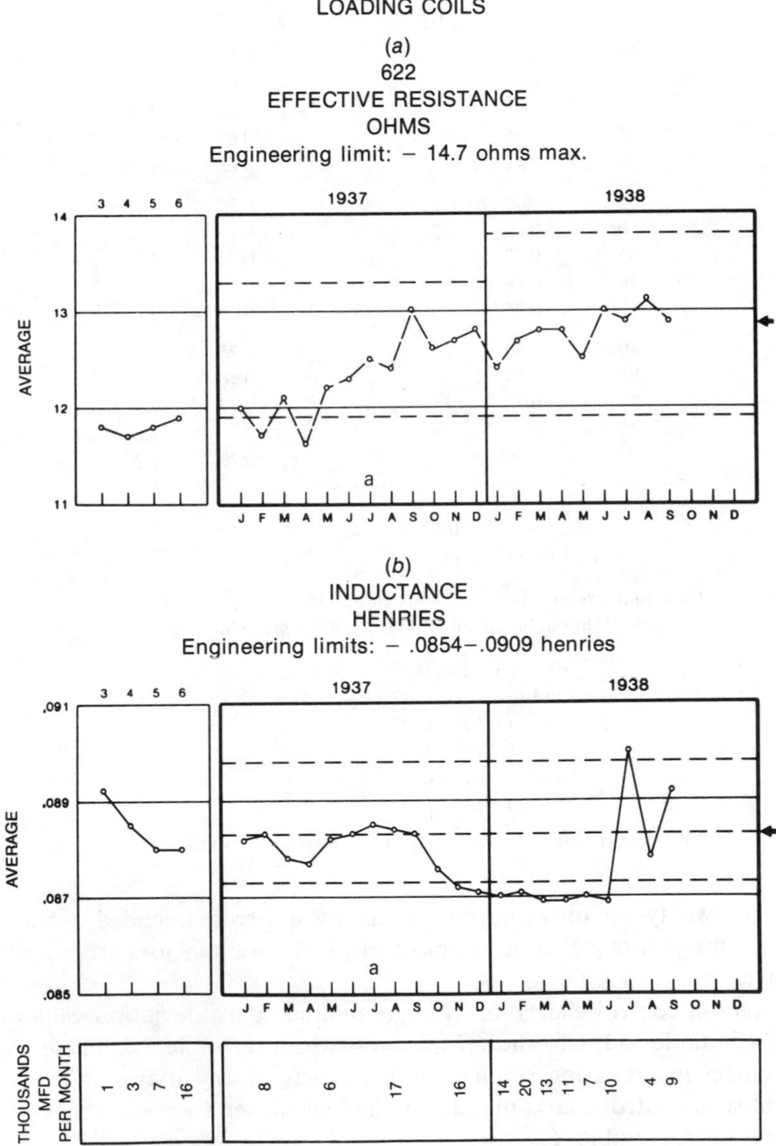

a – Preceding results cover No. 612.

Figure 6-2 Control charts for averages only, variability controlled.

Effective resistance values of Nos. 622 and 628 coils have been adjusted to the equivalent of a 10 foot 22 gauge stub cable.

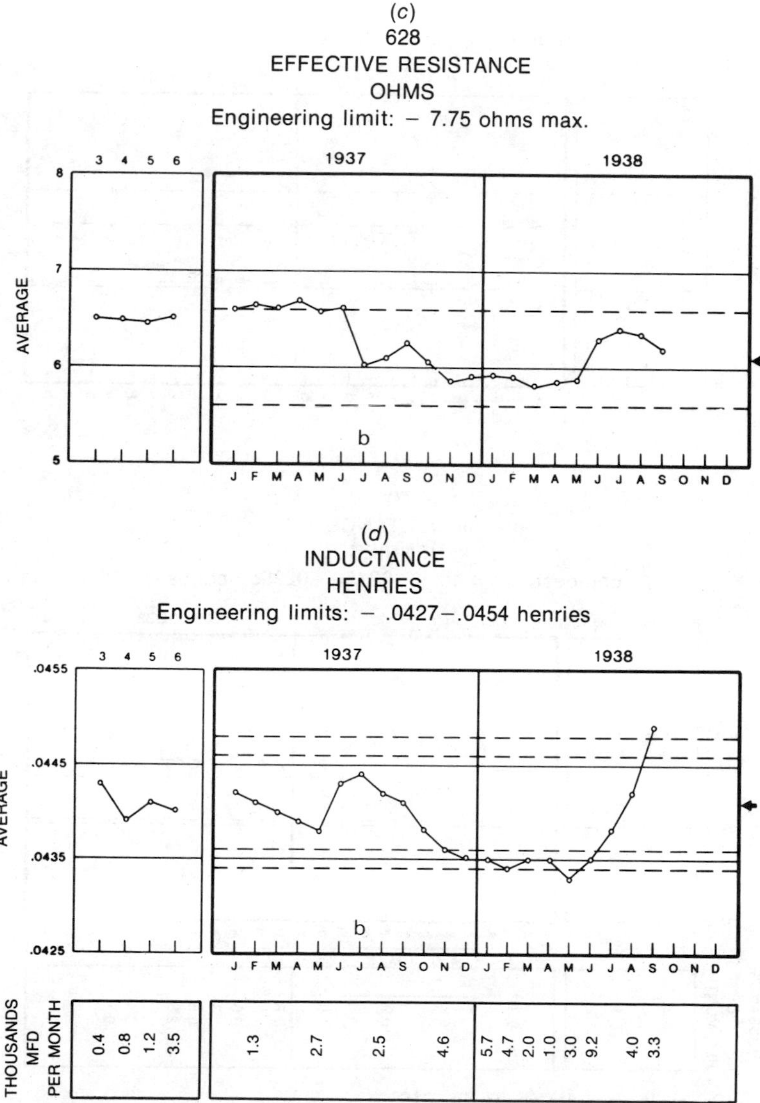

b – Preceding results cover No. 618.

Figure 6–2 Control charts for averages only, variability controlled.

Effective resistance values of No. 620 coil have been adjusted to the equivalent of coils as used in splice loading.

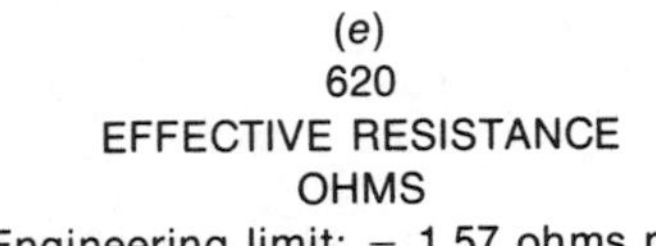

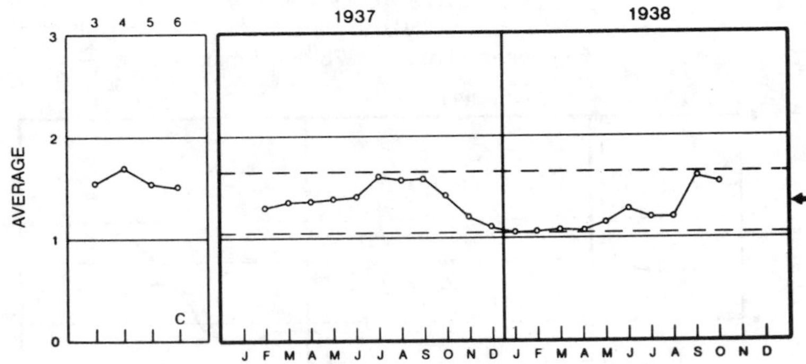

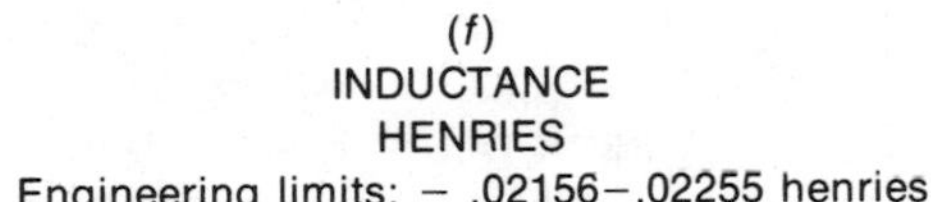

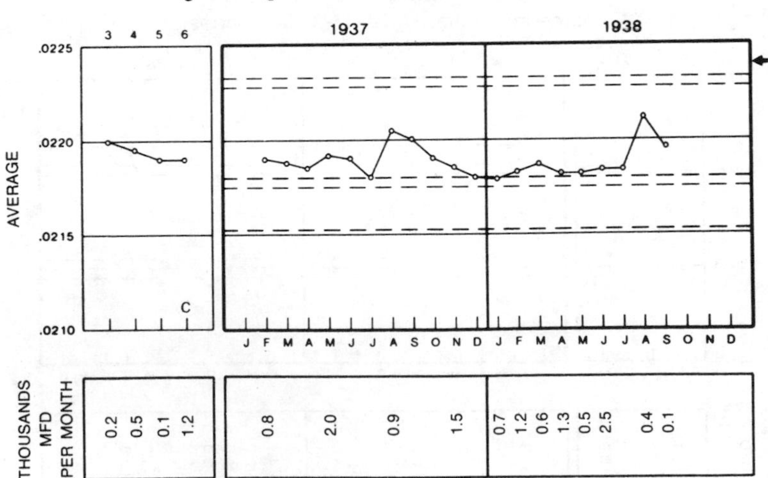

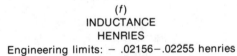

c – Preceding results cover No. 616.

Figure 6–2 Control charts for averages only, variability controlled.

Effective resistance values of M types have been adjusted to the equivalent of a 10 foot 19 gauge stub cable.

(*g*)
M1
CROSSTALK
TRUE CROSSTALK UNITS
PHANTOM TO SIDE
Engineering limit: – 40 true crosstalk units

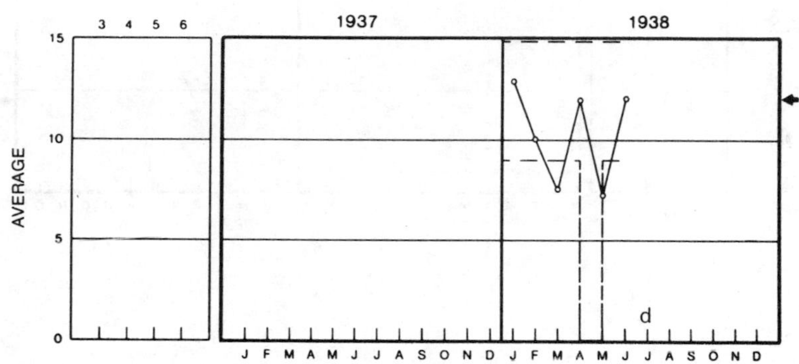

(*h*)
SIDE TO SIDE
Engineering limit: – 40 true crosstalk units

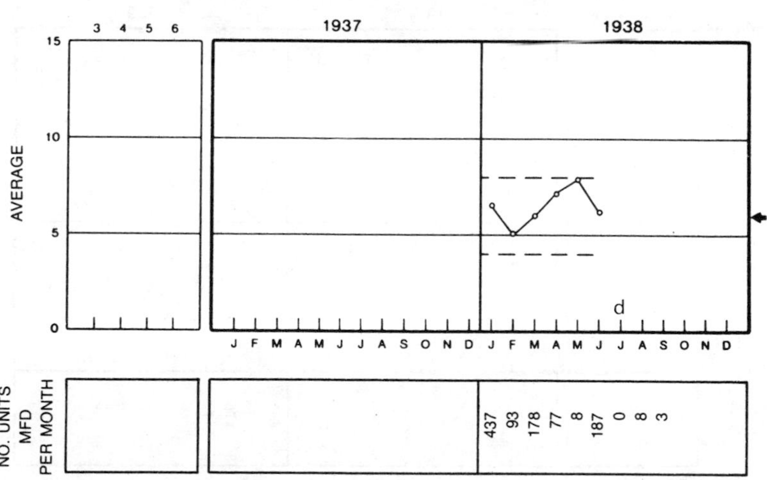

d – Preceding results cover P1B.

Figure 6–2 Control charts for averages only, variability controlled.

(*i*)
EFFECTIVE RESISTANCE
OHMS
PHANTOM CIRCUIT
Engineering limit: – 8.75 ohms max.

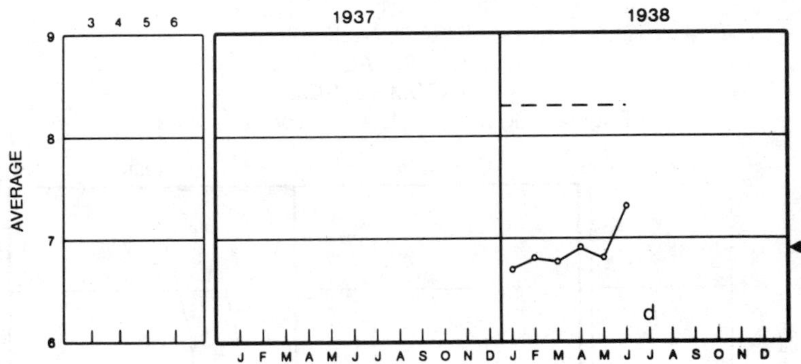

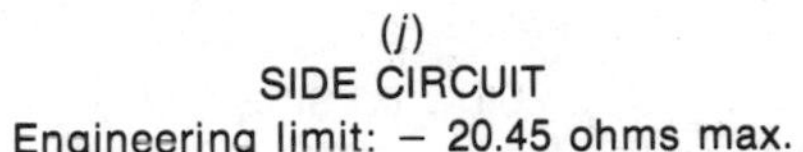

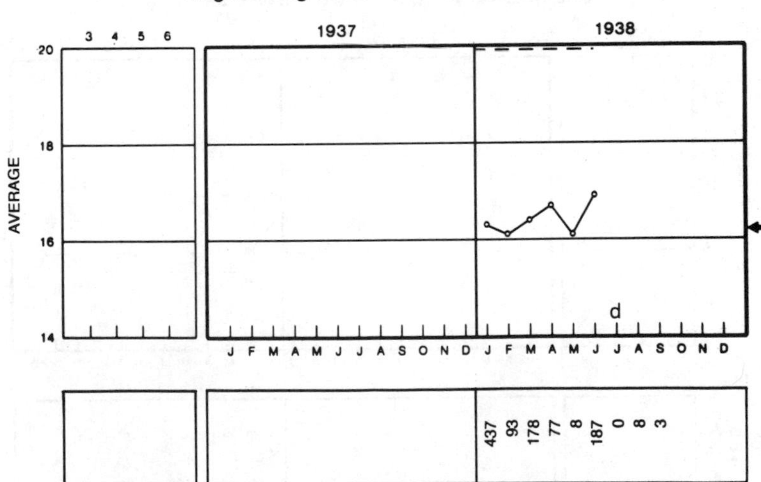

d – Preceding results cover P1B.

Figure 6–2 Control charts for averages only, variability controlled.

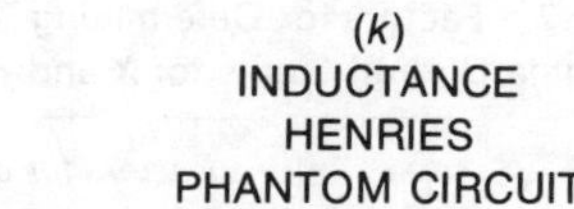

Engineering limits: – .0624–.0651 henries

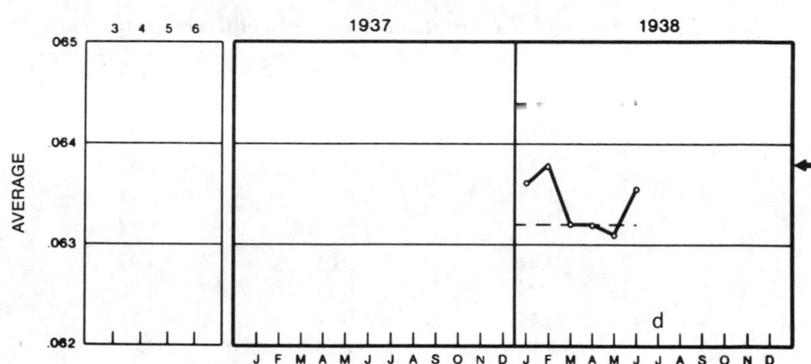

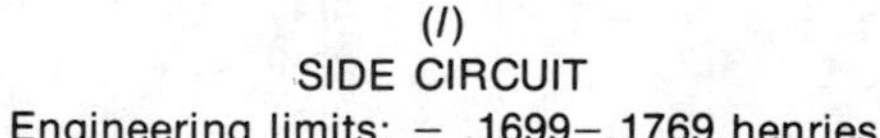

Engineering limits: – .1699–.1769 henries

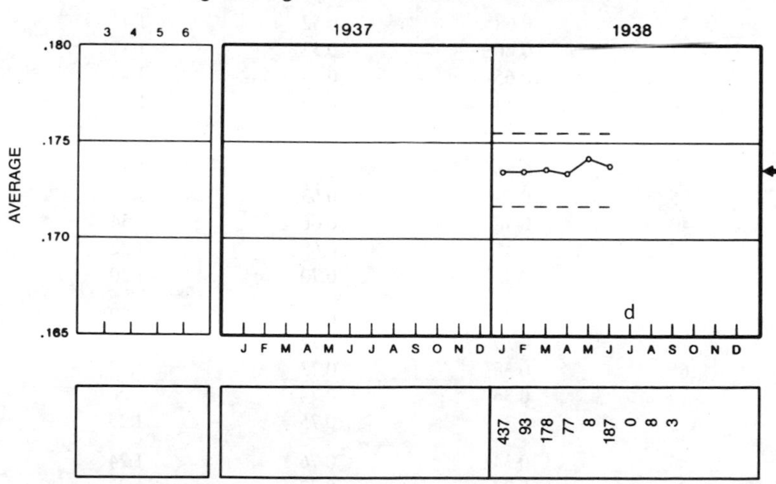

d – Preceding results cover P1B.

Figure 6–2 Control charts for averages only, variability controlled.

TABLE 6.7 Factors for Determining from $\bar{\sigma}$ the Three-sigma Control Limits for $\bar{X}$ and σ Charts

Number of Observations in Subgroup	*Factor for $\bar{X}$ Chart*	*Factors for σ Chart*	
		Lower Control Limit	*Upper Control Limit*
n	A_1	B_3	B_4
2	3.76	0	3.27
3	2.39	0	2.57
4	1.88	0	2.27
5	1.60	0	2.09
6	1.41	0.03	1.97
7	1.28	0.12	1.88
8	1.17	0.19	1.81
9	1.09	0.24	1.76
10	1.03	0.28	1.72
11	0.97	0.32	1.68
12	0.93	0.35	1.65
13	0.88	0.38	1.62
14	0.85	0.41	1.59
15	0.82	0.43	1.57
16	0.79	0.45	1.55
17	0.76	0.47	1.53
18	0.74	0.48	1.52
19	0.72	0.50	1.50
20	0.70	0.51	1.49
21	0.68	0.52	1.48
22	0.66	0.53	1.47
23	0.65	0.54	1.46
24	0.63	0.55	1.45
25	0.62	0.56	1.44
30	0.56	0.60	1.40
35	0.52	0.63	1.37
40	0.48	0.66	1.34
45	0.45	0.68	1.32
50	0.43	0.70	1.30
55	0.41	0.71	1.29
60	0.39	0.72	1.28
65	0.38	0.73	1.27
70	0.36	0.74	1.26
75	0.35	0.75	1.25
80	0.34	0.76	1.24
85	0.33	0.77	1.23
90	0.32	0.77	1.23
95	0.31	0.78	1.22
100	0.30	0.79	1.21

++

Upper Control Limit for $\bar{X} = UCL_{\bar{X}} = \bar{\bar{X}} + A_1\bar{\sigma}$
Lower Control Limit for $\bar{X} = LCL_{\bar{X}} = \bar{\bar{X}} - A_1\bar{\sigma}$

(If target or standard value $\bar{X}'$ is used rather than $\bar{\bar{X}}$ as the central line on the control chart, $\bar{X}'$ should be substituted for $\bar{\bar{X}}$ in the preceding formulas.)

Upper Control Limit for $\sigma = UCL_\sigma = B_4\bar{\sigma}$
Lower Control Limit for $\sigma = LCL_\sigma = B_3\bar{\sigma}$

All factors in table 6.7 are based on the normal distribution.

given in several texts, but is identical with Table E in the Grant and Leavenworth text.

The factors that are used for determining control charts from the average of the X values and also the average of the σ values, $\bar{\sigma}$, provided as aids for computing the three-sigma control limits, are listed in Table D from the Grant and Leavenworth text, reproduced here as table 6.7.

The following example illustrates the use of control charts for averages and standard deviations for small samples of unequal size. It also applies to the case where the samples are equal. Control limits shown in figure 6-3 are based on formulas given in table 6-3.

Example 1 *Control Charts for $\bar{X}$ and σ, Small Samples of Unequal Size, Standards Given for $\bar{X}$ and σ.* A manufacturer wished to control the resistance of a certain product after it had been operating for 100 hrs., where $\bar{X}' = 150$ ohms and $\sigma' = 7.5$ ohms. From each of 15 consecutive lots, he selected a random sample of 5 units and subjected them to the operating test for 100 hrs. Due to mechanical failures, some of the units in the sample failed before the completion of 100 hrs. of operation. Table 6.8 gives the averages and standard deviations for the 15 samples together with their sample sizes. Figure 6-3 gives the control charts for $\bar{X}$ and σ.

TABLE 6.8 Resistance in Ohms after 100-hr Operation, Lot by Lot Control Data

Sample	*Sample Size, n*	*Average, $\bar{X}$*	*Standard Deviation, σ*	*Sample*	*Sample Size, n*	*Average, $\bar{X}$*	*Standard Deviation, σ*
No. 1.........	5	154.6	12.20	No. 9.........	5	156.2	8.92
No. 2.........	5	143.4	9.75	No. 10........	4	137.5	3.24
No. 3.........	4	160.8	11.20	No. 11........	5	153.8	6.85
No. 4.........	3	152.7	7.43	No. 12........	5	143.4	7.64
No. 5.........	5	136.0	4.32	No. 13........	4	156.0	10.18
No. 6.........	3	147.3	8.65	No. 14........	5	149.8	8.86
No. 7.........	3	161.7	9.23	No. 15........	3	138.2	7.38
No. 8.........	5	151.0	7.24				

Central Lines

For $\bar{X}$: $\bar{X}' = 150.$

For σ:

$n = 3$:

$\bar{\sigma} = c_2\sigma' = (0.7236)(7.5) = 5.43.$

$n = 4$:

$\bar{\sigma} = c_2\sigma' = (0.7979)(7.5) = 5.98.$

$n = 5$:

$\bar{\sigma} = c_2\sigma' = (0.8407)(7.5) = 6.31.$

Control Limits

For $\bar{X}$:

$n = 3$:

$\bar{X}' \pm A\sigma' = 150 \pm 1.732\ (7.5),$
163.0 and 137.0.

$n = 4$:

$\bar{X}' \pm A\sigma' = 150 \pm 1.500\ (7.5),$
161.2 and 138.8.

$n = 5$:

$\bar{X}' \pm A\sigma' = 150 \pm 1.342\ (7.5),$
160.1 and 139.9.

For σ:

$n = 3$: $B_2\sigma'$ and $B_1\sigma' =$
(1.858) (7.5) and (0) (7.5),
13.94 and 0.

$n = 4$: $B_2\sigma'$ and $B_1\sigma' =$
(1.808)(7.5) and (0)(7.5),
13.56 and 0.

$n = 5$: $B_2\sigma'$ and $B_1\sigma' =$
(1.756) (7.5) and (0) (7.5),
13.17 and 0.+

Results Evidence of lack of control is indicated since samples from lots Nos. 5 and 10 have averages below their lower control limit. No standard deviation values are outside their control limits.

Where no standard is given and standards are derived from the past data, the following example taken from the ASA Standard—an enlargement of the ASTM presentation—gives a concrete example of such charts where three-sigma control

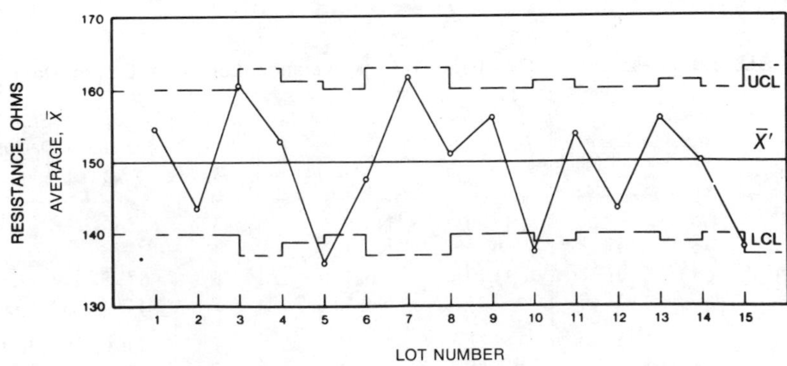

Figure 6–3 Control charts for $\bar{X}$ and σ. Small samples of unequal size, $n = 3, 4, 5$; $\bar{X}'$, σ' given.

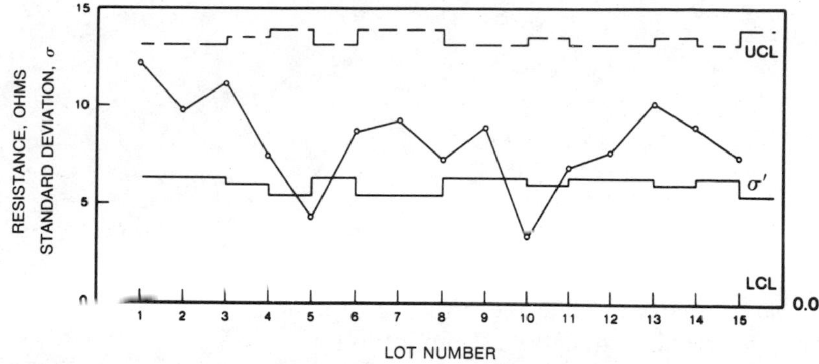

Figure 6-3 Control charts for $\bar{X}$ and σ. Small samples of unequal size, n = 3, 4, 5; $\bar{X}'$, σ' given.

limits apply. This is a case where the average breaking strength is seemingly uncontrolled. It is given to illustrate the fact that many times the control limits may be exceedingly narrow. It may be necessary in analyzing this case to provide another factor for different machine set-ups for this strand. Possibly the raw materials may vary with the weather or seasons; so the standard value for σ should be increased.

Example 2 *Control Charts for $\bar{X}$ and σ, Equal Small Samples, No Standard Given.* Table 6.9 gives breaking strength results on 10 lots of steel wire strand. A sample of $n = 4$ test specimens was taken per lot. Figure 6-4 shows control charts for $\bar{X}$ and σ.

TABLE 6.9 Breaking Strength, Steel Wire Strand

Lot	*Test Values*				*Average,* $\bar{X}$	*Standard Deviation,* σ	*Range,* R
	X_1	X_2	X_3	X_4			
No. 1	7490	7535	7455	7480	7490.0	28.94	80
No. 2	6550	6495	6525	6465	6508.75	31.90	85
No. 3	6995	6995	6970	6880	6960.0	47.30	115
No. 4	7045	7060	7095	7035	7058.75	22.74	60
No. 5	6715	6740	6780	6720	6738.75	25.59	65
No. 6	6585	6630	6675	6645	6633.75	32.48	90
No. 7	6600	6590	6610	6650	6612.5	22.78	60
No. 8	6665	6670	6630	6660	6656.25	15.56	40
No. 9	6440	6425	6460	6470	6448.75	17.46	45
No. 10	6660	6630	6605	6625	6630.0	19.69	55
Average					6773.75	26.44	69.5

+

Central Lines

For $\overline{X}$: $\overline{\overline{X}} = 6773.75.$

For σ: $\bar{\sigma} = \quad 26.44.$

Control Limits

For $\overline{X}$: $\overline{\overline{X}} \pm A_1\bar{\sigma} = 6773.75 \pm 1.880(26.44),$
6724.04 and 6823.46.

For σ: $B_3\bar{\sigma}$ and $B_4\bar{\sigma} = (0)(26.44)$ and
$(2.266)(26.44),$
0 and **59.9**. +

Results Charts indicate the presence of assignable causes of variation in average breaking strength, X, from lot to lot.

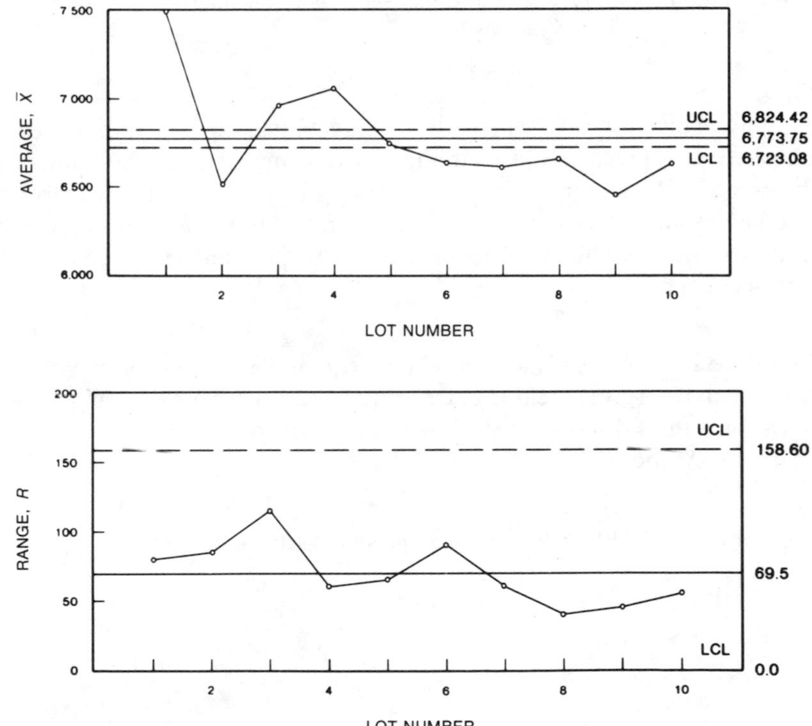

Figure 6–4 Control chart for $\overline{X}$ and σ; small equal samples, no standard given, $n = 4$.

The most modern techniques in quality control involve the use of the best statistics available. Process controls are obtained by the use of control charts for averages, $\overline{X}$, called *X-bar charts*, and also for standard deviations, σ. Such controls over variability or dispersion are also achieved by the use of control charts for ranges, R. The latter are the most popular as the values of R are determined by simply taking the difference between the largest and smallest observation in a sample. Unfortunately, when the sample sizes are large, the efficiency of the range is very poor, often as low as 75%. By low efficiency, we mean that the variation in a series of R values is very much greater than the variation that exists in the use of values of the standard deviation. Thus to obtain the same confidence in the controls using range, we will need a much larger sample than for standard deviations. The efficiency of the range decreases as the size of the sample increases, when compared with the standard deviation. In order to achieve the same discrimination (and possible error), more samples of the same size or smaller will be required when using the range for the control of variability rather than the standard deviation. Estimates of the true standard deviation value by use of range values is achieved by the use of m subsamples of size n^*, where $n = mn^*$. Determine m values of R and then obtain their average value $\bar{R}$. Then $\sigma'_e = \bar{R}/d_2$, where the value of d_2 used corresponds to n^* in the table of d_2 values. Economically, a judgment must be made whether to spend more for computing the standard deviation or to spend more for taking a larger number of samples. If an electronic computer is available and is properly set up to readily compute sigma values, these sigma charts may be less costly in the long run than corresponding control charts using ranges. Some courses in statistical quality control primarily stress the use of range charts.

Both will be discussed in detail in this book. Examples of control charts follow which include step-by-step procedures for preparing such control charts.

Example 3 *Step-by-Step Procedures for Preparing Control Charts for $\bar{X}$ and σ.* This example uses actual data to develop a step-by-step procedure for the preparation of standards to be used as the basis for control charts for the variables that best describe and define a distribution. These two statistics are the average $\bar{X}$ and the standard deviation σ. For controlling the variability an average of a group of standard deviation values is determined, giving the central value $\bar{\sigma}$ from which an estimate of σ', the true parameter, is obtained.

Table 6.10 presents ten subgroups of four units each which are tested in accordance with standard practices to give the weight of explosive charges in grains. These data provide weight values to three significant figures. To simplify the computations, the observed weights are reduced by thirty for each observed value. These much smaller numbers are used to determine average and standard deviation values for each of the ten subgroups. The data seem to be truly random and provide values for $\bar{\bar{X}}$, a grand average of the ten average ($\bar{X}$) values determined for the ten subgroups. The method used to obtain this standard is tabulated in successive steps. Standard deviation values are obtained for each of the ten subgroups. The procedures that most economically provide this final average value are noted. Variances and standard deviation values are found for each subgroup.

After detailing how to obtain the necessary standards for $\overline{X}$ and σ, ten steps are recorded; the tenth step covers the interpretation of the control charts together with a presentation of the complete control charts to be applied.

Control charts were first developed in 1924 by Dr. Walter A. Shewhart of the Bell Telephone Laboratories for use in the Bell System; after many different applications and developments, quarterly quality reports were issued by the Quality Assurance Department of BTL showing control charts for the most important items and characteristics used in communication. Such charts used standards that were established and reviewed yearly and covered, in some cases, as much as five years' data, on a monthly basis, quarterly basis, and yearly basis. Some samples during the various periods were equal and some were unequal. These practical applications may be applied to other industries very effectively. Their purpose was to indicate in which areas it would prove profitable to effect

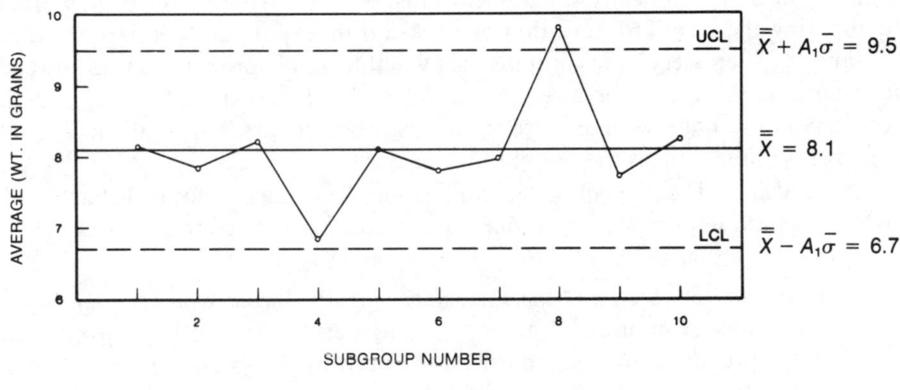

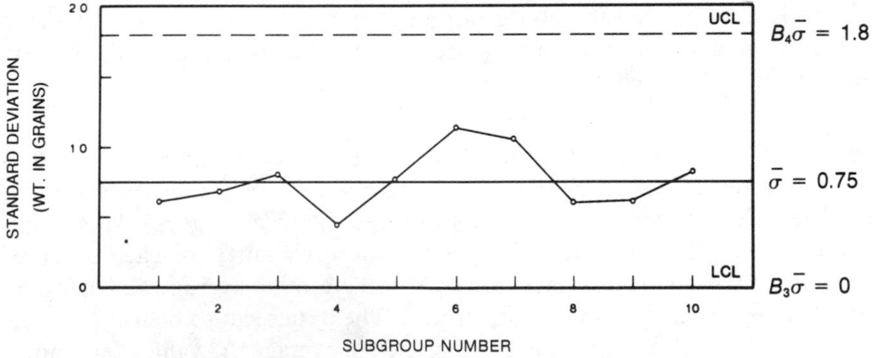

Figure 6–5 Procedure for constructing control charts for *average* and *standard deviation*. Some σ values for 10 subgroups of equal sample size.

TABLE 6.10 Weights of Explosive Charges in Grains Ten Subgroups of Four Units Each

Subgroup No.	*1*	2	3	4	5	6	7	*8*	9	10
Observed Values of Quality	38.4	37.4	39.5	37.4	38.0	36.1	38.7	39.5	38.1	39.0
Measured	37.1	37.3	37.4	37.1	39.2	37.6	38.2	39.2	37.8	38.3
	38.8	39.0	38.3	36.5	37.0	38.3	36.2	39.8	36.7	36.9
(Wt. in Grains)	38.5	37.7	37.7	36.3	38.2	39.2	38.8	40.8	38.3	38.8
Total	152.8	151.4	152.9	147.3	152.4	151.2	151.9	159.3	150.9	153.0

improvements in components and in the manufacturing processes. Figure 6-6 presents such a chart, showing the case where the monthly samples were of equal size. Note these charts cover two different characteristics on one of the types of handset receivers classified in the group called *Telephone Instruments.* Yearly values are shown for four years, while monthly values are given for eighteen months. The number of units manufactured per month is also shown.

Figure 6-7 shows two different types of units used in a given Teletypewriter, presenting control charts for two characteristics of each. Variable monthly sample sizes are given in this figure, covering control charts for average and standard

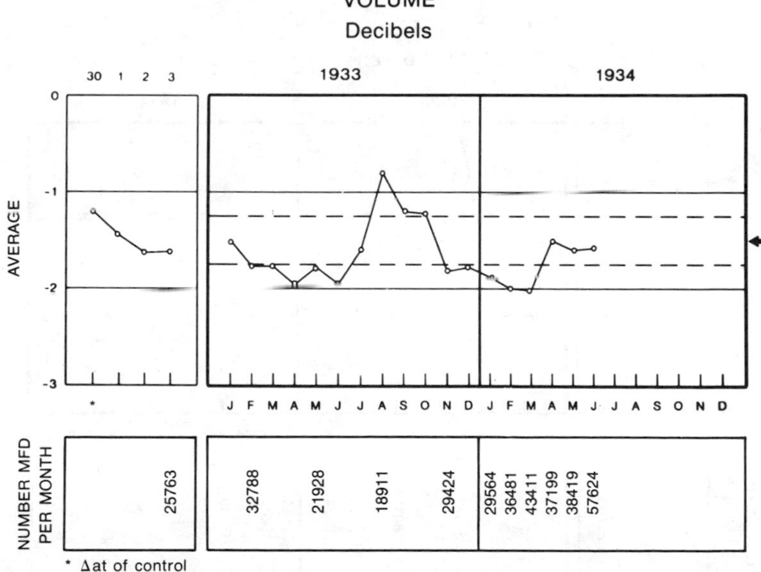

Figure 6–6 Example of control charts for $\bar{X}$ and σ; early applications by industry—1930–34, two characteristics; approximately equal samples.

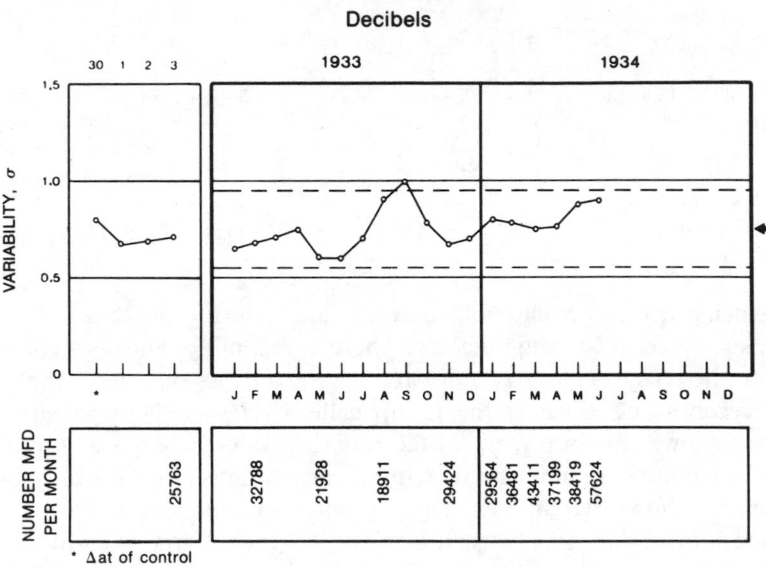

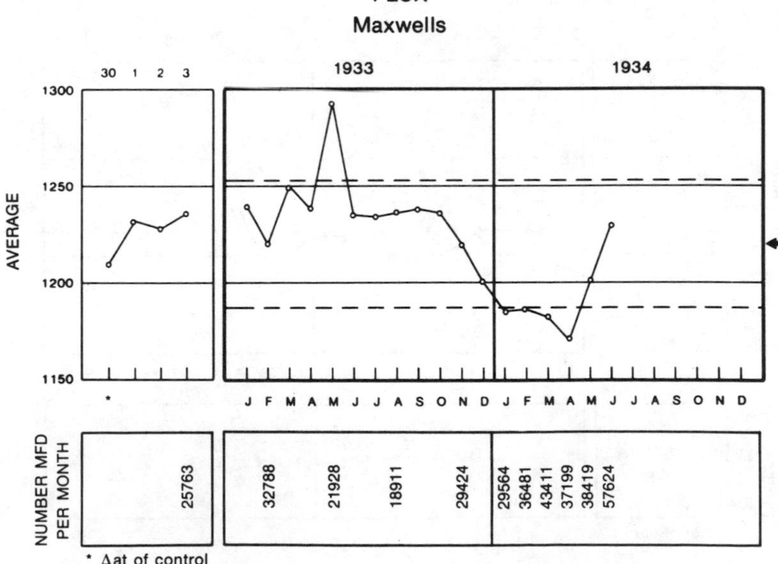

Figure 6-6 Example of control charts for $\bar{X}$ and σ; early applications by industry—1930-34, two characteristics; approximately equal samples.

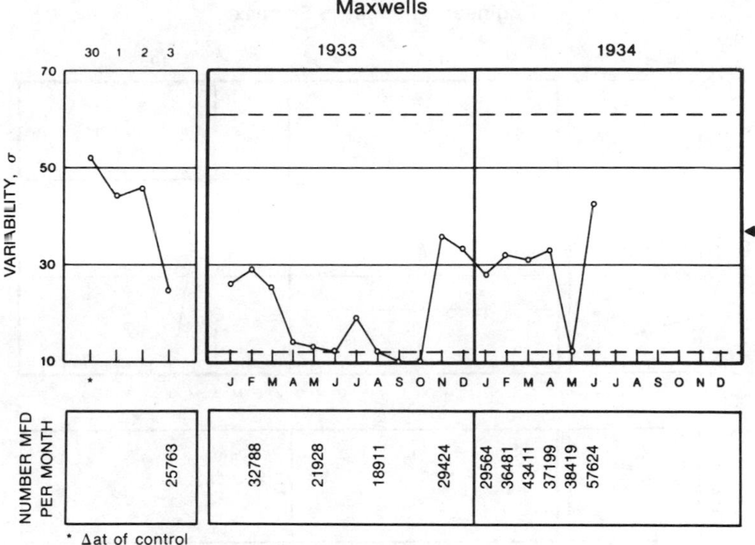

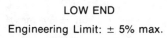

Figure 6-6 Example of control charts for $\overline{X}$ and σ; early applications by industry—1930-34, two characteristics; approximately equal samples.

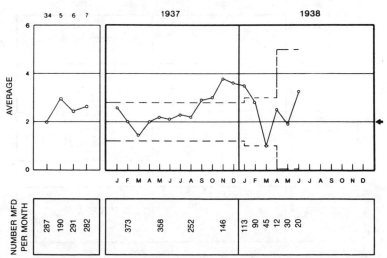

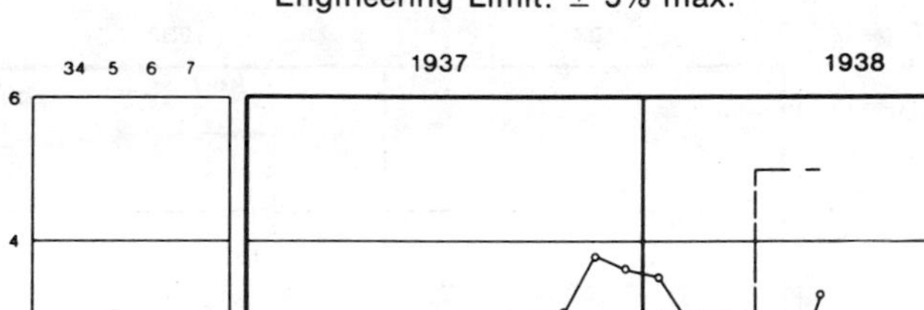

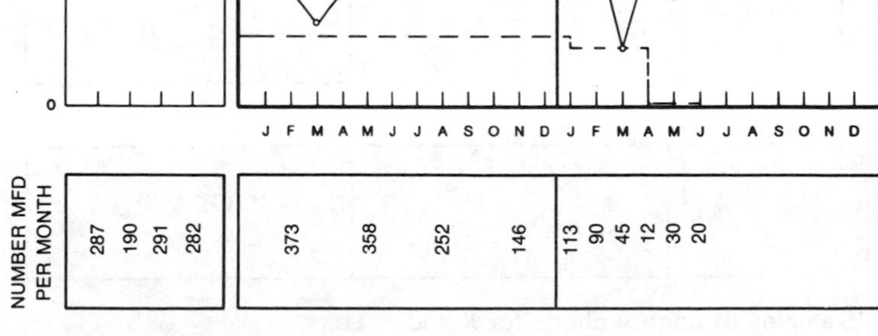

Figure 6–7 Examples of control charts for $\overline{X}$ and σ. Later applications by industry.

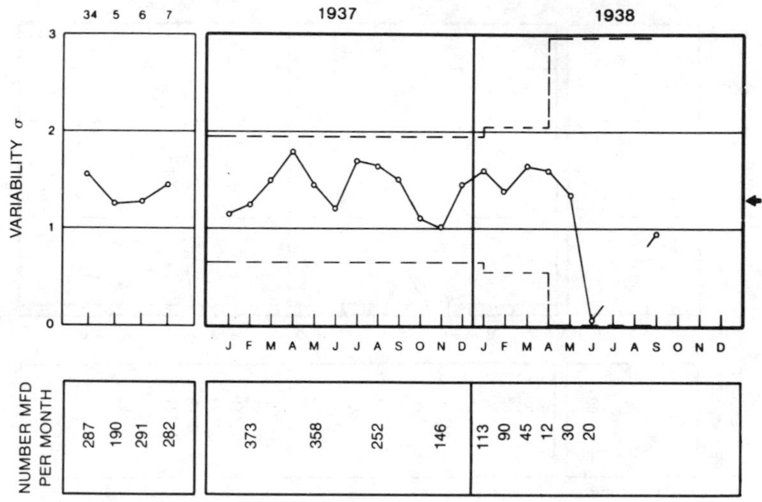

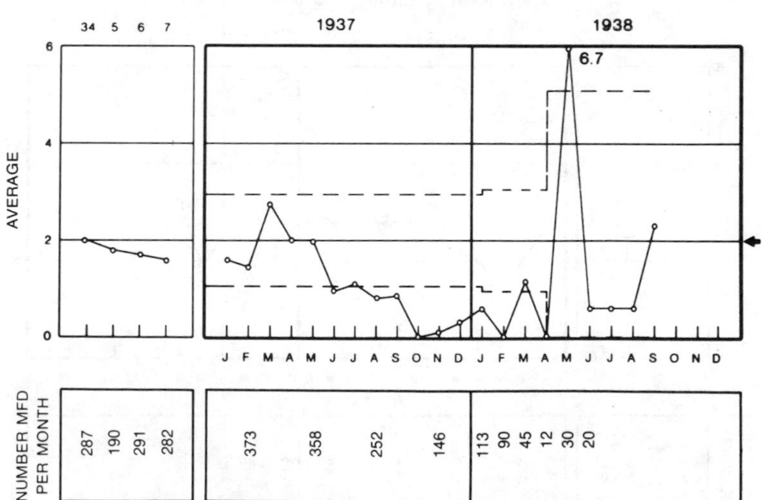

Figure 6-7 Examples of control charts for $\bar{X}$ and σ. Later applications by industry.

HIGH END

Engineering Limit: ± 5% max.

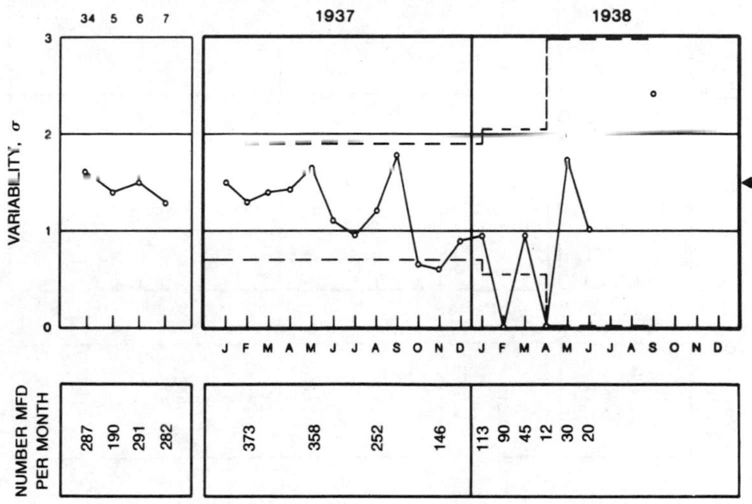

Engineering Limit: 72% min.

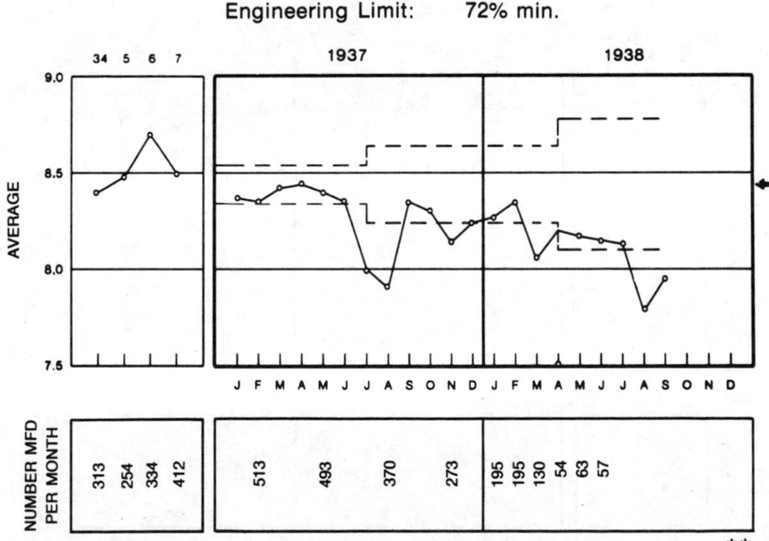

Figure 6-7 Examples of control charts for $\bar{X}$ and σ. Later applications by industry.

Engineering Limit: 72% min.

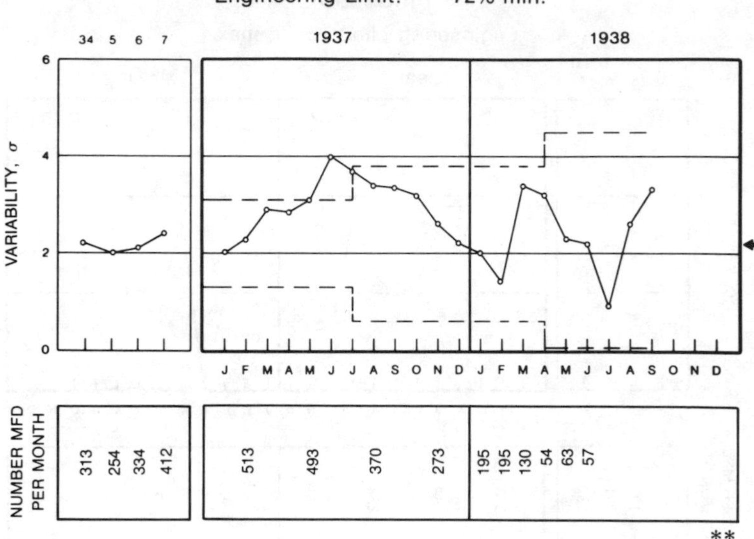

BIASED SIGNAL RECEPTION In Percent
Engineering Limit: 40% min.

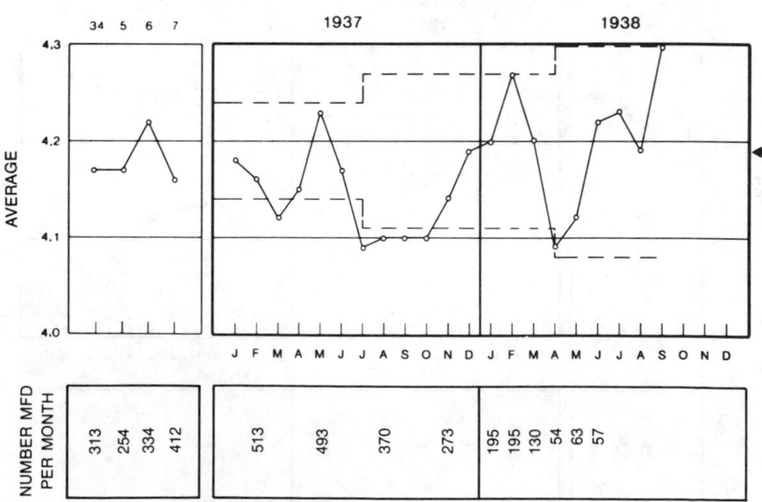

Figure 6-7 Examples of control charts for $\overline{X}$ and σ. Later applications by industry.

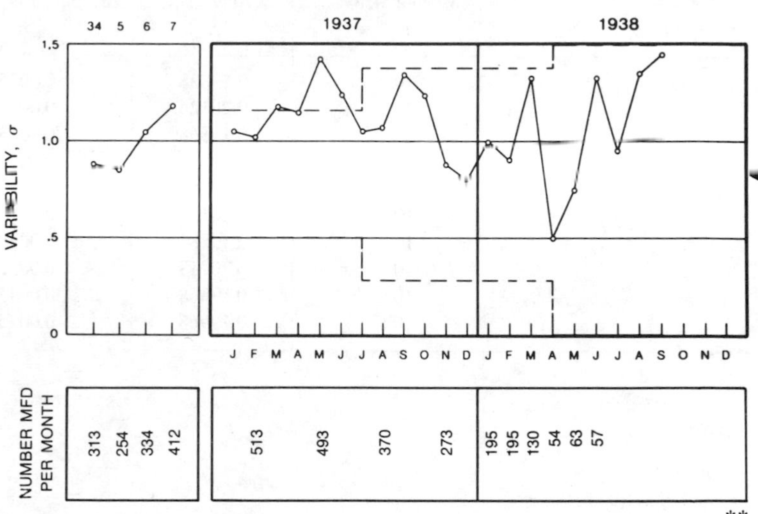

Figure 6-7 Examples of control charts for $\bar{X}$ and σ. Later applications by industry.

deviation values with standards specified. This figure covers a later quality report period, which serves to show that such charts were extremely valuable as they were continued over the years. Those studying the use of statistical controls will find such applications extremely profitable if they are properly prepared and applied in areas where the best possible controls must be exerted over processes.

We can see from figure 6-6 that where monthly values were found to be outside their respective control limits, within a few months the process was brought back into control. The processes are well-controlled in most months.

Each of the control charts in figure 6-7 (where monthly sample sizes vary) shows some months out of control for short periods, sometimes for average values and sometimes for variability, as shown by the standard deviation charts.

Another case, typified by example 4, arises where the standards are given and the samples taken are small and equal.

Example 4 *Control Charts for $\bar{X}$ and σ, Small Samples of Equal Size, Standard Given.* For this product and characteristic, it is desired to control the diameter of this product with respect to sample variations during each day, since samples of ten were taken at definite intervals each day. The desired level is $\bar{X}' =$ 0.20000 in. with $\sigma' = 0.00300$ in. Table 6.11 gives observed values of $\bar{X}$ and σ for ten samples of ten each taken during a single day. Figure 6-8 gives the control charts for $\bar{X}$ and σ.

TABLE 6.11 Control Data for One Day's Product

Sample	*Sample Size,* n	*Average,* $\bar{X}$	*Standard Deviation,* σ
No. 1	10	0.19838	0.00350
No. 2	10	0.20126	0.00304
No. 3	10	0.19868	0.00333
No. 4	10	0.20071	0.00337
No. 5	10	0.20050	0.00159
No. 6	10	0.20137	0.00104
No. 7	10	0.19883	0.00299
No. 8	10	0.20218	0.00327
No. 9	10	0.19868	0.00431
No. 10	10	0.19968	0.00356

Central Lines

For $\bar{X}$: $\bar{X}' = 0.20000.$

$n = 10$:

For σ: $c_2\sigma' = (0.9227)(0.00300) =$
0.00277

Control Limits

$n = 10$:

For $\bar{X}$: $\bar{X}' \pm A\sigma' =$
$0.20000 \pm (0.949)(0.00300)$,
0.20285 and 0.19715.

For σ: $B_2\sigma'$ and $B_1\sigma' =$
(1.584)(0.00300) and
(0.262)(0.00300),
0.00475 and 0.00079. +

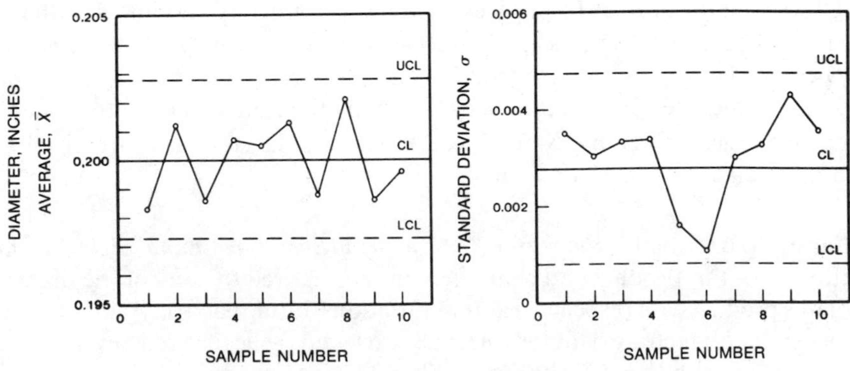

Figure 6–8 Control charts for $\bar{X}$ and σ. Small samples of equal size, $n = 10$, σ given.

Results No lack of control is indicated.

A set of examples showing different conditions under which control charts for averages $\bar{X}$ and standard deviations σ are given for guidance. Note that some cover the case where the standard is given; and others show situations where no standard has been specified, but the data are used to obtain a satisfactory standard. Example 5 covers the case with a standard given with large samples of unequal size.

Example 5 *Control Charts for $\bar{X}$ and σ, Large Samples of Unequal Size, Standard Given.* For a product it was desired to control a certain critical dimension, the diameter, with respect to day to day variation. Daily sample sizes of 30, 50, or 75 were selected and measured, the number taken depending on the quantity produced per day. The desired level was $\bar{X}' =$ 0.20000 in. with $\sigma' = 0.00300$ in. Table 6.12 gives observed values of $\bar{X}$ and σ for the samples from ten successive days' production. Figure 6-9 gives the control charts for $\bar{X}$ and σ.

TABLE 6.12 Diameter in Inches, Control Data

Sample	*Sample Size,* n	*Average,* $\bar{X}$	*Standard Deviation,* σ
No. 1	30	0.20133	0.00330
No. 2	50	0.19886	0.00292
No. 3	50	0.20037	0.00326
No. 4	30	0.19965	0.00358
No. 5	75	0.19923	0.00313
No. 6	75	0.19934	0.00306
No. 7	75	0.19984	0.00299
No. 8	50	0.19974	0.00335
No. 9	50	0.20095	0.00221
No. 10	30	0.19937	0.00397

Central Lines

For $\bar{X}$: $\bar{X}' = 0.20000$.
For σ: $\bar{\sigma} = \sigma' = 0.00300$.

Control Limits

For $\bar{X}$: $\bar{X}' \pm 3\dfrac{\sigma'}{\sqrt{n}}$.

$n = 30$:

$$0.20000 \pm 3\frac{0.00300}{\sqrt{30}} =$$

0.20000 ± 0.00164,
0.20164 and 0.19836.

$n = 50$:
0.20127 and 0.19873.

$n = 75$:
0.20104 and 0.19896.

For σ: $\bar{\sigma} \pm 3 \dfrac{\sigma'}{\sqrt{2n}}$.

$n = 30$:

$0.00300 \pm 3 \dfrac{0.00300}{\sqrt{60}} =$

0.00300 ± 0.00116,
0.00416 and 0.00184.

$n = 50$:
0.00390 and 0.00210.

$n = 75$:
0.00373 and 0.00227. +

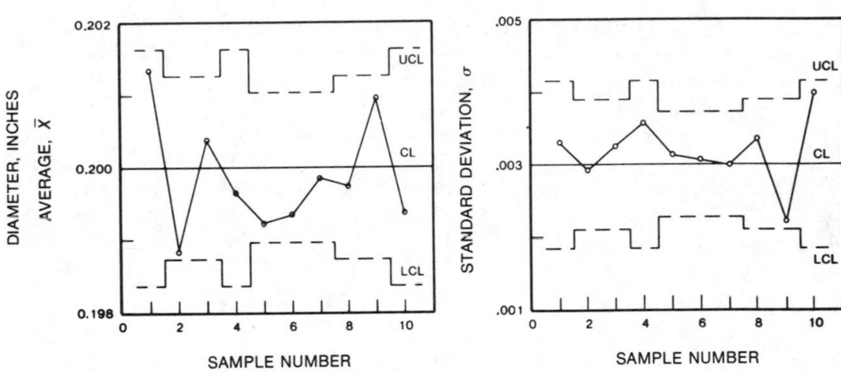

Figure 6–9 Control charts for $\bar{X}$ and σ. Large samples of unequal size; standard given, $\bar{X}'$, $\bar{\sigma} = \sigma'$.

Results The charts give no evidence of significant deviations from standard values.

Example 6 covers the case in which no standard is given and the standards are derived from the data. In particular, it illustrates the case for large samples of equal size where control exists for both averages and standard deviations.

Example 6 *Control Charts for $\bar{X}$ and σ, Large Samples of Equal Size, No Standard Given.* A manufacturer wished to determine if his product exhibited a state of control. In this case the central lines and control limits were based solely on the data. Table 6.13 gives observed values of $\overline{X}$ and σ for daily samples of $n = 50$ observations each for ten consecutive days. Figure 6-10 gives the control charts for $\overline{X}$ and σ.

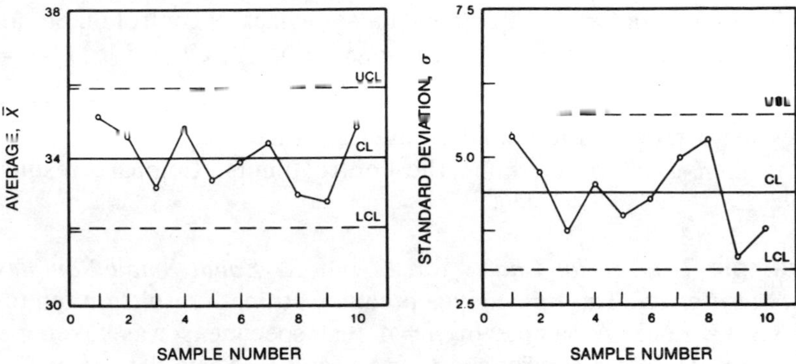

Figure 6–10 Control charts for $\overline{X}$ and σ. Large samples of equal size; no standard given.

TABLE 6.13 Operating Characteristic, Daily Control Data

Sample	*Sample Size,* n	*Average,* $\overline{X}$	*Standard Deviation,* σ
No. 1	50	35.1	5.35
No. 2	50	34.6	4.73
No. 3	50	33.2	3.73
No. 4	50	34.8	4.55
No. 5	50	33.4	4.00
No. 6	50	33.9	4.30
No. 7	50	34.4	4.98
No. 8	50	33.0	5.30
No. 9	50	32.8	3.29
No. 10	50	34.8	3.77
Total	500	340.0	44.00
Average	...	34.0	4.40

Central Lines

For $\overline{X}$: $\overline{\overline{X}} = 34.0$.

For σ: $\bar{\sigma} = 4.40$.

Control Limits

$n = 50$:

For $\overline{X}$: $\overline{\overline{X}} \pm 3\frac{\bar{\sigma}}{\sqrt{n}} = 34.0 \pm 1.9,$

35.9 and 32.1.

For σ: $\bar{\sigma} \pm 3 \frac{\bar{\sigma}}{\sqrt{2n}} = 4.40 \pm 1.32,$
5.72 and 3.08. +

Results The charts give no evidence of lack of control. With standards set at $\bar{X}' = 35.00$ and $\sigma' = 4.20$, same data show lack of control on 8th and 9th day for $\bar{X}$. For $\bar{X}: UCL = 36.8; LCL = 33.2$. For $\sigma: UCL = 5.46; LCL = 2.94$.

Example 7 covers the case where lack of control is very evident. It involves the use of data to obtain an average value for the ten range values, which is then used to determine the control limits. Compare results with example 2.

Example 7 *Control Charts for $\bar{X}$ and R, Equal Small Samples, No Standard given*. Table 6.14 gives breaking strength results on ten test lots of steel strand. A sample of $n = 4$ test specimens was taken per lot. Figure 6–11 shows control charts for $\bar{X}$ and R. Same data as in Example 2, table 6.9. Comparison between use of $\bar{R}$ rather than $\bar{\sigma}$.

TABLE 6.14 Breaking Strength, Steel Wire Strand

Lot	*Test Values*				*Average,* $\bar{X}$	*Standard Deviation,* σ	*Range,* R
	X_1	X_2	X_3	X_4			
No. 1	7490	7535	7455	7480	7490.0	28.94	80
No. 2..........	6550	6495	6525	6465	6508.75	31.90	85
No. 3..........	6995	6995	6970	6880	6960.0	47.30	115
No. 4..........	7045	7060	7095	7035	7058.75	22.74	60
No. 5..........	6715	6740	6780	6720	6738.75	25.59	65
No. 6..........	6585	6630	6675	6645	6633.75	32.48	90
No. 7..........	6600	6590	6610	6650	6612.5	22.78	60
No. 8..........	6665	6670	6630	6660	6656.25	15.56	40
No. 9..........	6440	6425	6460	6470	6448.75	17.46	45
No. 10..........	6660	6630	6605	6625	6630.0	19.69	55
Average					6773.75	26.44	69.5

Central Lines

For $\bar{X}$: $\bar{\bar{X}} = 6773.75$.
For $\bar{R}$: $\bar{R} = 69.5$

Control Limits

For $\bar{X}$: $\bar{\bar{X}} \pm A_2\bar{R} = 6773.75 \pm 0.729(69.5)$
6723.08 and 6824.42.
For R: $D_3\bar{R}$ and $D_4\bar{R} = (0)(6.95)$ and $(2.282)(6.95)$, 0 and 158.60.

Results Charts indicate the presence of assignable causes of variation in average breaking strength, $\bar{X}$, from lot to lot.

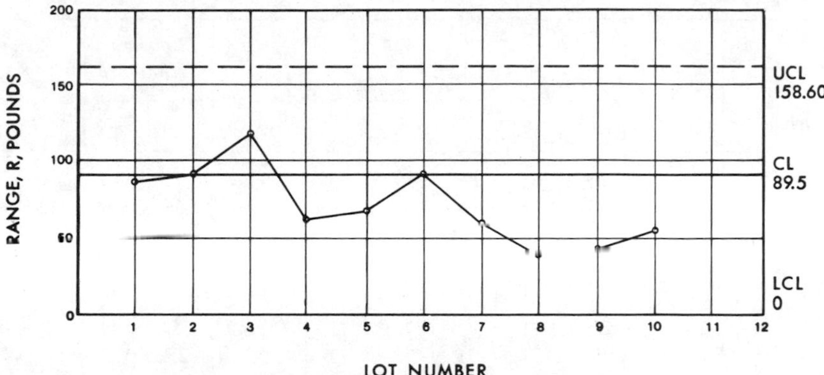

Figure 6–11 Control Chart for $\bar{X}$ and R, Small Equal Sample Sizes, $n = 4$; No Standard Given. Compare with Figure 6–4(2).

In the example 7, the central lines and control lines were determined from the relations in table 6.5. Since $\bar{\sigma}$ is determined, the factors used as multipliers are taken from table 6.1 for $n = 4$. Example 8 has unequal, small samples, so use must be made of weighted values, using the n sizes as weights. The relations used are in accordance with the relations in table 6.5 for each subgroup having the same sample size. Having obtained a weighted average, the factors in table 6.1 may be used for each different sample size as noted. In example 7, if factors are taken from table 6.7 with only three significant figures for B_4, i.e. $B_4 = 2.27$, then UCL for σ is 60.02.

Example 8 *Control Charts for $\bar{X}$ and σ, Small Samples of Unequal Size, No Standard Given.* Table 6.15 gives interlaboratory calibration check data on twenty-one horizontal tension testing machines. The data represent tests on No. 16 wire. The procedure is similar to that given in example 7, but indicates a suggested method of computation when the samples are not equal in size. Figure 6-12 gives control charts for $\bar{X}$ and σ.

TABLE 6.15 Interlaboratory Calibration, Horizontal Tension Testing Machines

Machine	*Number of Tests*	*Test Value* 1	2	3	4	5	*Average,* $\bar{X}$	*Standard Deviation,* σ $n = 4$	$n = 5$	*Range,* R $n = 4$	$n = 5$
No. 1..........	5	73	73	73	75	75	73.8	....	0.98	....	2
No. 2..........	5	70	71	71	71	72	71.0	....	0.63	....	2
No. 3..........	5	74	74	74	74	75	74.2	....	0.40	....	1
No. 4..........	5	70	70	70	72	73	71.0	....	1.26	....	3
No. 5..........	5	70	70	70	70	70	70.0	....	0	....	0

Machine	Number of Tests	Test Value 1	2	3	4	5	Average, $\bar{X}$	Standard Deviation, σ $n = 4$	$n = 5$	Range, R $n = 4$	$n = 5$
No. 6..........	5	65	65	66	69	70	67.0	....	2.10	....	5
No. 7..........	4	72	72	74	76	—	73.5	1.66	....	4	....
No. 8..........	5	69	70	71	73	73	71.2	....	1.60	....	4
No. 9..........	5	71	71	71	71	72	71.2	....	0.40	....	1
No. 10..........	5	71	71	71	71	72	71.2	....	0.40	....	1
No. 11..........	5	71	71	72	72	72	71.6	....	0.49	....	1
No. 12..........	5	70	71	71	72	72	71.2	....	0.75	....	2
No. 13..........	5	73	74	74	75	75	74.2	....	0.75	....	2
No. 14..........	5	74	74	75	75	75	74.6	....	0.49	....	1
No. 15..........	5	72	72	72	73	73	72.4	....	0.49	....	1
No. 16..........	4	75	75	75	76	—	75.3	0.43	....	1	....
No. 17..........	5	68	69	69	69	70	69.0	....	0.63	....	2
No. 18..........	5	71	71	72	72	73	71.8	....	0.75	....	2
No. 19..........	5	72	73	73	73	73	72.8	....	0.40	....	1
No. 20..........	5	68	69	70	71	71	69.8	....	1.17	....	3
No. 21..........	5	69	69	69	69	69	69.0	....	0	....	0
Total........	103							2.09	13.69	5	34
		Weighted average $\bar{\bar{X}} = 71.65$									

$$\sigma_e = \frac{1}{21}\left(\frac{2.09}{0.7979} + \frac{13.69}{0.8407}\right) = 0.900$$

Central Lines

For $\bar{X}$: $\bar{\bar{X}} = 71.65$.

For σ: $n = 4: \bar{\sigma} = c_2\sigma_e = (0.7979)(0.900) = 0.718.$

$n = 5: \bar{\sigma} = c_2\sigma_e = (0.8407)(0.900) = 0.757.$

Control Limits

For $\bar{X}$: $n = 4$: $\bar{\bar{X}} \pm A_1\bar{\sigma} =$ $71.65 \pm (1.880)(0.718)$, 73.0 and 70.3.

$n = 5$: $\bar{\bar{X}} \pm A_1\bar{\sigma} =$ $71.65 \pm (1.596)(0.757)$, 72.9 and 70.4.

For σ: $n = 4$: $B_4\bar{\sigma}$ and $B_3\bar{\sigma} =$ (2.266)(0.718) and (0)(0.718), 1.63 and 0.

$n = 5$: $B_4\bar{\sigma}$ and $B_3\bar{\sigma} =$ (2.089)(0.757) and (0)(0.757), 1.58 and 0.+

Results The calibration levels of machines were not controlled at a common level; the averages of six machines are above and the averages of five machines

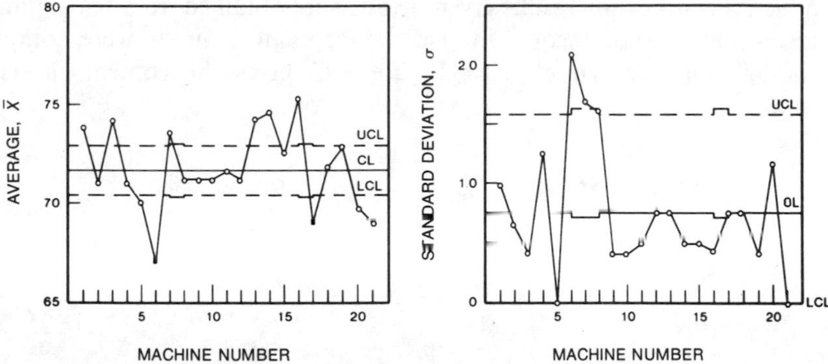

Figure 6–12 Control chart for $\bar{X}$ and σ. Small samples of unequal size, $n = 4, 5$; no standard given.

are below control limits. Likewise, there is an indication that the variability *within* machines is not in statistical control, since three machines, Nos. 6, 7, and 8, have standard deviations outside control limits.

For many processes, control charts for averages and standard deviations involve large samples of unequal size. When standards are not specified and must be determined from available data, we use techniques like those illustrated in example 9. This example covers the case where lack of control exists, where no standards are given, and where samples are large and unequal in size.

Example 9 *Control Charts for $\bar{X}$ and σ, Large Samples of Unequal Size, No Standard Given.* To determine whether there existed any assignable causes of variation in quality for an important operating characteristic of a given

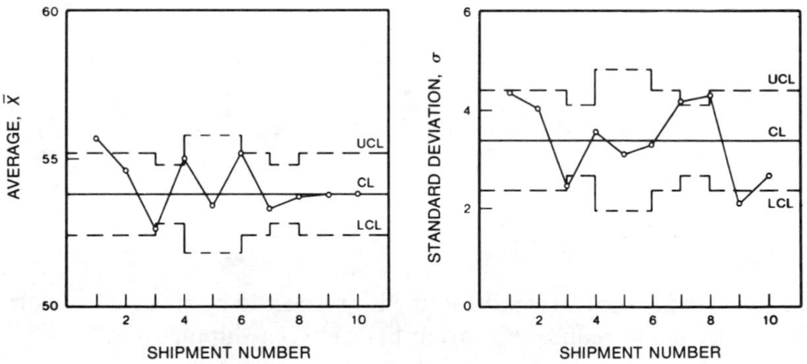

Figure 6–13 Control charts for $\bar{X}$ and σ. Large samples of unequal size; no standard given.

product, the inspection results given below were obtained from ten shipments whose samples were unequal in size; hence, control limits were computed separately for each sample size. Figure 6-13 gives the control charts for $\overline{X}$ and σ.

TABLE 6.16 Operating Characteristic, Mechanical Part

Shipment	*Sample Size,* n	*Average,* $\overline{X}$	*Standard Deviation,* σ
No. 1	50	55.7	4.35
No. 2	50	54.6	4.03
No. 3	100	52.6	2.43
No. 4	25	55.0	3.56
No. 5	25	53.4	3.10
No. 6	50	55.2	3.30
No. 7	100	53.3	4.18
No. 8	50	52.3	4.30
No. 9	50	53.7	2.09
No. 10	50	54.3	2.67
Total	550	$\Sigma n\overline{X} = 29590.0$	$\Sigma n\sigma = 1864.50$
Weighted average	...	53.8	3.39

Central Lines

For $\overline{X}$: $\overline{\overline{X}} = 53.8.$

For σ: $\bar{\sigma} = 3.39.$

Control Limits

For $\overline{X}$: $\overline{\overline{X}} \pm 3\dfrac{\bar{\sigma}}{\sqrt{n}} = 53.8 \pm \dfrac{10.17}{\sqrt{n}},$

$n = 25$: 55.8 and 51.8,
$n = 50$: 55.2 and 52.4,
$n = 100$: 54.8 and 52.8.

For σ: $\bar{\sigma} \pm 3\dfrac{\bar{\sigma}}{\sqrt{2n}} = 3.39 \pm \dfrac{10.17}{\sqrt{2n}},$

$n = 25$: 4.83 and 1.95,
$n = 50$: 4.41 and 2.37,
$n = 100$: 4.11 and 2.67. +

Results Lack of control is indicated with respect to both $\overline{X}$ and σ. Corrective action is needed to reduce the variability between shipments.

In this section, we have given tables of factors and relations that have been developed to make the construction of control charts for averages and standard deviations very simple, even when the data given is composed of results based on sets of widely different sample sizes. Table 6.1 gives most of these factors. Other tables cover the case where σ' as well as $\bar{X}'$ have been specified. Another table covers the case where no standard is given, but the average of many different σ values is used as the basis for a standard and c_2 factors are given to relate $\bar{\sigma}$ to σ'. These factors may be taken directly from the appropriate tables as illustrated by the examples.

The next section covers the use of ranges and interchanging factors for standard deviation values with factors for ranges. This inter-relationship is shown in the following summary table of formulas for central lines and control limits where the standards $\bar{X}'$ and σ' are given. These are the transition relations that relate ranges to standard deviation values.

TABLE 6.17 Formulas for Central Lines and Control Limits

Control with Respect to a Given Standard (X', σ' given)		
	Central Line	*Control Limits*
Averages	$\bar{X}'$	$\bar{X}' \pm A\sigma'$
Standard deviations	$c_2\sigma'$	$B_2\sigma'$ and $B_1\sigma'$
Ranges	$d_2\sigma'$	$D_2\sigma'$ and $D_1\sigma'$

The ASTM *Manual* presents a separate table for the factors A, c_2, B_1, and B_2, together with those values of d_2, D_1, and D_2 which apply to control charts for ranges. They are not repeated here as they are included in the factors given in table 6.1. This section is self-sufficient with respect to all such control charts.

6.5 Control Charts for Averages and Ranges

When sample sizes are small, say twenty-five or less, use may be made of the range for each sample rather than computing its standard deviation. Since the range R is the difference between the largest observed value in a sample and the smallest value, it is very easily determined from the formula $R = X_M - X_m$, where X denotes the variable under consideration. The range is used as a measure of variability or dispersion. It may also be used to estimate the true standard deviation, of one of the parameters of the characteristic involved. Thus it may be used to determine the three-sigma control limits for averages.

As noted in the previous section, it is necessary to cover in detail the two cases (1) standard given and (2) no standard given for large and small samples, which may be of equal or unequal size. When dealing with the case where the standards $\bar{X}'$ and σ' are given, theoretical factors based on the assumption of a normal distribution are used. These factors have been used for almost fifty years and have been proven to be practical in providing three-sigma control limits for making valid decisions concerning the existence or nonexistence of assignable causes of changes in the processes. In the previous section, the expected value of sigma is determined by using c_2 as a multiplying term. Values of c_2 for different sample sizes were tabulated in table 6.1 for values of n from 2 to 25. Correspondingly, the expected value of R may be determined as $\bar{R}'$ by using d_2 as a multiplying factor. Table 6.1 also gives these values of d_2 for values of n from 2 to 25. Table 6.18 extends the range of these c_2 and d_2 values for values of n from 2 to 100.

Table 6.19 summarizes the three factors A_2, D_3, and D_4 used for establishing control limits from an $\bar{R}$ value based on R values determined from m samples of equal size n for a range of values of n from 2 to 20, to two significant figures. It is not recommended to use range values for larger samples than 20 directly from a table; hence table 6.19 does not give factors for values of n larger than 20. These tabulated values are actually extracted from table 6.1, as were the values of d_2 and c_2 listed in table 6.18.

In many cases, standard values are specified for the central value $\bar{X}'$ and for the variability or dispersion σ', from which for the range R may be determined by assuming a normal distribution standard values and by using the factor d_2 given in table 6.18. In establishing control charts for averages and ranges ($\bar{X}$ and R) where standards are already specified, the relations for determining the control limits must be determined and simplified so that it is only necessary to multiply the standards by appropriate factors to secure the control limits needed to control the process for any important characteristic. The basic formulas for determining these control chart limits are given in table 6.20. It is necessary to use the standard deviation of the range. The factor d_3 used as a multiplier of σ' has a different value for each sample size, as indicated in the tabulation of d_3 in table 6.1. The complete formula for d_3 is given in the ASTM *Manual.* The factors used to provide three-sigma control limits for $\bar{X}$ and R when standards are given are in table 6.21. The use of these factors is illustrated by the examples that are included in this section.

The most popular sample sizes when controlling processes by the use of range values together with average values are 4, 5, and 10. If the median (M_e) rather than the average is used, odd sample sizes such as 3, 5, 7, and 9 are preferred. For destructive tests, using a sample size of two units per lot is preferred, since the units measured are destroyed in the test used to measure some critical characteristic. When only two units are in the sample, the efficiency of the range is 100%, the same efficiency as when the standard deviation (σ) is used. Where standards are given for $\bar{X}$ and σ as $\bar{X}'$ and σ', the formulas for central lines and control limits are given in table 6.20. The factors used in computing the necessary values are given in table 6.21.

The use of control charts for small samples involving standard values is illustrated by example 10, which applies a small sample of five units to the same problem covered in example 6, where samples of fifty units were used. In example 6, it was noted that the manufacturer desired control at standard levels

TABLE 6.18 Factors for Estimating σ' from $\bar{R}$ or $\bar{\sigma}$

Number of Observations in Subgroup n	*Factor for Estimate from* $\bar{R}$ $d_2 = R/\sigma'$	*Factor for Estimate from* $\bar{\sigma}$ $c_2 = \bar{\sigma}/\sigma'$
2	1.128	0.5642
3	1.693	0.7236
4	2.059	0.7979
5	2.326	0.8407
6	2.534	0.8686
7	2.704	0.8882
8	2.847	0.9027
9	2.970	0.9139
10	3.078	0.9227
11	3.173	0.9300
12	3.258	0.9359
13	3.336	0.9410
14	3.407	0.9453
15	3.472	0.9490
16	3.532	0.9523
17	3.588	0.9551
18	3.640	0.9576
19	3.689	0.9599
20	3.735	0.9619
21	3.778	0.9638
22	3.819	0.9655
23	3.858	0.9670
24	3.895	0.9684
25	3.931	0.9696
30	4.086	0.9748
35	4.213	0.9784
40	4.322	0.9811
45	4.415	0.9832
50	4.498	0.9849
55	4.572	0.9863
60	4.639	0.9874
65	4.699	0.9884
70	4.755	0.9892
75	4.806	0.9900
80	4.854	0.9906
85	4.898	0.9912
90	4.939	0.9916
95	4.978	0.9921
100	5.015	0.9925

++

Estimate of $\sigma' = \dfrac{\bar{R}}{d_2}$ or $\dfrac{\bar{\sigma}}{c_2}$.

These factors assume sampling from a normal universe.

TABLE 6.19 Factors for
Determining the Three-sigma Control Limits for $\bar{X}$ and R Charts from $\bar{R}$

Number of Observations in Subgroup n	*Factor for* $\bar{X}$ *Chart* A_2	*Factors for R Chart* *Lower Control Limit* D_3	*Upper Control Limit* D_4
2	1.88	0	3.27
3	1.02	0	2.57
4	0.73	0	2.28
5	0.58	0	2.11
6	0.48	0	2.00
7	0.42	0.08	1.92
8	0.37	0.14	1.86
9	0.34	0.18	1.82
10	0.31	0.22	1.78
11	0.29	0.26	1.74
12	0.27	0.28	1.72
13	0.25	0.31	1.69
14	0.24	0.33	1.67
15	0.22	0.35	1.65
16	0.21	0.36	1.64
17	0.20	0.38	1.62
18	0.19	0.39	1.61
19	0.19	0.40	1.60
20	0.18	0.41	1.59

$$\text{Upper Control Limit for } \bar{X} = UCL_{\bar{X}} = \bar{\bar{X}} + A_2\bar{R}$$
$$\text{Lower Control Limit for } \bar{X} = LCL_{\bar{X}} = \bar{\bar{X}} - A_2\bar{R}$$

(If aimed-at or standard value $\bar{X}'$ is used rather than $\bar{\bar{X}}$ as the central line on the control chart, $\bar{X}'$ should be substituted for $\bar{\bar{X}}$ in the preceding formulas.)

$$\text{Upper Control Limit for } R = UCL_R = D_4\bar{R}$$
$$\text{Lower Control Limit for } R = LCL_R = D_3\bar{R}$$

All factors in table 6.19 are based on the normal distribution. ++

of 35.00 for $\bar{X}'$ with $\sigma' = 4.20$. For these standards with $n = 50$, the control limits for the ten values of $\bar{X}$ and σ shown in table 6.13 were: for $\bar{X}$, UCL = 36.8 and LCL = 33.2; and for σ, UCL = 5.46 and LCL = 2.94. All the standard deviation values were within their control limits, but on the eighth and ninth days samples 8 and 9 had $\bar{X}$ values of 33.0 and 32.8 respectively, both less than 33.2, the lower control limit. This was noted in the comments on the results in example 6, which showed this process was controlled at a different level than the standards given.

TABLE 6.20 Formulas for Central Lines and Control Limits Including Basic Formula for Ranges

Control with Respect to a Given Standard ($\bar{X}'$, σ' given)

	Central Line	Control Limits
Averages........................	$\bar{X}'$	$\bar{X}' \pm A\sigma'$
Standard deviations............	$c_2\sigma'$	$B_2\sigma'$ and $B_1\sigma'$
Ranges	$d_2\sigma$	$D_2\sigma'$ and $D_1\sigma'$

	Central Line	Control Limits	
		Simplified Formula Using Factors in Table 6.21	Basic Formula
For range, R.....................	$d_2\sigma'$	$D_2\sigma'$ and $D_1\sigma'$	$d_2\sigma' \pm 3d_3\sigma'$

Use table 6.21 for factors d_2, D_1, and D_2.
Factors d_2, d_3, D_1, and D_2 are defined in Appendix 2. +

TABLE 6.21 Factors for Computing Control Chart Lines—Standard Given

Number of Observations in Sample, n	Chart for Averages	Chart for Standard Deviations			Chart for Ranges		
	Factors for Control Limits	Factor for Central Line	Factors for Control Limits		Factor for Central Line	Factors for Control Limits	
	A	c_2	B_1	B_2	d_2	D_1	D_2
2..........	2.121	0.5642	0	1.843	1.128	0	3.686
3..........	1.732	0.7236	0	1.858	1.693	0	4.358
4..........	1.500	0.7979	0	1.808	2.059	0	4.698
5..........	1.342	0.8407	0	1.756	2.326	0	4.918
6..........	1.225	0.8686	0.026	1.711	2.534	0	5.078
7..........	1.134	0.8882	0.105	1.672	2.704	0.205	5.203
8..........	1.061	0.9027	0.167	1.638	2.847	0.387	5.307
9..........	1.000	0.9139	0.219	1.609	2.970	0.546	5.394
10.........	0.949	0.9227	0.262	1.584	3.078	0.687	5.469
11.........	0.905	0.9300	0.299	1.561	3.173	0.812	5.534
12.........	0.866	0.9359	0.331	1.541	3.258	0.924	5.592
13.........	0.832	0.9410	0.359	1.523	3.336	1.026	5.646
14.........	0.802	0.9453	0.384	1.507	3.407	1.121	5.693
15.........	0.775	0.9490	0.406	1.492	3.472	1.207	5.737

	Chart for Averages	Chart for Standard Deviations			Chart for Ranges		
	Factors for Control Limits	Factor for Central Line	Factors for Control Limits		Factor for Central Line	Factors for Control Limits	
Number of Observations in Sample, n	A	c_2	B_1	B_2	d_2	D_1	D_2
16..........	0.750	0.9523	0.427	1.478	3.532	1.285	5.779
17..........	0.728	0.9551	0.445	1.465	3.588	1.359	5.817
18..........	0.707	0.9576	0.461	1.454	3.640	1.426	5.854
19..........	0.688	0.9599	0.477	1.443	3.689	1.490	5.888
20..........	0.671	0.9619	0.491	1.433	3.735	1.548	5.922
21..........	0.655	0.9638	0.504	1.424	3.778	1.606	5.950
22..........	0.640	0.9655	0.516	1.415	3.819	1.659	5.979
23..........	0.626	0.9670	0.527	1.407	3.858	1.710	6.006
24..........	0.612	0.9684	0.538	1.399	3.895	1.759	6.031
25..........	0.600	0.9696	0.548	1.392	3.931	1.804	6.058
Over 25..........	$\frac{3}{\sqrt{n}}$	....	*	**	....	....	....

* $1 - \frac{3}{\sqrt{2n}}$ ** $1 + \frac{3}{\sqrt{2n}}$

The variability seems too large, so this next example shows an attempt to use small samples to check whether the methods applied really do reduce the variability.

The effectiveness of control charts is apparent in example 6 where $n = 50$. In example 10, where $n = 5$, there are two apparent trends. The average seems to be drifting towards a level of 30.0, while the variability is increasing to a range of 20. Controls must be added to keep this operating characteristic within the desired limits to reduce nonconformances.

Example 10 *Control Charts for $\bar{X}$ and R, Small Samples of Equal Size, Standard Given.* Consider the same problem as in example 6 where $\bar{X}' =$ 35.00 pounds and $\sigma' = 4.20$ pounds, found to be controlled at $\bar{X} = 34.0$ and $\bar{\sigma} = 4.40$ on figure 6-10. The manufacturer wished to control variations in quality from lot to lot by taking a small sample from each lot. Table 6.22 gives observed values of $\bar{X}$ and R for samples of $n = 5$ each, selected from ten consecutive lots. Since the sample size n is less than 10, actually 5, he elected to use control charts for $\bar{X}$ and R rather than for $\bar{X}$ and σ. Figure 6-14 gives the control charts for $\bar{X}$ and R.

TABLE 6.22 Operating Characteristic, Lot by Lot Control Data

Lot	*Sample Size,* n	*Average,* $\overline{X}$	*Range,* R
No. 1	5	36.0	6.6
No. 2	5	31.4	0.5
No. 3	5	39.0	15.1
No. 4	5	35.6	8.8
No. 5	5	38.8	2.2
No. 6	5	41.6	3.5
No. 7	5	36.2	9.6
No. 8	5	38.0	9.0
No. 9	5	31.4	20.6
No. 10	5	29.2	21.7

Central Lines

For $\overline{X}$: $\overline{X}' = 35.00.$

$n = 5:$

For R: $d_2\sigma' = 2.326(4.20) = 9.8.$

Control Limits

$n = 5:$

For $\overline{X}$: $\overline{X}' \pm A\sigma' = 35.00 \pm (1.342)(4.20),$
40.6 *and* 29.4.

For R: $D_2\sigma'$ and $D_1\sigma' =$
(4.918)(4.20) and (0)(4.20),
20.7 and 0. +

Results Lack of control at the standard level is indicated by results for lots Nos. 6 and 10. Corrective action is required both with respect to averages and with respect to variability within a lot.

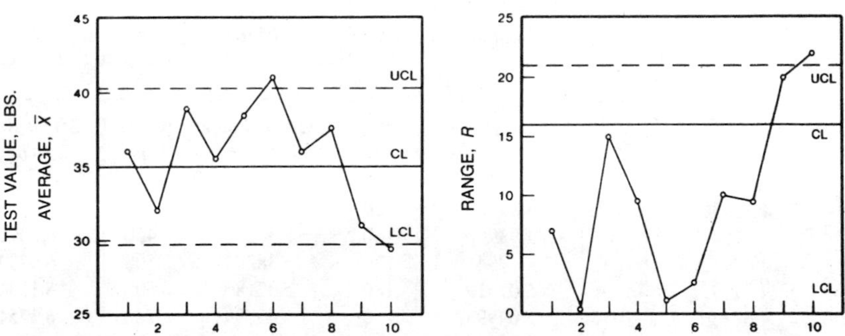

Figure 6–14 Control charts for $\overline{X}$ and R. Small samples of equal size, $n = 5$; $\overline{X}'$, σ' given.

In all cases, the range for a sample is based on only two values, the largest and the smallest. In units of standard deviation, the range for a normal law distribution (as shown in figure 6-15) includes $d_2\sigma'$ units. A plus and minus three-sigma range occurs only when n is large (about 450 units). Table 6.23 tabulates these d_2 values to six significant figures for a practical range of n values from 2 to 1000, giving values by units up to $n = 40$.

Since range values rather than standard deviation values are applied in the majority of cases to check control of variability, it is necessary to fully understand the relations that must be applied. When the standard is given in terms of sigma as σ', then for a given sample size n an $\bar{R}'$ can be determined by using the proper value of d_2. Such values can readily be determined from figure 6-15 or table 6.23. Tables 6.1, 6.18, and 6.21 also include d_2 values, as such values are used in deriving their accompanying factors to cover particular cases. The following example illustrates how to simplify data when constructing control charts for averages and ranges for small equal samples.

TABLE 6.23 Ratio of the Mean Range to Standard Deviation, d_2

The ratio of mean range of samples of size n to σ of the normal population from which they are drawn

The Ratio of Mean Range of Samples of Size n to σ of the Normal Population from which they are Drawn

n	Mean Range / σ	n	Mean Range / σ	n	Mean Range / σ	n	Mean Range / σ
0	....	10	3.07751	20	3.73495	30	4.08552
1	....	11	3.17287	21	3.77834	31	4.11293
2	1.12838	12	3.25846	22	3.81938	32	4.13934
3	1.69257	13	3.33598	23	3.85832	33	4.16482
4	2.05875	14	3.40676	24	3.89535	34	4.18943
5	2.32593	15	3.47183	25	3.93063	35	4.21322
6	2.53441	16	3.53198	26	3.96432	36	4.23625
7	2.70436	17	3.58788	27	3.99654	37	4.25855
8	2.84720	18	3.64006	28	4.02741	38	4.28018
9	2.97003	19	3.68896	29	4.05704	39	4.30117

n	Mean Range / σ	n	Mean Range / σ	n	Mean Range / σ	n	Mean Range / σ
40	4.32156	85	4.89789	150	5.29849	400	5.93636
45	4.41544	90	4.93940	160	5.34244	450	6.00903
50	4.49815	95	4.97841	170	5.38344	500	6.07340
55	4.57197	100	5.01519	180	5.42186	600	6.18340
60	4.63856	105	5.04997	190	5.45799	700	6.27510
65	4.69916	110	5.08295	200	5.49209	800	6.35358
70	4.75472	120	5.14417	250	5.63837	900	6.42211
75	4.80598	130	5.19996	300	5.75553	1000	6.48287
80	4.85355	140	5.25118	350	5.85302	...	....

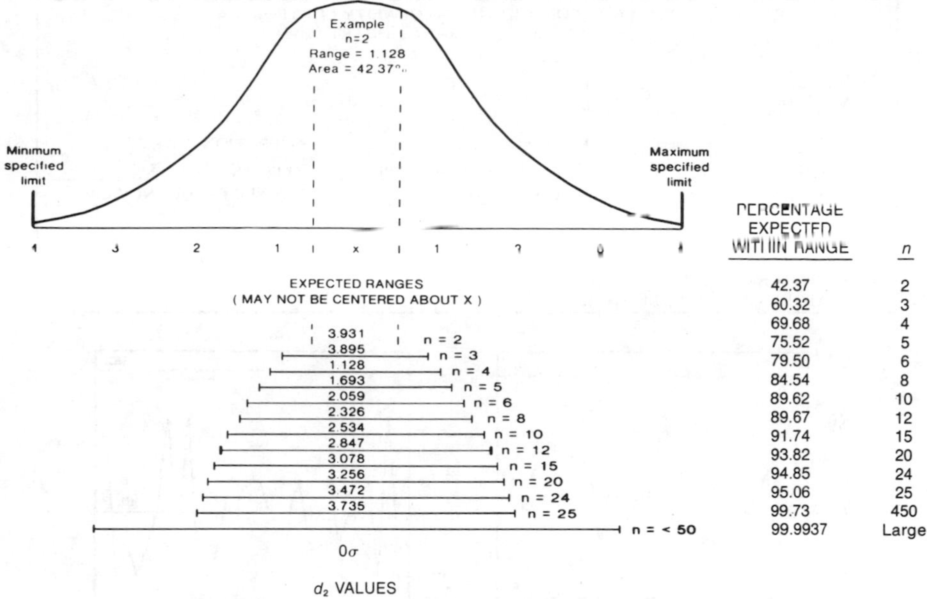

Figure 6–15 Method of variables—normal law universe. Number of σ' values within range for different n values. d_2 values for estimating σ' where $\sigma_e' = \bar{R}/d_2$.

Example 11 In 1958, the John Doe Corporation set up controls over the operation of welding on a frame assembly at one of their plants. Figure 6-16 gives the details about the process capability and shows the control charts used to control this process. The specified requirement is 5.070 ± 0.045. For these limits, 1% can be tolerated outside these limits. Experience with the process showed that reasonable standards would be $\bar{X}' = 5.072$, with $\sigma' = 0.0172$. Using normal law theory with these values, the band $\bar{X}' \pm 2.576\sigma'$ will contain 99% of the product in order for the 1% specified tolerance to be satisfied. The specified tolerance of 0.045 is also satisfied as $2.576(0.0172) = 0.0443$. In order to provide small numbers for practical use, $\bar{X}'$ is set at 0.20 rather than 5.0720. Thirty samples of five units each were obtained and are plotted in figure 6-16, which shows these values as plus or minus deviations from 5.07 with a unit of measure of 0.01. Readings have been recorded as deviations from 5.07. That is, the actual readings for the five values in sample 1 are really 5.06, 5.07, 5.08, 5.09, and 5.09 but are listed as -1, 0, $+1$, $+2$, and $+2$. Their sum is $+4$, with an average of 0.8 as plotted. Using d_2 from table 6.18 and D_4 from table 6.19 gives $\bar{R} = 2.326(0.0172) = 0.040$ (plotted as 4.0) and $\text{UCL} = 2.11(4.0) = 8.44$.

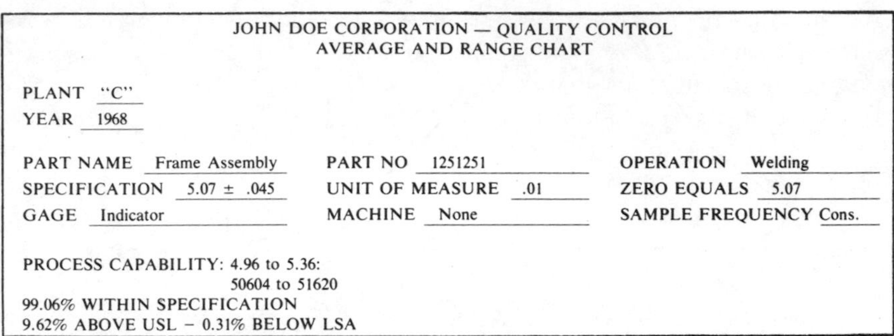

JOHN DOE CORPORATION — QUALITY CONTROL
AVERAGE AND RANGE CHART

PLANT "C"
YEAR 1968

PART NAME Frame Assembly PART NO 1251251 OPERATION Welding
SPECIFICATION 5.07 ± .045 UNIT OF MEASURE .01 ZERO EQUALS 5.07
GAGE Indicator MACHINE None SAMPLE FREQUENCY Cons.

PROCESS CAPABILITY: 4.96 to 5.36:
50604 to 51620
99.06% WITHIN SPECIFICATION
9.62% ABOVE USL – 0.31% BELOW LSA

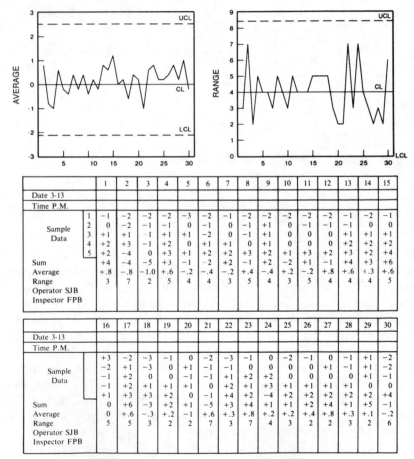

		1	2	3	4	5	6	7	8	9	10	11	12	13	14	15
Date 3-13																
Time P.M.																
Sample Data	1	−1	−2	−2	−2	−3	−2	−1	−2	−2	−2	−2	−2	−1	−2	−1
	2	0	−2	−1	−1	0	−1	0	−1	+1	0	−1	−1	−1	0	0
	3	+1	+1	−1	+1	+1	−2	0	−1	+1	0	0	0	+1	+1	+1
	4	+2	+3	−1	+2	0	+1	+1	0	+1	0	0	0	+2	+2	+2
	5	+2	−4	0	+3	+1	+2	+2	+3	+2	+1	+3	+2	+3	+2	+4
Sum		+4	−4	−5	+3	−1	−2	+2	−1	+2	−2	+1	−1	+4	+3	+6
Average		+.8	−.8	−1.0	+.6	−.2	−.4	−.2	+.4	−.4	+.2	−.2	+.8	+.6	+.3	+.6
Range		3	7	2	5	4	4	3	5	4	3	5	4	4	4	5
Operator SJB																
Inspector FPB																

		16	17	18	19	20	21	22	23	24	25	26	27	28	29	30
Date 3-13																
Time P.M.																
Sample Data		+3	−2	−3	−1	0	−2	−3	−1	0	−2	−1	0	−1	+1	−2
		−2	+1	−3	0	+1	−1	−1	0	0	0	0	+1	−1	+1	−2
		−1	+2	0	0	−1	−1	+1	+2	+2	0	0	0	0	+1	−1
		−1	+2	+1	+1	+1	0	+2	+1	+3	+1	+1	+1	+1	0	0
		+1	+3	+3	+2	0	−1	+4	+2	−4	+2	+2	+2	+2	+2	+4
Sum		0	+6	−3	+2	+1	−5	+3	+4	+1	+1	+2	+4	+1	+5	−1
Average		0	+.6	−.3	+.2	−1	+.6	+.3	+.8	+.2	+.2	+.4	+.8	+.3	+.1	−.2
Range		5	5	3	2	2	7	3	7	4	3	2	2	3	2	6
Operator SJB																
Inspector FPB																

Figure 6–16 Control charts for averages and ranges; standards given for $\bar{X}'$ and σ'; equal small samples, $n = 5$; $d_2 = 2.326$ (See Table 6–18 and 6–21); $D_3 = 0$; $D_4 = 2.11$ (see Table 6–10).

As indicated previously, the range R of a sample is the difference between the largest observation and the smallest observation. When $n \leq 10$, simplicity and economy of effort can be obtained by using control charts for $\bar{X}$ and R in place of control charts for $\bar{X}$ and σ. Although many concerns use the range values for samples as large as twenty-five, it is not recommended for samples of more than ten observations since it rapidly becomes less effective than the standard deviation as a detector of assignable causes for variability as n increases beyond this value. To cover all feasible cases, however, the relations and factors cover values of n up to twenty five.

The cases covered previously were those in which standards for $\bar{X}$ and σ were given as prime values. Relations and factors were provided in tables where standards were given. When no standards are given, use is made of standards based upon the data obtained from what is believed to be a controlled process. Table 6.24 lists the formulas for central lines and control limits where the range R is to be used. The least difficult case is the one in which small samples of equal size are used. However, if small samples of unequal size occur during the periods covered, then certain rules must be followed carefully to make such control limits correct for all the different sample sizes involved.

For small samples of unequal size, formulas (16) and (17) (or corresponding formulas) can be used for computing the control chart lines. Similarly, the average value must also be weighted, using the different n values as weighting

TABLE 6.24 Formulas for Central Lines and Control Limits Primarily Applicable to Ranges

		Control Limits	
	Central Line	*Simplified Formula Using Factors in Table 6.26*	*Basic Formula*
For averages, $\bar{X}$	$\bar{\bar{X}}$	$\bar{\bar{X}} \pm A_2\bar{R}$	$\bar{\bar{X}} \pm 3\dfrac{\bar{R}}{d_2\sqrt{n}}$ **(16)**
For ranges, R	$\bar{R}$	$D_4\bar{R}$ and $D_3\bar{R}$	$\bar{R} \pm 3\dfrac{d_3\bar{R}}{d_2}$ **(17)**

where:

$\bar{\bar{X}}$ = the grand average of observed values of X for *all* samples,
$\bar{R}$ = the average value of range R for the k individual samples,

$$= \frac{R_1 = R_2 + \cdots + R_k}{k} \qquad \textbf{(18)}$$

and factors d_2, d_3, A_2, D_3 and D_4 are given in table 6.1 and table 6.26 and d_2 in table 6.23 and table 6.18.

factors. This was described previously, but will be repeated here using all $\overline{X}$ values based on unequal sample sizes for a series of samples obtained under controlled conditions. For such a grand average used as a standard, the relation is

$$\overline{\overline{X}} = \frac{n_1\overline{X}_1 + n_2\overline{X}_2 + n_3\overline{X}_3 + \cdots + n_k\overline{X}_k}{n_1 + n_2 + n_3 + \cdots + n_k}, \tag{19}$$

where the subscripts $1, 2, 3, \ldots, k$ refer to the k subgroups.

Table 6.25 summarizes the formulas for central lines and control limits for control charts covering averages using sigma, averages using ranges, and standard deviations using the average of a set of sigma values, $\bar{\sigma}$ or ranges, $\overline{R}$. The equation numbers that apply to the terms used in these relations are given. These relations are also numbered, as they are also essentially basic formulas for the factors listed.

For samples of equal size, the computations are relatively simple. However, where groups with different sample sizes are used, computations are more difficult but may be simplified by combining all samples having the same sample size n in separate groups. Control limits then may be determined separately for

TABLE 6.25 Formulas for
Central Lines and Control Limits—No Standard Given; Small Samples of Equal Size

Control—No Standard Given ($\overline{X}'$, σ', Not Given)—Small Samples of Equal Size			
	Central Line	*Control Limits*	
Averages using σ	$\overline{\overline{X}}$	$\overline{\overline{X}} \pm A_1\bar{\sigma}$....... ($\bar{\sigma}$ as given by Eq. 12)	**(20)**
Averages using R	$\overline{\overline{X}}$	$\overline{\overline{X}} \pm A_2\overline{R}$...... ($\overline{R}$ as given by Eq. 18)	**(21)**
Standard deviations	$\bar{\sigma}$	$B_4\bar{\sigma}$ and $B_3\bar{\sigma}$ ... ($\bar{\sigma}$ as given by Eq. 12)	**(22)**
Ranges	$\overline{R}$	$D_4\overline{R}$ and $D_3\overline{R}$ .. ($\overline{R}$ as given by Eq. 18)	**(23)**

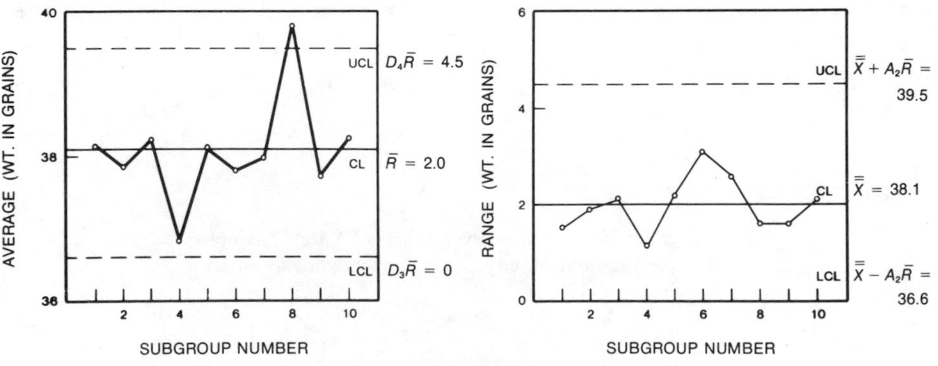

Figure 6–17 Instruction sheet 2—pair of control charts.

each new sample group. Whereas table 6.25 gives formulas for the factors, table 6.26 gives the numerical values of the factors for values of n from 2 to 25. Figure 6-17 presents a complete procedure for constructing control charts for the average and the range in the form of an instruction sheet.

TABLE 6.26 Factors for Computing Control Chart Lines No Standard Given

Number of Observations in Sample, n	*Chart for Averages*		*Chart for Standard Deviations*			*Chart for Ranges*		
	Factors for Control Limits		*Factor for Central Line*	*Factors for Control Limits*		*Factor for Central Line*	*Factors for Control Limits*	
	A_1	A_2	c_2	B_3	B_4	d_2	D_3	D_4
2..........	3.760	1.880	0.5642	0	3.267	1.128	0	3.267
3..........	2.394	1.023	0.7236	0	2.568	1.693	0	2.575
4..........	1.880	0.729	0.7979	0	2.266	2.059	0	2.282
5..........	1.596	0.577	0.8407	0	2.089	2.326	0	2.115
6..........	1.410	0.483	0.8686	0.030	1.970	2.534	0	2.004
7..........	1.277	0.419	0.8882	0.118	1.882	2.704	0.076	1.924
8..........	1.175	0.373	0.9027	0.185	1.815	2.847	0.136	1.864
9..........	1.094	0.337	0.9139	0.239	1.761	2.970	0.184	1.816
10..........	1.028	0.308	0.9227	0.284	1.716	3.078	0.223	1.777
11..........	0.973	0.285	0.9300	0.321	1.679	3.173	0.256	1.744
12..........	0.925	0.266	0.9359	0.354	1.646	3.258	0.284	1.716
13..........	0.884	0.249	0.9410	0.382	1.618	3.336	0.308	1.692
14..........	0.848	0.235	0.9453	0.406	1.594	3.407	0.329	1.671
15..........	0.816	0.223	0.9490	0.428	1.572	3.472	0.348	1.652
16..........	0.788	0.212	0.9523	0.448	1.552	3.532	0.364	1.636
17..........	0.762	0.203	0.9551	0.466	1.534	3.588	0.379	1.621
18..........	0.738	0.194	0.9576	0.482	1.518	3.640	0.392	1.608
19..........	0.717	0.187	0.9599	0.497	1.503	3.689	0.404	1.596
20..........	0.697	0.180	0.9619	0.510	1.490	3.735	0.414	1.586
21..........	0.679	0.173	0.9638	0.523	1.477	3.778	0.425	1.575
22..........	0.662	0.167	0.9655	0.534	1.466	3.819	0.434	1.566
23..........	0.647	0.162	0.9670	0.545	1.455	3.858	0.443	1.557
24..........	0.632	0.157	0.9684	0.555	1.445	3.895	0.452	1.548
25..........	0.619	0.153	0.9696	0.565	1.435	3.931	0.459	1.541
Over 25..........	$\frac{3}{\sqrt{n}}$	....	....	*	**	....	....	....

* $1 - \frac{3}{\sqrt{2n}}$ ** $1 + \frac{3}{\sqrt{2n}}$

Following the procedures given in figure 6-17, Instruction Sheet 2, the following examples illustrate the case where no standard is given. Example 12 covers the case where the samples are small and of equal size. Example 13 covers the same conditions, except that the samples are of unequal size.

Example 12 *Control Charts for $\overline{X}$ and R, Small Samples of Equal Size, No Standard Given.* Table 6.27 gives the width in inches to the nearest 0.0001 inch, measured prior to exposure, for ten sets of corrosion test specimens of Grade BB zinc, where six measured values are recorded for each of the ten sets. Two groups of five sets each were selected from a large number of sets of test specimens for illustrative purposes; each set consisted of six specimens used in atmosphere exposure tests sponsored by ASTM. In each of the two groups, the five sets correspond to five different millings that were employed in the preparation of the specimens. The table also includes average, standard deviation, and range values for each set, as well as the overall values for these statistics used as standards for the control charts. The central lines and control limits for $\overline{X}$ and R are tabulated following these data.

Although the excessive size of the average values for sets 5 and 6 indicates lack of control for those sets, the average values for $\overline{X}$ and R are still used as standards. The resultant statistics used and the control charts for $\overline{X}$ and R are given in figure 6-18.

TABLE 6.27 Width in Inches, Test Specimens of Grade BB Zinc

Set	Measured Values						Average, $\overline{X}$	Standard Deviation, σ	Range, R
	X_1	X_2	X_3	X_4	X_5	X_6			
Group 1									
No. 1..........	0.5005	0.5000	0.5008	0.5000	0.5005	0.5000	0.50030	0.00032	0.0008
No. 2..........	0.4998	0.4997	0.4998	0.4994	0.4999	0.4998	0.49973	0.00016	0.0005
No. 3..........	0.4995	0.4995	0.4995	0.4995	0.4995	0.4996	0.49952	0.00004	0.0001
No. 4..........	0.4998	0.5005	0.5005	0.5002	0.5003	0.5004	0.50028	0.00024	0.0007
No. 5..........	0.5000	0.5005	0.5008	0.5007	0.5008	0.5010	0.50063	0.00032	0.0010
Group 2									
No. 6..........	0.5008	0.5009	0.5010	0.5005	0.5006	0.5009	0.50078	0.00018	0.0005
No. 7..........	0.5000	0.5001	0.5002	0.4995	0.4996	0.4997	0.49985	0.00026	0.0007
No. 8..........	0.4993	0.4994	0.4999	0.4996	0.4996	0.4997	0.49958	0.00020	0.0006
No. 9..........	0.4995	0.4995	0.4997	0.4992	0.4995	0.4992	0.49943	0.00018	0.0005
No. 10..........	0.4994	0.4998	0.5000	0.4990	0.5000	0.5000	0.49970	0.00038	0.0010
Average..........							0.49998	0.00023	0.00064

Central Lines

For $\bar{X}$: $\bar{\bar{X}} = 0.49998$.
For R: $\bar{R} = 0.00064$.

Control Limits
$n = 6$:

For $\bar{X}$: $\bar{\bar{X}} \pm A_2\bar{R} =$
$0.49998 \pm (0.483)(0.00064)$,
0.50029 and 0.49967.

For R: $D_4\bar{R}$ and $D_3\bar{R} =$
$(2.001)(0.00064)$ and
$(0)(0.00064)$, 0.00128 and 0.

A. Computed Values.

B. Control Charts for $\bar{X}$ and R.
Small samples of equal size, $n = 6$; no standard given.+

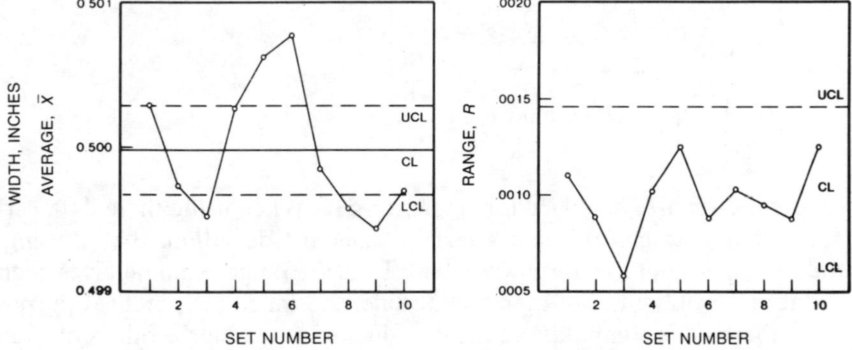

Figure 6–18 Central lines, control limits, with control charts for $\bar{X}$ and R; for samples of equal size, $n = 6$ for example 6-12 data.

Results Average values for sets 1, 5 and 6 are larger than their respective control limits. The last four sets of values, however, are within their control limits and seem to be scattered by chance around the central line for averages. The range values appear to be well controlled at their average value.

The next example illustrates the case in which the sample sizes are unequal. It is necessary to obtain an estimate for the standard deviation from the range values observed in the different subgroups, combining results based on a single sample size n in each subgroup. The procedure in Instruction Sheet 2 for obtaining control charts for $\bar{X}$ and R is followed. Central lines and control limits are obtained for each different sample size as noted in the solution.

Example 13 *Control Charts for $\bar{X}$ and R, Small Samples of Unequal Size, No Standard Given.* Use will be made of the data from example 8, in which table 6.15 presented test values taken from twenty-one machines, four each from machines numbered 7 and 16, and five each from the remaining nineteen machines. Control charts for $\bar{X}$ and σ have already been presented in figure 6-12. Here control charts will be based on range values rather than σ values. The weighted average $\bar{\bar{X}}$ is the same as in example 8, i.e., 71.65 based on 103 tests, where the sum of the X values is 7380. Hence the grand average $\bar{\bar{X}}$ is $\frac{7380}{103} = 71.65$. In dealing with the range values to estimate the standard deviation, the relation $\sigma = \bar{R}/d_2$ is applied first to the $\bar{R}$ value for the two R values based on four observations each and then to the $\bar{R}$ value for the nineteen R values based on five observations each. This gives the relation:

$$\sigma_e = \frac{1}{21}\left(\frac{4+1}{2.059} + \frac{2+2+1+3+0+5+4+1+1+1+2+2+1+1+2+2+1+3+0}{2.326}\right)$$

$$= \frac{1}{21}\left(\frac{5}{2.059} + \frac{34}{2.326}\right) = \frac{1}{21}(2.42836 + 14.61737)$$

$$= \frac{1}{21}(17.04573) = 0.811701 \textit{ or } 0.812.$$

Thus the estimated standard for sigma is 0.812. When using these data earlier for determining control charts for the standard deviation, the $\bar{\sigma}_e$ using c_2 values rather than d_2 values was 0.900. Thus the range estimate gives slightly tighter control limits, but they do not differ too much for practical purposes. Note that in this computation, the d_2 values were read for n values of 4 and 5 from any of the tables giving d_2 values.

Figure 6-19 shows the central lines, control limits, and control charts for $\bar{X}$ and R for these twenty-one observed results, modifying them to cover the two different sample sizes of four and five, respectively.

Control charts for averages and ranges are used universally. Figure 6-18 is an American control chart set for $\bar{X}$ and R based on equal sample size samples of six units each, while figure 6-19 covers unequal sample sizes. Figure 6-20 presents a similar case used in Japan showing control charts for $\bar{X}$ and R for ten sets of five units each, where the derived standards are $\bar{X}'_e = 4051.6$, with an $\bar{R}$ value of 2.4. The sample size used is five for each set. The upper and lower control lines for averages are based on $\bar{X}' \pm A_2\bar{R}$, where, for $n = 5$, $A_2 = 0.577$. This value is determined from table 6.26. For the chart for ranges, the D_3 and D_4 factors are 0 and 2.115, respectively. When multiplied by $\bar{R} = 2.4$, the UCL and LCL values shown on the range chart are 0 and 5.09, respectively.

$$\sigma_e = \frac{1}{21}\left(\frac{5}{2.059} + \frac{34}{2.326}\right) = 0.812.$$

Central Lines

For $\bar{X}$: $\bar{\bar{X}} = 71.65.$

For R: $n = 4: \bar{R} = d_2\sigma_e =$
$(2.059)(0.812) = 1.67.$

$n = 5: \bar{R} = d_2\sigma_e =$
$(2.326)(0.812) = 1.89.$

Control Limits

For $\bar{X}$: $n = 4: \bar{\bar{X}} \pm A_2\bar{R} =$
$71.65 \pm (0.729)(1.67),$
72.9 and $70.4.$

$n = 5: \bar{\bar{X}} \pm A_2\bar{R} =$
$71.65 \pm (0.577)(1.89),$
72.7 and $70.6.$

For R: $n = 4: D_4\bar{R}$ and $D_3\bar{R} =$
$(2.282)(1.67)$ and
$(0)(1.67)$, 3.8 and 0.

$n = 5: D_4\bar{R}$ and $D_3\bar{R} =$
$(2.115)(1.89)$ and
$(0)(1.89)$, 4.0 and 0.

A. Computed Values.

B. Control Charts for $\bar{X}$ and R.
Small samples of unequal size, $n = 4, 5$; no standard given.

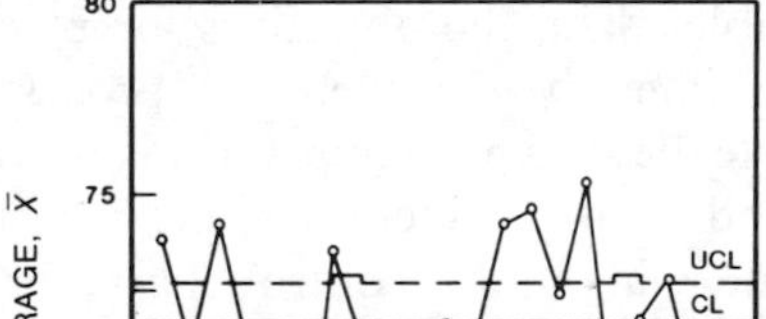

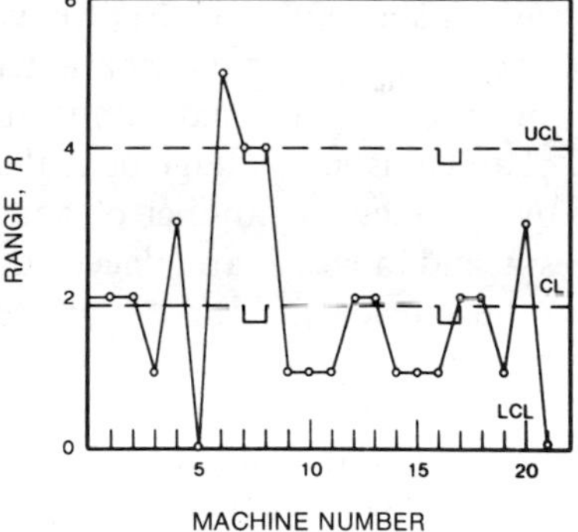

Figure 6–19 Central lines, control limits and control charts for $\bar{X}$ and R; no standards given, samples of unequal size.

Results Lack of control for both averages and ranges.

The same pattern appears in figure 6-19, where the average for the sixth entry is out of control and the subsequent sample results show that the action taken to restore control at the desired level was fairly successful, as the next few values are within their various respective control limits. Lack of control at the sixth entry also occurs for the range. The corrective measures to remove assignable causes seem to have been more successful with variability than with respect to the desired

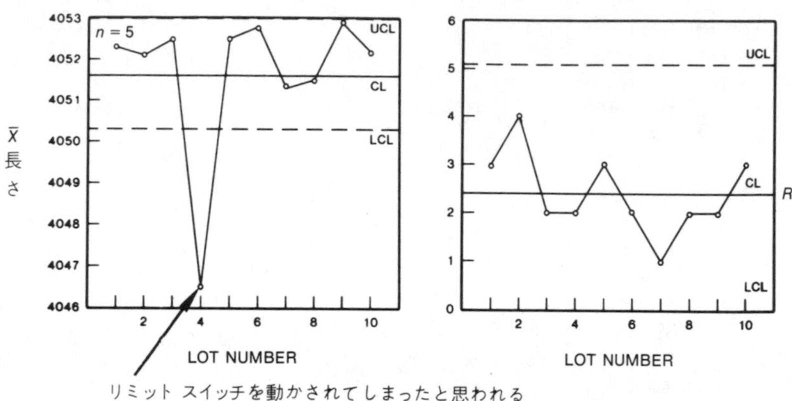

Figure 6–20 Universality of control charts for averages and ranges.

level, as several subsequent average values are outside their respective control limits.

The control charts in figure 6-20 show the fourth entry out of control for averages, with good control showing for range values. Control has been attained in this chart for averages for subsequent entries for averages.

In using these control charts for variables data, the objectives for placing a control chart on a particular characteristic must be considered. A process may seem to be producing too many units outside the specified limits for this particular critical characteristic. Management demands that production reduce the losses caused by an excessive number of nonconforming units. Control charts for both averages $\overline{X}$ and ranges R are placed in effect. In operating such charts, a point is found to be outside the three-sigma control limit. This indicates the possible existence of an assignable cause that should be improved or eliminated. While seeking this assignable cause, a second sample may be taken; its average may be found to be within its control limits. Based on a normal distribution of sample averages, the probability of being wrong in deciding that the average has shifted when such an average is outside the control limits is approximately 3 in 1,000, as previously indicated. The probability measured by the area between the plus and minus three-sigma limits for a normal distribution is 0.9973; hence the probability of being outside is $1 - 0.9973 = 0.0027$ or twenty-seven in ten thousand. Figure 6-21 illustrates such a case.

In this figure, the observed value is assumed to be at the two-sigma level for the succeeding second sample. It seems likely that the point found outside its UCL value is a maverick rather than a true indicator of lack of control. The values in the figure show that the probability of no change in the average central value is very small. Thus, even if the second average is in control, the probability that the average has not shifted is less than 7 in 100,000. Therefore there is much more

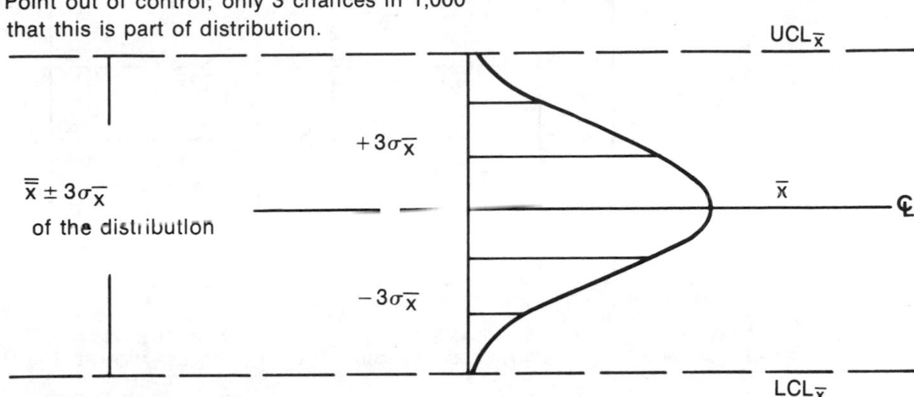

Assuming a second sample average is at the two-sigma level and on the same side of $\overline{\overline{X}}$ as the first, what is the probability now that there has been a shift in the average?

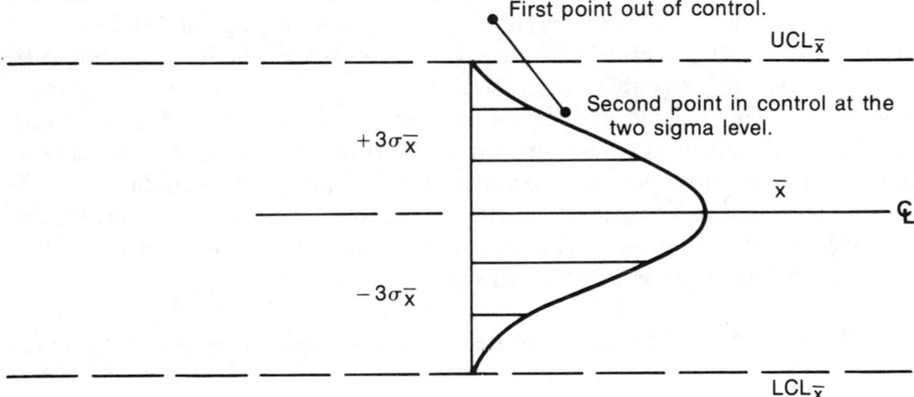

Figure 6–21 Lack of control for an average.

assurance of a shift in the average on the basis of the two points, even if the second is in control, than on the basis of the first sample results alone.

The above case showed an average value out of control. The process average may shift, yet both average and range control charts may show control because the variability has not increased sufficiently to show lack of control. Figure 6-22 shows such a condition for average and range values.

If it appears that the process average has shifted, since the results for range values tend to stay consecutively above the expected $\overline{R}$ value set as a tentative standard, even though no points are above their respective control limits, a check should be made for an assignable cause. The second range chart gives positive indications that lack of control exists and that there should be an assignable

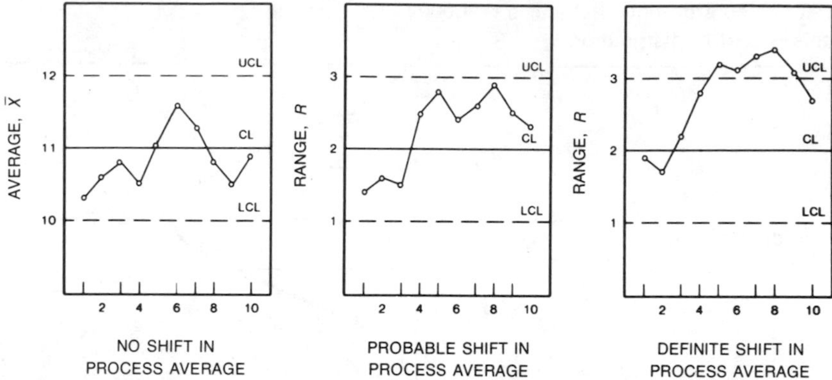

Figure 6–22 Nature of probable shifts in process average—three charts.

cause for such lack of control with respect to variability. In addition, there are some general rules to follow in deciding if the process average has shifted. Such guides are generally accepted in industry. They indicate when action should be taken to look for assignable causes of variation in the process, thus causing a probable unfavorable shift in the process average. At times the process average may be out of control in a favorable direction. If the process average for a large number of consecutive lots and samples is significantly low, standards can be recomputed and charts prepared at the new levels to truly indicate an improvement in quality. When the following conditions occur one may be sufficiently sure that the process average has shifted to warrant analysis.

1. When seven successive points are on the same side of the process average. The process average for fraction defective is $\bar{p}$; for defects per unit it is $\bar{u}$; for averages it is $\bar{X}$; and for ranges it is $\bar{R}$. For other measures the process average would be considered as the expected value, often expressed as $E(X)$.
2. When ten points out of eleven are on the same side of the process average.
3. When twelve points out of fourteen are on the same side of the process average.
4. When fourteen points out of seventeen are on the same side of the process average.
5. When sixteen points out of twenty are on the same side of the process average.

6.6 Case Study: Example of $\bar{X}$ and R Charts

Example 14 This example deals with the construction of a control chart to monitor the 0.500 ± 0.008 inch diameter on the stud shown in figure 6-23.

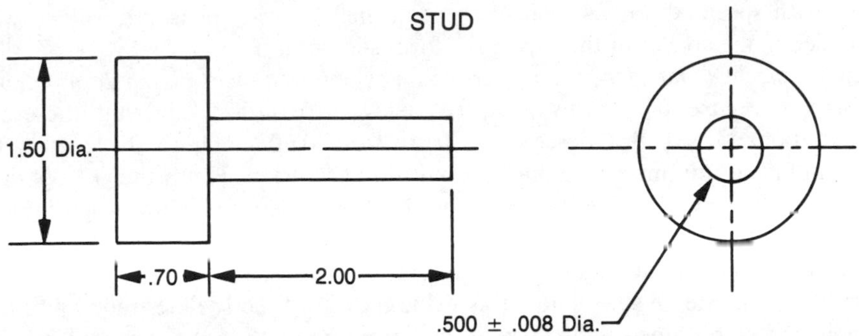

Figure 6–23 Stud dimensions.

The stud is produced on an automatic machine. A step-by-step set of instructions for preparing such control charts for averages and ranges for this important characteristic is provided, together with the history of the case and an analysis of the results obtained by repeated measurements. A frequency distribution of 100 measurements is given and tallied. The twenty samples measured consisted of five units each. Directions are included showing how to establish process limits. An analysis is made and the study concludes with a diagram showing nominal specification values, control limits for averages, ranges, and finally process limits. This case illustrates how effective the control chart techniques may be in obtaining a quality product.

Steps for Constructing Control Charts for Averages and Ranges with Standards Derived from Observed Data: Diameter of Stud

Step 1 *Making lots available for tests.* The control charts shown in figure 6-25 for averages and ranges cover the critical diameter 0.500 ± 0.008 inch for the stud shown in figure 6-23. Twenty lots, made up of N units each, produced successively on an automatic machine are made available for inspection and test.

Step 2 *Taking random samples.* A history of the process was secured and was substantiated by taking a sample of five units each from each of the twenty available lots. These samples were selected at random from each lot and represent the process for a series of twenty lots produced from successive runs from all manufacturing shifts.

Step 3 *Obtaining data from a seemingly controlled process.* In step 1, twenty successive lots containing N units each (N might be 100 to 500 studs produced by one automatic machine) were made available for test and measurements. In step 2, five studs were selected successively at random from each such lot. In this step, each of these five units is measured for the critical dimension, diameter of stud, with specified values of 0.500 ± 0.008 inch. These measured values were recorded in the spaces at the top of the form shown in figure 6-24.

Step 4 *Establishing a frequency distribution by ordering and tallying data obtained in step 3.* Figure 6-24 shows the frequency distribution covering these 100 observations tallied in a descending array from 0.508 inch to 0.492 inch, the maximum and minimum diameters specified in accordance with the ±0.008-inch tolerance allowed. All values tallied are well within the specified limits for diameter for this particular stud. This distribution closely approximates a normal law distribution. This figure also shows the overall average for the 100 observations as 0.5015 inch. Step 5 shows how this value may be directly determined and also how it may be obtained by the use of smaller numbers than those recorded.

Step 5 *Computation of overall average, variance, standard deviation, and average range for twenty samples of five units each.* Arrange the data in a frequency distribution with the X values tabulated in a descending array with a cell interval of 0.001 and using 0.497, the smallest value of X for which an observation was obtained, as the origin. For ease of computation, use a Y scale with zero equivalent to 0.497, 1 to 0.498, and so on as noted. In the longer method, the actual X values are squared to obtain the variance and the corresponding standard deviation σ, which is the square root of the variance v. In the shorter method, the Y values are squared and the same relations as generally used with the actual observations are applied to obtain values with Y. These are $\bar{Y}$ (its average value) and σ_Y (its standard deviation). Where i represents the width of the interval for the original X frequency distribution and X_0 denotes the X value corresponding to zero (the first Y value for the Y distribution), then $\bar{X}$ and σ_X may be determined from the following relations.

Usual relations:

$$\bar{X} = \frac{\Sigma f_j(X_j)}{n}; \quad \sigma_X = \sqrt{\frac{\Sigma f_j(X_j - \bar{X})^2}{n}} = \sqrt{\frac{\Sigma f_j X_j^2}{n} - \bar{X}^2} \tag{24}$$

Y-scale relations:

$$\bar{Y} = \frac{\Sigma f_j Y_j}{n}; \quad \sigma_Y = \sqrt{\frac{\Sigma f_j Y_j^2}{n} - \bar{Y}^2} \tag{25}$$

Determination of X statistics from the Y statistics:

$$\bar{X} = X_0 + i\bar{Y}; \quad \sigma_X = i\sigma_Y, \tag{26}$$

where the X-cell width or interval is i, and the origin corresponding to $Y = 0$ is X_0.

Figure 6-24 lists the 100 observations obtained in measuring the stud diameter, tabulated in twenty groups of five units each. A tally of these observations is given in figure 6-25. This frequency distribution for X values is used to obtain the average and standard deviation values. The shorter method also is given using Y values.

TABLE 6.28 Computations of $\overline{X}$ and $\overline{Y}$ Values and σ_X and σ_Y Values for Stud Diameter

Observed X_j	*Frequency* f_j	$f_j(X_j)$	$f_j(X_j^2)$	*New Scale* Y_j	$f_j(Y_j)$	$f_j(Y_j^2)$
0.497	1	0.497	0.247009	0	0	0
0.498	2	0.996	0.496008	1	2	2
0.499	11	5.489	2.739011	2	22	44
0.500	16	8.000	4.000000	3	10	144
0.501	18	9.018	4.518018	4	72	288
0.502	25	12.550	6.300100	5	125	625
0.503	15	7.545	3.795135	6	90	540
0.504	9	4.536	2.286144	7	63	441
0.505	3	1.515	0.765075	8	24	192
Sum	100	50.146	25.146500	Sum	446	2276

$$\overline{X} = \frac{50.146}{100} = 0.50146; \quad \sigma_X^2 = \frac{25.1465}{100} - (0.50146)^2 = 0.25146500 - 0.2514621316 =$$

$$0.0000028684 = \sigma_X^2; \quad \sigma_X = 0.001694.$$

$$\overline{Y} = \frac{446}{100} = 4.46; \quad \overline{X} = 0.497 + 0.001(4.46) = 0.50146; \quad \sigma_Y^2 = \frac{2276}{100} - (4.46)^2 =$$

$$22.7600 - 19.8916 = 2.8684; \quad \sigma_Y = 1.694; \quad \sigma_X = 0.001(1.694) = 0.001694.$$

Figure 6-25 presents a tally of the data given in figure 6-24 for stud diameter. It also includes a comparison of the estimates of standard deviation obtained from $\overline{R}$, derived from the twenty R values for samples of five obtained by using equation (18). Using the d_2 value for $n = 5$, the computed σ and σ_e based on the range agree to two significant figures.

Step 6 *Graphing data and preparing control charts for averages and ranges.* Using a graph paper form designed for a composite chart—shown in figure 6-24, where the measured values of the stud diameter are tabulated—fill in the totals, compute the average values for each of the twenty groups of data, and determine and record the range for each group. These values were used in step 5 to compute the statistics for these 100 observed values. List the best possible values for the y ordinates for the average ($\overline{X}$) and range (R) values. For averages, these were found by using intervals of 0.0005 with values listed for $\overline{X}$ from 0.4985 to 0.5045. Since average values are to be plotted, the specified limits for individual values need not be on the chart itself but should be noted. Draw in the central control line and also the upper and lower control limits for average values and then repeat the process for range values.

Step 7 *Plotting points.* On the graphs prepared in step 6, plot the twenty average values given in figure 6-24. Next plot the twenty range values that have been

EQUATION:

$\bar{\bar{X}} = 0.5015\ (0.50146)$ $\quad \bar{R} = 0.004\ (0.00405)$ $\quad UCL_{\bar{X}} = \bar{\bar{x}} + .577\bar{R}$ $\quad UCLR = 2.115\bar{R}$

$LCL_{\bar{X}} = \bar{\bar{x}} - .577\bar{R}$ $\quad LCLR = 0$

DATE		STUD DIAMETER (0.500 ± 0.008″)										
SAMPLE		1	2	3	4	5	6	7	8	9	10	
	1	.498	.504	.500	.499	.503	.503	.502	.502	.504	.504	
	2	.501	.502	.499	.503	.502	.501	.499	.502	.502	.503	
	3	.504	.505	.501	.502	.500	.504	.502	.504	.501	.503	
	4	.502	.503	.502	.503	.501	.501	.503	.502	.503	.499	
	5	.503	.500	.504	.502	.501	.500	.503	.500	.503	.498	
TOTALS		2.508	2.514	2.506	2.509	2.507	2.509	2.509	2.510	2.513	2.507	
$\bar{\bar{X}}$		.5016	.5028	.5012	.5018	.5014	.5018	.5018	.5020	.5026	.5014	
R		.006	.005	.005	.004	.003	.004	.004	.004	.003	.006	Sum
SAMPLE		11	12	13	14	15	16	17	18	19	20	Σ
	1	.501	.499	.499	.501	.505	.504	.501	.502	.501	.499	
	2	.502	.501	.500	.500	.505	.502	.502	.501	.499	.503	
	3	.500	.501	.502	.502	.500	.499	.504	.502	.503	.497	
	4	.500	.502	.500	.500	.501	.499	.500	.499	.502	.502	
	5	.501	.502	.501	.500	.502	.500	.503	.502	.500	.501	
TOTALS		2.504	2.505	2.502	2.503	2.513	2.504	2.510	2.506	2.505	2.502	50.146
$\bar{\bar{X}}$		.5008	.5010	.5004	.5006	.5026	.5008	.5020	.5012	.5010	.5004	10.0292
R		.002	.003	.003	.002	.005	.005	.004	.003	.004	.006	.081

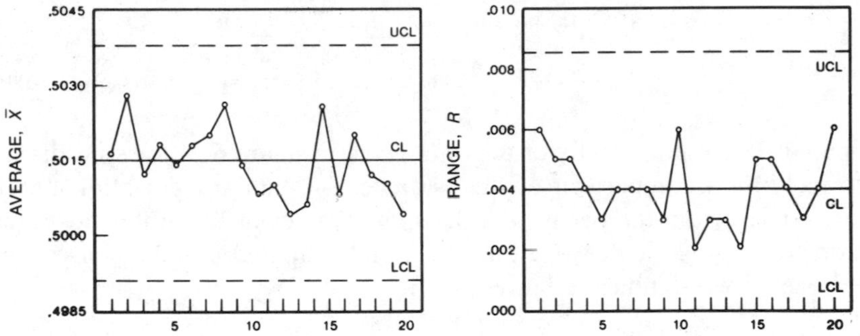

PART NUMBER	PART NAME	CHARACTERISTIC	DEPT. NO	OPERATION NO.	MACHINE NO.	CHART NO.
8640-9419	STUD	0.500 ± 0.008 DIAM.	41	2	13	1

Figure 6–24 Case study: stud diameter; data and control charts for $\bar{X}$ and R.

determined and tabulated in figure 6-24. Since these twenty groups of five units each are being used to establish standards, a second chart should be prepared, following the steps above for preparing control charts. This second form will continue the control charts and should have the same *y* ordinates, central lines and control limits as shown in figure 6-24.

Step 8 *Analysis and evaluation.* Check the values as plotted and determine if any average or range values are outside their respective control limits. Since none are outside these limits and the process appears to be in excellent control, the standards

0.500 ± 0.800 Dia	Specified Values TALLY	TOTAL
0.508		
0.507		
0.506		
0.505	X X X	3
0.504	X X X X X X X X X	9
0.503	X X X X X X X X X X X X X X X	15
0.502	X X X X X X X X X X X X X X X X X X	18
0.501	X X X X X X X X X X X X X X X X X X X X X X X X X	25
0.500	X X X X X X X X X X X	11
0.499	X X	2
0.498	X	1
0.497		
0.496		
0.495		
0.494		
0.493		
0.492		

$\overline{X} = \frac{50.146}{100} = 0.50146;\ \sigma_x^2 = \frac{\Sigma X^2}{n} - \overline{X}^2$ Total Readings 100

$\overline{X} = \frac{\Sigma x}{n} = 0.5015;\ \sigma_x^2 = \frac{25.1465}{100} - (0.50146)^2 = 0.251465 - 0.2514621316$

$\sigma_x = 0.001694;\ \sigma_x^2 = 0.0000028684$

$n = 5,\ m = 20,\ \Sigma n = 20 \times 5 = 100.\ \ \Sigma R = 0.081,\ \overline{R} = \frac{\Sigma R}{m} = \frac{0.081}{20} = 0.00405$

$\sigma_e' = \frac{\overline{R}}{d_2} = \frac{0.00405}{2.326} = 0.0017411.$ (Good estimate for $\sigma' = 0.001694$ as computed from 100 units in Table 6-27.)

Figure 6–25 Case study: tally of frequencies for 100 observed values stud diameter. Comparison: two estimates of standard deviation.

established from these data may be used for the continuation of the operations. Continue measuring the diameters of the five studs selected as a sample from each lot and record these data. Determine the average and range values for each sample and plot them on the average and range control charts. If any value of $\overline{X}$ or R is outside its respective control limits, stop production and determine the assignable cause for lack of control. When found, correct the process.

This case and the step-by-step procedure for setting up standards and control charts for $\overline{X}$ and R provide guides for the determination of the most economical standards of quality and process averages for the critical characteristics of any product similar to these studs. Consider the specified engineering limits for the diameter of this stud and the data obtained from random samples from this manufacturing process. It can be seen from figure 6-26 that the central tendency of the turning process is shifted somewhat to the right, but the process limits are

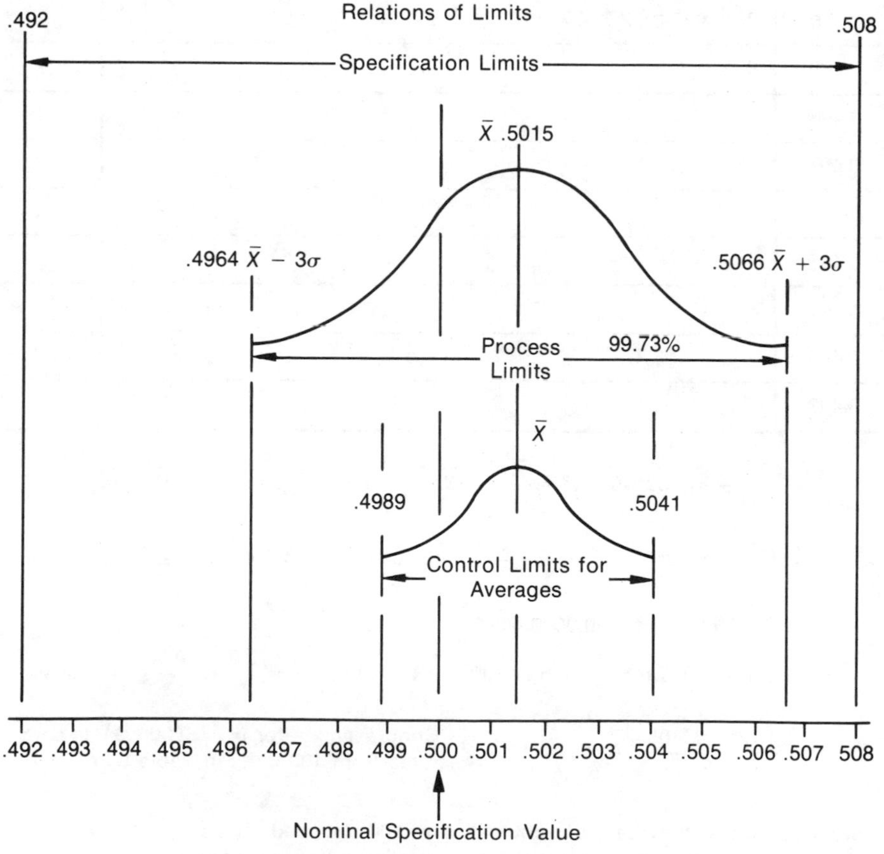

Figure 6–26 Case study: comparison of specified limits.

still within the specification limits. The variation in the turning process is within the specification limits.

Among the various process variations that might occur, consider these two cases: (1) the process limits are too wide; and (2) the process limits are too narrow. Figure 6-27 depicts the first case.

The above process has too much variation to meet the specification limits. If control limits were accepted as shown, defective parts would be produced. There are several possible alternatives.

1. Improve the process. For the diameter of studs, control the turning process more stringently.
2. Widen the specification limits if it will not affect the quality of the product.
3. If the specification cannot be changed, transfer the work to a machine having tighter controls.
4. It can be recognized as part of the job cost that, if no change can be made, some scrap will be inevitable. In many cases this may be the most economical solution. Solution 3 seems excellent, but the cost of a better machine may be so high and its use so limited that the overall costs will be increased by its use rather than being decreased.

The second case, where the process limits appear to be too tight, is shown in figure 6-28. The process is so tight that both individual as well as average values are well within all specification and control limits.

Where the automatically or manually controlled machine produces units that are well within the specification limits but with quality much better than specified, this may not be profitable. In many processes, tight controls may be very desirable as it may be more economical to eliminate the control charts, which are useless for a process that is always in control, that is, well within its respective three-sigma control limits. Other considerations must also be made.

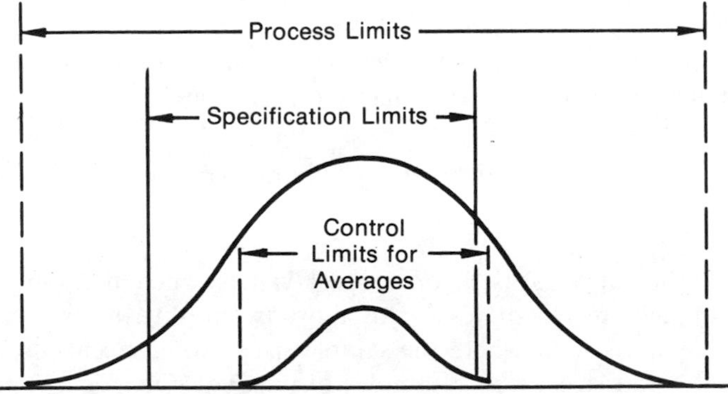

Figure 6–27 Case study: Case 1—Process limits too wide.

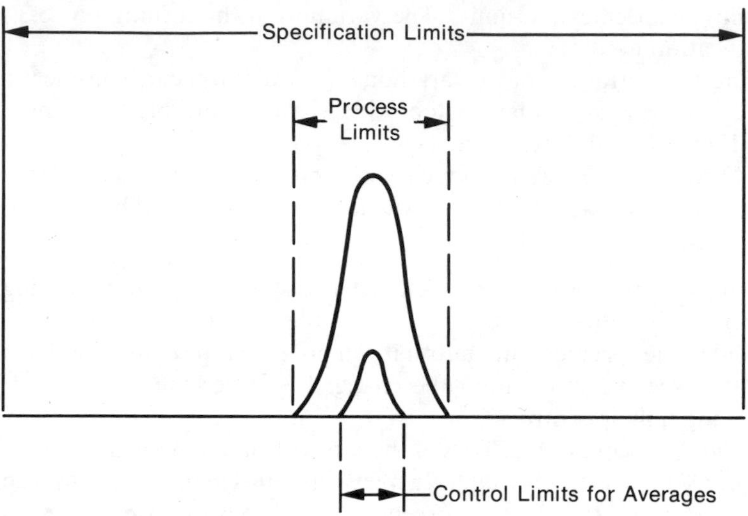

Figure 6–28 Case study: Case 2—Process limits too narrow.

1. The specification limit can be narrowed if this will tend to produce a better and more profitable product. Customers may be willing to pay more for units with much narrower limits and smaller tolerances.
2. The control limits can be widened by some factor beyond the process limits. In many instances it may be found uneconomical to reset a tool or improve a process condition every time sample results show out-of-control conditions to exist.
3. Without impairing the quality of the product with such wide specification limits, a less expensive process or machine may be utilized.

Control charts are a useful tool, but should be used only where their application will stabilize the process and result in producing quality products at levels dictated by customer demands. The next few sections will show a few additional features that may be incorporated in control charts for variables.

6.7 Use of Range for Controlling Variability When Samples Are Large

Generally, the range is used for control values when the sample sizes for successive samples are ten or less or at most twenty-five units in a few cases. Two conditions may occur where the sample sizes exceed twenty-five. These are (1) samples of equal size, and (2) samples of unequal size. Also, standards may be specified or they may be determined from process data. The latter case is one that needs particular attention and requires specific methods to obtain the most efficient use for range control charts; where the samples from lot to lot are different, samples of equal size should be segregated and analyzed. It is then possible to set up standards by weighting the results, using the number of units in each group. The methods previously described for combining data from groups where the sample sizes are unequal should be followed. The most important feature described here is using range values for a large sample more efficiently than would be done following the methods prescribed for small samples of equal size.

Where the size of successive samples selected from a series of lots continuously exceeds twenty-five, using a range value to estimate the variability of the process is not very efficient, since only two observed values (the largest and smallest) are used to determine the range R. For such cases, many prefer to use control charts for standard deviation values. However, better controls may be achieved by systematizing the inspection and recording processes. Divide the n units selected at random as a sample from each lot into m groups of n^* units, where $n^* = 10$, so that $mn^* = n$. The portions of the lot from which the n^* subsamples are selected for inspection or test should be adequately identified, so that if any subsample of n^* units gives results outside its control limits, that portion of the lot from which it was selected may be completely checked for possible occurrences of poor quality product. This possibility results when a control chart covering ranges from samples of size n^* is used with the central line $\bar{R}$ corresponding to the n^* sample size, and corresponding control limits are used to check the process.

For the lot as a whole, an estimated value for the standard deviation σ_e may also be determined from the relation $\bar{R}/d_2 = \sigma_e$. A control chart for the total sample n may also be established corresponding to such σ_e values.

There are many ways of dividing a sample of n units into smaller, equal subgroups. For example, when the sample consists of forty-eight units, it is possible to have twenty-four subgroups of two units each, sixteen subgroups of three units each, twelve subgroups of four units each, eight subgroups of six units each, six subgroups of eight units each, or four subgroups of twelve units each. For a sample of fifty units the breakdown might be twenty-five subgroups of two units each, ten subgroups of five units each, five subgroups of ten units each, or two subgroups of twenty-five units each. The latter is not recommended, since the smaller the n^* value is, the more efficient the measure of variability. The following example covers the case where the large sample is thirty units per lot.

Example 15 *Control Charts for Averages and Ranges, Large Equal Samples, No Standard Given.* A manufacturer is producing six lots of resistors per day, under continuous production. The critical characteristic of resistors is their resistance in ohms with a specified value of 10.00 ± 0.5 ohms. A sample of thirty units for making measurements on units is selected at random from each lot. It is desired to use the range rather than the standard deviation to establish controls over their variations. This choice simplifies the operations and reduces the time required for computations. A large company would have a computer available to use in computing the standard deviations for these thirty units. However, a smaller company would generally have to use computations obtained by their statistician or one of their engineers and might prefer to use range values on the production line.

Carrying out this example completely requires a great deal of computation, so only part of the data will be used to illustrate the application of the proper techniques for utilizing subgroups and their ranges. If the first five units in each sample of thirty units from each lot is used in conjunction with succeeding samples from the other five lots produced during a day, we have a total of thirty units in a sample for a day's production. For this illustrative example, with large samples of equal size, control charts for average and range values ($\bar{X}$ and R) are computed and listed covering the five days in a week. This illustrates the use of six subgroups from a day's product with a random sample of five units each selected from each subgroup. Thus an $\bar{R}$ value may be determined for $n^* = 5$ units from six R values, and control charts for averages and ranges may be established for these subgroups. Control charts may also be set up for averages and ranges based on the total sample of thirty units for each day's production. Standards for averages and ranges may be readily established for these conditions, and will prove to be much more efficient than using only basic standards. The average for each total sample of thirty units each is readily determined by summing the thirty X values and dividing their sum by the total sample size for the day. The range for the thirty units may be used with an $\bar{R}$ based on the average of ranges obtained for the total sample of thirty units. This is not very efficient, so an estimate of σ_e may be obtained by using the $\bar{R}$ derived from the six R values per day for $n^* = 5$ units per subgroup and dividing this $\bar{R}$ by the d_2 factor corresponding to $n^* = 5$, i.e., $d_2 = 2.326$, the correct value of d_2 as read from table 6.18 $n = mn^* = 6(5) = 30$.

The applicable control charts should be set up by preparing graphs on coordinate paper with five or ten spaces marked per inch. These σ_e values are plotted on the control chart for standard deviation values derived from the set of six range values. The central line for this σ_e control chart is $\bar{\sigma}_e$, the average of all σ_e values determined from random samples which were selected from a product believed to have been produced under controlled conditions. The three-sigma control limits for such σ_e values are based on the relation $\bar{\sigma} \pm 3\,\sigma'/\sqrt{m}$. Since $\bar{\sigma}_e$ has been determined from the data, its standard value may be determined from the relation $\sigma' = \bar{\sigma}_e/c_2$, where the c_2 value is read from table 6.18. For $n = 30$, $c_2 = 0.9748$. Then the control limit lines are

$$\text{UCL} = \bar{\sigma}_e + 3\,\frac{\bar{\sigma}_e}{c_2\sqrt{m}}$$

and (27)

$$\mathrm{LCL} = \bar{\sigma}_e - 3\,\frac{\sigma_e}{c_2\sqrt{m}}$$

This example uses $n^* = 5$ with $m = 6$ subgroups, so $n = 30$. The thirty units in the sample might also be divided into other subgroups, such as fifteen subgroups of two units each, ten subgroups of three units each, or five subgroups of six units each. Thus the method provides many choices depending on the product and the methods of sampling, testing, and recording the observed data selected for use from a practical and profitable point of view.

The tables tabulate and summarize a week's data. Thirty observations are recorded for the five working days in a week. The specified limits for individual units of resistance are 10.0 ± 0.5 ohms, i.e., 9.5 ohms minimum and 10.5 ohms maximum. For the 150 observations recorded, only one nonconforming unit was observed, in the second lot on Friday. It shows a value of 9.4 ohms, less than the specified lower limit for individual units of 9.5 ohms. Thus all the data are included in setting the standards proposed. Table 6.29 gives the 150 observed values used in this example, while table 6.30 gives a summary of average and range values for the data in table 6.29.

Table 6.29 has summarized the data with respect to average and range values in such a form that the techniques covered in the discussion of the use of the analysis of variance methods may be readily applied. What factor contributes most to the total variation in the resistance value? When the control charts show lack of control and a search must be made for its cause, the breakdown in table 6.29 shows how much variability is contributed by variations within samples, variations between lots, and variations from day to day during the week. Control charts for averages and ranges can be made for an n^* value of six rather than five, where six represents the number of lots made per day. Since these data are seemingly well controlled at desired levels, control charts are not needed for controlling variations within lots, since adding more control charts increases the costs.

The central lines (CL) and the three-sigma control lines based on these data are given below.

Control Charts for Subgroups of $n^* = 5$ Units
Central Lines

$$\text{Averages:}\quad \bar{\bar{X}} = \frac{\Sigma X}{n} = \frac{1500.0}{150} = 10.00 \text{ ohms}$$

$$\text{or}\quad \bar{\bar{X}} = \frac{\Sigma \bar{X}}{m} = \frac{300.00}{30} = 10.00 \text{ ohms}$$

$$\text{Ranges:}\quad \bar{R} = \frac{\Sigma R}{m} = \frac{16.2}{30} = 0.54$$

TABLE 6.29 Weekly Measurements of Resistance; $n^* = 5$ per Lot; 6 Lots per Day Resistor, Engineering Limits: 10.0 ± 0.5 Ohms

Sample Number	*Resistance Measured to Nearest 0.1 Ohm; Lot Numbers* 1	2	3	4	5	6	*Sum*	*Range*
				MONDAY				
1	9.8	10.1	9.9	10.2	10.3	9.7	60.0	0.6
2	9.7	10.2	10.1	10.0	10.1	9.8	59.9	0.5
3	10.1	9.8	10.2	9.9	10.3	9.5	59.8	0.8
4	10.2	9.7	10.3	10.3	9.9	10.1	60.5	0.6
5	9.9	10.3	9.8	10.1	9.8	9.9	59.8	0.5
Sum	49.7	50.1	50.3	50.5	50.4	49.0	300.0	3.0
Average	9.94	10.02	10.06	10.10	10.08	9.80	60.00	0.60
Range	0.5	0.6	0.5	0.4	0.5	0.6	3.1	$\bar{R} = 0.62$
				TUESDAY				
6	10.0	10.2	9.9	10.1	9.9	9.7	59.8	0.5
7	9.7	10.1	10.2	9.9	9.6	10.3	59.8	0.7
8	9.6	9.9	10.3	9.8	10.2	10.2	60.0	0.7
9	10.1	9.6	10.0	10.0	10.1	10.5	60.3	0.9
10	10.0	9.7	9.8	10.2	9.8	10.6	60.1	0.9
Sum	49.4	49.5	50.2	50.0	49.6	51.3	300.0	3.7
Average	9.88	9.90	10.04	10.00	9.92	10.26	60.00	0.74
Range	0.5	0.6	0.5	0.4	0.6	0.9	3.5	$\bar{R} = 0.70$
				WEDNESDAY				
11	10.2	9.9	10.3	9.9	9.7	10.1	60.1	0.6
12	9.8	10.1	9.9	10.1	9.9	9.9	59.7	0.3
13	9.7	9.7	10.2	10.3	10.0	10.3	60.2	0.6
14	10.1	10.2	9.7	9.8	9.8	9.7	59.3	0.5
15	10.0	10.3	10.1	10.0	10.1	10.2	60.7	0.3
Sum	49.8	50.2	50.2	50.1	49.5	50.2	300.0	2.3
Average	9.96	10.04	10.04	10.02	9.90	10.04	60.00	0.46
Range	0.5	0.6	0.6	0.5	0.4	0.6	3.2	$\bar{R} = 0.64$
				THURSDAY				
16	10.2	9.7	10.0	9.7	10.2	10.1	59.9	0.5
17	10.3	10.1	9.8	10.2	9.9	10.3	60.6	0.5
18	9.9	10.0	9.6	9.9	9.7	9.9	59.0	0.4
19	10.1	9.8	10.1	10.0	10.0	10.0	60.0	0.3
20	10.2	9.6	10.3	9.8	10.2	10.4	60.5	0.8
Sum	50.7	49.2	49.8	49.6	50.0	50.7	300.0	2.5
Average	10.14	9.84	9.96	9.92	10.00	10.14	60.0	0.50
Range	0.4	0.5	0.7	0.5	0.5	0.5	3.1	$\bar{R} = 0.62$

Sample Number	*Resistance Measured to Nearest 0.1 Ohm; Lot Numbers* 1	2	3	4	5	6	Sum	Range
				FRIDAY				
21	10.1	9.7	10.2	9.9	10.0	10.5	60.4	0.8
22	10.0	10.1	10.3	10.1	9.9	10.1	60.5	0.4
23	10.2	9.9	10.1	10.3	9.8	10.2	60.5	0.5
24	10.3	9.5	9.8	9.8	10.0	10.0	59.4	0.8
25	9.8	9.4	9.7	9.7	10.2	10.4	60.2	1.0
Sum	50.4	48.6	50.1	49.8	49.9	51.2	300.0	3.5
Average	10.08	9.72	10.02	9.96	9.98	10.24	60.0	0.70
Range	0.5	0.7	0.6	0.6	0.4	0.5	3.3	$\bar{R} = 0.66$
				TOTAL FOR WEEK				
Sum, $\bar{X}$	50.00	49.52	50.12	50.00	49.88	50.48	300.00	$\bar{R}_{\bar{X}} = 0.328$
Sum, R	2.4	3.0	2.9	2.4	2.4	3.1	16.2	$\bar{R}_R = 0.648$
Average, $\bar{X}$	10.000	9.904	10.024	10.000	9.976	10.096	60.000	0.192
Range, $\bar{R}$	0.48	0.60	0.58	0.48	0.48	0.62	3.24	0.14

Control Lines (Reference: Table 6.19)

Averages: $\text{UCL} = 10.00 + 0.58(0.54) = 10.00 + 0.3132 = 10.31$

$A_2 = 0.58$

$\text{LCL} = 10.00 - 0.58(0.54) = 10.00 - 0.3132 = 9.69$

Ranges: $\text{UCL} = 2.11(0.54) = 1.1394 = 1.14$

$D_1 = 2.11$

$D_2 = 0$ $\quad \text{LCL} = 0(0.54) = 0$

Control charts for the data for the resistors are given in figure 6-29. These are the only control charts that would be applied, for all practical purposes.

Most tables covering range values do not go beyond $n = 20$ or $n = 25$, so if $n = 30$, we cannot find values in a table. For these larger sample sizes, the standard deviation is generally used. To complete this illustrative example, control charts for $\bar{X}$ and R based on $\bar{R}$ for $n = 30$ are developed here to use as a guide when preparing similar control charts. From the data for resistors in table 6.29, where $n = 30$, five values are listed for the average values that are tabulated for each of the working days in a week. The values that occur in this example have all been arbitrarily made equal for simplification, and would probably never occur when obtaining actual measured values. Each day has an average of *exactly* 10.00 ohms since the sum of each day's thirty observations is 300.00 ohms. The

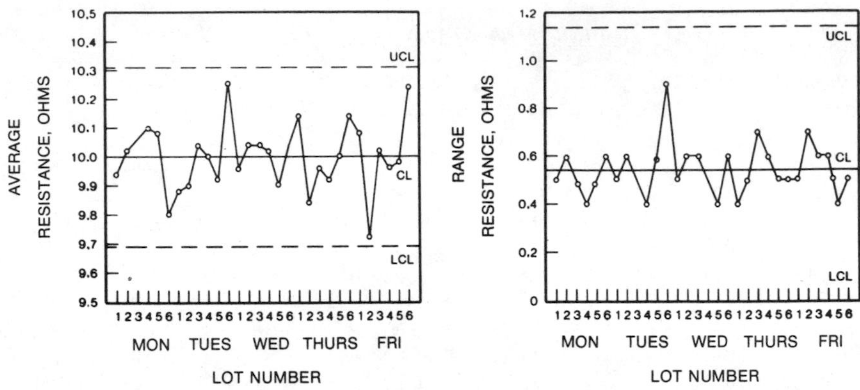

Figure 6–29 Control charts for $\bar{X}$ and R by subgroups, $n^* = 5$, $n = 30$: resistors.

data for ranges is found each day by subtracting the minimum observed value from the maximum observed value in each set of thirty readings of the resistance of these resistors. The data for the averages $\bar{X}$ and ranges R for $n = 30$ are as follows.

TABLE 6.30 Average and Range Values for $n = 30$ Resistors

Day	*Average,* $\bar{X}$	*Range R (Max. − Min.)*
Monday	10.00 ohms	10.3 − 9.5 = 0.8 ohms
Tuesday	10.00 ohms	10.6 − 9.6 = 1.0 ohms
Wednesday	10.00 ohms	10.3 − 9.7 = 0.6 ohms
Thursday	10.00 ohms	10.4 − 9.6 = 0.8 ohms
Friday	10.00 ohms	10.5 − 9.4 = 1.1 ohms
Sum	50.00	4.3
Average	$\bar{\bar{X}} = 10.00$ ohms	$\bar{R} = 0.86$ ohm

Use methods previously given for determining the three-sigma control limit lines for both $\bar{X}$ and R, where $\bar{R}$ is derived from the observed data. The equations that apply are given in table 6.24 as equations (16) and (17). Table 6.1 gives values of A_2, D_3, and D_4, which apply when $\bar{R}$ is known or computed. It also gives values of d_2 and d_3, but only for numbers up to and including $n = 25$. Table 6.19 gives A_2, D_3, and D_4 for numbers up to and including $n = 20$, and table 6.23 shows values of d_2 for some numbers less than or equal to 1000. For $n = 30$, table 6.23 gives $d_2 = 4.08552$, to six significant figures, whereas table 6.18 gives $d_2 = 4.086$, to only four significant figures. To obtain values for D_3 and D_4, it is necessary to estimate a value for d_3. Good estimates for d_3, D_3, and D_4 are derived from the information in table 6.1, using extrapolation, as follows.

$$A_2 = \frac{3}{d_2\sqrt{n}}$$

For $n = 30$,

$$\sqrt{30} = 5.4772 \quad \text{and} \quad d_2 = 4.08552$$

hence

$$A_2 = \frac{3}{(4.08552)(5.4772)} = \frac{3}{22.37721} = 0.134065$$

From equation (17), $D_3 = 1 - 3d_3/d_2$, and $D_4 = 1 + 3d_3/d_2$. Only four significant figures need to be used, since d_3 can only be estimated to three significant figures. From table 6.1, by extrapolation, $d_3 = 0.695$. Thus the factor $d_3/d_2 = 0.695/4.086 = 0.170093 = 0.170$. Hence, for $n = 30$, the best estimates for D_3 and D_4 are: $D_3 = 1 - 3(0.170) = 1 - 0.510 = 0.490$ and $D_4 = 1 + 3(0.170) = 1 + 0.510 = 1.510$. Using table 6.1 to extrapolate directly gives the same values for D_3 and D_4.

Control charts based on $\bar{R}$ for $n = 30$ are given in figure 6-30, with values in ohms.

Center Lines Averages: $\bar{\bar{X}} = \dfrac{50.00}{5} = 10.00$; Ranges: $\bar{R} = \dfrac{4.3}{5} = 0.86.$

Averages: UCL $= 10.00 + (0.1341)(0.86) = 10.00 + 0.1153 = 10.115$

Control Lines LCL $= 10.00 - (0.1341)(0.86) = 10.00 - 0.1153 = 9.8847$

Ranges: UCL $= 1.510(0.86) = 1.299$;
LCL $= 0.490(0.86) = 0.421$

Using these range values for the complete sample of thirty resistors shows no lack of control, and indicates very little variation in the quality of the units and daily results. The recommended set of charts is an excellent pair of charts. One high and one low average value is shown, along with one high range value, but the results indicate that the process is well controlled even though one nonconforming unit was observed in the total sample of 150 units for the week. In contrast to the use of range values, standard deviation values will next be computed

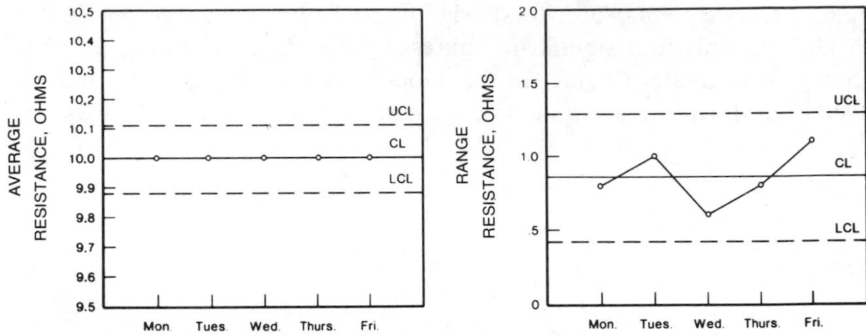

Figure 6–30 Control charts for $\bar{X}$ and R for $n = 30$ by days for resistors.

and presented for comparison purposes. The procedure will show how to obtain repeated estimates of standard deviation values by the use of ranges in conjunction with proper applicable d_2 factors.

Standard Deviation Values Derived from Range Values

Assuming a normal law distribution for the population or universe, standard deviation values may be estimated from the relation $\sigma'_e = \bar{R}/d_2$, where the d_2 values depend on the sample size. For the entire sample of thirty units, $\bar{R} = 0.86$ as the sum of the five R values for the five working days of the week is 4.3. Thus $\sigma'_e = 0.86/4.086 = 0.210475$, where d_2 was obtained from table 6.18. Next determine values of σ'_e for $n = 30$ from each of the sets of six subgroups, the six lots produced during a working day. Each of these contains $n^* = 5$ units. The daily estimate of σ_e is shown in table 6.31, where $d_2 = 2.326$ from table 6.18.

TABLE 6.31 Estimated Daily σ_e Values for Resistors

Monday	Sum $R = 3.1$	hence $\bar{R} = 0.62$	$\sigma'_e = \dfrac{0.62}{2.326} = 0.2665520$
Tuesday	Sum $R = 3.5$	hence $\bar{R} = 0.70$	$\sigma'_e = \dfrac{0.70}{2.326} = 0.3009458$
Wednesday	Sum $R = 3.2$	hence $\bar{R} = 0.64$	$\sigma'_e = \dfrac{0.64}{2.326} = 0.2751505$
Thursday	Sum $R = 3.1$	hence $\bar{R} = 0.62$	$\sigma'_e = \dfrac{0.62}{2.326} = 0.2665520$
Friday	Sum $R = 3.3$	hence $\bar{R} = 0.66$	$\sigma'_e = \dfrac{0.66}{2.326} = 0.2837489$
			Sum $= 1.3929492$
			$\bar{\sigma}_e = 0.2785898$

Since σ'_e was based on five samples of thirty units each, it is really based on only ten of the 150 observations, two for each day of the week, which is not a very efficient measure of the actual variability. The $\bar{\sigma}_e$ derived from the subgroup ranges is based on sixty of the 150 observations and thus provides a better estimate of the true standard deviation for this process. Since it is an average value, it should be corrected by the use of the c_2 factor used to derive σ' from $\bar{\sigma}$ for the sample size involved. Table 6.5 gives the relations that apply. Table 6.7 gives the values of A_1, B_3, and B_4 that are used as multiplying factors for $\bar{\sigma}$. For $n^* = 5$, their values are $A_1 = 1.60$, $B_3 = 0$, and $B_4 = 2.09$. Control limits for each of the thirty subgroups may be determined from the $\bar{\sigma}$ value, 0.2786. The control limits obtained by using these values of B_3 and B_4 will apply to the following σ'_e values for subgroups.

For $n^* = 5$, $c_2 = 0.8407$ (from table 6.1); hence $\sigma'_e = \dfrac{0.2785898}{0.8407} = 0.3314$.

Control chart values for $n^* = 5$ for estimated σ_e based on ranges for subgroups are:

Central Value: $\bar{\sigma}_e = 0.2786$.

Control Line Limits: $\text{UCL} = B_4\sigma_e = 2.09(0.2786) = 0.5823$

$\text{LCL} = B_3\sigma_e = 0(0.2786) = 0$.

The largest range value listed for $n^* = 5$ in table 6.28 is 0.9. For this R value, $\sigma_e = R/d_2 = 0.9/2.326 = 0.3869$; hence all subgroup σ_e values are within these control limits. The above estimate of σ', denoted by σ_e, includes variations between subgroups. Using the σ'_e based on the five daily range values for $n = 30$ gives $\sigma'_e = 0.2105$. Using this estimate provides tighter controls on the variability. Control limit lines are next developed for n^* and n values of five and thirty, respectively. These limits may then be used to check for control without drawing the charts, as all points in most cases are well within their respective control limits.

Control chart values for $n^* = 5$ for estimated σ_e based on ranges for the total daily sample, with the standard assumed being $\sigma'_e = 0.2105$, are given below. Factors for $n^* = 5$ from tables 6.7 and 6.1 are also given.

Central Value: $\bar{\sigma}_e = d_2\sigma' = 0.8407(0.2105) = 0.1770$, with

$A_1 = 1.60$, $B_3 = 0$, and $B_4 = 2.09$.

Control Line Limits: $\text{UCL} = B_4\bar{\sigma}_e = 2.09(0.170) = 0.3637$

$\text{LCL} = B_3\bar{\sigma}_e = 0(0.170) = 0$

If σ'_e is used, then the factors for $n^* = 5$ from tables 6.1 and 6.6 are $A = 1.34$, $B_1 = 0$, and $B_2 = 1.76$. Using these factors gives $\text{UCL} = B_2\sigma' = 1.76(0.2105) = 0.3705$ and $\text{LCL} = B_1\sigma'_e = 0(0.2105) = 0$. These two methods of computation are given to show that, even when using four significant figures for these factors, the limits may only be good to only two significant figures. Limit values and probabilities associated with them agree within a small area of doubt, but may not always agree identically unless one carries the factors and computations out to a large number of significant figures.

Since the data originally were compiled in terms of ranges, the factors for ranges based on the standard σ'_e are $D_1 = 0$ and $D_2 = 4.92$, from these same tables.

Control limit lines for ranges are UCL $= D_2\sigma'_e = 4.92(0.2105) = 1.036$ and LCL $= 0$. Actually, table 6.1 gives D_2 as 4.918. Using this factor gives UCL $=$ 1.0352. These tables do not give a factor by which to multiply the average standard deviation, $\bar{\sigma}_e$, but one may be obtained by using the c_2 factor. Thus a D_2^* value is given by D_2/c_2. For $n^* = 5$, this gives D_2^* as 4.918/0.8407 or 4.918(1.1894), from table 6.1. Using division gives D_2^* as 5.8498870 and using multiplication gives D_2^* as 5.8494692. Using 5.849 together with the average value 0.1770 gives UCL $= 5.849(0.1770) = 1.035273$, while using 5.850 gives 1.03545. Thus the UCL value to be used is 1.04. Since recorded ranges are given only to the tenth place, then 1.0 is within limits and 1.1 is a point out of control.

Even with the narrower limits for the measures of variability, the largest range for these data is only 0.9, well within the control limits. Such is not the case when estimates of σ_e derived from the ranges are charted against these tighter control limits. Values of an estimate of the standard deviation for the thirty observations are given in table 6.31 for each working day of the week. These values will be checked against the tighter standard and the control limits based on that standard.

Control chart values for $n = 30$ for estimated daily σ_e values based on $\bar{R}$ for $m = 6$ subgroups, with $n^* = 5$ for each and with $d_2 = 2.326$ are given next.

Factors for n = 30 from tables 6.6 and 6.18

$c_2 = 0.9748$; $A = 0.55$; $B_1 = 0.59$; and $B_2 = 1.36$ for σ' values.

Standard: $\sigma'_e = 0.2105$.

Central Line: $\bar{\sigma}_e = \dfrac{0.2105}{0.9748} = 0.215942$

Control Line Limits: UCL $= 1.36(0.2105) = 0.2863$

LCL $= 0.59(0.2105) = 0.1242$

Analysis: For these tighter control limits the σ_e value of 0.30095 for Tuesday's sample of thirty units is just outside the UCL value of 0.2863. Hence production results for the manufacturing process in operation on Tuesday should be studied to determine if there is an assignable cause for this larger value for the total variability on that day.

NOTE: To complete this illustrative example, use will be made of the more efficient measure of variability, the variance and standard deviation. This study will help those examining this method of analysis to determine whether the range values are sufficiently valid to justify use in place of the more costly and complex computations with standard deviation values. When computer facilities are available, the standard deviation control charts are generally used. However, in some auto industries, only control charts for ranges are utilized. Summaries of computations for the standard deviation values will be given, rather than all the detailed computations.

The Standard Deviation Control Charts for Resistor Data for σ'_e Values given in table 6.31 is presented in figure 6-31. These data are very uniform.

The use of standard deviation values for control charts is considerably more efficient than use of range values, possibly even indicating lack of control earlier than would be shown by the use of ranges. To check this assumption, control charts based on actual computed standard deviation values derived from the data for this resistor example are presented for comparison purposes, and also to show how best to prepare such control charts. Standard deviation values are computed for the thirty subgroups with $n^* = 5$ and also for the five daily samples of thirty units each; as a check, an overall standard deviation value is also computed from the total of 150 resistors.

Values of X and X^2 are first tabulated for each of the thirty subgroups. These values, when summed, are used to compute the variance and the standard deviation for each subgroup, for the daily samples, and for all of the 150 observations. Table 6.32 presents one of these computations made for each subgroup of five units in detail.

It is not only necessary for quality control personnel to know how to set up the best possible control charts in trouble areas, but also to be able to analyze these charts and determine where to seek the assignable causes for poor quality. When a period of poor quality is indicated by the preliminary analysis of such data, other statistical techniques may be helpful. In this example, the level of quality is maintained at the specified value of 10.00 ohms, but the variability in some

TABLE 6.32 Example of Computations for Variance and Standard Deviation Subgroup of Resistor Values in Ohms, $n^* = 5$

Sample Number	*Resistance, X*	*X Values Squared,* X^2
1	9.8	96.04
2	9.7	94.09
3	10.1	102.01
4	10.2	104.04
5	9.9	98.01
Sum	49.7	494.19
Average, $\bar{X}$	9.94	98.8380
Range, R	0.5	$\bar{X}^2 =$ 98.8036
		$v =$ 0.0344
Standard Deviation, $\sigma'_e = \dfrac{\bar{R}}{d_2}$	0.2150	$\sigma =$ 0.1855

NOTE: For an n^* value of 5, the d_2 factor is obtained from table 6.1, table 6.18, table 6.21, table 6.23 and table 6.26 as 2.326.

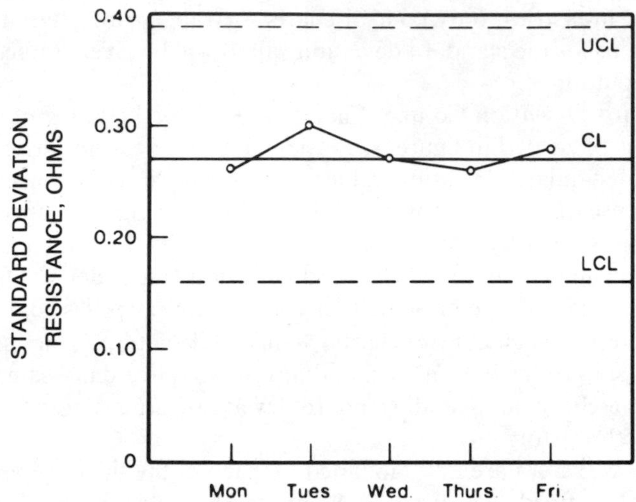

Resistance R, ohms	Monday		Tuesday		Frequencies Wednesday		Thursday		Friday		Week	
9.4									I	1	I	1
Min. 9.5	I	1							I	1	II	2
9.6			III	3			II	2			IIII	5
9.7	III	3	III	3	𝍸	5	III	3	III	3	𝍸 𝍸 𝍸 II	17
9.8	𝍸	5	III	3	III	3	III	3	IIII	4	𝍸 𝍸 𝍸 III	18
9.9	𝍸	5	IIII	4	𝍸	5	IIII	4	III	3	𝍸 𝍸 𝍸 𝍸 I	21
10.0	I	1	IIII	4	III	3	𝍸	5	IIII	4	𝍸 𝍸 𝍸 II	17
10.1	𝍸 I	6	IIII	4	𝍸 I	6	IIII	4	𝍸	5	𝍸 𝍸 𝍸 𝍸 𝍸	25
10.2	IIII	4	𝍸	5	IIII	4	𝍸	5	IIII	4	𝍸 𝍸 𝍸 𝍸 II	22
10.3	𝍸	5	II	2	IIII	4	III	3	III	3	𝍸 𝍸 𝍸 II	17
10.4							I	1	I	1	II	2
Max. 10.5			I	1					I	1	II	2
10.6			I	1							I	1
		30		30		30		30		30		150

Figure 6–31 Control chart for estimates of σ' from range values ($m = 6, n^* = 5, —n = 30$); σ'_e values for daily samples in one week listed in Table 6–31.

cases appears to be excessive. Is the distribution of resistance values satisfactory from day to day or is the variability excessive on some particular day of the week? Using subgroups as a breakdown, is the variability controlled lot by lot or is there a radical change in variability at different times of the day? A tally of the various possible distributions is a useful guide. Figure 6-32 presents the sample distributions to show the spread from day to day.

It may be possible that the time of the day causes excessive variations in the resistance values produced by the manufacturing process. Six different lots were made each day, per schedule. Figure 6-32 presents the sample distributions, lot by lot, to facilitate this study. This shows variations during a day.

Resistance R, ohms	Lot 1		Lot 2		Lot 3		Lot 4		Lot 5		Lot 6		Total 6 Lots	
9.4			I	1									I	1
Min. 9.5			I	1							I	1	II	2
9.6	I	1	II	2	I	1			I	1			~~IIII~~	5
9.7	III	3	~~IIII~~	5	II	2	II	2	II	2	III	3	~~IIII~~ ~~IIII~~ ~~IIII~~ II	17
9.8	III	3	II	2	IIII	4	IIII	4	IIII	4	I	1	~~IIII~~ ~~IIII~~ ~~IIII~~ III	18
9.9	II	2	III	3	III	3	~~IIII~~	5	~~IIII~~	5	III	3	~~IIII~~ ~~IIII~~ ~~IIII~~ ~~IIII~~ I	21
10.0	IIII	4	I	1	II	2	IIII	4	IIII	4	II	2	~~IIII~~ ~~IIII~~ ~~IIII~~ II	17
10.1	~~IIII~~	5	~~IIII~~	5	IIII	4	IIII	4	III	3	IIII	4	~~IIII~~ ~~IIII~~ ~~IIII~~ ~~IIII~~ ~~IIII~~	25
10.2	~~IIII~~	5	III	3	IIII	4	III	3	IIII	4	III	3	~~IIII~~ ~~IIII~~ ~~IIII~~ ~~IIII~~ II	22
10.3	II	2	II	2	~~IIII~~	5	III	3	II	2	III	3	~~IIII~~ ~~IIII~~ ~~IIII~~ II	17
10.4											II	2	II	2
Max. 10.5											II	2	II	2
10.6											I	1	I	1
Sum:		25		25		25		25		25		25		150

Figure 6–32

TABLE 6.33 Summary of $\overline{X}$ and σ Values: $m = 30$ Subgroups with $n^* = 5$ Observed Resistance Values in Ohms for Week's Production of Resistors

Lot Number:	†1	†2	†3	†4	†5	†6	*All*
			MONDAY				
Sum ΣX	49.7	50.1	50.3	50.5	50.4	49.0	300.0
Sum ΣX^2	494.19	502.27	506.19	510.15	508.24	480.40	3,001.44
Average, $\overline{X}$	9.94	10.02	10.06	10.10	10.08	9.80	10.00
Variance, v	0.0344	0.0436	0.0344	0.0200	0.0416	0.0400	0.0480
Standard Deviation, σ	0.18547	0.20881	0.18547	0.14142	0.20396	0.20000	0.21909
			TUESDAY				
Sum ΣX	49.4	49.5	50.2	50.0	49.6	51.3	300.0
Sum ΣX^2	488.26	490.31	504.18	500.10	492.26	526.83	3,001.94
Average, X	9.88	9.90	10.04	10.00	9.92	10.26	10.00
Variance, v	0.0376	0.0520	0.0344	0.0200	0.0456	0.0984	0.06466
Standard Deviation, σ	0.19391	0.22804	0.18547	0.14142	0.21354	0.31369	0.25430
			WEDNESDAY				
Sum ΣX	49.8	50.2	50.2	50.1	49.5	50.2	300.00
Sum ΣX^2	496.18	504.24	504.24	502.15	496.15	504.24	3,001.20
Average, $\overline{X}$	9.96	10.04	10.04	10.02	9.90	10.04	10.00
Variance, v	0.0344	0.0464	0.0464	0.0296	0.0200	0.0464	0.0400
Standard Deviation, σ	0.1853	0.21541	0.21541	0.17205	0.14142	0.21541	0.20000
			THURSDAY				
Sum ΣX	50.7	49.2	49.8	49.6	50.0	50.7	300.0
Sum ΣX^2	514.19	484.30	496.30	492.18	500.18	514.27	3,001.42
Average, $\overline{X}$	10.14	9.84	9.96	9.92	10.00	10.14	10.00
Variance, v	0.0184	0.0344	0.0584	0.0296	0.0360	0.0344	0.04733
Standard Deviation, σ	0.13565	0.18547	0.24166	0.17205	0.18974	0.18547	0.21756
			FRIDAY				
Sum ΣX	50.4	48.6	50.1	49.8	49.9	51.2	300.0
Sum ΣX^2	508.18	472.72	502.27	496.24	498.09	524.46	3,001.96
Average, $\overline{X}$	10.08	9.72	10.02	9.96	9.98	10.24	10.00
Variance, v	0.0296	0.0656	0.0536	0.0464	0.0176	0.0344	0.06533
Standard Deviation, σ	0.17205	0.25612	0.23152	0.21541	0.13266	0.18547	0.25560
			TOTAL FOR WEEK				
Sum ΣX	250.0	247.6	250.6	250.0	249.4	252.4	1,500.0
Sum ΣX^2	2501.00	2453.84	2513.18	2500.82	2488.92	2550.20	15,007.96
Average, $\overline{X}^*$	10.000	9.904	10.024	10.000	9.976	10.096	(60.000) 10.000
Average, $\overline{X^2}$	100.040000	98.153600	100.527200	100.032800	99.556800	102.008000	100.05306667
Subtract, $\overline{X}^{*2}$	−100.000000	−98.089216	−100.480576	−100.000000	−99.520576	−101.929216	−100.00000000
Variance, v	0.040000	0.064384	0.046624	0.032800	0.036224	0.078784	0.05306667
Standard Deviation, σ	0.20000	0.25373	0.21593	0.18111	0.19033	0.28068	0.230362

To completely analyze these data, a table giving the X and X^2 values for each of the thirty subgroups was compiled and all the above standard deviation values

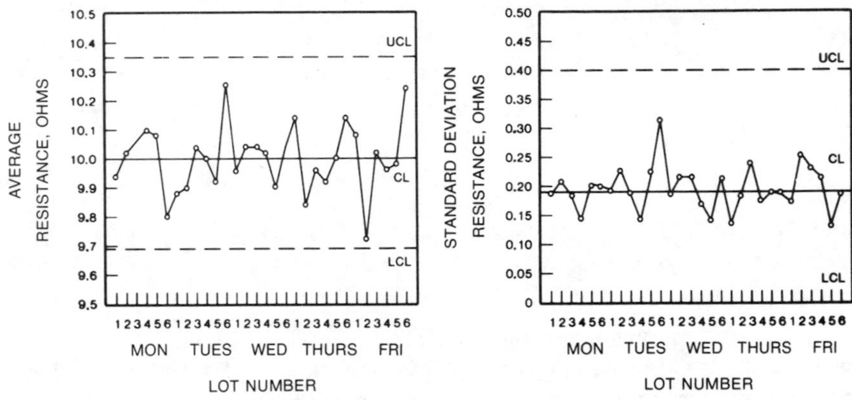

Figure 6–33 Control charts for $\bar{X}$ and $\bar{\sigma}$ values, resistance in ohms (Table 6–33).

TABLE 6.34 Simplified Computation of Standard Deviation Values Using Y Scale for 150 Resistance Values by Days and for Entire Week Specified: Resistance $R = 10.0 \pm 0.5$ Ohms; X-Scale Interval $i = 0.1$; Y-Scale Interval $i = 1$; Origin $Y = 0$ is $X_0 = 9.4$ Ohms

$$\bar{X} = X_0 + i\bar{Y}; \quad \sigma_X = i\sigma_Y; \quad \sigma_Y = \quad v_Y; \quad v_X = \sigma_X^2$$

Res.	New Scale	Square	Monday			Tuesday			Wednesday			Thursday			Friday			Week		
X	Y	Y^2	f	$f(Y)$	$f(Y^2)$	f	$f(Y)$	$f(Y^2)$	f	$f(Y)$	$f(Y^2)$	f	$f(Y)$	$f(Y^2)$	f	$f(Y)$	$f(Y^2)$	f	$f(Y)$	$f(Y^2)$
9.4	0	0													1	0	0	1	0	0
9.5	1	1	1	1	1										1	1	1	2	2	2
9.6	2	4				3	6	12				2	4	8				5	10	20
9.7	3	9	3	9	27	3	9	27	5	15	45	3	9	27	3	9	27	17	51	153
9.8	4	16	5	20	80	3	12	48	3	12	48	3	12	48	4	16	64	18	72	288
9.9	5	25	5	25	125	4	20	100	5	25	125	4	20	100	3	15	75	21	105	525
10.0	6	36	1	6	36	4	24	144	3	18	108	5	30	180	4	24	144	17	102	612
10.1	7	49	6	42	294	4	28	196	6	42	294	4	28	196	5	35	245	25	175	1225
10.2	8	64	4	32	256	5	40	320	4	32	256	5	40	320	4	32	256	22	176	1408
10.3	9	81	5	45	405	2	18	162	4	36	324	3	27	243	3	27	243	17	153	1377
10.4	10	100										1	10	100	1	10	100	2	20	200
10.5	11	121				1	11	121							1	11	121	2	22	242
10.6	12	144				1	12	144										1	12	144
	SUM		30	180	1224	30	180	1274	30	180	1200	30	180	1222	30	180	1276	150	900	6196
Averages $\bar{Y}$			6			6			6			6			6			6		
$\Sigma\bar{Y}^2$					40.8000			42.4667			40.0000			40.7333			42.5333			41.306667
Subtract $\bar{Y}^2$					−36.0000			−36.0000			−36.0000			−36.0000			−36.0000			−36.00000
Variance (Y), u_Y					4.8000			6.4667			4.0000			4.7333			6.5333			5.306667
Standard Deviation, σ_Y					2.1909			2.5430			2.0000			2.1766			2.5560			2.30362
$\bar{X} = 9.4 + 0.1\bar{Y}$					10.00			10.00			10.00			10.00			10.00			10.00
$\sigma_X = 0.1\sigma_Y$					0.21909			0.25430			0.20000			0.21756			0.25560			0.230362

were evaluated. From this detailed table, the pertinent data required to find averages, variances, and standard deviations for these data daily and by lots has been summarized in table 6.33. These results are then presented on control charts in the same form as those previously used to measure variability with range values.

When processing any data, one of the most important steps is to devise a method to check the results obtained for accuracy. This is especially true when utilizing computer programs, as the printed results are only as good as the data that has been entered into the computer program. Also, when determining standard deviation values, a simpler method of manual as well as computer evaluation is provided by using another scale in place of the larger scale value involved in obtaining the measurements or observations. This may be termed a Y scale, starting with 0 with an interval i of 1. Table 6.34 illustrates the use of this method for these resistance values.

There are many different methods of obtaining the best estimate of the true standard deviation for this population of resistors for the characteristic resistance, measured in ohms. These are tabulated in table 6.35 and the best estimate is selected for use in preparing control charts for standard deviations.

TABLE 6.35 Different Estimates of σ' for Resistance Data for $m = 30$ Subgroups of $n^* = 5$ Resistors by Days (5) and Lots (6)—One Week's Production

Method	*Number of Subgroups, m*	*Units per Subgroup, n**	*Average Standard Deviation,* $\bar{\sigma}$	*Factor* c_2 *Value*[(a)]	*Estimated Standard Deviation,* $\sigma' = \frac{\bar{\sigma}}{c_2}$
1	30	5	0.19499*	0.8407	0.23194*
2	5 (Days)	30	0.22931	0.9748	0.23524[(c)]
3	6 (Lots)	25	0.22030	0.9696	0.22720* 0.23435[(d)]
4	1 (Week)	150	0.23036	0.9950[(b)]	0.23152

NOTES: (*a*) For assumed normal distribution for the parent population, the distribution of standard deviations differs slightly from normal, and c_2 is the factor used for determining σ' from $\bar{\sigma}$, where c_2 varies with n and is determined from the relation:

$$c_2 = \sqrt{\frac{2}{n}}\frac{\left(\frac{n-2}{2}\right)!}{\left(\frac{n-3}{2}\right)!} = \sqrt{\frac{2}{n}}\frac{\Gamma\left(\frac{n}{2}\right)}{\Gamma\left[\left(\frac{n-2}{2}\right)+\frac{1}{2}\right]} = \sqrt{\frac{2}{n}}\frac{\Gamma\left(\frac{n}{2}\right)}{\Gamma\left(\frac{n-1}{2}\right)}, \quad \text{since} \quad \left(\frac{n-3}{2}\right) = \Gamma\left(\frac{n-1}{2}\right)$$

c_2 is given in table 6.18 for n values of 2 through 100; hence above equation was used to obtain c_2 for $n = 150$ as noted under (b).

(*b*) For $n = 150$, c_2 is determined as follows:

$$c_2 = \sqrt{\frac{2}{150}}\,\frac{\Gamma(75)}{\Gamma(74 + \frac{1}{2})} = \frac{\sqrt{3}}{15}\left(\frac{3.30788544 \times 10^{107}}{3.8388487 \times 10^{106}}\right)$$

$$= \left(\frac{1.73205081}{15}\right)(8.616868) = 0.11547054(8.616868) = 0.9949902 = 0.9950$$

In the above, the values of $\Gamma(n)$ have been taken from table 6.3, p. 273, *Handbook of Mathematical Functions with Formulas, Graphs, and Mathematical Tables,* National Bureau of Standards, Applied Mathematics Series 55, U.S. Government Printing Office, Washington, D.C., March, 1965.

(*c*) All daily averages $\bar{X}$ are equal to 10.00 as in table 6.33, so the variations between averages is zero.

(*d*) Four of six average lot values differ as in table 6.33, so variance between lots is 0.0032973, determined from averages. The average variance within lots is 0.0516216; hence the total variance is their sum, which is 0.0549190. The best estimate of the standard deviation for this method is 0.234348, its square root.

* Average standard deviation value and expected standard, $\bar{\sigma}$ and σ', are deemed the best estimate of the true values for the process. Used in the control charts in figure 6.33.

Analysis of above table: It should be noted that there is practically no difference between the estimates of the standard deviation to three significant figures. These values are 0.232, 0.235, 0.234, and 0.232. Thus methods 1 and 4 have the same value for σ'. The values of $\bar{\sigma}$ and σ' determined by method 1 are used below in determining the central lines and the three-sigma control limits using σ' as a standard. The center line (CL) and the three-sigma control lines based on this standard value of σ' are given below.

The following information is used in the control charts for subgroups of $n^* = 5$ units.

References

Formulas: Tables 6.3, 6.5 and 6.20

Factors: Tables 6.1, 6.6, 6.7, 6.21 and 6.26

Center Lines

Averages: $\bar{\bar{X}} = \frac{\Sigma X}{n} = \frac{1500.0}{150} = \frac{300.00}{30} = 10.00$ ohms

Standard Deviation: $\bar{\sigma} = 0.195$ ohm (value given in table 6.35 for method 1, where $\sigma' = 0.232$)

Control Lines

Averages:

Factors: For use with σ': $A = 1.342$

For use with $\bar{\sigma}$: $A_1 = 1.596$

$\text{UCL} = 10.00 + 1.342(0.232) = 10.00 + 0.311 = 10.31$ ohms or

$\text{UCL} = 10.00 + 1.596(0.195) = 10.00 + 0.311 = 10.31$ ohms

$\text{LCL} = 10.00 - 1.596(0.195) = 10.00 - 1.342(0.232) = 9.69$ ohms

$$\text{Standard Deviations}\begin{cases}\text{Factors:} & \text{For use with } \sigma'\text{: } B_1 = 0,\ B_2 = 1.756\\ & \text{For use with } \bar{\sigma}\text{: } B_3 = 0,\ B_4 = 2.089\\ \text{UCL} = 1.756(0.232) = 0.4074 \text{ ohm or} & \\ \text{UCL} = 2.089(0.195) = 0.4074 \text{ ohm} & \\ \text{LCL} = 0(0.195) = 0(0.232) = 0 \text{ ohm} & \end{cases}$$

Control charts for the resistor data, given below in figure 6-34, should be compared with those in figure 6-29 which were based on ranges. These charts use the center lines and control limit lines given above.

In the previous presentation using range values, figure 6-30 showed graphical control charts for averages and ranges where statistics based on thirty observations per day taken from six consecutive lots produced during the day were used. For comparison, where standard deviation values are computed for the larger sample sizes combining subgroups, control charts are given by days for $n = 30$ resistors using standard deviation values. Since all the previous quality control charts for averages for these resistors show the averages are controlled within very narrow limits, which is deemed more than satisfactory, the next set of control charts presented here cover only standard deviation values for the larger groups of data. In place of the average chart previously compiled for average values, a control chart is given covering possible control with respect to time of day for the production of successive lots, using twenty-five observations per week per lot for the six lots produced at different times of the day.

The lot-by-lot control chart often is very valuable, as it may indicate a change in the process due to changes in temperature, humidity, or worker fatigue during an average day or week. If the fatigue factor tends to greatly reduce the quality of the last lot produced during a day, it may indicate that the work hours are

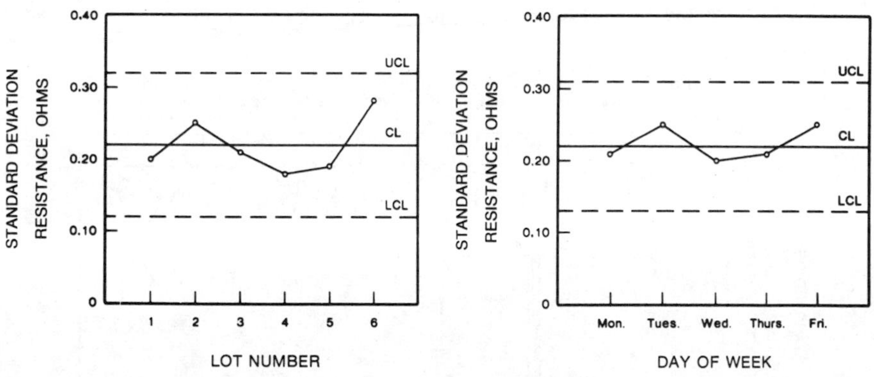

Figure 6–34 Two charts showing standard deviation, resistance in ohms: by lot number and by days of the week.

excessive. This would be especially true if the last lot were produced during overtime. In other cases, these lots may have been made successively by two or even three different shifts. For instance, the night shift could be composed of less-experienced workers, which might lead to a greater variability in the quality of the outgoing product. Figure 6-35 gives a control chart covering the six lots as well as a chart for the five days of the week. The necessary data for control charts for standard deviations by lots and by days for resistor production with 150 resistance observations per week and lot samples of twenty-five resistors per week and daily samples of thirty resistors per week; specified values: 10.00 ± 0.50 ohms.

References

Formulas: (Table 6.3) $\bar{\sigma} = c_2\sigma'$ for center line; $\bar{\sigma} \pm \dfrac{3\sigma'}{\sqrt{n}}$ for control lines

Factors: Tables 6.1, 6.6, and 6.18

Factors used in computing Center Lines and Control Lines

$$\text{Standard Deviations}\begin{cases} n = 25: c_2 = 0.9696;\ B_1 = 0.55,\ B_2 = 1.39 \\ n = 30: c_2 = 0.9748;\ B_1 = 0.59,\ B_2 = 1.36 \end{cases}$$

Center Line $n = 25: \bar{\sigma} = 0.225$ ohm; $n = 30: \bar{\sigma} = 0.226$ ohm

Control Lines $n = 25$: UCL $= 1.39(0.232) = 0.3225$ ohm

LCL $= 0.55(0.232) = 0.1276$ ohm

$n = 30$: UCL $= 1.36(0.232) = 0.3155$ ohm

LCL $= 0.59(0.232) = 0.1369$ ohm

where $\sigma' = 0.232 = \bar{\sigma}/c_2$ *for above factors.*

Using these values, two control charts for lots and days covering standard deviation values are presented in figure 6-35. The second chart should be compared with a similar chart where the variability is measured by the use of range values. Figure 6-30 indicates that the daily variations are well controlled.

Analysis: More variability in resistance values for these resistors seems to occur the last part of the day. This indicates that the human factor of fatigue might be a possible assignable cause, as the machines

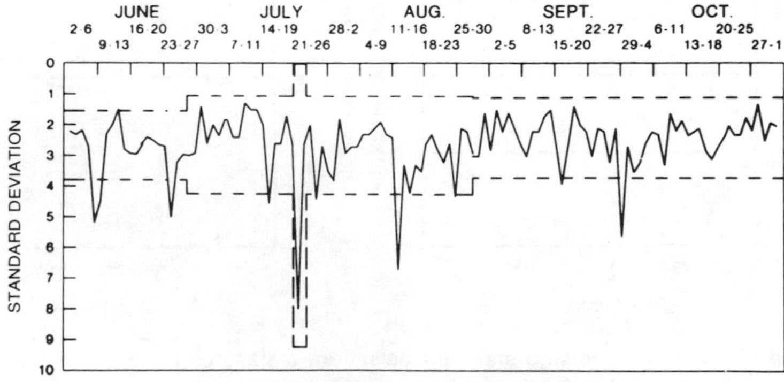

Figure 6–35 Control spoilage for electrical part *X, individual units.*

used in production should not change, but may need minor adjustments during the day. This study thus might indicate that it is undesirable to increase production by overtime operations, as the quality of the outgoing product may be affected adversely with respect to increased variability in resistance values.

6.8 Control Charts for Individuals for 100% Inspection for Several Characteristics

For many expensive items, it is desired to maintain control of the process at an economical level. Hence the best control is to use a control chart covering the successive inspection results covering these characteristics. An illustrative example of this case is given in the American War Standard ASA Z1.3, 1942. The product involved was a certain type of electrical apparatus; checks were made on each unit for four important, specified electrical characteristics measurable on a test set. A complete account of the efforts to control the process is given in Z1.3. The first control charts were daily and monthly control charts based on the principles presented in chapter 5, *Control Charts for Attributes.* Additional controls were conducted based on results for individual units. This illustrates how control charts for attributes and control charts for variables may be used together to gain control of a process.

Control charts for daily values of p were used as aids to disclose either of two conditions: (1) the occasional presence of assignable causes in the manufacturing process, or possibly in the inspection operations, and (2) the inherent inability of the existing manufacturing process to turn out the quality of work demanded by the specification tolerances. Figure 6-36 presents this control chart for individual units.

In this illustrative example, the first standard p' value was established at 2.65%. In September, a tighter standard of 2.40% was selected, based on an analysis of the prior data omitting uncontrolled results. It was found in this case that when excessive p values occurred, it was usually caused by faulty workmanship. By

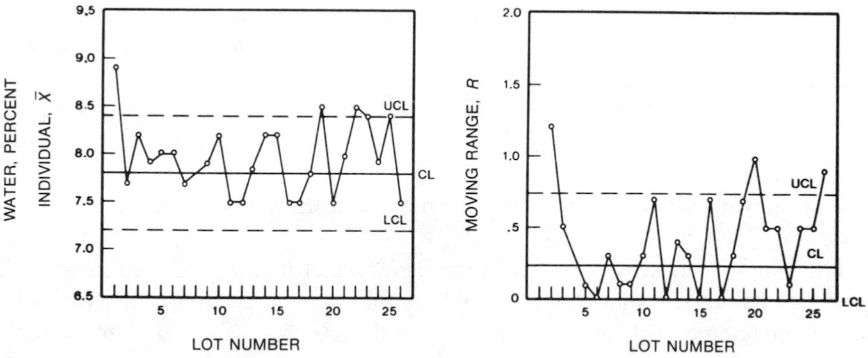

Figure 6-36 Control charts for water content in denatured alcohol, percent.

instituting training programs, the loss of these expensive individual units was reduced to an economic level.

6.9 Control Charts for Individuals and Moving Ranges ($n = 2$)

When individual observations are plotted one by one on a specific control chart, changes in the process may be detected much earlier than when using averages, standard deviations, or ranges. Use may also be made of moving range values, where successive ranges from sample to sample are applied. These controls are generally applied when:

1. Sampling or testing is destructive,
2. Costly chemical analyses or physical tests are involved, or
3. The material sampled at any one time (such as a batch or lot) is normally quite homogeneous, as for a well-mixed fluid or aggregate.

The purpose of such control charts is to discover whether the individual, observed values differ from the expected value by an amount greater than that which should be attributed to chance.

When there is some definite rational basis for grouping the batches, the test results, or observations into rational subgroups (such as four successive batches in a single shift), the following method involving rational subgroups may be followed. In this method, the control chart for individuals is merely an adjunct to the usual charts, but will react more quickly to a sharp change in the process than the $\bar{X}'$ chart. This applies when batches are very costly.

When there is no definite basis for grouping the data, the control limits may be based on the variation between batches. One of the measures used to control such possible variations is obtained from moving ranges of two observations (the successive differences between individual observations which are arranged in chronological order). This latter method should be used with caution if the distribution of the individual values is markedly asymmetrical. A control chart for moving ranges is a companion to the chart for individuals. In such charts, it must be noted that adjacent moving ranges are correlated, as they have one observation in common.

As discussed in prior sections, two cases may occur when preparing these control charts for individuals or moving ranges. They are (1) standard given and (2) no standard given. An illustrative example of each of these two possible conditions is included. These examples may be followed when preparing similar charts for industry.

The following tables present the formulas and factors that are used in compiling control charts for rational subgroups where the size of such subgroups varies from two to ten. Somewhat similar formulas and factors are included to cover the conditions where moving ranges are the best form of control charts. Since some industries prefer to use range values rather than standard deviation values in setting up their control charts, the formulas and factors are given for both cases. When standards are given, since the standard deviation does not vary with sample size, then σ' is usually specified; $\bar{R}'$ values are generally derived from the standard deviation value for a specific sample size and will be different for a different sample size value. The E_1 and E_2 factors used vary with sample sizes because they are functions of c_2 and d_2 (used in determining the center lines), respectively.

Two cases also occur when using moving ranges for controlling the process. When a standard is given, the formulas and factors are related to σ' rather than any value of the range R. However, the central lines and control limits that are compiled, although computed in terms of the standard deviation, apply to the observed or compiled range values obtained from successive data. The manner in which these are used will be readily seen when the examples given are studied.

When moving ranges are used for control purposes, table 6.38 presents the formulas for such ranges where (1) standard is given and (2) no standard is given.

Table 6.37 gives values of E_1 and E_2 for samples of $n = 10$ or less. More complete values are given in table 6.1.

TABLE 6.36 Formulas for Control Chart Lines for Individuals, *X*, Using Rational Subgroups

FORMULAS FOR CONTROL CHART LINES			
Chart for Individuals—Associated with Chart for σ or R Having Sample Size n			
		Control Limits	
Nature of Data	*Central Line*	*Simplified Formula Using Factors in Table 6.37*	*Basic Formula*
Standard Given			
Samples of Equal or Unequal Size	$\bar{\bar{X}}'$		$\bar{\bar{X}}' \pm 3\sigma'$
No Standard Given			
Samples of Equal Size:			
Based on $\bar{\sigma}$	$\bar{\bar{X}}$	$\bar{\bar{X}} \pm E_1\bar{\sigma}$	$\bar{\bar{X}} \pm 3\dfrac{\bar{\sigma}}{c_2}$
Based on $\bar{R}$	$\bar{\bar{X}}$	$\bar{\bar{X}} \pm E_2\bar{R}$	$\bar{\bar{X}} \pm 3\dfrac{\bar{R}}{d_2}$
Samples of Unequal Size: σ_e computed from observed values of $\bar{\sigma}$ per equation (15) or from observed values of $\bar{R}$ per Example 13	$\bar{\bar{X}}$		$\bar{\bar{X}} \pm 3\sigma_e$

TABLE 6.37 Factors for Control Chart Lines for Individuals Using Rational Subgroups

FACTORS FOR COMPUTING CONTROL LIMITS

Chart for Individuals—Associated with Chart for σ or R Having Sample Size n

No. of Observations in Samples of Equal Size (from which $\bar{\sigma}$ or $\bar{R}$ has been determined)	2	3	4	5	6	7	8	9	10
Factors for control limits:									
E_1	5.318	4.146	3.760	3.568	3.454	3.378	3.323	3.283	3.251
E_2	2.660	1.772	1.457	1.290	1.184	1.109	1.054	1.010	0.975

TABLE 6.38 Formulas for Control Chart Lines for Moving Ranges

Control Chart for Individuals—Using Moving Ranges

(1) *Standard Given* When $\bar{X}'$ and σ' are given, the control chart lines are as follows:

FORMULAS FOR CONTROL CHART LINES

	Central Line	*Control Limits*
For individuals	$\bar{X}'$	$\bar{X}' \pm 3\sigma'$
For moving ranges of two observations..........	$d_2\sigma'$	$D_2\sigma'$ and $D_1\sigma' = 3.69\sigma'$ and 0

(2) *No Standard Given* Here the control chart lines are computed from the observed data. In this section the symbol R is used to signify the moving range. The control chart lines are as follows:

FORMULAS FOR CONTROL CHART LINES

Chart for Individuals—Using Moving Ranges

	Central Line	*Control Limits*
For individuals	$\bar{\bar{X}}$	$\bar{\bar{X}} \pm E_2\bar{R} = \bar{\bar{X}} \pm 2.66\bar{R}$
For moving ranges of two observations..........	$\bar{R}$	$D_4\bar{R}$ and $D_3\bar{R} = 3.27\bar{R}$ and 0

where:

$\bar{\bar{X}}$ = the average of the individual observations,

$\bar{R}$ = the mean moving range, the average of successive differences between the individual observations, and

$n = 2$ for determing E_2, D_3 and D_4.

The ASTM *Manual on Quality Control of Materials*, together with the ASA War Standards, present the preparation of control charts for individual values, X, and moving ranges in great detail. Two of these examples are presented to cover the two cases (1) standard values of X, denoted by $\bar{X}'$, and σ' given, and (2) no standard given. These two illustrations provide sufficient information with applications for use in the preparation of similar charts in most industries. The two cases cover the water content of successive lots of denatured alcohol and the methanol content of successive lots of denatured alcohol. Somewhat similar problems will be provided in the review exercises, covering such items as the silicon content of heats of manganese steel and coating weights of instrument pins.

Example 16 *Control Charts for Individuals, X, and Moving Range, R, of Two Observations, Standards Given, Based on* $\bar{X}'$ *and* σ'. With data from a distilling plant, which was distilling and blending batch lots of denatured alcohol in a large tank it was desired to control the percentage of water for this process. The variability of sampling within a single lot was found to be negligible, so it was decided to take only one observation per lot and to set control limits for individual values, X, and for the moving range, R, of successive lots with $n = 2$ where $\bar{X}' = 7.800$ percent and $\sigma' = 0.200$ percent. Table 6.39 gives a summary of the water content of twenty-six consecutive lots of the denatured alcohol and the twenty-five values of the moving range, R. Figure 6-36 gives control charts for individuals, X, and for the moving range, R.

TABLE 6.39 Water Content of Successive Lots of Denatured Alcohol and Moving Range for $n = 2$

Lot	*Percentage of Water, X*	*Moving Range, R*	*Lot*	*Percentage of Water, X*	*Moving Range, R*
No. 1	8.9	—	No. 14	8.2	0.3
No. 2	7.7	1.2	No. 15	8.2	0
No. 3	8.2	0.5	No. 16	7.5	0.7
No. 4	7.9	0.3	No. 17	7.5	0
No. 5	8.0	0.1	No. 18	7.8	0.3
No. 6	8.0	0	No. 19	8.5	0.7
No. 7	7.7	0.3	No. 20	7.5	1.0
No. 8	7.8	0.1	No. 21	8.0	0.5
No. 9	7.9	0.1	No. 22	8.5	0.5
No. 10	8.2	0.3	No. 23	8.4	0.1
No. 11	7.5	0.7	No. 24	7.9	0.5
No. 12	7.5	0	No. 25	8.4	0.5
No. 13	7.9	0.4	No. 26	7.5	0.9
			Total	207.1	10.0
			Number of Values	26	25
			Average	7.965	0.400

Central Lines

For X: $\bar{X}' = 7.800$.

$n = 2$:

For R: $d_2\sigma' = (1.128)(0.200)$,
0.23.

Control Limits

For X: $\bar{X}' \pm 3\sigma' =$
$7.800 \pm 3(0.200)$,
8.4 and 7.2.

$n = 2$:

For R: $D_2\sigma'$ and $D_1\sigma' =$
$(3.686)(0.200)$ and
$(0)(0.200)$, 0.74 and 0. +

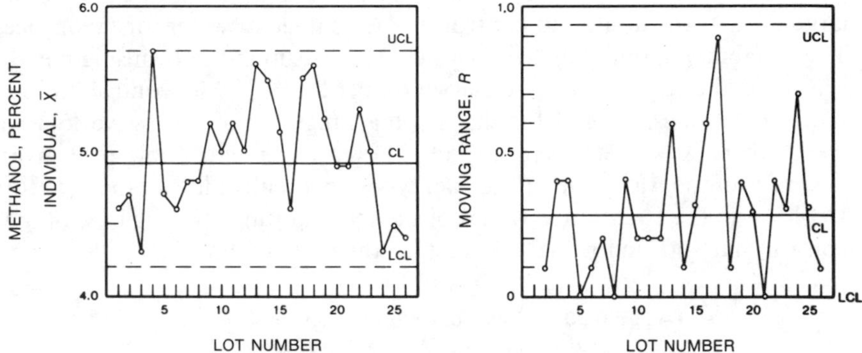

Figure 6–37 Control charts for methanol content in denatured alcohol, percent.

Results Lack of control at desired levels is indicated with respect to both the individual readings and the moving range. These results indicate corrective measures should be taken to reduce the level in percent and to reduce the variation between lots.

Example 17 covers the case where no standard is given. Standards to be used are derived from the sampling results and observations recorded. Thus control charts may be based on either standard deviation values or ranges or any other measure of variability. Mean deviation estimates of variability might even be used, but such values are not as efficient as the standard deviation. For simplicity, ranges are preferred.

Example 17 *Control Charts for Individuals, X, and Moving Range, R, of Two Observations, No Standard Given, Based on $\bar{\bar{X}}$ and $\bar{R}$, the Mean Moving Range.* A distilling plant was distilling and blending batch lots of denatured alcohol in a large tank. It was desired to control the percentage of methanol for this process. The variability of sampling within a single lot was found to be negligible, so it was decided feasible to take only one observation per lot and to set control limits on the basis of the moving range of successive lots. Table

6.40 gives a summary of the methanol content, X, of 26 consecutive lots of the denatured alcohol and the 25 values of the moving range, R, the range of successive lots with $n = 2$. Figure 6-37 gives control charts for individuals, X, and the moving range, R.

TABLE 6.40 Methanol Content of Successive Lots of Denatured Alcohol and Moving Range for $n = 2$.

Lot	*Percentage of Methanol, X*	*Moving Range, R*	Lot	*Percentage of Methanol, X*	*Moving Range, R*
No. 1..........	4.6	—	No. 14.........	5.5	0.1
No. 2..........	4.7	0.1	No. 15.........	5.2	0.3
No. 3..........	4.3	0.4	No. 16.........	4.6	0.6
No. 4..........	4.7	0.4	No. 17.........	5.5	0.9
No. 5..........	4.7	0	No. 18.........	5.6	0.1
No. 6..........	4.6	0.1	No. 19.........	5.2	0.4
No. 7..........	4.8	0.2	No. 20.........	4.9	0.3
No. 8..........	4.8	0	No. 21.........	4.9	0
No. 9..........	5.2	0.4	No. 22.........	5.3	0.4
No. 10..........	5.0	0.2	No. 23.........	5.0	0.3
No. 11..........	5.2	0.2	No. 24.........	4.3	0.7
No. 12..........	5.0	0.2	No. 25.........	4.5	0.2
No. 13..........	5.6	0.6	No. 26.........	4.4	0.1
			Total......	128.1	7.2

Central Lines

For X: $\bar{\bar{X}} = \frac{128.1}{26} = 4.927.$

For R: $\bar{R} = \frac{7.2}{25} = 0.288.$

Control Limits

$n = 2$:

For X: $\bar{\bar{X}} \pm E_2\bar{R} = \bar{\bar{X}} \pm 2.660\bar{R} =$
$4.927 \pm (2.660)(0.288)$,
5.693 and 4.161

For R: $D_4\bar{R}$ and $D_3\bar{R} =$
(3.267)(0.288) and
(0)(0.288), 0.94 and 0. +

Results The trend pattern of the individuals and their tendency to crowd the control limits suggest that better control may be attainable.

The next section covers control charts for midranges combined with range values, which is followed by a section covering control charts for medians. These methods provide the majority of the types of control charts used in industry. Those applying them should select the most efficient and effective applicable charts.

6.10 Control Charts for Midranges and Ranges

Midranges are often used as a satisfactory measure of the Central value of a group of observations. An excellent discussion of this measure and a comparison between it and the median of the distribution is given in detail in the *Introduction to Statistical Analysis,* by Wilfrid J. Dixon and Frank J. Massey, Jr., latest edition published by McGraw-Hill Book Company, Inc. It includes a series of tables referenced in the text and included in the section containing tables, especially the Table 8 set. The midrange is often used as an estimate of the true average value, termed μ or $\bar{X}'$ whereas the range is a good estimate of the true standard deviation σ'. These estimates are both computed from the same two values, the maximum and the minimum observations in the sample. The efficiency of the midrange decreases rapidly for samples greater than 5.

Detailed information for preparing control charts for Ranges and Midranges were presented by Enoch B. Ferrell, Bell Telephone Laboratories, in a brief departmental memorandum. To maintain a reasonable efficient use of these measures factors are given only for small samples. In line with the prior presentation on the use of subgroups this memorandum also recommends this procedure. Given measurements on a number of manufactured items, supposedly alike, or a number of repetitive observations, divide these into small subgroups, of n^* each, according to the time of production, the lot of raw material, or any other variable that may be considered to have a possible significance. For each of these subgroups compute the range R, which is the difference between the two extreme values, and the midrange M, which is the average of these two extremes. Compute the average of all the ranges, $\bar{R}$, and the average of all the midranges, $\bar{M}$. Then $\bar{M}$ is used as an estimate of $\bar{X}'$, the average or nominal value for the whole manufacturing or measuring process. As given previously $\bar{R}/d_2$ is an estimate of σ', the RMS (Root Mean Square) or standard deviation of the process about that average.

Computation of Control Charts:

Central Values, Center Line (CL or ℄):

Midrange: $\bar{M}$; Range: $\bar{R}$.

Three-sigma Control Limits:

Midrange: Upper Control Limit, UCL $= \bar{M} + A_4\bar{R}$,
Lower Control Limit, LCL $= \bar{M} - A_4\bar{R}$.

Range: Upper Control Limit, UCL $= D_4\bar{R}$,
Lower Control Limit, LCL $= D_3\bar{R}$.

If any M or R value is found outside these control limits, it is worthwhile to examine the process for an identifiable disturbance or assignable cause of nonconformance. If no M or R value in 25 consecutive subgroups lies outside their respective limits, there is reason to believe that the process is stable and capable of producing items substantially within these limits:

$$\bar{X}' \pm 3\sigma' = \bar{M} \pm 3\bar{R}/d_2.$$

The memorandum by Enoch B. Ferrell contained the following table:

TABLE 6.41 Factors for six n^* values for Control Limits for M and R

n^*	d_2	A_4	D_3	D_4
2	1.13	1.88	0	3.27
3	1.69	1.07	0	2.57
4	2.06	0.80	0	2.28
5	2.33	0.66	0	2.11
6	2.53	0.57	0	2.00

6.11 Control Limits for the Median

Many prefer to use the median as a measure of central values as it is so easy to obtain from a group of data. When the sample size is odd the median will be one of the observations, whereas when the sample size is even the median is a hypothetical value, half-way between the two central observations. Where n is the sample size, the median, sometimes designated as M_e, is the $(n - 1)/2$ value observed and recorded for ordered data. Thus when n is 5, the 3rd observation in an ordered array is the median. However, if there are 6 observations the value for the median is half-way between the 3rd and 4th observation for ordered data.

Confidence Limits for the Median are discussed in the "Introduction to Statistical Analysis" by Dixon and Massey, previously referenced. For an informative discussion of the median it should be consulted. It notes that a confidence interval for the median of the population can be obtained immediately from the observations arranged in order of magnitude. No assumption is necessary about the population except that the observations are being taken for a continuous variable. The order used is usually the smallest first, followed in order by observations equal to or greater than the preceding recorded value of X. Table A-25 in the back of the Dixon and Massey text presents Confidence Intervals for the Median for n values from 6 to 65. Means are therein provided to obtain confidence intervals for probability values of 0.90 and 0.95. Other limits may be determined by the application of the proper methods of computation.

The symbol W or w is often used to designate the range in many texts. The expected Median Range is represented as $W\sigma'$. Control Chart Limits based on this statistic have been summarized by Dr. Paul S. Olmstead, when with the Bell Telephone Laboratories in an informal memorandum dated 13 November 1947. These factors to be used in computing Control Chart Limits using the Median

Range R_M as a measure of dispersion were based on a normal distribution and were first developed in articles by T. Hojo and K. Pearson in 1931 and developed for practical use by E. S. Pearson in 1942. These articles appeared in the Biometrics journal published in those years. The median term varies and differs in form when n is even or odd, hence these factors reflect this difference. The table below could be arranged without showing this difference but it is just as useful in the form shown.

TABLE 6.42 Factors for Control Chart Limits Based on Medians (Using Median Range); Sample Sizes Given as Odds and Evens: 2–20

Sample Size n	Median Range $= W\sigma$ W	$\bar{X} \pm A_3 R_M$ A_3	$X_M \pm A_4 R_M$ A_4	$R_{LCL} = D_5 R_M$ D_5	$R_{UCL} = D_6 R_M$ D_6
ODD					
3	1.5878	1.091	1.266	0	2.745
5	2.2568	0.594	0.711	0	2.179
7	2.6454	0.429	0.521	0.078	1.967
9	2.9155	0.343	0.419	0.187	1.850
11	3.1206	0.290	0.356	0.260	1.773
13	3.2851	0.253	0.311	0.313	1.718
15	3.4216	0.226	0.279	0.353	1.676
17	3.5384	0.206	0.255		
19	3.6398	0.189	0.234		
EVEN					
2	0.9538	0.224	2.224	0	3.865
4	1.9784	0.758	0.828	0	2.375
6	2.4717	0.495	0.562	0	2.055
8	2.7909	0.380	0.441	0.139	1.901
10	3.0243	0.314	0.370	0.227	1.809
12	3.2068	0.270	0.321	0.289	1.744
14	3.3563	0.239	0.286	0.334	1.696
16	3.4822	0.215	0.259		
18	3.5907	0.197	0.238		
20	3.6859	0.182	0.221		

Exercises

1. Describe the difference between the use of control charts for attributes data and control charts applied to variables data.

2. List three kinds of control charts that are used for attributes data and three kinds of control charts applied to variables data.

3. Determine the three-sigma control limits for $\bar{X}$ and σ covering the standards given as $\bar{X}' = 10.0$ ohms and $\sigma' = 0.5$ ohm for the following sample sizes.

(a) $n = 4$ (c) $n = 10$
(b) $n = 5$ (d) $n = 25$

4. For the case where $\bar{X}' = 10$ ohms and $\sigma' = 0.5$ ohm, determine the expected value of R, $E(R) = R$, and the three-sigma control limits for R for the following sample sizes.
(a) $n = 4$ (c) $n = 10$
(b) $n = 5$ (d) $n = 25$

5. In exercise 4, control limits for the sample size $n = 25$ are considered very inefficient. If the sample of size $n = 25$ is divided into five subgroups of five units each, so that five R values may be found in each complete sample of twenty-five units, what three-sigma control limits should be used for each case?
(a) The subgroup samples each containing five units each?
(b) The $\bar{R}$ calculated for the five R values derived from each set of five subgroups of five units each?

When answering (a), determine three-sigma control limits for the five $\bar{X}$ values obtained for each sample of five subgroups and also the five R values.
(*NOTE:* As an aid in answering part (b) correctly, note that each $\bar{R}$ found for a sample of twenty-five units divided into five rational subgroups is an average value and that $\sigma'_{\bar{X}} = \dfrac{\sigma'}{\sqrt{n}}$; hence $\sigma'_{\bar{R}} = \dfrac{\sigma'_R}{\sqrt{m}}$, where m is the number of subgroups in each sample.)

6. The data in table 6.43 were obtained for the length of a shaft for the first week of production.

TABLE 6.43 Sampling Results for Shaft Length: Week 1
$n = 5$, Number measured: Specified: 12.00 ± 0.10 inches

Sample No.	*Lot 1*	*Lot 2*	*Lot 3*	*Lot 4*	*Lot 5*
i	X_i	X_i	X_i	X_i	X_i
1	11.95	11.94	12.03	11.90	12.01
2	12.05	12.02	11.96	11.95	11.98
3	12.02	12.00	11.97	12.05	12.00
4	11.98	11.98	12.00	12.10	11.99
5	12.00	12.06	12.04	12.00	12.02
Sum	60.00	60.00	60.00	60.00	60.00

(a) For these data, determine estimated standards for $\bar{X}$ and σ to be used in preparing control charts for averages $\bar{X}$ and standard deviations σ.
(b) Determine three-sigma control limits for $\bar{X}$ and σ for $n = 5$ and prepare a graph showing the five average and standard deviation values on the two control charts. Show values selected from the appropriate tables in this chapter or computed and used in determining these control limits.

7. (a) For the data in exercise 6, determine R for each lot and $\bar{R}$ for the five R values.
(b) Plot the $\bar{X}$ and R values for the five lots listed in exercise 6.

(c) Using the applicable values, given in table 6.1 or 6.19, determine the three-sigma control limits for $\bar{X}$ and R and place these on the graph prepared in (b). Show all the computations.

(d) Are any points outside their respective control limits? Is this process controlled? Would you purchase parts from this supplier?

8. In addition to the data given in exercise 6, the data in table 6.44 were obtained for the last two weeks of production. Although other data have been obtained since the data for the first week were taken, the prior data are not considered as representative of the true process. These data are for week 10 and week 11.

TABLE 6.44(a) Sampling Results for Shaft Length: Week 10 $n = 5$, Number measured: Specified: 12.00 ± 0.10 inches

Sample No.	*Lot 1*	*Lot 2*	*Lot 3*	*Lot 4*	*Lot 5*
i	X_i	X_i	X_i	X_i	X_i
1	11.75	11.25	10.30	10.40	11.20
2	11.25	11.00	10.20	10.45	11.60
3	11.60	10.90	10.00	10.55	11.75
4	11.40	11.10	9.70	11.00	11.50
5	11.50	10.75	9.80	11.10	11.95
Sum	57.50	55.00	50.00	53.50	58.00

TABLE 6.44(b) Sampling Results for Shaft Length: Week 11 $n = 5$, Number measured: Specified: 12.00 ± 0.10 inches

Sample No.	*Lot 1*	*Lot 2*	*Lot 3*	*Lot 4*	*Lot 5*
i	X_i	X_i	X_i	X_i	X_i
1	12.01	11.99	12.00	11.99	12.01
2	11.99	12.02	12.01	11.97	11.98
3	12.00	11.98	11.98	12.00	12.00
4	12.02	12.00	12.02	12.02	12.01
5	11.98	12.01	11.99	12.02	12.00
Sum	60.00	60.00	60.00	60.00	60.00

(a) Determine $\bar{X}$ and σ for each of these ten lots. Prepare a graph showing the three-sigma control limits for the data in exercise 6, as well as for the data in table 6.44. Use estimated standards $\bar{X}'_e$ and σ'_e derived only from the data given in exercise 6. Note what values are outside these control limits. Do you consider the process controlled?

(b) Eliminating lots that are deemed out of control, determine new standards for $\bar{X}$ and σ. Use these new standards and replot the prior two control charts. What weeks are deemed under control? Discuss the results.

9. It is often less costly to use control charts for midranges and ranges. Use the data given for production weeks 1, 10, and 11 in exercises 6 and 8.

(a) Determine the midranges and ranges for these fifteen lots.

(b) Graph the fifteen values of midranges on a control chart and determine and graph the upper control limit (UCL) and the lower control limit (LCL) for sample size $n = 5$.

(c) Graph the fifteen values of ranges on a control chart and graph the UCL and LCL for sample size $n = 5$.

(d) What factors were used to determine the UCL and LCL values used?

10. (a) Using the data in exercises 6 and 8, determine the median for each of fifteen samples of five units each.

(b) Prepare a control chart for medians and plot the fifteen medians obtained in (a) together with three-sigma control limits that apply.

(c) Three measures of central tendency have been computed for these fifteen sets of data. Tabulate these. Which measure do you prefer? Give reasons for your choice. The three statistics are (i) mean, the arithmetic average, (ii) midrange, and (iii) median.

11. A choice of the best method for measuring variability or dispersion may be made.

(a) In solving exercises 6 and 8, standard deviation values were computed. If these exercises have not been assigned, compute the fifteen σ values for weeks 1, 10, and 11 and tabulate.

(b) For the fifteen samples for these data, compute the mean deviation for the fifteen sets of data and list these on the table of σ values.

(c) For the fifteen samples for these data, determine the range for each sample and tabulate these values on the table prepared in (a) corresponding to the following captions: week 1 values listed as 1–1, 1–2, 1–3, 1–4, 1–5; week 10 values listed as 10–1, 10–2, 10–3, 10–4, 10–5; and week 11 values listed as 11–1, 11–2, 11–3, 11–4, and 11–5.

(d) Determine the average values for σ from the fifteen computed σ values and estimate σ' by using the c_2 value for $n = 5$.

(e) Determine the correlation between σ and $\left(\sqrt{\frac{\pi}{2}} = 1.25331414\right)$ (mean deviation from mean) for $n = 4$ shown on page 288 of Shewhart and the average value for the fifteen mean deviation from mean values; then obtain the best estimate of σ. Use as this estimate the approximate value $\sigma'_e \dfrac{1.25\,\overline{\text{M.D.}}}{c_2}$, using c_2 for $n = 5$ for normal distribution.

(f) Determine the average value for the fifteen range values. Obtain an estimate of σ' by dividing this $\bar{R}$ value by the d_2 value for $n = 5$ given for a normal distribution.

(g) Which of these three estimates of σ' would you select? State reasons for your choice.

(h) Dixon and Massey shows that the mean deviation from median (M.D.*) is a more efficient measure of dispersion than the mean deviation from mean. Determine fifteen median values; using these determine fifteen mean deviations from median values. Using the average of these M.D.* values, estimate σ' by the same method as (e). Is this estimate of σ' better than (e) value?

12. Where the data given in exercises 6 and 8 have been completely analyzed and many sample results were indicated as having been made by an uncontrolled process, make the following determinations.

(a) Determine the best estimate of central value $\bar{X}'$, tabulating estimated values from samples from the controlled process periods for (i) arithmetic mean, (ii) median, and (iii) midrange.
(b) Determine the best estimate of variability or dispersion for (i) standard deviation values, (ii) range, and (iii) mean deviation.
(c) Note the new standards $\bar{X}'$ and σ' selected from results in (a) and (b).

13. A more efficient measure of dispersion compared with the mean deviation is the mean deviation from the median.
(a) For the controlled samples selected for exercise 12, determine mean deviation from the median values.
(b) Compute the best estimate of σ' from the average of the m values of M.D. (median) values.
(c) For the five m units given in samples assumed to have been taken from a controlled process, determine the overall σ value. Estimate σ' from this value by multiplying σ by $\sqrt{\dfrac{5m}{5m-1}}$.
(d) Two more estimates of σ' have been obtained. Compare these values with the σ' standard established in 12(c).

14. Two different canneries process frozen apricots. The drained weight in ounces depends on the concentration of syrup used and also on the differences in the syrup composition. Possible concentrations of syrup used are designated as 30, 40, 50, and 65, while the syrup composition used may be (i) all sucrose, (ii) $\frac{2}{3}$ sucrose and $\frac{1}{3}$ corn syrup, (iii) $\frac{1}{2}$ sucrose and $\frac{1}{2}$ corn syrup, or (iv) all corn syrup. The drained weight minimum in ounces is 28 ounces. Plant A uses concentration 40 and composition (ii), while Plant B uses concentration 50 with composition (iii). During the first week of processing apricots each plant took five samples of ten units each day. The data in terms of drained weight are tabulated in table 6.45.

TABLE 6.45 Characteristic: Drained Weight in Ounces for Frozen Apricots. Sample Results for Two Different Plants for First Week

PLANT A

Sample Number	*Monday*	*Tuesday*	*Wednesday*	*Thursday*	*Friday*
1	29.00	29.05	29.35	29.45	29.10
2	29.10	29.12	29.15	29.00	29.10
3	29.40	29.25	28.50	29.10	29.40
4	29.60	29.40	28.70	28.90	28.90
5	29.25	29.08	29.30	28.60	28.40
6	29.15	28.70	29.40	29.20	28.70
7	28.90	28.50	29.10	28.80	29.30
8	28.70	28.40	28.70	28.30	29.20
9	29.10	29.00	29.10	29.70	28 90
10	27.80	29.50	28.70	28.95	29.00
Sum	290.00	290.00	290.00	290.00	290.00

Table 6.45 (continued)

PLANT B

Sample Number	*Monday*	*Tuesday*	*Wednesday*	*Thursday*	*Friday*
1	28.50	28.70	28.50	29.00	28.30
2	28.40	29.10	29.00	28.70	28.50
3	29.10	28.80	28.70	28.40	28.40
4	28.90	28.20	28.20	28.60	29.00
5	28.50	28.30	28.30	29.10	28.70
6	28.30	28.50	28.40	28.30	28.30
7	28.40	28.60	28.70	28.20	28.60
8	28.80	28.25	28.50	28.70	28.80
9	28.50	28.35	28.30	28.30	29.10
10	28.60	29.20	28.40	28.70	28.30
Sum	286.00	286.00	286.00	286.00	286.00

(a) Using $\overline{X}' = 29.00$ ounces and $\sigma' = 0.3$ ounces, prepare control charts for $\overline{X}$ and R for each plant. Are any values out of control? If so, designate values of $\overline{X}$ or R that are outside their respective control limits.

(b) From the results found in (a), which plant has a controlled process? If both are considered to have a controlled process, at what levels are they controlled? Which plant has more variability in its process?

(c) If a new processing plant is to be added, would you use the same concentration and composition as used by one of the plants or would you try a different set of values? Explain the reasons for this decision.

15. (a) Use the data in exercise 14 and determine σ values for the ten sets of samples and tabulate the results for each plant by days.

(b) Prepare control charts for $\overline{X}$ and σ for the standard values $\overline{X}' = 29.00$ ounces and $\sigma' = 0.3$ ounces.

(c) Are the σ values indicated as well-controlled as the R values plotted on control charts for R in exercise 14? Which plant has the best process or are the processes equally well-controlled? Justify your answer.

(d) Should the standard be revised? Give reasons for your answer.

16. (a) For the data in exercise 14, assuming that no standards are given for $\overline{X}$, σ, and R, determine standards for $\overline{X}$ and R based on the data for both plants. If any day's production is deemed out of control for any reason, omit such data in arriving at new standards. If all data are considered satisfactory, base new standards on all 100 values.

(b) Prepare control charts for $\overline{X}$ and R using the new standards obtained in (a). Are any values outside these new limits? If so, list them.

(c) For the data in exercise 14, using the $\overline{X}$ and σ values computed previously, determine new standards for $\overline{X}$, σ, and R. Omit any data that are deemed out of control and hence are not truly representative of the processes.

(d) Prepare control charts for $\overline{X}$ and σ using the new standards found in (c). Are any values outside these new limits? If so, list them.

(e) Is the minimum of 28.00 ounces a reasonable limit? If it is unrealistic, what value should be used? If it is satisfactory, are the processes at Plants A and B controlled at proper levels for such a minimum value?

17. Tensile strength is one of the most important characteristics for cable. The data listed in table 6.46 gives tensile strength for one type of steel cable used in constructing bridges and in other types of construction. Since the samples tested are destroyed, only four tests per lot are made. The specified engineering minimum is 10,000 P.S.I. (pounds per square inch).

(a) The data in table 6.46 give average values for each lot and the overall average for all forty observations. Determine and tabulate (i) the range for each lot, (ii) the standard deviation for each lot, and (iii) the overall standard deviation for all forty values.

(b) Using the overall $\bar{X}$ and $\bar{R}$ values for the forty test results, establish approximate standards and make a control chart for $\bar{X}$ and R. Note any values outside their control limits, if any.

(c) Determine tentative standards for $\bar{X}$ and σ using the overall $\bar{X}$ and the $\bar{\sigma}$ value found for the ten sets of tests. Make control charts for these statistics. Are there any lot results out of control? If so, list them.

Table 6.46 Tensile Strength Test Results X for Steel Cable Expressed in PSI. Specified Minimum: 10,000 PSI

Lot Numbers

Sample Number	*1*	*2*	*3*	*4*	*5*	*6*
1	22,000	15,000	25,000	100,000	100,000	30,000
2	40,000	47,000	40,000	80,000	20,000	15,000
3	25,000	72,000	65,000	70,000	15,000	20,000
4	53,000	26,000	70,000	30,000	85,000	15,000
Sum	140,000	160,000	200,000	280,000	220,000	80,000
$\bar{X}$	35,000	40,000	50,000	70,000	55,000	20,000

Lot Numbers (Continued)

Sample Number	*7*	*8*	*9*	*10*	*All Lots Combined*
1	55,000	40,000	30,000	50,000	467,000
2	45,000	20,000	15,000	40,000	362,000
3	20,000	18,000	35,000	20,000	360,000
4	30,000	12,000	40,000	50,000	601,000
Sum	150,000	90,000	120,000	160,000	1,600,000
$\bar{X}$	37,500	22,500	30,000	40,000	40,000

18. The characteristic tensile strength may be represented by a log normal distribution rather than linear normal. The data in exercise 17 are given in table 6.47 in terms of four-place logarithms for analysis.

TABLE 6.47
Strength Test Results for Steel Cable Expresses as Log X P.S.I.
Specified Minimum: Log X = 4,000 P.S.I.

Lot Numbers

Sample Number	*1*	*2*	*3*	*4*	*5*	*6*
1	4.3424	4.1761	4.3979	5.0000	5.0000	4.4771
2	4.6021	4.6721	4.6021	4.9031	4.3010	4.1761
3	4.3979	4.8573	4.8129	4.8451	4.1761	4.3010
4	4.7243	4.4150	4.8451	4.4771	4.9294	4.1761
Sum	18.0667	18.1205	18.6580	19.2253	18.4065	17.1303
$\overline{\text{Log } X}$	4.5167	4.5301	4.6645	4.8063	4.6016	4.2826
$\bar{X}$	32,862	33,892	46,189	64,014	39,955	19,170

Lot Numbers (Continued)

Sample Number	*7*	*8*	*9*	*10*	*All Lots Combined*
1	4.7404	4.6021	4.4771	4.6990	45.9121
2	4.6532	4.3010	4.1761	4.6021	44.9889
3	4.3010	4.2553	4.5441	4.3010	44.7917
4	4.4771	4.0792	4.6021	4.6990	45.4244
Sum	18.1717	17.2376	17.7994	18.3011	181.1171
$\overline{\text{Log } X}$	4.5429	4.3094	4.4498	4.5753	4.5279
$\bar{X}$	34,908	20,390	28,173	37,609	33,723

(a) The averages of the logarithms are listed for all sets of data expressed as logarithms to the base ten and also for all ten sets combined. For each lot, determine the range R and obtain tentative standards for $\bar{X}$ and R for these log values; then note if any lot sample results are outside their respective control limits.

(b) For each lot and for all ten lots combined, determine the standard values, σ. Determine $\bar{\sigma}$ for the ten σ values computed and establish tentative standards for $\bar{X}$ and σ. Prepare control charts for $\bar{X}$ and σ for the log values and note if any value of $\bar{X}$ and σ are outside their respective three-sigma control limits.

(c) Estimate the σ' for the distribution of the logarithms of tensile strength values by the following methods: (i) using $\sigma'_e = \frac{\bar{R}}{d_2}$; (ii) using $\sigma'_e = \frac{\bar{\sigma}}{c_2}$, and (iii) using the overall σ for the forty test values, σ_0, correcting this estimate by using $n - 1$ instead of obtaining the s estimate of σ'. Hence $\sigma'_e = \sqrt{\frac{40}{39}}\,\sigma_0$. Tabulate these three values and determine from each estimate of σ'_e by probabilities read from the normal table in Appendix A. What percentage of the distribution is less than the specified engineering limit, 10,000 P.S.I., whose $\log_{10}$ is 4,000, the minimum for log values?

19. In using control charts, particularly for individual values, it is often desirable to determine the nature of the distribution. Is it a linear normal distribution, a log normal, a rectangular, a right triangular, an isosceles triangular, a J-shaped, or one of the many other forms of distribution? Appendix A shows how to check an observed distribution for "goodness of fit" to a theoretical distribution such as the normal. The data for tensile strength in exercises 17 and 18 are summarized in table 6.48 as forty independent values, each value listed, combined in a number of cells of equal width. The distributions shown cover actual measured values and also their logarithms. This exercise requires two checks to determine whether the distribution is linear normal or log normal using the method for checking such hypotheses given in Appendix A.

(a) For distribution II, determine its $\bar{X}$, σ, and skewness k values.
(b) Fit distribution II with a normal law distribution, whose theoretical frequencies are derived from the $\bar{X}$ and σ values found in (a).
(c) Using the χ^2 test determine the probability for goodness of fit.
(d) The second approximation distribution will probably be a better fit for distribution II. Find the theoretical frequencies for the second approximation distribution using $\bar{X}$, σ, and k values obtained in (a). Using the χ^2 test determine the probability for goodness of fit.
(e) For distribution IV, determine its $\bar{X}$, σ, and skewness k values.

TABLE 6.48 Distributions of Tensile Strength of Steel Cable
$n = 40$, Specified Minimum 10,000 P.S.I.; Log 10,000 = 4.0000

Observed X Value	*Log X*	*Frequency*	*Cum. Freq.*	*Observed X Value*	*Log X*	*Frequency*	*Cum. Freq.*
12,000	4.0792	1	1	50,000	4.6990	2	30
15,000	4.1761	5	6	53,000	4.7243	1	31
18,000	4.2553	1	7	55,000	4.7404	1	32
20,000	4.3010	5	12	65,000	4.8129	1	33
22,000	4.3424	1	13	70,000	4.8451	2	35
25,000	4.3979	2	15	72,000	4.8573	1	36
26,000	4.4150	1	16	80,000	4.9031	1	37
30,000	4.4771	4	20	85,000	4.9294	1	38
35,000	4.5441	1	21	100,000	5.0000	2	40
40,000	4.6021	5	26				
45,000	4.6532	1	27	Sum		40	
47,000	4.6721	1	28	Number less than 10,000 P.S.I. = 0			

(f) Fit distribution IV with a normal law theoretical distribution using the $\bar{X}$ and σ values obtained in (e). Using the χ^2 test, determine the probability for goodness of fit.

(g) Which is the best theoretical distribution? Give reasons for your answer.

20. Control charts may be used in many ways to control processes or indicate when to search for assignable causes for poor quality. The text covers most types of control charts. It also covers moving averages and individual values. It covers in detail the derivation of three-sigma charts for various items, along with their characteristics and their defining statistics such as averages, midranges, medians, ranges, mean deviations, and standard deviations. Discuss where the various types of control charts for variables may be used most effectively.

TABLE 6.49 Possible Distributions for Observed X Values

Distribution I			*Distribution II*		
Cell Boundaries	*Mid-Cell*	*Frequency*	*Cell Boundaries*	*Mid-Cell*	*Frequency*
10,000– 21,000	15,500	12	10,000– 24,000	17,000	13
21,000– 32,000	26,500	8	25,000– 39,000	32,000	8
32,000– 43,000	37,500	6	40,000– 54,000	47,000	10
43,000– 54,000	48,500	4	55,000– 69,000	62,000	2
54,000– 65,000	59,500	2	70,000– 84,000	77,000	4
65,000– 76,000	70,500	3	85,000– 99,000	92,000	1
76,000– 87,000	81,500	2	100,000–114,000	107,000	2
87,000– 98,000	92,500	0	Sum		40
98,000–109,000	103,500	2			
Sum		40			

Possible Distributions for Logarithms of Observed X Values

Distribution III			*Distribution IV*		
Cell Boundaries	*Mid-Cell*	*Frequency*	*Cell Boundaries*	*Mid-Cell*	*Frequency*
4.0000–4.1000	4.0500	1	4.0000–4.1250	4.0625	1
4.1000–4.2000	4.1500	5	4.1250–4.2500	4.1875	5
4.2000–4.3000	4.2500	1	4.2500–4.3750	4.3125	7
4.3000–4.4000	4.3500	8	4.3750–4.5000	4.4375	10
4.4000–4.5000	4.4500	5	4.5000–4.6250	4.5625	6
4.5000–4.6000	4.5500	1	4.6250–4.7500	4.6875	5
4.6000–4.7000	4.6500	9	4.7500–4.8750	4.8125	4
4.7000–4.8000	4.7500	2	4.8750–5.0000	4.9325	2
4.8000–4.9000	4.8500	4	Sum		40
4.9000–5.0000	4.9500	4			
Sum		40			

FOOTNOTES

[1] This parenthetical reference was added editorially in September, 1954.

[2] For samples of n greater than 25, consider $c_2 = 1$.

[3] Formula **(8)** is an approximate formula suitable for most practical purposes. The values of B_1 and B_2 given in the tables are computed from the exact equation for σ_σ.

[4] Formula **(14)** is an approximate formula suitable for most practical purposes. The values of B_3 and B_4 given in the tables are computed from the exact equation for σ_σ.

+ Reproduced with permission of the American Society for Testing and Materials from STP-15C, *Manual on Quality Control of Materials*.

++ Reproduced with permission of authors and McGraw-Hill Book Co., from Grant and Leavenworth, *Statistical Quality Control*, 4th ed., 1972.

CHAPTER SEVEN

LINEAR CORRELATION

7.1 Objective

The object of quality control is to control processes to avoid the production of nonconforming units. If the percentage of units deemed unsatisfactory by consumers is kept to a minimum, the product can be sold at a profit in line with customer demands. There are many tests that may be used to assure the production of units that will always be within their specification limits. Some of these tests may injure the units tested, while other inspections and tests may be extremely costly. Such tests may also be difficult to conduct, require special testing facilities, or be very time consuming. The question is raised: Is there not some satisfactory test that is nondestructive or less expensive? Generally some nondestructive tests can be found to replace the more destructive or expensive tests that are sometimes specified by engineering. On the other hand, one might wonder if the test results of a nondestructive, inexpensive test can reflect the quality of the characteristic that is supposed to be tested directly by the specified destructive or costly test and if it will prevent the acceptance of nonconforming units. If so, what means and relations should be specified and used to provide the quality assurance desired for such critical characteristics?

It is the purpose of this chapter to answer the questions raised above and to provide methods and techniques that may be readily applied. The primary topic, linear correlation, provides the simplest method for relating two variables directly, so the value observed for one type of test may be used to provide a corresponding related value for the actual characteristic specified. For some specified items, nonlinear correlation techniques might provide more closely related results; more advanced texts cover such cases and should be consulted. The majority of cases that arise in practice may be resolved by the methods that are given in this chapter.

Linear correlation measures how closely two variables X and Y are related by means of a straight line in one plane. Means will be used to relate these two variables X and Y and to determine how closely they are related. Methods are provided to evaluate the two sets of observed values and determine the value of the coefficient of correlation, r_{XY}, which is used to measure the extent of dependence of one variable on the second variable. It will also be shown how to extend such correlation methods to three or more variables. The chapter covering the analysis of variance covers these questions in more detail.

After these methods are developed, examples of their use will be given, allowing anyone with even a very limited knowledge of algebra to obtain the correct answers and to conduct the necessary tests and computations necessary to make a valid decision concerning the conformance or nonconformance of the product submitted for acceptance.

7.2 Statistics Required in Correlation Studies

When two characteristics X and Y are to be checked to determine whether they are correlated or independent, it is necessary to consider the relationship between the basic statistics describing the frequency distributions of each. The population or universe from which values of X are taken need not be normal; however, it should be able to be represented by its arithmetic mean $\bar{X}$ (indicating its central value and its variance v_X) or, better yet, by its standard deviation σ_X, the best measure of its dispersion or variability. The same is also true for the universe U_Y from which corresponding values of Y are taken.

Values of the respective arithmetic means and variances for the two universes U_X and U_Y may already be known or given as standards. Their true values are called *parameters* in contrast to values computed from observed values in samples, which are called *statistics*. When these measures of central tendency and variability are known, they may be used directly in the relations developed in this chapter to provide direct measures of the extent of independence for the two universes under consideration. Again, it must be emphasized that the same two conditions encountered when preparing control charts generally exist: (1) standard given (parameters known) or (2) no standard given (statistics derived from sample values).

In most correlation studies, the statistics for the two variables X and Y will have to be computed from n pairs of values. Each of the X values and each of the corresponding Y values must be in the same unit to make these correlation results valid. When n pairs of X and Y values have been measured, their respective means and measures of variability are computed from the following relations.

$$\bar{X} = \frac{\Sigma X_i}{n} \tag{1}$$

$$v_X = \frac{\Sigma(X_i - \bar{X})^2}{n} = \frac{\Sigma X_i^2}{n} - \bar{X}^2 \tag{2}$$

$$\sigma_X = \sqrt{v_X} = \sqrt{\frac{\Sigma(X_i - \bar{X})^2}{n}} = \sqrt{\frac{\Sigma X_i^2}{n} - \bar{X}^2} \tag{3}$$

$$\bar{Y} = \frac{\Sigma Y_i}{n} \tag{4}$$

$$v_Y = \frac{\Sigma(Y_i - \bar{Y})^2}{n} = \frac{\Sigma Y_i^2}{n} - \bar{Y}^2 \tag{5}$$

$$\sigma_Y = \sqrt{v_Y} = \sqrt{\frac{\Sigma(Y_i - \bar{Y})^2}{n}} = \sqrt{\frac{\Sigma Y_i^2}{n} - \bar{Y}^2} \tag{6}$$

It should be possible to obtain a pair of values of X and Y values from each unit, each measured by a different method. When one method is considered to give a direct measure of the characteristic under consideration, then the other gives a correlated value; the second method is possibly nondestructive, while the method originally specified may destroy the usefulness of the unit. Another situation is when the newly proposed method costs much less per test than the original method. Are these common, recorded, measured values dependent or independent? If they are independent, their coefficient of correlation value is considered as zero; if they are dependent, it is hoped their dependency is great enough so that the observed value from a less expensive test may be used to estimate the value that might be found had a more costly test been applied. If the X and Y values are 100% dependent, their correlation value r_{XY} is either $+1$ or -1, depending on the slope of the linear relation used to relate their values.

The linear relation between them is represented as

$$Y = a + bX \tag{7}$$

and

$$X = c + dY \tag{8}$$

If the correlation between them is either $+1$ or -1, these two lines coincide. The two linear relations may also be written in terms of the basic statistics for the distributions of U_X and U_Y as

$$Y - \bar{Y} = r_{XY}\frac{\sigma_Y}{\sigma_X}\cdot(X - \bar{X}) \tag{9}$$

and

$$X - \bar{X} = r_{XY}\frac{\sigma_X}{\sigma_Y}\cdot(Y - \bar{Y}). \tag{10}$$

The task of determining the value of r_{XY} involves a mathematical relation between X and Y. This is the product of the deviation of each pair of observed values from their respective means, summed and divided by the sample size n, which gives a mean value called the *covariance* of X and Y. Expressed as an equation, the covariance is determined from the following equation.

$$\text{Cov.}\,(X,Y) = \frac{\Sigma(X_i - \bar{X})(Y_i - \bar{Y})}{n} = \frac{\Sigma x_i \cdot y_i}{n} \tag{11}$$

where

$$x_i = X_i - \bar{X} \quad \text{and} \quad y_i = Y_i - \bar{Y} \tag{12}$$

Note that observed values are written as X and Y, sometimes called *uppercase terms*, whereas deviations from mean values are written as x and y, called *lower-case letters*. Some texts also attempt to standardize notation by using only Greek letters for the true values, called *parameters*, and reserving the alphabet to represent the statistics derived from observed values. Others prefer to designate the parameters with a prime notation such as $\bar{X}'$ for the true mean of U_X, while those using the Greek alphabet use μ (Mu) as the true mean.

The covariance of X, Y may also be determined directly from the values of the observations themselves in a form similar to those used in equations (2) and (5). Where observed values are continually being added to prior results, it is not wise to use deviations from mean values, x_i and y_i, as the mean values are continually changing with each computation; rather, it is better to use the sum of the X and Y values, as well as the sum of the squares of such values, to reduce the time required for computations. Relations for the covariance of X, Y are given to simplify calculations. For each case, select those relations that are workable and easiest to use. In determining the two lines of regression, it will be easier in many cases to use the Cov. (X, Y) values, together with the standard deviations σ_X and σ_Y, rather than the coefficient of correlation, r_{XY}.

$$\begin{aligned} \text{Cov. }(X,Y) &= \frac{\Sigma(X_i - \bar{X})(Y_i - \bar{Y})}{n} = \frac{\Sigma(X_i Y_i - \bar{X} Y_i - X_i \bar{Y} + \bar{X}\bar{Y})}{n} \\ &= \frac{\Sigma X_i Y_i}{n} - \frac{\Sigma \bar{X} Y_i}{n} - \frac{\Sigma X_i \bar{Y}}{n} + \frac{\Sigma \bar{X}\bar{Y}}{n} \\ &= \frac{\Sigma X_i Y_i}{n} - \bar{X}\bar{Y} - \bar{X}\bar{Y} + \bar{X}\bar{Y} = \frac{\Sigma X_i Y_i}{n} - \bar{X}\bar{Y}, \end{aligned} \tag{13}$$

since $\dfrac{\bar{X}\Sigma Y_i}{n} = \bar{X}\bar{Y}$, $\dfrac{\Sigma X_i \bar{Y}}{n} = \bar{X}\bar{Y}$, and $\dfrac{\Sigma \bar{X}\bar{Y}}{n} = \dfrac{n\bar{X}\bar{Y}}{n} = \bar{X}\bar{Y}$.

The linear coefficient of correlation r_{XY} is defined as

$$r_{XY} = \frac{1}{n}\sum \frac{(X_i - \bar{X})}{\sigma_X}\frac{(Y_i - \bar{Y})}{\sigma_Y} = \frac{\text{Cov. }(X,Y)}{\sigma_X \sigma_Y} \tag{14}$$

This relation may be substituted in the relations for the two lines of regression given as equations (9) and (10), giving relations that are easier to use.

$$Y - \bar{Y} = \frac{\text{Cov. }(X,Y)}{\sigma_X \sigma_Y} \cdot \frac{\sigma_Y}{\sigma_X}(X - \bar{X}), \quad \text{or} \quad Y - \bar{Y} = \frac{\text{Cov. }(X,Y)}{\sigma_X^2}(X - \bar{X}) \tag{15}$$

$$X - \bar{X} = \frac{\text{Cov. }(X,Y)}{\sigma_X \sigma_Y} \cdot \frac{\sigma_X}{\sigma_Y}(Y - \bar{Y}), \quad \text{or} \quad X - \bar{X} = \frac{\text{Cov. }(X,Y)}{\sigma_Y^2}(Y - \bar{Y}) \tag{16}$$

7.3 Lines of Regression

When n pairs of X and Y values are listed and one is to be treated as the independent variable while the other is considered as the dependent variable, a preliminary line of best fit to these n pairs of values plotted as points on a graph may be estimated by several different crude methods. One very popular method is to estimate the line that will best fit the data by eye and draw such a line. A somewhat better, though not too exact, method is to divide the range of values into five to ten equal parts and determine average values of X and Y for each such segment. These average values serve as guides for estimating the line of best fit by eye. A relation for such a line is desired and may be obtained by relations given in analytical geometry texts. Since two points determine a straight line, two such points may be selected at the two extremes of the line.

Example 1 Twenty-five pairs of X, Y values have been found during a given year covering changes in the resistance of a particular type of coil with a nominal resistance value of 115 ohms, designated as Y, when subjected to different humidity conditions in percent, designated by X. Table 7.1 presents these data, slightly modified, taken in sequence and ordered by months rather

TABLE 7.1 Coil Resistance (Ohms) vs. Humidity (%)
Twenty-five Values Listed in Order with Respect to Time; One Year

Humidity in %, X	*Resistance in Ohms, Y*	*Humidity in %, X*	*Resistance in Ohms, Y*	*Humidity in %, X*	*Resistance in Ohms, Y*	*Humidity in %, X*	*Resistance in Ohms, Y*
50	125	5	103	30	112	40	115
10	100	48	120	42	117	12	102
36	117	35	118	47	123	22	112
15	108	18	110	14	103	44	115
45	120	45	118	40	120	25	114
20	107	43	120	25	110	46	119
43	122						

than by numerical values as recorded. Month-by-month data are given covering one year. Actual variations in resistance values are usually much smaller than those listed in this example; variations in these resistance values have been increased about tenfold so that the method in this example may be better understood. Humidity values do actually vary even more than listed, though only a range from 5% to 50% is used. As noted above, humidity will be represented by X, called *abscissa values,* while resistance measurements will be represented by Y, called *ordinate values*. This follows the usual practice where cartesian coordinates are used. The original time-ordered data are given in table 7.1.

These twenty-five values of (X, Y) are graphed in figure 7-1. Since all lines of regression must pass through the average point $(\overline{X}, \overline{Y})$ computed from the data, this point $(\overline{X}, \overline{Y}) = (32, 114)$ is also plotted. This point is obtained from the sums of X and Y values given in table 7.2, which shows the above data arranged as an ascending array of the X values, together with values and sums of X, Y, XY, X^2, Y^2, x, y, xy, x^2, and y^2. Figure 7-1 also shows an estimated line of regression described later.

Figure 7-1 shows the twenty-five data points (X, Y) and also the computed average point $(\overline{X}, \overline{Y}) = (32, 114)$. A line of regression passing through two selected extreme points on the graph, $(X, Y)_{min.} = (6, 100)$ and $(X, Y)_{max.} = (60, 129)$, as well as $(\overline{X}, \overline{Y})$, is fitted by eye. The equation for this estimated line is given on the graph. Its derivation is described later.

TABLE 7.2 Coil Resistance (Ohms), Y, vs. Humidity, X

Sample Number	Humidity $X\%$	Resistance in Ohms, Y	XY	X^2	Y^2	$X - \overline{X}$ $X - 32$ x	$Y - \overline{Y}$ $Y - 114$ y	xy	x^2	y^2
1	5	103	515	25	10609	−27	−11	297	729	121
2	10	100	1000	100	10000	−22	−14	308	484	196
3	12	102	1224	144	10404	−20	−12	240	400	144
4	14	103	1442	196	10609	−18	−11	198	324	121
5	15	108	1620	225	11664	−17	−6	102	289	36
6	18	110	1980	324	12100	−14	−4	56	196	16
7	20	107	2140	400	11449	−12	−7	84	144	49
8	22	112	2464	484	12544	−10	−2	20	100	4
9	25	114	2850	625	12996	−7	0	0	49	0
10	25	110	2750	625	12100	−7	−4	28	49	16
11	30	112	3360	900	12544	−2	−2	4	4	4
12	35	118	4130	1225	13924	3	4	12	9	16
13	36	117	4212	1296	13689	4	3	12	16	9
14	40	120	4800	1600	14400	8	6	48	64	36
15	40	115	4600	1600	13225	8	1	8	64	1
16	42	117	4914	1764	13689	10	3	30	100	9
17	43	120	5160	1849	14400	11	6	66	121	36
18	43	122	5246	1849	14884	11	8	88	121	64
19	44	115	5060	1936	13225	12	1	12	144	1
20	45	118	5310	2025	13924	13	4	52	169	16
21	45	120	5400	2025	14400	13	6	78	169	36
22	46	119	5474	2116	14161	14	5	70	196	25
23	47	123	5781	2209	15129	15	9	135	225	81
24	48	120	5760	2304	14400	16	6	96	256	36
25	50	125	6250	2500	15625	18	11	198	324	121
Sum	800	2850	93442	30346	326094	0	0	2242	4746	1194

The statistics derived from the above data are given below. Using these values, the line of best fit is derived for comparison with the relation derived from the estimated best line, as shown in figure 7-1.

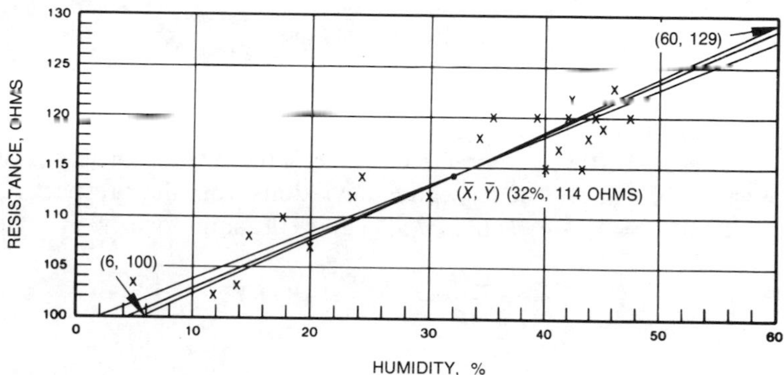

1. Est. equation for line of regression: $Y = 96.778 + 0.537X$
2. Line of regression: $Y = f(X) = Y = 98.88 + 0.472X$
3. Line of regression: $X = g(Y) = X = 182.06 + 1.877Y$
4. Coefficient of correction: $r_{XY} = 0.842$

Figure 7–1 Line of regression estimated by eye; resistance varies with humidity.

$$n = 25; \bar{X} = \frac{800}{25} = 32; \frac{\Sigma X^2}{n} = \frac{30346}{25} = 1213.84; \bar{X}^2 = (32)^2 = 1024$$

Using equations (2) and (3), we have $v_X = 1213.84 - 1024.00 = 189.84$ and $\sigma_X = \sqrt{v_X} = \sqrt{189.84} = 13.78$.

Sums are also given in table 7.2 for Y, Y^2, x, and x^2 values for the twenty-five values of resistance. Sums are also given for the possible correlation between humidity and resistance. These are the XY and xy values. From these values, we have the following statistics for these combined distributions.

$$n = 25: \bar{Y} = \frac{2850}{25} = 114 \text{ ohms}; \quad v_Y = \frac{326{,}094}{25} - (114)^2 = 13{,}043.76 - 12{,}996.00$$

$$= 47.76; \quad \sigma_Y = \sqrt{v_Y} = \sqrt{47.76} = 6.911$$

The coefficient of correlation $r_{XY} = \dfrac{\text{Cov.}(X, Y)}{\sigma_X \sigma_Y}$, where the covariance of XY is determined by the relation

$$\text{Cov.}(X, Y) = \frac{\Sigma(X_i - \bar{X})(Y_i - \bar{Y})}{n} = \frac{\Sigma XY}{n} - \bar{X}\bar{Y}$$

Using the sums given in table 7.2,

$$\text{Cov.}(X, Y) = \frac{93{,}442}{25} - (32)(114) = 3737.68 - 3648.00 = 89.68$$

Using this value of Cov. (X, Y),

$$r_{XY} = \frac{89.68}{(13.78)(6.91)} = \frac{89.68}{95.2198} = 0.942$$

Here the coefficient of correlation r_{XY} is positive, although the value of r may vary between -1 and $+1$. It is good practice to check these values where possible by using the values of x and y, the respective deviations from their respective means. $x_i = X_i - \bar{X}$ and $y_i = Y_i - \bar{Y}$. Table 7.2 also gives the sums for x, y, xy, x^2, and y^2.

$$v_X = \frac{\Sigma x_i^2}{n} = \frac{4746}{25} = 189.84$$

and

$$v_Y = \frac{\Sigma y_i^2}{n} = \frac{1194}{25} = 47.76$$

Also $\Sigma y_i = 0$. Cov. $(X, Y) = \Sigma x_i y_i / n = 2242/25 = 89.68$; all these values agree with those given earlier.

We wished to obtain a linear relation by which the resistance of a unit in ohms might be determined from a value of humidity given as a percentage value. Figure 7-1 showed such a line fitted by eye. The equation for such a line is determined by the following expression using two points (X_1, Y_1) and (X_2, Y_2), which fall on the chosen line. We can then check this relation to make certain that the line passes through the average point $(\bar{X}, \bar{Y})$. Two points determine a straight line on a plane. We can actually determine a linear equation for the line that passes through two known points by the relation

$$\frac{Y - Y_1}{X - X_1} = \frac{Y_2 - Y_1}{X_2 - X_1}, \quad \text{or} \quad Y = Y_1 + \frac{(X - X_1)(Y_2 - Y_1)}{(X_2 - X_1)} \tag{17}$$

The point on figure 7-1 selected at the lower end of the line is (6,100). This is the point (X_1, Y_1). The point at the upper end of the line is (60,129). This is the point (X_2, Y_2). The point used as a check on our equation is the two averages $(\bar{X}, \bar{Y}) = (32, 114)$. Substituting these values in relation (17) gives

$$Y = 100 + \frac{(X - 6)(129 - 100)}{(60 - 6)} = 100 + 0.537(X - 6) = 100 + 0.537X - 3.222;$$

$$Y = 96.778 + 0.537X.$$

This is the equation shown in figure 7-1. Its validity is now checked by substituting $\bar{X} = 32$ in the equation, giving $\bar{Y} = 96.778 + 17.184 = 113.962$, or about 114. The slight difference of 0.038 could be accounted for by using a more accurate approximation of the points (X_1, Y_1) and (X_2, Y_2), but the data do not warrant such accuracy. The line is only an estimate. The line of best fit derived from relations based on the method of least squares is given later and will be the best one to use. The line given here is just the first estimated line.

To find the line of best fit, it is necessary to determine values of a and b which make the distances $(Y - Y_t)_i$ a minimum when squared, for all values of Y_i for $i = 0, 1, 2, \ldots, n$. The corresponding Y_{t_i} values are the computed theoretical values of these Y_i values and are determined from the corresponding X_i values using the equation $Y = a + bX$. For X_i, then $Y_{t_i} = a + bX_i$. Y_{t_i} corresponds to X_i for theoretical values, whereas Y_i is the observed value for X_i.

There are actually two possible lines of regression or lines of best fit. The one discussed is of the form $Y = f(X)$. The second line of regression is denoted by $X = g(Y)$. This last equation is expressed as $X = c + dY$. To obtain the line of best fit, the differences used are $(X - X_t)$, (value of X observed minus the theoretical value of X derived from the relation $X = c + dY$). We make the sum of the squares of such differences a minimum by the relations used to compute the values of c and d to be substituted in the above equation. Both of these lines of regression will pass through the point $(\bar{X}, \bar{Y})$. If there exists 100% correlation, so that the coefficient of correlation r_{XY} is either plus one or minus one, then the two lines will coincide.

Let us first consider the derivation of the function $Y = f(X)$. The best theoretical values of a and b for the line of best fit by the method of least squares is based on the theory of errors. The subscript t has been placed on the Y value derived from the function $Y = f(X)$ as noted previously. There will be n of these Y_t values derived from the observed n values of X obtained in the sample on n units. The relation to be evaluated is

$$L_Y = \sum_{i=1}^{i=n} (Y - Y_t)_i^2, \tag{18}$$

where L_Y is a minimum. Appendix B shows in detail the derivation of the best values of a and b which satisfy the requirement stated in equation (18). The factors required to obtain these best values, based on the sums of the usual factors that must be computed to obtain the basic statistics from a set of data, are as follows.

$$a = \frac{(\Sigma Y \Sigma X^2 - \Sigma X \Sigma XY)}{[n\Sigma X^2 - (\Sigma X)^2]}$$
$$b = \frac{(n\Sigma XY - \Sigma X \Sigma Y)}{[n\Sigma X^2 - (\Sigma X)^2]} \tag{19}$$

We can use these values to modify equation (18) to obtain the best values of a and b to make L_Y a minimum.

$$L_Y = \sum_{i=1}^{i=n} [Y - (a + bX)]^2 \tag{20}$$

The relations in equation (19) provide the best values of a and b to use in securing the most accurate equation for the line of regression $Y = f(X)$. They must be computed from the sums of the values derived from n sets of points (X, Y). However, if the line of regression desired is for the relation $X = g(Y)$, then the relation expressed as a linear function is $X = c + dY$. Using the theory of errors, the line of best fit in this case using the method of least squares makes use of the relation

$$L_X = \sum_{i=1}^{i=n} (X - X_i)^2 = \sum_{i=1}^{i=n} [X - (c + dY)]^2, \tag{21}$$

where L_X is a minimum. Using relation (21), the derivation of the best values of c and d are described in detail in Appendix B. This derivation yields the relations below for computing the best values for c and d using the sums of the factors derived from n sets of points (X, Y). These factors are also used to obtain the other statistics used in controlling any desired characteristic at specified values.

$$\begin{aligned} c &= \frac{(\Sigma X \Sigma Y^2 - \Sigma Y \Sigma XY)}{[n\Sigma Y^2 - (\Sigma Y)^2]} \\ d &= \frac{(n\Sigma XY - \Sigma X \Sigma Y)}{[n\Sigma Y^2 - (\Sigma Y)^2]} \end{aligned} \tag{22}$$

These relations will be applied in a continuation of the example involving coil resistance versus humidity, whose data are given in table 7.2. All the sums needed to determine lines of best fit are listed there.

Example 2 Find the two lines of regression for the data given in table 7.2. Values of X and Y for 25 observations are listed in table 7.1. Figure 7-1 shows a graph of these values and a line fitted by eye to these data. The first solution provides values of a and b as well as an equation that may be compared with the first rough estimate of the best line of regression.

A summary of the sums required to obtain the lines of regression for this example as previously detailed follows.

$n = 25$; $\Sigma X = 800$; $\Sigma X^2 = 30{,}346$; $\Sigma Y = 2{,}850$; $\Sigma Y^2 = 326{,}094$; $\Sigma XY = 93{,}442$.

Substituting these values in equation (19) provides the necessary values of a and b that are used in equation (7).

$$a = \frac{[(2{,}850)(30{,}346) - (800)(93{,}442)]}{[(25)(30{,}346) - (800)^2]} = \frac{(86{,}486{,}100 - 74{,}753{,}600)}{(758{,}650 - 640{,}000)} = \frac{11{,}732{,}500}{118{,}650}$$
$$= 98.88327.$$

$$b = \frac{[(25)(93{,}442) - (800)(2{,}850)]}{[(25)(30{,}346) - (800)^2]} = \frac{(2{,}336{,}050 - 2{,}280{,}000)}{(758{,}650 - 640{,}000)} = \frac{56{,}050}{118{,}650}$$
$$= 0.4723978.$$

Based on these values, the line of best fit is

$$Y = 98.88 + 0.472X$$

rounding off the values of a and b to reasonable values.

This linear equation for the line of best fit may now be checked by the use of equations (9) and (15). To use these relations, it is first necessary to obtain some additional information, which may be determined from table 7.2 and from the computations made in the paragraphs below this table. The necessary information is

$$n = 25;\ \overline{X} = 32,\ \sigma_X^2 = v_X = 189.84,\ \sigma_X = 13.78;$$

$$\overline{Y} = 114,\ \sigma_Y^2 = v_Y = 47.76,\ \sigma_Y = 6.911;$$

$$\text{Cov.}\ (X, Y) = 89.69;\ r_{XY} = 0.942.$$

The first check will be made by substituting the above values in equation (9).

$$Y - 114 = \frac{(0.942)(6.911)}{13.78}(X - 32)$$

$$Y = 114 + \frac{6.510162}{13.78}(X - 32)$$

$$= 114 + 0.47244(X - 32)$$

$$= 114 + 0.47244X - 15.11808$$

$$= 98.88 + 0.472X.$$

The next check is to substitute values from above in equation (15).

$$Y - 114 = \frac{89.69}{189.84}(X - 32)$$

$$Y = 114 + 0.47245(X - 32)$$

$$= 114 + 0.472X - 15.1184$$

$$= 98.88 + 0.472X$$

Evaluating all three relations results in the same final equation for the line.

This line of best fit does not differ very much from the line obtained by fitting a line to the data by eye. This theoretical line of best fit based on the method of least squares has been drawn in as a dashed line on figure 7-1. In practice, the line of best fit is usually computed rather than estimated as the data are analyzed very thoroughly; all the necessary factors are computed and need only be substituted in one of these theoretical relations to obtain the desired line of regression.

For this example, the coefficient of correlation r_{XY} differs very little from 1 since it is 0.942. This second line of regression, $X = g(Y)$, will now be evaluated in the same way that $Y = f(X)$ was obtained. In actual practice, only the easiest relation to compute would be selected for the necessary substitutions; we will evaluate all three as a complete example of these computations. The relations to be evaluated are tied in with equations (8), (10), and (16). The same data will be used as before, so you may consult the summary listings above for these values. The values of c and d needed to determine the line of best fit as represented by equation (8), $X = c + dY$, are found from the relations in equation (22). Note that they are the same as for a and b except that the X terms and Y terms are reversed. Values for c and d are

$$c = \frac{[(800)(326{,}094) - (2{,}850)(93{,}442)]}{[(25)(326{,}094) - (2{,}850)^2]}$$

$$= \frac{(260{,}875{,}200 - 266{,}309{,}700)}{(8{,}152{,}350 - 8{,}122{,}500)}$$

$$= -\frac{5{,}434{,}500}{29{,}850} = -182.0603.$$

$$d = \frac{[(25)(93{,}442) - (800)(2{,}850)]}{[(25)(326{,}094) - (2{,}850)^2]}$$

$$= \frac{(2{,}336{,}050 - 2{,}280{,}000)}{(8{,}152{,}350 - 8{,}122{,}500)}$$

$$= \frac{56{,}050}{29{,}850} = 1.877722.$$

$$X = g(Y) = -182.06 + 1.878Y.$$

Equation (16) also may be used to obtain the second line of regression, $X = g(Y)$. Substituting the values listed previously gives

$$X - 32 = \frac{89.69}{47.76}(Y - 114)$$

$$X = 32 + 1.8779313(Y - 114)$$

$$= 32 + 1.878Y - 214.0842$$

$$= -182.084 + 1.878Y.$$

Another check is to substitute the correct computed terms from the example in equation (16). This gives the relation

$$X - 32 = \frac{89.69}{47.76}(Y - 114)$$

$$X = 32 + 1.8779313(Y - 114)$$

$$= 32 + 1.878Y - 214.08417$$

$$= -182.08 + 1.878Y.$$

The two lines of regression are:

(1) $Y = 98.88 + 0.472X$ and
(2) $X = -182.1 + 1.878Y$.

Both of these lines must pass through the average, the point $(\overline{X}, \overline{Y}) = (32, 114)$. Checking (1) gives $Y = 98.88 + 0.472(32) = 98.88 + 15.10 = 114$. Checking (2) gives $X = -182.1 + 1.878(114) = -182.1 + 214.092 = 32$. Both check. These two lines of regression are plotted in figure 7-1.

7.4 A Simple Technique to Obtain Best Linear Relation for Correlated Data

Calculating machine manuals on general statistics and quality control usually contain examples showing how to use Litton Ind's. computers to obtain the best linear relations for data that seem to be correlated. Such presentations give several excellent examples; one of these, with considerable modifications, is given below. Simple manual computations can be used to obtain these best lines of regression. As outlined in the previous section, it is necessary to list the data that are considered to be correlated as paired values of X and Y, which may be graphed as points on coordinate paper. For making the computations, the squares X^2 and Y^2 are tabulated, as well as the cross product XY. When summed, these values are used in conjunction with the number of points n to determine the factors used in obtaining the lines of regression and all the basic statistics for the two variables or characteristics involved.

Example 3 Complete a linear regression study covering six months' data listing the amount of production, Y, per month (given in thousands) for the monthly average temperature, X, in degrees Fahrenheit. These data are tabulated below, together with values of X^2, Y^2, and XY. These values are plotted in figure 7-2 with the lines of best fit $Y = f(X)$ and $X = g(Y)$ shown.

Correlation of X versus Y: X, Average Temperature, Degrees Fahrenheit (°F); Y × 10³, Units Produced per Month for Six Months

Month	Temp. °F X	Unit × 10^3 Y	X^2	Y^2	XY
March	60	133	3,600	17,689	7,980
April	65	124	4,225	15,376	8,060
May	76	100	5,776	10,000	7,600
June	81	83	6,561	6,889	6,723
July	85	78	7,225	6,084	6,630
August	89	72	7,921	5,184	6,408
Sum	456	590	35,308	61,222	43,401

$$n = 6: \ \overline{X} = \frac{456}{6} = 76.00; \ \sigma_X^2 = v_X = \frac{35308}{6} - (76)^2$$

$$= 5884.6667 - 5776 = 108.6667;$$

$$\overline{Y} = \frac{590}{6} = 98.3\dot{3}; \ \sigma_Y^2 = v_Y = \frac{61222}{6} - (98.3\dot{3})^2 = 10203.6667 - 9669.4443$$

$$= 534.2224;$$

$$\text{Cov.}\,(X, Y) = \frac{43401}{6} - (76.00)(98.33) = 7233.500 - 7473.3333 = -239.8333;$$

$$\sigma_X = \sqrt{108.6667} = 10.424$$

$$\sigma_Y = \sqrt{534.2224} = 23.113$$

$$r_{XY} = \frac{\text{Cov.}\,(X, Y)}{\sigma_X \sigma_Y}$$

$$= -\frac{239.8333}{(10.424)(23.113)} = -\frac{239.8333}{240.92991} = -0.99545.$$

Note that the coefficient of correlation is negative in this case, while in the previous example it is positive. Equation (15) gives the best relation to be used in obtaining the line of best fit.

$$Y - \overline{Y} = \frac{\text{Cov.}\,(X, Y)}{\sigma_X^2}(X - \overline{X})$$

$$Y - 98.33 = -\frac{239.8333}{108.6667}(X - 76)$$

$$Y = 98.33 - 2.2070542(X - 76)$$

$$= 98.33 - 2.207X + 167.73612$$

$$= 266.07 - 2.2071X, \quad \text{or} \quad Y = 266 - 2.21X$$

Note that in the above computations, the products and quotients were retained to about eight significant figures. However, the basic data are given only to three significant figures, so the final numbers in the equation most apt to be used are given to three significant figures. This line is shown on the graph in figure 7-2, which shows the basic six points given in this example. Recall that when the coefficient of correlation is plus one or minus one ($r_{XY} = +1$ or -1), the two lines of regression coincide. This example has almost perfect correlation—as indicated by the negative value -0.99545—so there will be little difference between the two lines of regression. The second line will be determined next using $X = g(Y)$ rather than $Y = f(X)$.

The corresponding second line of regression is evaluated below. Equation (16) will be used in its evaluation.

$$X - \bar{X} = \frac{\text{Cov. }(X, Y)}{\sigma_Y^2}(Y - \bar{Y})$$

$$X - 76.00 = -\frac{239.8333}{534.2224}(Y - 98.33)$$

$$X = 76.00 - 0.4489391(Y - 98.33)$$

$$= 76.00 \quad 0.4489391Y + 44.144182$$

$$= 120.14 - 0.44894Y, \quad \text{or} \quad X = 120 - 0.449Y$$

These two lines of regression should be checked by determining the values of a, b, c, and d. The reader should try to compute these values using the equations in (19) for a and b and the equations in (22) for c and d. Then check your answers against the values given below. Values of a and b are as follows.

$$a = \frac{(\Sigma Y \Sigma X^2 - \Sigma X \Sigma XY)}{n\Sigma X^2 - (\Sigma X)^2}$$

$$= \frac{(590)(35{,}308) - (456)(43{,}401)}{6(35{,}308) - (456)^2}$$

$$= \frac{(20{,}831{,}720 - 19{,}790{,}856)}{211{,}848 - 207{,}936}$$

$$= \frac{1{,}040{,}864}{3{,}912} = 266.06953$$

$$b = \frac{(n\Sigma XY - \Sigma X \Sigma Y)}{n\Sigma X^2 - (\Sigma X)^2}$$

$$= \frac{6(43{,}401) - (456)(590)}{6(35{,}308) - (456)^2}$$

$$= \frac{(260{,}406 - 269{,}040)}{211{,}848 - 207{,}936}$$

$$= -\frac{8{,}634}{3{,}912} = -2.2070552$$

Since $Y = a + bX$, then $Y = 266 - 2.21X$. This agrees with the previous evaluation.

The values of c and d are determined in the same manner.

$$c = \frac{(\Sigma X \Sigma Y^2 - \Sigma Y \Sigma XY)}{n\Sigma Y^2 - (\Sigma Y)^2}$$

$$= \frac{(456)(61{,}222) - (590)(43{,}401)}{6(61{,}222) - (590)^2}$$

$$= \frac{(27{,}917{,}232 - 25{,}606{,}590)}{(367{,}332 - 348{,}100)}$$

$$= \frac{2{,}310{,}642}{19{,}232} = 120.14569$$

$$d = \frac{(n\Sigma XY - \Sigma X \Sigma Y)}{n\Sigma Y^2 - (\Sigma Y)^2}$$

$$= \frac{6(43{,}401) - (456)(590)}{6(61{,}222) - (590)^2}$$

$$= \frac{(260{,}406 - 269{,}040)}{(367{,}332 - 348{,}100)}$$

$$= -\frac{8{,}634}{19{,}232} = -0.4489393$$

The value of $X = g(Y)$ may be determined by substituting these values of c and d in the relation $X = c + dY$, giving $X = 120 - 0.449Y$. This is the same as the relation given earlier. These two regression lines are shown on figure 7-2. The two lines are almost the same, as the correlation value of -0.99545 is very close to -1. Note that this correlation is negative; hence the slopes of the lines of regression are negative, as contrasted with the previous example.

Correlations of this linear type are required in many different fields other than quality control and engineering. Those who develop nondestructive testing to replace costly destructive methods find that regression equations like these will provide the necessary observations to determine whether certain critical characteristics meet their requirements. If positive evidence is obtained that the product either fails or does not fail to meet the critical tolerances, then an immediate judgment may be made to reject or accept the units involved. If there is a

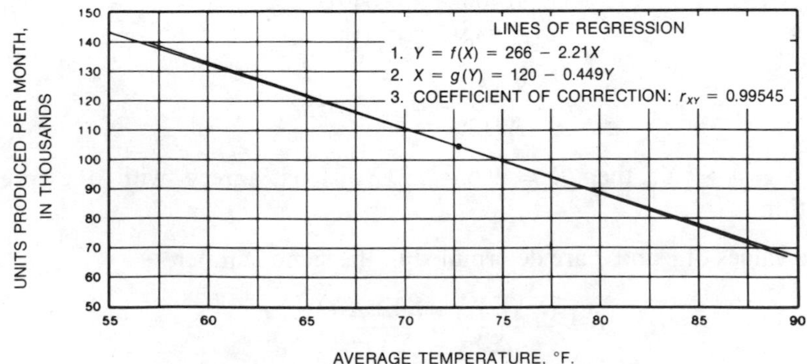

Figure 7–2 Lines of regression: average temperature per month *vs.* units produced per month for six months.

questionable result, it may be necessary to actually perform a few additional destructive tests for the characteristic in question. For this example covering average temperature versus production in terms of units produced, the possible conclusion might be to install temperature controls in the production area.

7.5 Extension of Correlation Techniques Based on Theory of Errors

In certain phases of quality control work, lines of best fit are found and checked for goodness of fit by the Chi-square test for critical variables. For example, for smog control the two most important constituents may be represented by a daily linear relation. We then ask what the most probable value for the week is, as derived from such a set of lines. An analysis of the assignable causes may be made with the objective of reducing the amount of pollution in the future. Some lines may be based on a large quantity of data and others may be based on fewer data. It is possible to obtain the most probable value from such lines weighted by the amount of data utilized in each analysis for each line. Appendix B covers the theoretical development of a solution based upon weighted values as well as items of equal weight. In this section, it will be assumed that the lines are of equal value to best illustrate the method of applying these techniques. Only those relations requiring simple computations to obtain the normal equations are presented; from such relations, the desired most probable value based on the theory of least squares can also be found.

This problem arises when there are n observed relations covering m variables, where n is greater than m ($n > m$) as compared with the case where $n = m$. All such linear relations must be treated in obtaining the most probable solution. For the simplest case involving only two variables x and y, the relations would be of the form $a_1x + b_1y + c_1 = 0$, $a_2x + b_2y + c_2 = 0$, and $a_3x + b_3y + c_3 = 0$. In the above, there are n observed linear equations using m variables, where n is 3 and m is 2, so that n is greater than m. There are also three constants given in each equation.

The generalized form treated in the appendix is as follows.

$$\begin{array}{c} a_1x_1 + b_1x_2 + c_1x_3 + \cdots + f_1x_m + k_1 = 0 \\ a_2x_1 + b_2x_2 + c_2x_3 + \cdots + f_2x_m + k_2 = 0 \\ \cdots\cdots\cdots\cdots\cdots\cdots\cdots\cdots\cdots\cdots \\ a_nx_1 + b_nx_2 + c_nx_3 + \cdots + f_nx_m + k_n = 0 \end{array} \tag{23}$$

The unknown residual of error is designated as v_r in the rth equations corresponding to the true values of $x_1, x_2, \ldots, x_m$, given as

$$v_r = a_rx_1 + b_rx_2 + \cdots + f_rx_m + k_r, \qquad r = 1, 2, 3, \ldots, n \tag{24}$$

Evaluating this relation, as shown in the appendix, results in the two simple tables used to obtain the normal equations. For two variables x and y the relation is

$$ax + by + k = 0 \tag{25}$$

where a set of a, b, and k values may be found for each observed or derived equation. An example for this simple case will follow after the two tables giving the relations used to determine the normal equations that are to be solved. These tables cover the case where the number of variables, m, is three, but may be readily expanded to cover any m value. The equations covered are of the form: $ax + by + cz + k = 0$.

TABLE 7.3 Form for Tabulation of Coefficients equals Sum of Coefficients and Constants $s = a + b + c + k$

First Tabulation	*a*	*b*	*c*	*k*
Equation 1:				
Equation 2:				
Equation 3:				
Equation 4:				
....				
Equation n:				

TABLE 7.4 Form for Determining Coefficients from Normal Equations that Result in Most Probable Values of Variables

Equation Number	*aa*	*ab*	*ac*	*ak*	*as*	*bb*	*bc*	*bk*	*bs*	*cc*	*ck*	*cs*
1												
2												
3												
4												
5												
⋮												
n												
Sum												

Use Sums of Products of Coefficients Below:

Normal Equations: $\Sigma aax + \Sigma aby + \Sigma acz + \Sigma ak = 0$;
$\Sigma bax + \Sigma bby + \Sigma bcz + \Sigma bk = 0$;
$\Sigma cax + \Sigma cby + \Sigma ccz + \Sigma ck = 0$.

Check on Results:

$\Sigma aa + \Sigma ab + \Sigma ac + \Sigma ak = \Sigma as$;
$\Sigma ba + \Sigma bb + \Sigma bc + \Sigma bk = \Sigma bs$;
$\Sigma ca + \Sigma cb + \Sigma cc + \Sigma ck = \Sigma cs$.

NOTE: Σab is equal to Σba, Σac is equal to Σca, and Σbc is equal to Σcb.

This technique is used for a series of linear relations that have somewhat similar slopes and gives the most probable value for such a series. An interesting case is found when there are three linear equations with two variables and the three lines intersect. Sometimes the average of the three intersecting x values and the average of the three corresponding y values will be the same as the most probable value. Examples have been found where this does occur. Two examples will be presented showing the use of these techniques. Both will use only two variables, x and y, although the first will use four equations and the second will use three linear equations that intersect (forming a triangle). These linear equations will be graphed to show the desirability of using these techniques in obtaining the most probable values for the variables involved. Few texts present this method, but it is a very valuable tool in quality control work

Example 4 Determine the most probable values of x and y for the following four observed relations by the techniques outlined.

(1) $x + y - 4 = 0$ (2) $2x + y - 1 = 0$
(3) $x + 2y - 2 = 0$ (4) $3x + y - 3 = 0$

Solution Using table 7.3 as a guide, the coefficients of x and y and the constants k and s, the sum of the coefficients and the constant term are tabulated.

Tabulation of Terms

Relation	*a*	*b*	*k*	*s*
(1)	1	1	−4	−2
(2)	2	1	−1	2
(3)	1	2	−2	1
(4)	3	1	−3	1

$s = a + b + k.$

Values from the above tabulation are next set up in the form given in table 7.4.

Determination of Two Normal Equations

Relation	*aa*	*ab*	*ak*	*as*	*bb*	*bk*	*bs*
(1)	1	1	−4	−2	1	−4	−2
(2)	4	2	−2	4	1	−1	2
(3)	1	2	−2	1	4	−4	2
(4)	9	3	−9	3	1	−3	1
Sum	15	8	−17	6	7	−12	3

Normal Equations: I. $15x + 8y - 17 = 0$; Check: $15 + 8 - 17 = 6 = \Sigma as$.
II. $8x + 7y - 12 = 0$; Check: $8 + 7 - 12 = 3 = \Sigma bs$.

Values of x and y found by obtaining a common solution for equations I and II will give the desired most probable values for these two variables based on these four observed relations. There are two means of finding this common solution.

Method 1 Multiply equation I by 7 gives: $105x + 56y - 119 = 0$
Multiply equation II by 8 gives: $64x + 56y - 96 = 0$
Subtracting II from I gives: $41x + 0y - 23 = 0$
Thus $41x = 23$ and $x = \frac{23}{41} = 0.561$

Multiply equation I by 8 gives: $120x + 64y - 136 = 0$
Multiply equation II by 15 gives: $120x + 105y - 180 = 0$
Subtracting II from I gives: $0x - 41y + 44 = 0$
Thus $-41y = -44$ and $y = \frac{44}{41} = 1.073$.

Method 2 The general solution for the two linear equations $a_1x + b_1y = k_1$ and $a_2x + b_2y = k_2$ by determinants follows.

$$x = \frac{\begin{vmatrix} k_1 & b_1 \\ k_2 & b_2 \end{vmatrix}}{\begin{vmatrix} a_1 & b_1 \\ a_2 & b_2 \end{vmatrix}} = \frac{k_1b_2 - k_2b_1}{a_1b_2 - a_2b_1} \quad \text{and} \quad y = \frac{\begin{vmatrix} a_1 & k_1 \\ a_2 & k_2 \end{vmatrix}}{\begin{vmatrix} a_1 & b_1 \\ a_2 & b_2 \end{vmatrix}} = \frac{a_1k_2 - a_2k_1}{a_1b_2 - a_2b_1}$$

Normal Equations

I. $15x + 8y = 17$
II. $8x + 7y = 12$

Solution

$$x = \frac{\begin{vmatrix} 17 & 8 \\ 12 & 7 \end{vmatrix}}{\begin{vmatrix} 15 & 8 \\ 8 & 7 \end{vmatrix}} = \frac{17(7) - 12(8)}{15(7) - 8(8)} = \frac{119 - 96}{105 - 64} = \frac{23}{41} = 0.561$$

$$y = \frac{\begin{vmatrix} 15 & 17 \\ 8 & 12 \end{vmatrix}}{\begin{vmatrix} 15 & 8 \\ 8 & 7 \end{vmatrix}} = \frac{15(12) - 8(17)}{15(7) - 8(8)} = \frac{180 - 136}{105 - 64} = \frac{44}{41} = 1.073$$

This type of solution can be programmed on a computer; then it is necessary only to provide values for the coefficients and constants for the n relations and the computer will provide almost immediately a set of values for the most probable values for the m variables.

The next example has been selected to show a probable value for three linear relations that intersect at three points, where this probable value is also the same point on the graph as the average values of the three x and y values found for the points of intersection of these three lines. Thus this point is similar to the center of gravity (CG) of this system of lines. This relationship occurs in many cases; where it does not occur, the probable value will be in the neighborhood of the average value. Various central points within the triangle can be found from the three intersecting lines. For example, three perpendicular bisectors can be drawn to the given lines, providing a point of intersection within the triangle; such a point is similar to the center of gravity of this system. Another point within the triangle is obtained by drawing lines from the midpoints of the three sides of the triangle to its vertices. Yet another may be obtained by drawing three angle bisectors. Where the three intersecting lines form an equilateral triangle, all these points will coincide. This is a special case which might occur frequently.

In quality control work, the cases that occur involve n relations that have quite similar slopes. Figure 7-3 shows the four linear relations covered in example 4. The two normal relations found for these four relations are shown as dotted lines on this graph, along with the probable value obtained as their intersection.

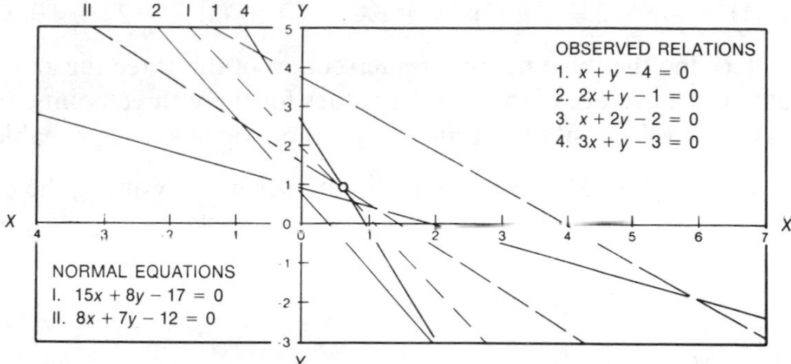

Figure 7–3 Probable value (x, y) for four observed relations with two variables.

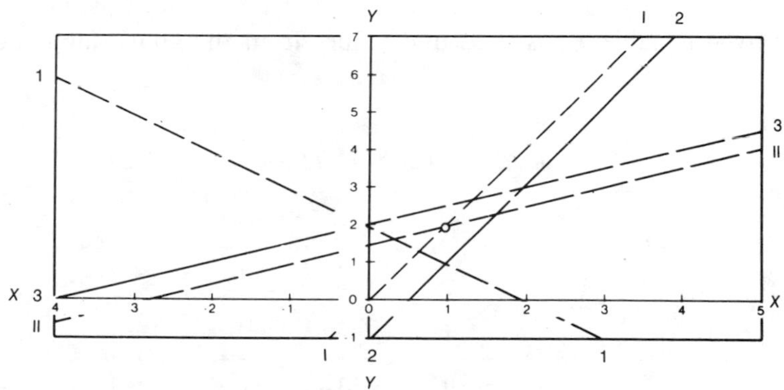

Figure 7–4 Probable value (x, y); another set of relationships and variables.

Example 5 illustrates the case where three lines intersect. The probable value found by the techniques based on the method of least squares is identical with the average x and y values obtained from the three points of intersection. Figure 7-4 shows these three relations as solid lines and their resultant two normal relations as dotted lines. The point of intersection of the dotted lines gives the values of x and y which are considered to be their most probable values. Other values will have a larger residual error.

Other somewhat similar cases where the averages of the intersecting lines do not equal the probable value of x and y obtained by the techniques based on the method of least squares should be studied.

Example 5 Determine the two normal equations and the most probable values of x and y for the following three observed relations which intersect at three points, using the techniques outlined earlier.

$$(1)\ x + y - 2 = 0; \quad (2)\ 2x - y - 1 = 0; \quad (3)\ x - 2y + 4 = 0.$$

Also determine the three points of intersection of the three linear equations and obtain the average of the x and y values for these three points. Compare these average values with the x and y values obtained as the probable values.

Solution Using table 7.3 as a guide, the coefficients of x and y, the constants k and s, and the sum of the coefficients and the constant term are tabulated.

Tabulation of Terms

Relation	a	b	k	s
(1)	1	1	−2	0
(2)	2	−1	−1	0
(3)	1	−2	4	3

$s = a + b + k.$

The form given in table 7.4 is used and values from the above tabulation are entered.

Determination of Two Normal Equations

Relation	aa	ab	ak	as	bb	bk	bs
(1)	1	1	−2	0	1	−2	0
(2)	4	−2	−2	0	1	1	0
(3)	1	−2	4	3	4	−8	−6
Sum	6	−3	0	3	6	−9	−6

General Form of Normal Equations

I. $\Sigma aax + \Sigma aby + \Sigma ak = 0$

II. $\Sigma bax + \Sigma bby + \Sigma bk = 0,\ ab = ba$

Normal Equations

I. $6x - 3y + 0 = 0$; Check: $6 - 3 + 0 = 3$

II. $-3x + 6y - 9 = 0$; Check: $-3 + 6 - 9 = -6$

or

I. $2x - y = 0$

II. $x - 2y = -3$

Solution of Normal Equations

$$\begin{array}{r} 4x - 2y = 0 \\ -x + 2y = 3 \\ \hline 3x + 0y = 3 \end{array}$$

$x = 1$; since $y = 2x$ (from I), $y = 2$. These are the probable values.

Figure 7-4 provides a graphical solution for the three points of intersection, (1, 1), (2, 3), and (0, 2). These values may be found algebraically, as shown below.

$$\begin{array}{lr} (1) & x + y - 2 = 0 \\ (2) & 2x - y - 1 = 0 \\ \hline \text{Add:} & 3x + 0y - 3 = 0 \end{array} \qquad \begin{array}{lr} (1) & 2x + 2y - 4 = 0 \\ (3) & x - 2y + 4 = 0 \\ \hline \text{Add:} & 3x + 0y + 0 = 0 \end{array} \qquad \begin{array}{lr} (2) & 4x - 2y - 2 = 0 \\ (3) & x - 2y + 4 = 0 \\ \hline \text{Subtract:} & 3x + 0y - 6 = 0 \end{array}$$

Points of intersection: $x = 1$ | $x = 0$ | $x = 2$

$y = 2 - x = 2 - 1 = 1$ | $y = 2 - x = 2 - 0 = 2$ | $y = 2x - 1 = 4 - 1 = 3$

The sum of these three x intersecting values is $1 + 0 + 2 = 3$, so the average is $\bar{x} = 1$. The sum of these three y intersecting values is $1 + 2 + 3 = 6$, so the average is $\bar{y} = 2$. These agree with the most probable value (1, 2) determined earlier.

7.6 Results of Correlation Studies

Correlation methodology is generally applied in quality control work to provide nondestructive testing for destructive tests. When a stipulation is made that requires the destruction of the part tested, units in lots classed as nonconforming cannot be subjected to 100% inspection. Such screening must be performed by some correlated test that does not injure the units inspected or tested. Great strides have been made in recent years in securing many different types of tests to cover important characteristics that are nondestructive in nature. Rockwell Hardness tests replace tests for tensile strength which required the test specimens to be destroyed. The statistical techniques which can be applied to determine the degree of correlation between two such related tests have been presented. Linear correlation techniques will be found applicable in the majority of cases. There are, however, many cases where nonlinear correlation techniques should be used. Data previously secured for checks on possible correlations may be found which will provide a valid measure of such correlations and provide the range of values already obtained for the coefficient of correlation. Confidence in such tests will thus be gained.

EXERCISES

1. (a) Arrange the following data covering two variables in an ascending pattern, starting with the smallest value of X. Tabulate the corresponding Y values, which will not be ordered unless there is perfect correlation.

	X	Y	X	Y
	9	13	5	9
	7	12	10	13
	11	14	2	5
	0	3	4	6
	3	8	9	17
Sum	30	50	30	50

(b) Graph these ten points on coordinate graph paper.

2. For the data in exercise, determine (a) the averages or arithmetic means, (b) the variances, and (c) the standard deviations for X and Y respectively.

3. (a) Determine the covariance for the ten points in exercise 1. (b) Determine the coefficient of correlation, r_{XY}, for the ten points in exercise 1 from the relation: $r_{XY} = \dfrac{\text{Cov. }(X, Y)}{\sigma_X \sigma_Y}$, where the Cov. $(X, Y) = \dfrac{\Sigma(X_i - \bar{X})(Y_i - \bar{Y})}{n}, \dfrac{\Sigma x_i y_i}{n}$, or $\dfrac{\Sigma XY}{n} - \bar{X}\bar{Y}$.

4. Use the data in exercise 1. (a) Determine the two lines of regression by finding the values of a and b for the relation $Y = a + bX$ and the values of c and d for the relation $X = c + dY$.
(b) Check the two lines of regression found in (a) against the two lines of regression obtained from the relations $X - \bar{X} = \dfrac{\text{Cov. }(X, Y)}{\sigma_Y^2} \cdot (Y - \bar{Y})$, and

$$Y - \bar{Y} = \frac{\text{Cov. }(X, Y)}{\sigma_X^2} \cdot (X - \bar{X}).$$

5. (a) Determine ten values of $Z = X + Y$ for the ten values of X and Y given in exercise 1 and then find (1) the average or arithmetical mean, (2) the variance, and (3) the standard deviation value for Z.
(b) Determine the variance of Z from the previously determined values of σ_X^2, σ_Y^2 and r_{XY} using the relation: $\sigma_{Z=X+Y}^2 = \sigma_X^2 + \sigma_Y^2 + 2r_{XY}\sigma_X\sigma_Y = \sigma_X^2 + \sigma_Y^2 + 2 \text{ Cov. }(X, Y)$.
6. (a) Using the ten values of X and Y given in exercise 1, determine ten values of $W = Y - X$ and then find the (1) average, (2) variance, and (3) standard deviation for W.
(b) Check the variance found in (a) using the relation

$$\sigma_{W=Y-X}^2 = \sigma_Y^2 + \sigma_X^2 - 2r_{XY}\sigma_X\sigma_Y = \sigma_Y^2 + \sigma_X^2 - 2 \text{ Cov. }(X, Y).$$

7. If these X and Y values are treated as independent values, then the sum of all possible random values, $Z = X + Y$ for $10 \times 10 = 100$ possible sums should have an average equal to the sum of the X and Y values and a variance value equal to the sum of the variances of X and Y since, if independent, $r_{XY} = 0$. Check this theorem by arranging the 100 values of Z in an ordered distribution and then determining the average and variance of this distribution of 100 Z values. Check both results against the statements that both average values of X and Y and variance values of X and Y are additive and will give the same respective values.
8. (a) If the possible differences between Y and X (assuming all possible 100 random values of $W = Y - X$ where Y is assumed to be independent of X) are found and arranged in an ordered distribution, then determine (1) the average and also (2) the variance. (As a guide the first twelve values with a few of the unordered but sequential differences as obtained from the data in exercise 1 are: 4, 6, 2, 13, 10, 8, 3, 11, 9, 4, 3, 5,... ; 8, 10, 6, 17, ..., 13, 8. If such a pattern is followed, no values will be omitted in determining the 100 W values. The last two shown above were obtained by listing $17 - 4 = 13$, and $17 - 9 = 8$.
(b) Check the values of $\bar{W}$, the average, and the variance σ_W^2 against the theoretical values determined from the relations: $\bar{W} = \bar{Y} - \bar{X}$ and $\sigma_W^2 = \sigma_Y^2 + \sigma_X^2$.

9. (a) Determine the two normal equations for the two variables x and y for the linear expressions (1) $x - y - 1 = 0$, (2) $x + y - 1 = 0$, and (3) $x - 2y - 1 = 0$. Use the techniques involving the expressions in tables 7.3 and 7.4.
(b) Obtain the values of x and y for the intersection of the two normal relations. This point $(x, y)_p$ is the most probable value for this system of observed relations.

10. (a) Determine the two normal equations for the variables x and y for the linear relations (1) $x + y - 1 = 0$, (2) $x - y - 3 = 0$, and (3) $x - 2y + 2 = 0$.
(b) From the two normal equations obtained in (a), determine the most probable value $(x, y)_p$.

11. (a) Determine the two normal equations for the linear relations (1) $2x - y - 1 = 0$, (2) $x + y - 4 = 0$, and (3) $x - 2y - 1 = 0$.
(b) From the two normal equations obtained in (a), determine the most probable value $(x, y)_p$. This value is to be compared with the average values of x and y found in (c).
(c) Determine both graphically and algebraically the intersection values (x, y) for the three relations in (a). Determine the average $\bar{x}$ for the three x values and the average $\bar{y}$ for the three values of y. Compare $(\bar{x}, \bar{y})$ with $(x, y)_p$ which is the most probable value (x, y) determined in (b).

12. (a) Determine the two normal equations in terms of x and y for the following observed relations: (1) $x + y - 1 = 0$, (2) $x - y + 2 = 0$, (3) $2x - y - 3 = 0$, (4) $2x - 3y + 1 = 0$, and (5) $2x - 3y + 4 = 0$.
(b) Determine the most probable value of x and y, $(x, y)_p$, from the two normal relations determined in (a).

13. Graph the five observed relations given in exercise 12 (a) and also the two normal equations determined in 12 (a) on coordinate graph paper. Note on this graph the most probable value $(x, y)_p$, the intersection of the normal relations.

14. (a) Determine the two normal equations in terms of x and y for the following observed relations (1) $x + y - 1 = 0$, (2) $x - y - 1 = 0$, (3) $x + 3y - 3 = 0$, and (4) $3x + 3y - 5 = 0$.
(b) Plot the four observed relations and the two normal relations determined in (a) above on coordinate graph paper.
(c) Determine the most probable value of x and y for the four observed relations using the two normal equations determined in (a). Mark this point $(x, y)_p$ on your graph.

15. The following values of X and Y have been obtained and are thought to be correlated. Only five points have been given. These are:

$$X:\ 0,\ 2,\ 1,\ 4,\ 3 \quad \text{and}$$
$$Y:\ 2,\ 0,\ 4,\ 2,\ 7.$$

(a) Graph these five points (X, Y).
(b) Determine the coefficient of correlation r_{XY} for these five pairs of values.
(c) Determine and graph the two lines of regression.
(d) Give the equations for these two lines of regression.
(e) Are these values sufficiently correlated to use as a basis for future tests?

16. (a) What information that is useful for quality control work may be obtained by using the method of linear correlation?
(b) What may be learned from the determination of the most probable value for a set of observed relations?

17. Three methods are now being used for controlling the quality of manufactured products:

(1) The method of control charts;

(2) The method of correlation (both linear and nonlinear); and
(3) The method termed the analysis of variance.

(a) Which of these methods do you believe is most effective? Give reasons for your answer.
(b) All three methods have areas where they are most effective. Discuss the possibility of using all methods so as to have the most efficient operations employing all the best statistical techniques.

CHAPTER EIGHT

DESIGN OF EXPERIMENTS

8.1 Objective

One of the most powerful statistical tools that can be applied to quality control is the analysis of variance technique. It was first developed by R. A. Fisher for use in agriculture, but has been found extremely helpful in analyzing variations in quality that occur in production and all phases of management, especially in data processing. Its effectiveness depends on having available for analysis good data. Such data are obtained by the application of the best designs of experiments. These designs are a great improvement over the older classical designs, in which all variables except one were held constant successively for the characteristics under study while carrying out the experiment or test.

It is the purpose of this chapter to cover the most efficient applications of these techniques. We will indicate how to obtain and record data in such a way that the most appropriate statistical methods may be applied to the data. By proper computations, the results obtained will provide valid results that, in turn may be used in making important decisions. In most companies, these techniques are introduced by either quality control or the statistical group.

Many different engineering designs may be developed to secure a complex system that functions in accordance with customer demands. It is then necessary to select the design which is the best, the most economical and which will result in the most reliable products. A final judgment is rendered only when an analysis has been made of the critical characteristics of the system. In obtaining the data necessary for use in such an analysis, it is usually wise to provide the most effective design, such as is discussed in this chapter. Analysis of variance techniques are presented in basic forms with examples of their use. It will be shown how to make decisions after completing the analysis that should result in maximum profits and minimum costs.

The difference between the classical method and the factorial design method is also discussed. By comparing these methods, the best possible designs of experiments may be developed. This chapter presents the techniques of the analysis of variance method, which can be used in most cases. Only about 5% to 10% of the situations encountered will require the more complex techniques covered in texts devoted entirely to the analysis of variance. Special attention will be paid to the proper use of the *Fisher test* (called the *F-test*). The best method of analysis is given and illustrated by examples showing how to select the factors contributing most to the end results from an adequate experimental design. Fundamental designs will be presented to check whether significant differences exist and whether they fall into one of the following three categories.

1. Lack of control for dispersion or an extremely large variability. This may result in many nonconforming units, whereas the methods considered have essentially the same central value for the critical characteristics of the product or method under consideration.
2. Lack of control for both central values and dispersion. This condition results in many unexpected occurrences of nonconforming units. There will be found a lack of homogeneity in the data for the various characteristics studied.
3. Lack of control for central values when variability is well controlled within desired limits and has little effect on the wide differences noted. Most texts consider only this case.

TABLE 8.1 Random Sampling Numbers Part 1 Lines 1–25

Group	*A*					*B*					*C*					*D*					*E*				
Column / *Line*	1	2	3	4	5	6	7	8	9	10	11	12	13	14	15	16	17	18	19	20	21	22	23	24	25
1	68	30	22	50	75	28	82	03	62	14	86	52	20	36	01	26	14	91	76	60	24	77	21	48	97
2	00	57	99	63	85	05	25	32	92	53	99	71	32	77	51	32	19	67	85	15	69	36	56	82	12
3	35	73	84	25	97	59	83	45	49	24	34	28	70	58	35	12	45	63	97	28	72	47	73	66	48
4	40	69	18	22	61	85	73	23	71	53	74	78	99	79	87	81	13	95	61	11	96	39	75	23	17
5	54	19	88	37	16	03	91	57	41	13	38	60	34	13	33	58	70	01	16	87	12	60	47	00	84
6	23	40	25	57	42	62	33	79	58	70	60	03	43	71	67	35	18	44	61	51	39	46	67	36	92
7	06	86	74	89	96	36	56	80	44	18	93	27	97	07	89	03	59	10	96	83	09	75	35	74	47
8	39	69	49	96	07	58	88	10	69	59	66	04	80	53	53	83	56	52	07	90	46	41	30	86	29
9	30	20	96	89	10	83	32	98	25	84	21	17	44	12	77	48	05	87	53	56	16	07	72	37	64
10	49	35	93	85	53	54	44	79	08	62	65	23	69	93	46	18	22	06	10	21	72	88	63	51	81
11	80	72	54	28	33	94	95	70	90	05	71	85	06	88	73	62	72	91	33	74	52	40	55	01	54
12	78	84	64	63	03	39	00	89	52	72	45	15	79	09	47	52	86	33	03	51	87	74	18	68	18
13	50	14	38	09	92	77	78	42	30	17	94	81	65	12	21	77	93	30	88	65	42	94	52	27	27
14	27	63	57	10	85	34	42	80	66	93	81	10	92	91	09	34	81	19	85	96	71	15	62	40	13
15	64	54	21	07	08	67	04	37	97	81	68	48	96	18	90	44	92	05	08	14	67	77	09	45	64
16	37	15	43	61	25	98	82	56	49	92	80	95	80	84	17	42	44	29	51	32	55	47	14	43	48
17	27	59	29	76	68	60	38	15	71	44	90	20	90	15	42	16	29	28	60	53	26	93	16	67	22
18	74	27	89	01	04	29	91	78	49	29	22	68	36	82	84	74	00	75	94	25	87	64	86	99	01
19	32	91	76	51	59	90	54	59	51	13	64	06	43	98	14	05	04	82	10	88	06	04	95	50	94
20	73	49	16	48	98	29	65	01	59	04	75	11	45	07	94	31	26	99	09	50	27	56	33	89	37
21	26	20	46	66	36	31	50	61	03	75	35	24	69	41	26	73	86	00	02	37	31	02	34	08	78
22	47	17	22	15	77	38	12	02	95	31	79	66	55	83	43	57	34	46	55	28	37	76	26	24	99
23	30	43	93	28	58	57	39	41	23	11	68	08	40	50	76	23	62	98	19	11	24	58	11	75	02
24	19	20	38	05	11	98	55	46	06	99	41	67	55	63	45	99	87	00	97	31	21	99	39	83	68
25	48	47	17	70	13	02	61	24	65	08	66	78	83	02	40	90	94	26	20	73	70	31	65	08	41

The best statistical tests should be made to determine which of these three chief possible reasons for lack of control exist. One should be able to state with confidence that lack of control does not exist. These tests are covered, as well as the best elemental designs of experiments. Modern statistical methods result in less error by using measures based on degrees of freedom for these tests rather than the number n measured. This concept is treated herein so that the designs and tests used, together with the computations, are in proper form to make use of the printed tables prepared to evaluate these tests in terms of probability values or whatever measures have been used in the analysis.

8.2 Random Numbers

In inspection, samples must be selected at random for inspection results to be effective. All samples selected for experiments and tests, as well as for inspection, should be truly representative. These random samples are considered to be representative samples, also called *unbiased samples.* Many costly experiments are complete failures because the samples used were not selected correctly under

TABLE 8.1 Random Sampling Numbers Part 2 Lines 26–50

Group	*A*					*B*					*C*					*D*					*E*				
Column / *Line*	1	2	3	4	5	6	7	8	9	10	11	12	13	14	15	16	17	18	19	20	21	22	23	24	25
26	87	38	88	54	46	40	49	71	58	26	68	72	00	32	36	50	61	79	96	29	07	10	80	86	48
27	76	67	42	78	03	62	03	66	35	28	09	97	53	82	22	79	22	80	30	80	61	09	06	98	92
28	17	88	75	40	08	75	56	13	46	15	93	33	65	81	97	33	14	96	25	47	75	86	57	33	84
29	18	56	52	02	51	41	48	78	50	61	25	81	83	90	07	85	08	34	00	73	44	58	65	75	46
30	92	13	53	90	23	01	23	39	76	14	28	34	47	52	79	26	24	07	94	37	70	63	77	50	19
31	00	38	84	73	32	20	43	88	87	73	99	72	03	77	00	53	13	91	82	93	56	14	35	85	38
32	79	67	30	05	22	98	40	03	98	61	37	71	28	46	55	68	70	39	32	28	36	91	02	03	95
33	82	28	82	91	81	41	66	35	54	36	12	31	88	12	25	04	55	63	77	27	40	67	37	62	41
34	51	15	59	39	30	37	20	34	71	22	30	45	69	65	52	53	59	95	44	43	95	26	34	69	05
35	01	64	21	46	76	87	74	18	36	63	85	68	05	76	88	66	72	01	25	97	56	78	51	93	19
36	20	96	84	49	60	60	22	66	89	58	81	23	10	13	01	14	82	98	50	19	88	02	87	48	02
37	52	27	31	62	43	69	93	68	53	76	10	09	50	19	44	12	09	68	33	90	20	85	27	92	11
38	74	10	67	07	40	16	99	40	94	99	43	76	34	66	63	49	45	42	00	97	52	97	17	84	37
39	14	39	34	69	19	66	18	23	16	45	52	21	39	06	09	17	99	17	71	58	30	61	39	46	35
40	21	60	19	83	72	59	88	26	04	11	79	86	50	81	61	84	04	68	95	06	00	11	60	55	26
41	63	18	29	92	35	60	84	11	27	89	97	95	60	21	15	62	79	54	62	54	14	42	04	09	41
42	11	23	33	15	87	86	25	94	77	74	83	33	15	83	64	47	45	83	65	42	21	96	23	38	78
43	58	94	65	13	17	24	74	55	48	91	24	71	49	44	07	29	00	94	80	12	75	68	94	95	31
44	16	57	86	16	73	42	49	80	53	24	98	95	60	11	86	64	10	73	06	45	18	10	59	41	83
45	77	38	30	48	89	25	96	43	32	29	62	70	12	85	57	81	54	44	57	56	58	53	38	15	55
46	12	25	04	73	96	72	93	08	90	70	98	80	17	90	64	44	85	51	65	64	21	32	56	87	50
47	82	08	24	70	91	02	54	51	89	65	71	06	31	27	42	05	92	25	11	78	01	03	31	41	26
48	93	36	50	47	69	06	64	59	37	38	07	57	20	20	05	27	73	04	35	90	12	92	36	05	78
49	29	67	72	32	48	63	38	89	76	24	97	65	08	74	18	13	77	29	02	74	55	85	67	09	31
50	70	47	99	22	16	54	47	55	49	33	01	77	26	75	91	64	51	45	32	89	29	08	47	43	89

controlled conditions, resulting in more variability in the samples than that under study. For example, a number of brass companies selected groups of samples of different types of brass and sent sets of such samples to all parts of the United States to check degradation and corrosion due to weathering. After five years of testing, the data were sent to laboratories for analysis of the preliminary results. Quality control personnel at the laboratories, who were also trained in statistics, found that the variation in the original test samples was greater than the corrosive effects being evaluated, so the tests had to be discarded and replaced by another series of tests based on truly random samples. Over $10,000 was wasted on the first set of invalid results. The analysis of variance technique has been found to be most effective when randomization of the data has been made an integral part of the designs of experiments.

A truly random sample is obtained when each unit available for test has an equal chance of being selected as part of the sample. To secure the best random samples, use is made of tables of random numbers. L. H. C. Tippett published one of the

TABLE 8.2 Frequency of Occurrences of Random Numbers Given in Table 8.1 By Individual Groups and All Groups Combined. Part 1 : Numbers 01–25 and 26–50

Number	*A*	*B*	*C*	*D*	*E*	*ALL*	*Number*	*A*	*B*	*C*	*D*	*E*	*ALL*
01	2	2	3	2	3	12	26	1	2	2	4	5	14
02	1	3	1	2	5	12	27	5	1	2	2	4	14
03	2	5	2	2	2	13	28	3	2	3	4	0	12
04	2	3	1	4	2	12	29	2	4	0	5	2	13
05	2	2	2	4	2	12	30	6	1	1	2	2	12
06	1	2	4	4	2	13	31	1	2	2	2	5	12
07	3	0	5	2	2	12	32	3	3	2	4	1	13
08	3	3	2	1	3	12	33	2	2	3	4	2	13
09	1	0	5	2	5	13	34	1	2	4	3	2	12
10	3	0	3	4	2	12	35	3	2	2	2	3	12
11	2	3	2	3	4	14	36	2	3	3	0	4	12
12	1	1	5	3	2	12	37	2	3	1	2	5	13
13	3	3	2	3	1	12	38	5	3	1	0	3	12
14	2	2	1	4	3	12	39	3	4	1	1	5	14
15	4	2	4	2	2	14	40	4	3	2	0	3	12
16	5	2	0	2	2	11	41	0	4	2	0	6	12
17	4	1	3	2	2	12	42	2	3	2	3	2	12
18	3	3	2	2	3	13	43	3	2	4	1	2	12
19	4	1	1	3	2	11	44	0	3	3	6	1	13
20	4	2	4	1	1	12	45	0	2	4	5	1	12
21	3	0	4	1	4	12	46	3	2	2	1	4	12
22	5	2	2	2	1	12	47	4	0	2	2	5	13
23	3	4	2	1	2	12	48	4	2	1	1	5	13
24	1	5	2	1	3	12	49	4	6	1	1	0	12
25	4	4	2	4	0	14	50	3	1	2	3	3	12
Sum	68	55	64	61	60	308	Sum	66	62	52	58	75	313

Total Number of above Sets: 308 + 313 = 621, differs by 4 from expected 625.

first tables of random numbers.[1] Many other tables have been computed and tested for randomness. If no tables are available, the numbers in a telephone directory may be used as a close approximation.

Table 8.1 provides such a table of random numbers. It consists of two parts: the horizontal lines in part 1 are numbered from 1 to 25, successively, while the horizontal lines in part 2 are numbered from 26 to 50, successively. Two digits are given in each column and the columns are numbered from 1 to 25, successively. Thus this table consists of 50 × 25 × 2 = 2500 numbers, consisting of 1250 pairs of values.

Table 8.2 gives the frequency of occurrence in the table of random numbers from 01 to 99, including 00, which represents 100. This Random Sampling Numbers Table, table 8.1, is divided into five groups of five columns each, designated respectively as A, B, C, D, and E. The frequency of occurrence of numbers from 01 to 100 is given in four sets, listed as 01–25, 26–50, 51–75, and 76–100. Similar results are tabulated for all the 1250 pairs of values. In certain portions of such random

TABLE 8.2 Frequency of Occurrences of Random Numbers Given in Table 8.1 By Individual Groups and All Groups Combined. Part 2: Numbers 51–75 and 76–00

Number	*A*	*B*	*C*	*D*	*E*	*ALL*	*Number*	*A*	*B*	*C*	*D*	*E*	*ALL*
51	3	2	1	5	2	13	76	5	3	3	1	1	13
52	2	2	4	2	3	13	77	2	2	4	3	3	14
53	2	4	3	4	1	14	78	2	3	2	1	4	12
54	4	5	0	3	1	13	79	1	2	5	3	0	11
55	0	3	3	2	5	13	80	1	3	4	3	1	12
56	1	4	0	3	5	13	81	1	1	6	3	1	12
57	4	3	2	3	2	14	82	3	2	2	3	1	11
58	2	4	1	2	3	12	83	1	2	5	3	2	13
59	3	6	1	2	1	13	84	4	2	2	1	3	12
60	2	3	4	2	2	13	85	3	1	3	4	3	14
61	2	5	1	3	2	13	86	2	1	3	2	4	12
62	1	3	1	4	2	11	87	2	2	1	2	4	11
63	4	2	2	2	2	12	88	3	3	3	2	2	13
64	3	1	3	3	3	13	89	4	5	1	1	2	13
65	1	3	5	3	2	14	90	1	3	5	4	0	13
66	1	4	4	1	1	11	91	3	3	2	3	1	12
67	4	1	2	1	4	12	92	3	2	1	2	4	12
68	2	1	5	3	3	14	93	3	3	3	2	2	13
69	4	2	3	0	2	11	94	1	3	2	4	3	13
70	3	3	2	2	2	12	95	0	2	3	3	4	12
71	0	4	6	1	1	12	96	5	1	1	4	2	13
72	3	2	2	2	3	12	97	1	1	5	4	2	13
73	5	2	1	5	1	14	98	1	5	3	2	1	12
74	3	3	2	3	2	13	99	2	3	3	3	2	13
75	1	2	2	1	6	12	00	2	1	2	6	2	13
Sum	60	74	60	62	61	317	Sum	56	59	74	69	54	312

Total Number of above Sets: 317 + 312 = 629, differs by +4 from expected 625.
Total for all four Sets: 308 + 313 + 317 + 312 = 1250.

order tables, some numbers may be repeated in the section selected for use. In such cases, the repetition is deleted from the numbers designating the random sample. Also, if only twenty-five units are to be selected when the number found listed in the section designating the sample is greater than 25, such an observed number is omitted as there are only twenty-five units available from which a sample can be selected for test. Instead, select at random a section of the table beginning with a number less than 26. Methods for using the table are given later in this chapter.

The number of pairs listed vary from 0 to 6 in each group for the four sets 01–25, 26–50, 51–75, and 76–00. The frequency of occurrences for such values are tabulated in table 8.3.

TABLE 8.3 Frequency of the Number of Occurrences Listed in Table 8.2 By Individual Groups: A, B, C, D, and E and All Groups Combined

Part 1 : 4 Sets of 25 Units Each

No. of Occurrences	*01–25*						*26–50*						*51–75*						*75–00*					
	Groups						*Groups*						*Groups*						*Groups*					
	A	*B*	*C*	*D*	*E*	*All*	*A*	*B*	*C*	*D*	*E*	*All*	*A*	*B*	*C*	*D*	*E*	*All*	*A*	*B*	*C*	*D*	*E*	*All*
0	0	4	1	0	1	6	3	1	1	4	2	11	2	3	2	1	0	8	1	0	0	0	2	3
1	5	3	4	5	2	19	3	3	6	5	3	20	5	7	6	4	6	28	8	6	4	4	6	28
2	6	8	10	10	13	47	5	10	11	6	6	38	6	7	7	8	10	38	6	8	6	6	8	34
3	7	6	3	4	5	25	7	7	4	3	4	25	6	5	4	8	5	28	6	9	8	9	4	36
4	5	2	4	6	2	19	4	3	3	4	3	17	5	2	2	2	1	12	2	0	2	5	5	14
5	2	2	3	0	2	9	2	0	0	2	6	10	1	1	3	2	2	9	2	2	4	0	0	8
6	0	0	0	0	0	0	1	1	0	1	1	4	0	0	1	0	1	2	0	0	1	1	0	2
Sum	25	25	25	25	25	125	25	25	25	25	25	125	25	25	25	25	25	125	25	25	25	25	25	125

Part 2: 4 Sets Combined—100 Units

No. of Occurrences	*01–00 All Groups Combined*					
	A	*B*	*C*	*D*	*E*	*All*
0	6	8	4	5	5	28
1	21	19	20	18	17	95
2	23	33	34	30	37	157
3	26	27	19	24	18	114
4	16	7	11	17	11	62
5	7	5	10	4	10	36
6	1	1	2	2	2	8
Sum	100	100	100	100	100	500

The above frequency distributions illustrate one type of statistical analysis that must be utilized by those working in quality control. Variations occur at all times in manufacturing, in troubleshooting for assignable causes of excessive variability, and in the analysis of related reports and cost analyses. To properly evaluate the above distributions, the best statistical techniques require that averages and standard deviations be computed. Table 8.3 is given in terms of four groups of twenty-five units each, i.e., 1–25, 26–50, 51–75, and 76–00 (00 denotes 100), and in five groups of five pairs each, i.e., A, B, C, D, and E. Tables 8.4 and 8.5 summarize these statistics for analysis.

For most groups of data, three statistics usually provide all the necessary information required for quality control to use in its analysis. Quality standards

TABLE 8.4 Statistics Derived from Table 8.3, By Sets 01–25, 26–50, 51–75, and 76–00

	SETS				
Statistic	*01–25*	*26–50*	*51–75*	*76–00*	*All Sets Combined*
n	125	125	125	125	500
$\bar{X}$	2.472	2.504	2.344	2.496	2.454
v	1.577216	1.617984	1.873664	1.641984	1.835884
σ	1.256	1.272	1.369	1.281	1.355
$\bar{X} - \bar{\bar{X}}$	0.018	0.050	−0.110	0.042	0
$(\bar{X} - \bar{\bar{X}})^2$	0.000324	0.002500	0.012100	0.001764	0.016688
$v_{\bar{X}} = \sigma_{\bar{X}}^2$					0.004172
$\sigma_{\bar{X}}$					0.064591
$\dfrac{(\bar{X} - \bar{\bar{X}})}{\sigma_{\bar{X}}}$	0.279	0.774	−1.703	0.650	0

TABLE 8.5 Statistics Derived from Table 8.3, By Groups A, B, C, D, and E

	GROUPS					
Statistic	*A*	*B*	*C*	*D*	*E*	*All Groups Combined*
n	100	100	100	100	100	500
$\bar{X}$	2.500	2.250	2.510	2.500	2.510	2.454
v	1.890000	1.607500	1.949900	1.730000	1.409900	1.835884
σ	1.375	1.268	1.396	1.315	1.187	1.355
$\bar{X} - \bar{\bar{X}}$	0.046	−0.204	0.056	0.046	0.056	0
$(\bar{X} - \bar{\bar{X}})^2$	0.002116	0.041616	0.003136	0.002116	0.003136	0.052120
$v_{\bar{X}} = \sigma_{\bar{X}}^2$						0.010424
$\sigma_{\bar{X}}$						0.102098
$\dfrac{(\bar{X} - \bar{\bar{X}})}{\sigma_{\bar{X}}}$	0.451	−1.998	0.548	0.451	0.548	0

may then be set and upper and lower control limits established for controlling processes. These three statistics are (1) the sample size n used in obtaining the data to be analyzed which represents the number of observations taken, (2) the arithmetic average $\overline{X}$, called the mean, the measure of the desired central value, and (3) the variance, a measure of the dispersion or variability, which is generally used to obtain the standard deviation, the square root of the variance. The computations used to obtain the average and standard deviation are shown below.

Example 1 *Computations.* Determine the average, variance, and standard deviation for the first distribution in table 8.3 designated 01–25.

TABLE 8.6 Statistics for Set 01–25 of Table 8.3

No. of Occurrences X	No. of Observations, Frequency Listed f	$f(X)$	$f(X^2)$
0	6	0	0
1	19	19	19
2	47	94	188
3	25	75	225
4	19	76	304
5	9	45	225
Sum	125	309	961

Example 1: Computation of Statistics

$$n = 125$$

$$\overline{X} = \frac{\Sigma f(X)}{n} = \frac{309}{125} = 2.472 \text{ Average}$$

$$v = \frac{\Sigma f(X^2)}{n} - \overline{X}^2$$

$$= \frac{961}{125} - (2.472)^2$$

$$= 7.688 - 6.110784$$

$$= 1.577216 \text{ Variance}$$

$$\sigma = \sqrt{v} = \sqrt{1.577216} = 1.256 \text{ Standard Deviation}$$

Having found a set of average values for a series of measurements, quality control personnel need to determine whether there are any significant differences between any of these samples. This is called a *test for significant differences between means.* This test is easier if the sample size for each sample included in the series is the same. When the sample sizes are unequal, more complex methods, in which we weight the results by the various sample sizes, must be used. Other texts should be consulted to cover this case. When the experiment is well-designed, the sample sizes are kept equal to simplify the analysis and also to make results truly random.

Are there any significant differences between the various sections of this table of random numbers? One criterion used for such a test is based on the extent to which any average or mean differs from the expected value or the overall average value for the series of values. The analysis of variance technique uses the standard deviation as a measure of such differences. The distribution of such differences between averages is essentially normal, so that probabilities based on the normal law apply. As shown earlier in the discussion of control charts, assignable causes of variation may usually be found if any set of values has a mean greater than three standard deviation units from the overall mean. For a normal law distribution derived from random sampling, referred to as *randomization,* 99.73% of the observations are expected to be within three-sigma control limits. When such a condition exists, the confidence level is considered to be at 99.73%, based on this three-sigma criterion. If any mean differs more than $3\sigma_{\bar{X}}$ from the standard, that group is considered to be significantly different from the other averages.

Many managers or quality control personnel desire a tighter criterion. They may use two-sigma control limits rather than the usual three-sigma control limits. The confidence level for such two-sigma control limits, based on the assumption of a normal law distribution, is 95.45%. Others may desire confidence levels such as 80%, 90%, 95%, 98%, or 99%. Multiples of the standard deviation $z\sigma$ may be obtained from normal law tables corresponding to areas under the normal law curve for $\bar{X}' \pm z\sigma'$. Such confidence levels are set on the assumption that the process may be controlled with the chance system of causes in operation remaining constant for a considerable interval of time.

Results in various areas differ. In each particular area, the effects measured are due to the operation of a chance system of causes. Variations in the results measured will be found and tabulated as a frequency distribution. Variations observed in clerical operations may be due to worker fatigue, amount of actual illumination provided, or the nature of the data being processed. Room temperature may also affect the effectiveness of the workers. In manufacturing operations, the inherent ability of the operators, their training, the condition of the machines used in the operations, and the environment under which the employees work all play a part in providing the quality desired. Control limits may be established that take these possible causes of variation into account. Professor Jerzy Neyman, head of the statistical laboratory at the University of California in Berkeley, has introduced the term *fiducial limits* based on the fiducial distribution introduced by R. A. Fisher in 1930. This distribution represents the confidence provided by the best possible estimation, based on the distribution of estimators rather than on current data only. Numerically, the values found for the usual confidence limits agree with those based on estimators. Hence most texts used the term *confidence limits* for both kinds of limits. Such limits are usually determined from probability distribution functions such as the normal law or binomial and similar distributions.

Where a series of averages are obtained and an overall average is computed as the present level for these data, a standard deviation for averages may be computed directly from these m averages, where each average is based on the same number of observations, n. (More advanced texts cover the case where the sample sizes are not equal.) In the designs of experiments described in this text, more effective results are obtained by keeping all sample sizes equal.

The experiment has been designed so that a check may be made for a significant difference between averages. The amount by which each average in the series of average values for these random number frequency distributions differs from the overall average indicates whether the experiment has been made under well-controlled conditions. Unless an experiment or manufacturing process is in a state of statistical control, valid predictions cannot be made concerning future results. Determining the degree of variation in terms of the standard deviation for averages, $\sigma_{\bar{X}}$ in terms of z values, where $z_i = \dfrac{|\bar{X}_i - \bar{\bar{X}}|}{\sigma_{\bar{X}}}$, provides a means to determine which set, if any, differs significantly from the overall mean and hence may differ significantly from the other sets. As noted previously, if this z_i value is greater than 3, a significant difference is indicated. The example below illustrates this technique.

Example 2 *Test for Significant Difference for Means*
The average values listed in table 8.7 were taken from the summarized data for random numbers and give the average number of occurrences of numbers, successively, in groups A, B, C, D, and E. Are any of these five averages significantly different from the overall average?

TABLE 8.7 Example 2: Data and Statistics for Summary Results

Series i	Group	Sample Size, n	Average $\bar{X}$	$\bar{X}_i - \bar{\bar{X}}$	$(\bar{X}_i - \bar{\bar{X}})^2$	z_i	Computations
1	A	100	2.500	0.046	0.002116	0.451	$m = 5, n = 100$
2	B	100	2.250	−0.204	0.041616	1.998*	$\bar{\bar{X}} = \dfrac{\Sigma \bar{X}_i}{m}$
3	C	100	2.510	0.056	0.003136	0.548	$= \dfrac{12.270}{5}$
4	D	100	2.500	0.046	0.002116	0.451	$= 2.454$
5	E	100	2.510	0.056	0.003136	0.548	$v_{\bar{X}} = \dfrac{\Sigma(\bar{X}_i - \bar{\bar{X}})^2}{m}$
All	Sum	500	12.270	0	0.052120	0	$= 0.010424$
Average		100	2.454	0	0.010424		$\sigma_{\bar{X}} = \sqrt{0.010424} = 0.102098$
							$z_i = \dfrac{\lvert \bar{X}_i - \bar{\bar{X}} \rvert}{\sigma_{\bar{X}}}$

* Questionable. For $P = 0.95$ criterion, assuming normal law, z_i maximum value is 1.960; hence using this criterion, this value might be considered significantly different.

This test shows that only group B is questionable. It has the largest z_i value as $z_2 = 1.998$, just less than 2.000, which is the limiting criterion for a confidence level of 95.45%. The group B average value of 2.250 is only slightly less than the desired value of 2.500. This analysis shows that, when using the table of random numbers, a slightly poorer distribution of random numbers is provided within group B numbers than has been found in the other four groups.

The random numbers given in table 8.1 for 1250 pairs of values from 01 to 00 (100) provide very close to an equal choice for each of these 100 numbers. This is depicted in table 8.8, which shows the distribution for the number of occurrences for each of the 100 numbers for which a total of 1250 pairs is given. For this particular table of random numbers, the expected number of occurrences is $\frac{1250}{100} = 12.5$. This fractional value will not occur in the table. The average for the table is actually 12.54, which differs very little from the expected value of 12.500. The standard deviation for this distribution is small, showing the values in the table to be very uniform.

TABLE 8.8 Frequency of Occurrence of Pairs of Numbers

X No. of Occurrences	*Frequency, f*					*Computations*			
	Set 01–25	*Set 26–50*	*Set 51–75*	*Set 76–00*	*All Sets 01–00*	$f(X)$	$f(X^2)$	$x = X - \bar{X}$ x	$f(x^2)$
11	2	0	3	3	8	88	968	−1.54	18.9728
12	16	15	4	9	44	528	6336	−0.54	12.8304
13	4	7	12	11	34	442	5746	0.46	7.1944
14	3	3	6	2	14	196	2744	1.46	29.8424
Sum	25	25	25	25	100	1254	15794	—	68.8400
Average						12.54	15.79		0.688400

Expected Value:

$$\bar{X}' = \frac{1250}{100} = 12.500$$
$$\bar{X} = \frac{1254}{100} = 12.540 \quad \text{(the average)}$$
$$v = \sigma^2 = \frac{\Sigma f x^2}{n} - \bar{X}^2$$
$$= \frac{15794}{100} - (12.54)^2$$
$$= 157.9400 - 157.2516$$
$$= 0.6884$$
$$\sigma = \sqrt{v} = 0.83 \quad \text{(the standard deviation)}$$

A check may also be made by using the squares of the deviations from the average: $v = \sigma^2 = \dfrac{\Sigma f x^2}{n} = \dfrac{68.8400}{100} = 0.6884$. This variance agrees with the same value above.

For a normal law distribution, the limits for a three-sigma range corresponding to a probability of 0.9973 and based on the above computed values are $12.54 \pm 3(0.83) = 12.54 \pm 2.49$. This gives 10.05 and 15.03 for the lower control limit and the upper control limit respectively. Since a frequency of 0 occurred in table 8.8 for 10 and 15, this random number table provides very close to an equal chance for the selection of values from 1 to 100 when using the entire table.

The table of random sampling numbers, table 8.1, as shown by the above analysis satisfies the statistics and the criteria for true randomness. Paired sets of values have practically an equal chance for their occurrence. They may be used to select samples for tests at random or to select areas to visit for making self-audits or for surveying vendors. Their use is practically unlimited where randomization is desired. For effective analysis by the use of analysis of variance techniques, randomization is a must.

8.3 Why Experimental Tests are Necessary

Those working in quality control and reliability engineering need to know how to conduct simple experiments in order to properly evaluate many of the failure reports that are sent to them. In most cases, such evaluations will cost a great deal and may not provide sufficient evidence to reach a valid decision concerning the cause of the failure and how to eliminate future failures. Most feel that they do not have sufficient knowledge concerning the proper statistical techniques to provide a clear-cut answer.

In order to make a good simple analysis of such situations, it is necessary to know how to set up a series of tests that will provide the necessary data for applying the best techniques for analyzing the case. One example is the selection of two size D dry cell batteries for operating a flashlight. Complaints have been made that the given flashlight appears to operate for only a short period of time with the two cells sold at the time the flashlight was purchased. The company selling the flashlight uses cells made to their specifications and believes from the preliminary tests made that these cells should give a satisfactory bright light under intermittent operation for at least three months. Some customers complain that the flashlight provides a very dim light after only one month of operation. Is this short life due to the cells provided or could it be due to poor contacts in the switch or at the point of contact with either the bottom of the cells or the base of the flashlight bulb? After a series of tests the cause of the weak light was deemed to be primarily the dry cells.

Most manufacturers of dry cells make two types: (1) those with short lives that sell at a low price; and (2) a type that costs much more and is supposed to have a much longer life than the cheaper cell, even as much as ten times the life of the cheaper cell when used in activating electrically operated toys or even a flashlight. However, some make a medium-priced cell that is supposed to have about three times the life of the ordinary cell.

What kind of an experiment should be used to determine whether to change the specification for the batteries being sold, change the switching device in the flashlight, improve the contacts made by the dry cells and also the life of the bulb, or insist on providing a more expensive dry cell that has a longer life? The problem is turned over to a group of design and research engineers or to the quality control department, which often establishes the standards of performance for the company. To set up a valid experiment, some basic principles should be first established.

8.4 Fundamentals of Experimentation

Randomization

It has been repeatedly pointed out that the greatest improvement in the designs of experiments resulted from the introduction of *Randomization.* Before this, research and engineering departments ran many experiments upon which good decisions could be based, but often were later found to be wrong because the samples used were biased, that is, they were not selected under truly random conditions. There is a tendency to select samples in the easiest manner possible, which tends to give samples that are not truly representative of the product or the process which produced them. However, it is necessary to select samples to be tested in a random manner from the population of which they are a part. It is also desirable to have the samples of the brands of products selected for testing randomized. Sometimes this is difficult to achieve or is too expensive. In any case before conducting the experiment, a definite plan for obtaining the samples to be tested should be made.

The cases of flashlight batteries was selected to include the two areas of randomization that must be covered to obtain a valid experiment. There are a large number of brands of flashlights of varying costs available. Costs per unit vary greatly from brand to brand, and there may be found a wide spread in the time such flashlights will actually operate satisfactorily. In some cases, the batteries used may have been stored too long before being used. Dry cells selected for test must have been received from their manufacturer only a short time prior to purchase for test to make the tests valid.

Suppose $200 has been allotted for the cost of testing the samples. This fund must be distributed between different manufacturers and their respective life characteristics. One supplier's catalog features ordinary batteries, triple-life batteries, alkalines which are supposed to render longer service than ordinary batteries, and rechargeable batteries. In general, however, the rechargeable batteries are rather special and will be eliminated from this experiment. That leaves three different types. This same catalog also has three standard, well-known brands in addition to their own. That gives twelve different types to check for one supplier. Another supplier may also have batteries made or ordered to their specifications. Such a company will probably also have the same three standard brands as the other supplier for sale. Most of the cut-rate stores will also have available similar batteries that might be obtained for test.

How should a randomized sample be obtained? To obtain equal coverage for the batteries produced for a particular supplier, it will be necessary to obtain as many units of these batteries for the different types as the number of different suppliers selected at random for supplying the samples for test. For this example, select five different suppliers. Since there are three different life levels, fifteen batteries should be selected to represent the supplier's own brand; for the three well-known brands, three batteries each, totaling nine batteries, must be selected, so we have twenty-four batteries to purchase from each of the five suppliers.

Replication

After making one set of tests, there may be some question as to the validity of these tests. To cover such a situation, texts on designs of experiment recommend that a certain number of replicate tests be made to provide results that are deemed to be significant. When the tests are very costly and the results are considered very important, such tables covering the desired number of replicates should be consulted.[2] In practice, the number of replications used is two, although such tables cover from two to fifty replications, depending on the true difference found, considered as a percentage of the mean for either a one-tailed or two-tailed distribution with the following criteria:

Test of significance at 5% level, probability 80%,
Test of significance at 5% level, probability 90%, and
Test of significance at 1% level, probability 95%.

The costs of purchasing these batteries would be between \$50 and \$75 for the 120 batteries selected for test. If a replicate set is desired, the cost would be doubled; if a third replicate is desired, the cost is still within the allocated \$200 budget. For practically all designs of experiment, although only one set of tests is originally planned, allowance should be made in the budget for the possibility of having to duplicate the test at least once with the possibility that a third or fourth replicate set of tests may be required. In many electrical life tests, changes in power used, power failures, or errors in taking readings may occur. Replicate tests provide a means to provide the necessary assurance that the tests are valid.

8.5 Samples

The random samples thus selected for the first set of life tests are distributed as follows. A, B, C, D, and E denote the five different suppliers and J, K, and L denote the three well-known manufacturers. D_1 represents the ordinary 1.5 volt flashlight battery of size D, D_3 represents a similar battery with three times the life of the first, while D_{10} represents a battery with ten times the life of the ordinary inexpensive battery. Table 8–9 indicates the nature of the first complete sample.

TABLE 8.9 Number of Different Kinds of Batteries in Sample

Supplier	*Supply Brand*			*Brand J*			*Brand K*			*Brand L*			*Total*
	D_1	D_3	D_{10}	D_1	D_3	D_{10}	D_1	D_3	D_{10}	D_1	D_3	D_{10}	
A	5	5	5	1	1	1	1	1	1	1	1	1	24
B	5	5	5	1	1	1	1	1	1	1	1	1	24
C	5	5	5	1	1	1	1	1	1	1	1	1	24
D	5	5	5	1	1	1	1	1	1	1	1	1	24
E	5	5	5	1	1	1	1	1	1	1	1	1	24
Total	25	25	25	5	5	5	5	5	5	5	5	5	120

It is advisable to use randomization in selecting the sets of five batteries each for the supplier's brands from each supplier. Use may be made of a table of random numbers such as table 8.1. When selecting only one battery from each supplier of brands J, K, and L, a random and representative battery may readily be selected from each lot of N batteries by the use of table 8.1, as described and illustrated by examples in succeeding paragraphs.

8.6 Tables of Random Numbers—Usage

It is desired to give each unit an equal chance of being selected from the universe being sampled. To obtain an unbiased sample, units available for inclusion in the sample may be numbered 1 to N, where N is the total number available. In some receiving inspection departments, a large metal or wooden table whose top is ruled into squares and numbered 1 to 100 or 1 to 1,000 is used. The units in a lot submitted for inspection are individually placed on these squares or spaces and thus are temporarily serialized. With such temporary identification, two cases may occur and methods for them are developed in the examples.

Example 3 *Selection of Random Sampling Numbers for Two Cases with the Aid of Temporary Serialization Tables:*
I. 1–1,000 squares or spaces; II. 1–100 squares or spaces

Case 1: $N \leqq 100$; Example (A) with $n = 5$, and Example (B) with $n = 10$.
Case 2: $N > 100$; Example (C) with $n = 10$, and Example (D) with $n = 20$.

Case 1. Example (A) with $n = 5$. Select any row or column covering two digits in table 8.1, which is often called a table of random numbers. In the first example, only five random numbers are required. Let 00 denote the 100th unit. Use column 14. Go down the column and record the first five different numbers found; in this case they are 36, 77, 58, 79, and 13. The units already placed on these numbered places on the temporary serialization table are picked as the sampling test units from this lot furnished for acceptance-rejection tests by a particular supplier. To illustrate the case where duplicate units may be designated, select line 44 on part 2 of table 8.1. This line gives 16, 57, 86, (16), 73, and 42. Since a second 16 was in this line, it is marked in parentheses and the next two-digit number in line 44 takes its place.

Example (B) with $n = 10$. For the first five random numbers, use the first set obtained from column 14 (see Example (A)). Then include the next five numbers from this column. They are 71, 07, 53, 12, and 93. A check for duplicate numbers is provided by arranging the ten consecutive numbers in column 14 as an ascending ordered array. The ten random two-digit numbers thus arranged are 07, 12, 13, 36, 53; 58, 71, 77, 79, and 93. There are no duplicates, so no additional selection is necessary. To obtain a second random sample of ten units, use line 44 to obtain five additional numbers 49, 80, 53, 24, and 98. No duplicates are found in these last five numbers. Order all ten numbers as 16, 24, 42, 49, 53; 57, 73, 80, 86, and 98. There are no duplicates.

Case 2: ($N > 100$.) Suppose that there are only 900 batteries of this type in inventory. We will first cover the first condition in this example, I. 1,000 squares or spaces on the temporary identification table often referred to as the sampling random table. Since the submitted lot contains only 900 batteries, only the 900 available batteries are placed on this table so the spaces numbered from 901 to 1,000 have no units on them. Variations in this method may be provided by omitting any of the 1,000 available spaces at random. Accountability is made easier by omitting any block of 100 spaces rather than blocks of 10 units or even single units. The random numbers selected must be a space on which a unit has been placed. The second condition is where II. 100 squares or spaces only are provided by the sampling random table. This condition requires definite procedures as outlined below.

Condition I. 1,000 spaces on sampling random table.

Example (C) with $n = 10$. Since the units on the random sampling table are now identified by the numbers 001 to 900, the random sampling numbers to be selected are three-digit numbers. First use any combination of column headings from 1 to 25, using one column heading and half of the next two-digit column. In this example, use column (11) and first part of (12). Start selection at line 1, giving 148, 539, 243, 537, 133; 706, 189, 596, 842, and 626. Arranging these numbers in an ascending array will show there are no duplicates. The units to be taken from the sampling random table for testing are 133, 148, 189, 243, 537; 539, 596, 626, 706, and 842.

The procedure for selecting random three-digit random sampling numbers may use consecutive three-digit values line by line rather than by columns. Numbers that exceed 900 or duplicate numbers should be omitted and replaced by another selection. Using line 39 gives the following numbers: 143, (934), 691, (966), 182, 316, 455; 221, 390, 609, 179, (917), and 715. The ten units to be included in the sample when arranged in an ascending array, omitting the units in parentheses, are as follows: 143, 179, 182. 221, 316; 390, 455, 609, 691, and 715.

Example (D) with $n = 20$. To obtain a sample of twenty units continue the process above for columns and then by lines. Only ten more units need to be numbered. From line 39 go to line 41; table 8.10, part 2 lists these.

The procedure used in example (C) is continued until no additional random numbers are found. In example (C), no numbers exceeding 900 occurred, nor were there any duplicate numbers. When such numbers occur, it is necessary to continue the selection until twenty different units are selected. Where numbers are to be omitted, they are noted below by parentheses. The next ten numbers found from columns 10 (1 and 2) and 11 (1) are: 057, 724, 179, (938), 816, (928), 449; 292, 136, 047, 753, and 317. These numbers, together with the previous ten, are ordered to check for possible duplicates. When duplicates are found, additional numbers are selected as outlined before until n different numbers are listed. When ordered, the twenty random sampling numbers are:

047, 057, 133, 136, 148; 179, 189, 243, 292, 317;
449, 537, 539, 596, 626; 706, 724, 753, 816, 842

There are no duplicates. Units on the random sampling table number 1 to 900 are tested in accordance with the standard test procedures provided. The same procedure for selecting random three-digit sampling numbers may use consecutive five-digit values line by line rather than by consecutive columns.

Using sufficient adjacent digits in one or more columns, each containing two digits, is the simplest way to use table 8.1. Random numbers can be selected from three adjacent columns for a lot containing as many as 1,000,000 units. For example, if $n = 5$, using part 2, lines 26 on and columns 16, 17, and 18 gives:

$$506, 179; \quad 792, 280; \quad 331, 496; \quad 850, 834; \quad 262, 407.$$

The above procedure will be satisfactory to most and is considered sufficiently random, thus providing each unit with an equal chance to be selected.

Many who play bridge and other games where cards are selected at random for each player feel the more the cards are shuffled, the fairer the deal. Many more complex random selections may be developed and applied to these random numbers. Numbered lines may be selected rather than numbered columns. Receiving areas may have a table with only 100 spaces marked on it. How could such a table be used when the lot size $N = 900$? It is utilized nine times in succession. Case 2, example (C) where $n = 10$ will be covered by a procedure using a random line to designate the random sampling numbers. To simulate repeated shuffling of a deck of cards, select a random number from a selected line (such as line 39) where the sublots of 100 units are numbered 1 to 9. Since $n = 10$, ten two-digit numbers are retained. The first nine can indicate the space number successively. How do we select the location of the tenth unit? Arbitrarily, the procedure might be to select the tenth unit from subgroup 1 or some other selected subgroup. To avoid possible bias use this procedure: After nine two-digit numbers have been selected, use the first digit in the line from column 10 to designate the number of the subgroup and the two-digit number in column 11 as the random space to be used for the tenth unit. The random sampling numbers with 1–9 designating successive subgroups from line 39 are:

1–14, 2–39, 3–34, 4–69, 5–19; 6–66; 7–18; 8–23; 9–16; 4–52.

If this procedure is followed using line 23, the random sampling numbers would be:

1–30, 2–43, 3–93, 4–28, 5–58; 6–57, 7–39, 8–41, 9–23, 1–68.

To simulate double randomization for this example, since each of the twenty-five columns contains a two-digit number and there are fifty different lines, select a two-digit number from 01 to 25 denoting columns from a line number selected at random. For procedure A, select the line in part 1 from 1 to 25 to designate the random sampling number and for procedure B the line in part 2 from 26 to 50 adding 25 to the column number used. Designate the subgroup number 1 to 9 by the successive digits in the two-digit numbers. Using this procedure and line 39 and 40, the designated columns for $n = 10$ are:

Line 39: 14, (39), (34), (69), 19, (66), 18, 23, 16, (45), (52);
Line 39: 21, (39), 06, 09, 17, (99), (17), (71), (58), (30), (61), (39), (46), (35);
Line 40: (21), (60), (19), (83), (72), (59), (88), (26), 04.

Numbers greater than 25 and duplicates have been placed in parentheses and are not to be used. The location for the ten random sampling numbers are:

Procedure A, Part 1, Lines 01–25

Subgroup No. Line 39	1	4	3	9	3	4	6	9	1	9
Random No. Location	14–14	19–19	18–18	23–23	16–16	21–21	06–06	09–09	17–17	04–04
Random Sampling No.	1–91	4–10	3–75	9–11	3–42	4–31	6–62	9–25	1–29	9–22

Procedure B, Part 2, Lines 26–50

Subgroup No. Line 39	6	6	9*	2	3	1	6	4	5	2
Random No. Location#	14–39	19–44	18–43	23–48	16–41	21–46	06–31	09–34	17–42	04–29
Random Sampling No.	6–06	1–06	8–94	2–36	3–62	1–21	6–20	4–71	5–45	2–02

***1 + 8 = 9 used. #25 added to first 2 digits for second 2 digits.**

Note that in using this procedure for selecting subgroups some may be omitted. This method provides a random sample for the lot, but not necessarily for a representative sample for each subgroup. If a sample is to be selected from each subgroup, just use subgroup numbers 1, 2, 3, 4, 5, 6, 7, 8, 9 for each of the first nine samples tested and select the tenth from the sublot having a value outside or closest to the tolerance limits. This introduces a bias in the sample, but is a practical approach.

For example (D) where $n = 20$, the next set of ten units under procedures *A* and *B* are found by continuing the selection of columns and corresponding lines from line 40 on. These are:

(68), (95), 06*, 00**, 11, (60), (55), (26), (63), 18*, (29), (92), (35), (60), (84), 11*
(27), (89), (97), (95), (60), 21*, 15, (62), (79), (54), (62), (54), 14*, (42), 04*, 09.

* For a repeated number, under procedure *A*, instead of using the random number under column x, line x, use column x, line $x + 25$ and under procedure *B*, use column x and instead of line $x + 25$, use line x.

** 00 denotes 100, but in this case, consider it as $10 - 10$ and also as designating subgroup 1.

The additional ten random sampling numbers are tabulated below. Continue selecting subgroup numbers from single successive digits in line 39 starting with column 2 omitting zero and repetitions.

Procedure A: Part 1, Lines 01–25, except for starred items for which a part 2, line 25 units larger is used

Subgroup No. Line 39	2	1	3	9	6	9	1	7	9	9
Selected Random No.	6*	10	11	18*	11*	21*	15	14*	04*	09*
Random No. Location#	6–31	10–10	11–11	18–43	11–36	21–46	15–15	14–39	4–29	9–34
Random Sampling No.	2–20	1–62	3–71	9–80	6–81	9–21	1–90	7–06	9–02	9–71

#31 = 6 + 25; 43 = 18 + 25; 36 = 11 + 25; 46 = 21 + 25; 39 = 14 + 25; 29 = 4 + 25; 34 = 9 + 25.

Procedure B: Part 2, Lines 26–56, except for starred items for which a part 1 line as noted is used

Subgroup No. Line 39	1	7	7	1	5	8	3	6	1	4*
Subgroup No.	6*	10	11	18*	11*	21*	15	14*	04*	09*
Random No. Location#	6–6	10–35	11–36	18–18	11–11	21–21	15–40	14–14	4–4	9–9
Random Sampling No.	1–62	7–63	7–81	1–75	5–71	8–31	3–61	6–91	1–22	4–25

*4 selected arbitrarily. Line position had too many repetitions of 1, 7, 6, and 9.

#35 = 10 + 25; 36 = 11 + 25; 40 = 15 + 25; the addition of 25 is arbitrary.

The random sampling numbers for these two cases are summarized in table 8–10 and are ordered in an ascending array to simplify the selection of the random samples that should be used.

TABLE 8.10 Summary of Random Units Selected for Two Different Cases Two Sample Sizes per Case, Ordered Array

Two Sample Sizes per Case, Ordered Array
Case 1: N = 100
Example (A): n = 5

Sample Number:	1	2	3	4	5					
Random Number: (a)	13	36	58	77	79					
(b)	07	12	53	71	93					

Example (B): n = 10

Sample Number:	1	2	3	4	5	6	7	8	9	10
Random Number:	07	12	13	36	53	58	71	77	79	93

Case 2: N = 900
I. Random Table Top with 1000 Spaces
Part 1. Using Numbers in Adjacent Columns 10(1, 2) + 11(1)
Example (C): n = 10

Sample Number:	1	2	3	4	5	6	7	8	9	10
Random Number: (a)	133	148	189	243	537	539	596	626	706	842
(b)	047	057	136	179	292	317	449	724	753	816

Example (D): n = 20

Sample Number:	1	2	3	4	5	6	7	8	9	10
Random Number:	047	057	133	136	148	179	189	243	292	317
Sample Number (Cont'd)	11	12	13	14	15	16	17	18	19	20
Random Number:	449	537	539	596	626	706	724	753	816	842

Part 2, Using Numbers in Successive Lines 39, 41
Example (C); n = 10

Sample Number:	1	2	3	4	5	6	7	8	9	10
Random Number: (a)	143	179	182	221	316	390	455	609	691	715
(b)	021	235	278	299	318	356	411	608	613	830

Example (D): n = 20

Sample Number:	1	2	3	4	5	6	7	8	9	10
Random Number:	021	143	179	182	221	235	278	299	316	318
Sample Number:	11	12	13	14	15	16	17	18	19	20
Random Number:	356	390	411	455	608	609	613	691	715	830

TABLE 8.11 Random Table Top with 100 Spaces (Used 9 Times)
9 Subgroups of 100 Units Each. Designated 1, 2, 3, 4, 5, 6, 7, 8, and 9
A. Simple Randomization
Example (C): n = 10

Sample Number:	1	2	3	4	5	6	7	8	9	10
					(a) Line 39					
Random Number:	1–14	2–39	3–34	4–69	4–52	5–19	6–66	7–18	8–23	9–16
					(b) Line 23					
Random Number:	1–30	2–43	3–93	4–28	5–58	6–57	7–39	8–41	9–23	1–68

Example (D): n = 10
Use the Two Different Sets for Example (C)
B. Double Randomization
Example (C): n = 10

Sample Number:	1	2	3	4	5	6	7	8	9	10
					a. Procedure A, 6 Lines 39 & 40					
Random Sampling No.:	1–29	1–91	3–42	3–75	4–10	4–31	6–62	9–11	9–22	9–25
					b. Procedure B, Lines 39 & 40					
Random Sample No.:	1–06	1–21	2–02	2–36	3–62	4–71	5–45	6–06	6–20	8–94
					c. Procedure A, Line 40 on					

Random Sample No.:	1–62	1–90	2–20	3–71	6–68	7–06	9–62	9–21	9–71	9–80
				d. Procedure B, Line 4 on						
Random Sample No.:	1–22	1–62	1–75	3–61	4–25	5–71	6–91	7–63	7–81	8–31

Example (D): n = 20

Use any 2 sets of 10 units from the 4 different samples of n = 10.

These are ab, ac, ad, bc, bd, and cd, six possible samples for n = 20.

These may be ordered to determine if there are any duplicates. The ad combination is given below as an ordered array.

n = 20, a & d above combined

Sample Number:	1	2	3	4	5	6	7	8	9	10
Random Sampling No.	1–22	1–29	1–62	1–75	1–91	3–61	3–75	3–92	4–10	4–25
Sample Number:	11	12	13	14	15	16	17	18	19	20
Random Sampling No.:	4–31	5–71	6–62	6–91	7–63	7–81	8–31	9–11	9–22	9–25

For the well-known brands, by using only one battery from each supplier, these methods should provide random samples unless all have received shipments simultaneously from one production lot.

8.7 Random, Representative, Unbiased, Biased, and Other Samples

It is important that unbiased samples be selected for all phases of quality assurance work including receiving inspection, production inspection, quality control charts, reliability engineering, significant tests, analysis of variance, configuration management, etc. Valid decisions depend upon valid data, which must be obtained from truly random samples. This use of randomization is the recent breakthrough that has made it possible to reduce research time, use smaller samples to obtain results at desired confidence levels, and make better use of modern statistical techniques. It provides the basis for replacing the classical design of experiments by the factorial form, thus reducing research time by months and years.

Inspection by the use of truly random samples has been presented in previous chapters, which refer to this section for information covering the proper methods and techniques for selecting the samples to be used in all the various inspection plans, either by the method of attributes or by the method of variables.

Representative samples rather than randomly selected samples are often desired. Lots submitted for acceptance or rejection may consist of a number of sublots. As far as possible, the same number of units should be selected from each sublot, if they are of equal size, or the number may be directly proportional to the size of the various sublots. Where sublots are of equal size, the selection of the proper number of units in each subsample is easier and the criterion applied to each is easier to determine. Where sublots vary considerably in size, there are differences of opinion concerning whether the sample size should be selected on a first-degree linear basis, since many feel that the proportions should be based on the square root of the number of units in each sublot since the standard deviation for averages is $\sigma = \frac{\sigma}{\sqrt{n}}$, not σ. This allocation of samples is supposed to be better, since it provides the same order of discrimination for all subgroups.

Example 4 A lot consists of ten 100-unit boxes of product A. The sample to be used is $n = 100$ units. On a linear basis, ten units should be selected from each box of 100 units. If one or more nonconforming units are found in a subsample of ten units, the balance of the units in that box are inspected 100%. All nonconforming units are discarded and arrangements are made for the supplier to replace such nonconforming units with conforming units. However, if no nonconforming units are found in the sample of ten units from any single box, that box is accepted without additional inspections.

Example 5 A lot consists of 1,000 units submitted in sublots of 50, 200, 350, and 400 units respectively. The total sample size for the lot is 100 units. How should the sample sizes for the various sublots be determined? On a linear basis, since 100 is 10% of the lot of 1,000 units, the sample sizes would be, respectively, 5, 20, 35, and 40. Many believe that a sample of only 5 from a sublot of 50 units is too small. The approximate square roots of the sublots' sizes are respectively 7, 14, 19, and 20. Their sum is 60. Using this information, the sample sizes would be respectively, for $N = 50$, $n = \frac{7}{60} \times 100 = \frac{700}{60} = 12$; for $N = 200$, $n = \frac{14}{60} \times 100 = \frac{1400}{60} = 23$; for $N = 350$, $n = \frac{19}{60} \times 100 = \frac{1900}{60} = 32$; and for $N = 400$, $n = \frac{20}{60} \times 100 = \frac{2000}{60} = 33$. Summarizing, the n_i are 12, 23, 32, and 33. Their total is 100. If the acceptance number c is 1, 100% inspection would be required since $\frac{1}{12} = 8\frac{1}{3}\%$, which exceeds 5%. If two or more nonconforming units were found in the total sample of 100 units, the entire lot of 1,000 units would be rejected. If one nonconforming unit was observed in any of the other subsamples of size 23, 32, or 33, they need not be screened as $\frac{1}{23} = 4.3\% < 5.0\%$, $\frac{1}{32} = 3.1\% < 5.0\%$, and $\frac{1}{33} = 3.0\% < 5.0\%$.

A random sample is considered an unbiased, representative sample. However, some representative samples are not random. Many inspectors want at least one sample from every sublot. Liquids in barrels, containers, or tanks may have their lighter constituents at the top and their heavier elements at the bottom. In this case, representative samples are obtained by taking so-called *thief* samples. A sampling device may consist of a container with a valve or opening that can only be actuated by an outside lever. In a ten-foot-deep tank a different sample might be selected every two feet cumulatively, or five samples might be selected successively from depths of two feet, four feet, six feet, eight feet, and ten feet. This design thus provides a means of obtaining the variation within a sample at the same depth and also the variation between the five averages obtained from five samples at each depth, giving two different measures of variability.

In some cases, the individuals taking the samples or making measurements on each unit in a sample may be biased. Some prefer to read even numbers and others prefer odd numbers. In thickness of plating, measurements between the two metals involved is a grey area containing a mixture of the two metals. An individual may read the maximum value, the average value, or the minimum value, as seen through a microscope.

In destructive inspections, the number of units inspected per each lot is kept as small as possible. Often in controlled operations, samples are selected for check only periodically (such as every fifth or tenth lot), resulting in 20% or 10% selection of lots to be inspected. Sometimes only a sample of one unit is selected for destruction. When there is no knowledge that the process is controlled, such a sample should be representative and not merely selected at random. If controlled, any random sample would provide valid results. Past history plus results from the current lot may provide all the information required.

8.8 Degrees of Freedom

In statistics and in the theory of gases, *degrees of freedom* (d.f.) often are used to obtain the most valid results. In the earlier work in statistics, the sample size n was used in obtaining means, variance, standard deviations, and in many other types of computations. In engineering and calculus, many statistical forms are explained in terms of moments, and there are many direct analogies between physical events and these statistical measures. For example, the *center of gravity* (c.g.) of a system is usually its central value or mean and is determined from the relation

$$\bar{X} = \frac{\sum_{i=1}^{n} X_i}{n} \quad \text{or} \quad \bar{X} = \frac{\sum_{i=1}^{m} f_i X_i}{\sum f_i}, \tag{1}$$

where X_i is the ith observation, Σ is the capital Greek letter sigma representing summation, n is the number of observations (often called the sample size), m is the number of different X values, and $\bar{X}$ (X bar) is the symbol for the average or arithmetical mean. In engineering, the zero moment μ_0 (mu zero) denotes the sample size, while the first moment μ_1 (mu one) denotes the mean. μ_1 is often used to represent the true mean of a universe or population, the parameter of the population, whereas $\bar{X}$ is the best estimate of the true average derived from the sample using equation (1). In terms of estimation, $\bar{X}$ has been found to be the best estimate of the true value μ_1. Two weights W_1 and W_2 are placed on the ends of a board of length $X = L$, which is supported near its center by a sharp edge. If W_1 is at a distance X_1 from the sharp edge and W_2 is at a distance of X_2 from the sharp edge, with $L = X = X_1 + X_2$, then the board will balance if $W_1 X_1 = W_2 X_2$. This is equivalent to $W_1 X_1 = W_2(L - X_1)$. The point on the board above the sharp edge is the center of gravity of the system. Texts on calculus and physics covering the theory of moments give more detailed explanations. Other statistics associated with moments are the variance related to μ_2 (mu two) and the skewness k associated with both μ_3 and μ_2, and so on. Most engineering texts use sample size n denoting the number of X values in their computations rather than $n - 1$ for d.f., the number of degrees of freedom.

In the theory of estimation, it has been found that using degrees of freedom for many computations reduces the error of estimation. In engineering, the variance is given by the relations

$$v = \sigma^2 = \frac{\Sigma(X_i - \bar{X})^2}{n}, \quad \text{or} \quad \sigma^2 = \frac{\Sigma f_i X_i^2}{\Sigma f_i} - \bar{X}^2 \tag{2}$$

with the standard deviation σ derived from the above as

$$\sigma = \sqrt{v} = \sqrt{\frac{\Sigma(X_i - \bar{X})^2}{n}}, \quad \text{or} \quad \sigma = \sqrt{\frac{\Sigma X_i^2}{n} - \bar{X}^2} \tag{3}$$

However, in the theory of estimation, the best estimate of the true standard deviation of the universe is given by the relation

$$s = \sqrt{v_s} = \sqrt{\frac{\Sigma(X_i - \bar{X})^2}{(n - 1)}}, \quad \text{or} \quad s = \sqrt{\frac{n}{(n - 1)}} \cdot \sigma, \tag{4}$$

where the degrees of freedom (d.f.) $= n - 1$.

In using even the simplest form of the analysis of variance, the squared deviations are related to the degrees of freedom for each part to obtain valid measures of their probability of occurrence.

The term *degrees of freedom* may best be explained as being the number of independent values needed in addition to the statistics, n, $\bar{X}$, σ, etc., given to reproduce the original set of observations. If n and $\bar{X}$ are known as well as $(n - 1)$ values of X_i, then all n values of X_i may be determined. If the standard deviation σ is also known, then only $(n - 2)$ values of X_i are required to reproduce the original set of X_i values.

Example 6 $X_1 = 5$, $X_2 = 7$, $X_3 = 4$, $X_4 = 16$, and $n = 4$; $\bar{X} = 8$ is also given. Then only three values of X_i are needed to reproduce all the four X_i values and d.f. $= n - 1 = 4 - 1 = 3$.

From equation (1), $\bar{X} = \dfrac{\Sigma X_i}{n} = \dfrac{(X_1 + X_2 + X_3 + X_4)}{4} = \dfrac{32}{4} = 8.$

If we have $X_1 = 5$, $X_3 = 4$, $X_4 = 16$, $n = 4$, and $\bar{X} = 8$, can we find X_2?

Solution $X_1 + X_3 + X_4 = 5 + 4 + 16 = 25$

$$\overline{X} = \frac{(25 + X_2)}{4} = 8$$

Hence $25 + X_2 = 4 \times 8 = 32$

$X_2 = 32 - 25 = 7$

Example 7 $X_1 = 5, X_2 = 7, X_3 = 4, X_4 = 16, n = 4, \overline{X} = 8$, and $v = \sigma^2 =$ 22.5 are given. $n - 2 =$ d.f. $= 4 - 2 = 2$. If $X_1 = 5$ and $X_2 = 7$, determine X_3 and X_4.

Solution With $n = 4$ and $\overline{X} = 8$ from relation (1), $X_1 + X_2 + X_3 = 4 \times 8 =$ 32, $\overline{X}^2 = 8^2 = 64$

$5 + 7 + X_3 + X_4 = 32$

$X_3 + X_4 = 32 - 12 = 20$

$$\frac{X_1^2 + X_2^3 + X_3^2 + X_4^2}{4} - \overline{X}^2 = \frac{25 + 49 + X_3^2 + X_4^2}{4} - \overline{X}^2 = 22.5$$

$74 + X_3^2 + X_4^2 = 4(22.5 + 64) = 4(86.5) = 346.0$

$X_3^2 + X_4^2 = 346 - 74 = 272.$

We know $X_3 = 20 - X_4$

$(20 - X_4)^2 + X_4^2 = 272$

$400 - 40X_4 + X_4^2 + X_4^2 = 272$

$2X_4^2 - 40X_4 + (400 - 272) = 0$

$2X_4 - 40X_4 + 128 = 0$

$X_4^2 - 20X_4 + 64 = 0$

$(X_4 - 4)(X_4 - 16) = 0$

Hence $X_4 = 4$ or 16 and $X_3 = 16$ or 4, since $X_3 + X_4 = 20$.

An alternate means of solving $X_4^2 - 20X_4 + 64$ is to use the quadratic formula.

For $aX^2 + bX + c = 0$, $X = \dfrac{-b \pm \sqrt{b^2 - 4ac}}{2a}$.

In $X_4^2 - 20X_4 + 64 = 0$, $a = 1$, $b = -20$, and $c = 64$. Hence

$$X_4 = \frac{-(-20) \pm \sqrt{(-20)^2 - 4(1)(64)}}{2(1)} = \frac{20 \pm \sqrt{400 - 256}}{2} = \frac{20 \pm \sqrt{144}}{2}$$

$$= \frac{20 \pm 12}{2}. \text{ Then } X_4 = \frac{32}{2} = 16, \text{ or } \frac{8}{2} = 4.$$

8.9 General Tests for Significant Difference

Most texts discuss only variables data checking for the difference between two means or the difference between several means. For quick tests, tests for any two sets of data may be made by treating for significant differences between any two sets of data. Random sets of differences generally should result in as many negative differences as positive differences, so that the resultant distribution of differences is symmetrical and has a mean of zero. The generalized distribution might approach normality or have some of the features of other symmetrical distributions. Some have used t to represent this measure and others z. Since the t may be confused with the *"Student's" t-distribution,* we will determine the differences from the relation

$$z = \frac{|\theta_1 - \theta_2|}{\sigma_{\text{diff}\cdot(\theta_1 - \theta_2)}} = \frac{|\theta_1 - \theta_2|}{\sqrt{\sigma_{\theta_1}^2 + \sigma_{\theta_2}^2}} \tag{5}$$

In this relation, θ may represent any variable for which such a test is desired. When the method of attributes is used, then $\theta_1 = p_1$ and $\theta_2 = p_2$. The difference $(\theta_1 - \theta_2)$ can readily be evaluated from the theorem covering the determination of the variances of sums or differences. This may be stated as

$$\sigma_{\theta_1 \pm \theta_2}^2 = \sigma_{\theta_1}^2 + \sigma_{\theta_2}^2 \pm 2r_{\theta_1\theta_2}\sigma_{\theta_1}\sigma_{\theta_2} \tag{6}$$

When θ_1 and θ_2 are independent, then $r_{\theta_1\theta_2} = 0$, and

$$\sigma_{\theta_1 - \theta_2}^2 = \sigma_{\theta_1}^2 + \sigma_{\theta_2}^2. \tag{7}$$

Then equation (5) becomes

$$z = \frac{|\theta_1 - \theta_2|}{\sqrt{\sigma_{\theta_1}^2 + \sigma_{\theta_2}^2}} = \frac{|p_1 - p_2|}{\sqrt{\sigma_{p_1}^2 + \sigma_{p_2}^2}} \tag{5'}$$

For this test for a high degree of belief, P_b, consider θ_1 to be significantly different from θ_2 if $z > 3$. The probability associated with 3, according to Tchebycheff's inequality, cannot be less than 88.9% and might be as great as almost 100%, but should at least be around 95%. For more liberal tests, use 2 instead of 3, with a minimum probability of 75% associated with this limit. (Tchebycheff's inequality gives $1 - \frac{1}{t^2} = 1 - \frac{1}{2^2} = 1 - \frac{1}{4} = \frac{3}{4} = 75\%$.) From the Camp-Meidel inequality, $1 - \frac{1}{2.25t^2}$, we have a lower limit which is 88.89%, since $1 - \frac{1}{2.25(2)^2} = 1 - \frac{1}{9} = \frac{8}{9} = 0.8888 = 88.89\%$ for $t = z = 2$.

It should be noted that use is made of the correct relation for the standard deviation or variances in these relations. If the distributions are truly binomial, then $\sigma_p = \sqrt{\frac{p(1-p)}{n}}$, but for a Poisson Exponential, $\sigma_{pn} = \sqrt{pn}$, where pn is known but not p or n independently. If defects for a binomial are covered, then $\sigma_{pn} = \sqrt{pn(1-p)}$.

Example 8 *Binomial Distribution—Equal Sample Sizes*
Two methods of production are being tested to determine which is superior to the other. The conforming values, in table 8.12, expressed as percentages, were found for the two methods.

TABLE 8.12

Sample Nos.	1	2	3	4	5	6	7	8	9	10	Total
Method A $n = 100$ per sample	5	4	1	0	10	9	3	2	6	10	50
Method B $n = 100$ per sample	7	8	15	9	11	6	8	4	5	12	85

$$\theta_A = p_A = \frac{50}{1{,}000} = 0.050;\ \sigma^2_{p_A} = \frac{0.050(0.950)}{1{,}000} = \frac{0.047500}{1{,}000} = \frac{0.47500}{10{,}000}$$

$$\text{Sum} = \frac{1.25275}{10{,}000}$$

$$\theta_B = p_B = \frac{85}{1{,}000} = 0.085;\ \sigma^2_{p_B} = \frac{0.085(0.915)}{1{,}000} = \frac{0.077775}{1{,}000} = \frac{0.77775}{10{,}000}$$

$$z_{AB} = \frac{|0.050 - 0.085|}{\sqrt{\dfrac{1.25275}{10{,}000}}} = \frac{0.035}{(\frac{1}{100})\sqrt{1.25275}} = \frac{0.035}{0.0112} = 3.13 > 3.00$$

This large z value indicates that there exists a significant difference between the two methods.

The test above used $\theta_1 = p_A$ and $\theta_2 = p_B$, with sample sizes of n_1 and n_2 respectively. Since $n_1 = n_2$, the test could have been made on the basis of the number of defects observed on the average in each sample of 100 units. However, a quick approximate test when the total sample sizes used for each of two methods is the same is to neglect the $(1 - p)$ factors and use $v_A = \Sigma d_A = \Sigma p_A n_A = 50$ and $v_B = \Sigma d_B = \Sigma p_B n_B = 85$.

Then $$z_{AB} = \frac{|\Sigma d_A - \Sigma d_B|}{\sqrt{\Sigma d_A + \Sigma d_B}} = \frac{|50 - 85|}{\sqrt{50 + 85}} = \frac{35}{\sqrt{135}} = \frac{35}{11.62} = 3.01,$$

which is greater than 3. If this z_{AB} value had been slightly less than 3, it would be a borderline case and require the addition of the $(1 - p)$ factors. Then, since $p_A = 0.05$, $1 - p_A = 0.95$, and $p_B = 0.085$, $1 - p_B = 0.915$. Adding these $(1 - p)$ values in both cases gives

$$z_{AB} = \frac{|50 - 85|}{\sqrt{50(0.95) + 85(0.915)}} = \frac{35}{\sqrt{125.275}} = \frac{35}{11.2} = 3.13,$$

the same value as found using the significant test for p_A and p_B.

Example 9 *Poisson Distribution—Average Values*
Three different methods for insulating wire were tested to determine which should be used as the standard method. Tests for leakage were given by successively placing 1,000 feet of each type of wire in a water tank and determining how many leakage points occurred in each 1,000 feet of wire. Varying amounts of these three different kinds of insulation were available for these crucial tests. Eight, ten, and twelve lengths were finally tested. The results are tabulated in table 8.13.

TABLE 8.13 Leakage Tests on Insulated Wires
Defects Noted per 1,000 feet Lengths—Three Methods of Insulation

Test No.	1	2	3	4	5	6	7	8	9	10	11	12	Total
Method A	2	3	6	7	8	1	4	1	—	—	—	—	32
Method B	1	0	2	3	4	0	1	0	2	1	—	—	14
Method C	0	1	3	2	1	0	1	0	2	1	0	1	12

This is a case where the fraction defective p is not known, nor is the number of possible occurrences n, the sample size, known, but pn is known in each length of 1,000 feet of wire. The standard deviation for such a Poisson distribution of pn values is $\sigma_{pn} = \sqrt{pn}$. A different number of lengths was available for these tests for determining whether method A was significantly different from method B or from method C, or whether method B is significantly different from method C. These pn values are now treated as variables and an average pn value found for each method. For the method of variables, the standard deviation for m average values is $\dfrac{\sigma}{\sqrt{n}}$, where the number of lengths taken is considered as the sample size. Three tests for significant difference in levels may be made, where $\theta_A = \overline{pn}_A$, $\theta_B = \overline{pn}_B$, and $\theta_C = \overline{pn}_C$, the average values to be tested. The variances for the three methods are respectively

$$v_A = \frac{\overline{pn}_A}{m_A}, \quad v_B = \frac{\overline{pn}_B}{m_B}, \quad \text{and} \quad v_C = \frac{\overline{pn}_C}{m_C}$$

From these data, the values used in the test are as follows.

$$\overline{pn}_A = \frac{32}{8} = 4.0; \quad \overline{pn}_B = \frac{14}{10} = 1.4; \quad \overline{pn}_C = \frac{12}{12} = 1.0$$

$$v_A = \frac{4.0}{8} = 0.50; \quad v_B = \frac{1.4}{10} = 0.14; \quad v_C = \frac{1.0}{12} = 0.0833$$

$$z_{AB} = \frac{|\theta_A - \theta_B|}{\sqrt{v_A + v_B}} = \frac{|4.0 - 1.4|}{\sqrt{0.50 + 0.14}} = \frac{2.6}{\sqrt{0.64}} = \frac{2.6}{0.8} = 3.25$$

Since 3.25 > 3.00, method A is significantly poorer than method B, resulting in more defects per 1,000 feet.

$$z_{AC} = \frac{|\theta_A - \theta_C|}{\sqrt{v_A + v_C}} = \frac{|4.0 - 1.0|}{\sqrt{0.50 + 0.0833}} = \frac{3.0}{\sqrt{0.5833}} = \frac{3.0}{0.764} = 3.93$$

Since 3.93 > 3.00, method A is significantly poorer than method C, resulting in more defects per 1,000 feet.

$$z_{BC} = \frac{|\theta_B - \theta_C|}{\sqrt{v_B + v_C}} = \frac{|1.4 - 1.0|}{\sqrt{0.14 + 0.0833}} = \frac{0.4}{\sqrt{0.2233}} = \frac{0.4}{0.473} = 0.85$$

Since 0.85 is considerably less than 3.00, there is no significant difference between method B and method C. The final decision would be to use either method B or method C, whichever will result in more profit.

Example 10 *Binomial Distribution—Unequal Sample Sizes*
As indicated in example 2, the number of tests do not have to be equal in order to carry out a test for the difference between the fraction defective or percent defective found for components received from two suppliers of similar types of products. Supplier A has submitted 100 units of his product for test and supplier B has submitted 400 units of his product for test. In the first supplier's units, two nonconforming units were observed, giving a tentative process average of 2%. In a similar test of supplier B's units, twenty-eight nonconforming units were observed, giving a tentative process average of 7%. There is a 5% (2%:7%) difference in these results. Is this result significantly different?

Solution

$$\theta_A = p_A = 0.02, \text{ with } v_A = \frac{0.02(0.98)}{100} = 0.000196$$

$$\theta_B = p_B = 0.07, \text{ with } v_B = \frac{0.07(0.93)}{400} = 0.00016275$$

$$z_{AB} = \frac{|0.02 - 0.07|}{\sqrt{0.000196 + 0.00016275}} = \frac{0.05}{\sqrt{0.00035875}} = \frac{0.05}{0.01894} = 2.64$$

If z_{AB} must exceed 3 to state positively that there is a significant difference between the two suppliers, either supplier should be used. However, some prefer to use 2 as the limiting criterion. Then a significant difference between the two suppliers is indicated by the z_{AB} value of 2.64. Although this distribution of differences is not necessarily normal, it is close enough that normal law probability values are used as a guide in selecting the criterion to use for these tests. For the normal law within $\pm 3\sigma$ control limits, the area is 0.9973, while within $\pm 2\sigma$ control limits, the area is 0.9545. Since this z_{AB} value of 2.64 seems to be a borderline case, it appears questionable whether supplier B should be used as well as supplier A or in place of supplier A. A second solution is to have supplier B furnish another sample for test. In all fairness, however, supplier A should furnish some more units for test since originally he furnished only 100 units. The 100 units might have been a very selective sample; the degree of belief in supplier A's process average of 2%, the best value, is not as great as it is for supplier B with a process average of 7%. The best solution is to obtain equal samples and sufficient additional samples from each supplier to provide positive assurance that one of them is actually much better than the other.

8.10 Significant Difference Between Two Means and Two Variances

In all the different industries and economic areas, there may arise many cases where two or more methods, parts, components, or procedures should be compared to determine if there is any significant difference between them. Statistical texts go into great detail to cover the differences between two means and between several means. Experiments are designed to handle these cases and many are prepared so they may be programmed for different varieties of computers. The simple z test just presented covers a great majority of these cases. Also, many desire to know whether the dispersions or spreads of the various universes are similar or significantly different. The z test gives quick answers for these tests and may be applied initially. If it indicates that the differences may be slight, then the more rigorous statistical tests described in other references should be used.

It is desired to determine whether two sets of data are significantly different with respect to central values and their variabilities or dispersions. The two tests to be used are

$$z_{12} = \frac{|\bar{X}_1 - \bar{X}_2|}{\sqrt{\dfrac{\sigma_1^2}{n_1} + \dfrac{\sigma_2^2}{n_2}}}, \tag{8}$$

and

$$z_{12}^* = \frac{\sigma_1 - \sigma_2}{\sqrt{\dfrac{\sigma_1^2}{2n_1} + \dfrac{\sigma_2^2}{2n_2}}}. \tag{9}$$

This last relation for the difference between the two standard deviation values is only a rough approximation to more exact tests, but gives a quick indication regarding differences in the spreads of the two universes being tested. Somewhat more refined tests are given in later sections.

Example 11 Most automobiles have resistors in series with their horns. The following resistance values (purely empirical) might represent two different brands of resistances. Are they significantly different with respect to level or variability?

These data are shown in table 8.14 listing measured values of resistance for five groups of five units each for brand 1 and four groups of ten units each for brand 2. The data are set up so that these same data may be used later for other tests.

TABLE 8.14 Resistance Values for Two Brands of Resistors

Brand 1: R_1 Values = X Values										
	Sample Numbers									
Test No.	*1*		*2*		*3*		*4*		*5*	
	X	X^2	X	X^2	X	X^2	X	X^2	X	X^2
1	10	100	9	81	8	64	10	100	11	121
2	9	81	8	64	10	100	9	81	12	144
3	11	121	11	121	12	144	12	144	9	81
4	10	100	10	100	11	121	7	49	10	100
5	10	100	9	81	10	100	11	121	11	121
Sum	50	502	47	447	51	529	49	495	53	567
$\bar{X}, \bar{X}^2$	10.0	100.00	9.4	88.36	10.2	104.04	9.8	96.04	10.6	112.36

$\Sigma X = 50 + 47 + 51 + 49 + 53 = 250;\quad X = \frac{250}{25} = 20.0,\ n_i = 5,\ m = 5,\ n = 5 \times 5 = 25.$

$\Sigma X^2 = 502 + 447 + 529 + 495 + 567 = 2540;\quad \sigma_X^2 = \frac{2540}{25} - (10.0)^2 = 101.60 - 100.00 = 1.60$

$\Sigma \bar{X}^2 = 100.00 + 88.36 + 104.04 + 96.04 + 112.36 = 500.80;\quad \sigma_X = \sqrt{1.60} = 1.2649.$

$$\sigma_{\bar{X}}^2 = \frac{500.80}{5} - (10.0)^2 = 100.16 - 100.00 = 0.16;$$

Variation between samples $\sigma_{\bar{X}} = \sqrt{0.16} = 0.4000.$

Varation Within Samples

$\sigma_{11}^2 = \frac{502}{5} - (10.0)^2 = 100.40 - 100.00 = 0.40 \qquad \sigma_{12}^2 = \frac{447}{5} - (9.4)^2 = 89.40 - 88.36 = 1.04$

$\sigma_{13}^2 = \frac{529}{5} - (10.2)^2 = 105.80 - 104.04 = 1.76 \qquad \sigma_{14}^2 = \frac{495}{5} - (9.8)^2 = 99.00 - 96.04 = 2.96$

$\sigma_{15}^2 = \frac{567}{5} - (10.6)^2 = 113.40 - 112.36 = 1.04$

Summary

$$\sigma_{11} = 0.6325,\ \sigma_{12} = 1.0198,\ \sigma_{13} = 1.3266,\ \sigma_{14} = 1.7205,\ \sigma_{15} = 1.0198;\ \bar{\sigma}_1 = \frac{5.7192}{5} = 1.14384.$$

c_2 values from table X: $c_{2,5} = 0.8407,\ c_{2,25} = 0.9696;\qquad \sigma'_{1,25} = \frac{1.2653}{0.9696} = 1.3050.$

$$\sigma_{W_1}^1 = \frac{\bar{\sigma}_1}{c_{25}} = \frac{1.14384}{0.8407} = 1.3606;$$

$\sigma_{\bar{X}_1} = 0.4000, \; \sigma^1_{b_1} = \dfrac{0.4000}{0.8407} = 0.4758$

$(\sigma^1_1)^2 = \sigma^2_{W_1} + \sigma^2_{b_1} = (1.3606)^2 + (0.4758)^2 = 1.85123236 + 0.22638564 = 2.07761800,$
$\sigma^1_1 = \sqrt{2.07761800} = 1.4414.$

Brand 2: R_2 Values = Y Values

Test No.	*Sample Numbers* 1		2		3		4	
	X	X^2	X	X^2	X	X^2	X	X^2
1	11	121	14	196	12	144	15	225
2	9	81	10	100	13	169	11	121
3	12	144	9	81	14	196	10	100
4	10	100	10	100	10	100	12	144
5	8	64	9	81	11	121	9	81
6	11	121	13	169	10	100	8	64
7	10	100	14	196	12	144	10	100
8	12	144	13	169	12	144	9	81
9	9	81	9	81	13	169	12	144
10	12	144	10	100	11	121	11	121
Sum	104	1100	111	1273	118	1408	107	1181
$\bar{X}, \bar{X}^2$	10.4	108.16	11.1	123.21	11.8	139.24	10.7	114.49

$\Sigma X = 104 + 111 + 118 + 107 = 440; \quad \bar{X} = \frac{440}{40} = 11.0 \quad n_i = 10, m = 4, n = 4 \times 10 = 40$
$\Sigma X^2 = 1100 + 1273 + 1408 + 1181 = 4962; \quad \sigma^2_X = \frac{4962}{40} - (11.0)^2 = 124.05 - 121.00 = 3.05$
$\Sigma \bar{X}^2 = 108.16 + 123.21 + 139.24 + 114.49 = 485.10; \quad \sigma_X = \sqrt{3.05} = 1.7464$
$\sigma^2_{\bar{X}} = 485.10/4 - (11.0)^2 = 121.275 - 121.000 = 0.275;$
Variation between samples $\sigma_{\bar{X}} = \sqrt{0.275} = 0.5244.$

Variation Within Samples

$\sigma^2_{21} \frac{1100}{10} - (10.4)^2 = 110.0 - 108.16 = 1.84; \qquad \sigma^2_{22} = \frac{1273}{10} - (11.1)^2 = 127.30 - 123.21 = 4.09$
$\sigma^2_{23} = \frac{1408}{10} - (11.8) = 140.80 - 139.24 = 1.56; \quad \sigma^2_{24} = \frac{1181}{10} - (10.7)^2 = 118.10 - 114.49 = 3.61$

Summary

$\sigma_{21} = 1.3565, \sigma_{22} = 2.6224, \sigma_{23} = 1.2490, \sigma_{24} = 1.9000; \quad \bar{\sigma}_2 = \dfrac{6.5279}{4} = 1.6320.$

c_2 values from table X; $c_{2,10} = 0.9227, \; c_{2,40} = 0.9811; \sigma^1_{2,40} = \dfrac{1.7464}{0.9811} = 1.7800$

$\sigma^1_{W_2} = \dfrac{\bar{\sigma}_2}{c_{2,10}} = \dfrac{1.6320}{0.9227} = 1.7687;$

$\sigma_{\bar{X}_2} = 0.5244, \; \sigma^1_{b_2} = \dfrac{0.5244}{0.7979} = 0.6572$

$(\sigma^1_2)^2 = \sigma^2_{W_1} + \sigma^2_{b_2} = (1.7687)^2 + (0.6572)^2 = 3.12829969 + 0.43191184 = 3.56021153.$
$\sigma^1_2 = \sqrt{3.56021153} = 1.8869.$

Test for Difference Between Means

$$z_{12} = \frac{|10.0 - 11.0|}{\sqrt{\dfrac{1.60}{25} + \dfrac{3.05}{40}}} = \frac{1.0}{\sqrt{0.0640 + 0.07625}} = \frac{1.0}{\sqrt{0.14025}} = \frac{1.0}{0.3745} = 2.6702$$

Test for Difference Between Standard Deviations

$$z_{12}^{*} = \frac{|1.265 - 1.746|}{\sqrt{\dfrac{1.60}{50} + \dfrac{3.05}{80}}} = \frac{0.481}{\sqrt{0.0320 + 0.038125}} = \frac{0.481}{\sqrt{0.070125}} = \frac{0.481}{0.2648} = 1.8165$$

Final Decision Using 3 as the criterion for significant differences, these results with $z_{12} = 2.67$ for averages indicate no significant differences; however, if $z_{\text{Max.}} = 2.00$ is the criterion, then brand 1 is significantly better than brand 2 for central values. For variability, $z_{12}^{*} = 1.82$, so there is no significant difference between the variability of the two brands.

8.11 Experimental Arrangements

If an automobile manufacturer wishes to check the effectiveness of four different carburetors placed in a particular model of car, it is desirable to arrange an experiment to determine whether there is any significant difference between these carburetors. Designate these carburetors as A, B, C, and D and install each carburetor on a different car. The results to be compared might be in terms of miles per gallon achieved by the operation of this particular model of automobile with each different carburetor. To avoid possible differences shown being due to the cars rather than the carburetor, use the same four cars for each of the four carburetors. This might give the following results.

Example 12 *Mileage Results in Miles per Gallon*

TABLE 8.15 Carburetor Type

	Carburetor Type			
Car No.	*A*	*B*	*C*	*D*
1	20.2	19.0	21.3	18.9
2	19.6	21.2	22.5	20.7
3	20.5	22.7	24.8	23.1
4	19.7	21.1	23.4	25.3
Sum	80.0	84.0	92.0	88.0
Average	20.0	21.0	23.0	22.0

The data above may be analyzed in many different ways. One of the best experimental designs is the Latin square.

8.12 Latin Square

The Latin square is an arrangement used by many statisticians to set up many research experiments. It permits at least two factors (other than the one being studied) to vary during the experiment, while excluding the principal component of their variation from the basic error of the experiment. In the above case covering mileage per gallon for automobiles, the two factors which might affect such results might be the difference in the adjustment of the carburetor by different auto mechanics and the difference in the automobiles in which the carburetors are installed. The four carburetors are denoted by A, B, C, and D, so the possible Latin square is given by table 8.16.

TABLE 8.16

		Automobile			
		1	*2*	*3*	*4*
Mechanic	1	D	B	A	C
	2	C	A	D	B
	3	A	C	B	D
	4	B	D	C	A

Some like to use the simpler design in table 8.17.

TABLE 8.17

		Automobile			
		1	*2*	*3*	*4*
Mechanic	1	A	B	C	D
	2	B	C	D	A
	3	C	D	A	B
	4	D	A	B	C

The completely randomized experiment makes it possible to consider the variations among the means of gasoline mileage of carburetors and the unallocable variations of individual observations about the respective means of carburetors, which represent the variation within carburetors of the same kind. This covers all sources of variation for the sixteen observations about the grand mean.

A Latin square excludes only the variation among the row and column means from experimental error. In order to cover any kind of data, values recorded horizontally along one single line are called row values while those recorded vertically are termed column data. There are variations within rows and between rows, also variations within columns and between columns. This makes it possible to present the methods used to compute the various kinds of variability to treat the variables just as column values or row values. When using a Latin square experimental model, a ten by ten square should be the maximum used. Too small a Latin square also has a large error in the estimates obtained from it. When as few as three or four items of the same kind are to be compared, more than one Latin square must be used.

8.13 Experimental Models—Classical versus Factorial Designs

In the experiments first used, the classical method made a model that kept all but one variable constant while the variable studied is tested and the data obtained analyzed. The second step is to keep all but a second factor constant while the second factor is analyzed. This method required a large number of tests.

The modern method is to use a randomized sample along with a model such as the Latin square or another model given in references covering the analysis of variance method of analysis in detail. As noted above, the contribution of each factor to the total variability is found by analyzing these randomized variable results. However, before making an analysis which finally determines significance between means, two different methods of analysis are used as a check to determine whether the data are *homogeneous* or not. The latter situation is sometimes termed *heterogeneous*. The first simple set of tests are the L_0 and L_1 tests described by H. A. Freeman in *Industrial Statistics*,[3] which also gives tables of L_0 and L_1 based on the approximations for these distributions developed by Jerry Neyman and Egan Pearson, with tables which were prepared by P. C. Mahalanobis.[4] A modified form of these tables is included in this text, together with one form of the F-table for use in making the F-test. Tests for homogeneity should be made just before using the F-test.

The second test used to check for homogeneity is the Bartlett test, which is presented in the more advanced texts on statistics. Both are easy to use and are described in sufficient detail in the next section, so that they may readily be used by those engaged in quality control analysis.

8.14 L_0 and L_1 Tests for Homogeneity

The following questions are answered by the L_0, L_1, and F tests.

1. Could the samples belong to normal populations having the same mean and the same variance? (Use L_0 test.)

2. Could the samples belong to normal populations with the same variance with no restrictions placed on the mean? (Use L_1 test.)
3. Could these samples belong to normal populations whose means are practically the same and whose variances are assumed to be the same? (Apply the F test if the L_0 and L_1 tests are satisfied; otherwise the F test gives a false indication concerning significance of means.)

The two functions devised by Neyman and Pearson are respectively:

$$L_0 = \left(\frac{\sigma_1^2 \sigma_2^2 \sigma_3^2 \ldots \sigma_i^2 \ldots \sigma_k^2}{\sigma_0^2 \sigma_0^2 \sigma_0^2 \ldots \sigma_0^2 \ldots \sigma_0^2} \right)^{1/k}, \tag{10}$$

and

$$L_1 = \left(\frac{\sigma_1^2 \sigma_2^2 \sigma_3^2 \ldots \sigma_i^2 \ldots \sigma_k^2}{\sigma_a^2 \sigma_a^2 \sigma_a^2 \ldots \sigma_a^2 \ldots \sigma_a^2} \right)^{1/k}, \tag{11}$$

where

$$\sigma_1^2 = \frac{\sum_1^{n_1} (X_{1i} - \bar{X}_1)^2}{n_1}, \sigma_2^2 = \frac{\sum_1^{n_2} (X_{2i} - \bar{X}_2)^2}{n_2}, \ldots, \sigma_k^2 = \frac{\sum_2^{n_k} (X_{ki} - \bar{X}_k)^2}{n_k}, n_1 = n_2 = \ldots$$

$$= n_k \text{ and } \sigma_0^2 = \frac{\sum_1^{n} (X_i - \bar{X})^2}{n}, \sigma_a^2 = \frac{\sum_1^{k} \sigma_i^2}{k}, n = \sum_1^{k} n_i = kn_k.$$

Here σ_1^2, σ_2^2, etc., are the within-sample variances, whereas σ_0^2 is the variance based on the deviation of all the n observations about the overall mean $\bar{X}_1$ and σ_a^2 is the average or mean of the within-sample variances.

Table 8.18 gives values of L_0 for both 5% and 1% values for eight values of k and ten values of n_k, the sample size for each group, while table 8.19 gives values of L_1 for both 5% and 1% values for eight values of k and ten values of n_k, the sample size for each group. Note for these tables, values of n_k and k are used for entering these tables rather than degrees of freedom. Entries for tables for the F test are made in terms of degrees of freedom. Tables for the F test are given in those texts that cover the analysis of variance. The Fisher tables cover 5% and 1% for degrees of freedom for the numerator from 1 to 500 and ∞ and the denominator from 1 to 1,000 and ∞.

Most tables in this text are included within the chapters describing their applications. Those that apply in a larger number of different conditions, such as the normal law probability table, are given in the appendix. Random numbers, which are used most effectively in obtaining truly random results for the analysis of variance, are included in table 8.1. Such random sampling numbers should also be selected by those in charge of inspection and test. In receiving inspection, in particular, it is wise to have true random samples where less than 100% inspection is used. Samples should always be selected randomly on the production line to make certain that the process is controlled at desired levels. In the following study of gasoline mileage results, it is assumed that the data are random and representative of the products.

TABLE 8.18 L_0 Values[4]

L_0

Five percent Values

Values of k (number of samples)	Values of n (size of samples) 2	3	4	5	10	15	20	30	40	50
2	0.0190	0.1719	0.3277	0.4424	0.7071	0.8028	0.8515	0.9007	0.9254	0.9403
3	0.0217	0.1745	0.3205	0.4290	0.6977	0.7950	0.8450	0.8960	0.9216	0.9372
4	0.0258	0.1846	0.3328	0.4416	0.7008	0.7968	0.8463	0.8967	0.9222	0.9376
5	0.0301	0.1946	0.3421	0.4511	0.7057	0.8000	0.8488	0.8983	0.9234	0.9384
10	0.0470	0.2296	0.3792	0.4857	0.7262	0.8142	0.8595	0.9057	0.9294	0.9432
20	0.0656	0.2640	0.4149	0.5193	0.7549	0.8358	0.8766	0.9183	0.9383	0.9511
25	0.0721	0.2744	0.4204	0.5338	0.7635	0.8422	0.8816	0.9210	0.9408	0.9519
50	0.0878	0.3036	0.4644	0.5731	0.7865	0.8550	0.8891	0.9275	0.9449	0.9554

One percent Values

Values of k (number of samples)	2	3	4	5	10	15	20	30	40	50
2	0.0023	0.0590	0.1804	0.2856	0.5870	0.7135	0.7811	0.8516	0.8875	0.9097
3	0.0024	0.0856	0.2053	0.3112	0.6043	0.7253	0.7900	0.8575	0.8922	0.9133
4	0.0065	0.1031	0.2293	0.3353	0.6219	0.7382	0.8001	0.8644	0.8975	0.9176
5	0.0092	0.1180	0.2478	0.3558	0.6367	0.7490	0.8086	0.8702	0.9018	0.9210
10	0.0229	0.1679	0.3093	0.4171	0.6804	0.7809	0.8335	0.8877	0.9154	0.9321
20	0.0422	0.2166	0.3656	0.4736	0.7286	0.8180	0.8632	0.9098	0.9316	0.9443
25	0.0495	0.2315	0.3814	0.4954	0.7428	0.8285	0.8710	0.9142	0.9356	0.9473
50	0.0688	0.2729	0.4389	0.5464	0.7727	0.8486	0.8833	0.9243	0.9422	0.9531

TABLE 8.19 L_1 Values[4]

L_1

Five percent Values

Values of k (number of samples)	Values of n (size of samples) 2	3	4	5	10	15	20	30	40	50
2	0.0723	0.3107	0.4782	0.5842	0.7985	0.8673	0.9014	0.9349	0.9512	0.9612
3	0.0704	0.3040	0.4696	0.5755	0.7925	0.8632	0.8980	0.9325	0.9495	0.9598
4	0.0753	0.3152	0.4800	0.5849	0.7970	0.8662	0.9005	0.9341	0.9506	0.9608
5	0.0825	0.3278	0.4915	0.5950	0.8025	0.8699	0.9032	0.9358	0.9519	0.9618
10	0.1135	0.3738	0.5341	0.6318	0.8228	0.8813	0.9135	0.9427	0.9573	0.9659
20	0.1472	0.4191	0.5697	0.6658	0.8417	0.8961	0.9227	0.9498	0.9619	0.9694
25	0.1578	0.4320	0.5841	0.6747	0.8453	0.8989	0.9250	0.9508	0.9630	0.9697
50	0.1878	0.4723	0.6278	0.7137	0.8688	0.9150	0.9365	0.9584	0.9672	0.9730

One percent Values

Values of k (number of samples)	2	3	4	5	10	15	20	30	40	50
2	0.0126	0.1361	0.2818	0.3855	0.6782	0.7821	0.8359	0.8902	0.9171	0.9340
3	0.0169	0.1615	0.3138	0.4291	0.6992	0.7976	0.8476	0.8981	0.9234	0.9388
4	0.0233	0.1876	0.3414	0.4594	0.7194	0.8118	0.8586	0.9056	0.9291	0.9434
5	0.0285	0.2101	0.3703	0.4838	0.7350	0.8228	0.8645	0.9113	0.9334	0.9470
10	0.0624	0.2838	0.4483	0.5556	0.7791	0.8537	0.8908	0.9273	0.9458	0.9565
20	0.0997	0.3524	0.5138	0.6142	0.8131	0.8768	0.9082	0.9404	0.9546	0.9633
25	0.1129	0.3718	0.5304	0.6287	0.8201	0.8817	0.9121	0.9415	0.9565	0.9640
50	0.1517	0.4328	0.5915	0.6672	0.8576	0.9077	0.9307	0.9548	0.9643	0.9697

The data in the example concerning mileage results in miles per gallon is summarized in table 8.20 so that the L_0 and L_1 tests may be made. The sum of the X values is given and, since there are only four observations per carburetor type, their averages are also given.

TABLE 8.20 Carburetor Type, n_k

	A	B	C	D
$X =$	80.0	84.0	92.0	88.0
$\overline{X} =$	20.0	21.0	23.0	22.0

Using these $\overline{X}$ values and the individual X values previously given, then variances are given in table 8.21. Here, $x_i = X_i - \overline{X}$.

TABLE 8.21

Car No.	x_1	x_1^2	x_2	x_2^2	x_3	x_3^2	Σx	Σx^2
1	0.2	0.04	−2.0	4.00	−1.7	2.89	−3.1	9.61
2	−0.4	0.16	0.2	0.04	−0.5	0.25	−1.3	1.69
3	0.5	0.25	1.7	2.89	1.8	3.24	1.1	1.21
4	−0.3	0.09	0.1	0.01	0.4	0.16	3.3	10.89
Sum	0	0.54	0	6.94	0	6.54	0	23.40
Variances		0.135		1.735		1.635		5.850

The information above gives the variances within the carburetor samples. The overall variance for all four carburetors is computed in table 8.22. For obtaining the overall variance, use $x = X - \overline{X}, \overline{X} = 21.5$ and the X values given under A, B, C and D in tables 8.23 and 8.24.

TABLE 8.22

Car No.	A		B		C		D		Total	
	x	x^2	x	x^2	x	x^2	x	x^2	Σx	Σx^2
1	−1.3	1.69	−2.5	6.25	−0.2	0.04	−2.6	6.76	−6.6	14.74
2	−1.9	3.61	−0.3	0.09	1.0	1.00	−0.8	0.64	−2.0	5.34
3	−1.0	1.00	1.2	1.44	3.3	10.89	1.6	2.56	5.1	15.89
4	−1.8	3.24	−0.4	0.16	1.9	3.61	3.8	14.44	3.5	21.45
Total	−6.0	9.54	−2.0	7.94	6.0	15.54	2.0	24.40	0.0	57.42

The above computations provide the overall sum of squares value used in the analysis of variance table prepared for and in making the F test. The form in which it is computed may be used in making similar computations. The same variance values are computed in several different ways, to provide a check on these computations. Averages and standard deviation values are found as follows for the data in this example.

TABLE 8.23

Car No.	Carburetor Type							
	A	A^2	$A-\bar{A}$	$(A-\bar{A})^2$	B	B^2	$B-\bar{B}$	$(B-\bar{B})^2$
1	20.2	408.04	+0.2	+0.04	19.0	361.00	2.0	4.00
2	19.6	384.16	0.1	+0.16	21.2	449.44	0.2	0.04
3	20.5	420.25	+0.5	+0.25	22.7	515.29	1.7	2.89
4	19.7	388.09	−0.3	+0.09	21.1	445.21	0.1	0.01
Sum	80.0	1600.54	0	0.54	84.0	1770.94	0	6.94
Average	20.0	400.1350		0.1350	21.0	442.7350		1.7350
(Averages)^2		−400.0000				441.0000		
Variance		0.1350				1.7350		

TABLE 8.24

Car No.	Carburetor Type							
	C	C^2	$C-\bar{C}$	$(C-\bar{C})^2$	D	D^2	$(D-\bar{D})$	$(D-\bar{D})^2$
1	21.3	453.69	−1.7	2.89	18.9	357.21	−3.1	9.61
2	22.5	506.25	−0.5	0.25	20.7	428.49	−1.3	1.69
3	24.8	615.04	1.8	3.24	23.1	533.61	1.1	1.21
4	23.4	547.56	0.4	0.16	25.3	640.09	3.3	10.89
Sum	92.0	2122.54	0	6.54	88.0	1959.40	0	23.40
Average	23.0	530.6350		1.6350	22.0	489.8500		5.8500
(Averages)^2		529.0000				484.0000		
Variance		1.6350				5.8500		

TABLE 8.25

Carburetor Type	Average Values	$(\bar{X})^2$	Within sample Variance σ^2	X^2	$(\bar{X}-\bar{\bar{X}})$	$(\bar{X}-\bar{\bar{X}})^2$
A	$\bar{X}_A = 20.0$	400.00	0.135	1600.54	−1.5	2.25
B	$\bar{X}_B = 21.0$	441.00	1.735	1770.94	−0.5	0.25
C	$\bar{X}_C = 23.0$	529.00	1.635	2122.54	1.5	2.25
D	$\bar{X}_D = 22.0$	484.00	5.850	1959.40	0.5	0.25
Sum	86.0	1854.00	9.355	7453.42	0	5.00*
Average	21.5	463.50	2.33875	465.83875		1.25
(Averages)^2		462.25				

$$\Sigma X^2 = 465.83875$$
$$-\bar{X}^{n_2} = -462.25000$$
$$\overline{};\ \bar{\bar{X}} = 21.5$$
$$\sigma_0^2 = 3.58875$$

$$L_0 = \left(\frac{\sigma_A^2\sigma_B^2\sigma_C^2\sigma_D^2}{\sigma_0^2\sigma_0^2\sigma_0^2\sigma_0^2}\right)^{1/4} = \left(\frac{(0.135)(1.735)(1.635)(5.85)}{(3.58875)^4}\right)^{1/4} = \left(\frac{(2.2403036)}{(3.58875)^4}\right)^{1/4}$$

$$= \left(\frac{2.2403036}{165.87190}\right)^{1/4} = (0.0135062)^{1/4}$$

$$= (0.1162)^{1/2} = 0.3409$$

$$L_0 = \frac{1.224}{3.58875} = 0.34107$$

or

$$L_0 = [(0.0376175)(0.4834552)(0.4555903)(1.630094)]^{1/4}$$

$$= [(0.0181864)(0.742655)]^{1/4} = (0.0135062)^{1/4} = 0.341$$

The L_0 table for $k = 4$, $n = 4$ gives 0.3328 for the 5% value and 0.2293 for the 1% value. For perfect homogeneity, $L_0 = 1$, 0.341 is only slightly larger than 0.3328 for 5%; hence it may be considered barely homogeneous with respect to means and variance.

$$L_1 = \left(\frac{\sigma_A^2\sigma_B^2\sigma_C^2\sigma_D^2}{\sigma_a^2\sigma_a^2\sigma_a^2\sigma_a^2}\right)^{1/4} = \left(\frac{(0.135)(1.735)(1.635)(5.85)}{(2.33875)^4}\right)^{1/4}$$

$$= \left(\frac{2.2403036}{29.918182}\right)^{1/4}$$

$$= (0.074881)^{1/4}$$

$$= (0.27365)^{1/2} = 0.5231$$

or

$$L_1 = [(0.0577231)(0.7418492)(0.6990913)(2.501336)]^{1/4}$$

$$= [(0.0428218)(1.7486622)]^{1/4} = (0.0748809)^{1/4} = 0.5231$$

For $n = 4$ and $k = 4$, the L_1 table gives 0.4800 for 5% and 0.3414 for 1%. Since $L_1 = 0.5231$, the L_1 hypothesis is upheld. Since both the L_0 value and the L_1 tests show no significance, the F test is a valid test. If this L_1 test had failed, it would have shown that the variances are not from the same or similar distributions. Carburetor D has a variance of 5.85, whereas carburetor A has a variance of only 0.135, widely different, but judged by these tests to be due only to chance causes. Carburetor A appears to have the least variability from car to car, but gives the least mileage. Carburetor C gives 23.0 miles per gallon, the best, and its variability has a variance of 1.635. The three sigma ranges for these four carburetors are respectively:

Type A: $20.0 \pm 3\sqrt{0.135} = 20.0 \pm 3(0.367) = 20.0 \pm 1.101 = 18.90$ to 21.10
Type B: $21.0 \pm 3\sqrt{1.735} = 21.0 \pm 3(1.317) = 21.0 \pm 3.951 = 17.05$ to 24.95
Type C: $23.0 \pm 3\sqrt{1.635} = 23.0 \pm 3(1.279) = 23.0 \pm 3.837 = 19.16$ to 26.84 (Best)
Type D: $22.0 \pm 3\sqrt{5.850} = 22.0 \pm 3(2.419) = 22.0 \pm 7.257 = 14.74$ to 29.26

8.15 Analysis of Variance

When the experiment is completely randomized, the analysis that is best considers the variation within samples and the variation between samples. In setting up an analysis of variance table to aid in the computations, the data is placed in columns and in rows as shown in the previous data for the four types of carburetors and the four different cars. In this example, the variation within and between columns cover the four different carburetors. The general form of such an analysis of variances table is presented in most texts discussing the analysis of variance. The engineering approach given in the Freeman text is the simplest and is given with slight modification in table 8.26.

TABLE 8.26 Simple Analysis of Variance Design

Source of Variation	*Sum of Squares*	*Degrees of Freedom*	*Mean Square*
Among K columns	$n_k \Sigma(\bar{X}_c - \bar{X})^2$	$k - 1$	$\sigma_1^2 = n_k \dfrac{\Sigma \bar{X}_c - \bar{X}}{k - 1}$
Within K columns	$\Sigma(X - \bar{X}_c)^2$	$n - k$	$\sigma_2^2 = \dfrac{\Sigma(X - \bar{X}_c)^2}{n - k}$
Total	$\Sigma(X - \bar{X})^2$	$n - 1$	$\sigma^2 = \dfrac{\Sigma(X - \bar{X})^2}{n - 1}$

n = number of units in each sample; k = number of columns.

The analysis of variance may be expanded to show in detail many other factors. For example, for the search for the best carburetor there are other factors that should be added, such as (1) operators who adjust the carburetor, (2) difference in engines of the same power due to differences in design (an extreme difference is the difference between the rotary engine and the piston-type engine), and (3) difference in gasolines (such as regular or high-test, different octane ratings, or different oil company products).

Advanced texts in the analysis of variance should be consulted to make the most efficient use of this technique. If there are four different factors, A, B, C, and D, then consideration should be given to the following:

Variation within A values in a sample;
Variation between A values between several samples;
Variation within B values;
Variation between B values;
Variation within C values;
Variation between C values;
Variation within D values;
Variation between D values;
Interactions as follows: AB, AC, AD, BC, BD, CD, ABC, ABD, ACD, BCD, ABCD.

The interaction effects are often very important. In systems engineering, the system may consist of a large number of subsystems. If this number is only three, sometimes called *black boxes*, each subsystem may meet all its requirements and each is checked and inspected by quality control personnel and accepted. However, when connected as a system, the total system will not operate. Hence inspection must set up a system that operates, and then check interactions by replacing an operative subsystem by the newly manufactured similar subsystem. If the system fails to operate, the new unit may be readjusted so that the interactions are positive rather than negative and so that the system becomes satisfactory with the inclusion of the new unit. Other designs of experimental tests may be made so that adequate checks may be made on such subsystems and systems. These are features covered in systems engineering techniques.

8.16 *F* Test

The Fisher test, named for its originator Sir Ronald A. Fisher, used in the analysis of variance method, is called the F test. It is obtained by taking the ratio of the mean square obtained from the last column of the analysis of variance table for one of the sources of variation to the mean square for the last row. When only two sources of variation are given,

$$F = \frac{\text{mean square among columns}}{\text{mean square within columns}}. \tag{12}$$

For more complex tables, the mean square for the residual error is usually taken as the denominator. The F distribution covers such ratios in terms of the number of degrees of freedom for both the numerator and the denominator. Such an F table usually covers only 5% and 1% points for the distribution of F, with the degrees of freedom for the greater mean square in the ratio entered horizontally as the first row of the table, while the degree of freedom for the lesser mean square is entered vertically on the first column of the table. Table 8.27 is a brief extract from such a table, illustrating the magnitude of values that might occur. One part of the table covers the 5% points and the second part covers the corresponding 1% points indicated in boldface type.

There are many extensive tables for the F distribution. One gives the 1%, the 10%, the 5%, and the 2.5% values. Most of these were given in Volume 1 of *Biometrika Tables for Statisticians*,[5] edited by E. S. Pearson and H. O. Hartley. Pearson and Hartley have done much original work in these areas. The first design of experiments and techniques for their use are attributed to Sir Ronald A. Fisher.[6] Applicable tables are given in the Fisher and Yates tables,[7] providing excellent tables for the F test.

To obtain a better conception of the use of the F test and when it may be applied, these data will be presented as an example, although there is a lack of homogeneity for the data for the four values. The data are given in table 8.28.

TABLE 8.27 *F* Distribution Table, page 1*

Degrees of Freedom for Lesser Mean Square	*Degrees of Freedom for Greater Mean Square*																							
	1	*2*	*3*	*4*	*5*	*6*	*7*	*8*	*9*	*10*	*11*	*12*	*14*	*16*	*20*	*24*	*30*	*40*	*50*	*75*	*100*	*200*	*500*	∞
1	161	200	216	225	230	234	237	239	241	242	243	244	245	246	248	249	250	251	252	253	253	254	254	254
	4052	**4999**	**5403**	**5625**	**5764**	**5859**	**5928**	**5981**	**6022**	**6056**	**6082**	**6106**	**6142**	**6169**	**6208**	**6234**	**6258**	**6286**	**6302**	**6323**	**6334**	**6352**	**6361**	**6366**
2	18.51	19.00	19.16	19.25	19.30	19.33	19.36	19.37	19.38	19.39	19.40	19.41	19.42	19.43	19.44	19.45	19.46	19.47	19.47	19.48	19.49	19.49	19.50	19.50
	98.49	**99.01**	**99.17**	**99.25**	**99.30**	**99.33**	**99.34**	**99.36**	**99.38**	**99.40**	**99.41**	**99.42**	**99.43**	**99.44**	**99.45**	**99.46**	**99.47**	**99.48**	**99.48**	**99.49**	**99.49**	**99.49**	**99.50**	**99.50**
3	10.13	9.55	9.28	9.12	9.01	8.94	8.88	8.84	8.81	8.78	8.76	8.74	8.71	8.69	8.66	8.64	8.62	8.60	8.58	8.57	8.56	8.54	8.54	8.53
	34.12	**30.81**	**29.46**	**28.71**	**28.24**	**27.91**	**27.67**	**27.49**	**27.34**	**27.23**	**27.13**	**27.05**	**26.92**	**26.83**	**26.69**	**26.60**	**26.50**	**26.41**	**26.30**	**26.27**	**26.23**	**26.18**	**26.14**	**26.12**
4	7.71	6.94	6.59	6.39	6.26	6.16	6.09	6.04	6.00	5.96	5.93	5.91	5.87	5.84	5.80	5.77	5.74	5.71	5.70	5.68	5.66	5.65	5.64	5.63
	21.20	**18.00**	**16.69**	**15.98**	**15.52**	**15.21**	**14.98**	**14.80**	**14.66**	**14.54**	**14.45**	**14.37**	**14.24**	**14.15**	**14.02**	**13.93**	**13.83**	**13.74**	**13.69**	**13.61**	**13.57**	**13.52**	**13.48**	**13.46**
5	6.61	5.79	5.41	5.19	5.05	4.95	4.88	4.82	4.78	4.74	4.70	4.68	4.64	4.60	4.56	4.53	4.50	4.46	4.44	4.42	4.40	4.38	4.37	4.36
	16.26	**13.27**	**12.06**	**11.39**	**10.97**	**10.67**	**10.45**	**10.27**	**10.15**	**10.05**	**9.96**	**9.89**	**9.77**	**9.68**	**9.55**	**9.47**	**9.38**	**9.29**	**9.24**	**9.17**	**9.13**	**9.07**	**9.04**	**9.02**
6	5.99	5.14	4.76	4.53	4.39	4.28	4.21	4.15	4.10	4.06	4.03	4.00	3.96	3.92	3.87	3.84	3.81	3.77	3.75	3.72	3.71	3.69	3.68	3.67
	13.74	**10.92**	**9.78**	**9.15**	**8.75**	**8.47**	**8.26**	**8.10**	**7.98**	**7.87**	**7.79**	**7.72**	**7.60**	**7.52**	**7.39**	**7.31**	**7.23**	**7.14**	**7.09**	**7.02**	**6.99**	**6.94**	**6.90**	**6.88**
7	5.59	4.74	4.35	4.12	3.97	3.87	3.79	3.73	3.68	3.63	3.60	3.57	3.52	3.49	3.44	3.41	3.38	3.34	3.32	3.29	3.28	3.25	3.24	3.23
	12.25	**9.55**	**8.45**	**7.85**	**7.46**	**7.19**	**7.00**	**6.84**	**6.71**	**6.62**	**6.54**	**6.47**	**6.35**	**6.27**	**6.15**	**6.07**	**5.98**	**5.90**	**5.85**	**5.78**	**5.75**	**5.70**	**5.67**	**5.65**
8	5.32	4.46	4.07	3.84	3.69	3.58	3.50	3.44	3.39	3.34	3.31	3.28	3.23	3.20	3.15	3.12	3.08	3.05	3.03	3.00	2.98	2.96	2.94	2.93
	11.26	**8.65**	**7.59**	**7.01**	**6.63**	**6.37**	**6.19**	**6.03**	**5.91**	**5.82**	**5.74**	**5.67**	**5.56**	**5.48**	**5.36**	**5.28**	**5.20**	**5.11**	**5.06**	**5.00**	**4.96**	**4.91**	**4.88**	**4.86**
9	5.12	4.26	3.86	3.63	3.48	3.37	3.29	3.23	3.18	3.13	3.10	3.07	3.02	2.98	2.93	2.90	2.86	2.82	2.80	2.77	2.76	2.73	2.72	2.71
	10.56	**8.02**	**6.99**	**6.42**	**6.06**	**5.80**	**5.62**	**5.47**	**5.35**	**5.26**	**5.18**	**5.11**	**5.00**	**4.92**	**4.80**	**4.73**	**4.64**	**4.56**	**4.51**	**4.45**	**4.41**	**4.36**	**4.33**	**4.31**
10	4.96	4.10	3.71	3.48	3.33	3.22	3.14	3.07	3.02	2.97	2.94	2.91	2.86	2.82	2.77	2.74	2.70	2.67	2.64	2.61	2.59	2.56	2.55	2.54
	10.04	**7.56**	**6.55**	**5.99**	**5.64**	**5.39**	**5.21**	**5.06**	**4.95**	**4.85**	**4.78**	**4.71**	**4.60**	**4.52**	**4.41**	**4.33**	**4.25**	**4.17**	**4.12**	**4.05**	**4.01**	**3.96**	**3.93**	**3.91**
11	4.84	3.98	3.59	3.36	3.20	3.09	3.01	2.95	2.90	2.86	2.82	2.79	2.74	2.70	2.65	2.61	2.57	2.53	2.50	2.47	2.45	2.42	2.41	2.40
	9.65	**7.20**	**6.22**	**5.67**	**5.32**	**5.07**	**4.88**	**4.74**	**4.63**	**4.54**	**4.46**	**4.40**	**4.29**	**4.21**	**4.10**	**4.02**	**3.94**	**3.86**	**3.80**	**3.74**	**3.70**	**3.66**	**3.62**	**3.60**
12	4.75	3.88	3.49	3.26	3.11	3.00	2.92	2.85	2.80	2.76	2.72	2.69	2.64	2.60	2.54	2.50	2.46	2.42	2.40	2.36	2.35	2.32	2.31	2.30
	9.33	**6.93**	**5.95**	**5.41**	**5.06**	**4.82**	**4.65**	**4.50**	**4.39**	**4.30**	**4.22**	**4.16**	**4.05**	**3.98**	**3.86**	**3.78**	**3.70**	**3.61**	**3.56**	**3.49**	**3.46**	**3.41**	**3.38**	**3.36**
13	4.67	3.80	3.41	3.18	3.02	2.92	2.84	2.77	2.72	2.67	2.63	2.60	2.55	2.51	2.46	2.42	2.38	2.34	2.32	2.28	2.26	2.24	2.22	2.21
	9.07	**6.70**	**5.74**	**5.20**	**4.86**	**4.62**	**4.44**	**4.30**	**4.19**	**4.10**	**4.02**	**3.96**	**3.85**	**3.78**	**3.67**	**3.59**	**3.51**	**3.42**	**3.37**	**3.30**	**3.27**	**3.21**	**3.18**	**3.16**
14	4.60	3.74	3.34	3.11	2.96	2.85	2.77	2.70	2.65	2.60	2.56	2.53	2.48	2.44	2.39	2.35	2.31	2.27	2.24	2.21	2.19	2.16	2.14	2.13
	8.86	**6.51**	**5.56**	**5.03**	**4.69**	**4.46**	**4.28**	**4.14**	**4.03**	**3.94**	**3.86**	**3.80**	**3.70**	**3.62**	**3.51**	**3.43**	**3.34**	**3.26**	**3.21**	**3.14**	**3.11**	**3.06**	**3.02**	**3.00**
15	4.54	3.68	3.29	3.06	2.90	2.79	2.70	2.64	2.59	2.55	2.51	2.48	2.43	2.39	2.33	2.29	2.25	2.21	2.18	2.15	2.12	2.10	2.08	2.07
	8.68	**6.36**	**5.42**	**4.89**	**4.56**	**4.32**	**4.14**	**4.00**	**3.89**	**3.80**	**3.73**	**3.67**	**3.56**	**3.48**	**3.36**	**3.29**	**3.20**	**3.12**	**3.07**	**3.00**	**2.97**	**2.92**	**2.89**	**2.87**
16	4.49	3.63	3.24	3.01	2.85	2.74	2.66	2.59	2.54	2.49	2.45	2.42	2.37	2.33	2.28	2.24	2.20	2.16	2.13	2.09	2.07	2.04	2.02	2.01
	8.53	**6.23**	**5.29**	**4.77**	**4.44**	**4.20**	**4.03**	**3.89**	**3.78**	**3.69**	**3.61**	**3.55**	**3.45**	**3.37**	**3.25**	**3.18**	**3.10**	**3.01**	**2.96**	**2.89**	**2.86**	**2.80**	**2.77**	**2.75**
17	4.45	3.59	3.20	2.96	2.81	2.70	2.62	2.55	2.50	2.45	2.41	2.38	2.33	2.29	2.23	2.19	2.15	2.11	2.08	2.04	2.02	1.99	1.97	1.96
	8.40	**6.11**	**5.18**	**4.67**	**4.34**	**4.10**	**3.93**	**3.79**	**3.68**	**3.59**	**3.52**	**3.45**	**3.35**	**3.27**	**3.16**	**3.08**	**3.00**	**2.92**	**2.86**	**2.79**	**2.76**	**2.70**	**2.67**	**2.65**
18	4.41	3.55	3.16	2.93	2.77	2.66	2.58	2.51	2.46	2.41	2.37	2.34	2.29	2.25	2.19	2.15	2.11	2.07	2.04	2.00	1.98	1.95	1.93	1.92
	8.28	**6.01**	**5.09**	**4.58**	**4.25**	**4.01**	**3.85**	**3.71**	**3.60**	**3.51**	**3.44**	**3.37**	**3.27**	**3.19**	**3.07**	**3.00**	**2.91**	**2.83**	**2.78**	**2.71**	**2.68**	**2.62**	**2.59**	**2.57**
19	4.38	3.52	3.13	2.90	2.74	2.63	2.55	2.48	2.43	2.38	2.34	2.31	2.26	2.21	2.15	2.11	2.07	2.02	2.00	1.96	1.94	1.91	1.90	1.88
	8.18	**5.93**	**5.01**	**4.50**	**4.17**	**3.94**	**3.77**	**3.63**	**3.52**	**3.43**	**3.36**	**3.30**	**3.19**	**3.12**	**3.00**	**2.92**	**2.84**	**2.76**	**2.70**	**2.63**	**2.60**	**2.54**	**2.51**	**2.49**
20	4.35	3.49	3.10	2.87	2.71	2.60	2.52	2.45	2.40	2.35	2.31	2.28	2.23	2.18	2.12	2.08	2.04	1.99	1.96	1.92	1.90	1.87	1.85	1.84
	8.10	**5.85**	**4.94**	**4.43**	**4.10**	**3.87**	**3.71**	**3.56**	**3.45**	**3.37**	**3.30**	**3.23**	**3.13**	**3.05**	**2.94**	**2.86**	**2.77**	**2.69**	**2.63**	**2.56**	**2.53**	**2.47**	**2.44**	**2.42**
21	4.32	3.47	3.07	2.84	2.68	2.57	2.49	2.42	2.37	2.32	2.28	2.25	2.20	2.15	2.09	2.05	2.00	1.96	1.93	1.89	1.87	1.84	1.82	1.81
	8.02	**5.78**	**4.87**	**4.37**	**4.04**	**3.81**	**3.65**	**3.51**	**3.40**	**3.31**	**3.24**	**3.17**	**3.07**	**2.99**	**2.88**	**2.80**	**2.72**	**2.63**	**2.58**	**2.51**	**2.47**	**2.42**	**2.38**	**2.36**
22	4.30	3.44	3.05	2.82	2.66	2.55	2.47	2.40	2.35	2.30	2.26	2.23	2.18	2.13	2.07	2.03	1.98	1.93	1.91	1.87	1.84	1.81	1.80	1.78
	7.94	**5.72**	**4.82**	**4.31**	**3.99**	**3.76**	**3.59**	**3.45**	**3.35**	**3.26**	**3.18**	**3.12**	**3.02**	**2.94**	**2.83**	**2.75**	**2.67**	**2.58**	**2.53**	**2.46**	**2.42**	**2.37**	**2.33**	**2.31**
23	4.28	3.42	3.03	2.80	2.64	2.53	2.45	2.38	2.32	2.28	2.24	2.20	2.14	2.10	2.04	2.00	1.96	1.91	1.88	1.84	1.82	1.79	1.77	1.76
	7.88	**5.66**	**4.76**	**4.26**	**3.94**	**3.71**	**3.54**	**3.41**	**3.30**	**3.21**	**3.14**	**3.07**	**2.97**	**2.89**	**2.78**	**2.70**	**2.62**	**2.53**	**2.48**	**2.41**	**2.37**	**2.32**	**2.28**	**2.26**
24	4.26	3.40	3.01	2.78	2.62	2.51	2.43	2.36	2.30	2.26	2.22	2.18	2.13	2.09	2.02	1.98	1.94	1.89	1.86	1.82	1.80	1.76	1.74	1.73
	7.82	**5.61**	**4.72**	**4.22**	**3.90**	**3.67**	**3.50**	**3.36**	**3.25**	**3.17**	**3.09**	**3.03**	**2.93**	**2.85**	**2.74**	**2.66**	**2.58**	**2.49**	**2.44**	**2.36**	**2.33**	**2.27**	**2.23**	**2.21**
25	4.24	3.38	2.99	2.76	2.60	2.49	2.41	2.34	2.28	2.24	2.20	2.16	2.11	2.06	2.00	1.96	1.92	1.87	1.84	1.80	1.77	1.74	1.72	1.71
	7.77	**5.57**	**4.68**	**4.18**	**3.86**	**3.63**	**3.46**	**3.32**	**3.21**	**3.13**	**3.05**	**2.99**	**2.89**	**2.81**	**2.70**	**2.62**	**2.54**	**2.45**	**2.40**	**2.32**	**2.29**	**2.23**	**2.19**	**2.17**
26	4.22	3.37	2.89	2.74	2.59	2.47	2.39	2.32	2.27	2.22	2.18	2.15	2.10	2.05	1.99	1.95	1.90	1.85	1.82	1.78	1.76	1.72	1.70	1.69
	7.72	**5.53**	**4.64**	**4.14**	**3.82**	**3.59**	**3.42**	**3.29**	**3.17**	**3.09**	**3.02**	**2.96**	**2.86**	**2.77**	**2.66**	**2.58**	**2.50**	**2.41**	**2.36**	**2.28**	**2.25**	**2.19**	**2.15**	**2.13**

*Note: Five percent points are in regular type; 1% points are in boldface type.

(Continued on next page)

TABLE 8.27 *F* Distribution Table, page 2*

Degrees of Freedom for Lesser Mean Square	Degrees of Freedom for Greater Mean Square																							
	1	2	3	4	5	6	7	8	9	10	11	12	14	16	20	24	30	40	50	75	100	200	500	∞
27	4.21	3.35	2.96	2.73	2.57	2.46	2.37	2.30	2.25	2.20	2.16	2.13	2.08	2.03	1.97	1.93	1.88	1.84	1.80	1.76	1.74	1.71	1.68	1.67
	7.68	**5.49**	**4.60**	**4.11**	**3.79**	**3.56**	**3.39**	**3.26**	**3.14**	**3.06**	**2.98**	**2.93**	**2.83**	**2.74**	**2.63**	**2.55**	**2.47**	**2.38**	**2.33**	**2.25**	**2.21**	**2.16**	**2.12**	**2.10**
28	4.20	3.34	2.95	2.71	2.56	2.44	2.36	2.29	2.24	2.19	2.15	2.12	2.06	2.02	1.96	1.91	1.87	1.81	1.78	1.75	1.72	1.69	1.67	1.65
	7.64	**5.45**	**4.57**	**4.07**	**3.76**	**3.53**	**3.36**	**3.23**	**3.11**	**3.03**	**2.95**	**2.90**	**2.80**	**2.71**	**2.60**	**2.52**	**2.44**	**2.35**	**2.30**	**2.22**	**2.18**	**2.13**	**2.09**	**2.06**
29	4.18	3.33	2.93	2.70	2.54	2.43	2.35	2.28	2.22	2.18	2.14	2.10	2.05	2.00	1.94	1.90	1.85	1.80	1.77	1.73	1.71	1.68	1.65	1.64
	7.60	**5.52**	**4.54**	**4.04**	**3.73**	**3.50**	**3.33**	**3.20**	**3.08**	**3.00**	**2.92**	**2.87**	**2.77**	**2.68**	**2.57**	**2.49**	**2.41**	**2.32**	**2.27**	**2.19**	**2.15**	**2.10**	**2.06**	**2.03**
30	4.17	3.32	2.92	2.69	2.53	2.42	2.34	2.27	2.21	2.16	2.12	2.09	2.04	1.99	1.93	1.89	1.84	1.79	1.76	1.72	1.69	1.66	1.64	1.62
	7.56	**5.39**	**4.51**	**4.02**	**3.70**	**3.47**	**3.30**	**3.17**	**3.06**	**2.98**	**2.90**	**2.84**	**2.74**	**2.66**	**2.55**	**2.47**	**2.38**	**2.29**	**2.24**	**2.16**	**2.13**	**2.07**	**2.03**	**2.01**
32	4.15	3.30	2.90	2.67	2.51	2.40	2.32	2.25	2.19	2.14	2.10	2.07	2.02	1.97	1.91	1.86	1.82	1.76	1.74	1.69	1.67	1.64	1.61	1.59
	7.50	**5.34**	**4.46**	**3.97**	**3.66**	**3.42**	**3.25**	**3.12**	**3.01**	**2.94**	**2.86**	**2.80**	**2.70**	**2.62**	**2.51**	**2.42**	**2.34**	**2.25**	**2.20**	**2.12**	**2.08**	**2.02**	**1.98**	**1.96**
34	4.13	3.28	2.88	2.65	2.49	2.38	2.30	2.23	2.17	2.12	2.08	2.05	2.00	1.95	1.89	1.84	1.80	1.74	1.71	1.67	1.64	1.61	1.59	1.57
	7.44	**5.29**	**4.42**	**3.93**	**3.61**	**3.38**	**3.21**	**3.08**	**2.97**	**2.89**	**2.82**	**2.76**	**2.66**	**2.58**	**2.47**	**2.38**	**2.30**	**2.21**	**2.15**	**2.08**	**2.04**	**1.98**	**1.94**	**1.91**
36	4.11	3.26	2.86	2.63	2.48	2.36	2.28	2.21	2.15	2.10	2.06	2.03	1.99	1.93	1.87	1.82	1.78	1.72	1.69	1.65	1.62	1.59	1.56	1.55
	7.39	**5.25**	**4.38**	**3.89**	**3.58**	**3.35**	**3.18**	**3.04**	**2.94**	**2.86**	**2.78**	**2.72**	**2.62**	**2.54**	**2.43**	**2.35**	**2.26**	**2.17**	**2.12**	**2.04**	**2.00**	**1.94**	**1.90**	**1.87**
38	4.10	3.25	2.85	2.62	2.46	2.35	2.26	2.19	2.14	2.09	2.05	2.02	1.96	1.92	1.85	1.80	1.76	1.71	1.67	1.63	1.60	1.57	1.54	1.53
	7.35	**5.21**	**4.34**	**3.86**	**3.54**	**3.32**	**3.15**	**3.02**	**2.91**	**2.82**	**2.75**	**2.69**	**2.59**	**2.51**	**2.40**	**2.32**	**2.22**	**2.14**	**2.08**	**2.00**	**1.97**	**1.90**	**1.86**	**1.84**
40	4.08	3.23	2.84	2.61	2.45	2.34	2.25	2.18	2.12	2.07	2.04	2.00	1.95	1.90	1.84	1.79	1.74	1.69	1.66	1.61	1.59	1.55	1.53	1.51
	7.31	**5.18**	**4.31**	**3.83**	**3.51**	**3.29**	**3.12**	**2.99**	**2.88**	**2.80**	**2.73**	**2.66**	**2.56**	**2.49**	**2.37**	**2.29**	**2.20**	**2.11**	**2.05**	**1.97**	**1.94**	**1.88**	**1.84**	**1.81**
42	4.07	3.22	2.83	2.59	2.44	2.32	2.24	2.17	2.11	2.06	2.02	1.99	1.94	1.89	1.82	1.78	1.73	1.68	1.64	1.60	1.57	1.54	1.51	1.49
	7.27	**5.15**	**4.29**	**3.80**	**3.49**	**3.26**	**3.10**	**2.96**	**2.86**	**2.77**	**2.70**	**2.64**	**2.54**	**2.46**	**2.35**	**2.26**	**2.17**	**2.08**	**2.02**	**1.94**	**1.91**	**1.85**	**1.80**	**1.78**
44	4.06	3.21	2.82	2.58	2.43	2.31	2.23	2.16	2.10	2.05	2.01	1.98	1.92	1.88	1.81	1.76	1.72	1.66	1.63	1.58	1.56	1.52	1.50	1.48
	7.24	**5.12**	**4.26**	**3.78**	**3.46**	**3.24**	**3.07**	**2.94**	**2.84**	**2.75**	**2.68**	**2.62**	**2.52**	**2.44**	**2.32**	**2.24**	**2.15**	**2.06**	**2.00**	**1.92**	**1.88**	**1.82**	**1.78**	**1.75**
46	4.05	3.20	2.81	2.57	2.42	2.30	2.22	2.14	2.09	2.04	2.00	1.97	1.91	1.87	1.80	1.75	1.71	1.65	1.62	1.57	1.54	1.51	1.48	1.46
	7.21	**5.10**	**4.24**	**3.76**	**3.44**	**3.22**	**3.05**	**2.92**	**2.82**	**2.73**	**2.66**	**2.60**	**2.50**	**2.42**	**2.30**	**2.22**	**2.13**	**2.04**	**1.98**	**1.90**	**1.86**	**1.80**	**1.76**	**1.72**
48	4.04	3.19	2.80	2.56	2.41	2.30	2.21	2.14	2.08	2.03	1.99	1.96	1.90	1.86	1.79	1.74	1.70	1.64	1.61	1.56	1.53	1.50	1.47	1.45
	7.19	**5.08**	**4.22**	**3.74**	**3.42**	**3.20**	**3.04**	**2.90**	**2.80**	**2.71**	**2.64**	**2.58**	**2.48**	**2.40**	**2.28**	**2.20**	**2.11**	**2.02**	**1.96**	**1.88**	**1.84**	**1.78**	**1.73**	**1.70**
50	4.03	3.18	2.79	2.56	2.40	2.29	2.20	2.13	2.07	2.02	1.98	1.95	1.90	1.85	1.78	1.74	1.69	1.63	1.60	1.55	1.52	1.48	1.46	1.44
	7.17	**5.06**	**4.20**	**3.72**	**3.41**	**3.18**	**3.02**	**2.88**	**2.78**	**2.70**	**2.62**	**2.56**	**2.46**	**2.39**	**2.26**	**2.18**	**2.10**	**2.00**	**1.94**	**1.86**	**1.82**	**1.76**	**1.71**	**1.68**
55	4.02	3.17	2.78	2.54	2.38	2.27	2.18	2.11	2.05	2.00	1.97	1.93	1.88	1.83	1.76	1.72	1.67	1.61	1.58	1.52	1.50	1.46	1.43	1.41
	7.12	**5.01**	**4.16**	**3.68**	**3.37**	**3.15**	**2.98**	**2.85**	**2.75**	**2.66**	**2.59**	**2.53**	**2.43**	**2.35**	**2.23**	**2.15**	**2.06**	**1.96**	**1.90**	**1.82**	**1.78**	**1.71**	**1.66**	**1.64**
60	4.00	3.15	2.76	2.52	2.37	2.25	2.17	2.10	2.04	1.99	1.95	1.92	1.86	1.81	1.75	1.70	1.65	1.59	1.56	1.50	1.48	1.44	1.41	1.39
	7.08	**4.98**	**4.13**	**3.65**	**3.34**	**3.12**	**2.95**	**2.82**	**2.72**	**2.63**	**2.56**	**2.50**	**2.40**	**2.32**	**2.20**	**2.12**	**2.03**	**1.93**	**1.87**	**1.79**	**1.74**	**1.68**	**1.63**	**1.60**
65	3.99	3.14	2.75	2.51	2.36	2.24	2.15	2.08	2.02	1.98	1.94	1.90	1.85	1.80	1.73	1.68	1.63	1.57	1.54	1.49	1.46	1.42	1.39	1.37
	7.04	**4.95**	**4.10**	**3.62**	**3.31**	**3.09**	**2.93**	**2.79**	**2.70**	**2.61**	**2.54**	**2.47**	**2.37**	**2.30**	**2.18**	**2.09**	**2.00**	**1.90**	**1.84**	**1.76**	**1.71**	**1.64**	**1.60**	**1.56**
70	3.98	3.13	2.74	2.50	2.35	2.32	2.14	2.07	2.01	1.97	1.93	1.89	1.84	1.79	1.72	1.67	1.62	1.56	1.53	1.47	1.45	1.40	1.37	1.35
	7.01	**4.92**	**4.08**	**3.60**	**3.29**	**3.07**	**2.91**	**2.77**	**2.67**	**2.59**	**2.51**	**2.45**	**2.35**	**2.28**	**2.15**	**2.07**	**1.98**	**1.88**	**1.82**	**1.74**	**1.69**	**1.62**	**1.56**	**1.53**
80	3.96	3.11	2.72	2.48	2.33	2.21	2.12	2.05	1.99	1.95	1.91	1.88	1.82	1.77	1.70	1.65	1.60	1.54	1.51	1.45	1.42	1.38	1.35	1.32
	6.96	**4.88**	**4.04**	**3.56**	**3.25**	**3.04**	**2.87**	**2.74**	**2.64**	**2.55**	**2.48**	**2.41**	**2.32**	**2.24**	**2.11**	**2.03**	**1.94**	**1.84**	**1.78**	**1.70**	**1.65**	**1.57**	**1.52**	**1.49**
100	3.94	3.09	2.70	2.46	2.30	2.19	2.10	2.03	1.97	1.92	1.88	1.85	1.79	1.75	1.68	1.63	1.57	1.51	1.48	1.42	1.39	1.34	1.30	1.28
	6.90	**4.82**	**3.98**	**3.51**	**3.20**	**2.99**	**2.82**	**2.69**	**2.59**	**2.51**	**2.43**	**2.36**	**2.26**	**2.19**	**2.06**	**1.98**	**1.89**	**1.79**	**1.73**	**1.64**	**1.59**	**1.51**	**1.46**	**1.43**
125	3.92	3.07	2.68	2.44	2.29	2.17	2.08	2.01	1.95	1.90	1.86	1.83	1.77	1.72	1.65	1.60	1.55	1.49	1.45	1.39	1.36	1.31	1.27	1.25
	6.84	**4.78**	**3.94**	**3.47**	**3.17**	**2.95**	**2.79**	**2.65**	**2.56**	**2.47**	**2.40**	**2.33**	**2.23**	**2.15**	**2.03**	**1.94**	**1.85**	**1.75**	**1.68**	**1.59**	**1.54**	**1.46**	**1.40**	**1.37**
150	3.91	3.06	2.67	2.43	2.27	2.16	2.07	2.00	1.94	1.89	1.85	1.82	1.76	1.71	1.64	1.59	1.54	1.47	1.44	1.37	1.34	1.29	1.25	1.22
	6.81	**4.75**	**3.91**	**3.44**	**3.13**	**2.92**	**2.76**	**2.62**	**2.53**	**2.44**	**2.37**	**2.30**	**2.20**	**2.12**	**2.00**	**1.91**	**1.83**	**1.72**	**1.66**	**1.56**	**1.51**	**1.43**	**1.37**	**1.33**
200	3.89	3.04	2.65	2.41	2.26	2.14	2.05	1.98	1.92	1.87	1.83	1.80	1.74	1.69	1.62	1.57	1.52	1.45	1.42	1.35	1.32	1.26	1.22	1.19
	6.76	**4.71**	**3.88**	**3.41**	**3.11**	**2.90**	**2.73**	**2.60**	**2.50**	**2.41**	**2.34**	**2.28**	**2.17**	**2.09**	**1.97**	**1.88**	**1.79**	**1.69**	**1.62**	**1.53**	**1.48**	**1.39**	**1.33**	**1.28**
400	3.86	3.02	2.62	2.39	2.23	2.12	2.03	1.96	1.90	1.85	1.81	1.78	1.72	1.67	1.60	1.54	1.49	1.42	1.38	1.32	1.28	1.22	1.16	1.13
	6.70	**4.66**	**3.83**	**3.36**	**3.06**	**2.85**	**2.69**	**2.55**	**2.46**	**2.37**	**2.29**	**2.23**	**2.12**	**2.04**	**1.92**	**1.84**	**1.74**	**1.64**	**1.57**	**1.47**	**1.42**	**1.32**	**1.24**	**1.19**
1000	3.85	3.00	2.61	2.38	2.22	2.10	2.02	1.95	1.89	1.84	1.80	1.76	1.70	1.65	1.58	1.53	1.47	1.41	1.36	1.30	1.26	1.19	1.13	1.08
	6.66	**4.62**	**3.80**	**3.34**	**3.04**	**2.82**	**2.66**	**2.53**	**2.43**	**2.34**	**2.26**	**2.20**	**2.09**	**2.01**	**1.89**	**1.81**	**1.71**	**1.61**	**1.54**	**1.44**	**1.38**	**1.28**	**1.19**	**1.11**
∞	3.84	2.99	2.60	2.37	2.21	2.09	2.01	1.94	1.88	1.83	1.79	1.75	1.69	1.64	1.57	1.52	1.46	1.40	1.35	1.28	1.24	1.17	1.11	1.00
	6.64	**4.60**	**3.78**	**3.32**	**3.02**	**2.80**	**2.64**	**2.51**	**2.41**	**2.32**	**2.24**	**2.18**	**2.07**	**1.99**	**1.87**	**1.79**	**1.69**	**1.59**	**1.52**	**1.41**	**1.36**	**1.25**	**1.15**	**1.00**

*Note: Five percent points are in regular type; 1 % points are in boldface type.

TABLE 8.28 Application of *F* Test for Analysis of Variance in a Designed Experiment

Source of Variation	*Sum of Squares*	*Degrees of Freedom*	*Mean Square*
Among Carburetors	20.00	3	6.6667
Within Carburetors (error)	37.42	12	3.1183
Total	57.42	15	. . .

$F = \dfrac{6.6667}{3.1183} = 2.138$. Table gives for d.f. = 3, 12: 5% $F = 3.49$; 1% $F = 5.95$. No significant difference in means is indicated by this test.

8.17 Additional Checks for Homogeneity

Most texts covering the use of the analysis of variance techniques for determining whether there exists a significant difference between two or more different items present the F test, but fail to provide tests for homogeneity. By this we mean that the cause of the difficulties encountered affecting its operations may not be due to a shift in the mean, but may be due to enormous changes in variability. If its variance is uncontrolled, the distribution is assumed to be nonhomogeneous, or nonuniform. Quality control personnel are responsible for the quality of outgoing products and need to assist production, as well as engineering and purchasing, in monitoring all aspects of quality. They need to know how to determine where the greatest effort must be exerted to secure a product produced under controlled conditions. The precept of quality control is that valid predictions concerning outgoing quality cannot be made unless the tests and measurements covering the product indicate that a state of statistical control exists.

When tests do indicate that there is a lack of homogeneity in the product, what practical steps can be taken to cure this ill? An actual example will show how quality control may function effectively. In a well-known company, there was a need for an effective small relay. A small manufacturing operation was established and relays were made according to the design, but unfortunately many failed to operate satisfactorily. The quality control director conducted sufficient tests, including tests for homogeneity, and found the cause was uncontrolled variability. One of the raw materials used was a certain grade of bar stock obtained from an outside supplier. Checks on these bar stocks and the way they were produced indicated a change in quality might exist in lengths supplied. A one-foot length was cut off the ends of each twelve-foot length, leaving 10 feet of usable material. When only this bar stock was used, the variance was reduced and was found to be in control for the features measured. This illustrates the need to know how to apply the tests for homogeneity, such as the L_0 and L_1 tests, prior to making an F test. Additional tests recommended in only a few of the more recent texts are Bartlett's test and Cochran's test for homogeneity, but in general there is a deterioration in carrying out those tests. One recent text states two important assumptions covering a t test of a difference are (1) that the populations sampled are normal and (2) the population variances are homogeneous, σ^2 having the same value for each population. It is noted that of these two, the homogeneity of variances is the most important but criticizes the older texts suggesting separate tests for homogeneity when it is now stated that, "the most modern authorities suggest that this is not really worth the trouble involved." The text indicates this position is taken because these tests are generally poor for the small samples involved and the small number of different sample sizes used. The text also makes one good recommendation to help cure some of these errors: *when in doubt use samples of equal size.* This permits the use of the L_0 and L_1 tests with small errors. If samples are of unequal size, then the tests given below apply.

Herein is emphasized the techniques and methods that have been applied effectively in industry and many other fields. Consideration is given to the fact that there is a big gap between theory and actual results. With rising costs in labor and raw materials, quality in many areas has deteriorated. The techniques often given are also not practical and give a false sense of security. The general public suffers from products of poorer quality which are highly variable with less reliability and life expectancies, but which cost much more. Applications of the simple tests provided herein should effectively aid in alleviating these conditions.

8.18 Bartlett's Test

Natural logarithms are used in the computations of Bartlett's test. This test is made to determine if the variances of k normally distributed populations are equal. This test was presented in 1932.[8]

Most populations may differ greatly from normality. As indicated previously, the distribution of practically all mean values for four sets of samples of four or more have been shown to be normal whether their parent populations are normal or not. Hence, for means, this assumption is valid and will be approximately valid for distributions of individual values. Let n_i be the sample size of the ith sample with k different samples included in the experiment. n_i designates the sample size where $n = \Sigma n_i = n_1 + n_2 + \cdots + n_k$. If equal sample sizes are used, then $n = \Sigma n_i = kn_i$. The hypothesis to be tested is that the variances of k normally populations are equal. It has been determined that σ_i^2 is the variance of the ith sample. An estimate of the variance for the population is designated as σ_p^2 and is determined from the relation

$$\sigma_p^2 = \frac{\Sigma(n_i - 1)\sigma_i^2}{n - k} \tag{13}$$

Four different terms, A, b, f_1, and f_2, whose values are determined from the equations listed in equation (14) are used to define the value of F considered as a sampling distribution, found to be approximately $F(f_1, f_2)$, the F distribution for which 5% and 1% points are available in a great many texts and even 2.5% points in a few texts. This provides criteria for testing homogeneity, where f_1 and f_2 denote the two values for degrees of freedom for columns and rows.

$$\begin{aligned} A &= \frac{1}{3(k-1)}\left[\Sigma\left(\frac{1}{n_i - 1}\right) - \frac{1}{n-k}\right] \\ f_1 &= k - 1 \\ f_2 &= \frac{k+1}{A^2} \end{aligned} \tag{14}$$

$$b = \frac{f_2}{\left(1 - A + \frac{2}{f_2}\right)}$$

$$M = (n - k) \cdot \ln(\sigma_p^2) - \Sigma[(n_i - 1)\ln(\sigma_i^2)]$$

$$F = \frac{f_2(M)}{f_1(b - M)},$$

where ln denotes a logarithm to the base e, often written $\log_e$. f_2 may not be an integer; hence interpolation in the F table may be required, using reciprocals of the degrees of freedom rather than linear interpolation.

An example showing how to use Bartlett's test is given in the Dixon and Massey text.[9] A summary of this example is given in example 13.

Example 13 Do the following four populations have equal variances? (1) $n_1 = 3$, $\sigma_1^2 = 6.33$, (2) $n_2 = 3$, $\sigma_2^2 = 1.33$, (3) $n_3 = 3$, $\sigma_3^2 = 4.33$, (4) $n_4 = 4$, $\sigma_4^2 = 4.33$, $n = 13$, $k = 4$, $n - k = 9$.

Solution $n = \Sigma n_i = 3 + 3 + 3 + 4 = 13,$

$$\sigma_p^2 = \frac{[2(6.33) + 2(1.33) + 2(4.33) + 3(4.33)]}{13 - 4} = 4.11; \quad \sigma_p = 2.2027$$

where $n = 3 + 3 + 3 + 4 = 13, \sigma_p^2 = \dfrac{(12.66 + 2.66 + 8.66 + 12.99)}{9} = \dfrac{36.97}{9} = 4.11;$
$\ln(4.11) = 1.413$, $\ln(6.33) = 1.846$, $\ln(1.33) = 0.284$, $\ln(4.33) = 1.466$.

Using the above numerical values, $A = 0.1914, f_1 = 3, f_2 = 136.6, \ b = 165.9$ and $M = 1.127$. The observed value if $F \ \dfrac{136.5(1.127)}{3(165.9 - 1.127)} = 0.31$, $F(f_1, f_2) = F(3, 136.6)$. Table 8.27 gives $F(3, 125) = 2.68$, $F(3,150) = 2.67$ for $f = 5^0{}_0$ and $F(3, \infty) = 2.60$. By interpolation, $F(3.136.6) = 2.67$. Since $F = 0.31$ is less than 2.67, the hypothesis is accepted.

8.19 Cochran's Test

When one variance is very much larger than the remainder of the variances, this may invalidate the analysis of variance test for means. Cochran has devised a simple test for this case. Its relation is

$$C = \frac{\text{largest } \sigma_i^2}{\Sigma \sigma_i^2}. \tag{15}$$

For criteria, *Percentile 95* and *Percentile 99* tables were given originally in chapter 15 of the text, *Techniques of Statistical Analysis*, by C. Eisenhart, M. W. Hastay, and W. A. Wallis.[10] This table reproduced as table A–17, pp. 438–439 of the Dixon and Massey text previously mentioned. The two-page table gives the 5% and 1% levels of significance and should be sufficient to cover most cases. The hypothesis of equal variances is rejected if the computed value of the statistic C exceeds the value in the table. This test is actually only critical when the sample variances are based on the same sample size and degrees of freedom $f_1 = n_i - 1$ with $f_2 = k$, the number of samples.

Example 14 *Use of the Bartlett and Cochran Tests*
The data for the four different types of carburetors used in four different cars gives $n_1 = n_2 = n_3 = n_4 = 4$ and $k = 4$, with $f_1 = n_i - 1 = 3$ for the Cochran test. The σ^2 values for this example are shown in table 8.29 and 8.21.

TABLE 8.29 Carburetor Types

Variances	*A*	*B*	*C*	*D*
σ_i^2	0.135	1.735	1.635	5.850

$$\sigma_p^2 = \frac{3(0.135) + 3(1.735) + 3(1.635) + 3(5.850)}{16 - 4}$$

$$= \frac{0.405 + 5.205 + 4.905 + 17.550}{12} = \frac{28.065}{12} = 2.338750$$

$$A = \frac{1}{3(3)}\left(\frac{1}{3} + \frac{1}{3} + \frac{1}{3} + \frac{1}{3} - \frac{1}{12}\right) = \frac{1}{9}\left(\frac{4}{3} - \frac{1}{12}\right) = \frac{1}{9}\frac{(15)}{(12)} = \frac{15}{108} = 0.13889$$

$$f_1 = k - 1 = 4 - 1 = 3$$

$$f_2 = \frac{k+1}{A^2} = \frac{5}{(0.13889)^2} = \frac{5}{0.01929043} = 259.1959$$

$$b = \frac{259.20}{(1 - 0.13889) + (2/259.20)} = \frac{259.20}{0.86111 + 0.007716} = \frac{259.20}{0.86883} = 2.98332$$

In the following computation for M, ln stands for log to the base e. Values must be read from the natural logarithm table in the appendix.

$$M = 12\ \ln(2.33875) - [3 \cdot \ln(0.135) + 3 \cdot \ln(1.735) + 3 \cdot \ln(1.635) + 3 \cdot \ln(5.850)]$$
$$= 12(0.84958) - [3(-2.00248) + 3(0.55101) + 3(0.49164) + 3(1.76644)]$$
$$= 10.19496 - (-6.00744 + 1.65300 + 1.47492 + 5.29932)$$
$$= 10.19496 - (-6.00744 + 8.42727)$$
$$= 10.19496 - 2.41983 = 7.77513$$

Using these constants, F can be readily determined.

$$F = \frac{(259.1959)(7.77513)}{(3)(259.1959 - 7.77513)} = \frac{2015.291452}{3(251.42077)}$$

$$= \frac{2015.291451}{754.26231} = 2.67187$$

Hence, $F(3, 259) = 2.6719$.

The F table (8.27) gives $F(3, 200) = 2.65$ as the 5% point and $F(3, 200) = 3.88$ as the 1% point, and also $F(3, 400) = 2.62$ as the 5% point and $F(3, 400) = 3.83$ as the 1% point. No interpolation is required. This F test indicates no significant difference between the variances. The second edition of the Dixon and Massey text, in table A-7c, gave values of F for $F(3, 120)$ and $F(3, \infty)$ respectively of 3.23 and 3.12, and 2.68 for the 0.95 probability point (5% criterion) and ∞ for the 0.90 probability point (10% criterion). Thus, although linear interpolation does not apply, the $F(3, 259) = 3.99$ is at approximately the 5% point, and possibly a significant difference.

Since the Bartlett test is possibly satisfied for a 5% criterion, the F test for means may be considered valid. However, the variance for the equal samples is slightly questionable. Since the variance for carburetor D is larger than the other three, while the variance for carburetor A is extremely small, Cochran's test should also be used.

Cochran's Test for Example 12 For the four carburetor types, the σ_i^2 values computed from $n_i = 4$ values are shown in table 8.30.

TABLE 8.30

Carburetor Types	*A*	*B*	*C*	*D*	*Total*
σ_i^2 within sample	0.135	1.735	1.635	5.850	9.355

$$C = \frac{\sigma_i^2 \text{ (largest)}}{\Sigma\sigma_i^2} = \frac{5.850}{9.355} = 0.625334$$

$f_1 = n_i - 1 = 4 - 1 = 3$ degrees of freedom with $k = 4$. Using table A.17 from Dixon and Massey,[9] for the 5% point, $C = 0.6841$, and for the 1% point, $C = 0.7814$. Since the computed value of C is less than the 5% point, this test indicates no significant differences in these sample variances.

8.20 Compilations and Applications for Designs of Experiments with Applicable Analysis Tests

A brief presentation has been given in this chapter of the simpler forms to be used in designing experimental tests. The nature of such experiments is discussed, along with the necessity of using randomization to make such experimental tests most efficient as contrasted with the older, classical methods of varying only one factor at a time. The factorial design is presented, including the basic Latin square design. Tests are given to determine the significant factor in obtaining current quality and what improvements may be made to improve the quality of the product, improve its design, reduce the fatigue factors for workers, and improve all events where the final results are considered unsatisfactory.

Tests for significant differences between means or variances are given. These tests cover the L_0 and L_1 tests, the Bartlett and Cochran tests, and the Fisher F test. A complete example has been presented so that those reading this chapter may readily design critical experiments and evaluate them correctly by the required tests.

EXERCISES

1. When selecting samples for inspection, use is made of random numbers. Units are placed in rectangular squares or spaces numbered consecutively from 1 to 100, in blocks of 10. A sampling plan for inspecting each lot of 100 relays requires a random sample of 20 units which are to be inspected and tested to determine whether to accept or reject the lot. Acceptance or rejection of the lot is based on the observed results. In single sampling, only one sample is selected at random from each lot; if a major defect is found in the random sample of $n = 20$, the lot is rejected. If not more than 1 minor defect is found in the sample, the lot is accepted. Using the random sampling numbers table, table 8.1, part 1, line 25 and, if necessary, line 26 in part 2 (where duplicate numbers occur and 20 different numbers are not found when using line 25), list the 20 random numbers.

(a) Tabulate the numbers as read from the table directly.

(b) Order the 20 random numbers in an ascending array.

(c) List the duplicate numbers found before the 20th different random number was found.

(d) Was it necessary to use line 26 in part 2?

NOTE: Only two-digit numbers are to be selected for the sample.

2. For the sampling plan noted in exercise 1, a different random sample is desired when a second lot of 100 units is submitted for acceptance. Place the 100 units on the 100 consecutively numbered spaces on the sampling table. To determine which units should be included in the sample, find 20 random numbers as follows.

(a) Read 20 two-digit numbers from column 15, starting with line 1. Tabulate and mark any duplicate numbers with parentheses for the second or third duplicates.

(b) Order the 20 different random numbers as an ascending array.

(c) List any duplicate numbers that must be omitted when they occur.

3. For the sampling plan in exercise 1, a third lot of 100 units is submitted for acceptance. Select a third set of random numbers for the third sample.

(a) Using table 8.1, select 20 different random numbers from line 4 and line 5, if necessary. Place duplicate values in parentheses.

(b) Order the 20 different random numbers as an ordered, ascending array.

(c) For each of the 1, 2, and 3 sets of 20 random numbers, note how many duplicate two-digit numbers occurred.
(d) Do you believe the random sampling numbers table, table 8.1, gives true random numbers? Give reasons for your statements.

4. Select 15 different four-digit numbers from the random sampling numbers from table 8.1.
(a) Use lines 31 and 32, with, respectively, columns 1 and 2 together, then columns 3 and 4 together, etc. Tabulate as read from the table.
(b) Order the 15 four-digit numbers as an ascending array, listing the smallest number in your 15 selected numbers first.
(c) Are there any duplicate numbers? If so, list them.
(d) Why are duplicate numbers less likely to occur when listing four-digit numbers than when listing two-digit numbers?

5. A sampling device used in receiving inspection to obtain unbiased random samples is a table 5 feet by 10 feet with 100 6-inch by 12-inch rectangles painted on it; small units of the same type from a lot submitted for acceptance are placed at random on the table as unpacked. These 100 spaces are numbered 1 to 100, respectively. Using table 8.1, determine the units for the desired random sample for each of the following.
(a) $n = 10$. Use column 8 under letter *B*, which gives two-digit numbers to be used when only 100 units are in the lot. List the necessary 10 different random numbers. When any duplicates occur, indicate the replicate by parentheses. Continue your selection until you have 10 different numbers.
(b) $n = 10$. Select your own column or line and select another set of 10 different random numbers. List your numbers as read from the table.
(c) Order the random numbers from (a) as an ascending array. Do the same for the 10 random numbers found in (b). Do you find that the use of this method gives a truly random sample for use in inspecting the lots submitted for acceptance by the receiving department? Would 100% inspection be used in all cases?

6. Where a lot consists of 1,000 units, determine three-digit random numbers for (i) $n = 10$ and (ii) $n = 25$, using the columns or lines specified.
(a) *Case 1:* Use column 15 and the first part of column 16 for (i) 10, and (ii) 25, recording values as read from the columns in table 8.1. If any duplicates occur, indicate numbers not used by placing them in parentheses.
(b) *Case 2:* Use lines 11, 12, etc., as needed, using successive three-digit numbers, list as read in table 8.1, and place all duplicates not used in parentheses. Cover (i) $n = 10$, and (ii) $n = 25$.
(c) Order the two sets of random numbers selected in (a). Record the smallest number first to obtain an ascending array.
(d) Order the two sets of random numbers selected in (b) as ascending arrays.
(e) Are these four sets of random numbers truly representative samples?

7. (a) What is meant by a random number?
(b) How are random numbers obtained?
(c) What is meant by a representative sample? a representative number?
(d) When is a sample considered biased?
(e) How would you obtain an unbiased sample? an unbiased number to be used in selecting a unit in a sample?

8. (a) What is the most important requirement or condition to be realized in ordering or arranging numbers in a table of random numbers? In answering this question, write the accepted definition of a random number or random unit which is to be selected from a set of numbers or units.
(b) Statistical analyses as conducted for years accomplished little in research, agriculture, and industrial processes. What important feature did R. A. Fisher add which made the analysis of variance a powerful tool, reducing the time to obtain valid evidence used in making efficient decisions effective almost immediately?
(c) How is a factorial-designed experiment conducted? How is a Latin square design of experiment conducted? Consider the three variables A, B, and C in answering these questions. Use a graph to show your answers.

9. Random numbers for more than two digits may be difficult to select if lines are selected at random rather than columns for a set of numbers. For example, using line 21, 5 four-digit random numbers are (1) 2620, (2) 4666, (3) 3631, (4) 5061, and (5) 0375. If only 5 three-digit random numbers are needed, using line 38 gives (1) 741, (2) 067, (3) 074, (4) 016, and (5) 994.
(a) For $n = 10$, using line 17 and line 18 if necessary, list 10 three-digit random sampling numbers selected from table 8.1. List these numbers as read and then order them in an ascending array. Are there any duplicates? If so, note them.
(b) For $n = 10$, using line 41 and lines 42 and 43 if necessary, list 10 four-digit random sampling numbers as read from table 8.1. Order these 10 random numbers as an ascending array. Was it necessary to use more than one line?
(c) Automatic machines turn out pins, small screws, and many small parts by the millions. Each column gives two-digit numbers. Using columns 14, 15, and 16, list 10 six-digit random numbers. List as read and then order the numbers as an ascending array.
(d) How would you use successive lines to obtain six-digit random numbers?

10. The text obtains and uses random sampling numbers for a lot of 900 units, where the numerically marked spaces on the random sampling table give only 100 equal spaces, while the lots consist of more than 100 units. If a lot consists of only 500 units, indicate the following.
(a) The steps in setting up a procedure to obtain 25 three-digit numbers for a lot size that consists of $N = 500$ units.
(b) Give an example stating each step in the procedure for obtaining the three-digit numbers where the table accommodates only two-digit numbers. List the random numbers as selected from table 8.1, the columns and lines used in their selection, and the random numbers ordered in an ascending array.

11. An oil tanker has many compartments with cylinders with curvilinear sides and some with linear sides forming cubes rather than cylinders. The contents in these compartments will contain oil whose density will vary in proportion to the depth of the various tanks, since the heavier oils will sink to the bottom of the tanks and the lighter components will be at the surface. Thus the specific gravity of such contents will differ theoretically for a tank of height h, varying possibly in accordance with a relation such as $g_t = k(1 + ah)$. The theoretical specific gravities for the oils carried by this tanker are believed to be $g_t = 0.80(1 + 0.004h)$, where $k = 0.80$ sometimes termed g^*. To obtain a truly representative sample a "thief" sample is taken. The method consists of lowering a

container equipped with an opening at the bottom that may be opened and closed as desired. Thief samples are taken in a set of three rectangular 30-foot tanks. The specific gravity of each sample is obtained and is recorded in table 8.31, together with theoretical values.

TABLE 8.31

Depth in feet, h	*Specific Gravities for Samples*			
	First Tank	*Second Tank*	*Third Tank*	*Theoretical, g_t^**
5	0.810	0.820	0.730	0.816
10	0.840	0.845	0.742	0.832
15	0.850	0.859	0.767	0.848
20	0.860	0.876	0.781	0.864
25	0.880	0.890	0.800	0.880
Sum	4.240	4.290	3.820	4.240
Average	0.848	0.858	0.764	0.848

*General equation used for these g_t values based on $g_t = 0.80\,(1 + 0.0032\,h)$.

(a) Determine the variance and standard deviation values for the four sets of data.

Determine whether there is a significant difference in the means for (i) first tank vs. second tank, (ii) first tank vs. third tank, and (iii) second tank vs. third tank. When making this test, let the criterion be as follows. If the value of t in the relation below is greater than 3, then the test indicates that the two samples have means so different that their parent populations are assumed to be significantly different.

$$t = \frac{|X_1 - X_2|}{\sigma_{\text{difference}}}, \text{ where } \sigma^2_{\text{difference}} = \frac{\sigma_1^2}{n_1} + \frac{\sigma_2^2}{n_2}$$

(b) Another check for determining whether any of these three $\bar{X}$ values found for the three tanks are significantly different from the theoretical standard values of $\bar{X}'$ and σ' is to determine three-sigma control limits about $\bar{X}'$ using $\sigma'_{\bar{X}} = \frac{\sigma'}{\sqrt{n}}$. Make such a control chart for the average values and also make a similar control chart for the standard deviation values, σ computed in (a).

(c) The g^* or k value used for the theoretical specific gravity of this oil is 0.80. What are the corresponding k or g^* values for the results for the three tanks? Compute #. List the computed value for each tank. Using 15 feet as the mid-point depth of the 30-foot tanks, what specific gravity values should be given for this depth as the best estimate of the specific gravity of the oil in each tank, respectively? # Use relation $g_t = 0.80\,(1 + 0.0040\,h)$.

12. (a) Using table 8.1, select 25 four-digit numbers, starting with line 26 of columns 4 and 5. List these 25 values and order them in an ascending array. Are there any duplicates? If so, use line 26 again with columns 6 and 7.

(b) Using table 8.1, select 25 four-digit numbers, starting with column 1 of lines 16, 17, and 18, if necessary. List the numbers as read and order in an ascending array.
(c) Determine average, variance, and standard deviation values for the two sets of 25 random numbers each ordered in (a) and (b). List these $\bar{X}$, v, and σ values.
(d) Make a test for significant differences between the two means found in (a), (b), and (c) and also the two sigma values found in (c). Use 3 as a criterion for the maximum allowable z value.

13. (a) Name five different kinds of samples, particularly a random sample and a thief sample. Define each and give an example of each.
(b) Describe what is meant by degrees of freedom, sometimes designated as d.f. To illustrate what is meant by d.f. solve the following problem. Given that $n = 5$ units in sample, arithmetic mean $\bar{X} = 5$, variance or $\sigma^2 = 6$, $X_1 = 5$, $X_2 = 7$, and $X_3 = 4$, determine values for X_4 and X_5, where the number of degrees of freedom is d.f. $= n - 2 = 5 - 2 = 3$.
(c) What is the value of the number of degrees of freedom d.f. for a sample of 20 units, where its average $\bar{X}$, its variance v, and standard deviation $\sigma = \sqrt{v}$, skewness k based on the third moment, and its kurtosis β_2 are also given? In this case, four other statistics for the sample are given besides the sample size.

14. For a production operation, two brands of machines are being considered. Machine A is operated for a week of five days with daily outputs as noted in table 8.32, while machine B is also operated during the same period with daily outputs also recorded in table 8.32.

TABLE 8.32

Daily Outputs of Two Machines		
Day of Week	*Machine A*	*Machine B*
Monday	260	325
Tuesday	240	330
Wednesday	235	320
Thursday	230	315
Friday	235	310
Week	1200	1600

(a) Using a 2-σ rather than a 3-σ criterion for significant differences, determine if the two machines are significantly different with respect to average daily output.
(b) If an eight-hour day were used, so that hourly rates of production are readily obtained, would you feel that an hourly test for significant differences would prove more efficient, effective, and representative than the daily test?
(c) If it is known that machine A was five years older than machine B, and actually was available for operating only an average of six hours per day, being down for repairs an average of two hours per day, would this fact modify your answer to (b)?

(d) Change the data to an hourly rate and, with the adjusted data for each machine, determine if there is a significant difference between the means for the two machines on an hourly production basis. State conclusion and reasons for any change in your conclusion.

15. (a) When making a test for selecting the most effective and efficient method of operation or recording outputs from two different machines, when there are available two sets of data for two different conditions and their respective average and variance values are available, and when lack of control for the test exists or differences in the available statistics noted appears to exist, what three different kinds of differences between the two may exist? Name these three and the tests such as the L_0 and L_1 tests used to detect the difference.
(b) Gasoline is available in different grades, leaded or unleaded, with various octane ratings. The higher the octane rating, the better the level of performance is the usual experience of car owners if the carburetors are adjusted properly for the fuel being used. Using gasoline as an example, (i) what would be the effect on the performance of your automobile when a difference occurred in the rating of the gasoline you usually put in your tank? (Such a difference may be positive or negative.) (ii) What effect would you expect when there is a large increase in the variability of the gasoline you buy from tank load to tank load during any given period?
(c) Why does industry demand uniformity in its products? In buying gasoline, which would you prefer: (i) an increase in the average for miles per gallon or (ii) a marked decrease in the variability of the gasoline you purchase so you consistently know within 5% error what mileage per gallon your brand of gasoline will give your car?

16. A product is submitted in lots of 250 units each to a customer. Where a 10% sample, consisting of 25 units for each lot, is selected as the size of the first sample in a double sampling plan of inspection, perform the following tasks. (a) Using the table of random sampling numbers, determine the first sample of 25 units using columns 14 and 15 (first part). List these numbers and order them as an ascending array. Determine the average, variance, and standard deviation values for this set of numbers.
(b) Using lines 16, 17, 18, etc., in table 8.1, determine 25 random numbers to be used in selecting the second equal sample for this double sampling plan of inspection. List these as read and order them as an ascending array.
(c) Determine the average, variance, and standard deviation values for this second set of random numbers.

17. Use the two sets of random numbers for the first sample found in 16(a) and the second set of 25 random numbers found in 16(b) and their statistics consisting of average, variance, and standard deviation values.
(a) Determine whether there is a significant difference in their sample number averages, $\bar{X}_1$ and $\bar{X}_2$, using equation (5) in the text. Determine z and state your conclusions.
(b) The difference between $\bar{X}_1$ and $\bar{X}_2$ may be considered as a range for a sample of two average values. Using the d_2 factor for a sample of two, determine an estimate of the standard deviation between samples (i.e., averages). When squared, this number is a measure of the variance between samples. Compare this value with the two variances found for the first sample and the second sample, respectively.
(c) Make a rough determination for the possible significant difference between the two

standard deviation values found for the first sample and the second sample. For this test, the standard deviation of differences is $\sqrt{2}$ times the standard deviation for differences for the mean, $\sqrt{2}\sigma_{\text{difference}}$.

18. Five different versions of the same component were checked for an important characteristic, and the average $\bar{X}$ and variance v values shown in table 8.33 were obtained.

TABLE 8.33 Test Results: Characteristic A; 5 Suppliers

Sample No.	*Sample Size*	*Average,* $\bar{X}$	*Variance,* v	*Standard Deviation,* σ
1	4	53.7	6.3	2.51
2	4	46.5	5.7	2.39
3	4	47.8	3.1	1.76
4	4	53.4	2.4	1.55
5	4	48.6	4.2	2.05
Combined	20	50.0	15.48	3.93

(a) Before making any test for a significant difference between the above means, use the L_0 and L_1 test for homogeneity of the variances as presented in the text. Note for the 1% and 5% values, the applicable values corresponding to five different suppliers, where the sample number above designates the different suppliers. These values are to be compared with the computed values of L_0 and L_1 computed from the data above.
(b) Test the hypothesis that the mean values for these five suppliers are equal. The true value for $\bar{X}_1$ is denoted as $\mu_{1,1} = \mu_1$, while the true value for $\bar{X}_2$ is $\mu_{1,2} = \mu_2$, and so on. Here the subscripts, 1, 2, 3, 4, and 5 denote the sample number, not the moment number. The hypothesis to be tested is that $\mu_1 = \mu_2 = \mu_3 = \mu_4 = \mu_5$, assuming homogeneity of these variances by the Bartlett's test. Show all the values used in this test, where $\Sigma n_i = 20$, using the relation

$$F = \frac{f_2 M}{f_1(b - M)}$$

(c) Since 6.3 is much larger than the other variances, use Cochran's test for the homogeneity of variances, as given in this chapter.

19. (a) For the five different samples and data in exercise 18, prepare a control chart for the five average and σ values. Determine standards for $\bar{X}$ and σ from the data and show how they were determined. Show a graph of these control charts.
(b) Assuming that the variances have been found to be homogeneous by the various tests for homogeneity, i.e., all five suppliers are essentially uniform, use the analysis of variance test to check whether there is any significant difference between the means using the F test. The analysis of variance test for one variable, termed the F test, is given below. All you need to do is to use the proper table to determine applicable F values for 0.95 and 0.99 confidence levels and compare them with the F ratio you have computed from the mean square values provided in the table.

TABLE 8.34 Analysis of Variance

Variations	*Sum of Squares*	*df*	*Mean Square*	*F-ratio*
Between means	44.20	4	11.05	$F =$ ______?
Within samples	66.00	15	4.40	$F_{0.95}(4, 15) =$ ______?
				$F_{0.99}(4, 15) =$ ______?
Total	110.20	19	5.80	

(c) What conclusion can be drawn from the F test?

20. When preparing a design for an important experiment, designs may be made in many different ways. A 4 × 4 Latin square is one form of design and may be made in the following form.

	I	*II*	*III*	*IV*
1	A	B	C	D
2	D	A	B	C
3	C	D	A	B
4	B	C	D	A

This design may represent the case where a number of children are divided into four equal groups and four lists of words are divided into four tests of different types. The scores are the number of words each group spells correctly in each test which were spelled incorrectly previously. Let A, B, C, and D represent the separate tests in each list. The words were all spelled from dictation in the previous test. The four tests are as follows.

A, multiple choice
B, second dictation
C, wrongly spelled word
D, skeleton word

The above is called a 4 × 4 Latin square. The possible number of such designs is $(4!) \times (4!) = 24 \times 24 = 576$.

A research program for reducing rejects of tile was condensed to 3 months by using a similar design of experiment covering the characteristic modulus of rupture of green (prior to firing) tile utilizing four different tests for four different clays, four different talcs, and four different quantities of water.

(a) Prepare a similar 2 × 2 Latin square design.
(b) How many such 2 × 2 Latin squares may be designed?
(c) Prepare a similar 3 × 3 Latin square design.
(d) How many such 3 × 3 Latin squares may be designed?
(e) Give a concrete example for a single characteristic that is to be measured by one form of Latin square. Use letters A, B, C, etc., to denote an item you use in your example.

FOOTNOTES

[1] *Tracts for Computers No. XV, Random Sampling Numbers,* arranged by L. H. C. Tippett (Cambridge, Massachusetts: Cambridge University Press, 1927). Reprinted by photographic process, 1950. Edited by E. S. Pearson. *Tracts for Computers No. XXIV, Tables of Random Sampling Numbers,* by M. G. Kendall and B. Bobington Smith (Cambridge, Massachusetts: Cambridge University Press, 1946). Edited by E. S. Pearson.

[2] William G. Cochran and Gertrude M. Cox, *Experimental Designs* (New York: John Wiley & Sons, Inc., 1957), Table 2.1.

[3] H. A. Freeman, *Industrial Statistics* (New York: John Wiley & Sons, Inc., 1956).

[4] P. C. Mahalanobis, "L_0 and L_1 Tables," *Sankhya* (*The Indian Journal of Statistics*), 1933. Also issued later in pamphlet form, reproduced as Tables IX and X in the Freeman text on pages 174 and 175.

[5] *Biometrika Tables for Statisticians,* E. S. Pearson and H. O. Hartley, eds.

[6] R. A. Fisher, *Statistical Methods for Research Workers,* 13th edition.

[7] R. A. Fisher and Frank Yates, *Statistical Tables.*

[8] M. S. Bartlett, *Properties of Sufficiency and Statistical Tests,* Proc. Royal Soc. A., 160, 1932, pp. 268–82.

[9] Wilfred J. Dixon and Frank J. Massey, Jr., *Introduction to Statistical Analysis,* 2nd édition (New York: McGraw-Hill Book Co., Inc., 1957). Example given on pp. 179–180, for text material, pp. 388–403 for Table A.7, F distribution on pp. 438–439, Cochran's test.

[10] C. Eisenhart, et al., *Techniques of Statistical Analysis.*

CHAPTER NINE

RELIABILITY AND MAINTAINABILITY ASSURANCE

9.1 Objective

During recent years, there has been growing general concern about product reliability. Many product applications need high standards, and safe and reliable performance. Very simply defined, *reliability* is the probability that a product will perform in accordance to expectation for a predetermined period of time in a given environment.

This definition satisfies the usual engineering requirements, in that probability can be expressed numerically. However, in order for the number to be meaningful when applied to a specific product, operating parameters must be specified, the criteria of satisfactory performance must be defined, the period of time must be stated, and the conditions of use must be specified. The performance aspect of product reliability involves planning, designing, manufacturing, testing, and maintaining the product to achieve the desired reliability.

The reliability of a product depends in great part on how well reliability has been planned into the product in early planning stages. Criteria about how long and how well a product is expected to perform are needed for design.

Once the design has been accepted as having met all reliability requirements, it is the job of manufacturing, quality engineering, and quality control personnel to make sure that the reliability characteristics that are designed into the products are not compromised during fabrication and assembly phases. After an article has been qualified for production, appropriate process controls must be implemented to ensure that the product is built to meet all approved drawings and specifications. This chapter deals with the functions and disciplines required to achieve product reliability.

Setting Reliability Levels

In a competitive society, it is virtually impossible to economically manufacture products that will be totally safe under all conditions of use. Neither is it possible for a manufacturer to build a product which will always operate successfully, that is, have a probability of success of one. As the probability of success approaches one, costs approach infinity.

In modern industry, managers always must make certain burdensome decisions pertaining to optimum reliability levels. They realize that the consequences of producing a product with a reliability that is too low can be as great as, if not greater than, the consequences of producing one with a reliability that is too high. If a reliability level is set too low, a company's reputation as a quality producer may suffer; perhaps of even more significance, if a user of a substandard article is injured, ensuing litigation may be extremely costly to the manufacturer. On the other hand, if a large amount of capital is spent on developing techniques and devices to produce products that are exceptionally reliable, it may be difficult for the manufacturer to hold a profitable position in the competitive market. Given these parameters, managers must arrive at a compromise between reliability and cost. Figure 9-1 illustrates the point of optimum reliability.

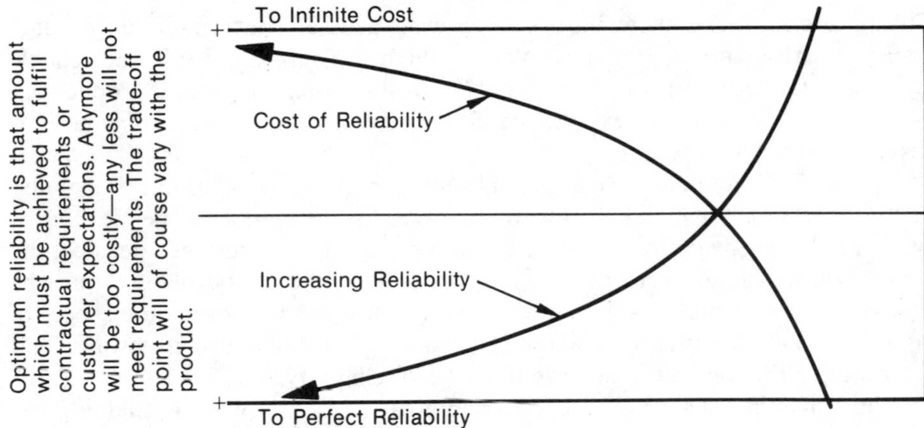

Figure 9–1 Reliability-Cost Trade-off.

Testing for Reliability

Ever since the beginning of mass production technology, there has been the chance that some parts or products would fail sooner than expected, and consumers in the past have more or less accepted this fact. In recent years, however, there has been an increasing awareness and apprehension among both consumer and contractor that chances of failure are real, and that these chances tend to increase if certain precautionary measures are not taken.

When equipment is to be built for the government or used for commercial purposes, the buyer submits specifications that govern quality. These are sundry military or governmental specifications or performance criteria relevant to the products being produced. For consumer goods, the customer depends essentially on a competitive industry to provide safe and reliable products since he cannot submit such specifications. It is, therefore, incumbent upon industry to conduct adequate tests not only to develop reliable products, but also to confirm quality levels before shipment.

Many executives have learned that the probabilities of product failure can be reduced if adequate testing programs are implemented, and if test results lead to improvements. Component and system testing provides information needed either to improve reliability during development stages or to prove that the products do indeed conform to planned levels of reliability in various stages of manufacture. The testing procedure involves the collection and evaluation of performance data obtained through simulated service testing of a component or product. These collected data provide criteria upon which judgments may be based regarding product compliance with planned or accepted standards.

The ultimate purpose of reliability testing is to provide an estimate of the probability that a component or product in question will adequately perform its function for the specified time when used in a specific environment. Thus, reliability tests permit one to estimate statistically the reliability of a product.

Designing for Reliability

The importance of the design function in achieving reliable products can be realized from the fact that the design itself is the "blueprint" by which the product will be manufactured and inspected. Once the design has been conceived, completed, and issued, it becomes the all-important document to production and inspection personnel. Reliability cannot be inspected into a product. Neither testing to determine reliability characteristics, nor evaluating to determine product effectiveness can enhance the ultimate soundness of a product. After production has begun, unless there is a design change, reliability cannot be increased; it can only be sacrificed.

After all the designs have been released to production, the only way that inspection personnel can *increase* product reliability is to motivate design changes by means of feedback information pertaining to manufactured quality. For example, if an inspector discovers that two parts will not mate properly due to wrong tolerances, feedback data recorded on a rejection form will prompt the design department to make the necessary design changes. Only after the design has been corrected can a new higher level of reliability be created for the parts.

Another source of motivation to raise the reliability level of a product, after the designs have been completed, is the customer. Customer feedback by means of complaints about product performance may also trigger design changes. A good example is the automobile industry in which thousands of cars have been called back because of sundry quality problems. These quality problems were revealed by the consumer through actual service conditions long after the vehicles had left the assembly plants. In these cases, the customer performed the feedback service that should have been performed by a quality function within the company during early stages of qualification testing.

Normally a first article is built, based on the released design documentation, then subjected to various tests. The results of these tests (often referred to as *qualification tests*) provide feedback to the designer about the degree of reliability achieved in the design. But, unless the designer is an extraordinary genius, or is unusually blessed by good luck, he or she will need to revise the design to correct for certain deficiencies. This is the reason that drawing changes normally are necessary to achieve the desired level of designed reliability before production begins.

After a product has been marketed, design changes frequently still are necessary. When customer complaints about product performance indicate a trend of substandard parts, the engineering department should be as interested as other departments in finding the source of the trouble and implementing corrective action. Design problems requiring corrective action may take such forms as a poor choice of materials, improper mating of parts, system incompatibility, or an understressed part. Some design faults are not revealed until after a part has been placed into service, when it is found that the product did not measure up to reliability standards. Most design errors or deficiencies that could cause product failure, however, are detected prior to production runs either before design release or during first article inspection.

Safety in Design

A major mission of any manufacturing company in modern society is to design and market a product that will render both reliable and safe service for the consumer. The safety aspect of product design is concerned with the *inherent* safety of a product and accounts for all possible end uses. To design a product that will perform safely under unusual service conditions is relatively costly, but it is folly not to take such safety precautions. Costs incurred by one liability suit because of inferior product design can be sufficiently penalizing to bankrupt a company. Numerous court actions during recent years have indicated that either the manufacturer or seller can be held liable if a product fails and causes bodily injury to the consumer. Inferior design is the origin of many such failures. In modern industry the designer must anticipate unconventional usages or applications of products before design documentation are released to production departments. Unintended use of a product or negligence on the part of the user are poor defenses for manufacturers should litigation occur.

The need for safety in product design is not unique to such well-known products as automobiles. Safety factors must be considered in the design of both consumer goods and commercial products. If an injury can be attributed to faulty design of such articles as lawn mowers, ladders, or even household appliances, the manufacturers or sellers may be held liable. For example, a recent court case involved a man who collected $70,000 from a vineyard after he was blinded by a cork that prematurely shot out of a champagne bottle. An inherent safety hazard existed and the container was not labeled to forewarn the user. Design deficiencies such as a chain breaking below its advertised load, or a hoisting device breaking because of unforeseen side loads also are examples of design inferiority that have in the past caused bodily injuries to users and have resulted in costly liability actions.

Failures also have been reported in the use of hospital equipment. There have been instances where designers of hospital equipment did not anticipate all the ways that a medical technician or a doctor would connect and use certain equipment. And, as a result of such unintended use, a patient either died unnecessarily or his progress was appreciably retarded. Anticipation by the designer that either poor human judgment or human error may cause a consumer to use equipment in an unusual manner or incorrectly has become an important design consideration. Maintainability factors must also be considered when designing products that will render safe service. Where a product will require field maintenance and repair operations, a certain predictable amount of human error must be anticipated in the design. Especially if the maintenance could affect a function and result in a critical failure, special preventive design measures must be taken.

In addition to being able to predict future product usage, the designer must be aware of current safety codes. In product liability litigation, it is significant if a product has been designed in ignorance by some design engineers who fail to consider all of the current and applicable states in which the product will be sold and used. Lawsuits reveal that many design engineers fail to use all of the current and applicable technical safety requirements relating to the products for which they are responsible. Some do not know what safety factors constitute the mandatory minimum for design and test purposes or what special safety features are now required by law. Moreover, they are unaware of the design and test criteria contained in all of the applicable trade standards, and may overlook the protective measures that are recommended in various manuals, handbooks, and supplier catalogs.

Unfortunately the responsibility of the design department for safe design does not end when all of the drawings and pertinent design changes have been released to production departments. Records of drawings, specifications, and all design changes must be kept for an indefinite period of time. Should a failure result in a lawsuit, a complete set of design and test records are necessary to construct a case for the defense. Without such documentation, the case for the defense is extremely weak. Safety in design should not be an occasional or cursory endeavor, but should start when the basic design concepts are originated and continue as a systematic activity throughout product development, detail design, modification, testing, fabrication, maintenance, and finally during the life of the product.

9.2 System Design

A good design contains all the necessary reliability characteristics that will enable the unit when built to perform satisfactorily for its predicted period of time. Such a design accounts for factors such as tolerances of mating parts, operational conditions of components and systems, sizes and weights of materials and parts, and capabilities of materials and components for substitution and interchangeability.

A good designer will select components and circuits that have been tried and proven to be reliable, and will avoid the use of unproven design methods. Poor design methods invariably embody circuits and components which have marginal characteristics as well as unnecessary parts and mechanisms.

If it were possible to manufacture a product with perfect reliability (probability of no failure) the value of the reliability would be 1. The highest reliability attained however is a 0.9 repeating decimal approaching 1 (e.g. 0.999999). Probability is the basis of reliability calculations. To reason that perfect reliability can be achieved is to infer that all *chance* of failure can be eliminated.

When designing for reliability, there are several fundamental methods of achieving the appropriate reliability level in a given product.

Series Design

The smallest number of components should be used without compromising performance, particularly if the design of a system is basically a *series* design. As additional parts are added in series, the *total* reliability decreases. This point is illustrated in the following figures.

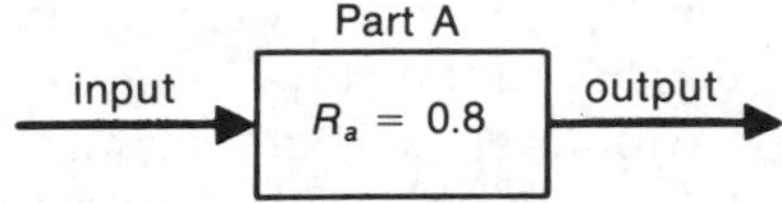

Figure 9–2 Input—Output, part A.

A reliability of 0.8 for part A means that it will *probably* perform satisfactorily 80% of the time for a certain operating period. It can also be stated that it will probably fail 20% of the time within the given period.

It should be understood that it does not necessarily follow that in 100 operations the system will perform satisfactorily exactly 80 times and fail 20 times. It may fail 40 or 50 times in 100 trials, or it may not fail at all in 100 trials. One of the phenomena of probability is that over a large number of trials the ultimate outcome will approach 80% success and 20% failure as limiting values.

Now, if additional elements were added in series, even though they may have greater reliabilities, overall system reliability would become progressively less. For example, figure 9-3 illustrates the addition of part B, which has a reliability of 0.9, in series with part A. The combined reliability of the parts is 0.72. This is given by the expression

$$R_s = R_a R_b = (0.8)(0.9) = 0.72,$$

where R_s is system reliability and R_a and R_b are the respective component reliabilities. Notice that as parts are added in series, the output reliability becomes increasingly smaller.

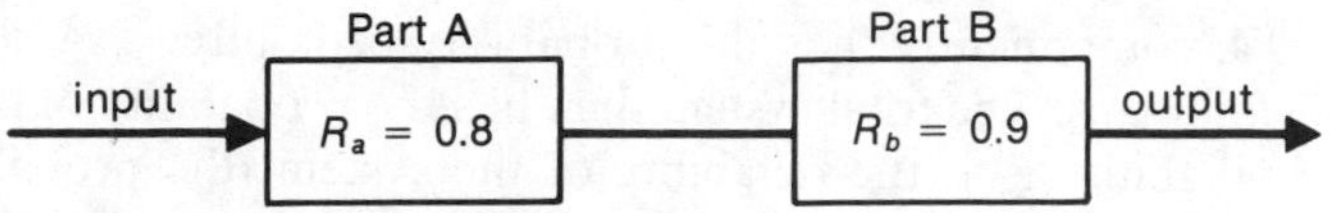

Figure 9-3 Input—Output, parts A and B.

System reliability can be drastically reduced by combining a large number of elements in a series arrangement. If a single part functions properly 99 times out of 100, it has 99% reliability (0.99). However, if the system contained 400 parts all in series with each part being 99% reliable, the overall reliability of the system would be

$$R_s = R_1 \cdot R_2 \cdot \cdots \cdot R_n, \quad \text{then} \quad R_s = 0.99^{400} = 0.018 = 1.8\%.$$

This means simply that the system likely will not function satisfactorily more than 1.8% of the time. In a series arrangement, the total system's reliability is the product of its component's reliabilities. This is known as the product rule.

Parallel Design

In reliability engineering, designing units in parallel (utilizing redundant systems or components) is defined as the existence of more than one means for achieving a stated level of performance; all paths must fail before the system will fail. In such a design, the probability of failure plus the probability of success is equal to one, where Q is the probability of failure and R is the reliability or the probability of success.

$$Q + R = 1$$

Further, the probability of failure is given symbolically as

$$Q = q_1 q_2$$

where q_1 and q_2 are the respective probabilities of the two elements of a simple system.

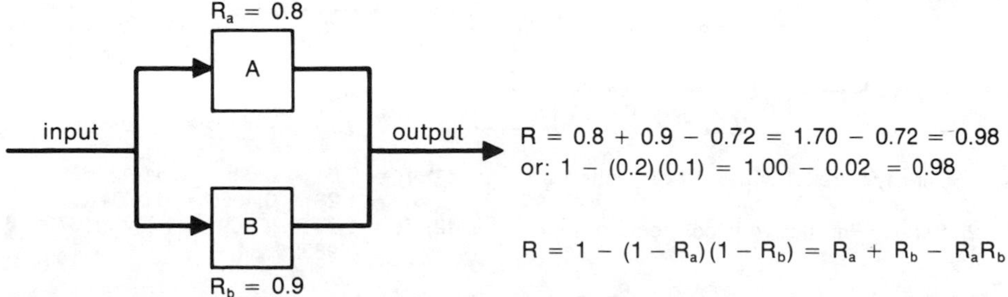

Figure 9-4 Input—Output, (parallel).

In figure 9-4, component A has the probability of failure q_1 and B has the probability of failure q_2. The total system then has the probability of failure q_1q_2. Since perfect reliability is 1, the reliability of the system (the probability of *no* failure) therefore is $1 - Q$, or $1 - q_1q_2$. For example, if it is known that A has a reliability (R_1) of 0.95 and B has a reliability (R_2) of 0.91, the unreliability (or probability of failure) of the system may be calculated as follows.

$$1 - R_1 = 0.05$$

$$1 - R_2 = 0.09$$

The probability of failure is (0.05)(0.09) = 0.0045. Hence the reliability of the system is

$$R_s = 1 - 0.0045 = 0.9955$$

Such a parallel arrangement has a higher combined reliability than either of the component parts functioning singly.

R_s may also be calculated by the following method.

$$R_s = R_1 + R_2 - R_1R_2 = 0.95 + 0.91 - (0.95 \times 0.91) = 1.8600 - 0.8645 = 0.9955$$

As parallel elements are added to such a redundant system, the reliability increases because each new element provides a different route or bypass that may be used should other routes fail. As the number of bypasses increases, the probability of success also increases.

Figure 9-5 illustrates how the reliability of a system can be doubled quite easily.

In a system of four like components (e.g., A, B, C, and D, as illustrated in figure 9-5), the reliability could be greatly improved by adding a bypass like line *ab*.

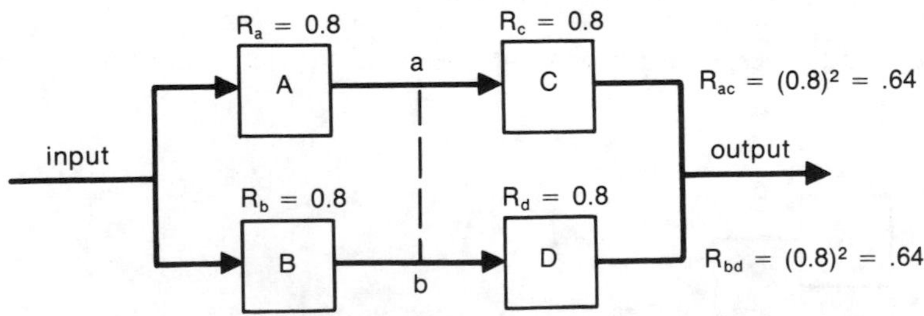

1. Series/Parallel without connection ab
2. Series/Parallel with connection ab

(1) $R = 0.64 + 0.64 - (0.64)^2 = 1.28 - 0.4096 = 0.8704$

(2) $R = 1 - (0.1296)^2 = 1 - 0.01679616 = 0.98320384$

Figure 9–5 Input—Output, parts A, B, C, and D.

System design usually becomes more complex as redundancy measures are taken. As additional elements are included, they influence the operating characteristics of other elements. Factors of ambient operating conditions and packaging in turn become more complex. These are some of the reasons that high reliability and the costs to achieve such reliability are directly proportional. As system reliability approaches one, costs increase at a greater rate. Often the operating reliability values increase or decrease where interactions occur during actual operations due to interactions between parts. The effects of such interactions must be evaluated to obtain accurate reliability values.

Example In figure 9-5, two cases will be considered. A, B, C, and D components will be assumed to have equal reliability values (*a*) 0.90 and (*b*) 0.95. Two components in series are necessary to obtain a satisfactory output. Without redundancy, A and C in series have a joint reliability obtained by the product law $R_A \cdot R_C = R_{AC}$ or $R_B \cdot R_D = R_{BD}$. For (*a*), $R_i = 0.9$, so $R_{AC} = R_{BD} = 0.9 \times 0.9 = 0.81$. For (*b*), $R_i = 0.95$, so $R_{AC} = R_{BD} = 0.95 \times 0.95 = 0.9025$. With simple redundancy, $R = 1 - (1 - 0.81)^2 = 1 - (0.19)^2 = 1 - 0.0361 = 0.9639$. When connection *ab* is added, four circuit paths rather than two are available. Hence, $R = 1 - (0.81)^4 = 1 - (0.19)^4 = 1 - 0.00130321 = 0.99869679$. Thus the reliability for only two in series is increased from 0.81 to 0.9639 by simple redundancy and to $R = 0.99869679$ by adding line *ab*. Similarly, for case (*b*) where $R_A = R_B = 0.95$, $R = 0.95 \times 0.95 = 0.9025$. With redundancy, $R = 1 - (1 - 0.9025)^2 = 1 - (0.0975)^2 = 1 - 0.00950625 = 0.99049375$. If line *ab* is added, then $R = 1 - (1 - 0.9025)^4 = 1 - 0.0000903687890625 = 0.99990963$.

Derating

Derating techniques can be applied to reduce the failure rates below the averages. When weight, space, and cost limitations permit, system reliability can also be increased by designing components with operating safety margins. For example, derating may be applied in structural design by designing a 10,000-pound load capability into a device when the maximum specification is 1,000 pounds. In electronic design, it means to derate electronic parts until they are being used to 10% or 15% of their rated capabilities. In hydraulic or pneumatic designs, it means designing a pressure vessel which will withstand 1,000 psi (pounds per square inch) when the design maximum specified pressure is 100 psi. This design technique is very effective when design constraints permit its use. Derating involving overdesign is merely the practice of providing for a large safety margin in the operation of the part.

Any reliability program must also include a well-planned program of testing and inspection. Incoming materials, as well as parts fabricated in-house, must meet prescribed quality standards and pass certain quality tests before they can be delivered. Qualification tests are performed during development and design stages to make certain that the design does indeed contain the planned reliability. Results of such tests provide data to verify that the design concepts used will ultimately yield the desired reliability.

Once the design has been accepted as having met all reliability requirements, it is the job of manufacturing, quality engineering, and quality control personnel to make sure that the reliability characteristics that are designed into the products are not compromised during fabrication and assembly phases. After an article has been qualified for production, appropriate process controls must be implemented to ensure that the product is built to meet all prescribed drawings and specifications.

After production begins, an increased number of chance factors are introduced which can decrease the ultimate probability of successful product operation. Therefore, miscellaneous materials and processes controls, accurate feedback of quality status, and corrective actions are mandatory.

9.3 Achieving High Reliability in Certain Products

Achieving maximum reliability of products that are used to prolong human life, for example, is a subject of much interest among certain manufacturers, doctors, and hospitals. One would not question the need to have the greatest possible reliability for such articles as artificial organs or similar items that might extend an otherwise shortened lifespan. Modern technology is constantly put to the test to design and build such units with a high prediction of satisfactory service.

An example of one of these items is the *pacemaker*. For quite some time, pacemakers have served to keep certain heart patients alive who otherwise could not have survived. Figure 9-6 illustrates one of these units being placed into an

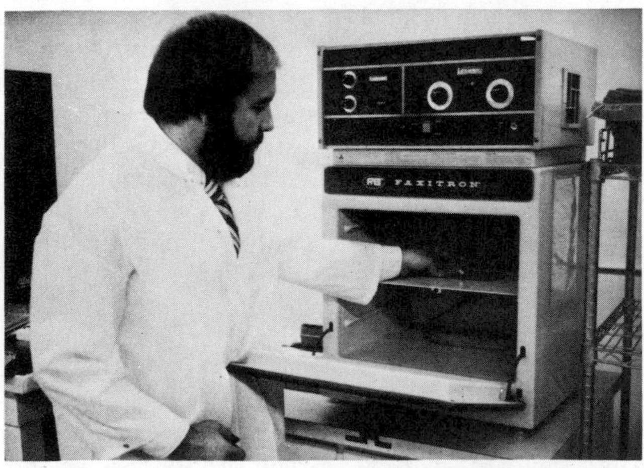

Figure 9–6 Unit in an x-ray machine.

x-ray machine for final examination. Considerable care and attendant manufacturing reliability must be exercised to provide maximum assurance that no defective units are shipped. Such units receive 100% functional test and x-ray examination to verify that all components and circuitry are in proper working order before shipment. Figure 9-7 is an enlarged photo of one of the x-rays taken. The actual size of the pacemaker which is surgically implanted in the patient just below the rib cage is approximately one inch by two inches by one inch. Recent reliability tests by one manufacturer indicate the mean time before failure of his pacemaker is 400 years.

9.4 The Failure Rate

An important factor affecting the reliability function is the failure rate. Failure rate may be thought of as the average proportion of failures per unit of time. As an example, if 1,000 components are placed in operation for one hour and 100 of these fail before the hour has elapsed, the system failure rate can be expressed as approximately 10% per hour or as 0.10 per hour, on a per unit basis. If all other factors are held constant, the failure rate may vary with the age of the system. A typical curve of failure rate versus age of equipment is shown in figure 9-8.

Early Failure

Deficiencies originating in materials and manufacturing processes often show up very early in the life of a product. Some components have relatively high

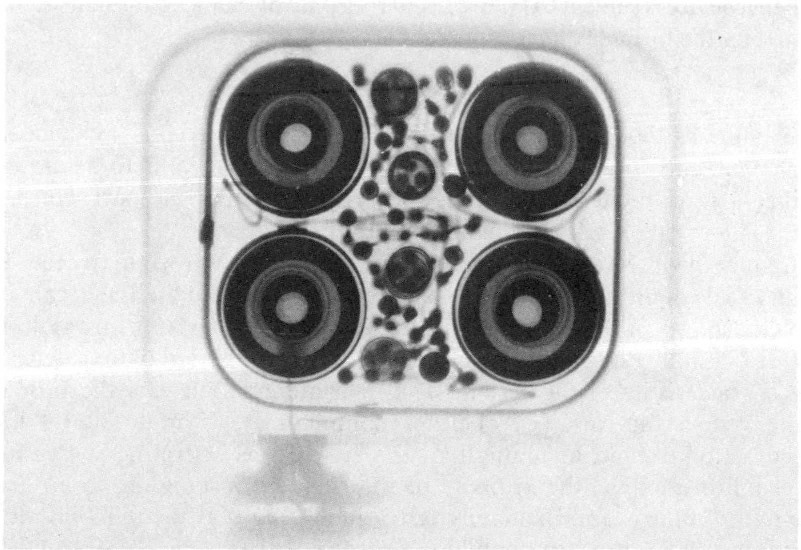

Figure 9-7 Photo of a pacemaker (x-ray).

mortality rates, but once they survive this initial stage, the probability of normal performance is much greater. *Debugging* or *burn-in* tests are run to ascertain whether or not there are workmanship defects that exist in various components and assemblies.

The burn-in process theoretically involves operating a number of components under simulated conditions for a number of hours, and then using the components that survive for the assembly of the equipment. If a number of small subsystems—such as printed circuit cards—are required for a given system, they too may require burn-in tests. This process reduces the probability of total system failure by increasing the probability of component success.

Many consumer products do not receive adequate burn-in testing before being sold. And, in some instances, the consumer is relegated the task of burning-in his own products. Some manufacturers rely on customer feedback to service agencies regarding early failures instead of performing this service before the products are shipped. Warranties usually cover this service, but often not without much inconvenience to the consumer.

Chance Failure

Latent defects sometimes escape early failure. These are called *chance failures* because they are completely unpredictable and are difficult to trace. They may be caused by the myriad conditions that occur during the normal use of the product. These failures are not caused by component deterioration; they occur randomly and happen only by chance. Such failures often occur suddenly, and are sometimes referred to as *catastrophic failures.*

When a device is subject to failure occurring only by chance causes, its reliability is defined by the formula

$$R(t) = e^{-\lambda t}, \tag{1}$$

where e is the base of natural logarithm (2.71828), λ (lambda) is a chance failure rate constant, and t is an operating period for which one wants to determine the reliability $R(t)$ of the item. Thus R is the probability that the part which has a constant failure rate λ will not fail in time t.

A frequently observed idealized reliability function is shown in figure 9-9. The reliability scale of ordinates extends from zero to one, while the time scale in this example is shown in units of time. In an actual case, unity on this scale might represent 1 minute, 1 hour, 13.2 hours, or any other unit period of time determined by the characteristics of the system. The ordinate, reliability, is the probability that the system survives (i.e., operates continuously without failure) for the specified period of time, assuming that the system was operating successfully at time zero. For example, the ordinate of the curve corresponding to an abscissa of one unit of time is approximately 0.368, indicating that the reliability for one time unit is 0.368 = 36.8% probability of success.

For example, if a part has a normal life of 1,000 hours, the reliability can be predicted for any operating period within the 1,000-hour span. This is true because

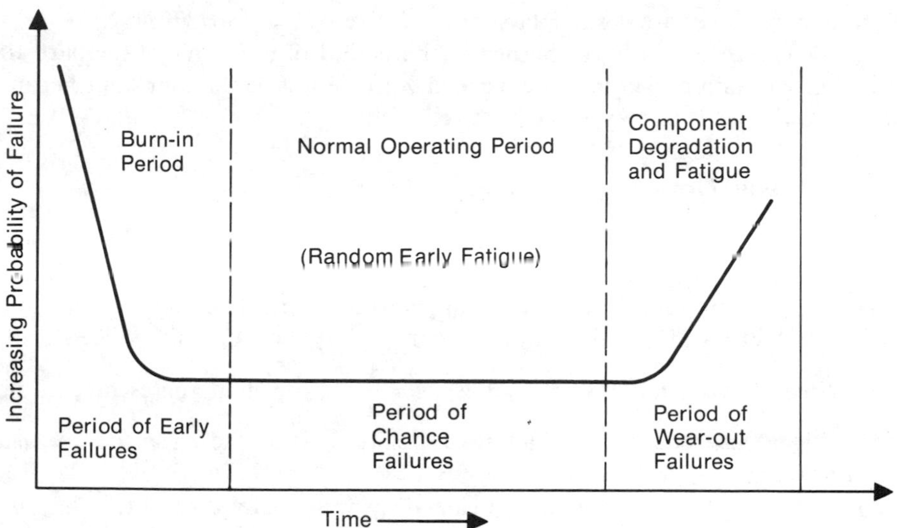

Figure 9–8. Periods in which products can fail.

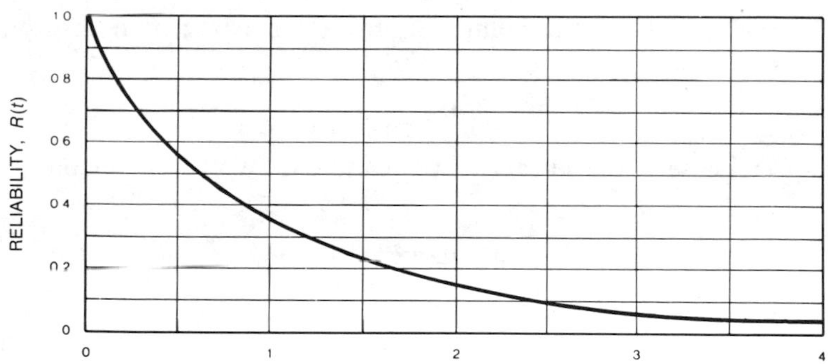

Figure 9–9 Graph of component reliability.

(as figure 9-8 illustrates for the normal operating period) the probability of success is relatively stable throughout the normal operating period. If a part, for example, has a 1,000-hour useful life and has a constant failure rate of $\lambda = 0.001$ per hour, under controlled environmental conditions, its reliability for 10 hours of operation within the 1,000 hour period is calculated as follows.

$$R = e^{-0.001 \times 10} = e^{-0.01} = 0.99 +$$

Similarly, the probability that the part will survive during its normal life of 1,000 hours is

$$R = e^{-0.001 \times 1000} = e^{-1.0} = \frac{1}{e} = 0.368$$

(Where more places are desired, tables of e^{-x} give $e^{-1} = 0.3678794412$.)

If 1,000 hours has been established as the period of useful life of the part, the probability of failure will increase markedly above this 1,000-hour limit because wear-out will begin to play a role in its reliability.

The Mean Time Between Failures

Closely connected with the failure rate is the concept of mean time between failures (MTBF). This is simply the average (or expected) time between failures which can be approximated by dividing the total operating time by the total number of failures. If the failure rate λ is constant, it is reciprocally related to the mean time between failures m. That is, $m = \frac{1}{\lambda}$. If the item represented is not repairable, mean time between failures is referred to as the *mean life,* or *mean time to failure.*

The above relations apply in the case of exponentially distributed times-to-failure. The failure rate λ in any period of time can be computed by taking the ratio of the failures f during the operating period to the number of equipments N at the start of the operating period, that is $\lambda t = \frac{f}{N}$. This formula (equality) is sometimes referred to as the failure hazard. The exponential distribution is expressed as

$$f(t) = \lambda e^{-\lambda t} \tag{2}$$

and is a special case of the so-called two-parameter Weibull probability density function

$$f(t) = \alpha \lambda t^{\alpha - 1} e^{-\lambda t^{\alpha}}, \tag{3}$$

when $\alpha = 1$.

Extreme care must be used in handling such problems in reliability. The failure rate λ can be any variable and integrable function of the time t. $R(t)$ describes reliability in a most general way and applies to all possible kinds of failure distributions. For this case, the general expression for λ is a function of the derivative of R with respect to t and is

$$\lambda = -\frac{1}{R}\frac{dR}{dt} \tag{4}$$

The hazard rate or instantaneous failure rate, denoted in some texts as $z(t)$, is defined as the limit of the failure rate as the interval length approaches zero. The hazard rate is sometimes written as

$$z(t) = -\frac{1}{R(t)}\frac{dR(t)}{dt} = \frac{f(t)}{R(t)} \tag{5}$$

which can also be written as

$$z(t) = -\frac{d \ln R(t)}{dt} \tag{6}$$

This failure rate or hazard r is expressed in terms of failures per unit of time, such as failures per hour or failures per 100 or 1,000 hours. It is computed as a simple ratio of the number of failures f during a specified test interval t which is used to indicate a small time interval, T as the sum of all test intervals t. When more than one unit is under test, this sum should be multiplied by n to obtain the total test time T. The equation for r is

$$r = \frac{f}{T}, \tag{7}$$

where r = failure rate, failures per hour (fph),
f = total number of failures for the test interval, and
T = total test hours.

Where the number of survivors in a reliability test is s and the duration of the survival time of each during the test interval t in hours equals the total number of test hours T, the average number of survivors is $\bar{s}$, and the test interval is t, then

$$r = \frac{f}{\bar{s}t} \tag{8}$$

When a design is mature, this failure rate is fairly constant during the operating or service life period.

An explanation of hazard rate and failure rate is given by the following analogy. If one completes an automobile trip of 150 miles in 3 hours, the average rate is $\frac{150}{3} = 50$ mph, although the car was sometimes driven at only 20 miles per hour and other times at 55 miles per hour. The 50 mph is analogous to the failure rate and the speed at any point of the trip is analogous to the hazard rate or instantaneous failure rate.

Statistical data on the failure-free performance of parts with the respective periods of operation are gathered and tabulated. This is accomplished by observing a number of the units in operation, measuring the time of failure-free performance, and counting the number of failures during the observation period. When sufficient data on times to failure are taken, the mean time to failure or mean time between failures can be closely estimated.

During the operating time of the part, the mean time between failures is the ratio of the total operating time to the total number of failures. As noted previously this is the reciprocal of the constant failure rate and is given by the expressions

$$m = \frac{1}{\lambda}, \quad \text{and} \quad R_t = e^{-\frac{t}{m}} \quad \text{or,} \quad R(t) = e^{-\frac{t}{\text{MTBF}}} \tag{9}$$

Mean time between failure should not be confused with mean life. While mean life is used to describe a case in which the arithmetic mean of the time to failure is calculated, the mean time between failure describes components that are replaced upon failure and is a ratio of the total operating time to the total number of failures. MTBF has real meaning only as a replacement model.

Wear-out Failures

Products are similar to human beings: they are created, they function for a period of time, and then they wear out. Like humans, there is no escaping the fact that products ultimately fail or wear out. Products inevitably depreciate and wear to the point that they can no longer be used for their intended purposes. This type of failure is caused either by the normal wear of parts or by fatigue.

The time that it takes a component or product to wear out varies with the product and conditions of service. An electric iron, for example, may last ten years or even longer if it is always used the way it should be. But if it were subjected to severe operating conditions, such as repeated dropping or long periods of idleness at a high temperature, it would probably have a shortened useful life. Also, if a machine that was designed to operate ten years did not have sufficient lubrication and maintenance, its life would be appreciably shortened. The automobile may be cited as another example. Even the novice realizes that servicing a car is mandatory if it is to perform for a reasonable period of time. It is also known that the life of a car is dependent on the treatment it is subjected to, and that parts such as batteries, lights, tires, and brakes need periodic replacement. Thus, early failure can be brought about in products through negligence, abuse, and misuse.

Maintainability

Relationship of Maintainability to Reliability

Maintainability, defined in a generic sense, is that combination of design characteristics of a product that will permit or enhance the accomplishment of maintenance by personnel of average skill under conditions in which the equipment will operate. While reliability is concerned with *how long* a part will remain effective, maintainability involves essentially the restoration of a product or component back to usefulness. Reliability and maintainability are interrelated; an adequate program of maintenance will add to the probability that the equipment will reach its lifetime expectancy.

Types of Maintainability

Maintainability programs may apply either to the machinery which is used to fabricate products, or to the products themselves. Such programs are implemented to (1) maintain machines and processes which are used to manufacture the products and (2) to maintain finished products during periods of use and storage. Much equipment requires scheduled and systematic replacement of parts to achieve reliability assurance.

Maintainability may be broken down into two major categories, (1) preventive maintenance, and (2) corrective maintenance. Preventive maintenance may be further classified into *ongoing maintenance,* which is required for the normal operation of the equipment and *replacement maintenance,* requiring periodic replacement of parts to preclude failure. An example of ongoing maintenance is the frequent oiling of a machine by the operator to keep it operating at the desired degree of accuracy. Another example is the regular servicing of an automobile to prevent excessive wear of parts. Replacement maintenance involves the planned temporary shutdown of an operation or even an entire plant for the purpose of replacing worn parts with new parts before a failure occurs.

The life expectancy of some parts is less than for others in any given system. The performance lives of components differ because of the many variations in design, materials and processes of manufacture, workmanship, and conditions under which the parts are used. Consequently, in order to attain the highest degree of reliability, a program of preventive maintenance may be necessary to provide a procedure and method whereby parts having low reliabilities can be replaced by parts of longer life expectancy.

Some quality programs are concerned essentially with the quality of units undergoing repair and refurbishment. For example, the shipyards across the country have very large and detailed programs of maintainability. Ships of many varieties must be periodically drydocked and must undergo numerous tests of quality and attendant repair. This repair work covers a multitude of tasks, varying from replacing engines or guidance systems to repairing certain sections of the deck or hull. Occasionally the giant propellers of the ships also need repair. The photograph in figure 9-10 illustrates a portion of a propeller blade that was found to be in need of repair. Such parts must be restored according to strict standards which govern their performance.

Preventive maintenance is mandatory for such agencies as airlines. Parts replacement in airplanes is done in strict accordance with a thoroughly planned program of preventive maintenance. Tires on the DC-8, for example, are replaced regularly after approximately 110 to 120 flights in cold weather and after approximately 70 to 80 flights in hot weather, whether they appear to need it or not.

Corrective maintenance involves corrective action after a failure has occurred. This type of maintenance ordinarily has cost consequences. An example might be the failure of a bearing in a very critical machine. This type of failure can result in the idleness of many people in the plant. If the machine is part of the production line, for example, the entire line may have to be shut down during the corrective action. The need to implement a preventive maintenance program should be carefully weighed against the probability of failure and consequent costs of corrective action.

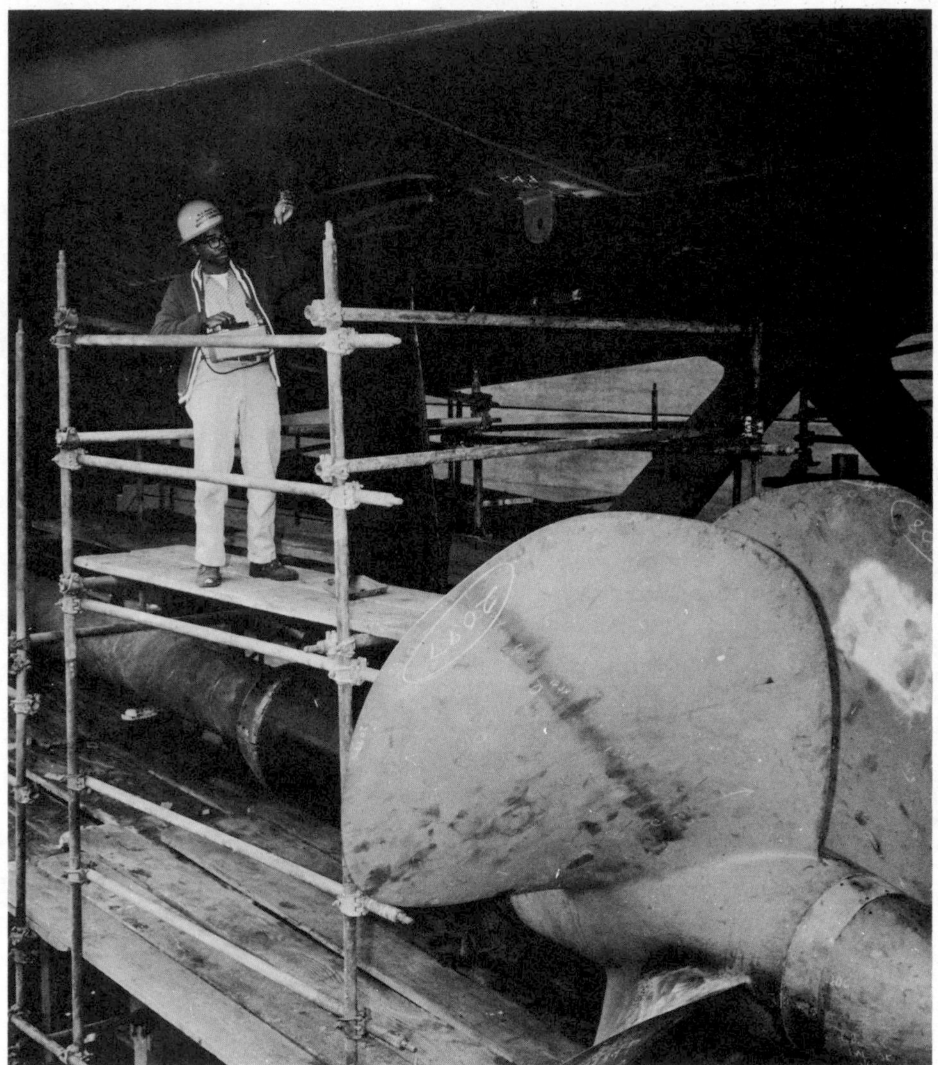

Figure 9–10 Propeller in need of repair.

Characteristics of Maintainability

Present-day trends in liability suits make it imperative that an organized program of preventive maintenance be established for many products. Under today's liability laws, a single failure can bankrupt a company, especially when the loss of human lives is involved. Airline corporations, for example, maintain highly organized maintainability programs to preclude aircraft failure and consequent litigation.

Maintainability is so important to the satisfactory operation of some products that maintenance test articles may be an integral portion of equipment design. Such a design enables scheduled tests to be made with the built-in preventive maintenance equipment. Also, tests may be made to detect sources of trouble in the parent system. The cost justification for such built-in testing apparatus is found in the fact that it is primarily a cost avoidance measure. Such equipment can be designed so that it not only can be operated without a high degree of skill, but it also can be used to detect problems which, if not detected, would result in substantial corrective maintenance costs.

9.5 The Role of Statistics in Reliability

It has been correctly stated that the reliability of a product or system is a parameter inherent in the design of the item. Since system design techniques have not yet reached perfection from the reliability standpoint, it is generally necessary to conduct system reliability tests. These tests, which may be conducted independently or in conjunction with other engineering tests, are usually proposed to investigate possible design deficiencies or to demonstrate reliability. Field maintenance reports also provide a source of reliability information which may be applied to increase the field reliability of equipment.

Information from tests or actual operations must be systematically organized and analyzed in a scientific manner if optimum reliability benefits are to be gained. The results of such a reliability analysis provide a sound basis for the evaluation, prediction, and improvement of reliability. Through the detailed analysis of reliability data, a study is made of:

1. Environmental conditions,
2. Operating and maintenance procedures,
3. Modes of failure,
4. Component and part behavior, and
5. Design considerations.

In order to inspire confidence, a reliability analysis should be designed and executed with scientific accuracy and objectivity. Many reliability data are highly variable and show unexpected and complex relationships, making it necessary to make a systematic collection and classification of facts on the basis of relative number or occurrence as a ground for the inference of general truths about the system. The above phrase is one definition of *statistics*.

As an elementary example of a case in which the statistician can aid the technologist, consider the problem of estimating the reliability of a weapon from firing tests. A random selection of five weapons of a particular kind is made from the manufacturer's production lot. As a test, the five weapons are fired immediately following a successful checkout, and it is found that four are successful, while one is unsuccessful. The estimated reliability is 0.8. However, it is not unlikely that if more samples of five were fired, all five weapons of the sample would be successful, or that perhaps three out of five would be successful. If the results are examined critically, questions arise concerning the best estimate of reliability, the limits within which the estimate is likely to vary, and the confidence that can be placed on the limits. The statistician can help the engineer give answers to such questions based on objective, rigorous, mathematical logic.

The example cited above is only one of the many types of problems in which statistical methods may be profitably employed. However, these problems all have one important common factor, i.e., an attempt to make inferences about a population based on a sample that is chosen to be representative of the population.

In order to make a statistical analysis of reliability data, a complete description of the reliability characteristics of the system under investigation is desired. The following are the more important types of data which are typically required.

1. The geographical location in which the system is employed.
2. The identification of the installation including the serial number by which the system is uniquely identified.
3. Total system cumulative operating time at the occurrence of failure.
4. A description of failure symptoms including performance measurements.
5. Detailed information concerning the repair, including a full description of

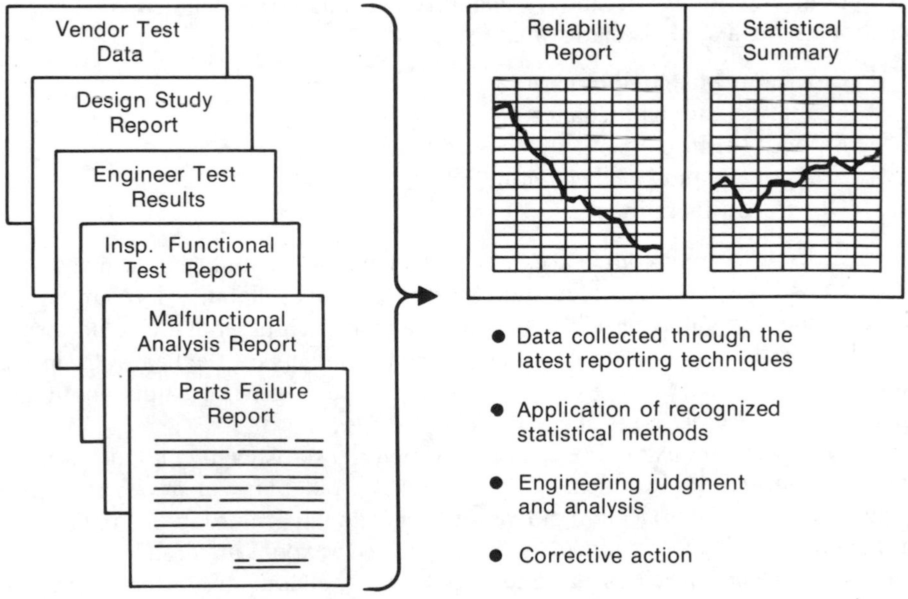
● Basically a program consists of four steps—including comprehensive and controlled evaluation of performance data and expedient corrective action
Vendor Test Data
Design Study Report
Engineer Test Results
Insp. Functional Test Report
Malfunctional Analysis Report
Parts Failure Report
Reliability Report
Statistical Summary
● Data collected through the latest reporting techniques
● Application of recognized statistical methods
● Engineering judgment and analysis
● Corrective action

Figure 9–11 Steps for a reliability program.

the parts replaced, adjustments made, and exact location of the fault in the system.

6. A record of checkout measurements.

Figure 9-11 indicates in a general manner how a reliability program might function. It points out especially that when failure reports are made, corrective action should be taken.

Figure 9-12 indicates the flow of data from the field to the central data processing function. It indicates what output covering field evaluation studies

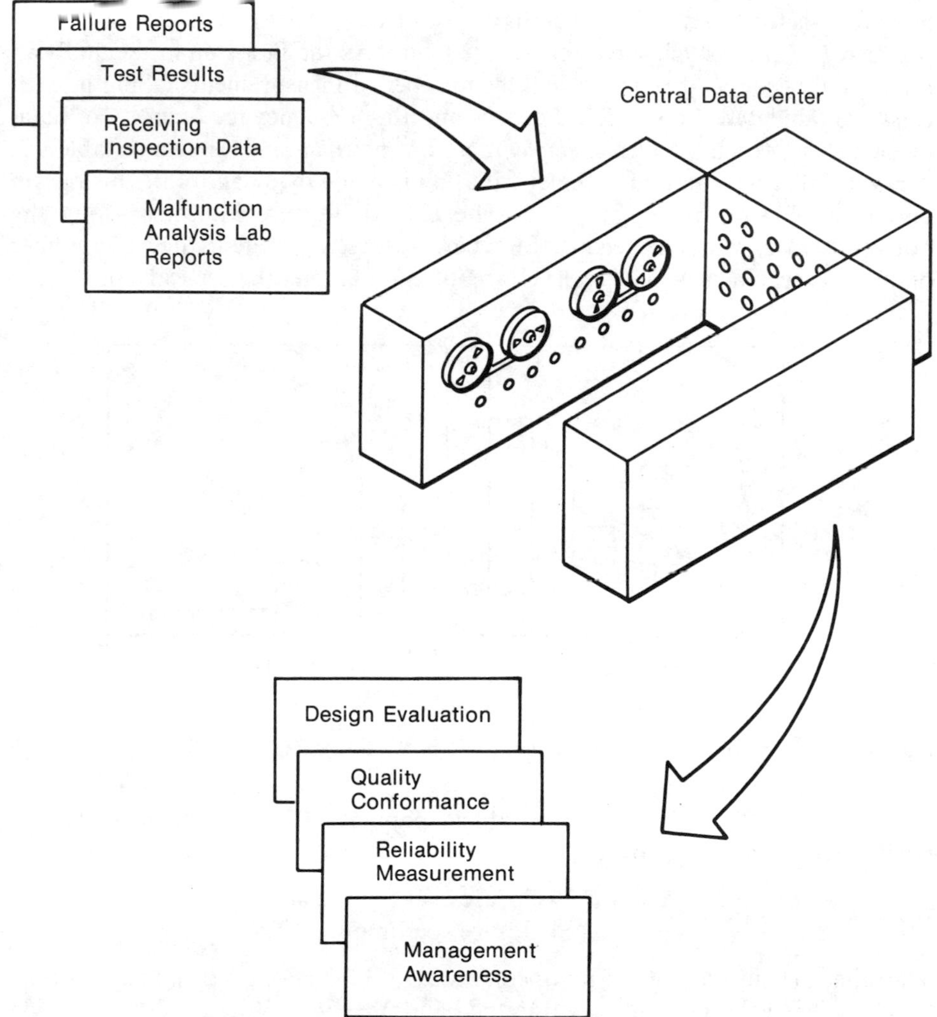

Figure 9–12 Data processing and analysis.

should be provided to top management to provide maximum reliability for products now operating and those currently being made by production.

9.6 Frequency and Probability Distributions

Normally, one of the first steps in analyzing the sample is to determine a simple frequency distribution. This process can be described by the example about the valves.

Table 9.1 shows the measured repetition rates of a random sample of 119 valves drawn from the problem population previously mentioned. An examination of the table reveals little, beyond the fact that most of the measurements fall in a range between 100 and 120 closures per minute (cpm). As the first step in the analysis, the data are grouped by classes, and the number of measurements falling in each class are tabulated. This series of classes and the frequency (or quantity of data) in each class, which is called a *simple frequency distribution,* is shown in table 9.2. A graphical representation of the distribution is made by means of the histogram or bar-graph shown in figure 9-13. The class limits are indicated along the horizontal axis, while the heights of the bars, representing the frequency (number of occurrences) in each class interval, are measured along the vertical axis.

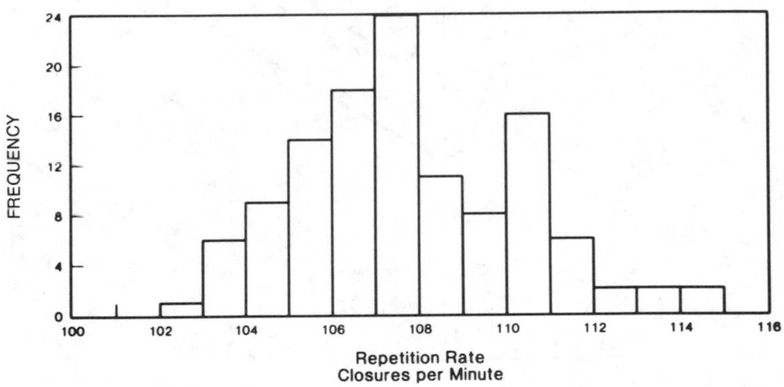

Figure 9–13 Histogram of frequency distribution of valve data, $n = 119$.

For these 119 valves from the problem population, the sample statistics are completed, giving the following average and standard deviation values.

$$\bar{X} = 107.76 \text{ closures per minute and}$$
$$\sigma = \quad 2.54 \text{ closures per minute.}$$

The range in values for the 119 numbers is 102.1 to 114.9. For a normal distribution, 99.73% of the values should be within the band $\bar{X} \pm 3\sigma = 107.76 \pm 3(2.54)$, giving a theoretical range of 100.14 to 115.38. Since failure reports indicated that failures tended to occur when a valve failed to have at least 110 closures per minute,

TABLE 9.1 Repetition Rates of Valves Sampled

Repetition Rates of Valves Sampled Closures Per Minute n = 119							
107.7	109.4	105.2	110.6	103.3	107.4	110.9	109.5
108.2	104.4	108.3	105.0	111.9	105.3	113.5	107.8
105.4	106.1	109.6	105.1	110.1	107.8	110.6	104.4
104.8	107.3	109.9	110.4	104.4	110.7	106.9	107.2
108.6	108.9	111.2	112.5	104.5	111.3	105.1	110.0
107.2	108.6	111.3	109.3	103.3	107.8	108.1	113.7
108.3	104.1	105.7	110.7	110.5	106.8	103.6	110.9
105.0	107.2	108.8	106.1	107.7	110.6	110.9	106.5
112.8	106.0	106.8	108.6	109.7	108.5	113.7	106.5
110.1	109.8	105.8	103.7	102.1	103.5	106.0	105.7
109.6	104.5	111.6	111.1	110.6	104.3	107.9	107.8
106.6	107.6	106.6	107.8	106.7	107.8	106.0	107.2
114.4	106.2	107.5	107.2	107.1	109.6	114.9	107.7
107.4	104.7	107.7	105.2	105.8	107.7	106.7	106.1
110.2	110.4	108.6	106.0	106.9	113.7	103.7	

TABLE 9.2 Simple Frequency Distribution of Valve Sample Data

Repetition Rate—Closures per Minute n = 119	
Cell Boundaries	
Class (cpm)	*Frequency (Number)*
102–103	1
103–104	6
104–105	9
105–106	14
106–107	18
107–108	24
108–109	11
109–110	8
110–111	16
111–112	6
112–113	2
113–114	2
114–115	2
Total	$n = 119$

these data had an average value less than 110. Hence, to improve the reliability of these valves whose production samples had a standard deviation value of 2.5, corrective action should be taken to increase the average by 12 units to 110 + 4(2.5 = 120 closures per minute, 12.24 units larger than the current average of 107 : 76 units.

A further examination of the frequency distribution histogram indicates that the data are scattered about the central value within a range of approximately 7 cpm on either side of 108 cpm. As brought out in previous chapters, the statistic most commonly used to describe this dispersion or spread of the data is the standard deviation, which is expressed by the formula

$$\sigma_X = \sqrt{\frac{1}{n}\sum_{i=1}^{n}(X_i - \bar{X})^2}$$

After design engineering had modified the specifications for production and after manufacturing changes were in effect, a sample of 100 modified valves were checked, giving the following statistics.

$$\bar{X} = 120.5 \text{ and}$$
$$\sigma = 2.36$$

These 100 valves were then tested to failure and provided an MTBF value of 1200 hours. Average testing time was 50 days with operation of 24 hours per day. The complete operation required about 60 days, under a rush schedule for design engineering and manufacturing.

This example emphasizes the need to have reliability designed into the product and then verified through qualification testing. Sufficient functional testing should be completed to assure the reliability expected. In the case of these valves, the customer desired a mean life of 1,000 hours of failure-free operation. The modified design provided 1200 hours as the MTBF with a small standard deviation value of about 70 MTBF, so that the lower three-sigma limit in terms of mean time between failures was 1200 − 3(70) = 990 hours, only 10 hours less than the desired absolute minimum of 1,000 hours.

One other factor related to the evaluation of reliability is required. What confidence do the consumer and the producer have that the reliability values as determined are correct and will be obtained in future products? Confidence levels, often termed the degree of belief, P_b, are established from sample life test results for desired confidence levels such as 98%, 99%, 99.73%, or 99.99%. For example, for space missions $P_b = 99.99\%$ was desired for $R = 99.99\%$. This gave a possibility of 16,000 minor failures for this mission, using exceedingly complex systems. In the flight, only four errors occurred. This actual flight result increased the confidence level to $P_b = 99.99999\%$. This reliability result is equivalent to the occurrence of only one failure in the usual type of automobile occurring after 35 years of operation under standard driving conditions.

EXERCISES

1. Define *reliability*. Explain the relation between reliability and maintainability. What is the difference between reliability and quality control?

2. Discuss the position that reliability engineering has with design engineering.

3. How are reliability levels achieved? If perfect reliability could be achieved, what would this mean?

4. Discuss the validity and implications of the following statements.
   (a) Quality is *designed* into a product.
   (b) Quality is *built* into a product.
   (c) Quality is *inspected* into a product.

5. What is meant by the expression *safety in design*?

6. In system design, with the same number of components, is reliability increased most by series design or redundant design?

7. If parts R_1, R_2, and R_3 in a system have respective reliabilities of 0.78, 0.85, and 0.98, what is the system reliability with the parts in series? In parallel? What is the system reliability if parts R_1 and R_2 were in series and R_3 in parallel?

8. Compared to the normal operating period, is the probability of failure more or less during the burn-in period? During the wear-out period? Explain your answer.

9. Utilizing the exponential reliability function, if the failure rate is $\lambda = 0.0001$, and the normal life of the part is 3,000 hours, what is its reliability after 200 hours of operation? What is the MTBF?

10. Performance observations of a system indicate that 175 failures occur in 1,475 total hours of operation. What is the approximate MTBF? If the failure rate is constant, over the 1,475 hours of operation, what is the estimated failure rate?

11. Calculate system reliability from the following data.

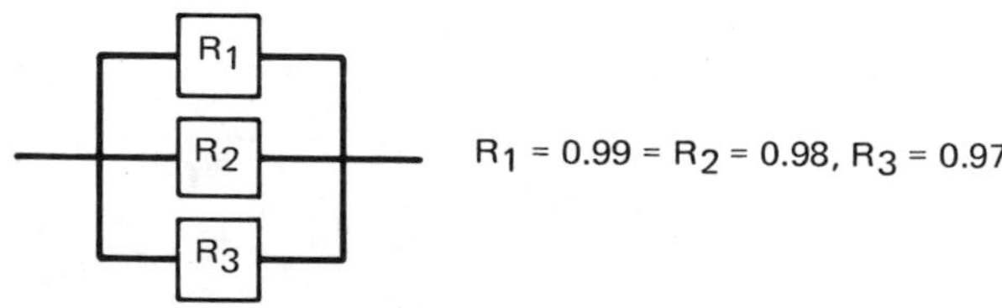

12. If the components of exercise 11 were placed in the following arrangement, what would R_s be?

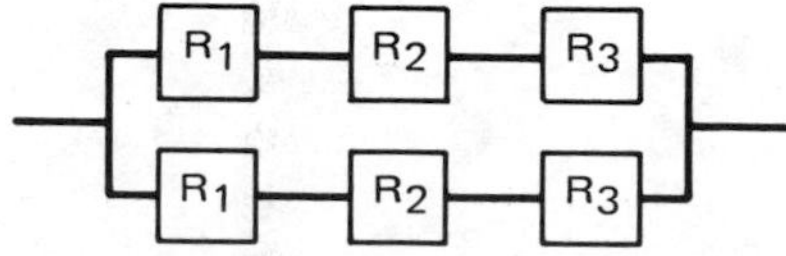

13. If a system reliability of 0.998 is required, what reliability of two identical components in series is required?

14. Given mean time to failure of 200 hours for each of two components, what is the probability of failure if both components operate in series for one hour?

15. If a test is run for 500 hours and five failures are observed during this period, what is the mean time between failures?

PART TWO
MANAGERIAL CONCEPTS

Introduction

This part covers those aspects of a company in which management decision weighs so heavily on the efficacy of the quality system. From the time that a contract is negotiated, during design and manufacturing stages and through customer relations, this management influence on quality is felt.

Understanding and applying statistical concepts to quality control work are of the utmost importance in many companies. Any student of modern quality control should be sufficiently competent in statistical concepts not only to understand statistical theory and how it relates to quality control and reliability, but also to know when, where, and how much of this theory should be applied to certain work. However, statistics is primarily a tool used by management in decision making, and there are many broader issues with which management is continuously confronted that a student of quality control should also understand. This chapter and those that follow deal with management functions as they pertain to quality control. They cover quality objectives and how they are economically met, and present management philosophy and attendant practices that should be exercised in managing a business. These are very broad concepts which can be broken down into two principal categories.

1. *The extent to which there exist good relations between manager-employee, and top management-midmanagement as they pertain to policies, budgets and attitudes.* Policy statements about quality are evidences of the philosophy or attitudes top management has regarding quality expectations. If policy statements are in any way inadequate or if they are ambiguous, this is the first step toward the development of quality problems.

   The more thorough the management is in generating policy statements and making certain that these are followed by other appropriate communications (directives, specifications, interoffice memoranda and procedures, etc.), the greater the chance that quality-mindedness will be developed in the organization and good quality delivered to customers. Policy statements and directives on quality issued by management are, in essence, standards to which management expects employees ultimately to work. Such written forms of communication set the scene for the kinds of attitudes employees have about quality and efficiency with which quality objectives are achieved.

Also, management support of quality organizations is clearly evidenced by the operating budgets which are allocated to the quality departments. Without appropriate budgets, quality departments may encounter serious obstacles, but often must make the best of the situation.

2. *The extent to which management exercises their functions of planning, organizing, leading, and controlling activities.* Top management must take into account the need for quality planning, and see to it that adequate budgets are provided. It is sometimes easy to slight functions that have been created primarily for the purpose of planning activities. Management often gets caught up into the vicious cycle of "pushing parts out the door" and devoting almost all their time to corrective action and answering complaints from customers rather than calmly planning to avoid the need for corrective action. This preventive perspective, however, can only be attained through proper organization and effective leadership. An organized system must be set into motion that will allow quality functions to successfully accomplish their missions. A measure of success of a company is a measure of success of its quality organization. The success of both is dependent in great part upon how well the management organizes and leads the company successfully in collecting and evaluating quality costs; planning, implementing, and supporting quality audits; and conjuring in the minds of all the employees the general attitude of "doing the job right the first time."

CHAPTER TEN

ORGANIZATION AND MANAGEMENT FOR PRODUCT ASSURANCE

10.1 Objective

The purposes of this chapter are fourfold. Discussed subsequently in detail, they provide the basic foundations for the material in part 2 of this text, covering management concepts and quality systems. An important aspect in the training of any student of quality control is a fundamental understanding of industrial organization. The student should be familiar with the principles of industrial organization and how the organization provides the means to achieve quality goals. He or she should also have some knowledge of the various planning and communications media, and how they fit into the total organizational structure. In addition, a student of quality control should have a general understanding of the management aspects of running a business. This entails such factors as styles of leadership, human relations in the various operations, and modern motivational theory. Many of the issues that confront a manager under normal operating conditions are bewildering at best, and a student going into any phase of industrial quality control should have a fundamental understanding of the scope, complexity, causes, and approaches to the solutions of these problems.

10.2 Organization for Product Assurance

Organizational Factors

Organizational factors always influence product quality. Marketing and sales departments, research, development and design departments, quality control and inspection departments, and manufacturing departments all must be organized so that their respective jobs can be completed efficiently. The total system can only be as efficient as the functional elements that comprise the total system. Efficiency is maximized when both established quality levels are achieved, and costs are minimized.

Organization Scope

Whenever an activity or business gets too large for one individual to properly manage it, help from others must be sought so that the details of operation needed to get results can be shared. As the number of tasks that must be completed in a company increases, the size of the organization also must increase.

Difficulties of directing and controlling activities, however, are concomitants of organizational growth. The larger an organization becomes, the more remote top management is from the worker. And, in order for a top manager to be successful, he cannot be of a run-of-the-mill caliber. For example, when the business is a large manufacturing industry, particularly when it deals with metal products of great precision, the manager has to possess a very broad and relevant professional experience, as well as executive ability of a high order, to attain success in modern industry.

As the number of people and activities that must be controlled rises, the difficulties of communication and control increase as well. When instructions and information have to pass through many hands between the point of origin and the point at which action will result, there are delays and sometimes mistakes. One way of avoiding this is to break the organization down into smaller units, giving the manager of each unit more freedom of action—within defined limits—than would be the case if there were just one large unit.

The Organizational Unit

When the departments that will carry out the various functions have been set up, each will have a departmental head, such as a quality control manager, a production manager, a personnel director, etc. Within each department, responsibilities will be divided into sections and subsections. If one identifies the departmental head by the letter X and those in charge of sections and subsections by the letters Y, Z, and so on, a pyramidal organizational structure is formed. This structure is illustrated in figure 10-1, in which X has two subordinates of equal rank or status, Y and Z; Y has two subordinates, A and B; and Z has one sub-

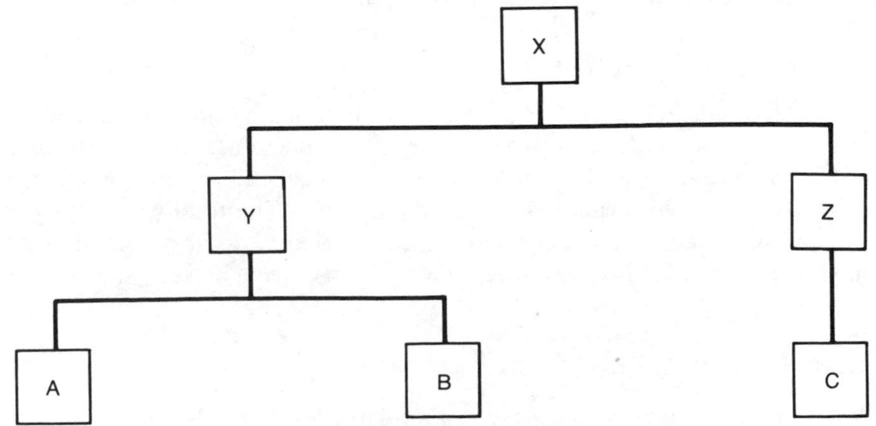

Figure 10–1 Organization chart: pyramidal diagram.

ordinate, C. It will be clear from this diagram that if Z gives orders to A, there is going to be confusion; A's superior is Y, so A could find himself being given contradictory instructions from Y and Z. He will not know which instruction to follow, and he will not be helped by the fact that Z is higher than he is in status; however, Z is not his superior. Again, X may give B an instruction that conflicts with the instructions given by Y.

The following statements illustrate two very important principles in organization.

1. Each person should have one and only one superior from whom he will take his instructions under all normal circumstances (A and B from Y; Y and Z from X).
2. Any person having subordinates may give instructions to them and to them alone, and will give orders only to immediate subordinates under normal circumstances (X to Y and Z; Y to A and B).

These relationships are called line relationships; thus A has line authority over Y and Z, Y over A and B, and Z over C. Other relationships which might exist will be considered later.

In the example given, it was assumed that the structure illustrated one department containing two sections and that X was the head of that department. The next step is to consider two separate departments, in which X has charge of one and D has charge of the other. Both X and D are responsible to a superior, R. The diagram now takes the form shown in figure 10-2. From what has been stated

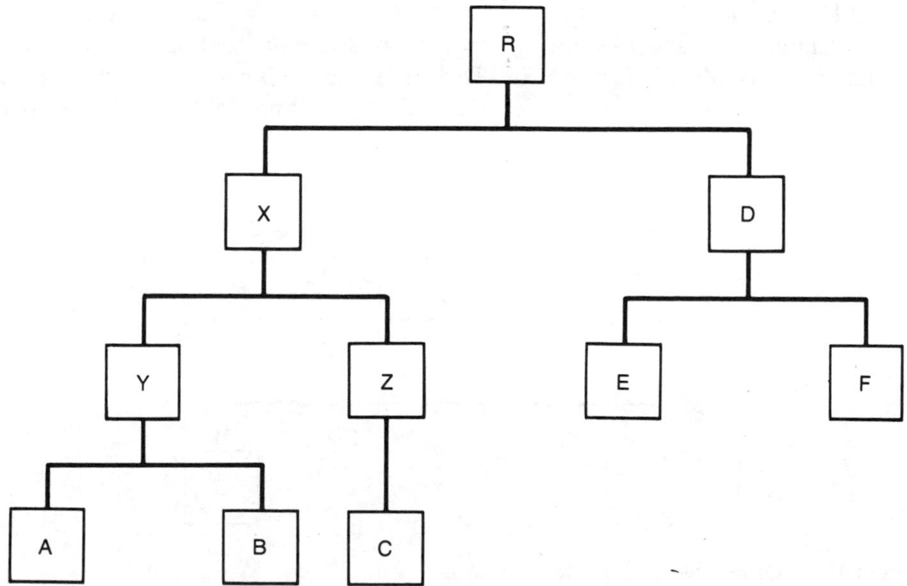

Figure 10–2 Organization chart: two-fold structure.

already, it will be clear that R's line authority follows the lines of the diagram.

If R is in charge of the production function, X is responsible for a workshop (subfunction), and D is in charge of inspection (subfunction), clearly X has no authority over D's subordinates, nor D over X's. Even so, the inspectors may work in the workshop and in close cooperation with X's subordinates. Suppose a disagreement arises. For example, X states that a component is satisfactory and D states that it is not acceptable to inspection. This can be resolved by referring the dispute to R, who has the authority to decide. But, in most cases, it is unsatisfactory to take such disagreements to R, and is made unnecessary in most cases by the adoption of a simple rule. Since D is in charge of the inspection subfunction, his decision must be accepted in all matters affecting inspection. In other words, he bears functional responsibility and his department provides an expert service for the workshop with respect to inspection. Only if X does not accept an inspection decision must he appeal for a ruling to R, who is both X's and D's superior. X cannot overrule D in any but the most exceptional circumstances. Naturally, the same applies in the reverse situation.

This is a functional relationship: the head of a functional department has line authority over his subordinates but none over those working in other departments.

Some managers or supervisors have assistants. For example, a foreman may have a clerk to assist in the orderly issue of work to the operators. A managing director may have a personal assistant to help in the task of coordinating the work of the various functional departments. In neither of these cases is the assistant a deputy; the assistant has no authority over the superior's subordinates. Diagrammatically, the assistant T is shown as in figure 10-3. T may transmit R's orders to X and D on occasion, or pass information from them to R. T may also plan the coordination of X's and D's work in order to relieve R of routine, but he or she has no authority whatever over X and D. The relationship with X and D is a *staff* relationship. If T were R's *deputy,* then the diagram would look like figure 10-4.

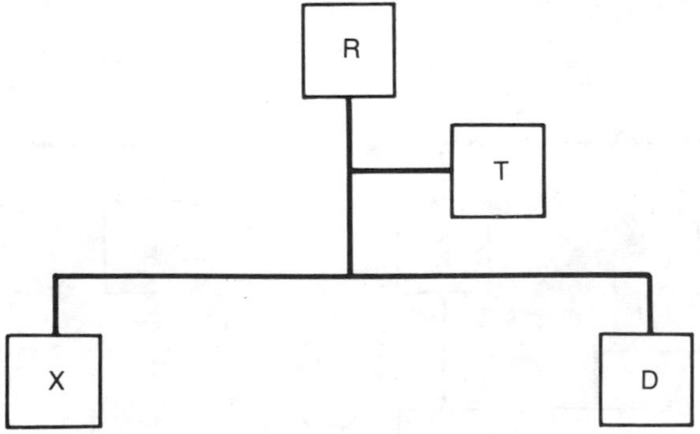

Figure 10–3 Organization chart with assistant.

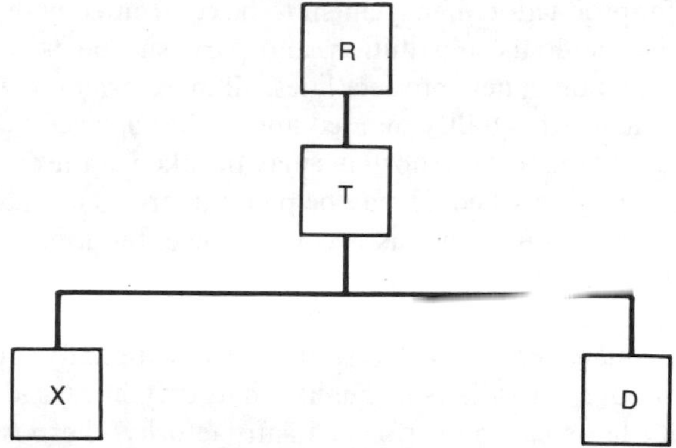

Figure 10-4 Organization chart with deputy position.

Organizing by Functional Concept

Under the functional group concept, the work is represented by objectives to be accomplished. Division of the work is accomplished by establishing functions and subfunctions (or smaller components) to actually execute the tasks.

Specific assignments are then made so that a task is equal to an individual's ability to perform a segment of the work. Measurements are adopted to determine the success or lack of success of each function and each assignment. Finally, controls are instituted so that the measurements can be established upon reported facts and substantiated with as much information as needed in order to assist in defining problems and to indicate corrective action.

The leader is responsible for the results of the work group and for knowing its objectives, functions, assignments, key measurement areas, and control procedures. He or she must know the time allotted for accomplishing the work, the relationship of the work group to other work groups, and the effects of the group's output in relation to the output of other groups. The leader must take corrective action and make changes as required by changes in objectives, shifts in functions, and the need to split or combine work groups.

Organizational Positions of Quality Functions

There is a positive relationship between the quality of a total organization and the quality of quality organizations. A total organization without character leaves little doubt that quality functions will likewise lack certain needed characteristics, since the quality structure is integrally tied to total organization.

In a plant where tasks are primarily manufacturing and where stringent quality standards are required, quality departments should be separate from production. Quality may be compromised when production management is responsible for it, unless there is a prevailing attitude among the employees to do high quality work.

It is not unusual for production management to be confronted with schedule crises, equipment failures, materials substitution, and parts shortages, and to be aggravated by the introduction of new product lines, all in a normal day's work. Unless the production manager is quality-minded and makes a special effort to uphold the quality control system, certain shortcuts may be taken at the expense of quality. The immediate production schedule may be met, but errors in quality may not be detected for quite some time, and, as a consequence, the long-range reputation of the company as a quality producer may be threatened.

There is a trend toward quality departments reporting directly to the vice-president or plant manager. With this status organizationally, quality functions have more control over the affairs of quality than they have had in the past. In order that quality tasks can be performed satisfactorily, the position of quality functions in the organization must be one in which objective analyses are always possible. Statistical quality control methodology, for example, rests in great part upon the ability of quality personnel to maintain impersonal and objective points of view, and their organizational positions are significant determinants of this ability.

Quality functions may be placed in different positions on the organization charts, as illustrated in figures 10–5, 10–6, 10–7, and 10–8. Each may be satisfactory, provided that counterpart groups are sufficiently quality-minded to ensure that the objectives of quality are achieved.

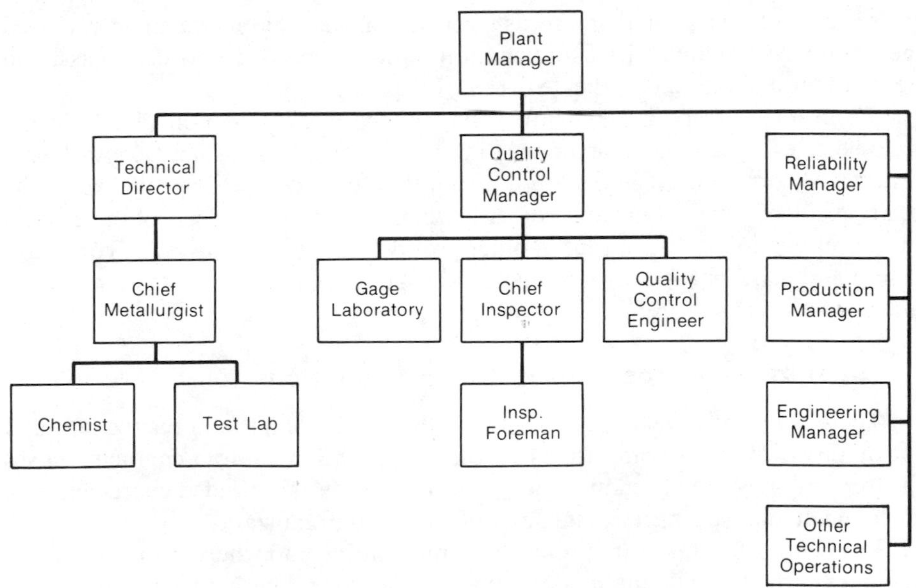

Figure 10–5 Quality control shown organizationally on an equal basis with reliability, production, engineering, and other technical operations.

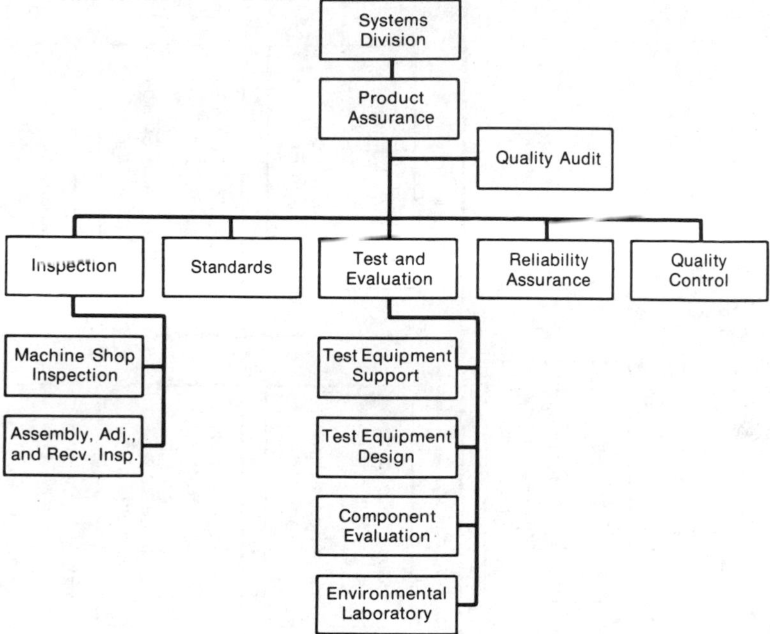

Figure 10–6 Quality control shown reporting to product assurance.

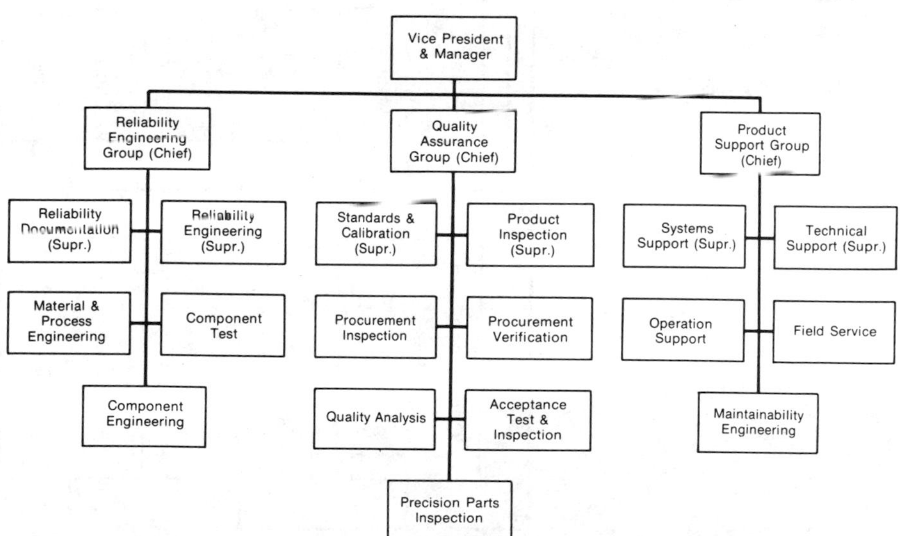

Figure 10–7 Quality assurance reporting to the vice president.

Figure 10–8 Example of a quality control organization on the basis of programs and functions.

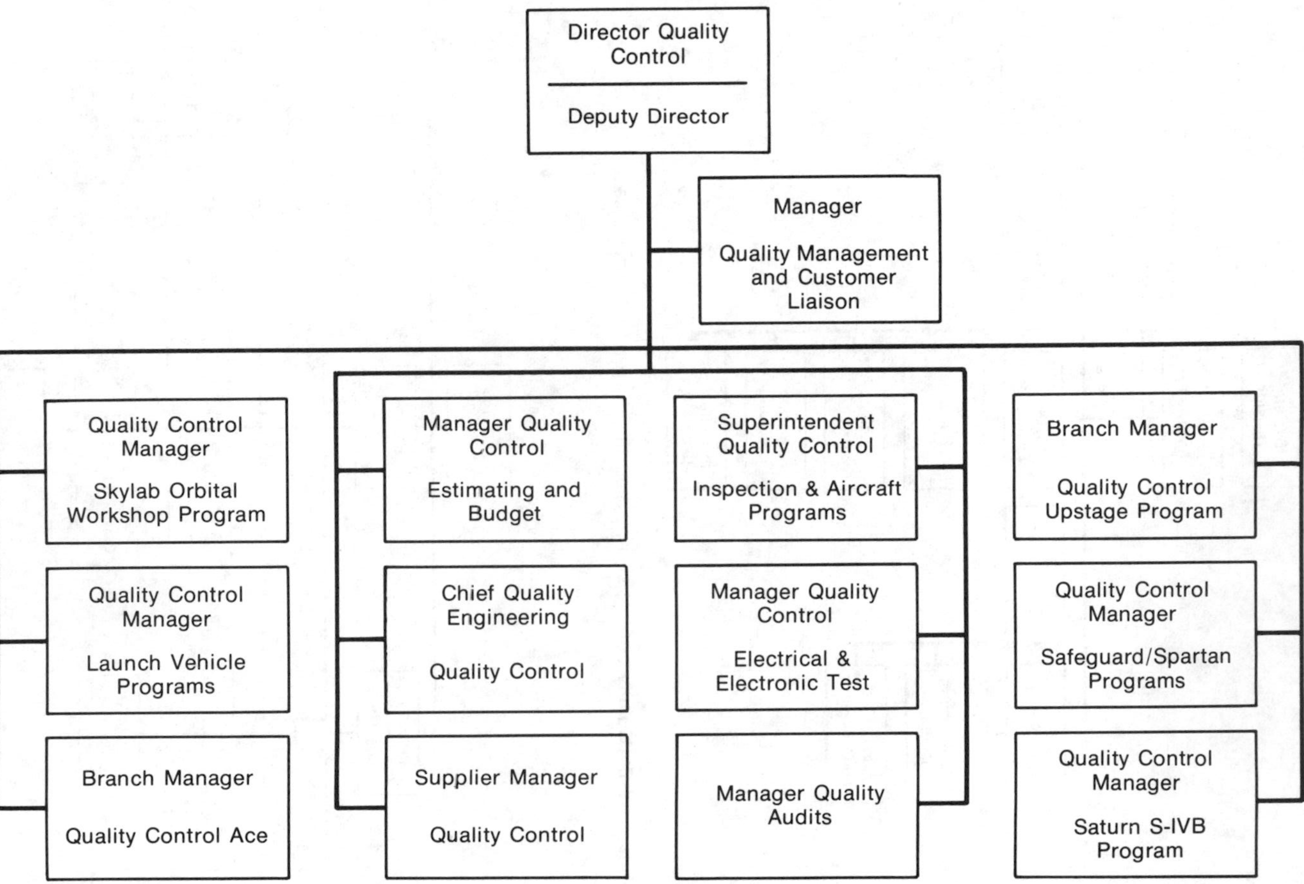

10.3 Responsibilities of Quality Control Personnel

The detailed operation of a quality control department will vary from plant to plant, depending on such variables as plant size, layout, facilities, the product, and degree of automation. Generally speaking, however, it is usually agreed that the following are the primary functions of a quality control operation.

1. Develop effective receiving, in-process, and outgoing inspection, based on running quality or requirements. Classify parts, assemblies, and characteristics subject to inspection according to their inspection complexity, and prepare and keep current inspection instruction sheets.
2. Determine current significant[1] defects based on an analysis of warranty, scrap, repair and rework costs, customer dissatisfaction criteria, and company audit results. Periodically publish a list of these defects to bring them to the attention of management and effect corrective action.
3. Devise and install a system of suitable inspection plans, and provide regular and routine inspection data such as percent defective, defects per unit, and percent acceptance. Provide criteria for measuring and reporting the quality performance of production departments and plant staff departments, and make regular evaluations of such performance.
4. Witness, monitor, and appraise vendor systems and procured articles to safeguard quality standards.
5. Analyze significant quality defects on a preventive, appraisal, and failure cost basis to (*a*) make recommendations and assign departmental responsibilities for correction, (*b*) permit cost decisions to be made intelligently, and (*c*) provide evidence of cost savings attributed to the quality control department.
6. Use recognized quality control charts, process capability studies, and other accepted quality control techniques.
7. When necessary establish, conduct, and attend periodic quality meetings to review quality progress and originate quality committees on unresolved significant quality defects.
8. Establish quality standards.
9. Maintain a gauge control program.
10. Apprise the plant manager of total annual plant quality costs in sufficient detail, and maintain "scoreboards" indicating the performance being achieved in quality improvement and quality cost reduction. Orient plant management on the general objectives and policies of the quality control system, and use persuasion effectively to sell the program.
11. Coordinate the quality activities of other departments and make every effort to have each department carry out its responsibilities for quality.
12. Obtain the support and concurrence of the plant manager in establishing critical quality standards and responsibility for corrective action on significant defects, and in defining the quality functions of other departments.

Keep the plant manager informed on current quality levels (the "big picture," not a mass of undigested data), and predict future quality trends.

13. Eliminate "firefighting" and "troubleshooting" on quality problems by quality control, production, and other personnel as much as possible by reporting and analyzing significant defects.
14. Obtain industrial engineering and plant management approval of quality control manpower requirements (including inspection) by justifying the operation on a cost basis.
15. Comply with corporate and group quality control procedures and recommendations.
16. Provide for quality control orientation of plant supervisory and staff personnel.
17. Reevaluate the plant quality control system on a continuing basis to incorporate necessary improvements.
18. Request technical assistance in the installation of the most effective quality control system from group or corporate quality control functions, if necessary.

While inspection is, and probably always will be, an essential part of quality control, there is a lot more to quality control than inspection. In fact, without good quality control, it is virtually impossible to have good inspection. Quality standards, inspection instructions, determination of which characteristics to inspect, sampling plans, reporting methods, sampling error, and data reliability must all be determined in advance before an effective inspection system can be established. Typically, the development of such an inspection system is a function of the quality engineering section.

The Need for Overall Teamwork

In dealing with work groups, teamwork is a vital factor in increasing productivity and improving quality. There are four essential conditions to successful teamwork.

1. Members of the group must have and work toward a common goal.
2. Members of the group must have good methods to be followed in pursuit of the objectives.
3. The organization must be designed so that (*a*) authority and responsibility are clearly defined, (*b*) the person or people best fitted to perform a particular task or function are assigned to it, and (*c*) instructions are clearly given in advance and fully understood.
4. The organization and work are balanced so that there is continuity between the elements of the groups and fairness among team members.

When these conditions are met, the greatest harmony and smoothness of work is attained, waste is reduced to the minimum, quality improves, and production reaches its highest level.

When an organization is planned, manned, and managed so that it develops a team spirit in the minds of its employees, it may be said to be a successful organization. To be successful, it does not need to be a vast industry with many thousands of employees, general offices in New York, and plants scattered over the country. As a matter of fact, the large organizations are often those that find it most difficult to stimulate team spirit, and it is these that have had to do the most extensive work in the field of developing personnel management. With the small plant, it should be easy for the executives to create an atmosphere of working together and to build up a team spirit that will yield greater efficiency and increased output.

If an organization does not meet these conditions for teamwork, production as a whole will be kept down to the level of the production of the weakest department. Unless each element entering into a product is ready to take its place in the manufacturing operation at exactly the time it is required, the rate of production will slow down, bottlenecks will develop, the chance of inferior quality will increase, delivery will be delayed, and the inevitable result—if such a practice becomes frequent—will be decreased sales, lowered profits, and direct hardship to all concerned in the production.

Even so small a thing as a missing screw or a delayed bolt has been known to hold up a big job, resulting in serious loss. The department or person responsible for getting that small part to the machine failed to meet the schedule and, as a consequence, the production was held back and a promised delivery date was not met. In addition to departments concerned in processing the products, the departments such as the purchasing department or the inspection department that may be considered as contributory departments have responsibilities in this connection also. The purchasing department must not let production be hampered by its tardiness in procuring a needed material or tool, no matter how small or seemingly incidental the needed article may be. The inspection department must not allow a fine manufacturing record to be spoiled by its failure to inspect and report problems promptly.

Intelligent direction is the secret of building a successful organization. The factory team is developed not through haphazard growth, but through careful planning and guidance. Thought is given to the selection of the workers; attention is given to placing them where they will do the most productive work; and pains are taken to train people for leadership. A factory team formed in this way is not something that simply emerges without direction, but is rather a balanced, smooth-running, efficient production machine. Every part of it is essential; every part is in the right place.

10.4 The Working Climate

Atmosphere

Most people would agree that the quality and volume of work in a workplace are influenced very much by the atmosphere that exists among the people who work there. If there is a general feeling of discontent, there is little desire among the workers to do a good job.

Much of a supervisor's time is spent in discussing real or imagined grievances. Personal animosities develop in an organization that can lead to situations where mistakes will have compounding effects. For example, if one employee holds a grudge against another, there is a temptation to allow that person to walk into trouble, even though the outcome is known. Petty grievances among employees always increase operating costs and add to the difficulties in meeting quality standards in one way or another.

Every individual reacts according to the way his experience in his environment makes him feel. If he feels comfortable mentally and physically, he will react favorably; if he feels uncomfortable, his reaction will be unfavorable. Individuals who are unhappy or discontented cannot produce their best work, and if the unhappiness or discontent arises because of an unsatisfactory climate of work, it is the duty of management to do all that is possible to improve matters.

The personality of a department is a vital factor in whether or not a department functions smoothly, rationally, and in an organized manner. This personality is manifested by the strength of bond between the superior and subordinates. Mutual cooperation between individuals is the foundation of confidence and the basis of permanent growth, as well as being the living spirit of an organization. Dominating every business enterprise is a controlling force, an executive whose personality stimulates others to action and guides the whole working force. Such a person should have character and strength, combined with a helpful attitude toward subordinates. He or she should keep in touch with the personnel and be ready to discuss any differences which may arise. Impartiality in dealing with employees is a virtue. Nothing fosters discontent, creates friction, and throws the working force into confusion more quickly than favoritism. Irrational behavior destroys enthusiasm, interest, and loyalty, and has no place in any business aiming at improving workmanship and increasing efficiency. The success of an organization depends largely upon the choice of the proper head, a person who has the needed character and strength to guide the organization effectively. No matter what kind of business undertaking, success depends, in great measure, upon the proper relationship existing between the management and the employees.

Attitude

The proper relationship between superior and subordinate helps to generate enthusiasm and instill a sense of loyalty in the working force. There is a direct relationship between the degree to which enthusiasm and loyalty exist in an organization and the degree that quality objectives can be met economically. The amount of work which any person may do is subject to various conditions, but intellect, feeling, and self-discipline should work together in order to obtain the best results. Where there is no feeling about the work, a serious handicap to quality work exists, even if intellect and self-discipline are strained to the utmost. The worker who is not loyal to the company usually renders only halfhearted service.

The proper treatment to obtain employees' cooperation and to arouse their interest, loyalty, and enthusiasm is one of the most difficult problems confronting every management, but its successful solution paves the way for improved quality and increased efficiency.

The attitude which employees have toward a business is governed very largely by their feelings toward the person who directs them from day to day. It should not be forgotten that people are not bits of machinery, but possess certain rights which should be respected. Recognizing the rights of workers and making them feel that they are integral parts of an organization prevents friction with an outcome of greater efficiency. A measure of efficiency is the extent to which the cooperation and the enthusiasm of the working force is sustained throughout an organization.

If foremen and superintendents know that the manager is genuinely interested in their efforts, approving, supporting, and sparing them whenever possible, they will tend to place their energy and enthusiasm in their work in achieving the greatest possible results. Similarly, if workers know that their superintendent is interested in them and aware of the quality of the work being done, they are more apt to work more industriously and have an interest in the success of the business. To secure efficiency, empathy, and mutual understanding of the person above with the person below is necessary.

10.5 Organizing and Planning Activities

Policy Determination

Policies are guidelines for action; statements of policy reflect the major objectives of the company. They are general statements in writing which stipulate preferred methods of dealing with a situation or responsibility. A policy is not an order; it is not a directive; it provides no answer to a specific problem; but it does serve to guide the application of judgment, and by so doing eases the burden of decision making. Figure 10-9 illustrates the exchange of policy information from the division manager to the quality manager.

Policies are made known throughout an organization by a myriad of communicative methods, such as those listed below.

1. Procedures manuals and instructions books.
2. Directives originating from management.
3. Miscellaneous company publications.
4. Bulletin board announcements.
5. Various verbal instructions.
6. Interoffice correspondence.

Irrespective of the media used, policies will be most successful if they possess the following characteristics.

Quality Manager
Incorporates Product Improvement Changes as Indicated by Performance.
Forwards Quality Performance Reports to Division Manager.
Division Manager
Directs Division Policy.
Informs General Offices of Progress.

Figure 10–9 Management evaluation and decisions.

1. They should be carefully formulated and recorded in writing.
2. They should be consistently enforced.
3. They should be effectively made known to all persons who should be guided by them.
4. They should be stable, yet flexible enough to accommodate unusual and unforeseen conditions.

Use of Directives

There are situations in which the exercise of judgment on the part of subordinates is not appropriate. Quality considerations sometimes dictate explicit action and preclude the desirability of alternative decisions. At other times, it is essential that an explicit directive be issued in order to secure synchronized initiation of several independently performed but interrelated actions. In such a situation, the manager is well advised to dictate just what is to be done.

For example, in an agreement between a customer and the manufacturer, it could be specified that a certain maximum number of defectives were allowable in

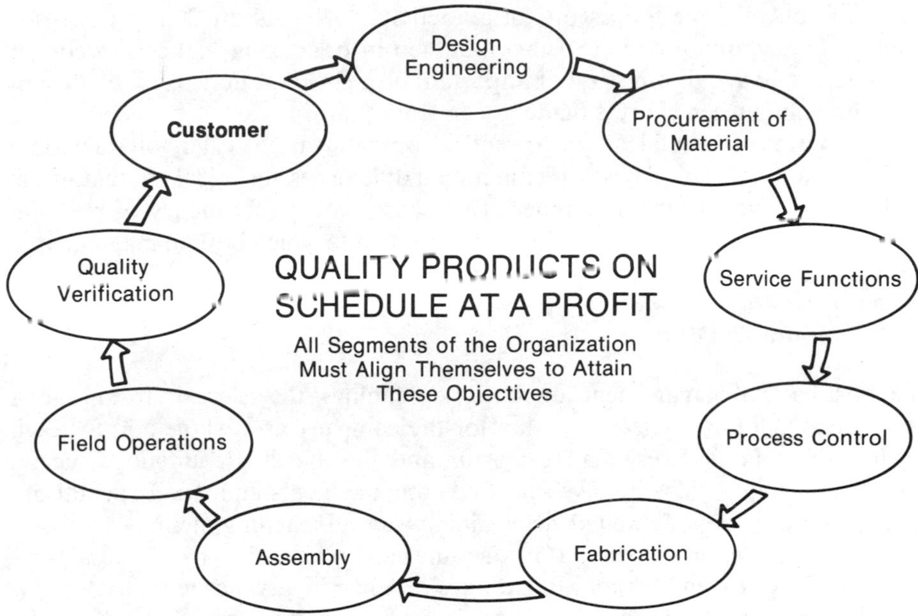

Figure 10–10 Management objectives.

all orders. Because of an urgent need for a material, the customer might be willing to accept an order as is and take his chances with the quality of the lot. A directive from top management may then order the quality organization to ship a certain number of lots with a minimum amount of inspection. Of course, such actions must be fully documented by both the customer and the management.

10.6 Organizing the Job

The task of organizing the activities so that quality products will be delivered on schedule at a reasonable profit is large in scope. This begins with top management, by whom specific objectives are set forth. Figure 10-10 illustrates the general scope of activities relevant to these tasks. Work organization and planning go hand in hand. Planned activity must be organized so that it will result in efficient action. The organizing element of managing involves a number of successive steps, such as those listed below.

1. Explicit delineation of the total activity to be organized.
2. Subdivision of the total activity to be organized.
3. Preparation of clear specifications for each job created by the subdivision process.
4. Preparation of a system of feedback so that performance can be measured.
5. Selection of people and their assignments to specific areas of responsibility.

Too frequently, the total scope of an activity to be subdivided is taken for granted. Thoughtful attention to this first step in organizing makes subsequent steps easier and avoids omission of important elements that may cause confusion and even failure when effort is made to carry out plans.

Subdivision of the total task into practical, operating units will involve a variety of considerations. Typical bases are functional differences, technical content of the work, geographic influences, number of persons involved, frequency of problem occurrence, management philosophy, and the extent to which both managerial and nonmanagerial work is required.

10.7 Planning Work

The most basic of management functions is planning—the selection from among alternatives of future courses of action for the company as a whole and for each department within it. Every manager plans, and all subordinate functions depend upon his planning. Plans involve selecting company goals and departmental objectives and programs, as well as determining ways of reaching them.

A plan predetermines action. It bridges the gap between the position at a point in time and the desired position. Planning is deciding in advance what to do, how to do it, where to do it, and who is to do it. It provides a rational scheme by which things happen that would not happen otherwise. Output can never be completely independent of chance factors, but inadequate planning will most certainly contribute to the rapid increase of problems.

To do an effective overall job of planning, whether at the department level or at the top executive level, the manager must always start with a clear-cut knowledge of the objectives of his particular part of the organization. Until these objectives are clearly defined, known and understood by all, his planning will be hit-and-miss, whether it is short-range or long-range. The president of a company cannot expect his factory superintendent to plan effectively and as desired, unless both the superintendent and the president have clear and explicit knowledge of what the superintendent's objectives are. The more this requirement of definitive objectives is common practice throughout all levels of the organization, the better the organization will function.

Many planning functions have failed because the planners have worked without a plan that defined the task and set dates for the completion of the work. A good first step, therefore, is to make an assessment of the status of planning within the company and determine what end result is wanted, what work is required, who should do the work, and how long it should take. Good business involves the art of selecting probabilities, while poor business results from taking chances on mere possibilities.

Sound concepts, visions, forecasts of coming events or needs, or estimates of conditions by leaders in the company are fundamentals in business preparedness. Experience shows that the most successful companies are those in which the least number of factors have been left to chance. Lack of preparedness is always rooted in lack of foresight or inaccurate estimates. It is not known how many poor predictions of the future are made, on the average, by professional forecasters or top management, but it is certain that in some companies, planning, preparedness, and clear thinking are not too prominent. Many industrial and business ventures fail early because of misguided objectives and poor planning. Such failures are sometimes concealed until capital has been hopelessly wasted upon a project; various more obvious but secondary reasons are then advanced for the collapse.

> I never allow myself to become discouraged under any circumstances. The three great essentials to achieve anything worthwhile are, first, hard work; second, stick-toitiveness; third, common sense.[2]
>
> Thomas Edison

10.8 Achieving Efficiency

The elimination of wastes of time, energy, or materials, no matter how slight, results in increasing efficiency. Efficiency is of special interest both to the man with a small business and to the many executives running a million-dollar corporation. Efficiency involves making a critical comparison of how things should be done with how they are done. It would appall the average proprietor or owner of a business if he or she were aware of the profits lost annually through ignorance of how the work is performed compared with how it should be performed. Every saving of scrap is a step toward greater efficiency and increased profits. Efficiency has assumed such importance that it is considered one of the fundamentals of the industrial system.

Meeting quality standards at lowest unit cost and efficiency are contiguous. Failure, waste, and the need for rework, by definition, oppose efficiency. Every time work must be redone, an element of inefficiency has already been introduced.

Inefficiency is introduced in a business organization in a multitude of ways. Traditionally, *method* has been the factor most often referred to when effort is made to improve efficiency. There are, however, many other variables in every business enterprise that influence the degree to which wastes are generated. These include leadership, communications, and attitudes of employees.

Methods

Everything else being equal, good methods contribute more to increased output than any other factor. Ironically, the methods found in many business enterprises are not the result of carefully and properly conducted investigation, but are instead those guessed to be best by the management and the workers. It frequently happens that a person, working as hard as possible, falls short of what could be done because of excessive delays and inferior methods in his work.

Every operation in a business enterprise may be performed in a number of ways, and it is evident that all are not equally efficient. As a rule, many are so inefficient that if only a slight investigation were made, they would be discarded at once.

There is usually one best way to do a piece of work and that way should be used in every business enterprise. Few workers know the best way of doing a task, and most have neither the time nor the ability to investigate different methods and select the one which is best. Not only the workers, but even the management, cannot randomly know the best method of doing a piece of work.

The presence of wrong methods means waste, lower quality, or higher costs. This is true with every kind of labor and with the performance of every kind of task. The aim of a business enterprise should be to produce stated quality with the greatest economy, with the preservation of human health, and with the least possible waste of energy or time to either man or machine.

The purpose of efficiency analysis is to eliminate waste, and this is the object of the scientific study of personnel, materials, and machines. Many businesspeople are blind to the extent of waste occurring in every business plant. Ignorance has been and is still the chief factor in causing high costs and failures. Some believe that efficiency is attained only when ideal conditions are reached. Such an ideal is not possible. Technology is dynamic; the discovery of new methods, processes, etc., continually raises standards. The pursuit of ideal conditions is an ongoing process; perfect efficiency can never be achieved, but should be diligently pursued.

System Analysis

Most companies employ either an operation analysis group or a system analysis group, or both, to study, make recommendations, and implement changes in methods. Operation analysis is an analytical process in which the factors that affect the method of performing an operation to achieve maximum overall economy are studied. The operation analysis technique consists of applying the questioning attitude separately to each part of an operation. A thorough examination is made of each of the following points of primary analysis.

1. Purpose of operation.
2. Design of part.
3. Process analysis.
4. Materials.
5. Quality requirements. (This includes both design and manufacturing.)
6. Workplace layout, tools, and equipment.
7. Materials handling.
8. Methods.
9. Working conditions.
10. Plant layout.

The operation analyst applies the questioning attitude to each of the points of primary analysis to determine as much information as possible. The information obtained through application of a questioning attitude with knowledge of possible alternatives is combined to develop suggestions for improvement. As the analyst conducts a study, suggestions for improvement are recorded on an analysis form; these suggestions are the basis for further action. Experience has shown that a thorough application of the operation analysis procedure will almost always uncover opportunities for improvement. However, the potential improvements must be acted upon before cost savings can be realized.

Utilizing Staff Personnel

A manager can often make his job run much more smoothly by utilizing the services of good staff personnel. A staff person can be a valuable aid to the quality control manager if he or she possesses the desirable attributes. The staff person can play a key role in assuring that his or her boss receives complete, accurate, and timely information for decision making. Staff personnel support the manager by supplying him or her with reports, proposals, letters ready for signature, or any other information that may be required for decision making. To be effective, however, staff personnel must have several very important personal qualifications.

1. *Staff personnel must be objective and energetic.* A staff person who is not inquiring, creative, and persistent cannot be effective in this role. A staff person must be confident that he or she has what it takes for the job. In so doing, he or she must be well versed in the general operations of the company and have the respect of coworkers. A staff person sometimes represents the second pair of eyes and ears of the manager, and as such, must have the ability to be objective and discerning about the information transmitted to the manager. Confidence in a staff person is lost rather quickly if the manager is the recipient of propaganda or too much irrelevant information from the hands of the staff person.

   A staff person must also be *persistent,* but not to the point of becoming pugnacious. Persistence and patience must be exercised in alternate cycles; that is, persistence must be followed by a period for response. Without sufficient time for understanding of the proposal to take place, an important proposal may never be approved. Too much persistence without patience can result in negative reaction, and thus can be a liability rather than an asset. Dealing with and obtaining the proper responses from other personnel is sometimes an awesome task for a staff person. This pressure can cause a novice staff person to be anxious and overly aggressive, resulting in a response completely opposite to that being sought. As a consequence, he or she may rapidly become ineffectual in this role and may never understand why. Someone has stated, "Before a person should proceed with a difficult or distasteful task, he should stop and think—then remember to get started again." This is always a good rule for a staff person to follow.
2. *Staff personnel must be able to follow through.* A staff member should work out the details of a problem as completely as possible before confronting

the manager with the problem. Only as the last resort should he or she consult the superior about the details of a problem. The term *completed action* is emphasized because there is some tendency among staff personnel to present a problem to a supervisor in a piecemeal or poorly thought out manner. It is much easier to simply ask the manager what to do in a particular situation than it is to struggle with the details. This impulse should be vigorously resisted. If additional information is needed for a report, proposal, or project, outside sources or other staff personnel should first be consulted. The staff member's job is to study, write, restudy, and rewrite until a single proposed best course of action has evolved. Then, and only then, should the package be presented to the manager for approval. (However, these tasks should not take so long that the superior becomes justifiably impatient.)

Moreover, one should not concern his boss with lengthy explanations and memoranda. The art of listening is one of the most important attributes a staff person can have. Also, writing a memorandum to a superior does not in itself constitute completed staff work, but writing a memorandum that is ready for signature (so that copies can be immediately distributed) does represent completed staff work. If the proper result is achieved, the manager usually will recognize it at once; if he wants further explanation, study, or action, he then will ask for it. At this stage, the first cycle of staff work is complete, and if the manager chooses a different course of action or requests additional work, it is his prerogative. However, the manager should recognize that the initial staff work has been completed. Completed staff work does not preclude a rough draft per se, but the rough draft must be complete insofar as the requisite concept or scope is concerned. Under no circumstances should a rough draft be used by a staff member to shift the burden of defining the details and formulating the action to the manager. Depending upon the scope of the project, completed staff work may not necessarily terminate with a completed report. If the original assignment is a report that is followed by action, set in motion by the manager's endorsement, then follow-up action by the staff person is usually a final phase that must be finished before the entire job can be considered complete. Such follow-up means that the implementation of a project may need to be monitored and usually involves submitting periodic progress reports so that the manager is apprised of all important trends.

10.9 Management-Worker Relationships

There are countless conditions that either aid management in reaching quality objectives or else inhibit it. It is not the intent here to attempt a detailed discussion of such conditions, but for purposes of illustration some may be grouped and classified.

Figure 10-11 illustrates some of the conditions relevant to manager-worker relationships that tend to preclude high quality. Conversely, figure 10-12 shows

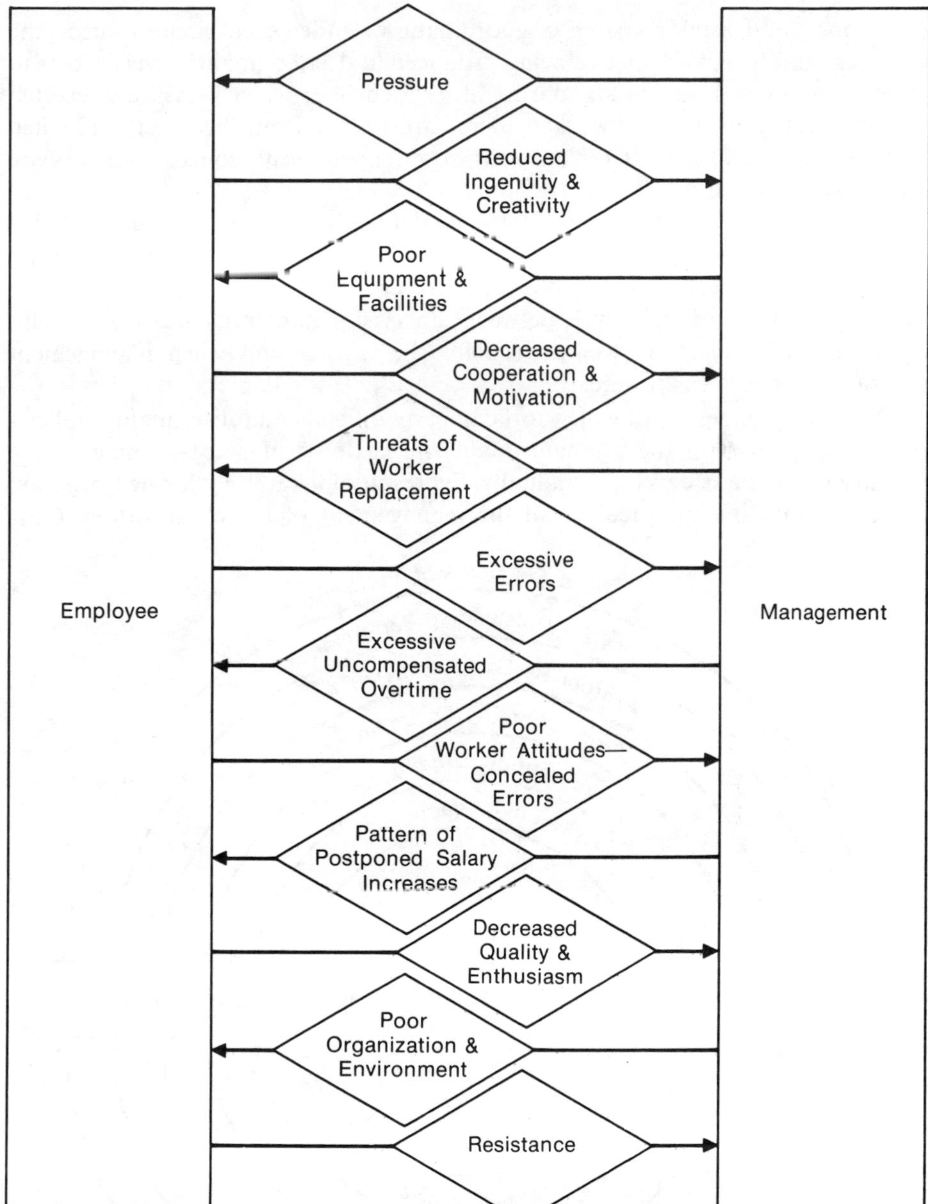

Figure 10–11 Conditions leading to poor quality— indirect and opposing responses between management and employee result in decreasing team effort and reduced overall product quality.

some of the conditions that encourage high quality. As shown in figure 10-11, the product is in the center of a poorly organized system, a poor management philosophy, and a poor system of coordination. Under such circumstances, the product has a far less chance of being produced at desired quality levels. Costs to produce to a given quality standard will be excessive; when pressure is exerted by management against the worker, there is resistance from the latter, and when there are threats of worker replacement from management, concealed errors are inevitable.

However, within the framework of well-defined objectives, a quality-minded organization, and an effective administration, a greater number of quality characteristics can be expected in the product at a lower unit cost. Figure 10-12 illustrates that the direction-response cycle between supervision and employees is more efficient when objectives are well-defined for the worker and when management portrays a supportive attitude.

The thoroughness with which top company officials establish quality policies plays a large part in the ultimate quality-mindedness of a total organization. Quality-mindedness develops gradually, the result of a carefully formed program of quality that is supported by all the management of the organization. Only

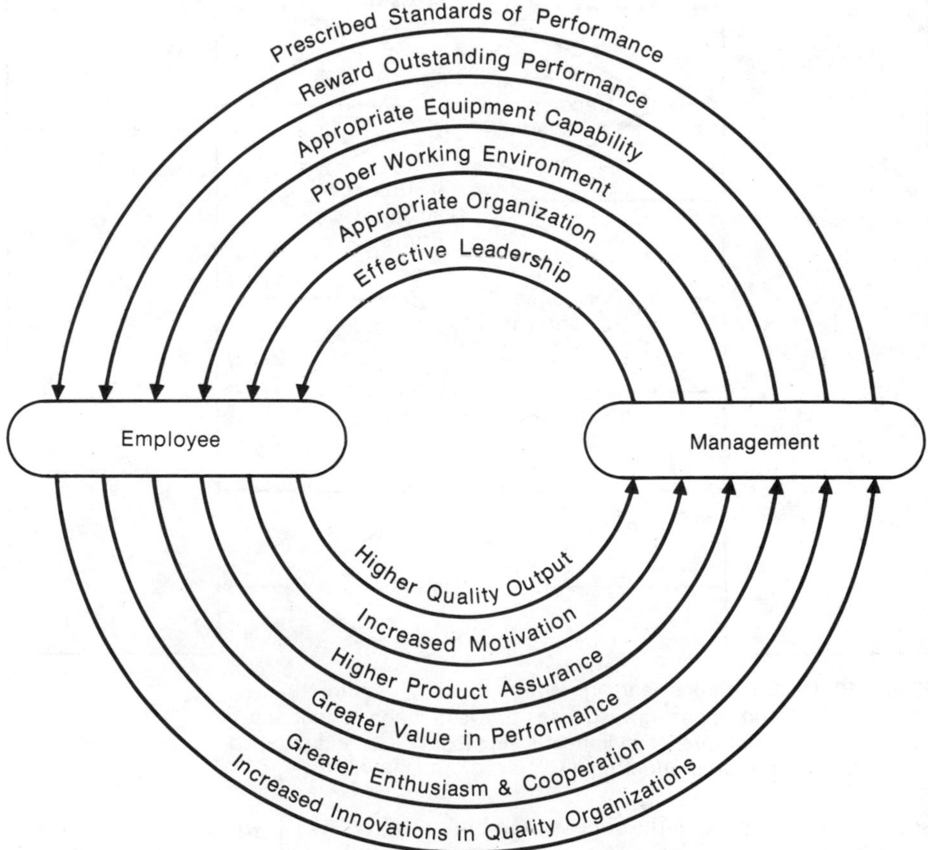

Figure 10–12 Effective management induces high product quality.

when management provides such support can habits of quality be learned by other employees. The habits of doing a job well and on schedule are learned in companies where the quality philosophy begets quality-mindedness.

Delegating Authority

The manager makes his contribution to the success of a business enterprise through other people. The manager, together with his or her employees, plans the work and organizes activities. The manager motivates subordinates and integrates their activities and evaluates the results in order that he or she may replan where necessary, reorganize, and better motivate others for whose work he or she is responsible.

Authority is delegated in an organization when power is given to a subordinate by a superior. The process of delegation involves the assignment of a task, the assignment of authority for completing the task, and the fixation of responsibility for accomplishing the task. This implies two important points: (1) the superior cannot delegate authority which he does not have, and (2) authority must be relinquished to be delegated. Potential degrees of authority are vested in the organizational levels within the hierarchial structure, but it can be delegated by those higher in the organizational hierarchy to subordinates at any given level in this structure. Of perhaps more significance is the willingness to delegate authority, as well as the willingness to accept authority, which are the first requisites for true delegation of authority.

Some managers find it very difficult to delegate authority and seem unable to enlist the aid of others. When such a situation exists, it is usually the result of a lack of confidence in subordinate personnel on the part of the manager, or the manager's fear of loss of status. In either case, the responsibility rests with management. Any situation that prevents genuine delegation of authority should be corrected, as delegation is essential to the fair distribution of tasks within an enterprise. Planned quality cannot be achieved without including a system in which some tasks are delegated to personnel below the levels of top management. Delegating is much more than giving orders. To delegate effectively, one must supply accurate information, have assurance that the responsibility is willingly accepted, and make certain that everyone with related interests understands the scope of the delegation. This is an achievement that calls for high skill and much practice in the use of that skill.

The modern industrial manager faces increasing pressures and demands. He can no longer do everything himself. If he is to be a successful manager, he has no choice but to delegate authority to others so that many of the tasks can be shared. A manager who possesses talent and skill in abundance but lacks the ability to choose competent people, motivate them, and develop their skills by proper delegation can do no more than a mediocre job. On the other hand, a manager who has modest abilities but has an outstanding ability in choosing competent people, motivating them, and developing their skills through proper leadership and delegation techniques will usually do an outstanding job. Only through proper delegation can one build a quality control organization that can effectively handle the demands made by today's consumer. A manager who cannot or will not delegate, unwittingly compromises his position. Some of the ways this happens are listed below.

1. He has no time to plan for the future, reeducate himself, and broaden his skills. This marks him as a *status quo* manager.
2. He gets mired in so much detail that he eventually loses the ability to separate the important from the routine.
3. He may lose a chance for promotion because he has not groomed a successor and, therefore, cannot make himself available. A man chosen for promotion must be able to make himself available; when he does not, he does a disservice to the company, himself, and his subordinates.
4. He loses the respect and damages the morale of his subordinates because of his inability to put trust and confidence in them.

The notion that delegation of authority requires only the issuance of an oral or written statement is a mistake. The extent and scope of the delegated authority must also be completely clear. Delegation actually has been accomplished only when there is assurance of understanding and willing acceptance of the responsibility by the person to whom authority is being delegated.

A manager who has not learned the art of delegation cannot be regarded as a leader, as delegation of authority is a requisite of leadership. The management practice of expecting subordinates to perform outside the limits of authority delegated to them is false leadership. Only through the appropriate delegation of authority can leadership actually exist.

Assigning Work

The supervisor should discuss the content of a job with his employees. This includes the importance of the tasks and how these tasks fit into the overall mission of the organization. Jointly, they set some specific and intermediate objectives that will lead to the realization of overall organization goals. The two most important aspects of this discussion are to (1) allow the employee the opportunity of participating in setting his objectives as well as planning how he will pursue and meet them, and (2) make certain that the employee understands the importance of meeting his objectives and how the realization of these objectives coincides with or is related to others in the organization.

The employee should draw up a program of performance targets for the immediate period ahead. This period can be as short as a week or as long as a year, its length depending on the nature of the work. This list of objectives should be realistic, attainable, and challenging. It should represent improvements and always lead to established overall goals.

The supervisor should review the plan, but the discussion should center around the plan the employee has formulated rather than the supervisor's ideas. At this stage, employee enthusiasm can be appreciably reduced if the supervisor exercises strong control and veto power rather than creating a genial, cooperative attitude. Both the supervisor and the employee will learn more about the problems at hand if the discussion is oriented toward joint considerations and mutual decisions rather than *orders* from management, i.e., the supervisor. This does not mean, however, that the supervisor never must insist that certain changes be made in the employee's objectives or the approaches to these objectives. On the contrary, pressing organizational needs may dictate changes in the direction that certain work must take.

The subordinate together with the supervisor should also define specific checkpoints, points at which progress can be measured against planned action, for assessing progress. A checkpoint may be a specific completion date of a project, or it may be an event that is highlighted because of its importance.

The number of such checkpoints will vary with the longevity of the project. In any case, checkpoints should be spaced so that if an appraisal indicates rework, or a change of pace, mode, or direction, the change can be implemented with the least sacrifice of resources.

Effectiveness of the individual can be optimized when he or she can monitor his or her own performance. Unfortunately, many workers are relatively unaware of what proportion of good or bad work they are producing. The results of their work may not be established until the end of the production process or during the final inspection procedure. By this time, however, much waste has been generated.

A supervisor must, therefore, consider the ways in which subordinates can be made aware of what is required of their work, and thus introduce the necessary procedures to obtain and maintain control of quality at desired levels. This can be done by providing guides, patterns, or gauges for the work. Simple pictures which are diagrams clearly differentiating between what is acceptable and what is not are extremely powerful tools. That part of a specification relevant to the work can also be prominently displayed for guidance. The relation of the subordinates' jobs to subsequent processes or to parallel processes in an assembly, illustrated by visual aids or samples, is also very important in arousing and maintaining interest and providing a competitive atmosphere.

Encouraging Innovation

Supervisory personnel often must deal with those who reject anything not fully understood on the ground that it is unlikely to be of any value. The argument usually follows the line, "We have done without it in the past, why do we need it now?"

Fundamentally, the success in competition and, hence, the survival of a company will depend upon the economy with which its affairs are conducted. If quality can be improved or cost can be reduced by introducing a new technique, then there can be little question that this should be done. Like every other supervisor, the quality supervisor has a personal interest in the success and strength of the firm which employs him and recognizes that it is foolish to resist improvements because of ignorance or prejudice.

Often, the forward-thinking supervisor will find himself advocating techniques which will be resisted by his superiors. He or she should not withdraw merely on that account, but should try to prove the virtues of the innovation by every legitimate means available. Progress might be slow, but the end result will be worthwhile. It is the business of the persistent and creative supervisor to be so well informed about new techniques in use in his or her field that he or she can conduct a campaign on the basis of complete and accurate information.

Frequently, managers express a wish that their people would take more initiative. There is little doubt that there is too often hesitancy on the part of subordinates to initiate action and to develop and try out new ideas. One reason for this is that employees have learned from past experience that, in general, the taking of initiative does not pay. Ideas are often rejected in such a way that only negative reenforcement can take place. Managers may say that they want subordinates to take initiative, but too often managers are suspicious of new methods which are departures from ways that have been successful. Managers are essentially the same as other people when it comes to resisting change. It is more safe and secure to remain with the status quo, resisting the use of unproved methods. Fear of reprisal, embarrassment, and loss of status are great inhibitors of innovation.

Good managers do not stifle creativity. They recognize that without the freedom to make mistakes and learn from them, there is no engendering the will to innovate. Progress depends on innovation.

Recognizing Individual Differences

Individual differences always exist in physical capacities, training, or aptitudes for certain types of work among personnel. Irrespective of the combinations of these differences, their manifestations occur for the most part by chance, and can be represented by the normal curve.

Good management practices attempt to minimize these differences, as well as the effects of these differences. Various techniques of job enrichment, careful selection and training of employees, and a variety of motivation programs are examples of measures used to minimize differences.

The extent of these individual differences in terms of output has been variously estimated. An average ratio of 1 to 2 is often given as the range more likely to be found in groups of more than twenty people. This means that in such large groups, the best performer may produce twice as much as the lowest performer during any given period. However, this range of individual differences in mass production work can be reduced considerably by implementing good methods, training personnel in the use of these methods, and then monitoring the use of the methods. The reliability of this estimate is not as great for groups of less than fifteen people.

For a large group of equally motivated employees selected at random, the frequency distribution of the group output is expected to approximate the form of the normal curve. In terms of operator performance, the variability will be determined by the selection, training, practices, etc., in effect during production. The symbol we have used to designate the amount of variability is sigma (σ). The average is commonly designated by X-bar($\bar{X}$). In the normal distribution curve, the percent of the total area beneath the curve is as noted in the prior chapters covering statistical concepts and principles.

Limits	*Percent of total area within limits*
$\bar{X} \pm \sigma$	68.26
$\bar{X} \pm 2\sigma$	95.45
$\bar{X} \pm 3\sigma$	99.73

Thus is can be predicted that fewer than three cases in 1,000 would be expected to fall outside the three-sigma limits. Figure 10-13 presents such a normal law distribution.

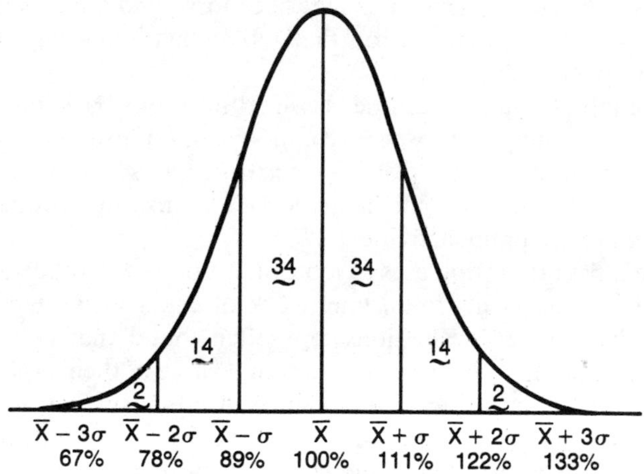

Figure 10–13 Normal law distribution.

Assume as an example that the ratio of the least capable ($X - 3\sigma$) to the most capable operator ($\bar{X} + 3\sigma$) is 1 to 2 on a given operation. The limits may be drawn on the normal curve, together with values for sigma and the number of persons predicted to be found in each of the areas. With a mean ($\bar{X}$) of 100%, sigma equals 11%, $\bar{X} - 3\sigma$ is 67%, and $\bar{X} + 3\sigma$ is 133%. The $\bar{X} - 3\sigma$ to $\bar{X} + 3\sigma$ ratio is 1 to 2. For a group of 100 workers, approximately sixty-eight would be expected to perform between 89% and 111%. Approximately fourteen would fall into the bracket 78% to 89%, and the same number would fall between 111% and 122%. Two would fall below 78% and two above 122%. The number of workers in each section of the diagram corresponds to the area under the curve.

With a group of workers who are well motivated through an incentive plan, the average performance is expected to be above 100%. Because the employees are usually selected to fit a particular job and a weeding-out process eliminates the misfit or the very poor performer, both the mean and the dispersion will be altered. However, in cases where the operator wishes to restrict his output, his production may fall below the lower limits.

10.10 Job Evaluation

Job evaluation is a necessity if management is to have a reasonable degree of objectivity in promoting personnel and uniformity in giving merit increases. A properly prepared job evaluation can serve as an invaluable tool to simplify personnel control by providing a uniform basis for comparing employees to determine how to allocate merit increases.

Moreover, with typical present-day confrontations between management and labor unions, a sound basis for rating employees is essential. Since World War II, industry has witnessed increased union activities and repeated demands for higher wages, accompanied by union stewards eagerly seeking causes for grievances. This has served to further confirm the need for sound job evaluations. Today it can be stated without contradiction that job evaluation is an integral part of any progressive personnel policy.

The uses of job evaluations can be classified into four basic groups: (1) specifications for the screening of prospective employees, (2) norms for the transfer of employees to new tasks, (3) controls for merit increases and upgrading, and (4) standards for establishing a simplified functional organization through elimination of duplicate and overlapping activities.

One of the most interesting uses of job evaluation is the reduction of inequitable wages for employees accomplishing work of equal value. Upon analysis of jobs and establishment of evaluations, it is often found that certain employees are receiving remuneration in excess of the actual value of their tasks, while others are underpaid. This is a normal consequence of establishing wages without an objective analysis of work content and the attendant skills needed for the work. Also, without such a method, merit increases are more apt to be given according to the personal opinions of supervisory personnel. After all jobs have been evaluated, it is possible to remedy the situation concerning underpaid employees, although it is usually impractical to attempt to correct the situation regarding overpaid employees. However, once a sound job-evaluation system is established, there should be no reason for repetition of inequitable wage and salary values.

Figure 10-14 illustrates the relationships between points, salary grades, and salaries. Each salary grade has specific criteria for point value which, in turn, has a commensurate wage. Such charts can be designed in a number of ways. For example, this chart illustrates that a certain number of merit increases can be earned within the salary grades. It may be more suitable to expand the scope so that more merit increases can be achieved in each salary grade, making it possible

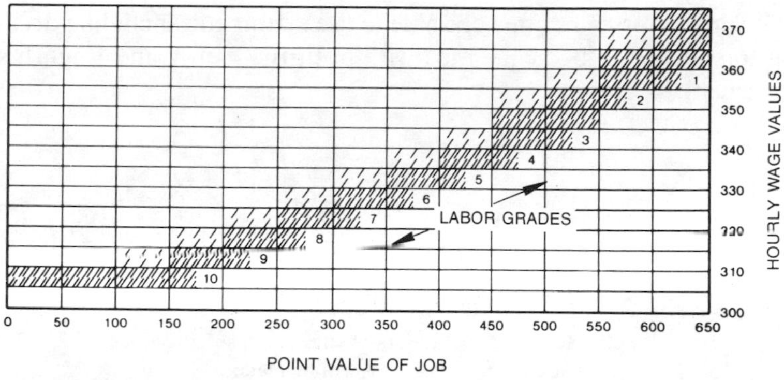

Figure 10–14 Relationship of point values to labor grades and wages.

to grant merit increases as a reward for exceptional performance without necessarily reclassifying or upgrading the employee. In any case, the important point in job evaluation is to set forth objective qualifications for each labor grade and specific standards for advancement.

10.11 Job Descriptions

Job descriptions state personal qualifications and other criteria needed by an employee to adequately perform a job. They describe the scope of the duties and the nature of the responsibility involved in a job. Examples of a job description and of a position description are given below. The job description is in concert with figure 10-14 and describes the job of a laborer, grade number four.

Example, Job description

Tools and Equipment

Quality control engineers, technicians, and inspectors need to be familiar with all types of electrical and mechanical precision testing equipment, such as precision measuring instruments, gauges and test equipment, fixtures and templates, and inspection stamps, as well as surface-finish analyzers and all forms of inspection equipment to perform their functions most effectively.

Knowledge and Ability

Quality control personnel must know receiving inspection methods and procedures, including use of drawing prints, specifications, catalogues, and standards handbooks. They must have the knowledge and ability to recognize any defect that may exist and must be acquainted with the peculiarities of items purchased from different vendors. They must be able to use arithmetic, including decimal and common fractions, and be acquainted with both the metric and English systems of measurement.

Factor	*Degree*	*Points*
Knowledge	Interpret drawing prints. Solve mathematical problems of moderate complexity	80
Responsibility	Follow company policies, procedures, and specifications so that a minimum of error will be made	40
Mental Application	Very close mental application	40
Physical Application	Continuous light physical exertion	20
Job Conditions	No disagreeable elements	15
Unavoidable Hazards	Little accident or health hazard	5
Experience	Minimum 2 years	220
	Total	420

Figure 10–15 Job evaluation.

Example, Position description

1. *The position of Quality Assurance Auditor* is located in the Quality Assurance Division as an independent (singular) function and on an equivalent level with QA Branch Chiefs. Incumbent analyzes government directives, written procedures, develops audit plans and checklists, programs internal and other required audits, displays results for Division Chief review, identifies courses of action, recommends corrective actions, and monitors the Division QA Program for adequacy. Incumbent also serves as the Deputy for the QA Division Chief.

2. The purpose of this position is to serve as the QA Division Auditor by developing, performing, and managing the QA Division Internal Audit Program to assure the overall effectiveness of all QA Branches in performing required mission functions and obtaining established objectives.

Duties and Responsibilities

1. Develops audit plans, audit checklists, organizes and directs the performance of QA Division internal audits.

2. Conducts in-depth periodic internal audits of all QA Division Branches to determine degree of effectiveness and progress toward projected goals, compliance with procedures, regulations, directives.

3. Identifies inadequacies in the QA Division's operations, procedures, practices.

4. Finalizes all audit findings, ascertains causes of all inadequacies found, and makes recommendations for correction of these inadequacies to the Division Chief.

5. Keeps the Division Chief informed of audit progress, findings, problems, at all times.

6. Reviews all incoming IG, DPMR, or other survey reports received by the AFPRO (from other government activities) for possible existence of reported deficiencies at this detachment.

7. Initiates positive action to correct all deficiencies found during audits and investigates all suspected problems as a result of IG, DPMR, or reports received from other activities.

8. Informs the Division Chief of specific instances where corrective action is not forthcoming for various reasons.

9. Monitors the QA Division Training Program and makes recommendations when a need for training exists. This may be the result of an audit finding or a random observation by the auditor.

10. Serves as the primary point of contact for Government Survey Teams, i.e., AFCMD, IG, DPMR, etc.

11. Reviews QA Management Data compiled by the Quality Evaluation Branch to identify need for special audits when data reveals trends that may indicate ineffective management of function or significant quality problems. Either problem could reduce the effectiveness of the applicable Branch.

12. Performs audit follow-ups to assure that accepted audit deficiencies are in fact corrected.

13. Constantly reviews contractual requirements, quality delegations, directives, regulations, to keep abreast of all requirements, thereby assuring the continued effectiveness of the QA Division's efforts.

14. Performs other duties as assigned.

15. Conducts or participates in material, industrial, Air Force, and other Government Agency surveys.

Controls Over Work

Incumbent receives administrative supervision from the QA Division Chief. Full authority is extended to the incumbent in performing required duties in an independent manner and for making decisions necessary to assure optimum effectiveness. Results of incumbent's efforts are reviewed by the Division Chief.

Extent of research, methods of solution, and technical aspects are determined on own initiative, predicated on a comprehensive knowledge of procurement practices, QA policies, applicable directives, regulations and/or other requirements.

Other Signicant Facts

This position requires independent judgment and is reserved for individuals of demonstrated capacity and ability to meet changing conditions and situations, keeping established objectives in mind. The individual must have a good knowledge of all AF functions, procedures, audit procedures and techniques, and should be able to apply modern QA principles to the accomplishment of all required tasks. Technical and administrative background is necessary to assure satisfactory performance. Grade structure is not subservient to other Branch Chiefs in the Quality Assurance Division.

10.12 Motivating Personnel

Motivating personnel as a management function requires the development and practice of a varied set of skills. These skills and their effective use are probably of the highest order of managing ability. It is doubtful that perfection in all the varied applications of these skills can be achieved by any one person, but the rewards for striving for some measure of perfection are great. Not the least of these is the satisfaction of seeing others develop and become more productive.

If it were possible to select that part of managerial work of first importance, probably the choice would be the manager's responsibility for motivating the people for whom he or she is responsible and for integrating their efforts. This involves far more than the relatively more simple task of persuading people to work hard. There are many qualities that a leader must possess and many conditions that must be satisfied to best motivate people in industry. Among the important factors are the ability to communicate, leadership, expertise, and appropriate working conditions and climate.

Communication

An important factor always present in motivating subordinates is skill in communication. The need for the ability to explain and to clarify, both verbally and in writing, long has been recognized. Speaking and writing abilities are essential for executive success. Listening—the other half of the communication concept—has received far too little attention. An effective manager, although often trained very effectively in speaking, usually must develop listening expertise on the job. It can be safely stated that every *effective* manager has learned the art of listening. Verbal information can be very difficult to understand, even if listening takes place. This can occur as shown in figure 10-16 if too many people are giving orders at the same time.

In some companies, often despite concerted efforts to improve internal communications, some quality managers (as well as other managers) are almost totally insulated from what is actually taking place in their organizations. The feedback they receive, including formal reports, is all too often incomplete or slanted. Some managers assume that the supervisory hierarchy provides a clear channel of vertical communication, either upward or downward, and that horizontal interdepartmental communication is equally reliable. In fact, it is not usually difficult to find that some levels of supervision are more communication barriers than communi-

Figure 10–16 Potential communication problems.

cation centers. Also, certain company functions, such as production and purchasing, can be less inclined to be cooperative allies than to be rivals for power, recognition, and executive favor. Many departments adjunctive to quality control are prolific sources of information, but this does not mean that the intelligence that they provide is complete, accurate, and coordinated.

Not all quality managers are capable of accepting and assimilating information which conflicts with their personal opinions and predilections. Consequently, projects of critical significance to the achievement of quality objectives are sometimes undertaken on the basis of incomplete, inadequate, or incorrect information. Without knowing it, the manager is in the position of being unaware of the seriousness of a situation until confronted with a disaster. This is not infrequently the cause of quality problems even in a presumably well-run business.

Managers who will not see what they wish to see or who instinctively avoid the disagreeable and the troublesome parts of business and daily contacts are the people who are unfair to themselves and will seldom possess the truth about the issues at hand. However able a manager may be, without the truth he or she is like a captain without a compass; he or she may sail on many seas but will never reach the destination. Those decisions that are made will not be based on facts and hence often will be wrong.

Misleading information has many origins and causes. Some may be attributed to willful misleading and others to purely unintentional causes. There are three important reasons, however, that the quality manager may not receive accurate and complete information. These may be summarized as follows.

1. In vertical hierarchy, subordinates may be inclined to withhold information that tends to discredit them. Thus, information transmitted undergoes a screening process which allows only the positive to be reported. In horizontal communication, where quality is being appraised, if rejects, scrap or rework, and attendant blame are expected outcomes, information sometimes is slanted or incomplete, resulting in more serious problems in the future.
2. It is not long before subordinates discover the kind of boss they have to work with. There is a tendency to tell a supervisor (particularly the authoritarian type) what he or she wants to hear, shielding the negative. This practice results in concealed errors and avoidable delays and costs.
3. An incumbent manager is not always surrounded by allies. In a typical organization, there exists competition and rivalry for the higher positions. Despite overt manifestations of loyalty, a few people in every organization seem ready and willing to create a situation of embarrassment, or to manipulate the manager into a compromising position. The manager is thus placed in the position of devoting too much time to making excuses to top management for certain actions rather than to the job of running the department. It is sometimes necessary to replace well-intentioned, but undependable, subordinates by loyal and efficient helpers. Decisions of this nature require a cool evaluation of the situation. The decisions reached should be such that the results are beneficial to both the company and the workers affected.

Sustained Motivation

One of the most important challenges that confronts management is how to both sustain and increase internal motivation in the work group. Knowledge of fundamental human relations on the part of the manager is important. The uniqueness of the individual and the necessity to tailor leadership to the needs of individuals are significant. Although many people have limitations, attributes, and similar qualities that characterize their personalities in common, many needs are quite different among individuals and should be dealt with on an individual basis.

The manager should also recognize that people do have certain needs in common, which may often be met in basically the same way. For example, two such common needs are (1) that of being needed, and of (2) being treated with dignity and self-respect.

The personal attitudes and values of a manager are decidedly influential factors in his or her attempts to create a work environment in which the workers have sustained motivation. For real motivation of subordinates, changes in managerial attitudes are frequently necessary. If the firm does not allow people to achieve and grow, and if the manager's attitudes are negative, the best motivational efforts and techniques may be useless.

Effective managers must have confidence in both their subordinates and in themselves. More effective managers believe in their subordinates and trust them to a greater degree than do less effective leaders. This trust is closely related to the ability of a manager to avoid close and anxious supervision. Workers tend to respond to and respect the manager who knows their capabilities, who is fair and consistent, and who respects them as individuals. Moreover, no manager can sustain the motivation of subordinates if they are not allowed to motivate him or her. The best way to influence an employee's thinking and behavior is to be open to his or her influence.

Leadership

If one phrase could be used to collectively describe how quality goals and efficiency are best obtained, the phrase would be *through the processes of leadership.* All that we have discussed as management principles, work organization, work assignment, delegation of authority, and the working climate are interrelated with the exercise of leadership.

Leadership is primarily a human relations activity. In simple terms it may be defined as the art of motivating, guiding, and directing people. No system of organization, no aggregation of manpower, no set of procedures, and no plant facilities can possess the vigor and coordination needed for efficient output without leadership.

An organization should look after and take care of the personnel who compose it, because their bodily and mental development is an important factor bearing upon production of quality goods and services. Loyalty, enthusiasm, and cooperation of workers in a business enterprise are needed for success and efficiency, and every manager should strive for their presence in his organization.

These three requisites—loyalty, enthusiasm, and cooperation—cannot be obtained unless the management inspires confidence by the assurance of proper reward for all services, of suitable workplaces and tools, and of fair operations and proper treatment. An organization should have genial, resourceful leaders, assisted by a well-trained and enthusiastic staff. There should be a close contact between management and employees, bringing with it a close cooperation and willingness to work for the success of the business enterprise.

Recognizing the rights of workers and making them feel that they are integral parts of an organization prevent friction and contribute toward efficiency. Workers should have some share in devising methods and plans, be made to feel that they are important parts of an organization, be consulted concerning difficulties, and be encouraged to suggest ways of overcoming these difficulties. Working together with the interest of the enterprise at heart is the proper spirit of workers, one that should be sought by every management. Cooperation has two sides. However, the management frequently sees only one, sometimes believing that workers should cooperate to produce efficient results, while being blind to the fact that management should cooperate with the workers to assist them to obtain better working conditions, methods, etc. In every form of business, true cooperation is more than a theory; it is a necessity, and its importance is gradually being impressed upon all managers.

10.13 The Quality Manager

Leadership roles of quality control managers are broad in scope and normally complex. Traditionally, leadership pertains in great part to the vertical chain of command. But quality managers may make their greatest contributions as managers in the liaison role, making contacts and maintaining good relations with personnel outside their chain of command. Quality control managers devote as much time to interpersonal contacts with peers and people outside their units as they do with their own subordinates. This is as it should be—managers without liaison contacts lack external information. As a result, they can neither disseminate the information their employees need nor make decisions that adequately reflect external conditions.

Attributes of Successful Quality Managers

There are numerous attributes with which quality managers should be liberally endowed if they are to be fully successful. Correspondingly, there are many activities with which quality managers are concerned that require the exercise of these attributes. There are eight principal categories into which these attributes and functions may be grouped.

1. **Motivating subordinates** It is through leadership and attendant delegation of authority that the detailed tasks of the organization are completed. The quality manager is instrumental in setting goals and monitoring performances of the group for which he or she is responsible. The manager must inspire and encourage employees, somehow reconciling their individual needs with the goals of the organization. In virtually every contact the quality manager has with employees, subordinates seek leadership clues from his or her actions. In nearly every dealing, the conscientious employee is covertly asking questions such as, "Does the manager *really* approve of this report?" or "Is this letter what he or she *really* wants?"
2. **Developing and maintaining peer relationships** Quality organizations are in the business of helping to prevent the design and manufacture of defective merchandise, detecting problems once they do occur, and seeing to it that

corrective action is taken when needed. In performing these jobs, much of the quality manager's time is devoted to interpersonal relationships with key personnel in other departments such as engineering, marketing, manufacturing, and purchasing. The ability of quality managers to maintain good peer relations determines in great measure their effectiveness in their roles.

3. **Establishing networks for the dissemination of information** The processing of information is a key part of any quality manager's job. Studies have shown that executives, in general, spend approximately 40% of their contact time on activities devoted to the transmission of information. The quality manager does not leave a meeting or hang up the telephone in order to get back to work. These forms of communication *are* his work. The manager screens incoming information (both verbal and written) and then passes that portion which is deemed relevant, needed, and appropriate on to subordinates, upper management, or peers.
4. **Carrying out negotiations** Quality managers also spend much time in negotiations: the company's vice-president delegates the authority to negotiate in a litigation proceeding involving quality; the quality manager negotiates with a customer about quality problems; the quality manager works with marketing and government officials in contract negotiations; the quality manager also frequently gets involved in labor negotiations. Negotiations are an integral part of quality executives' jobs. Only they have the authority to commit organizational resources to such activities, and only they have the information that important negotiations require.
5. **Resolving conflicts** Although the quality manager is in a decision-making capacity and is a voluntary initiator of changes, he also must act on an involuntary basis in handling disturbances when the need arises. He must act in certain instances because the pressures of the situation are too severe to be ignored. Budgets have been drastically cut and layoffs are forthcoming; a strategic supplier of high reliability components has canceled a contract; data records and failure analysis reports must be supplied in a costly liability case.

   Disturbances arise not only because managers ignore situations until they reach crisis proportions, but also because they cannot anticipate many of the consequences of the actions they take.

   Most quality managers have many projects they are supervising at any given time, and the task of resolving conflicts often takes important time away from principal objectives. Nevertheless, handling disturbances must be done and done well.
6. **Securing and allocating resources** To ensure adequate operating budgets for the quality organization, the manager must not only be an expert negotiator, but must also have a general knowledge of the operating expenses of other departments. It is difficult indeed for most quality managers to acquire the needed budgets for their departments, but this is an important responsibility that they must shoulder.

If the quality manager is not on top of this fiscal problem, the department is soon unable to adequately solve the myriad issues that pertain to the prevention and detection of quality problems.

The responsibility of allocating resources in the quality control department also falls to the quality manager. He or she must make certain that the available resources are fairly and properly distributed throughout the functional units; indeed, the pattern of formal relationships that determines how work is to be divided and coordinated is an ongoing responsibility of the quality manager.

A quality manager is faced with very complex choices. The impact of each decision on other decisions as well as on the organization's strategy must be considered. The manager not only must be confident that a decision will be acceptable to those who have important influences on the organization, but also ensure that resources will not be overextended. A manager's time is extremely valuable; the judgment of subordinates must be relied upon if it is to be used wisely. Some subordinates earn the trust of their managers more than others, and thus are given more responsibility. However, this should not be used by the manager as a simple dodge.

7. **Making decisions** If there is one attribute a successful quality manager must have, it is the ability to make good judgments. Complex decisions under conditions of extreme ambiguity must often be made. In dealing with such complex issues, the manager has much to gain from close relationships with specialists in the organization. Opinions of subordinates must be utilized because the time is not available for personally probing complex issues.

   Informational and decisional roles are inseparable. The quality manager who wishes to innovate often initiates a project and obligates others to report status; the manager who needs certain information about operations establishes channels that will keep him or her informed. The manager cannot make good decisions without accurate information.

   Effectiveness at decision-making is also significantly influenced by the manager's insight into his or her own work. The ability to make good judgments depends in great part on how well one understands and responds to the pressures and dilemmas of the job. Managers who are introspective about their work are more likely to consistently make better decisions than those who are not realistic.

8. **Making effective use of time** Time is one of the most precious commodities of a quality manager. However, in spite of this fact, there are countless situations that seem to arise that leave little time for productive work. Six important time thieves that a quality manager should avoid are (1) failure to think in terms of delegation; (2) lack of confidence that the organization will meet its goals; (3) devoting too much time to trivia instead of moving ahead to meet primary objectives; (4) permitting a contrary desire to weaken principal purposes; (5) indecision; and (6) dwelling on what has been missed rather than on what can be gained.

The qualities that make the successful leader are often difficult to measure. Insofar as value is concerned, there is no complete list of leadership attributes upon which authorities completely agree. Manifestly, the demand for different qualities depends on the given conditions—the kind of work to be directed, the kind of people to be dealt with, and the character of the environment.

Needless to say, a group of scientists in a research laboratory would require a leadership emphasis on intellectual achievements, while a group of laborers on a construction site would require more emphasis on scheduling work, keeping activities moving, and assimilating knowledge concerning ways to carry out the necessary construction. A group of assemblers in the shop also would take a different style of leadership than an engineering group of designers. Some specific fundamental human attributes that are also needed by quality managers are listed below. The optimum situation would be for the manager to possess these characteristics in large measure, but it is folly to expect that any one person can continuously demonstrate all of these traits.

1. Congeniality.
2. Strength of character.
3. Knowledge and wisdom.
4. Creativity.
5. The ability to communicate effectively (writing, speaking, and listening).
6. Patience.
7. Fairness.
8. Persistence.
9. Honesty.
10. Decisiveness.
11. Resourcefulness and enthusiasm.
12. Discernment.
13. Good mental and physical health.
14. Compassion.

Some statements that compare the characteristics of a boss to those of a leader are given in figure 10-17.

In a generic sense, motivating employees and supervisory leadership are also inseparable. A principal goal of leadership is to motivate subordinates to meet planned objectives. But since employees differ vastly in ability, knowledge, skills, aptitudes, attitudes, needs, etc., leadership styles must also vary.

Managers have discovered that in order to effectively motivate employees, they must use several leadership styles. Some situations call for a *telling* style of leadership. On occasion, certain employees need to be told explicitly what to do. Other employees respond to a *selling* style of leadership in which the manager attempts to sell an idea or persuade his workers that a certain change should be implemented. Still other employees respond to a *consulting* style of leadership in which the manager obtains employees' opinions before reaching a specific decision. However, the manager should not go so far as to join the consensus of the group in

The boss drives his men; the leader coaches them.
The boss depends on authority, the leader on goodwill.
The boss inspires fear; the leader inspires enthusiasm.
The boss says "I", the leader says "We".

The boss says: "Get here on time"; the leader gets there ahead of time.
The boss fixes blame for a problem; the leader finds solutions to the problem.
The boss says "Go", the leader says "Let's Go".

The boss uses people; the leader develops them.
The boss dwells on yesterday and sees today; the leader also looks at tomorrow.
The boss commands; the leader asks.
The boss never has enough time; the leader makes time for things that count.

The boss is concerned with things; the leader is concerned with people.
The boss lets his people know where he stands; the leader also lets his people know where they stand.
The boss works hard to produce; the leader works hard to help his people produce.
The boss takes the credit; the leader gives it.

Figure 10–17 Boss or leader?

order to avoid controversy. This is called the *joining* style of leadership. Effective managers realize that different styles must be used with different employees at different times and according to different conditions. The emotional characteristics of people as well as conditions change from one day to the next, making it necessary for a manager to respond by varying his or her style of leadership. Getting to know traits of the individuals in his or her employ is usually difficult for a manager, but it is always important.

As in every kind of work, it takes certain natural qualities of mind to make a good judge of human values. The manager must be such a person, having a wide experience and acquaintance with different types of personalities, able to detect them readily, appraise them, and place them where they can function most effectively with other people and functions. Prejudice and personal bias are fatal barriers in management. Being successful in a managerial position also requires the following attributes.

1. Being sensitive to changes in attitudes and performance among the personnel in his or her employ.
2. Being willing to delegate authority and to make assignments that are commensurate with worker abilities, plant facilities, employee training, and organizational objectives.
3. Taking every possible opportunity to make fair, attainable, and challenging assignments to all employees.
4. Being sensitive to improved performances within his or her group, then giving appropriate recognition.

5. Accepting responsibility for his or her mistakes.
6. Aiding subordinates in taking corrective action when honest mistakes are made.
7. Setting an example for employees and being consistent in day-to-day activities.
8. Keeping subordinates informed about company policies and relevant issues.
9. Reviewing subordinates, regularly letting them know (in advance) the basis upon which they will be judged, and keeping them apprised of performances and ratings made.
10. Exhibiting a positive outlook and seeing value in achievement.
11. Being responsive to the needs of subordinates, including working conditions, budgets, salaries, and facilities.

10.14 Research on Motivation

Research in the United States pertaining to employee behavior in the industrial environment essentially began shortly before the beginning of the great depression in 1929. Beginning during the late 1920's and continuing through the 1930's, Elton Mayo and his colleagues at the Harvard Business School conducted a study at the Hawthorne Works, a division of Western Electric Company.

The results of this study left countless unanswered questions and opened up many new areas for industrial research. Two important points were revealed in this study.

1. Group behavior has a powerful influence upon individual members. The work group is a significant factor, either *for* or *against* productivity, being largely influenced by the management's ability to effectively lead the work force.
2. The work group is a social group which fulfills certain human needs on the job. Up to this time, these needs were considered to be fulfilled in the home, church, and organizations away from the working environment.

One of the primary objectives of the study was to determine the effect of illumination on productivity. However, it was later discovered that with lower illumination, output continued to increase. The study actually revealed a far more important and insightful factor—so long as people are treated as human beings, giving due consideration to individual needs, they tend to cooperate in increasing productivity.

The Hawthorne studies were probably as important for the things they didn't find as the things they did find. They exposed many unanswered questions about manager-worker relations and stimulated much further study into human relations in industry. Thus the Hawthorne studies served to attract the attention of behavioral scientists to the industrial environments.

Later, during World War II, Abraham Maslow conducted industrial research pertaining to human needs.[3] In his study, he presented a hierarchy of needs ranging from survival needs (food, air, water, shelter, etc.) to self-actualization needs (becoming what one can become). Maslow's theory affirmed the view that individuals are motivated to lower-order needs until these are relatively satisfied, but higher-order needs must be satisfied to sustain satisfaction. His hierarchy of needs progress from basic needs to security needs to belonging needs to status needs to self-actualization. The message in this study to modern management suggests that more emphasis should be placed on higher-order needs for most employees.

During the mid 1950's, Douglas McGregor began to introduce his new theory, which he called theory X and theory Y, to his students at the Massachusetts Institute of Technology. Probably no single concept has generated so much interest among behaviorists and had so much widespread influence as this now-famous theory.[4] McGregor contended that traditional management practices were rooted in certain basic negative assumptions about people that were rarely openly stated. These are that people, by nature:

1. Are fundamentally lazy and desire to work as little as possible,
2. Avoid responsibility,
3. Lack integrity,
4. Are not interested in achievement,
5. Are incapable of directing their own behavior,
6. Are indifferent to organizational needs,
7. Prefer to be directed by others,
8. Avoid making decisions whenever possible, and
9. Are not very bright.

McGregor advanced the theory that the exercise of theory X and of strong direction and control are concomitant activities. If theory X assumptions are correct, management must tell subordinates, as explicitly as possible, how and when a job must be done.

On the other hand, McGregor suggested that such negative, traditional concepts can be effectively changed for the better by exercising the management practices embodied in what he labeled theory Y ideas. Theory Y contained the following important points.

1. The expenditure of physical effort in work is as natural as play or rest. The average human being does not inherently dislike work. Depending upon controllable conditions, work may be a source of satisfaction (and will be voluntarily performed) or a source of punishment (and will be avoided if possible).
2. External control and the threat of punishment are not the only means for bringing about effort toward organizational objectives. Man will exercise self-direction and self-control in the service of objectives to which he is committed.

3. *Commitment to objectives* is a function of the rewards associated with their achievement. The most significant of such rewards, e.g., the satisfaction of ego and self-actualization needs, can be direct products of effort directed toward organization objectives.
4. The average human being learns, under proper conditions, not only to accept but to seek responsibility. Avoidance of responsibility, lack of enthusiasm, and emphasis on security are generally consequences of experience and are not an inherent human characteristic.
5. The capacity to use a relatively high degree of imagination, ingenuity, and creativity in the solution of organizational problems is widely, not narrowly, distributed in the population.
6. Under conditions of modern industrial life, only a small portion of the intellectual potential of the average human being is utilized.

McGregor viewed management's job as one in which working conditions are created so that individuals can establish and integrate goals with the organization. Given this proper working climate, both the individual's and the organization's goals can be mutually achieved. In many modern companies, it is still very difficult to find many of the theory Y concepts actively pursued. Certain traditional aspects of theory X are unfortunately applied rather extensively in some companies.

Soon after the revealing studies of McGregor, Frederick W. Herzberg and his colleagues at Western Reserve Institute conducted studies on the motivation to work. This research, which was originally performed using engineers and accountants, revealed that workers were best motivated through a hierarchy of satisfiers. First, the most important outside influences, called *extrinsic satisfiers*, must be experienced. Extrinsic motivators are such factors as fringe benefits, salary, working conditions, status symbols, and other factors exterior to the work itself. Second, important internal influences, called *intrinsic satisfiers*, must be experienced in order to achieve a more sustained motivation. Intrinsic motivators originate from (1) recognition (the type that results naturally from meeting a work objective itself), (2) a sense of achievement, (3) satisfaction from the work itself, and (4) advancement and the attendant sense of responsibility.[5]

Figure 10-18 illustrates the importance of active organized teamwork in the quality control system. The quality-oriented activities of planning, verifying, and eliminating are more successfully accomplished through cooperation and team effort.

Training Employees to Do Quality Work

Executives are aware of the critical importance of having thoroughly trained employees perform operations where product quality is at stake. Many companies have implemented extensive training and apprenticeship programs in order to meet their production goals and to reduce substandard work and attendant costs. Unless people are adequately trained to perform the jobs they are assigned, they

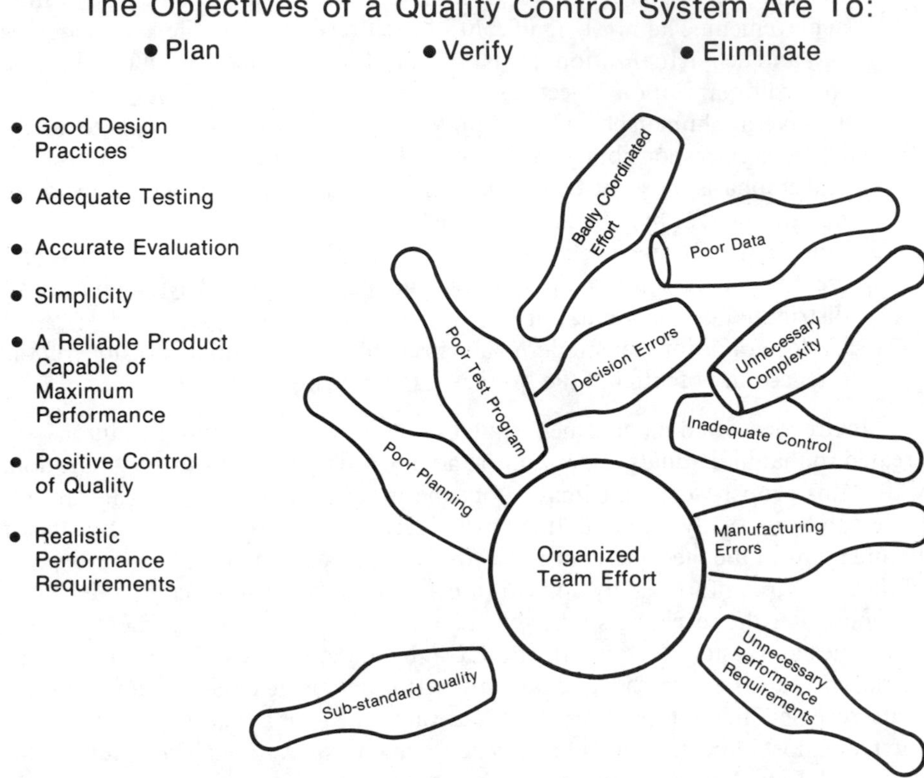

Figure 10–18 Objectives of a quality control system.

are not only safety hazards to themselves and to coworkers, but also are slow performers, inaccurate performers, and costly performers.

Good training is a planned and ordered process where the trainee is guided along a path of learning, moving logically step-by-step from the known to the unknown to the new known. This means that a supervisor must ensure that those who are to teach new entrants are themselves clear about their duties and that the process of training is properly supervised.

The New Employee

When a person takes a new job, he or she faces many unknown conditions. The new employee must become familiar with new surroundings, with perhaps strange equipment, and with new coworkers. Also, skill must be developed in performing assigned operations, together with an understanding of what the new employer expects. Such development may take much longer for some than for others.

It is very unwise for a trainee to be left to fend for himself or herself, picking up duties and job knowledge from whomever will spare the time to help. Often, those who will help in these circumstances are those whose own skills and attitudes are of such quality that supervisors and management have no wish for them to be passed on. Avoidance of this situation is only possible if the supervisor takes an interest and gives clear instructions regarding which skilled people shall be responsible for training each newcomer.

Training the New Employee

The instructor in any training activity should not only be informed about the subject being taught, but must also possess the attributes of a teacher. It is not enough for the instructor to be an expert in a particular field; he or she must also know how to impart this expertise to others. This involves both patience and the desire to help others. A problem frequently arises when a foreman attempts to train a new employee; the foreman may know the job well, but may have neither the time nor patience to instruct a person about the details of a job. Under these circumstances, an employee can become discouraged, and the training may take longer than it should.

There are questions that should be answered concerning the breadth of employee training: Should employees be given training only with reference to the immediate problems of the job? Should they be trained to understand and handle the kinds of problems that may be faced in the future? Should they be given training in the general operation of the company? The answers to these questions must be made on the basis of prevailing company policies, conditions, and trends. It is not possible to give a categorical answer to questions of this type. In any case, the initial training given an employee should be sufficiently concrete to enable him or her to apply it on his or her current job.

Quality assurance is not achieved simply by inspecting something after it has been assembled. For many products in today's state of the art, quality assurance can be achieved only by very carefully trained and skilled hands assembling miniature components into intermediate assemblies. Modern-day computers, for example, are designed to utilize thousands of tiny ferrite cores in their memory systems. Figure 10-19 is a photograph of an inspector in a plant individually inspecting many of these cores after they have been strung in rows in an assembly. These cores, illustrated in figure 10-20, vary somewhat in size, but the ones being inspected here are 0.018 inch in diameter.

Establishing Training Needs

The kinds of training needed to best meet a firm's commitments must be determined before launching into a full-fledged training program. First, it must be decided where training is most needed. Training personnel frequently discover that everyone believes in training, but questions about the validity of, need for, and extent of training sometimes are not adequately pursued and answered.

Delineation of training needs must come before the preparation of course content, selection of materials and aids, teaching methods, and even before concrete plans for a training program. It may be decided, based upon information gained

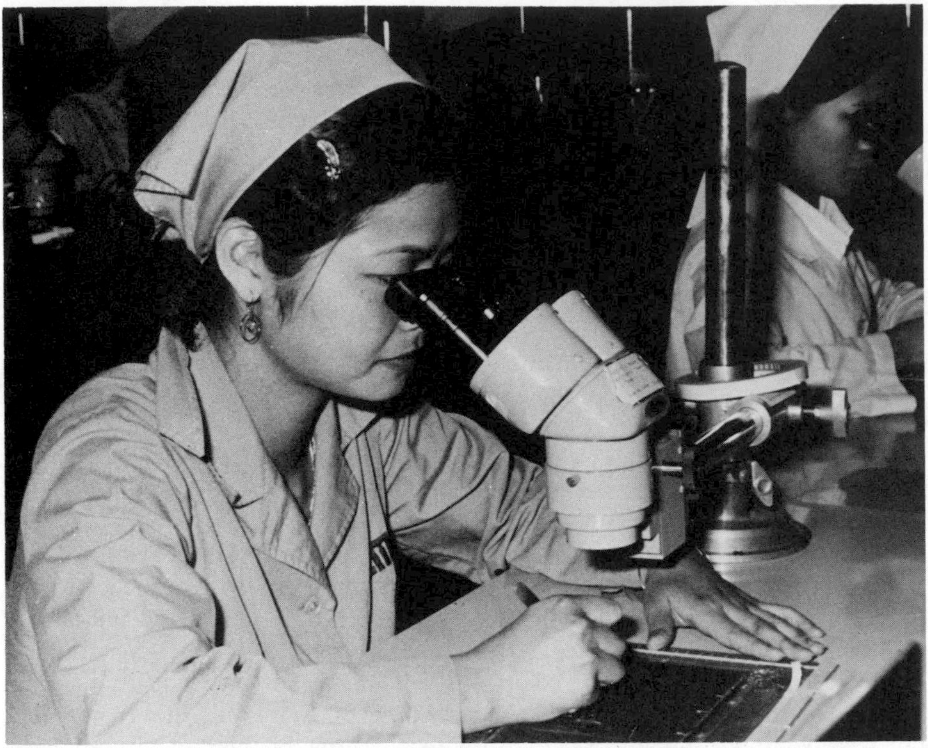

Figure 10–19 Inspecting ferrite cores.

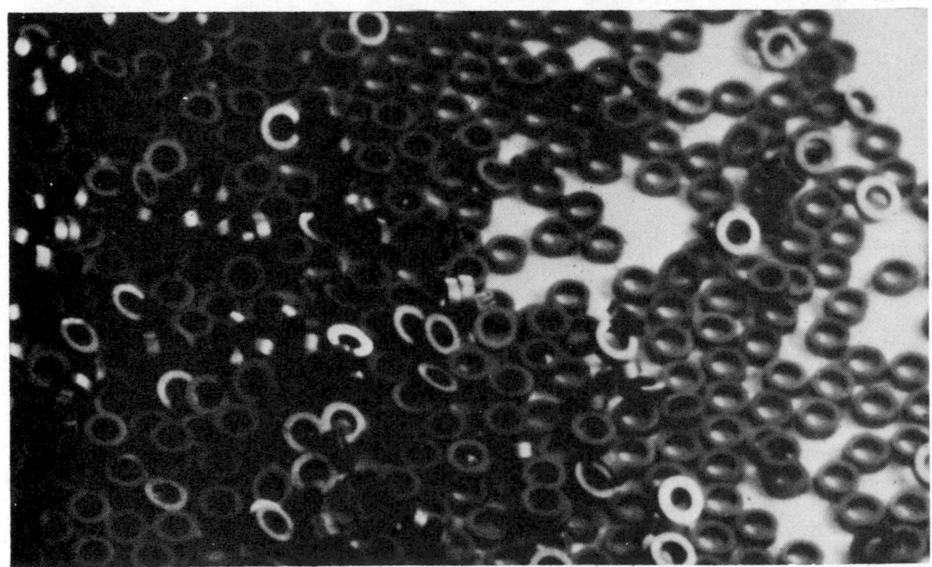

Figure 10–20 Ferrite cores.

in the investigation of training needs, that no training of a formal sort is needed. Sometimes, for example, it is more feasible to engage the services of university professors to conduct specific courses than to implement an ongoing training program. On the other hand, the company may be contractually obligated to establish an extensive training program through which its employees become certified in a variety of skills.

The preparation for good training involves job analysis, training analysis, curriculum construction, and frequent evaluation of the course content. This is just as true in clerical and shop training as it is in supervisorial training. Such preparation may involve a great amount of work, but the outcome and the returns on the investment will be commensurably greater if proper preparation has been made. To maximize benefits, all the courses in the training program must be periodically assessed to determine compatibility with current training needs.

Training needs are dynamic; conditions change in a company that influence the need for training. A surge in hiring, changes in product lines, seasonal fluctuation, increases in employee turnover and retirement, changes in machinery and equipment, reorganization of departments, new specifications, and new contracts are all factors that from time to time can cause training needs to change. Thus, these factors become sources of information needed by the firm and should be periodically evaluated.

The audit procedure is commonly used to make this evaluation. Using checklists of pertinent criteria, a representative from the quality organization examines training operations to detect conditions diverging from established policies and procedures, and any other conditions that detract from meeting training objectives. The results of these audits provide valuable information about the effectiveness of the training program and should point out areas of training needs. The subject of quality audits is covered in chapter 16.

Training Principles and Incentives

Training is the primary method used by management to develop increased capability in job performance. It is also a means of advancing personnel to more complex job assignments and higher pay schedules. Training is a continuing process that includes effort by both the trainer and the trainee toward the goal of acquiring new information, attitudes, and skills on the part of the trainee.

All training involves transmitting some type of information; before an attitude can be changed or a skill learned, new information must be received by the trainee. Attitude changes in the trainee are also important, for even under ideal training conditions a skill cannot be learned if the trainee does not want to learn. The attitude of the unmotivated learner must be altered before reception of information needed in a new skill can occur. Skill training involves improving a person's capability to perform a certain task, and different skills require different training techniques. Mastering the skills of inspection required to perform dimensional measurements using precision gauge blocks, for example, differs considerably from that involved in learning to interpret a radiograph.

Positive reinforcement may be an excellent incentive to learning, but it will be more effective if supported by encouragement from the trainer. Indeed, the social climate of the whole training department can be a great incentive to learning if it is one of empathy, friendly competition, and challenge. It is important to challenge the trainee, though much of this can be built into the training procedure. Continual success, in however small a way, through skillful design of the stages of learning can scarcely be equaled as an incentive to continued learning.

While the individual's need to learn is a motivating force which determines his speed of learning, these needs must be real to the trainee. A wise trainer will encourage the need to learn before proceeding with each aspect of training. This can be done, for example, by asking the learner why any given exercise is necessary, and by explaining or demonstrating its relevance.

Some aspects of training can be directly related to what the learner feels important to him: his need for recognition, for achievement, or for advancement and corresponding salary increases. To present information in a stimulating way can make learning fun. A reduction in the resistance to learning in this and other ways has the same effect as enhancing the need for such training.

There are six important underlying principles which can be used to enhance the effectiveness of training.

1. Objectives should be expressed in *performance terms* as much as possible.
2. Learners should *respond actively* to the material in a way which is relevant to the training purpose.
3. Learners should receive *immediate feedback* in understandable terms about the correctness of their responses.
4. Training programs must be *audited and validated,* then modified if they do not achieve their objectives.
5. Training programs must be *adapted to the individual student* as much as possible.
6. Learners must be *involved* by having the material expressed in ways that are directly relevant and related to their interests and needs; feelings of anxiety and failure should be prevented if possible.

10.15 Training Deterrents

It is relatively easy for a teacher to say "On your mark, get set, go" when beginning a class. However, just because the teacher feels that he is prepared to *present* certain information does not mean that the trainees are ready to *receive* the information.

Many people have a resistance to learning new things and training specialists need to be aware of this tendency. Unwillingness to learn may not be manifested directly; the trainee may not even realize that he or she is defensive about training. Some employees may feel that being asked to participate in a training program carries some implication of unsatisfactory job performance. In addition, they may feel apprehensive about taking on an unknown task, fear that they might not perform well in front of their peers, or fear that their comparative progress may not merit complete approval by their supervisors. Attitudes of the trainee play an extremely important role in ability and speed of learning. These attitudes are also usually evidenced indirectly. A poor attitude can be dealt with if the training specialist is alert to individual differences in the classroom. Some trainees are unwilling to participate; some may appear to be bored; others may be impudent and overbearing. These are all roadblocks to learning, but they usually can be handled. For example, providing an atmosphere in which the trainee can express opinions may result in more determination to learn on the part of the trainee. However, the experienced teacher realizes that the classroom is not a place for bull sessions and that training objectives must be constantly kept in mind.

Employees are sometimes reticent about asking questions because of fear of appearing dumb. As shown in figure 10-21, it is better to ask questions that may appear to be dumb than to create a need for consequent corrective action.

DON'T
BE AFRAID
TO ASK
DUMB QUESTIONS
THEY'RE
EASIER TO
HANDLE THAN
DUMB MISTAKES

Figure 10–21 Advice to employees.

Fear and anxiety are ever-present deterrents to learning and can freeze performance and immobilize skills. Skills form an important part of personality; to a great degree, people are what skills make them. They think, talk, act, and prosper largely according to their skills. A learner, therefore, tends to be vulnerable to fear of failure and anxiety-producing situations.

These can be significantly reduced and brought under control through the design of the training program and procedures: for instance, by slowing down the pace; by reducing the possibility of being overlooked or singled out as a slow learner; or by giving the learner a chance to develop sufficient skills and achieve adequate success before reaching the critical, anxious stages of learning. Sympathetic and supportive relationships between instructors and learners are essential to reduce fear and anxiety. Such relationships should include a constructive tolerance for mistakes.

Another deterrent to learning with which training specialists are confronted is that supervisory personnel frequently resent the fact that a training program takes their employees away from the immediate job. They sometimes feel that a training program interferes with their ability to get their jobs done. When key people are scheduled to be away in a class, it is more difficult to meet schedules and maintain a smoothly operating department. Moreover, if the supervisor is involved in a training activity, he may not be confident that the work will go smoothly if he is not on hand, despite any arrangement that he may have made in delegating responsibility. It may take time for supervisory personnel to realize that training has the preventive function of keeping the norm of the work force in concert with business needs. When employees attempt to perform tasks for which they have not been adequately trained, quality objectives cannot be economically reached. Proper training reduces both errors in quality and operating costs.

An example of what might be included in a training program for inspectors is given in figure 10-22. Inspectors must not only be thoroughly familiar with the prevailing procedures but also indoctrinated with the value of following established standards.

10.16 Training to Reduce Workmanship Defects

There are three general conditions that lead to workmanship defects: (1) lack of skill or training, (2) misunderstanding instructions, or (3) carelessness. Workmanship failures of various types are known causes of major failures, and companies

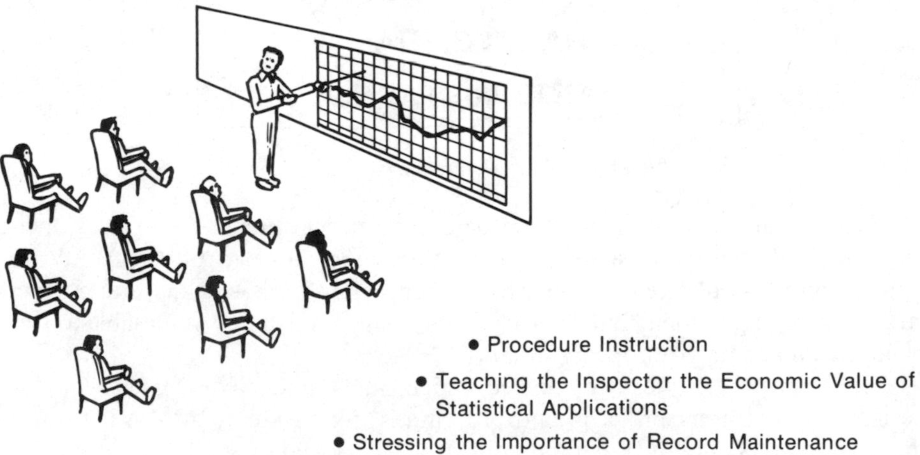

• Procedure Instruction
• Teaching the Inspector the Economic Value of Statistical Applications
• Stressing the Importance of Record Maintenance
• Making the Inspector a Team Member in the Quality Program
• Stressing the Concept of Conformance to Established Quality Standards

Figure 10–22 Inspector training.

must make certain that employees are provided the level of training that is commensurate with job complexity. Where high quality workmanship is mandatory, employees must be certified that they can perform to required standards. This certification usually encompasses the following.

1. Pre-hiring qualifications: (a) education and experience in the area, and (b) satisfactory scores on aptitude and performance tests.
2. Post-hiring training: (a) concentrated training program (usually 40 to 120 hours), (b) satisfactory grades on knowledge and performance tests after the completion of the training program, and (c) special training for specific tasks such as soldering, x-ray analysis, welding, and penetrant evaluation.

A training program should also focus on the proper use of company procedures and practice at following instructions. Every company uses a variety of paperwork, each having its unique forms and other means of transmitting written information. Familiarization with such documents is a necessary part of a training activity. Murphy's law states that "If anything can go wrong, it will go wrong" and this is certainly applicable in the area of following instructions. There is a tendency to read unintended meanings in a set of instructions, irrespective of how well the instructions have been written. An indoctrination program providing orientation and practice at following instructions will help to curb this problem.

Carelessness is often the result of a poor attitude about the job. However, a poor attitude is frequently a symptom of other problems in the working environment. Unfortunately, a training program often corrects only the symptom, while the causes go unchecked. The complex topic of worker attitudes, affected by countless variables, cannot be dealt with in depth here. However, a training program that meets its total objective will identify poor attitudes and either attempt to correct them or recommend reassignment of the employee to a job more suitable to his or her aptitudes and interests. Defects due to carelessness can often be reduced by a properly instituted job enrichment program which has as a principal objective a positive change in worker attitudes.

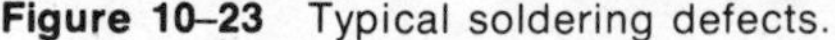

Figure 10–23 Typical soldering defects.

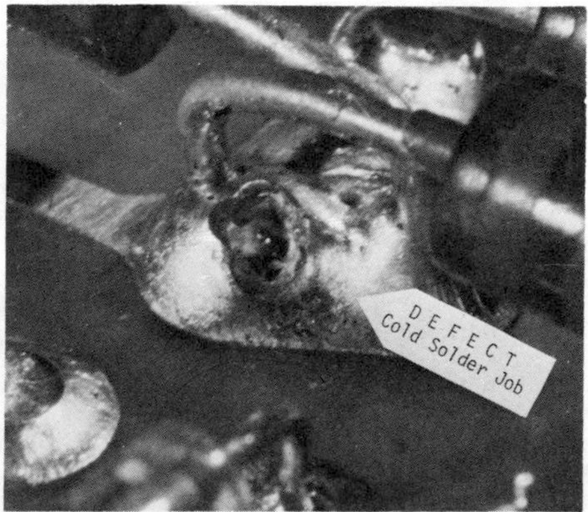

Figure 10–24 Typical soldering defects.

Figures 10-23 and 10-24 illustrate two examples of workmanship involving soldering defects that were found in an electronics manufacturing company. Figure 10-23 shows a misplaced drop of solder on a circuit card, which caused a short circuit. Figure 10-24 illustrates a poorly soldered terminal of a component. These types of workmanship defects almost always can be traced to one of the causes discussed earlier, i.e., lack of soldering experience or to poor training.

10.17 Some Major Training Guidelines

There are several broad guidelines that should be considered in developing an industrial training program. Industrial training should:

1. Continuously educate all levels in each of three fundamentally important areas: skill, knowledge, and attitudes needed to do quality work. (One can be guided in determining what to teach by recognizing that long-range plans should contain courses and other training devices of sufficient kind and variety to continuously educate everyone in each of the three major areas.)
2. Place a great emphasis on education in the desire and ability to cooperate, in mutual understanding, and in social skills of working harmoniously together. (These are the factors which most influence the effectiveness of industry today and the security and satisfaction of its personnel.)
3. Provide for continuous and cumulative learning. (Training should never be considered complete. Therefore, one can be guided in determining what to teach by recognizing that long-range plans should provide subject matter for continuous development of all levels of personnel.)
4. Include all levels of personnel in industry, from the custodian to the president. (The company can be guided in determining what to teach by recognizing that long-range plans must eventually include the instruction of all levels of personnel, the kind and amount depending on both immediate responsibilities and assignments and future potential promotions to positions requiring more skills and knowledge.)

EXERCISES

1. What is the relationship of company organization to quality organization?

2. Where should quality control appear on the organization chart?

3. What is meant by the functional type of organization?

4. Is it acceptable to have quality control subordinated to the production department organizationally? If so, under what conditions? Discuss the pros and cons of this practice.

5. Of the responsibilities discussed in this chapter, which do you believe are the most important? Support your answer.
6. Discuss some of the factors that will influence a worker's attitude toward building quality products.
7. Several authors have defined the major functions of management as planning, organizing, leading, and controlling. In a two-page report, explain these four functions. (More information on the control function is presented in the following chapter.)
8. What is meant by delegation of authority? How is this related to leadership?
9. What do behavioral scientists do? Discuss some of the work that these researchers have done that pertains to worker attitudes toward doing quality work.
10. Name five training principles. Discuss some guidelines that should be used in setting up an industrial training program.
11. List the primary abilities that an effective quality control manager must possess.
12. Discuss briefly the proper relation between a supervisor and those reporting directly to him or her.
13. What employee incentives are necessary to make a training program successful?
14. The study at the Hawthorne Works Division of General Electric covered the actual operations in industry. Describe the results of this study and its effect on industry.
15. What training programs should be provided for personnel in quality control? Explain how to develop quality-mindedness in all personnel in an industrial operation.

FOOTNOTES

[1] The significance of a defect is defined in terms of either the severity or frequency of its occurrence. In other words, a significant defect is a costly defect.

[2] Mack R. Douglas, *Success Can Be Yours* (Grand Rapids, Michigan: Zondervan Publishing House, 1968).

[3] A. H. Maslow, "A Theory of Human Motivation," *Psychological Review*, Vol. 50, 1943.

[4] D. McGregor, *The Human Side of Enterprise* (New York: McGraw-Hill Book Company, 1960).

[5] F. Herzberg, B. Mausner, and B. Snyderman, *The Motivation to Work*, 2nd edition (New York: John Wiley and Sons, Inc., 1959).

CHAPTER ELEVEN

SYSTEMS AND PROCEDURES

11.1 Objective

The efficient transmission of meaningful and accurate information is a vital factor in the economic control of quality in any plant. If information is inaccurate, misunderstood, or not available where and when it is needed, quality standards are costly to maintain. Errors in specifications, drawings, interdepartmental correspondence, purchase orders, test reports, and inspection procedures are examples of information systems problems. Systems and procedures must be carefully planned, accurately implemented, and periodically monitored while in use to avoid such problems.

This chapter is concerned with techniques of communicating data and information and the analysis of these techniques. This material is included (1) to focus the attention of the reader on the importance of maintaining an efficient communications system as a significant part of achieving overall quality control, and (2) to present current information pertaining to systems analysis and techniques.

11.2 Industrial Systems

The general manager of a modern business is in charge of a number of different systems, each of which performs different functions. In a manufacturing organization, a complex system of machines and personnel is devoted to the production of the company's goods. Scheduling machines to do particular jobs and determining when and by whom a task will be completed are difficult jobs and require a thorough knowledge of the entire production system. A second system is the communications system that involves telephones, messengers, and perhaps teletype connections between facilities that are geographically separated. A third system pertains to managing goods, preparing invoices, shipping the goods, and perhaps following up the order to help the customer make best use of what he has purchased. Still another system is concerned with billing the customer, determining what credit to extend to the customer, analyzing discount procedures, making adjustments, and so forth.

The study of business-information systems shows an organization as a large system of activities designed to satisfy the goals of the business. Each of these activities—production, filling orders, billing customers, information flow, and so forth— is itself a system. Ideally, the individual systems within the whole complement each other. The information system indicates to the production system what to produce and in what quantities to best satisfy the customers. The customer-billing system aids the accounting and financial systems to determine the flow of funds and the marketing system by providing reports of customer activities. The marketing system complements the production system by determining not only what can be sold but what can be both sold and profitably produced.

An *open loop* (a break in the flow of information) and consequent misunderstanding in any one of these systems invariably will have direct or indirect negative effects upon either product quality or costs or both.

11.3 The Information System

Definition of a System

A *system* is a logical and organized combination of parts that comprises the total. The opposite of a system is disorganization and inefficiency. A company information system is designed to fulfill the requirements of management for the needed data to plan, direct, communicate, control, and evaluate business.

A systems analysis group is usually needed in large companies to investigate, plan, design, and implement efficient methods for handling data for business transactions. Investigation, analysis, and planning phases necessitate providing written plans including flow charts, schedules of changes, and a description of the technical devices needed to implement a system. The system function in modern business is concerned not only with accounting and financial aspects of the business, but also with information system efficiency in departments such as production, quality control, procurement, marketing, contracts, program control, and engineering, all of which either directly or indirectly influence the control of quality.

Information, as used in an industrial organization, is a commodity that should maximize the organization's use of resources such as raw materials, labor, and physical facilities—and should achieve the goals of the organization in the most efficient manner. Like other resources available to the organization, information is not a free commodity. Its overuse in some companies, however, might lead one to believe that it is.

As more and more information becomes available, the organization finds it increasingly difficult to make as much use of it as was possible with the first few items of data. Thus, as the amount of information available to an organization increases, the usefulness of each additional unit of information decreases. It follows that it is possible for a business organization to have more information than it can use. Unfortunately, this is not only possible, but true in many companies.

The use of computers during the last two decades has, in some instances, compounded information problems instead of solving them. Few things are more expensive than processing data at computer speeds that do not need processing at all. Automation should never precede work simplification to reduce the total work element and optimize the needs of the various departments. Only with work simplification will the computer come closer to processing only those data that are *required* in the normal course of business. (A further discussion of computer applications is presented later in this chapter.)

Procedures

In systems work, use is often made of the term procedure. A *procedure* is a series of logical steps for accomplishing a job. For example, the procedure for starting the engine of an automobile equipped with an automatic transmission might be (1) place transmission in park, (2) insert key into ignition, (3) press accelerator pedal to the floor once and release, (4) turn ignition key clockwise and hold key in this position until engine starts, (5) release key, and (6) put transmission in the position desired. Procedures that are formally specified are very important for most manufacturing operations. For example, the steps that a worker on a production line must take to accomplish a task may be set forth in a manner designed to help train future workers to do the same work, and to provide the basis for an analysis of what actions are required. In quality organizations, inspection procedures which describe the steps to be followed during the inspection task are usually needed. Maintainability programs also provide procedures for replacement or repair of systems. In this case, procedures describe precisely how certain components or subassemblies must be replaced in order to achieve the predicted reliability.

Work Instructions

Work instructions, like procedures, describe the steps of operations, but usually contain considerably more detail than procedures. Work instructions have different names in different plants and sometimes even in different departments of the same plant. Among the names used are *production control books, production control releases, job tickets, manufacturing control sheets, work orders,* and other various inspection instructions. Such instructions ordinarily tell how a job will be done, the order in which actions are accomplished, set-up information, speeds and feeds, associated drawings and specifications, and other pertinent information.

Instructions that state how work is to be done affect quality in many departments. For example, inadequate instructions for packaging a product will lead to

Figure 11–1 Operation instruction sheet.

Operation Instruction Sheet				
	Part Number 552-8572-002 Description Terminal Board Next Assy 552-8547-004	Drawing Revision B Operation Instruction Revision Date System		
Sequence	Operation	Quan.	Min./ Cycle	Total Time
1.	Mount CRI on slotted terminals 1 and 2, polarity per sketch below.			
	1-353-2885-00 diode 1N663			
2.	Mount resistor R1 on slotted terminals 3 and 4.			
	1-745-3337-00 resistor 470Ω			
3.	Mount resistor R2 on terminals 5 and 6.			
	1-745-3278-00 resistor 180Ω			
4.	Bus wire to terminals as follows:			
	Term. 8 to 7 Term. 9 to 10			
5.	7 to 9 6 to 12 (clear teflon tubing, this wire)			
	Solder all connections			
6.	Apply decal to back of board per sketch below			
	1-552-8557-002 decal			
7.	Inspection for Workmanship			

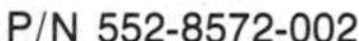

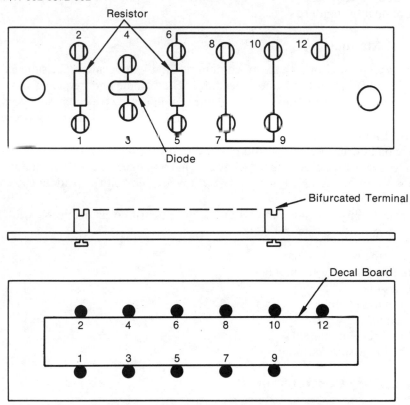

Figure 11–2 Assembly sketch used with operation instruction sheet (Figure 11–1).

inferior packaging, which, in turn, may result in damage to the item during transportation. Also, improper instructions for the assembly of units will result in defective units. An example of an operation instruction sheet and the attendant sketch for the assembly of components are illustrated in figures 11-1 and 11-2. On such an instruction sheet, explicit steps of the assembly are set forth to classify the desired procedure. Without such instructions, there is a high probability of error.

It is of prime importance that the events that make possible the fabrication of a product follow a systematic, unvarying sequence of work operations. For this reason, work instructions are necessary, regardless of whether a contractor's facilities and organization are considered to be small or large. Of course, for large enterprises. documented work instructions are an absolute necessity for communication purposes because of the large number of people involved. However, smaller organizations have no less need for appropriately documented work instructions to achieve quality standards.

Use of Manuals

Manuals represent one means of communicating management decisions concerning organization, policies, and procedures. The volume and frequency of such decisions are increasing in modern companies, and progressive enterprises regard their organizational structures, policy statements, and procedural practices as elements of administration that can and should change as often as required to capitalize on new business opportunities and to meet competition.

This concept of management has somewhat changed the role of manuals. Manuals are now designed with a view toward flexibility, readability, and simplicity.

There are many kinds of manuals in use in industrial organizations. A few of the most common are listed here.

1. Drafting room manual
2. Industrial relations manual
3. Sales manual
4. Training manual
5. Finance manual
6. Procurement manual
7. Quality assurance manual

The Quality Control Manual

In a manner similar to other manuals, the quality control manual sets forth the overall quality control activities that must be implemented throughout the design, build, and test phases of hardware development. A quality control manual should be written, used, and kept up to date regardless of the size of the company or the nature of the products. No organized system can function properly without a plan; no group of people can be organized and function smoothly without guidelines and a plan for action. The quality control manual is the "bible" for the department and contains such information as

Discussion of the quality organization.
Definitions, abbreviations, and acronyms.
Quality costs definition and data collection.
Definition and disposition of nonconforming materials.
Acceptance and rejection criteria.
Corrective action procedures.
Supplier controls.
Tooling control and certification.

In-process and final inspection procedures.
Equipment calibration and control.
Sampling procedures and statistical control.
Administrative policies.
Audits.
Reliability and maintainability.
Testing procedures.
Government furnished equipment (GFE).

11.4 Influences on System Performance

A system is composed of three principal components: people, equipment, and information. Thus, conditions that influence these three factors will influence system efficiency.

Personal Factors

When attempting to assign causes of human error, *personal factors* are often very complex. Countless physiological and psychological variables constantly influence a person's ability to perform. Only when the human component is replaced by a mechanical device can these variables be removed from the system.

Principles

1. Maximize worker motivation and job satisfaction. This is best accomplished when (a) the operator feels a sense of achievement and responsibility for maintaining system efficiency, and (b) objectives have been set, preferably allowing the workers to participate in the planning tasks.
2. Set up regular rest periods, particularly for routine or monotonous jobs, and discourage overtime.
3. Establish an employee-certification program, and assign appropriate jobs to the employees.
4. Select workers who are less sensitive to such conditions where disturbing conditions at or near the work place are unavoidable.

System Design Factors

System design factors refer to any overall system design conditions which can eventually reduce the reliability of the human element. This includes all conditions which do not aid in completing manual activities in the desired time with no errors.

Principles

1. Sufficient time must be provided to complete a given activity.
2. An accurate and meaningful feedback must be provided to the worker about status.

3. An organizational structure should be established which assigns the responsibility of system success to one individual, together with effective lines of reporting with stated degrees of responsibility at each level.
4. System outputs in the format required by the system user should be achieved.
5. Input forms should be laid out in a manner consistent with the way data are being received by the system.

Documentation Factors

It is necessary that complete procedures be prepared and used so that design decisions can be communicated to the user. The operator must know exactly what he is to do if he is to meet system objectives. It follows that this documentation must be organized and written so that the operator can completely understand its contents.

Principles

1. Complete, clear, and accurate procedures must be written and used.
2. A program for efficient and continuous documentation revision must be implemented.
3. New documentation should complement and be consistent with existing procedures.
4. Supervisory personnel should insist that documentation be followed.
5. Complete and well-organized reference materials must be available.
6. Useful and clear memory aids should be provided.

Training Factors

It is an important fact that having an operator completely trained is not the same as having complete and updated training materials. Even if the system is well designed and adequately documented, the probability of error will be high if employees are not trained concerning exactly what they are to do and how to do it best.

In order to acquire all the knowledge and skills necessary to work efficiently and accurately, both formal classroom training and on-the-job training are usually required. Competency is developed primarily through application of the principles.

Principles

1. Provide adequate classroom training to effectively teach what needs to be taught.
2. Measurable objectives to assess progress must be used.
3. Follow-up action to insure that skills are developing correctly should be conducted.
4. A continuous program of training should be implemented to account for "change" factors.

5. Operators must have the minimum knowledge and skill required to increase their levels of understanding and benefit from training programs.

Environmental Factors

Factors relating to working conditions in a facility always affect the accuracy of performance in some way. Included among these conditions are room temperature, noise, lighting, or traffic passing back and forth in front of work stations.

Principles

1. At least 100 footcandles of light should be provided at the work surface for tasks involving sight problems. (Unfortunately, the energy crunch has resulted in a compromise of this principle in many companies.)
2. Eliminate distracting noise, especially of unexpected or intermittent character.
3. Room temperatures and relative humidities should be maintained from 70° to 75°F and from 40 to 50%, respectively.
4. A social environment acceptable to the operators should be provided.
5. Adequate work space for each operator must be provided.
6. Visual distractions should be minimized.

11.5 Criteria for System Success

The efficacy with which information can be transmitted and utilized will be in direct proportion to the degree in which certain fundamental principles are satisfied. Among the most important of these are the following

1. The application of systems and procedures and their analyses must be dynamic; changing conditions usually call for changes in systems and procedures.
2. The policies, scope, objectives, and responsibilities of the company's systems and procedures program must be clearly documented.
3. Management, in general, must be knowledgeable about the company and the systems and procedures in operation.
4. Responsibility for the technical aspects of the systems and procedures program must properly be placed with specialists who have the expertise to best perform this work.
5. The improvement of systems and procedures, through simplification, modernization, or standardization, must not be viewed as an intermittent campaign; it is a continuous, repetitive function that can pay off in a host of beneficial results, with only a few of these results being of a spectacular nature.
6. Last, and perhaps most important, top management must give such a function its full support.

11.6 Information for Management Decisions

Both policy-making and operating levels of management must have accurate and relevant information in order to construct future plans and control day-to-day activities. Policy-level planning involves defining objectives of the organization, deciding the resources to be used in meeting these objectives, and creating policies that govern these actions. The operating level of planning is more transaction-oriented; more detail must be generated by data processing at this level, the amount depending on the nature of the organization and the level of managerial usage. Top management does not need the information detail that is needed to plan and control effectively at lower levels of management. In either case, however, management control is achieved through the process of assuring that available men, materials, and machines are utilized effectively in meeting the organization's commitments. The efficient transmittal of information is a vital factor in achieving this control.

11.7 How Control is Achieved

The Meaning of Control

Any control function involves objectives, planning, and appraisal; it embraces those activities by which the company's operations are motivated and guided to accomplish stated goals.

Control is achieved through the exercise of the following disciplines and activities.

1. Control begins with planning: the determination of objectives through the medium of profit, goals, work programs, procedures, quality standards, and the like.
2. The process of control includes the appraisal of performance by those who have delegated authority and are responsible for seeing that the job is done properly.
3. On the basis of appraisal, it is possible to ascertain the points at which performance has varied from planned objectives or standards, and to determine the reasons for variance. Either performance has been inadequate or the goals were incorrectly set.
4. The cycle is completed with the planning function, again receiving new information for direction.
5. Once decisions have been made and the job is being done, these management tools and objectives permit the individual to better accomplish the task at hand and to gain the inner satisfaction which comes with meeting an objective.

This management cycle of planning and control can be described in terms of *goals, planning, review, evaluation,* and *corrective action.*

Goals and Planning

Goals are established for the organization as a whole, as well as for every one of its components. Available resources are examined to determine whether they permit the realization of these targets. This establishes the best way by which the objectives can be reached under the prevailing conditions.

A decision among possible alternative plans is made. Necessary instructions are discussed with all concerned. Activities proceed under the direction of management and as closely in harmony with the plans as possible.

Review and Evaluation

While planning looks ahead to determine what should be done, review and evaluation looks back to determine what actually did happen. Review and evaluation requires (1) the observation of operations, (2) recording results, and (3) evaluating the results.

Corrective Action

Results of the evaluation activities in the review and evaluation phase dictate the nature of the corrective action to be taken.

Figure 11-3 shows the relationship of all these terms, and figure 11-4 shows the details of the cycle. Once plans have been carried out, the degree to which the plans become operative must be reviewed and evaluated, then corrective action taken if necessary. Correspondingly, the corrective action may result in a change in the original planning and the cycle may begin anew.

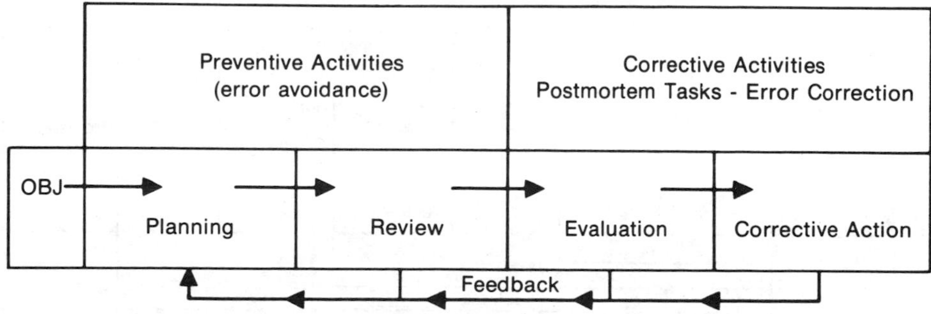

Figure 11–3 Cycle of planning and corrective action.

The Importance of Feedback

Feedback provides the means by which the planning and control cycle works. To the degree that feedback is accurate and timely, planning and control will be effective.

Once a plan has been formulated, its efficient ongoing implementation is based on accurate reviews and evaluation as the plan progresses through its various stages. A plan predetermines action; it is a road map for future work. There are many roadblocks, however, that can occur along the way that could not be predicted when the plan was put into effect. Hence, quick and accurate feedback are needed to plot new courses of action or to plan the best means of detouring around the unplanned roadblocks.

Program progress and status, which are needed for control, are gleaned through feedback information. Program status reporting involves a system which:

1. permits management to maintain overall status identity of the program compared to the program plan;
2. permits decision making on the basis of integrated management data;
3. permits quick and complete evaluation of program progress; and
4. permits rapid adjustment of plans to meet changing conditions when required.

Feedback for Quality Control

Review, evaluation, and corrective action documentation are forms of reporting quality. Miscellaneous inspection reports, change orders, failure reports, and customer complaints are examples of quality feedback information. Figure 11-3

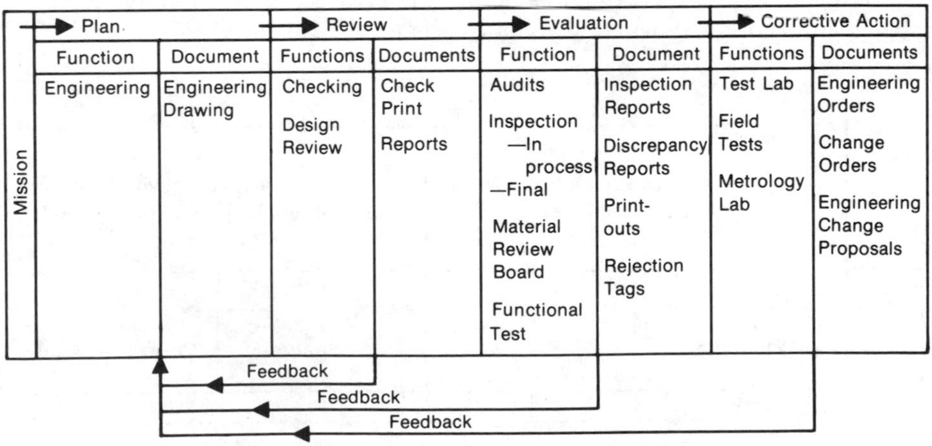

Mission

Plan		Review		Evaluation		Corrective Action	
Function	Document	Functions	Documents	Function	Document	Functions	Documents
Engineering	Engineering Drawing	Checking Design Review	Check Print Reports	Audits Inspection —In process —Final Material Review Board Functional Test	Inspection Reports Discrepancy Reports Print-outs Rejection Tags	Test Lab Field Tests Metrology Lab	Engineering Orders Change Orders Engineering Change Proposals

Feedback
Feedback
Feedback

Figure 11–4 Illustration of a cycle of planning and corrective action.

shows an example of a planning and control cycle which shows feedback as a vital factor in the cycle. Feedback information is that essential ingredient which enables management to assess conformance of the implementation of a plan with the plan itself. Figure 11-4 is a flow diagram of such a system in which plans are conceived and carried out, and by which control is achieved through feedback.[1]

The link between reviewing past operations and planning for the future is frequently weak. Feedback depends upon the communications media and decisions are based on these communications reports. It is incumbent on the systems engineer to take every precaution to close all loops in the information system. Inadequate development of the communication system can be manifested as follows. (1) A systems man makes a change that he thinks will improve the system, but does not communicate the nature of the change to the various levels that should know about it. (2) Programs that are created, tested, and become operational will require changes that could involve any number of programs and an exhaustive reprogramming effort. (3) Reports containing erroneous information could be going to management, which might be making decisions based upon this information. The outcomes could be disastrous.

Figure 11-5 illustrates how feedback for control is integrated into the total information system. As goals (milestones) are achieved or as rework becomes necessary, feedback of status information is required. Feedback of failure data is also needed by design engineering and production departments. Appropriate design change action and production improvements are consequences of effective feedback of failure data.

The closed-loop system is shown in figure 11-6.

Success in a system requires cooperation between the systems personnel and the operating people that are to use the system. Proper lines of communication, used continuously, will go far toward enhancing the chance of success. Conversely, improper lines of communication could well result in failure, despite the presence of all other elements of success. With proper communications, operating personnel are more likely to feel that they are part of the system. Then they will speak freely of their needs and make definitive contributions to the system effort.

11.8 Some Reasons for Loss of Control

Countless reasons can be given for poor control in a company, but *open loops* in the information system will certainly contribute to the problems. Open loops will foster delays either in issuing information to a work station, or in receiving performance data back from an operation. Breaches in the flow of information will also jeopardize a manager's ability to transmit and receive accurate information.

The tendency toward open loops in an information system is directly related either to receiving too little relevant information for decision making, or to receiving too much irrelevant information. If needed data are not readily available to the user, timely decisions cannot be made. On the other hand, if specific information

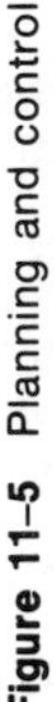

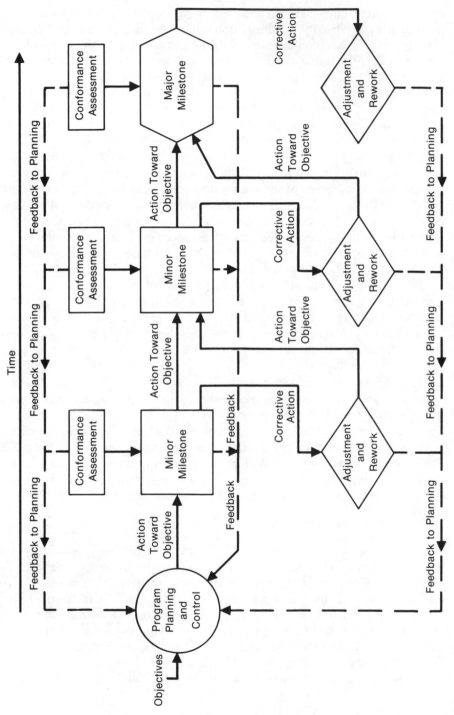

Figure 11–5 Planning and control.

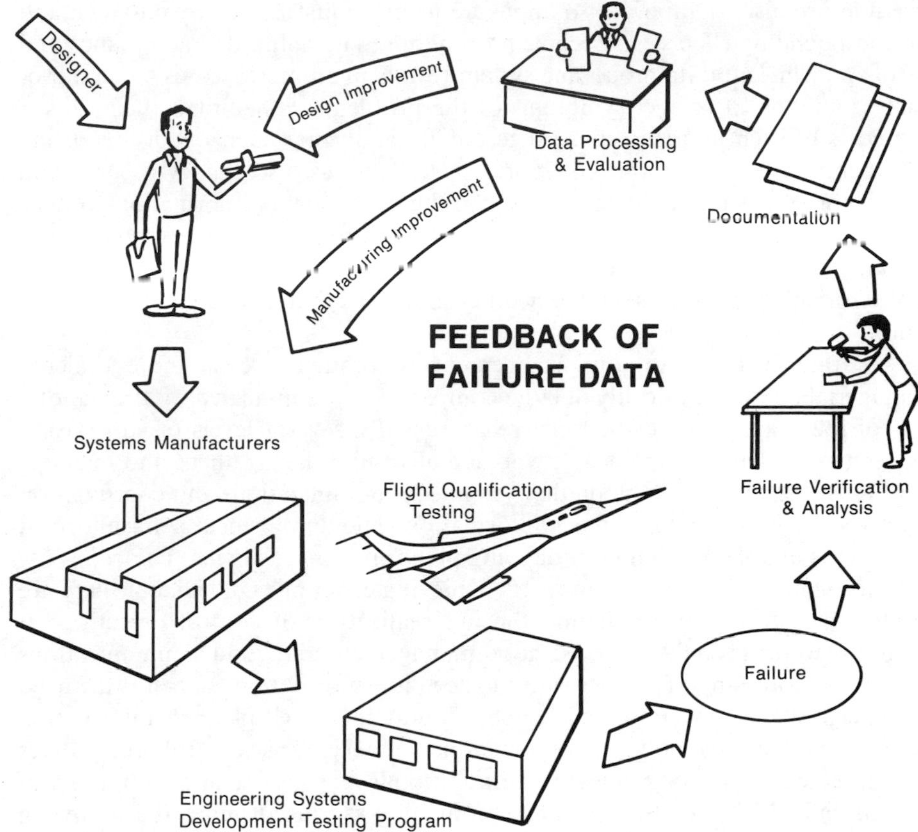

Figure 11–6 Feedback of failure data.

is needed, it should not be necessary for the user to waste time in deciphering and extracting the information from a conglomeration of unwanted data. Personnel should not receive information unless it is needed or relevant to their objectives. To receive accurate and timely data for decision making is both important and necessary, but to receive correspondence and data that serve only to annoy the recipient results in confusion and wastefulness. When the recipients of miscellaneous documents develop the attitude that certain data are perfunctory or inadequate to render required judgments, a change in the system is justified and should be made.

An ineffectual flow of information has compounding consequences. Avoidable (but often hidden) costs are always incurred when quality information is in an uncontrolled condition. Varying amounts of corrective action ultimately will be needed to meet planned commitments, and the attendant costs will usually exceed normal expectations. In striving to stay within budget allocations and keep schedule promises, temporary solutions frequently must be hastily initiated, and the compounding effects can become horrendous. The continued acceptance and use of an inefficient data processing system results in an increased use of inappropriate solutions to correct symptoms of the problems rather than their causes. The costs of such actions can be detected by analyzing such quality-reporting documents as rework and scrap reports, miscellaneous discrepancy reports, and sundry corrective action documents. When there is a lack of information control, it is impossible to efficiently achieve expected profit margins. Moreover, customer apprehension and criticism tend to increase commensurably with the diversity of quality-oriented problems and schedule slippages that accompany corrective action.

Accurate feedback to top management is frequently even more difficult. Managerial control, especially in large companies, is complicated by the remoteness of the manager's position. There are usually several levels of supervision between executives and the people who actually build the products, and management must depend heavily upon the system of communications and coordination to be assured of accurate feedback information. The uninformed or misinformed executive is unable to administer ongoing plans and can easily lose control.

Thorough planning is a requisite for achieving economic control, but there are additional factors that can inhibit the full realization of control objectives. If economic control is to be achieved, good management and good communications must be concomitants. Together with the need for information control is the need to manage effectively. Potential benefits found in a well-planned information system can be realized only if management personnel exercise control prerogatives as well as leadership principles. Some additional reasons for and symptoms of control difficulties are also presented. Control is sacrificed under the following conditions.

1. The philosophy in a company shifts from preventive action to corrective action. If this occurs, emphasis is placed on what can be done to correct errors instead of what can be done to prevent errors. Management conditions the employees to think in terms of rework or corrective action by planning *for* these activities instead of planning *against* them. Reliance for product assurance is placed on correcting quality instead of planning and building quality. This philosophy creeps into an organization very subtly, and usually only top management is in the position to make desired changes. If the top officials of the company are convinced that economic control can be attained through preventive planning, they can be the source of stimulus needed to keep planning and control activities in the proper proportion.
2. There is no effective program for improving the methods of correcting system deficiencies. Most control functions in a company sorely need methods studies at the system level. Often procedures are developed over a long period of time and certain segments may overlap and become redundant.

Unwarranted procedures and miscellaneous corrective actions may *appear* to be needed because of the lack of overall system visibility. If there is no central authority in the organization to implement needed changes in the system, tasks are performed, open loops in the control system develop, corrective action flourishes, more "band aids" are needed to patch up problems, and costs soar.

3. Supervisory personnel sanction deviation from procedures instead of using channels to effect formal changes. The practice of taking shortcuts to meet an immediate objective may jeopardize full realization of another objective, and will often lead to additional corrective action.

11.9 Overcoming Loss of Control

There are several measures that an executive may take to either avoid or correct the situation when loss of control has occurred.

1. Implement and support a systems planning and analysis function with both the authority and expertise needed to detect and correct system deficiencies. The head of this function must report to the plant manager and be given clear authority to effect approved changes. The mission of such a function would be to implement changes that would avoid excessive corrective action.

It is important to be aware of a company's procedure and to be able to exercise reasonable control over it. If management does not provide a properly chartered systems department, informality will tend to rule and individuals and departments will do things more or less as they please.

2. The quality control organization should take a leadership role and assume more responsibility for the jobs that directly involve quality. A specifically defined inspection and test planning function is desirable. The type of planning referred to here relates to inspection and test methods and procedures as well as scheduling. Costs that are often accepted as inherent are only hidden and can be reduced by implementing a planning function which defines test and inspection steps much like manufacturing planners plan the steps of manufacture. Better control and fewer trial-and-error methods are results of good inspection methods. The costs to achieve these objectives should be much less than the hidden costs incurred without such planning.
3. Managers of the company should work closely with supervisors before problems occur, not just when corrective action is needed. As shown in figure 11-7, time is usually planned for reworking but may not be allowed for avoiding problems. By taking concrete steps to assist supervisors in planning their tasks, corrective action frequently can be reduced.

WHY IS IT
THAT THERE IS NEVER
ENOUGH TIME
TO DO IT RIGHT?
BUT THERE IS ALWAYS
ENOUGH TIME TO DO IT
OVER!

Figure 11–7 Why is it . . .?

11.10 Forms Design and Control

Definition of a Form

A form is nothing more than a source of printed, constant information with spaces for the entry of variable information. It is generally printed on paper and reproduced by a variety of processes such as carbon, ditto, computer printouts, zerox, etc.

Some of the more common types of forms with which almost every person is familiar are employment applications, payroll checks, and income-tax reports. In a manufacturing company, forms such as bills for materials, corrective-action requests, engineering change requests, and various inspection forms are commonplace. (Numerous examples of forms are presented in Chapter 12.)

In form design, it is necessary to know how data will be gathered or entered, and how they will be used in succeeding process steps. Will data be typed or key-punched or read by optical scanners or by other means? Mechanical equipment of the data-capturing set often must be considered in the design procedure.

There is also the matter of future reference. Will the form be retrieved at some future date? If so, for what purposes? What will be the key or keys by which this form is retrieved? During this period, how will the form be stored? Further, will there be archival retention during long future periods?

Proper Use of Forms

The proper use of forms sometimes calls for training to some extent, but unfortunately this is frequently ignored. If the system of which the form is a part is to be adequately understood and operated, then it is important that the form and its operation be incorporated into the overall systems definition. This includes training or refresher training in the requirements of the form and all related aspects, if necessary. Such training sometimes requires the use of procedures manuals and instructional directives, which together provide the steps necessary for effective operation.

The study of systems steps has reached a high level of refinement in many large companies. In computer programs, for example, there can be pages of flow charts to diagram precisely everything that can and should or should not occur. By studying and simplifying information structures, one can present a diagram of the underlying flow process. Such training devices can be valuable in understanding complex aspects of a large data handling system.

Training in the use of forms is also important in small companies where the information system should not be complex and unwieldy. However, misinterpretation and consequent mistakes do occur often simply because someone did not know how to fill out a form correctly. A few minutes devoted to the preventive measure of training personnel in the use of forms will avoid perhaps hours or even days of correcting mistakes caused by a misunderstanding or by errors made in filling out a form.

Forms Control

With the wide variety of products and activities intrinsic to modern industry, correct and current data are essential to cogent quality analysis. When planning a data system, the planner must keep in mind one of the most important purposes of the system: that of evaluating quality status from feedback data. Often, efficiency can be improved either by modifying existing forms for data collection or by creating new forms that better meet the objectives.

Effective forms control can be achieved by applying good business practices to the forms control function within the organization. This begins with the assignment of responsibility, authority, and resources for the program to an appropriate part of the organization. This may or may not include a professional forms design group within the company.

The form itself should have a direct relationship to the data flow preceding and following it. This relationship requires sufficient analysis to reveal the procedure or process from start to finish. A rigorous review of this total beginning-to-end process and the specific part that the form plays should be initiated at the form's inception, and repeated periodically during its life and at times of major change in the process.

This review should ensure that all the form's interfaces are appropriate and adequate, including such considerations as timing, collateral information, links to coordinate or parallel files, proper treatment of duplicating or overlapping functions that may be identified, proper arrangement of succeeding or dependent actions, storage and retrieval methods, and authentication or authorizations that may be required.

The cost of forms can vary considerably. For example, 1000 standard IBM punched cards may be purchased for approximately $2.00, but an eight-carbon hardback form may cost as much as .50 to .75c per copy. Forms for collecting data and communicating information should be examined on the basis of the following goals.

1. Eliminate unnecessary data collection devices. Redundant forms increase costs, sources of errors, and confusion.

2. Combine certain data segments of the forms to provide for better flow of information. If information should be included on a particular form, then measures must be taken to include such information. If data are not relevant to a given document, then the information should be evaluated for inclusion on a different form. If certain data are not useful, they should not be collected and reported.
3. Change the order in which segments of the forms are organized.

A forms control group should be organized to make certain that the forms are properly designed and available to those who need them and at the time they are needed. The forms control group is responsible for (a) ascertaining that each form fulfills a basic requirement of an approved operating procedure, (b) designing each form so that it will perform its purpose efficiently and effectively, (c) specifying the most economical method of manufacture for each form, and (d) establishing a system of stock control and replenishment that will make each form available when needed, in economic quantities and at advantageous prices.

This means that the forms control group is normally responsible for controlling the design, revision, specifications, nomenclature, numbering, classification, provisioning, and obsolescence of all company forms. However, the forms control specialist does not necessarily approve the application of a form; this is normally the systems analyst's function. The latter determines whether a proposed new form is essential to carrying out an approved procedure before turning it over to forms personnel for action. Likewise, the forms person refers any procedural problem relative to a form that has come to his or her attention to the systems man.

11.11 Prevention vs. Correction

System analysts should fully understand the concept of *preventive action* to avoid *corrective action* when planning and implementing a data processing system. The overall costs that are generated while planning and controlling activities (including corrective action) will be less if adequate preventive measures are taken in the initial stages of the design of a data processing system. This point is illustrated in figures 11-8 and 11-9. Ongoing control of quality is largely dependent on the amount of preventive action taken when planning the information system. Proper preventive controls (e.g., the use of in-line control charts as shown in figure 11–10) will result in a higher average outgoing quality at a reduced cost.

Costs of control can be reduced with an information system that:

1. is thoroughly planned;
2. provides for the efficient flow of information *to* and *from* the respective work centers;
3. ensures that all the information needs for effecting quality plans and reporting quality levels and trends are accounted for;

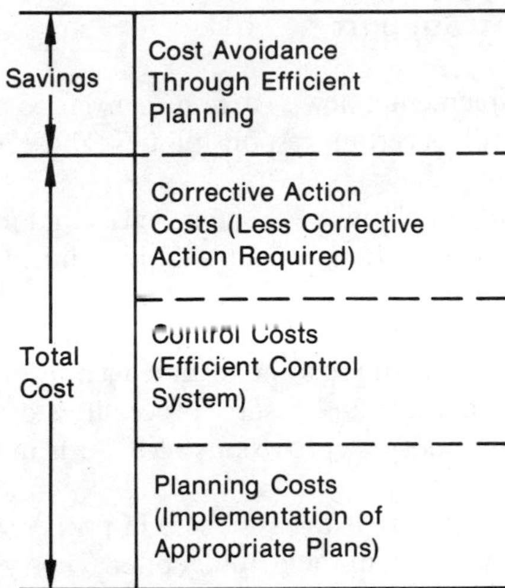

Figure 11–8 Savings and total cost.

4. is designed so that if the information system must be circumvented, there is a *planned* method for doing so;
5. is sufficiently flexible and versatile to accommodate changes as required; and
6. is sufficiently stable and reliable to earn the confidence of personnel throughout the organization.

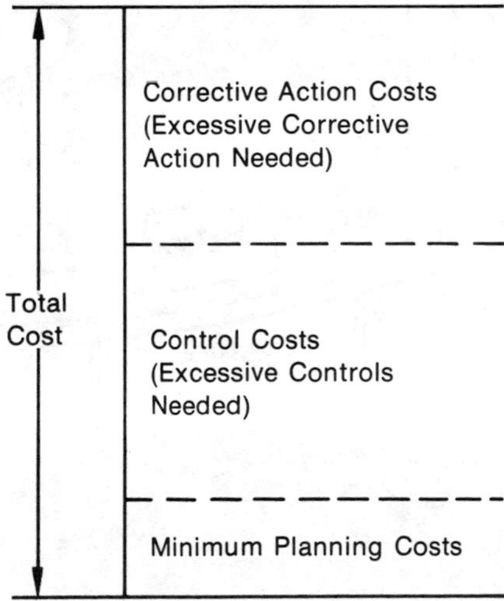

Figure 11–9 Total cost.

11.12 Management Support

Once the decision to implement a new system or convert to a different system has been made, management has certain responsibilities. These are outlined below.

1. Communication channels must be established so that management is alerted when difficulties arise. Management should confirm that scheduling has been properly set up for testing new on-line and off-line procedures; that sufficient hours have been provided for paralleling (a secondary method) before conversion; that there is good documentation during this period, including various control and restart procedures, operating route sheets, and other records; and that provisions have been made to retain records and history files.
2. The user should be sure that the system is in proper working order before accepting the turnover from the manufacturer. The system should be completely field-tested by the manufacturer, who does this by running certain diagnostic tests after the machine has been installed. The manufacturer's engineering staff should be on call during the initial period.
3. After installation, everyone concerned should be included in discussions of what must take place. People who have been trained for this period should

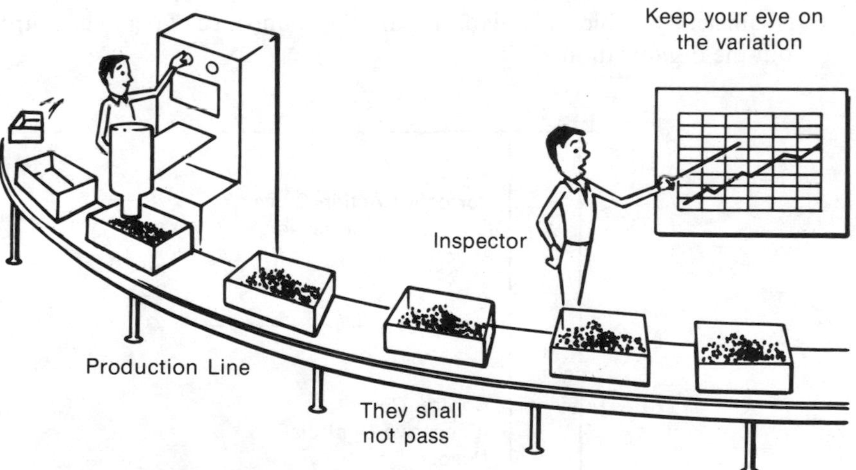

- Improve Methods and Procedures
- Speed up of Production
- Reduced Cost
- Higher Quality

Figure 11–10 Preventive controls development.

be given a final training session to make certain that nothing has been left out. Management should be available while this is taking place.

4. Management must make certain that backup facilities are available in case of machine malfunction or unforeseen failures in planning.

Management has both a right and a need to rely on the accuracy of the information being provided by the system. However, it does not pay to spend ten dollars to provide checks and balances that verify a transaction involving one dollar. Many systems practitioners institute controls as an auditing concept without regard to practicality or economy.

The systems person must be sure that the manager realizes that methods of handling data which were not previously feasible may now be feasible. The manager must be aware of the rapid changes that have taken and will take place in equipment capabilities, making previously impossible things not only practical and feasible, but also desirable. The systems person should also suggest that managers periodically resubmit requests previously denied; new equipment may have made the denial obsolete. Managers should be encouraged to request not only everything they need, but also everything they would like to have from the systems group. If line managers ask only for what they must have, they may unknowingly do without things that could easily be provided by the systems group.

11.13 Role of Computers

Computer Applications

Applications of computers in industry have burgeoned during the past twenty years. Many tasks that once had to be completed manually can now be done more accurately and on a much faster basis with the use of computers. Five important benefits found in the use of computers are given in figure 11-11.

1. HUGE MASSES OF DATA CAN BE COMPILED FOR EASY ANALYSIS.
2. THE NECESSARY MATHEMATICS CAN BE QUICKLY COMPUTED WITH COMPUTER SYSTEMS.
3. COMPUTER USE ENABLES MANY TYPES OF REPORTS TO BE ISSUED.
4. REPORTS CAN BE PREPARED AND DISTRIBUTED ON A VERY CURRENT BASIS.
5. DATA CAN BE ORGANIZED AND REPORTED FOR SPECIFIC PURPOSES AND FOR SPECIFIC USERS.

Figure 11–11 From manual to computerized data.

The following points were brought out in a survey of 8,000 different organizations conducted in 1969.

1. Most firms using computers use them for such routine jobs as payroll, accounts receivable, and general bookkeeping. Sixty-eight percent of the respondents indicated that they operated their own in-house computer system, and only 28% of these users indicated that their own systems were paying off.
2. Results of the survey indicated that 90% of the computers used in industry were either overqualified or underemployed. *Overqualified* means that the computer possesses far more processing power than is necessary for the job to which it is put, while *underemployed* means that the system stands idle unjustifiably or is not put to the sort of uses for which it was designed to perform most efficiently.
3. The most-often named course of action to increase the efficiency of computer use was better planning and preparation.

Some of the reasons that computer applications have not been as effective as they might be are given below.

1. Equipment was purchased that was too elaborate for the company's needs. This can happen when a company is heavily influenced by advertising claims. The desire for status also may be a factor.
2. Equipment that is not sophisticated enough for the business purpose was brought in. The result is that the demands made of the equipment are excessive and cannot be met.
3. Improper planning resulted in installation costs—such as programming, debugging, and paralleling—that are considerably over the initial estimate, even though the equipment is appropriate. In addition, the conversion might be poorly planned.
4. The initial decision to mechanize was erroneous. Very often the work can be done more economically manually than with elaborate equipment. Perhaps it might have been better to mechanize at a later date. Very often companies treat data processing equipment like a new toy, so that a short-run job completed in seconds on a computer takes many minutes in handling and setup time, and is therefore not economically sound.
5. Fear and indecision lead to undermechanizing. Miscalculations or temporary problems may force an improper reevaluation of mechanization needs. Perhaps the desire to bring the result within budgetary limits causes the manager to compromise his principles or settle for a misleading short-run benefit.

Computers should be used in the way that they are best qualified to work. The basic computer system should be directed to obtain maximum performance from the electronic computing equipment. It is certainly not true that computers should be programmed to do work the way humans have in the past. Although computers and humans perform many of the same tasks, their relative efficiencies and economic advantages are quite different. To arbitrarily make the computer follow the same routines, steps, or processes as humans is illogical.

If any of the pitfalls enumerated above overtake a manager, the effect upon top management is usually the same. The image of data processing is needlessly damaged. Confidence in automated data processing (ADP) and its potential is lost long before it has been given a fair chance, and it may never again get a fair trial in the company.

The Integrated Automatic System Approach

The keystone of an integrated data processing system is a complete network of managerial intelligence. This does not mean kilometers of wires strung between buildings and departments nor does it mean a computer per se. An integrated automatic data processing system is one in which data are manually recorded at their source on some type of machine-readable media so that all further processing can be handled by machines. It is a systematic network of people and equipment integrated in order to process information.

True integration follows lines of information flow and cuts both vertically and horizontally through an organization. Data upon which management bases its decisions must be the result of a planned system of indicators. For example, quality control information in the inspection and quality engineering departments should be integrated with—not superimposed on—other functions within the organization. Quality costs in engineering, production, inspection, and purchasing, for example, can be matched together deliberately, not coincidentally.

By having all the information processes linked together inside the computer, it is unnecessary for each department or group to duplicate the others' files. For instance, independent cost files of material lists, blueprints, and planning records for every part and assembly would no longer have to be maintained. This elimination of file redundancy would be felt in many indirect labor activities. This means that all procedures should be planned carefully, involving not only the kind of measurement devices needed, but also methods of collection and interpretation, frequency and form of the resulting reports, and the scope and speed of their distribution.

Computers in Management Control

Computers have two vital functions in management control.

1. They can mechanize the functions of the management control cycle. At the present time, it is not economical to mechanize all data processing systems since, in some instances, clerical help and semiautomatic devices are still

cheaper than electronic computers. Computers are useful where highly repetitive, high-volume, or extremely complex applications exist. Within a few years, however, computer technology is expected to bring devices inexpensive enough to permit mechanization of almost all computational procedures in this area. As shown in figure 11.12, compiling data manually is often time-consuming and costly compared to using a computer.

2. Computers provide the only available tool for investigating decision-making processes. This is done by programming the computer to simulate the complex decision situation and its environment. The fruits of this research should lead to significant changes in business management and organization procedures.

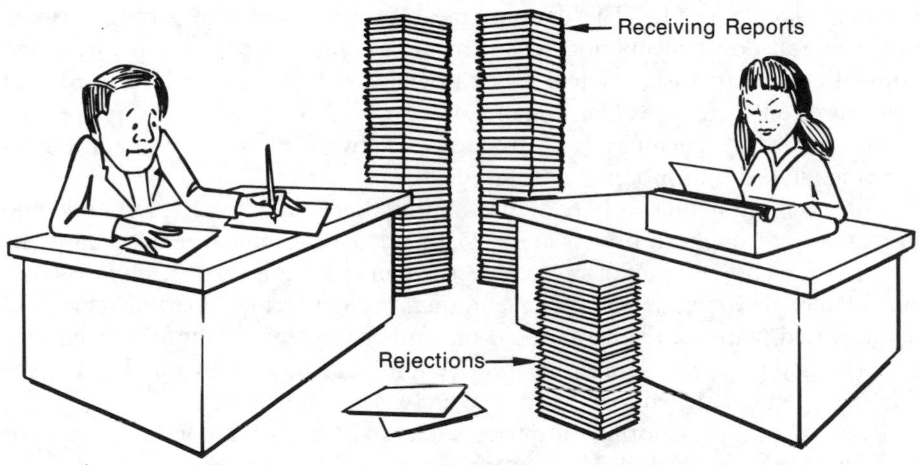

Figure 11–12 A manual system is burdensome and usually slow.

The following are some important conditions for efficient operation of a management information system.

1. The system should provide relevant, integrated, nonredundant information, and these factors should be viewed as a design objective. There is often a considerable duplication of information in the data base that can be originated for technical convenience, or from the need for specialized information. It should always be an objective to achieve a system design in which source data are accumulated and recovered only once and then placed in a data base accessible to all those who have a need for the information.
2. The system should support top management, as well as other levels of management. Most critical decisions of a company take place at the apex of the organizational pyramid, and management must have the correct

and appropriate information to make these decisions, albeit there is concomitant need for information at intermediate levels of management. The principal objective of a management informational system should be to serve all levels of the organization.

3. A data system functions at its best when it can deal with the physical characteristics of data and not with the underlying meaning and implications of the data. It converts, sorts, and distributes information at high speed; it is a great "mailbox" of stored and forwarded information. As a communication device, the computer can facilitate the interpersonal communications of many planners. It can solicit, store, and display the semi-formulated ideas of planners for further definition and interaction. Speeding up data processing and, hence, the timeliness of the information collected, analyzed, and distributed is also a most important advantage of computerized information systems.
4. The system should cross organizational lines. Functional units such as inspection, purchasing, and design, as well as finance, should be served. Actually, if the management information system is to satisfy the goal of efficiently providing information for decision, such functional information must be included. Accurate decision making at policy levels of management cannot take place without information from functional areas. Often top management decisions are influenced considerably by certain operational costs and conditions.
5. The system should possess flexibility and versatility. It should be responsive to requests for information. An effective management information system permits the retrieval of information from a data base in response to requests where parameters have not been entirely prescribed.

In-Line Computer Applications

While it is entirely feasible to install very large-scale data processing systems at central locations to handle increased work loads, the basic problem becomes essentially one of moving large masses of data from many reporting locations to the data processing center, not just the use of more powerful computers. In a rapidly expanding company, the systems planner must always consider that a data processing plan which resolves the information processing requirements of a company at the present time may be quite inadequate where the information processing requirements of the business reach a critical volume.

In a large production or assembly plant (such as an automobile assembly plant), information control is particularly important, yet difficult to achieve. Complete control of quality in such a plant is complicated by several factors, like those given below.

1. The great mass of data must be handled and analyzed.
2. The wide area over which this data originates.

3. The great number of people originating this data.
4. The need for early detection of defect trends as they develop.
5. The need for quick notification to allow immediate corrective action.
6. The need for a defect summary report giving management a gauge of the effectiveness of the quality control program.

In the case of an automobile, for example, there are approximately 4,000 separate defects that could be encountered during the assembly. Normally, during full operation, assembly lines are geared to produce from forty to sixty cars per hour. This production rate is often maintained during two shifts per day. On the basis of this production, 30,000 defects could hypothetically be reported on any given day.

The defect data are detected by many different inspectors spread over the entire plant floor. The defects may be repaired over this same wide area. This means that quality control data originate with as many as several hundred different people. The detection of the defect by the inspector and the repair effected by the repairman must both be reported. These reports are gathered from the actual assembly line, which may stretch over a distance of several miles. The actual gathering of this quality data is complicated by the need to know the status of a defect (that is, repaired or unrepaired) as it leaves the department in which it originated. This knowledge is important to management, since it is indicative of the repair cost involved. For example, in the assembly of automobiles, a pit in body joint solder can be repaired in the body fabrication department for a few cents. If it is not repaired until after the paint line, however, the defect area has to be resoldered and repainted. If, in addition, the unit goes through the trim area prior to repair, the correction may require removal or masking of trim pieces, removal of interior fabric, resoldering, repainting, and reinstallation of the removed parts. The repair that might have cost only a few cents would now cost several dollars. If this defective car is sent to a dealership, its repair cost increases manyfold. At this point, the same repairs could have been done at the factory for a small percentage of the current cost.

At a typical production rate of forty to sixty cars per hour, failure to detect a trend for an extended period of time can create the need for repair on a large number of cars. In fact, if the defect condition lasts for only one hour, there will be enough defective cars to fill most of the repair facilities available within the factory area. It is very important, therefore, that trends be spotted as quickly as possible and that the people responsible for initiation of corrective action be notified immediately.

To guide management in evaluating the effectiveness of the quality control program, a report showing the volume of defects encountered and their status is desirable. Figures that allow management to compare the present quality picture with that of the past will make this report still more valuable. However, a report that recaps up to 30,000 possible daily defects in 4,000 different classes along with comparative figures could be so lengthy that no one would have the time to extract the usable facts needed to make effective use of it.

11.14 Dynamic Quality Control

There are two basic concepts behind the design of a dynamic quality control system.

1. The rapid gathering of data pertaining to specific defects.
2. Automatic counting of defects and quick reporting of defect trends.

Historically, quality control has consisted mainly of policing production and analyzing defects statistically in an attempt to spot defect trends. This information, although valuable, has assumed the status of history by the time it has been gathered and processed. The results can be used only as a guide for future operations in an attempt to avoid repeating the defects that have recently occurred. Dynamic quality control, on the other hand, makes the defect trend data available in time to allow corrective action to be taken immediately.

In a dynamic quality control system, it is very important for production and quality control people to agree upon and establish a minimum defect frequency point (MDFP) for each type of defect, which will be indicative of the possible beginning of a trend for that particular defect. The MDFP can be established on the basis of a specific period of time or on a given number of units produced (lot). Then as defects are corrected and reported, a count is kept by type, and the total for each type is compared with its respective MDFP. If the total count exceeds the established trend indicator point, the production area in which the defect is occurring is notified so that immediate corrective action can be taken. The total count of defects is, in effect, set to zero at the end of each time period or lot. This figure is accumulated only for comparison purposes within the lot, and a separate count is kept of total defects per shift or a given period.

The first prerequisite of this system is the ability to rapidly gather defect data as it is detected. To accomplish this, the input units must be placed along the assembly line, preferably at points where the assembly is changing hands—that is, where another department is accepting the unit. The positioning of these input stations is vital to the success of the entire program. Positioning hinges on the operator's ability to report the defects quickly and accurately, and from the proper location on the assembly line. By placing the data collection stations at points where units are leaving one department to enter another, the relinquishing department has an opportunity to repair all of its defects before transferring the unit. Departmental repairs should be completed at this point so that the reporting of unrepaired defects has greater significance.

In large departments, it is often necessary to have additional input stations in order to reduce the number of defects that must be reported at any one station. Usually there are natural breakoff points within the department for the installation of these additional input stations. For example, in the automotive industry, these points are at the completion of electrical inspection and repair or body water test. The number of defects per unit that might be reported at any one station will determine the number of variable input keyboards needed at each station.

Additional factors, such as those outlined below, must be considered in selecting the final sites for the quality input stations.

1. The stations must be beyond the repair area, so that repairmen will not interfere with the station's operator.
2. The distance the operator must travel to get the information from the car must be kept to a minimum.
3. The information must be easily accessible to the operator.
4. There must be enough time for the operator to return the documents to the production unit, prior to removal of the car by overhead conveyor, etc. (Placement of input stations is also important from the viewpoint of additional applications that may be installed.)

The actual data transmitted from an input station depends on the desired output and possibly on the additional applications that may be tied to this system. In any event, the serial number is usually transmitted, along with the input station number, defect codes, some indication of status of the reported defects (repaired or unrepaired), and a code indicating first or second transmission or no defect. From some departments, it may also be helpful to send the jig or fixture number on which the defective unit was assembled to aid in the detection of defective fixtures. All of the above data, with the possible exception of the serial number, is variable and is readily transmitted through the use of the input keyboards. The serial number may not be needed unless a defect history of each individual unit is being kept for future warranty purposes, or unless an allied application, such as assembly line broadcasting, is being handled by the computer.

It should not be necessary for inspectors to operate the input stations. Factory clerks should be capable of handling the job after the operations have been fully explained. Their function is to report the defects marked on the inspection sheets by the inspectors via the data gathering system. Time spent educating clerks for this job should result in a smoothly operating system.

The last link in the gathering of the data is the actual defect code and coding sheet. By combining the previously mentioned input station number (which denotes reporting department) with a three-digit defect code, it is possible to represent all of the defects that can be encountered in a department. To aid the inspectors in marking the proper codes and to aid the clerks in reporting them, an inspection sheet must be designed.

It is also necessary to have a computer system with random access storage in order to rapidly count the defects being transmitted, store the totals generated, and control remote typing stations. This will provide the ability to quickly notify production managers of defect trends. Random access storage is utilized to store totals by defect code and by various meaningful breakdowns, such as:

1. units with no defects, by station;
2. defects by code, by station;
3. defects unrepaired, by station;
4. defects by code per lot;
5. units built; and
6. units built, no defects.

As the computer system accumulates these or similar totals, the new defect total is compared against the minimum defect frequency point (MDFP). When the defect total exceeds this point, a message is transmitted to the remote typing station in the office of the superintendent of the responsible department, alerting him to this possible defect trend. This system spots defect trends quickly and alerts the proper people so that corrective action can be initiated immediately. The message shows the defect code, a full description of the defect, intensity code (average cost of repair for this defect), and total number of this defect. The defect codes can be defined specifically to enable the management to identify the work station causing the defects. These warning messages can be triggered by various means, such as unrepaired defects going out of a department, unrepaired defects reaching the end of the final line, or defect totals exceeding the trend indicator points.

At the conclusion of the day's production, the defect data generated and stored throughout the operating day can be printed for management review. Since the full details would be too cumbersome to handle, the report should be in summary form so that management can evaluate the data quickly.

Valuable cost information for management action can also be gleaned for such a system. Inputs and outputs of data can be designed so that a summary of significant defects are presented. Frequencies and average repair costs classified by defect and the responsible department can be obtained.

11.15 Requirements for the System

For a quality control information system as described, the following features are required.

1. **Multiple input units,** with the ability to read prepunched cards and accept variable information (quality defects and indicative information about an assembly) from positions along the assembly lines.
2. **Remote typing/inquiry stations,** offering the ability to notify the proper people quickly when a defect trend develops, and allowing free access to all the information stored in the random access storage, such as the option status information.

3. **Random access storage,** providing quick storage and retrieval of voluminous amounts of information, such as the totals of the defects and the options of the units to be built, in a completely random manner.
4. **Real-time operation,** providing direct entry of data to the computer, instantaneous processing and analysis, and immediate reaction to out-of-control conditions, such as the automatic and timely notification that a defect trend is developing.
5. **Remote printing stations,** placed along the assembly lines to print assembly line unit broadcast sheets.

EXERCISES

1. Explain why *information* in general is such an important factor in meeting quality objectives.
2. What is an open loop? How is one created? What are some consequences of open loops?
3. If an operator states that he knows how to do a certain job, is it advisable to still give him written instructions? Explain your answer.
4. What is the quality control manual? Is it necessary? Explain your answer.
5. Name four different kinds of written documentation found in a typical manufacturing company.
6. Explain the meaning of control. What are the elements in achieving control? Explain.
7. How is feedback related to achieving quality control?
8. Discuss some of the ways in which control can be lost. Give an example of how this can cause defective hardware.
9. Explain how you would attempt to correct the conditions that lead to poor control.
10. Explain how the misuse of a form can result in defective hardware. Discuss ways that such problems can be reduced.
11. Explain the principle of *preventive action to avoid corrective action.*
12. Explain the use of in-line computers. What are some applications where benefits would be significant?

FOOTNOTES

[1] Glenn E. Hayes, *Quality Assurance: Management and Technology.* Revised Edition, Charger Productions, Inc., Capistrano Beach, California, 1976.

CHAPTER TWELVE

PROCUREMENT QUALITY CONTROL

12.1 Objective

The purpose of this chapter is to describe the relationship of and the need for quality control functions in the procurement of raw materials and components and in subcontract buying. A student of quality control should understand the integral association of quality and purchasing functions.

Most of the products sold on today's markets consist of components made by more than one manufacturer. Raw materials such as bar stock and tubing, components such as transistors and resistors, and clerical supplies such as staplers or pencil sharpeners, all must be purchased; countless subassemblies are subcontracted to other manufacturers, while maintenance materials and supplies, such as cutters for production machinery and parts and supplies for normal maintenance, must be bought and kept on hand. In large companies, millions of dollars' worth of procurement contracts are signed every twenty-four hours.

12.2 The Procurement Function

Procurement is a necessary part of any industrial enterprise. Before manufacturing processes can begin, materials that meet quality requirements must be on hand, and there must be assurance of a continuing supply to meet schedules and production needs. Failure in this area will generate hidden costs in the production process, contribute to inferior products, result in broken delivery promises, and can be the cause of loss of goodwill among customers. In order to maintain a favorable competitive selling position and satisfactory profits, the materials must be purchased at the lowest cost consistent with quality and service requirements.

A census published by the United States Department of Commerce indicates that, on the average, more than half of the total dollar income from the sale of products is spent on the purchase of materials, supplies, and miscellaneous equipment needed to produce the products. Also, in the majority of manufacturing companies, materials costs are found to be approximately one-half of total product cost. In special cases, however, purchases may range widely beyond these limits, depending on the type of business and the kinds of materials used.

In some continuous types of production, the ratio of purchased material cost to total product cost is even greater. The automobile industry, for example, buys batteries and tires, carburetors, bumpers, completely wired dashboard assemblies, and many other parts from specialized makers of such products, to be incorporated into the finished car. The prices paid for these items by the automobile manufacturer include the supplier's labor, his indirect charges, and his profits. For the automobile manufacturer, these prices represent the actual purchased material costs.

Since procurement represents such a large portion of total manufacturing costs, top management has an obligation to insist that not only shall each part function properly, but that it shall make every possible contribution to profit objectives.

12.3 Buying the Proper Quality

Defining Quality before Procurement

Quality may be contemporarily defined as the composite of the properties inherent in a material or product. Although quality characteristics are often difficult to state accurately, their clear definition is a requisite in order for a purchasing agent or contracting officer to know precisely what to ask a supplier to furnish. This definition of quality, in greater or lesser detail, becomes the ordering description for all materials, supplies, components, and other articles.

Quality must be defined and expressed in such a way that

1. The purchasing department knows exactly what is required;
2. The purchase order or contract is made out with a proper description of what is desired;
3. The supplier is completely informed of the buyer's quality requirements;
4. Proper means of inspecting and testing can be applied to verify that delivered items meet the stated standards of quality; and
5. Delivered goods will be acceptable to the buyer.

The Purchase Requisition

The purchase requisition authorizes the buyer to procure the goods and services described. It combines a statement of the need for certain goods with a request to purchase them. The purchasing department must make certain that the individual who signs the requisition has adequately checked against the purchase budget to make certain that the purchase is authorized financially. In some companies, the requisitions are edited or reviewed to see if the items requested are available in the storeroom, or if satisfactory lower-cost standard items cannot be substituted. A flow chart showing the key steps in the purchase request procedure is shown in figure 12-1.

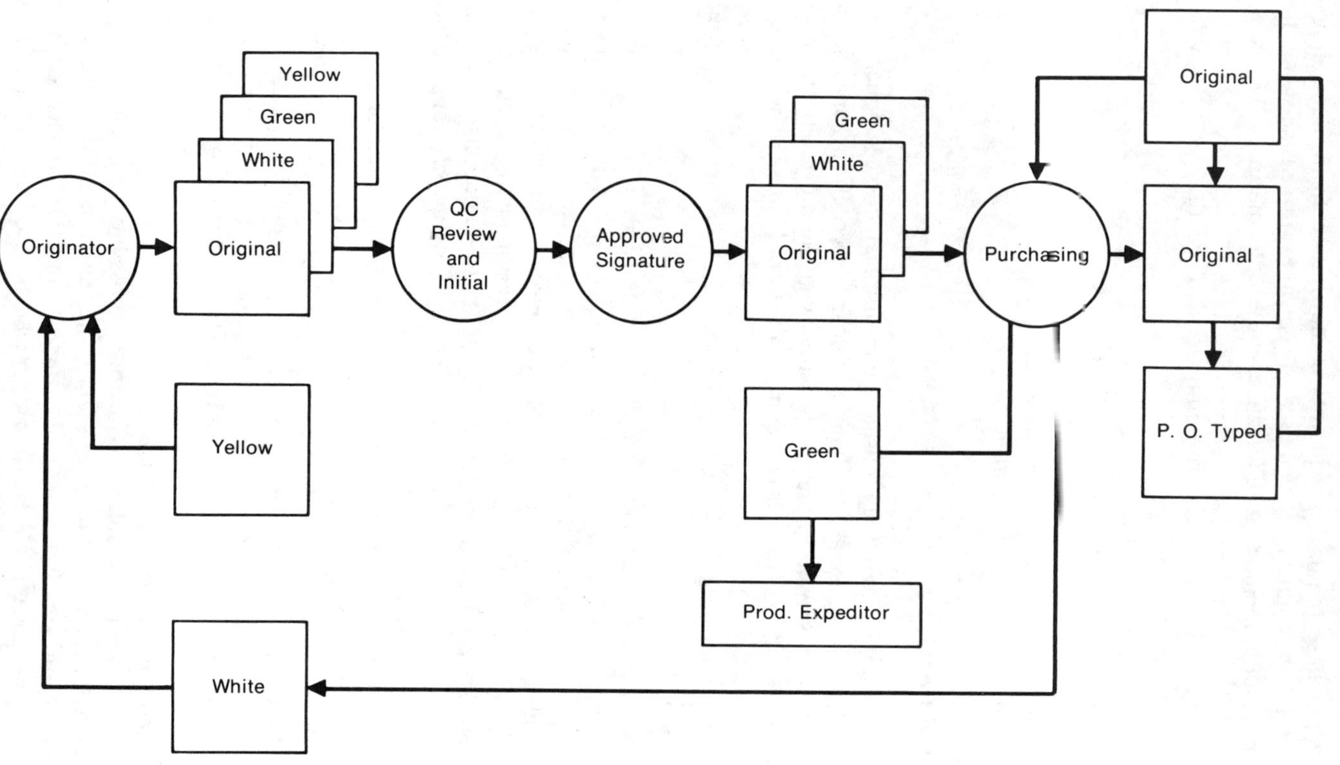

Figure 12–1 A purchase request.

The purchase requisition will vary somewhat in form, depending upon its origin and the accounting system used. A typical example is shown in figure 12-2. The form should include the following essential information.

1. Name and accurate description of goods needed.
2. Quality and quantity needed.
3. Date required or desired.
4. Account to which goods are to be charged.
5. Statement of need or record of use justifying requisition.
6. Point of delivery of the goods within the plant.
7. Authority for the requisition.

Specifications

Information about quality is usually communicated to a supplier by means of a *specification.* Dimensional, functional, and cosmetic criteria are specified so that the supplier will know as accurately as possible what he must deliver. Specifications, therefore, are especially important communication documents when items of high reliability are being procured.

There are several criteria that a good specification should meet. Among these are the following.

1. A specification should describe what is required in concise terms. Unnecessary tolerances or details result in confusion and additional costs.
2. A specification is of value only if it is clear and accurate. Inaccurate or ambiguous specifications motivate burdensome clarification and invite costly errors. Such specifications can result in the receipt of an unsatisfactory product. If production changes become necessary, this may cause delays and attendant rises in costs. And, of even worse consequence, failures of in-service systems could occur.

   An invitation for bid may need to be amended or even canceled if specifications are not made clear. If parameters of a requirement can be legitimately interpreted differently by bidders, there is no common basis for the evaluation of the bids. For example, if a specification called for "special test equipment as required," a wide range of interpretations among bidders could be generated, making bid evaluations very difficult or even impossible. Loss of time and needless expense and inconvenience to both the customer and the bidders are consequences.
3. A specification should be as flexible as possible. An author of a specification may inadvertently incorporate a nonessential condition into the specification and, in doing so, make the specification unnecessarily restrictive. For instance, a specification could be phrased so that a connector must have special features. This requirement, although not really necessary, either

PURCHASE REQUEST **P.R. №**

SUGGESTED VENDOR:

JOB NUMBER	ACCOUNT NUMBER	REQUESTED BY
DELIVERY DATE REQUIRED		APPROVED BY
DATE		INSPECTION REQUIRED

RECEIVING DEPT. DELIVER TO:

ITEM NO.	QUANTITY	UNIT	DESCRIPTION AND PART NUMBER	APPROX. UNIT PRICE	PRICE	TOTAL	PURCHASING REMARKS
REQUESTER REMARKS:					TOTAL AMOUNT		

VENDOR	F.O.B.	SHIP VIA	TERMS
	DELIVERY DATE		DATE PLACED
	TAXABLE YES ☐ NO ☐	CONFIRMING YES ☐ TO	NO ☐
PHONE NO.		P. O. No.______	
REMARKS			

Figure 12–2 Purchase request form.

1. PURCHASE ORDER CONTROL AT THE PLANNING LEVEL TO INSURE ADEQUATE INFORMATION BEING PLACED ON THE PURCHASE ORDER FOR THE SUPPLIER TO FOLLOW
2. CHECK OF PURCHASE ORDER FOR COMPLIANCE AND APPROVAL OF SAME
3. ADEQUATE SURVEY OF VENDORS TO INSURE CAPABILITIES TO DO THE JOB
4. DETAIL DOCUMENTATION OF QUALITY REQUIREMENTS FOR READY REFERENCE WITH LITTLE NEED FOR INTERPRETATION
5. MONITORING OF SUPPLIER FACILITY BY ACTUAL SURVEILLANCE INSPECTION UTILIZING OBSERVATION OF SYSTEMS TO PREVENT PROBLEMS
6. EVALUATION OF SUPPLIERS' RESULTS BY ACTUAL INSPECTION
7. SECURING OF NECESSARY CORRECTIVE ACTION WHEN RESULTS ARE UNSATISFACTORY
8. PERFORMING DIVERSIFIED LIAISON ACTION AT THE SUPPLIERS' FACILITY
9. CONDUCT VENDOR CONFERENCES TO BRING BETTER UNDERSTANDING AND GENERATE CLOSER LIAISON BETWEEN SUPPLIER AND CUSTOMER
10. EVALUATE AND RATE VENDOR LONG RANGE PERFORMANCE THROUGH PERIODIC ANALYSIS AND REPORTING

Figure 12–3 Ten point vendor quality control program.

could preclude many potentially good bidders from bidding on the work, or could force a bidder to include unreasonably high contingencies in its prices. A specification must be sufficiently flexible to allow capable suppliers to bid, but rigid enough to ensure that all requirements are set forth.

There are four important points to remember when writing a specification where quality is concerned. The specification should be:

1. **Clear and concise** Misunderstandings about the meaning and content of specifications are costly. Unnecessary detail in a specification also results in confusion and additional costs.
2. **Accurate and complete** A specification is of value only if it is accurate. It must be checked for accuracy and completeness. It must include copies of the latest blueprints, tests required, referenced specifications and data to be furnished.
3. **Reasonable for specified tolerances** Unnecessary exactitude not only limits sources, but is also costly. The tolerances specified must be in line with

current standards. The quality provided must be in accordance with or at standards of good workmanship.

4. **Flexible** A specification should be flexible enough to allow improvements, but sufficiently rigid to ensure the desired quality. The usual warranties and/or guarantees must be furnished. Where necessary, measures of reliability should be included.

Listed in figure 12-3 are ten important points in a vendor quality control program. The extent to which these should be followed depends on the scope of work and experience with a supplier.

Describing Quality

Unit quality is predicated on some standard of measurement that is understood by the supplier as well as the buyer. There are countless methods of describing quality that are applicable, depending upon the nature of the item being procured. In any case, quality characteristics must be completely understood. Figure 12-4 illustrates how requirements can be misinterpreted.

The following are by no means an exhaustive accounting of the ways quality can be measured, but should give the reader some idea of the complexity of this problem.

1. Design specifications define an item in such a way that it can be manufactured by any competent subcontractor. Such specifications are normally necessary to ensure operating and quality characteristics of a product. Design specifications may be developed either by a major contractor or a subcontractor. Quality is designed into the product by stating certain tolerances and other parameters to which the product will be fabricated. Such specifications are applicable to any or all of the seven basic units of measurement—length, mass, time, electric current, temperature, amount of substance, and luminous intensity. Thus, permissible quality can be stated in terms of tolerances applied to any of the units of measurement listed.
2. Physical and chemical properties are also measures of quality. Physical tests provide a measurement of quality with respect to such properties as the tensile and shearing strength of metals, the bursting, folding, and tearing strengths of paper, dielectric properties, elasticity, ductility, opacity, resistance to abrasion, resistance to sunlight or moisture, resistance to shock and many others. Testing machines have been devised for accurate measurement of these properties in terms of standard units. Accelerated tests under controlled conditions can also be used to simulate the effects of use over long periods of time.

   The chemical composition of a material predetermines many of its physical properties. Consequently, chemical analyses are also important measures of quality.

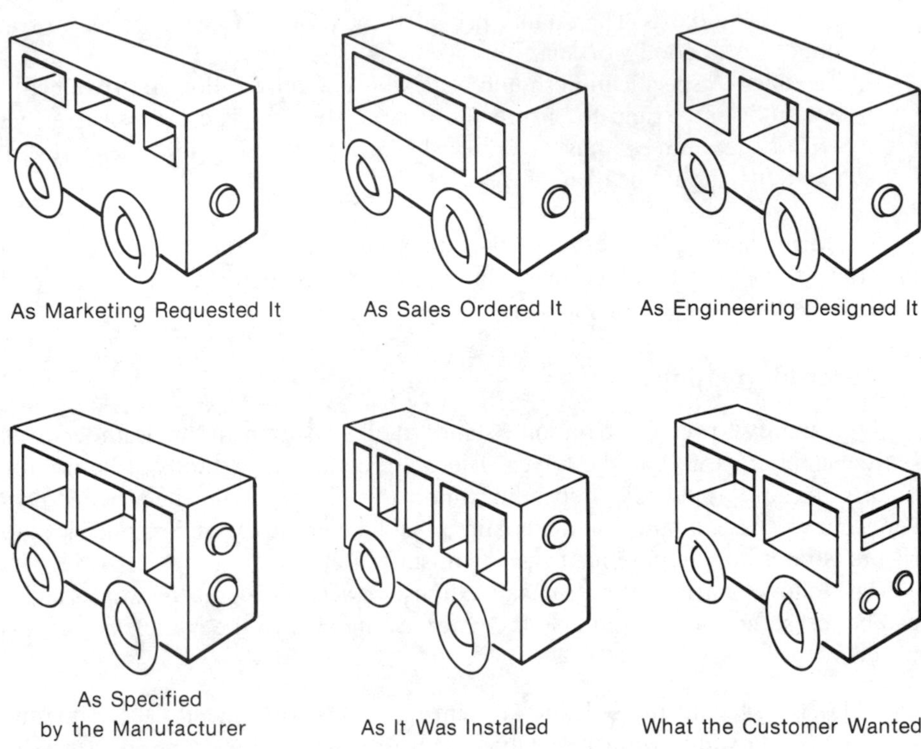

Figure 12–4 Communicating accurate information is sometimes difficult.

3. Performance or guaranteed output may also be considered as basic measures of quality. Dimensions, cosmetics, and physical properties are meaningless if the purchased unit is not reliable, safe, or otherwise suited for its purpose. Frequently, it is necessary to procure an item on the basis of guaranteed or stated quality.

   Performance specifications define such factors as function or capacity, leaving much of the detail up to the subcontractor. Development contracts, for example, are generally placed on the basis of performance specifications, since general characteristics and performance objectives are about all that can be defined. When several firms have relatively equal capabilities to produce a certain product, although with considerable variation in details, a performance specification ensures the greatest degree of competition. When complex equipment is involved, it is usually desirable to leave design detail to the technically competent firm, where the latest technological improvements can be incorporated into the design.

Price is sometimes considered a measure of quality, but it is not always a valid measure. The assumption that a higher price itself denotes higher quality has been disproved many times. Often an identical material can be purchased at varying prices from different sources. The old adage, "You get what you pay for," is only a half-truth.

The quality definition may be very simple or very complex, according to the item involved, but it must be sufficiently specific to provide an accurate and adequate ordering description.

Procurement Planning

Procurement planning in a company should embrace the entire procurement process from the inception of a program to the completion of a contract. Planning activities must be integrated with all procurement functions if they are to be effective. Especially when major contracts are involved, such planning must begin long before a contract is awarded. By participating in early planning conferences with potential subcontractors, a course toward cooperation, a better understanding of suppliers, and knowledge about the many influential factors affecting quality can be charted.

Issues pertaining to the advisability of utilizing single sources, the urgency of certain end items, and management relationships all must be adequately considered. Procurement planning helps to forestall procurement delays, clarify responsibilities, and provides a definite route by which contractual activities can be efficiently conducted. Early procurement planning always reduces the potential of both procurement and quality problems that may occur later in a program.

In both pre-solicitation and subsequent contract negotiation phases, rather complex teamwork is often needed. In some instances, computer technology and other analytical tools are needed to aid contracting officers, management, quality assurance, and engineering personnel in this effort. However, even under conditions of low-cost procurements in which the nature of the procurement does not require sophisticated management tools, planned teamwork is a preventive requisite for the avoidance of subsequent quality and cost problems. Irrespective of whether the contract is for a major weapons system or a low-reliability production item, effective procurement rests on adequate planning at all stages of contract negotiations. Good business transactions, timely contract awards, and effective contract administration are by-products of efficient procurement planning.

Multiple-Source Buying

The procurement policy of most companies involves purchasing from multiple sources. Conditions that affect quality, schedules, and price continuously vary from one supplier to another because of circumstances they encounter. Multiple-source buying will help to minimize the effects of these conditions and at the same time provides certain quality safeguards for the buyer. As illustrated conceptually in figure 12-5 any one of price, quality, or schedule can take precedence over the other two. Facts and conditions surrounding the specific need will determine the proper decision. Inputs from quality personnel are vital elements in this decision-making process and should never be omitted. The following are advantages of multiple-source buying.

RATINGS NOT COMPARABLE

WHICH IS THE BETTER PROCUREMENT SOURCE?

		VENDOR A	VENDOR B
PRICE	$	8.00	6.00
QUALITY	%	4.0	9.0
SCHEDULE		O.K.	O.K.

ADD:

APPLES + ORANGES = FRUIT SALAD

Figure 12–5 Selection of procurement sources must be made with adequate information.

1. **Quality protection** Alternate sources can be used if temporary quality difficulties are being experienced.
2. **Price competition** By providing the buyer with alternate sources, competitive quotations can be solicited.
3. **Delivery protection** Alternate sources allow the buyer flexibility in placing orders. Large orders can be split to prevent overloading and to prevent production stoppage in case of a strike or other problems.
4. **Expertise** Alternate sources allow the buyer to choose a company with known capabilities.

The Technical Proposal

A technical proposal stating all the conditions under which the bidder will perform the work or service is submitted by the *bidder* when he is asked to bid on certain work. Usually a contract is awarded to the subcontractor who best meets the criteria of price, quality, and schedule, although the quality of the proposal itself can either strengthen or weaken the position of a potential subcontractor.

The proposal must be written completely and accurately, including certification plans, equipment and manpower development and allocation, facility plans, etc. A potentially well-qualified source can be disqualified on the basis of an inferior proposal. The intrinsic quality of the proposal itself, together with its technical competence, are significant factors in selecting sources from which to purchase materials.

Writing Procurement Specifications

Procurements are initiated and contracts are placed at several points in the life span of an item, from the initial research and development stages through production and in-service use, until the item is finally disposed of as obsolete or excess to the company's material needs. As an item progresses from research and development into production, it can be described more definitively and precisely. Research investigations, for example, are commonly purchased on the basis of work descriptions that provide considerable latitude for the subcontractor in his research effort. During early developmental stages, work descriptions and performance specifications must be written in comparatively general terms to permit sufficient flexibility and creativity on the part of the subcontractor. When the production stage is reached, it is expected that firm plans and specifications will be developed and released so that production quantities can be procured competitively.

Many factors, both technical and contractual, must be considered by a company in planning for and timing the release of production-type specifications. It is sometimes advantageous to delay the release of specifications as long as possible to ensure that all changes are accurate and complete. However, while delaying the release of specifications tends to reduce the amount of change necessary in the original document and in the contract after award, it also has a disadvantage. Assuming a fixed date for delivery of production items, the longer the release of specifications is delayed, the shorter will be the procurement lead time. When contractual lead times are restrictive, competitive bids may be impossible, and initial production units may have to be procured from a single source. This has the technical advantage of permitting any necessary engineering and testing to continue concurrently with actual production, but has a cost disadvantage since lack of competition may force a subcontractor to pay higher prices for initial quantities. Development suppliers should be able to produce items at fair and reasonable prices because of their past experience with, and understanding of, the item involved, but this is not always the case. Development subcontractors are frequently high-cost suppliers.

Responsibility for Defining Quality

The responsibility for defining quality requirements rests with design engineering, quality control, and other similar groups. The purchasing responsibility is to procure stated quality at the lowest cost. However, the purchasing agent's idea of the right quality often starts with the minimum acceptable quality. Therefore, it is mandatory that minimum quality standards not be left open to judgment unless the quality level warrants such judgment. A buyer may not actually purchase the minimum quality item, even though in some instances this would be the proper choice to make. Superior quality may be desirable, although not actually essential. Sometimes the buyer can find higher quality at no additional cost, or at merely a nominal increase that represents better value received for the expenditure. If premium prices are paid for quality in excess of the need, the extra dollars spent are sheer waste. If, for any reason, it seems desirable to modify the basic definition of quality, this is done only with the approval of design, quality control, and the department needing the articles. In the preparation of formal specifications, even though they are primarily of a technical nature, the best practice is to approach the matter as a joint project of technical, manufacturing, and purchasing personnel, so that all phases of quality, use, and procurement may be considered at the outset.

The Supplier Survey

When selecting suppliers to produce certain assemblies or components, an evaluation of their facilities, quality assurance system, and production methods is often necessary. A team of specialists may visit a prospective supplier to witness operations in the company and make an overall assessment of the company's potential to produce quality articles.

Survey information is acquired from the following sources.

1. Past history of supplier reports.
2. Previous survey information.
3. Supplier ratings from other divisions of the company.
4. Government agency data.

There are two types of surveys, the *desk survey* and the *physical survey*. The type used is determined by the nature of the product to be built.

The desk survey is used only in cases of noncritical parts or where the supplier's quality history for similar parts has been outstanding. The desk survey usually involves submitting a "quality system questionnaire" to be filled out and returned to the contractor.

If a physical survey is required, a quality assurance representative, together with members of engineering, purchasing, and production, visits the companies for the purpose of evaluating all conditions which would affect product quality. These include (1) the capability and condition of equipment, (2) facilities that would be used, and (3) systems design of all the quality-oriented functions.

At the beginning of the physical survey, survey personnel should be given copies of the supplier's quality control manual and other written procedures or inspections. The size and content will vary with the size of the supplier and the product manufactured. The important point is that anyone attempting to supply parts for government-sponsored projects must have some sort of a quality control plan or manual. This manual itself then may provide answers to some of the survey questions.

Not all suppliers have quality control manuals, but there should be at least a set of written quality directives and a plan for quality. The scope of such a plan is governed by the size of the supplier's facility and the complexity of his operation. Any plan should show an organization chart delineating the line of authority and the relationship between production and quality control. While no attempt should be made to prescribe the precise level of quality control in the organization, quality control should be in an organizational position to have access to top management in resolving interdepartmental problems affecting quality. It is essential that quality control personnel have freedom to make decisions without pressure or bias.

Other important criteria relate to record keeping. Incoming inspection records should show clearly the sampling plan used and testing results. Records also must be maintained which show long-time performances of suppliers. Equally important are the identification and disposition of rejected materials.

Inspection test equipment should have planned recalibration and maintenance schedules. The record, showing actual dates involved, should be visible on the equipment.

Survey teams should be skeptical when they are told that a company employs 100% inspection on everything. Unless a company is very small or produces only small job lot quantities, sampling procedures usually exist. Sampling inspection normally is accomplished in accordance to MIL–STD–105, MIL–STD–414, or the Dodge-Romig tables; as long as these tables are used, the team knows what percentage defectives are being allowed.

Records of final inspection results are also critical, and products should be clearly identified when shipped to facilitate tracing if necessary.

Rating techniques vary from company to company but the following scale is typical.

1. Required and not being done.
2. Required and being done in a substandard or marginal manner.
3. Satisfactory with only minor departures from quality standards.
4. Meets quality standards in all respects.

A score is recorded for each one of the questions in the survey. When this has been accomplished, the scores are totaled and an average score is calculated.

An example of a questionnaire used in conducting a supplier audit is presented in figure 12-6.

Conditions found to be substandard can usually be grouped under five categories. Negative reports are typically based on these factors.

1. An organized system of quality control is not documented or is not in use.
2. Records of poor past performances exist and there are no indications of improvements.
3. Conditions that are known to lead to poor quality are currently in evidence.
4. The size or capability of the company is inadequate to handle the proposed work.
5. The financial condition of the company is poor or unstable.

Compatibility of team members and their ability to communicate with the prospective company officials are also important factors. The purposes of the survey may not be fulfilled if for any reason wrong judgments are made or invalid data are obtained.

Once a supplier or a subcontractor has been fully accepted as a source, an agreement can be reached. After the contract has been signed, the respective companies begin the task of work planning. A letter of intent often precedes the formal contract and allows some work to begin.

SUPPLIER QUALITY EVALUATION SURVEY

SUPPLIER ID NUMBER:	DATE:	REQUEST NUMBER:
SUPPLIER:		
ADDRESS:		
CITY:	STATE:	ZIP CODE:
AREA CODE:	TELEPHONE:	

EVALUATED BY:	DIVISION:	REQUESTED BY:	DIVISION:

GOVERNMENT SOURCE INSPECTION AGENCY

☐ DCAS ☐ NASA ☐ A.F. ☐ ARMY ☐ NAVY ☐ OTHER

		PROC.		CONF.	
A	ADMINISTRATIVE				
B	PROCUREMENT CONTROL				
C	RECEIVING CONTROL				
D	MATERIAL STORAGE & HANDLING				
E	IN - PROCESS CONTROL				
F	FINAL INSPECTION/TEST				
G	PACKAGING & SHIPPING				
H	DRAWING CHANGE CONTROL				
I	TOOL & GAGE CONTROL				
J	NON - CONFORMING MATERIAL CONTROL				
K	SAMPLING INSPECTION				
L	CORRECTIVE ACTION				

MANAGEMENT PERSONNEL CONTACTED:

NAME:	TITLE:
NAME:	TITLE:
NAME:	TITLE:
NAME:	TITLE:

NUMBER OF EMPLOYEES:

ADMIN.	ENGR.	REL.	Q.C.	PROD.	INSP	OTHER	TOTAL

SUPPLIER RATING

☐ APPROVED ☐ WITHHELD ☐ DISAPPROVED

SPECIFICATION						
CAPABILITY CODE						

SPECIAL SUPPLIER CAPABILITIES

WELDING (MIL - T - 5021)

"X" APPLICABLE BLOCK		I STEEL	II CRES	III cu Ni	IV Al.	V MAG.	VI TITANIUM
	GAS - TORCH						
	ARC						
	ARC - SUBMERGED						
	INERT GAS-TUNG.						
	INERT GAS - ROD						
	ATOMIC						
	SPOT						
	SEAM						
	FLASH						

WELDING (NAVSHIPS 250 - 1500)

PROCESS	MATERIAL (B NO.)	MATERIAL THICK	SPECIAL WELDS	REMARKS

WELDING (ASME CODE SECTION IX)

PROCESS	MATERIAL (P NO.)	MATERIAL THICK	SPECIAL WELD	REMARKS

PROCESS	SPEC	PROCESS	SPEC
ANODIZE - CHROMIC		HOT TIN - DIP	
ANODIZE - HARDCOAT		HOT ZINC	
ANODIZE - SULFURIC		IMPREGNATION	
BLACK OXIDIZING		IRIDIUM PLATING	
CADMIUM PLATING		LEAD - TIN PLATING	
CHROMATE - AL.		NICKEL - ELECTROLESS	
CHROMATE - MAG		NICKEL PLATING	
CHROME PLATING		PAINTING	
COLOR -DYE		PALLADIUM PLATING	
COPPER PLATING		PHOSPHATE COATING	
DRY LUBRICANT		PLATINUM PLATING	
ELECTROPOLISHING		RHODIUM PLATING	
GOLD PLATING		SAND BLASTING	
HEAT TREAT - AL.		SHOT PEENING	
HEAT TREAT - CUBE		SILVER PLATING	
HEAT TREAT - MAG		TIN PLATING	
HEAT TREAT - STEEL		ZINC PLATING	
HEAT TREAT - OTHER			

FACILITIES	CONTROL YES	CONTROL NO	FACILITIES	CONTROL YES	CONTROL NO
ACOUSTICS			PENETRANT INSP.		
ALTITUDE			RADIOGRAPHIC		
CENTRIFUGE			RADIOINTERFERENCE		
CHEMICAL TEST			SALT SPRAY		
COMBUSTION			SAND & DUST		
ELECTRICAL CALIB.			SHOCK		
FUNGUS			TEMPERATURE		
HUMIDITY			ULTRASONIC		
MAGNETIC PARTICLE			VIBRATION		
MECHANICAL CALIB.			WIND		
METALLURGICAL TEST					

SURVEYED BY ____ DATE ____ EVALUATED BY ____ DATE ____ APPROVED BY ____ DATE ____

Figure 12–6 Supplier quality evaluation survey.

12.4 Negotiating a Contract

The Contract

A contract of purchase is signed by authorized agents of *both* the buyer and seller. A formal contract usually has not been consummated unless a purchase order is issued by the buyer and accepted by the supplier. Acknowledgment copies of a

A. ADMINISTRATIVE

1. Does the facility have a Quality Control Manual and/or Inspection Plan? ☐☐☐☐
2. Are procedures adequate to maintain a level of quality commensurate with General Dynamics programs? ☐☐☐☐
3. Are the Quality Procedures reviewed and upgraded at at pre-determined intervals? ☐☐☐☐
4. Is the Quality Control Manual and/or Inspection plan approved by Company management? ☐☐☐☐
5. Is responsibility and authority for product quality assigned to personnel with sufficient management stature to resolve problems effectively? ☐☐☐☐
6. Is the Quality Control function [illegible] MIL-Q-9858, as revised, or applicable specifications? ☐☐☐☐
7. Does the company maintain a single standard quality system? ☐☐☐☐
8. Is the ratio of Quality personnel to other departments sufficient to maintain control? ☐☐☐☐
9. Are personnel familiar with instructions and procedures contained in the Quality Control Manual or plan? ☐☐☐☐
10. Do the articles currently manufactured reflect workmanship capabilities required by General Dynamics? ☐☐☐☐

B. PROCUREMENT CONTROL

1. Are adequate, written procedures in use for the quality control of purchased materials and services? ☐☐☐☐
2. Does Quality Control review procurement documents for the inclusion of quality requirements? ☐☐☐☐
3. Do procurement documents reflect drawing and/or specification requirements? ☐☐☐☐
4. Are customer requirements reflected on the Company's procurement documents? ☐☐☐☐
5. Are certified test reports or certificates of compliance required by procurement documents? ☐☐☐☐
6. Are records available to substantiate an adequate Supplier Quality rating system? ☐☐☐☐
7. Are supplier's quality programs evaluated by personal audit? ☐☐☐☐
8. Are inspection records used to evaluate suppliers? ☐☐☐☐
9. Is an approved suppliers list utilized? ☐☐☐☐

C. RECEIVING CONTROL

1. Does Receiving Inspection check incoming shipments to requirements of the Purchase Order, referenced specifications, and applicable drawings? ☐☐☐☐
2. Is a list of company and customer-approved sources maintained in Receiving Inspection? ☐☐☐☐

C. RECEIVING CONTROL (Continued)

3. Are incoming materials identified to the applicable Purchase Order or material certification? ☐☐☐☐
4. Is material, when accepted on test reports and/or certificates of conformance, subjected to verification testing? ☐☐☐☐
5. Are test reports or certificates of chemical and physical analysis maintained on file? ☐☐☐☐
6. Are classification of characteristics utilized during visual and dimensional inspections? ☐☐☐☐
7. Do Receiving Inspection records indicate [illegible] incoming material? ☐☐☐☐
8. Do Receiving Inspection records reflect the reason for rejections? ☐☐☐☐
9. Are records maintained to adequately reflect a supplier's quality conformance rating? ☐☐☐☐
10. Are records of receiving activities properly stored? ☐☐☐☐
11. Are adequate controls for the handling and protection of received materials in use? ☐☐☐☐
12. Are inspected items properly segregated from material awaiting inspection? ☐☐☐☐
13. Are received items properly handled and stored prior to inspection? ☐☐☐☐
14. Are controls adequate to prevent entry of uninspected materials into stock or manufacturing? ☐☐☐☐
15. Is inspected material adequately identified as to acceptance or rejection? ☐☐☐☐
16. Is rejected material adequately controlled? ☐☐☐☐
17. Are age-controlled items inspected for date of manufacture and expiration date? ☐☐☐☐
18. Is raw sheet and bar stock adequately identified? ☐☐☐☐
19. Are facilities and equipment adequate? ☐☐☐☐

D. MATERIAL STORAGE & HANDLING

1. Are procedures for the control and issuance of material adequate? ☐☐☐☐
2. Are stock rooms and material storage areas restricted to authorized personnel? ☐☐☐☐
3. Are materials properly handled and stored to prevent damage, contamination and/or loss? ☐☐☐☐
4. Is "open" stock adequately maintained and controlled? ☐☐☐☐
5. Does Quality Control periodically inspect stock rooms? ☐☐☐☐
6. Are records of stockroom inspection available? ☐☐☐☐
7. Are commercial and military contract suppliers properly segregated? ☐☐☐☐

Figure 12–6 (continued)

purchase order are normally sent to the vendor for his signature, which implies his acceptance of the order. In an ordinary purchase contract, the seller agrees to sell and deliver and the buyer agrees to purchase certain items or services under stated terms and conditions. Default by either party can become a cause for litigation.

A contract is normally awarded directly to a bidder who can meet all contractual requirements (including quality) at the lowest price. The contract type is usually a negotiable item encompassing such major factors as price, delivery, and quality. Thus, contract negotiation entails (1) reaching an agreement with a proposed contractor or subcontractor on the pricing, quality, and delivery terms and other provisions that will influence his performance; and (2) setting forth the terms

D. MATERIAL STORAGE & HANDLING (Continued)

8. Are materials properly identified as to their contents or chemical/physical characteristics to preclude error during issuance? □□□□
9. Are chemical compounds rotated while in stock to prevent chemical separation? □□□□
10. Are materials traceable to the chemical/physical analysis, certifications of compliance, test documents, or purchase orders? □□□□
11. Are "age controlled" items properly identified? □□□□
12. Are castings and forgings identified by heat or melt numbers and material specifications? □□□□
13. Is bar and sheet stock identified? □□□□
14. When material is issued from stock, is the shop traveler/stock order, etc., identified with the certification of material, test reports or purchase order? □□□□
15. Is "first in – first out" stock rotation practiced? □□□□
16. Does the supplier practice "good housekeeping" in stock areas? □□□□

E. IN - PROCESS CONTROL

1. Are written procedures adequate for the in-process control of fabrication and services? □□□□
2. Are in-process inspections pre-planned in such a manner as to be compatible with manufacturing operations? □□□□
3. Are assembly and inspection operations and tests performed in accordance with approved written instructions? □□□□
4. Are in-process inspections documented in such a manner as to provide a positive inspection status of the material? □□□□
5. Are assembly and inspection operations and test results documented and validated by Inspection on a traveler, work order or other identifying document? □□□□
6. Are values and/or readings obtained during first article and in-process inspection recorded? □□□□
7. Is material, and/or supporting documentation, identifiable to the manufacturing and inspection personnel responsible for the operation? □□□□
8. Is product identity maintained throughout the manufacturing operation? □□□□
9. Are in-process items protected and handled in such a manner as to preclude damage or loss? □□□□
10. Are inspection stations sufficient in number and located in adequate areas to provide maximum control? □□□□
11. Are adequate in-process inspection facilities, instructions and specifications available and adequate for the type of work being accomplished? □□□□
12. Is surplus material properly identified, inspected, and promptly returned to stock? □□□□

E. IN-PROCESS CONTROL (Continued)

13. Is nonconforming material promptly identified and segregated? □□□□
14. Is "good housekeeping" maintained in the manufacturing and inspection areas? □□□□

F. FINAL INSPECTION ACCEPTANCE AND/OR TEST

1. Is final inspection, acceptance and/or test performed either by, or under the surveillance of, Quality Control? □□□□
2. Does Quality Control review and approve acceptance and test procedures for adequacy to assure contractual compliance? □□□□
3. Do acceptance and test procedures reflect the approved test equipment required to perform acceptance tests? □□□□
4. Do acceptance and test procedures reflect the product configuration and reference engineering document configuration? □□□□
5. Are functional test procedures adequately detailed to minimize operator error? □□□□
6. Are records of inspection and test data maintained? □□□□
7. Does the product and/or its associated inspection test records reflect the test operator and/or inspector performing the detailed operations? □□□□
8. Do these records reflect actual measurement values obtained during inspection and testing? □□□□
9. Does the company demonstrate and maintain records of interchangeability? □□□□
10. Are products properly protected and handled to prevent inadvertent damage? □□□□
11. Does the supplier maintain "good housekeeping" practices in the final acceptance and test area? □□□□

G. PACKAGING AND SHIPPING

1. Are adequate controls in use to assure good commercial packaging? □□□□
2. Does the facility have equipment and controls for packaging to Military Specifications? □□□□
3. Are adequate written instructions covering packaging, packing, marking and shipping utilized by Shipping and/or Inspection personnel? □□□□
4. Are customer P.O. packaging, shipping and marking requirements incorporated by written instructions? □□□□
5. Is a check list used to verify shipping requirements and documentation to be enclosed in the shipment? □□□□
6. Is product configuration verified prior to shipment? □□□□
7. Do packing and shipping records reflect the individuals performing and inspecting the shipping operations? □□□□

Figure 12–6 (continued)

in a procurement document that technically, contractually, and legally protects the company's interests and will ensure delivery of acceptable items in time to meet operating needs.

A contracting officer (or buyer) normally has the primary responsibility for negotiating the contract. However, the success of his efforts will depend largely on the accuracy and completeness of the information obtained during early planning and request for bid stages. An example of a typical purchase order is illustrated in figure 12-7.

One of the most important aspects of any negotiated procurement is the selection of the proper type of contract and appropriate contract terms. The primary

G. PACKAGING AND SHIPPING (Continued)

8. Are adequate storage facilities available and in use to safeguard the quality of the product between final acceptance and shipping?

H. DRAWING AND CHANGE CONTROL

1. Does the company have adequate written procedures governing an Engineering Change Control system?
2. Are adequate contorls in effect to assure applicable engineering drawings, change notices and specifications are in use by production and inspection at the time and place of production/inspection operation?
3. Do drawings, change orders and specifications reflect:
   (a) Change letters/numbers?
   (b) Adequate dimensioning?
   (c) Adequate general and specific notes?
   (d) Reason/authority for changes?
   (e) Product effectivity?
4. Are records maintained which reflect a history of change incorporation?
5. Do change control records reflect the following:
   (a) Date of change/revision?
   (b) Point of effectivity?
   (c) Disposition of items already produced?
   (d) Tooling effectivity?
   (e) Specification compliance verification?
6. Are tool drawings adequately controlled?
7. Is an adequate system in effect to control customer furnished drawings and specifications?
8. Obsolete, marked up, or illegible drawings/specifications are not in use by either Production or Inspection

I. TOOL AND GAGE CONTROL

1. Are adequate procedures in effect to contorl tools, gages and test equipment?
2. Does the system adequately provide for mandatory recall of all calibrated/inspected tools, gages, and test equipment?
3. Are controls in effect to prevent production items from being used as a gage or test equipment?
4. Is an adequate tool checkout and accountability system in effect?
5. Are customer-furnished tools, gages and test equipment adequately controlled?
6. Are employee-owned tools and gages subject to same controls as company owned tools?
7. Are detailed procedures used for inspection and calibration of tools, gages and test equipment?
8. Are new or reworked tools "proven" prior to usage?

I. TOOL AND GAGE CONTROL (Continued)

9. Are tools, gages and test equipment traceable to the National Bureau of Standards?
10. Do calibration/inspection records reflect:
    (a) Item identity number and name?
    (b) Frequency of calibration?
    (c) Procedure for calibration/inspection?
    (d) Date calibrated/inspected and date due for calibration/inspection?
    (e) Personnel performing calibration/inspection?
    (f) Identity of "master" used to perform calibration or the certification document identity?
    (g) Deviation from standard values?
    (h) Engineering configuration (as required)?
11. Are tools, gages and test equipment identified in a manner to reflect:
    (a) Date calibrated/inspected and/or date due for calibration/inspection?
    (b) Personnel responsible for calibration/inspection?
    (c) Item identity or serial number?
12. Are inactive standards identified as "inactive" or "calibration not required"?
13. Do standards currently in calibration have certifications on file that are traceable to the National Bureau of Standards?
14. Are calibration adjustments sealed after certification?
15. Are adequate facilities used for transportation, storage and calibration of all tools, gages and test equipment?

J. NONCONFORMING MATERIAL CONTROL

1. Do written procedures provide for:
   (a) Rejection forms?
   (b) Identification of discrepant material?
   (c) Segregation of nonconforming material from normal production?
   (d) Review of authorized (MRB) repair?
   (e) Record maintenance?
   (f) Review of repetitive discrepancies?
   (g) Corrective action?
   (h) "Incomplete" material?
   (i) Periodic management review of deficiency level?
   (j) Control of scrap material?
   (k) Control of materials review activity?
2. Is defective and "incomplete" material identified and documented as to inspection status?
3. Is a bonded area used for nonconforming materials?
4. Is nonconforming material identified to the applicable rejection document?
5. Is Quality Control represented in the materials review activity?
6. Is material, accepted by materials review, identified as to its acceptance and the authorizing acceptance documentation?
7. Are management reports on nonconforming products published and acted upon?

Figure 12–6 (continued)

responsibility for making this selection rests with the contracting officer, who must see that the provisions of every contract adequately protect the company's interests and comply with purchasing regulations. Procurement personnel should be thoroughly conversant with the contract forms and terms used in purchasing since, under each contract, the specific form and terms not only set forth the obligations and responsibilities of both the supplier and the contractor, but also provide the regulatory framework within which all procurement action must take place. Conversely, the nature of the procurement requirement, as established and defined by the company, directly affects the type of contract that must be selected to fulfill the requirement.

J. NONCONFORMING MATERIAL CONTROL (Continued)

8. Do records of non-conformances and materials review action reflect adequate descriptions of deficiencies, corrective action and dispositions? ☐☐☐☐
9. Are records reviewed and analyzed for repetitive discrepancies? ☐☐☐☐
10. Is an adequate system in effect to control, investigate and correct Customer complaints? ☐☐☐☐

K. SAMPLING INSPECTION

1. Do inspection personnel have instructions covering sampling inspection? ☐☐☐☐
2. Do instructions provide for tightened or reduced inspection when results warrant? ☐☐☐☐
3. Is sampling performed to MIL-STD-105, MIL-STD-414. AMC 74-23, Dodge-Romig Tables, or other statistically correct sampling plans? ☐☐☐☐
4. Are Classification of Defects used? ☐☐☐☐
5. Do inspection records show lot size, sample size, and lot identity? ☐☐☐☐
6. Is tightened inspection required on resubmitted lots? ☐☐☐☐
7. Are different inspection indications used to show sampling vs detailed inspection? ☐☐☐☐

K. SAMPLING INSPECTION (Continued)

8. Are control charts maintained . . . used to indicate product performance? ☐☐☐☐
9. Are process averages maintained? ☐☐☐☐
10. Are control charts used to reduce inspection? ☐☐☐☐

L. CORRECTIVE ACTION

1. Does the supplier maintain an adequate corrective action system? ☐☐☐☐
2. Are defective products and related data analyzed to determine cause and extent of discrepant condition? ☐☐☐☐
3. Is inspection data collected and analyzed to establish quality levels in processes and work performance? ☐☐☐☐
4. Is corrective action initiated when an unsatisfactory trend is indicative? ☐☐☐☐
5. Are corrective action requests issued to a supplier when a quality problem exists? ☐☐☐☐
6. Is corrective action required within a prescribed time limit? ☐☐☐☐
7. Does the company maintain a follow-up system of control on corrective action taken? ☐☐☐☐

COMMENTS: ____________________

Figure 12–6 (continued)

Contract Types

1. **Firm Fixed-Price Contract** A firm fixed-price contract contains an agreement to pay a specified price upon the delivery and acceptance of items or services specified. Unless performance is affected by other clauses, the supplier must perform for this price regardless of the cost experienced, or the supplier may be liable for breach of contract. Firm fixed-price contracts best reflect accepted industrial practices. The supplier assumes all risks of, and responsibility for, performance at a specified price. Suppliers' profits depend on their ability to produce the items called for and to control the cost of production; profit will be higher if production is efficient, and lower if

VENDOR

SHIP TO

PHONE NO.

REQUEST NO.	JOB NUMBER	ACCOUNT NUMBER	TERMS	DATE
F.O.B.	SHIP VIA		DELIVERY COMMITMENT	

ITEM NUMBER	QUANTITY	DESCRIPTION	UNIT PRICE	AMOUNT
			TOTAL AMOUNT	

CONTRACT NO.	PRIORITY	CERTIFICATIONS REQUIRED YES ☐ NO ☐
DELIVER TO	COMP. EVAL. ☐	SPECIAL INSTRUCTIONS

TAXABLE YES ☐ NO ☐ RESALE PERMIT NO. CONFIRMING NO ☐ YES ☐ TO:

ITEM	DATE	REF.	QTY.	B/O	REJ.	P/S	QTY. DUE	ITEM	DATE	REF.	QTY.	B/O	REJ.	P/S	QTY. DUE

Figure 12–7 Purchase order.

costs are high. This type of contract gives the supplier the maximum incentive to avoid waste and to devise production and procurement methods that will save labor and materials.

2. **Fixed-Price Contract with Escalation** Escalation clauses may be inserted in fixed-price contracts for the purpose of removing specific contingencies beyond the subcontractor's control from a procurement. For example, if aluminum prices were fluctuating and the subcontractor proposed to include a substantial allowance in his price for possible future price increases, an

escalation clause might be used to provide that the contractor would raise the contract price if and when any increases took place.

3. **Fixed-Price Redeterminable Contracts** Redeterminable contracts provide a means of shifting certain risks from the supplier to the buyer, to exclude contingency allowances from the initially negotiated price. Redetermination is usually applied to procurements in which (1) adequate estimates of material and labor quantities are not initially available, (2) existing specifications are not accurate enough to set a firm fixed price for the life of the contract, or (3) sound initial estimates of the total cost of performance cannot be made for other reasons. When a redeterminable-type contract is used, the contract price can be adjusted either upward or downward at some point during the performance of the contract.
4. **Fixed-Price Incentive Contracts** The objective of an incentive contract is to motivate a supplier to increase efficiency and reduce costs, while still producing the best possible item. Incentive provisions may cover such areas as higher value or better delivery schedules, negotiated by the company and the supplier. Value engineering clauses are often applicable in such contracts.
5. **Prospective Price Redetermination at a Stated Time** This type of contract provides for a firm fixed price during the initial phase of contract performance, after which the price is redetermined prospectively at a stated point during the remaining life of the agreement. Redetermination may be either upward to a fixed level or downward. This contract type is used for quantity production procurements, when a fair and reasonable firm fixed price can be negotiated for initial work but not for later work.
6. **Firm Target** During early contract negotiations, a target cost, a target profit, and a ceiling price are established. Then an adjustment formula is agreed upon. The formula is generally expressed as a ratio (such as 50/50 or 75/25) and provides for the proportionate division of cost over-runs or under-runs between the supplier and the buyer. If the final negotiated cost is less than the target cost (under-run), application of the formula gives the buyer a share of the savings. His total profit will thus be proportionately greater than the target profit. Conversely, when, final cost is more than the target cost (over-run), his profit will be reduced, since he must share in the loss. When other incentives are also used, the formula will give the subcontractor greater profits when his overall performance, in terms of all the goals established—delivery schedule, costs, and end-item performance—is better than the targets set initially. His profits will be lower if he fails to reach the target goals, depending upon relative weights assigned to each target area (cost, quality, delivery). A target incentive contract is most appropriate if targets that are reasonably free of contingencies and provide a fair and reasonable incentive can be established during initial negotiations.
7. **Successive Targets** In this contract type, the company and the supplier negotiate (1) an initial target cost, (2) an initial target profit, (3) a price ceiling,

(4) a formula for establishing the firm target profit, and (5) a point in production when the formula will be applied (generally prior to first item completion) at the outset. When this point is reached, the firm target cost is negotiated, and the firm target profit is determined.

8. **Cost Reimbursement Type Contracts** Under cost reimbursement contracts, the company pays allowable contract costs. These contracts are primarily used in the absence of a sound basis for estimating reasonable performance costs.

   Cost reimbursement contracts impose a large administrative burden on both the company and the supplier, requiring careful surveillance and cost control. The basis types are (a) cost-plus-incentive-fee contracts, (b) cost and cost-sharing contracts, and (c) cost-plus-fixed-fee contracts.

9. **Letter Contract** A letter contract is a preliminary contractual instrument, used when a subcontractor must be given a binding commitment to begin work immediately, although a formal contract cannot be negotiated in time to meet the procurement requirement. It should be emphasized that the letter contract is only an interim procedure that should never be used as a substitute for careful procurement planning; it should be converted to a formal contract at the earliest practicable date.

Selecting the Contract

There are myriad products, materials, equipment, services, etc., that are purchased, and this great variety requires that there be a variety of contract types in order to meet all the procurement requirements. Contract types used differ principally in the amount of responsibility (or risk) assumed by a subcontractor in performance of the contract and the amount or type of incentive provided for accomplishing the prescribed objectives. In the firm fixed-price contract, where the supplier must perform the work at the price originally agreed upon regardless of his costs, he must assume full risk. At the same time, he may keep all reductions, thus giving him great incentive to perform efficiently. On the other hand, since a supplier is reimbursed for all allowable costs in a cost-plus-fixed-fee contract, he encounters less risk, and has little motivation to perform within the estimated price; therefore, incentive to reduce cost is almost nonexistent.

There are a number of redeterminable and incentive-type contracts between these two extremes. In redeterminable contracts, a portion of the risk is shifted to the contractor, while incentive-type contracts provide an opportunity for increased profit as an incentive for the contractor to reach or exceed specific price, delivery, or quality goals. A number of special contractual devices also have been designed for specific procurement situations.

No one contract type is suitable for all procurement situations; each has advantages and limitations that must be considered in each situation.

Many factors may govern selection of the most desirable type of contract for a given procurement. These include the following.

1. The existing degree of competition.
2. The urgency of the situation.
3. The company's prior experience with the supplier.
4. The overall period of required performance.
5. The nature and complexity of the item in question.
6. The degree of risk involved for both vendor and vendee.
7. The administrative costs involved.
8. The supplier's attitude about certain types of contracts.
9. The difficulty of accurately estimating a supplier's performance costs.
10. The availability of valid data upon which contract contingencies can be established.

12.5 Evaluating Contractual Progress

While the subcontractor has primary responsibility for the timely and satisfactory performance of a contract, the contractor may find it necessary to monitor the performance of contracts to ensure satisfactory progress and to identify problems that either threaten to delay production or sacrifice quality. When problems arise that the supplier cannot resolve himself, such as obtaining a material in short supply, the buyer may provide him with assistance.

The importance of obtaining timely and accurate progress information from suppliers, of carefully evaluating this information, and of communicating this information to all interested personnel cannot be overemphasized. Monitoring contract progress serves several important purposes.

1. It permits purchasing personnel to anticipate potential areas of difficulty, and, in turn, take appropriate remedial action to avoid more serious subsequent problems.
2. It provides information concerning completion of required supplies or services.
3. It provides information on costs incurred in specific phases of the contract. This information is important for cost, price, and profit analysis.
4. It provides information about interim payments that may be made to the subcontractor for work performed.
5. Under component development contracts, it enables early decisions concerning when and how many components may be incorporated in major systems to be made.

Source Inspection

After the decision has been made to purchase components or other articles, it often is necessary to monitor the subcontractor's work on the parts. This surveillance ranges from having an itinerant inspector drop in occasionally to having several quality engineers in residence.

The degree of involvement in source inspection activities depends upon the size of the task and the degree of assurance necessary for conformance to the contract. To gain this assurance, it may be necessary not only to place several inspectors at the source to witness tests and to give their approvals on hardware, but also to place a resident quality control engineer in the company to monitor the vendor's quality control system. By making programmed random checks and subsequently reporting the findings to the prime contractor, management can plot a course of action to change those subcontractor activities that are deviating from contract compliance.

Although the cost of maintaining a source inspection program may not be justified in the manufacture of some products, after careful analysis management may find that long-range benefits overshadow short-range costs.

If the decision is made to employ some degree of source inspection, the optimum amount is measured in terms of maximum inspection assurance of contract conformance at the least cost to the prime contractor. Arriving at and maintaining this balance is a continuous problem of quality management.

Quality organizations, in cooperation with procurement personnel, establish the requirement for source inspection by an evaluation of the following factors.

1. Complexity of inspections and test required.
2. Availability of the required measuring and testing equipment for receiving inspection.
3. Inspection cost and program schedule considerations.
4. Supplier's quality performance.

When source inspection is a requirement, as indicated on the procurement document, special care must be taken to prepare parts for such inspection. Most source inspectors must inspect a wide variety of materials and parts, and it is important to clearly document specifications so that they are not ambiguous or difficult to interpret. If parameters negotiated by engineering are not covered by specifications, the source inspector's job is needlessly difficult. Nebulous specifications often mean negative interpretation and consequent rejection of parts. Many source inspectors are convinced that good source inspection allows no deviation from the specifications. Not infrequently one finds that parts of superior quality have been rejected merely because of a small processing variation, or the misinterpretation of a dimension. On the other hand, if the source inspection is not performed vigorously, there may be instances when substandard parts are accepted as meeting the quality requirements, when in fact they can cause serious subsequent failures of major systems.

Beginning at the time of the supplier survey, rapport should be established between quality personnel and the supplier. The quality communications and coordination system of the supplier should be such that there can be a free exchange of information between the source inspectors and the supplier. A simple explanation or the mere clarification of a process or procedure can prevent the rejection of acceptable parts. This philosophy applies whether the source inspector represents the government or a major contractor. In the case of government inspections, government specifications provide the authority. Inspection parameters for government source inspection personnel are expressed explicitly in certain government documents. These documents also state that these government inspectors (quality assurance representatives, often called DCAS for Defense Contract Administration Services) will take work in the subcontractor facility to review and monitor quality progress of pertinent parts.

Requirements of source inspection in many companies involve more than just verifying a few critical dimensions at final inspection. The electronics industry, for instance, has become convinced that process control is just as important as, if not more important than, final checkout. In such companies the source inspector's job can be complex. He might have the following duties.

1. To monitor the entire production process to ensure that the product qualified is actually what is being built, and that process deviations are made per the change process and are performed to only required specifications.
2. To monitor final tests to ensure that all tests have been performed per specification.
3. To make certain that all data requirements are met and are in proper form so that receiving inspection at the original equipment manufacturer's (O.E.M.) facility is efficient.
4. To give advance warning of schedule slippage to O.E.M. procurement.
5. To conduct a continuous quality improvement campaign at the supplier.
6. To make certain that field failures are analyzed and result in corrective action.

The above assignments can be accomplished in several ways. The most widely used method is the analysis of inspection records to gain assurance that tests were actually performed. Most original equipment manufacturers now require prior notice of anticipated testing of their parts, so that source inspectors can be present during the tests. Care must be taken, however, to coordinate the time for such

1. SURVEY VENDORS' FACILITIES FOR COMPLIANCE WITH REQUIREMENTS.
2. ALERTS VENDOR TO PROBLEM AREAS.
3. WITNESSES TESTS AND CONDUCTS SYSTEM INSPECTIONS.
4. REPRESENTS THE COMPANY IN GENERAL.

Figure 12–8 The company's outside quality control representative.

tests with the representatives, because entire production lines can be shut down awaiting the arrival of the inspectors.

Some companies find that it is a good practice to employ a quality control representative (QCR), located in the subcontractor's facility, for the duration of a contract. In this capacity, the representative can perform a valuable service for both the vendor and vendee. Typical functions of the QCR are outlined in figure 12-8.

Material Review Board (MRB)

Most companies have either a formal or informal procedure for disposition of nonconforming materials. A material review procedure provides for the review, control, evaluation, disposition, and documentation of production materials which depart from applicable drawings, specifications, and contract requirements.

Material review boards are established in most companies for the purpose of accomplishing the aforementioned tasks. Members of the board are usually from the following organizations and are in a decision-making capacity.

1. A government representative.
2. Engineering.
3. Quality assurance.

The quality assurance organization is responsible in such matters for the following.

1. Assuring proper consideration of the quality and workmanship aspects of the disposition.
2. Assuring that the final disposition is properly carried out.
3. Assuring that quality or reliability has not been degraded in the process of repair.
4. Taking appropriate corrective action to eliminate assignable causes leading to the creation of nonconforming materials.

Acceptance of Nonconforming Articles

The decision is sometimes made to accept articles that do not meet the prescribed standards of quality. Top management may elect to waive a certain quality requirement in lieu of a schedule crisis if it can be shown that the nonconforming material is not seriously defective. For example, if a buyer discovers that a major job will be significantly delayed because a purchased device fails to meet certain minor quality standards that the buyer can readily correct, the buyer might elect to absorb the cost of bringing the unit up to quality standards rather than incur a far greater cost waiting for the vendor to finish the work.

Also, on occasion, there are some quality standards higher than those which can be produced by modern processes. Very large and complex castings or forgings, for example, may need final repair in the form of welding or other special processes by the customer in order to render such units fully usable. These situations should not result in serious problems because they should occur only occasionally. If such conditions can be defined in advance, they would be incorporated into the original purchase order specifications which outline the limits of responsibility of both parties.

Nonconforming parts or materials must be identified and classified according to their condition and status, then diverted from normal manufacturing channels. Companies should provide a special area where nonconforming materials can be staged and where the business of evaluation and disposition of the nonconforming material can be satisfactorily conducted. An example of a form used by a review board is shown in figure 12-9.

Nonconforming materials are usually classified as minor, major, or critical. These are discussed in detail in chapter 14. Nonconforming materials can originate in the factory of the original manufacturer or with the subcontractor. Most of the materials that do not comply with specifications are detected and segregated at the supplier through regular process controls and source inspection. However, some nonconforming parts always reach the point of assembly before they are discovered. This is also true for materials and subsystems fabricated and assembled at the original manufacturer. In spite of a great amount of process controls and testing, some defective parts are known to be installed on major assemblies.

Receiving Inspection

Receiving inspection, like source inspection, is an expense to the account of the buyer. It is obviously poor practice to incur an expense of this sort out of proportion to the value of the purchased articles. Receiving inspection to some degree is needed when judgment indicates that any of the following might occur *without* such inspection.

1. Manufacturing efficiency will be adversely affected.
2. Large amounts of labor will be expended on the material in fabrication processes.
3. Expenses will be multiplied with the use of other parts in the assembly.
4. There is a high probability of defectives in the order.
5. Personal safety of workers is involved.
6. Outgoing quality will be lower.

The receiving inspection procedure is normally correlated with the receiving routine. The decision about what and how much to inspect usually is made before an order is placed and generally follows an established policy with respect to the units purchased.

When the shipment arrives, the inspection or testing department is promptly notified by the receiving department. Ordinarily the goods are received, identified by purchase order number, and checked for quantity, then segregated for inspection before being placed into general stores for subsequent issue and use.

MATERIAL REVIEW BOARD

S/N__________
DATE__________

Part Name __________
Part No. __________
Part S/N __________
Job No. __________ Contract No. __________
Quantity Rej. __________ of __________

DESCRIPTION OF THIS DISCREPANCY

INSPECTOR __________ DATE __________

RECOMMENDED REWORK: __________

CORRECTIVE ACTION TAKEN: __________

FINAL DISPOSITION __________

DCASR Rep. __________ Quality Mgr. __________
Customer's Rep. __________ Project Engr. __________

Figure 12–9 Material review board.

Materials rejected from vendors are recorded on a vendor inspection report such as the one illustrated in figure 12-10. The form is then routed to a procurement group (sometimes procurement quality control) for coordination with the supplier. This document should be designed to fulfill the needs of purchasing and quality control engineering, as well as providing for materials control and for dealing with the supplier. A daily receiving inspection report like the one in figure 12-11 should be maintained.

Responsibilities of Receiving Inspection

Receiving inspection has the basic responsibility of controlling the quality of all material purchased by the company. This is accomplished through examination of all items received by the company to determine conformance to applicable purchase orders and ancillary specifications. The normal functions of receiving inspection include determining the acceptability of (1) raw-stock material purchased from vendors, (2) parts and assemblies purchased from vendors, (3) parts and assemblies manufactured by outside production sources, and (4) items which have been withdrawn from stores but not used and which require reinspection before being returned to stores.

Specific duties of receiving inspection personnel are outlined in the following statements.

1. Segregate received materials and place in the proper area provided.
2. Follow inspection procedures as necessary to assure a complete inspection.
3. Check the purchase order for special requirements to assure that all of the purchase stipulations have been met.
   (a) If government source inspection is a requirement, the department verifies that all parts and documentation are properly identified with the government acceptance stamp.
   (b) If the company's source inspection is a requirement, the department verifies that all parts and required documentation have been accepted by the source inspector.
   (c) If test data, laboratory reports, or certificates of compliance are required, inspection personnel verify that the appropriate documents have been submitted and that they provide satisfactory evidence of conformance to specification requirements.
   (d) Raw materials are frequently accompanied by test reports or physical and chemical analysis reports that are checked against the applicable material specifications for verification of material quality. Such data must be positively identifiable with the raw material. Where large quantities of parts are involved, periodic verification of material quality is often performed by a predetermined sampling plan.
   (e) If first article inspection is a requirement for castings, forgings, extrusions, etc., inspection personnel check the receiving record to verify that such actions have been successfully completed.

VENDOR INSPECTION REPORT

VENDOR		PART NAME	C-E PART NO.		REV.
INSPECTOR'S NAME	DATE	Q-E VERIFICATION	DATE	PURCH. ORDER NO.	

INSTRUCTIONS: 1. COMPLETE THIS FORM FOR EACH LOT SHIPPED.
2. PLACE FORM IN PACKAGE WITH MATERIAL.
3. MARK OR TAG EACH PART MEASURED WITH A NUMBER AND THE RESULTS ENTERED BELOW.

		SERIAL/LOT NO. →												
ITEM	CHARACTERISTIC	ZONE	MEASUREMENT		MEASUREMENT		MEASUREMENT		MEASUREMENT		MEASUREMENT		MEASUREMENT	
			VENDOR	Q-E	VENDOR	Q-E	VENDOR	Q-E	VENDOR	Q-E	VENDOR	Q-E	VENDOR	Q-E

Figure 12–10 Vendor inspection report.

Figure 12–11 Daily receiving inspection report.

DAILY RECEIVING INSPECTION REPORT

DATE ______________

SHEET ______ OF ______

JOB NO.	P.O. NO.	PART NAME	PART NO.	VENDOR (MFG.)	DISTR.	QTY.	NO. ACC.	NO. REJ.	INSP. STP.	DATE OUT	REJECTION (QCR) NO. AND REASON	IF HELD, REASON

4. Perform the test and inspection sequences outlined on the inspection checklist.
5. Accept material that has successfully completed all applicable receiving inspection criteria and processes, and complete the following.
   (a) Complete the appropriate entries on all inspection records.
   (b) Identify acceptable material and release the material for use.
   (c) Segretate the documentation and transmit copies to the appropriate organizations.
6. Reject any material that does not conform to specification or purchase order requirements and processes, and complete the following.
   (a) Complete appropriate entries on all inspection records.
   (b) Prepare a nonconformance report describing the reason for rejection and forward the material and paperwork to materials review.

While the basic function of receiving inspection involves examination of all purchased material upon arrival at the company's receiving department, there are sometimes additional responsibilities assigned to receiving inspection in the interest of reducing costs through consolidation of similar functions.

Nondestructive testing (NDT), for example, sometimes is a responsibility of receiving inspection. This may include ultrasonic, radiography, magnetic-particle inspection, penetrant inspection, and eddy current testing. It may be necessary for receiving inspection to accomplish NDT(inspection.)on the basis that, while NDT equipment is primarily needed for receiving inspection, this need may not require full-time operation. NDT(inspection) required during or following fabrication and assembly operations also can be routed through receiving inspection to obtain full utilization of the equipment and avoid additional cost for duplicate equipment and personnel.

Receiving inspection may also be responsible for performance testing all items (such as hydraulic valves or electric motors) that require special tests, whether as a receiving or a production operation. In other cases, this may be the duty of the inspection laboratory or of a production process control group.

Applicable Criteria

An important function of receiving inspection is the complete identification of each incoming item with full knowledge of the requirements for the item, its quality history, and its intended use. Thus the receiving department should have complete copies of all purchase orders and pertinent specifications. In addition, inspectors should have ready access to files of industry and military specifications and standards. Copies of pertinent drawings often are located in the receiving departments or can be requisitioned by the departments.

Supplier test results accompanying each shipment can permit a company to substitute sample testing for 100% testing. The better a company's knowledge of supplier inspection systems or quality programs, the more accurate its adjustments of receiving inspection.

Companies usually detect flaws in raw materials by appropriate laboratory tests. Because the mechanical properties and composition of metals, the chemical composition of fluids, and the physical and chemical properties of a host of other raw materials usually cannot be fully determined once manufacturing or processing begins, a company should analyze and test raw materials as soon as possible after receipt.

Following inspection of a given shipment, an inspection report is issued that states what conditions have been found and what quantities have been received, accepted, and rejected. This is transmitted to the receiving department, the material control functions, and purchasing functions, where it becomes the authority for payment to the vendor supplying the items.

It is a good policy to accept only shipments authorized by a purchase order in the receiving department. Each purchase order package (including specifications related to quality) must provide complete information on what should be received in a given shipment. It is only necessary for inspection to indicate their findings regarding the corresponding shipment on the appropriate form, and a complete receiving report is created.

Identifying stocks of raw material and keeping untested, uninspected material separate from that already tested must be done very carefully—the inadvertent release to production of wrong or defective raw material can be disastrous.

Incoming inspection should employ a method in which traceability of incoming parts can be achieved. A control log for procured parts and materials that require traceability should be maintained. This log must include the following minimum information.

1. Nomenclature of thc item.
2. Project name.
3. Purchase order or contract number under which the parts or materials are manufactured.
4. Date manufactured, received, or tested, as applicable.
5. Manufacturer's lot or serial numbers.
6. Part number and revision of drawing to which each article is manufactured.
7. Cross-reference of manufacturer's lot or serial number with traceability lot number assigned in-house.

Need for Prompt Inspection

A major goal of receiving inspection is to inspect incoming material to provide the production department with materials and parts that meet quality specifications within the schedule that has been established. One of the responsibilities of quality control management is to see that incoming materials are promptly inspected. Ideally, articles should be inspected the same day on which they arrive, but this is seldom possible where large amounts and varieties of components and parts are being received. In any case, every effort must be made not to hold incoming materials more than three to four days before they are inspected. If, under *normal* operating conditions, articles wait in receiving inspection more than one week before action is initiated, management should examine the entire situation to determine the causes and take the necessary corrective action. Many reasons can be attributed to a backlog of uninspected items in receiving: overloads, conflicting priorities, insufficient number of personnel, absenteeism, equipment breakdown, etc. However, when a pattern of delay is created, resulting in delays of longer than a week, hidden adjunctive costs mount. Some effects of such delays are given below.

1. **Production Problems** Especially in companies where inventory turnover is rapid, parts coming into the plant are usually scheduled for production with very little lead time. Although it is possible for an expeditor to exert pressure to move material through the system and onto the production floor, this is an extra cost that need not be incurred if materials are promptly processed. Further, the effects of such delays compound. When production people find that material takes too long to go through receiving inspection, they tend to order using a longer lead time. Such practices result in a larger inventory which, in turn, add to costs of inventory.
2. **Defective or Damaged Articles** If incoming material is not promptly inspected, responsibility for material damage or other kinds of defects is difficult to assign. If the damage appears to be the fault of the delivering carrier, he may object to accepting the responsibility. He can logically argue that damage occurred after delivery. If the damage appears to be due to a vendor's faulty packaging, he too may make the same argument. If a rejection is due to failure of the supplier to comply with purchase order requirements, it is easier to obtain satisfaction if faulty material is promptly returned to the vendor. Some vendors set a time limit after which they will not accept a rejection except for latent defects. Although these vendors may back down on their policy, they usually do so only after costly discussion or argument.
3. **Replacement of Defective Parts** The need for repair or replacement of unacceptable goods is as important as (and often more important than) the above reasons for prompt inspection of incoming materials. If there is not a smooth and orderly completion of receiving inspection tasks, there is the added danger of shortages in the production department. Moreover, it is not uncommon to insist that a vendor work extra hours to replace defective parts in order to meet a production schedule. Such unusual steps as interrupting the vendor's normal flow of work to produce new parts, working overtime, and using premium transportation to deliver the parts may be necessary when production lead times are short, resulting in extra cost. This problem is compounded when articles are held by the buyer too long. It becomes incumbent upon the quality manager to ensure that the receiving inspection

function is provided with the necessary procedures, personnel, and equipment to expedite the tasks of receiving inspection. The quality manager must also point out the contributing causes of inspection delays to other departmental managers (for example, purchasing). A paperwork problem, such as the lack of an appropriate form or document, is too often the cause of a delay.

4. **Paperwork Costs** A further consequence of delayed receiving inspection is paperwork, particularly with respect to accounts payable. Some companies pay for goods only after acceptance by inspection. If inspection is delayed, trade discounts may be lost. If payment is delayed too long, the company's reputation for prompt payment may suffer. Moreover, some companies charge interest on overdue payments.

Normally, purchased parts must be inspected after being received by the company. The inspector shown in figure 12-12 has removed a sample from the shipment

Figure 12–12 Example of inspection by sampling.

and is verifying that certain dimensions are within the specifications that accompanied the purchase order package. In this particular instance, the inspector is checking the diameter of the housing.

For certain critical measurements, it is sometimes more economical, quicker, and accurate to utilize air gauges. The inspector shown in figure 12-13 is measuring the inside diameter of an aluminum flange with an air gauge. A plug is used containing orifices through which air escapes between the outside diameter of the plug and the inside diameter of the part. The air pressure differences generated during the test, which are read directly on the instrument, are the basis for the measurement. Notice the circular standards lying on the surface plate. The instrument is calibrated by inserting the plug into such known standards.

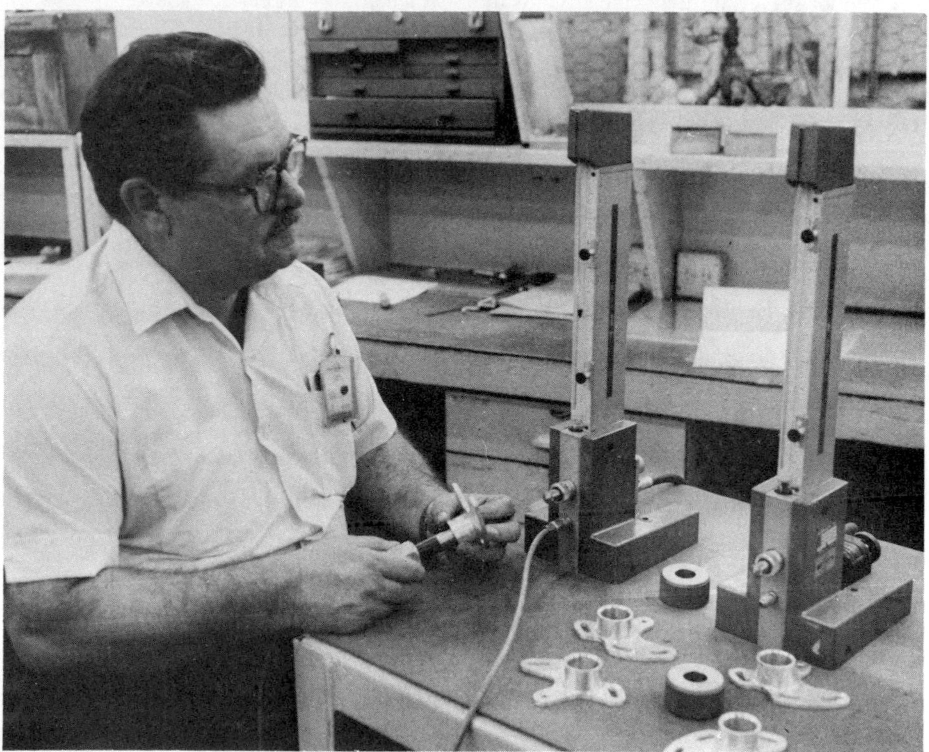

Figure 12–13 Example of inspection by sampling.

EXERCISES

1. Should quality control personnel be interested in procurement? Why?

2. What are the differences between a purchase requisition and a purchase order?

3. Explain the value of the purchase specification insofar as quality control is concerned.

4. Discuss the pros and cons of the adage, "You get what you pay for."

5. What are some of the different kinds of criteria that one might need to cover in a procurement specification covering quality?

6. What are some values of multiple source buying?

7. What is a technical proposal?

8. What is a supplier survey? Explain the differences between the desk survey and the physical survey.

9. Write a one-page report on the types of information that should be obtained during a vendor survey, including the grounds upon which you would reject a source.

10. What are the chief differences between a firm fixed-price contract and a firm target contract?

11. What is an escalation clause in a contract?

12. What is the significance of an incentive-type contract?

13. When do you think it advisable to utilize source inspection?

14. Does the use of source inspection reduce the need for receiving inspection?

15. What are the principal purposes of a material review board (MRB)?

16. If vendor surveys and source inspections are conducted, is there a need for receiving inspection? Explain your answer.

17. What are some typical problems associated with receiving inspection?

CHAPTER THIRTEEN

STANDARDS FOR QUALITY

13.1 Objective

The objective of establishing standards is to provide a uniform base for performing certain work. Standards may be thought of as plans against which work is appraised. Thus, a standard not only carries with it the connotation of expectation of how some activity is to be completed, but also the concept of conformance.

It is beyond the scope of this book to describe the many aspects of standardization, but some of the more important topics discussed have to do with: dimensional standardization to secure interchangeability; concentration on the optimum number of types, sizes, and grades of products; specifications as a basis of purchase; methods of making acceptance tests for materials and apparatus; safety codes for the protection of workers via the Occupational Safety and Health Administration (OSHA); building codes; and nomenclature, the definition of terms commonly used in specifications and contracts.

While there have been adverse opinions about standardization, this movement does offer certain benefits for quality control. Most of the criticisms that have been directed against standardization have been based upon the misconception that standardization results in stagnation. Sound standardization is dynamic, not static. By facilitating the flow of products through industry and commerce, standards help to maintain what an engineer would call *dynamic stability* in industrial processes. The danger of stagnation lies not in the use of standards, but in taking a fixed mental attitude instead of always being open to new ideas.

13.2 The Importance of Standards

Industrial Standardization

Industrial standardization consists of distinguishing between products and materials; deciding upon the properties, dimensions, and performance of these products; and focusing attention upon these factors in design, in production, and in use, so that the greatest possible industrial efficiency can be attained.

Standard Designs and Parts

Company standard designs and parts are those that have been standardized to eliminate unnecessary duplication of engineering work and blueprint release.

A standard design establishes a uniform method of accomplishing a certain fabrication or assembly operation and simplifies drawings by eliminating repetition of elaborate notes. Examples of one type of standard design are lightening holes, rivet-installation data, and electrical-cable-assembly information.

A standard part differs from other parts in that it is not identified with any one particular model but can be used universally over a variety of models.

Drawings of company standard designs and parts are normally contained in a standards handbook issued by the engineering department. These are referred to whenever the drawing for an item being inspected calls out a standard part or design. Designs should be standardized only after quality considerations have been given; then, the use of such standards helps considerably in the control of quality in design.

Standard Specifications

A standard specification implies standard methods of testing and usually implies standard definitions. In some instances, methods of testing are incorporated within a materials specification, while in other cases some standardizing agencies establish standard methods of testing separately from the materials specifications and make reference to the test methods.

Properly devised and administered, standard specifications can be of immense value to a company. Some of the advantages that may be cited for standard specifications for materials are as follows.

1. They give the manufacturer a standard of production and help to maintain a uniform product. They also aid in reducing the number of required varieties of stock, and consequent waste and cost.
2. They help to achieve the required quality levels through the use of standard parts of known quality.
3. They lower unit costs by making possible the mass production of standardized articles.
4. They permit the consumer to use a specification that has been tried and proven.
5. They normally represent the combined knowledge of the producer and consumer and provide a basis of common understanding.
6. They permit the designer to select materials that are reasonably available.
7. They simplify the preparation of special-use specifications because standard specifications can be incorporated by reference.
8. They aid the purchasing agent in securing truly competitive bids and in comparing bids.

9. They set standards of testing procedure in commercial testing and hence permit comparison of test results obtained from different laboratories.

Importance of Quality Standards

Little is accomplished by setting up standard methods of operation which do not result in output of satisfactory quality. When one refers to *satisfactory* quality, quality *measurement* is implied. Measurement is only possible in terms of some predetermined standard. Control of quality should not be attempted by using the experience of a foreman or an inspector as a sufficient standard by which to judge the quality of output. It is much better to carefully define quality requirements and document these requirements in specifications and procedures. Inspection requirements thus can be also thought of as standards for quality.

Unless definite quality standards are carefully formulated, quality measurement becomes a matter of human judgment, and quality is sure to suffer. Formulating standards involves several important factors: defining definite standards for quality measurement, fixing definite responsibility for quality of output, establishing procedures to ensure uniform measurement of results, systematically determining responsibility for any failure to meet quality standards, determining causes of any failure to meet quality standards as early as possible, and acting promptly to remedy these causes and prevent their recurrence.

Performance Standards

One of the best and often most important criteria for deciding whether or not a product has the desired quality is simply that of performance. If standards of performance can be established, against which outgoing quality can be measured, this is often sufficient. Operating characteristics such as safety and reliability are evidenced by the actual performance of the product. Performance standards sometimes are set forth in contracts, but it is normally just good business to establish suitable performance criteria for the products, then compare the performance of the products with these criteria as they are built.

Figure 13-1 is an example of a performance test in which a light-sensitive speed trap and electronic timer provides records of velocities of toy racing cars under a variety of conditions. In the tests shown, different wheel, axle, and bearing designs are being tested to determine which design gives the greatest speed out of the loop when the cars are started from the same height on the ramp. This same basic setup can be used in evaluating curve efficiency of banked turns. This type of equipment can be used to measure the velocity of many different toys, as long as the technician is capable of repeatedly passing the toy through the two light beams which activate the timer.

The low-speed wind tunnel shown in figure 13-2 provides performance data on various wing and fuselage configurations of toy airplaines; transducers are used

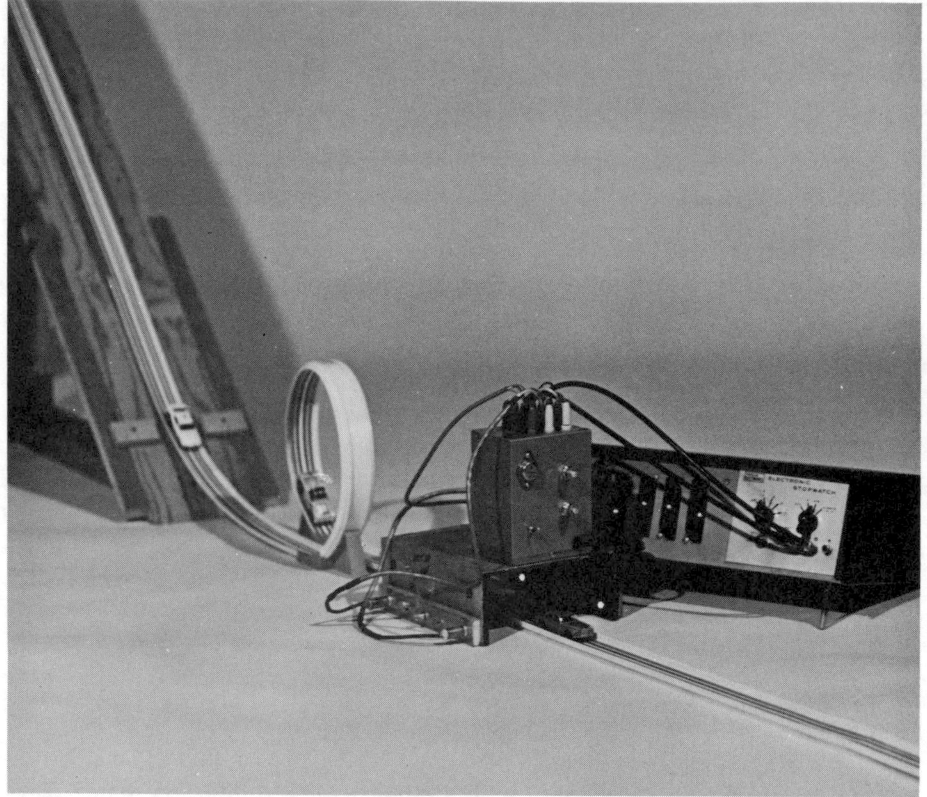

Figure 13–1 Light-sensitive speed trap.

to evaluate the lift and drag characteristics. An inclined manometer is used to accurately establish the pressure differential within the tunnel, thus establishing the air velocity. This tunnel has a velocity range of ten to forty feet per second. As dramatized by the technician's blowing hair, the tunnel is currently in operation. During normal operation the technician would observe the plane through a clear plastic door, thus not disturbing or altering the air pressure differential.

Another example that illustrates the importance of standards is the manufacture of golf clubs. Those who frequently play golf know that the balance of the club is a very important factor in the precision with which one can play the game. Although some players are not aware of it, each golf club undergoes a *swing weight test* for balancing characteristics. The swing weight is the ratio of the weight of the head of the club to the length of the shaft. Figure 13-3 illustrates a golf club being tested for its swing weight so that the exact amount of weight can subsequently be added to the head to attain the correct balance. Figure 13-4 shows the procedure of inserting lead shot into the head end of the club to achieve the correct balance.

Figure 13–2 Low speed wind tunnel.

Figure 13–3 Testing balance of golf clubs.

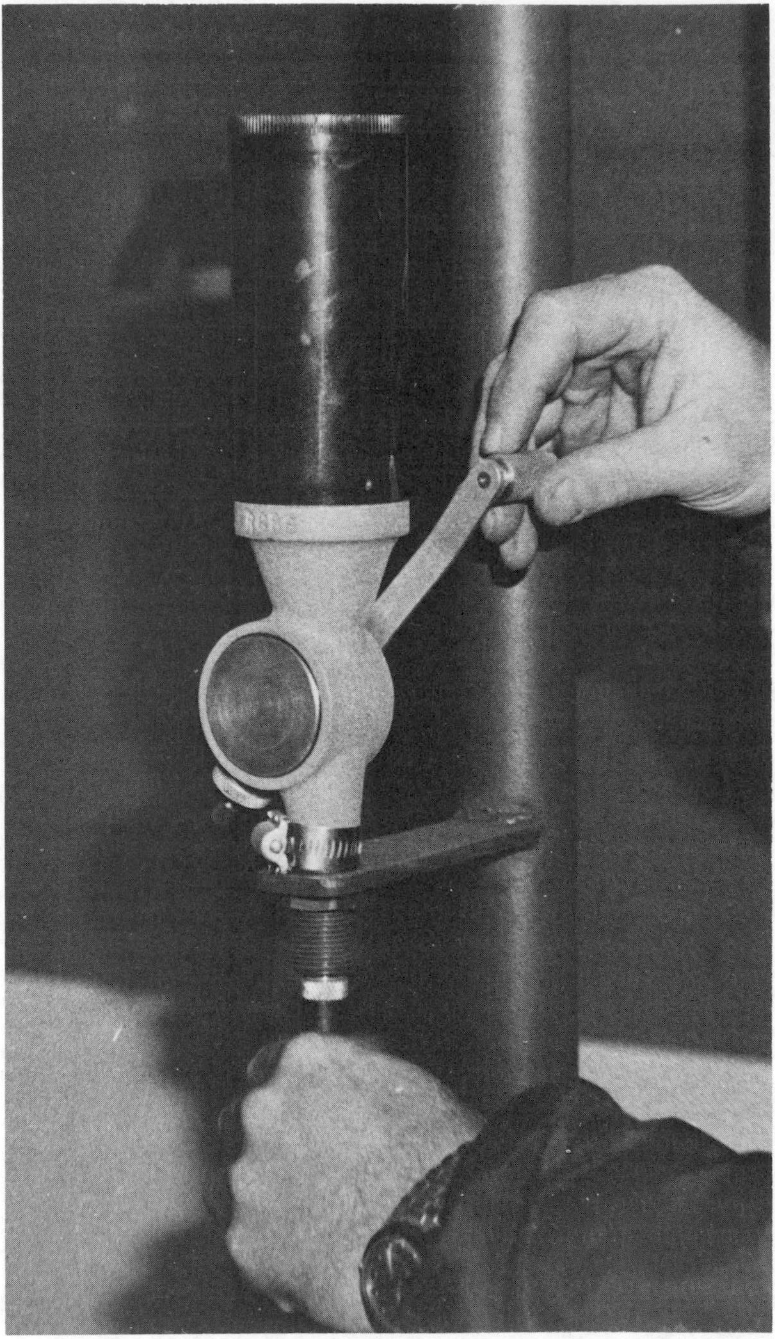

Figure 13–4 Adjusting balance of golf clubs.

13.3 Workmanship and Rework Standards

Countless workmanship standards are set forth and used in various industries. Such standards usually carry with them the need to qualify employees to meet the prescribed standards. Certification programs are instituted primarily for this purpose.

Among the most common of these certification endeavors are various training programs in *soldering*. Since many products contain electromechanical devices, and since most of this work must be done by hand, it is imperative that (1) accurate

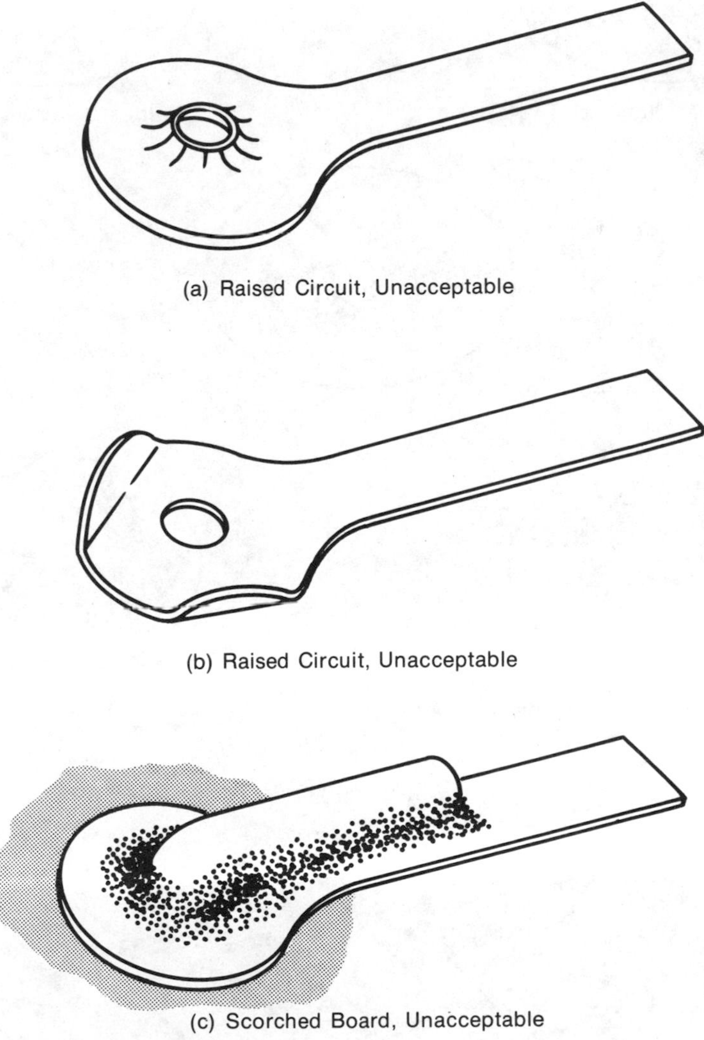

(a) Raised Circuit, Unacceptable

(b) Raised Circuit, Unacceptable

(c) Scorched Board, Unacceptable

Figure 13–5 Damaged circuits or boards.

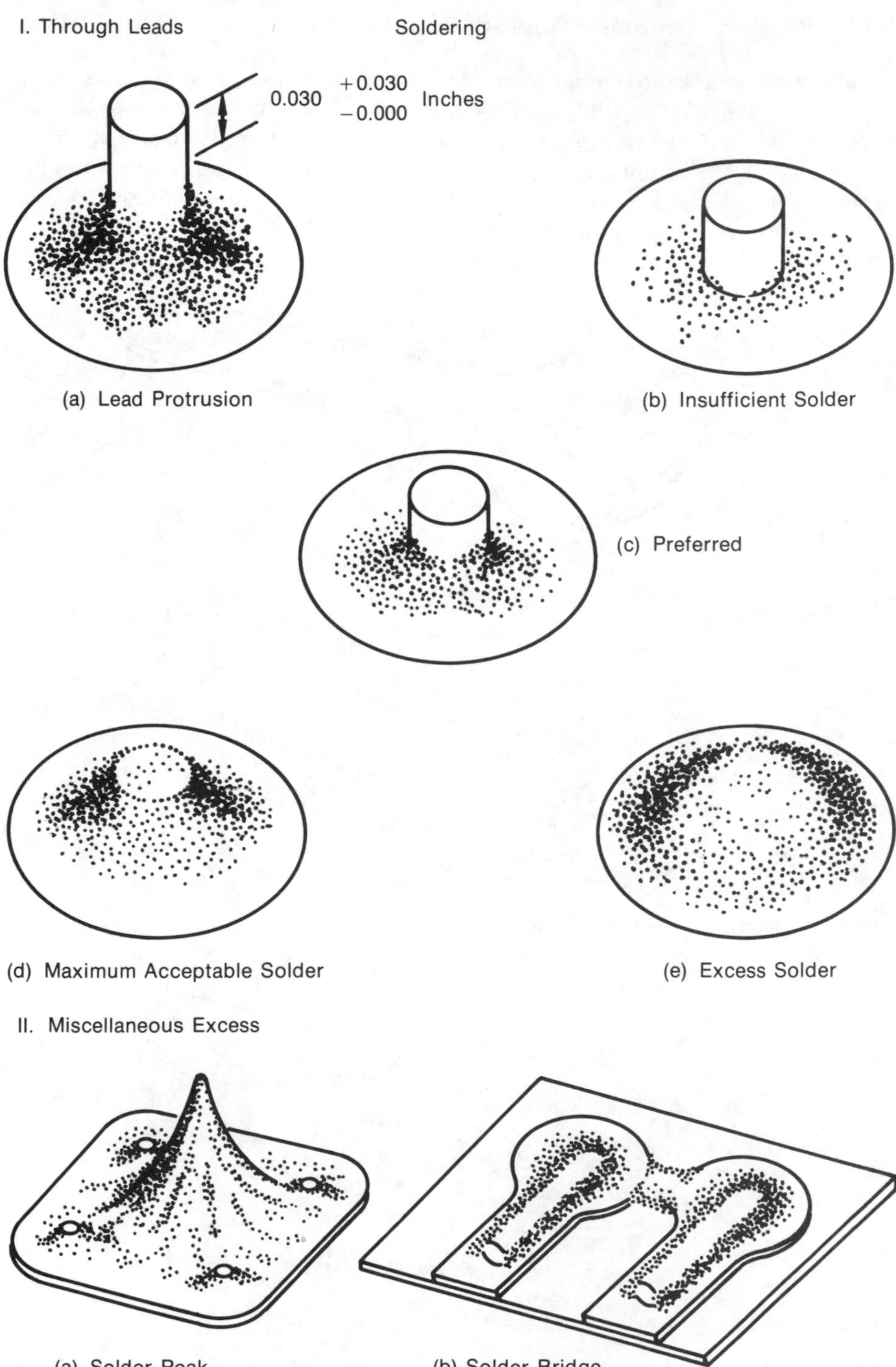

Figure 13–6 Standards for soldering.

and unambiguous workmanship standards be set forth, (2) personnel be trained in both the meaning of these standards and how they are to be met, and (3) personnel have the necessary skills, tools, and materials to meet these standards (this includes both manufacturing and inspection personnel). Examples of such workmanship standards are presented in figures 13-5 through 13-7.

After work has been completed, either at various stages of in-process manufacture or final assembly, an inspector will visually inspect the units using either

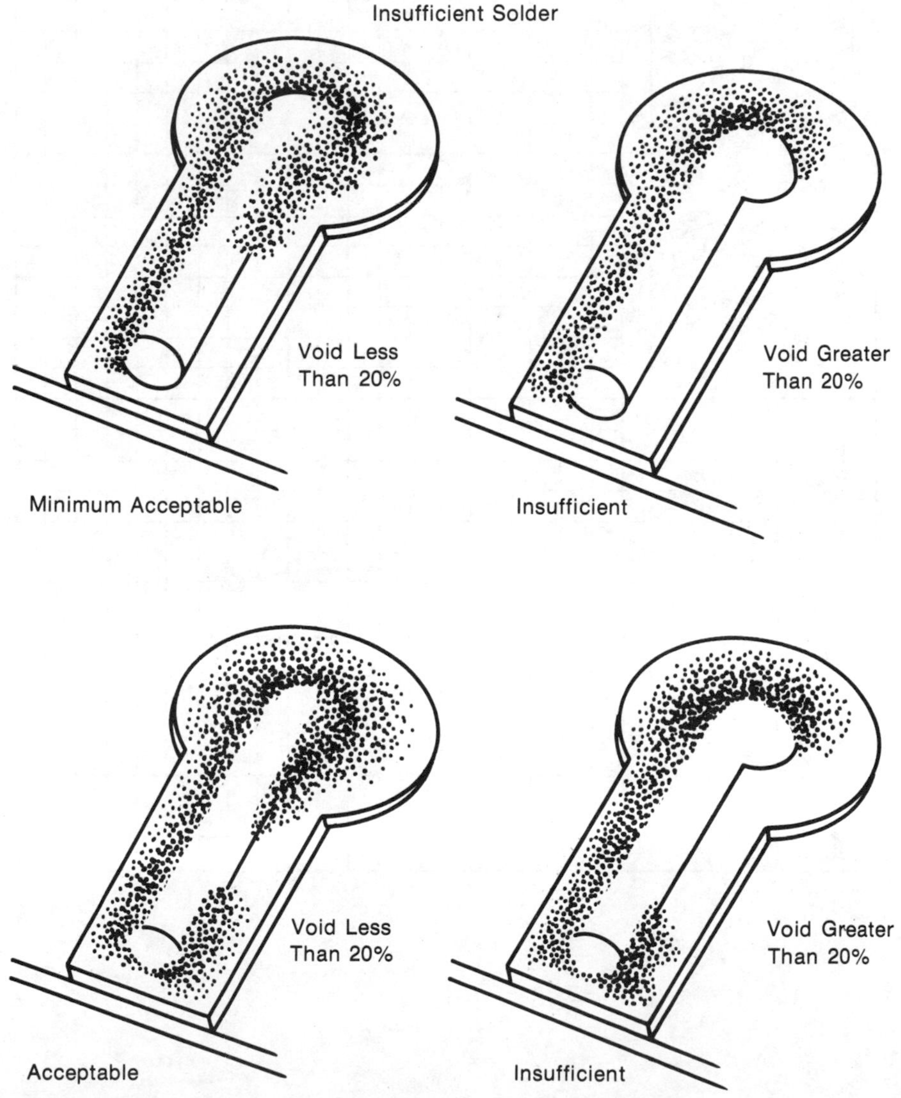

Figure 13–7 Standards for Soldering

Figure 13–8 Form for circuit card assembly inspection.

________ CIRCUIT CARD ASSEMBLY INSPECTION

INSPECTOR NO. ________

	CIRCUIT CARD ASSY.								SOLDER DEFECTS								COMPONENT & MECHANICAL DEFECTS												
																	COMPONENTS												
	DATE	PART NUMBER	S/N	LOT/ SAMPLE	QTY REJ	IN PROCESS	FINAL	TEST	NOT SOLDERED	DISTURB, FRACTURED, COLD JT.	VOIDS	DEWETTING	EXCESS/INSUFF. SOLDER	LEAD OFF-PAD	CLEANLINESS	OTHER (USE BACK OF SHT)	DAMAGED	MISSING	REVERSED	WRONG	MARKINGS ILLEGIBLE/MISSING	NO STRESS RELIEF	RIVETS LOOSE/DAMAGED	DAMAGED BOARD/CIRCUITRY	I. D. MARKINGS	CONNECTOR	COATING	OTHER (EXPLAIN ON BACK SHT)	REMARKS
1																													
2																													
3																													
4																													
5																													
6																													
7																													
8																													
9																													
10																													
11																													
12																													
13																													
14																													
15																													
16																													
17																													
18																													
19																													
		TOTALS																											

a sampling procedure or by 100 percent inspections. Figure 13-8 illustrates an example of an inspection status sheet on which inspection data are collected.

Rework and Repair

Workmanship standards pertaining to *rework* and *repair* also are issued to help ensure that when a unit undergoes rework, it will meet all quality standards. Figures 13-9 through 13-13 show examples of how a damaged conductor may be repaired. Such standards, of course, apply to all kinds of products.

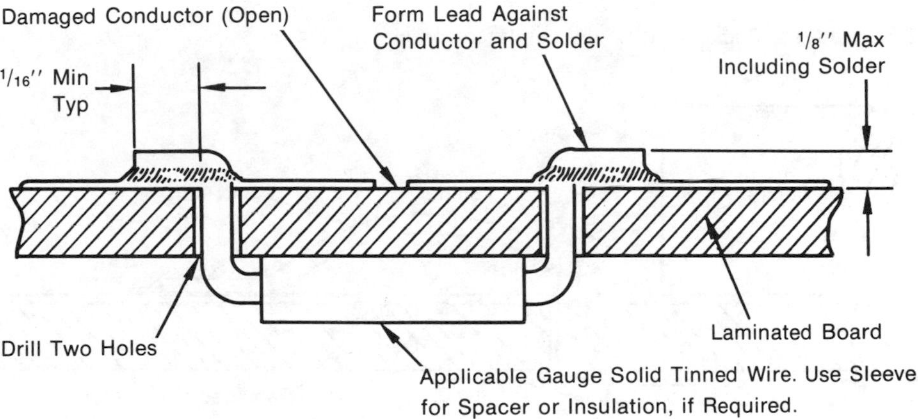

Figure 13–9 Repair of damaged conductor on circuit card.

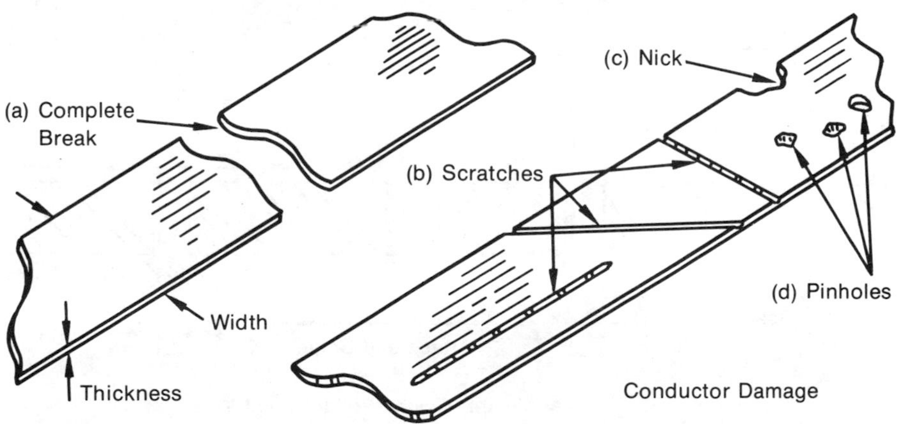

Figure 13–10 Complete break in conductor.

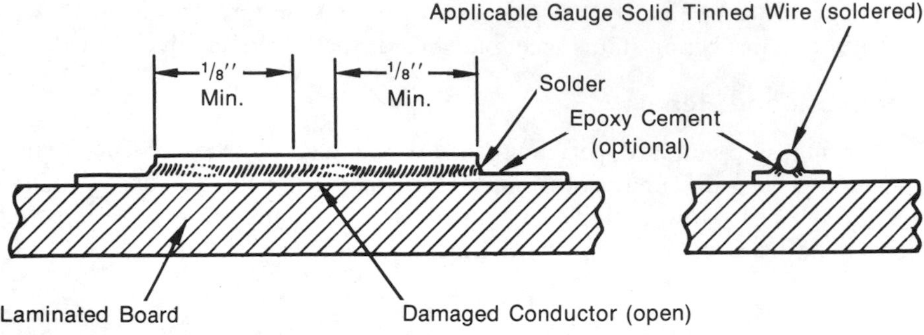

Figure 13–11 Repair of damaged conductor on circuit card.

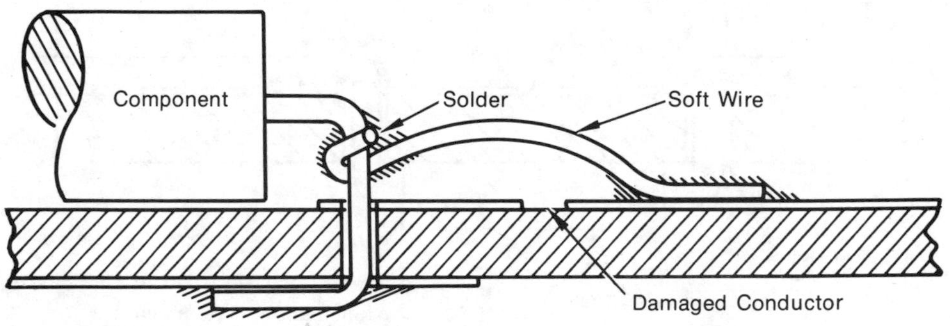

Figure 13–12 Repair of damaged conductor.

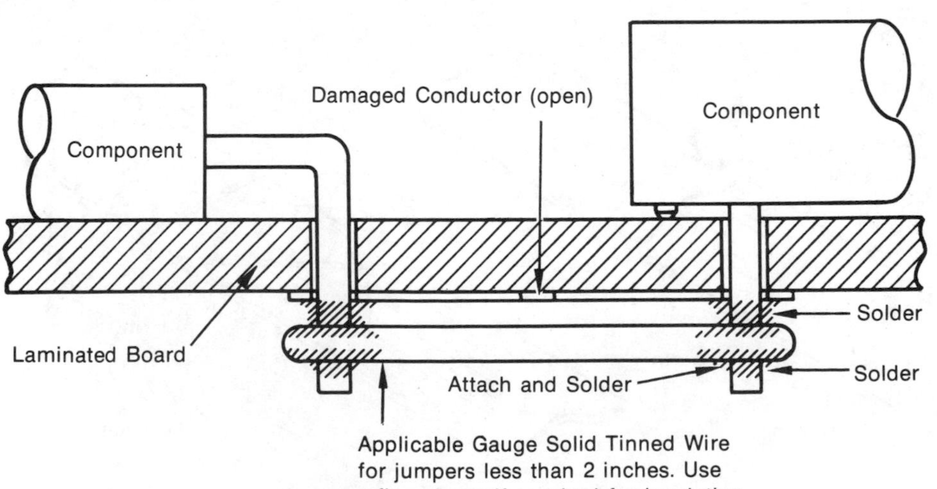

Figure 13–13 Repair of damaged conductor.

13.4 Expressing Quality Standards

Drawings and Specifications

A product's quality is determined by the characteristics it possesses. It is necessary for the manufacturer (often together with the customer) to decide what the characteristics of his product should be, and then have the engineers design a product which embodies these characteristics. The engineers must describe the product's design or characteristics in language that can be understood in fabrication and assembly departments. And the engineers must set the limits of acceptability for deviations. This is accomplished by the use of *specifications* and *tolerances* that the designer decides will best meet quality and cost criteria.

Before an order for material or parts can be issued and even before a preliminary estimate can be prepared, it is essential that the exact character of the material or components be fully and clearly defined. Any production department must have directions which can be followed before products of specified quality can be made. Quality instructions usually take the form of drawings and specifications. The drawings show dimensions and configurational information. Specifications describe the physical and chemical properties that are required in the product. It would not be feasible to attempt to add all the necessary information regarding such factors as performance requirements to the drawings, so this information is provided by specifications.

It would also not be practical to attempt to describe all tolerances and dimensional criteria in specifications. Drawings and specifications complement each other. Drawings give dimensional data used in fabricating the parts; specifications describe post-fabrication characteristics of the part. Drawings and specifications are separate pieces of documentation, but become an integral part of a contract for subcontracted parts.

Tolerances and Allowances

An engineering drawing is the graphic language used in the industrial world by engineers and designers to express the information necessary for the fabrication of any apparatus. The drawings usually show size and contour of the parts to a specified scale and are dimensioned accordingly.

Upper and lower limits must be specified in some way for every dimension of every part. The purpose of dimensioning is not to make a part to an exact size, since no two parts are ever exactly the same; rather, its purpose is to define limits of acceptability.

All specified dimensions must have tolerances, even if they are expressed as basic dimensions. Dimensional tolerances represent the total amount that a given dimension may vary from the nominal size. Tolerances, therefore, define the permissible variation in the size of the part. In the specification 2.000 ± 0.005, 2.000 is the nominal dimension and $+0.005$ and -0.005 are the upper and lower tolerance limits respectively. An acceptable part could thus have any dimension between 1.995 and 2.005.

A continuous problem in product design is establishing tolerances and specifications that are appropriate for performance standards of the products. In cases where the specifications are too limiting, production costs cut into profit margins and are prohibitive. In cases where they are not sufficiently limiting for performance requirements, the reliability levels will not meet customer needs.

Many parts must be designed so that they will fit with other parts. The prescribed tolerances on the drawings permit the fabrication and processing of parts so that interchangeability of the items can be achieved. The functional objectives of many assemblies can only be accomplished by careful control of the dimensions of mating parts. Figure 13-14 illustrates an extruded plastic tube, designed so the die cast cap will snap into the ends of the extrusion, producing a container. A slight out-of-tolerance condition in either part would render the parts useless unless the parts were carefully matched. In actuality, however, the dimensions of such extruded products are very accurately controlled by the manufacturing process and auxiliary tooling, so that once a first article has been produced and the accuracy

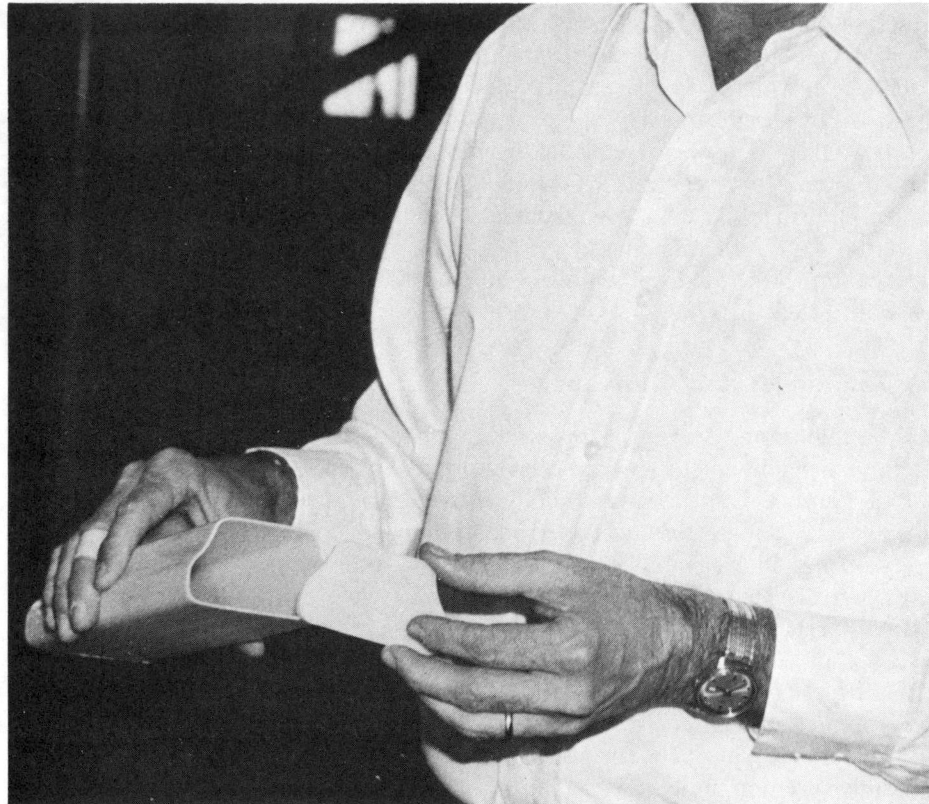

Figure 13–14 Mating parts—tolerances controlled by manufacturing processes.

and precision of tooling and processes verified, the job will run with minimum difficulty. Thus, the most significant factor in assuring the ultimate quality is specifying the correct tolerances on the part so that the tooling in turn can be made to accurately produce the respective parts.

Geometrical and Positional Tolerancing

In recent years, the drafting standard *Dimensioning and Tolerancing for Engineers,* ANSI Y 14.5 has been adapted by many companies. The symbols for this method are illustrated in figure 13-15. Geometrical and positional tolerancing has several features that can benefit the overall quality control system.[1]

1. Positional tolerancing is not restricted to precision parts; the conceptual advantage applies to any level of dimensional accuracy.
2. Positional tolerancing is a logical tolerancing technique, which denotes basic exact position. It eliminates possible tolerance buildup and permits manufacturing to exceed tolerance limits where anything less than the maximum material conditions exists.
3. The delineation of feature relationships in parts, together with functional tolerancing, provides for more efficient product control by simplifying inspection techniques. Inspection equipment can be used efficiently to evaluate functional criteria, and sound quality decisions can be made in less time.
4. By utilizing an allowable tolerance zone for mating parts, tolerance calculations are simplified.
5. Positional tolerancing of parts is efficient on a low-volume basis as well as on a high-volume basis.
6. Under the concept of positional tolerancing, drawings require less overall drafting hours, and consequently, less liaison and consultation for clarification.

Symbol	Form	Symbol	Form
▱	Flatness	⊥	Perpendicularity
—	Straightness	∠	Angularity
○	Roundness	‖, //	Parallelism
⌭	Cylindricity	⌯	Symmetry
⌒	Profile of Line	◉, ◎	Concentricity
⌓	Profile of Surface	⌖	True Position
/	Runout		

Figure 13–15 Symbols for geometrical tolerancing.

7. The use of positional tolerancing reduces costs of corrective action and scrap.
8. Positional tolerancing provides a more efficient means of communicating design information than conventional methods.

Hierarchy of Responsibility for Quality

The highest order of responsibility for quality rests with top management, for without first having the proper budgets, policies, and general support, a company struggles unsuccessfully to achieve and maintain quality standards. Policies and directives issued by top management, in essence, are standards against which quality, employee conduct, safety, and similar factors are monitored.

The next order of responsibility for quality rests with engineering. Since the design (drawings and ancillary specifications) is the standard against which all manufacturing work is compared, it has the second order of importance. If this standard is inaccurate, manufacturing work and inspection work in turn will be incorrect.

Given a design that is accurate and complete, the next order of responsibility for quality rests with manufacturing personnel. The quality of design predetermines manufactured quality, but once the design package is released, manufacturing has the responsibility for quality of conformance.

This leaves the role of all quality assurance, quality control, and inspection people technically as one of assistance, monitoring performances, safeguarding quality standards, conducting audits and providing confidence that quality objectives are being achieved.

It should be understood that quality assurance is a company-wide *philosophy,* not a narrow set of controls planned and monitored by a quality department. Personal attitudes of all the employees in the company about quality are far more important than a single department which merely detects problems and recommends corrective action after problems have been encountered.

13.5 Observance of Standards

Standards should simplify and increase the accuracy of quality control activities. However, these objectives will be achieved only when personnel in the company in general, as well as quality control personnel are convinced of the necessity of strict observance of standards. This can be achieved by educating them to understand the value of standards and defining the responsibilities in such a way that standards can be observed without confusion. This is especially true of quality control personnel.

All managers should make certain that supervisors under their jurisdiction have all standards applicable to the respective areas, maintain these in an up-to-date condition, and acquaint all inspectors with standards requirements. Keeping standards current is a matter that should not be left to individual inspectors using the information. Experience has shown that personnel using standards books, drawing prints, and other reference data tend to neglect prompt updating of books with revised pages, change notices, etc., with the result that the reference material can quickly become obsolete.

This problem can be remedied by assigning one person in the inspection area the responsibility for keeping all standards up to date. This person should have the responsibility of receiving all new and revised standards, obtaining a sufficient quantity of each, and immediately placing these in the standards books. Superseded pages must also be removed at the same time. New or revised critical information should be called directly to the attention of the holder of the book affected, and his or her inspection stamp should be affixed to the pages as evidence of knowledge of the change.

Each inspection supervisor should review all new and revised standards to determine those applicable to the work performed by his or her group. A copy of each applicable standard should be circulated among the inspection personnel to be read. A periodic check should be made of all standards books used by the inspectors to make certain that all are up to date and fully understood by the personnel.

Whenever a supervisor finds that a standard is incorrect, incomplete, or inadequate, he should immediately send a written request to his superior for the necessary correction, addition, or revision.

Inspectors should analyze and thoroughly understand each standard received from their supervisor. Any provision that is not entirely clear, either as to its necessity or its meaning, should be questioned and discussed with the supervisor.

Correction of Specifications

Changes in dimensions, processing, and assembly requirements often become necessary during manufacture of a product. While these are often undesirable from a manufacturing or scheduling standpoint, they are nonetheless unavoidable. Such changes are the result of engineering errors, changes in production methods, and changing customer requirements. Inspection's responsibility in these matters is to insure that all items are manufactured in accordance with the proper revisions of drawings and specifications, as listed on such documents as sales orders, shop orders, assembly orders, and drawing change orders.

Drawing changes issued through normal, routine channels should seldom cause difficulty, because the system is geared to accommodate such changes. Normal procedure identifies each changed version of a drawing by a letter or a number, and this is shown on the shop or assembly order. The inspector simply makes certain that the items are manufactured in accordance with the proper revision.

More serious difficulties are often encountered when changes are "bootlegged" through the system. Open loops in communications are created, frequently resulting in confusion, redundant effort, and hidden costs.

The need for correcting the amount of tolerance and the location of the dimensions, as well as the inclusion of information which may have been omitted, may become apparent as the product is inspected. Whether or not these corrections are made depends largely upon the inspection policy and on the intimacy of the relations between quality control people and the design group. In plants where these relations are not close, an agreement is often made between the inspection organization and the production group to ignore certain parts of the specifications which are manifestly incorrect. The design group, unaware of these agreements, continues to make the same mistakes.

This condition can be brought about as the result of a poor attitude on the part of either quality control or design engineering personnel. In either case, individual egos are usually involved. A cleft that breaks good communications between the two departments should be discerned and rectified. Management involvement or even a training seminar may be required to resolve conflicts. When controversies develop between design engineering and quality control, their origin can often be traced to ambiguous policy statements, specifications, job descriptions, and procedures, or lack of these documents altogether. Such written communications should leave no doubt as to what must be done, and who has the responsibility to accomplish the work.

These kinds of issues, however, can develop into delicate situations, because they can be rooted in conflicts at the manager level. In this instance, top management must recognize this problem and reconcile the differences.

As far as the inspection function itself is concerned, if the policy is to accept all parts that meet current specifications and definitely reject all parts that do not, then mistakes and omissions will ultimately come to light. If the rejected parts are fully adequate for the service they must render, then the specifications should be revised to cover them. If some requirement other than the one specified is needed to make serviceable parts, then the specifications also should be corrected accordingly.

13.6 Standard Units of Measurement

In 1968, an international standard system (SI) of units of measurement was established. The final authority for standards rests with this internationally based system of units. This system classifies measurements into seven distinct categories, referred to as basic units of measurement in the metric system.

1. **Length (meter)** The meter is defined as 1,650,763.73 wavelengths in a vacuum of the radiation corresponding to the transition between the levels $2p_{10}$ and $5d_5$ of the krypton-86 atom.
2. **Time (second)** The second is defined as the duration of 9,192,631,770 cycles of the radiation associated with a specific transition of the cesium-55 atom as it passes through a system of magnets and a resonant cavity into a detector. The number of periods or cycles per second is called *frequency*. The SI unit for frequency is the hertz (one cycle per second).

3. **Mass (kilogram)** The standard for the unit of mass, the kilogram, is a cylinder of platinum iridium alloy kept in a vault by the international bureau of weights and measures near Paris, at Sèvres, France. A duplicate in the custody of the National Bureau of Standards serves as the mass standard for the United States. This is the only base unit still defined by an artifact. Closely allied to the concept of mass is that of *force*. The SI unit of force is the newton (N). A force of one newton when applied for one second will give an acceleration of one meter per second to a one kilogram mass.
4. **Temperature (Kelvin)** The thermodynamic or Kelvin scale of temperature has its origin or zero point at absolute zero. The Kelvin unit is the fraction 1/273.16 of the thermodynamic temperature of the triple point of water. The Celsius scale is derived from the Kelvin scale. The triple point is defined as 0.01°C on the Celsius scale, which is approximately 32.02°F on the Fahrenheit scale. The relationship of Kelvin, Celsius, and Fahrenheit temperature scales is shown below.

	Kelvin	*Celsius*	*Fahrenheit*
Water boils	373.16°	100°	212°
Body temperature	310.16°	37°	98.6°
Water freezes	273.16°	0°	32°

5. **Electric current (ampere)** The ampere is defined as the magnitude of the current that, when flowing in opposite directions through each of two long parallel wires separated by one meter in free space, results in a force between two wires (due to their magnetic fields) of 2×10^{-7} newtons for each meter of length. The SI unit for electrical resistance is the ohm.
6. **Light (candela)** The candela is defined as the luminous intensity of 0.00006 square meter of a radiating cavity at a temperature of freezing platinum (2042 K). The SI unit light flux is the lumen (lm). A source having an intensity of 1 candela in all directions radiates a light flux of 4π lumens (an 100-watt light bulb emits approximately 1700 lumens).
7. **Amount of substance (mole)** The mole is the amount of substance of a system which contains as many elementary entities as there are carbon atoms in 0.012 kg of carbon-12. The elementary entities must be specified and may be atoms, molecules, ions, electrons, photons, other particles, or specified groups of such particles.

13.7 The Industrial Application

It is the task of quality control to set up standards and allowable variations for use by inspection and manufacturing departments. Given these standards and allowable variations, it is the responsibility of inspection to determine the acceptability of the part, and it is the duty of the workers to fabricate the part as close to the standard as their ability and tools will allow.

The control of the dimensions of a product, such as width, length, diameter, and concentricity, requires the use of many types of measuring devices. Common instruments for these measurements are the steel rule, calipers, vernier calipers, and micrometers. For greater accuracy, precision gauge blocks, pneumatic air gauges, and electrical and optical devices are used.

The greater percentage of an inspector's time is ordinarily spent in measurement—in comparing a given characteristic to a standard. The basis for this comparison is the science of measurement called *metrology*.

When a characteristic is measured, the dimension being measured is compared to a standard. The standard may be a yardstick, a pair of calipers, or even a set of gauge blocks, but they all represent some criteria against which a measurement of an object is compared.

Linear standards are easier to define and describe if they are divided into functional levels. There are five such levels in which standards are usually described.

1. **Working Level** This level includes, for example, gauges used at the work center.
2. **Calibration Standards** These are standards to which working-level standards are calibrated.
3. **Functional Standards** This level of standards is used only in the metrology laboratory of the company for measuring precision work and calibrating other standards.
4. **Reference Standards** These standards are certified directly to the U.S. Bureau of Standards and are used in lieu of national standards.
5. **National and International Standards** This is the final authority of measurement to which all standards are traceable.

Since the continuous use of national standards is neither feasible nor possible, other standards are developed for various levels of functional utilization. National standards are taken as the central authority for measurement accuracy, and all levels of working standards are traceable to this primary standard.

In order for some parts, such as screw threads and gears, to function properly, their profiles or shapes must meet rather high standards of quality. It is often necessary to check the contours of such parts on an optical comparator to determine the degree to which they meet standards. By magnifying and projecting a shadow image of the part on the screen upon which a standard profile is also placed, a comparison can be made between the part and the standard. Figure 13-16 shows a technologist studying a screw thread for the purpose of improving the standard.

A suitable standard is essential for any test. Unless the results of a test can be compared with some known quantity, the measurements are relatively meaningless. In figure 13-17, the technologist is using an ultrasonic digital thickness gauge to measure the thickness of the section shown. Every material has a specific velocity through which ultrasonic waves are propagated; therefore, the instrument must be adjusted for each material with calibration blocks such as those shown in the foreground.

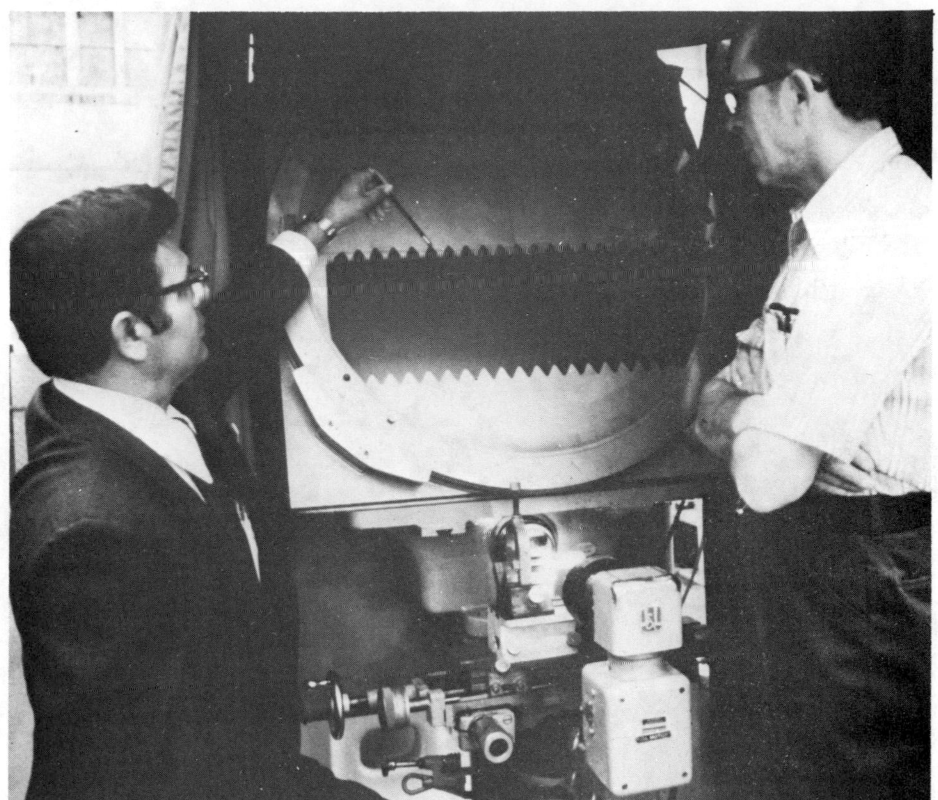

Figure 13–16 Studying standard for screw thread.

13.8 Defining Accuracy and Precision

When an object is measured or compared to a standard, there is always the possibility of error regardless of the accuracy of the instruments. A measurement is accurate to the degree that it agrees with the true value of the measured quantity.

If a primary meter is sent to the Bureau of Standards for calibration, the amount that it differs from the standard meter will be detected. If it does not differ by any appreciable amount, say 0.0000 cm, then its error to four decimal places is zero. However it might differ by −0.000008 cm, called the error. It would be called *accurate* to −0.000008 cm per meter.

It is possible to calibrate many testing devices on the job since measurements are relative. Many laboratories use primary standards for calibration and then use secondary standards for calibrating the working standards. Thus care is taken not to use a standard so much that it is affected by wear or time.

Precision, on the other hand, is affected by both men and equipment. Precision is the capability of reproduction of a measurement. If, for example, Operator A

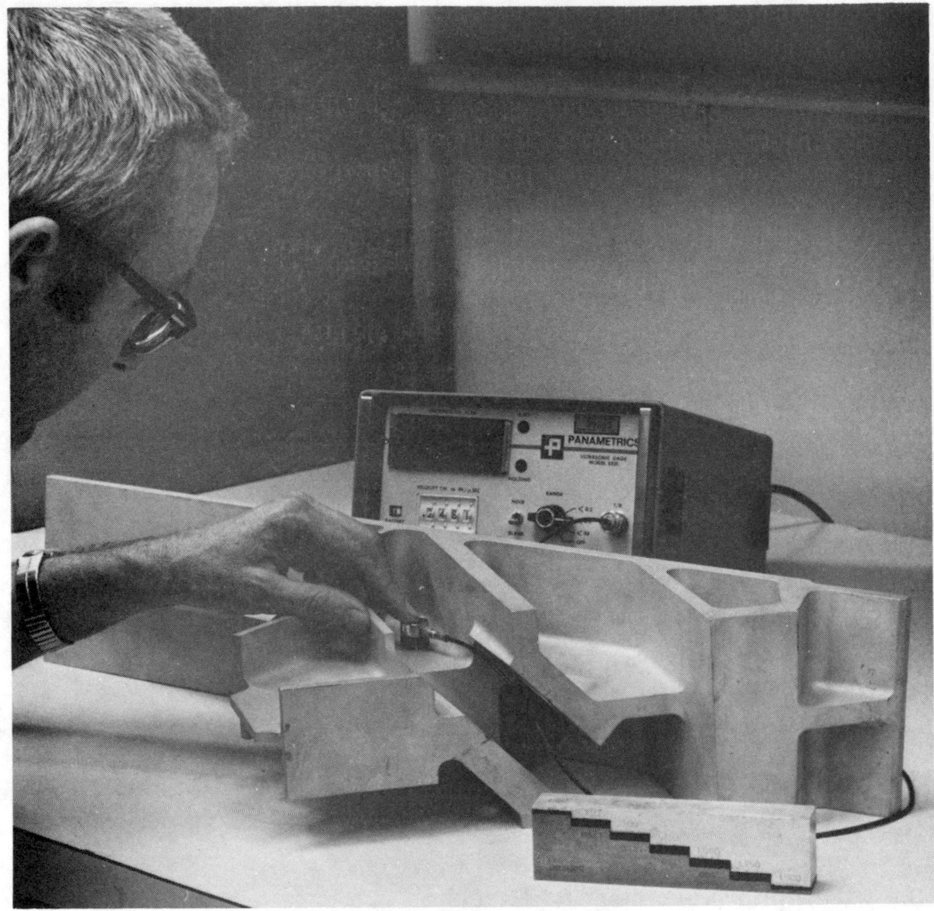

Figure 13–17 Ultrasonic digital thickness gauge.

measures a part and states that its length is 1.225 inch, will Operator A obtain the same length every time he measures this part? Assuming the part is not affected by its environment, if Operator A reads 1.224 inch a second time, 1.226 inch a third time, and continues to read in the range 1.224 inch to 1.226 inch, then his precision may be determined by computing his average and standard deviation, and establishing the distribution of his readings. The true value might be 1.220 inch or 1.230 inch, but this does not affect his precision. However, if a gauge were dropped, causing it to be inaccurate, and if it were used in the inaccurate condition, the inaccurate measurement would be repeated very precisely. Such a gauge can possess a high degree of precision because it will repeat nearly the same measurement over and over again, while still having a relatively low degree of accuracy.

The calibration of measuring instruments is necessary to maintain accuracy, but calibration does not necessarily increase precision.

13.9 Calibration

Calibration is the comparison of a measurement standard or instrument of known accuracy with another standard or instrument to detect, correlate, report, or eliminate by adjustment any variation in the accuracy of the item being compared. Calibration tasks are performed to ensure accuracy of measurement and therefore help to ensure that measurement standards are maintained. Electrical and mechanical measuring instruments frequently are easy to knock out of calibration, which means that they will not measure to the required accuracy. A systematic procedure must be inaugurated in a company to ensure that the instruments used for measurement are periodically checked to determine if they are measuring within the prescribed limits. If they are not, the proper adjustments must be made. If they are verified to be accurate, their continued use is permitted. The calibration procedure always involves a comparison of the instrument being calibrated with a standard having a higher accuracy level. Figure 13-18 shows a calibration report form like those used in most companies.

Figure 13-19 illustrates an inspector calibrating a height gauge to a standard of higher accuracy, traceable directly to the international standard. He is performing this operation prior to inspecting the part shown on the surface plate.

A company should provide and maintain gauges and other measuring and testing devices necessary to assure that supplies conform to technical requirements.

The desired calibrated accuracy of the measurement standards should be ten times the accuracy of the inspection and test equipment under calibration, and as a minimum, a four-to-one accuracy ratio should be maintained when direct measurements are being performed. Exceptions due to practical limitations, excessive costs, or other reasons sometimes are made. A ten-to-one accuracy ratio gives better than 99.2% assurance that *no* out-of-tolerance items will be accepted. The four-to-one ratio provides measurements which are in error less than 3% of the time.

In most plants, definite procedures are established and are in operation for periodically calibrating all measuring devices. Micrometers should be calibrated any time one is dropped. Some instruments should be calibrated immediately before being used, as they vary considerably from day to day, even during temporary storage. Others are calibrated weekly or monthly as required to maintain accuracy. A good tool and gauge laboratory will maintain a card system to cover each measuring device. Each card will give the history of a particular device from the time of purchase, including any repairs that may have been required. Also, any special changes in calibration will be emphasized on the card. Such a historical record helps to maintain instrumentation accuracy in a cost-effective manner. Many large companies utilize the computer as the basis for an organized recall

CONTROL NO. ____________

INSTRUMENT CALIBRATION RECORD

DESCRIPTION ____________

ACCURACY REQUIREMENT ____________

____

CYCLE CHECK REQUIRED ____________

LOCATION ____________

CALIBRATION TEST PROCEDURE ____________

____

CALIBRATION DATE	SCHEDULED RE-CALIBRATION	PRE-CALIBRATION CONDITION	CALIBRATED CONDITION	CALIBRATED BY

Figure 13–18 Instrument calibration report.

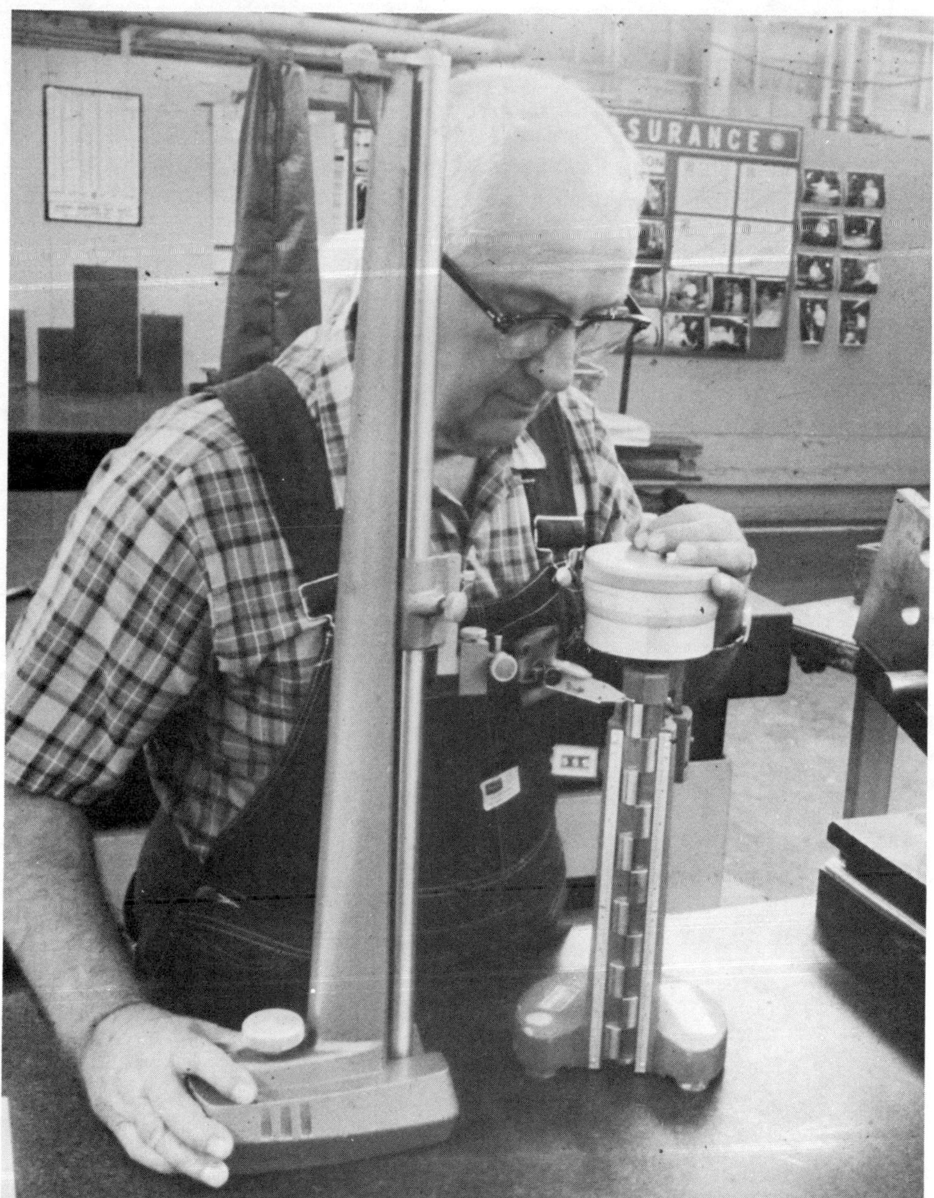

Figure 13–19 Calibrating a height gauge.

program. In any case the overall system should assure the direct or indirect traceability of a company's calibration standards through an unbroken chain of calibrations to the international system of standards.

13.10 Making Accurate Measurements

Surface Plates

To make accurate and precise dimensional measurements, one must have a reference plane or starting point. Such a plane actually is theoretical, since perfect measurement is impossible. Accurate measurements to some determinable degree are the best that can be achieved.

Since a true reference plane does not exist, nor can it be created, a compromise has been made. This compromise resulted in the use of reference surfaces, such as surface plates.

Most "setups" for inspection are made on surface plates, many of which are for calibration of working standards. It is imperative, therefore, that the surface plate itself be maintained so that its accuracy is much greater than that of the measuring tool. Figure 13-21 shows the use of a large surface plate on which a very accurate measurement (to 0.00010 inch) is being made. This laser setup is capable of precise measurement of 0.00005 inch in 60 inches and 0.0010 inch in 300 feet. Frequently, laser potential cannot be fully realized because of variables other than the laser itself.

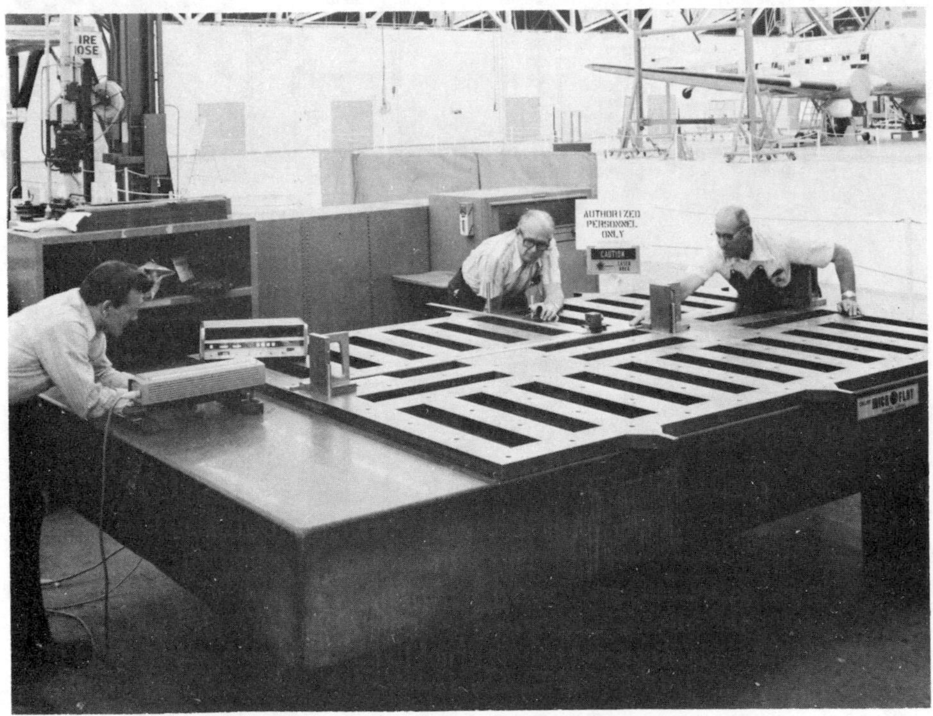

Figure 13–20 Calibration of a surface plate.

Gauging

When there is the need to inspect large quantities of products, it is advantageous to use gauges which have been made or adjusted to the limits required, thus allowing quick checks of products for conformance to the required dimensions. In interchangeable manufacturing, different types of gauges must be used to check the linear and angular dimensions, amount of taper, roundness, concentricity, parallelism, and contour. Interchangeable manufacturing depends not only on tolerances, but also upon precise and efficient measuring or gauging instruments for checking established tolerances.

Gauge Blocks

It has been pointed out that the international standard of length is based on the krypton-86 isotope. Light waves provide an excellent means for making extremely accurate measurements in the laboratory. Unfortunately, their use as a measuring instrument in the shop is often not feasible. Gauge blocks, on the other hand, are one of the most accurate physical representations of the light wave standard of length available today in terms of millionths of an inch. Hence they constitute a practical means whereby the standard inch can be subdivided, multiplied, and used as a shop tool—an everyday tool that can be handled, used, and then discarded.

The surfaces of the blocks are ground and lapped to such a fine finish that the sum of combined blocks equals the sum of the values of individual blocks when various sizes are combined. The procedure of sliding gauge blocks together is known as *wringing*. When they are properly wrung together, air space between them is virtually eliminated.

Standards for gauge blocks are defined in terms of accuracy grades. They are listed in table 13.1.

TABLE 13.1

Federal Accuracy Grades		*Accuracy in length*
New designation	*old designation*	
0.5	*AAA*	±0.000001
1	*AA*	±0.000002
2	*A*+	+0.000004 −0.000002
3	*A & B*	+0.000006 −0.000002

Attributes Measurement and Inspection

An *attribute* is a characteristic or property which is appraised in terms of its existence with respect to a given standard. An attribute clearly exists or does not exist, and is discerned frequently by a single observation. The purpose of attribute inspection is simply to accept or reject on the basis of the attribute, not to determine the exact measurement. Go, no-go gauging is a good example of attribute inspection, as shown by figure 13-21. Part A is acceptable and part B is unacceptable, as evidenced by the gauge. Inspection by attributes is inspection in which either a product or characteristic is judged simply as defective or nondefective with respect to a drawing or specification.

Attributes inspection is more commonly used, therefore, when inspecting items for visual defects, workmanship defects, or incorrect configuration (when checked with fixed-limit gauges), and when examining marking and packaging. It is used in those instances when the objective is to determine solely whether a unit or characteristic meets or does not meet an established requirement.

Variables Measurement and Inspection

A variable is a characteristic or property which is appraised in terms of scalar values on a continuous scale, such as inches, centimeters, pounds, or liters.

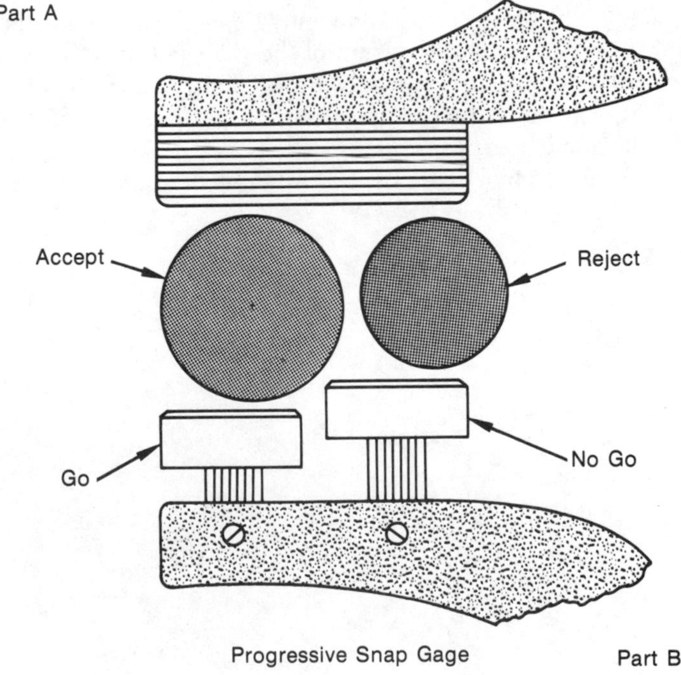

Figure 13–21 Go, no-go gauge.

A measurement, which is a precise point along the scale, is then recorded. Where attribute inspection is concerned with whether or not a part passes, inspection by variables is concerned with the degree or margin by which a part is passed or rejected. If the measurement of a characteristic is involved, this is called variables inspection.

Therefore, inspection by variables is used whenever the quality of any given characteristic of a unit is determined in quantitative or measurable terms. Examples of variables inspection include such characteristics as a specific tensile strength, hardness, or a measured dimension. Following is a specific example of variables inspection.

The outside diameter dimension of a rotor shaft was 2.495 ± 0.002. This dimension (characteristic) of every part was measured with micrometers to determine the degree to which the measurements were between 2.493 and 2.497. Inspection by variables was performed on each shaft, because they were subsequently matched with bushings which also had been inspected by variables.

Examples of devices used in variables measuring are micrometers and vernier height gauges. Figure 13-22 illustrates a variables inspection job being performed. A micrometer is being used to measure the thickness of an extruded polystyrene

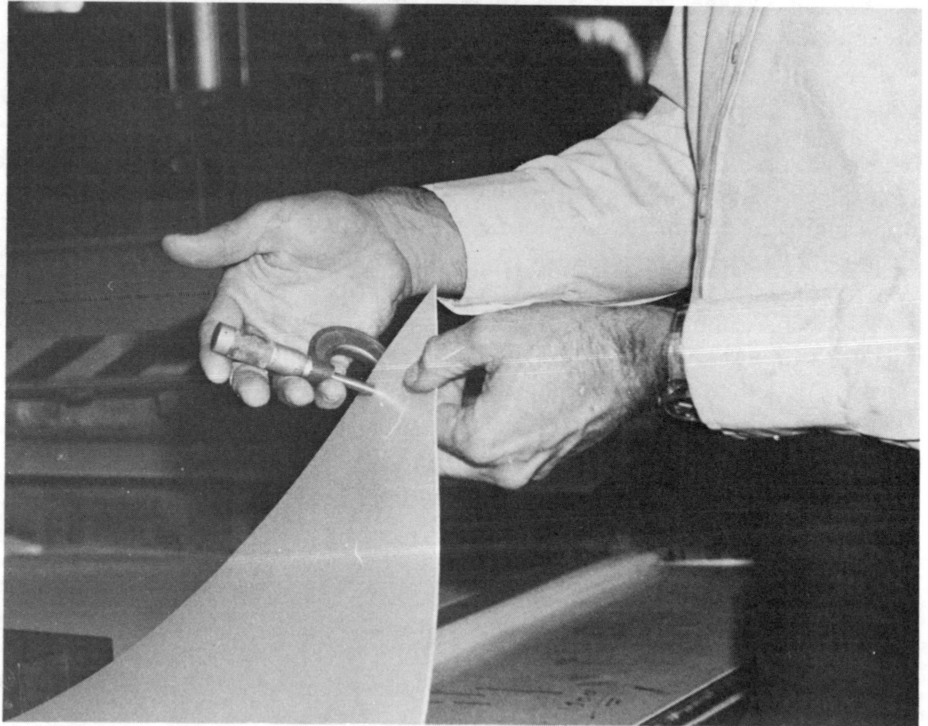

Figure 13–22 Using a micrometer.

plastic sheet. The running thickness of such extruded stock is usually controlled by the process itself, but periodically a variables measurement with micrometers must be made to verify that the process is within acceptable tolerance limits. The allowable tolerance in this instance was 0.002. Such instruments measure the degree to which a part conforms or does not conform to a standard. (Such a standard is generally the engineering drawing on which dimensions and tolerances are presented.) Many inspection devices, such as optical comparators and pneumatic gauges can be used either for inspection of attributes or variables.

Hardness standards and measurements of materials hardness are also very prevalent in modern industry. In most cases, the hardness of a material is positively correlated with other important quality characteristics such as compressive or tensile strengths, and hardness standards and tests are often used as a measure of such quality characteristics. Figure 13-23 illustrates a Rockwell hardness test being performed on a spline where torsion and tensile properties were critical.

Government Specifications

As technology advances, it becomes a necessity to specify the requirements that are desired in a product. These requirements are set forth in the form of specifications by the customer who desires to have an item produced, and then are used by the producer of the product to ensure that customers' wishes or requirements are met.

The government, one of the largest of these customers, has set forth not only specifications for products they wish to have manufactured, but also have developed specifications and certain standards for the organization and operation of quality assurance systems. Any student of quality should take advantage of opportunity to obtain quality documents published by the U.S. Government Printing Office in Washington, D.C. Much relevant and excellent information can be purchased from this office for a very nominal fee.

Following are some of the government specifications commonly applied to quality assurance systems. There are many others that should be named, but space does not permit a complete listing.

MILITARY STANDARDS AND SPECIFICATIONS

1. Quality Assurance Terms and Definitions	MIL–STD–109
2. Quality Program Requirements	MIL–Q–9858
3. Inspection System Requirements	MIL–I–45208
4. Calibration System Requirements	MIL–C–45662
5. Quality Control System Requirements (Technical Data)	MIL–T–50301
6. Quality Assurance Provisions for Government Agencies	NHB–53004
7. Supplier Quality Assurance Program Requirements	MIL–STD–1535 USAF

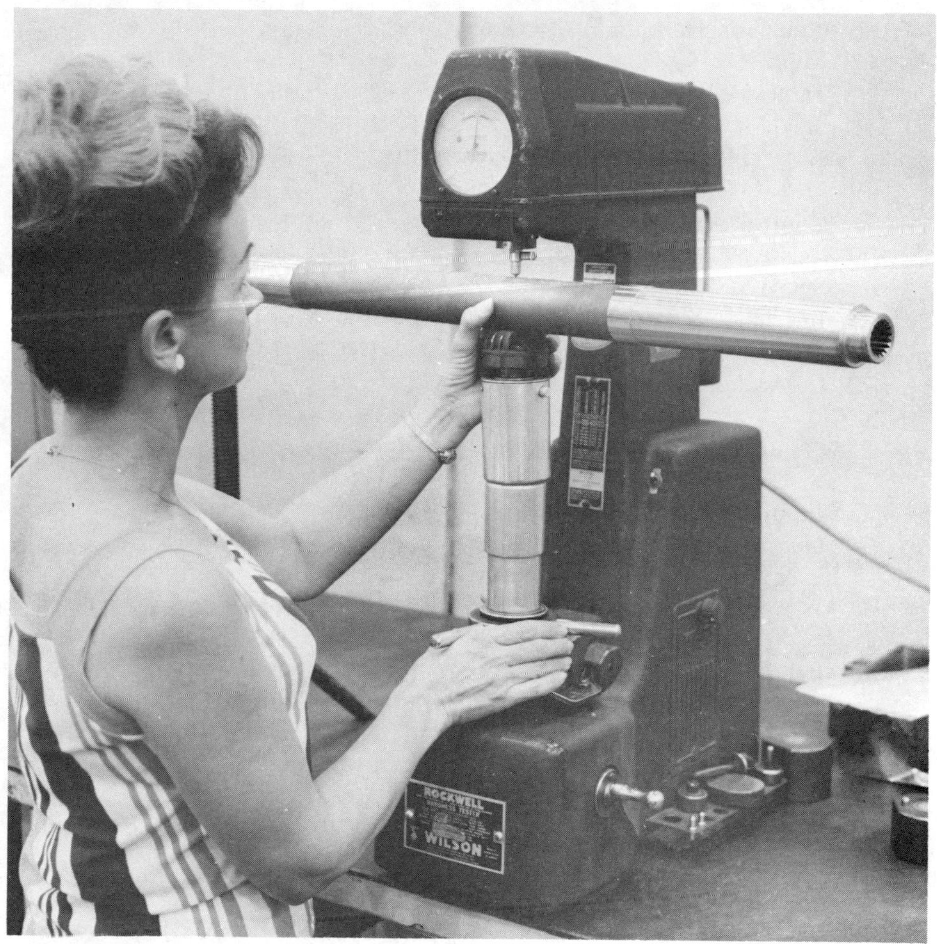

Figure 13–23 The Rockwell hardness test.

8.	Sampling Procedures and Methods for Quality Assurance	DSAM 8260.1
9.	Handbook of Quality Assurance Forms and Procedures	DSAH 8230.1
10.	Magnetic Inspection Units	MIL–M–6867
11.	Sampling Procedures and Tables for Inspection by Attributes (International Designations)	MIL–STD–105
12.	Sampling Procedures and Tables for Inspection by Variables for Percent Defective	MIL–STD–414
13.	Evaluation of Contractors Quality Program	Handbook 50
14.	Evaluation of Contractors Inspection System	Handbook 51
15.	Evaluation of Contractors Calibration System	Handbook 52

16. Guide for Sampling Inspection	Handbook 53
17. Multi-level Continuous Sampling Procedures and Tables for Inspection by Attributes	Handbook 106
18. Single-level Continuous Sampling Procedures and Tables for Inspection by Attributes	Handbook 107
19. Quality Program Provisions for Space System Contractors	NHB 5300.1
20. Quality Program Provisions for Aeronautical and Space System Contractors	NHB 5300.4
21. Inspection System Provisions for Supplier of Space Materials, Parts, Components and Services	NHB 5300.2
22. Control of Manufacturing Supplies	USAF Spec. Bulletin 515
23. Quality Assurance Testing and Inspection of Aircraft Crew Emergency Escape Propellant Equipment	MIL–STD–1550
24. Quality Control of Gaseous and Liquid Aviators Breathing Oxygen at Aircraft Contract Facilities	MIL–STD–1551
25. Quality Standards for Aircraft Pneumatic Tires and Inner Tubes	MIL–STD–698
26. Quality Control of Chemicals	MIL–Q–7640
27. Quality Control General Specifications	MIL–Q–14461
28. Quality of Wood Member Containers	MIL–STD–731
29. Quality Control Requirements General Equipment	MIL–Q–5923
30. Reliability Report	MIL–STD–1304
31. Reliability Prediction	MIL–STD–756
32. Reliability Test Exponential Distribution	MIL–STD–781
33. Reliability Requirements for Weapons Systems (superseded by MIL–R–27542)	MIL–26674
34. Reliability Assurance Program for Electrical Equipment (superseded by MIL–T–27542 USAF)	MIL–R–25717
35. Reliability Assurance Program for Electronic Parts Spec.	MIL–STD–790
36. Reliability Assurance for Production Acceptance of Avionic Equipment General Spec. (superseded by MIL–STD–781A)	MIL–23094
37. Reliability Program for Systems and Equipment Development and Production	MIL–STD–785
38. Reliability Requirements for Design of Electrical Equipment or Systems (superseded by MIL–STD–785)	MIL–R–22256
39. Reliability Index-Determination for Avionic Equipment Control General Spec.	MIL–R–22973

40. Reliability Prediction and Demonstration for Airborne Surveillance Systems (Multipurpose MQM 58A) — MIL–R–55413
41. Reliability and Quality Assurance Requirements for Established Parts General Spec. — MIL–R–38100
42. Reliability Evaluation from Demonstration Data — MIL–STD–757
43. Reliability Requirements for Development of Electrical Subsystems for Equipment Use (MIL–STD–781) — MIL–R–26484
44. Reliability Requirements for Development of Ground Electrical Equipment (superseded by MIL–STD–785) — MIL–R–27070
45. Reliability Requirements for Electrical Ground Checkout Equipment — MIL–R–27173
46. Reliability Requirements for Shipboard Electrical Equipment — MIL–R–22732
47. Reliability Requirements for Shipboard Electronic Equipment — MIL–R–22732
48. Reliability of Production of Electronic Equipment, General Spec. — MIL–R–19610
49. Reliability Prediction of Monolithic Integrated Circuits — MIL–STD–1600
50. Life Cycle Product Quality Program Requirements — OD 46574

EXERCISES

1. What is the underlying purpose of standardization? Discuss the pros and cons of standardizing. Name some of the forms standardization can take.
2. Discuss some benefits of standardization as related to the control of quality.
3. Are good standards important to quality control? If so, give three examples. If not, explain.
4. Are drawings and specifications forms of standards? Explain.
5. What is a tolerance? Why are tolerances needed?
6. Name seven standard international units of measurement. Why are these necessary?
7. What is a calibration standard? Where are calibration standards normally used?
8. Explain the differences between accuracy and precision. Is the task of calibrating an instrument related closer to accuracy than to precision? Explain your answer.
9. What is a gauge block? How are gauge blocks used?

10. What is the difference between checking for attributes and checking for variables? Give an example of an attribute checking device and a variables checking device.

FOOTNOTES

[1] Used with permission from *Quality Assurance: Management and Technology*, Revised Edition. Glenn E. Hayes. Charger Productions, Capistrano Beach, California, 1976.

CHAPTER FOURTEEN

INSPECTION PRINCIPLES AND PRACTICES

14.1 Industrial Inspection

Definition and Development

Inspection is defined as the examination and testing of supplies and services (including, when appropriate, raw materials, components, and intermediate assemblies) to determine whether or not they conform to specified requirements.

Because inspection has safeguarding and maintaining product quality as its ultimate objective, one may conclude that inspection has existed as long as people have lived—for people have always examined the things they have made to determine their fitness for use.

However, industrial inspection is of relatively recent origin. It arose as a result of problems brought about by mass production, which created a need for interchangeable parts. During the period when craftspeople created their own products, separate inspection operations were not required; the craftspeople produced the entire article and were responsible for its quality. If parts did not fit properly, they made the necessary adjustments. There was no need for separate inspection, because each person was responsible for the fabrication, the assembly, and the inspection of the articles. No two parts were alike, but there was no practical reason why they should be.

This independent, hand-fit method has only limited use. Modern industrial economy requires the low-cost methods of mass production. Such an economy is possible only when men and machines are specialized for the performance of certain operations. It has been necessary, therefore, to divorce the worker from all-round craft work and to supplant hand-fit methods with interchangeable manufacture.

The transition from crude machines to better-designed and more powerful mechanisms was not possible without the simultaneous development of accurate and reliable inspection instruments and methods. Intricate machines and devices are both the cause and the effect of more accurate and efficient inspection. Improvements in metallurgy and in raw materials manufacturing could not have come about were it not for process control, a principal portion of which inspection has the responsibility for exercising. Production itself has been expedited by efficient inspection, which often eliminates tooling bottlenecks and poor processing before these lead to needless rejections. Industrial inspection has emerged as a powerful tool in the hands of management, helping to ensure that a competitive, quality product can be produced in volume.

Purposes and Scope

The following are the principal purposes of inspection.

1. To determine which units conform to established requirements.
2. To identify and separate acceptable goods from those which are not acceptable.
3. To report deficiencies as soon as possible after detection.

The inspection criteria used to determine whether or not quality requirements are met are stated in such documents as drawings and specifications, inspection instructions, purchase specifications, technical orders and bulletins, military specifications, and various other project documents.

The scope of inspection will vary with the company and the kinds of products, but some type of inspection is normally needed from the time that the selection of a vendor for purchased parts is made to the time after the product is placed into service. The inspection system may be subdivided into three broad phases: (1) procurement of parts, (2) in-house fabrication of parts and assemblies, and (3) post-fabrication. These are described in figure 14-1.

Materials and parts frequently are inspected at the vendor's facility by the buyer's source inspector before a shipment is made. The parts may again be inspected (together with those that have not had source inspection) by receiving

PROCUREMENT OF PARTS AND PRE-FABRICATION	FABRICATION	POST-FABRICATION
• Vendor Certification • Source Inspection • Receiving Inspection	• Tooling Inspection • In-process Inspection • Assembly Inspection • Final Inspection • Rework Inspection	• Packaging • Shipping • Maintenance and Field Service

Figure 14–1 Stages of AQL inspection of a product.

inspectors at the buyer's facility when the parts are received. Later, during various stages of product manufacture, parts and assemblies are inspected to verify that the final articles actually have all the desired quality characteristics before they are delivered. Further, during the life of a product, inspection may be necessary when parts are being maintained or replaced.

Inspection and Quality Control

The roles of inspection and quality control in the overall job of management are often vital for the sound functioning of the company. Although production has resources such as personnel, machinery, and materials, it cannot be certain of what it is getting in the way of resources or of the level of results it is achieving when converting its resources into saleable articles. Inspection, inserted throughout the production sequence, is required as a screening activity. Unless the unit quality from an operation itself can be guaranteed, some amount of inspection is essential to ensure that raw materials, tools, gauges, and produced units conform to specifications. Inspection is always concerned with the degree of success attained by production in converting incoming resources to satisfactory parts and assemblies.

In a strict sense, inspection does not create quality characteristics, because it neither adds nor subtracts those features for which the customer is paying. Quality is added only by production itself, through fabrication, assembly, and rework processes. Product characteristics are created prior to inspection; therefore, the inspector can influence the value of the products only indirectly. By performing the job satisfactorily, he or she contributes indirectly to cost values by helping to assure optimum costs. The inspector also contributes indirectly to use values by helping to ensure that the delivered products meet specifications which have been established for each of the products.

Inspection results must be tabulated, classified, and critically examined for trends in quality. This analysis is normally performed by quality control engineering. Quality originating from various processes varies with the quality of workers, material, and machinery. This necessitates constant reappraisal, together with effective managerial action, to eliminate unsatisfactory conditions, preferably before they occur. The combined efforts of inspection and quality control give management the necessary data upon which preventive and intelligent remedial actions can be based.

14.2 Classifying Defects

A defect is any nonconformance **unit with respect to** a single quality characteristic, while a defective is a unit with one or more defects, possibly involving the deficiency of a number of quality characteristics. For example, a single solder joint not meeting workmanship standards is a defect, but should the circuit board also have a missing component, contain a short circuit, etc., it would be classified as a defective. Either a defect or a defective involves failure to meet a prescribed specification. Defects and defectives are classified in accordance with their seriousness. The main classifications are described in the following paragraphs.

1. **Critical Defect** A critical defect is one that judgment and experience indicate will *surely*: (*a*) result in hazardous or unsafe conditions for individuals using, maintaining, or depending upon the product, and (*b*) prevent performance of the tactical function of a major product such as a ship, aircraft, tank, missile, space vehicle, cost accounting system, inventory control system, or similar administrative system.
2. **A Major Defect** A major defect is one that is not critical, but that is *likely* to result in failure, or to materially reduce the usability of the unit for its intended purpose.
3. **A Minor Defect** A minor defect is one that is not likely to materially reduce the usability of the unit for its intended purpose, nor will it have any bearing on the effective use or operation of the unit. (It is important to realize, however, that a minor defect in one material for one application may be a major defect for another, and vice versa.)

14.3 Inspection Planning

Inspection planning is necessary for most manufacturing operations, whether it is done by manufacturing planners or inspection personnel. If manufacturing planners have the capability needed, are aware of the importance of the inspection tasks, and fully coordinate their efforts with the quality control department, inspection checkpoints may be satisfactorily designated by manufacturing planners at the time that manufacturing planning is accomplished. However, additional inspection information may be required which can best be designated by inspection personnel. Together with inspection point definition, methods of inspection should be prescribed. Issuing blueprints at random to inspectors to inspect miscellaneous items can be very inefficient. It is usually more economical to plan the steps of the inspection procedure in detail. These planning tasks must be accomplished by an inspection planner who is (1) skilled in the use of the inspection equipment, and (2) knowledgeable about the inspection steps that best meet quality objectives in a cost-effective manner.

An example of an inspection planning sheet that could be used with such a procedure is shown in figures 14-2 and 14-3. The detail drawing of part 2-159100, showing the characteristics to be inspected, is illustrated in figure 14-2 and the operation instruction sheet describing the steps of manufacture and inspection is given in figure 14-3. Both manufacturing and inspection planning can be accomplished on the same planning sheet, giving specific steps of each procedure. Note

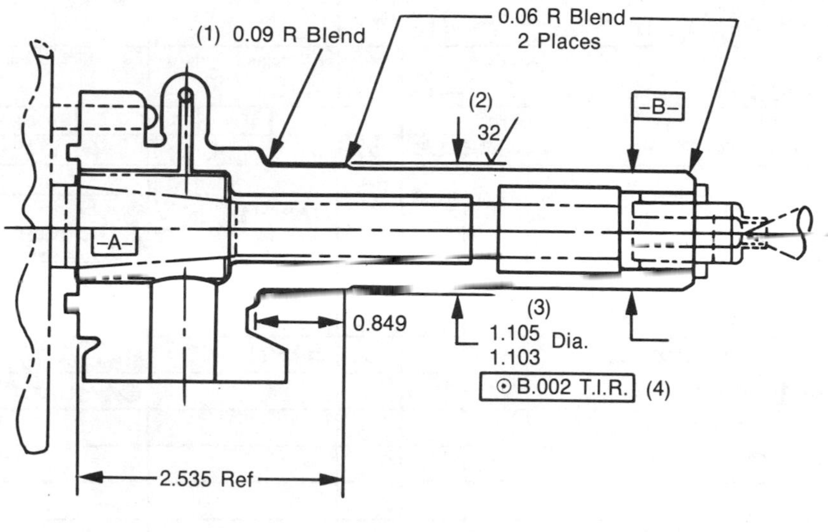

Inspection Note:
Development of common Axis -A- allows functional acceptance of all concentricities of diameters generated relative to -A-

Figure 14–2 Detailed drawing of part 2-159100.

that inspection steps 1 through 5 are listed on the drawing. This helps to avoid confusion about which characteristics should be inspected.

Inspection planning may need to take another form where *system* inspection is involved. If a large number of inspection check points need to be covered, a planning sheet listing all the inspection points helps to insure that certain characteristics or assemblies are not missed during inspection. Figure 14-4 illustrates such a guide sheet.

Selecting Inspection Points and Locations

There are two basic arrangements of inspection work centers. One arrangement provides for a central inspection point, to which materials and parts are delivered for inspection. Figure 14-5 illustrates a centralized inspection center to which parts flow from the respective operations.

In this example, three product lines are directed to the same inspection work station where the inspector (1) appraises the degree of the conformance of the products, (2) makes a disposition of the defectives, and (3) makes a disposition of acceptable parts, and (4) fills out the appropriate forms or tickets.

The second arrangement utilizes inspection points directly in the line of product flow. The frequency of the inspection points within the total manufacturing cycle

Operation Instruction Sheet				Sheet 1 of 2
Part Name HOUSING-MACHINED	Part No. 2-159100	Configuration	Issue No.	Oper. No.

Operation Description	NC Tape No.	Set up	Parts/	STD Hours/	Surface Speed	RDS Effective
TURN SEAL DIA		4.0	10	.10		

Machine Name	Mfg. Engineer	Date	Eng.	Appd. Q. C.		Appd. M. E.	
ENGINE LATHE #9360	F. LAWRENCE	11/21/66	[illegible]	[illegible]	1-9-66	[illegible]	1/6/67

ITEM	Description	Total Length of Cut	R.P.M.	Feed	Time in Min.	Tools (Appd. by [illegible] 8-27-66)	Gages (Appd. by)
	SET UP						① .06/.12 RAD. GAGE 1/P
							② PROFILOMETER V
							③ 914646 1/P
	MOUNT PART ON				.01	SA-7104629	④ PROCESS CONTROLLED 1/P
	ARBOR & USE						⑤ VISUAL 1
	TAILSTOCK CENTER						
	MACHINE						
	TURN 1.103/1.105 DIA				.05	INSERT #10-661	
	X .849 DIM & BLEND					HOLDER #22-271	
	TO .09 R						
	BLEND .06 RADIUS						
	(2) PLACES						

Revisions					Quality Control Revisions		
No	Description	By	Allow to Change Feed,		No	Description	By
			Total Operation Time	.06			
	STATION NB WAS	F.L.	Position Tools @				
	9221 & TURN DIA		Check Dims @	.01			
	WAS GRIND DIA		Total	.07			
			Machine & Tool	.01			
			Rest & Delay	.02			
			Total Allowable Time	.10			

Figure 14–3 Manufacturing and inspection planning sheet.

INSPECTION CHARACTERISTICS LIST — GUIDE SHEET

1. Check lockbolts for pin protrusion and swaging, using gages.
2. Lockbolts in sealant application areas do not show evidence of sealant in locking grooves.
3. Check Hi-locks for protrusion and bottoming, using gages. Verify use of self-aligning nuts and washers on tapered surfaces as required.
4. Check bolt and screw protrusion.
5. Check mating parts for gap/preloaded, twisted, or distorted condition.
6. Tooling holes plugged.
7. Verify contour waviness and mismatch requirements.
8. Proper orientation of attachments.
9. Temporary attachments identified.
10. No sealant build-up between structural members.
11. Minimum clearances between structures prior to application of sealant.
12. Design gaps and bend relief cutouts are not in excess of limitations of sealant to seal.
13. Verify presence of faying surface seals.
14. Temporary attachments are installed at end of sealant area where permanent attachments will be installed at later date.
15. No burrs or sharp edges on parts.
16. Check around titanium holes for discoloration which indicates over heating. Discoloration is cause for rejection.
17. Check for damage after removal from assembly jig.
18. Electrical plugs tight and safetied when required.
19. Wire bundles not constricted by structure or adjacent installation.
20. Non-terminated wires identified and stowed.

Figure 14–4 Check points for system inspection.

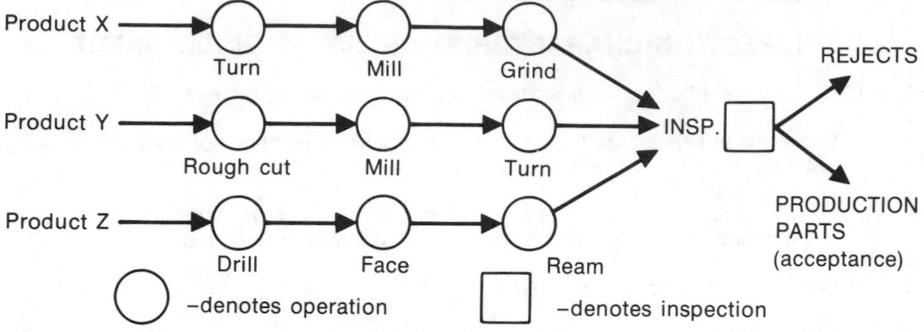

Figure 14–5 Centralized inspection.

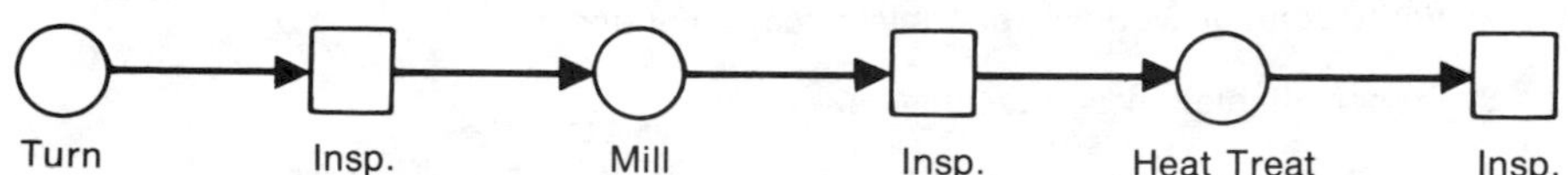

Figure 14–6 In-line inspection.

is determined by the nature of the product and the operational costs for its fabrication. Figure 14-6 illustrates the use of an inspection station after each operation.

In this case, the inspection function is required after each successive operation to prevent subsequent work on defective parts.

Often inspection stations are not required until several operations have been performed. This method will normally be used under the following conditions.

1. There is a large number of a given product to produce.
2. There are high manufacturing costs involved in each successive operation.
3. There is the tendency toward a large number of defective units originating from the previous process.

Product specifications not only dictate the type of inspection and test equipment needed, but also play a large part in determining the physical positions of the inspection stations. For example, a noncritical plastics product may require little more than visual inspection throughout the inspection points in the manufacturing cycle. The physical positions of the inspection stations and required tools would be based on this need. On the other hand, electronic components which have high reliability requirements may require dimensional verification, electronic testing, and environmental testing all during the manufacturing cycle. Under these conditions, suitable inspection and testing stations should be placed near specified manufacturing operations.

While either centralized or decentralized inspection may predominate in a plant, in practically every case the two plans will be combined. The heterogeneous nature of most manufacturing companies usually makes one type necessary in one manufacturing area and the second type necessary in another. The decision regarding which one to inaugurate is made by determining the least cost required to safeguard the desired level of quality.

When inspection stations are inserted in the production sequence as shown in figure 14-6, a patrolling inspector usually makes spot checks of parts at designated points in the manufacturing cycle. He may work from a sampling plan, in which case he would inspect a given number of parts to determine the pattern of variability and the trends of the processes.

Another instance of in-line inspection is when the inspector must inspect at least one characteristic of each part. Every part that is passed to him from the previous operation may need to be inspected or tested. He must determine whether or not the item conforms to product standards, and then either accept or reject the part. (This is one level of 100% inspection.)

The integrity of fabrication and assembly inspection rests on the following conditions. The inspection system should

1. preclude possibilities of bypassing the inspection work centers,
2. have a balanced flow in and out of the inspection stations,
3. have correct standards for measuring conformance of the parts,
4. provide for the correct use of a sampling plan if one has been designated,
5. account for qualified inspectors, and
6. provide for adequate inspection equipment.

An example of an in-process test is illustrated in figure 14-7. This is a photograph of an X-ray technician placing the film on a welded honeycomb ring subassembly. The radiographs will reveal if any unbonded areas exist in the honeycomb structure.

14.4 Characteristics of a Lot

A lot (sometimes referred to as a *batch*) may be defined as a collection of individual pieces from a common source, possessing a common set of quality characteristics, and offered as a homogeneous group for inspection and acceptance at one time. These pieces may be parts, partial assemblies, or finished units of product. For purposes of inspection, it is desirable that a lot be composed of pieces that all have been produced under what are judged to be the same basic conditions. Accordingly, attempts should be made to avoid grouping batches of product that are likely to differ in quality because of differences in the raw materials used or differences in manufacturing methods or conditions. For inspections made in a manufacturing plant, particularly where production is continuous (as with conveyor systems), the time element may often be the deciding factor in fixing the size of a lot, and such items as **convenient** in handling and stocking or shipping facilities may make it desirable to take an hour's, a half-day's, or a day's production as the quantity to be considered as a lot for inspection purposes.

Figure 14–7 In-process testing.

14.5 Quantity of Inspection

One of the first decisions that must be made when writing inspection procedures is whether all of the units of a product should be inspected (100% inspection), or only a part of the units should be inspected (sampling inspection).

One Hundred Percent Inspection

One hundred percent inspection is the inspection of every unit produced. Each unit is accepted or rejected individually, for the quality characteristics concerned. For certain quality characteristics (e.g., critical), 100% inspection or inspection of relatively large sample sizes is usually required to ensure quality standards.

When one conducts 100% inspection, it may involve inspecting a variety of characteristics, such as dimension, physical qualities, chemical composition, hardness, or color, or it could involve only one characteristic. One should be specific about characteristics when stating the need for 100% inspection, because if more than one characteristic is inadvertently included, inspection costs can be much more than anticipated. It should be remembered 100% inspection usually is done for only *significant* characteristics.

In many cases, 100% inspection may be necessary to provide the greatest assurance that all defectives are discovered. Experience has shown, however, that 100% inspection does not guarantee a perfect product. Human error, the lack of desire on the part of the inspector to do an adequate job, faulty inspection equipment, wrong or misused quality standards, and numerous other factors can prevent the detection of all defectives.

If 100% inspection is called for, it follows that the aforementioned conditions should be avoided as much as possible. This may necessitate specific training and certification programs for inspectors, as well as the control of other conditions that tend to cause inspector errors.

In most mass production operations, 100% inspection is neither practical nor necessary. Any product that warrants mass production techniques generally requires concerted efforts to minimize costs. Inspection methods are an integral portion of this cost structure. *Overinspection* can be as costly as *underinspection.*

Acceptance Sampling

Sampling procedures and plans are covered in greater detail in the following chapter, but a few statements of definition will serve to introduce the topic. Acceptance sampling is used as an economical measure. In any lot, the cost goes up as the percentage of parts inspected increases. It is not economical to inspect all parts if the quality characteristics of the total group of parts can be predicted to be acceptable. The concept of sampling is based on the probability that if a representative sample of a lot is examined, it will infer characteristics of the entire lot. The percent defective found in the sample is assumed to be the same percent defective found in the total lot. Thus, if a very large quantity of parts is produced, the cost of inspection can be appreciably reduced by not having to inspect every part of the lot.

14.6 Quality Standards

The need for creating and maintaining definite standards of quality in the products that are manufactured should be self-evident. A reputation for uniformity and dependability of product quality is one of the most important assets a business can have. Appreciation of the value of goodwill has caused many manufacturers to build quality reputations and then endeavor to maintain them. This, of course, implies an attendant need for good advertising and marketing.

Two primary goals of most companies are to build consumer confidence and a quality reputation and to prevent the production of any units that fail to meet quality standards. This dual-purpose approach to the quality function involves several essentials: specific standards for quality measurement, definite fixing of responsibility for quality of output, a routine to ensure regular measurement of

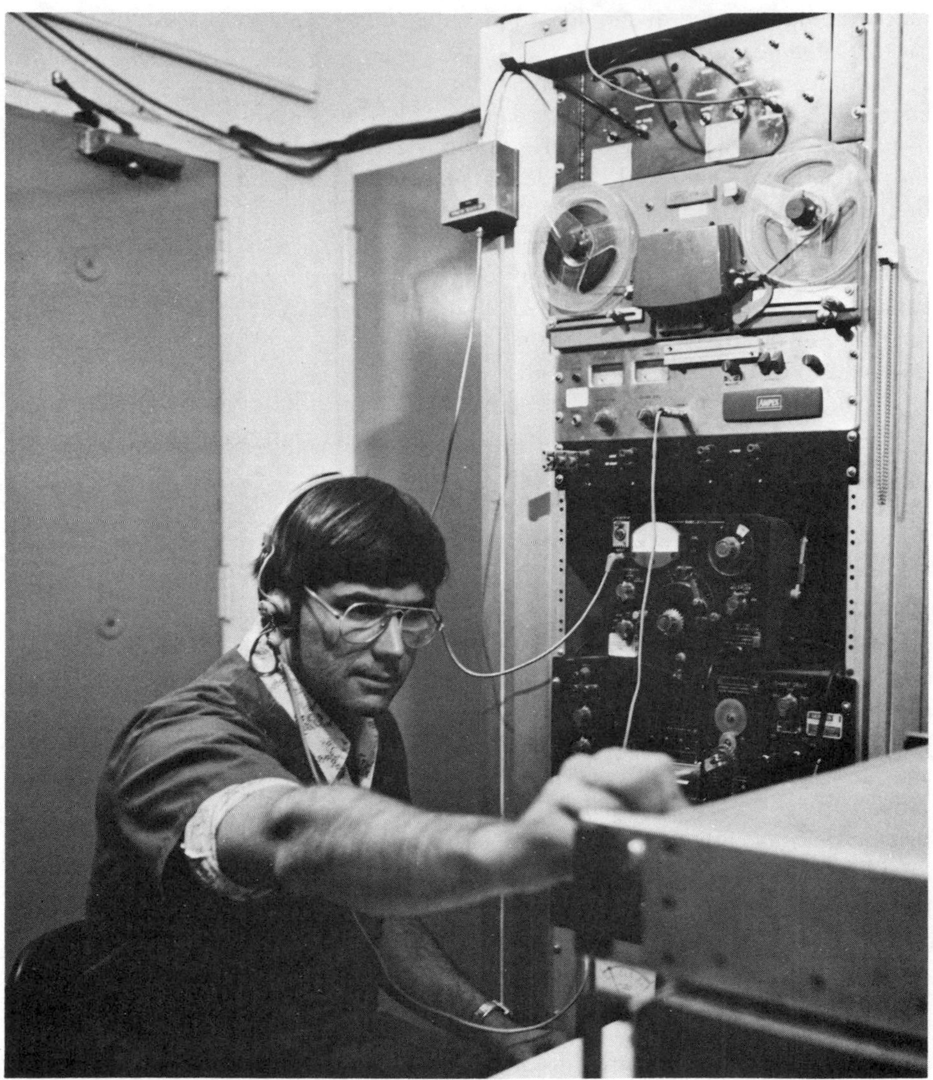

Figure 14–8 Toys being tested.

results, systematic determination of responsibility for any failure to meet quality standards, early determination of causes of any failure to meet quality standards, and prompt action to remedy these causes and prevent their recurrence.

In building a quality reputation, the kinds of inspection needed may be quite varied. In the toy manufacturing industry, for example, among the many types of inspections performed are those to measure sound characteristics of products. In certain instances, such characteristics can be very critical to consumer safety and

Figure 14–9 Toys being tested.

satisfaction. Toys such as those that simulate tools often must be checked to ensure that noise levels are safe. Figures 14-8 and 14-9 show several toys being operated in an *anechoic* chamber (one which is essentially free from echoes and reverberations).

While the technician operates these children's toys in the anechoic chamber, the results are recorded by the acoustical engineer on the control panel. The

Figure 14–10 Inspection of a shaft.

technician measures the sound pressure levels of the toys to determine if their sound output is adequately high, but still safe. Meanwhile, the acoustical engineer records the toy's sound output on tape, or photographs the wave form on an oscilloscope. The frequency spectrum of the sound can be determined by analyzing the tape, and undesirable peaks in the toy's output can be isolated and eliminated.

Quality standards for other products may be considerably different. Illustrated in figures 14-10 and 14-11, for example, is a part being inspected for very high *dimensional* accuracy.

These photographs illustrate the inspection of a beryllium shaft used in an earth-orbiting satellite mechanism. Because of the high accuracy requirements, the measurements must be made in a room where cleanliness, temperature, and humidity are controlled. The inspector must wear the appropriate garments (gloves, cap, and smock) to preclude contamination while making the appraisal. The Indi-Ron machine is applied here to measure roundness, parallelism, and concentricity; the inspector is shown tracing the concentricity of one surface of the shaft to another surface. Each division on the circular chart represents 0.000050 of an inch. In this instance, measurements are being read to 0.000010 of an inch.

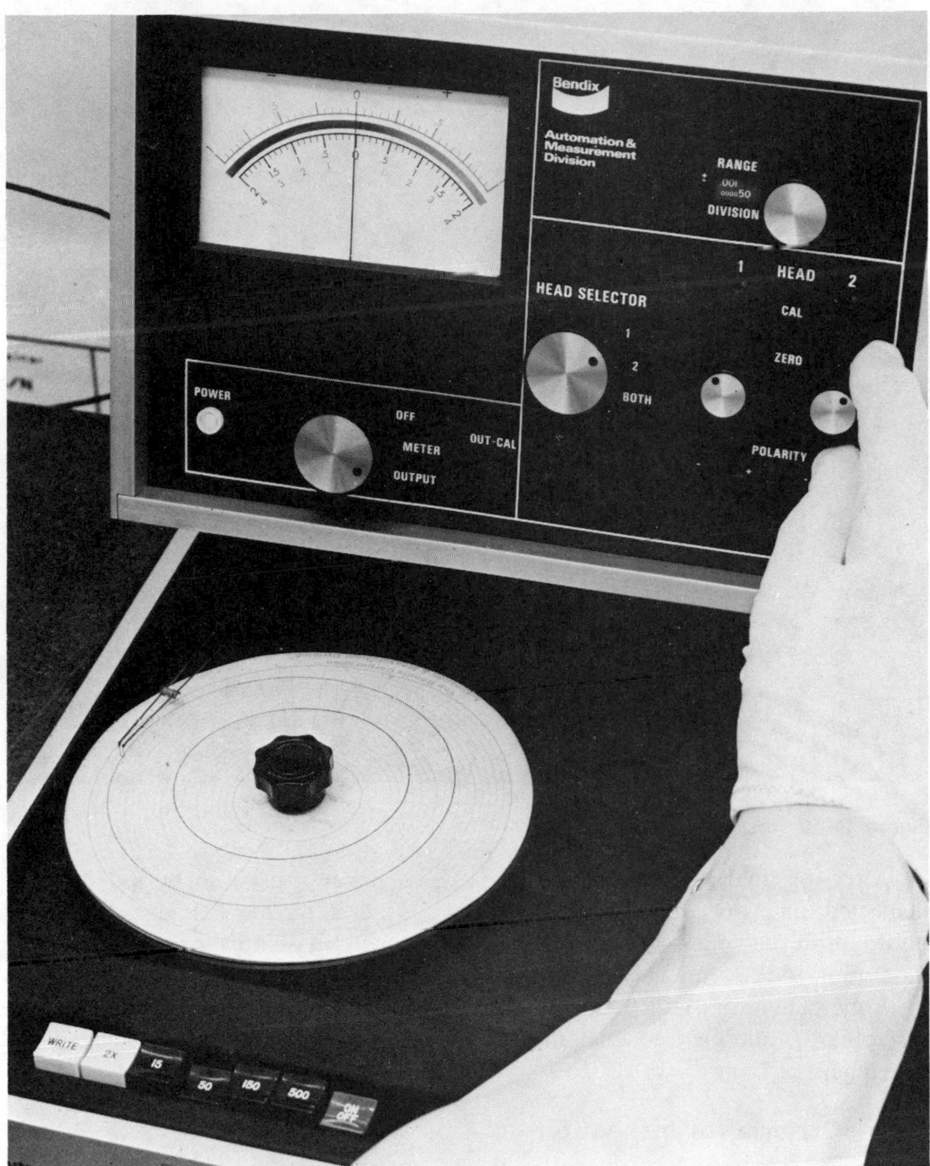

Figure 14–11 Inspection of a shaft.

Another kind of example where high measurement accuracy is required is in the manufacture of organs due to the complexity of the solid state circuitry in modern organs, it is very critical that all components relating to keyboard assembly be 100% inspected before final assembly. (Here, 100% means only significant characteristics.)

Figure 14–12 Inspection of an organ.

After the final assembly of a keyboard, each key must also be individually inspected for proper tension and electrical contact adjustment. Figure 14-12 is a photograph showing a technician adjusting the switch assembly for proper tension in relation to the sequence of sounds to be blended electronically.

Tone generators and frequency meters are used extensively in the final line assembly to tune the frequency modulation of each note by means of electronic instruments.

14.7 Criteria for Inspection

Change Control

Design change is a normal part of the development of any product. Such change activity is essential in order to eventually achieve a design which meets all criteria. Certain changes may continue to be instituted even after first-article acceptance, although at this stage of manufacture the number of changes should diminish.

Change control is not a quality control function organizationally, nor should it be. The responsibility for change control normally rests with either design engineering or configuration management. However, in either case the control of engineering changes is of critical interest to quality organizations, because quality can be built into a product only if all the drawings are accurate, complete, and in use.

Design changes are desirable in that their objective is product improvement, but are undesirable if they are not controlled and lead to error and redundancy of effort. Someone has said, "If a change is not necessary, then it is necessary not to make the change." It would be ideal if the designer could predict all the fabrication and assembly problems, and make all necessary design adjustments in the initial design. Unfortunately, this is usually not possible. As the complexity of the product or system being designed increases, so does the tendency to require more design change.

With the large number of engineering changes that must be made when designing complicated systems, a system of change control must be instituted in order to accurately identify, classify, and incorporate the changes in hardware. Those responsible for change control have a number of responsibilities. They (1) review and classify changes, (2) evaluate the significance and impact of changes, (3) determine the effect of changes on the program, (4) determine at what point in the program changes will be incorporated, and (5) establish a plan of action for incorporating the changes. Many companies impose what are commonly called *design freezes*, after which time changes cannot be incorporated in the production unit in question. The automobile industry, for example, includes certain design change schedule limits in their planning network in order to meet deadlines for the yearly changing of models. The aerospace industry also uses the terms *design freezes, base lines*, and *change points* to identify certain milestones or phases of vehicle design and manufacture for points of identification and reference. Change control begins at the point of initial release of engineering drawings and specifications relating to procurement, fabrication, and test. A control group is typically organized and assigned the task of ensuring that release documentation is applicable to the intended project, and copies are disseminated to the appropriate functions. The duties of the control group are outlined as follows.

1. To assure that the requested change is adequately described.
2. To assure that the design or specification concerned is correctly identified.
3. To assure that the change is routed to all concerned groups within a predetermined time period.

Blueprint Reading

Every inspector engaged in mechanical work, especially in a machine shop or pattern shop, should know how to read blueprints or drawings. The expression *reading a drawing* simply means *understanding* the drawing. The designer of a device, by means of mechanical drawings, shows the person in the shop the form and proportions of the different parts. Some drawings also show the relation of these parts when they are assembled in the completed machine or mechanism.

Drawings also provide records, so that a given part or mechanism can be reproduced readily at any future time.

The inspector who cannot read drawings is handicapped almost as much as though he could not read or write. In order to read mechanical drawings, it is necessary to understand certain basic principles underlying the arrangement of such drawings. In other words, if a worker knows what the different views of a drawing represent, and understands the methods of dimensioning drawings, as well as the meaning of certain commonly used terms, abbreviations, or symbols, then he or she is capable of obtaining the information required for the job from a a drawing. One does not simply become proficient in making mechanical drawings. It requires practice and dexterity in the use of instruments, as well as a knowledge of machine or tool design in case the drawn part represents the development of some original type of mechanical device. It is evident that ability to read a book does not necessarily mean that the reader could write one, but he must know the language. Similarly, reading a drawing requires a knowledge of the special line and symbol language employed in the mechanical industries.

Use of Shop Drawings

A procedure should be maintained concerning the adequacy, the completeness, and the currentness of drawings and the control of changes in design. The company must assure that requirements for the effectivity point of changes are met and that obsolete drawings and change requirements are removed from all points of issue and use. Some means of recording the effective points should be employed and made available for management visibility.

A procedure should be maintained to provide for the evaluation of the engineering adequacy of drawings as well as of proposed changes. The evaluation encompasses both standard engineering and design practices, together with the design and purpose of the product to which the drawings relate.

Process instructions, production engineering instructions, industrial engineering instructions, and work instructions relating to a particular design must all work in concert to be efficient. The quality program must provide complete coverage of all information necessary to produce an article in complete conformity with requirements of the design.

At times, work is attempted from drawings alone, without work instructions. Sometimes changes are developed on the shop floor and not entered in the instructions. At other times, an attempt is made to use an unsuitable general instruction on new work operations. Also, changes in machines, tools, work locations, or conditions may not be reflected properly in the work instructions. These practices should be avoided because they lead to misunderstanding and error.

Just as drawings are used by designers, engineers, customers, machine operators, and many others, so work instructions are used by inspectors, supervisors, and managers, as well as by production personnel. Supervisors or others responsible for quality improvement often find manufacturing details that need to be changed in the work instructions. Whenever a drawing is changed, a work instruction change is likely; however, many work instruction changes do not require drawing changes.

Since work instructions are so numerous and varied, have such wide use, and are subject to much change, both controllable and uncontrollable, it is necessary that the company periodically review the work instruction system to assure that it provide accurate and complete instructions, as well as being followed.

Document Control

Drawings normally are used in engineering departments, production control departments, purchasing departments, and such shop floor areas as machining, fabrication, and assembly. Assurance that everyone is using correct and current drawings can best be obtained by using procedures which provide for immediate recall of obsolete drawings and issuance of revised or new ones.

Just as important as having the correct drawing in the right place at the proper time is having drawings that are up to standard; that is, drawings that contain the correct delineation of tolerances and notes essential for manufacturing acceptable parts or items. Each drawing must convey a complete design, suitable in all respects for the specific object depicted and its particular purpose. Since design engineers, like other employees, are subject to human failings and have varying capabilities, many companies provide checks and balances to assure design adequacy from each engineer or designer creating the drawings. Frequently, supervisory engineers review the work of project engineers to make certain that drawings are accurate and of sufficiently high quality to give a workable and satisfactory design. Accurate drawings are of paramount importance to effective design and manufacturing efforts.

In addition to making sure that drawings and specifications are accurate, suitable files must be established for copies of such documents as purchase orders, engineering drawings, specifications, engineering orders (EO's), and change orders (CO's). Specific responsibility for the maintenance of these files should be assigned, and inspection personnel desiring the use of these data should always obtain the required documents from the person in charge of these files. Unless this is done, documents soon become disorganized, misplaced, or even destroyed, and there is constant danger of working from wrong or obsolete information.

Inspection Records

Inspection and testing must be prescribed by clear, complete, current instructions. These instructions pertain to the inspection and test of materials, work in progress, and completed articles as required by specifications. In addition, criteria for approval and rejection of a product must be included.

A company must maintain adequate records of all inspections and tests. Such records indicate the nature and number of observations made, the number and type of deficiencies found, the quantities approved and rejected, and the nature of corrective action taken, where appropriate.

14.8 Handling Rejections

Rework and Scrap

Mention has been made of rejections and rework of items that have fallen short of meeting existing quality standards in some way. Such items should be reworked when the error can be corrected by proper application of normal manufacturing processes on an economical basis. Some types of rework can be easily accomplished, so that costs do not exceed the point at which scrapping the item is more feasible. For instance, a turned shaft found to be oversize can normally be returned to the responsible department for rework, but rework of an undersize shaft may not be possible under normal manufacturing methods, making the cost of rework far in excess of the value of the shaft. In any case, however, before scrapping an item, those in charge should be positive that the unit deviates from specifications in a manner that will not permit correction on a cost-effective basis.

To be acceptable after rework, the item must (1) perform its intended function, (2) interchange with an identical item manufactured without reworking, (3) conform to dimensions, material, processes, and other pertinent specifications applying to the item, and (4) meet all strength requirements.[1]

The Material Review Board

Disposition of nonconforming materials (those departing from specifications) involves decisions beyond the control of inspection in cases of deviation, special rework, or repair; inspection is concerned only with determining that items are within allowable specification limits. To accomplish disposition of nonconforming items, it is usually necessary to utilize the collective knowledge of quality control, manufacturing engineering or planning, and design engineering. Further, it may be necessary to obtain assistance from purchasing when procured units are involved, and approval from the customer's representative when the items are being manufactured under contract to a government agency.

Normally the minimum requirements for a material review board include one representative each from quality control or inspection, manufacturing engineering or planning, purchasing, and a government or customer representative. The board is established as a formal group, with each member making a contribution in his or her area of expertise. The board should have regular and alternate representatives from each function, and should hold regularly scheduled meetings. In a large company, it may be necessary to hold meetings daily, but weekly meetings are usually sufficient for a small company. It is sometimes necessary to call special meetings to review items that are likely to cause a critical shortage or have an important impact on quality.

Reporting Nonconformances

Nonconformances generated in the company are recorded on a nonconformance report such as the one illustrated in figure 14-13. After it is legibly, accurately, and completely filled out, the report is given to the manufacturing supervisor for corrective action, then processed by a quality control material review representative. The procedure for handling must provide for rework planning, a nonconforming corrective action statement, engineering disposition, customer coordination if required, and a method of recording charges resulting from the rework. In-process corrective actions should be kept separate from vendor-responsible problems for adequate cost control of rework activities. When rework is to be performed, a rework instruction form should be used to identify the work to be performed so that costs can be correlated with the activity. An example of such a form is shown in figure 14-14.

Frequently, logbook records for complicated assembly operations, such as those used in the manufacture of aircraft, guidance systems, or engines, must contain a complete record of the inspection of each assembly operation. Where the same worker is responsible for a variety of dissimilar work operations, inspecting and recording his or her compliance with work instructions often is necessary to properly protect quality.

The value of any failure or rejection record is increased considerably if it can help prevent repetition of the same error which caused the defects. Such prevention is best achieved by having the failure record show (1) the cause of the error, (2) how the error was corrected, and (3) the action necessary to prevent a recurrence. Many factories record such information on job tickets and rejection tags. Examples of three types of inspection dispositions are shown in figure 14-15. Materials, components, and assemblies can be accepted, rejected, or held for a particular reason. Any other disposition should not be necessary.

It is difficult to consolidate individual items of logbook data into a record which permits a broad-scale judgment of the quality of whole groups of a specific item. For instance, the logbook record completely tells the quality of one engine, vehicle, or aircraft. However, it is very difficult to tell the prevailing quality of a whole year's production of engines, vehicles, or aircraft from the logbooks. Because few companies manage production and quality control on a one-item-at-a-time basis, it is necessary to collate, tabulate, and consolidate all similar or identical quality or deficiency information. From this properly organized and consolidated data, a supervisor or manager can evaluate the general quality of the product and its individual parts. For large quantities of data, the use of a computer is especially helpful.

Use of Manufacturing Orders and Travelers

Regardless of the type of product a manufacturer is producing, a system for positive identification of inspection status should be maintained. The manufacturing order (sometimes called the shop order) is issued to authorize manufacture of

TITLE	CEI/EI	ASSEMBLY	SUBASSEMBLY	COMPONENTS
NAME				
PART NO.				
SERIAL NO.				
LOT NO.				
DRAWING NO.				
P.O. NO.		VENDOR		

PROBLEM DESCRIPTION:

ATTACHMENT ☐ ____________

REFERENCE: ____________ INSPECTOR: ____________ DATE: ____________

PROBLEM DISPOSITION:

☐ MRB
☐ VMRR/DIR
☐ MR
☐ REWORK
☐ REPLACE

PARTS DISPOSITION:

☐ SCRAP
☐ IMPOUND
☐ FORWARD TO ____________

CUSTOMER QAR: ____________ ENGR: ____________ B&C QAR: ____________ DATE: ____________

REWORK PERFORMED:

COST CENTER: ____________

TECHNICIAN: ____________ INSPECTED: ____________ B&C QAR: ____________ DATE: ____________

CORRECTIVE ACTION:

RESPONSIBILITY:

☐ SUPPLIER
☐ MANUFACTURING
☐ ENGINEERING
☐ PRODUCT ASSURANCE
☐ OTHER: ____________

	YES	NO	REFERENCE
PREVIOUS OCCURRENCE	☐	☐	____________
DRAWING/SPECIFICATION CHANGE	☐	☐	____________
C.A.R. WRITTEN	☐		____________
C.A.R. ORAL	☐		____________

B&C QAR: ____________ DATE: ____________

WHITE = QA FILE YELLOW = DATA PACKAGE GREEN = PARTS GOLD = ORIGINATOR

Figure 14–13 Nonconformance report.

INSPECTION DISCREPANCY REPORT
MILITARY PRODUCTS DIVISION

PART NUMBER DASH	REV.	DESCRIPTION	MAKE	PROJECT	UNIT	PLANT	ORIG.DEPT	QTY. REC.	QTY. REJ.	% DEF.	DATE REJ.

VENDOR	V CODE	P.O. OR SHOP ORDER	QTY. P.O.	P.O. REV.	REV. DATE	REC. TICKET	SOURCE INSP.		ISSUED BY
							YES	NO	

PRELIMINARY REVIEW BY	DATE P.R.	USE AS IS	REWORK	R.T.V.	SCRAP	OBSOLETE QTY.	FWD. P.R. PROC.	FWD. MRB	PREVIOUS REJECTIONS	NOTIFY VENDOR	CORRECT V. RATING	DEBIT MEMO NO.
							YES	YES	YES	YES	YES	

MATERIAL REVIEW

QUALITY CONTROL			DATE
USE AS IS	REWORK	R.T.V.	SCRAP

ENGINEERING			DATE
USE AS IS	REWORK	R.T.V.	SCRAP

CUSTOMER			DATE
USE AS IS	REWORK	R.T.V.	SCRAP

RWK. ORDER #	PLANNING BY	DATE

QTY.SPLIT	REF. I.D.R.	DATE

COMPLETED REWORK DISPOSITION			
ACCEPT	REWORK	SCRAP	DATE

ITEM	ITEMIZE EACH DISCREPANCY BELOW – "BE SPECIFIC"

FORM 32-26/REV. 12-76

Figure 14–14 Inspection discrepancy report.

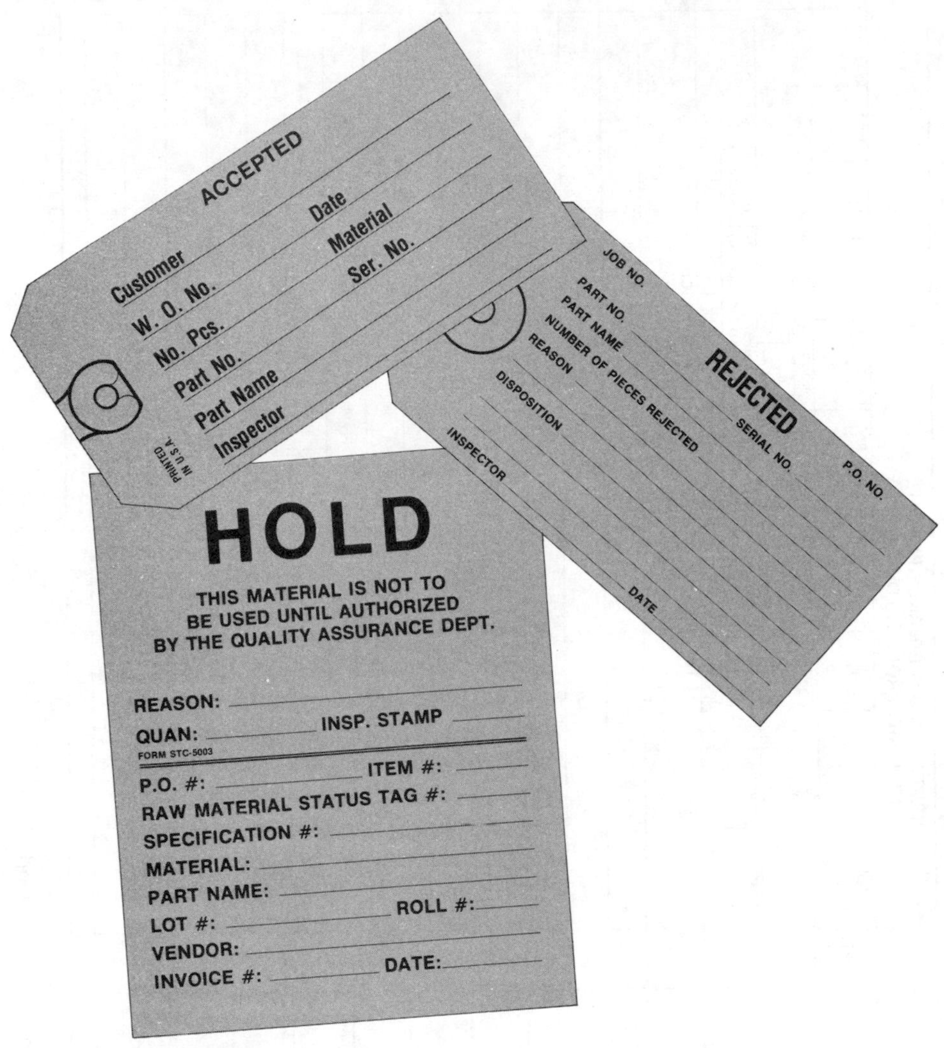

Figure 14–15 Inspection dispositions.

a particular lot of items. However, it can serve a dual purpose; if properly designed, it also can be used as the record of inspection action on each operation during fabrication or assembly. This is readily accomplished when the order lists each operation required to produce the item, and provides a place for inspection notations and stampings.

A quality control person should review each manufacturing order prior to examining the items to ascertain that all required preceding inspections have been "stamped off," and that the operations for which the items are now represented for inspection are in accordance with the order and with all applicable drawings and specifications.

An accurate count should be made of the items, and this quantity should be compared with that specified on the order. If some of the items have been rejected on preceding examinations, the actual quantity will of course be less than that specified on the order. Following a count and inspection, the quantities received, accepted, and rejected are noted on the order.

After all inspection work is completed, the inspector stamps the order at the side of the inspection operation entry, prior to forwarding the accepted items to the next operation. Items requiring rework are segregated and a rework tag noting the required action is attached. The rework items are returned to the appropriate department for accomplishment of the required correction, and the accepted units are either held for the return of the reworked units, or processed immediately, depending upon the urgency for the items. It may be decided by the material review board that the rework of certain rejected units is not feasible, and these will be scrapped or held for other purposes.

Some companies utilize the inspection traveler procedure in which a traveler form "travels" with the work being processed. This procedure provides current information about quality status as the unit or product progresses from one operation to another. An ongoing accounting of inspection is thus generated. An example of such a traveler is shown in figure 14-16. The inspector uses his or her stamp (containing a number which identifies it as his or hers) to indicate whether the items are accepted or rejected.

INSPECTION TRAVELER						QTY REC	
PART NO.			REV.	VENDOR		QTY INSP	
P.O. NO.			R/S NO.			TOTAL QTY REJ	
NO. OF BOXES			SAMPLE PLAN			QTY REJ CRITICAL	SAMPLE SIZE
INSPECTOR					DATE	QTY REJ MAJOR A	
OK TO STOCK	QTY.	ST	OK TO STOCK AS IS	QTY.	ST	QTY REJ MAJOR B	
ADD WORK REQ.	QTY.	ST	WITH-HELD	QTY.	ST	QTY REJ MINOR	

Figure 14–16 Inspection traveler.

Application and Control of Stamps

Most companies prefer inspection stamps to other identification methods, both because of their permanence and because they can be applied directly to products. Material handlers know better what to do with parts by the presence or absence of inspection stamps and, of course, by the nature of the stamp. Stamping also simplifies required-part segregation.

Inspection stamps are considered an essential part of an inspector's operating equipment and should be in his or her possession, or locked up at all times during working hours. Each inspector is responsible for the safekeeping of the stamps assigned to him or her. The stamps must be in good condition at all times and be turned in to the inspection department upon leaving the company or the department.

Each stamp should bear a serial number to identify the inspector to whom it is issued. Stamps should never be used by any other person than the inspector to whom the stamp is assigned. Under no circumstances should a stamp be loaned, even to another inspector. Unless this practice is rigidly followed, it becomes impossible to fix responsibility for improper inspection work.

Application of an acceptance stamp to an item or to its accompanying document signifies that inspection has determined that the item is in accordance with applicable drawings and specifications or that it is acceptable under an existing

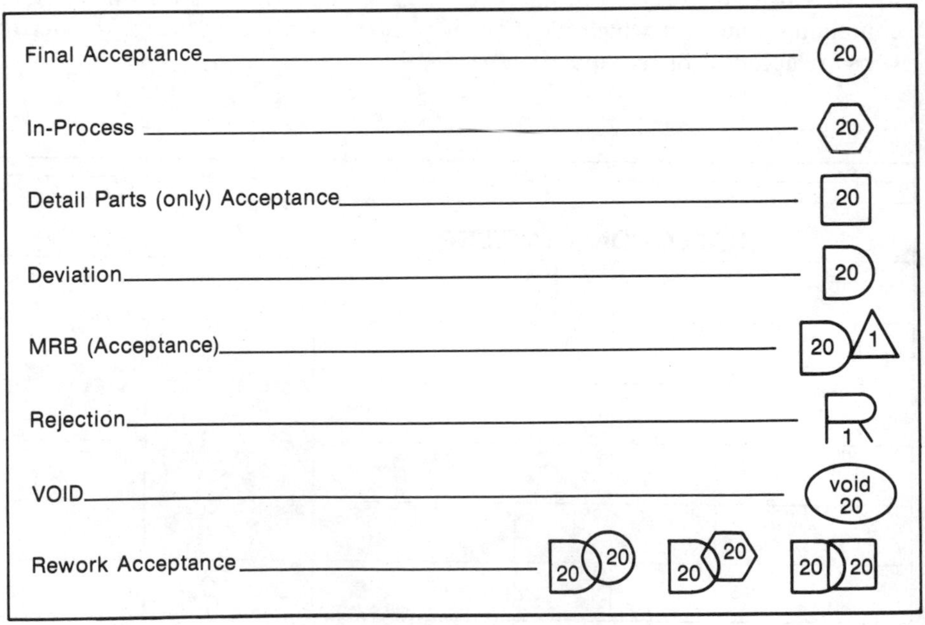

Final Acceptance ____ 20

In-Process ____ 20

Detail Parts (only) Acceptance ____ 20

Deviation ____ 20

MRB (Acceptance) ____ 20 1

Rejection ____ R 1

VOID ____ void 20

Rework Acceptance ____ 20 20 20 20 20 20

Figure 14–17 Stamp description and configuration.

engineering deviation, standard rework, or the material review board's disposition. Applying the stamp opposite an inspection entry on an order signifies that the listed operations are in accordance with applicable drawings and specifications. In any case the stamp must be applied in a legible manner.

A list of inspection stamp assignments should be prepared and issued to inspection personnel. This list should contain the type and the serial numbers of all stamps assigned to each inspector, together with his employee number and work station. This list should be maintained in an up-to-date condition by issuing revised pages whenever an assignment change occurs.

A record of stamp assignments is useful in a variety of ways. It provides a means of accurate periodic inspection of stamps and a check on the return of proper stamps upon the termination of employment. During inspection examinations, it provides a rapid means for an inspector to locate a suspicious item, and to contact the person responsible for earlier inspection acceptance. The inspector responsible for acceptance or rejection of any item or record bearing an inspection stamp can be immediately identified through reference to the assignment record.

Completed Corrective Action.

A corrective action request, such as the one illustrated in figure 14-18, should be utilized to communicate a need for such action. The write-up must be legible, accurate, and complete. Likewise, the corrective action itself must be positive and complete. It should never be gibberish merely to fulfill paper requirements. A good quality control department with the authority to transcend departmental boundaries is the major key in the initiation and follow-up of corrective action measures. If the errors are caused by inspection or shop personnel, quality control should require written instructions to prevent recurrence of the deficiencies and then audit the use of the instructions. The following corrective action reply was received from a supplier.

> The characteristic in question was not checked in production or by inspection. We have prepared written instructions to check the characteristic at final inspection. We also have established this as a controlled parameter during processing and have provided the operator with gauging equipment to check the characteristic.

This is positive corrective action. The cause was determined and a system established that will not only provide control, but will be rechecked by inspection to assure that control is obtaining the expected results.

If corrective action has not been completed within a reasonable time, follow-up action should be taken. This period may be as short as one day or even longer than two weeks, depending upon the kind of problem and the policies of the company. However, once an allowed time for corrective action has been established, it should be enforced. Figure 14-19 illustrates an example of a form used for corrective action follow-up.

CORRECTIVE ACTION REQUEST

To: ______________________ Date ______________________

Part/Assem. No. ________ Part/Assem. Disc. ______________________

Job No. __________ Contract No. __________ P.O. No. __________

Condition Requiring Corrective Action: ______________________

____

____

____

____

____

No. Insp. ______ No. Defective _____ No. Previous Rejections ____

The above condition requires prompt, effective corrective action to prevent recurrence of the defect.

You are requested to investigate the cause of this condition and submit a letter report (in triplicate) within five days, setting forth your findings and the course of corrective action to be taken. This report should include the effectivity of the action and means of identifying items on which action has been incorporated. Corrective action correspondence should be addressed to the Manager, Quality Assurance, (COMPANY NAME).

____

Manager,
Quality Assurance

Copy to:

Figure 14–18 Corrective action request.

14.9 Responsibility for Quality

Inspection should be conducted as an independent function. Production is responsible for producing units that meet all quality standards; inspection measures its achievement. Engineering design, production, and quality control should rank

CORRECTIVE ACTION REQUEST
FOLLOW-UP

To: ______________________ Date ______________________

Part/Assem. No. __________ Part/Assem. Disc. ______________

Job No. ____________ Contract No. ________ P.O. No. __________

Condition Requiring Corrective Action: ______________________

____

____

____

____

____

The above condition was brought to your attention by our Corrective Action Request dated__________. As of this date, there has been no response to this request.

We are obligated to our Customer to provide corrective action and follow-up on discrepant conditions, which may affect our efficiency or ability to produce a quality item. This letter is being directed to you for completion of the originally requested action.

Your reply (in triplicate) should be addressed to the Manager, Quality Assurance, (COMPANY NAME). Your failure to respond will necessitate a visit by one of our representitives.

____
Manager,
Quality Assurance

Copy to:

Figure 14–19 Corrective action request follow-up.

equally as independent functions. This concept is illustrated in the organization chart shown on page 444.

Inspection departments can be satisfactorily subjugated to production departments only if there exists quality-mindedness in the organization and if the production manager places quality in its proper perspective. However, under such organizational circumstances, there is the continual danger that a wrong decision can be made to compromise quality for the sake of expediency.

The inspection department's relation to the whole organization is *judicial* rather than *creative*. It is responsible to the management for detecting failures in quality, and thus it bears a heavy responsibility for the maintenance of standards. The inspection department does not produce defectives. Therefore, when poor work is produced, the production department cannot shift the blame to the inspection department. The production department should realize that it is itself responsible for the quality of its product—it does the work right or it does it wrong. If the production force is organized by process or function, each operator should feel that he is responsible for the quality of his work.

The philosophy about quality can shift without management being fully aware of it. If the philosophy of the design and production departments is principally one under which every employee strives to "do the job right the first time," then the role of inspection becomes one of *verification*. On the other hand, if the philosophy shifts away from a quality-minded attitude to one which rests on the belief that the inspector will right any wrong that has been done, the role of the inspector becomes one of *detection*. It should not take the reader very long to realize that operating under the verification concept is considerably less costly than operating under the detection concept. The company will profit by the avoidance of costs associated with corrective action, rework, and scrap.

Discovery Inspection

The earlier in the manufacturing processes that responsibility for quality can be fixed, the less need there will be for corrective action. Since defectives are essentially produced by personnel who fabricate and assemble the products, these operators should bear some of the responsibility for the quality of their work.

Some companies have been very successful in improving outgoing quality and reducing corrective action costs by having each operator inspect his or her own work. It has often been demonstrated that it is good quality assurance policy to provide immediate feedback to an operator about the quality of his or her work. Such information tends to build a positive attitude about doing the job right the first time, and increases operator motivation to raise performance levels.

Some companies have adopted the technique of *discovery sampling*.[2] This procedure involves placing the responsibility for quality primarily in the hands of those who create quality. Discovery sampling is fundamentally the use of 100% inspection followed by sampling inspection. This procedure is unique in that the 100% inspection is accomplished not by the quality control department, but by the direct labor force. This technique involves a judgment about quality at a very meaningful control point—the time at which an operation is being performed. In addition, this method can help to integrate the efforts of the machine operators and quality control personnel to provide the characteristics desired. Quality-mindedness is extended to every employee in the shop by involving the production force in quality-oriented tasks. This helps to focus attention on the fact that quality is built in, not inspected in, the products. It must be emphasized at this point that this procedure may be too costly if 100% inspection is not warranted for the work in question.

The following are the general points of a discovery inspection program.

1. 100% inspection of the characteristic being generated by the operator responsible for it. (This may be cosmetic or dimensional.)
2. Segregation of discrepant parts for inspection disposition by the operator.
3. Variables inspection sampling performed on the parts, consistent with the quantity in the lot and standard time.
4. Screening of parts performed on lots discovered (by inspection) to be suspect after the operation evaluation.

Such a program usually consists of a three-step control: 100% inspection by the operator, an inspection audit, and inspection screening. This provides a reliable method of dealing with quality improvement of the processes where the normal percent of defectives is below 5%.

When changing from a conventional inspection program to discovery inspection, a training or orientation program is usually needed. The objectives of such a program are improved operator attitude and job satisfaction, improved product quality, decreased schedule problems, and reduced corrective action and costs. Specifically, this training will help in several ways.

1. To train shop operators so that proficiency in the use of measurement tools could be expected.
2. To emphasize that an operator's responsibility would be expanded to include the accuracy and proficiency for measurement of his or her own works.
3. To provide a motivational program for increasing shop quality standards.
4. To improve communications between management and shop personnel.

The content of the training program should include the following elements.

1. Program introduction and purpose.
2. Traveler and operation instruction sheet review.
3. Basic drafting practice interpretation, including metrics and positional tolerancing.
4. Fundamental review of shop safety.
5. Comparing a part against a standard.
6. Disposition system for nonconforming parts.
7. Standard inspection tool review and use.
8. Basic machine operation and theory.
9. Measurement laboratory.
10. Examination: written and practical.
11. Group critique.

Upon completion of this program, each operator is issued a stamp, identified as his, to be used as follows.

1. The operator sets up the job, or has the job set up in accordance with established planning.
2. The operator performs a first piece check to verify the setup.
3. The operator verifies that all the processes are in accord with specification requirements during the entire production run.
4. If discrepancies are found, the operator identifies them and sets them aside for inspection verification and disposition. If discrepancies are (a) material type defects, (b) have occurred during prior operations, (c) are the result of process drift, or (d) are caused by other factors, the operator must screen the parts for nonconforming characteristics.
5. The operator stamps all parts, good and bad, with the operator stamp. This procedure makes it possible to accumulate worker and machine capability data for computer reports.

The inspection task is altered to an audit-type procedure. Inspectors are assigned to various operations and their functions outlined as follows.

1. Inspectors verify that a first piece check has been made by the operator.
2. Itinerant inspectors are assigned to machines throughout the shift. Visits are scheduled on the basis of production rates and generally are no more frequent than once each hour and no less than two times during each shift. In the event of short runs, a minimum of one visit is required.
3. In preparation for taking the first sample, a check of the traveler is made to determine the quantity to be run and the time required to complete each unit. On subsequent samples, the inspector determines the number of pieces produced since the last discovery sample and makes a check for characteristics generated in the operation. He then takes a random sample from only those parts accepted by the operator.
4. If discrepancies are detected, inspectors screen all parts completed since the last "discovery sample" on the nonconforming characteristic.
5. Inspectors verify all nonconformances set aside by the operator and stamp each item.
6. Inspectors complete the necessary forms.
7. Inspectors record the results of each visit on the process control inspection tag.

The total implementation of discovery sampling requires extensive coordination throughout the organization. Meetings must be conducted with manufacturing engineering to establish timetables for changing manufacturing travelers to reflect the use of discovery sampling. Forms may need to be revised and developed to complement both the system and the tasks to be performed. Computer programs can be constructed which yield reports meaningful to managerial personnel in the shops, in manufacturing engineering, and quality engineering. These should be developed only after extensive meetings have been held to define the user's interest and need.

Under all circumstances, it must be understood that inspection costs money, and a careful analysis must be made to accurately determine comparative costs before old programs are scrapped or new ones inaugurated.

14.10 Pitfalls for Inspectors

There are two major factors to be considered in the performance of inspectors' duties. Inspectors must, of course, be as unbiased and accurate as possible in reporting quality status. They must also guard against making decisions that are not defined in their jobs. One of the pitfalls that inspectors sometimes fall into is acting as supervisors to production personnel. Inspectors are often promoted from the ranks of production workers and this may carry with it the "buddy syndrome." The close association of an inspector with certain operators sometimes places an inspector in the position of helpfulness, which can result in considerable time being devoted to instructing production personnel about specific elements of their jobs. This may not be altogether bad, provided that there is a prescribed method of controlling the activity.

An inspector who instructs an operator about how he should perform his job, or decides whether or not a deviation from standard can be tolerated, may place not only his job but also that of certain members of management on the line. Unless it is clearly defined in his job description, it is dangerous for an inspector to assume that he can make decisions about things outside the scope of his responsibilities. Even though the inspector may believe that he is right and feel a certain sense of obligation to correct a condition (e.g., by telling an operator to change a setup), he is devoting his time to tasks outside those for which quality assurance budgets have been allocated. This makes cost control and accurate budget forecasting very difficult to accomplish. Also, if in working outside his scope the inspector should make an error in judgment, there can be even more serious effects. Regardless of how insignificant a deviation might appear, outcomes can have severe consequences. The inspector generally is not in the position to understand all the ramifications of a procedure, specification, or dimension and, therefore, should not take it upon himself to make decisions outside the scope of his assigned duties unless explicit authority has been delegated to him to do so. Then, the responsibility for any errors in judgment shifts to those who have delegated the authority.

Inspectors must also realize that in the inspection role they no longer produce parts; they safeguard quality levels. This means that they should be uncompromising insofar as quality standards are concerned. Particularly in a situation where production operators are not as well trained as they might be, bias and compromising attitudes about quality can be generated.

Inspectors must also possess or develop the attitude of conformance. It should not be the prerogative of the inspector to decide that if a part is only a "little" out of tolerance, it can be permitted to pass. Decisions about the severity of nonconformances and their dispositions are dealt with by others (e.g., a material review board). Inspector judgments about quality pertain only to whether or not a part conforms to specifications. In case of a systems inspector, his or her task is restricted to monitoring the steps taken in a job not directing the project.

14.11 Quality Control of Tooling

Tool engineering functions play a vital role in product assurance. Once products have been designed, various tools must be provided so that fabrication and assembly operations can be accomplished efficiently. Tools such as jigs, fixtures, and dies directly affect the accuracy with which an article is fabricated or assembled. Jigs and fixtures hold parts securely and accurately while operations are being performed or while the parts are being assembled; dies are constructed so that parts can be accurately formed, pierced, blanked, forged, or molded. Tooling helps to achieve the objectives of quality assurance by controlling important dimensions of the parts, thereby assuring that every part will meet the required dimensional accuracy.

Tooling Inspection and Control

Tooling inspection is accomplished by visual and dimensional examination of production tooling to detect unsafe, worn, loosened, broken, or otherwise defective tooling. Periodic checks of production tooling are required when such tooling is used. Regularly scheduled calendar intervals should be established to inspect production tooling such as inspection gauges, assembly jigs, small tools and dies, rigging fixtures, and installation fixtures that control interchangeable parts and assemblies, or the interface of mating assemblies.

The major activities of tooling inspection involve the following.

1. Inspection, acceptance, release for use of (a) company fabricated tooling, (b) purchased tools, (c) perishable tools, and (d) all cutting tools which have been modified, reground, etc.
2. Control and disposition of nonconforming tools and tooling materials through tooling material review board action.
3. Liaison with tool design, tool control, tool planning, and tool fabrication.
4. Maintenance of records of receiving reports, purchase orders, tool completion reports, tooling historical records, tool rejection actions, and tool review board actions.

Numerically Controlled Equipment

Numerical control is a technique by which numbers are used for the direct control of machines and processes. Numerical information is translated into a coded form that the machine can understand, and directs the fundamental operations of the machine. The numerical commands given to the machine may be in a variety of forms, such as punched cards, magnetic tape, punched tape, etc., and may include spindle speeds, tool changes, movement of machine members along an axis, and coolant on or off.

Numerically controlled systems represent a complete departure from conventional methods of operation, in which machine operators study engineering drawings and manually guide the tools to form the desired parts. When using conventional methods, the measuring devices may include small rules, micrometers, calipers, scales, etc.; however, there is either potential error involved, or an unnecessary amount of "down time" spent checking dimensions. The efficient operation of a conventional machine depends largely upon the skill of the individual operator.

In numerical control, the drawings are studied by a part programmer, who translates the information into numbers. These numbers represent all of the various movements, speeds, and actions that the machine tool must execute to properly form the workpiece. The complete sequence of numbered codes necessary to complete the part is called the *part program.* The responsibility for the correct machining of the piece is thus shifted from the operator or machinist to the part programmer, who controls the machine tools movements and functions by means of a program.

Maintaining Quality Levels with Tape-Controlled Equipment

The manufacturing department should submit all first articles produced on numerical equipment to the inspection department for evaluation. Since the tapes used on numerically controlled (N/C) machines essentially predetermine and control the characteristics of the parts fabricated on the N/C machines, a first article should be inspected to verify the accuracy of the tape. Once the accuracy of the first article has been shown to meet all dimensional criteria, proof has been rendered regarding the accuracy of the tape. Manufacturing personnel should not proceed without quality assurance approval of the control tape. Modifications of a tape that have previously been accepted also should have a first piece inspection of the affected dimensions.

After a first piece inspection has been performed, all down time of numerically controlled machines resulting from maintenance or adjustments to machines, changeover of tools, or resetting of cutters should be coordinated with quality assurance personnel. The personnel assigned this responsibility can then determine whether or not to inspect a new first article.

After it has been verified that the tapes meet all the prescribed standards, they must be properly identified and stored. They should be identified by part number, engineering change letter, and engineering order number. Tape containers should be identified with a reference number traceable to a tape history index that gives all pertinent information regarding tape status. Tapes should be well organized for storage and carefully handled during use. Use of either a wrong or defective tape can be very costly.

The following steps should be taken when inspecting parts fabricated on numerically controlled machines.

1. Inspect the first article visually and dimensionally to determine conformance to drawings and specifications, and to verify that the tape is accurate.
2. Inspect one in-process part (usually about the midpoint of the production lot) to verify that the operation is under control. (If the lot is very large, more than one part may need to be inspected to make certain that tools and cutters are functioning properly.)
3. Inspect the last piece produced in the lot visually and dimensionally to ensure that no changes have been made to the tape program or tooling, and that neither cutter nor tool wear has caused out-of-tolerance variations in the part.
4. If the first article has been accepted and either the in-process part or last piece is rejected for any reason, the entire lot should be inspected for the discrepant characteristics.

14.12 Quality Control after Assembly Inspection

Some products are more susceptible to damage and deterioration than others, and control of articles during handling, storage, and delivery is an important aspect of satisfactory quality programs. Manufacturers and users of such products must carefully plan for their preservation, packaging, packing, and storage. Regularly scheduled inspections of all stored material should be conducted. In many cases, the date of manufacture or receipt of a material is marked on incoming materials so that they can be used in order of receipt and thus spend minimum time in storage.

Shipping and storage control departments should develop documented work and inspection instructions for handling, storing, preserving, packaging, marking, and shipping materials to prevent damage, loss, deterioration, substitution, degradation, or any other quality defects. The extent to which such procedures should be maintained is based on quality requirements, contract clauses, and product characteristics.

Packaging the Products

Packaging factors are sometimes not given the attention they deserve in quality control programs. Safeguarding quality does not stop with the final inspection. Some of the most serious quality problems experienced by manufacturers have been attributed to improper packaging, followed by abusive handling. Large amounts of resources are normally utilized in building acceptable products; it is folly to waste these efforts through substandard packaging methods.

Several packaging principles should be considered when providing containers to protect products during shipment. Each product, component, or material may have a unique configuration, weight, and quality standard; thus packaging will be more or less tailored to these factors.

First, the enclosure must be suitable to protect the product from outside elements such as dust, dirt, heat, cold, insects, moisture, pilferage, or foreign bodies. Containers often look sturdy initially, but it is not unusual to find containers subjected to hazards of handling, storing, and shipping that cause them to rupture before they have fulfilled their intended purpose.

Containers must be strong enough to prevent outside loads from affecting the contents. During shipment and storage, containers are frequently stacked one upon another, producing a tremendous external force that may not have been accounted for in the design of the container.

Items in the container should be prevented from moving and shifting during shipment. If the items are fragile they may require cushioning against shock and vibration; since too much movement will result in damage, it may be better to restrain certain items to preclude movement. Experience in the use of certain container designs and testing various applications help one to gain the confidence that a particular container is satisfactory.

Instructions on packages should also be utilized. Especially fragile or dangerous items must be so labeled. Precautionary labels also are frequently needed. For example, if an item must be kept in one position only, it must be so labeled. Material handling people do not always follow the instructions on packages, but instructions will certainly help to avoid mishandling.

The following considerations should be given when packaging materials.

1. Use containers of a standard size and construction where possible.
2. To reduce the number of container sizes needed to accommodate a wide range of products, use pads, fillers, and inserts in standard boxes.
3. Before establishing packing specifications, determine all the conditions to be met. Often a less costly package will meet all objectives. The packaging industry is constantly developing new containers and new packaging materials, and the engineer should determine the best one for each specific application.
4. It is usually more economical to put a larger number of units in one container than to package each one separately.
5. Investigate the applicability of other types of packaging material.
6. It may be desirable to conduct environmental tests on certain containers to verify their adequacy and estimate their service capacity.
7. Review applicable packing specifications for foreign and domestic markets.

Shipping Inspection

After the end item is completely assembled and inspected, it is either forwarded to a stockroom to await shipment to the customer, or sent directly to shipping.

Inspection has guarded the product's quality throughout the production cycle of receiving, fabrication, assembly, and final test. When end items are packaged immediately after completion of the production cycle, inspection observes that the basic packaging is properly accomplished without damage to the contents and that each container is properly marked to identify its contents.

Inspection also has another obligation—that of making certain that the final preparation for shipment is accurately accomplished, with the proper quantity of the correct items prepared for forwarding, and that each shipment is delivered to the carrier in an undamaged condition. While an important function of shipping inspection is to verify that the proper items are correctly packaged for shipment, a second important responsibility is verifying that all raw-stock material, components, and assemblies are properly shipped to outside production sources. This latter duty is important when extensive outside production is purchased by the company; only when the proper quantity of material is shipped to the outside sources can completed end items have all the needed quality characteristics.

The function of shipping inspection is to insure that all items forwarded by the company shipping department meet all established quality standards and conform to the description and quantities shown on packing sheets or other instructions. This function can be broken down into the following duties.

1. Verify that all units are complete, have received final inspection acceptance, conform to the requirements of the customer's purchase order, are properly packed to avoid damage or deterioration in transit, and are correctly identified and addressed.
2. Determine that all spare parts conform to the customer's purchase order and company service department's instructions, are properly packaged to avoid damage in transit, and are correctly identified and addressed.
3. Inspect all raw-stock material shipped to outside production sources to insure conformance with the type and quantities shown on packaging sheets or other shipping instructions.
4. Verify that all semifinished and completely fabricated items shipped to outside production sources have received required inspection prior to preparation for shipment and in conformance with the description and quantities shown on packing sheets or other shipping instructions.
5. Verify that all procedures, instructions, specifications, warranties, and labels are included with the shipment. (This should fulfill requirements of the DD-250 for shipments made to government agencies.)

In each case, shipping inspection will follow one of three basic courses of action. Shipments meeting all requirements will be accepted. Those which are found deficient in a manner that permits correction will be returned for rework. Shipments (or portions thereof) that cannot be corrected by the shipping department will be rejected for further disposition.

EXERCISES

1. Define *inspection*. How does inspection differ from quality control?
2. Name the three important functions that an inspector is expected to perform.
3. What is the difference between a critical defect and a major defect?
4. What is inspection planning? What is its scope? Who does it?
5. What is the difference between in-line inspection and centralized inspection?
6. What is the difference between 100% inspection and acceptance sampling? Which is better? Qualify your answer.
7. Explain the importance of having effective change control in relation to the inspection function.
8. Describe some personal qualifications that an inspector should have to be effective in his job.
9. Why is documentation of inspection results so important?
10. Does quality control stop after final inspection? If not, what are some of its tasks?
11. Would the concept of "doing the job right the first time" tend to reduce inspection or increase it? Explain your answer.
12. Discuss the pros and cons of discovery sampling.
13. Is it normally the inspector's responsibility to make sure that corrective action (rework) has been accomplished? If not, who has the responsibility?
14. Why is it important for an inspector to understand fully the limits of his responsibilities?
15. Why should there be quality control of production tooling?
16. Discuss the duties of a receiving inspector. Compare these duties in a large company with those in a small company.

FOOTNOTES

[1] *Inspection Organization and Management.* James E. Thompson, McGraw Hill, N.Y.,

[2] The term, "Discovery Sampling," was used in the 1950's to describe a specific type of sampling techniques applied first in the inspection of metal plate. Several papers covered these procedures, the first written and presented by Ray Crawford.

CHAPTER FIFTEEN

INSPECTION BY SAMPLING

15.1 Objective

The primary objectives of this chapter are to acquaint the readers with inspection by sampling methods, familiarize them with some of the problems, procedures, and applications of sampling, and explain the essential elements of the MIL–STD–105, the Dodge-Romig Sampling tables, and other sampling techniques used in quality control.

We will discuss how to select the sampling plans that best fit each situation. The data, studies, and analyses necessary to secure the most economical sampling plans as well as ways to obtain the desired protection for the quality levels desired are described. In addition, inspection by continuous sampling, sequential sampling, and variables sampling plans are presented. Emphasis is placed on developing the ability to obtain from sampling inspection tables now available those plans that are suited to the production process, testing areas, and other areas such as accounting, clerical departments, research and development, and design that are most effective and economical.

15.2 Sampling Concepts

It is possible to obtain the necessary information for the acceptance or rejection of submitted products and for controlling the manufacturing process at the desired level by examining each piece of a batch of parts; but 100% inspection is costly, often unnecessary, and at times physically impossible. Consider the feasibility of testing every straight pin in a box for sharpness, tasting each piece of candy before it is packaged, or inspecting each inch of coils of wire secured for industrial use. Obviously, the practical procedure is to take a sample and infer the quality characteristics of the entire population from the observed characteristics of the sample.

A sample is defined as a part shown to present and prove the quality of the whole. However, to know the quality of the whole does not necessarily imply that the sample must be a duplicate in miniature of the whole. It does mean that the sample must be *representative* of the whole in order for inferences about the total group to be reliable.

Thus, the underlying principle of sampling is that if there is a sufficiently large population of units and from this population there is taken a sufficient number of randomly selected sample units, the sample will infer the characteristics of the entire population. For example, say a bowl contains 5,000 white and 5,000 red marbles thoroughly mixed together. If a number of samples were taken from the bowl, the average of the samples taken would reflect the characteristics of the total population, that is, 50% white and 50% red. Moreover, to carry this example one step further, if an unknown number of black marbles were added to the contents of the bowl, then mixed thoroughly, and new samples examined, the percentage of red, white, and black in the total population would be reflected by the sample. An estimate or prediction could be made with regard to the total number of black marbles in the bowl based on the contents of the sample. If repeated samples were taken, an average would show that, if 500 black marbles were added, the black marbles would approach 10% of either the red or white ones (or approximately 5% of the total population) in the samples. Thus, sampling can be used to estimate, predict, or infer unknown characteristics of a much larger group.

The same principles apply to inspecting hardware. Sampling inspection is defined simply as that type of inspection wherein a sample of one or more units of product is selected at random from the production process output, and examined for one or more quality characteristics. When a large number of parts is produced by a certain process, it is usually more economical to inspect sample units from the lot and draw inferences about the quality of the entire group than to inspect every piece. However, a sample does not always reflect the true characteristic of the lot. Several problems in the design and implementation of an acceptance sampling procedure must be overcome before satisfactory results can be attained. These problems are discussed subsequently.

15.3 One Hundred Percent Inspection vs. Acceptance Sampling

The terms used in particular cases in quality control have specific meanings. The terms *sample* and *sampling* may refer to only one unit, a portion of the units in a lot, or all the units in a lot. Any unit submitted for inspection is a sample. Where n units are selected as a sample from a lot containing N units, the n units are considered as a sample from the lot. Sampling may mean inspecting only one unit from a lot or the first article made by a new process, or it may mean inspecting a portion of the units in the lot. The usage will be clear from the context in which the terms are used. *Acceptance sampling* is normally to designate the inspection of less than 100% of the units in the lot or batch of material submitted for acceptance or rejection, although some prefer to use the term *sampling inspection* for less than 100% inspection.

There are three principal reasons that acceptance sampling is used. The most important reason is reduced inspection cost. Provided that the sampling plan has proven validity and the correct plan and procedures are followed, sampling is far less costly than 100% inspection, albeit on occasion good lots are rejected and bad lots are accepted. (Among those plans which are well established and have withstood the test of time are the MIL–STD–105 and the Dodge-Romig tables.) A second benefit of acceptance sampling is that it can improve workmanship quality. If in-process acceptance sampling is not carried out, there is the tendency of some employees to adopt the philosophy of letting the inspector find a faulty unit rather than tightening their own standards of workmanship. Especially if an operator knows his work will not be evaluated until final inspection, the importance of doing the job right the first time may not be fully realized. On the other hand, if in-process acceptance sampling and attendant control chart procedures are used, the operators can have immediate feedback about the quality of their work. This procedure has the potential of more inherent quality control and the possibility of not accepting too many defective units.

A third reason for implementing acceptance sampling is that, since the quality of many products can be judged only by destroying them, some form of sampling procedure is mandatory. Ammunition is an example. (There may be a number of stages of in-process inspection, however, where components undergo 100% inspection prior to final assembly.) In many cases, electric motors are given an operation test before being mounted in a system; also all automobile engines are block operated prior to delivery to customers.

Often, there is more than one characteristic of a unit that must be appraised by the inspector. At other times, only one characteristic needs to be inspected. In any case, so-called 100% inspection does not consistently yield complete protection. Screening all items in a lot may be only 85% to 95% effective. Inspectors are like other human beings; they can be fatigued, bored, distracted, and even emotionally upset, all of which lead to errors in judgment. When a large quantity of parts is to be inspected, even repeated inspections may not render full protection against the acceptance of a few defective parts. Acceptance sampling procedures can provide effective quality control, but when high reliability requires that all elements of risk be removed from the inspection process, various redundant inspection techniques may be required to provide the greatest possible quality protection.

There are many variations possible in inspection procedures. Adequate verification of product quality may be achieved merely by a cursory spot check of parts, or by inspecting every part several times. The following considerations should be made when prescribing the degree and method of inspection.

1. The end use of the product.
2. The complexity of the product.
3. The number of units produced in a given period of time.
4. The number of quality characteristics in each unit to be appraised.
5. A cost analysis of inspection and test versus performance requirements of the product.

6. The number of components and subassemblies in a given final assembly.
7. The quality history of the process or producer.

15.4 Criteria for Successful Inspection Sampling

Establishing Procedures

Procedures should be established and followed regarding the manner in which production runs will be sampled for inspection. Some companies have no definite rules regarding sample sizes and sampling frequency, leaving these decisions largely to the discretion of the inspector. The fallacy in this management practice is that inspectors may have neither the knowledge nor the initiative to effect satisfactory acceptance sampling.

The history of how a process has been running also yields important statistical information. If, during a given period, the quality of material received from a certain vendor were consistently high, sampling would continue to be of high quality. However, should an incoming order of material happen to contain an unusually high percentage of defectives, a tightened inspection procedure would probably be used until such time that quality assurance at the desired standard level of quality was regained.

When there is assurance of very high quality, skip lot sampling is sometimes used. Under skip lot inspection sampling, samples may be drawn on a fractional basis, such as from every other lot, every third lot, three lots out of twenty-five, every tenth lot, or some other fraction of the submitted lots. The main purpose of skip lot sampling is to decrease the frequency of inspection sampling and thus reduce total inspection costs. A factor in deciding whether or not to permit skip lot sampling is the ability of the supplier to submit products of consistently high quality as indicated by the quality history of the product.

One of the limitations of inspection sampling, in general, is that people sometimes fail to fully realize that the judgment made on the basis of a sample is based purely on chance factors and not on complete facts obtained by perfect, 100% inspections. For this reason, it is imperative that the sampling plans in use be reliable. Fortunately, several of these plans have been validated. One source of those inspection sampling plans most widely used is the MIL–STD–105. This standard has been established for use by all government agencies involved in such inspection activities. It provides ready-to-use sampling tables which give precise sample sizes for a given inspection level and lot size. The Dodge-Romig tables for sampling also have wide acceptance and usage in industry. Both the MIL–STD–105 and the Dodge-Romig tables depict sampling criteria which, if used, avoid a great deal of confusion, statistical problems, and consequent cost. Dodge-Romig, when applied for the going process average, result in desired quality at minimum costs. These tables apply to attributes sampling. Variables sampling plans are used less frequently but may be applied very effectively to many important characteristics.

Choosing a Representative Sample

There are numerous sampling problems associated with acceptance sampling inspection which can detract from the potential value of a given plan. Making sure that the sample selected is truly representative of the entire lot is sometimes more difficult than it may appear on the surface. For example, a process may have performed satisfactorily during the fabrication of 95% of a lot, but begun to run out of control during the last 5%. If the inspector should sample only the last 5%, the results obviously would not be a true representation of the characteristics of the entire lot, and a perfectly good lot might be rejected. On the other hand, it is possible for a process to produce defective parts for some time, then suddenly begin to produce acceptable parts. In this instance, the inspector might accept a lot which actually should be rejected, or might reject a lot which actually should be accepted.

These types of sampling errors would not happen if the procedure for taking the sample included assurance of randomness. A random sample contains items which have the same probability of being selected from a lot or batch for inspection as those that were not selected. In other words, when true randomness is achieved, there are no factors that influence the selection of units other than pure chance. Sampling should be random and representative enough to overcome the effects of stratification or bunching of parts. This means that for a given batch of items from which a random sample is to be selected, the parts at the bottom and sides of the batch must have the same chance of being chosen as those on the top. For this reason, when acceptance sampling is performed by an itinerant inspector, the interval between sample inspections should be evaluated, established, and controlled. This interval of time will vary with the speed of the process, the degree of inspection required, the number of characteristics to be inspected on each unit, and the sampling plan used.

Sometimes, however, it is not practical to mix the units thoroughly because of their physical dimensions, or for other reasons. In some instances, the best that can be done in drawing a sample is to avoid any type of obvious bias. For example, if the units are stacked in layers, bias would result if the entire sample is drawn from only the top layer. It is possible to reduce bias by avoiding such pitfalls as drawing units from the same position in containers, stacks, or piles; selecting units from the output of one machine and not others; or selecting units which appear to be defective or nondefective. If such biased sampling procedures are avoided, it will be easier to obtain a sample that approaches a random sample and will better reflect the overall quality of the lot.

A table of random numbers, such as table 8.1 in chapter eight may be used to draw a random sample of units from the lot. Each unit in the lot must be identified by a distinctly different number. This can be done by placing the units in racks or trays where the rows and columns in the racks are numbered. If the units have serial numbers, these serial numbers can be used. The three-dimensional positions of each unit (row, column, depth) in a large grouping can also be used.

Then a table of random numbers, such as shown in table 8.1, can be used to select the random sample:

Tables of random numbers should provide numbers with enough digits to be at least as large as the number of units in the inspection lot. Two digits will be sufficient for lots having fewer than 100 units. Five digits will be sufficient for lots having fewer than 100,000 units. For larger lot sizes, such a table can still be used by ignoring the break between columns. For example, if a series of six-digit random numbers is desired, three lines or three columns of two digits each may be used. The two digits in a column may be connected to the first digit of the adjacent column together with the digits in the third column; or any set of two digits in a column may be connected to the first two digits of the adjacent column, and so on; if lines are selected rather than columns, use three successive lines for any designated column of two digits; then proceed to the next column, and so on.

Sample Size

Sample size is also a very important factor in assuring both the validity of inferences made and optimum cost for a given quality level. For example, if four cards were drawn from a well-shuffled deck of cards, the selection would theoretically consist of one diamond, one club, one spade, and one heart. However, any person who plays cards knows that the odds are against selecting a card from each suit in any given draw. Now, if diamonds were considered to be defectives and the procedure were repeated several times, there would be a number of instances in which no diamonds (or defectives) would appear. In these instances, the sample inferring characteristics of the lot (deck of cards) would contain less defects than really exist.

As a rule of thumb, large lots require proportionately small samples and small lots require proportionately large samples for a given degree of confidence. The risk of accepting bad lots depends far more on the size of the sample than it does on the percentage of the total lot that is contained in the sample. As the sample size increases, the diagnosis becomes more accurate, and the risk inherent in the sampling procedure is reduced. It is good practice to select a sample size which is of such proportion to the lot size that it allows a minimum of inspection and expense, yet provides the greatest reliable inference. Although the chance factor in sampling varies, it can be estimated by means of mathematical calculations. The upper and lower limits of accuracy in sampling can be established with the use of the formula below. (Note that this is the same formula used in calculating upper and lower control limits for attribute control charts in chapter 5.)

$$\text{Limits} = p \pm 3\sqrt{\frac{p(1-p)}{n}} \tag{1}$$

As an example, assume that a random sample of 500 pieces is selected from a batch of parts containing 8,500 pieces, and that 30 defects are found in the sample.

The percent defective in the sample is determined by dividing 30 by 500; in this case it is

$$p = \frac{30}{500} = 0.06 \quad \text{or} \quad 6\%.$$

The limits of sampling error may then be calculated from the formula.

$$\begin{aligned}
\text{Limits} &= p \pm 3\sqrt{\frac{p(1-p)}{n}} \\
&= 0.06 \pm 3\sqrt{\frac{0.06(1-0.06)}{500}} \\
&= 0.06 \pm 3\sqrt{\frac{0.06 \times 0.94}{500}} \\
&= 0.06 \pm 3\sqrt{\frac{0.0564}{500}} \\
&= 0.06 \pm 3\sqrt{0.0001128} \\
&= 0.06 \pm 3(0.010621) \\
&= 0.06 \pm 0.031863 \\
&= 0.060 \pm 0.032 \\
&= 2.8\% \text{ and } 9.2\%
\end{aligned}$$

The sampling error for samples of 500 units each may vary from 3% to 9% defective, even though the single test showed the lot to be 6% defective.

Size of Lots

A lot should be as large as possible since the cost of inspection is not only comparatively less, but large lots are also more uniform and statistically sound. There are instances when very large lots may be undesirable, since they may create an expensive storage problem or disrupt the flow of a product to the consumer on a fixed delivery schedule. If rejection occurs, other problems can also be generated. For large lots, inaccessibility to all units in the lot may make it more difficult to obtain a random sample. Under certain conditions, this problem can be minimized by dividing the lot into sublots for purposes of inspection sampling. For example, if the lot represents a full week of production, each inspection sublot may consist of one day's production. Each sublot may be sampled by applying a single sampling plan individually, or a single sample based upon the grand lot apportioned by taking one-fifth of the sample from each sublot. The acceptance/rejection criteria are then applied to the inspection results accumulated over the week.

Establishing Rational Lots

The average quality level (AQL) will be higher if inspection lots are formed without creating a heterogeneous mixture of products of different quality. It is, therefore, advisable to establish rational lots if possible. A rational lot is a group of parts, all originating essentially from the same material process, etc., and following a similar manufacturing sequence. Units of product subjected to a specific inspection should be of a single type, grade, class, size, and composition, manufactured under similar conditions and during the same time period, and also should be selected at random from the process. By establishing rational lots, greater homogeneity of parts in a given lot is assured. Several ways that homogeneity of parts in lots can be achieved are described as follows.

1. By the same assembly line and process using the same jigs, fixtures, dies, personnel, etc., for producing the parts.
2. By choosing parts from the same batches of raw materials or subassemblies.
3. By choosing parts during the same unit of time (e.g., hour or week).

Establishing rational lots also helps to isolate problems. Should inspection reveal a high degree of defectives in a lot, the source of the trouble can be more readily located if all parts and materials used in the manufacturing process can be identified, i.e., if there is a reasonable degree of traceability of every phase of the process manufacture of parts in the lot. Inferences with regard to the cause system which produced the parts has far more meaning if the origin of all the parts in the lot is the same and the parts have progressed through the manufacturing system under very similar conditions.

15.5 Acceptance Sampling Plans

MIL–STD–105

The MIL–STD–105 sampling plans were developed during World War II and were first computed and established as sampling tables for military use by the U.S. Army Ordnance, first appearing as M608-8. They cover inspection by attributes, where "the unit of product is classified simply as defective or nondefective." They were modified to a small degree by the Navy, who put out their own version as Appendix X. Then the Columbia University Statistical Research Group was asked to prepare a manual on sampling by the Navy Bureau of Ordnance in February 1945, and used these tables as a basis for their book, *Sampling Inspection,* published in 1948. In a modified form, these became first a JAN specification and then the MIL–STD–105 set of tables. The tables were recently modified again as MIL–STD–105D, or ABC–STD–105D, so that they might be a standard for America (A), Britain (B), and Canada (C). The primary change was made in the Double Sampling Tables, where the second sample size was modified to equal the first sample size rather than being double its size. These tables are now being considered as International Standards to be designated as an ISO document.

Acceptable Quality Level (AQL)

Under this method, a producer has good protection against rejection of submitted lots from a process that is at the acceptable quality level (AQL) or better. On the other hand, this type of classification does not specify anything about the protection the consumer has against the acceptance of a lot worse than the AQL. Acceptance procedures based on the acceptable quality level generally make use of the process average to determine the sampling plan to be used. The AQL may be viewed as the highest percent defective that is acceptable as a process average. In normal sampling, a lot at AQL quality will have a high probability of acceptance. The probability of acceptance $P_a = 1 - \alpha$ is usually set near the 95% point, where α is known as the *Producer's Risk*. Where modifications were made in the tables by the various committees, acceptance numbers were changed to have the probability of acceptance P_a as close to 0.95 as possible.

Type of Inspection

Use of the MIL–STD–105 (the current revision is the *D* revision) is based on the following known information.

1. Severity of inspection (usually normal inspection, level II).
2. Type of sampling (single, double, or multiple).
3. Lot size.
4. Acceptable quality level (AQL).

The MIL–STD–105 sampling inspection plans provide for three degrees of severity of inspection—normal, tightened, and reduced—at three different levels of inspection—I (less discrimination), II (usual), and III (more discrimination). These degrees of severity are applied in all three general inspection levels. These procedures, plans, and applications are discussed in the following sections.

Normal Inspection

Normal inspection is used when there is no evidence that the quality of product being submitted is better or poorer than the specified quality level. Normal inspection is usually used at the start of inspection, and is continued as long as there is evidence that the quality is consistent with specified requirements.

Tightened Inspection

Under tightened inspection, the sampling inspection plan requires more stringent acceptance criteria. Such a plan is instituted when it becomes evident that quality is deteriorating. Tightened inspection is accomplished by decreasing either the number of defectives or defects per hundred units permitted in the sample for acceptance or by increasing the sample size using the same criteria (acceptance number values) as were used for the smaller normal inspection plan. When it is evident that quality has improved, normal inspection may be reinstated when five consecutive lots or batches have been considered acceptable on original inspection.

Reduced Inspection

Under reduced inspection, the plans allow a smaller sample to be taken than under normal inspection. Reduced inspection may be implemented when it is evident that quality is running unusually well, as indicated by at least ten previous lots being accepted on original inspection plus other criteria indicating process control. The requirements for switching from normal to reduced inspection are more involved than for switching from normal to tightened inspection. A proven quality history for the product is essential in deciding to switch from normal to reduced inspection. Switching from normal to tightened inspection is usually a mandatory requirement, but switching from normal to reduced inspection is permissive only under certain conditions. When product quality shows evidence of deterioration, changing from reduced to normal inspection is mandatory.

Inspection Level

The inspection level defines the relationship between the lot or batch size and the sample size. The inspection level to be used for any particular requirement will be prescribed by the responsible authority. The three inspection levels set forth in MIL–STD–105 are I, II, and III. These are listed in table 15.1, together with four special inspection levels. Unless otherwise specified, inspection level II is used and is termed the normal level. Inspection level I may be specified, however, when less discrimination is needed, or level III may be specified for greater discrimination. The four additional special levels, S-1, S-2, S-3, and S-4, are given in the same table and may be used where relatively small sample sizes are necessary for destructive or extremely costly inspections and large sampling risks can or must be tolerated.

Single Sampling

A single sampling plan is one in which the inspection results for a single sample yield judgment criteria for either accepting or rejecting a given lot. Based upon the plan used, the lot from which the sample was drawn is accepted when the number of defectives found in the sample is equal to or less than the acceptance number called for by the table. On the other hand, if the number of defectives is equal to or greater than the rejection number, the lot is rejected. Apply table 15.2 for normal inspection using simple sampling. For example, for an acceptable quality level (AQL) of 2.5 (percent or defects per 100) and a lot size (N) of 500 parts, using inspection level II (shown in table 15.1), the sample size code letter is H and the sample size (n) is 50. Reading from the table again, the acceptance number (Ac) is 3 and the rejection number (Re) is 4.

TABLE 15.1 Table I of MIL–STD–105D: Code Letters for Sample Sizes

Lot or Batch Size	*Special Inspection Levels*				*General Inspection Levels*		
	S-1	S-2	S-3	S-4	I	II	III
2 to 8	A	A	A	A	A	A	B
9 to 15	A	A	A	A	A	B	C
16 to 25	A	A	B	B	B	C	D
26 to 50	A	B	B	C	C	D	E
51 to 90	B	B	C	C	C	E	F
91 to 150	B	B	C	D	D	F	G
151 to 280	B	C	D	E	E	G	Ⓗ
281 to 500	B	C	D	E	F	Ⓗ	J
501 to 1200	C	C	E	F	G	J	K
1201 to 3200	C	D	E	G	Ⓗ	K	L
3201 to 10000	C	D	F	G	J	L	M
10001 to 35000	C	D	F	Ⓗ	K	M	N
35001 to 150000	D	E	G	J	L	N	P
150001 to 500000	D	E	G	J	M	P	Q
500001 and over	D	E	Ⓗ	K	N	Q	R

In another example, if the acceptable quality level is 15.0, the inspection level is I, and the lot size is 1,000 parts, then from table 15.1, the sample size code letter is G; from table 15.2, the sample size is 32, the acceptance value is 10, and the rejection value is 11.

Double Sampling

Double sampling plans are similar to single sampling plans except that they involve two samples and consequently two acceptance numbers and two rejection numbers. When the number of defectives found in the first sample is equal to or less than the first acceptance number in the sampling plan, the lot is accepted. If the number of defectives found in the first sample is equal to or greater than the first rejection number, the lot must be rejected. If, however, the number of defectives found in the first sample is *between* the first acceptance and rejection numbers, a second sample must be examined. If the *sum* of the defectives found in the first and second samples is equal to or less than the second acceptance number, the lot is accepted. If the cumulative number of defectives is equal to or greater than the second rejection number, the lot must be rejected. A flow chart depicting this procedure is presented in figure 15-1.

Although two samples of material may need to be examined, the double sampling plan has several advantages.

TABLE 15.2 Table II–A of MIL–STD–105D: Normal Single Sampling

Sample size code letter	Sample size	Acceptable Quality Levels (normal inspection)																																																			
		0.010		0.015		0.025		0.040		0.065		0.10		0.15		0.25		0.40		0.65		1.0		1.5		2.5		4.0		6.5		10		15		25		40		65		100		150		250		400		650		1000	
		Ac	Re	Ac	Re	Ac	Re	Ac	Re	Ac	Re	Ac	Re	Ac	Re	Ac	Re	Ac	Re	Ac	Re	Ac	Re	Ac	Re	Ac	Re	Ac	Re	Ac	Re	Ac	Re	Ac	Re	Ac	Re	Ac	Re	Ac	Re	Ac	Re	Ac	Re	Ac	Re	Ac	Re	Ac	Re	Ac	Re
A	2	↓		↓		↓		↓		↓		↓		↓		↓		↓		↓		↓		↓		↓		↓		0	1	↓		↓		1	2	2	3	3	4	5	6	7	8	10	11	14	15	21	22	30	31
B	3	↓		↓		↓		↓		↓		↓		↓		↓		↓		↓		↓		↓		↓		0	1	↑		↓		1	2	2	3	3	4	5	6	7	8	10	11	14	15	21	22	30	31	44	45
C	5	↓		↓		↓		↓		↓		↓		↓		↓		↓		↓		↓		↓		0	1	↑		↓		1	2	2	3	3	4	5	6	7	8	10	11	14	15	21	22	30	31	44	45	↑	
D	8	↓		↓		↓		↓		↓		↓		↓		↓		↓		↓		↓		0	1	↑		↓		1	2	2	3	3	4	5	6	7	8	10	11	14	15	21	22	30	31	44	45	↑		↑	
E	13	↓		↓		↓		↓		↓		↓		↓		↓		↓		↓		0	1	↑		↓		1	2	2	3	3	4	5	6	7	8	10	11	14	15	21	22	30	31	44	45	↑		↑		↑	
F	20	↓		↓		↓		↓		↓		↓		↓		↓		↓		0	1	↑		↓		1	2	2	3	3	4	5	6	7	8	10	11	14	15	21	22	↑		↑		↑		↑		↑		↑	
G	32	↓		↓		↓		↓		↓		↓		↓		↓		0	1	↑		↓		1	2	2	3	3	4	5	6	7	8	10	11	14	15	21	22	↑		↑		↑		↑		↑		↑		↑	
(H)	50	↓		↓		↓		↓		↓		↓		↓		0	1	↑		↓		1	2	2	3	(3)	(4)	5	6	7	8	10	11	14	15	21	22	↑		↑		↑		↑		↑		↑		↑		↑	
J	80	↓		↓		↓		↓		↓		↓		0	1	↑		↓		1	2	2	3	3	4	5	6	7	8	10	11	14	15	21	22	↑		↑		↑		↑		↑		↑		↑		↑		↑	
K	125	↓		↓		↓		↓		↓		0	1	↑		↓		1	2	2	3	3	4	5	6	7	8	10	11	14	15	21	22	↑		↑		↑		↑		↑		↑		↑		↑		↑		↑	
L	200	↓		↓		↓		↓		0	1	↑		↓		1	2	2	3	3	4	5	6	7	8	10	11	14	15	21	22	↑		↑		↑		↑		↑		↑		↑		↑		↑		↑		↑	
M	315	↓		↓		↓		0	1	↑		↓		1	2	2	3	3	4	5	6	7	8	10	11	14	15	21	22	↑		↑		↑		↑		↑		↑		↑		↑		↑		↑		↑		↑	
N	500	↓		↓		0	1	↑		↓		1	2	2	3	3	4	5	6	7	8	10	11	14	15	21	22	↑		↑		↑		↑		↑		↑		↑		↑		↑		↑		↑		↑		↑	
P	800	↓		0	1	↑		↓		1	2	2	3	3	4	5	6	7	8	10	11	14	15	21	22	↑		↑		↑		↑		↑		↑		↑		↑		↑		↑		↑		↑		↑		↑	
Q	1250	0	1	↑		↓		1	2	2	3	3	4	5	6	7	8	10	11	14	15	21	22	↑		↑		↑		↑		↑		↑		↑		↑		↑		↑		↑		↑		↑		↑		↑	
R	2000	↑		↑		1	2	2	3	3	4	5	6	7	8	10	11	14	15	21	22	↑		↑		↑		↑		↑		↑		↑		↑		↑		↑		↑		↑		↑		↑		↑		↑	

↓ = **Use first sampling plan below arrow. If sample size equals, or exceeds, lot or batch size, do 100 percent inspection.**

↑ = **Use first sampling plan above arrow.**

Ac = **Acceptance number.**

Re = **Rejection number.**

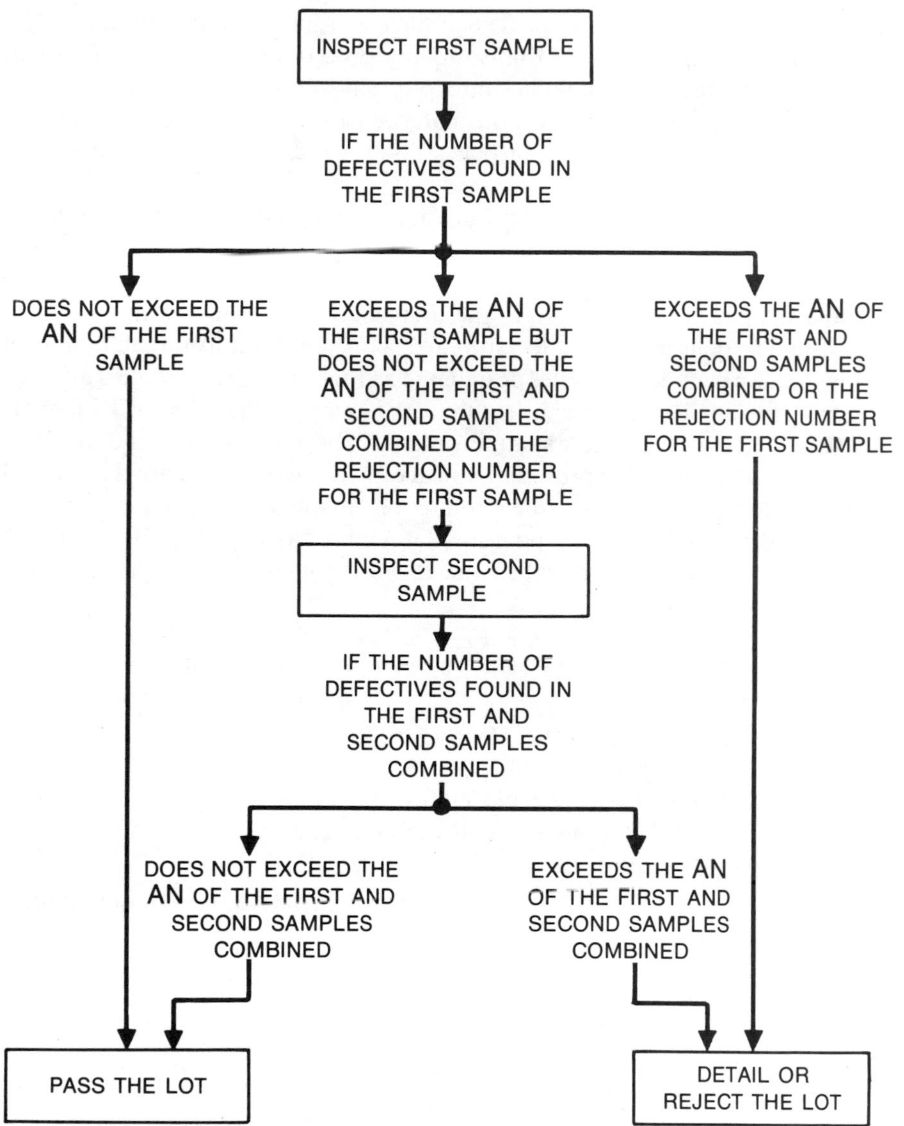

AN = Acceptance Number

Figure 15–1 Flow chart for double sampling.

1. If appraisal of the first sample clearly shows that the lot is either acceptable or rejectable, immediate disposition can be made without taking a second sample. (This sample is smaller, compared to a single sampling plan, for a given AQL.)

2. There is a certain psychological advantage in using a double sampling plan. Most inspectors are aware that sampling procedures are based on laws of chance, and they sometimes hesitate to reject or accept material on the basis of a single sample, especially if the material passes or is rejected by a narrow margin. The double sampling plan allows a second chance for marginal material.
3. When either good or bad running quality is evidenced, it is more economical to use a double sampling plan than a comparable single sampling plan because a decision to accept or to reject can be made on the basis of the first sample. For a given AQL, the first sample in a double sampling plan is smaller than in the single sampling plan. The total average amount of inspection per lot, sometimes designated as I for the current process average, will generally be very much less than the comparable value of I in single sampling. Thus the double sampling plan will be much more economical. To substantiate this, if the probability of acceptance (P_a) curves are determined and graphed for comparable production in single and double sampling plans, the double sampling plan simulates more closely the ideal probability of the acceptance curve (called the operating characteristic curve) where 100% inspection applies.

An example of how the double sampling plan works is given below.

II = Inspection Level
N = Lot Size = 500
H = Sample size code letter (from table 15.1)
n_1 = First sample = 32 (from table 15.3)
n_2 = Second sample = 32 (from table 15.3)
AQL = Acceptable Quality Level = 2.5% 2.5 defects per hundred units

From table 15.3

Ac = c_1 = Acceptance number 1 (Ac_1) for first sample = 1
Ac = c_2 = Acceptance number 2 (Ac_2) for first and second = 4 (samples combined)
Re = r_1 = Rejection number 1 (Re_1) for first sample = 4
Re = r_2 = Rejection number 2 (Re_2) for first and second = 5 (samples combined)

Referring to Tables I and III–A of MIL–STD–105D, if the desired AQL is 2.5 and 500 parts were submitted for acceptance or rejection at inspection level II, the first sample n_1 would be 32. If by the first criteria, Ac_1 and Re_1, there were 1 or less defectives found in the sample, the lot would be accepted without going further. And, if there were 4 or more defectives found in the sample (n_1), 4 = Re_1, the lot would be rejected without going further. However, if there were between 1 and 4

TABLE 15.3 Table III–A of MIL–STD–105D: Normal Double Sampling

Sample size code letter	Sample	Sample size	Cumulative sample size	Acceptable Quality Levels (normal inspection)																									
				0.010	0.015	0.025	0.040	0.065	0.10	0.15	0.25	0.40	0.65	1.0	1.5	2.5	4.0	6.5	10	15	25	40	[illegible]	00	150	250	400	650	1000
				Ac Re	Ac Re	Ac Re	Ac Re	Ac Re	Ac Re	Ac Re	Ac Re	Ac Re	Ac Re	Ac Re	Ac Re	Ac Re	Ac Re	Ac Re	Ac Re	Ac Re	Ac Re	Ac Re	Ac Re	Ac Re	Ac Re	Ac Re	Ac Re	Ac Re	Ac Re
A				↓	↓	↓	↓	↓	↓	↓	↓	↓	↓	↓	↓	↓	↓	•	↓	↓	•	•	•	•	•	•	•	•	•
B	First	2	2	↓	↓	↓	↓	↓	↓	↓	↓	↓	↓	↓	↓	↓	•	↑	↓	0 2	0 3	1 4	2 5	3 7	5 9	7 11	11 16	17 22	25 31
	Second	2	4																	1 2	3 4	4 5	6 7	8 9	12 13	18 19	26 27	37 38	56 57
C	First	3	3	↓	↓	↓	↓	↓	↓	↓	↓	↓	↓	↓	↓	•	↑	↓	0 2	0 3	1 4	2 5	3 [illegible]	5 9	7 11	11 16	17 22	25 31	↑
	Second	3	6																1 2	3 4	4 5	6 7	8 [illegible]	12 13	18 19	26 27	37 38	56 57	
D	First	5	5	↓	↓	↓	↓	↓	↓	↓	↓	↓	↓	↓	•	↑	↓	0 2	0 3	1 4	2 5	3 7	5 [illegible]	7 11	11 16	17 22	25 31	↑	↑
	Second	5	10															1 2	3 4	4 5	6 7	8 9	12 [illegible]	18 19	26 27	37 38	56 57		
E	First	8	8	↓	↓	↓	↓	↓	↓	↓	↓	↓	↓	•	↑	↓	0 2	0 3	1 4	2 5	3 7	5 9	7 [illegible]	11 16	17 22	25 31	↑	↑	↑
	Second	8	16														1 2	3 4	4 5	6 7	8 9	12 13	18 [illegible]	26 27	37 38	56 57			
F	First	13	13	↓	↓	↓	↓	↓	↓	↓	↓	↓	•	↑	↓	0 2	0 3	1 4	2 5	3 7	5 9	7 11	11 [illegible]	↑	↑	↑	↑	↑	↑
	Second	13	26												1 2	3 4	4 5	6 7	8 9	12 13	18 19	26 [illegible]						
G	First	20	20	↓	↓	↓	↓	↓	↓	↓	↓	•	↑	↓	0 2	0 3	1 4	2 5	3 7	5 9	7 11	11 16	↑	↑	↑	↑	↑	↑	↑
	Second	20	40												1 2	3 4	4 5	6 7	8 9	12 13	18 19	26 27							
(H)	First	32	32	↓	↓	↓	↓	↓	↓	↓	•	↑	↓	0 2	0 3	1 4	2 5	3 7	5 9	7 11	11 16	↑	↑	↑	↑	↑	↑	↑	↑
	Second	32	64											1 2	3 4	4 5	6 7	8 9	12 13	18 19	26 27								
J	First	50	50	↓	↓	↓	↓	↓	↓	•	↑	↓	0 2	0 3	1 4	2 5	3 7	5 9	7 11	11 16	↑	↑	↑	↑	↑	↑	↑	↑	↑
	Second	50	100										1 2	3 4	4 5	6 7	8 9	12 13	18 19	26 27									
K	First	80	80	↓	↓	↓	↓	↓	•	↑	↓	0 2	0 3	1 4	2 5	3 7	5 9	7 11	11 16	↑	↑	↑	↑	↑	↑	↑	↑	↑	↑
	Second	80	160									1 2	3 4	4 5	6 7	8 9	12 13	18 19	26 27										
L	First	125	125	↓	↓	↓	↓	•	↑	↓	0 2	0 3	1 4	2 5	3 7	5 9	7 11	11 16	↑	↑	↑	↑	↑	↑	↑	↑	↑	↑	↑
	Second	125	250								1 2	3 4	4 5	6 7	8 9	12 13	18 19	26 27											
M	First	200	200	↓	↓	↓	•	↑	↓	0 2	0 3	1 4	2 5	3 7	5 9	7 11	11 16	↑	↑	↑	↑	↑	↑	↑	↑	↑	↑	↑	↑
	Second	200	400							1 2	3 4	4 5	6 7	8 9	12 13	18 19	26 27												
N	First	315	315	↓	↓	•	↑	↓	0 2	0 3	1 4	2 5	3 7	5 9	7 11	11 16	↑	↑	↑	↑	↑	↑	↑	↑	↑	↑	↑	↑	↑
	Second	315	630						1 2	3 4	4 5	6 7	8 9	12 13	18 19	26 27													
P	First	500	500	↓	•	↑	↓	0 2	0 3	1 4	2 5	3 7	5 9	7 11	11 16	↑	↑	↑	↑	↑	↑	↑	↑	↑	↑	↑	↑	↑	↑
	Second	500	1000					1 2	3 4	4 5	6 7	8 9	12 13	18 19	26 27														
Q	First	800	800	•	↑	↓	0 2	0 3	1 4	2 5	3 7	5 9	7 11	11 16	↑	↑	↑	↑	↑	↑	↑	↑	↑	↑	↑	↑	↑	↑	↑
	Second	800	1600				1 2	3 4	4 5	6 7	8 9	12 13	18 19	26 27															
R	First	1250	1250	↑	↑	0 2	0 3	1 4	2 5	3 7	5 9	7 11	11 16	↑	↑	↑	↑	↑	↑	↑	↑	↑	↑	↑	↑	↑	↑	↑	↑
	Second	1250	2500			1 2	3 4	4 5	6 7	8 9	12 13	18 19	26 27																

↓ = Use first sampling plan below arrow (refer to continuation on following page where necessary). If sample size equals or exceeds lot or batch size, do 100 percent inspection.
↑ = Use first sampling plan above arrow.
Ac = Acceptance number.
Re = Rejection number.
· = Use corresponding single sampling plan for alternate, use multiple sampling plan below, where available.
+ + = Use corresponding double sampling plan for alternate, use multiple sampling plan below, where available.

defectives, a second sample must be taken. A second sample of 32 is then examined and the number of defectives found in the first sample and the second sample are totaled. For illustrative purposes, suppose that the number of defectives found in the first sample is 2 and in the second sample is 4, should the lot be accepted or rejected? Since 6 defectives were observed in the first and second samples combined, which is more than the second acceptance number 4 ($c_2 = 4 = \text{Ac}_2; r_2 = 5 = \text{Re}_2$), the lot must be rejected. On the other hand, if the number of defectives found in the first sample is 2, and in the second sample the number of observed defectives is 1, the total of 3 defectives would be less than the second acceptance number 4 and the lot would be accepted.

Multiple Sampling

Multiple sampling is a type of sampling in which a decision to accept or reject an inspection lot may be reached after one or more samples from the inspection lot have been inspected, and will always be reached after not more than a designated number of samples have been inspected, generally a maximum of 7 samples in MIL–STD–105D. The procedure is similar to that described for double sampling, except that the number of successive samples required to reach a decision to accept or reject may be more than two. (As noted previously, seven samples of equal size are generally allowed.)

The following is an example of an application of the multiple sampling plan.

Data for the example:

1. The lot size is 500 units, $N = 500$.
2. General inspection level II applies.
3. From table 15.1 (table I of MIL–STD–105D), the sample size code letter is H.
4. Normal inspection (level II) is to be used.
5. An AQL value of 1.5% defective is specified.

Based on these data, the following equivalent multiple sampling plan is obtained: 13 units are selected at random from the lot. If two or more defectives are found, reject the lot; if one or no defective is found, select a second sample of 13 units at random from the lot (for this example, acceptance of the lot is not possible on the basis of the first sample). If in the first two samples (cumulative sample size of 26 units) no defectives are found, accept the lot; if three or more defectives are found, reject the lot; if one or two defectives are found in the two samples combined, select a third sample of thirteen units at random from the lot and inspect each unit in this third sample, and so on. Seven samples of thirteen units each or a cumulative sample of ninety-one units may be selected at random and inspected, if necessary, to obtain a final decision covering acceptance or rejection of the submitted lot of 500 units. This process is repeated for each lot of

TABLE 15.4 Table IV–A of MIL–STD–105D: Normal Multiple Sampling Acceptable Quality; Levels (Normal Inspection)

Sample size code letter	Sample	Sample size	Cumulative sample size	Acceptable Quality Levels (normal inspection)																									
				0.010	0.015	0.025	0.040	0.065	0.10	0.15	0.25	0.40	0.65	1.0	1.5	2.5	4.0	6.5	10	15	25	40	65	100	150	250	400	650	1000
				Ac Re	Ac Re	Ac Re	Ac Re	Ac Re	Ac Re	Ac Re	Ac Re	Ac Re	Ac Re	Ac Re	Ac Re	Ac Re	Ac Re	Ac Re	Ac Re	Ac Re	Ac Re	Ac Re	Ac Re	Ac Re	Ac Re	Ac Re	Ac Re	Ac Re	Ac Re
A				↓	↓	↓	↓	↓	↓	↓	↓	↓	↓	↓	↓	↓	↓	·	↓	↓	·	·	·	·	·	·	·	·	·
B				↓	↓	↓	↓	↓	↓	↓	↓	↓	↓	↓	↓	↓	·	↑	↓	++	++	++	++	++	++	++	++	++	++
C				↓	↓	↓	↓	↓	↓	↓	↓	↓	↓	↓	↓	·	↑	↓	++	++	++	++	++	++	++	++	++	++	↑
D	First	2	2	↓	↓	↓	↓	↓	↓	↓	↓	↓	↓	↓	·	↑	↓	# 2	# 2	# 3	# 4	0 4	0 5	1 7	2 9	4 12	6 16	↑	↑
	Second	2	4															# 2	0 3	0 3	1 5	1 6	3 8	4 10	7 14	11 19	17 27		
	Third	2	6															0 2	0 3	1 4	2 6	3 8	6 10	8 13	13 19	19 27	29 39		
	Fourth	2	8															0 3	1 4	2 5	3 7	5 10	8 13	12 17	19 25	27 34	40 49		
	Fifth	2	10															1 3	2 4	3 6	5 8	7 11	11 15	17 20	25 29	36 40	53 58		
	Sixth	2	12															1 3	3 5	4 6	7 9	10 12	14 17	21 23	31 33	45 47	65 68		
	Seventh	2	14															2 3	4 5	6 7	9 10	13 14	18 19	25 26	37 38	53 54	77 78		
E	First	3	3	↓	↓	↓	↓	↓	↓	↓	↓	↓	↓	·	↑	↓	# 2	# 2	# 3	# 4	0 4	0 5	1 7	2 9	4 12	6 16	↑	↑	↑
	Second	3	6														# 2	0 3	0 3	1 5	1 6	3 8	4 10	7 14	11 19	17 27			
	Third	3	9														0 2	0 3	1 4	2 6	3 8	6 10	8 13	13 19	19 27	29 39			
	Fourth	3	12														0 3	1 4	2 5	3 7	5 10	8 13	12 17	19 25	27 34	40 49			
	Fifth	3	15														1 3	2 4	3 6	5 8	7 11	11 15	17 20	25 29	36 40	53 58			
	Sixth	3	18														1 3	3 5	4 6	7 9	10 12	14 17	21 23	31 33	45 47	65 68			
	Seventh	3	21														2 3	4 5	6 7	9 10	13 14	18 19	25 26	37 38	53 54	77 78			
F	First	5	5	↓	↓	↓	↓	↓	↓	↓	↓	↓	·	↑	↓	# 2	# 2	# 3	# 4	0 4	0 5	1 7	2 9	↑	↑	↑	↑	↑	↑
	Second	5	10													# 2	0 3	0 3	1 5	1 6	3 8	4 10	7 14						
	Third	5	15													0 2	0 3	1 4	2 6	3 8	6 10	8 13	13 19						
	Fourth	5	20													0 3	1 4	2 5	3 7	5 10	8 13	12 17	19 25						
	Fifth	5	25													1 3	2 4	3 6	5 8	7 11	11 15	17 20	25 29						
	Sixth	5	30													1 3	3 5	4 6	7 9	10 12	14 17	21 23	31 33						
	Seventh	5	35													2 3	4 5	6 7	9 10	13 14	18 19	25 26	37 38						
G	First	8	8	↓	↓	↓	↓	↓	↓	↓	↓	·	↑	↓	# 2	# 2	# 3	# 4	0 4	0 5	1 7	2 9	↑	↑	↑	↑	↑	↑	↑
	Second	8	16												# 2	0 3	0 3	1 5	1 6	3 8	4 10	7 14							
	Third	8	24												0 2	0 3	1 4	2 6	3 8	6 10	8 13	13 19							
	Fourth	8	32												0 3	1 4	2 5	3 7	5 10	8 13	12 17	19 25							
	Fifth	8	40												1 3	2 4	3 6	5 8	7 11	11 15	17 20	25 29							
	Sixth	8	48												1 3	3 5	4 6	7 9	10 12	14 17	21 23	31 33							
	Seventh	8	56												2 3	4 5	6 7	9 10	13 14	18 19	25 26	37 38							
(H)	First	13	13	↓	↓	↓	↓	↓	↓	↓	·	↑	↓	# 2	# 2	# 3	# 4	0 4	0 5	1 7	(2) (9)	↑	↑	↑	↑	↑	↑	↑	↑
	Second	13	26											# 2	0 3	0 3	1 5	1 6	3 8	4 10	7 14								
	Third	13	39											0 2	0 3	1 4	2 6	3 8	6 10	8 13	13 19								
	Fourth	13	52											0 3	1 4	2 5	3 7	5 10	8 13	12 17	19 25								
	Fifth	13	65											1 3	2 4	3 6	5 8	7 11	11 15	17 20	25 29								
	Sixth	13	78											1 3	3 5	4 6	7 9	10 12	14 17	21 23	31 33								
	Seventh	13	91											2 3	4 5	6 7	9 10	13 14	18 19	25 26	37 38								
J	First	20	20	↓	↓	↓	↓	↓	↓	·	↑	↓	# 2	# 2	# 3	# 4	0 4	0 5	1 7	2 9	↑	↑	↑	↑	↑	↑	↑	↑	↑
	Second	20	40										# 2	0 3	0 3	1 5	1 6	3 8	4 10	7 14									
	Third	20	60										0 2	0 3	1 4	2 6	3 8	6 10	8 13	13 19									
	Fourth	20	80										0 3	1 4	2 5	3 7	5 10	8 13	12 17	19 25									
	Fifth	20	100										1 3	2 4	3 6	5 8	7 11	11 15	17 20	25 29									
	Sixth	20	120										1 3	3 5	4 6	7 9	10 12	14 17	21 23	31 33									
	Seventh	20	140										2 3	4 5	6 7	9 10	13 14	18 19	25 26	37 38									

↓ = Use first sampling plan below arrow (refer to continuation on following page where necessary). If sample size equals or exceeds lot or batch size, do 100 percent inspection.

↑ = Use first sampling plan above arrow.

Ac = Acceptance number.

Re = Rejection number.

· = Use corresponding single sampling plan for alternate, use multiple sampling plan below, where available.

++ = Use corresponding double sampling plan for alternate, use multiple sampling plan below, where available.

Samples required to reach a decision is seven. The following table represents the complete multiple sampling table.

Sample No.	Sample Size	Cumulative Sample Size Σ_n	Acceptance Number, A_c	Number, R_e
1	13	13	*	2
2	13	26	0	3
3	13	39	0	3
4	13	52	1	4
5	13	65	2	4
6	13	78	3	4
7	13	91	4	5

*Acceptance is not possible for the first sample because the cumulative size is not large enough to assure the desired product quality (AQL).

Figure 15–2 Multiple sampling plan for code letter *H*, lot size $N = 500$, AQL = 1.5, Mil STD-105D.

500 units until a decision to accept or reject each such lot is ultimately reached. The maximum number of samples required to reach a decision is seven. Figure 15-2 presents the complete multiple sampling table extracted for an AQL of 1.5% and code letter H, using table 15.4.

Table 15.1* gives the military table in MIL–STD–105D covering sampling code letter H. It gives the sampling plans used as examples for single sampling, double sampling, and multiple sampling. Table 15.6, chart H shows the probability of acceptance (P_a) curves, called operating characteristic curves, that cover only P_a values for all possible incoming process average levels for single sampling. Such OC curves should be studied in detail to make certain that the risks taken in sampling inspections are reasonable. The results on such OC curves for single sampling may be extended to cover selected double and multiple sampling by extensive mathematical operations. Such operations may be programmed on many of the most common computers and actual P_a curves may be determined for comparison purposes. These will show that the OC curve for double sampling is superior to the corresponding P_a curve for single sampling. However, the OC curve for multiple sampling will be slightly superior to the corresponding double sample OC curve.

*Code letters for samples sizes per Table 1 of MIL-STD 105D given for 7 inspection levels. Level II, H covers later batch size 281 to 500.

TABLE 15.5 Table X–H–2 from MIL–STD–105D for Sample Size Code Letter H

Type of Sampling Plan	Cumulative Sample Size	Less than 0.25	0.25	0.40	X	0.65	1.0	1.5	2.5	4.0	6.5	X	10	X	15	X	25	Higher than 25	Cumulative Sample Size
		Ac Re	Ac Re	Ac Re	Ac Re	Ac Re	Ac Re	Ac Re	Ac Re	Ac Re	Ac Re	Ac Re	Ac Re	Ac Re	Ac Re	Ac Re	Ac Re	Ac Re	
Single	50	▽	0 1	Use Letter G	Use Letter K	Use Letter J	1 2	2 3	3 4	5 6	7 8	8 9	10 11	12 13	14 15	18 19	21 22	△	50
Double	32	▽	*				0 2	0 3	1 4	2 5	3 7	3 7	5 9	6 10	7 11	9 14	11 16	△	32
	64						1 2	3 4	4 5	6 7	8 9	11 12	12 13	15 16	18 19	23 24	26 27		64
Multiple	13	▽	*				† 2	† 2	† 3	† 4	0 4	0 4	0 5	0 6	1 7	1 8	2 9	△	13
	26						† 2	0 3	0 3	1 5	1 6	2 7	3 8	3 9	4 10	6 12	7 14		26
	39						0 2	0 3	1 4	2 6	3 8	4 9	6 10	7 12	8 13	11 17	13 19		39
	52						0 3	1 4	2 5	3 7	5 10	6 11	8 13	10 15	12 7	16 22	19 25		52
	65						1 3	2 4	3 6	5 8	7 11	9 12	11 15	14 17	17 20	22 25	25 29		65
	78						1 3	3 5	4 6	7 9	10 12	12 14	14 17	18 20	21 23	27 29	31 33		78
	91						2 3	4 5	6 7	9 10	13 14	14 15	18 19	21 22	25 26	32 33	37 38		91
Acceptable Quality Levels (tightened inspection)		Less than 0.40	0.40	X	0.65	1.0	1.5	2.5	4.0	6.5	X	10	X	15	X	25	X	Higher than 25	

Column group heading (normal inspection): *Acceptable Quality Levels (normal inspection)*

△ = Use next preceding sample size code letter for which acceptance and rejection numbers are available.
▽ = Use next subsequent sample size code letter for which acceptance and rejection numbers are available.
Ac = Acceptance number
Re = Rejection number
* = Use single sampling plan above (or alternatively use letter L)
† = Acceptance not permitted at this sample size

TABLE 15.6

(Curves for double and multiple sampling are matched as closely as practible)

CHART H—MIL–STD–105D—Operating Characteristic Curves for Single Sampling Plans.

PERCENT OF LOTS EXPECTED TO BE ACCEPTED (P_a)

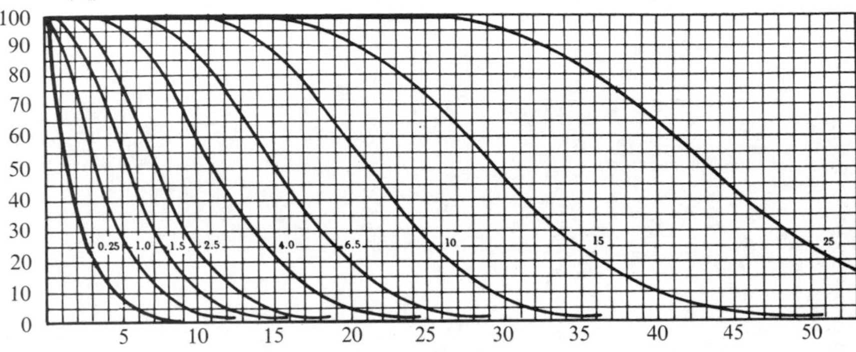

QUALITY OF SUBMITTED LOTS
(p, in percent defective for AQL's ≤ 10; in defects per hundred units for AQL's > 10)

Note: Figures on curves are Acceptable Quality Levels (AQL's) for normal inspection.

15.6 Probability Frequency Distributions for Attributes Inspection

The proper selection of the best possible sampling inspection plan depends on several factors. The plan selected must provide the type and amount of protection desired (such as lot protection) and average quality protection at minimum costs. To evaluate these features, three basic probability frequency distributions are used. For finite lots, where lot sizes are small, the hypergeometric relation is used. Where lot sizes are fairly large, the p binomial probability distribution usually applies. Tables for the p binomial are limited in their coverage. The third probability distribution is the Poisson exponential, which is often referred to as the *true* distribution, and is used as an approximation for the other two distributions, the hypergometric and the p binomial. Tables of the Poisson exponential binomial limit are available, covering individual and cumulative frequencies. Graphs of these probability values are available and usually present cumulative probability values. Figure 15-3 shows such a graph, which is used in determining probability values used in examples in succeeding sections.

TABLE 15.6.2 Probability of Acceptance Values

Table X–H–1 from MIL–STD–105D for Single Sampling Plans = Tabulated Values for Operating Characteristic Curves

P_a	Acceptable Quality Levels (normal inspection)																			
	0.25	1.0	1.5	2.5	4.0	6.5	×	10	0.25	1.0	1.5	2.5	4.0	6.5	×	10	×	15	×	25
	p (in percent defective)								p (in defects per hundred units)											
99.0	0.020	0.306	0.888	1.69	3.66	6.06	7.41	11.1	0.020	0.298	0.872	1.65	3.57	5.81	7.01	9.[illegible]4	12.2	15.0	20.7	25.1
95.0	0.103	0.712	1.66	2.77	5.34	8.20	9.74	12.9	0.103	0.710	1.64	2.73	5.23	7.96	9.39	12.[illegible]	15.4	18.5	24.9	29.8
90.0	0.210	1.07	2.23	3.54	6.42	9.53	11.2	14.5	0.210	1.05	2.20	3.49	6.30	9.31	10.9	14.0	17.3	20.6	27.3	32.5
75.0	0.574	1.92	3.46	5.09	8.51	12.0	13.8	17.5	0.576	1.92	3.45	5.07	8.44	11.9	13.7	17.2	20.8	24.5	31.8	37.4
50.0	1.38	3.33	5.31	7.30	11.3	15.2	17.2	21.2	1.39	3.36	5.35	7.34	11.3	15.3	17.3	21.6	25.3	29.3	37.3	43.3
25.0	2.74	5.30	7.70	10.0	14.5	18.8	21.0	25.2	2.77	5.39	7.84	10.2	14.8	19.4	21.6	26.0	30.4	34.8	43.5	49.9
10.0	4.50	7.56	10.3	12.9	17.8	22.4	24.7	29.1	4.61	7.78	10.6	13.4	18.6	23.5	26.0	30.8	35.6	40.3	49.5	56.4
5.0	5.82	9.13	12.1	14.8	19.9	24.7	27.0	31.6	5.99	9.49	12.6	15.5	21.0	26.3	28.9	33.9	38.9	43.8	53.4	60.5
1.0	8.80	12.5	15.9	18.8	24.3	29.2	31.7	36.3	9.21	13.3	16.8	20.1	26.2	32.0	34.8	40.3	45.6	50.9	61.1	68.7
	0.40	1.5	2.5	4.0	6.5	×	10	×	0.40	1.5	2.5	4.0	6.5	×	10	×	15	×	25	×
	Acceptable Quality Levels (tightened inspection)																			

Note: Binomial distribution used for percent defective computations; Poisson exponential binomial limit used for defects per hundred units.

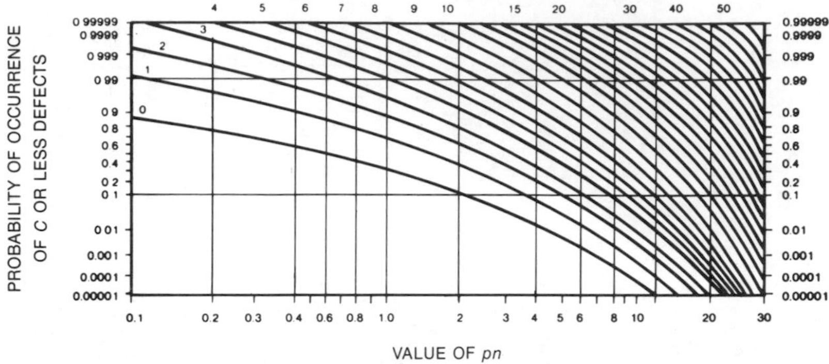

Figure 15–3 Cumulative probability curves of the Poisson exponential distribution (a modification of a chart given by Miss F. Thorndike in *The Bell System Technical Journal,* October, 1926). These curves may be used for determining the probability of occurrence of *c* or less defects in a sample of *n* pieces selected from an infinite universe in which the fraction defective is *p*. They may also be used as an approximation under certain conditions for determining the probability of occurrence of *c* or less *defectives* for a given *p* and *n*. Further, they serve as a generalized set of OC curves for simple sampling plans, when the Poisson distribution is applicable.

15.7 Features of MIL–STD–105 Sampling Plans

The next section covers the average outgoing quality limit (AOQL) and the lot tolerance percent defective (LTPD) concepts which are the basis of the Dodge-Romig Sampling Inspection Tables. Possible values of AOQL which can be realized by the use of sampling plans based on the MIL–STD–105D sampling plans have again been included in the last revision. Table 15.7 gives Table V–A, average outgoing quality limit factors for normal inspection (single sampling), which makes it possible to determine approximately what AOQL values may be obtained by using these MIL–STD–105D sampling plans for any specific lot size, for which value the correct code letter is obtained from table 15.1 (Table I of MIL–STD–105D), designating the sample sizes that apply for the selected AQL value.

The example given earlier specified $N = 500$, for which the code letter H is given in table 15.1. This gives a sample size of 50 units for single sampling. For an AQL value of 2.5%, the acceptance number is 3 and the rejection number is 4. For code letter H, sample size 50 and acceptable quality level 2.5, the multiplying factor given in table 15.7 is 3.9. Then the AOQL value (P_L) will be approximately

TABLE 15.7 Table V–A of MIL–STD–105D:
Average Outgoing Quality Limit Factors for Normal Single Sampling Inspection

Code Letter	Sample Size	Acceptable Quality Level																									
		0.010	*0.015*	*0.025*	*0.040*	*0.065*	*0.10*	*0.15*	*0.25*	*0.40*	*0.65*	*1.0*	*1.5*	*2.5*	*4.0*	*6.5*	*10*	*15*	*25*	*40*	*65*	*100*	*150*	*250*	*400*	*650*	*1000*
A	2															18			42	69	97	150	220	330	470	730	1100
B	3														12			28	46	65	110	150	220	310	490	720	1100
C	5													7.4			17	27	39	63	90	130	190	290	430	660	
D	8												4.6			11	17	24	40	56	82	120	180	270	410		
E	13											2.8			6.5	11	15	24	34	50	72	110	170	250			
F	20										1.8			4.2	6.9	9.7	16	22	33	47	73						
G	32									1.2			2.6	4.3	6.1	9.9	14	21	29	46							
(H)	50								0.74			1.7	2.7	3.9	6.3	9.0	13	19	29								
J	80							0.46			1.1	1.7	2.4	4.0	5.6	8.2	12	18									
K	125						0.29			0.67	1.1	1.6	2.5	3.6	5.2	7.5	12										
L	200					0.18			0.42	0.69	0.97	1.6	2.2	3.3	4.7	7.3											
M	315				0.12			0.27	0.44	0.62	1.00	1.4	2.1	3.0	4.7												
N	500			0.074			0.17	0.27	0.39	0.63	0.90	1.3	1.9	2.9													
P	800		0.046			0.11	0.17	0.24	0.40	0.56	0.82	1.2	1.8														
Q	1250	0.029			0.067	0.11	0.16	0.25	0.36	0.52	0.75	1.2															
R	2000			0.042	0.069	0.097	0.16	0.22	0.33	0.47	0.73																

Note: For the exact AOQL, the above values must be multiplied by $\left(1 - \dfrac{\text{Sample size}}{\text{Lot or Batch size}}\right)$

$$P_L = 3.9\left(1 - \frac{50}{500}\right) = 3.9(1 - 0.1) = 3.9(0.9) = 3.51, \quad \text{i.e. } 3.51\%$$

This checks very closely with the more exact value determined from theoretical relations in the Dodge-Romig Sampling Inspection Tables on pages 37 and 39 of the second edition.

$$P_L = y\left(\frac{1}{n} - \frac{1}{N}\right), \quad \text{where } y = 1.942 \text{ for } c = 3, \quad \text{so} \tag{2}$$

$$P_L = 1.942\left(\frac{1}{50} - \frac{1}{500}\right) = 1.942(0.020 - 0.020) = 1.942(0.018) = 0.034956$$

or 3.50%

This example illustrates the use of this table. Such an AOQL value assumes that all rejected lots are inspected 100% and all defective units found are replaced by conforming units. If we call these factors F, the equation used with such tables is

$$P_L = F\left(1 - \frac{n}{N}\right), \text{ where } n = \text{sample size and } N \text{ is the lot size.} \tag{3}$$

Similar factors are not included in MIL–STD–105D for double sampling and multiple sampling. However, a rough approximation to possible AOQL values for all plans is to use the next higher AQL value in the tables as the AOQL value. Thus, for an AQL of 25%, the AOQL should be 4.0% or less. The actual value is 3.5%. If 6.5% is the AQL value specified, the AOQL value will be in the neighborhood of 10.0%.

Other features of the MIL–STD–105D tables are provisions for the use of the AQL values as lot tolerance percent defective (LTPD) values or corresponding defects per hundred units in conjunction with consumer risk values of either 5% or 10%. These are in addition to the tables for reduced inspection and tightened inspection. Table 15.8 presents Table VI–A, which provides quality expressed as the percent defective for which $P_a = 10\%$, that is $P_C = 0.10$, the consumer's risk associated with lot tolerance percent defective (LTPD) value in many other tables.

Table 15.9 covers Table VII–B, which provides limiting quality (LQ) values in defects per hundred units, for which the consumer's risk is 5%. For code letter H, sample size is 50 with the AQL = 2.5%; the limiting quality is 13%, which may also be read from the applicable OC curve given on table 15.6 for curve 4. Similarly for AQL = 2.5 defects per hundred units, the limiting quality shown on table 15.9 is 16 defects per hundred units. The OC curve in table 15.6 shows 15 defects per hundred units. In MIL–STD–105D, when the AQL is expressed as percent defective, the corresponding LQ value is 15%, which agrees exactly with the OC curve. The difference in these two values is due to the application of the binomial distribution for percent defective values and the Poisson exponential distribution

TABLE 15.8 Table VI–A of MIL–STD–105D:
LQ (LTPD) Values for $P_a = P_C = 0.10$, based on Pn (Poisson Exponential Probability Values)

Code Letter	Sample Size	*Acceptable Quality Level*															
		0.010	*0.015*	*0.025*	*0.040*	*0.065*	*0.10*	*0.15*	*0.25*	*0.40*	*0.65*	*1.0*	*1.5*	*2.5*	*4.0*	*6.5*	*10*
A	2															68	
B	3														54		
C	5													37			58
D	8												25			41	54
E	13											16			27	36	44
F	20										11			18	25	30	42
G	32									6.9			12	16	20	27	34
(H)	50								4.5			7.6	10	13	18	22	29
J	80							2.8			4.8	6.5	8.2	11	14	19	24
K	125						1.8			3.1	4.3	5.4	7.4	9.4	12	16	23
L	200					1.2			2.0	2.7	3.3	4.6	5.9	7.7	10	14	
M	315				0.73			1.2	1.7	2.1	2.9	3.7	4.9	6.4	9.0		
N	500			0.46			0.78	1.1	1.3	1.9	2.4	3.1	4.0	5.6			
P	800		0.29			0.49	0.67	0.84	1.2	1.5	1.9	2.5	3.5				
Q	1250	0.18			0.31	0.43	0.53	0.74	0.94	1.2	1.6	2.3					
R	2000			0.20	0.27	0.33	0.46	0.59	0.77	1.0	1.4						

TABLE 15.9 Table VII–B of MIL–STD–105D: LQ (LTPD) Values for $P_a = 0.05$

Code Letter	*Sample Size*	*Acceptable Quality Level*																									
		0.010	*0.015*	*0.025*	*0.040*	*0.065*	*0.10*	*0.15*	*0.25*	*0.40*	*0.65*	*1.0*	*1.5*	*2.5*	*4.0*	*6.5*	*10*	*15*	*25*	*40*	*65*	*100*	*150*	*250*	*400*	*650*	*1000*
A	2															150			240	320	390	530	660	850	1100	1500	2000
B	3														100			160	210	260	350	440	570	730	1000	1400	1900
C	5													60			95	130	160	210	260	340	440	610	810	1100	
D	8												38			59	79	97	130	160	210	270	380	510	710		
E	13											23			37	48	60	81	100	130	170	230	310	440			
F	20										15			24	32	39	53	66	85	110	150						
G	32									9.4			15	20	24	33	41	53	68	95							
H	50								6.0			9.5	13	16	21	26	34	44	61								
J	80							3.8			5.9	7.9	9.7	13	16	21	27	38									
K	125						2.4			3.8	5.0	6.2	8.4	11	14	18	24										
L	200					1.5			2.4	3.2	3.9	5.3	6.6	8.5	11	15											
M	315				0.95			1.5	2.0	2.5	3.3	4.2	5.4	7.0	9.6												
N	500			0.60			0.95	1.3	1.6	2.1	2.6	3.4	4.4	6.1													
P	800		0.38			0.59	0.79	0.97	1.3	1.6	2.1	2.7	3.8														
Q	1250	0.24			0.38	0.50	0.62	0.84	1.1	1.4	1.8	2.4															
R	2000			0.24	0.32	0.39	0.53	0.66	0.85	1.1	1.5																

for defects per hundred units. Cumulative probabilities for this latter distribution are given in figure 15-3. In MIL–STD–105D, Table VI–A and VII–B provide LQ values for a consumer's risk value of $P_C = P_a = 10\%$, while Tables VII–A and VII–B cover the case where $P_a = 5\%$. For an acceptance number $c = 3$, using the cumulative probability curves of the Poisson exponential (presented later as figure 15-3), for $P_a = 0.10$, $pn = 6.6$, so $p = 6.6/50 = 13.2$ defects per hundred units; for $P_a = 0.05$, $pn = 7.8$, so $p = 7.8/50 = 15.6$ defects per hundred units, which rounds off to 16. This is the value for code letter H, where the value for AQL $= 2.5\%$ is given as 16 defects per hundred units; this is the LQ value of table 15.6, rounded off to a whole number.

Another feature of the MIL–STD–105D tables is a summary table of sampling plans for sample size code letter H, presented in tables 15.5 and 15.6. Values from these tables have already been used in the examples presented herein. An important feature of these tables for the various sample size code letters are the operating characteristic curves for single sampling plans covered by the code letter. Operating characteristics give probability of acceptance values for incoming quality p. The operating characteristic curve for AQL $= 2.5\%$ on this table gives the LQ values discussed above. These values are listed as quality of submitted lots in percent defective, or defects per 100 units corresponding to $P_a = 0.05$ and 0.10. Table VI–B in MIL–STD–105D covers $P_a = 0.10$ and gives LQ as 13 for AQL $= 2.5$ defects per hundred units, corresponding to the 13.2 calculated above from the Poisson exponential graph and the value of 13 read on table 15.6 for $P_a = 0.10$.

15.8 The Dodge-Romig Tables

Although acceptance sampling procedures and plans have had numerous contributors, there are probably none who have contributed more than Harold F. Dodge and Harry G. Romig. They were not only among the early developers of the MIL–STD–105 (1942), but many years before (1928) had developed their well-known Dodge-Romig sampling tables while employed at the Bell Telephone Laboratories. Nearly every company engaged in the fabrication of mechanical and electrical equipment and hardware uses either the MIL–STD–105 or the Dodge-Romig tables, or both.

The Dodge-Romig sampling tables were designed primarily to minimize the total amount of inspection for current process average levels considering total sampling inspection and screening inspection of rejected lots. Their works contain four sets of tables, listed below.

1. Single sampling lot tolerance percent defective (LTPD) tables.
2. Single sampling average outgoing quality limit (AOQL) tables.
3. Double sampling lot tolerance percent defective (LTPD) tables.
4. Double sampling average outgoing quality limit (AOQL) tables.

Before illustrating the tables themselves, some of the purposes and concepts of the plans should be understood as well as certain points noted about the Dodge-Romig tables. First, they are unique to programs that submit the rejected lots to 100% inspection. Second, for the most effective use of the tables, some knowledge must already have been obtained about the average fraction defective of the incoming material, called the process average, $\bar{p}$. When new material is first being inspected, the quality of the incoming material is checked by the sampling plan corresponding to the largest process average (the last column of the Dodge-Romig tables) until a good determination of the process average is made from one or more preliminary samples or from data provided by the producer. The average results of the manufacturing and inspection processes of the supplier are needed. After the program has been in operation for a time, the inspection office may be able to estimate this process average reasonably well from the data it has collected. These subsequent calculations may lead to the adoption of a new plan, based on the substantiated process average value $\bar{p}$, which is used in conjunction with p_t to determine $k = p/p_t$. This designates the sampling plans which will result in the minimum average amount of inspection for the case in question and also provide the desired quality protection.

15.9 Determination of Probabilities Involved in Sampling

Sampling tables provide sampling plans that provide average protection against the acceptance of unsatisfactory lots. The criteria provided in the usual attributes plans presented herein and the criteria given for variables inspection plans are based on probability frequency distributions. The probability values obtained from these are given in tables or are graphed. For the variables plans, the usual distribution is the normal law distribution, given in other sections and described in detail. For attributes sampling plans, the criteria are usually given in terms of maximum allowable number of defects or defectives allowed, shortened to an acceptance number, and symbolically represented as c or Ac. It is assumed that all samples are taken at random and may be considered as representative and unbiased samples. For infinite lots where the size of the submitted lots is not considered, the probability of acceptance values (called P_a) usually are based on the p binomial relation which may be approximated by the Poisson exponential binomial limit shown in figure 15-3. Where the percent defective and the sample size are not known, but their product is known, such as defects per 1000 feet of wire, the Poisson distribution truly represents this condition. Figure 15-3 presents this distribution in graphical form. For c values from 0 to 50, inclusive, the graph presents the probability of occurrences of c or less defects for pn values from 0 to 30. Tables giving individual values and cumulative probabilities are available. In a more restricted sense, tables of the p binomial are also available. These tables are listed in the bibliography. As noted previously, when N is finite and is considered, the hypergeometric relation applies and must usually be computed, but may be roughly approximated by the Poisson exponential distribution.

15.10 Average Outgoing Quality (AOQ)

It is the usual practice of industry to screen rejected lots and resubmit the lots to the receiver after replacing all defective units with good ones. The screened lots that are resubmitted, together with other accepted lots, improve the average quality of all lots ultimately accepted by reducing the average quality originally accepted by the sampling plan. An example will serve to illustrate how the AOQ can be calculated. Referring to figure 15-3, suppose that in all submitted lots 3% of the items are defective, and it is found from the Poisson exponential curve showing the probability of acceptance value for P_n and c that about 85% of such lots will be accepted. If 100 of these lots are received, 85 would be accepted and 15 rejected. The 85 accepted would be 3% defective. The 15 returned to the supplier for screening before acceptance would supposedly contain no defectives when finally accepted. The average percent defective in the combined lot (the AOQ) is approximately

$$P_A = \frac{85 \times 3 + 15 \times 0}{100} = 2.55\%.$$

Thus, on an average, P_A, the average outgoing quality (AOQ) is obtained by screening (100% inspection) all rejected lots and replacing all defective units by satisfactory units. Plans based on this concept provide average quality protection for product in inventory rather than individual lot protection as provided by the LTPD plans. Each plan does retain within itself and also provides individual lot protection, which is tabulated in the Dodge-Romig tables for each sampling plan.

Average Outgoing Quality Limit (AOQL)

The AOQL concept is unique because it is based on the fact that for values of incoming quality p_I for some value of p, a maximum value exists for the average outgoing quality p_A; this is symbolically designated as p_L or AOQL.

It should be noted that when the units found to be defective are not replaced, then this AOQL value will be increased slightly. Inspection costs may be reduced by having the more highly paid and experienced inspectors do the first inspections, determining when a lot should be accepted or rejected. When a lot must be rejected, it should then be subjected to 100% screening by production inspectors or less-skilled inspectors who sort out the good units from the bad. Such inspections may also be charged against the supplier or be performed under proper supervision by the supplier's representative at the purchaser's plant. The same procedure may also be established for lots inspected under MIL–STD–105 sampling plans. It can be seen that the AOQL for MIL–STD–105 plans will be roughly at the next higher level of quality as noted in the previous sections.

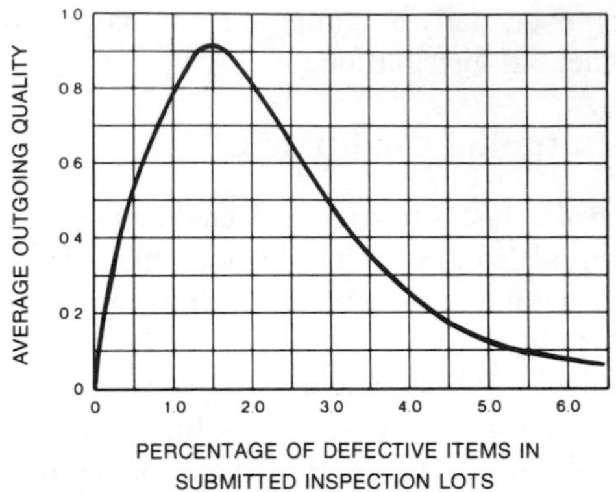

Figure 15–4 Graph of defective items in inspection lots in relation to average outgoing quality.

Under the AOQL procedure, the average outgoing quality control limit method does not refer to a definite point on the OC curve, but rather to the upper limit on outgoing quality that may be expected in the long run when all rejected lots are subjected to 100% inspection, with all defective articles removed and replaced by good articles. The average outgoing quality limit (AOQL) thus is related to the acceptable quality level (AQL) according to the formula

$$\text{Max}\,(\text{AOQ}) = \text{AOQL} \tag{4}$$

Curves can be plotted which designate the limit for a given AOQ curve. Such a curve is shown in figure 15-4, indicating the limit for the outgoing quality curve for values of incoming quality from 0 to 6.0%.

Under a given sampling plan, if the AOQ's were calculated for each possible percent defective in the lots originally submitted and if their values were plotted, the result would be known as an AOQ curve.

One should note that this curve has a maximum point. The AOQ curve of any sampling plan will have such a limit. This maximum value on the AOQ curve is known as the average outgoing quality limit of the sampling plan (AOQL). It may be simply defined as the maximum average percent of defective items in the product that is finally accepted if all rejected lots are screened and resubmitted for acceptance and all rejected units are replaced by satisfactory units.

The AOQL also provides other information. Whenever rejected parts are screened and returned, the AOQL provides (1) assurance about the lowest quality of the accepted product, and (2) assurance that the average quality accepted is never worse than the prescribed percent defective.

If submitted lots are badly out of statistical control, so that the screened lots are generally much worse than the unscreened lots, the screening may result in an important improvement in quality. If the submitted product is in good statistical control and few lots are screened, the outgoing quality will not differ greatly from incoming quality. In any event, the AOQ will nearly always be considerably better than the AOQL.

The supplier attempts to make sure that delivered products are better than the acceptable quality level, AQL, and then the average outgoing quality will be less than this limit.

Lot Tolerance Percent Defective (LTPD)

This procedure usually refers to that incoming quality level above which there is a small chance that a lot will be accepted. This probability is usually near the 10% point. When a consumer inspects lots submitted from a process that is at the LTPD or worse, there is a small probability of accepting such lots. This probability is known as the consumer's risk (P_C). However, this method does not render protection for the producer against the rejection of lots better than the LTPD.

In order to use the Dodge-Romig single sampling inspection tables, it is necessary to know the process average percent defective and the number in the lot; it is necessary to choose (on a technical basis) the lot tolerance percent defective corresponding to a consumer's risk of 0.10, or the average outgoing quality limit. The tables then give the values of n and c that minimize the total amount of inspection. Moreover, if the lot tolerance is chosen, the corresponding AOQL is given and vice versa.

Some selected sample Dodge-Romig tables illustrating the four categories of plans are presented in tables 15.10 and 15.11.

Sequential Sampling

Sequential sampling involves a unit-by-unit plan in which the sample units are selected one at a time. After each unit is inspected, the decision is made to accept, to reject, or to inspect another unit. Sampling terminates when the cumulative inspection results of the sample unit indicate that the acceptance or rejection decision can be made. The sample size is not fixed in advance, but depends on actual inspection results. It may be possible to continue sampling under the sequential plan until all units are inspected. From a practical standpoint, this is not desirable and is seldom required. In most sequential sampling plans, either an acceptance or rejection decision is made after a specified number of units have been inspected. It should be emphasized that for a large majority of lots, the total sample size under sequential sampling will be smaller than under single or double sampling.

Continuous Sampling by Attributes (Single Level)

Where the MIL–STD–105 is applicable to a definable lot or group of parts, continuous sampling is applicable to moving parts submitted by a conveyor, or

TABLE 15.10 Dodge-Romig Sampling Inspection Tables

A: Single Sampling Table for Average Outgoing Quality Limit (AOQL) = 2.0%

Lot Size	*Process Average 0 to 0.04%*			*Process Average 0.05 to 0.40%*			*Process Average 0.41 to 0.80%*			*Process Average 0.81 to 1.20%*			*Process Average 1.21 to 1.60%*			*Process Average 1.61 to 2.00%*		
	n	c	p_t%	n	c	p_t%	n	c	p_t%	n	c	p_t%	n	c	p_t%	n	c	p_t%
1–15	All	0		All	0	—	All	0	—	All	0	—	All	0	—	All	0	—
16–50	14	0	13.6	14	0	13.6	14	0	13.6	14	0	13.6	14	0	13.6	14	0	13.6
51–100	16	0	12.4	16	0	12.4	16	0	12.4	16	0	12.4	16	0	12.4	16	0	12.4
101–200	17	0	12.2	17	0	12.2	17	0	12.2	17	0	12.2	35	1	10.5	35	1	10.5
201–300	17	0	12.3	17	0	12.3	17	0	12.3	37	1	10.2	37	1	10.2	37	1	10.2
301–400	18	0	11.8	18	0	11.8	38	1	10.0	38	1	10.0	38	1	10.0	60	2	8.5
401–500	18	0	11.9	18	0	11.9	39	1	9.8	39	1	9.8	60	2	8.6	60	2	8.6
501–600	18	0	11.9	18	0	11.9	39	1	9.8	39	1	9.8	60	2	8.6	60	2	8.6
601–800	18	0	11.9	40	1	9.6	40	1	9.6	65	2	8.0	65	2	8.0	85	3	7.5
801–1000	18	0	12.0	40	1	9.6	40	1	9.6	65	2	8.1	65	2	8.1	90	3	7.4
1001–2000	18	0	12.0	41	1	9.4	65	2	8.2	65	2	8.2	95	3	7.0	120	4	6.5
2001–3000	18	0	12.0	41	1	9.4	65	2	8.2	95	3	7.0	120	4	6.5	180	6	5.8
3001–4000	18	0	12.0	42	1	9.3	65	2	8.2	95	3	7.0	155	5	6.0	210	7	5.5
4001–5000	18	0	12.0	42	1	9.3	70	2	7.5	125	4	6.4	155	5	6.0	245	8	5.3
5001–7000	18	0	12.0	42	1	9.3	95	3	7.0	125	4	6.4	185	6	5.6	280	9	5.1
7001–10,000	42	1	9.3	70	2	7.5	95	3	7.0	155	5	6.0	220	7	5.4	350	11	4.8
10,001–20,000	42	1	9.3	70	2	7.6	95	3	7.0	190	6	5.6	290	9	4.9	460	14	4.4
20,001–50,000	42	1	9.3	70	2	7.6	125	4	6.4	220	7	5.4	395	12	4.5	720	21	3.9
50,001–100,000	42	1	9.3	95	3	7.0	160	5	5.9	290	9	4.9	505	15	4.2	955	27	3.7

Continued on next page

TABLE 15.10 (continued)

B: Single Sampling Table for Lot Tolerance Per Cent Defective (LTPD) = 2.0%

Lot Size	*Process Average 0 to 0.02%*			*Process Average 0.03 to 0.20%*			*Process Average 0.21 to 0.40%*			*Process Average 0.41 to 0.60%*			*Process Average 0.61 to 0.80%*			*Process Average 0.81 to 1.00%*		
	n	*c*	*AOQL* %	*n*	*c*	*AOQL* %	*n*	*c*	*AOQL* %	*n*	*c*	*AOQL* %	*n*	*c*	*AOQL* %	*n*	*c*	*AOQL* %
1–75	All	0	0	All	0	0	All	0	0	All	0	0	All	0	0	All	0	0
76–100	70	0	0.16	70	0	0.16	70	0	0.16	70	0	0.16	70	[illegible]	0.16	70	0	0.16
101–200	85	0	0.25	85	0	0.25	85	0	0.25	85	0	0.25	85	[illegible]	0.25	85	0	0.25
201–300	95	0	0.26	95	0	0.26	95	0	0.26	95	0	0.26	95	0	0.26	95	0	0.26
301–400	100	0	0.28	100	0	0.28	100	0	0.28	160	1	0.32	160	1	0.32	160	1	0.32
401–500	105	0	0.28	105	0	0.28	105	0	0.28	165	1	0.34	165	1	0.34	165	1	0.34
501–600	105	0	0.29	105	0	0.29	175	1	0.34	175	1	0.34	175	1	0.34	235	2	0.36
601–800	110	0	0.29	110	0	0.29	180	1	0.36	240	2	0.40	240	2	0.40	300	3	0.41
801–1000	115	0	0.28	115	0	0.28	185	1	0.37	245	2	0.42	305	3	0.44	305	3	0.44
1001–2000	115	0	0.30	190	1	0.40	255	2	0.47	325	3	0.50	380	4	0.54	440	5	0.56
2001–3000	115	0	0.31	190	1	0.41	260	2	0.48	385	4	0.58	450	5	0.60	565	7	0.64
3001–4000	115	0	0.31	195	1	0.41	330	3	0.54	450	5	0.63	510	6	0.65	690	9	0.70
4001–5000	195	1	0.41	260	2	0.50	335	3	0.54	455	5	0.63	575	7	0.69	750	10	0.74
5001–7000	195	1	0.42	265	2	0.50	335	3	0.55	515	6	0.69	640	8	0.73	870	12	0.80
7001–10,000	195	1	0.42	265	2	0.50	395	4	0.62	520	6	0.69	760	10	0.79	1050	15	0.86
10,001–20,000	200	1	0.42	265	2	0.51	460	5	0.67	650	8	0.77	885	12	0.86	1230	18	0.94
20,001–50,000	200	1	0.42	335	3	0.58	520	6	0.73	710	9	0.81	1060	15	0.93	1520	23	1.0
50,001–100,000	200	1	0.42	335	3	0.58	585	7	0.76	770	10	0.84	1180	17	0.97	1690	26	1.1

TABLE 15.11 Dodge-Romig Sampling Inspection Tables

A: Double Sampling Table for Average Outgoing Quality Limit (AOQL) = 2.0%

Lot Size	Process Average 0 to 0.04%						Process Average 0.05 to 0.40%						Process Average 0.41 to 0.80%					
	Trial 1		Trial 2				Trial 1		Trial 2				Trial 1		Trial 2			
	n_1	c_1	n_2	$n_1 + n_2$	c_2	p_t %	n_1	c_1	n_2	$n_1 + n_2$	c_2	p_t %	n_1	c_1	n_2	$n_1 + n_2$	c_2	p_t %
1–15	All	0	—	—	—	—	All	0	—	—	—	—	All	0	—	—	—	—
16–50	14	0	—	—	—	13.6	14	0	—	—	—	13.6	14	0	—	—	—	13.6
51–100	21	0	12	33	1	11.7	21	0	12	33	1	11.7	21	0	12	33	1	11.7
101–200	24	0	13	37	1	11.0	24	0	13	37	1	11.0	24	0	13	37	1	11.0
201–300	26	0	15	41	1	10.4	26	0	15	41	1	10.4	29	0	31	60	2	9.1
301–400	26	0	16	42	1	10.3	26	0	16	42	1	10.3	30	0	35	65	2	9.0
401–500	27	0	16	43	1	10.3	30	0	35	65	2	9.0	30	0	35	65	2	9.0
501–600	27	0	16	43	1	10.3	31	0	34	65	2	8.9	35	0	55	90	3	7.9
601–800	27	0	17	44	1	10.2	31	0	39	70	2	8.8	35	0	60	95	3	7.7
801–1000	27	0	17	44	1	10.2	32	0	38	70	2	8.7	36	0	59	95	3	7.6
1001–2000	33	0	37	70	2	8.5	33	0	37	70	2	8.5	37	0	63	100	3	7.5
2001–3000	34	0	41	75	2	8.2	34	0	41	75	2	8.2	41	0	84	125	4	7.0
3001–4000	34	0	41	75	2	8.2	38	0	62	100	3	7.3	41	0	89	130	4	6.9
4001–5000	34	0	41	75	2	8.2	38	0	62	100	3	7.3	42	0	88	130	4	6.9
5001–7000	35	0	40	75	2	8.1	38	0	62	100	3	7.3	44	0	116	160	5	6.4
7001–10,000	35	0	40	75	2	8.1	38	0	62	100	3	7.3	45	0	115	160	5	6.3
10,001–20,000	35	0	40	75	2	8.1	39	0	66	105	3	7.2	45	0	115	160	5	6.3
20,001–50,000	35	0	40	75	2	8.1	43	0	92	135	4	6.6	47	0	148	195	6	6.0
50,001–100,000	35	0	45	80	2	8.0	43	0	92	135	4	6.6	85	1	185	270	8	5.2

TABLE 15.11 (continued)

B: Double Sampling Table for Lot Tolerance Percent Defective (LTPD) = 2.0%

Lot Size	Process Average 0 to 0.02%						Process Average 0.03 to 0.20%						Process Average 0.21 to 0.40%					
	Trial 1		Trial 2			AOQL in %	Trial 1		Trial 2			AOQL in %	Trial 1		Trial 2			AOQL in %
	n_1	c_1	n_2	$n_1 + n_2$	c_2		n_1	c_1	n_2	$n_1 + n_2$	c_2		n_1	c_1	n_2	$n_1 + n_2$	c_2	
1–75	All	0	—	—	—	0	All	0	—	—	—	0	All	0	—	—	—	0
76–100	70	0	—	—	—	0.16	70	0	—	—	—	0.16	70	0	—	—	—	0.16
101–200	85	0	—	—	—	0.25	85	0	—	—	—	0.25	85	0	—	—	—	0.25
201–300	115	0	50	165	1	0.29	115	0	50	165	1	0.29	115	0	50	165	1	0.29
301–400	120	0	60	180	1	0.32	120	0	60	180	1	0.32	120	0	60	180	1	0.32
401–500	125	0	65	190	1	0.33	125	0	65	190	1	0.33	125	0	120	245	2	0.37
501–600	125	0	70	195	1	0.34	125	0	70	195	1	0.34	125	0	130	255	2	0.39
601–800	130	0	75	205	1	0.35	130	0	75	205	1	0.35	130	0	135	265	2	0.41
801–1000	135	0	75	210	1	0.36	135	0	140	275	2	0.42	135	0	40	275	2	0.42
1001–2000	135	0	85	220	1	0.38	135	0	155	290	2	0.45	135	0	220	355	3	0.50
2001–3000	140	0	85	225	1	0.39	140	0	155	295	2	0.46	140	0	285	425	4	0.56
3001–4000	140	0	85	225	1	0.40	140	0	225	365	3	0.52	140	0	290	430	4	0.57
4001–5000	140	0	160	300	2	0.47	140	0	230	370	3	0.53	140	0	360	500	5	0.61
5001–7000	140	0	160	300	2	0.48	140	0	230	370	3	0.54	140	0	365	505	5	0.62
7001–10,000	140	0	160	300	2	0.48	140	0	235	375	3	0.54	225	1	350	575	6	0.66
10,001–20,000	140	0	165	305	2	0.49	140	0	235	375	3	0.54	225	1	415	640	7	0.71
20,001–50,000	140	0	165	305	2	0.49	140	0	305	445	4	0.59	225	1	480	705	8	0.75
50,001–100,000	140	0	165	305	2	0.49	140	0	305	445	4	0.60	225	1	545	770	9	0.78

some other continuous material-handling method. The primary advantage of continuous sampling is that it provides a method of accepting or rejecting a product as it moves past the inspection station. This feature eliminates the necessity for recall, disassembly, and reinspection of rejected material. Secondary advantages are the reduction of storage problems and fewer production bottlenecks resulting from in-process stages, transporting, and rehandling of material. Handbook H-107 documents three types of continuous sampling plans. They are CSP–1, CSP–2, and CSP–A. These plans are most applicable when (1) 100% inspection is performed by the supplier and all sampling is performed by the consumer, and (2) 100% inspection is performed by the supplier and the consumer wishes to utilize audit procedures.

Continuous sampling is based on the principle that if a certain number of parts are inspected with no occurrence of defectives, the odds are against the future occurrence of defectives as the process progresses. This probability allows reduced inspection from 100% to sampling. However, should defects begin to occur, more severe inspection must again be resumed.

TABLE 15.12 Sampling Frequency Code Letters

*Number of Units of Product Produced in a Production Interval**	*Inspection Intervals*			
	I	*II*		*III*
	CSP–1 & CSP–2	*CSP–1 & CSP–2*	*CSP–A*	*CSP–1 & CSP–2*
2–8	C	B	A′	A
9–25	D	C	B′	A
26–65	E	D	C′	B
66–110	F	E	D′	B
111–180	F	E	E′	C
181–300	G	E	F′	C
301–500	G	F	G′	D
501–800	G	F	H′	E
801–1300	H	F	I′	E
1301–3200	H	G	J′	F
3201–8000	I	H	K′	G
8001–22,000	J	I	L′	H
22,001–110,000	K	J	M′	I
110,001–up	K	K	N′	J

*The production interval is the period of time, usually a shift or a day, during which a number of units of product or a homogeneous batch of product is produced. The choice of the number of units of product or of the duration of the production interval must be estimated from prior information.

The general procedure is as follows. A given number of consecutive parts *i* are inspected from the moving line. If no defects are found, a sampling procedure may begin. The products are sampled in accordance with the sampling frequency table 15.12 and the ratio documented in handbook H-107. The steps taken in single level continuous sampling are explained by the flow charts in figures 15-5, 15-6, and 15-7.

Multilevel Continuous Sampling

Multilevel continuous sampling, which is the subject of handbook H-106, is essentially increasing or decreasing the levels of inspection, depending on the

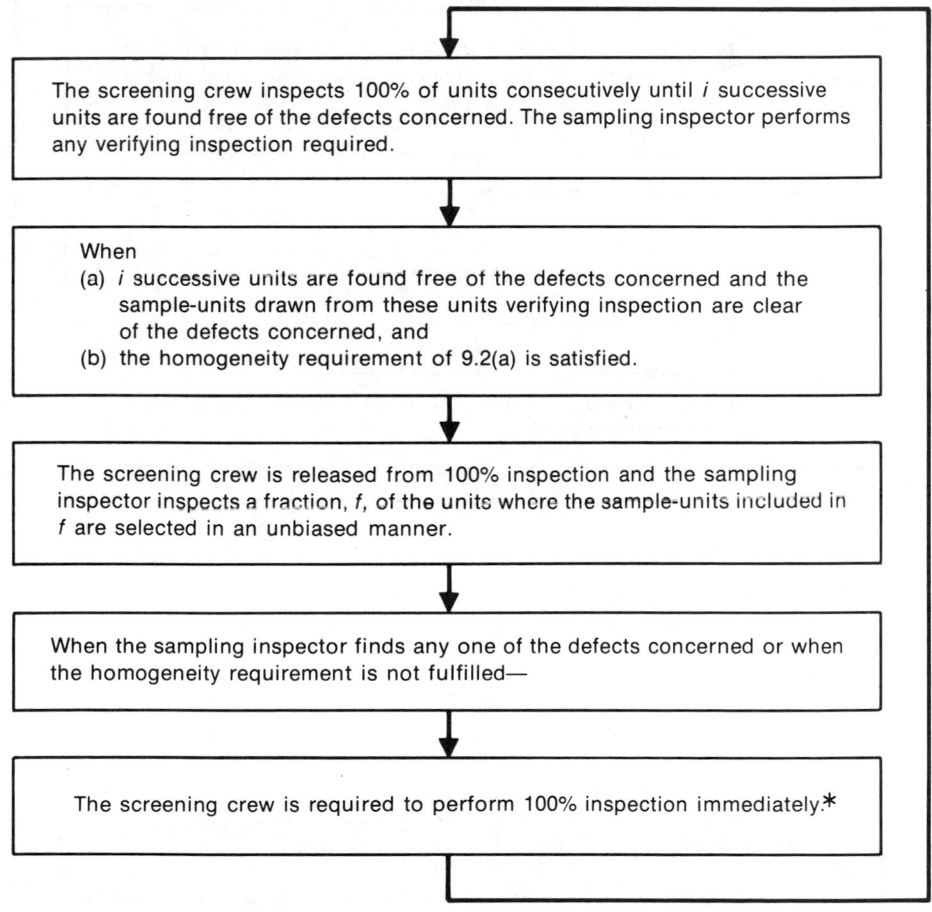

The screening crew inspects 100% of units consecutively until i successive units are found free of the defects concerned. The sampling inspector performs any verifying inspection required.
When
(a) i successive units are found free of the defects concerned and the sample-units drawn from these units verifying inspection are clear of the defects concerned, and
(b) the homogeneity requirement of 9.2(a) is satisfied.
The screening crew is released from 100% inspection and the sampling inspector inspects a fraction, f, of the units where the sample-units included in f are selected in an unbiased manner.
When the sampling inspector finds any one of the defects concerned or when the homogeneity requirement is not fulfilled—
The screening crew is required to perform 100% inspection immediately.*

*For critical defects, screening should begin with the unit of product just after the last defect-free sample-unit.

Figure 15–5 Procedure for CSP-1 plans.

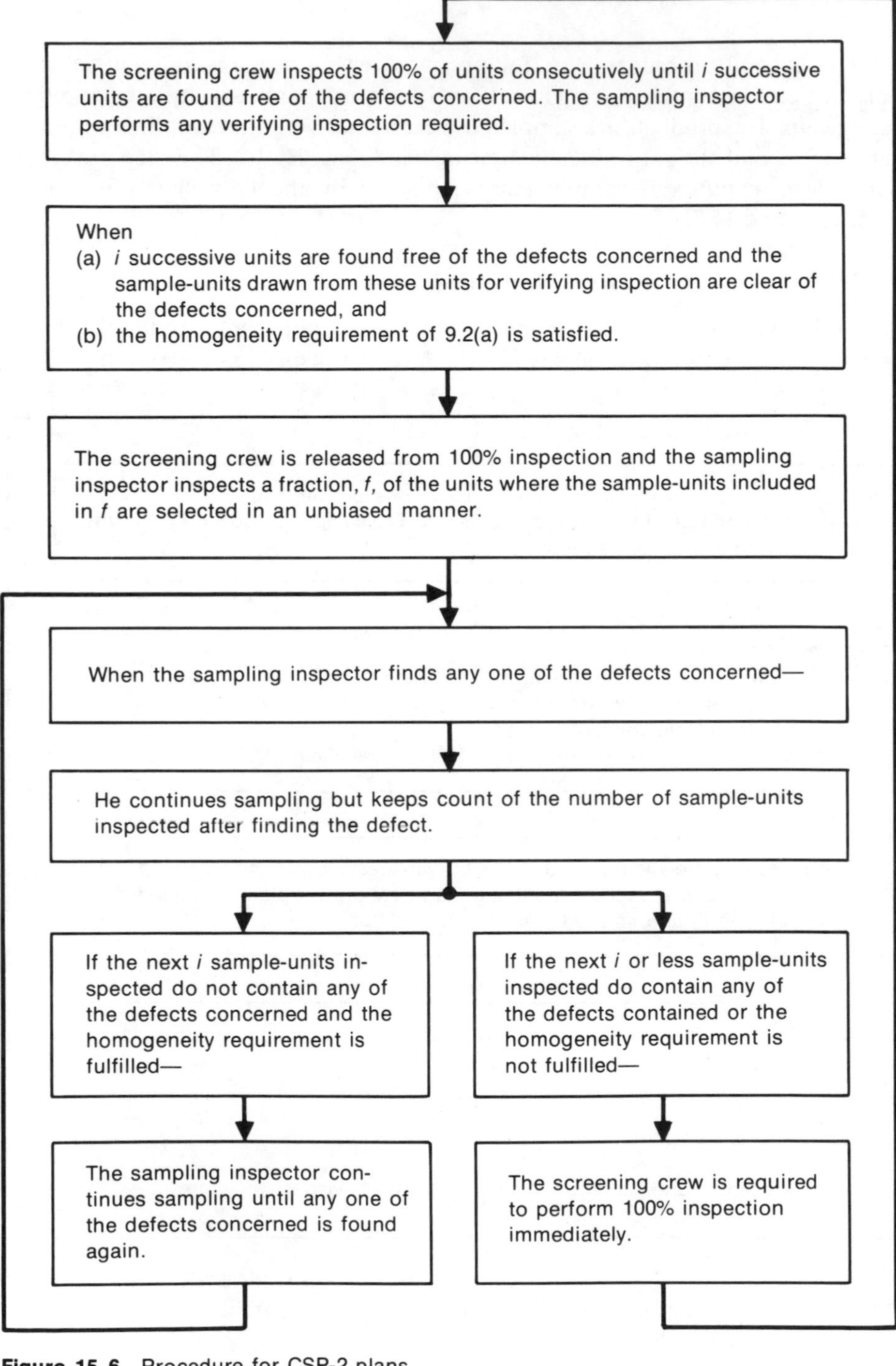
The screening crew inspects 100% of units consecutively until i successive units are found free of the defects concerned. The sampling inspector performs any verifying inspection required.
When
(a) i successive units are found free of the defects concerned and the sample-units drawn from these units for verifying inspection are clear of the defects concerned, and
(b) the homogeneity requirement of 9.2(a) is satisfied.
The screening crew is released from 100% inspection and the sampling inspector inspects a fraction, f, of the units where the sample-units included in f are selected in an unbiased manner.
When the sampling inspector finds any one of the defects concerned—
He continues sampling but keeps count of the number of sample-units inspected after finding the defect.
If the next i sample-units inspected do not contain any of the defects concerned and the homogeneity requirement is fulfilled—
If the next i or less sample-units inspected do contain any of the defects contained or the homogeneity requirement is not fulfilled—
The sampling inspector continues sampling until any one of the defects concerned is found again.
The screening crew is required to perform 100% inspection immediately.

Figure 15–6 Procedure for CSP-2 plans.

running quality of the units. Like the single-level plan, the inspection level begins at 100%. If there are no defects found after i units are inspected or tested, a fraction f is inspected; if the operation continues with no defectives, a still lower f_2 number

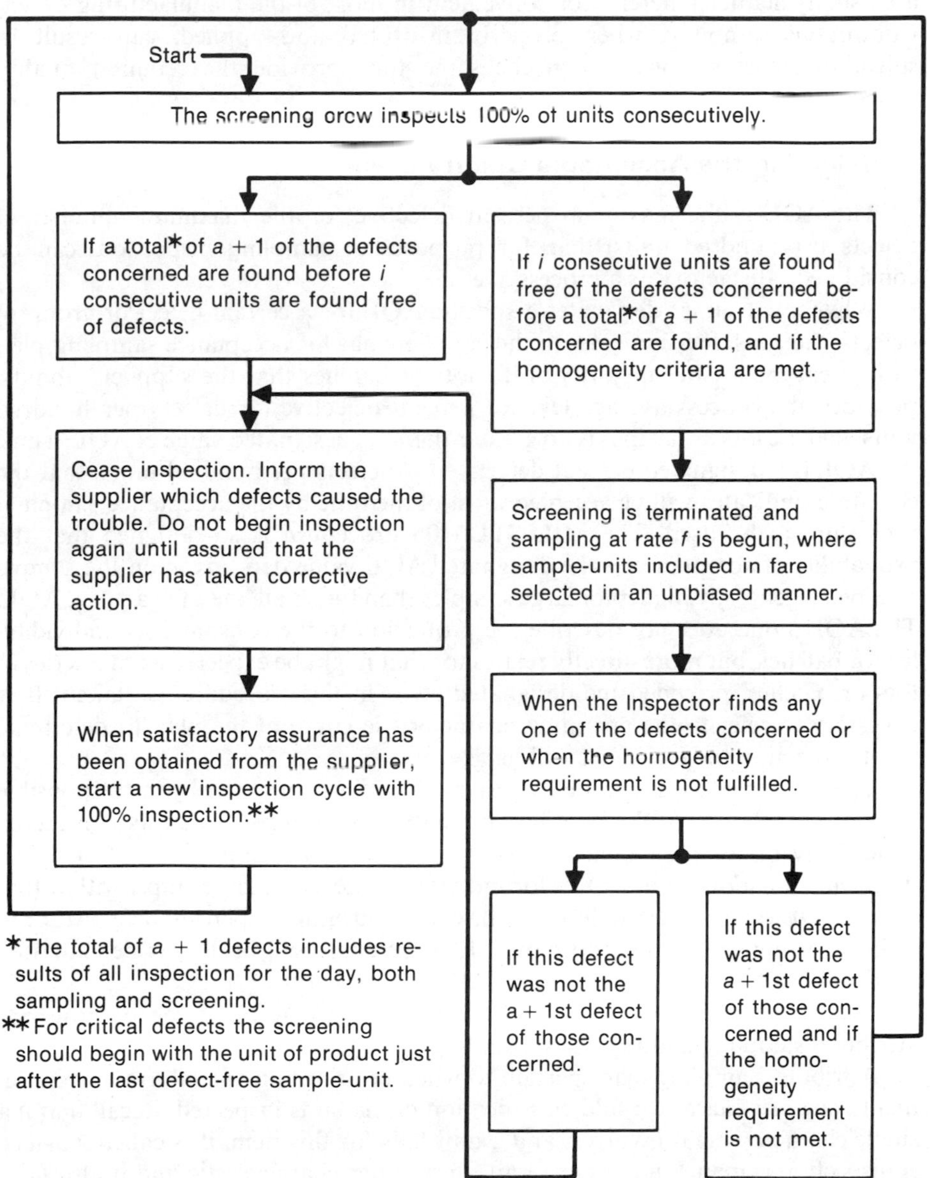

Figure 15–7 Figure procedure for CSP-A plans.

of units is inspected. This procedure is continued through several levels of reduced or increased inspection, depending on the running quality level.

Continuous acceptance sampling is an excellent method in some manufacturing plants. Where units of product are manufactured on an assembly line, lot quantities are usually neither inherent nor convenient in most of the manufacturing cycles. Continuous sampling, when properly instituted and applied, can result in substantial cost savings and at the same time provide the required quality protection.

Selecting the Acceptable Quality Level

The AQL is the maximum percent defective (or the maximum number of defects per hundred units) that, for purposes of sampling inspection, can be considered satisfactory as a process average.

When a consumer designates a specific AQL for a certain defect or group of defects, the consumer indicates to the supplier that his acceptance sampling plan will accept the greater majority of the lots or batches that the supplier submits, provided the process average level of percent defective (or defects per hundred units) in these lots or batches is no greater than the designated value of AQL. Thus, the AQL is a designated percent defective (or defects per hundred units) that the consumer indicates will be accepted most of the time by the acceptance sampling procedure to be used. The MIL–STD–105 procedure is so designed that the probability of acceptance at the designated AQL value depends upon the sample size, being generally higher for large samples than for small ones, for a given AQL. The AQL alone does not describe the protection to the consumer for individual lots or batches, but more directly relates to what might be expected from a series of lots or batches, provided the designated steps in the procedure are taken. It is necessary to refer to the operating characteristic curve of the plan to determine what protection the consumer will have.

The AQL to be used is normally designated in the contract or by the responsible authority. Different AQLs may be designated for groups of defects considered collectively or for individual defects. An AQL for a group of defects may be designated in addition to AQL's for individual defects, or subgroups, within that group. AQL values of 10.0 or less may be expressed either in percent defective, or in defects per hundred units; those over 10.0 are expressed in defects per hundred units only.

There are two broad categories into which sampling plans can be grouped: attributes sampling and variables sampling.

Attributes sampling plans pertain to whether or not units conform to requirements, and are thus a two-fold classification of the units inspected. Recall that if a single characteristic is involved, and a unit fails for this item, it is called a *defect.* If inspection is made on the same unit for another characteristic and it also fails, then there are now two defects on the same unit. This nonconforming unit is called a *defective* because it contains more than one defect. Attributes sampling plans may be set upon the basis of defective units or in terms of defects per 100 units. In the latter case, all defects observed are counted, even if several occur on a single unit. This method allows controls to be established on all characteristics so that the expected level of quality may be compared with the running level.

Although many types of sampling plans may be used, from an economical standpoint, sampling plans with desired protection either for a series of lots (AOQL) or for a single lot (Lot Tolerance Percent Defective—Consumer's Risk Concept), the Dodge-Romig single and double sampling tables have been found to be the most suitable.

Variables sampling plans usually permit the use of much smaller sample sizes to provide the same protection that the attributes sampling plans may furnish. Acceptance criteria may be based upon allowable averages, where the variability is fairly well controlled, or may be based upon both averages and ranges, or averages and standard deviations. The first variables sampling plan was placed in the field in 1934 for copper tie wire. Plans may be made for lot tolerance–consumer risk values, average outgoing quality (AOQL) values, acceptable quality level (AQL) values, or combinations of these. Operating characteristics may be computed for each and every plan. Such OC curves provide some information as to the severity and variability of each plan. In actual operations, combinations of all these various sampling plans will prove most effective and result in maximum profits for the company involved.

15.11 Sampling Risks and Operating Characteristic Curves

If 100% inspection is performed, statistics per se are not involved; the appropriate action is purely a technical question. However, data obtained from wuch 100% inspections are often utilized to establish standard quality levels and control charts for both attributes and variables data. Statistics enter into the picture when the quality of the lot is appraised on the basis of a representative sample drawn from the lot. If action is taken on the basis of the sample result, there is inevitably a risk that the action may not be appropriate; the probability (or lack of it) that is associated with these risks is a statistical matter.

Any lot-by-lot sampling plan has as its primary purpose the acceptance of good lots and the rejection of bad lots. What distinguishes a good lot from a bad lot varies with the part, with the customer, and with the manufacturer. The customer would naturally like all of the parts he receives to be free of defectives. The manufacturer, however, might incur large additional costs most of which would have to be borne by the customer in order to prevent the shipment of possibly a small number of defectives. Performing 100% inspection—particularly on high-volume production parts—is costly and should be avoided, if possible. If screening inspection (100% inspection) is mandatory, the cost of inspection obviously adds to the selling price of the item. The manufacturer and consumer usually reach an agreement on what constitutes acceptable quality. If lots are submitted at the agreed quality level or better, the lots would be accepted; otherwise, they would be rejected.

Whenever sampling is involved, there is always the risk that some good lots may be rejected and some bad lots accepted. An ideal sampling plan is one which rejects all lots worse than the standard, and accepts all lots equal to or better than the standard. Such an ideal is normally impossible in acceptance sampling, since the procedure is based on laws of chance. However, if an ideal plan could be designed, its performance could be diagrammed, giving a result like the one shown in figure 15-8.

For example, suppose that an ideal sampling plan could be devised so that all lots with less than 4% defective would be accepted and all lots with more than 4% defective would be rejected. A sampling plan with this capability is shown graphically in figure 15-9. However, no sampling plan actually exists that can discriminate between good and bad lots all of the time. Even 100% inspection under highly controlled and ideal conditions may not accomplish this goal.

The capability of a given plan to distinguish between varying degrees of good and bad quality can be accurately calculated. The fact that these risks can be quantified makes it possible to state the risks in advance and describe with a very high degree of mathematical accuracy the quantities of product that will be accepted if the quality standard is met, and the quantity rejected if the standard is not met. Such calculations—based on the mathematical theory of probability—provide the basis for the curve shown in figure 15-9. As in the case of the ideal sampling plan, performance of any sampling plan can be shown graphically by these curves. Figure 15-9 compares the single sampling plan with sample size 80 and acceptance number equal to 3 to the theoretical ideal sampling plan.

Each sampling plan has an unique risk pattern which is represented by an operating characteristic (OC) curve for the plan. Therefore, each OC curve is distinctly different, a property which provides an effective means for ascertaining the effect of changes in sample sizes and acceptance numbers on the acceptance or

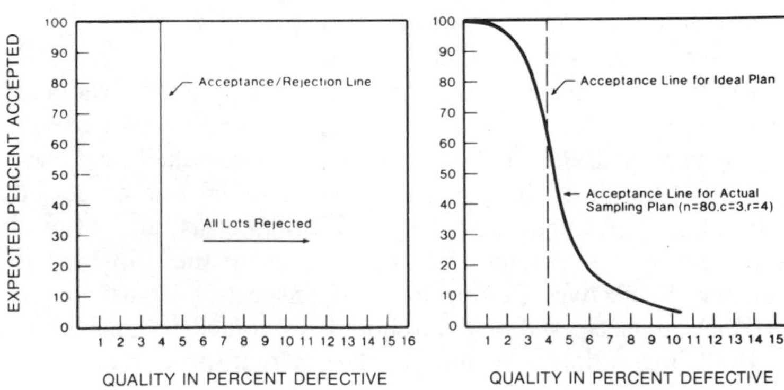

Figure 15–8 Performance diagram for an ideal sampling plan.

Figure 15–9 Comparing an ideal plan with an actual plan.

rejection of lots. The proper sampling plan can be determined from studying the OC curve for each plan under consideration. By studying the OC curves, it is possible to compare the relative risks of two or more sampling plans for a given sampling situation. By virtue of the OC curve, sampling tables can be constructed to depict the risks of incorrect decisions in advance, making it possible to select plans which will have risk factors that are acceptable from the viewpoint of both the supplier and the consumer.

In selecting a suitable sampling plan, it is beneficial to have specific knowledge of their operating characteristics. This information can best be presented by the operating characteristic curve for each plan.

Another typical OC curve for a sampling plan is illustrated in figure 15-10. Each point on this curve shows the percentage of submitted inspection lots for their particular percent defective that will be accepted by the plan. For example, if a number of lots containing 0.65% defective items were submitted to the plan, 95% of them would be accepted, according to this OC curve. This property of the plan can be expressed another way: if a lot containing 0.65% defective items were submitted, the probability is 0.95 that it would be accepted. If lots with 3.6% of the items defective were submitted, the curve shows that only 10% of them would be accepted.

15.12 Operating Characteristic (OC) Curves

Although many sampling tables include operating characteristic curves for the sampling plans given in their tables, most such curves are only given for single sampling plans, since probability of acceptance values for double sampling plans

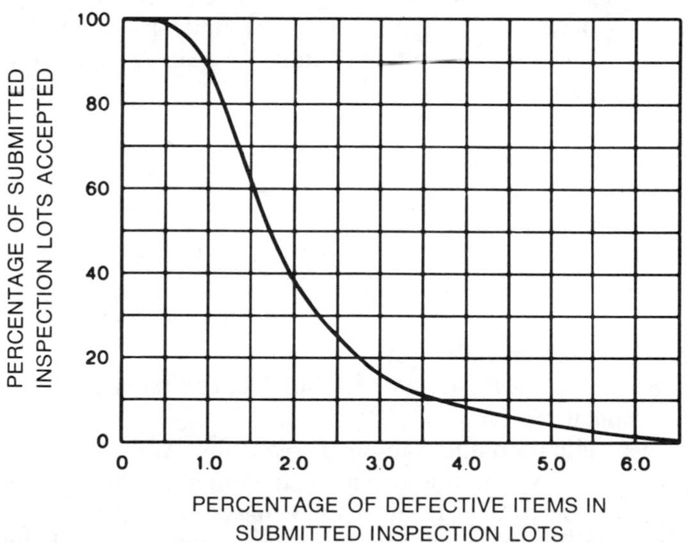

Figure 15–10 OC curve of a sampling plan.

and multiple sampling plans require a large number of compound probabilities. We will give a few examples showing how to determine such OC curves. More advanced texts on statistical quality control cover such OC curves for the more complex sampling plans. Probability of acceptance (P_a) values may be determined for percent defective plans by use of the p binomial. For defects per hundred units, the Poisson exponential based on pn values is generally used. In general, these Poisson probability values may be readily obtained from tables or roughly from the graph in figure 15-3.

Many sampling plans permitting two or more samples, such as double sampling and multiple sampling, use only acceptance numbers and include no possible early rejection values such as are included in the double and multiple sampling plans in MIL–STD–105D. The basis for comparing probability of acceptance values for the two systems is provided by the following sampling plans using sample sizes per code letter H of MIL–STD–105D. For single sampling, both systems use the same mathematical expression for computing P_a values. In double sampling, where a smaller rejection number is used in the first sample than is permitted when no rejection values are listed for sampling plans, the P_a value is decreased slightly. In multiple sampling plans with Re values included in the criteria specified, the P_a equation omits many possible combinations for acceptance applicable when no Re values are noted. In single sampling in all cases, P_a for any p value is the same for both systems and is the sum of all possible probabilities from 0 to c possible defects in the sample, where c is the acceptance number.

When the P_a equation has terms that cover more than zero defects or defectives, cumulated probability values may be obtained from the tables rather than by summing individual terms. These cumulated values are best illustrated by the probabilities obtained for P_a in single sampling. A single sampling plan from MIL–STD–105D illustrates this point. Using sample size code letter H, with inspection level II specified, where lots contain between 281 and 500 units each corresponding to code letter H and an AQL value of 2.5% or 2.5 units per hundred defective, the single sampling plan per table 15.2 is $n = 50$, $c = \text{Ac} = 3$, and $r = \text{Re} = 4$. The latter value is not needed for this example. Probability of acceptance values are determined from

$$P_a = \sum_{i=0}^{i=3} P_{i,n} = P_{0,n} + P_{1,n} + P_{2,n} + P_{3,n} = P_{0,50} + P_{1,50} + P_{2,50} + P_{3,50} \qquad (5)$$

For any selected p value, tables listing cumulated values for the Poisson exponential provide either P_a values directly or may be cumulated in the reverse order, giving P_r values. Then $P_a = 1 - P_r$ should be tabulated, corresponding to the p value used in the computations for pn.

The corresponding double sampling plan for $\text{AQL} = 2.5\%$ is $n_1 = 32$, $c_1 = 1$; $n_2 = 32$, $c_2 = 4$. For this commercial sampling plan with no rejection numbers given, P_a is determined from the following equation. Terms in parentheses are to be read from Poisson exponential tables for cumulated probabilities, while single terms are to be read from tables giving individual probability values.

$$P_a = (P_{0,n_1} + P_{1,n_1}) + P_{2,n_1}(P_{0,n_2} + P_{1,n_3} + P_{2,n_2}) + P_{3,n_1}(P_{0,n_2} + P_{1,n_2}) + P_{4,n_1}P_{0,n_2} \quad (6)$$

where $n_1 = 32$ and $n_2 = 32$. Where p binomial probability values are to be used instead of the Poisson exponential, binomial tables are available for many values of n that give both individual and cumulated probability values. When tables are used properly, the time for computing the desired P_a values is greatly reduced.

In the following examples, which show how to compute operating characteristic (OC) curves, it is also shown how to obtain sufficient P_a values for sets of p values by the proper use of individual and cumulated terms. An example is given for the exact plan given in MIL–STD–105D, including the use of rejection numbers. The desired P_a value for AQL = 2.5% is 0.95. For the single sampling plan, the Poisson exponential cumulated value for $pn = 0.025(50) = 1.25$ is found by interpolation to be $1 - 0.038432 = 0.961568$, slightly greater than the desired value of 0.95. Interpolated values are often slightly in error; computing the exact value gives 0.961731. The difference is negligible. Interpolation was between $pn = 1.2$ and $pn = 1.3$, using a value midway between the values in the tables. Values for the p binomial for $p = 0.02$ and $p = 0.03$ are 0.982242 for 0.02 and 0.937240 for 0.03. Linear interpolation gives $P_a = 0.959741$ for 0.025, while computing probability values by a ten-place logarithmic table gives $P_a = 0.963796$. This comparison shows that interpolated values are accurate enough for these computations.

For the double sampling plan, $n_1 = n_2 = 32$ with $p = 0.025$, $pn_1 = pn_2 = 0.80$. For this pn value, Poisson exponential tables give individual and cumulated terms directly and no interpolation is needed. Using equation (6) gives

$$P_a = 0.808792 + 0.143785(0.952577) + 0.038343(0.808792) + 0.007669(0.449329)$$

$$= 0.808792 + 0.136966 + 0.031012 + 0.003446 = 0.980216$$

For this case, MIL–STD–105D uses the double sampling plan $n_1 = 32$, Ac = 1, Re = 4; $n_2 = 32$, Ac = 4, Re = 5; hence the last term in equation (6) does not apply. Consequently the applicable $P_a = 0.976770$, is slightly greater than the stipulated 0.95 value. Table 15.6 gives the p values for single sampling that result in a P_a value of 0.95. For the AQL value of 2.5%, this table gives 2.77% as the p value for which $P_a = 0.95$. Similarly, for double sampling the p value for $P_a = 0.95$ is about 2.8% rather than exactly 2.5%.

The number of terms used to obtain P_a values for multiple sampling plans is much greater than those for double sampling. To illustrate this, the corresponding multiple sampling plan for AQL = 2.5% given for sample size code letter H in table 15.5 taken from MIL–STD–105D is reproduced as table 15.13.

Particular attention should be paid to the fact that in this multiple sampling plan, two samples must be inspected before the lot can be accepted, even though the first sample contains no defectives. Rejection can be determined and placed in effect if three or more defects or defectives are found in the first sample of thirteen units, thus stopping the inspection early when a nonconforming lot is found.

TABLE 15.13

Sample Size Code Letter	*Sample*	*Sample Size*	*Cumulative Sample Size*	*AQL* = 2.5% *Ac*	*– Re*
H	First	13	13	†	3
	Second	13	26	0	3
	Third	13	39	1	4
	Fourth	13	52	2	5
	Fifth	13	65	3–	6
	Sixth	13	78	4	6
	Seventh	13	91	6	7

† = Acceptance not permitted at this sample size.

A better understanding of how to apply all types of sampling plans is to outline in tabular form all the ways a lot may be accepted. When such a table is prepared, the complete equation for obtaining P_a values for any p value may be readily written. It may be better to also tabulate the various probability values that apply for all the possible ways to accept a lot. Table 15.14 does both for the above multiple

TABLE 15.14 Determination of P_a for AQL = 2.5 % for Multiple Sampling Plan per Sample Code Letter H of MIL–STD–105D Using Poisson Exponential Probability Values

Multiple Sampling Plan AQL = 2.5%, *Code Letter H*

Sample No.		*Sample Size*	*Cum. Samples*	*Ac*	*Re*
1	n_1	13	13	†	3
2	n_2	13	26	0	3
3	n_3	13	39	1	4
4	n_4	13	52	2	5
5	n_5	13	65	3	6
6	n_6	13	78	4	6
7	n_7	13	91	6	7

† = Acceptance not permitted at this sample size.

Possible Ways to Meet Criteria for Acceptance

Ref. No.	$n_1 + n_2$			$n_3 + n_4$		$n_4 + n_5$		$n_5 + n_6$		$n_6 + n_7$	
	n_1	n_2	n_3		n_4		n_5		n_6		n_7
1	0										
2	1		0								
3	1		1		0						
4	1		1		1		0				
5	1		1		1		1		0		
6	1		1		1		1		1		0, 1
7	1		1		1		2			0, 1	
8	1		1		2			0			
9	1		1		2			1			0, 1
10	1		2			0					
11	1		2			1			0		
12	1		2			1			1		0, 1
13	2			0							
14	2			1			0				
15	2			1			1		0		
16	2			1			1		1		0, 1
17	2			1			2			0, 1	
18	2			2				0			
19	2			2				1			0, 1

For $p = 2.5\%$ or 0.025

	$n = 13, pn = 0.325$	$n = 26, pn = 0.650$
P_0	0.722527	0.522046*
P_1	0.234821	0.339330*
P_2	0.038158	0.110282*
P_0+P_1	0.957348	0.861376*

Probabilities Based on Poisson's Exponential Binomial Limit.
* Probabilities for 2 Samples Combined, $n_i + n_{i+1} = 13 + 13 = 26$.

Row No.	$n_1 + n_2$	n_3	$n_3 + n_4$	n_4	$n_4 + n_5$	n_5	$n_5 + n_6$	n_6	$n_6 + n_7$	n_7	Contribution to P_a
1	0.522046*										0.522046
2	0.339330*	0.722527									0.245175
3	0.339330*	0.234821		0.722527							0.057572
4	0.339330*	0.234821		0.234821		0.722527					0.013519
5	0.339330*	0.234821		0.234821		0.234821		0.722527			0.003175
6	0.339330*	0.234821		0.234821		0.234821		0.234821		0.957348	0.000988
7	0.339330*	0.234821		0.234821		**0.038158**			0.861376*		0.000615
8	0.339330*	0.234821		0.038158			0.522046*				0.001587
9	0.339330*	0.234821		0.038158			0.339330*			0.957348	0.000988
10	0.339330*	0.038158			0.522046*						0.006760
11	0.339330*	0.038158			0.339330*			0.722527			0.003175
12	0.339330*	0.038158			0.339330*			0.234821		0.957348	0.000988
13	0.110282*		0.522046*								0.057572
14	0.110282*		0.339330*			0.722527					0.027038
15	0.110282*		0.339330*			0.234821		0.722527			0.006349
16	0.110282*		0.339330*			0.234821		0.234821		0.957348	0.001975
17	0.110282*		0.339330*			**0.038158**			0.861376*		0.001230
18	0.110282*		0.110282*				0.522046*				0.006349
19	0.110282*		0.110282*				0.339330*			0.957348	0.003951
											P_a = 0.961652

sampling plan. It provides a good format to use when quality engineers must evaluate P_a values to aid in selecting the most economical sampling plans.

This example covering multiple sampling shows when additional samples may be taken and also indicates when two sample size units must be combined to secure possible results that will permit acceptance of the lot. The many Re values provide for early rejections when an excessive number of defects have been observed in the first few samples. Table 15.14 presents all the terms necessary to determine a P_a value for any p value between 0 and 1.00 for the above multiple sampling plan. It covers all the P_i values that should be used in obtaining the operating characteristic curve for this multiple sampling plan where AQL is 2.5% or 2.5 units per hundred defective.

Many P_a values are required to graph an OC curve. For the single sampling plans $n = 50$, Ac = 1, Re = 2 and $n = 50$, Ac = 3, Re = 4, table 15.15 gives sufficient P_a values to graph their OC curves. Table 15.2 shows nine sets of Ac and Re values for sample size code letter H with a sample size of 50 specified. In single sampling, Re values are redundant and only Ac = c values need be listed. The nine SS plans have the following c values for the specified AQL values listed.

AQL%	0.25	1.0	1.5	2.5	4.0	6.5	10	15	25
c	0	<u>1</u>	2	<u>3</u>	5	7	10	14	21

The underlined *c* values are used as examples in the text.

Chart H on table 15.6 presents OC curves for these nine plans. Curves 2 and 4 provide graphs of the P_a values given in detail in table 15.15. Table X–H–1 lists the corresponding *p* values determined from Poisson exponential tables for nine P_a values (1.0 to 0.99), whereas table 15.15 uses a set of *p* values and computes exact P_a values for such points on the graph. Both systems provide sufficient data to draw the OC curve for any single sampling plan. The second procedure used in presenting examples in this text is easier to apply for making the necessary computations for all types of sampling plans for attributes inspection.

TABLE 15.15 Data for Construction of OC Curve Based on Poisson Table for Sample Size of 50 and Acceptance Numbers of 1 and 3

Fraction Defective in Lot (p')	*Expected Average No. of Defectives in Sample of 50* (np')	*Probability of Acceptance of Lot According to Acceptance No. of 1*	*Probability of Acceptance of Lot According to Acceptance No. of 3*
0.002	0.10	0.995	1.000
0.004	0.20	0.982	1.000
0.006	0.30	0.963	1.000
0.007	0.35	0.951	1.000
0.008	0.40	0.938	0.999
0.010	0.50	0.910	0.998
0.016	0.80	0.809	0.991
0.018	0.90	0.772	0.987
0.020	1.00	0.736	0.981
0.022	1.10	0.699	0.974
0.024	1.20	0.663	0.966
0.025	1.25	0.645	0.962
0.026	1.30	0.627	0.957
0.030	1.50	0.558	0.934
0.032	1.60	0.525	0.921
0.034	1.70	0.493	0.907
0.036	1.80	0.463	0.891
0.038	1.90	0.434	0.875
0.040	2.00	0.406	0.857
0.044	2.20	0.355	0.819
0.048	2.40	0.308	0.779
0.052	2.60	0.268	0.736
0.056	2.80	0.231	0.692
0.060	3.00	0.199	0.647
0.080	4.00	0.091	0.433
0.100	5.00	0.040	0.265
0.120	6.00	0.017	0.151
0.160	8.00	0.003	0.042

The OC curves constructed from table 15.15 are shown in figure 15-11. The data for the table are obtained as follows. Various fraction defectives are assumed for incoming lots (left-hand column). A sufficient number must be tabulated to locate points for constructing the OC curve. To find the average number of defectives in submitted lots of a given fraction defective (column two), the fraction defective is multiplied by the sample size, which is 50 in this case. Column two values are then looked up in the Poisson table to obtain the probabilities of acceptance.

The table tabulated is interpreted in the following manner. If random samples of 50 were taken from submitted lots that were 0.01 (1%) defective, we would expect the average number of defectives in the samples to be 0.01 (50) or 0.50. With an average of ½ defective per sample and an acceptance number of 1 (1 defective allowed while still accepting the lot) we would expect to accept such lots 91% of the time. Other probability values selected from the tabulated table are illustrated below.

For an Acceptance Number of 1 and a Rejection Number of 2:

1. Accept lots that are 0.2% defective 99.5% of the time.
2. Accept lots that are 3.0% defective 55.8% of the time.

For an Acceptance Number of 3 and a Rejection Number of 4:

1. Accept lots that are 3.0% defective 93.4% of the time.
2. Accept lots that are 12.0% defective. 15.1% of the time.

For the acceptance number of 1, the OC curve of figure 15-11 tells us that if a supplier were to submit a large number of shipments that were 2% defective, we would expect to accept 74% of the shipments.

If the supplier submitted a large number of shipments that were 4% defective, we could expect to accept 41% of them, and to reject the remaining 59%.

Shipments that were 6% defective would be 20% accepted and 80% rejected.

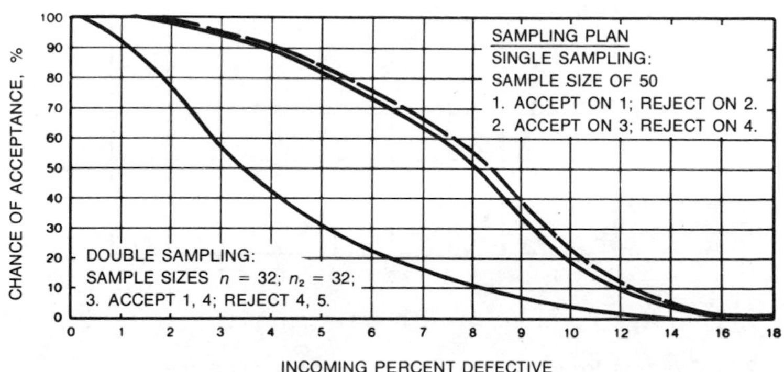

Figure 15–11 OC curve of a sampling plan.

If a supplier submitted a particular shipment that was 3% defective, its chance for acceptance would be 56%.

For the acceptance number of 3, the probability of acceptance values for the levels discussed above are much larger, whereas this sampling plan for $c = 1$ usually would be used when we have decided that we are willing to accept material 0.7% defective. It is called a 0.7% AQL plan, as it provides the 0.95 probability of acceptance value stipulated for MIL–STD–105D sampling plans for AQL values. However, if a supplier were to submit material 0.7%, we would reject approximately 5% of the shipment. This is the risk taken by the supplier when material is submitted at the AQL percent defective level of quality. Of course, if better material were submitted, there would be less risk of rejection. However, note that where the AQL was set at 2.5%, then for $c = 3$ the probability of acceptance is 0.962, which is very close to the desired value of 0.95. Integral values of sample sizes and acceptance numbers often make it impossible to obtain a P_a value of 0.95 exactly. The series of lot sizes, sample sizes, and AQL values were originally selected on the basis of several preferred number scales. This reduces the size of the sampling tables to one that is practical to use.

Figure 15-12 shows the OC curves for varying sample sizes and acceptance and rejection numbers, all with about the same AQL values. The same acceptance and rejection numbers $c = 3$ and $r = 4$ as used for AQL = 2.5% with $n = 50$ are

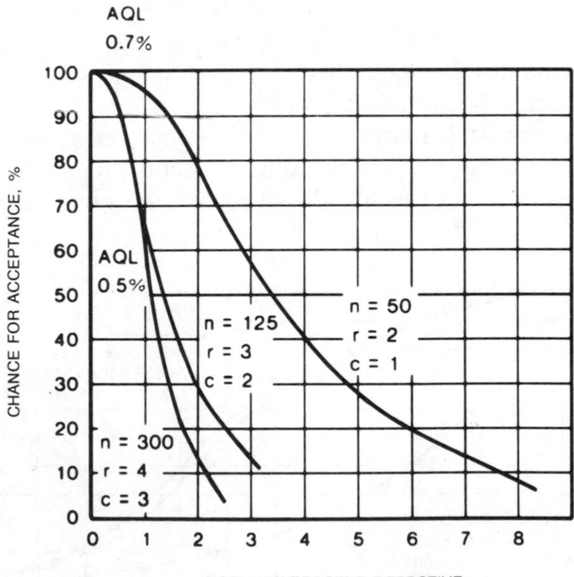

Figure 15–12 OC curves for varying sample sizes and acceptance and rejection numbers.

shown in the graph, with $n = 300$ rather than 50. Its OC curve shows that for a consumer's risk of about 10%, the LTPD value is about 2.5%. For the same quality level of 2.5% and acceptance and rejection numbers of $c = 3$ and $r = 4$, one plan favors the producer with $P_a = 0.95$ and the other favors the consumer with $P_a = 0.10$.

Operating characteristic curves based on P_a values for double sampling require many compound and cumulated probabilities, as noted previously. They can best be computed by a programmed computer. One example is sufficient to indicate how they must be determined. The MIL–STD–105D code letter H double sampling plan for AQL = 2.5% is used as an example. Fortunately, the two samples have the same sample size of 32. The corresponding single sampling P_a value is for $n = 50$, $c = \text{Ac} = 3$, $r = \text{Re} = 4$, while for double sampling the plan is shown:

*Double Sampling Plan for **AQL** = 2.5%*

Sample Size	*Cumulative Sample Size*	*Acceptance Number*	*Rejection Number*
32	32	1	4
32	64	4	5

No rejection numbers are given in the Dodge-Romig sampling inspection tables; only acceptance numbers are tabulated as noted previously. The relation for P_a must eliminate for the MIL–STD–105D the first sample for which the Rejection Number for the first sample is different than the Rejection Number for the second sample. The value of P_a in terms of cumulated probabilities and for the above sampling plan is as follows.

$$P_a = (P_{0,n_1} + P_{1,n_1}) + P_{2,n_1}(P_{0,n_2} + P_{1,n_2} + P_{2,n_2}) + P_{3,n_1}\,(P_{0,n_2} + P_{1,n_2}) \qquad (7)$$

Although the acceptance number is four for the first and second samples combined, when four nonconforming units occur in the first sample the lot is immediately rejected.

Table 15.16 summarizes the items that need to be considered in computing P_a values for a series of p values in order to graph the OC curve for a particular sampling plan. Only items involved in single and double sampling are listed. Table 15.14 adequately covers the corresponding multiple sampling plan.

The double sampling plan has an OC curve with slightly larger P_a values than those obtained for the corresponding single sampling plan. (See figure 15-11.) If desired, the student may also draw these two OC curves for single sampling and double sampling. If more points are desired, they may be readily computed by adding more p values in table 15.16.

TABLE 15.16 Summarizes the items that need to be considered in Computing P_a Values for a Series of p Values in Order to Graph the OC Curve for a particular Sampling Plan. Only Items involved in Single and Double Sampling are Listed. Table 15.14 Adequately Covers the Corresponding Multiple Sampling Plan

Sample Size Code Letter H; Acceptable Quality Level AQL = 2.5%		
	Single Sampling	*Double Sampling*
Sample Size	$n = 50$	$n_1 = 32, n_2 = 32; n_1 + n_2 = 64$
Acceptance No.	$Ac = 3$	$Ac_1 = 1, Ac_2 = 4$
Rejection No.	$Re = 4$	$Re_1 = 4, Re_2 = 5$
pn Values	$pn = p \times 50$	$pn_1 = p \times 32 = pn_2 = p \times 32$
P_a equation	$P_a = P_{0,n_1} + P_{1,n} + P_{2,n}$	$P_a = (P_{0,n_1} + P_{1,n_1}) + P_{2,n_1}(P_{0,n_2} + P_{1,n_2} + P_{2,n_2}) + P_{3,n_1}(P_{0,n_2} + P_{1,n_2})$

Double Sampling: $n_1 = n_2 = 32$

(1) p	(2) pn	(3) $P_{0,n_1} + P_{1,n_1}$	(4) P_{2,n_1}	(5) $P_{0,n_2} + P_{1,n_2} + P_{2,n_2}$	(6) (4) × (5)	(7) P_{3,n_1}	(8) $P_{0,n_2} + P_{1,n_2}$	(9) (7)(8)	(5) + (6) + (8) Pa	Single Sampling $n = 50, c = 3$ ph	Pa
0.025	0.80	0.809	0.144	0.953	0.1372	0.038	0.809	0.0307	0.977	1.25	0.962
0.05	1.60	0.525	0.258	0.783	0.2020	0.138	0.525	0.0724	0.799	2.50	0.758
0.075	2.40	0.308	0.262	0.570	0.1493	0.209	0.308	0.0644	0.522	3.75	0.484
0.100	3.20	0.171	0.209	0.380	0.0794	0.223	0.171	0.0381	0.288	5.00	0.265
0.125	4.00	0.092	0.146	0.238	0.0347	0.195	0.092	0.0179	0.145	6.25	0.130
0.150	4.80	0.048	0.095	0.143	0.0136	0.151	0.048	0.0072	0.069	7.50	0.059

15.13 Variables Inspection vs. Attributes Inspection

Variables inspection plans may be used in many cases where actual measurements may be taken. They have the disadvantage that separate criteria must be available for each characteristic. This disadvantage may be minimized by using the same sample size for each characteristic covered. Some products may have several critical characteristics requiring that exact data be recorded for each observed test or they may be automatically recorded. On the other hand, the sample size used for the same protection may often be much smaller than that required by attributes inspection. The simplest variables plan has criteria based only on averages. Such plans may be evaluated by the use of the operating characteristic for the plan used. Those desiring to use a large number of variables inspection plans should consult other sources for a more comprehensive coverage.

The examples that follow cover only single sampling plans for attributes and variables sampling plans based on lot quality protection with average outgoing quality limit (AOQL) values determined and presented for comparison purposes. The AOQL concept is discussed first. As noted below, all units in rejected lots must be inspected and defective units replaced. This is called *Condition 2*, where 100% screening of lots that are questionable is required.

Example 1 Average Outgoing Quality Limit, (AOQL)

Where a consumer is purchasing a product continuously from a single supplier or the producer wishes to control the fraction nonconforming in his product held in stock at or below some specified value, sampling plans may be set up under Condition 2 that give adequate assurance that the average outgoing quality P_A after inspection does not exceed some specified limiting value P_L, termed the average outgoing quality limit (AOQL). Such sampling plans assume

1. that all pieces in nonconforming lots are inspected for the quality characteristic under consideration, and
2. that all nonconforming pieces found in inspection are removed or corrected.

The average outgoing quality (AOQ), P_A, is defined as the expected fraction nonconforming in outgoing product after the elimination of nonconforming pieces found during the inspection process when the quality characteristic of the submitted product is controlled at p. In practice, each nonconforming piece found by inspection is removed and is usually replaced by a conforming piece. The average outgoing quality limit (AOQL), P_L, is defined as the

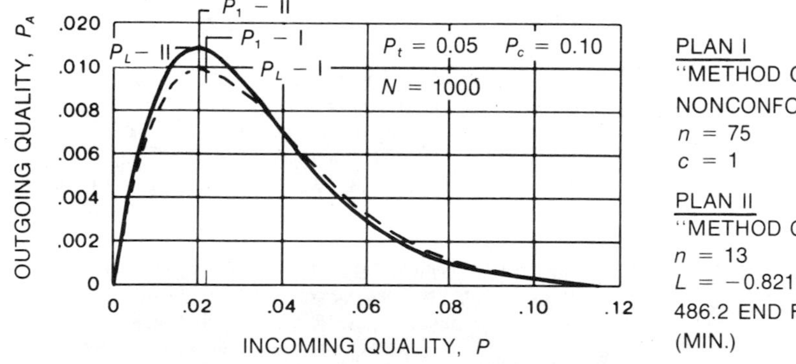

Figure 15–13 Average outgoing quality (AOQ), p_A, and average outgoing quality limit (AOQL), p_L.

maximum expected value of fraction nonconforming in the outgoing product or the maximum value of P_A that occurs when $p = p_1$.

Table 15.17 indicates the similarities and differences between the assumptions, criteria, and procedure for the determination of fraction nonconforming for the two methods under discussion, *method of fraction nonconforming* and *method of averages*.

TABLE 15.17 Comparison Between Assumptions, Criteria and Nature of Fraction Nonconforming Used in Setting Up Two Different Sampling Plan for a Single Quality Characteristic

"Method of Fraction Nonconforming"	*"Method of Averages"*
Universes	
Any distribution.	Distributions are normal with the same standard deviation for each "universe" in the set of "universes" under consideration.
Lots Selected from Universe	
Lots of size N	
Samples Selected from Lot	
All samples must be random samples.	
Single Sampling: Sample of size n. Double Sampling: Sample of size n_1 for first sample. Sample of size n_2 for second sample. Multiple Sampling (Number of samples $= i$): Samples of size n_1 for first sample. Sample of size n_j for jth sample. ($j = 1, 2, \ldots, i$.)	
Criteria for Classifying Lots as Conforming or Nonconforming	
Maximum allowable number of nonconforming pieces c in sample n. When number of nonconforming pieces observed in sample n exceeds c, the lot is classed as nonconforming.	Limiting value for observed average L for sample n, termed allowable average. When the average of n observations is less than L for minimum engineering limit or exceeds L for maximum engineering limit, the lot is classed as nonconforming.
Fraction Nonconforming, p	
Plan based directly on the statistic p. Selected values of the fraction nonconforming p are used directly in setting up sampling plans, where p is the fraction outside engineering limits and is considered as the probability of the occurrence of a nonconforming piece.	Plan based on statistic $\bar{X}$, with p values determined indirectly. Selected values of the average $\bar{X}$ are used to indicate fraction nonconforming p values used in setting up sampling plans, where p is the fraction outside engineering limits as determined from normal law integral tables corresponding to t values, which measure the distances of the engineering limits L_e from the average $\bar{X}$ in units of standard deviation σ. Thus p may be considered as the correlative of $\bar{X}$ since a one-to-one correspondence exists between them and the p value thus determined is the probability of the occurrence of a nonconforming piece for a quality characteristic in a state of statistical control at level $\bar{X}$, with standard deviation σ, for a normal universe.

Example 2 Probability of Acceptance Curves for Two Different Sampling Plans

The concepts of "Probability of Acceptance and Probability of Rejection" and "Average Outgoing Quality Limit" indicate the necessity of obtaining probability of acceptance P_a values for a series of p values. In evaluating the protection afforded by any sampling plan it is not sufficient to consider only the consumer's risk and the producer's risk. It is desirable to know the exact nature of the P_a curve for all possible p values rather than two P_a values corresponding respectively to $p = p_t$ and $p = \bar{p}$. Figure 15-14 presents two such P_a curves, both derived from single sampling plans, where only the results of a single initial sample are used in determining nonconformance ($i = 1$), based on a lot tolerance $p_t = 0.05$, a consumer's risk $P_C = 0.10$, and a lot size $N = 1000$.

The P_a curve denoted as Curve I corresponds to Plan I, the "method of fraction nonconforming," that results in a minimum average amount of inspection per lot I_m for a quality characteristic having a process average fraction nonconforming $\bar{p} = 0.24$ percent (the process average value for illumination). Curve II corresponds to Plan II, the "method of averages," which results in a minimum average amount of inspection per lot I_m for $\bar{p} = 0.24$ percent. By definition, I is the average amount of inspection per lot for a quality characteristic in a state of statistical control at $\bar{X}$ such that the probability of the occurrence of a nonconforming piece is p and I_m is the minimum value of I. In practice, values of I and I_m are usually determined for $p = \bar{p}$ but in certain cases a series of I values may be given for various values of p and this particular case is distinguished from other possible cases where $p \neq \bar{p}$, by using the symbols $\bar{I}$ and $\bar{I}_m$ when $p = \bar{p}$.

It is practically impossible to set up two different sampling plans that will give identical P_a curves for all values of p. The two curves of figure 15-14 differ very little, so that for all practical purposes the two plans may be said to classify about the same proportion of lots as conforming for any value of p, the

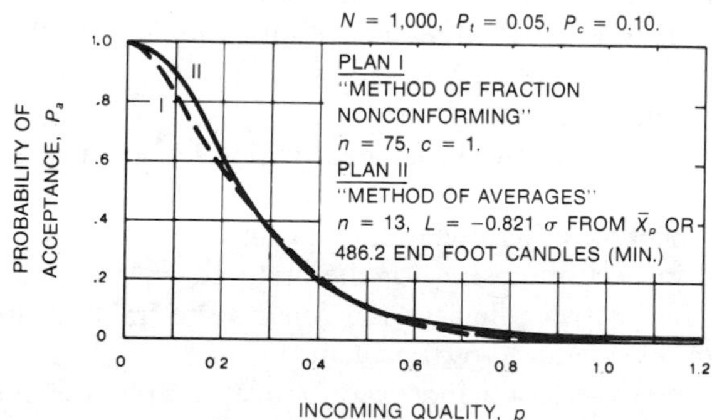

Figure 15–14 Probability of acceptance curves comparing two sampling plans.

fraction nonconforming in submitted product. The P_a curve for the method of averages has been computed on the assumption that the distribution of the quality characteristic is normal and the standard deviation remains the same for every "universe" of the quality characteristic regardless of the value of $\bar{X}$. It would be a different curve for every different assumed "universe," while the P_a curve for the "method of fraction nonconforming" is the same for any distribution of a quality characteristic. Compensating for this limitation is the fact that Plan II, method of averages, requires only 1.5 percent of the product of $\bar{p}$ quality inspected while Plan I, method of fraction nonconforming, requires 8.9 percent of $\bar{p}$ quality product inspected, almost 6 times that required by Plan II.

Both sampling plans give almost the same protection for tolerance quality product $p = p_t = 0.05$, but Plan II rejects fewer lots than Plan I when p is less than 0.025. The two plans reject approximately the same proportion of lots when p is equal to or greater than 0.025. The average outgoing quality limit based on Plan II, method of averages, is slightly higher ($p_L = 1.14$ percent as compared with $p_L = 1.04$ percent) than the AOQL based on Plan I, method of fraction nonconforming. The p_L value for Plan II may be made identical with Plan I, by changing the criterion L (minimum limit for average) and making it larger in magnitude so that its distance from $\bar{X}_p$ is less. The entire P_a curve for Plan II would be modified by this change, as it is impossible to make two P_a curves identical. As a result the P_C value would be less for the specified p_t value than the consumer's risk for Plan I.

Economic Advantage through Decreased Inspection Costs

What are the economic advantages of one method over the other? The commercial justification for developing the "method of averages" is the fact that its use in a large number of cases may result in a reduction in inspection costs. Figure 15-14 gives probability of acceptance values and figure 15-13 presents the expected average outgoing fraction nonconforming values for that sampling plan for each of the two methods that results in a minimum average amount of inspection per lot $\bar{I}_m$ for product of process average fraction nonconforming quality $\bar{p} = 0.0024$. Any other single sampling plan for each method satisfying the stipulated conditions would result in a larger value of $\bar{I}$.

The difference between the two values of I in table 15.18 indicates that if the cost of inspecting each unit at every step in the inspection procedure is the same for both methods, then inspection costs under the specified conditions may be reduced 83.7%. If the unit inspection cost c_1 for the first and only sample $n_1 = n$ for the "method of averages" is twice that for the "method of fraction nonconforming," inspection costs may be reduced 69.0 percent.

When it is desired to select the most economical sampling plan for the method of averages, it is necessary to determine the average cost of inspection per lot C for each sampling plan satisfying the stipulated conditions and to select that plan

TABLE 15.18 Determination of P_a for OC Curve

Conditions: Lot Size $N = 1{,}000$; Process Average Fraction Nonconforming $\bar{p} = 0.0024$; Lot Tolerance $p_i = 0.05$; Consumer's Risk $P_C = 0.10$

Method	*Sample Size*	*Criterion for Judging Lot Nonconforming*	*Average Amount of Inspection per Lot*	*Average Outgoing Quality Limit*
	n		I	$\bar{p}_L$
I. Fraction Nonconforming	75	Max. No. of Nonconforming Pieces in Sample $c = 1$	88.83	0.0104
II. Averages.........	13	Min. Limit for Average $= -0.821\sigma$ from $\bar{X}_p = 486.2$ end foot candles (Min.)	14.51	0.0114

which results in a minimum average cost of inspection per lot C_m for a quality characteristic where the probability of the occurrence of a nonconforming piece is $\bar{p}$. In developing these cost equations, c_r is defined as the unit inspection cost for inspecting the remainder of any lot indicated as nonconforming by the sampling criteria, while c_j is the unit inspection cost for the jth sample, where $j = 1, 2, \ldots, i$. For the method of fraction nonconforming, c_r, which is usually smaller than the various c_j values, is frequently the average unit inspection cost for each piece in the sample or series of samples as well as for each piece in the remainder of a lot that requires each piece to be inspected. A simpler relation for determining the most economical sampling plan is given by an equation covering costs, when $c_1 = c_2 = \cdots = c_i = ac_r$. This relation applies, when the cost of measuring or testing each piece and recording the result for a given quality characteristic is the same at every step in the inspection procedure for the "method of averages" except the step where each piece in the remainder of a lot is inspected by the "method of attributes," such as by a go no-go gauge, at which step the inspection cost per unit c_r is usually less than c_j ($j = 1, 2, \ldots, i$) and $a > 1$. For a quality characteristic of $\bar{p}$ quality, the sampling plan that results in a minimum value of C, C_m, is the most economical sampling plan.

Although there are many different inspection plans available in many texts, this text has presented only a survey of those most used. Figures 15-13 and 15-14 show a comparison between comparable attributes and variables sampling plans. It covers lot quality protection. For a lot size of 1,000 units, this compares two systems (attributes vs. variables) with an LTPD value of $p_t = 5.0\%$ and a consumer's risk of 0.10 for the two single sampling plans. The attributes plan uses a sample of seventy-five units, whereas for almost the same OC curve, the variables plan uses only thirteen units. If measurement time is almost the same as inspection time for the characteristic being checked, the variables inspection might cost only 30% or

$\frac{1}{5}$ of the corresponding inspection costs for attributes inspection. Other variables sampling plans might be found even more economical. More variables sampling plans should be used in industry.

In conclusion, this section has given a survey of the best and simplest common sampling plans now being used. It provides sufficient information to make it possible for quality control and inspection personnel to be able to select sampling plans that provide protection against shipment or acceptance of unsatisfactory product at minimum costs.

EXERCISES

1. Discuss the basic sampling concepts in quality control.
2. Describe the procedures required in the applications of sampling inspection.
3. What are the the principles used in selecting samples? Differentiate between biased and unbiased samples, defining in particular random and representative samples.
4. What principles are used in selecting the best size of lots for (a) production and (b) for consumers?
5. (a) Describe sampling inspection by the *method of attributes.* (b) Describe sampling inspection by the *method of variables.*
6. Describe briefly the different applications of sampling inspection. Give two concrete examples.
7. Name and describe the two most popular sampling tables used in the method of attributes and give examples of each.
8. Name and describe the three different continuous sampling plans covered in the text and give examples of each.
9. MIL–STD–105D provides sampling plans for many different levels including several special levels. (a) Name these levels and indicate where they might be used. (b) Describe the difference between (1) normal inspection, (2) reduced inspection, and (3) tightened inspection.
10. In both the method of attributes and the method of variables, nonconforming units are classified according to their seriousness. (a) Describe the following: (1) Critical defect; (2) Major defect; and (3) Minor defect. (b) Some companies inspect all critical defects 100% or even inspect each unit several times for these critical items. They then use Major A, Major B, Minor C, and Minor D as their classification. Define and differentiate between these four classes. (c) In some cases the classification *Incidental* is used for insignificant errors that are reported but do not affect the acceptance or rejection of units. Discuss such defects and give an example.
11. Describe the demerits per unit method of rating quality and give an example. (*Note*: The chapter covering control charts for attributes gives supplementary information that will aid in answering the above.)

12. MIL–STD–105D (a) For successive lots of 2,000 units each for Inspection Level I, what sample size code letter designates the sampling plan to apply? (b) Using the sample size code letter obtained in (a) where the AQL value is specified as either 4% or 4 defects per 100 units, list in detail the sampling plan that applies for (1) single sampling; (2) double sampling; and (3) multiple sampling. (c) Using table 15.6, draw the correct operating characteristic (OC) curve for the single sampling plan found above, listing the probability values for assumed p values used in constructing this curve.

13. MIL–STD–105D (a) For Special Inspection Level S–4, what sample size code letter designates the sample sizes that should be used in the selected sampling plan? (b) For an acceptable quality level (AQL) of 4% list the single sampling (SS) plan that applies in detail. (c) If after several weeks the sampling inspection results are unsatisfactory and tightened inspection must be authorized, what is the SS plan that must be applied? Give sample size and Ac and Re values. (d) Using table 15.7 in text, determine for both normal inspection and tightened inspection the average outgoing quality limit (1) factors and (2) exact AOQL values per equation at bottom of table.

14. MIL–STD–105D (a) For the single sampling plans obtained in exercises 11 and 12 using table 15.8 in the text, determine the LQ values for $P_a = 10\%$. (b) These LQ values are equivalent to what named percent defective or fraction defective values used in other sampling tables and noted in the Dodge-Romig tables?

15. The Dodge-Romig sampling tables were designed to provide quality protection at minimum costs. List the special features in these tables that are used to achieve this goal.

16. Dodge-Romig sampling tables: Lot protection is provided by the LTPD tables. Where the LTPD or p_t value is 2.0% the lot sizes in all cases $N = 2{,}500$ and the process average p is 1.0%. (a) What sampling plan should be used for (1) single sampling and (2) double sampling? (b) What are the listed AOQL values for the two sampling plans found in (a)?

17. Dodge-Romig sampling tables: Average quality protection is provided by the AOQL tables. Where the AOQL value is 2.0%, the process average $\bar{p}$ is 1.0% and the lots offered for inspection each contain $N = 2{,}500$ units. (a) What sampling plan should be used for (1) single sampling and (2) double sampling? (b) What are the listed p_t = LTPD values for the two sampling plans found in (a)?

18. Where all lots contain exactly 1,000 units each and the single sampling plan stipulated is $n = 100$, $c = 1$. (a) Determine probability of acceptance values assuming that the distribution is a Poisson exponential so that such probability values may be read directly from cumulative Poisson exponential tables given in this text. For such P_a values and other parts of this exercise use p values at least from the following: $p = 0.000, 0.005, 0.010, 0.015, 0.020, 0.025, 0.030, 0.040, 0.05$ and any other p values necessary to obtain answers to the exercises below. (b) Determine probability of rejection values where $P_r = 1 - P_a$ or $P_a = 1 - P_r$. Some Poisson exponential cumulative tables give P_r directly and others give P_a values or where the table gives only individual values, then $P_a = P_0 - P_1$, using pn values obtained in (a). (c) Determine the actual AOQL value for this sampling inspection plan. Select additional values of p to determine the correct answer, the exact AOQL value. (d) The answers to the above can best be obtained by preparing a table using the headings: $p, pn, P_r, P_a = 1 - P_r$, average amount of inspection per lot, I, where $I = n + (N - n)P_r$, $N - I$, and $p_A = AOQ = p\dfrac{(N - I)}{N}$. (e) Graph the operating characteristic curve from

the P_a values found in the table per (d). (f) Graph the AOQ curve and show the AOQL value.

19. This text gives table 15.13 showing the P_a values for the MIL–STD–105D sampling plan: $n_1 = 32$: $Ac = 1$, $Re = 4$; $n_2 = 32$: $Ac = 4$, $Re = 5$. When the Re values are not given and the double sampling plan is given as mentioned in the text as: $n_1 = 32$, $c_1 = 1$; $n_2 = 32$, $c_2 = 4$, determine the P_a values for the p values listed in table 15.13. (a) List these P_a values listed in table 15.13 in one column; add any additional probability values found in your computations. (b) Finally list the revised P_a values for the complete sampling plan. (c) List a fourth column showing the percentage change due to the added probability of acceptance value.

20. Variables sampling plans were first developed in 1934 with a formal discussion published in 1939 using a single variables criterion, the allowable average assuming control of the variability measured by the standard deviation or range. Mention was made in this presentation that a criterion for dispersion or variability might be added if uncontrolled. Thus criteria for a characteristic might be based on (1) Averages $\bar{X}$ and standard deviation σ or (2) Average $\bar{X}$ and range R. (a) Give an example where such variables sampling plans might be applied. (b) What are the advantages of variables sampling plans when compared with comparable attributes sampling plans providing equal quality protection? (c) What are the disadvantages of such variables sampling plans? (d) Variables sampling plans are presented in several texts. Where would one find such a presentation of variables sampling plans for both commercial use and also for products made for the military? List names of such documents and where used.

CHAPTER SIXTEEN

INTERNAL QUALITY AUDITS

16.1 Need for Quality Audits

It has become generally accepted that measuring the level of product quality is one of the primary functions of quality assurance. This is customarily accomplished by inspecting and testing the product to ascertain the degree to which it complies with the requirements. However, what is to be said about the integrity of the systems that influence product quality? Some method is needed to monitor the effectiveness of the internal operations of the organization so that there is confidence that the operating system does indeed lead to the economic achievement of quality goals.

Like many large police departments which have internal investigators to check on the activities of other police personnel, a quality system needs quality audits to provide a measure of effectiveness and integrity to the system.

In an internal quality audit, a person with an objective attitude makes representative sample evaluations of both software and hardware items to determine if a performance or procedure actually reflects plans and intentions. This means that the auditor must be as unbiased as possible and possess knowledge of the activity being audited. A record is made of deviations found during the audit, and their significance is assessed in relation to the importance of the activity and the degree of departure from the specified procedure. Internal audits are a measure of managerial control, since the efficiency of the quality system depends on the prescribed policies and procedures being followed.

16.2 Purposes of Auditing

Many reasons are given in modern organizations for management errors. Among those popularly referred to is failure to communicate. Oral and written communications describe desired activities for personnel. In order for these communications to be effective, the recipients must, in fact, (1) get the message, (2) understand the message, (3) be motivated to carry out the action, and (4) make certain the stipulated action is completed correctly. The sources of some well-known profit leaks are when someone doesn't get the message, or does not understand the message, or does not agree with the message and does not take action, or does not care enough to take action, or completes the action incorrectly.

A glaring example of what can happen without a check on actual performance is provided by the following story.

> A platoon commander who had been in charge of a tank division was asked why, when abandoning his tanks, he had not made them inoperable. He fully believed and insisted that he had done so. When he was taken back to the area and shown them to be intact and in perfect fighting order, he could not understand it. The mission must have been carried out. *He had told somebody to do it.*

Several specific purposes of internal audits are given below. When such audits are adequately supported and properly conducted, the results will provide valuable data to

1. Measure the efficiency of quality systems.
2. Evaluate the effectiveness of company policy implementation.
3. Ascertain whether company objectives and customer requirements are being satisfied.
4. Improve cost effectiveness.
5. Evaluate the effectiveness of people in the implementation of quality plans.
6. Identify potential problem areas.
7. Provide the company with documentation, for customer assurance, that necessary controls are implemented, and are performing satisfactorily.
8. Predict customer reaction to quality.
9. Reduce customer complaints.

Some Typical Consequences of Not Auditing

Numerous *hidden* conditions that detract from quality objectives usually exist and go undetected without the feedback provided by the quality audit. Results of audits have shown the existence of the following conditions in varying amounts in a typical company.

1. Without management's knowledge, misinterpretation of instructions result in far different operating practices than planned or anticipated.
2. Without management's knowledge, actual operating practices are often quite different than those defined in written instructions.
3. Without management's knowledge, profit drain occurs because departments and divisions tend to move in their own directions without regard for each other's needs and problems.
4. Customer representatives sometimes see certain problems long before management recognizes them, which is a source of irritation and embarass-ment. (This pertains primarily to government-funded programs.)

Major Steps in Conducting an Audit———

In performing an audit, there are several important general criteria that should be followed to maximize their value.

1. A schedule of audits must be followed in order to ensure that all elements of the quality system are reviewed at least once a year. (Some will require much shorter intervals.) The schedule is prepared before the audit is conducted.
2. Audits are performed using checklists for applicable quality system elements. (Examples of these are illustrated in later sections.
3. Results of audits are recorded and distributed to appropriate personnel for their visibility and/or action.
4. Follow-up actions must be taken to verify or assure that deficiencies noted during the audit have been or will be corrected within a designated time.

Specific Criteria———

There are several specific criteria that also should be met in order to properly conduct an internal quality audit.

1. **Maintain an audit schedule.** This is required to be sure that all areas are reviewed in a given time. Selecting the area to be audited and setting the schedule should not be made difficult. The frequency with which observations and verifications are made varies with the nature of the function being audited. The interval can range from one week to one year.
2. **Choose an auditor from an entirely different function.** One group that can be assigned to perform audits is the group that is responsible for preparing the quality manual. Since this group developed the basic system, it is familiar with the written system, as well as the intent behind the written work. It can perform an unbiased audit of the quality functions and evaluate the extent to which these functions are carried out.
3. **Conduct the audits without announcements.** In order to get a realistic picture of the actual practices rather than one that is cleaned up because the audit is anticipated, the amount of advance notice of the audit should be kept to a minimum. However, the area foreman should be notified in sufficient time just prior to the audit so that he or she or a delegate will be available during the audit. In all cases, the first audit should be definitely scheduled. Succeeding verification audits may be unannounced.
4. **The foreman of the area being surveyed or his designated representative should accompany the auditor during an audit.** This will eliminate many arguments later concerning what really was noted or occurred at the time of the audit.
5. **The same person should not conduct audits for more than six months at a time.** It is true that people usually have their own standards and blind spots. Changing the auditors periodically minimizes biased reports on the area audited, and results in a broader and more effective audit program.

6. **All operating shifts must be audited.** The second and third shifts must not be overlooked since other work shifts do not necessarily operate the same as the day shift.
7. **An item either conforms to the written requirements or it is rejected.** The auditor should not be permitted to use his or her judgment in not reporting an apparently small deviation. For example, if a gauge became overdue for calibration the day before the audit, this is classed as a deficiency. However, the closeness or defect severity is taken into consideration in determining corrective action requirements to support the program.
8. **Corrective action should depend on the severity and extent of the deficiency.** This is where good judgment must be used. Someone other than the auditor should review the audit results and then decide the degree of corrective action that is necessary. If the deficiency appears to be minor or isolated, correcting it on the spot may be satisfactory. If the deficiency is widespread or in complete violation, written corrective action should be required to be submitted to the auditor within approximately five days of the audit. (The five-day limit will vary somewhat with the company, agency, and type of problem. Some critical deficiencies must be corrected immediately.)
9. **Foremen or supervisors of the function being audited should have two principal obligations.** They should be cooperative in rendering assistance during the audit, and they should take the necessary action to correct the substandard condition detected during the audit within the time allowed.

Requirements of the Quality Audit

When implementing a quality assurance audit program, several important points should be reviewed. Some of these are described as follows.

1. Verifying the use of accurate and complete software (i.e., drawings, specifications, design memos, test memos, etc.) is as essential as verifying that the manufacturing and inspection processes are satisfactory.
2. A successful quality audit program must include the actual witnessing of physical processes being performed and an inspection of a sample of the end product in order to assure that procedures and instructions truly describe the work being performed or already completed.
3. Audit attributes must be carefully chosen so that they are commensurate with the correct requirements in sufficient breadth and scope to prevent overlooking deficiencies and presenting a picture of erroneous results.
4. Information must be as unbiased as possible and organized to provide specific information to management.
5. Audits must be efficient; they must provide information that has greater value than the cost of running the audit program through collecting data, processing information, and performing the analysis.

6. Auditors need not be engineers or technical specialists, but they should have a detailed knowledge of the requirements for the process or area of audit, be inquisitive by nature, and be well trained in the conduct of a meaningful audit. It is especially important to impress upon them the fact that their inquiry is not necessarily limited to the attributes of the audit plan, but that they can pursue new paths if the facts indicate that it is necessary.
7. All mathematical and statistical techniques must be sound. Necessary approximations and inferences should be skillfully evaluated to assure their applicability and validity.
8. Information about deficiencies must be gathered, analyzed, and reported in a timely manner, so that quick corrective action is also possible.
9. A comprehensive follow-up system for corrective action must be implemented.

Audits of Products

The product audit involves inspecting a sample of parts that previously has been inspected and accepted by normal inspection methods. The immediate goal of the product audit is to determine the degree of compliance of inspection to established requirements. The validity of the requirements is not questioned in the product audit. The inspectors' duties or procedures themselves are not monitored, but the effectiveness of the inspectors' performances is assessed. Functions and methods appraisals are accomplished by such methods as process certification and procedures audits.

In a typical product audit procedure, a certain minimum number of audits are required from each inspection point (work center) to enable meaningful statistical estimates to be made. The number of such audits will vary with the requirement. The items selected for audit are chosen at random from those inspected. Under certain conditions, it is desirable to stratify the audit. For example, the emphasis on certain products, inspection points, or characteristics may be increased, but the samples from these strata must be randomly selected in order to allow the use of valid statistical inference techniques to be applied to the data. The size of the sample is usually small and may include as few as four units. However, larger samples may be needed when a particular operation is being questioned, or when statistical inference calls for a larger sample.

Inherent in the audit procedure is the fact that inspectors' performances are constantly questioned. Personnel who are assigned audit responsibility, therefore, should have the respect of the inspectors. Accordingly, audit personnel are frequently selected from the ranks of well-qualified inspectors.

Product audits may be performed at a variety of stages in hardware manufacturing. They may take place as the components are being fabricated, or at the end of a product or assembly line. The decision regarding where and when audits are performed rests with management, but is based primarily on the volume of parts evolving from an inspection point and the criticalness of the inspection operation. Usually the quality audit must result in approval of the sample before the lot from which it was drawn can be released for further processing or shipment.

In most companies, when defects are found by the auditors, the articles are subject to review by both quality engineering and inspection supervision. Defects found by inspection and audit are classified according to their estimated effect on product performance. Some companies use the following method of classification.

Class A
Defects that will result in the failure of a product to perform its intended function.
Class B
Defects which could result in the failure of a product.
Class C
Defects which cannot result in the failure of the product.
Class P
Paperwork discrepancies.

If a nonconformance is discovered during the audit and is found to be outside the scope of the responsibility of the inspector whose work is being audited, the defect should not be used in the computation of inspection accuracy, but should be used in the computation of the process quality level.

Benefits of the Product Audit

Some important benefits that are derived from the quality audit are summarized below. The quality audit:

1. Provides routine calibration of the physical (as opposed to functional test) inspection system.
2. Helps to stabilize quality levels.
3. Provides basic data which may be used by quality assurance management to (a) optimize inspection skill versus cost, (b) compare the quality levels of different products to assign appropriate emphasis and quality efforts, and (c) detect violations of established quality budgets.
4. Shows the effects of changes in the quality planning and other management changes.

There are several means for evaluating the worth of product quality audits. A few of these are listed below.

1. The knowledge of low or high accuracy should result in the redistribution of inspection labor, and there should be a decrease in required inspection-to-manufacturing man-hour support ratios.

2. Inspection planning should change as the results of audit indicate areas where inspection complexity and work load prevent achieving required accuracy.
3. The cost of finding defects and their causes should be small compared to overall cost avoidance.
4. The maintenance cost of operating an audit program should be decreased periodically to determine if the benefits are substantially more than the cost.

Actions to Avoid in Performing an Audit

1. Do not make deals with certain personnel. The auditor must personally verify, examine, or witness the activity, and must not rely on hearsay.
2. Do not conduct an audit with the deliberate attempt to catch someone in error or to find something wrong. Although audits should be unannounced in most cases, they should be conducted objectively, courteously, and in the presence of a spokesman for the function being audited.
3. Do not have the same auditor constantly audit the same functions. This practice can generate either positive or negative bias.
4. Do not allow an audit function to continue indefinitely without the corrective action loop being complete, or without the support of top management. Any audit practice becomes perfunctory and ineffectual if infractions become meaningless, or if the management does not support the audit function and enforce corrective actions.
5. Do not assume that an audit is finished without objective evidence that the proper corrective action has been completed.
6. Do not assume that an audit can be conducted effectively without first planning the procedure properly. Audit checklists must be completed, qualified personnel must conduct the audit, and proper intervals for auditing an activity must be established.

The purposes and flow diagrams of five typical types of internal quality audits used in industry are shown in figures 16-1 through 16-5. these are

Type I Quality Program Management Audit,
Type II Systems Effectiveness Audit,
Type III Policy Implementation Audit,
Type IV Functional Operations Audit, and
Type V Inspection Effectiveness Audit.

Reporting Audit Results

Completed audits are reported on forms designed to permit management to quickly and effectively identify significant information about the area audited. To

Figure 16–1 Type I: quality program management audit.

PHASE 1

PURPOSE:
To improve the quality assurance capability for effectively negotiating proposals. This involves providing negotiators with a record of past performances of quality activities that have contributed to loss of profit.

PHASE 2

PURPOSE:
To determine if the program quality plans have been translated into clear and accurate work instructions and to determine if the performing organizations have received these instructions.

CONTRACT

ASSURANCE OPERATING QUALITY PLAN

EVALUATION BY THE QUALITY ASSURANCE FUNCTION

FUTURE COMPANY PROPOSALS

MANAGEMENT OF FUNCTION BEING AUDITED

PROGRAM QUALITY INSTRUCTIONS

- QUALITY ASSURANCE PROCEDURES & DIRECTIVES
- PROGRAM PROCUREMENT QUALITY REQUIREMENTS
- PROGRAM QUALITY INSTRUCTIONS

EVALUATION BY QUALITY ASSURANCE DEPT. REPRESENTATIVE

EVALUATION SUM– MARY TO QUALITY ASSURANCE MANAGEMENT

INTERPRETATION SUMMARY TO TOP MANAGEMENT

PURPOSE:
To assure that Quality Assurance procedures and directives accurately reflect, define, and express company policy in such a manner that it is a solid base for developing economic, clear, concise working instructions, in accordance with contract criteria.

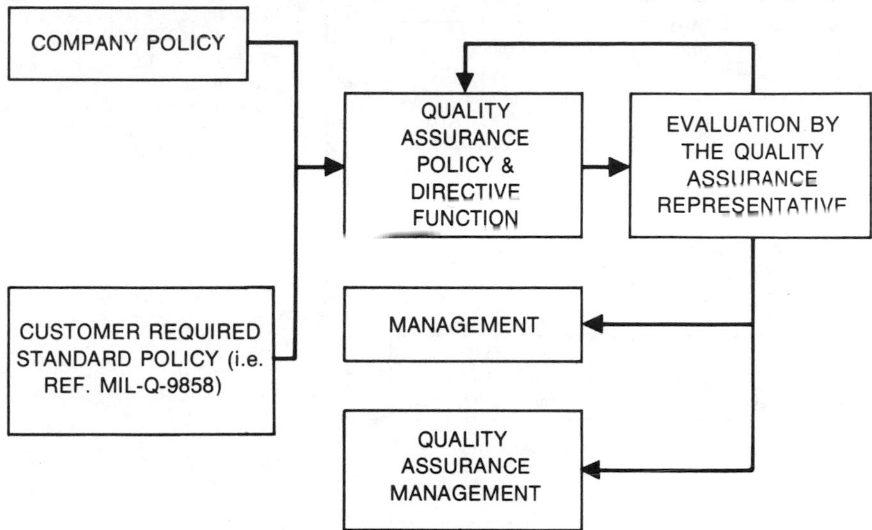

Figure 16–2 Type II: systems effectiveness audit.

PURPOSE:
To provide assurance that divisional quality procedures and instructions reflect stated quality policies and, when implemented, result in practices which are within the policy framework.

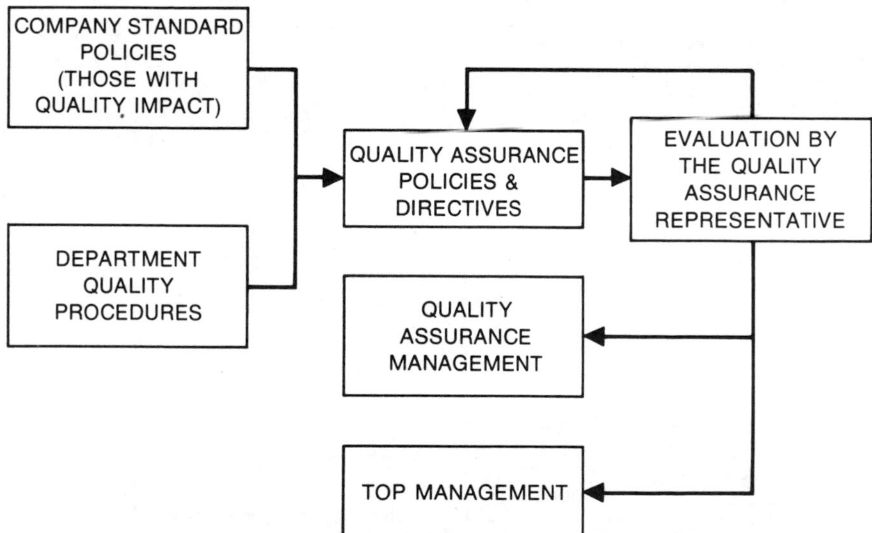

Figure 16–3 Type III: policy implementation audit.

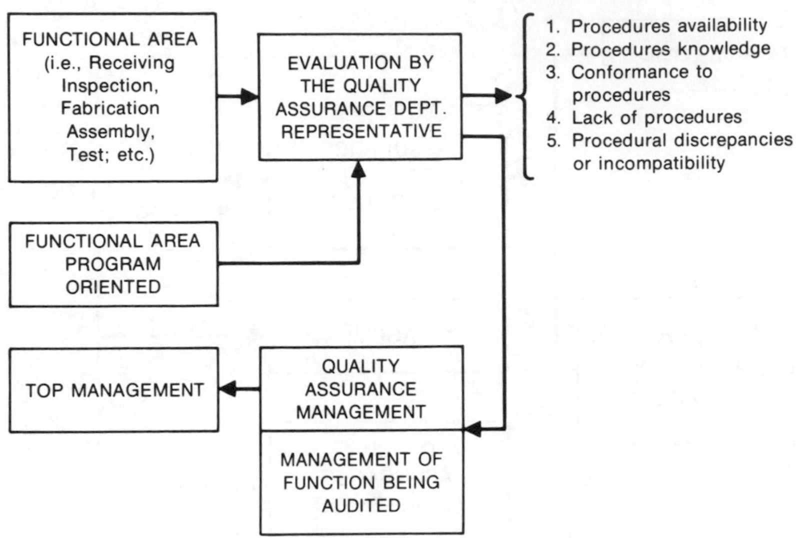

Figure 16–4 Type IV: functional operations audit.

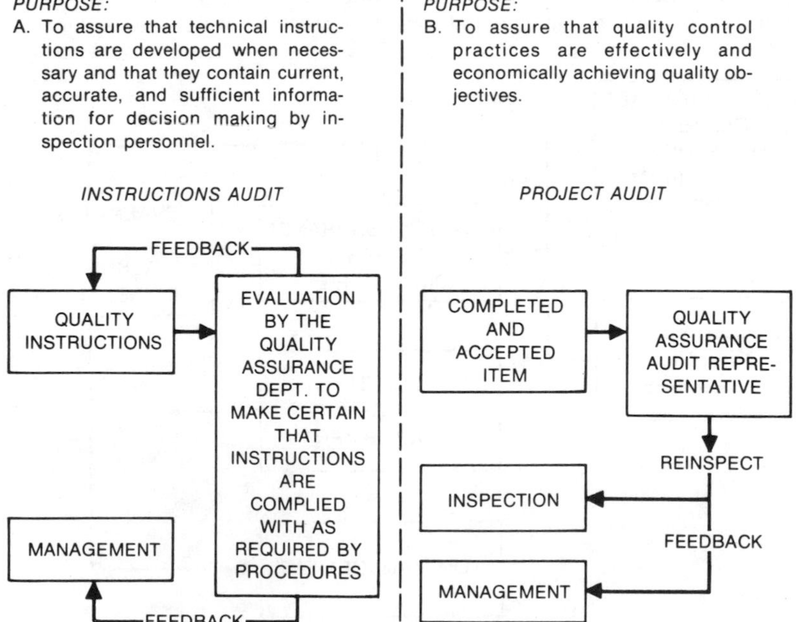

Figure 16–5 Type V: inspection effectiveness audit.

get the desired results, the audit report must be issued to a sufficiently high level of management to assure that the required action can be attained. The following should be followed in preparing the report.

1. Prepare preliminary report of audit findings.
2. Meet with the management of the areas affected by the audit to discuss the report.
3. Prepare final audit report, including corrective action assignments with due dates as determined in the meeting.
4. Distribute the report to the quality assurance manager, operative Quality Assurance Office, all department chiefs and section heads, and all other affected department managers.

Summarizing the Findings and Results

One of the most important aspects of conducting an effective audit is to properly summarize the findings and results. This feedback information, properly organized and summarized, is essential in order for management to see the actual impact of the problems revealed. Regular reports should be issued on the basis of the following criteria.

1. Weekly, monthly, or quarterly summaries of audit activities should be prepared. These summaries will include
   (a) the number of audits performed, (b) a concise description of audit findings, and (c) the status of corrective action.
2. The summaries will be distributed to cognizant managers (including those outside of quality assurance).
3. Each summary should be an audit report describing the status of quality systems and practices for the company.

Audit Follow-up

It is essential that accurate and complete records of corrective action be maintained in order to close the loop. A satisfactory follow-up system cannot depend solely on written replies to audit findings, but must include spot checks and occasional re-auditing of the particular area in order to verify proper and complete correction of the deficiency. A follow-up system must be devised to assure that corrective measures are instituted as required. The following follow-up steps should be taken.

1. Notify inspection surveillance personnel of corrective action commitments obtained during post-audit meetings so that they can verify correction during routine activities.
2. Secure a written statement of corrective action implementation from the area responsible for the action prior to the commitment date.

3. Close the audit when a satisfactory written statement of corrective action implementation is received. However, during the next scheduled audit the actions must be verified.
4. Contact the responsible area management to determine why the actions were not taken if a written statement is not received on time.
5. Initiate formal corrective action in the form of a corrective action request when no agreements can be reached with the responsible area management.

Audit Checklists

To prepare for conducting internal audits, checklists are prepared for each of the specific categories or functions being audited. These lists should be a series of questions that probe the accomplishments of each of the specific requirements in each overall procedure. For instance, for inspection records, questions such as the following should be prepared.

1. Is the lot number recorded?
2. Is the sampling plan noted?
3. Did the inspector stamp the record?
4. Are the number of pieces that were accepted and rejected recorded?
5. Are records available for the last 12 months?

Similar lists for each written procedure in the quality manual should also be prepared. With these questions, working checklists should be prepared for each of the areas to be audited. This can be done by pulling from the basic list of questions those that apply to the particular area.

The remainder of this chapter lists examples of questions and specific areas of concern in performing internal audits. By no means is this an exhaustive list, but it will serve as a guide in developing such a list.

The letters listed in the "Evaluation Action" columns of the following audit checklists are defined below. These are the actions required to be accomplished by the auditor.

V Verified the adequacy of the stated requirement by actual observation.
A Activity meets applicable specifications.
F Follow-up for further verification (i.e., at another location).
W Witnessed the performance of the operation.
R Requested personnel to provide a service, information, documents, etc.
C Comments by the auditor regarding a particular requirement or condition.

Samples to be used in these audits are noted. In all cases, samples selected should be obtained by a truly random process. This ensures representative, unbiased results and a fair evaluation of each area.

NO.	*QUALITY PLANNING, DATA ANALYSIS AND REPORTS*	**EVAL. ACTION*
1	Discussion by quality supervision of the planning, data analysis and reports	R
2	Operating procedures are available for use and are adequate	V
3	Data are received from all the operating functions, including incoming, in-process, assembly and final inspection and test operations, material review and suppliers	V
4	Tabulation and reports such as (Sample—2 or more of each type, if available.)	
	a. Production inspection reports	V
	b. Production discrepancy reports	V
	c. Usage and failure rates	V
	d. Process inspection reports	V
	e. Process test reports	V
	f. Failure summaries for trends	V
	g. Test summaries for trends	V
	h. Life expectancy summaries for maintenance	V
	i. Control charts depicting trends	V
5	Tabulation data and reports analysis are distributed to the operating departments (Sample—distribution list)	V
6	Adequacy of data to be provided as objective evidence for this contract (Sample—all data collected)	V
7	Inspection and test planning is evident	C
8	Quality planning is adequate to assure compliance to requirements	C

Figure 16–6 Audit checklist (quality, planning, analysis and reports).

NO.	*QUALITY COSTS*	**EVAL. ACTION*
1	Discussion by quality supervisor regarding the collection of quality cost data	R
2	Operating procedures are available for use and are adequate	V
3	Cost records, both labor and material, are available on nonconforming materials (Sample—all records)	V
	a. Scrap	V
	b. Rework	V

NO.	*QUALITY COSTS*	**EVAL. ACTION*
	c. Repair	V
	d. Reinspection	V
	e. Retest	V
	f. Analysis	V
4	Cost records are maintained for analysis of supplier quality effort	V
5	Cost records are available for the cost of the prevention of defects (Sample—all records)	V

Figure 16–7 Audit checklist (quality costs).

16.3 Typical Deficiencies Encountered— Quality Assurance Functions

A detailed evaluation of the quality assurance functions reveals the following most frequent deficiencies.

1. Quality planning is not adequate.
2. The audit function is not performed.
3. Audits are restricted only to quality functions.
4. There is no adequate program for defects analysis.
5. Defects status reports are not made available to operating personnel.
6. Replies to quality audit reports do not go to management higher than the quality director.
7. Audit findings are tampered with before management review.
8. Quality cost data are not collected or are not complete.
9. Quality does not review all change orders.
10. Quality control's review of changes is made after the fact.

NO.	*CHANGE CONTROL*	**EVAL. ACTION*
1	Discussion by change control supervisor	R
2	Change control procedures are available for use and are adequate	V
3	Engineering change orders (C.O.) include:	
	a. Effectively point (Sample 4 C.O.)	V
	b. Quality review (Sample 4 C.O.)	V
	c. Signatures of approval (Sample 4 C.O.)	V

4	Drawing numbers and revision collected agree with current revisions (Sample—those collected)	V
	a. Receiving	V
	b. Fabrication	V
	c. Assembly	V
	d. Final assembly and test	V
5	The distribution system provides for:	
	a. Record of drawings issued and to whom	V
	b. Record of removal of obsolete drawings	V
6	All the changes issued are within the scope of authority for this contract (Sample 10 or more)	V
7	No more than 6 changes are attached to a drawing (Sample 5 drawings)	V
8	Procedures provide for all changes affecting a supplier are forwarded to procurement (or whichever organization handles changes to suppliers) for dissemination (Sample 4 recent changes and check with purchasing)	F
	Check the inspection and test instructions and the specifications for latest revisions. If more than one deficiency is found in each area, check all other collected documents.	
9	Discussion by document change control supervisor	R
10	Document change control procedures are available for use	V
11	Document numbers and revisions collected agree with current revisions	V
	a. Inspection instructions	V
	b. Test procedures	V
	d. Fabrication work instructions	V
	e. Assembly work instructions	V
	f. Process instructions	V
	Check all available data.	
12	The distribution system provides for:	
	a. Record of documents issued and to whom	V
	b. Record of removal of obsolete documents	V
13	All changes issued are within the scope of authority for this contract (Sample 3 of each type)	V
14	All changes affecting a supplier are forwarded to the organization disseminating such data (Sample 4 recent changes for check at the control point)	F

Figure 16–8 Audit checklist (Change control—drawing and specifications, and revision documents).

16.4 Typical Deficiencies Encountered—Change Control Functions

The following list of deficiencies represents those most frequently found during evaluation of the change control functions of a quality control program.

1. The drawing change control system does not provide for the orderly disposition and removal of obsolete drawings.
2. Obsolete drawings and documents are found in manufacturing areas.
3. The system does not provide for the quality function to review necessary change requests before the fact.
4. Design engineering management are not fully cooperative in the conduct of the audit.

NO.	*PURCHASING*	**EVAL. ACTION*
1	Discussion by purchasing manager or a buyer of the purchasing function	R
2	Purchasing department procedures are available for use and are adequate	V
3	Adequacy of purchase order (P.O.) package (Sample 3 significant suppliers)	V
	a. Technical requirements—drawings, engineering changes, specifications, tests required, special instructions and procedures, special inspection and test equipment	V
4	Adequacy of detailed quality requirements	
	a. Government inspection requirement	V
	b. Source inspection	V
	c. Raw material physical and chemical certification	V
	d. Objective evidence to be submitted and specific characteristics inspected and tested	V
	e. Age dated items and materials	V
	f. Resubmitted rejected items identification by supplier	V
	g. Corrective action regarding deficiencies in the performance of the purchase order requirements	V
5	There is an indication that the quality group has reviewed purchase requests or orders prior to issue (Sample 4 P.O.)	V
6	There is an approved supplier list available for use	V
	a. No suppliers P.O. can be found that are not on the approved list (Sample 8 P.O.)	V
7	Records of supplier corrective actions are available	V
	a. Overdue replies are not excessive	V

	b. Follow-up corrective action notices are evident and prompt	V
	c. Replies by suppliers indicate timely and adequate corrective action (Sample 4)	V
8	Is there evidence that purchasing has purchased from "disapproved" suppliers?	C
9	Does purchasing personnel appear to adhere to quality objectives?	F

Figure 16–9 Audit checklist (procurement).

16.5 Typical Deficiencies Encountered— Procurement Function

The following list sets forth those deficiencies that most often are discovered during an audit of the procurement function.

1. Quality assurance does not review the purchase orders.
2. Quality assurance review of purchase orders has been bypassed.
3. Purchasing, when responsible, fails to send corrective actions recommended by the quality group or to follow up on delinquent suppliers.
4. Purchases are made from suppliers not on the approved supplier list without authorization by the quality control manager.
5. An approved supplier list is not generated.
6. Purchasing does not have a current approved supplier list.
7. No evidence of corrective action is shown in the file on poor quality suppliers.
8. Quality requirements are not included in some purchase order packages.
9. Purchase order does not include a revision or indicate the correct print revision.
10. Inadequate or inaccurate quality requirements are placed in purchase order specifications.

NO.	*CALIBRATION AND MEASURING EQUIPMENT*	**EVAL. ACTION*
1	Discussion by metrology personnel regarding calibration program	R
2	Operating procedures are available for use and are adequate	V
3	Adequacy of calibration records	V
	a. History of past calibrations	V
	b. Accuracy	V
	c. Location	V

NO.	*CALIBRATION AND MEASURING EQUIPMENT*	**EVAL. ACTION*
	d. Calibration intervals and due date	V
	e. Maintenance and repair details	V
	f. Name of manufacturer, model and serial number	V
	g. Name of calibration technician	V
	h. Date of calibration	V
	i. Serial number or identification of standard used to calibrate	V
	j. Number or name of procedure used to calibrate equipment	V
	k. Environmental conditions during calibration	V
	l. Variables data taken during calibration	V
4	Adequacy of procedures for calibration	V
	a. Specific equipment or group of equipments to which the procedure applies	V
	b. Identification of calibration points and environmental requirements	V
	c. Description of scope, principle of the methods of calibration	V
	d. List of all standards and other equipment in detail to perform the calibration	V
	e. Complete instructions for performing the calibration	V
	f. Specific instructions and data sheets for obtaining and recording test data	V
5	Intervals of calibration are based on stability, purpose and degree of use	V
6	There is supporting data to justify shortening and lengthening calibration intervals	V
7	Environmental controls are adequate for the laboratory	V
	a. Temperature	V
	b. Humidity	V
	c. Cleanliness	V
8	The instrument calibration dates collected from the operating areas agrees with the status records. Check all available data.	
9	Production tools calibration data collected from the operating areas agrees with status records. Check all available data	V
10	New and repaired instruments and gages are calibrated before use	V
11	Follow-up action is evident for overdue instruments for	

	calibration (Sample 8)	V
	a. Overdue instruments are minimal	V
12	Inspection equipment, within the state of the art, is 10 times more accurate than the characteristics being measured	V
13	Inspection equipment not ready for issue is tagged and segregated from ready for issue equipment	V
14	The recall system provides for the removal from the work area of inspection equipment after calibration expiration	V
15	Procedures are adequate and effective for the protection of gages and inspection equipment during handling in transit and storage (Sample—check operating methods)	V
16	Procedures are adequate for the control of instrument issued to suppliers	V
17	What actions are taken when inspection equipment is found to be out of tolerances?	C

Figure 16–10 Audit checklist (mechanical calibration and measuring equipment).

16.6 Typical Deficiencies Encountered—Measurement and Standards Functions

The following list relates deficiencies most often found during evaluation of the measurement and standards area.

1. Expired calibration dates are found on test equipment in use.
2. Calibration instructions are unavailable or inadequate.
3. Proper calibration records are not maintained.
4. Calibration intervals are revised without justification or authority.
5. Instruments are in use which should be included in the calibration system and are not.
6. The test equipment used does not adequately measure the product's characteristics.
7. Like instruments do not demonstrate reliable measurements. (Measurements from similar testing instruments differ more than they should.

NO.	*FABRICATION*	**EVAL. ACTION*
1	Discussion by inspection foreman regarding the operation of the shop	R

NO.	*FABRICATION*	**EVAL. ACTION*
2	Operating procedures for the fabrication area are available for us	V
3	Adequacy of fabrication work instruction or traveller that denotes and details the job (Sample 3)	V
	a. The function to be performed	V
	b. Sequence of operations	V
	c. Inspection points	V
	d. Set-ups, equipment and tools	V
	e. Speed, feeds, processes	V
	f. Drawing numbers and revision	V
	g. Sketches, working drawing	V
	h. Specifications	V
	i. Raw material, type and size	V
4	Adequacy of inspection work instructions (Sample 3)	V
	a. Define accept/reject criteria	V
	b. Tools, gages and inspection equipment	V
	c. Drawing No. and revision and nomenclature	V
	d. Workmanship criteria	V
	e. Details of the methods of inspections to be performed	V
	f. Characteristics to be inspected	
	1. Conditions at inspection point	V
	2. Tolerance limits	V
	g. Location of characteristic on drawing	V
	h. Data collected	V
	i. Environmental condition of inspection	V
	j. Precautions and safety, personnel, product and test equipment	V
	k. Inspection levels, AQL, Sample	V
5	Adequacy of drawing and document change control methods	V
	a. Removal of obsolete drawings (prints) or documents	V
	b. Records of current drawings or documents	V
	c. Drawing numbers and revisions (Sample 3)	F
	d. Fabrication work instruction numbers and revisions (Sample 3)	F
	e. Inspection work instruction numbers and revision (Sample 3)	F
6	No skipped inspection operations shown on traveller, fabrication or inspection work instruction (Sample 4)	V

7	Rejected material	
	a. Rejection tag attached to material	V
	b. Identification of material	V
	c. Removed from work area	V
8	Adequacy of material handling	V
	a. Containers	V
	b. Method	V
9	Adequacy of general housekeeping	V
10	Controls for production tooling, jigs and fixtures used for inspection (Sample 3 for verification in metrology)	F
11	Reject data summaries available for use	V
12	Change orders attached to working documents (Sample 5)	V
	a. Effectivity date or serial number	V
	b. Review by QA	V
	c. The number of change orders do not exceed 6 per drawing or document	
13	Unauthorized, marked-up, illegible or defaced production documents cannot be found (Sample 3 each)	V
	a. Fabrication work instructions	V
	b. Inspection work instructions	V
14	Reinspection of accepted parts (Sample 2 selected parts)	W
15	Inspection equipment calibration	
	a. Name, serial no. and dates (Sample 3)	F
	b. Current calibration dates (Sample 3)	V
16	Adequacy of inspection records (Sample 4)	V
	a. Part name and number and revision	V
	b. Lot identification	V
	c. Date of action	V
	d. Inspection performed	V
	e. Sample size	V
	f. Number of rejections	V
	g. Reason for rejection	V
	h. Indicates responsibility for corrective action	V
17	Adequacy of inspection status identification	V
	a. Identification of person to marking device	V
	b. Procedure controls use, care and replacement	V
	c. Stamps do not damage material	V
18	Adequacy of gage storeroom	V
	a. Discussion by storeroom man	R
	b. Recall system	V
	1. Issuring tag	V
	2. Calibration indication or system	V

NO.		**EVAL. ACTION*
	3. Delinquent gage tags or list	V
19	Adequacy of lot identification system	V
	a. Serialization and identification degree	V
	b. Traceability (Sample 3 parts)	V
20	Control charts are in evidence, such as X-bar ($\bar{X}$) and R charts, p and c charts?	V
21	Are there operations where production personnel do in-process verifications? If so, does QA audit by inspection? How?	C

Figure 16–11 Audit checklist (fabrication).

NO.	*FINAL ASSEMBLY AND TEST*	**EVAL. ACTION*
1	Operating procedures for the final assembly and test area are available for use and are adequate	V
2	Discussion by inspection foreman regarding the final assembly and test operations	R
3	Adequacy of assembly work instruction or traveller that denotes and details the job (Sample 3)	V
	a. The function to be performed	V
	b. Sequence of operations	V
	c. Inspection points	V
	d. Set-ups, equipment and tools	V
	e. Processes	V
	f. Drawing numbers and revisions	V
	g. Sketches, working drawing	V
	h. Specifications	V
	i. Assembly material	V
4	Adequacy of inspection work instructions (Sample 3)	V
	a. Define accept/reject criteria	V
	b. Tools, gages and inspection equipment	V
	c. Drawing No. and revisions and nomenclature	V
	d. Workmanship criteria	V
	e. Details of the methods and inspections to be performed	V
	f. Characteristics to be inspected	V
	1. Conditions at inspection point	V
	2. Tolerance limits	V
	g. Location of characteristic on drawing	V

	h. Data collected	V
	i. Environmental condition of inspection	V
	j. Precautions and safety, personnel, product and test equipment	V
	k. Inspection levels	V
5	Observe an inspection and test function (Sample 2 each)	W
	a. Select inspector or test operator	R
	b. Test equipment and inspection tools agree with instructions	V
	c. Calibration status of test equipment and inspection tools	V
	d. Workmanship standards available for inspection criteria	V
	e. Inspector or test operator checks instructions, materials and set-up for adequacy	V
	f. Adequacy of sampling plan and methods when used	V
	g. Inspector or test operator performs as instructions direct	W
	h. Inspector or test operator qualifications	
	1. Name and/or badge number	RF
	2. Training received (ask operator)	RF
6	Adequacy of drawing and document change control methods	V
	a. Removal of obsolete drawings (prints) or documents	V
	b. Records of current drawings (prints) or documents	V
	c. Drawing numbers and revisions (Sample 3)	F
	e. Inspection instruction numbers and revision (Sample 3)	F
	f. Test instructions, numbers and revisions (Sample 3)	F
7	No skipped inspection operations on traveller, fabrication or inspection work instruction (Sample 4)	V
8	Rejected material	
	a. Rejection tag attached to material	V
	b. Identification of material	V
	c. Removed from work area	V
9	Adequacy of material handling	V
	a. Containers	V
	b. Method	V
10	Adequacy of general housekeeping	V
11	Controls for assembly tooling, jigs and fixtures used for inspection (Sample 3 for verification in metrology)	A
12	Reject data summaries available for use	V
13	Change orders attached to working documents	V
	a. Effectivity date or serial number	V

NO.	*FINAL ASSEMBLY AND TEST*	**EVAL. ACTION*
	b. Review by QA	V
	c. The number of change orders do not exceed 6 per drawing or document	V
14	Unauthorized, marked up, illegible or defaced production documents cannot be found (Sample 10)	V
	a. Drawings (prints)	V
	b. Assembly work instructions	V
	c. Inspection instructions	V
	d. Test procedures	V
15	Visual work instructions (35 MM slides) are controlled (Sample 20% of available instructions)	
	a. Slides are traceable to the required drawing configuration	V
	b. All revisions to slides display approval by the appropriate planning and Quality personnel	V
	c. Slides in carousels are in the correct operational sequence	V
	d. Carousels in use are secured with a tamperproof device	V
16	Inspection and test equipment calibration	
	a. Name, serial no. and dates (Sample 3)	A
	b. Current calibration dates (Sample 20%)	V
17	Adequacy of inspection records (Sample 4)	V
	a. Assembly name, number and revision	V
	b. Lot identification	V
	c. Date of action	V
	d. Inspection performed	V
	e. Sample size	V
	f. Number of rejections	V
	g. Reason for rejection	V
	h. Indicates responsibility for corrective action	V
18	Adequacy of inspection status identification	V
19	Adequacy of lot identification system	V
	a. Serialization and identification degree	V
	b. Traceability (Sample 3 parts)	V
20	The configuration of the ''as built'' assembly can be traced	V
21	Adequacy of handling and storage to prevent damage or deterioration before shipping	W
22	Adequacy of test equipment controls for repair and adjustment seals are located so that there can be no unau-	

thorized entry into the equipment V
23 Control charts are evident V
24 When adjustments are made by final test personnel, how are they audited for accuracy? C
25 After completing final test, are other operations performed before packaging and shipment? C
26 Does Quality have the final authority to decide whether material in-process will move to the next operation? C
27 Are there operations the production personnel do in the verifications? If so, does QA audit by inspection and test? C
28 Reinspection of accepted parts (Sample 2 selected assemblies) V

Points to look for in reinspection of assembly:

a. Soldering thoroughness and acceptability
b. Marking of parts and assemblies
c. Freedom from burrs, sharp edges or damage
d. Mounting of parts is to specification
e. Cleaning that ensures parts from the possibility of inadequate operation, function or appearance
f. All added parts show no evidence of cross threading, detrimental or hazardous burrs or mutilation
g. All screw-type fasteners are tight to preclude movement of parts
h. Rivets are tightly seated to their bearing surface
i. Gear assemblies are properly aligned, meshed and operate as intended
j. Bearing assemblies are free of rust, discoloration, tool marks and other imperfections
k. Wiring and cabling is neat and sturdy and positioned so as not to become cut or damaged. Particular attention should be given to wire dressing, lacing, harnessing, insulation, splicing, clearance and shielding
l. Welds are free from harmful defects such as cracks, porosity, undercuts, voids, gaps and no burn through

Figure 16–12 Audit checklist (final assembly and test).

16.7 Typical Deficiencies Encountered—Manufacturing In-Process Operations

The following deficiencies are those most commonly observed during the evaluation of manufacturing in-process operations.

1. Inspection instructions are unavailable, inadequate, or incomplete.
2. Work instructions are not available or are inadequate.
3. Tools and equipment in use are not authorized or are misused.
4. Inspection stages are skipped or omitted.
5. Certain test equipment is not included in the calibration system.
6. Inspection and test equipment are overdue for calibration.
7. Obsolete drawings or documents are in use in the manufacturing operation.
8. Unauthorized changes are found in drawings, work instructions, or inspection instructions.
9. Operators are not certified.
10. Operators are not working to latest design changes.

NO.	*TRAINING AND CERTIFICATION*	**EVAL. ACTION*
1	Discussion by training personnel regarding programs provided	R
2	Training programs are provided for, such as:	
	a. Process and manufacturing techniques	V
	b. Machining operations	V
	c. Fabrication and assembly	V
	d. Use of production tooling and equipment	V
	e. Inspection instruments, techniques	V
	f. Quality methods and systems	V
	g. Statistical quality control and sampling	V
	h. Preservation, packaging and handling techniques	V
	i. Tests and check out	V
3	Each training course record indicates: (Sample 2 course outlines and programs)	
	a. Schedule	V
	b. Detail content	V
	c. Personnel attended	V
	d. Proficiency criteria	V
	e. Grades received	V
4	There is evidence that training needs are assessed periodically	V
5	Determine training received for personnel names collected in the functional areas	V
6	Does the training program meet the needs of the products manufactured?	R

NO.		**EVAL. ACTION*
1	Discussion by supervision regarding certification programs	R
2	Certification programs are provided as specifications indicate for, such as:	V
	a. Welding (ALL)	V
	b. Soldering	V
	c. Radiography	V
	d. Magnetic particle	V
	e. Dye penetrant	V
	f. Bonding	V
	g. Wire wrapping (solderless)	V
	h. Ultrasonic	V
	i. Heat treatment	V
	j. Potting and Encapsulation	V
	k. Brazing	G
	l. Plating	V
	m. Fungus—moisture proofing	V
	n. Chemical and anodic film	V
3	Adequate certification records	V

Figure 16–13 Audit checklist (training and certification).

16.8 Typical Deficiencies Encountered—Training Function

The following list of deficiencies are those most often discovered during an audit of a training function.

1. Classroom training courses are not provided.
2. Personnel are performing special operations without adequate certification.
3. Training programs do not provide a valid means of determining the proficiency of the trainee.
4. Training courses are not documented as to exact content.
5. Course outlines and lesson plans are inadequate.

16.9 Typical Deficiencies Encountered—Quality Corrective Action System

The following deficiencies depict those most generally found during the evaluation of a quality corrective action system.

1. There is no established corrective action system for the product in question.
2. The corrective action system is not fully defined or documented.
3. Corrective action due dates are not required.
4. Corrective action due dates are often delinquent.
5. The action taken does not always correct the cause of the problem, but only the symptom.
6. Established procedures are not followed in attempting corrective action.

NO.	*PRODUCT DEFICIENCY CORRECTIVE ACTION*	**EVAL. ACTION*
1	Discussion by supervisor of the product failure analysis function	R
2	Operating procedures are available for use	V
3	Adequacy of failure reporting, analysis and corrective action records	V
	a. Identify deficiency	V
	b. Description of deficiency	V
	c. Verification of deficiency	V
	d. Analysis to determine cause	V
	e. Prescribed time interval to take action	V
	f. Response of actions taken	V
	g. A review and approval to determine adequacy of actions taken	V
4	There is not an excessive number of delinquent corrective actions outstanding (Sample 8)	V
5	Corrective action reporting has been within the assigned time intervals	V
6	There is a follow-up system for overdue corrective action replies in operation (Sample—overdue file)	V
7	There is a report to higher management regarding open or delinquent corrective action replies (Sample—see reports)	V
8	Is a closed loop feedback corrective action system in full operation?	C

NO.	*QUALITY PROGRAM CORRECTIVE ACTION*	**EVAL. ACTION*
1	Discussion by supervisor of the corrective action program operation	R

2	Operating procedures are available for use and are adequate	V
3	Adequacy of quality program corrective action reporting records (Sample 4)	V
	a. Identification of program deficiency	V
	b. The program deficiency is stated in detail	V
	c. Status of corrective action is indicated	V
	d. Assignment of corrective action	V
	e. A due date has been assigned	V
	f. Approval of corrective action noted	V
4	There is not an excessive number of delinquent corrective actions outstanding (Sample 8)	V
5	The corrective action reporting is within the assigned due dates (Sample 8)	V
6	There is a follow-up system for overdue corrective action replies in operation (Sample—overdue file)	V
7	There is a report to higher management regarding open or delinquent corrective action replies	V
8	Is a closed loop feedback corrective action system in full operation?	C

Figure 16–14 Audit checklist (product deficiency corrective action, and quality program corrective action).

EXERCISES

1. What is the primary purpose of conducting an internal quality audit?
2. What tends to occur if audit techniques are not practical in a company?
3. Name the four major steps taken in an audit.
4. Discuss the pros and cons of conducting an audit unannounced. Under what conditions would it be better to announce an audit several days in advance?
5. Why are checklists used in conducting an audit?
6. Briefly describe some personal qualifications an auditor should have.
7. What is a product audit? How does it differ from inspection? How does it differ from a system audit?
8. Should audit assignments be rotated? If so, why?
9. Explain the five types of internal audits discussed in this chapter. Would these be applicable in any size of company? Why?
10. What part of the audit cycle do you feel is the most difficult to accomplish? Explain your answer.

11. Name the two principal responsibilities of those whose functions are being audited.

12. How could any quality audit be evaluated on a numerical scale? Give two examples.

13. If sample results for a particular audit indicated deficiencies that seemed to be excessive, should a second random sample be selected before making a final decision? Discuss briefly the basis of your evaluation.

14. When auditing purchase orders, how would a check be made against the original requisitions to make certain the respective purchase orders reflected the material, component, part, etc., requested on the requisition?

15. How frequently should audits be conducted? In answering this question, different intervals of time might be selected for different types of audits; hence, indicate the nature of at least two different types of audits with indicated time intervals and give valid reasons for your choice of different intervals.

CHAPTER SEVENTEEN

ECONOMICS OF QUALITY CONTROL

17.1 Quality Control for Profit

It is frequently said that the objective of management is making a profit. If by that is meant the ensuring of future profits, as well as the gaining of immediate returns, nearly everyone would agree. It is true that the modern method of measuring success of a business is by means of profit.

Profit margin, however, is a function of efficiency, and efficiency can be assessed only through cost analysis and control. Further, profit margins as well as cost trends can be accurately calculated only if accurate cost data are available.

Such information serves several purposes. It provides (1) a picture of cost status, (2) it provides a basis for decision making, and, equally important, (3) it helps to measure the effects of actions taken. When sensibly undertaken, the compilation of cost data often is neither excessively difficult nor expensive, and usually the values gained from a properly devised method far exceed the costs of collection.

Quality managers are greatly concerned with the cost of services and the value received as a result of those services. Top management reasonably expects that the results of the quality control department will be an improved relationship between cost and profit.

Many of the people whom a quality manager meets in industry communicate in accounting terms, so the manager should have an understanding of accounting fundamentals. The estimates he or she makes and the budget he or she lives under may be difficult to understand for one unfamiliar with accounting.

17.2 Cost Records as a Control Device

No attempt is being made in this chapter to consider the details of cost accounting. The importance of cost data as indicators of what should be done, as a yardstick of accomplishment, and as a means of fixing responsibility for results cannot be overlooked in any adequate introduction to the problem of quality control. The student who proposes to make a career for himself in the field of quality control should go further into methods and techniques of cost accounting and control.

Knowledge of current costs by types such as direct labor, materials used, supervision, maintenance, and the various quality costs is very useful. A proper combination of selected cost items can help the manager to judge and improve the methods of performing individual production operations. Other combinations can help in controlling department and production center costs. The use of properly selected cost information as one help in judging the effectiveness with which individual supervisors and executives discharge their responsibilities is increasing. Thus, understanding the nature of the wide range of factory costs, the methods of determining such costs, and the proper uses of cost information are essential equipment for today's quality manager.

Quality control is a management function; hence it is important that throughout any such study, the student of quality control retain a management point of view. To be valuable, a cost system should provide only *useful* information. This information should be in the form best suited to the particular objective and individuals served. The data which go to the foreman may well differ from the cost data provided the quality control department in both content and method of presentation. Consideration of matters such as the foregoing would often do much to convert costly, unwieldy, unusable cost systems, which are all too frequently regarded by production executives as nonrelevant statistical data, to useful devices invaluable to management. In this day and age, quality control that is not predicated on knowledge of costs is almost no control at all. On the other hand, an elaborate cost system all too frequently yields nothing except a feeling of self-righteousness on the part of a cost department, plus an increase in the cost of operations. The student of quality control will gain much by keeping this thought in mind while working through the intricacies of the techniques required for integrating cost accounts and quality control with management action.

Cost accounting methods and the accompanying data often fail to accomplish planned objectives because of a lack of understanding on the part of those who might use them to advantage. For this reason it is important that the names and terms used in connection with costs be those commonly understood in the shop and factory.

Cost Centers

In determining production costs, an important requisite is to divide the organization into units. It is sometimes advantageous to subdivide a department into smaller units for cost purposes, or even to combine departments which are closely associated. The subdivision finally selected is known as a *cost center.*

A cost center may be a subdivision of a department; in fact, it may be a still smaller unit and may include, for instance, three machines from one department and two from another, these five performing a production function of such a nature that they are conveniently grouped as a cost center. Another example of a cost center is a group of inspectors performing similar functions in an inspection area utilizing a surface plate or other inspection equipment. The basis for setting up a cost center may be the grouping of machines, methods, processes, operations, or other characteristics which segregate work activities having a common interest.

17.3 General Classification of Costs

The cost to produce a product (sometimes referred to as shop cost, factory cost, production cost, or manufacturing cost), the administrative expenses, and the cost to sell constitute the total cost of sales. An example of how these are subdivided and typically tabulated is as follows

Direct material		$400,000
Direct labor		200,000
Overhead charges:		
Indirect material	$150,000	
Indirect labor	200,000	
Fixed charges	100,000	
		450,000
Cost of production		1,050,000
Administrative expense		100,000
Selling expense		200,000
Cost of sales		$1,350,000

Cost of Labor

In cost control, it is necessary to distinguish between direct labor and indirect labor. Direct labor is all labor expended in manufacturing operations upon the product itself. Indirect labor, on the other hand, is subsidiary labor used in connection with the making of a manufactured product. It is not employed directly upon the product itself but contributes to its manufacture in some auxiliary manner.

Direct labor is one of the principal subdivisions of production cost. The expenditures for indirect labor occur through the overhead charges.

The tabulation of direct labor costs usually takes place on the time tickets or piece-work records. The amount of labor applied on a particular production or manufacturing order is recorded on these forms. The labor cost is posted to the cost sheet or production order.

Direct Cost of Materials

The direct cost of materials is that cost associated with the purchase price of the materials. For cost control purposes, these raw materials, subassemblies, or components are issued from a storeroom and are delivered on the authority of a requisition. The production and inventory control system, working on the basis of a balanced inventory, prepares coordinated schedules for the issue, use, and replenishment of these materials. Records of the cost for goods as they are used are maintained for cost accounting purposes.

Forms and methodology for direct materials cost control vary from company to company. In small companies, materials charges are often accumulated on the basis of material requisitions originating from manufacturing departments. As the materials are withdrawn from stock, the store's clerk sends a copy of the material requisitions to the cost accounting department. In other companies, where use is made of computers, daily, weekly, or monthly printouts are issued to provide information for cost control purposes. The cost accounting or financial department receives printouts of accumulated materials cost information for management visibility and decision making. (This, of course, is also true for other types of costs.)

Burden Costs

As a general rule, burden cost is the most difficult of all costs to ascertain. It cannot be determined with absolute accuracy, and it is particularly difficult to collect the many items of which it is composed until long after raw materials and labor costs are known.

Burden costs include a variety of unlike costs. Typical are machine maintenance, repair, depreciation, and power consumption. If the operation is carried out in leased property, rental costs are incurred. If the factory is owned, then taxes, maintenance, and improvements replace rental charges. Whether company-owned or not, there will be plant housekeeping, heat and light, and security costs involved. There are many indirect labor costs to be included: supervision, paid holidays, worker insurance, health services, unemployment supplements, investment and retirement funds, and others. Purchase price is not the only element in materials costs; storage expense, insurance, transport costs, deterioration, and taxes all add substantially to purchase price.

Some of these burden items are fixed in the sense that they do not vary with volume or rate of output; others increase or decrease with the production rate. Some change as the level of do not output changes, but vary constantly and in direct proportion to output. Some burden costs are partly variable and partly fixed. Some vary under certain conditions of change but remain fixed under other conditions. To exactly determine the burden costs involved in the production of a unit of output or of a line of products is usually impossible. However, to the extent that executive or supervisory action can have an effect on the costs of such burden items, it is important that those responsible be kept informed of the results of their decisions. Thus effort is made to establish a reasonable degree of control over the items of indirect manufacturing expense; otherwise they can become unreasonably excessive. A careful and accurate analysis of indirect costs will usually produce cost savings and thus areas to increase profit margins.

Fixed and Variable Costs

Fixed costs represent the minimum costs necessary to sustain operations at their lowest level. They do not vary with the rate of output. Such costs are independent of variables in production and are assessed on the basis of an original commitment. Fixed costs include salaries of key personnel, rental of facilities, minimum heating and lighting, and similar items. Machinery required for the production of products is another form of fixed costs. They may also include depreciation based upon time, interest, property taxes, and insurance. Fixed costs are expenditures arising from an investment for a particular purpose and cannot be recovered except for payment for the services rendered by the equipment.

A significant part of fixed costs normally can be attributed to capital equipment. For example, machines needed for the fabrication and inspection of products are classified as capital equipment. A considerable amount of equipment is normally required to provide manufacturing and inspection departments with the machines and apparatus needed for the tasks. Typical examples of capital equipment found in manufacturing departments are milling machines, lathes, drill presses, heat treat equipment, and similar items. Examples of capital equipment found in metrology and inspection departments are optical comparators, microscopes, surface plates, and calibration equipment.

Capital equipment may be designated as either *long term* or *short term*, depending upon the time for depreciation. The previous examples are all in the long-term category, since the life of such equipment (based upon original claims) ranges between six and twelve years. Short-term capital equipment (with a life of two or three years) that one would expect to find in manufacturing and inspection departments includes miscellaneous hand tools, magnifying glasses, certain types of accessory parts for machines, miscellaneous storage bins, and power distribution components, such as power panels.

Variable costs, however, vary with the rate of output and include such items as direct labor; direct material and supplies; depreciation based upon output, communication, and transportation costs; power; heat; light; and maintenance above the minimum levels. Variable costs are usually assumed to increase with the rate of operations on a straight line basis. This is shown by the break-even chart illustrated in figure 17-1.

The Break-Even Chart

Income from the sales of products is the primary source of income for a manufacturing company, although there may be minor sources such as rents, royalties from patents, and returns from securities. If the selling price of a product is fixed throughout the operating range and if output parallels sales, income from sales will increase in direct relation to output. This is illustrated by the income line in figure 17-1.

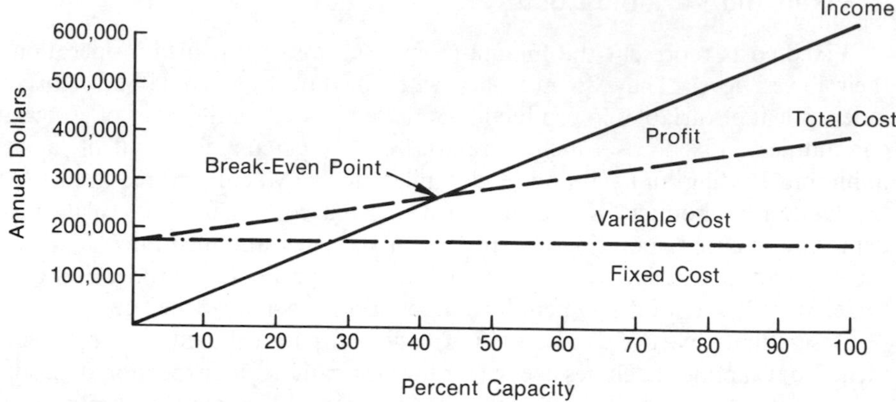

Figure 17–1 Break-even chart for a company.

The economic return experienced by a company is the excess of income over operating cost. In other words, economic return is realized at operating rates above the point where total cost and income are equal. This point is known as the break-even point for no gain or loss.

17.4 Cost Methods

There are two major types of cost methods distinguished by the basis of the costs that are accumulated, as follows.

1. Actual cost method.
2. Standard cost method.

Actual Cost Method

Methods of cost accounting that are set up on an actual cost basis seek to determine the actual cost of any item that is being manufactured. In accomplishing this, the following are included in the cost: (1) the cost of materials used in the production of the product, (2) the amount paid for direct or productive labor in manufacturing the product, and (3) an equitable proportion of other manufacturing expenses known by such terms as overhead, burden, and indirect. The term *overhead* is frequently used to designate indirect manufacturing expenses. The method of cost accounting on the actual basis accumulates the actual expenditures and charges. Thus, the cost is not determined until the product is produced. Because of the amount of work required and the expense involved, cost accounting methods utilizing the actual cost basis have been open to criticism. It is claimed that costs are determined too late to be of use in controlling cost, and that unnecessary effort is needed to determine the actual cost of similar products manufactured in the plant.

The Standard Cost Method

The standard cost method is based on five fundamentals which have persisted and are now generally accepted by both engineers and accountants, as listed below.

1. Determination of the proper cost before the article or service is produced.
2. Recognition of the fact that variations from standard costs will inevitably arise in practice.
3. Application of analytical procedures to these variations to determine their causes.
4. Application of the management principle of exceptions.
5. Application of the management principle of operating rates.

The point of departure between actual cost methods and standard cost methods is indicated by the first of these fundamentals. Standard cost methods seek to determine cost before the item is produced. Actual cost methods determine the cost after the item is produced.

The principal steps in the procedure for setting standard costs for an item are to (1) fix the standard quantities of materials, taking them from the engineering bills of material and pricing them at standard material costs, (2) determine standard labor costs, setting them from standard times for doing the work and standard wage rates, or from piece rates based on time study or predetermined standards, and (3) compute standard overhead charges on some basis that will allocate a fair amount of indirect expense to the item. These three costs, when summed, give the standard cost for the item of product. This cost can then be authoritatively established.

Steps in Establishing a Manufacturing Standard

There are ten fundamental steps in setting a standard which can be divided equally into two principal phases.

I. Analysis Phase (Motion Study)
   A. Select the job to be studied.
   B. Time and record the exact current method used by the operator.
   C. Divide the cycle of the operation into elements.
   D. Question the current method, using principles of motion economy.
   E. Implement the best method.
II. Standard Cost Phase
   A. Time new method.
   B. Compute average time of new method. (This is called the Base Time.)
   C. Level the time to low performance. (This is called the Normal Time.)

D. Apply allowances. (This is called the Allowed Time.)
E. Calculate standard cost. (This figure is based on both labor and overhead rates.)

After a standard has been implemented, it is certain that variations or variances can be observed between the actual cost and the standard cost. Some of the principal causes of these cost variations where standards are applied are

1. Unpredictable delays,
2. Allowances not properly evaluated,
3. Labor time and rate variations,
4. Changes in method,
5. Variations in rates of salaries paid,
6. Variations in personnel of the salaried staff,
7. Material price changes,
8. Material consumption changes,
9. Productivity efficiency changes, and
10. General creeping change.

In the application of the standard cost method, cost standards are set up for material, labor, and overhead expense. These standards are, therefore, rates of input and are closely analogous to time rates. It is self-evident that in the manufacture of an article, if the input of the cost factors can be controlled, the final cost of the article can be predetermined.

The preceding discussion of cost variations indicates a comparison between actual and standard costs, implying that actual costs are accumulated as a part of the procedure of cost control. While many authorities advocate this practice, instances can be found where actual costs are not accumulated, and the variations studied are those of *overall* factors, such as all of the material, labor, or overhead charges of a department. This practice is open to the general objection that the cost data so accumulated do not adequately satisfy the major purposes of cost analysis and control.

If the estimates for standard costs are well made, and revised to keep them in step with current changes in material and labor costs, the agreement between standard and actual costs may be close.

17.5 Quality Benefits of Standards

Methods time measurement (MTM) is one technique used in setting standards that often has special value in meeting quality objectives. The procedure of pre-establishing a better method allows quality characteristics to be considered and incorporated into the method and, consequently, into the overall standard. For example, operating instructions for a certain electronic assembly would include steps that the worker must follow for a given assembly. These steps would not only indicate predetermined time values required for the assembly, but encompass methods of inherent quality. Thus, quality methods derived from quality specifications can be integrated into the standard. This procedure has a degree of built-in quality control and has the effect of reducing the need for in-process inspection.

While MTM is not a panacea for every facet of a standard cost system, it does offer the following advantages for quality.

1. MTM permits methods to be properly determined before production, thus reducing the subsequent need for corrections.
2. Its design enables known quality characteristics to be incorporated into the prescribed method.
3. Explicit instructions are prescribed so that chances of error are reduced.
4. It provides management with a basis for comparing exceptional and substandard performance with standard performance.
5. It provides management with visibility regarding deviations from the prescribed standard, thus helping to pinpoint problem areas.

In some companies, the standard cost system is the basis for quality cost definition and evaluation. The accuracy of costs of work done on defective parts, inspection, and rework, and of general costs of quality activities is based largely upon the accuracy of the standard cost system. However, it is difficult, if not impossible, to accurately and reliably set standards on some types of quality activities. When establishing performance standards for quality personnel, questions of validity and reliability are always raised. Some indirect activities, such as witnessing tests, performing audits, and attending quality meetings, are difficult to quantify for purposes of setting performance standards. Numerous attempts to define work units or repeatable elements of such activities have been made without much success. Various techniques of indirect work measurement, utilizing work sampling and statistical methods, have been employed with some success, but it is generally agreed that reliable performance standards can be best established for operations that have repeating elements. In continuous production where tasks are very repetitive, specific elements and times for those elements can be prescribed.

Most quality activities are not repetitive in nature, and in order to establish and maintain an accurate method of reporting quality costs, careful attention must be given to how costs are reported by the individual performing the work, and how they are classified and grouped for accounting purposes.

17.6 Classifying and Reporting Quality Costs

Methods used for cost classification vary between companies, due to differences in company objectives. The quality cost structure in a company producing a variety of products on a short-term basis will normally be different than that in a mass production company. In the case of continuous production, the organization of quality costs would be product-line oriented, while in job-lot manufacture, cost control is often easier if quality costs are departmentalized. It is desirable, however, to maintain a system in which quality costs are classified and reported by both product and department.

Regardless of the type of company involved, quality costs should be segregated and reported in such a manner that preventive costs, appraisal (detection) costs, and failure costs can be evaluated. This is accomplished when the quality cost system provides for (1) the classification of all quality costs and (2) a method by which these costs are accurately reported. Quality cost trends can then be observed, the results evaluated by management, and adjustments made if needed.

Numerous methods of recording and accounting quality costs are in use. The technique of assigning numbers to various quality cost categories is sometimes used. The number of hours spent in performing a quality task is reported by an employee, by listing the time that was devoted to an assignment and the numbers that have been allocated for the particular kind of work performed, on a time card. Accounting personnel then tabulate these data and issue periodic reports to management personnel and other cognizant functions. There are numerous company documents that indicate quality trends and help to quantify quality costs. These include reports on rejections, scrap, receiving inspection, field service, maintainability, test and failure analyses, and others. Depending upon the company, these reports are issued weekly, bimonthly, or quarterly. Often both weekly and monthly reports are issued. Such quality cost information helps management and quality personnel to evaluate general efficiency and cost trends, establish budgets, detect problem conditions and effect corrective action, meet contractual requirements, maintain a quality improvement program, and reduce overall costs of quality.

All quality costs should be classified into categories similar to the following.

1. **Preventive** The costs associated with activities of planning and maintaining the quality system.
2. **Evaluation (Appraisal)** The costs associated with measuring, appraising or auditing products, components, and purchased materials to ensure conformance to quality standards and performance requirements.
3. **Pre-delivery (Internal) Failure** The cost associated with defective products, components, and materials that fail to meet quality requirements and result in manufacturing losses before being delivered to the customer.
4. **Post-delivery (External) Failure** The costs that result from defective parts or products after having been shipped to the customer.

Preventive Costs

Preventive costs are generated in the prevention of defective materials, components, and systems. There is some truth to the adage, "an ounce of prevention is worth a pound of cure," when discussing quality costs. If adequate preventive programs are not instituted, a far greater percentage of costs are developed in miscellaneous rework activities, not to mention increases in scrap. Too many preventive measures, however, can also become a cost burden. With inadequate preventive and appraisal measures, costs of failures tend to be high. Conversely, in order to achieve the position where few failures occur, costs of prevention and appraisal tend to be high. For every product, there are prevention and detection measures which, if taken, will minimize failure and corrective action costs. The point of optimum protection against failure varies with the product and, although probably never achieved, may be approached by (1) making sure that the cost recording method is complete and accurate, (2) analyzing the data, and (3) implementing the necessary adjustments and controls.

One of the most important preventive measures is planning. Planning tasks predetermine action, and if proper planning can be completed at the outset, subsequent problems can be avoided. However, many factors cannot be predetermined; they are intangible and unpredictable, and inevitably will be encountered during an implementation phase. These factors cannot be accurately incorporated into a plan, but they may have major influences on how well a plan can be implemented. A plan at any given time is only as good as the available facts and assumptions that are incorporated into its content.

The inability of managers to predict certain problems is a principal reason that failure costs tend to comprise the greatest percentage of quality costs. If problems could be predicted, chances of avoiding them through appropriate planning would be far greater, but if they cannot be predicted, their impacts can only be estimated and accordingly included into the plan.

Some of the major activities within a given company that fall into the category of error prevention are given below.

1. **Special Equipment Design** Special equipment may be required to produce parts with predictable quality. These costs are justified on the basis that fewer defectives will be produced on special equipment compared to those produced on standard equipment.
2. **Design Review** Design reviews are conducted to ensure that product designs reflect the necessary quality characteristics. Such reviews are preventive in nature.
3. **Supplier Evaluation** Supplier evaluations are conducted to reduce the probability of receiving inferior material. The results gathered from each survey indicate the feasibility of qualifying a certain supplier. This screening task is done to avoid purchase of defective parts.
4. **Equipment Calibration and Certification** All devices and instruments used for inspection and test must be calibrated in accordance with governing specifications. These calibration tasks are also done to avoid subsequent measuring and testing errors.
5. **Process Control** Quality assurance and quality control personnel design systems for monitoring quality progress, and also perform the task of assessing feedback information for further progress.

6. **Quality Planning** Customer requirements for product quality must be interpreted and documented in a plan, so that product design and manufacture reflect these criteria. Various types of quality planning personnel may be involved, including reliability engineers, quality control analysts, and engineers. Procurement quality analysts and quality engineering personnel also perform planning tasks.
7. **Employee Certification and Training** Many contracts specify that employees must be certified as capable of performing a certain operation to a definite quality standard. These costs of certification are preventive in nature.

Evaluation Costs

Evaluation costs (sometimes called *appraisal costs*) are generated while maintaining quality levels of a company. These are costs that are incurred by observing or measuring the conformance of activities to established standards, and pertain primarily to inspection-type activities. Some such functions are listed below.

1. **In-process Inspection** Checking, gauging, and testing parts (e.g., a circuit card) during various stages of production. All inspection tasks involve evaluation costs.
2. **Subassembly Inspection** Checking and testing subassemblies of components (e.g., a "drawer" for a computer, consisting of a group of circuit cards and other miscellaneous components).
3. **Assembly Inspection** System checkout or final inspection. Final appraisal of all performance and esthetic characteristics is made before shipment.
4. **Data Recordings** Records of inspections made by inspectors. These records are required for control.
5. **Quality System Audits** Periodic audits of a quality system made to appraise overall system integrity. (Some companies prefer to classify audits in the preventive category.)
6. **Data Review** Assessments of quality progress and trends. Data reviews are ongoing tasks in quality departments.

Failure Costs

Failure costs are incurred as the result of defective material. Some categories of this type of cost are given below.

1. **Failure Analysis Cost** Failure analysis involves both destructive and nondestructive testing. For example, parts may be subjected to tensile or compressive tests to determine their relative strengths. Nondestructive tests may also be performed to determine internal conditions of a material that failed in service.
2. **Corrective Action Cost** Disposition must be made of defective material.

An assessment is made regarding the seriousness of the failure, then a rework or scrap decision is made.

3. **Repair and Rework Cost** This is the cost generated while bringing the defective material or unit up to conformance standards.
4. **Scrap Cost** Scrap cost is associated with the value of the merchandise scrapped and with records and disposition.
5. **Liability Cost** Another failure-related cost causing increasing concern is the cost of liability. Substantial losses can be dealt a company by a single shipment of bad parts, especially if the defective parts are the cause of a failure in which bodily harm or loss of personal property occurred. Even if the company being sued wins the court case, the company must usually spend a considerable amount of money in putting together a good defense. Moreover, the cost of liability insurance also falls in this category.

Administrative Costs

Administrative costs are generated through the implementation and maintenance of a quality program. Much of the liaison and coordination between customer and manufacturer are aspects of general administrative costs. Some costs of supervision are also in this category.

A variation in the aforementioned method of classifying quality costs that works quite well is as follows.

1. **Prevention Costs**
   Quality engineering for implementation and product support
   Supplier evaluation, selection, and coordination
   Training and certification
   Quality audits and internal surveys
   Process capability surveillance
   Calibration
   Component qualification/requalification
   Sampling plans implementation and maintenance
   Quality data collection and reporting
2. **Evaluation Costs**
   Configuration verification
   Manufacturing inspection/test
   Source inspection/test
   Receiving inspection/test
   Final acceptance inspection/test
   In-process inspection/test
   Shipping inspection
3. **Scrap and Rework Costs**
   Engineering scrap and rework
   Vendor scrap and rework

Manufacturing scrap and rework from labor inputs (rework) from parts replacement

4. **Deficiency Costs**
   Disposition of nonconforming supplies
   Reinspection/retest
   Corrective action
5. **Administration Costs**
   Procedure manuals
   Supervision and management
   Quality cost analysis
   Proposal preparation
   Clerical/secretarial
   Budgeting and forecasting
   Quality expense items
   Miscellaneous administrative tasks

17.7 Implications of Quality Costs

Understanding the Functions

In order to create a better cost situation in any function, it is first necessary that the function itself be fully understood in terms of operations, relationship to other divisions of the firm, and its own cost structure. For example, the purchasing function is basic to the operation of the manufacturer or retailer. The cost of the materials procured and the cost of operating the department may in some cases amount to but a very small percentage of the total cost of the plant's operations. On the other hand, such costs may be the prime determinant of whether the firm is to operate at a profit or loss. The manufacturing division of the firm must also be measured in terms of its relative cost significance and the degree to which variations in the operations may serve to improve the company profits.

Insofar as the quality control department is concerned, it is a management function seeking to improve the profit margin of the company by lowering corrective action costs incurred by other departments. Only rarely, if at all, does a quality control function produce defective hardware. Instead, the mission of the quality control department is to safeguard the quality levels that have been established and *prevent* the manufacture of defective articles. Thus, in effect, quality organizations increase the profit margin of the company by

1. Making certain that planned quality is achieved,
2. Instituting various cost preventive measures such as control charts and sampling plans,
3. Reducing the number of man-hours associated with rework and other corrective actions,

4. Reducing the severity of defects through process controls,
5. Conducting failure analyses to prevent follow-on failures and improve outgoing quality levels, and
6. Analyzing customer complaints and taking or recommending appropriate action.

17.8 Pareto's Principle of Maldistribution

Vilfredo Pareto (1848–1923), an Italian sociologist and economist, discovered an analytical method that has come to have very important value in the economic control of quality. *Pareto's principle of maldistribution* is based on the fact that in the manufacture of hardware there are almost always a few kinds of defects that loom large both in severity and frequency of occurrence. In either case, these defects are significant because they are costly.

The very simplicity of this principle tends to make it difficult to accept. It states that a relatively few items will account for a disproportionately large amount of the total effect. It has been described as a method for distinguishing the "significant few" from the "trivial many." The importance of this is simply that on an average about 20% of the problems represent about 80% of the cost impact. Stated another way, about 20% of the problems deserve about 80% of the available attention. A high percentage of the remaining 80% of the problems either do not have readily assignable causes and would be very costly to evaluate, or occur only by chance, and do not have meaningful solutions.

Professor Pareto stated this general tendency in mathematical terms in his *Cours d'Economie Politique,* Vol. II, Book III, chapter I. It was applied first to economic problems and distributions as noted in many of the early texts covering the principles of economics, such as the 1915 text by F. W. Taussig, Harvard University. Applications of this principle to quality control appears to have been introduced by Joseph M. Juran, J. D., previously applied effectively in industrial engineering in reducing losses in manufacturing processes and production controls.

This principle is considered by many to be the single most important tool in the field of quality control. It, in itself, does not solve problems. It merely indicates where to direct one's efforts. But this alone is of tremendous benefit. For example, how should inspection manpower be utilized? Without applying Pareto's principle, it would be extremely difficult to allocate inspection manpower on a scientific basis. The result is likely to be that everything is inspected. But since there is never sufficient manpower to inspect everything adequately, the result is likely to be that some parts will receive more inspection than they need, while others need more inspection than they receive. Pareto's distribution should be the first step in any kind of analysis, whether it be of corporate audit, demerits, scrap, repair, rework, warranty, or any other quality problem.

If one assumes, for example, that a plant's scrap costs are getting out of hand and a decision is made that they must be drastically reduced, there are several

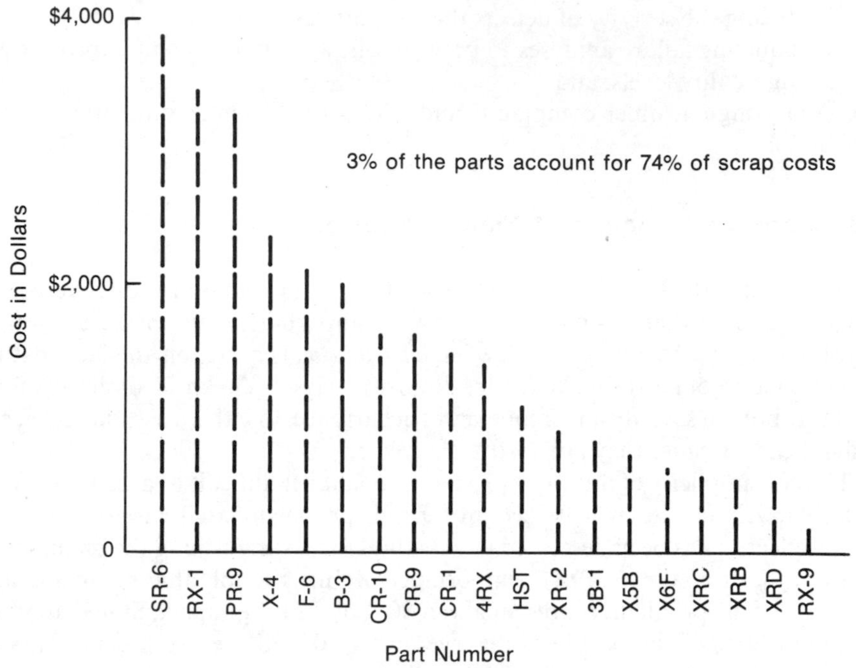

Figure 17–2 Pareto distribution example: scrap costs by part number.

approaches that might be used to achieve this objective. The plant manager or production manager might have a meeting with production superintendents, pointing out the rising costs and requiring that they take action to bring scrap figures in line. Scrap displays might be set up at various locations in the plant to highlight the scrap problem. The plant newspaper might run a series of articles to dramatize the importance of scrap reduction, attempting to enlist the cooperation of all employees.

Such methods may be effective, and they often produce the desired results. But frequently the improvement is short-lived and before long the scrap figures are back where they were. What is needed is analysis of scrap data by means of a Pareto distribution. This will permit concentration on the high part numbers, departments, causes, etc., so that corrective action can be taken in such a specific manner that high-cost scrap items will be reduced and will have a sizable effect on the total scrap picture. The size of the problem should be reduced to meaningful proportions.

To demonstrate how simple, yet effective, this technique can be, actual examples of Pareto distributions from a major automobile manufacturer are shown in figures 17-2 and 17-3.

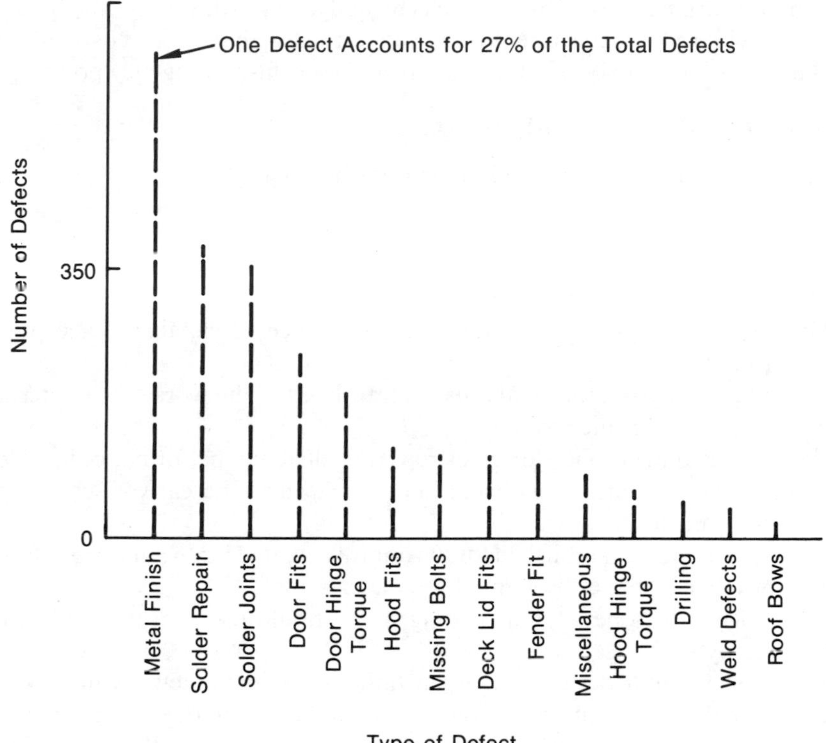

Figure 17–3 Pareto distribution example: body-in-white defects.

17.9 Budgeting for Quality

All quality managers must be concerned with fiscal budgeting. The quality control budget represents a consolidated estimate of what the department plans to do and how much it plans to do it. In a sense, it is a forecast of departmental activities, which is the basis for how the department can be expected to operate during the coming year. This forecast is an attempt to set up, in advance, the details of cost and operating expenses in each of the functions. It is established on a *dollar*, *time*, and *quantity* basis in order that the aspects of dollars, hours, and volume of work may be clearly depicted.

The budget may be thought of as a predetermined profit and loss statement for the department. It establishes cost limits which relate directly to income objectives. The budget procedure forces the quality control department, as well as other departments of the company, to recognize the significance of other operating departments. The interrelationship and the need for close cooperation in attaining expected profit margins is brought into focus by budgetary procedures. The budget procedure provides each department that is concerned with creating cost with an additional insight into its specific function from the profit-making viewpoint.

Criteria for Effective Budgeting

The following criteria can be used in planning a budget.

1. The budget must not be set up hastily.
2. Historical and current cost data must be available.
3. An adequate cost accounting system is assumed to be set up in the company.
4. Those who are to work the budget need to be people capable of accepting responsibility.
5. The budget is a goal; this goal must be translated to the work force in terms which have significance to them.
6. Provision should be made for quick reporting of actual performance in order to allow for comparison with the budget plan and the early discovery of any discrepancies.
7. A system should be established for the improvement of budgetary procedures and for the investigation of any discrepancies.
8. The budget has to be *worked*; management should not expect a budget to function by itself.
9. To the degree that the quality organization does its homework in making certain that it is adequately covered in the budget, the department can be effective. No quality control department can function well unless it has seen to it that it is properly budgeted. This is accomplished by carefully *evaluating* the needs of the department, *justifying* these needs, then *selling* the package to upper management.

For quality organization, these are sometimes awesome tasks. It takes only one year of operating on an inadequate budget to result in severe problems during forthcoming years. It becomes increasingly difficult to justify an increased budget for the coming year once the department has functioned with an inadequate budget for one year, in spite of the fact the department may have a strong justification for an adequate budget.

17.10 Measuring the Results of Quality Control

One can readily understand the potential benefits that can be derived through a quality control organization, but these are not always so easy to measure. One measure of effectiveness of a quality organization over a period of time could be the degree to which total quality costs are reduced—provided that such cost reduction could be attributed directly to efforts of quality control personnel. However, if this premise were valid, the antithesis would also have to be valid; that is, quality personnel would be blamed for *rising* quality costs. In most instances, quality control executives do not want to have the efficiency of their departments judged on the basis of rising or falling costs, because there are so many variables—uncontrollable by quality control personnel—that constantly affect product quality. These variables include such factors as a sufficient budget to operate an effective quality organization and the authority and freedom delegated to the quality organization to make necessary changes. On the other hand, some quality managers use such uncontrollable factors as excuses for not advocating a better structure for quality costs. Accurate quality cost reporting can be political dynamite for some quality executives.

The effectiveness of the quality organization is only as good as the support that top management gives it. It is true that such support is a two-way street—it should be pursued and earned by the quality organization. But, on the other hand, top management should be thoroughly familiar with the objectives and benefits of the quality organization and render support when and where needed. Without this support, regardless of the reason, the quality organization will always be confronted with more than its share of the problems.

Evaluating Quality Costs

To evaluate the effects of quality costs, management can apply them against several measurement bases: (1) a labor base—the cost of direct labor; (2) a cost base—manufacturing costs or added value; (3) a sales base—net sales billed; or (4) product base—number of units versus quality dollars. Of these, probably the most meaningful is the comparison of quality costs to sales, where quality costs are evaluated as a percentage of sales for the purpose of determining their effect on profits.

For example, if a company's profit column shows 3% of sales as a measure of profit, but the cost of product quality is 7% of sales, the company has something to worry about. A reduction in quality costs should be directly convertible to a contribution to profits. Thus, if quality costs of 7% of sales can be reduced to 4%, it should be convenient to convert the difference to profits and speak in terms of 6% profit and 4% quality costs.

In order for a company to make such comparisons, though, it must first determine how to organize its quality dollars. Failure costs (or corrective action costs), which generally represent the largest part of the quality dollar, can be as high as 65%. Costs for inspecting and sorting good work from bad—the second largest cost—often represent 33% of a company's quality dollars.

The problem in most quality systems is that little is spent for defect *prevention* in order to reverse the trend to higher quality costs and less reliable products. Sometimes as little as 1% to 3% of a company's quality dollar is spent on prevention. Yet, it is this area that has real potential for profit improvement.

In general, if preventive costs were to be increased from 1% to 3 % to 4% to 8% of total quality costs, corrective and failure costs should decline by from 10% to 15%. Furthermore, an attendant decline in appraisal costs of from 3% to 5% may

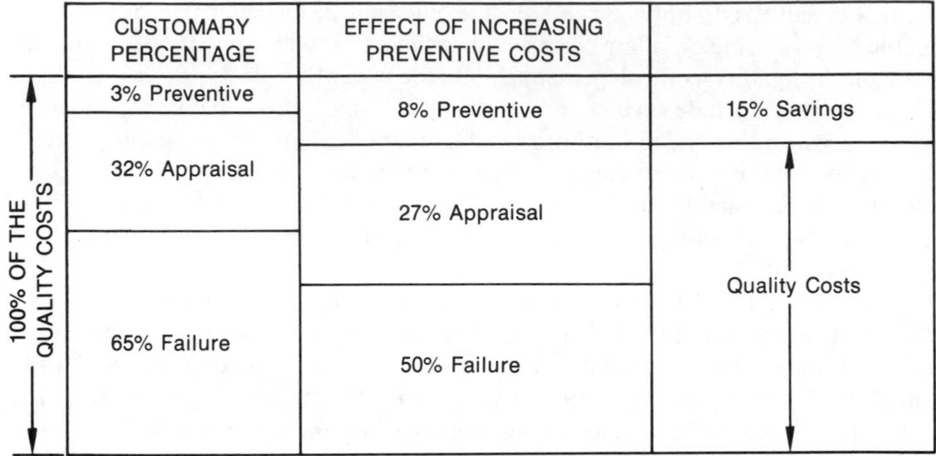

Figure 17–4 The effects of increasing preventive measures on total quality costs.

also be experienced, as illustrated in figure 17-4. The net reduction could result in as much as a 10% to 15% increase in net profit. A question that immediately comes to mind is: If a company can increase its profit margins this way, why doesn't it do it? The simple truth is that the effects of preventive action take place too late for management to recognize its value, and corrective action becomes the only recourse. Early in planning phases, when preventive activities are desperately needed, there are two concomitants that tend to occur between top management and quality control management. There are few tangible results from preventive actions taken by quality functions during early planning phases. When top management sees costs being generated without direct results, they become leery of such preventive objectives and begin to issue budget-restraining directives. To complicate this problem, quality control management often has not done its homework. They can have no case for a preventive budget unless they can demonstrate to top management that it will indeed ultimately reduce total quality costs. This fact can be very difficult to prove, but the best evidence can be accumulated if quality costs are reported so that the effect of preventive action can be measured against corrective action. By monitoring quality costs in preventive, evaluation (appraisal), and corrective action (failure) costs, then, and only then, will the picture of quality costs be clear.

Quality costs can also be viewed as illustrated in figure 17-5. Prevention and early detection of problems avoid compounding subsequent costs. The earlier that a quality control problem can be detected, the greater cost avoidance there will be. For example, a design error not detected by a checker or design review board may cause nonconformances in production, perhaps rework or scrap, extra labor of inspectors, and related functions; if the problem is not detected by the time it reaches the customer, analysis of complaints and returned articles must not only

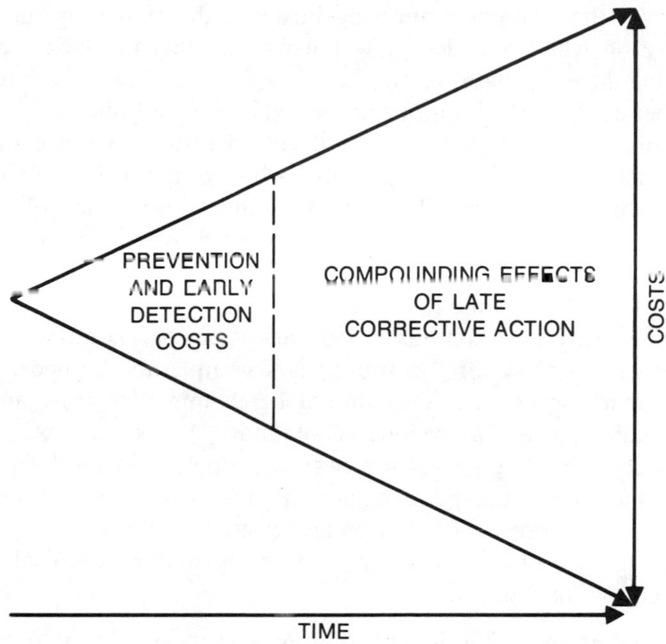

Figure 17–5 Funnel effect of compounding quality costs.

be performed, but liability can be involved as well. These add greatly to this "funnel effect" of quality costs.

A quality manager should consider the following seven points for periodic analysis. Some may need to be reviewed more frequently than others (perhaps biweekly), while others may not need to be examined on more than a monthly basis.

1. The manager must be able to thoroughly analyze cost and income, because profit is the goal in any business. With the computer, even custom or small-volume multiple-line businesses can now have timely profit-related data available for the manager in his prime areas of concern : engineering expense, material expense, direct labor costs, and net profit. Most convenient for the manager is a percentage breakdown of the costs that produce a satisfactory profit. In jobs where these percentages are greatly exceeded, a periodic review should be made.
2. The cost of each designed component must be measured against budget and the most recent forecasts. The budget is the best measure when the business climate is stable, but forecasts provide more meaningful guidance during unstable business conditions.
3. Staff size should also be measured against budget and forecast.
4. In-service failures should be charged against the engineering function

because, in the custom-engineering business, that function has the most influence on whether a design will work and has the best facilities for correcting the ones that do not.

5. Customer complaints should be measured in terms of number and dollars. The manager should give individual consideration to especially critical complaints, depending on what criteria his company uses to determine exactly which are critical. These may involve simply the dollar volume, the rate of expenditure, or the opinions of the field-service representatives, but the manager should certainly review any problems that may come to the attention of corporate management.

   In many cases, external failures or customer complaints will occur. An account should be set up for future years' complaints accrued against the current year's shipments. This should be examined at least annually to insure maintenance of a proper level of funds.
6. When a company has a cost-improvement program in the form of value-engineering teams, the performance of those teams should be checked monthly against pre-established budget costs.
7. The manager should check any periodic performance appraisals made on individuals in his unit.

The quarterly review should include opinion surveys of sales or service representatives and customers. These may tend to be subjective, but the sales and service organization can provide useful data for comparing various company units.

Value Engineering

In a competitive market, cost is always important. If the cost to design and build a product is beyond what it should be, profit margins will be lower than expected. Moreover, if sales of major product lines decline, management usually issues directives to reduce operating costs. Such directives frequently call for budget cuts and reductions in personnel. It is in this phase of the business cycle that there is a particular danger of compromise in product quality. If the cost reduction action creates an imbalance between fabricating departments and control functions, there is a greater chance that outgoing products will not measure up to all prescribed quality standards. The prime goal, therefore, is to somehow produce products with appropriate quality, and yet to produce them at minimum cost.

The exercise of value engineering principles pertains to the prevention of costs as well as the reduction of costs. Value engineering is a *discipline* which is principally function oriented in that it seeks to minimize cost by considering various methods of achieving the functional objectives of products. This approach often results in more ultimate cost savings than mere efforts to reduce cost would. By seeking better methods of achieving the functional objective, cost savings become a result rather than an objective.

At present there are several definitions of value engineering, but each has one central idea; that is, value engineering is a discipline that has the two objectives of cost reduction and quality improvement through better design and manufacturing methods. It is an analytical process which involves identification, selection, development, and implementation of an idea that will result in either increased product reliability (at no increase in cost) or reduced cost (with no sacrifice in reliability). Value engineering is a cost-quality oriented discipline that involves questioning, evaluating, and analyzing for the purposes of improving product quality and increasing company profits.

The value engineer has a creative role. By disciplining himself or herself to think creatively, the value engineer conceives new ideas that are used to create new designs and to improve existing methods. Through this discipline, he or she can identify a problem, speculate on many kinds of alternatives, and then select the best design or method. The discipline of value engineering involves both creativity and judgment. Creativity is a divergent process involving analysis of all possible alternatives to the solution of a given problem; judgment is a convergent process that involves synthesis or assembly of alternatives and selection.

Through a systematic problem solving process applied to a specific task, the value engineer seeks to do the following.

1. Select the best materials for the job.
2. Select the best manufacturing processes and equipment for product fabrication.
3. Identify and select the best design concepts.
4. Identify all cost and quality factors that reduce product value.
5. Replace poor design, poor methods, and inadequate specifications with ones of greater value.

In order to accomplish the objectives cited above, the value engineer must continually seek answers to six basic questions.

1. What is the part or function? (Identify)
2. What does it do? (Function)
3. What does it cost? (Cost)
4. What else will do the job? (Alternatives)
5. What would the alternative cost? (Alternative cost)
6. Would the alternative improve quality? (Alternative quality)

The value engineering methodology can be applied during the very first conceptual design stage and extended throughout the subsequent stages of design, development, manufacturing, test, and field operation. It can also involve personnel, facilities, procedures, and data associated with both software and hardware. Figure 17-6 shows the scope of activities in which value analysis and control can afford benefits to a company.[1]

A complete quality assurance program has no real purpose unless it is aimed at producing savings by reducing quality costs. The quality manager does not know where to direct his efforts or how to build a system until he can identify the areas of high cost.

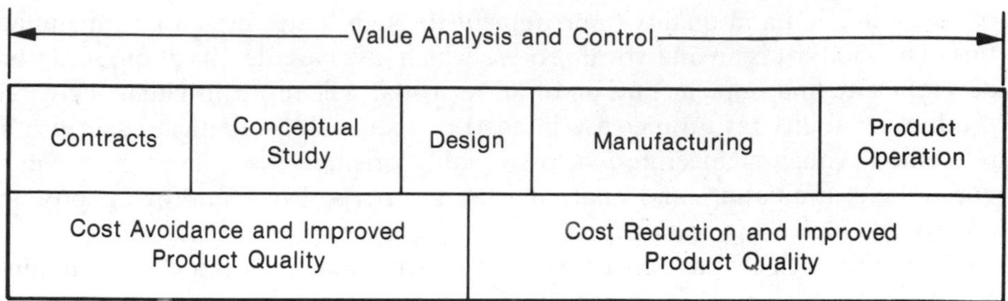

Figure 17–6 Illustration of value analysis and control.

For example, a plant once found that a large portion of its quality costs were caused by a single department in which scrap and rework on a particular component was unusually high. After identifying the area, management determined that they could do very little to improve the component because of a lack of experienced technical personnel. A further evaluation revealed that the item could be purchased from a specialist in that line at a considerable saving. This single element reduced the company's quality costs by 25%. This is a good example of the application of Pareto's principle.

Another company, after beginning a quality cost program, learned that the amount of money spent for prevention was negligible. They began a full-scale planning program for manufacturing operation, testing programs, and design review prior to production. They developed job instruction sheets that instructed the operators in how to set and adjust the processes. Characteristics were classified as to importance, and inspection frequency and inspection methods were documented. The process control engineers were trained in new technologies. They initiated a product and process audit to assure that the operators were performing as instructed. Given the proper tools and instructions, the operators were able to determine product quality. When quality began to drift, proper adjustments were made or the operators waited for further instructions.

The results were good. The amount of 100% inspection was reduced; sampling systems were employed; product quality increased; and scrap and rework costs were lowered.

Products can be nearly perfect as far as specifications are concerned, but still not satisfy a customer's expectations. The best quality image is reflected by a company which designs quality into a product at its conception, safeguards it in manufacture, and delivers it into the hands of a satisfied consumer for use through a normal life.

17.11 Benefits of a Quality Control Program

Benefits derived from quality control have been variously described. Like any other discipline, quality control must be applied correctly and appropriately to maximize benefits. Following are some of the categories in which quality control methodology can be effectively applied.

1. Reduce scrap and rework.
2. Improve the quality of both manufactured and assembled products.
3. Provide for more efficient use of inspection personnel.
4. Aid in rational design and selection of tolerances.
5. Assist in the choice of equipment and processes.
6. Increase the effectiveness of experimental investigations.
7. Furnish important aids in the selection and approval of incoming materials.
8. Lead to more satisfactory purchaser-vendor understanding.
9. Improve operator and supervisory morale.
10. Provide management with a new, effective, and impersonal basis for decisions.
11. Increase overall production and reduce overall costs.

This is a rather comprehensive list of benefits. It is doubtful whether each benefit stated will be accomplished in every case of quality control applications. For clarification, however, some basic benefits of quality control are considered.

Savings in Quality Costs

A sound, scientific approach to quality costs should bring about a sizable cost reduction, directly attributable to the quality control activity. Moreover, these savings should be much greater than the expense incurred in their accomplishment. For every $10 spent for quality cost reduction, the savings accomplished should be from $25 to $100. These figures are based on many years of actual experience in working with such programs, not on hypothetical projections.

Because of the potential savings involved, therefore, the cost reduction objective is a primary aim of the quality control organization. This does not mean, of course, that quality improvement is not an important objective. But often quality improvement brings about significant reduction in quality costs, such as scrap, repair and rework, warranty expense, inspection requirements, etc. Such improvements are also likely to lead to greater customer satisfaction as an added benefit.

Facts versus Opinion

Factual information is better than the personal opinion of the most knowledgeable person in the plant. Quality control has the advantage of providing a systematic and efficient method of gathering and maintaining information on important quality characteristics of products. It permits decisions to be made based on facts rather than opinion or memory. What is a process capable of producing? How good are our suppliers? What percent of defective items has been produced during the past month? How are the quality costs distributed? How accurate and reliable are the inspection findings? All of these questions seek answers, which efficient quality control organization should be able to provide. Decisions based on such a source of information are far more likely to be accurate because they should be devoid of personal opinion.

Improved Inspection Methods

When a quality control program is inaugurated, one of the first benefits that can be expected is improvement in inspection methods. This may include better defect reporting, better utilization of inspectors, improved inspection techniques, improved reliability of gauges and inspection data, etc.

While inspection improvements may provide inspection personnel needed for more complete inspection coverage, it is also possible that a complete review of the inspection system may actually bring about an increase in inspection personnel, at least temporarily. Where this is required, the expense of additional inspection should be offset by at least an accompanying decrease in failure costs, so that the total quality costs are no greater than before, and preferably less.

Quality Awareness

A well-organized quality control program, including appropriate analytical and reporting methods, will undoubtedly have a beneficial effect on everyone in the plant, from the plant manager to hourly personnel, from the standpoint of greater quality-awareness and incentive. The psychological benefit is often a byproduct of the quality control program. Knowing that work quality is important, that it is evaluated, and that supervisory personnel and the quality control department are interested in it, is very likely to instill a greater pride of workmanship in each hourly employee.

When quality control charts are used (these are discussed in detail in Chapters 4, 5, and 6), it is imperative that the foreman and the production employees concerned understand them. If they do not, or if they feel that the charts are unfair or unrealistic, the psychological effects can be negative instead of positive. To be advantageous, the charts must be of service. They must provide information which is beneficial and acted upon, or they become dormant, a waste of time to maintain, and actually worse than no charts at all.

Known Process Capabilities

One of the recognized quality control techniques is process capability studies. This is simply an evaluation of a manufacturing or assembly process to determine the tolerance limits within which it is capable of producing. Several different techniques are extant for such an analysis, including the average and range chart. Once the capability is known and is considered to be satisfactory, an average and range chart can be used to maintain the operation with a minimum amount of inspection and supervision.

It cannot be emphasized too strongly, however, that process capability studies and average and range charts should be used sparingly and only on those operations that are important enough to warrant them.

EXERCISES

1. What is a cost center? How does it differ from a work center?
2. What is the difference between direct labor and indirect labor? What are burden costs?
3. Compare fixed costs with variable costs.
4. Compare long-term capital with short-term capital.
5. What is the significance of standard costs? How can they benefit quality?
6. Why is it good practice to collect costs that involve quality? Explain.
7. Name the four broad categories of quality costs. Give three examples of activities that would be classified in each category.
8. In a typical company, which one of the four categories of quality costs usually comprises the greatest percentage? The lowest percentage?
9. Why is there a tendency in some companies not to maintain good quality cost records?
10. Obtain a copy of MIL–Q–9858A, and determine cost requirements set forth in this document. What are your conclusions?
11. Explain Pareto's *principle of maldistribution*. Why is it an important management tool?
12. Why is proper budgeting in quality-related organizations such an important factor in the economic control of quality?
13. How do the principles of value engineering apply to quality objectives and cost savings?

FOOTNOTE

[1] Glenn E. Hayes, *Quality Assurance: Manufacturing and Technology*, Revised Edition, Charger Productions, Inc., Capistrano Beach, California, 1976.

BIBLIOGRAPHY

Allen, Louis A., *Professional Management*, New York: McGraw-Hill Book Co., 1973.

American Society for Quality Control, "Annual Convention Transactions." (These paper-covered volumes, starting in 1951, typically contain several hundred pages and fifty or more papers.) Published annually by American Society for Quality Control, Inc., Milwaukee, Wis.

Amstadter, Bertram L. *Reliability Mathematics*, New York: McGraw-Hill Book Co. 1971.

Argyris, C., *Personality and Organization*, New York: Harper & Row, Publishers, Inc. 1957.

Arinc Research Corporation, *Reliability Engineering*, Englewood Cliffs, N.J.: Prentice Hall, Inc., 1964.

Barlow's *Tables of Squares, Cubes, Square Roots, Cube Roots and Reciprocals up to 12,500*, L. J. Comrie, editor, 4th Edition, Brooklyn, N.Y.: Chemical Publishing Co. Inc., 1950.

Barnes, Ralph M. *Motion and Time Study*, 5th Edition, New York: John Wiley & Sons, Inc., 1964.

Bazowsky, Igor, *Reliability: Theory and Practice*, Englewood Cliffs, N.J.: Prentice Hall, Inc., 1961.

Bittel, Lester R., *What Every Supervisor Should Know*, New York: McGraw-Hill Book Co., 1974.

Bowker, A. H., and Goode, H. P., *Sampling Inspection by Variables*, New York: McGraw-Hill Book Co., 1953.

Burr, I. W., *Engineering Statistics and Quality Control*, New York: McGraw-Hill Book Co., 1953.

Calabro, S. R., *Reliability Principles and Practices*, New York: McGraw-Hill Book Co., 1962.

Cangelosi, Vincent E., Taylor, Phillip H., and Rice, Philip F., *Basic Statistics: A Real World Approach*, Los Angeles, West Publishing Co., 1976.

Carter, C. L., Jr., *The Control and Assurance of Quality*, Dallas, Texas: C. L. Carter, Jr. & Associates, 1968.

Chao, Lincoln L., *Statistics: An Intuitive Approach*, Palo Alto, Calif.: Science Research Associates, 1974.

Cowden, D. J., *Statistical Methods in Quality Control*, Englewood Cliffs, N.J.: Prentice Hall, Inc., 1957.

Davis, Harmer E., Troxell, George E., and Wiskocil, Clement T., *The Testing and Inspection of Engineering Materials*, New York: McGraw-Hill Book Co., 1964.

Deming, W. E., *Some Theory of Sampling,* New York: John Wiley & Sons, Inc., 1966.

Dichter, Ernest, *Motivating Human Behavior*, New York: McGraw-Hill Book Co., 1971.

Dixon, W. J., and Massey, F. J., Jr., *Introduction to Statistical Analysis*, 3rd Edition, New York: McGraw-Hill Book Co., 1969.

Dodge, H. F., *A General Procedure for Sampling Inspection by Attributes—Based on the AQL Concept*, Technical Report No. 10, New Brunswick, N.J.: The Statistics Center, Rutgers the State University, 1959.

Dodge, H. F., and Romig, H. G., *Sampling Inspection Tables—Single and Double Sampling*, 2nd Edition, New York: John Wiley & Sons, Inc., 1959. (The complete Dodge–Romig tables, with an explanation of how they were derived, the OC curves of all AOQL plans, and an illustration of their use in Western Electric Company. Every inspection department in a mass-production industry should have a copy of this book.)

Duncan, A. J., *Quality Control and Industrial Statistics*, 3rd Edition, Homewood, Ill.: Richard D. Irwin, Inc., 1965.

Eisenhart, Churchill, Hastay, M. W., and Wallis, W. A. (eds.), *Techniques of Statistical Analysis,* New York: McGraw-Hill Book Co., 1947.

Enrick, N. L., *Quality Control and Reliability*, 5th Edition, New York: The Industrial Press, 1966.

Feigenbaum, A. V., *Total Quality Control—Engineering and Management*, New York: McGraw-Hill Book Co., 1961.

Feller, William, *An Introduction to Probability Theory and Its Applications*, 3rd Edition, Vol. I, New York: John Wiley & Sons, Inc., 1968.

Fetter, Robert B., *The Quality Control System,* Homewood, Ill.: Richard D. Irwin, Inc., 1967.

Fisher, R. A., *The Design of Experiments*, 3rd Edition, Edinburgh: Oliver & Boyd, Ltd., 1942.

Fisher, R. A., *Statistical Methods and Scientific Inference*, New York: Hafner Publishing Co., 1956.

Fisher, R. A., *Statistical Methods for Research Workers*, 13th Edition, New York: Hafner Publishing Co., Inc., 1958.

Freeman, H. A., *Introduction to Statistical Inference*, Reading, Mass.: Addison-Wesley Book Co., 1963.

Freeman, H. A., Friedman, Milton, Mosteller, Frederick, and Wallis, W. A. (eds.), *Sampling Inspection*, New York: McGraw-Hill Book Co., 1948.

Gellerman, S. W., *Management by Motivation*, New York: American Management Association, 1969.

Gellerman, S. W., *Motivation and Productivity*, New York: American Management Association, 1963.

Grant, E. L., and Leavenworth, R. S., *Statistical Quality Control*, 4th Edition, New York: McGraw-Hill Book Co., 1972.

Hansen, Bertrand L., *Quality Control: Theory and Applications*, Englewood Cliffs, N.J.: Prentice Hall, Inc., 1963.

Harris, D. H., and Chaney, F. B., *Human Factors in Quality Assurance*, New York: John Wiley & Sons, Inc., 1969.

Hayes, Glenn E., *Quality Assurance: Management and Technology*, Capistrano Beach, Calif.: Charger Productions, 1974.

Herzberg, F., Mausner, B., and Snyderman, B., *The Motivation to Work*, 2nd Edition, New York: John Wiley & Sons, Inc., 1959.

Howell, John M., and Gold, Ben K., *Elementary Statistics*, 2nd Edition, Dubuque, Iowa: Wm. C. Brown Book Co., 1965.

Juran, J. M. (ed.), *Quality Control Handbook*, 3rd Edition, New York: McGraw-Hill Book Co., 1974.

Juran, J. M., and Gryna, Frank M., Jr., *Quality Planning and Analysis*, New York: McGraw-Hill Book Co., 1970.

Kennedy, C. W., *Quality Control Methods*, Englewood Cliffs, N.J.: Prentice Hall, Inc., 1948.

Kennedy, C. W., and Andrews, D. E., *Inspection and Gaging*, New York: Industrial Press, Inc., 1967.

Kirkpatrick, E. G., *Quality Control for Managers and Engineers*, New York: John Wiley & Sons, Inc., 1970.

Kozich, S. S., *Quality Technology Syllabus*, Los Angeles, Calif.: Hanover Enterprises, 1970.

Lieberman, G. J., and Weon, D. B., *Tables of the Hypergeometric Probability Distribution*, Stanford, Calif.: Stanford University Press, 1961.

Mayo, Elton, *The Social Problems of an Industrial Civilization*, Boston, Mass.: Harvard Business School, 1945.

Mechtly, E. A., University of Illinois, *The International System of Units, Physical Constants and Conversion Factors*, Revised, NASA SP7012, 1969, 19 pages, Scientific and Technical Information Division, Office of Technology Utilization, National Aeronautics and Space Administration, U.S. Government Printing Office, Washington, D.C. 20402. (For Sale by the Superintendent of Documents, Price 30 cents.)

Miles, Lawrence D., *Techniques of Value Analysis and Engineering*, New York: McGraw-Hill Book Co., 1961.

Michelon, L. C., *Industrial Inspection Methods*, New York: Harper and Row Publishers, Inc., 1950.

Molina, E. C., *Poisson's Exponential Binomial Limit*, New York, N.Y.: Van Nostrand Co., Inc., 1949. (Molina's tables contain individual values and cumulative values of the Poisson, both to six decimal places.)

McClelland, D. C., Atkinson, J. W., Clark, R. A., and Lowell, E. L., *The Achievement Motive*, New York: Appleton-Century-Crofts, Inc., 1953.

Moroney, M. J., *Facts from Figures*, 3rd Edition, Harmondsworth, Middlesex, England, and Baltimore, Md.: Penguin Books, Ltd., 1956. (Paperback, a good introduction to statistics for the layman.)

Niebel, B. W., *Motion and Time Study*, 5th Edition, Homewood, Ill.: Richard D. Irwin, 1972.

Nixon, Frank, *Managing to Achieve Quality and Reliability*, New York: McGraw-Hill Book Co., 1971.

Ott, Ellis R., *Process Quality Control,* New York, McGraw–Hill Book Co., 1975.

Peach, Paul, *Industrial Statistics and Quality Control*, 2nd Edition, Raleigh, N.C.: Edwards & Broughton Co., 1947.

Pearson, E. S., and Hartley, H. O. (eds.), *Biometrika Tables for Statisticians*, Vol. I, 2nd Edition, 1958, and Vol. II, 1972. Cambridge, England: The University Press.

Peters, George A., *Product Liability and Safety*, Washington, D.C.: Coiner Publications, Ltd., 1971.

Product Quality Assurance Handbook H-57, Superintendent of Documents, Government Printing Office, Washington, D.C., 1969.

Quality Control and Reliability Handbook (Interim) H 108. "Sampling Procedures for Life and Reliability Testing" (Based on Exponential Distribution), Superintendent of Documents, Government Printing Office, Washington, D.C., 1960.

Quality Control and Reliability Handbook (Interim) H 109. "Statistical Procedures for Determining Validity of Suppliers Attributes Inspection," Superintendent of Documents, Government Printing Office, Washington, D.C., 1960.

Rand Corporation, *A Million Random Digits with 100,000 Normal Deviates*, New York: Glencoe Free Press Division of The Macmillan Co., 1955.

Roethlesberger, F. I., and Dickson, W. I., *Management and the Worker*, Cambridge, Mass.: Harvard University Press, 1939.

Romig, H. G., *Allowable Average in Sampling Inspection*, (Ph.D. thesis submitted to Columbia University, March, 1939. Can probably be borrowed from Columbia University Library.)

Shewhart, W. A., *Economic Control of Quality of Manufactured Products*, New York: D. Van Nostrand Co., Inc., 1931.

Shewhart, W. A., (edited by W. Edwards Deming) *Statistical Method from the Viewpoint of Quality Control*, Washington, D.C.: Graduate School, Department of Agriculture, 1939.

Simon, L. E., *An Engineer's Manual of Statistical Methods*, New York: John Wiley & Sons, Inc., 1941.

Smith, E. S., *Control Charts*, New York: McGraw-Hill Book Co., Inc., 1947.

Smith, J. G., and Duncan, A. J., *Elementary Statistics and Applications*, New York: McGraw-Hill Book Co., 1944.

Smith, J. G., and Duncan, A. J., *Sampling Statistics and Applications*, New York: McGraw-Hill Book Co., 1945.

United States Department of Commerce, Peter G. Peterson, Secretary, National Bureau of Standards/Lawrence M. Kushner, Acting Director. Special Publication 304A, Revised October, 1972, *Brief History of Measurement Systems with a Chart of the Modernized Metric System*, 1972, 4 pages. (For sale by the Superintendent of Documents, U.S. Government Printing Office, Washington, D.C., Price 25 cents.)

United States Department of Commerce, National Bureau of Standards, Applied Mathematics Series 23, *Tables of the Binomial Probability Distribution*, 344 pages, Washington, D.C.: U.S. Govt. Printing Office, 1950.

United States Department of Commerce, National Bureau of Standards, Applied Mathematics Series 6, *Tables of the Binomial Probability Distribution*, 387 pages, Washington, D.C.: U.S. Govt. Printing Office, 1950.

Vaughn, Richard C., *Quality Control*, Ames, Iowa: Iowa State University Press, 1974.

Whyte, W. F., *Money and Motivation*, New York: Harper & Row, Publishers, 1955.

———. Military Standard, *Sampling Procedures and Tables for Inspection by Variables for Percent Defective* (Mil-Std-414), Washington, D.C.: U.S. Government Printing Office, 1957.

———. *Multi-Level Continuous Sampling Procedures and Tables for Inspection by Attributes* (*H 106*). Inspection and Quality Control Handbook (Interim). Washington, D.C.: Office of the Assistant Secretary of Defense (Supply and Logistics), 1958.

———. *Single Level Continuous Sampling Procedures and Tables for Inspection by Attributes* (*H 107*). Inspection and Quality Control Handbook (Interim). Washington, D.C.: Office of the Assistant Secretary of Defense (Supply and Logistics), 1959.

———. *Evaluation of Contract or Quality Control Systems* (*H 110*). Quality Control and Reliability Handbook (Interim). Washington, D. C.: Office of the Assistant Secretary of Defense (Supply and Logistics), 1960.

———. Military Standard, *Sampling Procedures and Tables for Inspection by Attributes* (Mil-Std-105D). Washington, D.C.: U.S. Government Printing Office, 1963.

———. Military Specification, *Quality Control System Requirements* (Mil-Q-9858). Prepared by U.S. Air Force, Headquarters, Air Material Command, Wright-Patterson Air Force Base, Ohio. (A copy may be obtained from any military procurement activity.)

APPENDIX A

Appendix A: Fitting an Observed Distribution with the Best Theoretical Distribution together with Additional Tables Required for Quality Control

Many different tables are used in statistical evaluations. The one most often used for the evaluation of all kinds of data is the normal law. This is often called the *bell-shaped curve* and was apparently first discovered by De Moivre (1756) as the limiting form of the binomial distribution. It is sometimes called the Laplacian or the Second Law of Laplace, or the Gaussian Distribution. Texts in statistics often present two forms of the normal law tables. One form gives the ordinates for a complete range of z values, where z is used to measure values on the usual x-scale; the height of the curve is given as its frequency, as a percentage or fractional value, on the y-scale. These coordinates of the theoretical curve are plotted on Cartesian coordinate paper. This ordinate form is useful primarily for plotting directly the normal curve, where

$$y = \frac{1}{\sqrt{2\pi}} e^{-x^2/2}, \tag{A1}$$

with $y = 0.39894$ when $x = 0$. Here $x = X - \bar{X}$, where X is the observed value and $\bar{X}$ is the average of the distribution. The tabular values are based on the normal law theoretical values, where $\bar{X}' = 0$ and its standard deviation value $\sigma' = 1$. The other parameters for the normal law are its skewness k' which is zero; i.e., $k' = 0$, since the distribution is symmetric, or $\beta'_1 = \mu_3^2/\mu_2^3 = 0$. Its kurtosis or degree of peakedness is β'_2, which is equal to 3. These parameters may be determined from the moments of a given distribution taking into account the fact that the sum of the frequencies shown is 1 for a probability function and n or N for distributions based on n or N units in the sample.of units being tested or under consideration. The variance is the square of the standard deviation and is represented by μ_2, the second moment and $\beta_2 = \mu_4/\mu_2^2 = 3$ for the normal distribution. The true mean may be represented by μ'_1.

The general expression for this continuous frequency distribution with an infinite range is better defined by the equation:

$$dF = \frac{1}{\sigma\sqrt{2\pi}} e^{-\frac{1}{2}\left(\frac{x-m}{\sigma}\right)^2} dx, \; -\infty \leqq x \leqq \infty, \tag{A2}$$

where m is the mean and σ is the standard deviation. In this context, $m = \bar{X}$ and $x = X - \bar{X}$, and $x = X$ when $\bar{X} = 0$. The most useful form is the equation for determining the area under the curve and is written:

$$P_{a,b} = \frac{1}{\sqrt{2\pi}} \int_b^a e^{-x^2/2}\, dx. \tag{A3}$$

This is the form used for table A.1, which gives cumulative probability values. This table gives probability values for z values from -4.99 to $+4.99$ for intervals of z equal to 0.01, for most of the table. This is the most useful form for determining estimates of p values for characteristics with specified tolerances and for fitting a theoretical normal law curve to an observed distribution using the statistics $\bar{X}$ and σ as derived from the data to obtain a theoretical distribution with corresponding frequencies.

Many tolerances are expressed as $\bar{X} \pm$ (tolerance), where the tolerance can be measured by $z\sigma$; then the area between equal tolerance values about the mean is tabulated in table A.2. Another useful table for the normal law is given in table A.3, providing z values for definite probability area values under the normal law curve.

Table A.4 includes two tables, one for $F_1(z)$ and one for $F_2(z)$, used in evaluating the theoretical two-term Gram-Charlier series, where the normal law $F_1(z)$ is the generating function and $F_2(z)$ is the second term obtained by successive differentiations with the skewness k as its multiplier. This special case is sometimes called the Second Approximation. This relation may be used to cover observed distributions which may be skewed to the right or to the left depending on the value of the skewness k. Dr. Shewhart[1] gives the equation for this function as:

$$\int_0^x f(x)dx = \int_0^z \frac{1}{\sqrt{2\pi}} e^{-\frac{z^2}{2}} dz - k \frac{1}{6\sqrt{2\pi}} \left[1 - (1 - z^2) e^{-\frac{z^2}{2}}\right] = F_1(z) - kF_2(z).^1 \tag{A4}$$

Examples showing how these tables may be used are included in this appendix.

Many other theoretical distributions for variables are given in other texts and are also used and discussed in magazine articles or in papers presented at statistical conferences. One of the family of distributions used most frequently after the normal law distribution is that provided by a differential equation developed by Karl Pearson in England.[2] The normal equation is one of these and another is termed a Type III distribution. The Chi-squared distribution is one form of these distributions that is used in many areas. It is used here as a check for "goodness of fit" of a theoretical distribution to an observed distribution. Besides these distributions for variables data, there are also many distributions that are primarily used for attributes data as discussed in the text. The positive binomial distribution was one of these that seemed to apply most frequently for which the normal law was used as an approximation. Table A.5 gives a small table providing values that are most frequently applied where the distribution is a binomial. For such a distribution, the population is considered to be infinite and the universe or lot size is not involved in the mathematical relation for the binomial $(q + p)^n$, where n is the sample size. When N is finite, the applicable equation is the hypergeometric.

For this distribution, each case must be evaluated separately; general tables are not available since condensations in some formal way have never been realized. As an approximation to the hypergeometric, the binomial and some forms of the normal the Poisson exponential distribution are generally applied. Table A.6 gives some of the terms of this Poisson distribution. Since fractional events such as half-defects or quarter-defectives are meaningless, terms are given by integral values. Probabilities are compiled for individual terms and are also given as cumulative values. Where only one form of these tables is provided, such as cumulative probabilities, individual terms may be derived by successive subtractions. Conversely, where individual terms are given, cumulative probabilities may be obtained by addition. Separate tables for each are best.

TABLE A.1 The Cumulative Normal Distribution

$$\text{Part 1: } F(z) = \frac{1}{\sqrt{2\pi}} \int_{-\infty}^{z} e^{-x^2/2}\,dx \text{ for } -4.99 \leqq z \leqq -0.00$$

Example: (*1*) $F(-3.83) = 0.0^{4}641 = 0.0000641$; (*2*) $F(-6.00) = 0.0^{9}987 = 0.000000000987$

z	0.00	0.01	0.02	0.03	0.04	0.05	0.06	0.07	0.08	0.09
−4.9	$0.0^{6}479$	$0.0^{6}455$	$0.0^{6}433$	$0.0^{6}411$	$0.0^{6}391$	$0.0^{6}371$	$0.0^{6}353$	$0.0^{6}335$	$0.0^{6}318$	$0.0^{6}302$
−4.5	$0.0^{5}340$	$0.0^{5}324$	$0.0^{5}309$	$0.0^{5}295$	$0.0^{5}281$	$0.0^{5}268$	$0.0^{5}256$	$0.0^{5}244$	$0.0^{5}232$	$0.0^{5}222$
−4.0	$0.0^{4}317$	$0.0^{4}304$	$0.0^{4}291$	$0.0^{4}279$	$0.0^{4}267$	$0.0^{4}256$	$0.0^{4}245$	$0.0^{4}235$	$0.0^{4}225$	$0.0^{4}216$
−3.8	$0.0^{4}723$	$0.0^{4}695$	$0.0^{4}667$	$0.0^{4}641$	$0.0^{4}615$	$0.0^{4}591$	$0.0^{4}567$	$0.0^{4}544$	$0.0^{4}522$	$0.0^{4}501$
−3.6	$0.0^{3}159$	$0.0^{3}153$	$0.0^{3}147$	$0.0^{3}142$	$0.0^{3}136$	$0.0^{3}131$	$0.0^{3}126$	$0.0^{3}121$	$0.0^{3}117$	$0.0^{3}112$
−3.5	$0.0^{3}233$	$0.0^{3}224$	$0.0^{3}216$	$0.0^{3}208$	$0.0^{3}200$	$0.0^{3}193$	$0.0^{3}185$	$0.0^{3}178$	$0.0^{3}172$	$0.0^{3}165$
−3.4	$0.0^{3}337$	$0.0^{3}325$	$0.0^{3}313$	$0.0^{3}302$	$0.0^{3}291$	$0.0^{3}280$	$0.0^{3}270$	$0.0^{3}260$	$0.0^{3}251$	$0.0^{3}242$
−3.3	$0.0^{3}483$	$0.0^{3}466$	$0.0^{3}450$	$0.0^{3}434$	$0.0^{3}419$	$0.0^{3}404$	$0.0^{3}390$	$0.0^{3}376$	$0.0^{3}362$	$0.0^{3}349$
−3.2	$0.0^{3}687$	$0.0^{3}664$	$0.0^{3}641$	$0.0^{3}619$	$0.0^{3}598$	$0.0^{3}577$	$0.0^{3}557$	$0.0^{3}538$	$0.0^{3}519$	$0.0^{3}501$
−3.1	$0.0^{3}968$	$0.0^{3}935$	$0.0^{3}904$	$0.0^{3}874$	$0.0^{3}845$	$0.0^{3}816$	$0.0^{3}789$	$0.0^{3}762$	$0.0^{3}736$	$0.0^{3}711$
−3.0	$0.0^{2}1350$	$0.0^{2}1306$	$0.0^{2}1264$	$0.0^{2}1223$	$0.0^{2}1183$	$0.0^{2}1144$	$0.0^{2}1107$	$0.0^{2}1070$	$0.0^{2}1035$	$0.0^{2}1001$
−2.9	$0.0^{2}1866$	$0.0^{2}1807$	$0.0^{2}1750$	$0.0^{2}1695$	$0.0^{2}1641$	$0.0^{2}1589$	$0.0^{2}1538$	$0.0^{2}1489$	$0.0^{2}1441$	$0.0^{2}1395$
−2.8	$0.0^{2}2555$	$0.0^{2}2477$	$0.0^{2}2401$	$0.0^{2}2327$	$0.0^{2}2256$	$0.0^{2}2186$	$0.0^{2}2118$	$0.0^{2}2052$	$0.0^{2}1988$	$0.0^{2}1926$
−2.7	$0.0^{2}3467$	$0.0^{2}3364$	$0.0^{2}3264$	$0.0^{2}3167$	$0.0^{2}3072$	$0.0^{2}2980$	$0.0^{2}2890$	$0.0^{2}2803$	$0.0^{2}2718$	$0.0^{2}2635$
−2.6	$0.0^{2}4661$	$0.0^{2}4527$	$0.0^{2}4396$	$0.0^{2}4269$	$0.0^{2}4145$	$0.0^{2}4025$	$0.0^{2}3907$	$0.0^{2}3793$	$0.0^{2}3681$	$0.0^{2}3573$
−2.5	$0.0^{2}6210$	$0.0^{2}6037$	$0.0^{2}5868$	$0.0^{2}5703$	$0.0^{2}5543$	$0.0^{2}5386$	$0.0^{2}5234$	$0.0^{2}5085$	$0.0^{2}4940$	$0.0^{2}4799$
−2.4	$0.0^{2}8198$	$0.0^{2}7976$	$0.0^{2}7760$	$0.0^{2}7549$	$0.0^{2}7344$	$0.0^{2}7143$	$0.0^{2}6947$	$0.0^{2}6756$	$0.0^{2}6569$	$0.0^{2}6387$
−2.3	0.010724	0.010444	0.010170	0.009903	0.009642	0.009387	0.009138	0.008894	0.008656	0.008424
−2.2	0.013903	0.013553	0.013209	0.012874	0.012545	0.012224	0.011911	0.011604	0.011304	0.011011
−2.1	0.017864	0.017429	0.017003	0.016586	0.016177	0.015778	0.015386	0.015003	0.014629	0.014262
−2.0	0.022750	0.022216	0.021692	0.021178	0.020675	0.020182	0.019699	0.019226	0.018763	0.018309
−1.9	0.028717	0.028067	0.027429	0.026803	0.026190	0.025588	0.024998	0.024419	0.023852	0.023295
−1.8	0.035930	0.035148	0.034380	0.033625	0.032884	0.032157	0.031443	0.030742	0.030054	0.029379
−1.7	0.044565	0.043633	0.042716	0.041815	0.040930	0.040059	0.039204	0.038364	0.037538	0.036727
1.6	0.054799	0.053699	0.052616	0.051551	0.050503	0.049471	0.048457	0.047460	0.046479	0.045514
−1.5	0.066807	0.065522	0.064255	0.063008	0.061780	0.060571	0.059380	0.058208	0.057053	0.055917
−1.4	0.080757	0.079270	0.077804	0.076359	0.074934	0.073529	0.072145	0.070781	0.069437	0.068112
−1.3	0.096800	0.095098	0.093418	0.091759	0.090123	0.088508	0.086915	0.085343	0.083793	0.082264
−1.2	0.115070	0.113139	0.111232	0.109349	0.107488	0.105650	0.103835	0.102042	0.100273	0.098525
−1.1	0.135666	0.133500	0.131357	0.129238	0.127143	0.125072	0.123024	0.121000	0.119000	0.117023
−1.0	0.158655	0.156248	0.153864	0.151505	0.149170	0.146859	0.144572	0.142310	0.140071	0.137857
−0.9	0.184060	0.181411	0.178786	0.176186	0.173609	0.171056	0.168528	0.166023	0.163543	0.161087
−0.8	0.211855	0.208970	0.206108	0.203269	0.200454	0.197663	0.194895	0.192150	0.189430	0.186733
−0.7	0.241964	0.238852	0.235762	0.232695	0.229650	0.226627	0.223627	0.220650	0.217695	0.214764
−0.6	0.274253	0.270931	0.267629	0.264347	0.261086	0.257846	0.254627	0.251429	0.248252	0.245097
−0.5	0.308538	0.305026	0.301532	0.298056	0.294599	0.291160	0.287740	0.284339	0.280957	0.277595
−0.4	0.344578	0.340903	0.337243	0.333598	0.329969	0.326355	0.322758	0.319178	0.315614	0.312067
−0.3	0.382089	0.378280	0.374484	0.370700	0.366928	0.363169	0.359424	0.355691	0.351973	0.348268
−0.2	0.420740	0.416834	0.412936	0.409046	0.405165	0.401294	0.397432	0.393580	0.389739	0.385908
−0.1	0.460172	0.456205	0.452242	0.448283	0.444330	0.440382	0.436441	0.43251	0.428576	0.424655
−0.0	0.500000	0.496011	0.492022	0.488034	0.484047	0.480061	0.476078	0.472097	0.468119	0.464144

When more complete probability values are required based on the Normal Law, use should be made of the following tables from which these forms with less significant figures have been compiled.

1. The Staff of the Computation Library, *Tables of the Error Function and of its first Twenty Derivatives*, Cambridge, Massachusetts, Harvard University Press, 1952.
2. National Bureau of Standards, *Tables of Normal Probability Functions*, Applied Mathematics Series—23, issued June 5, 1953, U.S. Government Printing Office, Washington, D.C.

TABLE A.1 The Cumulative Normal Distribution

$$\text{Part 2: } F(z) = \frac{1}{\sqrt{2\pi}} \int_{-\infty}^{z} e^{-x^2/2}\, dx \text{ for } +0.00 \leqq z \leqq 4.99$$

Example: (1) $F(+4.57) = 0.9^5 756 = 0.99999756$; (2) $F(6.00) = 0.9^9 013 = 0.999999999013$

z	0.00	0.01	0.02	0.03	0.04	0.05	0.06	0.07	0.08	0.09
+0.0	0.500000	0.503989	0.507978	0.511966	0.515953	0.519939	0.523922	0.527903	0.531881	0.535856
+0.1	0.539828	0.543795	0.547758	0.551717	0.555670	0.559618	0.563560	0.567495	0.571424	0.575345
+0.2	0.579260	0.583166	0.587064	0.590954	0.594835	0.598706	0.602568	0.606420	0.610261	0.614092
+0.3	0.617911	0.621720	0.625516	0.629300	0.633072	0.636831	0.640576	0.644309	0.648027	0.651732
+0.4	0.655422	0.659097	0.662757	0.666402	0.670031	0.673645	0.677242	0.680822	0.684386	0.687933
+0.5	0.691462	0.694974	0.698468	0.701944	0.705402	0.708840	0.712260	0.715661	0.719043	0.722405
+0.6	0.725747	0.729069	0.732371	0.735653	0.738914	0.742154	0.745373	0.748571	0.751748	0.754903
+0.7	0.758036	0.761148	0.764238	0.767305	0.770350	0.773373	0.776373	0.779350	0.782305	0.785236
+0.8	0.788145	0.791030	0.793892	0.796731	0.799546	0.802338	0.805106	0.807850	0.810570	0.813267
+0.9	0.815940	0.818589	0.821214	0.823814	0.826391	0.828944	0.831472	0.833977	0.836457	0.838913
+1.0	0.841345	0.843752	0.846136	0.848495	0.850830	0.853141	0.855428	0.857690	0.859929	0.862143
+1.1	0.864334	0.866500	0.868643	0.870762	0.872857	0.874928	0.876976	0.879000	0.881000	0.882977
+1.2	0.884930	0.886861	0.888768	0.890651	0.892512	0.894350	0.896165	0.897958	0.899727	0.901475
+1.3	0.903200	0.904902	0.906582	0.908241	0.909877	0.911492	0.913085	0.914656	0.916207	0.917736
+1.4	0.919243	0.920730	0.922196	0.923642	0.925066	0.926471	0.927855	0.929219	0.930563	0.931888
+1.5	0.933193	0.934478	0.935744	0.936992	0.938220	0.939429	0.940620	0.941792	0.942947	0.944083
+1.6	0.945201	0.946301	0.947384	0.948449	0.949497	0.950528	0.951543	0.952540	0.953521	0.954486
+1.7	0.955434	0.956367	0.957284	0.958185	0.959070	0.959941	0.960796	0.961636	0.962462	0.963273
+1.8	0.964070	0.964852	0.965620	0.966375	0.967116	0.967843	0.968557	0.969258	0.969946	0.970621
+1.9	0.971283	0.971933	0.972571	0.973197	0.973810	0.974412	0.975002	0.975581	0.976148	0.976704
+2.0	0.977250	0.977784	0.978308	0.978822	0.979325	0.979818	0.980301	0.980774	0.981237	0.981691
+2.1	0.982136	0.982571	0.982997	0.983414	0.983823	0.984222	0.984614	0.984997	0.985371	0.985738
+2.2	0.986097	0.986447	0.986791	0.987126	0.987454	0.987776	0.988089	0.988396	0.988696	0.988989
+2.3	0.989276	0.989556	0.989830	0.990097	0.990358	0.990613	0.990862	0.991106	0.991344	0.991576
+2.4	$0.9^2 1802$	$0.9^2 2024$	$0.9^2 2240$	$0.9^2 2451$	$0.9^2 2656$	$0.9^2 2857$	$0.9^2 3053$	$0.9^2 3244$	$0.9^2 3431$	$0.9^2 3613$
+2.5	$0.9^2 3790$	$0.9^2 3963$	$0.9^2 4132$	$0.9^2 4297$	$0.9^2 4457$	$0.9^2 4614$	$0.9^2 4766$	$0.9^2 4915$	$0.9^2 5060$	$0.9^2 5201$
+2.6	$0.9^2 5339$	$0.9^2 5473$	$0.9^2 5604$	$0.9^2 5731$	$0.9^2 5855$	$0.9^2 5975$	$0.9^2 6093$	$0.9^2 6207$	$0.9^2 6319$	$0.9^2 6427$
+2.7	$0.9^2 6533$	$0.9^2 6636$	$0.9^2 6736$	$0.9^2 6833$	$0.9^2 6928$	$0.9^2 7020$	$0.9^2 7110$	$0.9^2 7197$	$0.9^2 7282$	$0.9^2 7365$
+2.8	$0.9^2 7445$	$0.9^2 7523$	$0.9^2 7599$	$0.9^2 7673$	$0.9^2 7744$	$0.9^2 7814$	$0.9^2 7882$	$0.9^2 7948$	$0.9^2 8012$	$0.9^2 8074$
+2.9	$0.9^2 8134$	$0.9^2 8193$	$0.9^2 8250$	$0.9^2 8305$	$0.9^2 8359$	$0.9^2 8411$	$0.9^2 8462$	$0.9^2 8511$	$0.9^2 8559$	$0.9^2 8605$
+3.0	$0.9^2 8650$	$0.9^2 8694$	$0.9^2 8736$	$0.9^2 8777$	$0.9^2 8817$	$0.9^2 8856$	$0.9^2 8893$	$0.9^2 8930$	$0.9^2 8965$	$0.9^2 8999$
+3.1	$0.9^3 032$	$0.9^3 065$	$0.9^3 096$	$0.9^3 126$	$0.9^3 155$	$0.9^3 184$	$0.9^3 211$	$0.9^3 238$	$0.9^3 264$	$0.9^3 289$
+3.2	$0.9^3 313$	$0.9^3 336$	$0.9^3 359$	$0.9^3 381$	$0.9^3 402$	$0.9^3 423$	$0.9^3 443$	$0.9^3 462$	$0.9^3 481$	$0.9^3 499$
+3.3	$0.9^3 517$	$0.9^3 534$	$0.9^3 550$	$0.9^3 566$	$0.9^3 581$	$0.9^3 596$	$0.9^3 610$	$0.9^3 624$	$0.9^3 638$	$0.9^3 650$
+3.4	$0.9^3 663$	$0.9^3 675$	$0.9^3 687$	$0.9^3 698$	$0.9^3 709$	$0.9^3 720$	$0.9^3 730$	$0.9^3 740$	$0.9^3 749$	$0.9^3 758$
+3.5	$0.9^3 767$	$0.9^3 776$	$0.9^3 784$	$0.9^3 792$	$0.9^3 800$	$0.9^3 807$	$0.9^3 815$	$0.9^3 822$	$0.9^3 828$	$0.9^3 835$
+3.6	$0.9^3 841$	$0.9^3 847$	$0.9^3 853$	$0.9^3 858$	$0.9^3 864$	$0.9^3 869$	$0.9^3 874$	$0.9^3 879$	$0.9^3 883$	$0.9^3 888$
+3.8	$0.9^4 277$	$0.9^4 305$	$0.9^4 333$	$0.9^4 359$	$0.0^4 385$	$0.9^4 409$	$0.9^4 433$	$0.9^4 456$	$0.9^4 478$	$0.9^4 499$
+4.0	$0.9^4 683$	$0.9^4 696$	$0.9^4 709$	$0.9^4 721$	$0.9^4 733$	$0.9^4 744$	$0.9^4 755$	$0.9^4 765$	$0.9^4 775$	$0.9^4 784$
+4.5	$0.9^5 660$	$0.9^5 676$	$0.9^5 691$	$0.9^5 705$	$0.9^5 719$	$0.9^5 732$	$0.9^5 744$	$0.9^5 756$	$0.9^5 768$	$0.9^5 778$
+4.9	$0.9^6 521$	$0.9^6 545$	$0.9^6 567$	$0.9^6 589$	$0.9^6 609$	$0.9^6 629$	$0.9^6 648$	$0.9^6 665$	$0.9^6 682$	$0.9^6 698$

TABLE A.2 Normal Probability Function

$$F(z) = \frac{1}{\sqrt{2\pi}} \int_{-x}^{+z} e^{-x^2/2}\,dx$$

Example: $F(6.00) = 0.9^{8}803 = 0.99999999803$

z	0.00	0.01	0.02	0.03	0.04	0.05	0.06	0.07	0.08	0.09
0.0	0.000000	0.007979	0.015957	0.023933	0.031907	0.039878	0.047844	0.055806	0.063763	0.071713
0.1	0.079656	0.087591	0.095517	0.103434	0.111340	0.119235	0.127119	0.134990	0.142847	0.150691
0.2	0.158519	0.166332	0.174129	0.181908	0.189670	0.197413	0.205136	0.212840	0.220522	0.228184
0.3	0.235823	0.243439	0.251032	0.258600	0.266143	0.273661	0.281153	0.288618	0.296055	0.303463
0.4	0.310843	0.318194	0.325515	0.332804	0.340063	0.347290	0.354484	0.361645	0.368773	0.375866
0.5	0.382925	0.389949	0.396936	0.403888	0.410803	0.417681	0.424521	0.431322	0.438085	0.444809
0.6	0.451494	0.458138	0.464742	0.471305	0.477827	0.484308	0.490746	0.497142	0.503496	0.509806
0.7	0.516073	0.522296	0.528475	0.534610	0.540700	0.546745	0.552745	0.558700	0.564609	0.570472
0.8	0.576289	0.582060	0.587784	0.593461	0.599092	0.604675	0.610211	0.615700	0.621141	0.626534
0.9	0.631880	0.637177	0.642427	0.647629	0.652782	0.657888	0.662945	0.667954	0.672914	0.677826
1.0	0.682689	0.687505	0.692272	0.696990	0.701660	0.706282	0.710855	0.715381	0.719858	0.724287
1.1	0.728668	0.733001	0.737286	0.741524	0.745714	0.749856	0.753951	0.757999	0.762000	0.765954
1.2	0.769861	0.773721	0.777535	0.781303	0.785025	0.788700	0.792331	0.795915	0.799455	0.802949
1.3	0.806399	0.809804	0.813165	0.816482	0.819755	0.822984	0.826170	0.829313	0.832413	0.835471
1.4	0.838487	0.841460	0.844392	0.847283	0.850133	0.852941	0.855710	0.858438	0.861127	0.863776
1.5	0.866386	0.868957	0.871489	0.873983	0.876440	0.878858	0.881240	0.883585	0.885893	0.888165
1.6	0.890401	0.892602	0.894768	0.896899	0.898995	0.901057	0.903086	0.905081	0.907043	0.908972
1.7	0.910869	0.912734	0.914568	0.916370	0.918141	0.919882	0.921592	0.923273	0.924924	0.926546
1.8	0.928139	0.929704	0.931241	0.932750	0.934232	0.935686	0.937114	0.938516	0.939892	0.941242
1.9	0.942567	0.943867	0.945142	0.946393	0.947620	0.948824	0.950004	0.951162	0.952296	0.953409
2.0	0.954500	0.955569	0.956617	0.957643	0.958650	0.959636	0.960601	0.961548	0.962474	0.963382
2.1	0.964271	0.965142	0.965994	0.966828	0.967645	0.968445	0.969227	0.969993	0.970743	0.971476
2.2	0.972193	0.972895	0.973581	0.974253	0.974909	0.975551	0.976179	0.976792	0.977392	0.977979
2.3	0.978552	0.979112	0.979659	0.980194	0.980716	0.981227	0.981725	0.982212	0.982687	0.983152
2.4	0.983605	0.984047	0.984479	0.984901	0.985313	0.985714	0.986106	0.986489	0.986862	0.987226
2.5	0.987581	0.987927	0.988265	0.988594	0.988915	0.989228	0.989533	0.989830	0.990120	0.990402
2.6	0.990678	0.990946	0.991207	0.991462	0.991709	0.991951	0.992186	0.992415	0.992638	0.992855
2.7	0.993066	0.993272	0.993472	0.993667	0.993856	0.994040	0.994220	0.994394	0.994564	0.994729
2.8	0.994890	0.995046	0.995198	0.995345	0.995489	0.995628	0.995764	0.995895	0.996023	0.996148
2.9	0.996268	0.996386	0.996500	0.996610	0.996718	0.996822	0.996924	0.997022	0.997118	0.997210
3.0	0.997300	0.997388	0.997472	0.997554	0.997634	0.997712	0.997787	0.997859	0.997930	0.997998
3.1	0.998065	0.998129	0.998191	0.998252	0.998311	0.998367	0.998422	0.998476	0.998527	0.998577
3.2	0.998626	0.998673	0.998718	0.998762	0.998805	0.998846	0.998886	0.998925	0.998962	0.998998
3.3	0.999033	0.999067	0.999100	0.999132	0.999162	0.999192	0.999221	0.999248	0.999275	0.999301
3.4	0.999326	0.999350	0.999374	0.999396	0.999418	0.999439	0.999460	0.999480	0.999499	0.999517
3.5	0.999535	0.999552	0.999568	0.999584	0.999600	0.999615	0.999629	0.999643	0.999656	0.999669
3.6	$0.9^{3}682$	$0.9^{3}694$	$0.9^{3}705$	$0.9^{3}717$	$0.9^{3}727$	$0.9^{3}738$	$0.9^{3}748$	$0.9^{3}757$	$0.9^{3}767$	$0.9^{3}776$
3.8	$0.9^{3}855$	$0.9^{3}861$	$0.9^{3}867$	$0.9^{3}872$	$0.9^{3}877$	$0.9^{3}882$	$0.9^{3}887$	$0.9^{3}891$	$0.9^{3}896$	$0.9^{3}900$
4.0	$0.9^{4}367$	$0.9^{4}393$	$0.9^{4}418$	$0.9^{4}442$	$0.9^{4}465$	$0.9^{4}488$	$0.9^{4}509$	$0.9^{4}530$	$0.9^{4}550$	$0.9^{4}569$
4.5	$0.9^{5}320$	$0.9^{5}352$	$0.9^{5}382$	$0.9^{5}410$	$0.9^{5}437$	$0.9^{5}464$	$0.9^{5}488$	$0.9^{5}512$	$0.9^{5}535$	$0.9^{5}557$
5.0	$0.9^{6}427$	$0.9^{6}456$	$0.9^{6}483$	$0.9^{6}510$	$0.9^{6}534$	$0.9^{6}558$	$0.9^{6}581$	$0.9^{6}602$	$0.9^{6}623$	$0.9^{6}642$

TABLE A.3 Inverse of the Normal Probability Distribution

Part 1: Table of z Deviates of the Normal Curve for each Permille (3 significant figures, per thousand) of Frequency

Permille	*0.000*	*0.001*	*0.002*	*0.003*	*0.004*	*0.005*	*0.006*	*0.007*	*0.008*	*0.009*	*0.010*	
0.00	∞	3.0902	2.8782	2.7478	2.6521	2.5758	2.5121	2.4573	2.4089	2.3656	2.3263	*0.99*
0.01	2.3263	2.2904	2.2571	2.2262	2.1973	2.1701	2.1444	2.1201	2.0969	2.0749	2.0537	*0.98*
0.02	2.0537	2.0335	2.0141	1.9954	1.9774	1.9600	1.9431	1.9268	1.9110	1.8957	1.8808	*0.97*
0.03	1.8808	1.8663	1.8522	1.8384	1.8250	1.8119	1.7991	1.7866	1.7744	1.7624	1.7507	*0.96*
0.04	1.7507	1.7392	1.7279	1.7169	1.7060	1.6954	1.6849	1.6747	1.6646	1.6546	1.6449	*0.95*
0.05	1.6449	1.6352	1.6258	1.6164	1.6072	1.5982	1.5893	1.5805	1.5718	1.5632	1.5548	*0.94*
0.06	1.5540	1.5464	1.5382	1.5301	1.5220	1.5141	1.5063	1.4985	1.4909	1.4833	1.4758	*0.93*
0.07	1.4758	1.4684	1.4611	1.4538	1.4466	1.4395	1.4325	1.4255	1.4187	1.4118	1.4051	*0.92*
0.08	1.4051	1.3984	1.3917	1.3852	1.3787	1.3722	1.3658	1.3595	1.3532	1.3469	1.3408	*0.91*
0.09	1.3408	1.3346	1.3285	1.3225	1.3165	1.3106	1.3047	1.2988	1.2930	1.2873	1.2816	*0.90*
0.10	1.2816	1.2759	1.2702	1.2646	1.2591	1.2536	1.2481	1.2426	1.2372	1.2319	1.2265	*0.89*
0.11	1.2265	1.2212	1.2160	1.2107	1.2055	1.2004	1.1952	1.1901	1.1850	1.1800	1.1750	*0.88*
0.12	1.1750	1.1700	1.1650	1.1601	1.1552	1.1503	1.1455	1.1407	1.1359	1.1311	1.1264	*0.87*
0.13	1.1264	1.1217	1.1170	1.1123	1.1077	1.1031	1.0985	1.0939	1.0893	1.0848	1.0803	*0.86*
0.14	1.0803	1.0758	1.0714	1.0669	1.0625	1.0581	1.0537	1.0494	1.0450	1.0407	1.0364	*0.85*
0.15	1.0364	1.0322	1.0279	1.0237	1.0194	1.0152	1.0110	1.0069	1.0027	0.9986	0.9945	*0.84*
0.16	0.9945	0.9904	0.9863	0.9822	0.9782	0.9741	0.9701	0.9661	0.9621	0.9581	0.9542	*0.83*
0.17	0.9542	0.9502	0.9463	0.9424	0.9385	0.9346	0.9307	0.9269	0.9230	0.9192	0.9154	*0.82*
0.18	0.9154	0.9116	0.9078	0.9040	0.9002	0.8965	0.8927	0.8890	0.8853	0.8816	0.8779	*0.81*
0.19	0.8779	0.8742	0.8705	0.8669	0.8633	0.8596	0.8560	0.8524	0.8488	0.8452	0.8416	*0.80*
0.20	0.8416	0.8381	0.8345	0.8310	0.8274	0.8239	0.8204	0.8169	0.8134	0.8099	0.8064	*0.79*
0.21	0.8064	0.8030	0.7995	0.7961	0.7926	0.7892	0.7858	0.7824	0.7790	0.7756	0.7722	*0.78*
0.22	0.7722	0.7688	0.7655	0.7621	0.7588	0.7554	0.7521	0.7488	0.7454	0.7421	0.7388	*0.77*
0.23	0.7388	0.7356	0.7323	0.7290	0.7257	0.7225	0.7192	0.7160	0.7128	0.7095	0.7063	*0.76*
0.24	0.7063	0.7031	0.6999	0.6967	0.6935	0.6903	0.6871	0.6840	0.6808	0.6776	0.6745	*0.75*
0.25	0.6745	0.6713	0.6682	0.6651	0.6620	0.6588	0.6557	0.6526	0.6495	0.6464	0.6433	*0.74*
0.26	0.6433	0.6403	0.6372	0.6341	0.6311	0.6280	0.6250	0.6219	0.6189	0.6158	0.6128	*0.73*
0.27	0.6128	0.6098	0.6068	0.6038	0.6008	0.5978	0.5948	0.5918	0.5888	0.5858	0.5828	*0.72*
0.28	0.5828	0.5799	0.5769	0.5740	0.5710	0.5681	0.5651	0.5622	0.5592	0.5563	0.5534	*0.71*
0.29	0.5534	0.5505	0.5476	0.5446	0.5417	0.5388	0.5359	0.5330	0.5302	0.5273	0.5244	*0.70*
0.30	0.5244	0.5215	0.5187	0.5158	0.5129	0.5101	0.5072	0.5044	0.5015	0.4987	0.4959	*0.69*
0.31	0.4959	0.4930	0.4902	0.4874	0.4845	0.4817	0.4789	0.4761	0.4733	0.4705	0.4677	*0.68*
0.32	0.4677	0.4649	0.4621	0.4593	0.4565	0.4538	0.4510	0.4482	0.4454	0.4427	0.4399	*0.67*
0.33	0.4399	0.4372	0.4344	0.4316	0.4289	0.4261	0.4234	0.4207	0.4179	0.4152	0.4125	*0.66*
0.34	0.4125	0.4097	0.4070	0.4043	0.4016	0.3989	0.3961	0.3934	0.3907	0.3880	0.3853	*0.65*
0.35	0.3853	0.3826	0.3799	0.3772	0.3745	0.3719	0.3692	0.3665	0.3638	0.3611	0.3585	*0.64*
0.36	0.3585	0.3558	0.3531	0.3505	0.3478	0.3451	0.3425	0.3398	0.3372	0.3345	0.3319	*0.63*
0.37	0.3319	0.3292	0.3266	0.3239	0.3213	0.3186	0.3160	0.3134	0.3107	0.3081	0.3055	*0.62*
0.38	0.3055	0.3029	0.3002	0.2976	0.2950	0.2924	0.2898	0.2871	0.2845	0.2819	0.2793	*0.61*
0.39	0.2793	0.2767	0.2741	0.2715	0.2689	0.2663	0.2637	0.2611	0.2585	0.2559	0.2533	*0.60*
0.40	0.2533	0.2508	0.2482	0.2456	0.2430	0.2404	0.2378	0.2353	0.2327	0.2301	0.2275	*0.59*
0.41	0.2275	0.2250	0.2224	0.2198	0.2173	0.2147	0.2121	0.2096	0.2070	0.2045	0.2019	*0.58*
0.42	0.2019	0.1993	0.1968	0.1942	0.1917	0.1891	0.1866	0.1840	0.1815	0.1789	0.1764	*0.57*
0.43	0.1764	0.1738	0.1713	0.1687	0.1662	0.1637	0.1611	0.1586	0.1560	0.1535	0.1510	*0.56*
0.44	0.1510	0.1484	0.1459	0.1434	0.1408	0.1383	0.1358	0.1332	0.1307	0.1282	0.1257	*0.55*
0.45	0.1257	0.1231	0.1206	0.1181	0.1156	0.1130	0.1105	0.1080	0.1055	0.1030	0.1004	*0.54*
0.46	0.1004	0.0979	0.0954	0.0929	0.0904	0.0878	0.0853	0.0828	0.0803	0.0778	0.0753	*0.53*
0.47	0.0753	0.0728	0.0702	0.0677	0.0652	0.0627	0.0602	0.0577	0.0552	0.0527	0.0502	*0.52*
0.48	0.0502	0.0476	0.0451	0.0426	0.0401	0.0376	0.0351	0.0326	0.0301	0.0276	0.0251	*0.51*
0.49	0.0251	0.0226	0.0201	0.0175	0.0150	0.0125	0.0100	0.0075	0.0050	0.0025	0.0000	*0.50*
	0.010	*0.009*	*0.008*	*0.007*	*0.006*	*0.005*	*0.004*	*0.003*	*0.002*	*0.001*	*0.000*	*Permille*

TABLE A.3 Inverse of the Normal Probability Distribution

Part 2: z Deviates of the Normal Distribution for P values 0.50 to 0.999999999 for most Practical Applications.

P	z	y	Q	P	z	y	Q
0.50	0.00000	0.39894	0.50	0.925	1.43953	0.14156	0.075
0.51	0.02507	0.39882	0.49	0.930	1.47579	0.13427	0.070
0.52	0.05015	0.39844	0.48	0.935	1.51410	0.12679	0.065
0.53	0.07527	0.39781	0.47	0.940	1.55477	0.11912	0.060
0.54	0.10043	0.39694	0.46	0.945	1.59819	0.11124	0.055
0.55	0.12566	0.39580	0.45	0.950	1.64485	0.10314	0.050
0.56	0.15097	0.39442	0.44	0.955	1.69540	0.09479	0.045
0.57	0.17637	0.39279	0.43	0.960	1.75069	0.08617	0.040
0.58	0.20189	0.39089	0.42	0.965	1.81191	0.07727	0.035
0.59	0.22754	0.38875	0.41	0.970	1.88079	0.06804	0.030
0.60	0.25335	0.38634	0.40	0.975	1.95996	0.05845	0.025
0.61	0.27932	0.38368	0.39	0.980	2.05375	0.04842	0.020
0.62	0.30548	0.38076	0.38	0.985	2.17009	0.03787	0.015
0.63	0.33185	0.37757	0.37	0.990	2.32635	0.02665	0.010
0.64	0.35846	0.37412	0.36				
0.65	0.38532	0.37040	0.35	0.991	2.36562	0.02431	0.009
0.66	0.41246	0.36641	0.34	0.992	2.40892	0.02192	0.008
0.67	0.43991	0.36215	0.33	0.993	2.45726	0.01949	0.007
0.68	0.46770	0.35761	0.32	0.994	2.51214	0.01700	0.006
0.69	0.49585	0.35279	0.31	0.995	2.57583	0.01446	0.005
0.70	0.52440	0.34769	0.30	0.996	2.65207	0.01185	0.004
0.71	0.55338	0.34230	0.29	0.997	2.74778	0.00915	0.003
0.72	0.58284	0.33662	0.28	0.998	2.87816	0.00634	0.002
0.73	0.61281	0.33065	0.27	0.999	3.09023	0.00337	0.001
0.74	0.64335	0.32437	0.26				
0.75	0.67449	0.31778	0.25	0.9991	3.12139	0.00306	0.0009
0.76	0.70630	0.31087	0.24	0.9992	3.15591	0.00274	0.0008
0.77	0.73885	0.30365	0.23	0.9993	3.19465	0.00243	0.0007
0.78	0.77219	0.29609	0.22	0.9994	3.23888	0.00210	0.0006
0.79	0.80642	0.28820	0.21	0.9995	3.29053	0.00178	0.0005
0.80	0.84162	0.27996	0.20	0.9996	3.35279	0.00145	0.0004
0.81	0.87790	0.27137	0.19	0.9997	3.43161	0.00111	0.0003
0.82	0.91537	0.26240	0.18	0.9998	3.54008	0.00076	0.0002
0.83	0.95417	0.25305	0.17	0.9999	3.71902	0.00040	0.0001
0.84	0.99446	0.24331	0.16				
0.85	1.03643	0.23316	0.15	0.99995	3.89059	0.00021	0.00005
0.86	1.08032	0.22258	0.14	0.99999	4.26489	0.00004	0.00001
0.87	1.12639	0.21155	0.13	0.999995	4.41717	0.00002	0.000005
0.88	1.17499	0.20004	0.12	0.999999	4.75342	0.00000	0.000001
0.89	1.22653	0.18804	0.11	0.9999995	4.89164	0.00000	0.0000005
0.900	1.28155	0.17550	0.10	0.9999999	5.19934	0.00000	0.0000001
0.905	1.31058	0.16902	0.095	0.99999995	5.32672	0.00000	0.00000005
0.910	1.34076	0.16239	0.090	0.99999999	5.61200	0.00000	0.00000001
0.915	1.37220	0.15561	0.085	0.999999995	5.73073	0.00000	0.000000005
0.920	1.40507	0.14867	0.080	0.999999999	5.99781	0.00000	0.000000001

TABLE A.4 Second Approximation Distribution

$$F(z) = F_1(z) - kF_2(z)$$

Table A. Values of $F_1(z) = \dfrac{1}{\sqrt{2\pi}} \displaystyle\int_0^z e^{-1/2z^2}\,dz$

z	$F_1(z)$	z	$F_1(z)$	z	$F_1(z)$	z	$F_1(z)$	z	$F_1(z)$	z	$F_1(z)$	z	$F_1(z)$
0.00	0.0000	0.45	0.1737	0.90	0.3160	1.35	0.4115	1.80	0.4641	2.25	0.4878	2.70	0.4966
0.01	0.0040	0.46	0.1773	0.91	0.3186	1.36	0.4131	1.81	0.4649	2.26	0.4881	2.71	0.4967
0.02	0.0080	0.47	0.1808	0.92	0.3212	1.37	0.4147	1.82	0.4656	2.27	0.4884	2.72	0.4968
0.03	0.0120	0.48	0.1844	0.93	0.3238	1.38	0.4162	1.83	0.4664	2.28	0.4887	2.73	0.4969
0.04	0.0160	0.49	0.1880	0.94	0.3264	1.39	0.4178	1.84	0.4671	2.29	0.4890	2.74	0.4970
0.05	0.0200	0.50	0.1915	0.95	0.3290	1.40	0.4193	1.85	0.4679	2.30	0.4893	2.75	0.4970
0.06	0.0239	0.51	0.1950	0.96	0.3315	1.41	0.4208	1.86	0.4686	2.31	0.4896	2.76	0.4971
0.07	0.0279	0.52	0.1985	0.97	0.3340	1.42	0.4222	1.87	0.4693	2.32	0.4899	2.77	0.4972
0.08	0.0319	0.53	0.2020	0.98	0.3365	1.43	0.4237	1.88	0.4700	2.33	0.4901	2.78	0.4973
0.09	0.0359	0.54	0.2054	0.99	0.3389	1.44	0.4251	1.89	0.4706	2.34	0.4904	2.79	0.4974
0.10	0.0399	0.55	0.2089	1.00	0.3414	1.45	0.4265	1.90	0.4713	2.35	0.4906	2.80	0.4975
0.11	0.0438	0.56	0.2123	1.01	0.3438	1.46	0.4279	1.91	0.4720	2.36	0.4909	2.81	0.4975
0.12	0.0478	0.57	0.2157	1.02	0.3462	1.47	0.4292	1.92	0.4726	2.37	0.4911	2.82	0.4976
0.13	0.0517	0.58	0.2191	1.03	0.3485	1.48	0.4306	1.93	0.4732	2.38	0.4914	2.83	0.4977
0.14	0.0557	0.59	0.2224	1.04	0.3508	1.49	0.4319	1.94	0.4738	2.39	0.4916	2.84	0.4978
0.15	0.0596	0.60	0.2258	1.05	0.3532	1.50	0.4332	1.95	0.4744	2.40	0.4918	2.85	0.4978
0.16	0.0636	0.61	0.2291	1.06	0.3555	1.51	0.4345	1.96	0.4750	2.41	0.4920	2.86	0.4979
0.17	0.0675	0.62	0.2324	1.07	0.3577	1.52	0.4358	1.97	0.4756	2.42	0.4923	2.87	0.4980
0.18	0.0714	0.63	0.2357	1.08	0.3599	1.53	0.4370	1.98	0.4762	2.43	0.4925	2.88	0.4980
0.19	0.0754	0.64	0.2389	1.09	0.3622	1.54	0.4382	1.99	0.4768	2.44	0.4927	2.89	0.4981
0.20	0.0793	0.65	0.2422	1.10	0.3644	1.55	0.4395	2.00	0.4773	2.45	0.4929	2.90	0.4982
0.21	0.0832	0.66	0.2454	1.11	0.3665	1.56	0.4406	2.01	0.4778	2.46	0.4931	2.91	0.4982
0.22	0.0871	0.67	0.2486	1.12	0.3687	1.57	0.4418	2.02	0.4783	2.47	0.4933	2.92	0.4983
0.23	0.0910	0.68	0.2518	1.13	0.3708	1.58	0.4430	2.03	0.4788	2.48	0.4935	2.93	0.4983
0.24	0.0949	0.69	0.2549	1.14	0.3729	1.59	0.4441	2.04	0.4793	2.49	0.4936	2.94	0.4984
0.25	0.0987	0.70	0.2581	1.15	0.3749	1.60	0.4452	2.05	0.4798	2.50	0.4938	2.95	0.4984
0.26	0.1026	0.71	0.2612	1.16	0.3770	1.61	0.4463	2.06	0.4803	2.51	0.4940	2.96	0.4985
0.27	0.1064	0.72	0.2643	1.17	0.3790	1.62	0.4474	2.07	0.4808	2.52	0.4942	2.97	0.4985
0.28	0.1103	0.73	0.2673	1.18	0.3810	1.63	0.4485	2.08	0.4813	2.53	0.4943	2.98	0.4986
0.29	0.1141	0.74	0.2704	1.19	0.3830	1.64	0.4495	2.09	0.4817	2.54	0.4945	2.99	0.4986
0.30	0.1179	0.75	0.2734	1.20	0.3850	1.65	0.4506	2.10	0.4822	2.55	0.4946	3.00	0.4987
0.31	0.1217	0.76	0.2764	1.21	0.3869	1.66	0.4516	2.11	0.4826	2.56	0.4948	3.10	0.4991
0.32	0.1255	0.77	0.2794	1.22	0.3888	1.67	0.4526	2.12	0.4830	2.57	0.4949	3.20	0.4993
0.33	0.1293	0.78	0.2823	1.23	0.3907	1.68	0.4535	2.13	0.4834	2.58	0.4951	3.30	0.4995
0.34	0.1331	0.79	0.2853	1.24	0.3925	1.69	0.4545	2.14	0.4838	2.59	0.4952	3.40	0.4997
0.35	0.1369	0.80	0.2882	1.25	0.3944	1.70	0.4555	2.15	0.4842	2.60	0.4954	3.50	0.4998
0.36	0.1406	0.81	0.2911	1.26	0.3962	1.71	0.4564	2.16	0.4846	2.61	0.4955	3.60	0.4999
0.37	0.1443	0.82	0.2939	1.27	0.3980	1.72	0.4573	2.17	0.4850	2.62	0.4956	3.70	0.4999
0.38	0.1481	0.83	0.2968	1.28	0.3997	1.73	0.4582	2.18	0.4854	2.63	0.4958	3.80	0.5000
0.39	0.1518	0.84	0.2996	1.29	0.4015	1.74	0.4591	2.19	0.4858	2.64	0.4959	3.90	0.5000
0.40	0.1554	0.85	0.3024	1.30	0.4032	1.75	0.4599	2.20	0.4861	2.65	0.4960	4.00	0.5000
0.41	0.1591	0.86	0.3051	1.31	0.4049	1.76	0.4608	2.21	0.4865	2.66	0.4961	∞	0.5000
0.42	0.1628	0.87	0.3079	1.32	0.4066	1.77	0.4617	2.22	0.4868	2.67	0.4962		
0.43	0.1664	0.88	0.3106	1.33	0.4083	1.78	0.4626	2.23	0.4872	2.68	0.4963		
0.44	0.1701	0.89	0.3133	1.34	0.4099	1.79	0.4633	2.24	0.4875	2.69	0.4965		

TABLE A.4 Second Approximation Distribution

$$F(z) = F_1(z) - kF_2(z)$$

Table B. Values of $F_2(z) = \frac{1}{6\sqrt{2\pi}}[1 - (1 - z^2)e^{-1/2z^2}]$

z	$F_2(z)$	z	$F_2(z)$	z	$F_2(z)$	z	$F_2(z)$	z	$F_2(z)$	z	$F_2(z)$	z	$F_2(z)$
0.00	0.00000	0.45	0.01857	0.90	0.05806	1.35	0.08848	1.80	0.09597	2.25	0.08798	2.70	0.07742
0.01	0.00001	0.46	0.01933	0.91	0.05894	1.36	0.08890	1.81	0.09590	2.26	0.08774	2.71	0.07722
0.02	0.00004	0.47	0.02011	0.92	0.05980	1.37	0.08930	1.82	0.09584	2.27	0.08749	2.72	0.07702
0.03	0.00009	0.48	0.02089	0.93	0.06066	1.38	0.08970	1.83	0.09576	2.28	0.08724	2.73	0.07682
0.04	0.00016	0.49	0.02168	0.94	0.06152	1.39	0.09008	1.84	0.09568	2.29	0.08699	2.74	0.07663
0.05	0.00025	0.50	0.02248	0.95	0.06236	1.40	0.09045	1.85	0.09559	2.30	0.08674	2.75	0.07644
0.06	0.00036	0.51	0.02329	0.96	0.06320	1.41	0.09080	1.86	0.09549	2.31	0.08650	2.76	0.07625
0.07	0.00049	0.52	0.02411	0.97	0.06404	1.42	0.09115	1.87	0.09539	2.32	0.08625	2.77	0.07606
0.08	0.00064	0.53	0.02494	0.98	0.06486	1.43	0.09148	1.88	0.09527	2.33	0.08600	2.78	0.07588
0.09	0.00081	0.54	0.02578	0.99	0.06568	1.44	0.09180	1.89	0.09516	2.34	0.08575	2.79	0.07569
0.10	0.00099	0.55	0.02662	1.00	0.06649	1.45	0.09211	1.90	0.09503	2.35	0.08550	2.80	0.07551
0.11	0.00120	0.56	0.02748	1.01	0.06729	1.46	0.09241	1.91	0.09490	2.36	0.08525	2.81	0.07534
0.12	0.00143	0.57	0.02833	1.02	0.06809	1.47	0.09269	1.92	0.09477	2.37	0.08500	2.82	0.07516
0.13	0.00167	0.58	0.02920	1.03	0.06887	1.48	0.09296	1.93	0.09463	2.38	0.08475	2.83	0.07499
0.14	0.00194	0.59	0.03007	1.04	0.06965	1.49	0.09322	1.94	0.09448	2.39	0.08450	2.84	0.07482
0.15	0.00222	0.60	0.03095	1.05	0.07042	1.50	0.09347	1.95	0.09433	2.40	0.08426	2.85	0.07465
0.16	0.00253	0.61	0.03183	1.06	0.07118	1.51	0.09371	1.96	0.09417	2.41	0.08401	2.86	0.07448
0.17	0.00285	0.62	0.03272	1.07	0.07193	1.52	0.09394	1.97	0.09401	2.42	0.08376	2.87	0.07432
0.18	0.00319	0.63	0.03361	1.08	0.07267	1.53	0.09415	1.98	0.09384	2.43	0.08352	2.88	0.07416
0.19	0.00355	0.64	0.03450	1.09	0.07340	1.54	0.09435	1.99	0.09366	2.44	0.08327	2.89	0.07400
0.20	0.00392	0.65	0.03540	1.10	0.07412	1.55	0.09454	2.00	0.09349	2.45	0.08303	2.90	0.07384
0.21	0.00432	0.66	0.03631	1.11	0.07483	1.56	0.09472	2.01	0.09330	2.46	0.08279	2.91	0.07369
0.22	0.00473	0.67	0.03721	1.12	0.07552	1.57	0.09489	2.02	0.09312	2.47	0.08255	2.92	0.07354
0.23	0.00516	0.68	0.03812	1.13	0.07621	1.58	0.09505	2.03	0.09293	2.48	0.08231	2.93	0.07339
0.24	0.00561	0.69	0.03904	1.14	0.07689	1.59	0.09519	2.04	0.09273	2.49	0.08207	2.94	0.07324
0.25	0.00607	0.70	0.03995	1.15	0.07756	1.60	0.09533	2.05	0.09253	2.50	0.08183	2.95	0.07309
0.26	0.00656	0.71	0.04086	1.16	0.07822	1.61	0.09546	2.06	0.09233	2.51	0.08159	2.96	0.07295
0.27	0.00705	0.72	0.04178	1.17	0.07886	1.62	0.09557	2.07	0.09213	2.52	0.08136	2.97	0.07281
0.28	0.00757	0.73	0.04270	1.18	0.07950	1.63	0.09567	2.08	0.09192	2.53	0.08112	2.98	0.07267
0.29	0.00810	0.74	0.04362	1.19	0.08012	1.64	0.09577	2.09	0.09170	2.54	0.08089	2.99	0.07254
0.30	0.00865	0.75	0.04453	1.20	0.08073	1.65	0.09585	2.10	0.09149	2.55	0.08066	3.00	0.07240
0.31	0.00921	0.76	0.04545	1.21	0.08133	1.66	0.09592	2.11	0.09127	2.56	0.08043	3.10	0.07118
0.32	0.00979	0.77	0.04637	1.22	0.08192	1.67	0.09599	2.12	0.09105	2.57	0.08020	3.20	0.07016
0.33	0.01038	0.78	0.04728	1.23	0.08250	1.68	0.09604	2.13	0.09082	2.58	0.07998	3.30	0.06933
0.34	0.01099	0.79	0.04820	1.24	0.08306	1.69	0.09608	2.14	0.09060	2.59	0.07975	3.40	0.06866
0.35	0.01161	0.80	0.04911	1.25	0.08361	1.70	0.09612	2.15	0.09037	2.60	0.07953	3.50	0.06813
0.36	0.01225	0.81	0.05002	1.26	0.08416	1.71	0.09614	2.16	0.09014	2.61	0.07931	3.60	0.06771
0.37	0.01290	0.82	0.05093	1.27	0.08468	1.72	0.09616	2.17	0.08991	2.62	0.07909	3.70	0.06739
0.38	0.01356	0.83	0.05183	1.28	0.08520	1.73	0.09616	2.18	0.08967	2.63	0.07888	3.80	0.06714
0.39	0.01424	0.84	0.05274	1.29	0.08571	1.74	0.09616	2.19	0.08943	2.64	0.07866	3.90	0.06696
0.40	0.01493	0.85	0.05363	1.30	0.08620	1.75	0.09615	2.20	0.08919	2.65	0.07845	4.00	0.06683
0.41	0.01564	0.86	0.05453	1.31	0.08668	1.76	0.09613	2.21	0.08895	2.66	0.07824	∞	0.0665
0.42	0.01635	0.87	0.05542	1.32	0.08715	1.77	0.09610	2.22	0.08871	2.67	0.07803		
0.43	0.01708	0.88	0.05631	1.33	0.08760	1.78	0.09606	2.23	0.08847	2.68	0.07782		
0.44	0.01782	0.89	0.05719	1.34	0.08805	1.79	0.09602	2.24	0.08823	2.69	0.07762		

TABLE A.5 Binomial Probability Distributions

Part 1: Individual Probabilities

Table entries are values of $\binom{n}{x}p^x q^{n-x}$. Items omitted are less than 0.00005.

$n = 5$

x	*0.1*	*0.2*	*0.3*	*0.4*	*0.5*	*0.6*	*0.7*	*0.8*	*0.9*
0	0.5905	0.3277	0.1681	0.0778	0.0312	0.0102	0.0024	0.0003	0.0000
1	0.3280	0.4096	0.3602	0.2592	0.1562	0.0768	0.0284	0.0064	0.0004
2	0.0729	0.2048	0.3087	0.3456	0.3125	0.2304	0.1323	0.0512	0.0081
3	0.0081	0.0512	0.1323	0.2304	0.3125	0.3456	0.3087	0.2048	0.0729
4	0.0004	0.0064	0.0284	0.0768	0.1562	0.2592	0.3602	0.4096	0.3280
5	0.0000	0.0003	0.0024	0.0102	0.0312	0.0778	0.1681	0.3277	0.5905

$n = 10$

x	*0.1*	*0.2*	*0.3*	*0.4*	*0.5*	*0.6*	*0.7*	*0.8*	*0.9*
0	0.3487	0.1074	0.0282	0.0060	0.0010	0.0001	0.0000	0.0000	0.0000
1	0.3874	0.2684	0.1211	0.0403	0.0098	0.0016	0.0001	0.0000	0.0000
2	0.1937	0.3020	0.2335	0.1209	0.0439	0.0106	0.0014	0.0001	0.0000
3	0.0574	0.2013	0.2668	0.2150	0.1172	0.0425	0.0090	0.0008	0.0000
4	0.0112	0.0881	0.2001	0.2508	0.2051	0.1115	0.0368	0.0055	0.0001
5	0.0015	0.0264	0.1029	0.2007	0.2461	0.2007	0.1029	0.0264	0.0015
6	0.0001	0.0055	0.0368	0.1115	0.2051	0.2508	0.2001	0.0881	0.0112
7	0.0000	0.0008	0.0090	0.0425	0.1172	0.2150	0.2668	0.2013	0.0574
8	0.0000	0.0001	0.0014	0.0106	0.0439	0.1209	0.2335	0.3020	0.1937
9	0.0000	0.0000	0.0001	0.0016	0.0098	0.0403	0.1211	0.2684	0.3874
10	0.0000	0.0000	0.0000	0.0001	0.0010	0.0060	0.0282	0.1074	0.3487

$n = 15$

x	*0.1*	*0.2*	*0.3*	*0.4*	*0.5*	*0.6*	*0.7*	*0.8*	*0.9*
0	0.2059	0.0352	0.0047	0.0005	0.0000	0.0000	0.0000	0.0000	0.0000
1	0.3432	0.1319	0.0305	0.0047	0.0005	0.0000	0.0000	0.0000	0.0000
2	0.2669	0.2309	0.0916	0.0219	0.0032	0.0003	0.0000	0.0000	0.0000
3	0.1285	0.2501	0.1700	0.0634	0.0139	0.0016	0.0001	0.0000	0.0000
4	0.0428	0.1876	0.2186	0.1268	0.0417	0.0074	0.0006	0.0000	0.0000
5	0.0105	0.1032	0.2061	0.1859	0.0916	0.0245	0.0030	0.0001	0.0000
6	0.0019	0.0430	0.1472	0.2066	0.1527	0.0612	0.0116	0.0007	0.0000
7	0.0003	0.0138	0.0811	0.1771	0.1964	0.1181	0.0348	0.0035	0.0000
8	0.0000	0.0035	0.0348	0.1181	0.1964	0.1771	0.0811	0.0138	0.0003
9	0.0000	0.0007	0.0116	0.0612	0.1527	0.2066	0.1472	0.0430	0.0019
10	0.0000	0.0001	0.0030	0.0245	0.0916	0.1859	0.2061	0.1032	0.0105
11	0.0000	0.0000	0.0006	0.0074	0.0417	0.1268	0.2186	0.1876	0.0428
12	0.0000	0.0000	0.0001	0.0016	0.0139	0.0634	0.1700	0.2501	0.1285
13	0.0000	0.0000	0.0000	0.0003	0.0032	0.0219	0.0916	0.2309	0.2669
14	0.0000	0.0000	0.0000	0.0000	0.0005	0.0047	0.0305	0.1319	0.3432
15	0.0000	0.0000	0.0000	0.0000	0.0000	0.0005	0.0047	0.0352	0.2059

$n = 20$

x	*0.1*	*0.2*	*0.3*	*0.4*	*0.5*	*0.6*	*0.7*	*0.8*	*0.9*
0	0.1216	0.0115	0.0008	0.0000	0.0000	0.0000	0.0000	0.0000	0.0000
1	0.2702	0.0576	0.0068	0.0005	0.0000	0.0000	0.0000	0.0000	0.0000
2	0.2852	0.1369	0.0278	0.0031	0.0002	0.0000	0.0000	0.0000	0.0000
3	0.1901	0.2054	0.0716	0.0123	0.0011	0.0000	0.0000	0.0000	0.0000
4	0.0898	0.2182	0.1304	0.0350	0.0046	0.0003	0.0000	0.0000	0.0000
5	0.0319	0.1746	0.1789	0.0746	0.0148	0.0013	0.0000	0.0000	0.0000

TABLE A.5 Binomial Probability Distributions

Part 1: Individual Probabilities

$n = 20$ (*continued*)

x	*0.1*	*0.2*	*0.3*	*0.4*	*0.5*	*0.6*	*0.7*	*0.8*	*0.9*
6	0.0089	0.1091	0.1916	0.1244	0.0370	0.0049	0.0002	0.0000	0.0000
7	0.0020	0.0545	0.1643	0.1659	0.0739	0.0146	0.0010	0.0000	0.0000
8	0.0004	0.0222	0.1144	0.1797	0.1201	0.0355	0.0039	0.0001	0.0000
9	0.0001	0.0074	0.0654	0.1597	0.1602	0.0710	0.0120	0.0005	0.0000
10	0.0000	0.0020	0.0308	0.1171	0.1762	0.1171	0.0308	0.0020	0.0000
11	0.0000	0.0005	0.0120	0.0710	0.1602	0.1597	0.0654	0.0074	0.0001
12	0.0000	0.0001	0.0039	0.0355	0.1201	0.1797	0.1144	0.0222	0.0004
13	0.0000	0.0000	0.0010	0.0146	0.0739	0.1659	0.1643	0.0545	0.0020
14	0.0000	0.0000	0.0002	0.0049	0.0370	0.1244	0.1916	0.1091	0.0089
15	0.0000	0.0000	0.0000	0.0013	0.0148	0.0746	0.1789	0.1746	0.0319
16	0.0000	0.0000	0.0000	0.0003	0.0046	0.0350	0.1304	0.2182	0.0898
17	0.0000	0.0000	0.0000	0.0000	0.0011	0.0123	0.0716	0.2054	0.1901
18	0.0000	0.0000	0.0000	0.0000	0.0002	0.0031	0.0278	0.1369	0.2852
19	0.0000	0.0000	0.0000	0.0000	0.0000	0.0005	0.0068	0.0576	0.2702
20	0.0000	0.0000	0.0000	0.0000	0.0000	0.0000	0.0008	0.0115	0.1216

$n = 30$

x	*0.1*	*0.2*	*0.3*	*0.4*	*0.5*	*0.6*	*0.7*	*0.8*	*0.9*
0	0.0424	0.0012	0.0000	0.0000	0.0000	0.0000	0.0000	0.0000	0.0000
1	0.1413	0.0093	0.0003	0.0000	0.0000	0.0000	0.0000	0.0000	0.0000
2	0.2277	0.0337	0.0018	0.0000	0.0000	0.0000	0.0000	0.0000	0.0000
3	0.2361	0.0785	0.0072	0.0003	0.0000	0.0000	0.0000	0.0000	0.0000
4	0.1171	0.1325	0.0208	0.0012	0.0000	0.0000	0.0000	0.0000	0.0000
5	0.1023	0.1723	0.0464	0.0041	0.0001	0.0000	0.0000	0.0000	0.0000
6	0.0474	0.1795	0.0829	0.0115	0.0006	0.0000	0.0000	0.0000	0.0000
7	0.0180	0.1538	0.1219	0.0263	0.0019	0.0000	0.0000	0.0000	0.0000
8	0.0058	0.1106	0.1501	0.0505	0.0055	0.0001	0.0000	0.0000	0.0000
9	0.0016	0.0676	0.1573	0.0823	0.0133	0.0006	0.0000	0.0000	0.0000
10	0.0004	0.0355	0.1416	0.1152	0.0280	0.0020	0.0000	0.0000	0.0000
11	0.0001	0.0161	0.1103	0.1396	0.0509	0.0054	0.0001	0.0000	0.0000
12	0.0000	0.0064	0.0749	0.1474	0.0805	0.0129	0.0005	0.0000	0.0000
13	0.0000	0.0022	0.0444	0.1360	0.1115	0.0269	0.0015	0.0000	0.0000
14	0.0000	0.0007	0.0231	0.1101	0.1354	0.0489	0.0042	0.0000	0.0000
15	0.0000	0.0002	0.0106	0.0783	0.1445	0.0783	0.0106	0.0002	0.0000
16	0.0000	0.0000	0.0042	0.0489	0.1354	0.1101	0.0231	0.0007	0.0000
17	0.0000	0.0000	0.0015	0.0269	0.1115	0.1360	0.0444	0.0022	0.0000
18	0.0000	0.0000	0.0005	0.0129	0.0805	0.1474	0.0749	0.0064	0.0000
19	0.0000	0.0000	0.0001	0.0054	0.0509	0.1396	0.1103	0.0161	0.0001
20	0.0000	0.0000	0.0000	0.0020	0.0280	0.1152	0.1416	0.0355	0.0004
21	0.0000	0.0000	0.0000	0.0006	0.0133	0.0823	0.1573	0.0676	0.0016
22	0.0000	0.0000	0.0000	0.0001	0.0055	0.0505	0.1501	0.1106	0.0058
23	0.0000	0.0000	0.0000	0.0000	0.0019	0.0263	0.1219	0.1538	0.0180
24	0.0000	0.0000	0.0000	0.0000	0.0006	0.0115	0.0829	0.1795	0.0474
25	0.0000	0.0000	0.0000	0.0000	0.0001	0.0041	0.0464	0.1723	0.1023
26	0.0000	0.0000	0.0000	0.0000	0.0000	0.0012	0.0208	0.1325	0.1771
27	0.0000	0.0000	0.0000	0.0000	0.0000	0.0003	0.0072	0.0785	0.2361
28	0.0000	0.0000	0.0000	0.0000	0.0000	0.0000	0.0018	0.0337	0.2277
29	0.0000	0.0000	0.0000	0.0000	0.0000	0.0000	0.0003	0.0093	0.1413
30	0.0000	0.0000	0.0000	0.0000	0.0000	0.0000	0.0000	0.0012	0.0424

TABLE A.5 Binomial Probability Distributions

Part 1: Individual Probabilities
$n = 50$

x	*0.1*	*0.2*	*0.3*	*0.4*	*0.5*	*0.6*	*0.7*	*0.8*	*0.9*
0	0.0052	0.0000	0.0000	0.0000	0.0000	0.0000	0.0000	0.0000	0.0000
1	0.0286	0.0002	0.0000	0.0000	0.0000	0.0000	0.0000	0.0000	0.0000
2	0.0779	0.0011	0.0000	0.0000	0.0000	0.0000	0.0000	0.0000	0.0000
3	0.1386	0.0044	0.0000	0.0000	0.0000	0.0000	0.0000	0.0000	0.0000
4	0.1809	0.0128	0.0001	0.0000	0.0000	0.0000	0.0000	0.0000	0.0000
5	0.1849	0.0295	0.0006	0.0000	0.0000	0.0000	0.0000	0.0000	0.0000
6	0.1541	0.0554	0.0018	0.0000	0.0000	0.0000	0.0000	0.0000	0.0000
7	0.1076	0.0870	0.0048	0.0000	0.0000	0.0000	0.0000	0.0000	0.0000
8	0.0643	0.1169	0.0111	0.0002	0.0000	0.0000	0.0000	0.0000	0.0000
9	0.0333	0.1364	0.0220	0.0005	0.0000	0.0000	0.0000	0.0000	0.0000
10	0.0152	0.1398	0.0386	0.0014	0.0000	0.0000	0.0000	0.0000	0.0000
11	0.0061	0.1271	0.0602	0.0035	0.0000	0.0000	0.0000	0.0000	0.0000
12	0.0022	0.1033	0.0838	0.0076	0.0001	0.0000	0.0000	0.0000	0.0000
13	0.0007	0.0755	0.1050	0.0147	0.0003	0.0000	0.0000	0.0000	0.0000
14	0.0002	0.0499	0.1189	0.0260	0.0008	0.0000	0.0000	0.0000	0.0000
15	0.0001	0.0299	0.1223	0.0415	0.0020	0.0000	0.0000	0.0000	0.0000
16	0.0000	0.0164	0.1147	0.0606	0.0044	0.0001	0.0000	0.0000	0.0000
17	0.0000	0.0082	0.0983	0.0808	0.0087	0.0003	0.0000	0.0000	0.0000
18	0.0000	0.0038	0.0772	0.0987	0.0160	0.0009	0.0000	0.0000	0.0000
19	0.0000	0.0016	0.0558	0.1109	0.0270	0.0020	0.0000	0.0000	0.0000
20	0.0000	0.0006	0.0370	0.1146	0.0419	0.0043	0.0000	0.0000	0.0000
21	0.0000	0.0002	0.0227	0.1091	0.0598	0.0084	0.0001	0.0000	0.0000
22	0.0000	0.0001	0.0128	0.0959	0.0788	0.0154	0.0002	0.0000	0.0000
23	0.0000	0.0000	0.0067	0.0778	0.0960	0.0259	0.0006	0.0000	0.0000
24	0.0000	0.0000	0.0032	0.0584	0.1080	0.0405	0.0014	0.0000	0.0000
25	0.0000	0.0000	0.0014	0.0405	0.1123	0.0584	0.0032	0.0000	0.0000
26	0.0000	0.0000	0.0006	0.0259	0.1080	0.0778	0.0067	0.0000	0.0000
27	0.0000	0.0000	0.0002	0.0154	0.0960	0.0959	0.0128	0.0001	0.0000
28	0.0000	0.0000	0.0001	0.0084	0.0788	0.1091	0.0227	0.0002	0.0000
29	0.0000	0.0000	0.0000	0.0043	0.0598	0.1146	0.0370	0.0006	0.0000
30	0.0000	0.0000	0.0000	0.0020	0.0419	0.1109	0.0558	0.0016	0.0000
31	0.0000	0.0000	0.0000	0.0009	0.0270	0.0987	0.0772	0.0038	0.0000
32	0.0000	0.0000	0.0000	0.0003	0.0160	0.0808	0.0983	0.0082	0.0000
33	0.0000	0.0000	0.0000	0.0001	0.0087	0.0606	0.1147	0.0164	0.0000
34	0.0000	0.0000	0.0000	0.0000	0.0044	0.0415	0.1223	0.0299	0.0001
35	0.0000	0.0000	0.0000	0.0000	0.0020	0.0260	0.1189	0.0499	0.0002
36	0.0000	0.0000	0.0000	0.0000	0.0008	0.0147	0.1050	0.0755	0.0007
37	0.0000	0.0000	0.0000	0.0000	0.0003	0.0076	0.0838	0.1033	0.0022
38	0.0000	0.0000	0.0000	0.0000	0.0001	0.0035	0.0602	0.1271	0.0061
39	0.0000	0.0000	0.0000	0.0000	0.0000	0.0014	0.0386	0.1398	0.0152
40	0.0000	0.0000	0.0000	0.0000	0.0000	0.0005	0.0220	0.1364	0.0333
41	0.0000	0.0000	0.0000	0.0000	0.0000	0.0002	0.0111	0.1169	0.0643
42	0.0000	0.0000	0.0000	0.0000	0.0000	0.0000	0.0048	0.0870	0.1076
43	0.0000	0.0000	0.0000	0.0000	0.0000	0.0000	0.0018	0.0554	0.1541
44	0.0000	0.0000	0.0000	0.0000	0.0000	0.0000	0.0006	0.0295	0.1849
45	0.0000	0.0000	0.0000	0.0000	0.0000	0.0000	0.0001	0.0128	0.1809
46	0.0000	0.0000	0.0000	0.0000	0.0000	0.0000	0.0000	0.0044	0.1386
47	0.0000	0.0000	0.0000	0.0000	0.0000	0.0000	0.0000	0.0011	0.0779
48	0.0000	0.0000	0.0000	0.0000	0.0000	0.0000	0.0000	0.0002	0.0286
49	0.0000	0.0000	0.0000	0.0000	0.0000	0.0000	0.0000	0.0000	0.0052
50	0.0000	0.0000	0.0000	0.0000	0.0000	0.0000	0.0000	0.0000	0.0000

TABLE A.5 Binomial Probability Distributions

Part 2: Cumulative Probabilities for Binomial Distributions $CP(x) = \sum_{k=0}^{n} \binom{n}{x} p\, q^{n-x}$

$n = 5$

x	0.1	0.2	0.3	0.4	0.5	0.6	0.7	0.8	0.9
0	0.5905	0.3277	0.1681	0.0778	0.0312	0.0102	0.0024	0.0003	0.0000
1	0.9185	0.7373	0.5283	0.3370	0.1874	0.0870	0.0308	0.0067	0.0004
2	0.9914	0.9421	0.8370	0.6826	0.5000	0.3174	0.1631	0.0579	0.0085
3	0.9995	0.9933	0.9693	0.9130	0.8124	0.6630	0.4718	0.2627	0.0814
4	0.9999	0.9997	0.9977	0.9898	0.9686	0.9222	0.8320	0.6723	0.4094
5	1.0000	1.0000	1.0000	1.0000	1.0000	1.0000	1.0000	1.0000	1.0000

$n = 10$

x	0.1	0.2	0.3	0.4	0.5	0.6	0.7	0.8	0.9
0	0.3487	0.1074	0.0282	0.0060	0.0010	0.0001	0.0000	0.0000	0.0000
1	0.7361	0.3758	0.1493	0.0463	0.0108	0.0017	0.0001	0.0000	0.0000
2	0.9298	0.6778	0.3828	0.1672	0.0547	0.0123	0.0015	0.0001	0.0000
3	0.9872	0.8791	0.6496	0.3822	0.1719	0.0548	0.0105	0.0009	0.0000
4	0.9984	0.9672	0.8497	0.6330	0.3770	0.1663	0.0473	0.0064	0.0001
5	0.9999	0.9936	0.9526	0.8337	0.6231	0.3670	0.1502	0.0328	0.0016
6	1.0000	0.9991	0.9894	0.9452	0.8282	0.6178	0.3503	0.1209	0.0128
7	1.0000	0.9999	0.9984	0.9877	0.9454	0.8328	0.6171	0.3222	0.0702
8	1.0000	1.0000	0.9998	0.9983	0.9893	0.9537	0.8506	0.6242	0.2639
9	1.0000	1.0000	0.9999	0.9999	0.9991	0.9940	0.9717	0.8926	0.6513
10	1.0000	1.0000	1.0000	1.0000	1.0000	1.0000	1.0000	1.0000	1.0000

$n = 15$

x	0.1	0.2	0.3	0.4	0.5	0.6	0.7	0.8	0.9
0	0.2059	0.0352	0.0047	0.0005	0.0000	0.0000	0.0000	0.0000	0.0000
1	0.5491	0.1671	0.0352	0.0052	0.0005	0.0000	0.0000	0.0000	0.0000
2	0.8160	0.3980	0.1268	0.0271	0.0037	0.0003	0.0000	0.0000	0.0000
3	0.9445	0.6481	0.2968	0.0905	0.0176	0.0019	0.0001	0.0000	0.0000
4	0.9873	0.8357	0.5154	0.2173	0.0593	0.0093	0.0007	0.0000	0.0000
5	0.9978	0.9389	0.7215	0.4032	0.1509	0.0338	0.0037	0.0001	0.0000
6	0.9997	0.9819	0.8687	0.6098	0.3036	0.0950	0.0153	0.0008	0.0000
7	1.0000	0.9957	0.9498	0.7869	0.5000	0.2131	0.0501	0.0043	0.0000
8	1.0000	0.9992	0.9846	0.9050	0.6964	0.3902	0.1312	0.0181	0.0003
9	1.0000	0.9999	0.9962	0.9662	0.8491	0.5968	0.2784	0.0611	0.0022
10	1.0000	1.0000	0.9992	0.9907	0.9407	0.7827	0.4845	0.1643	0.0127
11	1.0000	1.0000	0.9999	0.9981	0.9824	0.9095	0.7031	0.3519	0.0555
12	1.0000	1.0000	0.9999	0.9997	0.9963	0.9729	0.8731	0.6020	0.1840
13	1.0000	1.0000	1.0000	1.0000	0.9995	0.9948	0.9647	0.8329	0.4509
14	1.0000	1.0000	1.0000	1.0000	1.0000	0.9995	0.9952	0.9648	0.7941
15	1.0000	1.0000	1.0000	1.0000	1.0000	1.0000	1.0000	1.0000	1.0000

$n = 20$

x	0.1	0.2	0.3	0.4	0.5	0.6	0.7	0.8	0.9
0	0.1216	0.0115	0.0008	0.0000	0.0000	0.0000	0.0000	0.0000	0.0000
1	0.3918	0.0691	0.0076	0.0005	0.0000	0.0000	0.0000	0.0000	0.0000
2	0.6770	0.2060	0.0354	0.0036	0.0002	0.0000	0.0000	0.0000	0.0000
3	0.8671	0.4114	0.1070	0.0159	0.0013	0.0000	0.0000	0.0000	0.0000
4	0.9569	0.6296	0.2374	0.0509	0.0059	0.0003	0.0000	0.0000	0.0000
5	0.9888	0.8042	0.4163	0.1255	0.0207	0.0016	0.0000	0.0000	0.0000

More extensive tables of the Binomial are available. These tables were compiled from the following tables.

1. National Bureau of Standards, *Tables of the Binomial Probability Distribution,* Applied Mathematics Series—6, issued January 27, 1950, U.S. Government Printing Office, Washington, D.C. (Gives probability values to 7 figures

TABLE A.5 Binomial Probability Distributions

Part 2: Cumulative Probabilities, $n = 20$ (*continued*)

x	*0.1*	*0.2*	*0.3*	*0.4*	*0.5*	*0.6*	*0.7*	*0.8*	*0.9*
6	0.9977	0.9133	0.6079	0.2499	0.0577	0.0065	0.0002	0.0000	0.0000
7	0.9997	0.9678	0.7722	0.4158	0.1316	0.0211	0.0012	0.0000	0.0000
8	0.9999	0.9900	0.8866	0.5955	0.2517	0.0566	0.0051	0.0001	0.0000
9	1.0000	0.9974	0.9520	0.7552	0.4119	0.1276	0.0171	0.0006	0.0000
10	1.0000	0.9994	0.9828	0.8723	0.5881	0.2447	0.0479	0.0026	0.0000
11	1.0000	0.9999	0.9948	0.9433	0.7483	0.4044	0.1133	0.0100	0.0001
12	1.0000	1.0000	0.9987	0.9788	0.8684	0.5841	0.2277	0.0322	0.0005
13	1.0000	1.0000	0.9997	0.9934	0.9423	0.7500	0.3920	0.0867	0.0025
14	1.0000	1.0000	0.9999	0.9983	0.9793	0.8744	0.5836	0.1958	0.0114
15	1.0000	1.0000	1.0000	0.9996	0.9941	0.9490	0.7625	0.3704	0.0433
16	1.0000	1.0000	1.0000	0.9999	0.9987	0.9840	0.8929	0.5886	0.1331
17	1.0000	1.0000	1.0000	1.0000	0.9998	0.9963	0.9645	0.7940	0.3232
18	1.0000	1.0000	1.0000	1.0000	1.0000	0.9994	0.9923	0.9309	0.6084
19	1.0000	1.0000	1.0000	1.0000	1.0000	0.9999	0.9992	0.9885	0.8784
20	1.0000	1.0000	1.0000	1.0000	1.0000	1.0000	1.0000	1.0000	1.0000

$n = 30$

x	*0.1*	*0.2*	*0.3*	*0.4*	*0.5*	*0.6*	*0.7*	*0.8*	*0.9*
0	0.0424	0.0012	0.0000	0.0000	0.0000	0.0000	0.0000	0.0000	0.0000
1	0.1837	0.0105	0.0003	0.0000	0.0000	0.0000	0.0000	0.0000	0.0000
2	0.4114	0.0442	0.0021	0.0000	0.0000	0.0000	0.0000	0.0000	0.0000
3	0.6475	0.1227	0.0093	0.0003	0.0000	0.0000	0.0000	0.0000	0.0000
4	0.8246	0.2552	0.0301	0.0015	0.0000	0.0000	0.0000	0.0000	0.0000
5	0.9269	0.4275	0.0765	0.0056	0.0001	0.0000	0.0000	0.0000	0.0000
6	0.9743	0.6070	0.1594	0.0171	0.0007	0.0000	0.0000	0.0000	0.0000
7	0.9923	0.7608	0.2813	0.0434	0.0026	0.0000	0.0000	0.0000	0.0000
8	0.9981	0.8714	0.4314	0.0939	0.0081	0.0001	0.0000	0.0000	0.0000
9	0.9996	0.9390	0.5887	0.1762	0.0214	0.0007	0.0000	0.0000	0.0000
10	0.9999	0.9745	0.7303	0.2914	0.0494	0.0027	0.0000	0.0000	0.0000
11	1.0000	0.9906	0.8406	0.4310	0.1003	0.0081	0.0001	0.0000	0.0000
12	1.0000	0.9970	0.9155	0.5784	0.1808	0.0210	0.0006	0.0000	0.0000
13	1.0000	0.9992	0.9599	0.7144	0.2923	0.0479	0.0021	0.0000	0.0000
14	1.0000	0.9999	0.9830	0.8245	0.4277	0.0968	0.0063	0.0000	0.0000
15	1.0000	1.0000	0.9936	0.9028	0.5722	0.1751	0.0169	0.0002	0.0000
16	1.0000	1.0000	0.9978	0.9518	0.7076	0.2852	0.0400	0.0009	0.0000
17	1.0000	1.0000	0.9993	0.9788	0.8191	0.4212	0.0844	0.0031	0.0000
18	1.0000	1.0000	0.9998	0.9917	0.8998	0.5686	0.1593	0.0095	0.0000
19	1.0000	1.0000	0.9999	0.9970	0.9505	0.7082	0.2696	0.0256	0.0001
20	1.0000	1.0000	1.0000	0.9990	0.9785	0.8234	0.4112	0.0611	0.0005
21	1.0000	1.0000	1.0000	0.9998	0.9918	0.9057	0.5685	0.1287	0.0021
22	1.0000	1.0000	1.0000	0.9999	0.9973	0.9562	0.7186	0.2393	0.0079
23	1.0000	1.0000	1.0000	1.0000	0.9992	0.9825	0.8405	0.3931	0.0259
24	1.0000	1.0000	1.0000	1.0000	0.9998	0.9940	0.9234	0.5726	0.0733
25	1.0000	1.0000	1.0000	1.0000	0.9999	0.9981	0.9698	0.7449	0.1756
26	1.0000	1.0000	1.0000	1.0000	1.0000	0.9985	0.9906	0.8774	0.3527
27	1.0000	1.0000	1.0000	1.0000	1.0000	0.9998	0.9978	0.9559	0.5888
28	1.0000	1.0000	1.0000	1.0000	1.0000	1.0000	0.9996	0.9896	0.8165
29	1.0000	1.0000	1.0000	1.0000	1.0000	1.0000	0.9999	0.9989	0.9578
30	1.0000	1.0000	1.0000	1.0000	1.0000	1.0000	1.0000	1.0000	1.0000

for n values from 1 to 49 for p values from 0.01 to 0.50.)

2. Harry G. Romig, *50–100 Binomial Tables*, New York, N.Y., John Wiley & Sons, Inc. 1953. (Out of print, available from author.) (Gives probability values to 6 figures for p values from 0.01 to 0.50 in n values 50 to 100 given at intervals of 5.)

TABLE A.5 Binomial Probability Distributions

Part 2: Cumulative Probabilities
$n = 50$

x	*0.1*	*0.2*	*0.3*	*0.4*	*0.5*	*0.6*	*0.7*	*0.8*	*0.9*
0	0.0052	0.0000	0.0000	0.0000	0.0000	0.0000	0.0000	0.0000	0.0000
1	0.0338	0.0002	0.0000	0.0000	0.0000	0.0000	0.0000	0.0000	0.0000
2	0.1117	0.0013	0.0000	0.0000	0.0000	0.0000	0.0000	0.0000	0.0000
3	0.2503	0.0057	0.0000	0.0000	0.0000	0.0000	0.0000	0.0000	0.0000
4	0.4312	0.0185	0.0002	0.0000	0.0000	0.0000	0.0000	0.0000	0.0000
5	0.6161	0.0480	0.0007	0.0000	0.0000	0.0000	0.0000	0.0000	0.0000
6	0.7702	0.1034	0.0005	0.0000	0.0000	0.0000	0.0000	0.0000	0.0000
7	0.8779	0.1904	0.0073	0.0001	0.0000	0.0000	0.0000	0.0000	0.0000
8	0.9421	0.3073	0.0183	0.0002	0.0000	0.0000	0.0000	0.0000	0.0000
9	0.9755	0.4437	0.0402	0.0008	0.0000	0.0000	0.0000	0.0000	0.0000
10	0.9906	0.5836	0.0789	0.0022	0.0000	0.0000	0.0000	0.0000	0.0000
11	0.9968	0.7107	0.1390	0.0057	0.0000	0.0000	0.0000	0.0000	0.0000
12	0.9990	0.8139	0.2229	0.0133	0.0002	0.0000	0.0000	0.0000	0.0000
13	0.9997	0.8894	0.3279	0.0280	0.0005	0.0000	0.0000	0.0000	0.0000
14	0.9999	0.9393	0.4468	0.0540	0.0013	0.0000	0.0000	0.0000	0.0000
15	1.0000	0.9692	0.5692	0.0955	0.0033	0.0000	0.0000	0.0000	0.0000
16	1.0000	0.9856	0.6839	0.1561	0.0077	0.0001	0.0000	0.0000	0.0000
17	1.0000	0.9937	0.7822	0.2369	0.0164	0.0002	0.0000	0.0000	0.0000
18	1.0000	0.9975	0.8594	0.3356	0.0325	0.0005	0.0000	0.0000	0.0000
19	1.0000	0.9991	0.9152	0.4465	0.0595	0.0014	0.0000	0.0000	0.0000
20	1.0000	0.9997	0.9522	0.5610	0.1013	0.0034	0.0000	0.0000	0.0000
21	1.0000	0.9999	0.9749	0.6701	0.1611	0.0076	0.0000	0.0000	0.0000
22	1.0000	1.0000	0.9877	0.7660	0.2399	0.0160	0.0001	0.0000	0.0000
23	1.0000	1.0000	0.9944	0.8438	0.3360	0.0314	0.0003	0.0000	0.0000
24	1.0000	1.0000	0.9976	0.9022	0.4439	0.0573	0.0009	0.0000	0.0000
25	1.0000	1.0000	0.9991	0.9427	0.5561	0.0978	0.0024	0.0000	0.0000
26	1.0000	1.0000	0.9997	0.9686	0.6641	0.1562	0.0056	0.0000	0.0000
27	1.0000	1.0000	0.9999	0.9840	0.7601	0.2340	0.0123	0.0000	0.0000
28	1.0000	1.0000	1.0000	0.9924	0.8389	0.3299	0.0251	0.0001	0.0000
29	1.0000	1.0000	1.0000	0.9966	0.8987	0.4390	0.0478	0.0003	0.0000
30	1.0000	1.0000	1.0000	0.9986	0.9405	0.5535	0.0848	0.0009	0.0000
31	1.0000	1.0000	1.0000	0.9995	0.9675	0.6644	0.1406	0.0025	0.0000
32	1.0000	1.0000	1.0000	0.9998	0.9836	0.7631	0.2178	0.0063	0.0000
33	1.0000	1.0000	1.0000	0.9999	0.9923	0.8439	0.3161	0.0143	0.0000
34	1.0000	1.0000	1.0000	1.0000	0.9967	0.9045	0.4308	0.0308	0.0000
35	1.0000	1.0000	1.0000	1.0000	0.9987	0.9460	0.5532	0.0607	0.0001
36	1.0000	1.0000	1.0000	1.0000	0.9995	0.9720	0.6721	0.1106	0.0003
37	1.0000	1.0000	1.0000	1.0000	0.9998	0.9867	0.7771	0.1861	0.0010
38	1.0000	1.0000	1.0000	1.0000	1.0000	0.9943	0.8610	0.2893	0.0032
39	1.0000	1.0000	1.0000	1.0000	1.0000	0.9978	0.9211	0.4164	0.0094
40	1.0000	1.0000	1.0000	1.0000	1.0000	0.9992	0.9598	0.5563	0.0245
41	1.0000	1.0000	1.0000	1.0000	1.0000	0.9998	0.9817	0.7927	0.0579
42	1.0000	1.0000	1.0000	1.0000	1.0000	0.9999	0.9927	0.8095	0.1221
43	1.0000	1.0000	1.0000	1.0000	1.0000	1.0000	0.9975	0.8966	0.2298
44	1.0000	1.0000	1.0000	1.0000	1.0000	1.0000	0.9993	0.9520	0.3839
45	1.0000	1.0000	1.0000	1.0000	1.0000	1.0000	0.9998	0.9815	0.5688
46	1.0000	1.0000	1.0000	1.0000	1.0000	1.0000	1.0000	0.9943	0.7497
47	1.0000	1.0000	1.0000	1.0000	1.0000	1.0000	1.0000	0.9987	0.8883
48	1.0000	1.0000	1.0000	1.0000	1.0000	1.0000	1.0000	0.9998	0.9662
49	1.0000	1.0000	1.0000	1.0000	1.0000	1.0000	1.0000	1.0000	0.9948
50	1.0000	1.0000	1.0000	1.0000	1.0000	1.0000	1.0000	1.0000	1.0000

TABLE A.6 Poisson's Exponential Binomial Limit

Part 1: Individual Terms of the Poisson Formula, $\frac{e^{-m}m^x}{x!}$

$m = 0.001\text{–}2.0$, Small Values of m

x	$m = 0.001$	$m = 0.002$	$m = 0.003$	$m = 0.004$
0	0.9990005	0.9980020	0.9970045	0.9960080
1	0.0009990	0.0019960	0.0029910	0.0039840
2	0.0000005	0.0000020	0.0000045	0.0000080
	$m = 0.005$	$m = 0.006$	$m = 0.007$	$m = 0.008$
0	0.9950125	0.9940180	0.9930244	0.9920319
1	0.0049751	0.0059641	0.0069512	0.0079363
2	0.0000124	0.0000179	0.0000243	0.0000317
3			0.0000001	0.0000001
	$m = 0.009$	$m = 0.010$	$m = 0.02$	$m = 0.03$
0	0.9910404	0.9900498	0.9801987	0.9704455
1	0.0089194	0.0099005	0.0196040	0.0291134
2	0.0000401	0.0000495	0.0001960	0.0004367
3	0.0000001	0.0000002	0.0000013	0.0000044
	$m = 0.04$	$m = 0.05$	$m = 0.06$	$m = 0.07$
0	0.9607894	0.9512294	0.9417645	0.9323938
1	0.0384316	0.0475615	0.0565059	0.0652676
2	0.0007686	0.0011890	0.0016952	0.0022844
3	0.0000102	0.0000198	0.0000339	0.0000533
4	0.0000001	0.0000002	0.0000005	0.0000009
	$m = 0.08$	$m = 0.09$	$m = 0.10$	$m = 0.11$
0	0.9231163	0.9139312	0.9048374	0.8958341
1	0.0738493	0.0822538	0.0904837	0.0985418
2	0.0029540	0.0037014	0.0045242	0.0054198
3	0.0000788	0.0001110	0.0001508	0.0001987
4	0.0000016	0.0000025	0.0000038	0.0000055
5			0.0000001	0.0000001
	$m = 0.12$	$m = 0.13$	$m = 0.14$	$m = 0.15$
0	0.8869204	0.8780954	0.8693582	0.8607080
1	0.1064304	0.1141524	0.1217102	0.1291062
2	0.0063858	0.0074199	0.0085197	0.0096830
3	0.0002554	0.0003215	0.0003976	0.0004841
4	0.0000077	0.0000104	0.0000139	0.0000182
5	0.0000002	0.0000003	0.0000004	0.0000005

TABLE A.6 Poisson's Exponential Binomial Limit

Part 1: Individual Terms (*continued*) $m = 0.001\text{–}2.0$

x	$m = 0.16$	$m = 0.17$	$m = 0.18$	$m = 0.19$
0	0.8521438	0.8436648	0.8352702	0.8269591
1	0.1363430	0.1434230	0.1503486	0.1571222
2	0.0109074	0.0121910	0.0135314	0.0149266
3	0.0005817	0.0006908	0.0008119	0.0009454
4	0.0000233	0.0000294	0.0000365	0.0000449
5	0.0000007	0.0000010	0.0000013	0.0000017
6				0.0000001

x	$m = 0.20$	$m = 0.21$	$m = 0.22$	$m = 0.23$
0	0.8187308	0.8105842	0.8025188	0.7945336
1	0.1637462	0.1702227	0.1765541	0.1827427
2	0.0163746	0.0178734	0.0194210	0.0210154
3	0.0010916	0.0012511	0.0014242	0.0016112
4	0.0000546	0.0000657	0.0000783	0.0000926
5	0.0000022	0.0000028	0.0000034	0.0000043
6	0.0000001	0.0000001	0.0000001	0.0000002

x	$m = 0.24$	$m = 0.25$	$m = 0.26$	$m = 0.27$
0	0.7866279	0.7788008	0.7710516	0.7633795
1	0.1887907	0.1947002	0.2004734	0.2061125
2	0.0226549	0.0243375	0.0260615	0.0278252
3	0.0018124	0.0020281	0.0022587	0.0025043
4	0.0001087	0.0001268	0.0001468	0.0001690
5	0.0000052	0.0000063	0.0000076	0.0000091
6	0.0000002	0.0000003	0.0000003	0.0000004

x	$m = 0.28$	$m = 0.29$	$m = 0.30$	$m = 0.40$
0	0.7557837	0.7482636	0.7408182	0.6703200
1	0.2116194	0.2169964	0.2222455	0.2681280
2	0.0296267	0.0314645	0.0333368	0.0536256
3	0.0027652	0.0030416	0.0033337	0.0071501
4	0.0001936	0.0002205	0.0002500	0.0007150
5	0.0000108	0.0000128	0.0000150	0.0000572
6	0.0000005	0.0000006	0.0000008	0.0000038
7				0.0000002

x	$m = 0.5$	$m = 0.6$	$m = 0.7$	$m = 0.8$
0	0.606531	0.548812	0.496585	0.449329
1	0.303265	0.329287	0.347610	0.359463
2	0.075816	0.098786	0.121663	0.143785
3	0.012636	0.019757	0.028388	0.038343
4	0.001580	0.002964	0.004968	0.007669
5	0.000158	0.000356	0.000696	0.001227
6	0.000013	0.000036	0.000081	0.000164
7	0.000001	0.000003	0.000008	0.000019
8			0.000001	0.000002

TABLE A.6 Poisson's Exponential Binomial Limit

Part 1: Individual Terms (*continued*) $m = 0.001–2.0$

x	$m = 0.9$	$m = 1.0$	$m = 1.1$	$m = 1.2$
0	0.406570	0.367879	0.332871	0.301194
1	0.365913	0.367879	0.366158	0.361433
2	0.164661	0.183940	0.201387	0.216860
3	0.049398	0.061313	0.073842	0.086744
4	0.011115	0.015328	0.020307	0.026023
5	0.002001	0.003066	0.004467	0.006246
6	0.000300	0.000511	0.000819	0.001249
7	0.000039	0.000073	0.000129	0.000214
8	0.000004	0.000009	0.000018	0.000032
9		0.000001	0.000002	0.000004
10				0.000001

x	$m = 1.3$	$m = 1.4$	$m = 1.5$	$m = 1.6$
0	0.272532	0.246597	0.223130	0.201897
1	0.354291	0.345236	0.334695	0.323034
2	0.230289	0.241665	0.251021	0.258428
3	0.099792	0.112777	0.125511	0.137828
4	0.032432	0.039472	0.047067	0.055131
5	0.008432	0.011052	0.014120	0.017642
6	0.001827	0.002579	0.003530	0.004705
7	0.000339	0.000516	0.000756	0.001075
8	0.000055	0.000090	0.000142	0.000215
9	0.000008	0.000014	0.000024	0.000038
10	0.000001	0.000002	0.000004	0.000006
11				0.000001

x	$m = 1.7$	$m = 1.8$	$m = 1.9$	$m = 2.0$
0	0.182684	0.165299	0.149569	0.135335
1	0.310562	0.297538	0.284180	0.270671
2	0.263978	0.267784	0.269971	0.270671
3	0.149587	0.160671	0.170982	0.180447
4	0.063575	0.072302	0.081216	0.090224
5	0.021615	0.026029	0.030862	0.036089
6	0.006124	0.007809	0.009773	0.012030
7	0.001487	0.002008	0.002653	0.003437
8	0.000316	0.000452	0.000630	0.000859
9	0.000060	0.000090	0.000133	0.000191
10	0.000010	0.000016	0.000025	0.000038
11	0.000002	0.000003	0.000004	0.000007
12			0.000001	0.000001

TABLE A.6 Poisson's Exponential Binomial Limit

Part 1: Tables of $\frac{e^{-m}m^x}{x!}$: Individual Terms of Poisson's Exponential Expansion ("Law of Small Numbers").

B: m = 0.1–15.0

x	*m*										*x*
	0.1	*0.2*	*0.3*	*0.4*	*0.5*	*0.6*	*0.7*	*0.8*	*0.9*	*1.0*	
0	0.904837	0.818731	0.740818	0.670320	0.606531	0.548812	0.496585	0.449329	0.406570	0.367879	*0*
1	0.090484	0.163746	0.222245	0.268128	0.303265	0.329287	0.347610	0.359463	0.365913	0.367879	*1*
2	0.004524	0.016375	0.033337	0.053626	0.075816	0.098786	0.121663	0.143785	0.164661	0.183940	2
3	0.000151	0.001092	0.003334	0.007150	0.012636	0.019757	0.028388	0.038343	0.049398	0.061313	3
4	0.000004	0.000055	0.000250	0.000715	0.001580	0.002964	0.004968	0.007669	0.011115	0.015328	4
5	—	0.000002	0.000015	0.000057	0.000158	0.000356	0.000696	0.001227	0.002001	0.003066	5
6	—	—	0.000001	0.000004	0.000013	0.000036	0.000081	0.000164	0.000300	0.000511	6
7	—	—	—	—	0.000001	0.000003	0.000008	0.000019	0.000039	0.000073	7
8	—	—	—	—	—	—	0.000001	0.000002	0.000004	0.000009	8
9	—	—	—	—	—	—	—	—	—	0.000001	9

x	*1.1*	*1.2*	*1.3*	*1.4*	*1.5*	*1.6*	*1.7*	*1.8*	*1.9*	*2.0*	*x*
0	0.332871	0.301194	0.272532	0.246597	0.223130	0.201897	0.182684	0.165299	0.149569	0.135335	*0*
1	0.366158	0.361433	0.354291	0.345236	0.334695	0.323034	0.310562	0.297538	0.284180	0.270671	*1*
2	0.201387	0.216860	0.230289	0.241665	0.251021	0.258428	0.263978	0.267784	0.269971	0.270671	2
3	0.073842	0.086744	0.099792	0.112777	0.125510	0.137828	0.149587	0.160671	0.170982	0.180447	3
4	0.020307	0.026023	0.032432	0.039472	0.047067	0.055131	0.063575	0.072302	0.081216	0.090224	4
5	0.004467	0.006246	0.008432	0.011052	0.014120	0.017642	0.021615	0.026029	0.030862	0.036089	5
6	0.000819	0.001249	0.001827	0.002579	0.003530	0.004705	0.006124	0.007809	0.009773	0.012030	6
7	0.000129	0.000214	0.000339	0.000516	0.000756	0.001075	0.001487	0.002008	0.002653	0.003437	7
8	0.000018	0.000032	0.000055	0.000090	0.000142	0.000215	0.000316	0.000452	0.000630	0.000859	8
9	0.000002	0.000004	0.000008	0.000014	0.000024	0.000038	0.000060	0.000090	0.000133	0.000191	9
10	—	0.000001	0.000001	0.000002	0.000004	0.000006	0.000010	0.000016	0.000025	0.000038	*10*
11	—	—	—	—	—	0.000001	0.000002	0.000003	0.000004	0.000007	*11*
12	—	—	—	—	—	—	—	—	0.000001	0.000001	*12*

x	*2.1*	*2.2*	*2.3*	*2.4*	*2.5*	*2.6*	*2.7*	*2.8*	*2.9*	*3.0*	*x*
0	0.122456	0.110803	0.100259	0.090718	0.082085	0.074274	0.067206	0.060810	0.055023	0.049787	*0*
1	0.257159	0.243767	0.230595	0.217723	0.205212	0.193111	0.181455	0.170268	0.159567	0.149361	*1*
2	0.270016	0.268144	0.265185	0.261268	0.256516	0.251045	0.244964	0.238375	0.231373	0.224042	2
3	0.189012	0.196639	0.203308	0.209014	0.213763	0.217572	0.220468	0.222484	0.223660	0.224042	3
4	0.099231	0.108151	0.116902	0.125409	0.133602	0.141422	0.148816	0.155739	0.162154	0.168031	4
5	0.041677	0.047587	0.053775	0.060196	0.066801	0.073539	0.080360	0.087214	0.094049	0.100819	5
6	0.014587	0.017448	0.020614	0.024078	0.027834	0.031867	0.036162	0.040700	0.045457	0.050409	6
7	0.004376	0.005484	0.006773	0.008255	0.009941	0.011836	0.013948	0.016280	0.018832	0.021604	7
8	0.001149	0.001508	0.001947	0.002477	0.003106	0.003847	0.004708	0.005698	0.006827	0.008102	8
9	0.000268	0.000369	0.000498	0.000660	0.000863	0.001111	0.001412	0.001773	0.002200	0.002701	9
10	0.000056	0.000081	0.000114	0.000158	0.000216	0.000289	0.000381	0.000496	0.000638	0.000810	*10*
11	0.000011	0.000016	0.000024	0.000035	0.000049	0.000068	0.000094	0.000126	0.000168	0.000221	*11*
12	0.000002	0.000003	0.000005	0.000007	0.000010	0.000015	0.000021	0.000029	0.000041	0.000055	*12*
13	—	0.000001	0.000001	0.000001	0.000002	0.000003	0.000004	0.000006	0.000009	0.000013	*13*
14	—	—	—	—	—	0.000001	0.000001	0.000001	0.000002	0.000003	*14*
15	—	—	—	—	—	—	—	—	—	0.000001	*15*

TABLE A.6 Poisson's Exponential Binomial Limit

Part 1 (*continued*)

x	*m* 3.1	3.2	3.3	3.4	3.5	3.6	3.7	3.8	3.9	4.0	*x*
0	0.045049	0.040762	0.036883	0.033373	0.030197	0.027324	0.024724	0.022371	0.020242	0.018316	0
1	0.139653	0.130439	0.121714	0.113469	0.105691	0.098365	0.091477	0.085009	0.078943	0.073263	1
2	0.216461	0.208702	0.200829	0.192898	0.184959	0.177058	0.169233	0.161517	0.153940	0.146525	2
3	0.223677	0.222616	0.220912	0.218617	0.215785	0.212469	0.208720	0.204588	0.200122	0.195367	3
4	0.173350	0.178093	0.182252	0.185825	0.188812	0.191222	0.193066	0.194350	0.195119	0.195367	4
5	0.107477	0.113979	0.120286	0.126361	0.132169	0.137680	0.142869	0.147713	0.152193	0.156293	5
6	0.055530	0.060789	0.066158	0.071604	0.077098	0.082608	0.088102	0.093551	0.098925	0.104196	6
7	0.024592	0.027789	0.031189	0.034779	0.038549	0.042484	0.046568	0.050785	0.055115	0.059540	7
8	0.009529	0.011116	0.012865	0.014781	0.016865	0.019118	0.021538	0.024123	0.026869	0.029770	8
9	0.003282	0.003952	0.004717	0.005584	0.006559	0.007647	0.008854	0.010185	0.011643	0.013231	9
10	0.001018	0.001265	0.001557	0.001899	0.002296	0.002753	0.003276	0.003870	0.004541	0.005292	10
11	0.000287	0.000368	0.000467	0.000587	0.000730	0.000901	0.001102	0.001337	0.001610	0.001925	11
12	0.000074	0.000098	0.000128	0.000166	0.000213	0.000270	0.000340	0.000423	0.000523	0.000642	12
13	0.000018	0.000024	0.000033	0.000043	0.000057	0.000075	0.000097	0.000124	0.000157	0.000197	13
14	0.000004	0.000006	0.000008	0.000011	0.000014	0.000019	0.000026	0.000034	0.000044	0.000056	14
15	0.000001	0.000001	0.000002	0.000002	0.000003	0.000005	0.000006	0.000009	0.000011	0.000015	15
16	—	—	—	0.000001	0.000001	0.000001	0.000001	0.000002	0.000003	0.000004	16
17	—	—	—	—	—	—	—	—	0.000001	0.000001	17

x	4.1	4.2	4.3	4.4	4.5	4.6	4.7	4.8	4.9	5.0	*x*
0	0.016573	0.014996	0.013569	0.012277	0.011109	0.010052	0.009095	0.008230	0.007447	0.006738	0
1	0.067948	0.062981	0.058345	0.054020	0.049990	0.046238	0.042748	0.039503	0.036488	0.033690	1
2	0.139293	0.132261	0.125441	0.118845	0.112479	0.106348	0.100457	0.094807	0.089396	0.084224	2
3	0.190368	0.185165	0.179799	0.174305	0.168718	0.163068	0.157383	0.151691	0.146014	0.140374	3
4	0.195127	0.194424	0.193284	0.191736	0.189808	0.187528	0.184925	0.182029	0.178867	0.175467	4
5	0.160004	0.163316	0.166224	0.168728	0.170827	0.172525	0.173830	0.174748	0.175290	0.175467	5
6	0.109336	0.114321	0.119127	0.123734	0.128120	0.132270	0.136167	0.139798	0.143153	0.146223	6
7	0.064040	0.068593	0.073178	0.077775	0.082363	0.086920	0.091426	0.095862	0.100207	0.104445	7
8	0.032820	0.036011	0.039333	0.042776	0.046329	0.049979	0.053713	0.057517	0.061377	0.065278	8
9	0.014951	0.016805	0.018793	0.020913	0.023165	0.025545	0.028050	0.030676	0.033416	0.036266	9
10	0.006130	0.007058	0.008081	0.009202	0.010424	0.011751	0.013184	0.014724	0.016374	0.018133	10
11	0.002285	0.002695	0.003159	0.003681	0.004264	0.004914	0.005633	0.006425	0.007294	0.008242	11
12	0.000781	0.000943	0.001132	0.001350	0.001599	0.001884	0.002206	0.002570	0.002978	0.003434	12
13	0.000246	0.000305	0.000374	0.000457	0.000554	0.000667	0.000798	0.000949	0.001123	0.001321	13
14	0.000072	0.000091	0.000115	0.000144	0.000178	0.000219	0.000268	0.000325	0.000393	0.000472	14
15	0.000020	0.000026	0.000033	0.000042	0.000053	0.000067	0.000084	0.000104	0.000128	0.000157	15
16	0.000005	0.000007	0.000009	0.000012	0.000015	0.000019	0.000025	0.000031	0.000039	0.000049	16
17	0.000001	0.000002	0.000002	0.000003	0.000004	0.000005	0.000007	0.000009	0.000011	0.000014	17
18	—	—	0.000001	0.000001	0.000001	0.000001	0.000002	0.000002	0.000003	0.000004	18
19	—	—	—	—	—	—	—	0.000001	0.000001	0.000001	19

x	5.1	5.2	5.3	5.4	5.5	5.6	5.7	5.8	5.9	6.0	*x*
0	0.006097	0.005517	0.004992	0.004517	0.004087	0.003698	0.003346	0.003028	0.002739	0.002479	0
1	0.031093	0.028686	0.026455	0.024390	0.022477	0.020708	0.019072	0.017560	0.016163	0.014873	1
2	0.079288	0.074584	0.070107	0.065852	0.061812	0.057982	0.054355	0.050923	0.047680	0.044618	2
3	0.134790	0.129279	0.123856	0.118533	0.113323	0.108234	0.103275	0.098452	0.093771	0.089235	3

TABLE A.6 Poisson's Exponential Binomial Limit

Part 1—(*continued*)

x	*m* 5.1	5.2	5.3	5.4	5.5	5.6	5.7	5.8	5.9	6.0	*x*
4	0.171857	0.168063	0.164109	0.160020	0.155819	0.151528	0.147167	0.142755	0.138312	0.133853	4
5	0.175294	0.174785	0.173955	0.172821	0.171401	0.169711	0.167770	0.165596	0.163208	0.160623	5
6	0.149000	0.151480	0.153660	0.155539	0.157117	0.158397	0.159382	0.160076	0.160488	0.160623	6
7	0.108557	0.112528	0.116343	0.119987	0.123449	0.126717	0.129782	0.132635	0.135268	0.137677	7
8	0.069205	0.073143	0.077077	0.080991	0.084871	0.088702	0.092470	0.096160	0.099760	0.103258	8
9	0.039216	0.042261	0.045390	0.048595	0.051866	0.055192	0.058564	0.061970	0.065398	0.068838	9
10	0.020000	0.021976	0.024057	0.026241	0.028526	0.030908	0.033382	0.035943	0.038585	0.041303	10
11	0.009273	0.010388	0.011591	0.012882	0.014263	0.015735	0.017298	0.018952	0.020696	0.022529	11
12	0.003941	0.004502	0.005119	0.005797	0.006537	0.007343	0.008216	0.009160	0.010175	0.011264	12
13	0.001546	0.001801	0.002087	0.002408	0.002766	0.003163	0.003603	0.004087	0.004618	0.005199	13
14	0.000563	0.000669	0.000790	0.000929	0.001087	0.001265	0.001467	0.001693	0.001946	0.002228	14
15	0.000191	0.000232	0.000279	0.000334	0.000398	0.000472	0.000557	0.000655	0.000766	0.000891	15
16	0.000061	0.000075	0.000092	0.000113	0.000137	0.000165	0.000199	0.000237	0.000282	0.000334	16
17	0.000018	0.000023	0.000029	0.000036	0.000044	0.000054	0.000067	0.000081	0.000098	0.000118	17
18	0.000005	0.000007	0.000008	0.000011	0.000014	0.000017	0.000021	0.000026	0.000032	0.000039	18
19	0.000001	0.000002	0.000002	0.000003	0.000004	0.000005	0.000006	0.000008	0.000010	0.000012	19
20	—	—	0.000001	0.000001	0.000001	0.000001	0.000002	0.000002	0.000003	0.000004	20
21	—	—	—	—	—	—	—	0.000001	0.000001	0.000001	21

x	6.1	6.2	6.3	6.4	6.5	6.6	6.7	6.8	6.9	7.0	*x*
0	0.002243	0.002029	0.001836	0.001662	0.001503	0.001360	0.001231	0.001114	0.001008	0.000912	0
1	0.013682	0.012582	0.011569	0.010634	0.009772	0.008978	0.008247	0.007574	0.006954	0.006383	1
2	0.041729	0.039006	0.036441	0.034029	0.031760	0.029629	0.027628	0.025751	0.023990	0.022341	2
3	0.084848	0.080612	0.076527	0.072595	0.068814	0.065183	0.061702	0.058368	0.055178	0.052129	3
4	0.129393	0.124948	0.120530	0.116151	0.111822	0.107553	0.103351	0.099225	0.095182	0.091226	4
5	0.157860	0.154936	0.151868	0.148674	0.145369	0.141969	0.138490	0.134946	0.131351	0.127717	5
6	0.160491	0.160100	0.159461	0.158585	0.157483	0.156166	0.154648	0.152939	0.151053	0.149003	6
7	0.139856	0.141803	0.143515	0.144992	0.146234	0.147243	0.148020	0.148569	0.148895	0.149003	7
8	0.106640	0.109897	0.113018	0.115994	0.118815	0.121475	0.123967	0.126284	0.128422	0.130377	8
9	0.072278	0.075707	0.079113	0.082484	0.085811	0.089082	0.092286	0.095415	0.098457	0.101405	9
10	0.044090	0.046938	0.049841	0.052790	0.055777	0.058794	0.061832	0.064882	0.067935	0.070983	10
11	0.024450	0.026456	0.028545	0.030714	0.032959	0.035276	0.037661	0.040109	0.042614	0.045171	11
12	0.012429	0.013669	0.014986	0.016381	0.017853	0.019402	0.021028	0.022728	0.024503	0.026350	12
13	0.005832	0.006519	0.007263	0.008064	0.008926	0.009850	0.010837	0.011889	0.013005	0.014188	13
14	0.002541	0.002887	0.003268	0.003687	0.004144	0.004644	0.005186	0.005774	0.006410	0.007094	14
15	0.001033	0.001193	0.001373	0.001573	0.001796	0.002043	0.002317	0.002618	0.002949	0.003311	15
16	0.000394	0.000462	0.000540	0.000629	0.000730	0.000843	0.000970	0.001113	0.001272	0.001448	16
17	0.000141	0.000169	0.000200	0.000237	0.000279	0.000327	0.000382	0.000445	0.000516	0.000596	17
18	0.000048	0.000058	0.000070	0.000084	0.000101	0.000120	0.000142	0.000168	0.000198	0.000232	18
19	0.000015	0.000019	0.000023	0.000028	0.000034	0.000042	0.000050	0.000060	0.000072	0.000085	19
20	0.000005	0.000006	0.000007	0.000009	0.000011	0.000014	0.000017	0.000020	0.000025	0.000030	20
21	0.000001	0.000002	0.000002	0.000003	0.000003	0.000004	0.000005	0.000007	0.000008	0.000010	21
22	—	—	0.000001	0.000001	0.000001	0.000001	0.000002	0.000002	0.000003	0.000003	22
23	—	—	—	—	—	—	—	0.000001	0.000001	0.000001	23

TABLE A.6 Poisson's Exponential Binomial Limit

Part 2 (*continued*)

x	m 7.1	7.2	7.3	7.4	7.5	7.6	7.7	7.8	7.9	8.0	x
0	0.000825	0.000747	0.000676	0.000611	0.000553	0.000500	0.000453	0.000410	0.000371	0.000335	0
1	0.005858	0.005375	0.004931	0.004523	0.004148	0.003803	0.003487	0.003196	0.002929	0.002684	1
2	0.020797	0.019352	0.018000	0.016736	0.015555	0.014453	0.013424	0.012464	0.011569	0.010735	2
3	0.049219	0.046444	0.043799	0.041282	0.038889	0.036614	0.034455	0.032407	0.030465	0.028626	3
4	0.087364	0.083598	0.079934	0.076372	0.072916	0.069567	0.066326	0.063193	0.060169	0.057252	4
5	0.124057	0.120382	0.116703	0.113031	0.109375	0.105742	0.102142	0.098581	0.095067	0.091604	5
6	0.146800	0.144458	0.141989	0.139405	0.136718	0.133940	0.131082	0.128156	0.125171	0.122138	6
7	0.148897	0.148586	0.148074	0.147371	0.146484	0.145421	0.144191	0.142802	0.141264	0.139587	7
8	0.132146	0.133727	0.135118	0.136318	0.137329	0.138150	0.138783	0.139232	0.139499	0.139587	8
9	0.104249	0.106982	0.109596	0.112084	0.114440	0.116660	0.118737	0.120668	0.122449	0.124077	9
10	0.074017	0.077027	0.080005	0.082942	0.085830	0.088661	0.091427	0.094121	0.096735	0.099262	10
11	0.047774	0.050418	0.053094	0.055797	0.058521	0.061257	0.063999	0.066740	0.069473	0.072190	11
12	0.028267	0.030251	0.032299	0.034408	0.036575	0.038796	0.041066	0.043381	0.045736	0.048127	12
13	0.015438	0.016754	0.018137	0.019586	0.021101	0.022681	0.024324	0.026029	0.027794	0.029616	13
14	0.007829	0.008616	0.009457	0.010353	0.011304	0.012312	0.013378	0.014502	0.015684	0.016924	14
15	0.003706	0.004136	0.004603	0.005107	0.005652	0.006238	0.006867	0.007541	0.008260	0.009026	15
16	0.001644	0.001861	0.002100	0.002362	0.002649	0.002963	0.003305	0.003676	0.004078	0.004513	16
17	0.000687	0.000788	0.000902	0.001028	0.001169	0.001325	0.001497	0.001687	0.001895	0.002124	17
18	0.000271	0.000315	0.000366	0.000423	0.000487	0.000559	0.000640	0.000731	0.000832	0.000944	18
19	0.000101	0.000119	0.000141	0.000165	0.000192	0.000224	0.000259	0.000300	0.000346	0.000397	19
20	0.000036	0.000043	0.000051	0.000061	0.000072	0.000085	0.000100	0.000117	0.000137	0.000159	20
21	0.000012	0.000015	0.000018	0.000021	0.000026	0.000031	0.000037	0.000043	0.000051	0.000061	21
22	0.000004	0.000005	0.000006	0.000007	0.000009	0.000011	0.000013	0.000015	0.000018	0.000022	22
23	0.000001	0.000002	0.000002	0.000002	0.000003	0.000004	0.000004	0.000005	0.000006	0.000008	23
24	—	—	0.000001	0.000001	0.000001	0.000001	0.000001	0.000002	0.000002	0.000003	24
25	—	—	—	—	—	—	—	0.000001	0.000001	0.000001	25

x	8.1	8.2	8.3	8.4	8.5	8.6	8.7	8.8	8.9	9.0	x
0	0.000304	0.000275	0.000249	0.000225	0.000203	0.000184	0.000167	0.000151	0.000136	0.000123	0
1	0.002459	0.002252	0.002063	0.001889	0.001729	0.001583	0.001449	0.001326	0.001214	0.001111	1
2	0.009958	0.009234	0.008560	0.007933	0.007350	0.006808	0.006304	0.005836	0.005402	0.004998	2
3	0.026885	0.025239	0.023683	0.022213	0.020826	0.019517	0.018283	0.017120	0.016025	0.014994	3
4	0.054443	0.051740	0.049142	0.046648	0.044255	0.041961	0.039765	0.037664	0.035656	0.033737	4
5	0.088198	0.084854	0.081576	0.078368	0.075233	0.072174	0.069192	0.066289	0.063467	0.060727	5
6	0.119067	0.115967	0.112847	0.109716	0.106581	0.103449	0.100328	0.097224	0.094143	0.091090	6
7	0.137778	0.135848	0.133805	0.131659	0.129419	0.127094	0.124693	0.122224	0.119696	0.117116	7
8	0.139500	0.139244	0.138823	0.138242	0.137508	0.136626	0.135604	0.134446	0.133161	0.131756	8
9	0.125550	0.126866	0.128025	0.129026	0.129869	0.130554	0.131084	0.131459	0.131682	0.131756	9
10	0.101696	0.104031	0.106261	0.108382	0.110388	0.112277	0.114043	0.115684	0.117197	0.118580	10
11	0.074885	0.077550	0.080179	0.082764	0.085300	0.087780	0.090197	0.092547	0.094823	0.097020	11
12	0.050547	0.052993	0.055457	0.057935	0.060421	0.062909	0.065393	0.067868	0.070327	0.072765	12
13	0.031495	0.033426	0.035407	0.037435	0.039506	0.041617	0.043763	0.045941	0.048147	0.050376	13
14	0.018222	0.019578	0.020991	0.022461	0.023986	0.025565	0.027196	0.028877	0.030608	0.032384	14
15	0.009840	0.010703	0.011615	0.012578	0.013592	0.014657	0.015773	0.016941	0.018161	0.019431	15
16	0.004981	0.005485	0.006025	0.006604	0.007221	0.007878	0.008577	0.009318	0.010102	0.010930	16
17	0.002373	0.002646	0.002942	0.003263	0.003610	0.003985	0.004389	0.004823	0.005289	0.005786	17
18	0.001068	0.001205	0.001356	0.001523	0.001705	0.001904	0.002121	0.002358	0.002615	0.002893	18
19	0.000455	0.000520	0.000593	0.000673	0.000763	0.000862	0.000971	0.001092	0.001225	0.001370	19
20	0.000184	0.000213	0.000246	0.000283	0.000324	0.000371	0.000423	0.000481	0.000545	0.000617	20

TABLE A.6 Poisson's Exponential Binomial Limit

Part 2 (*continued*)

x	m: 8.1	8.2	8.3	8.4	8.5	8.6	8.7	8.8	8.9	9.0	x
21	0.000071	0.000083	0.000097	0.000113	0.000131	0.000152	0.000175	0.000201	0.000231	0.000264	21
22	0.000026	0.000031	0.000037	0.000043	0.000051	0.000059	0.000069	0.000081	0.000093	0.000108	22
23	0.000009	0.000011	0.000013	0.000016	0.000019	0.000022	0.000026	0.000031	0.000036	0.000042	23
24	0.000003	0.000004	0.000005	0.000006	0.000007	0.000008	0.000009	0.000011	0.000013	0.000016	24
25	0.000001	0.000001	0.000002	0.000002	0.000002	0.000003	0.000003	0.000004	0.000005	0.000006	25
26	—	—	—	0.000001	0.000001	0.000001	0.000001	0.000001	0.000002	0.000002	26
27	—	—	—	—	—	—	—	—	0.000001	0.000001	27

x	9.1	9.2	9.3	9.4	9.5	9.6	9.7	9.8	9.9	10.0	x
0	0.000112	0.000101	0.000091	0.000083	0.000075	0.000068	0.000061	0.000055	0.000050	0.000045	0
1	0.001016	0.000930	0.000850	0.000778	0.000711	0.000650	0.000594	0.000543	0.000497	0.000454	1
2	0.004624	0.004276	0.003954	0.003655	0.003378	0.003121	0.002883	0.002663	0.002459	0.002270	2
3	0.014025	0.013113	0.012256	0.011452	0.010696	0.009987	0.009322	0.008698	0.008114	0.007567	3
4	0.031906	0.030160	0.028496	0.026911	0.025403	0.023969	0.022606	0.021311	0.020082	0.018917	4
5	0.058069	0.055494	0.053002	0.050593	0.048266	0.046020	0.043855	0.041770	0.039763	0.037833	5
6	0.088072	0.085091	0.082154	0.079262	0.076421	0.073632	0.070899	0.068224	0.065609	0.063055	6
7	0.114493	0.111834	0.109147	0.106438	0.103714	0.100981	0.098246	0.095514	0.092790	0.090079	7
8	0.130236	0.128609	0.126883	0.125065	0.123160	0.121178	0.119123	0.117004	0.114827	0.112599	8
9	0.131683	0.131467	0.131113	0.130623	0.130003	0.129256	0.128388	0.127405	0.126310	0.125110	9
10	0.119832	0.120950	0.121935	0.122786	0.123502	0.124086	0.124537	0.124857	0.125047	0.125110	10
11	0.099133	0.101158	0.103090	0.104926	0.106661	0.108293	0.109819	0.111236	0.112542	0.113736	11
12	0.075176	0.077555	0.079895	0.082192	0.084440	0.086634	0.088770	0.090843	0.092847	0.094780	12
13	0.052623	0.054885	0.057156	0.059431	0.061706	0.063976	0.066236	0.068481	0.070707	0.072908	13
14	0.034205	0.036067	0.037968	0.039904	0.041872	0.043869	0.045892	0.047937	0.050000	0.052077	14
15	0.020751	0.022121	0.023540	0.025006	0.026519	0.028076	0.029677	0.031319	0.033000	0.034718	15
16	0.011802	0.012720	0.013683	0.014691	0.015746	0.016846	0.017992	0.019183	0.020419	0.021699	16
17	0.006318	0.006884	0.007485	0.008123	0.008799	0.009513	0.010266	0.011058	0.011891	0.012764	17
18	0.003194	0.003518	0.003867	0.004242	0.004644	0.005074	0.005532	0.006021	0.006540	0.007091	18
19	0.001530	0.001704	0.001893	0.002099	0.002322	0.002563	0.002824	0.003105	0.003408	0.003732	19
20	0.000696	0.000784	0.000880	0.000986	0.001103	0.001230	0.001370	0.001522	0.001687	0.001866	20
21	0.000302	0.000343	0.000390	0.000442	0.000499	0.000563	0.000633	0.000710	0.000795	0.000889	21
22	0.000125	0.000144	0.000165	0.000189	0.000215	0.000245	0.000279	0.000316	0.000358	0.000404	22
23	0.000049	0.000057	0.000067	0.000077	0.000089	0.000102	0.000118	0.000135	0.000154	0.000176	23
24	0.000019	0.000022	0.000026	0.000030	0.000035	0.000041	0.000048	0.000055	0.000064	0.000073	24
25	0.000007	0.000008	0.000010	0.000011	0.000013	0.000016	0.000018	0.000022	0.000025	0.000029	25
26	0.000002	0.000003	0.000003	0.000004	0.000005	0.000006	0.000007	0.000008	0.000010	0.000011	26
27	0.000001	0.000001	0.000001	0.000001	0.000002	0.000002	0.000002	0.000003	0.000004	0.000004	27
28	—	—	—	—	0.000001	0.000001	0.000001	0.000001	0.000001	0.000001	28
29	—	—	—	—	—	—	—	—	—	0.000001	29

x	10.1	10.2	10.3	10.4	10.5	10.6	10.7	10.8	10.9	11.0	x
0	0.000041	0.000037	0.000034	0.000030	0.000028	0.000025	0.000023	0.000020	0.000018	0.000017	0
1	0.000415	0.000379	0.000346	0.000317	0.000289	0.000264	0.000241	0.000220	0.000201	0.000184	1
2	0.002095	0.001934	0.001784	0.001646	0.001518	0.001400	0.001291	0.001190	0.001097	0.001010	2
3	0.007054	0.006574	0.006125	0.005705	0.005313	0.004946	0.004603	0.004283	0.003984	0.003705	3

TABLE A.6 Poisson's Exponential Binomial Limit

Part 2 (*continued*)

x	m										x
	10.1	10.2	10.3	10.4	10.5	10.6	10.7	10.8	10.9	11.0	
4	0.017811	0.016764	0.015773	0.014834	0.013946	0.013107	0.012313	0.011564	0.010856	0.010189	4
5	0.035979	0.034199	0.032492	0.030855	0.029287	0.027786	0.026350	0.024978	0.023667	0.022415	5
6	0.060565	0.058139	0.055777	0.053482	0.051252	0.049089	0.046991	0.044960	0.042995	0.041095	6
7	0.087387	0.084716	0.082072	0.079458	0.076878	0.074334	0.071830	0.069367	0.066949	0.064577	7
8	0.110326	0.108013	0.105668	0.103296	0.100902	0.098493	0.096072	0.093646	0.091218	0.088794	8
9	0.123810	0.122415	0.120931	0.119304	0.117720	0.116003	0.114219	0.112375	0.110475	0.108526	9
10	0.125048	0.124863	0.124559	0.124139	0.123606	0.122963	0.122215	0.121365	0.120418	0.119378	10
11	0.114817	0.115782	0.116633	0.117368	0.117987	0.118492	0.118882	0.119159	0.119323	0.119378	11
12	0.096637	0.098415	0.100110	0.101719	0.103239	0.104667	0.106003	0.107243	0.108386	0.109430	12
13	0.075080	0.077218	0.079318	0.081375	0.083385	0.085344	0.087248	0.089094	0.090877	0.092595	13
14	0.054165	0.056259	0.058355	0.060450	0.062539	0.064618	0.066683	0.068730	0.070754	0.072753	14
15	0.036471	0.038256	0.040071	0.041912	0.043777	0.045663	0.047567	0.049485	0.051415	0.053352	15
16	0.023022	0.024388	0.025795	0.027243	0.028729	0.030252	0.031810	0.033403	0.035026	0.036680	16
17	0.013678	0.014633	0.015629	0.016666	0.017744	0.018863	0.020022	0.021220	0.022458	0.023734	17
18	0.007675	0.008292	0.008943	0.009629	0.010351	0.011108	0.011902	0.012732	0.013600	0.014504	18
19	0.004080	0.004451	0.004848	0.005271	0.005720	0.006197	0.006703	0.007237	0.007802	0.008397	19
20	0.002060	0.002270	0.002497	0.002741	0.003003	0.003285	0.003586	0.003908	0.004252	0.004618	20
21	0.000991	0.001103	0.001225	0.001357	0.001502	0.001658	0.001827	0.002010	0.002207	0.002419	21
22	0.000455	0.000511	0.000573	0.000642	0.000717	0.000799	0.000889	0.000987	0.001093	0.001210	22
23	0.000200	0.000227	0.000257	0.000290	0.000327	0.000368	0.000413	0.000463	0.000518	0.000578	23
24	0.000084	0.000096	0.000110	0.000126	0.000143	0.000163	0.000184	0.000208	0.000235	0.000265	24
25	0.000034	0.000039	0.000045	0.000052	0.000060	0.000069	0.000079	0.000090	0.000103	0.000117	25
26	0.000013	0.000015	0.000018	0.000021	0.000024	0.000028	0.000032	0.000037	0.000043	0.000049	26
27	0.000005	0.000006	0.000007	0.000008	0.000009	0.000011	0.000013	0.000015	0.000017	0.000020	27
28	0.000002	0.000002	0.000003	0.000003	0.000004	0.000004	0.000005	0.000006	0.000007	0.000008	28
29	0.000001	0.000001	0.000001	0.000001	0.000001	0.000002	0.000002	0.000002	0.000003	0.000003	29
30	—	—	—	—	—	0.000001	0.000001	0.000001	0.000001	0.000001	30

x	11.1	11.2	11.3	11.4	11.5	11.6	11.7	11.8	11.9	12.0	x
0	0.000015	0.000014	0.000012	0.000011	0.000010	0.000009	0.000008	0.000008	0.000007	0.000006	0
1	0.000168	0.000153	0.000140	0.000128	0.000116	0.000106	0.000097	0.000089	0.000081	0.000074	1
2	0.000931	0.000858	0.000790	0.000727	0.000670	0.000617	0.000568	0.000522	0.000481	0.000442	2
3	0.003445	0.003202	0.002976	0.002764	0.002568	0.002385	0.002214	0.002055	0.001907	0.001770	3
4	0.009559	0.008965	0.008406	0.007879	0.007382	0.006915	0.006476	0.006062	0.005674	0.005309	4
5	0.021221	0.020082	0.018997	0.017963	0.016979	0.016043	0.015153	0.014307	0.013504	0.012741	5
6	0.039259	0.037487	0.035778	0.034130	0.032544	0.031017	0.029549	0.028137	0.026782	0.025481	6
7	0.062253	0.059979	0.057755	0.055584	0.053465	0.051400	0.049388	0.047432	0.045530	0.043682	7
8	0.086376	0.083970	0.081579	0.079206	0.076856	0.074529	0.072231	0.069962	0.067725	0.065523	8
9	0.106531	0.104496	0.102427	0.100328	0.098204	0.096060	0.093900	0.091728	0.089548	0.087364	9
10	0.118249	0.117036	0.115743	0.114374	0.112935	0.111430	0.109863	0.108239	0.106562	0.104837	10
11	0.119324	0.119164	0.118899	0.118533	0.118068	0.117508	0.116854	0.116110	0.115281	0.114368	11
12	0.110375	0.111220	0.111964	0.112607	0.113149	0.113591	0.113933	0.114175	0.114320	0.114363	12
13	0.094243	0.095820	0.097322	0.098747	0.100093	0.101358	0.102539	0.103636	0.104647	0.105570	13
14	0.074721	0.076656	0.078553	0.080409	0.082219	0.083982	0.085694	0.087350	0.088950	0.090489	14
15	0.055294	0.057236	0.059177	0.061110	0.063035	0.064946	0.066841	0.068716	0.070567	0.072391	15
16	0.038360	0.040065	0.041793	0.043541	0.045306	0.047086	0.048877	0.050678	0.052484	0.054293	16
17	0.025047	0.026396	0.027780	0.029198	0.030648	0.032129	0.033639	0.035176	0.036739	0.038325	17
18	0.015446	0.016424	0.017440	0.018492	0.019581	0.020706	0.021865	0.023060	0.024288	0.025550	18
19	0.009023	0.009682	0.010372	0.011095	0.011852	0.012641	0.013465	0.014322	0.015212	0.016137	19

TABLE A.6 Poisson's Exponential Binomial Limit

Part 2 (*continued*)

x	*m* 11.1	11.2	11.3	11.4	11.5	11.6	11.7	11.8	11.9	12.0	*x*
20	0.005008	0.005422	0.005860	0.006324	0.006815	0.007332	0.007877	0.008450	0.009051	0.009682	20
21	0.002647	0.002892	0.003153	0.003433	0.003732	0.004050	0.004388	0.004748	0.005129	0.005533	21
22	0.001336	0.001472	0.001620	0.001779	0.001951	0.002136	0.002334	0.002547	0.002774	0.003018	22
23	0.000645	0.000717	0.000796	0.000882	0.000975	0.001077	0.001187	0.001307	0.001435	0.001575	23
24	0.000298	0.000335	0.000375	0.000419	0.000467	0.000521	0.000579	0.000642	0.000712	0.000787	24
25	0.000132	0.000150	0.000169	0.000191	0.000215	0.000242	0.000271	0.000303	0.000339	0.000378	25
26	0.000057	0.000065	0.000074	0.000084	0.000095	0.000108	0.000122	0.000138	0.000155	0.000174	26
27	0.000023	0.000027	0.000031	0.000035	0.000041	0.000046	0.000053	0.000060	0.000068	0.000078	27
28	0.000009	0.000011	0.000012	0.000014	0.000017	0.000019	0.000022	0.000025	0.000029	0.000033	28
29	0.000004	0.000004	0.000005	0.000006	0.000007	0.000008	0.000009	0.000010	0.000012	0.000014	29
30	0.000001	0.000002	0.000002	0.000002	0.000003	0.000003	0.000003	0.000004	0.000005	0.000005	30
31	—	0.000001	0.000001	0.000001	0.000001	0.000001	0.000001	0.000002	0.000002	0.000002	31
32	—	—	—	—	—	—	—	0.000001	0.000001	0.000001	32

x	12.1	12.2	12.3	12.4	12.5	12.6	12.7	12.8	12.9	13.0	*x*
0	0.000006	0.000005	0.000005	0.000004	0.000004	0.000003	0.000003	0.000003	0.000002	0.000002	0
1	0.000067	0.000061	0.000056	0.000051	0.000047	0.000042	0.000039	0.000035	0.000032	0.000029	1
2	0.000407	0.000374	0.000344	0.000317	0.000291	0.000268	0.000246	0.000226	0.000208	0.000191	2
3	0.001641	0.001522	0.001412	0.001309	0.001213	0.001124	0.001042	0.000965	0.000894	0.000828	3
4	0.004966	0.004643	0.004341	0.004057	0.003791	0.003541	0.003307	0.003088	0.002882	0.002690	4
5	0.012017	0.011330	0.010679	0.010062	0.009477	0.008924	0.008400	0.007905	0.007436	0.006994	5
6	0.024233	0.023037	0.021892	0.020794	0.019744	0.018740	0.017781	0.016864	0.015988	0.015153	6
7	0.041889	0.040151	0.038467	0.036836	0.035258	0.033733	0.032259	0.030837	0.029464	0.028141	7
8	0.063358	0.061230	0.059142	0.057095	0.055091	0.053129	0.051212	0.049339	0.047511	0.045730	8
9	0.085181	0.083000	0.080828	0.078665	0.076515	0.074381	0.072266	0.070171	0.068100	0.066054	9
10	0.103069	0.101261	0.099418	0.097544	0.095644	0.093720	0.091777	0.089819	0.087849	0.085870	10
11	0.113376	0.112308	0.111168	0.109959	0.108686	0.107352	0.105961	0.104516	0.103023	0.101483	11
12	0.114321	0.114180	0.113947	0.113624	0.113215	0.112720	0.112142	0.111484	0.110749	0.109940	12
13	0.106406	0.107153	0.107811	0.108380	0.108860	0.109251	0.109554	0.109769	0.109897	0.109940	13
14	0.091965	0.093376	0.094720	0.095994	0.097197	0.098326	0.099381	0.100360	0.101263	0.102087	14
15	0.074185	0.075946	0.077670	0.079355	0.080997	0.082594	0.084143	0.085641	0.087086	0.088475	15
16	0.056103	0.057909	0.059709	0.061500	0.063279	0.065043	0.066788	0.068513	0.070213	0.071886	16
17	0.039932	0.041558	0.043201	0.044859	0.046529	0.048208	0.049895	0.051586	0.053279	0.054972	17
18	0.026843	0.028167	0.029521	0.030903	0.032312	0.033746	0.035204	0.036683	0.038183	0.039702	18
19	0.017095	0.018086	0.019111	0.020168	0.021258	0.022379	0.023531	0.024713	0.025925	0.027164	19
20	0.010342	0.011033	0.011753	0.012504	0.013286	0.014099	0.014942	0.015816	0.016721	0.017657	20
21	0.005959	0.006409	0.006884	0.007383	0.007908	0.008459	0.009036	0.009640	0.010272	0.010930	21
22	0.003278	0.003554	0.003849	0.004162	0.004493	0.004845	0.005216	0.005609	0.006023	0.006459	22
23	0.001724	0.001885	0.002058	0.002244	0.002442	0.002654	0.002880	0.003122	0.003378	0.003651	23
24	0.000869	0.000958	0.001055	0.001159	0.001272	0.001393	0.001524	0.001665	0.001816	0.001977	24
25	0.000421	0.000468	0.000519	0.000575	0.000636	0.000702	0.000774	0.000852	0.000937	0.001028	25
26	0.000196	0.000219	0.000246	0.000274	0.000306	0.000340	0.000378	0.000420	0.000465	0.000514	26
27	0.000088	0.000099	0.000112	0.000126	0.000142	0.000159	0.000178	0.000199	0.000222	0.000248	27
28	0.000038	0.000043	0.000049	0.000056	0.000063	0.000071	0.000081	0.000091	0.000102	0.000115	28
29	0.000016	0.000018	0.000021	0.000024	0.000027	0.000031	0.000035	0.000040	0.000046	0.000052	29
30	0.000006	0.000007	0.000009	0.000010	0.000011	0.000013	0.000015	0.000017	0.000020	0.000022	30
31	0.000002	0.000003	0.000003	0.000004	0.000005	0.000005	0.000006	0.000007	0.000008	0.000009	31
32	0.000001	0.000001	0.000001	0.000002	0.000002	0.000002	0.000002	0.000003	0.000003	0.000004	32
33	—	—	—	0.000001	0.000001	0.000001	0.000001	0.000001	0.000001	0.000002	33
34	—	—	—	—	—	—	—	—	—	0.000001	34

TABLE A.6 Poisson's Exponential Binomial Limit

Part 2 (*continued*)

x	*m* 13.1	13.2	13.3	13.4	13.5	13.6	13.7	13.8	13.9	14.0	*x*
0	0.000002	0.000002	0.000002	0.000002	0.000001	0.000001	0.000001	0.000001	0.000001	0.000001	0
1	0.000027	0.000024	0.000022	0.000020	0.000019	0.000017	0.000015	0.000014	0.000013	0.000012	1
2	0.000175	0.000161	0.000148	0.000136	0.000125	0.000115	0.000105	0.000097	0.000089	0.000081	2
3	0.000766	0.000709	0.000657	0.000608	0.000562	0.000520	0.000481	0.000445	0.000411	0.000380	3
4	0.002510	0.002341	0.002183	0.002035	0.001897	0.001768	0.001648	0.001535	0.001429	0.001331	4
5	0.006575	0.006180	0.005807	0.005455	0.005123	0.004810	0.004514	0.004236	0.003974	0.003727	5
6	0.014356	0.013596	0.012872	0.012183	0.011526	0.010902	0.010308	0.009743	0.009206	0.008696	6
7	0.026867	0.025639	0.024458	0.023322	0.022230	0.021181	0.020173	0.019207	0.018280	0.017392	7
8	0.043994	0.042304	0.040661	0.039064	0.037512	0.036007	0.034547	0.033132	0.031762	0.030435	8
9	0.064036	0.062046	0.060088	0.058161	0.056269	0.054410	0.052588	0.050802	0.049054	0.047344	9
10	0.083887	0.081901	0.079916	0.077936	0.075963	0.073998	0.072046	0.070107	0.068185	0.066282	10
11	0.099901	0.098281	0.096626	0.094940	0.093227	0.091489	0.089730	0.087953	0.086162	0.084359	11
12	0.109059	0.108109	0.107094	0.106017	0.104880	0.103687	0.102441	0.101146	0.099804	0.098418	12
13	0.109898	0.109773	0.109566	0.109279	0.108914	0.108473	0.107957	0.107370	0.106713	0.105989	13
14	0.102833	0.103500	0.104087	0.104595	0.105024	0.105373	0.105644	0.105836	0.105951	0.105989	14
15	0.089807	0.091080	0.092291	0.093439	0.094522	0.095539	0.096488	0.097369	0.098181	0.098923	15
16	0.073530	0.075141	0.076717	0.078255	0.079753	0.081208	0.082618	0.083981	0.085295	0.086558	16
17	0.056661	0.058345	0.060019	0.061683	0.063333	0.064966	0.066580	0.068173	0.069741	0.071283	17
18	0.041237	0.042786	0.044348	0.045920	0.047500	0.049086	0.050675	0.052266	0.053856	0.055442	18
19	0.028432	0.029725	0.031043	0.032385	0.033750	0.035135	0.036539	0.037962	0.039400	0.040852	19
20	0.018623	0.019619	0.020644	0.021698	0.022781	0.023892	0.025030	0.026193	0.027383	0.028597	20
21	0.011617	0.012332	0.013074	0.013846	0.014645	0.015473	0.016329	0.017213	0.018125	0.019064	21
22	0.006917	0.007399	0.007904	0.008433	0.008987	0.009565	0.010168	0.010797	0.011452	0.012132	22
23	0.003940	0.004246	0.004571	0.004913	0.005275	0.005656	0.006057	0.006478	0.006921	0.007385	23
24	0.002151	0.002336	0.002533	0.002743	0.002967	0.003205	0.003457	0.003725	0.004008	0.004308	24
25	0.001127	0.001233	0.001348	0.001470	0.001602	0.001744	0.001895	0.002056	0.002229	0.002412	25
26	0.000568	0.000626	0.000689	0.000758	0.000832	0.000912	0.000998	0.001091	0.001191	0.001299	26
27	0.000275	0.000306	0.000340	0.000376	0.000416	0.000459	0.000507	0.000558	0.000613	0.000674	27
28	0.000129	0.000144	0.000161	0.000180	0.000201	0.000223	0.000248	0.000275	0.000305	0.000337	28
29	0.000058	0.000066	0.000074	0.000083	0.000093	0.000105	0.000117	0.000131	0.000146	0.000163	29
30	0.000025	0.000029	0.000033	0.000037	0.000042	0.000047	0.000053	0.000060	0.000068	0.000076	30
31	0.000011	0.000012	0.000014	0.000016	0.000018	0.000021	0.000024	0.000027	0.000030	0.000034	31
32	0.000004	0.000005	0.000006	0.000007	0.000008	0.000009	0.000010	0.000012	0.000013	0.000015	32
33	0.000002	0.000002	0.000002	0.000003	0.000003	0.000004	0.000004	0.000005	0.000006	0.000006	33
34	0.000001	0.000001	0.000001	0.000001	0.000001	0.000001	0.000002	0.000002	0.000002	0.000003	34
35	—	—	—	—	—	0.000001	0.000001	0.000001	0.000001	0.000001	35

x	14.1	14.2	14.3	14.4	14.5	14.6	14.7	14.8	14.9	15.0	*x*
0	0.000001	0.000001	0.000001	0.000001	0.000001	—	—	—	—	—	0
1	0.000011	0.000010	0.000009	0.000008	0.000007	0.000007	0.000006	0.000006	0.000005	0.000005	1
2	0.000075	0.000069	0.000063	0.000058	0.000053	0.000049	0.000045	0.000041	0.000038	0.000034	2
3	0.000352	0.000325	0.000300	0.000277	0.000256	0.000237	0.000219	0.000202	0.000186	0.000172	3
4	0.001239	0.001153	0.001073	0.000999	0.000929	0.000864	0.000803	0.000747	0.000694	0.000645	4
5	0.003494	0.003275	0.003070	0.002876	0.002694	0.002523	0.002362	0.002211	0.002069	0.001936	5
6	0.008212	0.007752	0.007316	0.006902	0.006510	0.006139	0.005787	0.005454	0.005138	0.004839	6
7	0.016541	0.015726	0.014946	0.014199	0.013486	0.012804	0.012152	0.011530	0.010937	0.010370	7
8	0.029153	0.027913	0.026715	0.025559	0.024443	0.023367	0.022330	0.021331	0.020370	0.019444	8
9	0.045673	0.044040	0.042447	0.040894	0.039380	0.037907	0.036472	0.035078	0.033723	0.032407	9
10	0.064399	0.062537	0.060700	0.058887	0.057101	0.055343	0.053614	0.051915	0.050247	0.048611	10
11	0.082547	0.080730	0.078910	0.077089	0.075270	0.073456	0.071648	0.069850	0.068062	0.066287	11

TABLE A.6 Poisson's Exponential Binomial Limit

Part 2 (*continued*)

x	*m*										*x*
	14.1	*14.2*	*14.3*	*14.4*	*14.5*	*14.6*	*14.7*	*14.8*	*14.9*	*15.0*	
12	0.096993	0.095530	0.094034	0.092507	0.090951	0.089371	0.087769	0.086148	0.084510	0.082859	*12*
13	0.105200	0.104349	0.103437	0.102469	0.101446	0.100371	0.099247	0.098076	0.096862	0.095607	*13*
14	0.105951	0.105839	0.105654	0.105396	0.105069	0.104672	0.104209	0.103681	0.103089	0.102436	*14*
15	0.099594	0.100195	0.100723	0.101181	0.101567	0.101881	0.102125	0.102298	0.102402	0.102436	*15*
16	0.087768	0.088923	0.090021	0.091063	0.092045	0.092967	0.093827	0.094626	0.095361	0.096034	*16*
17	0.072795	0.074277	0.075724	0.077135	0.078509	0.079842	0.081133	0.082380	0.083581	0.084736	*17*
18	0.057023	0.058596	0.060158	0.061708	0.063243	0.064761	0.066259	0.067735	0.069187	0.070613	*18*
19	0.042317	0.043793	0.045277	0.046768	0.048264	0.049763	0.051263	0.052762	0.054257	0.055747	*19*
20	0.029834	0.031093	0.032373	0.033673	0.034992	0.036327	0.037678	0.039044	0.040422	0.041810	*20*
21	0.020031	0.021025	0.022045	0.023090	0.024161	0.025256	0.026375	0.027517	0.028680	0.029865	*21*
22	0.012838	0.013570	0.014329	0.015114	0.015924	0.016761	0.017623	0.018511	0.019424	0.020362	*22*
23	0.007870	0.008378	0.008909	0.009462	0.010039	0.010640	0.011264	0.011911	0.012584	0.013280	*23*
24	0.004624	0.004957	0.005308	0.005677	0.006065	0.006472	0.006899	0.007345	0.007812	0.008300	*24*
25	0.002608	0.002816	0.003036	0.003270	0.003518	0.003780	0.004057	0.004348	0.004656	0.004980	*25*
26	0.001414	0.001538	0.001670	0.001811	0.001962	0.002123	0.002294	0.002475	0.002668	0.002873	*26*
27	0.000739	0.000809	0.000884	0.000966	0.001054	0.001148	0.001249	0.001357	0.001473	0.001596	*27*
28	0.000372	0.000410	0.000452	0.000497	0.000546	0.000598	0.000656	0.000717	0.000784	0.000855	*28*
29	0.000181	0.000201	0.000223	0.000247	0.000273	0.000301	0.000332	0.000366	0.000403	0.000442	*29*
30	0.000085	0.000095	0.000106	0.000118	0.000132	0.000147	0.000163	0.000181	0.000200	0.000221	*30*
31	0.000039	0.000044	0.000049	0.000055	0.000062	0.000069	0.000077	0.000086	0.000096	0.000107	*31*
32	0.000017	0.000019	0.000022	0.000025	0.000028	0.000032	0.000035	0.000040	0.000045	0.000050	*32*
33	0.000007	0.000008	0.000009	0.000011	0.000012	0.000014	0.000016	0.000018	0.000020	0.000023	*33*
34	0.000003	0.000003	0.000004	0.000005	0.000005	0.000006	0.000007	0.000008	0.000009	0.000010	*34*
35	0.000001	0.000001	0.000002	0.000002	0.000002	0.000002	0.000003	0.000003	0.000004	0.000004	*35*
36	—	0.000001	0.000001	0.000001	0.000001	0.000001	0.000001	0.000001	0.000002	0.000002	*36*
37	—	—	—	—	—	—	—	0.000001	0.000001	0.000001	*37*

TABLE A.6 Poisson's Exponential Binomial Limit

Part 3: Cumulative Terms of the Poisson Formula, $P(x, m) = \sum_{x=0}^{\infty} \frac{m^x e^{-m}}{x!}$

$m = 0.001\text{–}0.15$

x	$m = 0.001$	$m = 0.002$	$m = 0.003$	$m = 0.004$
0	1.0000000	1.0000000	1.0000000	1.0000000
1	0.0009995	0.0019980	0.0029955	0.0039920
2	0.0000005	0.0000020	0.0000045	0.0000080
	$m = 0.005$	$m = 0.006$	$m = 0.007$	$m = 0.008$
0	1.0000000	1.0000000	1.0000000	1.0000000
1	0.0049875	0.0059820	0.0069756	0.0079681
2	0.0000125	0.0000179	0.0000244	0.0000318
3			0.0000001	0.0000001
	$m = 0.009$	$m = 0.01$	$m = 0.02$	$m = 0.03$
0	1.0000000	1.0000000	1.0000000	1.0000000
1	0.0089596	0.0099502	0.0198013	0.0295545
2	0.0000403	0.0000497	0.0001973	0.0004411
3	0.0000001	0.0000002	0.0000013	0.0000044
	$m = 0.04$	$m = 0.05$	$m = 0.06$	$m = 0.07$
0	1.0000000	1.0000000	1.0000000	1.0000000
1	0.0392106	0.0487706	0.0582355	0.0676062
2	0.0007790	0.0012091	0.0017296	0.0023386
3	0.0000104	0.0000201	0.0000344	0.0000542
4	0.0000001	0.0000003	0.0000005	0.0000009
	$m = 0.08$	$m = 0.09$	$m = 0.10$	$m = 0.11$
0	1.0000000	1.0000000	1.0000000	1.0000000
1	0.0768837	0.0860688	0.0951626	0.1041659
2	0.0030343	0.0038150	0.0046788	0.0056241
3	0.0000804	0.0001136	0.0001547	0.0002043
4	0.0000016	0.0000025	0.0000038	0.0000056
5				0.0000001
	$m = 0.12$	$m = 0.13$	$m = 0.14$	$m = 0.15$
0	1.0000000	1.0000000	1.0000000	1.0000000
1	0.1130796	0.1219046	0.1306418	0.1392920
2	0.0066491	0.0077522	0.0089316	0.0101858
3	0.0002633	0.0003323	0.0004119	0.0005029
4	0.0000079	0.0000107	0.0000143	0.0000187
5	0.0000002	0.0000003	0.0000004	0.0000006

Values of probabilities for Poisson's Binomial Limit, Individual and Cumulative Terms compiled (with permission) from the following:

1. Karl Pearson (editor), *Tables for Statisticians and Biometricians*, Part I, Second Edition, issued by the Biometric Laboratory, University College, London, 1924, Cambridge University Press, England, Table LI, pp. 113–121.
2. E. C. Molina, *Poisson's Exponential Limit*, Table I—Individual Terms; Part II—Cumulated Terms, New York, N.Y., 1949, D. Van Nostrand Company, Inc. (Very extensive table, probabilities to six places.)

Many different types of tables are included in this appendix, to cover problems in quality control involving problems covered by the material given in a number of different chapters in the text for which tables are not already included. Table A.7 gives probability values for the "Student" t-distribution. This table is used when checking for significant differences between two different sets of data obtained for two different methods or procedures. Where the parameters or true values of the two different possible distributions are not given and use must be made of observed values, this table may be used effectively.

As noted previously, another table used repeatedly for many types of problems and particularly in this text for checks for goodness of fit of theoretical distributions is the Chi-squared (χ^2) distribution. The table included herein covers a wide range of degrees of freedom values. It is designated as table A.8. Examples of its use are also included. The X value at the bottom of this table gives the z multipliers of σ in a normal law table for which the Q percentage points gives the area of the curve to the right of X.

Another check for goodness of fit is to plot cumulative distributions on linear or log probability graph paper. One possible theoretical evaluation uses this type of graph paper to indicate how skewed some distributions may be. Distributions for the Second Approximation are given as examples to aid in this adjudication by eye. Sufficient values for a wide range of skewness k values have been computed and a family of curves is provided for use in determining what value of skewness k is the best fit to the observed distribution as plotted.

The following set of figures shows in detail how to use table A.4, covering not only the normal distribution but both negative and positive skewed distributions where the normal law is used as the generating function. It is often necessary to find a distribution that theoretically represents an observed skewed distribution. Most texts ignore this case. Frequency probability distributions may have skewness values for k values from -2 to $+2$. Such distributions may be drawn and checked by eye against standard theoretical distributions.

TABLE A.7 *t*-Distribution—Two Forms and Different *P* Values

Part 1: Percentage Points of the *t*-Distribution
$\alpha = 0.25$ to 0.0005, Probability Values

Example
For $\phi = 10$ degrees of freedom:
$P[t > 1.812] = 0.05$
$P[t < -1.812] = 0.05$

ϕ \ α	0.25	0.20	0.15	0.10	0.05	0.025	0.01	0.005	0.0005
1	1.000	1.376	1.963	3.078	6.314	12.706	31.821	63.657	636.619
2	0.816	1.061	1.386	1.886	2.920	4.303	6.965	9.925	31.598
3	0.765	0.978	1.250	1.638	2.353	3.182	4.541	5.841	12.924
4	0.741	0.941	1.190	1.533	2.132	2.776	3.747	4.604	8.610
5	0.727	0.920	1.156	1.476	2.015	2.571	3.365	4.032	6.869
6	0.718	0.906	1.134	1.440	1.943	2.447	3.143	3.707	5.959
7	0.711	0.896	1.119	1.415	1.895	2.365	2.998	3.499	5.408
8	0.706	0.889	1.108	1.397	1.860	2.306	2.896	3.355	5.041
9	0.703	0.883	1.100	1.383	1.833	2.262	2.821	3.250	4.781
10	0.700	0.879	1.093	1.372	1.812	2.228	2.764	3.169	4.587
11	0.697	0.876	1.088	1.363	1.796	2.201	2.718	3.106	4.437
12	0.695	0.873	1.083	1.356	1.782	2.179	2.681	3.055	4.318
13	0.694	0.870	1.079	1.350	1.771	2.160	2.650	3.012	4.221
14	0.692	0.868	1.076	1.345	1.761	2.145	2.624	2.977	4.140
15	0.691	0.866	1.074	1.341	1.753	2.131	2.602	2.947	4.073
16	0.690	0.865	1.071	1.337	1.746	2.120	2.583	2.921	4.015
17	0.689	0.863	1.069	1.333	1.740	2.110	2.567	2.898	3.965
18	0.688	0.862	1.067	1.330	1.734	2.101	2.552	2.878	3.922
19	0.688	0.861	1.066	1.328	1.729	2.093	2.539	2.861	3.883
20	0.688	0.860	1.064	1.325	1.725	2.086	2.528	2.845	3.850
21	0.686	0.859	1.063	1.323	1.721	2.080	2.518	2.831	3.819
22	0.686	0.858	1.061	1.321	1.717	2.074	2.508	2.819	3.792
23	0.685	0.858	1.060	1.319	1.714	2.069	2.500	2.807	3.767
24	0.685	0.857	1.059	1.318	1.711	2.064	2.492	2.793	3.745
25	0.684	0.856	1.058	1.316	1.708	2.060	2.485	2.787	3.725
26	0.684	0.856	1.058	1.315	1.706	2.056	2.479	2.779	3.707
27	0.684	0.855	1.057	1.314	1.703	2.052	2.473	2.771	3.690
28	0.683	0.855	1.056	1.313	1.701	2.048	2.467	2.763	3.674
29	0.683	0.854	1.055	1.311	1.699	2.045	2.462	2.756	3.659
30	0.683	0.854	1.055	1.310	1.697	2.042	2.457	2.750	3.646
40	0.681	0.851	1.050	1.303	1.684	2.021	2.423	2.704	3.551
60	0.679	0.848	1.046	1.296	1.671	2.000	2.390	2.660	3.460
120	0.677	0.845	1.041	1.289	1.658	1.980	2.358	2.617	3.373
∞	0.674	0.842	1.036	1.282	1.645	1.960	2.326	2.576	3.291

Source: This table is abridged from Table III of Fisher & Yates: *Statistical Tables for Biological, Agricultural and Medical Research* published by Oliver & Boyd Ltd., Edinburgh, and by permission of the authors and publishers.

TABLE A.7 *t*-Distribution—Two Forms and Different *P* Values

Part 2: Percentage Points of the *t*-Distribution—Values of *t* in Terms of *A* and *v*, $A = 0.2$ to 0.0999999, Probability Values

v \ A	0.2	0.5	0.8	0.9	0.95	0.98	0.99	0.995	0.998	0.999	0.9999	0.99999	0.999999
1	0.325	1.000	3.078	6.314	12.706	31.821	63.657	127.321	318.309	636.619	6366.198	63661.977	636619.772
2	0.289	0.816	1.886	2.920	4.303	6.965	9.925	14.089	22.327	31.598	99.992	316.225	999.999
3	0.277	0.765	1.638	2.353	3.182	4.541	5.841	7.453	10.214	12.924	28.000	60.397	130.155
4	0.271	0.741	1.533	2.132	2.776	3.747	4.604	5.598	7.173	8.610	15.544	27.771	49.459
5	0.267	0.727	1.476	2.015	2.571	3.365	4.032	4.773	5.893	6.869	11.178	17.897	28.477
6	0.265	0.718	1.440	1.943	2.447	3.143	3.707	4.317	5.208	5.959	9.082	13.555	20.047
7	0.263	0.711	1.415	1.895	2.365	2.998	3.499	4.029	4.785	5.408	7.885	11.215	15.764
8	0.262	0.706	1.397	1.860	2.306	2.896	3.355	3.833	4.501	5.041	7.120	9.782	13.257
9	0.261	0.703	1.383	1.833	2.262	2.821	3.250	3.690	4.297	4.781	6.594	8.827	11.637
10	0.260	0.700	1.372	1.812	2.228	2.764	3.169	3.581	4.144	4.587	6.211	8.150	10.516
11	0.260	0.697	1.363	1.796	2.201	2.718	3.106	3.497	4.025	4.437	5.921	7.648	9.702
12	0.259	0.695	1.356	1.782	2.179	2.681	3.055	3.428	3.930	4.318	5.694	7.261	9.085
13	0.259	0.694	1.350	1.771	2.160	2.650	3.012	3.372	3.852	4.221	5.513	6.955	8.604
14	0.258	0.692	1.345	1.761	2.145	2.624	2.977	3.326	3.787	4.140	5.363	6.706	8.218
15	0.258	0.691	1.341	1.753	2.131	2.602	2.947	3.286	3.733	4.073	5.239	6.502	7.903
16	0.258	0.690	1.337	1.746	2.120	2.583	2.921	3.252	3.686	4.015	5.134	6.330	7.642
17	0.257	0.689	1.333	1.740	2.110	2.567	2.898	3.223	3.646	3.965	5.044	6.184	7.421
18	0.257	0.688	1.330	1.734	2.101	2.552	2.878	3.197	3.610	3.922	4.966	6.059	7.232
19	0.257	0.688	1.328	1.729	2.093	2.539	2.861	3.174	3.579	3.883	4.897	5.949	7.069
20	0.257	0.687	1.325	1.725	2.086	2.528	2.845	3.153	3.552	3.850	4.837	5.854	6.927
21	0.257	0.686	1.323	1.721	2.080	2.518	2.831	3.135	3.527	3.819	4.784	5.769	6.802
22	0.256	0.686	1.321	1.717	2.074	2.508	2.819	3.119	3.505	3.792	4.736	5.694	6.692
23	0.256	0.685	1.319	1.714	2.069	2.500	2.807	3.104	3.485	3.768	4.693	5.627	6.593
24	0.256	0.685	1.318	1.711	2.064	2.492	2.797	3.090	3.467	3.745	4.654	5.566	6.504
25	0.256	0.684	1.316	1.708	2.060	2.485	2.787	3.078	3.450	3.725	4.619	5.511	6.424
26	0.256	0.684	1.315	1.706	2.056	2.479	2.779	3.067	3.435	3.707	4.587	5.461	6.352
27	0.256	0.684	1.314	1.703	2.052	2.473	2.771	3.057	3.421	3.690	4.558	5.415	6.286
28	0.256	0.683	1.313	1.701	2.048	2.467	2.763	3.047	3.408	3.674	4.530	5.373	6.225
29	0.256	0.683	1.311	1.699	2.045	2.462	2.756	3.038	3.396	3.659	4.506	5.335	6.170
30	0.256	0.683	1.310	1.697	2.042	2.457	2.750	3.030	3.385	3.646	4.482	5.299	6.119
40	0.255	0.681	1.303	1.684	2.021	2.423	2.704	2.971	3.307	3.551	4.321	5.053	5.768
60	0.254	0.679	1.296	1.671	2.000	2.390	2.660	2.915	3.232	3.460	4.169	4.825	5.449
120	0.254	0.677	1.289	1.658	1.980	2.358	2.617	2.860	3.160	3.373	* 4.025	* 4.613	* 5.158
∞	0.253	0.674	1.282	1.645	1.960	2.326	2.576	2.807	3.090	3.291	3.891	4.417	4.892

$$A = A(t \mid v) = \left[\sqrt{v}B\left(\frac{1}{2}, \frac{v}{2}\right)\right]^{-1} \int_{-t}^{t} \left(1 + \frac{x^2}{v}\right)^{-[(v+1)/2]} dx$$

Reprinted from the *Handbook of Mathematical Functions with Formulas, Graphs and Mathematical Tables* (edited by Milton Abramowitz and Irene E. Stegn) National Bureau of Standards, Applied Mathematics Series 55, Mar 1965.

From E. S. Pearson and H. O. Hartley (editors), *Biometrika Tables for Statisticians,* vol. I. Cambridge Univ. Press, Cambridge, England, 1954 for *A* 0.999, from E. T. Federighi, Extended tables of the percentage points of Student's *t*-distribution, J. Amer. Statist. Assoc. **54,** 683–688, (1959) for *A* 0.999 (with permission).

TABLE A.8 χ^2 Probability Function

Part 1: $Q = 0.995$ to 0.25

Percentage Points of the χ^2-Distribution—Values of χ^2 in Terms of Q and ν

ν \ Q	0.995	0.99	0.975	0.95	0.9	0.75	0.5	0.25
1	(−5)3.92704	(−4)1.57088	(−4)9.82069	(−3)3.93214	0.0157908	0.101531	0.454937	1.32330
2	(−2)1.00251	(−2)2.01007	(−2)5.06356	0.102587	0.210720	0.575364	1.38629	2.77259
3	(−2)7.17212	0.114832	0.215795	0.351846	0.584375	1.212534	2.36597	4.10835
4	0.206990	0.297110	0.484419	0.710721	1.063623	1.92255	3.35670	5.38527
5	0.411740	0.554300	0.831211	1.145476	1.61031	2.67460	4.35146	6.62568
6	0.675727	0.872085	1.237347	1.63539	2.20413	3.45460	5.34812	7.84080
7	0.989265	1.239043	1.68987	2.16735	2.83311	4.25485	6.34581	9.03715
8	1.344419	1.646482	2.17973	2.73264	3.48954	5.07064	7.34412	10.2188
9	1.734926	2.087912	2.70039	3.32511	4.16816	5.89883	8.34283	11.3887
10	2.15585	2.55821	3.24697	3.94030	4.86518	6.73720	9.34182	12.5489
11	2.60321	3.05347	3.81575	4.57481	5.57779	7.58412	10.3410	13.7007
12	3.07382	3.57056	4.40379	5.22603	6.30380	8.43842	11.3403	14.8454
13	3.56503	4.10691	5.00874	5.89186	7.04150	9.29906	12.3398	15.9839
14	4.07468	4.66043	5.62872	6.57063	7.78953	10.1653	13.3393	17.1170
15	4.60094	5.22935	6.26214	7.26094	8.54675	11.0365	14.3389	18.2451
16	5.14224	5.81221	6.90766	7.96164	9.31223	11.9122	15.3385	19.3688
17	5.69724	6.40776	7.56418	8.67176	10.0852	12.7919	16.3381	20.4887
18	6.26481	7.01491	8.23075	9.39046	10.8649	13.6753	17.3379	21.6049
19	6.84398	7.63273	8.90655	10.1170	11.6509	14.5620	18.3376	22.7178
20	7.43386	8.26040	9.59083	10.8508	12.4426	15.4518	19.3374	23.8277
21	8.03366	8.89720	10.28293	11.5913	13.2396	16.3444	20.3372	24.9348
22	8.64272	9.54249	10.9823	12.3380	14.0415	17.2396	21.3370	26.0393
23	9.26042	10.19567	11.6885	13.0905	14.8479	18.1373	22.3369	27.1413
24	9.88623	10.8564	12.4011	13.8484	15.6587	19.0372	23.3367	28.2412
25	10.5197	11.5240	13.1197	14.6114	16.4734	19.9393	24.3366	29.3389
26	11.1603	12.1981	13.8439	15.3791	17.2919	20.8434	25.3364	30.4345
27	11.8076	12.8786	14.5733	16.1513	18.1138	21.7494	26.3363	31.5284
28	12.4613	13.5648	15.3079	16.9279	18.9392	22.6572	27.3363	32.6205
29	13.1211	14.2565	16.0471	17.7083	19.7677	23.5666	28.3362	33.7109
30	13.7867	14.9535	16.7908	18.4926	20.5992	24.4776	29.3360	34.7998
40	20.7065	22.1643	24.4331	26.5093	29.0505	33.6603	39.3354	45.6160
50	27.9907	29.7067	32.3574	34.7642	37.6886	42.9421	49.3349	56.3336
60	35.5346	37.4848	40.4817	43.1879	46.4589	52.2938	59.3347	66.9814
70	43.2752	45.4418	48.7576	51.7393	55.3290	61.6983	69.3344	77.5766
80	51.1720	53.5400	57.1532	60.3915	64.2778	71.1445	79.3343	88.1303
90	59.1963	61.7541	65.6466	69.1260	73.2912	80.6247	89.3342	98.6499
100	67.3276	70.0648	74.2219	77.9295	82.3581	90.1332	99.3341	109.141
X	−2.5758	−2.3263	−1.9600	−1.6449	−1.2816	−0.6745	0.0000	0.6745

$$Q(\chi^2 \mid \nu) = \left[2^{\nu/2}\Gamma\left(\frac{\nu}{2}\right)\right]^{-1} \int_{\chi^2}^{\infty} e^{-t/2} t^{\nu/2-1} dt$$

Reprinted from the *Handbook of Mathematical Functions with Formulas, Graphs and Mathematical Tables* (edited by Milton Abramowitz and Irene E. Stegn) National Bureau of Standards, Applied Mathematics Series 55, Mar 1965.

From E. S. Pearson and H. O. Hartley (editors), *Biometrika Tables for Statisticians,* Vol. I, Cambridge University Press, Cambridge, England, 1954 (with permission) for Q 70.0005.

TABLE A.8 χ^2 Probability Function

Part 2: $Q = 0.1$ to 0.0001
Percentage Points of the χ^2-Distribution—Values of χ^2 in Terms of Q and ν

ν \ Q	0.1	0.05	0.025	0.01	0.005	0.001	0.0005	0.0001
1	2.70554	3.84146	5.02389	6.63490	7.87944	10.828	12.116	15.137
2	4.60517	5.99147	7.37776	9.21034	10.5966	13.816	15.202	18.421
3	6.25139	7.81473	9.34840	11.3449	12.8381	16.266	17.730	21.108
4	7.77944	9.48773	11.1433	13.2767	14.8602	18.467	19.997	23.513
5	9.23635	11.0705	12.8325	15.0863	16.7496	20.515	22.105	25.745
6	10.6446	12.5916	14.4494	16.8119	18.5476	22.458	24.103	27.856
7	12.0170	14.0671	16.0128	18.4753	20.2777	24.322	26.018	29.877
8	13.3616	15.5073	17.5346	20.0902	21.9550	26.125	27.868	31.828
9	14.6837	16.9190	19.0228	21.6660	23.5893	27.877	29.666	33.720
10	15.9871	18.3070	20.4831	23.2093	25.1882	29.588	31.420	35.564
11	17.2750	19.6751	21.9200	24.7250	26.7569	31.264	33.137	37.367
12	18.5494	21.0261	23.3367	26.2170	28.2995	32.909	34.821	39.134
13	19.8119	22.3621	24.7356	27.6883	29.8194	34.528	36.478	40.871
14	21.0642	23.6848	26.1190	29.1413	31.3193	36.123	38.109	42.579
15	22.3072	24.9958	27.4884	30.5779	32.8013	37.697	39.719	44.263
16	23.5418	26.2962	28.8454	31.9999	34.2672	39.252	41.308	45.925
17	24.7690	27.5871	30.1910	33.4087	35.7185	40.790	42.879	47.566
18	25.9894	28.8693	31.5264	34.8053	37.1564	42.312	44.434	49.189
19	27.2036	30.1435	32.8523	36.1908	38.5822	43.820	45.973	50.796
20	28.4120	31.4104	34.1696	37.5662	39.9968	45.315	47.498	52.386
21	29.6151	32.6705	35.4789	38.9321	41.4010	46.797	49.011	53.962
22	30.8133	33.9244	36.7807	40.2894	42.7956	48.268	50.511	55.525
23	32.0069	35.1725	38.0757	41.6384	44.1813	49.728	52.000	57.075
24	33.1963	36.4151	39.3641	42.9798	45.5585	51.179	53.479	58.613
25	34.3816	37.6525	40.6465	44.3141	46.9278	52.620	54.947	60.140
26	35.5631	38.8852	41.9232	45.6417	48.2899	54.052	56.407	61.657
27	36.7412	40.1133	43.1944	46.9630	49.6449	55.476	57.858	63.164
28	37.9159	41.3372	44.4607	48.2782	50.9933	56.892	59.300	64.662
29	39.0875	42.5569	45.7222	49.5879	52.3356	58.302	60.735	66.152
30	40.2560	43.7729	46.9792	50.8922	53.6720	59.703	62.162	67.633
40	51.8050	55.7585	59.3417	63.6907	66.7659	73.402	76.095	82.062
50	63.1671	67.5048	71.4202	76.1539	79.4900	86.661	89.560	95.969
60	74.3970	79.0819	83.2976	88.3794	91.9517	99.607	102.695	109.503
70	85.5271	90.5312	95.0231	100.425	104.215	112.317	115.578	122.755
80	96.5782	101.879	106.629	112.329	116.321	124.839	128.261	135.783
90	107.565	113.145	118.136	124.116	128.299	137.208	140.782	148.627
100	118.498	124.342	129.561	135.807	140.169	149.449	153.167	161.319
X	1.2816	1.6449	1.9600	2.3263	2.5758	3.0902	3.2905	3.7190

$$Q(\chi^2 \mid \nu) = \left[2^{\nu/2} \Gamma\left(\frac{\nu}{2}\right) \right]^{-1} \int_{\chi^2}^{\infty} e^{-t/2} t^{\nu/2 - 1} \, dt$$

Reproduced (with permission) from pp. 984–5, Table 26.8, Milton Abromowitz and Irene E. Stegun (editors), *Handbook of Mathematical Functions with Formulas, Graphs and Mathematical Tables,* National Brueau of Standards, Applied Mathematical Series -55, Third Printing, March, 1965, U.S. Government Printing Office, Washington, D.C.

TABLE A.9 Logarithms of Factorials, $n! = \log \lfloor n$

1–250

log $\lfloor n$ from $n = 1$ to $n = 1000$

n	log $\lfloor n$	n	log $\lfloor n$	n	log $\lfloor n$	n	log $\lfloor n$	n	log $\lfloor n$
1	0.000 0000	51	66.190 6450	101	159.974 3250	151	264.935 8704	201	377.200 0847
2	0.301 0300	52	67.906 6484	102	161.982 9252	152	267.117 7139	202	379.505 4361
3	0.778 1513	53	69.630 9243	103	163.995 7624	153	269.302 4054	203	381.812 9321
4	1.380 2112	54	71.363 3180	104	166.012 7958	154	271.489 9261	204	384.122 5623
5	2.079 1812	55	73.103 6807	105	168.033 9851	155	273.680 2578	205	386.434 3161
6	2.857 3325	56	74.851 8687	106	170.059 2909	156	275.873 3824	206	388.748 1834
7	3.702 4305	57	76.607 7436	107	172.088 6747	157	278.069 2820	207	391.064 1537
8	4.605 5205	58	78.371 1716	108	174.122 0985	158	280.267 9391	208	393.382 2170
9	5.559 7630	59	80.142 0236	109	176.159 5250	159	282.469 3363	209	395.702 3633
10	6.559 7630	60	81.920 1748	110	178.200 9176	160	284.673 4562	210	398.024 5826
11	7.601 1557	61	83.705 5047	111	180.246 2406	161	286.880 2821	211	400.348 8651
12	8.680 3370	62	85.497 8964	112	182.295 4586	162	289.089 7971	212	402.675 2009
13	9.794 2803	63	87.297 2369	113	184.348 5371	163	291.301 9847	213	405.003 5805
14	10.940 4084	64	89.103 4169	114	186.405 4419	164	293.516 8286	214	407.333 9943
15	12,116 4996	65	90.916 3303	115	188.466 1398	165	295.734 3125	215	409.666 4328
16	13.320 6196	66	92.735 8742	116	190.530 5978	166	297.954 4206	216	412.000 8865
17	14.551 0685	67	94.561 9490	117	192.598 7836	167	300.177 1371	217	414.337 3463
18	15.806 3410	68	96.394 4579	118	194.670 6656	168	302.402 4464	218	416.675 8027
19	17.085 0946	69	98.233 3070	119	196.746 2126	169	304.630 3331	219	419.016 2469
20	18.386 1246	70	100.078 4050	120	198.825 3938	170	306.860 7820	220	421.358 6695
21	19.708 3439	71	101.929 6634	121	200.908 1792	171	309.093 7781	221	423.703 0618
22	21.050 7666	72	103.786 9959	122	202.994 5390	172	311.329 3066	222	426.049 4148
23	22.412 4944	73	105.650 3187	123	205.084 4442	173	313.567 3527	223	428.397 7197
24	23.792 7057	74	107.519 5505	124	207.177 8658	174	315.807 9019	224	430.747 9677
25	25.190 6457	75	109.394 6117	125	209.274 7759	175	318.050 9400	225	433.100 1502
26	26.605 6190	76	111.275 4253	126	211.375 1464	176	320.296 4526	226	435.454 2586
27	28.036 9828	77	113.161 9160	127	213.478 9501	177	322.544 4259	227	437.810 2845
28	29.484 1408	78	115.054 0106	128	215.586 1601	178	324.794 8459	228	440.168 2193
29	30.946 5388	79	116.951 6377	129	217.696 7498	179	327.047 6989	229	442.528 0548
30	32.423 6601	80	118.854 7277	130	219.810 6932	180	329.302 9714	230	444.889 7827
31	33.915 0218	81	120.763 2127	131	221.927 9645	181	331.560 6500	231	447.253 3946
32	35.420 1717	82	122.677 0266	132	224.048 5384	182	333.820 7214	232	449.618 8826
33	36.938 6857	83	124.596 1047	133	226.172 3900	183	336.083 1725	233	451.986 2385
34	38.470 1646	84	126.520 3840	134	228.299 4948	184	338.347 9903	234	454.355 4544
35	40.014 2326	85	128.449 8029	135	230.429 8286	185	340.615 1620	235	456.726 5223
36	41.570 5351	86	130.384 3013	136	232.563 3675	186	342.884 6750	236	459.099 4343
37	43.138 7369	87	132.323 8206	137	234.700 0881	187	345.156 5166	237	461.474 1826
38	44.718 5205	88	134.268 3033	138	236.839 9672	188	347.430 6744	238	463.850 7596
39	46.309 5851	89	136.217 6933	139	238.982 9820	189	349.707 1362	239	466.229 1575
40	47.911 6451	90	138.171 9358	140	241.129 1100	190	351.985 8898	240	468.609 3687
41	49.524 4289	91	140.130 9772	141	243.278 3291	191	354.266 9232	241	470.991 3857
42	51.147 6782	92	142.094 7650	142	245.430 6174	192	356.550 2244	242	473.375 2011
43	52.781 1467	93	144.063 2480	143	247.585 9535	193	358.835 7817	243	475.760 8074
44	54.424 5993	94	146.036 3758	144	249.744 3160	194	361.123 5835	244	478.148 1972
45	56.077 8119	95	148.014 0994	145	251.905 6840	195	363.413 6181	245	480.537 3633
46	57.740 5697	96	149.996 3707	146	254.070 0368	196	365.705 8742	246	482.928 2984
47	59.412 6676	97	151.983 1424	147	256.237 3542	197	368.000 3404	247	485.320 9954
48	61.093 9088	98	153.974 3685	148	258.407 6159	198	370.297 0056	248	487.715 4470
49	62.784 1049	99	155.970 0037	149	260.580 8022	199	372.595 8586	249	490.111 6464
50	64.483 0749	100	157.970 0037	150	262.756 8934	200	374.896 8886	250	492.509 5864

TABLE A.9 Logarithms of Factorials, $n! = \log \lfloor n$

Table of $\log \lfloor n$ from $n = 1$ to $n = 10000$ 251–500

n	$\log \lfloor n$	n	$\log \lfloor n$	n	$\log \lfloor n$	n	$\log \lfloor n$	n	$\log \lfloor n$
251	494.909 2601	301	616.964 3695	351	742.637 2813	401	871.409 5586	451	1002.893 0675
252	497.310 6607	302	619.444 3765	352	745.183 8240	402	874.013 7846	452	1005.548 2059
253	499.713 7812	303	621.925 8191	353	747.731 5987	403	876.619 0896	453	1008.204 3041
254	502.118 6149	304	624.408 6927	354	750.280 6020	404	879.225 4710	454	1010.861 3600
255	504.525 1551	305	626.892 9925	355	752.830 8303	405	881.832 9260	455	1013.519 3714
256	506.933 3950	306	629.378 7140	356	755.382 2803	406	884.441 4521	456	1016.178 3362
257	509.343 3282	307	631.865 8523	357	757.934 9485	407	887.051 0465	457	1018.838 2524
258	511.754 9479	308	634.354 4031	358	760.488 8316	408	889.661 7066	458	1021.499 1179
259	514.168 2476	309	636.844 3615	359	763.043 9260	409	892.273 4300	459	1024.160 9306
260	516.583 2210	310	639.335 7232	360	765.600 2285	410	894.886 2138	460	1026.823 6884
261	518.999 8615	311	641.828 4836	361	768.157 7357	411	897.500 0556	461	1029.487 3893
262	521.418 1628	312	644.322 6382	362	770.716 4443	412	900.114 9528	462	1032.152 0313
263	523.838 1185	313	646.818 1825	363	773.276 3509	413	902.730 9029	463	1034.817 6123
264	526.259 7225	314	649.315 1122	364	775.837 4523	414	905.347 9032	464	1037.484 1303
265	528.682 9683	315	651.813 4227	365	778.399 7452	415	907.965 9513	465	1040.151 5832
266	531.107 8500	316	654.313 1098	366	780.963 2262	416	910.585 0447	466	1042.819 9692
267	533.534 3612	317	656.814 1691	367	783.527 8923	417	913.205 1807	467	1045.489 2860
268	535.962 4960	318	659.316 5962	368	786.093 7401	418	915.826 3570	468	1048.159 5319
269	538.392 2483	319	661.820 3869	369	788.660 7665	419	918.448 5710	469	1050.830 7047
270	540.823 6121	320	644.325 5369	370	791.228 9682	420	921.071 8203	470	1053.502 8026
271	543.256 5814	321	666.832 0419	371	793.798 3421	421	923.696 1024	471	1056.175 8235
272	545.691 1503	322	669.339 8978	372	796.368 8851	422	926.321 4149	472	1058.849 7655
273	548.127 3129	323	671.849 1003	373	798.940 5939	423	928.947 7552	473	1061.524 6266
274	550.565 0635	324	674.359 6453	374	801.513 4655	424	931.575 1211	474	1064.200 4050
275	553.004 3962	325	676.871 5287	375	804.087 4968	425	934.203 5100	475	1066.877 0986
276	555.445 3052	326	679.384 7463	376	806.662 6846	426	936.832 9196	476	1069.554 7056
277	557.887 7850	327	681.899 2940	377	809.239 0260	427	939.463 3475	477	1072.233 2239
278	560.331 8298	328	684.415 1679	378	811.816 5178	428	942.094 7913	478	1074.912 6518
279	562.777 4340	329	686.932 3638	379	814.395 1570	429	944.727 2486	479	1077.592 9873
280	565.224 5920	330	689.450 8777	380	816.974 9406	430	947.360 7170	480	1080.274 2286
281	567.673 2984	331	691.970 7057	381	819.555 8655	431	949.995 1943	481	1082.956 3737
282	570.123 5475	332	694.491 8438	382	822.137 9289	432	952.630 6780	482	1085.639 4207
283	572.575 3339	333	697.014 2880	383	824.721 1277	433	955.267 1659	483	1088.323 3678
284	575.028 6523	334	699.538 0345	384	827.305 4589	434	957.904 6557	484	1091.008 2132
285	577.483 4971	335	702.063 0793	385	829.890 9196	435	960.543 1449	485	1093.693 9549
286	579.939 8631	336	704.589 4186	386	832.477 5069	436	963.182 6314	486	1096.380 5912
287	582.397 7450	337	707.117 0485	387	835.065 2179	437	965.823 1128	487	1099.068 1202
288	584.857 1375	338	709.645 9652	388	837.654 0496	438	968.464 5869	488	1101.756 5400
289	587.318 0354	339	712.176 1649	389	840.243 9992	439	971.107 0515	489	1104.445 8488
290	589.780 4334	340	714.707 6438	390	842.835 0638	440	973.750 5041	490	1107.136 0449
291	592.244 3264	341	717.240 3982	391	845.427 2406	441	976.394 9427	491	1109.827 1264
292	594.709 7092	342	719.774 4243	392	848.020 5267	442	979.040 3650	492	1112.519 0915
293	597.176 5768	343	722.309 7184	393	850.614 9192	443	981.686 7687	493	1115.211 9384
294	599.644 9242	344	724.846 2768	394	853.210 4154	444	984.334 1517	494	1117.905 6654
295	602.114 7462	345	727.384 0959	395	855.807 0125	445	986.982 5117	495	1120.600 2706
296	604.586 0379	346	729.923 1720	396	858.404 7077	446	989.631 8466	496	1123.295 7523
297	607.058 7943	347	732.463 5015	397	861.003 4982	447	992.282 1541	497	1125.992 1086
298	609.533 0106	348	735.005 0807	398	863.603 3813	448	994.933 4321	498	1128.689 3380
299	612.008 6818	349	737.547 9062	399	866.204 3542	449	997.585 6784	499	1131.387 4385
300	614.485 8030	350	740.091 9742	400	868.806 4142	450	1000.238 8910	500	1134.086 4085

TABLE A.9 Logarithms of Factorials, $n! = \log \lfloor n$

501–750

Table of $\log \lfloor n$ from $n = 1$ to $n = 1000$

n	$\log \lfloor n$	n	$\log \lfloor n$	n	$\log \lfloor n$	n	$\log \lfloor n$	n	$\log \lfloor n$
501	1136.786 2463	551	1272.848 0029	601	1410.881 1614	651	1550.721 4519	701	1692.229 8994
502	1139.486 9500	552	1275.589 9419	602	1413.660 7579	652	1553.535 6995	702	1695.076 2365
503	1142.188 5180	553	1278.332 6671	603	1416.441 0752	653	1556.350 6126	703	1697.923 1918
504	1144.890 9485	554	1281.076 1768	604	1419.222 1122	654	1559.166 1904	704	1700.770 7644
505	1147.594 2399	555	1283.820 4698	605	1422.003 8676	655	1561.982 4317	705	1703.618 9536
506	1150.298 3904	556	1286.565 5446	606	1424.786 3402	656	1564.799 3355	706	1706.467 7583
507	1153.003 3984	557	1289.311 3008	607	1427.309 3289	657	1567.616 9009	707	1709.317 1777
508	1155.709 2621	558	1292.058 0340	608	1430.353 4324	658	1570.435 1268	708	1712.167 2109
509	1158.415 9798	559	1294.805 4458	609	1433.138 0497	659	1573.254 0122	709	1715.017 8572
510	1161.123 5500	560	1297.553 6338	610	1435.923 3796	660	1576.073 5561	710	1717.869 1155
511	1163.831 9709	561	1300.302 5967	611	1438.709 4208	661	1578.893 7576	711	1720.720 9851
512	1166.541 2409	562	1303.052 3330	612	1441.496 1722	662	1581.714 6156	712	1723.573 4651
513	1169.251 3583	563	1305.802 8414	613	1444.283 6327	663	1584.536 1291	713	1726.426 5546
514	1171.962 3214	564	1308.554 1205	614	1447.071 8011	664	1587.358 2972	714	1729.280 2529
515	1174.674 1286	565	1311.306 1690	615	1449.860 6762	665	1590.181 1188	715	1732.134 5589
516	1177.386 7783	566	1314.058 9854	616	1452.650 2569	666	1593.004 5931	716	1734.989 4719
517	1180.100 2688	567	1316.812 5684	617	1455.440 5420	667	1595.828 7189	717	1737.844 9911
518	1182.814 5986	568	1319.566 9168	618	1458.231 5305	668	1598.653 4954	718	1740.701 1155
519	1185.529 7660	569	1322.322 0290	619	1461.023 2212	669	1601.478 9215	719	1743.557 8444
520	1188.245 7693	570	1325.077 9039	620	1463.815 6129	670	1604.304 9963	720	1746.415 1769
521	1190.962 6070	571	1327.834 5400	621	1466.608 7045	671	1607.131 7188	721	1749.273 1122
522	1193.680 2775	572	1330.591 9360	622	1469.402 4948	672	1609.959 0881	722	1752.131 6494
523	1196.398 7792	573	1333.350 0907	623	1472.196 9829	673	1612.787 1031	723	1754.990 7877
524	1199.118 1105	574	1336.109 0026	624	1474.992 1675	674	1615.615 7630	724	1757.850 5262
525	1201.838 2698	575	1338.868 6704	625	1477.788 0475	675	1618.445 0668	725	1760.710 8642
526	1204.559 2556	576	1341.629 0929	626	1480.584 6218	676	1621.275 0135	726	1763.571 8009
527	1207.281 0662	577	1344.390 2687	627	1483.381 8894	677	1624.105 6022	727	1766.433 3353
528	1210.003 7001	578	1347.152 1965	628	1486.179 8490	678	1626.936 8319	728	1769.295 4667
529	1212.727 1558	579	1349.914 8751	629	1488.978 4997	679	1629.768 7016	729	1772.158 1942
530	1215.451 4316	580	1352.678 3031	630	1491.777 8402	680	1632.601 2106	730	1775.021 5170
531	1218.176 5262	581	1355.442 4792	631	1494.577 8696	681	1635.434 3577	731	1777.885 4344
532	1220.902 4378	582	1358.207 4022	632	1497.378 5866	682	1638.268 1420	732	1780.749 9455
533	1223.629 1650	583	1360.973 0708	633	1500.179 9904	683	1641.102 5627	733	1783.615 0495
534	1226.356 7063	584	1363.739 4836	634	1502.982 0796	684	1643.937 6189	734	1786.480 7455
535	1229.085 0600	585	1366.506 6395	635	1505.784 8533	685	1646.773 3094	735	1789.347 0329
536	1231.814 2248	586	1369.274 5371	636	1508.588 3105	686	1649.609 6335	736	1792.213 9107
537	1234.544 1991	587	1372.043 1752	637	1511.392 4499	687	1652.446 5903	737	1795.081 3782
538	1237.274 9814	588	1374.812 5525	638	1514.197 2706	688	1655.284 1787	738	1797.949 4345
539	1240.006 5702	589	1377.582 6678	639	1517.002 7714	689	1658.122 3979	739	1800.818 0790
540	1242.738 9639	590	1380.353 5198	640	1519.808 9514	690	1660.961 2470	740	1803.687 3107
541	1245.472 1612	591	1383.125 1073	641	1522.615 8094	691	1663.800 7251	741	1806.557 1289
542	1248.206 1605	592	1385.897 4290	642	1525.423 3445	692	1666.640 8312	742	1809.427 5328
543	1250.940 9603	593	1388.670 4837	643	1528.231 5554	693	1669.481 5644	743	1812.298 5216
544	1253.676 5592	594	1391.444 2702	644	1531.040 4413	694	1672.322 9239	744	1815.170 0946
545	1256.412 9557	595	1394.218 7871	645	1533.850 0010	695	1675.164 9087	745	1818.042 2508
546	1259.150 1483	596	1396.994 0334	646	1536.660 2335	696	1678.007 5179	746	1820.914 9897
547	1261.888 1357	597	1399.770 0077	647	1539.471 1378	697	1680.850 7507	747	1823.788 3103
548	1264.626 9162	598	1402.546 7089	648	1542.282 7128	698	1683.694 6061	748	1826.662 2119
549	1267.366 4886	599	1405.324 1357	649	1545.094 9575	699	1686.539 0833	749	1829.536 6937
550	1270.106 8513	600	1408.102 2870	650	1547.907 8709	700	1689.384 1813	750	1832.411 7549

TABLE A.9 Logarithms of Factorials, $n! = \lfloor n$

Table of log $\lfloor n$ from $n = 1$ to $n = 1000$ — 751–1000

n	log $\lfloor n$	n	log $\lfloor n$	n	log $\lfloor n$	n	log $\lfloor n$	n	log $\lfloor n$
751	1835.287 3949	801	1979.790 7168	851	2125.649 5488	901	2272.784 2010	951	2421.123 8376
752	1838.163 6127	802	1982.694 8911	852	2128.579 9884	902	2275.739 4075	952	2424.102 4745
753	1841.040 4077	803	1985.599 6067	853	2131.510 9374	903	2278.695 0953	953	2427.081 5674
754	1843.917 7790	804	1988.504 8627	854	2134.442 3953	904	2281.651 2637	954	2430.061 1158
755	1846.795 7260	805	1991.410 6586	855	2137.374 3614	905	2284.607 9123	955	2433.041 1192
756	1849.674 2478	806	1994.316 9936	856	2140.306 8352	906	2287.565 0405	956	2436.021 5771
757	1852.553 3437	807	1997.223 8672	857	2143.239 8160	907	2290.522 6478	957	2439.002 4890
758	1855.433 0129	808	2000.131 2785	858	2146.173 3033	908	2293.480.7336	958	2441.983 8545
759	1858.313 2546	809	2003.039 2271	859	2149.107 2964	909	2296.439 2975	959	2444.965 6731
760	1861.194 0682	810	2005.947 7121	860	2152.041 7949	910	2299.398 3389	960	2447.947 9443
761	1864.075 4529	811	2008.856 7329	861	2154.976 7980	911	2302.357 8573	961	2450.930 6677
762	1866.957 4079	812	2011.766 2890	862	2157.912 3053	912	2305.317 8521	962	2453.913 8428
763	1869.839 9324	813	2014.676 3795	863	2160.848 3161	913	2308.278 3229	963	2456.897 4691
764	1872.723 0258	814	2017.587 0039	864	2163.784 8298	914	2311.239 2691	964	2459.881 5461
765	1875.606 6872	815	2020.498 1615	865	2166.721 8459	915	2314.200 6902	965	2462.866 0734
766	1878.490 9160	816	2023.409 8517	866	2169.659 3638	916	2317.162 5856	966	2465.851 0506
767	1881.375 7113	817	2026.322 0737	867	2172.597 3829	917	2320.124 9550	967	2468.836 4770
768	1884.261 0726	818	2029.234 8270	868	2175.535 9027	918	2323.087 7977	968	2471.822 3524
769	1887.146 9989	819	2032.148 1109	869	2178.474 9224	919	2326.051 1132	969	2474.808 6762
770	1890.033 4896	820	2035.061 9248	870	2181.414 4417	920	2329.014 9010	970	2477.795 4479
771	1892.920 5440	821	2037.976 2679	871	2184.354 4598	921	2331.979 1606	971	2480.782 6671
772	1895.808 1613	822	2040.891 1398	872	2187.294 9763	922	2334.943 8915	972	2483.770 3334
773	1898.696 3408	823	2043.806 5396	873	2190.235 9906	923	2337.909 0932	973	2486.758 4462
774	1901.585 0817	824	2046.722 4668	874	2193.177 5020	924	2340.874 7652	974	2489.747 0052
775	1904.474 3835	825	2049.638 9208	875	2196.119 5101	925	2343.840 9069	975	2492.736 0098
776	1907.364 2452	826	2052.555 9008	876	2199.062 0142	926	2346.807 5179	976	2495.725 4596
777	1910.254 6662	827	2055.473 4063	877	2202.005 0138	927	2349.774 5977	977	2498.715 3542
778	1913.145 6458	828	2058.391 4367	878	2204.948 5083	928	2352.742 1456	978	2501.705 6930
779	1916.037 1832	829	2061.309 9912	879	2207.892 4971	929	2355.710 1614	979	2504.696 4757
780	1918.929 2778	830	2064.229 0693	880	2210.836 9798	930	2358.678 6443	980	2507.687 7018
781	1921.821 9289	831	2067.148 6703	881	2213.781 9557	931	2361.647 5940	981	2510.679 3708
782	1924.715 1356	832	2070.068 7936	882	2216.727 4243	932	2364.617 0099	982	2513.671 4823
783	1927.608 8974	833	2072.989 4386	883	2219.673 3850	933	2367.586 8915	983	2516.664 0358
784	1930.503 2135	834	2075.910 6047	884	2222.619 8373	934	2370.557 2384	984	2519.657 0309
785	1933.398 0831	835	2078.832 2912	885	2225.566 7805	935	2373.528 0500	985	2522.650 4672
786	1936.293 5057	836	2081.754 4974	886	2228.514 2143	936	2376.499 3259	986	2525.644 3441
787	1939.189 4804	837	2084.677 2229	887	2231.462 1379	937	2379.471 0655	987	2528.638 6612
788	1942.086 0066	838	2087.600 4669	888	2234.410 5509	938	2382.443 2683	988	2531.633 4182
789	1944.983 0836	839	2090.524 2289	889	2237.359 4526	939	2385.415 9339	989	2534.628 6145
790	1947.880 7107	840	2093.448 5082	890	2240.308 8426	940	2388.389 0618	990	2537.624 2497
791	1950.778 8872	841	2096.373 3042	891	2243.258 7203	941	2391.362 6514	991	2540.620 3233
792	1953.677 6124	842	2099.298 6162	892	2246.209 0852	942	2394.336 7023	992	2543.616 8350
793	1956.576 8856	843	2102.224 4438	893	2249.159 9366	943	2397.311 2140	993	2546.613 7842
794	1959.476 7061	844	2105.150 7863	894	2252.111 2742	944	2400.286 1860	994	2549.611 1706
795	1962.377 0732	845	2108.077 6430	895	2255.063 0972	945	2403.261 6178	995	2552.608 9937
796	1965.277 9863	846	2111.005 0133	896	2258.015 4052	946	2406.237 5089	996	2555.607 2530
797	1968.179 4446	847	2113.932 8967	897	2260.968 1976	947	2409.213 8589	997	2558.605 9482
798	1971.081 4475	848	2116.861 2926	898	2263.921 4740	948	2412.190 6672	998	2561.605 0787
799	1973.983 9943	849	2119.790 2003	899	2266.875 2337	949	2415.167 9334	999	2564.604 6442
800	1976.887 0842	850	2122.719 6192	900	2269.829 4762	950	2418.145 6570	1000	2567.604 6442

From Table XLIX, pp. 98–101, *Tables for Statisticians and Biometricians*, Part I, Second Edition, edited by Karl Pearson, Biometric Laboratory, University College, London, Cambridge University Press, London, 1924 (with permission).

TABLE A.10 Logarithms of Numbers

N	*0*	*1*	*2*	*3*	*4*	*5*	*6*	*7*	*8*	*9*
10	0000	0043	0086	0128	0170	0212	0253	0294	0334	0374
11	0414	0453	0492	0531	0569	0607	0645	0682	0719	0755
12	0792	0828	0864	0899	0934	0969	1004	1038	1072	1106
13	1139	1173	1206	1239	1271	1303	1335	1367	1399	1430
14	1461	1492	1523	1553	1584	1614	1644	1673	1703	1732
15	1761	1790	1818	1847	1875	1903	1931	1959	1987	2014
16	2041	2068	2095	2122	2148	2175	2201	2227	2253	2279
17	2304	2330	2355	2380	2405	2430	2455	2480	2504	2529
18	2553	2577	2601	2625	2648	2672	2695	2718	2742	2765
19	2788	2810	2833	2856	2878	2900	2923	2945	2967	2989
20	3010	3032	3054	3075	3096	3118	3139	3160	3181	3201
21	3222	3243	3263	3284	3304	3324	3345	3365	3385	3404
22	3424	3444	3464	3483	3502	3522	3541	3560	3579	3598
23	3617	3636	3655	3674	3692	3711	3729	3747	3766	3784
24	3802	3820	3838	3856	3874	3892	3909	3927	3945	3962
25	3979	3997	4014	4031	4048	4065	4082	4099	4116	4133
26	4150	4166	4183	4200	4216	4232	4249	4265	4281	4298
27	4314	4330	4346	4362	4378	4393	4409	4425	4440	4456
28	4472	4487	4502	4518	4533	4548	4564	4579	4594	4609
29	4624	4639	4654	4669	4683	4698	4713	4728	4742	4757
30	4771	4786	4800	4814	4829	4843	4857	4871	4886	4900
31	4914	4928	4942	4955	4969	4983	4997	5011	5024	5038
32	5051	5065	5079	5092	5105	5119	5132	5145	5159	5172
33	5185	5198	5211	5224	5237	5250	5263	5276	5289	5302
34	5315	5328	5340	5353	5366	5378	5391	5403	5416	5428
35	5441	5453	5465	5478	5490	5502	5514	5527	5539	5551
36	5563	5575	5587	5599	5611	5623	5635	5647	5658	5670
37	5682	5694	5705	5717	5729	5740	5752	5763	5775	5786
38	5798	5809	5821	5832	5843	5855	5866	5877	5888	5899
39	5911	5922	5933	5944	5955	5966	5977	5988	5999	6010
40	6021	6031	6042	6053	6064	6075	6085	6096	6107	6117
41	6128	6138	6149	6160	6170	6180	6191	6201	6212	6222
42	6232	6243	6253	6263	6274	6284	6294	6304	6314	6325
43	6335	6345	6355	6365	6375	6385	6395	6405	6415	6425
44	6435	6444	6454	6464	6474	6484	6493	6503	6513	6522
45	6532	6542	6551	6561	6571	6580	6590	6599	6609	6618
46	6628	6637	6646	6656	6665	6675	6684	6693	6702	6712
47	6721	6730	6739	6749	6758	6767	6776	6785	6794	6803
48	6812	6821	6830	6839	6848	6857	6866	6875	6884	6893
49	6902	6911	6920	6928	6937	6946	6955	6964	6972	6981
50	6990	6998	7007	7016	7024	7033	7042	7050	7059	7067
51	7076	7084	7093	7101	7110	7118	7126	7135	7143	7152
52	7160	7168	7177	7185	7193	7202	7210	7218	7226	7235
53	7243	7251	7259	7267	7275	7284	7292	7300	7308	7316
54	7324	7332	7340	7348	7356	7364	7372	7380	7388	7396
N	*0*	*1*	*2*	*3*	*4*	*5*	*6*	*7*	*8*	*9*

TABLE A.10 Logarithms of Numbers

N	*0*	*1*	*2*	*3*	*4*	*5*	*6*	*7*	*8*	*9*
55	7404	7412	7419	7427	7435	7443	7451	7459	7466	7474
56	7482	7490	7497	7505	7513	7520	7528	7536	7543	7551
57	7559	7566	7574	7582	7589	7597	7604	7612	7619	7627
58	7634	7642	7649	7657	7664	7672	7679	7686	7694	7701
59	7709	7716	7723	7731	7738	7745	7752	7760	7767	7774
60	7782	7789	7796	7803	7810	7818	7825	7832	7839	7846
61	7853	7860	7868	7875	7882	7889	7896	7903	7910	7917
62	7924	7931	7938	7945	7952	7959	7966	7973	7980	7987
63	7993	8000	8007	8014	8021	8028	8035	8041	8048	8055
64	8062	8069	8075	8082	8089	8096	8102	8109	8116	8122
65	8129	8136	8142	8149	8156	8162	8169	8176	8182	8189
66	8195	8202	8209	8215	8222	8228	8235	8241	8248	8254
67	8261	8267	8274	8280	8287	8293	8299	8306	8312	8319
68	8325	8331	8338	8344	8351	8357	8363	8370	8376	8382
69	8388	8395	8401	8407	8414	8420	8426	8432	8439	8445
70	8451	8457	8463	8470	8476	8482	8488	8494	8500	8506
71	8513	8519	8525	8531	8537	8543	8549	8555	8561	8567
72	8573	8579	8585	8591	8597	8603	8609	8615	8621	8627
73	8633	8639	8645	8651	8657	8663	8669	8675	8681	8686
74	8692	8698	8704	8710	8716	8722	8727	8733	8739	8745
75	8751	8756	8762	8768	8774	8779	8785	8791	8797	8802
76	8808	8814	8820	8825	8831	8837	8842	8848	8854	8859
77	8865	8871	8876	8882	8887	8893	8899	8904	8910	8915
78	8921	8927	8932	8938	8943	8949	8954	8960	8965	8971
79	8976	8982	8987	8993	8998	9004	9009	9015	9020	9025
80	9031	9036	9042	9047	9053	9058	9063	9069	9074	9079
81	9085	9090	9096	9101	9106	9112	9117	9122	9128	9133
82	9138	9143	9149	9154	9159	9165	9170	9175	9180	9186
83	9191	9196	9201	9206	9212	9217	9222	9227	9232	9238
84	9243	9248	9253	9258	9263	9269	9274	9279	9284	9289
85	9294	9299	9304	9309	9315	9320	9325	9330	9335	9340
86	9345	9350	9355	9360	9365	9370	9375	9380	9385	9390
87	9395	9400	9405	9410	9415	9420	9425	9430	9435	9440
88	9445	9450	9455	9460	9465	9469	9474	9479	9484	9489
89	9494	9499	9504	9509	9513	9518	9523	9528	9533	9538
90	9542	9547	9552	9557	9562	9566	9571	9576	9581	9586
91	9590	9595	9600	9605	9609	9614	9619	9624	9628	9633
92	9638	9643	9647	9652	9657	9661	9666	9671	9675	9680
93	9685	9689	9694	9699	9703	9708	9713	9717	9722	9727
94	9731	9736	9741	9745	9750	9754	9759	9763	9768	9773
95	9777	9782	9786	9791	9795	9800	9805	9809	9814	9818
96	9823	9827	9832	9836	9841	9845	9850	9854	9859	9863
97	9868	9872	9877	9881	9886	9890	9894	9899	9903	9908
98	9912	9917	9921	9926	9930	9934	9939	9943	9948	9952
99	9956	9961	9965	9969	9974	9978	9983	9987	9991	9996
N	*0*	*1*	*2*	*3*	*4*	*5*	*6*	*7*	*8*	*9*

TABLE A.11 Natural Logarithms*

0.10–0.99

N	0.00	0.01	0.02	0.03	0.04	0.05	0.06	0.07	0.08	0.09
0.1	−2.303	−2.207	−2.120	−2.040	−1.966	−1.897	−1.833	−1.772	−1.715	−1.661
0.2	−1.609	−1.561	−1.514	−1.470	−1.427	−1.386	−1.347	−1.309	−1.273	−1.238
0.3	−1.204	−1.171	−1.139	−1.109	−1.079	−1.050	−1.022	−0.994	−0.968	−0.942
0.4	−0.916	−0.892	−0.868	−0.844	−0.821	−0.799	−0.777	−0.755	−0.734	−0.713
0.5	−0.693	−0.673	−0.654	−0.635	−0.616	−0.598	−0.580	−0.562	−0.545	−0.528
0.6	−0.511	−0.494	−0.478	−0.462	−0.446	−0.431	−0.416	−0.400	−0.386	−0.371
0.7	−0.357	−0.342	−0.328	−0.315	−0.301	−0.288	−0.274	−0.261	−0.248	−0.236
0.8	−0.223	−0.211	−0.198	−0.186	−0.174	−0.163	−0.151	−0.139	−0.128	−0.117
0.9	−0.105	−0.094	−0.083	−0.073	−0.062	−0.051	−0.041	−0.030	−0.020	−0.010

1.0–9.9

N	0.0	0.1	0.2	0.3	0.4	0.5	0.6	0.7	0.8	0.9
1.0	0.000	0.095	0.182	0.262	0.336	0.405	0.470	0.531	0.588	0.642
2.0	0.693	0.742	0.788	0.833	0.875	0.916	0.956	0.993	1.030	1.065
3.0	1.099	1.131	1.163	1.194	1.224	1.253	1.281	1.308	1.335	1.361
4.0	1.386	1.411	1.435	1.459	1.482	1.504	1.526	1.548	1.569	1.589
5.0	1.609	1.629	1.649	1.668	1.686	1.705	1.723	1.740	1.758	1.775
6.0	1.792	1.808	1.825	1.841	1.856	1.872	1.887	1.902	1.917	1.932
7.0	1.946	1.960	1.974	1.988	2.001	2.015	2.028	2.041	2.054	2.067
8.0	2.079	2.092	2.104	2.116	2.128	2.140	2.152	2.163	2.175	2.186
9.0	2.197	2.208	2.219	2.230	2.241	2.251	2.262	2.272	2.282	2.293

To obtain the natural logarithm of numbers above 10:
divide the number by 10 and add 2.303 to the ln obtained,
or divide the number by 100 and add 4.605 to the ln obtained,
or divide the number by 1,000 and add 6.908 to the ln obtained, etc.
To obtain the natural logarithm of numbers less than 0.1:
multiply the number by 10 and subtract 2.303 from the ln obtained,
or multiply by 100 and subtract 4.605 from the ln obtained,
or multiply by 1,000 and subtract 6.908 from the ln obtained, etc.

* A more detailed table of natural logarithms for this range of *N* values and one more decimal place for *N*, given to five numbers after the decimal point is provided by Table XXVI, pp. 96–97, with *N* values of 10–100 on pp. 98–99, in Fisher and Yates, *Statistical Tables for Biological, Agricultural and Medical Research*, Fourth Edition, 1953, Oliver and Boyd, London.

When it is desired to determine what theoretical relation fits a mass of observed values, the data are first plotted and a check is made *by eye* by drawing the theoretical curve on the same graph that was used for plotting the data. Sometimes the theoretical curve is determined from the statistics derived from the data and sometimes the standards are already given, the same as for control charts.

One of the most popular games of chance is "Craps." The probabilities are associated with the possible points for the sum of the pips when two dice are thrown simultaneously and come to rest. Some dice are very symmetric and provide an equal chance for the occurrence of any of its six faces, but others are "loaded," giving a biased result. Two dice used in this game were subjected to a check for possible bias by throwing them 360 times and recording the value of the point rolled. Table A.12 gives an analysis of this test. It gives the observed frequencies for each possible point and the corresponding theoretical values. A check for goodness of fit based on the Chi-squared distribution is given. The probability of fit is obtained from table A.8 in appendix A.

When analyzing data, it is necessary in many contracts to determine what theoretical distribution best fits the observed distribution. Definite procedures for determining possible parameters for such theoretical distributions have been developed in texts covering statistics. The purpose of the examples below is to present these statistical procedures showing how to obtain average and standard deviation values for the observed data, tabulate observed data in an observed frequency distribution, and compute a comparable theoretical distribution which

TABLE A.12 Test to Determine Whether Dice are Biased

Point Value	*No. Observed*	*Theoretical*			*Contribution to* χ^2
X	f	f_t	$f - f_t$	$(f - f_t)^2$	$(f - f_t)^2/f_t$
2	8	10	−2	4	0.400
3	16	20	−4	16	0.800
4	35	30	5	25	0.833
5	47	40	7	49	1.225
6	24	50	−26	676	13.520
7	80	60	20	400	6.667
8	44	50	−6	36	0.720
9	43	40	3	9	0.225
10	28	30	−2	4	0.133
11	25	20	5	25	1.250
12	10	10	0	0	0.000
Sum	360	360			25.773

Number of cells, $m = 11$.
Degrees of freedom, $df = m - 1 = 10$; $\chi^2_{0.05}(10) = 18.3070$; $\chi^2_{0.10}(10) = 15.9871$, from table A.8. For computed χ^2 value of 25.773, P for df of 10 is less than 0.005 since $\chi^2_{0.005}(10) = 25.188$ and $\chi^2_{0.001}(10) = 29.588$. Test shows dice are biased. Observed values for 6 and 7 total 104, compared with 110 for the theoretical value. Later it was found that the frequencies for these two points were tallied incorrectly. The correct observed frequencies were 6 − 46 and 7 − 58. Recomputing the contributions to χ^2 changes the 13.520 + 6.667 = 20.187 to

$$6: \quad f - f_t = 46 - 50 = -4, \quad \frac{(f - f_t)^2}{f_t} = \frac{16}{50} = 0.32 \quad \text{and}$$

$$7: \quad f - f_t = 58 - 60 = -2, \quad \frac{(f - f_t)^2}{f_t} = \frac{4}{60} = 0.067.$$

Their sum is 0.387. The error is 20.187 − 0.387 = 19.800; hence $\chi^2(10) = 5.973$. Table A.8 gives $\chi^2_{0.90}(10) = 4.865$ and $\chi^2_{0.75}(10) = 6.737$. Hence P is approximately 0.876. Thus the dice are unbiased.

best fits the observed distribution. Such distributions may be a normal law distribution, a second approximation distribution, with various measures of skewness, a Poisson exponential distribution, a binomial distribution, or one of many other types. The normal law fits many observed distributions and is used most frequently for variables data, whereas the binomial distribution is used most frequently for attributes data. The Poisson exponential approximates the normal law or binomial distribution and also represents directly many industrial cases.

Examples are given here which indicate exactly how to fit various types of data. To determine how well the theoretical curves fit the observed data, a Chi-squared test for goodness of fit will be used. These examples will suffice to show the general procedure to follow. Advanced texts should be consulted if the basis for these procedures is desired.

Figure 3-8 in chapter three presents the distribution for 100 observed values covering the diameters of 100 reamed oil pump shaft holes. These are tabulated in table A.13. This table also gives the necessary computations to find the average $\overline{X}$ and standard deviation σ for this distribution. Based on these values, theoretical frequencies are determined by finding the best theoretical normal law based on $\overline{X}$ and σ values. Normal law probability values are determined from table A.1. These values correspond to the boundary values of each cell expressed in standard deviation units.

TABLE A.13 Computing $\overline{X}$ and σ for Data in Table 3.1

Observed Frequency Distribution for Diameter of 100 Reamed Oil Pump Shaft Holes
Specified Values 0.5460 ± 0.0005 inch

		Short Method, Origin = 0.5465			*Usual Method*	
Measurement Inch, X	*Frequency f*	*Modified Scale Y*	fY	fY^2	fX	fX^2
0.5465	0	0	0	0	0	0
0.5466	1	1	1	1	0.5466	0.29877156
0.5467	8	2	16	32	4.3736	2.39104712
0.5468	12	3	36	108	6.5616	3.58788288
0.5469	24	4	96	384	13.1256	7.17839064
0.5470	18	5	90	450	9.8460	5.38576200
0.5471	14	6	84	504	7.6594	4.19045774
0.5472	10	7	70	490	5.4720	2.99427840
0.5473	12	8	96	768	6.5676	3.59444748
0.5474	1	9	9	81	0.5474	0.29964676
0.5475	0	10	0	0	0	0
Sum	100		498	2818	54.6998	29.92068458

Short Method: $i = 0.0001$
Origin $X_0 = 0.5465$
$\overline{Y} = 498/100 = 4.98$
$\overline{X} = X_0 + i\overline{Y} = 0.5465 + 0.0001(4.98) = 0.546998$
$\sigma_Y^2 = 2818/100 - (4.98)^2 = 28.1800 - 24.80040$
$\sigma_Y^2 = 3.3796;\quad \sigma_Y = 1.838369$
$\sigma_X = 0.0001\,(1.838369) = 0.0001838369842.$

Long Method:
$\overline{X} = 54.6998/100 = 0.546998$
$\sigma_X^2 = 29.92068458/100 = (0.546998)^2$
$= 0.2992068458 - 0.299206812004$
$= 0.000000033796$
$\sigma_X = 0.0001838368842$

TABLE A.14 Determination Goodness of Fit

Theoretical Normal Law based on $\bar{X}$ and σ Values for 100 Observations given in table 3.1—Diameter Reamed Oil Pump Shaft Hole

Base on χ^2 Test—$\chi^2 = \sum \frac{(f_0 - f_t)^2}{f_t}$

Midpoint X, Inch	*Observed Frequency,* f_0	*Theoretical Frequency,* f_t	*Difference* $f_0 - f_t$	*Diff. Squared* $(f_0 - f_t)^2$	*Contribution to* $\chi^2, (f_0 - f_t)^2/f_t$
0.5465	0	1	−1	1	1.00
0.5466	1	2	−1	1	0.50
0.5467	8	6	2	4	0.67
0.5468	12	12	0	0	0.00
0.5469	24	19	5	25	1.32
0.5470	18	21	−3	9	0.43
0.5471	14	18	−4	16	0.89
0.5472	10	12	−2	4	0.33
0.5473	12	6	6	36	6.00
0.5474	1	2	−1	1	0.50
0.5475	0	1	−1	1	1.00
Sum	100	100			12.64

$\bar{X} = 0.546998$; $k = 11, df = k - 3 = 8$.
$\sigma = 0.0001838$; $\chi^2_{0.05} = 15.5073$ from table A.9
$n = 100$. Accept at the 5 percent level of significance, the hypothesis that the distribution is normal as 12.67 is less than 15.51.

TABLE A.15 Determination of Theoretical Frequencies

Normal Law Calculation Sheet

Characteristic Inspected (a)	Diameter Shaft Hole
Units (b)	Inch

Subject		
Oil Pump	Calc. by H.G.R.	Report No. 101
Specified Values	Chk. by G.E.H.	Date March 19, 1976
0.5460 ± 0.0005″	App'd J.L.	
	2 Sheets Sheet 1	

$\bar{X}$	0.546998		
σ	0.000184		
N	100		

0	1	2	3	4	5	6	7	8	9	0
Cell No.	*Diameter* (a) *in Inches* (b)	*Cell Bound*	*Deviations from* $\bar{X}$ χ	z (χ/σ)	$F(z)$	*Diff.*	*Freq.*	*Approx. Freq.*	*Observed Freq.*	Cell No.
		0.54655	−0.000448	−2.43	0.00755*					
0	0.5466					0.02938	2.9	3	1	0
		0.54665	−0.000348	−1.89	0.02938					
1	0.5467					0.05913	5.9	6	8	1
		0.54675	−0.000248	−1.35	0.08851					
2	0.5468					0.12335	12.3	12	12	2
		0.54685	−0.000148	−0.80	0.21186					
3	0.5469					0.18557	18.6	18	24	3
		0.54695	−0.000048	−0.26	0.39743					
4	0.5470					0.21283	21.3	21	18	4
		0.54705	+0.000052	+0.28	0.61026					
5	0.5471					0.18647	18.7	19	14	5
		0.54715	+0.000152	+0.83	0.79673					
6	0.5472					0.11793	11.8	12	10	6
		0.54725	+0.000252	+1.37	0.91466					
7	0.5473					0.05727	5.7	6	12	7
		0.54735	+0.000352	+1.91	0.97193					
8	0.5474					0.02807	2.8	3	1	8
		0.54745	+0.000452	+2.46	0.99305†					
9										9
10										10
11										11
12										12
13										13
14										14
15										15
	Σ					1.00000	100.0	100	100	

TABLE A.16 Determination of Theoretical Frequencies

Normal Law Calculation Sheet

Characteristic Inspected (a)	Diameter Shaft Hole
Units (b)	Inch

Subject		
Oil Pump Shaft	Calc. by H.G.R.	Report No. 100
Diameter—Hole	Chk. by G.E.H.	Date March 19, 1976
Specified Values	App'd J.L.	
0.5460 ± 0.0005″	2 Sheets Sheet 2	

Sheet 1—table 3.1, chapter three
Diameter of 100 Reamed Oil Pump Shaft Holes

$\overline{X}$	0.546998		
σ	0.0001838		
N	100		

0	1	2	3	4	5	6	7	8	9	0
Cell No.	*Diameter (a) in Inches (b)*	*Cell Bound*	*Deviations from $\overline{X}$* χ	z (χ/σ)	$F(z)$	*Diff.*	*Freq.*	*Approx. Freq.*		Cell No.
		0.54645	−0.000548	−2.9815	0.001441[a]					
0	0.5465					0.007344	0.7	1		0
		0.54655	−0.000448	−2.4374	0.007344					
1	0.5466					0.022035	2.2	2		1
		0.54665	−0.000348	−1.8934	0.029379					
2	0.5467					0.059129	5.9	6		2
		0.54675	−0.000248	−1.3493	0.088508					
3	0.5468					0.120462	12.0	12		3
		0.54685	−0.000148	−0.8052	0.208970					
4	0.5469					0.188462	18.8	19		4
		0.54695	−0.000048	−0.2612	0.397432					
5	0.5470					0.212829	21.3	21		5
		0.54705	+0.000052	+0.2829	0.610261					
6	0.5471					0.186470	18.6	18		6
		0.54715	+0.000152	+0.8270	0.796731					
7	0.5472					0.117926	11.8	12		7
		0.54725	+0.000252	+1.3711	0.914657					
8	0.5473					0.057914	5.8	6		8
		0.54735	+0.000352	+1.9151	0.972571					
9	0.5474					0.020482	2.0	2		9
		0.54745	+0.000452	+2.4592	0.993053					
10	0.5475					0.006947	0.7	1		10
		0.54755	+0.000552	+3.0033	0.998650[b]					
11										11
12			Use only two digits after decimal							12
13			[a] Use 0.000000							13
14			[b] Use 1.000000							14
15										15
	Σ					1.000000	99.8	100		

Since the frequency distribution in table A.13 is very symmetric except for the larger values, a check is made below to determine whether the theoretical normal law distribution based on the observed $\overline{X}$ and σ values for these diameter measurements. Table A.14 presents the necessary computations in a form that simplifies the calculations. Table A.1 was used to determine the normal law probability area values corresponding to the z values, using only 2 values with 2 digits after the decimal point; thus the values in table A.1 may be used without using interpolation. Using cumulated probability values simplifies the problem, as theoretical frequencies for each cell are found by simply subtracting the probability for a z value for a cell boundary read from table A.1 from the probability for the z value for the next adjacent cell boundary. In this case, the theoretical frequencies were rounded to the closest integer. Some texts would use 0.7 rather than 1 or 18.8 rather than 19 for the theoretical frequency to test for goodness of fit. Rounded values are generally used, however.

When checking for goodness of fit the χ^2 (Chi-squared) value for the numbers of degrees of freedom is used to determine the probability value increases how closely the theoretical curve fits the observed distribution. This term, *goodness of fit*, refers to the comparison of some observed sample distribution with a theoretical frequency distribution. Actually most tests using χ^2 are problems of this type. A test is made of the hypotheses that the distribution has a selected type of distribution. In this case, the selected type is a normal distribution. Many texts cover such a test in great detail. One, using frequencies such as 10.4, also describes the number of degrees *df* that is correct as the number of categories $k - 3$, where k is the number of categories designating the number of cells used for the two distributions being compared. The statistics known for the observed distribution are n, $\bar{X}$ and σ. The texts on mathematical statistics use $\bar{X}$ and s, where s is determined from $n - 1$ degrees of freedom so

$$df = (k - 1) - (\text{degrees of freedom lost by statistics used}). \qquad \textbf{(A5)}$$

The criterion used is generally the χ^2 value corresponding to a 5% level of significance for the *df* involved. In table A.12, the χ^2 value corresponding to $df = 11 - 3 = 8$ for 0.05 is 15.5073. Confusion in the headings in the various χ^2 tables is caused by the use of different forms for defining χ^2. Table A.8 uses "percentage points" with $Q = 0.05$, whereas table A.6a of the Dixon and Massey text[3] uses "percentiles" where "95 percent value" corresponds to $Q = 1 - 0.95 = 0.05$.

In receiving inspection, ten lots of resistors were submitted for acceptance from Supplier A. Samples of fifty resistors were selected from each lot and measured for resistance. The specification required resistance values of 100.00 ± 1.00 ohm. Limits arc from 99.00 ohms to 101.00 ohms. The 500 measurements obtained are tallied and used in table A.17 to obtain $\bar{X}$ and σ values to check against the corresponding frequencies of the assumed best theoretical distribution.

TABLE A.17 Computations of $\overline{X}$ and σ for 500 Resistors

$m = 10, n = 50; mn = 500;$
Specified 100.00 ± 1.00 ohms

Part 1: Deviation of $\overline{X}$, σ and k (See figure A.3) — Part 2: Determination of goodness of fit

Resistance Value X	Observed Frequency f	Simplified Scale y	Computations fy	Computations fy^2	Computations fy^3	Theoretical Frequency f_t	Computations $f - f_t$	Computations $(f - f_t)^2$	Contribution to χ^2 $(f - f_t)^2/f_t$
99.0	1 } 3	0	0	0	0	0 } 1	2	4	4.00
99.1	2	1	2	2	2	1			
99.2	4	2	8	16	32	2	2	4	2.00
99.3	6	3	18	54	162	4	2	4	1.00
99.4	8	4	32	128	512	8	0	0	0
99.5	4	5	20	100	500	14	−10	100	7.14
99.6	12	6	72	432	2,592	20	−8	64	3.20
99.7	20	7	140	980	6,860	30	−10	100	3.33
99.8	30	8	240	1,920	15,360	45	−15	225	5.00
99.9	100	9	900	8,100	72,900	63	37	1,369	21.73
100.0	117	10	1,170	11,700	117,000	79	38	1,444	18.28
100.1	78	11	858	9.438	103,818	83	−5	25	0.30
100.2	50	12	600	7,200	86,700	71	−21	441	6.21
100.3	30	13	390	5,070	65,910	47	−17	289	6.15
100.4	20	14	280	3,920	54,880	24	−4	16	0.67
100.5	18	15	270	4,050	60,750	9	9	81	9.00
Sum, Σ	$n = 500$		5,000	53,110	587,678	500			88.01

$m = 0.1, X_0 = 99.0, \overline{X} = 99.0 + 0.1\,(5000/500) = \underline{100.0}$
${}_1\mu_2 = 53{,}110/500 = 106.22, \mu_2 = 106.22 - 100.00 = 6.22$
$\sigma = m\mu_2^{1/2} = 0.1(2.4940) = \underline{0.2494}$
${}_1\mu_1 = 5{,}000/500 = 10.0$
${}_1\mu_3 = 587{,}678/500 = 1{,}175.356$
$\mu_3 = 1{,}175.3560 - 3(10.0)(106.22) + 2(10.0)^3$
$\mu_3 = 1{,}175.3560 - 3{,}186.6000 + 2{,}000.000 = -11.244$
$k = \mu_3/\mu_2^{3/2} = -11.244/15.5126 = \underline{-0.72483}$

Values used in table A.18 for Second Approximation.

$m = 15, df = (m - 1) - b = 14 - 3 = \underline{11}.$
$b = 3$, since in addition to $n = 500$, $\overline{X}$, σ, and k were used for theoretical distribution.
Table A.8 gives $\chi^2_{0.0005}(11) = 33.137, \chi^2_{0.0001}(11) = 37.367$

Fit is very poor. It would be worse for a theoretical normal law distribution, hence process cannot be represented by the usual types of distribution and may be assumed not to be statistically controlled, although mean $\overline{X} = 100.00$ is at the desired central value 100.00 ± 1.00 ohms.

TABLE A.18 Development of Theoretical Frequencies

Second Approximation Calculation Sheet

Characteristic Inspected	Resistance
Units	Ohms

$\overline{X}$	100.0	n	500
σ	0.2494		
k	−0.7248		

Subject

Resistor
Specified
100.0 ± 1.0

Calc. by H.C.R.	Report No.
Chk. by	Date
App'd	
Sheets Sheet	

$P(\mp \chi) = \phi(t) \pm kf(t)$

0	1	2	3	4	5	6	7	8	9	10	11	12	0
Cell No.	*Mid-cell Value*	*Cell Boundary X*	*Deviation from $\overline{X}$* χ	(χ/σ) t	$\phi(t)$	$\pm f(t)$	$\pm kf(t)$	$\phi(t) \pm kf(t)$	*Difference*	*Freq*	*Theor. Approx. Freq.*	*Observed Freq.*	Cell No.
		98.95	−1.05	−4.21	0.5000	0.0665	0.0482	0.4518					
0	99.0								0.0002	0.10	0	1	0
		99.05	−0.95	−3.81	0.5000	0.06683	0.0484	0.4516					
1	99.1								0.0016	0.80	1	2	1
		99.15	−0.85	−3.41	0.4997	0.06861	0.0497	0.4500					
2	99.2								0.0037	1.85	2	4	2
		99.25	−0.75	−3.01	0.4987	0.07228	0.0524	0.4463					
3	99.3								0.0083	4.15	4	6	3
		99.35	−0.65	−2.61	0.4955	0.07931	0.0575	0.4380					
4	99.4								0.0160	8.00	8	8	4
		99.45	−0.55	−2.21	0.4865	0.08895	0.0645	0.4220					
5	99.5								0.0275	13.75	14	4	5
		99.55	−0.45	−1.80	0.4641	0.09597	0.0696	0.3945					
6	99.6								0.0408	20.40	20	12	6
		99.65	−0.35	−1.40	0.4193	0.09045	0.0656	0.3537					
7	99.7								0.0605	30.25	30	20	7
		99.75	−0.25	−1.00	0.3414	0.06649	0.0482	0.2932					
8	99.8								0.0898	44.90	45	30	8
		99.85	−0.15	−0.60	0.2258	0.03095	0.0224	0.2034					
9	99.9								0.1269	63.45	63	100	9
		99.95	−0.05	−0.20	0.0793	0.00392	0.0028	0.0765					
10	100.0								0.1586	79.30	79	117	10
		100.05	+0.05	+0.20	0.0793	0.00392	0.0028	0.0821					
11	100.1								0.1661	83.05	83	78	11
		100.15	+0.15	+0.60	0.2258	0.03095	0.0224	0.2482					
12	100.2								0.1414	70.70	71	50	12
		100.25	+0.25	+1.00	0.3414	0.06649	0.0482	0.3896					
13	100.3								0.0953	47.65	47	30	13
		100.35	+0.35	+1.40	0.4193	0.09045	0.0656	0.4849					
14	100.4								0.0488	24.40	24	20	14
		100.45	+0.45	+1.80	0.4641	0.09597	0.0696	0.5337					
15	100.5								0.0173	8.65	9	18	15
		100.55	+0.55	+2.21	0.4865	0.08895	0.0645	0.5510					
	Σ								1.0028	501.40	500	500	

The last example covers receiving inspection results using the usual type of sampling, inspection by the method of attributes. A series of tables covers the analysis of sampling results for 100 and 200 lots submitted by Supplier C. Various combinations are given to cover the primary possible causes for poor quality or lack of a controlled process.

Since the sampling plan with $n = 20$, $c = 3$ rejected 19 of the 100 lots of transistors submitted for acceptance by the supplier, quality control engineers worked with the engineers to introduce corrective measures to improve the process. After the process was improved, 200 lots were inspected using a single sampling plan with $n = 50$, $c = 8$. A summary of these data are given in table A.22.

TABLE A.19 Fitting Transistor Data by Binomial

$m = 200$ lots
Binomial, $p = 0.10$, $n = 50$

No. of Defects, d	*Observed Frequency* f_O	*Theoretical* Frequencies, Probability*	f_t *No.*	*Rounded Value*	$f_O - f_t$	$(f_O - f_t)^2$	*Contribution to* χ^2 $(f_O - f_t)^2/f_t$
0	4	0.0052	1.04	1	3	9	9.00
1	8	0.0286	5.72	6	2	4	0.67
2	12	0.0779	15.58	15	−3	9	0.60
3	29	0.1386	27.72	28	1	1	0.04
4	33	0.1809	36.18	36	−3	9	0.25
5	37	0.1849	36.98	37	0	0	0
6	27	0.1541	30.82	31	−4	16	0.52
7	25	0.1076	21.52	21	4	16	0.76
8	15	0.0643	12.86	13	2	4	0.31
9	6	0.0333	6.66	7	−1	1	0.14
10	2	0.0152	3.04	3	−1	1	0.33
11	1	0.0061	1.22	1	0	0	0
12	1	0.0022	0.44	1	0	0	0
13	—	0.0007	0.14	—			—
14	—	0.0002	0.04	—			—
15	—	0.0001	0.02	—			—
Sum	200	0.9999	199.98	200			12.62

$n = 50$ per lot, $mn = 200(50) = 10{,}000$
$\Sigma f_O d = 990$; $p = 990/10{,}000 = 0.099$, almost 10%
$k = 11$ categories or cells; $df = (k - 1) - 1 = 11 - 2 = 9$
Per table A.8 for $Q = 0.1$ and $v = df = 9$, $\chi^2 = 14.6837$
Computed value of $\chi^2 = 12.62$, which is much less than 14.68; hence fit is very good.

* Based on Binomial $(q + p)^n$, $p = 0.10$, $n = 50$. Values taken from *50–100 Binomial Tables,* Harry G. Romig, John Wiley & Sons, Inc., New York, 1953.

TABLE A.20 Receiving Inspection Results: 100 Lots Transistors

$n = 20$; $c = 3$; Process Average, $\bar{p} = 0.10$ for Supplier B

Group 1 Lot No.	*Observed Defects*	*Fraction Defective p*	*Group 2 Lot No.*	*Observed Defects*	*Fraction Defective p*	*Group 3 Lot No.*	*Observed Defects*	*Fraction Defective p*	*Group 4 Lot No.*	*Observed Defects*	*Fraction Defective p*
1	0	0	26	2	0.10	51	4*	0.20	76	4*	0.20
2	2	0.10	27	2	0.10	52	3	0.15	77	3	0.15
3	1	0.05	28	1	0.05	53	1	0.05	78	2	0.10
4	0	0	29	4*	0.20	54	1	0.05	79	3	0.15
5	0	0	30	6*	0.30	55	0	0	80	1	0.05
6	1	0.05	31	2	0.10	56	2	0.10	81	2	0.10
7	3	0.15	32	3	0.15	57	1	0.05	82	2	0.10
8	2	0.10	33	7*	0.35	58	2	0.10	83	1	0.05
9	1	0.05	34	6*	0.30	59	2	0.10	84	0	0
10	1	0.05	35	5*	0.25	60	1	0.05	85	0	0
11	1	0.05	36	5*	0.25	61	2	0.10	86	2	0.10
12	0	0	37	4*	0.20	62	4*	0.20	87	3	0.15
13	2	0.10	38	3	0.15	63	3	0.15	88	4*	0.20
14	4*	0.20	39	2	0.10	64	2	0.10	89	3	0.15
15	2	0.10	40	0	0	65	0	0	90	0	0
16	5*	0.25	41	0	0	66	0	0	91	1	0.05
17	0	0	42	1	0.05	67	1	0.05	92	2	0.10
18	0	0	43	1	0.05	68	2	0.10	93	2	0.10
19	0	0	44	3	0.15	69	3	0.15	94	1	0.05
20	1	0.05	45	5*	0.25	70	1	0.05	95	0	0
21	0	0	46	8*	0.40	71	0	0	96	1	0.05
22	2	0.10	47	6*	0.30	72	2	0.10	97	2	0.10
23	0	0	48	5*	0.25	73	1	0.05	98	0	0
24	1	0.05	49	4*	0.20	74	2	0.10	99	1	0.05
25	1	0.05	50	5*	0.25	75	0	0	100	0	0
Sum =	30	1.50		90	4.50		40	2.00		40	2.00
$\Sigma n = 500$			$\Sigma n = 500$			$\Sigma n = 500$			$\Sigma n = 500$		

Averages: *Groups 1*: $\bar{d} = 1.2, \bar{p} = 0.06$; 2: $\bar{d} = 3.6, \bar{p} = 0.18$; 3: $\bar{d} = 1.6, \bar{p} = 0.08$; 4: $\bar{d} = 1.6, \bar{p} = 0.08$

100 Lots: $\Sigma n = 2{,}000$; $\Sigma d = 200$; $\bar{d} = 2.0$; $\bar{p} = 0.10$.

* Greater than maximum allowable number of defects in sample, acceptance number $c = 3$ rejected lot.

† Average number of defects per sample per group.

TABLE A.21 Frequency Distribution

No. of Defects per Sample, $n = 20$

No. of Defects, d	*Observed Frequencies, f*					
	Group 1	*Group 2*	*Group 3*	*Group 4*	*Total*	*fd*
0	9	2	5	6	22	0
1	8	3	7	6	24	24
2	5	4	8	7	24	48
3	1	3	3	4	11	33
4	1	3	2	2	8	32
5	1	5			6	30
6		3			3	18
7		1			1	7
8		1			1	8
Sum	25	25	25	25	100	200

$\bar{d} = \frac{200}{100} = 2.0$; $\bar{p} = \frac{200}{2000} = 0.10$.

TABLE A.22 Frequency Distribution

No. Lots Rejected per Groups of 10 Submitted Lots

No. of Rejected Lots, L	*Frequency No. of Groups, G*	*Rejected Lots LG*	*Number of Accepted Lots* = 81.
0	2	0	
1	4	4	
2	2	4	
3	0	0	
4	0	0	
5	1	5	
6	1	6	
Sum	10	19	Lots Rejected = 19%

Average No. of Rejected Lots per Group of 10 Successive Submitted Lots = 1.0. Total number of lots = 100.

TABLE A.23 Sampling Results for Transistors; $n = 20$, $c = 3$

Test for Goodness of Fit by Binomial, $\bar{p} = 0.10$, 100 Lots

Individual Values	*Observed Values*					*Contribution to* χ^2
Theoretical Probabilities Binomial, $p = 0.10$, $n = 20$	*No. of Defects*	*Frequency,* f_0	*Theoretical Frequency,* f_t *Binomial,* $\bar{p} = 0.10$	$f_0 - f_t$	$(f_0 - f_t)^2$	$\frac{(f_0 - f_t)^2}{f_t}$
0.1216	0	22	12	10	100	8.33
0.2702	1	24	27	−3	9	0.33
0.2852	2	24	29	−5	25	0.86
0.1901	3	11	19	−8	64	3.37
0.0898	4	8	9	−1	1	0.11
0.0319	5	6	3	3	9	3.00
0.0089	6	3	1			
0.0020	7	1 } 5	0 } 1	4	16	16.00
0.0004	8	1	0			
Sum 1.0001		100	100			32.00

$k = 7$ categories or cells. Statistics used p only, hence $df = (k - 1) - 1 = 6 - 1 = 5$. Per table A.8, for $P = 0.0001$, $\chi^2(5) = 25.745$, hence binomial distribution does not fit data. Process appears to be out of control since $\chi^2 = 32.00 > 25.745$.

TABLE A.24 Sampling Results for Transistors; $n = 20$, $c = 3$, $\bar{p} = 0.10$

Test for Goodness of Fit by Poisson's Exponential Binomial Limit, $\bar{p}n = 2.00$

Individual Values	*Observed Values*					*Contribution to* χ^2
Theoretical Probabilities P.E., $\bar{p}n = 2.00$	*No. of Defects* d	*Frequency,* f_0	*Theoretical Frequency,* f_t *P.E.,* $\bar{p}n = 2.00$	$f_0 - f_t$	$(f_0 - f_t)^2$	$\frac{(f_0 - f_t)^2}{f_t}$
0.1353	0	22	13	9	81	6.23
0.2707	1	24	27	−3	9	0.33
0.2707	2	24	27	−3	9	0.33
0.1804	3	11	18	−7	49	2.72
0.0902	4	8	9	−1	1	0.11
0.0361	5	6	4	2	4	1.00
0.0120	6	3	1	2	4	4.00
0.0034	7	1 } 2	1 } 1	1	1	1.00
0.0009	8	1	0			
		100	100			15.72

$k = 8$ categories or cells, statistics used pn only, hence $df = (k - 1) - 1 = 7 - 1 = 6$. Per table A.8 for $P = 0.010$, $\chi^2 = 16.8119$, hence for 1% criterion fit is satisfactory. Usually 5% or more is desired, hence lack of control is indicated even for the Poisson Exponential.

FOOTNOTES

[1] Walter A. Shewhart, *Economic Control of Quality of Manufactured Product,* (New York: D. Van Nostrand Co., Inc., 1931), p. 89, Eq. 24.

[2] Type I to Type XII distributions. Basic equation:

$$\frac{df}{dx} = \frac{(x-a)f}{b_0 + b_1 x + b_2 x^2},$$

where f is the frequency function.

[3] Wilfred J. Dixon and Frank J. Massey, Jr., *Introduction to Statistical Analysis,* Second ed., (New York: McGraw-Hill Book Co., 1957), pp. 226–227, table A.6a for χ^2, page 385.

APPENDIX B

Appendix B: Derivations of Coefficients For Best Linear Lines of Regression

Chapter seven, in which the evaluation of the coefficient of linear correlation was discussed, noted that the derivation of the coefficients used in the equations, provided therein without proof, would be developed in an appendix. The values would be the best values to use, being determined to provide minimum differences between observed values and theoretical values based on the method of least squares. The derivations will cover two variables X and Y which may be correlated and related linearly by the expressions in equations (B1) and (B2).

$$Y = a + bX \quad \textbf{(B1)}$$

$$X = c + dY \quad \textbf{(B2)}$$

These derivations will be extended by analogy to cover the following second degree equations.

$$Y = a + bX + cX^2 \quad \textbf{(B3)}$$

$$X = d + eY + fY^2 \quad \textbf{(B4)}$$

Another feature of this appendix is the inclusion of the case in which a determination is made of indirectly observed quantities based on the theory of errors. When several unknown quantities are observed together, the results can usually be formulated as a set of linear relation equations for the unknowns, the number of equations usually being greater than the number of unknowns. When the equations are not compatible, the method of least squares can be used to find the most probable values of the unknowns. For these determinations there are m variables and n linear relations, $n > m$ or $n = m$; the latter being the case of the simple linear correlation of two variables X and Y, where $m = 2$ with the $n = 2$ linear relations given as equations (B1) and (B2).

Let us determine the best values of a and b by the theory of errors to determine the best line of regression $Y = a + bX$. For this line, where X_0 is the observed value of a variable characteristic A, the corresponding theoretical value for the correlated variable characteristic B is the Y value determined from $Y = a + bX_0$. However, there also exists by test an observed value Y_0 which may be equal to the computed theoretical value of Y or may differ from it by an amount

$$e = Y_0 - (a + bX_0) = Y_0 - Y \quad \textbf{(B5)}$$

The ith observation e_i is the difference in these two values of Y_i and is called its *error*. The theory of errors using the method of least squares gives the best values of a and b that make the sum of e_i^2 a minimum. Call such a sum of errors squared D.

$$D = E^2 = \Sigma\, e_i^2 \tag{B6}$$

$$D = \Sigma[Y - (a + bX)]^2 = \Sigma(Y^2 + a^2 + b^2X^2 - 2aY - 2bXY + 2abX) \tag{B7}$$

These e_i values are the discrepancies found between Y and Y_0 vertical distances, when plotted on graph paper. The sum of the squares is to be minimized. The method in calculus provides an equation giving a minimum or maximum value, its slope being zero for this case. This requires the derivative of Y with respect to X, dy/dx, which measures the value of the slope, given by the tangent of the angle between the graph of the linear relation and the X-axis. When this linear relation has a graph which is parallel to the X-axis, that point of inflection is either a minimum or a maximum. (See any text covering calculus for more details.) Here the values of the constants a and b are to be determined to make D a minimum, so partial derivatives are used and equated to zero.

$$\begin{aligned} \frac{\partial D}{\partial a} &= \Sigma(2a - 2Y + 2bX) = 0 \\ \frac{\partial D}{\partial b} &= \Sigma(2bX^2 - 2XY + 2aX) = 0 \end{aligned} \tag{B8}$$

Use n equal the number of units in sample, rather than the number of linear equations, when dealing with the case $n = m$ as covered in the texts dealing with this application of the theory of errors. Then $\Sigma a = na$ in the above expressions. The multiplier 2 appears in all six terms; since the two equations are equated to zero, both terms may be divided by 2, which gives a multiplier of 1. This results in two simple normal equations, from which the best values for a and b may be obtained.

$$\begin{aligned} na + \Sigma Xb &= \Sigma Y \\ \Sigma Xa + \Sigma X^2 b &= \Sigma XY \end{aligned} \tag{B9}$$

These expressions are ordered with respect to n, ΣX, ΣX^2, ΣY and ΣXY. Using standard algebraic methods with $\Sigma X^2 + \Sigma X$ as a multiplier, and subtracting the second modified relation from the first modified relation gives the following.

$$\begin{aligned} \Sigma X^2(na + \Sigma Xb) &= \Sigma X^2 \Sigma Y \\ - \Sigma X(\Sigma Xa + \Sigma X^2 b) &= \Sigma X \Sigma XY \\ \hline \Sigma X^2 na - \Sigma X \Sigma Xa &= \Sigma X^2 \Sigma Y - \Sigma X \Sigma XY \end{aligned}$$

Hence

$$a = \frac{\Sigma X^2 \Sigma Y - \Sigma X \Sigma XY}{n\Sigma X^2 - (\Sigma X)^2}. \tag{B10}$$

To obtain the best value of b, use ΣX and n as multipliers. This gives modified relations which, when subtracted, make the multiplier of a, called its coefficient, equal to zero.

$$\begin{array}{r} \Sigma X(na + \Sigma X b) = \Sigma X \Sigma Y \\ n(\Sigma X a + \Sigma X^2 b) = n\Sigma XY \\ \hline (\Sigma X)^2 b - n\Sigma X^2 b = \Sigma X \Sigma Y - n\Sigma XY \end{array}$$

Hence

$$b = \frac{\Sigma X \Sigma Y - n\Sigma XY}{(\Sigma X)^2 - n\Sigma X^2} = \frac{n\Sigma XY - \Sigma X \Sigma Y}{n\Sigma X^2 - (\Sigma X)^2} \tag{B11}$$

The denominators for a and b are identical. Those who have studied determinants will be able to write the solutions for a and b directly from equations (B9) as shown in equations (B12) and (B13).

$$a = \frac{\begin{vmatrix} \Sigma Y & \Sigma X \\ \Sigma XY & \Sigma X^2 \end{vmatrix}}{\begin{vmatrix} n & \Sigma X \\ \Sigma X & \Sigma X^2 \end{vmatrix}} = \frac{\Sigma Y \Sigma X^2 - \Sigma X \Sigma XY}{n\Sigma X^2 - (\Sigma X)^2} \tag{B12}$$

$$b = \frac{\begin{vmatrix} n & \Sigma Y \\ \Sigma X & \Sigma XY \end{vmatrix}}{\begin{vmatrix} n & \Sigma X \\ \Sigma X & \Sigma X^2 \end{vmatrix}} = \frac{n\Sigma XY - \Sigma X \Sigma Y}{n\Sigma X^2 - (\Sigma X)^2} \tag{B13}$$

This form makes it easy to write the best expressions for c and d to obtain the other line of regression, $X = c + dY$. Interchange X terms with Y terms and Y terms with similar X terms.

$$c = \frac{\begin{vmatrix} \Sigma X & \Sigma Y \\ \Sigma YX & \Sigma Y^2 \end{vmatrix}}{\begin{vmatrix} n & \Sigma Y \\ \Sigma Y & \Sigma Y^2 \end{vmatrix}} = \frac{\Sigma X \Sigma Y^2 - \Sigma YX \Sigma Y}{n\Sigma Y^2 - (\Sigma Y)^2} \tag{B14}$$

$$d = \frac{\begin{vmatrix} n & \Sigma X \\ \Sigma Y & \Sigma YX \end{vmatrix}}{\begin{vmatrix} n & \Sigma Y \\ \Sigma Y & \Sigma Y^2 \end{vmatrix}} = \frac{n\Sigma YX - \Sigma Y \Sigma X}{n\Sigma Y^2 - (\Sigma Y)^2} \tag{B15}$$

When computing the statistics for n values of each of the two correlated variables X and Y, the sample statistics are found for these two distributions from the sums of the X, Y, X^2, Y^2, and XY terms. Average values $\overline{X} = \Sigma X/n$, and $\overline{Y} = \Sigma Y/n$, variances $v_X = \Sigma X^2/n - \overline{X}^2$ and $v_Y = \Sigma Y^2/n - \overline{Y}^2$, and the covariance $\text{cov}(X, Y) = \Sigma XY/n - \overline{X}\overline{Y}$ provide values from which corresponding lines of regression may be written.

$$Y = \overline{Y} + \frac{\text{Cov}(X, Y)}{v_X}(X - \overline{X}), \qquad \textbf{(B16)}$$

$$X = \overline{X} + \frac{\text{Cov}(X, Y)}{v_Y}(Y - \overline{Y}) \qquad \textbf{(B17)}$$

Example 1 The simplest example is to obtain the two lines of regression for ten sets of X and Y values for which the necessary sums are given.

Sample No.	X	Y	XY	X^2	Y^2	$x = X - \overline{X}$	x^2	$y = Y - \overline{Y}$	y^2	xy
1	1	3	3	1	9	−3	9	−4	16	12
2	4	7	28	16	49	0	0	0	0	0
3	2	5	10	4	25	−2	4	−2	4	4
4	3	6	18	9	36	−1	1	−1	1	1
5	5	8	40	25	64	1	1	1	1	1
6	3	7	21	9	49	−1	1	0	0	0
7	7	9	63	49	81	3	9	2	4	6
8	6	10	60	36	100	2	4	3	9	6
9	4	7	28	16	49	0	0	0	0	0
10	5	8	40	25	64	1	1	1	1	1
Sum	40	70	311	190	526	0	30	0	36	31
Averages	4.0	7.0	31.1	19.0	52.6	0	3.0	0	3.6	3.1

$\overline{X} = 4.0$, $\overline{Y} = 7.0$, $\overline{X}\overline{Y} = 28.0$; $\text{Cov}(X, Y) = 31.1 - 28.0 = 3.1$; Checks using x, y, x^2, y^2, xy. $v_X = 19.0 - 16.0 = 3.0$, $v_Y = 52.6 - 49.0 = 3.6$; $v_X = 3.0$, $v_Y = 3.6$, $\text{Cov}(X, Y) = 3.1$.

Lines of Regression

Using equations (B12) and (B13):

$$a = \frac{70(190) - 40(311)}{10(190) - (40)^2} = \frac{13300 - 12440}{1900 - 1600} = \frac{860}{300} = 2.87$$

$$b = \frac{10(311) - 40(70)}{10(190) - (40)^2} = \frac{3110 - 2800}{1900 - 1600} = \frac{310}{300} = 1.03$$

$$Y = 2.87 + 1.03X$$

Using equations (B14) and (B15):

$$c = \frac{40(526) - 311(70)}{10(526) - (70)^2} = \frac{21040 - 21770}{5260 - 4900} = \frac{-730}{360} = -2.03$$

$$d = \frac{10(311) - 70(40)}{10(526) - (70)^2} = \frac{3110 - 2800}{5260 - 4900} = \frac{310}{360} = 0.86$$

$$X = -2.03 + 0.86Y$$

This solution is checked by the use of equations (B17) and (B18).

$$Y = 7.0 + \frac{3.1}{3.0}(X - 4.0)$$

$$Y = 7.0 + 1.03X - 4.12$$

$$Y = 2.88 + 1.03X$$

Using three significant figures, the difference in the values is 2.88 compared to 2.87. If four significant figures are used for 3.1/3.0, i.e., 1.033, 7.00 − 4.13 = 2.87.

$$X = 4.0 + \frac{3.1}{3.6}(Y - 7.0)$$

$$X = 4.0 + 0.86(Y - 7.0)$$

$$X = 4.0 + 0.86Y - 6.03$$

$$X = 2.03 + 0.86Y$$

This agrees exactly with equation found by the theory of least squares where 3.1/3.6 = 0.861 is used. Using only 0.86 gives $X = 2.02 + 0.86Y$.

Figure B1 shows these ten correlated values and the two lines of regression which must pass through $(\bar{X}, \bar{Y})$, i.e., (4.0, 7.0)

$$\bar{Y} = 2.88 + 1.03(4.0) = \quad 2.88 + 4.12 = 7.0$$

$$\bar{X} = 2.02 + 0.86(7.0) = -2.02 + 6.02 = 4.00$$

The linear coefficient of correlation

$$r_{XY} = \frac{\mathrm{Cov}(X, Y)}{\sigma_X \sigma_Y} = \frac{\mathrm{Cov}(X, Y)}{\sqrt{v_X v_Y}},$$

so r_{XY} for this example is

$$\frac{3.1}{\sqrt{3.0(3.6)}} = \frac{3.1}{\sqrt{10.8}} = \frac{3.1}{3.286335} = 0.9433.$$

The determinant solution provides the symmetric relations, giving a means to obtain values for the coefficients that provide the best possible lines of regression. Consider the relation for Y presented earlier.

$$Y = a + bX + cX^2 \tag{B3}$$

More advanced texts sometimes present these derivations in detail. By analogy, we can readily write the values due to the symmetric form of the equations for two variables.

$$a = \frac{\begin{vmatrix} \Sigma Y & \Sigma X & \Sigma X^2 \\ \Sigma XY & \Sigma X^2 & \Sigma X^3 \\ \Sigma X^2 Y & \Sigma X^3 & \Sigma X^4 \end{vmatrix}}{\begin{vmatrix} n & \Sigma X & \Sigma X^2 \\ \Sigma X & \Sigma X^2 & \Sigma X^3 \\ \Sigma X^2 & \Sigma X^3 & \Sigma X^4 \end{vmatrix}} \tag{B18}$$

$$b = \frac{\begin{vmatrix} n & \Sigma X & \Sigma X^2 \\ \Sigma X & \Sigma Y & \Sigma X^3 \\ \Sigma X^2 & \Sigma XXY & \Sigma X^4 \end{vmatrix}}{\begin{vmatrix} n & \Sigma XX^2 Y & \Sigma X^2 \\ \Sigma X & \Sigma X^2 & \Sigma X^3 \\ \Sigma X^2 & \Sigma X^3 & \Sigma X^4 \end{vmatrix}} \tag{B19}$$

$$c = \frac{\begin{vmatrix} n & \Sigma X & \Sigma Y \\ \Sigma X & \Sigma X^2 & \Sigma XY \\ \Sigma X^2 & \Sigma X^3 & \Sigma X^2 Y \end{vmatrix}}{\begin{vmatrix} n & \Sigma X & \Sigma X^2 \\ \Sigma X & \Sigma X^2 & \Sigma X^3 \\ \Sigma X^2 & \Sigma X^3 & \Sigma X^4 \end{vmatrix}} \tag{B20}$$

For the case where there are m unknown quantities related linearly in n equations, these expressions may be written as:

$$\left.\begin{array}{l} a_1 x_1 + b_1 x_2 + c_1 x_3 + \cdots + f_1 x_m + l_1 = 0 \\ a_2 x_1 + b_2 x_2 + c_2 x_3 + \cdots + f_2 x_m + l_2 = 0 \\ \cdots\cdots\cdots\cdots\cdots\cdots\cdots\cdots\cdots\cdots \\ a_n x_1 + b_n x_2 + c_n x_3 + \cdots + f_n x_m + l_n = 0 \end{array}\right\} \tag{B21}$$

and let $v_r = a_r x_1 + b_r x_2 + \cdots + f_r x_m + l_r$, where $r = 1, 2, 3, \ldots, n$, and v_r is the error in the rth equation corresponding to the true values of $x_1, x_2, \ldots, x_m$ and is called the unknown residual. Then the probability of the error v_r is proportional to $e^{-v_r^2/2\sigma^2}$, and the probability of the set of values v_r occurring simultaneously is proportional to $e^{-1/2\sigma^2 \Sigma v_r^2}$ or $e^{-1/2\sigma^2[vv]}$. Such a relation exists where the error takes into consideration an estimate of the variance σ^2, with $\bar{a}$ denoting the weighted mean with weights of a number of observations defined as a set of numbers inversely proportional to the variances of the n observations with

$$w_r = Kl\sigma_r^2 \tag{B22}$$

for $r = 1, 2, \ldots, n$; K being the same for all the observations and the observational equations are of equal weight. Observations may be considered equally reliable or unequally reliable with w_r defined as above. K may be taken equal to σ^2 then the error $(x_r - \bar{e})$ is proportional to $e^{-w_r(x_r - x)^2/2\sigma^2}$ and the probability of the set of values. $x_1, x_2, \ldots, x_r$ is proportional to $e^{-\Sigma w_r(X_n - x)^2/2\sigma^2}$. The most probable value of x is the weighted mean given by the following relation.

$$X = \frac{\Sigma w_r x_r}{\Sigma w_r} \tag{B23}$$

If $\bar{x}$ denotes the weighted mean, an estimate may be made of the variance σ^2 with which the n quantities $w_r^{1/2}(x_r - \bar{x})$ are distributed about zero, that is

$$\sigma^2 = \frac{1}{n-1} \sum_{r=1}^{n} w_r(x_r - \bar{x})^2 \tag{B24}$$

Using this relation for σ^2, the probability of the set of values v_r occurring simultaneously is proportional to $e^{-1/2^2 \Sigma v_r^2}$, or $e^{-1/2\sigma^2[vv]}$. The most probable set of values of the quantities $x_1, x_2, \ldots, x_m$ is the set which makes this probability a maximum, that is, the set which makes $[vv]$ a minimum.

To obtain such a minimum value of $[vv]$, equate to zero the m partial derivatives with respect to $x_1, x_2, \ldots, x_m$, formulating m normal equations from which the most probable values may be found for the m unknowns. The normal equation for x_1 is

$$\frac{\partial}{2x_1}[vv] = 0, \quad \frac{\partial}{2x_1}(v_1^2 + v_2^2 + \cdots + v_r^2) = 0$$

which gives

$$v_1 \frac{\partial v_1}{\partial x_1} + v_2 \frac{\partial v_2}{\partial x_1} + \cdots + v_r \frac{\partial v_n}{\partial x_1} = 0. \tag{B26}$$

Now from equation (B21)

$$\begin{aligned} v_1 \frac{\partial v_1}{\partial x_1} &= a_1(a_1 x_1 + b_1 x_2 + c_1 x_3 + \cdots + f_1 x_m + l_1 \\ v_2 \frac{\partial v_2}{\partial x_1} &= a_2(a_2 x_1 + b_2 x_2 + c_2 x_3 + \cdots + f_2 X_m + l_2) \end{aligned} \tag{B27}$$

$$v_n \frac{\partial v_n}{\partial x_1} = a_n(a_n x_1 + b_n x_2 + c_n x_3 + \cdots + f_n x_m + l_n)$$

These relations for all the derived normal equations are summarized below.

$$\begin{aligned}
[aa]x_1 + [ab]x_2 + [ac]x_3 + \cdots + [af]x_m + al = 0 \\
[ba]x_1 + [bb]x_2 + [bc]x_3 + \cdots + [bf]x_m + bl = 0 \\
[fa]x_1 + [fb]x_2 + [fc]x_3 + \cdots + [ff]x_m + fl = 0
\end{aligned} \qquad \textbf{(B28)}$$

These normal equations may be solved by the usual algebraic process or by the use of determinants. The solution provides the desired most probable value.

When the observational equations are of unequal weight, such as was noted as a possibility when discussing the evaluation of σ^2, then w values are inserted before each term in equation (B28), where $v_r(\partial v_r)/(\partial x_i)$ is multiplied by w_r.

These equations are applicable in a large number of practical cases. For smog control, the most probable value for each week may be desired, where a linear relation is obtained each day for two different contaminants. Then there will be seven equations using two unknowns.

A simple example with equal weights for every equation using only five linear equations, with $x_1 = x$ and $x_2 = y$, will show how to obtain solutions for any case that might be considered.

Example 2 Given the four linear equations shown in figure B2:

(1) $2x - y = 6$; (2) $x - y = 2$; (3) $x - 4y = 4$; (4) $x - y = -1$; (5) $2x - y = 2$. The equations in (B28) may be obtained more readily by writing the five given equations in the form $ax + by + 1 = 0$. As a check, let $S = a + b + 1$. Write the coefficients of these five equations using the headings noted.

Eq. No.	*a*	*b*	*l*	*s*
1	2	−1	−6	−5
2	1	−1	−2	−2
3	1	−4	−4	−7
4	1	−1	1	1
5	2	−1	−2	−1

Using these coefficients, the relations in equation (B28) may be written as shown, remembering that $ba = ab$.

Eq. No.	*aa*	*ab*	*al*	*as*	*bb*	*bl*	*bs*
1	4	−2	−12	−10	1	6	5
2	1	−1	−2	−2	1	2	2
3	1	−4	−4	−7	16	16	28
4	1	−1	1	1	1	−1	−1
5	4	−2	−4	−2	1	2	1
	11	−10	−21	−20	20	25	35

The two normal equations for this example are:

$$\Sigma aax + \Sigma aby + \Sigma al = 0; \qquad 11x - 10y = 21$$

$$\Sigma abx + \Sigma bby + \Sigma bl = 0; \quad -10x + 20^{y} = -25$$

Check:

$$\Sigma aa + \Sigma ab + \Sigma al = \Sigma as; \qquad 11 - 10 - 21 = -20 = \Sigma as = -20$$

$$\Sigma ab + \Sigma bb + \Sigma bl = \Sigma bs; \quad -10 + 20 + 25 = \quad 35 = \Sigma bs = \quad 35$$

The most probable values of x and y will be the solution of the above normal equations. Solving by determinants gives:

$$X = \frac{\begin{vmatrix} 21 & -10 \\ -25 & 20 \end{vmatrix}}{\begin{vmatrix} 11 & -10 \\ -10 & 20 \end{vmatrix}} = \frac{420 - 250}{220 - 100} = \frac{170}{120} = 1.4167$$

$$Y = \frac{\begin{vmatrix} 11 & 21 \\ -10 & -25 \end{vmatrix}}{\begin{vmatrix} 11 & -10 \\ -10 & 20 \end{vmatrix}} = \frac{-275 + 210}{220 - 100} = \frac{-65}{120} = -0.54167$$

Check: $11(1.4167) - 10(-0.54167) = 21$
$15.5837 + 5.4167 = 21.0004$
$-10(1.4167) + 20(-0.54167) = -25$
$-14.167 - 10.8334 = -25.0004$

Figure B2 presents a graph of the five equations in example 2 for which the most probable value has been determined as:

$$X = 1.41667,$$

$$\text{and } Y = -0.54167.$$

The two normal equations are also graphed. Their intersection is the most probable values of X and Y.

This method may be extended to more variables and any number of linear equations. When three lines intersect forming a triangle, the most probable values of X and Y may be the center of gravity of the system.

FOOTNOTE

[1] Lambe, C. G., *Elements of Statistics,* 1952, Longmans, Green and Co., London. (Portions of this derivation are given in Chapter IX, Theory of Errors, pp. 75–83.)

APPENDIX C

Appendix C: Mathematical Relations and Tables of Factors for Computing Control Chart Lines

The material in this Appendix C was originally written for the ASTM Manual on Quality Control of Materials in Supplements A and B. With some modifications for clarity, it is included here as an important complement for those who are using Control Charts. It is reproduced by permission of the American Society for Testing and Materials from copyright material STP-15C, which permission is gratefully acknowledged.

Scope

This appendix presents mathematical relations needed to develop the factors and formulas used particularly in chapter six. A tabulation of values of these factors, including reciprocal values of c_2 and d_2 and values of d_3, is given in table 6.1. This last factor is involved in the relations covering control charts for ranges. Factors used for control charts for attributes are given in chapter five and are included in this appendix.

Factors c_2, d_2, and d_3 (Values for $n = 2$ to 25, inclusive in table 6.1)

The relations given for factors c_2, d_2, and d_3 are based on sampling from a universe having a normal distribution.

$$c_2 = \sqrt{\frac{2}{n}} \frac{\left(\frac{n-2}{2}\right)!}{\left(\frac{n-3}{2}\right)!} \qquad \textbf{(C1)}^1$$

where the symbol ! as used indicates a factorial; for example, $4! = 4 \cdot 3 \cdot 2 \cdot 1 = 24$. For the relation $\frac{k}{2}!$, if k is even, $\frac{k}{2}! = \frac{k}{2} \cdot \frac{k-2}{2} \cdot \frac{k-4}{2} \cdots 1$, each number on the right-hand side being an integer; if k is odd, $\frac{k}{2}! = \frac{k}{2} \cdot \frac{k-2}{2} \cdot \frac{k-4}{2} \cdots \frac{1}{2} \cdot \sqrt{\pi}$, where $\left(-\frac{1}{2}\right)! = \sqrt{\pi}$ and $0! = 1$.

$$d_2 = \int_{-\infty}^{\infty} [1 - (1 - \alpha_1)^n - \alpha_1^n]\, dx_1 \qquad \text{(C2)}$$

where $\alpha_1 = \frac{1}{\sqrt{2\pi}} \int_{-\infty}^{x_1} e^{-x^2/2}\, dx$, $n =$ sample size[2]

$$d_3 = \left[2 \int_{-\infty}^{\infty} \int_{-0}^{x_1} [1 - \alpha_1^n - (1 - \alpha_n)^n + (\alpha_1 - \alpha_n)^n]\, dx_1 dx_n - d_2^2 \right]^{1/2} \qquad \text{(C3)}^3$$

where $\alpha_1 = \frac{1}{\sqrt{2\pi}} \int_{-\infty}^{x_1} e^{-x^2/2}\, dx, \alpha_n = \frac{1}{\sqrt{2\pi}} \int_{-\infty}^{x_n} e^{-x^2/2}\, dx$

$n =$ sample size[2] $d_2 =$ average range for a normal law distribution with standard deviation equal to unity. (In the original paper, Tippett[3] used w for range and w_2 for d_2.)[2]

The above relations for c_2, d_2, and d_3 are exact when the original universe is normal, but this does not limit their use in practice. They may, for most practical purposes, be considered satisfactory for use in control chart work even though the universe is not normal. Since the relations are involved and thus difficult to compute, values of c_2, d_2, and d_3 for $n = 2$ to 25, inclusive, are given in table 6.1. All values listed in the table were computed to enough significant figures so that when rounded off in accordance with standard practices the last figure shown in the table was not in doubt.

Standard Deviations of $\overline{X}$, σ, R, p, pn, u, and c

The standard deviations of $\overline{X}$, σ, R, p, etc., used in setting three-sigma control limits and designated $\sigma_{\overline{X}}$, σ_σ, σ_R, σ_p, etc., in part 3 of the ASTM *Manual on Quality Control of Materials,* are the standard deviations of the sampling distribution of $\overline{X}$, σ, R, p, etc., for subgroups (samples) of size n. They are not the standard deviations which might be computed from the subgroup values of $\overline{X}$, σ, R, p, etc., plotted on the control charts but are computed by formula from the quantities listed in table 6.1.

The standard deviations $\sigma_{\overline{X}}$, σ_σ, and σ_R computed in this way are unaffected by any assignable causes of variation between subgroups. Consequently, the control charts derived from them will detect assignable causes of this type.

The relations in equations (C4 to C16), inclusive, which follow, are all of the form: σ_y, where y is a subscript such as $\overline{X}$, σ, R, p, pn, u and c.

Standard deviation of the sampling distribution = A function of both the sample size, n, and universe value of

$$\sigma, p, u, \text{or } c.$$

For convenience, the universe values in the relations are designated simply by σ, p, u, or c and the quantities to be substituted for the cases "no standard given" and "standard given" are shown below immediately after each relation.

TABLE C.1 Basis of Standard Deviations for Control Limits

Control Chart for	*Standard Deviation Used in Computing 3-Sigma Limits is Computed From:*	
	Control—No Standard Given	*Control—Standard Given*
X	$\bar{\sigma}$ or $\bar{R}$	σ'
σ	$\bar{\sigma}$ or $\bar{R}$	σ'
R	$\bar{\sigma}$ or R	σ'
p	$\bar{p}$	p'
pn	$\bar{p}n$	p'
u	$\bar{u}$	u'
c	$\bar{c}$	c'

NOTE: $\bar{\sigma}$, $\bar{R}$, etc., are computed averages of subgroup values. σ', p', etc., are standard values.

Average, $\bar{X}$:

$$\sigma_{\bar{X}} = \frac{\sigma}{\sqrt{n}}, \tag{C4}$$

where σ is the standard deviation of the universe. For no standard given, substitute $\sigma = \dfrac{\bar{\sigma}}{c_2}$ or $\sigma = \dfrac{\bar{R}}{d_2}$; for standard given, substitute $\sigma = \sigma'$. Equation (C4) above does not assume a normal distribution.[4]

Standard Deviation,[5] σ:

$$\sigma_\sigma = \left[\frac{n-1}{n} - c_2^2\right]^{1/2} \sigma, \tag{C5}$$

or

$$\sigma_\sigma = [2(n-1) - 2nc_2^2]^{1/2} \frac{\sigma}{\sqrt{2n}}, \tag{C6}$$

(C6)[6]

where c_2 is defined in equation (C1), and σ is the standard deviation of the Normal universe sampled. For no standard given, $\sigma = \dfrac{\bar{\sigma}}{c_2}$ or $\dfrac{\bar{R}}{d_2}$; for standard given, $\sigma = \sigma'$. For control chart purposes the above relations may be used for distributions other than normal.

Approximations to above relation for σ_σ:

$$\sigma_\sigma = \left(\frac{1}{2n} - \frac{1}{8n^2} - \frac{3}{16n^3} - \cdots\right)^{1/2} \sigma$$

(C7)[7]

$$\sigma_\sigma = \left(1 - \frac{1}{8n} - \frac{25}{128n^2}\right) \frac{\sigma}{\sqrt{2n}} \tag{C8}$$

$$\sigma_\sigma = \frac{\sigma}{\sqrt{2n}} \tag{C9}$$

where σ is the standard deviation of the universe.[8]

The exact relation of equation (C5) or (C6) is used for control chart analyses involving σ_σ and for the determination of factors B_3 and B_4 and B_1 and B_2 of table 6.1. This makes $B_2 = \frac{1}{2}D_2$, and $B_4 = D_4$ for $n = 2$, which should be the case, since the range is merely twice the standard deviation for a subgroup of two.

When $n > 25$, equation (C9) is a good approximation for practical uses. In most cases, equation (C9) is good enough to use[9] when $n > 5$. For simplicity and ease of duplication this approximate relation was used previously in the *A S T M Manual on Presentation of Data,* Supplement B, Table I, for all values of n. Experience has indicated this choice to be satisfactory. However, the discrepancy introduced between B_4 and D_4, which are identically equal for $n = 2$, led to some confusion. Also for $n = 2$, $d_3 = [2 - 4c_2^2]^{1/2} = [2 - 4.1/\pi]^{1/2} = 0.853$, the multiplying factor of $\frac{\sigma}{\sqrt{2n}} = \frac{\sigma}{2}$ in equation (C6). To avoid confusion due to these slight discrepancies, the factors were recomputed using the exact relations rather than the simpler approximate relations previously used. Hence the tables now list the values based on computations including this additional correction factor for the tabulated values of n (2 to 25).

Range, R:

$$\sigma_R = d_3\sigma, \tag{C10}$$

where σ is the standard deviation of the universe. For no standard given, substitute $\sigma = \frac{\bar{\sigma}}{c_2}$ or $\sigma = \frac{\bar{R}}{d_2}$; for standard given, substitute $\sigma = \sigma'$.

The factor d_3 given in equation (C3) represents the standard deviation for ranges in terms of the true standard deviation of the Normal universe.[10]

Fraction defective, p:

$$\sigma_p = \sqrt{\frac{p(1-p)}{n}}, \tag{C11}$$

where p is the value of fraction defective for the universe. For no standard given, substitute $p = \bar{p}$; for standard given, substitute $p = p'$. When p is so small that the term $(1 - p)$ may be neglected, the following approximation is used:

$$\sigma_p = \sqrt{\frac{p}{n}} \tag{C12}$$

Number of defectives, pn:

$$\sigma_{pn} = \sqrt{pn(1-p)}, \tag{C13}$$

where p is the value of fraction defective for the universe. For no standard given, substitute $p = \bar{p}$; and for standard given, substitute $p = p'$. The function pn has been widely used to represent number of defectives (defective units) for one or more characteristics.

Both p and pn have a binomial distribution. Equations (C11) and (C13) are based on the binomial distribution in which the theoretical frequencies for $pn = 0, 1, 2, \ldots, n$ are given by the first, second, third, etc. terms of the expansion of the binomial $[(1 - p) + p]^n$, where p is the universe value. When p is so small that the term $(1 - p)$ may be neglected, the following approximation is used:

$$\sigma_{pn} = \sqrt{pn} \tag{C14}$$

Defects per unit, u:

$$\sigma_u = \sqrt{\frac{u}{n}}\,, \tag{C15}$$

where n is the number of units in sample, and u is the value of defects per unit for the universe. For no standard given, substitute $u = \bar{u}$; for standard given, substitute $u = u'$.

The number of defects found on any one unit may be considered to result from an unknown but large (practically infinite) number of points where a defect could possibly occur combined with an unknown but very small probability of occurrence at any one point. This leads to the use of the Poisson exponential distribution for which the standard deviation is the square root of the expected number of defects on a single unit. This distribution is likewise applicable to sums of such numbers, such as the observed values of c, and to averages of such numbers, such as observed values of u, the expected standard deviation of the averages being $1/n$ times that of the sums. Where the number of defects found on any one unit results from a known number of potential causes (relatively a small number as compared with the case described above), and the distribution of the defects per unit is more exactly a multinomial distribution, for practical purposes in most instances the Poisson exponential distribution, although an approximation may be used for control chart work.

Number of defects, c:

$$\sigma_c = \sqrt{un} = \sqrt{c}, \tag{C16}$$

where n is the number of units in sample, u is the value of defects per unit for the universe, and c is the number of defects in samples of size n for the universe. For no standard given, substitute $c = \bar{c} = \bar{u}n$; for standard given, substitute $c = c' = u'n$. The distribution of the observed values of c is discussed above.

Factors for Computing Control Limits

Note that all these factors are actually functions of n only and the constant 3 resulting from the choice of 3σ limits.

Averages:

$$A = \frac{3}{\sqrt{n}} \tag{C17}$$

$$A_1 = \frac{3}{c_2\sqrt{n}} \tag{C18}$$

$$A_2 = \frac{3}{d_2\sqrt{n}} \tag{C19}$$

NOTE: $A_1 = \frac{A}{c_2}$, $\quad A_2 = \frac{A}{d_2}$.

Standard deviations:

$$B_1 = c_2 - \frac{3}{\sqrt{2n}}[2(n-1) - 2nc_2^2]^{1/2} = c_2 - 3\left(\frac{n-1}{n} - c_2^2\right)^{1/2} \tag{C20}$$

$$B_2 = c_2 + \frac{3}{\sqrt{2n}}[2(n-1) - 2nc_2^2]^{1/2} = c_2 + 3\left(\frac{n-1}{n} - c_2^2\right)^{1/2} \tag{C21}$$

$$B_3 = 1 - \frac{3}{c_2\sqrt{2n}}[2(n-1) - 2nc_2^2]^{1/2} = 1 - \frac{3}{c_2}\left(\frac{n-1}{n} - c_2^2\right)^{1/2} \tag{C22}$$

$$B_4 = 1 + \frac{3}{c_2\sqrt{2n}}[2(n-1) - 2nc_2^2]^{1/2} = 1 + \frac{3}{c_2}\left(\frac{n-1}{n} - c_2^2\right)^{1/2} \tag{C23}$$

NOTE: $B_3 = \frac{B_1}{c_2}$, $\quad B_4 = \frac{B_2}{c_2}$.

Ranges:

$$D_1 = d_2 - 3d_3 \tag{C24}$$

$$D_2 = d_2 + 3d_3 \tag{C25}$$

$$D_3 = 1 - 3\frac{d_3}{d_2} \tag{C26}$$

$$D_4 = 1 + 3\frac{d_3}{d_2} \tag{C27}$$

NOTE: $D_3 = \frac{D_1}{d_2}$, $\quad D_4 = \frac{D_2}{d_2}$.

Individuals:

$$E_1 = \frac{3}{c_2} \tag{C28}$$

$$E_2 = \frac{3}{d_2} \qquad \text{(C29)}$$

Comparison of Symbols
Table of Some Symbols Used in This Text and Those Used in Other Statistical Texts

NOTE: This text uses the prime notation for universe parameters (or standard values), while other statistical texts are inclined to use Greek letters

Term	*Symbol Used in This Text*	*Symbol Commonly Used in Other Statistical Texts*
An observed value	X	X (or x)
Universe mean or average	$\bar{X}'$	μ
Sample size, or number of observations	n	n (or N)
Sample mean or average	$\bar{X}\left(=\frac{\Sigma X_i}{n}\right)$	$\bar{X}$ (or $\bar{x}$)
Universe standard deviation	σ'	σ
Sample standard deviation	$\sigma\left(=\sqrt{\frac{\Sigma(X_i-\bar{X})^2}{n}}\right)$	$s\left(=\sqrt{\frac{\Sigma(X_i-\bar{X})^2}{n-1}}\right)^a$
Universe variance	σ'^2, also v'	σ^2, also v
Sample variance	$\sigma^2\left(=\frac{\Sigma(X_i-\bar{X})^2}{n}\right)$	$s^2\left(=\frac{\Sigma(X_i-\bar{X})^2}{n-1}\right)^a$

[a] Some authorities feel the term "sample standard deviation" for s and the term "sample variance" for s^2 to be misapplied. In any case s^2 is the unbiased estimate of the universe variance.

Special Terms and Symbols Used in this Appendix

In general, the terms and symbols used in this appendix have the same meanings as in preceding parts of the text. In a few cases, which are indicated below, a more specific meaning is attached to them for the convenience of a portion or all of the mathematical definitions and derivations previously given.

A comparison of the symbols used in this text and those commonly used in other statistical texts is given above.

Special Terms

Unit One of a number of similar articles, parts, specimens, lengths, areas, etc., of a material or product.

Lot A specific quantity of similar material or collection of similar units from a common source; in inspection work, the quantity offered for inspection and acceptance at any one time. It may be a collection of raw material, parts, or subassemblies, inspected during production, or a consignment of finished product to be sent out for service.

Sample A portion of material or a group of units taken from a larger quantity of material or collection of units, which serves to provide information that can be used as a basis for action on the larger quantity or on the production process.

Subgroup One of a series of groups of observations obtained by subdividing a larger group of observations; alternatively, the data obtained from one of a series of samples taken from a series of lots or from a process. One of the essential features of the control chart method is to break up the inspection data into *rational subgroups,* that is, to classify the observed values into subgroups, *within* which variations may for engineering reasons be considered to be due to non-assignable chance causes only, but *between* which there may be differences due to assignable causes whose presence is considered possible.

Assignable Cause A factor contributing to the variation in quality, that it is economically feasible to identify.

Explanation of Symbols

Symbol	*General*	*Usage in Control Charts*
c	Number of defects or defective units; often used as the *acceptance number* in a single-sampling plan.	The *number of defects*; more specifically the number of defects in a sample (subgroup).
c_2	An adjustment factor for estimating σ'. In double-sampling plans where c is first *acceptance number* for n, first sample, c_2 is second *acceptance number*, the maximum allowable number of defectives in a total sample of $n_1 + n_2$ units.	A factor that is a function of n and expresses the ratio between the expected value of $\bar{\sigma}$ for a large number of samples of n observed values each and the σ' of the universe sampled. (Values of $c_2 = \bar{\sigma}/\sigma'$ are given in table 6.11 based on a normal distribution.)
d_2	An adjustment factor to estimate σ' from average range. By definition $d_2 = \bar{w}$.	A factor that is a function of n and expresses the ratio between the expected value of $\bar{R}$ for a large number of samples of n observed values each and the σ' of the universe sampled. (Values of $d_2 = \bar{R}/\sigma'$ are given in table 6.11, based on a normal distribution.)
d_3	Reciprocal of σ'_w, standard deviation of R.	Control Limits for ranges are obtained by using d_3.
df	Degrees of freedom.	The factor used in place of n for estimating σ'; used in analysis of variance computations.
k	Skewness k used to measure departure from normality or symmetry of a distribution.	The number of subgroups or samples under consideration.
n	The *number* of observed values (observations).	The subgroup or sample size, that is, the number of units or observed values in a sample or subgroup.

p	The *relative frequency or proportion*, the ratio of the number of occurrences to the total possible number of occurrences.	The *fraction defective*, the ratio of the number of defective units (articles, parts, specimens, etc.) to the total number of units under consideration; more specifically, the fraction defective of a sample (subgroup).
pn	The number of occurrences.	The *number of defectives* (defective units); more specifically, the *number of defectives* in a sample of n units.
R	The *range* of a set of numbers, that is, the difference between the largest number and the smallest number.	The range of the n observed values in a subgroup (sample). (The symbol R is also used to designate the mean moving range.)
σ (sigma)	The *standard deviation*, the root-mean-square (rms.) deviation of the observed values from their average.	The standard deviation of the n observed values in a subgroup (sample): $$\sigma = \sqrt{\frac{(X_1 - \bar{X})^2 + \cdots + (X_n - \bar{X})^2}{n}}$$ or expressed in a form more convenient for computation purposes, $$\sigma = \sqrt{\frac{X_1^2 + X_2^2 + \cdots + X_n^2}{n} - \bar{X}^2}$$
u	As used in control charts, $un = c$; the average number of units inspected by screening on continuous sampling.	The *defects per unit*, the number of defects in a sample of n units divided by n.
w	Relative *range*.	$w = R/\sigma'$
X	An observed value of a measurable characteristic; specific observed values are designated X_1, X_2, X_3, etc. Also used to designate a measurable characteristic.	
$\bar{X}$ (X bar)	The *average* (arithmetic mean); the sum of the n observed values divided by n.	The average of the n observed values in a subgroup (sample): $$\bar{X} = \frac{X_1 + X_2 + \cdots + X_n}{n}$$

Qualified Symbols

$\sigma_{\bar{X}}, \sigma_\sigma, \sigma_R, \sigma_p$, etc.	The standard deviation of values of $\bar{X}, \sigma, R, p$, etc.	The standard deviation of the sampling distribution of $\bar{X}, \sigma, R, p$, etc.
$\bar{\bar{X}}, \bar{\sigma}, \bar{R}, \bar{p}$, etc. (X double bar, sigma bar, etc.)	The *average of a* set of values of X, σ, R, p, etc. (the bar ($^-$) notation signifies an average value).	The average of the set of k subgroup (sample) values of X, σ, R, p, etc., under consideration. For samples of unequal size, an over-all or weighted average.
$\bar{X}', \sigma', p'$, etc. ($\bar{X}$-prime, sigma-prime, etc.)	The *true* or *objective* value of $\bar{X}$, σ, p, etc. for the universe sampled. (The prime (′) notation signifies the true or objective value as distinct from the observed value.)	The standard value of $\bar{X}, \sigma, p$, etc., adopted for computing control limits of a control chart for the case, control-standard given.

Explanatory Notes

NOTE 1 As explained in detail in chapter six, $\sigma_{\bar{X}}$ and σ_σ are computed from the observed variation of individual values *within* subgroups and the size n of a subgroup for the first use "(A) Control—No Standard Given," and from the adopted standard value of σ' and the size n of a subgroup for the second use "(B) Control with Respect to a Given Standard." Likewise, for the first use, σ_p is computed from the *overall* value of p, designated $\bar{p}$, and n, and for the second use from p' and n. The method for determining σ_R is outlined in this appendix.

NOTE 2 This is discussed fully in the Shewhart text. In some situations in industry in which it is important to catch trouble even if it entails a considerable amount of otherwise unnecessary investigation, two-sigma limits have been found useful. The necessary changes in the factors for control chart limits will be apparent from their derivation in the text and in this appendix. Alternatively, in process-quality-control work, probability control limits based on percentage points are sometimes used.

NOTE 3 From the viewpoint of the theory of estimation, if normality is assumed, an unbiased and efficient estimate of the standard deviation within subgroups is:

$$\frac{1}{c_2}\sqrt{\frac{n_1\sigma_1^2 + \cdots + n_k\sigma_k^2}{n_1 + \cdots + n_k - k + 1}}\ , \qquad \text{(C30)}$$

where c_2 is to be found from table 6.1, corresponding to $n = n_1 + \cdots + n_k - k + 1$. Actually c_2 will be very close to unity if the denominator $n_1 \cdots + n_k - k + 1$ is as large as 15 or more as it usually is, whether n_1, n_2, etc. be large, small, equal or unequal.

Equations (C4), (C6), and (C9), and the procedure provided for "Control—No Standard Given," have been adopted for use in the text with practical considerations in mind, equation (C6) representing a departure from that previously given. From the viewpoint of the theory of estimation they are unbiased or nearly so when used with the appropriate factors as described in the text and are nearly as efficient as equation (C30).

It should be pointed out that the problem of choosing a control chart criterion for use in "Control—No Standard Given" is not essentially a problem in estimation. The criterion is by nature more a test of consistency of the data themselves and must be based on the data at hand, including some which may have been influenced by the assignable causes which it is desired to detect. The final justification of a control chart criterion is its proved ability to detect assignable causes economically under practical conditions.

When control has been achieved and standard values are to be based on the observed data, the problem is more a problem in estimation, although in practice many of the assumptions made in estimation theory are imperfectly met and practical considerations, sampling trials, and experience are deciding factors.

In both cases, data are usually plentiful and efficiency of estimation a minor consideration.

NOTE 4 If most of the samples are of approximately equal size effort may be saved by first computing and plotting approximate control limits based on some typical sample size, such as the most frequent sample size, a standard sample size, or the average sample size. Then, for any point questionably near the limits, the correct limits based on the actual sample size for that point should be computed and also plotted, if the point would otherwise be shown in incorrect relation to the limits.

NOTE 5 Here it is of interest to note the nature of the statistical distributions involved, as follows:

(*a*) With respect to a characteristic for which it is possible for only one defect to occur on a unit, and, in general, when the result of examining a unit is to classify it as defective or nondefective by any criterion, the underlying distribution function may often usefully be assumed to be the binomial, where p is the fraction defective and n is the number of units in the sample (for example equation C14).

(*b*) With respect to a characteristic for which it is possible for two, three, or some other limited number of defects to occur on a unit, such as poor soldered connections on a unit of wired equipment, where we are primarily concerned with the classification of soldered connections, rather than units, into defective and nondefective, the underlying distribution may often usefully be assumed to be the binomial, where p is the ratio of the observed to the possible number of occurrences of defects in the sample and n is the possible number of occurrences of defects in the sample instead of the sample size (for example, equation C14), with n defined as number of possible occurrences per sample).

(*c*) With respect to a characteristic for which it is possible for a large but indeterminate number of defects to occur on a unit, such as finish defects on a painted surface, the underlying distribution may often usefully be assumed to be the Poisson distribution. (The proportion of defects expected in the sample, p, is indeterminate and usually small; and the possible number of occurrences of defects in the sample, n, is also indeterminate and usually large; but the product pn is finite. For the sample this pn value is c.) (For example, $\bar{c} \pm 3\sqrt{\bar{c}}$.)

For characteristics of types (*a*) and (*b*), the fraction p is almost invariably small, say less than 0.10, and under these circumstances the Poisson distribution may be used as a satisfactory approximation to the binomial. Hence, in general, for all these three types of characteristics, taken individually or collectively, we may use relations based on the Poisson distribution. The relations given for control limits for number of defects have accordingly been based directly on the Poisson distribution, and the relations for control limits for defects per unit have been based indirectly thereon.

NOTE 6 In the control of a process, it is common practice to extend the central line and control limits on a control chart to cover a future period of operations. This practice constitutes control with respect to a standard set by previous operating experience and is a simple way to apply this principle when no change in sample size or sizes is contemplated.

When it is not convenient to specify the sample size or sizes in advance, standard values of $\bar{X}'$, σ', etc. may be derived from past control chart data using the relations:

$$\bar{X}' = \bar{\bar{X}} \qquad p'n = \bar{p}n$$

$$\sigma' = \frac{\bar{R}}{d_2} \text{ or } \frac{\bar{\sigma}}{c_2} \qquad u' = \bar{u}$$

$$p' = \bar{p} \qquad c' = \bar{c}$$

where the values on the right-hand side of the relations are derived from past data. In this process a certain amount of arbitrary judgment may be used in omitting data from subgroups found or believed to be out of control.

NOTE 7 It may be of interest to note that, for a given set of data, the mean moving range as defined here is the average of the two values of $\bar{R}$ which would be obtained using ordinary ranges of subgroups of two, starting in one case with the first observation and in the other with the second observation. Also, where $n = 2$, $R = 2\sigma$, and $d_2 = 2c_2$ as listed in table 6.1.

The mean moving range is capable of much wider definition[11] but that given here has been the one used most in process quality control.

When a control chart for averages and a control chart for ranges are used together, the chart for ranges gives information which is not contained in the chart for averages and the combination is very effective in process control. The combination of a control chart for individuals and a control chart for moving ranges does not possess this dual property; all the information in the chart for moving ranges is contained, somewhat less explicitly, in the chart for individuals.

NOTE 8 In some texts on statistics, the term *standard deviation of a sample* is applied to the square root of the ratio of the sum of the squares of the deviations about the sample average to $n - 1$, where n is the sample size. This is the square root of an unbiased estimate of the universe variance based on the sample but is not an unbiased estimate of the universe standard deviation. It may be used in place of the rms. deviation provided the *equations,* and factors for control chart lines are suitably corrected by the factor $\sqrt{\frac{n-1}{n}}$, but this practice is not recommended in the interest of simplicity and uniformity.

Further, if an unbiased estimate is required at each point, $\frac{\sigma}{c_2}$, or $\frac{R}{d_2}$ may be plotted with the appropriate central lines and control limits but this will seldom, if ever, be worth the extra computation.

FOOTNOTES

[1] See Equation 66 of Shewhart text, p. 184.

[2] Editorially changed in September 1954.

[3] See pp. 368 to 370 of L.H.C. Tippit, "On the Extreme Individuals and the Range of Samples from a Normal Population." *Biometrika*, Vol. 17 (1925).

[4] See pp 180 and 181 of Shewhart text.

[5] Equation 64 on p. 184 of Shewhart text gives distribution of standard deviations for normal universe.

[6] Relations C5 and C6 were derived from Equation 12 on p. 390 of Frederick Mosteller, "On Some Useful 'Inefficient' Statistics," *The Annals of Mathematical Statistics*, Vol. XVII, No. 4, December, 1946, pp. 377–408.

[7] This equation was corrected editorially in September 1954.

[8] U. Romanovsky, "On the Moments of Standard Deviation and of Correlation Coefficient in Samples from Normal Population," *Metron*, Vol. 5, No. 4, 1925, pp. 3–46.

[9] Shewhart, p. 185, recommends the simple relation $\frac{\sigma}{\sqrt{2n}}$ for sample sizes greater than five, assuming that the Camp-Meidel inequality applies.

[10] Tippett, *loc. cit.*

[11] Paul G. Hoel, "The Efficiency of the Mean Moving Range," *The Annals of Mathematical Statistics*, Vol. XVII, No. 4, December 1946, p. 475.

INDEX

Acceptance sampling. *See* Inspection by sampling
American Society for Quality Control, 9
  training programs, 19
American Society for Testing and Materials, 7
Arithmetic mean, $\overline{X}$, formula for, 89–90
Arithmetic processes
  addition, 28–29
  arrays, 32–33
  casting out 9s, checking by, 40–43
  commutations and permutations, 54–56
  cube root, 35–36
  exponents, 29–30
  division, 30–31
  factorials, 53–54
  logarithms, 43–54
  multiplication, 28–29
  number systems, 30
  powers, 29–30, 33
  *n*th root, 35–36
  rounding off, 31–32
  sets, 32–33
  significant figures, 31–32
  square root, 33–38
  squares of numbers, 33
  tables of roots, 38–39
Array, 66–67, 69
ASTM Manual on Control of Materials, 7, 173–174, 220, 229–230
Attributes data vs. variables data, definitions of, 99–100
Attributes control charts
  c charts for defects per sample, 190–192, 196, 198–200
  construction of, steps in, 167
  control limits, 134–151, 157, 158, 163
  three-sigma limits, table of, 195
  data ordering for, 161–162
  defects, definitions and classifications of, 201–205
  defectives, definitions and classification of, 202–203
  D_u charts for demerits per unit, 201–210, 212–213
    control limits for, 209 (table 5.15B)
    demerit values for defects, 203–205
    formulas for, 206–207
    preparation of, 207–210
  formulas for central lines and control limits, 201, 202 (table 5.14)
  I charts for indexes, 211–215
    control limits for, 215
    formulas for, 211, 214–215
  p charts for fraction defective, 162–172
    construction of, steps in, 167
    control limits, 180–193
    for samples of equal size, 164, 166
    for samples of unequal size, 169–171, 186–190
    standard deviation, 163
    standard given, 163–167
    no standard given, 167–172
  pn or *d* charts for number of defectives, 172–182
    confidence level, 172
    control limits, 172–174
    as guide to show lack of control, 183–185
    for samples of unequal size, 174–177
    standard deviation for *p* binomial, 173
    standard given, 177–179

no standard given, 180–182
standards for, 158–159
standards, method to establish, 182–184
two-fold classification of data, 157
u charts for defects per unit, 193–198
Average, as measure of central tendency, 89

Barlow's tables of square roots, 33, 38–39
Bartky, R. Walter, 7
Bartlett's test for homogeneity, 398–399
Binomial table, 138–139 (table 4.7)
Bowker, Albert H., 9
Butterbaugh, Dr. Grant I., 9

Central tendency, measures of, 89–91
arithmetic mean, $\bar{X}$, 89–90, 92
median, M_e, 90
mid-range X_R, 90–91
mode, M_o, 90
Cochran's test for homogeneity, 399–401
Combinations, 54–56
Consumerism, 1
Contracts, purchase. *See* Procurement
Control charts. *See* also Attributes control charts; Variable control charts
applications of, 63–66, 115–118
clerical errors, reducing, 118
cost accounting, aid in, 116
food and drug products, maintaining purity of, 118
product quality levels, maintaining, 116
to show lack of control, 183–185
suppliers' product quality, evaluation of, 117–118
worker fatigue, measuring effects of, 130
basic techniques of, 130–134
confidence limits, 133–134
degree of belief (confidence coefficient), 133, 146
f binomial, 148, 149–150
fiduciary distribution, 133
hypergeometric distribution, 144–151
normal law probabilities, 133–134
normal law theory, 131
p binomial distribution, 134–139, 145, 148
Poisson exponential binomial limit, 140–144, 148–149
probability density function, 136
c charts for defects per sample, 190–192, 196, 198–200
control limits, 127–129, 134–151, 157
three-sigma limits, table of, 185
three sigma vs. two-sigma, 163
D_u charts (*see* Attributes control charts)
I charts for indexes, 211–215
for individual values (100% inspection), 307–308, 313
for midranges, *M*, and ranges, *R*, 314–315
monitoring charts, 124, 125
origin of, 7
p charts (*see* Attributes control charts)
pn or *d* charts (*see* Attributes control charts)
R charts for ranges (*see* Variables control charts)
sampling plans, selection, 152–154
terminology
assignable causes, 129, 131, 158, 161
chance causes, 161
characteristic, 160
defect, 159
defective, 159
fraction defective, 160
lot (batch), 160
percent defective, 160
system of causes, 160
tolerance, 159
work sampling, 130
types of, 119–120

u charts for defects per unit, 193–198
$\bar{X}$ charts for averages (*see* Variables control charts)
Correlation, linear, 327–352
abscissa values, 331
arithmetic means, 328–329
covariance, 329–330
dispersion or variability values, 328–329
linear coefficient of correlation, 329, 330, 333–334, 337–338
linear relation, 329, 334
two methods for, 345–346
lines of best fit, 331, 332–333, 335, 336–337, 338
by eye, 331, 332, 333
lines of regression, 331–339
simple computation technique for, 339–343
as method for relating two variables, 327–328
as nondestructive test method, 327, 329, 342
observed values (statistics), 328–329
ordinate values, 331
standards, given or not, 328
statistical techniques, 328–330
theory of errors technique, 343–349
true values (parameters), 328, 330
variances, 328–330
Costs of quality control. *See* Quality control, economics of

Defects, definitions and classifications, 201–205, 597–598, 700
Design of experiments
analysis of variance, 353–364, 393–394, 396 (table 8.28)
classical vs. factorial design, 387
experimental tests, purpose of, 364
replication, 366
F distribution table, 395–396
F-test, 21, 387, 388, 390, 394–396
homogeneity, tests for, 387–393, 397–401
Bartlett's test, 398–399
Cochran's test, 399–401
Latin square arrangement, 386–387
random sampling techniques, 355–364, 373–375
confidence limits, 361
degrees of freedom method, 375–377
fiducial limits, 361
normal law distribution, 361
random numbers, tables of, 354, 355, 356; frequency distributions of, 356, 357, 358; how to use, 367–373
randomization, 361, 364, 365, 373
representative samples, 373–374
statistics for quality standards, 359–360 (tables 8.4, 8.5, 8.6)
test for significant differences between means, 360, 361–364
three-sigma control criterion, 361
two-sigma control limits, 361
unbiased samples, 355, 375
significant difference, general tests for, 377–385
between two or several means, 377–382
between two means and two variances, 382–385
test factors to determine lack of control, 354–355
Dice game, probabilities in, 101–106
Dodge, Harold F., 7
Dodge-Romig sampling tables, 661–662, 663, 685
for double sampling plans, 668–669
for single sampling plans, 666–667
D_u charts. *See* Attributes control charts

Edwards, George DeForest, 7

Factorials, 53–54
Failure rates, computing, 51–52
F distribution table, 395–396
Fisher test (F-test), 21, 387, 388, 390, 394–396

Forms
  circuit card assembly inspection report, 570 (Fig. 13-8)
  inspection discrepancy report, 617 (Fig. 14-14)
  inspection stamp, 620 (Fig. 14-17)
  inspection traveler, 619 (Fig. 14-16)
  operation instruction sheet, 496 (Fig. 11-1), 600 (Fig. 14-1)
  material review board report, 551 (Fig. 12-9)
  purchase order, 543 (Fig. 12-7)
  purchase request, 529 (Fig. 12-2)
  receiving inspection report, 554 (Fig. 12-11)
  supplier quality evaluation survey report, 538–540 (Fig. 12-6)
  vendor inspection report, 553 (Fig. 12-10)
Frazee, C. N., 6
Freeman, Dr. H. A., 9
Frequency distributions
  chi-square, 110
  construction of, 66–67, 69–70
  cumulative, 70–72
    graphic representation of, 75–88
  fiduciary, 133
  Gram Charlier, 67–68, 111
  hypergeometric, 107, 144–151
  normal law, 67, 110, 111
  p binomial, 107–109, 134–139
  Poisson exponential binomial limit, 6, 48, 107–108, 140–144, 148–149
  probability, 106–107
  probability density functions, 67
  standard deviations of, 68, 91–93
  t-distribution, 110, 111
  triangular, 68–69

Graphic charts
  bar chart, 72, 73–78
  block diagram, 75
  distribution curve, 75–88
  frequency polygon, 72–74
  histogram, 75, 79 (Fig. 3-17), 87
  line charts, 72–74
Goode, Henry P., 9

Herzberg, Frederick W., 481
Historical background, 3–9
  Industrial Revolution and standardization, 4
  technology acceleration, 5–6
  producer-consumer cycle, growth of, 6
  statistical methods, origin of, 6–9

Information systems and procedures. *See* also Management; Organization, management
  computer applications in, 515
    defect data handling, 520–523
    in-line applications, 519
    management control and, 517–519
    pitfalls of, 516–517
    quality control and, 520–524
    survey results of, 516
    system requirements, 523–524
  control of, 502–509
    corrective action, 503, 508
    feedback, 504–505, 507 (Fig. 11-6), 508
    loss of control; corrective measures, 509; reasons for, 505–509
    open loops, 505–508
    preventive action, 503, 508
  forms, 510–512
    control, 511–512
    definition, 510
    design, 510
  as management decision-making tool, 502
  management support and, 514
  manuals, 498
  quality control and, 512–513
  system performance factors, 499–501
    design conditions, 499–500

documentation, 500
fundamental principles, 501
human component, 499
operator training, 500–501
working conditions, 501
systems definitions, 493–498
manuals, 498
procedures, 495
systems analysis, 494
work instructions, 495–498
Inspection, industrial. *See* also Inspection by sampling; Receiving inspection; Source inspection
acceptance sampling inspection, 605
after-assembly product inspection, 630
anechoic chamber tests, 607
batch inspection, 603
blueprint reading and, 611–612
centralized inspection station, 599, 602 (Fig. 14-5)
corrective action measures, 621–622
defects, classification of, 201–205, 597–598, 700
definition of, 595
design changes and, 577–578, 610–611
development, 585–596
dimensional accuracy, 608–610
discovery inspection, 624–627
inspection audit, 625, 626
operator identification stamp, 626
operator inspection, 625
program procedures, 625
training for, 625
in-line inspection stations, 599–602
inspection points and locations, selection of, 599–602
inspection role, limits of, 627–628
inspection stamps, 620–621
lot inspection, 603
manufacturing and inspection planning sheet, 600 (Fig. 14-3)
manufacturing order, 615–619
nonconforming products, disposition of, 614–615
material review board, 549–550, 551 (Fig. 12-9), 514
rejection record, 615
report of, 615
rework and scrap, 614
numerically controlled equipment and, 630
vs. conventional operation, 629
inspection procedures for, 630
one hundred percent inspection, 604–605, 609, 624–625
packaging inspection, 630–631
patrolling inspector, 603
phases of, 596–597
planning, 598–599
procedures, 598–603
product specifications and, 602
production tooling and, 628–630
purposes of, 596
quality control and, 10, 597
quality standards and, 605–610
records, 613
and responsibility for quality, 622–624
shipping inspection, 631–632
shop drawings, use of, 612–613
system inspection check points, 599, 601 (Fig. 14-4)
traveler form, 619
work instructions, 612–613
work sampling and, 130
Inspection by sampling
acceptable quality level (AQL)
acceptance procedures and, 643
for double sampling, 648, 649 (table 15.3)
for multiple sampling, 650, 651 (table 15.4), 652
selection of, 674–675
for single sampling, 644, 646 (table 15.2), 654 (table 15.6)
acceptance sampling vs. one hundred percent inspection, 636–638
acceptance sampling plans, 642–654
average outgoing quality limit (AOQL), 656–661, 663–665
consumer's risk, 665, 675, 691
continuous sampling by attributes, 665

multilevel, 671–674
definitions, 635–636
Dodge-Romig sampling tables, 661–662, 663, 685
for double sampling plans, 668–669 (table 15.11)
for single sampling plans, 666–667 (table 15.10)
lot tolerance percent defective (LTPD), 656, 658, 659 (table 15.8), 660 (table 15.9), 665
MIL-STD-105 sampling plans, 642–654, 656–661
Dodge-Romig sampling inspection tables and, 656, 661–662
levels of inspection, 643, 644
for multiple sampling, 650–654
for double sampling, 645–650
for single sampling, 644–645
types of inspection in, 643–644
operating characteristic (OC) curves, 652, 654 (table 15.6)
computing, 679–686
sampling risk pattern of, 676–677
probability of acceptance (P_a) values
computing, 678–686
tabulating for, 680–681, 683
probability frequency distributions for, 654–655, 662–663
producer's risk, 643
random sampling techniques, 355–364, 373–375
sampling accuracy, formula for limits of, 640
sampling error, formula for limits of, 641
sampling plans, selection of, 152–154
MIL-STD-105D, 154
sampling procedures, 638–642
attributes sampling, 638
Dodge-Romig tables, use of, 638
lot size, selection of, 641
MIL-STD-105, use of, 638
sample size, selection of, 640
random numbers table, use of, 639–640
rational lots, establishing, 642
representative sample, selection of, 639–640
skip lot sampling, 638
sampling risks, 675–677
variables inspection vs. attributes inspection, 686–692
average outgoing quality limit (AOQL) concept, 687–688
method of averages, 687 (Fig. 15-13)
method of fraction nonconforming, 687 (Fig. 15-13), 688, 690–691
probability of acceptance concept, 689–690
Inspection at source. *See* Source inspection
Institute of Electrical and Electronic Engineers, 9
Internal quality audits. *See* Quality audits, internal

Japanese circle approach, 16
Jones, Reginald, 7

Kurtosis, 74, 79 (Fig. 3-16)

Linear correlation. *See* Correlation, linear
Lines of regression, 61, 331–339
simple computation technique for, 339–343
Logarithms, 43–53
antilogarithms, 45, 52
common, 43, 48–52
conversion factors, 51
exponential, 48–52
how to use, 45–48
Naperian, 43, 51–52
natural, 43, 51–52

Maintainability programs, 426–429
corrective maintenance, 427
liability aspects of, 428–429
preventive maintenance, 427
relationship to reliability, 426
replacement maintenance, 427
types of, 426–428
Management. *See* also Organization, management; Information systems and procedures
delegating authority, 461
efficiency methods, devising, 455–458
functions, quality manager, 474–477
job evaluation, 466–470
job description, 467–468
position description, 468–470
leadership attributes, 477, 478–479
leadership styles, 477–478
management-worker relationships, 450–451, 458–461
encouraging innovation, 463–464
motivation research, 479–481
motivating subordinates, 470–472
communication and, 470–472
human relations and, 472–473
leadership and, 473–474, 477–478
motivation research, 479–481
operation analysis, 456–457
personnel
functions, quality control, 447–448
staff personnel qualifications, 457–458
teamwork, 448–449, 481, 482 (Fig. 10-18)
training programs, 481–490
working climate, 449–450
philosophy of, 437–438
planning functions, 438, 454–455
policy determination, 437–438, 451–453
work assignment procedures, 462–463
work organization, 453–454
worker performance evaluation, 463–466
frequency distribution of output, 464–466
individual differences ratio, 464
worker attitudes and workmanship defects, 488–490
Maslow, Abraham, 481
Mathematics, basic. *See* Arithmetic processes
May, Elton, 479
McGregor, Douglas, 480–481
Mean deviation, *M.D.*, formula for, 94–95
Mean time between failures (MTBF), 44, 424–426
Measures of central tendency. *See* Central tendency, measures of
Median, M_e, formula for, 90
Mid-range, X_R, formula for, 90–91
Military standards and specifications for quality assurance, list of, 590–593
MIL-STD-105D
definitions of defects and defectives, 201–203
sampling plans, 642–661
MIL-STD-109, definition of quality control, 10
Material review board, 549–550, 551 (Fig. 12-9), 614
Mode, M_o, formula for, 90
Molina, E. C., 7
Molina tables for *pn* values, 152
Motivation research, employee, 479–481
Maslow hierarchy theory, 480
McGregor theory X, theory Y, 480–481
Hawthorne studies, 479
Herzberg extrinsic and intrinsic satisfiers, 481

Operating characteristic (OC) curves, 6, 652, 654 (table 15.6)
computing, 677–686
sampling risk pattern of, 676–677
Organization, management. *See* Management; Information systems and procedures

assistant position, 442
charts, 442–446
deputy position, 442–443
functional group concept, 443
line relationships, 441
pyramidal unit, 440–441
quality functions status in company organization, 443–466
scope, 439–440
structure, 440–443
two-fold structure, 441

Pareto's principle of maldistribution, 739–741
Permutations, 54–56
Poisson exponential binomial limit, 6, 48, 140–144, 148–149
Probability
combinations, 98–99
definitions of, 95–96
formulas for laws of, 96–99
frequency distributions, 107, 654–655, 662–663
permutations, 98
probabilities of occurrence, 100–106, 107
Probability of acceptance (P_a) values
computing, 678–686
tabulating for, 680–681, 683
Probability frequency distributions, 107, 654–655, 662–663
Procedures. *See* Information systems and procedures
Procurement
contracts, 538–546
cost reimbursement type, 545
contract selection, 545–546
contract types, 542–546
contracting officer, 540–541
contractual progress, evaluating, 546
fixed-price type, 542–544
incentive type, 544
letter contract, 545
negotiation procedure, 539–541
purchase contract, 538–542
redeterminable type, 544
source inspection, 546–559
target type, 544–545
material review board, 549–550, 614
multiple-source buying, 533–534
nonconforming articles, acceptance of, 549–550
planning lead-time, 533
procurement function, 525–526
production-type specifications, 534–535
purchase requisition, 526–528, 529
quality control functions in, 525–526
quality specifications, 530–533, 535–536
receiving inspection, 550–559
specifications, 528–533
criteria for preparing, 528, 530
initiation of, 534–535
production-type, 534–535
quality requirements, 530–533, 535–536
standard, 562–563
supplier survey, 536–538
compatibility of survey team and supplier, 537
desk survey, 536
inspection records, 537
physical survey, 536
rating techniques, 537
supplier's quality control manual, 536
test equipment, 537
technical proposal, 534
vendor quality control program, 530 (Fig. 12-3)
Product inspection. *See* Inspection by sampling; Receiving inspection; Source inspection
Product reliability. *See* Reliability assurance, product

Quality audits, internal
checklists, code for evaluation, 706
checklists, examples of
calibration and measuring

equipment, 711–713
change control—drawing, specifications, and revision documents, 708–709
fabrication, 713–716
final assembly and test, 716–719
purchasing, 710–711
product deficiency correction action, 722
quality costs, 707–708
quality planning, data analysis, and reports, 707
quality program corrective action, 722–723
training and certification, 720–721
criteria for successful audit, 698–699
deficiencies encountered
in change control functions, 710
in manufacturing in-process operations, 719–720
in measurement and standards functions, 713
in procurement functions, 711
in quality assurance functions, 708
in quality corrective action system, 721–722
in training function, 721
feedback, benefits of, 696, 700
follow-up system, 705–706
inspectors' performances, assessment of, 699–700
personnel, qualifications of, 699
practices to avoid, 701
procedures, 697–698
purposes of, 695–696
product defects, classification of, 700
product quality audit points, 699–700
results, preparing reports of, 701, 705
samples selected for, 706
types of, flow diagrams of, 701–704
functional operations audit, 704 (Fig. 16-4)
inspection effectiveness audit, 704 (Fig. 16-5)
policy implementation audit, 703 (Fig. 16-3)
quality program management audit, 701 (Fig. 16-1)
systems effectiveness audit, 703 (Fig. 16-2)
working principles for conducting, 697–698
worth of, evaluating, 700–701
Quality assurance team concept, 15–16
circle approach, 16
training, 15
Quality definitions, 9, 62, 63
advertised quality, 13
experienced quality, 13–14
life-cycle, 10–11
real quality 12–13
stated quality, 11–12
Quality control, economics of
actual cost method, 730–731
budgeting procedures, 741–742
cost centers in production functions, 726–727
costs classification, 727–730
break-even point, 729–730
burden, 728
fixed, 729
labor, 727
materials, direct, 727–728
variable, 729
cost records as control device, 725–726
evaluating quality control effectiveness, 742–746
failure costs, 743
measurement bases, 743
periodic cost analysis, 745–746
preventive costs vs. profit margin, 743–745
methods of costing, 730–733
Pareto's principle of maldistribution and, 739–741, 748
quality assurance cost classification, 733–737
administrative, 737
alternative classification, 737–738
failure costs, 736–737
prevention costs, 734–736, 737
product evaluation costs, 736–737
recording and accounting methods, 734
standard cost method, 731–733

benefits for quality assurance, 732–733
cost variations, causes of, 732
manufacturing standards for, establishing, 731–732
principles of, 731
profit margin and quality control, 725, 738–739, 744
value engineering, 746–748
aims of, 746–747
definition of, 746–747
procedures, 747
Quality control, statistical
analysis of variance techniques, 129
benefits of, 748–751
cost reduction, 749
factual information for decisions, providing, 749–750
improved inspection methods, 750
measurable results from, list of, 749
process capabilities evaluation, 750–751
quality awareness and incentive, 750
concept of, 1–2
chronology of development, 8 (Fig. 1-2)
definition of, 10, 14, 62
method of attributes, 100–111
method of correlation, 120
method of variables, 99–100, 107–111
origin of, 6–9
organizing for, 18
personnel training for, 18–19
purposes of, 14–15, 115–118
scope of, 10
statistical tables, how to use, 21–22
Quality control techniques, 20–21
Quality standards. *See* Standardization

R charts (*see* Variable control charts)
Random numbers, tables of, 354, 355, 356
frequency distributions, 356, 357, 358
how to use, 367–373
Range, *R*, formula for, 93–94
Receiving inspection, 550–559
backlog, 557
control log, 556
daily receiving inspection report, 552, 554 (Fig. 12-11), 556
delayed inspection, consequences of, 557–558
functions of, 552–556
information requirements, 555–556
need for, 550
personnel duties, 552–556
procedures, 550, 552
promptness in, 556
rejected materials, handling, 552
vendor inspection report, 552, 553 (Fig. 12-10)
Regression analysis. *See* Correlation, linear
Reliability, definitions of, 17–18, 411
Reliability assurance, product. *See* Maintainability programs
definition, 17–18, 411
design function in, 413–419
customer feedback, 413
inspection feedback, 413
maintainability factors, 415
qualification test feedback, 413–414
safety factors, 414–415
failure rate, 421–426
chance failure, 422–424
early failure, 421–422
hazard rate, 424–425
mean time between failures, 424–426
wear-out failures, 426
levels of, setting, 411–412
maximum reliability products, 420–421
product rule, 417
statistical analysis in, 429
confidence levels, 434
data flow, 431
data for, types of, 430–431
frequency distributions, 432–434
system reliability, 415–420
derating techniques, 419–420

parallel arrangement, 417–419
probability of failure, 417–418
reliability levels, 417
series arrangement, 416–417
testing and inspection program, 412–413, 419–420
Reliability values, computing, 51–52
Romig, Dr. Harry G., 7

Sample selection, 107
parent populations, 108, 109–110
operating characteristic (OC) curve for, 71
probability of acceptance and cumulative distribution, 71
random sampling techniques, 355–364, 373–375
universes, 108, 109–110
Sampling inspection. *See* Inspection by sampling
Sequential analysis, 9
Shewhart, Dr. Walter A., 7, 69, 109–110, 131, 161
Skewness, 74, 77 (Fig. 3-15)
Source inspection, 546–559
government inspectors, 548
itinerant inspector, 546–548
requirements of, 547–548
resident quality control engineer, 547, 549
source inspector's duties, 548
Standard deviation, σ or s
for averages, 221–222
deriving from range values, 296–307
formulas for, 92–93
mean deviation as estimate of, 94–95
as measure of variability, 68, 91–93
Standardization
benefits of, 561
designs and parts, standard, 562
measurement standards, 579–587
accuracy and precision in, 581–583
attributes measurement and inspection, 568
calibration, 583–586
gauge blocks, 587
gauges, 587
instruments for, 580
levels of, 580
surface plates, 586
units of measurement, standard, 578–579
variables measurement and inspection, 588–590
performance standards, 565–566, 574
quality assurance systems, government standards for, 590–593
quality standards, establishing, 563, 573–578
drawings and specifications, 573; changes in, 577–578, 610–611; document control, 613
geometrical and positional tolerancing, 575–576
inspection policy, 578
responsibility for, 576–577
tolerances and allowances, 573–576
updating standards, 577
rework and repair standards, 571
specifications, standard, 562–563
workmanship standards, 567
Statistical quality control. *See* Quality control, statistical
Statistical techniques
application of, 63
central tendency, measures of, 89–95
chi-square distribution, 110
computers, use of, 26, 61
cumulative frequency distributions, 70–72
frequency distributions, 66–72, 107–111
graphical presentations, 72–88
Gram-Charlier distribution, 111
hypergeometric distribution, 107
method of attributes, 100–106
method of variables, 99–100
normal law distribution, 110, 111
p binomial distribution, 107–109
Poisson exponential binomial limit, 107–108

probability
definition of, 95–96
formulas for laws of, 96–99
probability frequency distributions, 106–107
reading accuracy, 26–28
sample selection, 107
parent populations, 108, 109–110
universes, 108, 109–110
t-distribution, 110, 111
triangular distributions, 68–59
System effectiveness, definitions of, 16–17
Systems, information. *See* Information systems and procedures

Training programs, industrial, 481–490
evaluation of, 483–485
guidelines for, 490
inspector training, 488
learning deterrents, 486–488
new employee and, 482–483
principles of, 486
trainee attitudes, 485–487
Thorndike, F., 6

u charts for defects per unit, 193–198

Variables data vs. attributes data, definitions of, 99–100
Variables control charts
applications of, 219–221
for averages, $\bar{X}$, 222–224
for averages, $\bar{X}$, and ranges, *R*, 242–243, 256–257, 261–288
central lines, 265–266 (table 6.20, 6.21), 271 (table 6.24), 272 (table 6.25), 273 (table 6.26)
construction of, steps in, 242–243, 261–266, 280–288
control limits, 261–262, 263 (table 6.18), 264 (table 6.19), 269 (table 6.20, 6.21), 271 (table 6.24), 272 (table 6.25), 273 (table 6.26), 287
mean range to standard deviation ratio, 268 (table 6.23)
normal law universe, 269 (Fig. 6-15)
points out of control, 278–280
range values for large samples, methods for, 288–296
small samples, equal size, 256–257, 266–271, 274–275
small samples, unequal size, 275–277
standards given, 266–271
no standards given, 256, 274–277
for averages, $\bar{X}$, and standard deviations, σ
central lines, 226 (table 6.1), 228 (table 6.3), 229 (table 6.5), 261 (table 6.17)
constructing, procedures for, 243–261
control limits, 225, 226 (table 6.1), 227 (table 6.2), 239; formulas for, 228, 229; three-sigma limits, 230–231 (table 6.6), 238 (table 6.7)
examples of, 232–237 (Fig. 6-2), 245–251
formula for averages, 227
large samples, equal size, 254–256
large samples, unequal size, 253–254, 259–260
small samples, equal sizes, 241, 251–253
small samples, unequal size, 229, 239, 240–241 (Fig. 6-3), 257–259
standard deviations, 224–225
standards given, 225, 239, 251, 253
no standard given, 225–227
conditions to be stipulated, 220
control limits, 221
based on medians, 315–316
for individual values (100% inspection), 307–308
for individuals, *X*, and moving range, *R*, 308–313

for midranges, *M*, and ranges, *R*, 314–315
standard deviation for averages, 221–222
standard deviation values deriving from range values, 296–307
Variability, measures of, 91–95
mean division, 94–95
range, 93–94
standard deviation, 68, 91–93
variance, 91
Variance, analysis of, 21, 120–129, 353–364, 393–394, 396 (table 8.28)
additive theorem, 120–121
average and variance values, 123
control limits, 127–129
overall variation, 122–123
ratio between variances, 125

Wald, Dr. Abraham, 9
Work sampling, 130